lonely planet

Central Europe

Susie Ashworth
Chris Baty
Neal Bedford
Andrew Bender

Yvonne Byron
Steve Fallon
Paul Greenway
Sarah Johnstone
Matt Lane

Alex Leviton
Craig MacKenzie
Rachel Suddart
Neil Wilson

LONELY PLANET PUBLICATIONS
Melbourne • Oakland • London • Paris

CENTRAL EUROPE

NORTH SEA

DENMARK

Zealand

Trelleborg

North Frisian Islands

Helgolander Bucht

Helgoland

Schleswig

Rodbyhavn

Rügen

Kiel

Kieler Bucht

Mecklenburger Bucht

Stralsund

Rostock

Uznam

West Frisian Islands

East Frisian Islands

Bremerhaven

Lübeck

Wismar

Hamburg

Schwerin

Groningen

Bremen

NETHERLANDS

GERMANY

Amsterdam

Hanover

Magdeburg

Potsdam

Berlin

The Hague

Rotterdam

Utrecht

Bielefeld

Eindhoven

Essen

Dortmund

Goslar

Göttingen

Halle

Leipzig

Meissen

Antwerp

Brussels

Düsseldorf

Kassel

Naumburg

Dresden

Gent

BELGIUM

Liège

Maastricht

Aachen

Cologne

Eisenach

Erfurt

Weimar

Chemnitz

Ústi Nab Labem

Charleroi

Bonn

Marburg

Teplice

Meuse

Koblenz

Karlovy Vary

LUXEMBOURG

Frankfurt/ Main

Cheb

Prague

Trier

Mainz

Würzburg

Plzeň

Luxembourg

Nuremberg

Metz

Saarbrücken

Regensburg

Klatovy

Nancy

Heidelberg

České Budějovice

FRANCE

Baden-Baden

Stuttgart

Český Krumlov

Strasbourg

Passau

Ulm

Linz

Dijon

Freiburg

Augsburg

Mulhouse

Munich

Steyr

Basel

Salzburg

Bad Ischl

Zürich

Kufstein

Kitzbühel

Neuchâtel

LIECHTENSTEIN

Vaduz

Innsbruck

AUSTRIA

Bern

Lucerne

Grossglockner (3797m)

Lausanne

SWITZERLAND

Interlaken

Chur

Lienz

Geneva

Sion

Klagenfurt

Annecy

Mt Blanc (4807m)

Lugano

Bolzano

Bled

Grenoble

ALPS

Como

ITALY

Trento

Udine

SLOVENIA

Milan

Ljubljana

Turin

Brescia

Trieste

Piran

Koper

Verona

Venice

Poreč

0   100   200km

0   50   100mi

SWEDEN

Bornholm

Pomeranian Bay

BALTIC SEA

Gulf of Gdańsk

Nemunas

RUSSIA

•Kaunas

LITHUANIA

Vilnius

Trakai•

Draskininkai•

Hrodna•

BELARUS

•Łeba

Gdynia•

Gdańsk•

•Kaliningrad

Suwałki•

Giżycko•

•Koszalin

•Malbork

Olsztyn•

Great Masurian Lakes

•Świnoujście

•Szczecin

Bydgoszcz•

•Toruń

Poznań• •Gniezno

•Frankfurt/Oder

POLAND

☆ Warsaw

Białystok•

•Brest

Pripet

•Zielona Góra

Görlitz•

•Zgorzelec

Sudeten Mountains

•Wrocław

•Liberec

Hradec Králové•

Łódź•

Radom•

•Lublin

•Zamość

Częstochowa•

Kielce•

•Nysa

Katowice•

Oświęcim•

•Kraków

•Rzeszów

50°N

UKRAINE

Kutná Hora•

Cieszyn•

Bielsko-Biała•

Przemyśl•

Lviv•

CZECH REPUBLIC

Ostrava•

•Olomouc

•Telč

•Brno

Žilina•

Zakopane•

Levoča•

•Prešov

•Košice

•Uzhhorod

Ivano-Frankivsk•

Dnister

CARPATHIAN MOUNTAINS

SLOVAKIA

Trenčín•

Banská Bystrica•

•Krems

St Pölten•

☆ Vienna

•Bratislava

Miskolc•

•Eger

•Nagykálló

Satu Mare•

Wiener Neustadt•

•Eisenstadt

•Sopron

Komárno•

•Esztergom

•Szentendre

Debrecen•

•Leoben

•Kőszeg

•Győr

☆ Budapest

Oradea•

Cluj-Napoca•

•Graz

Szombathely•

Székesfehérvár•

Kecskemét•

ROMANIA

Keszthely•

HUNGARY

•Maribor

Nagyatád•

Paks•

•Szeged

•Arad

Alba Iulia•

•Varaždin

Novo Mesto

Barcs•

•Pécs

•Subotica

☆ Zagreb

CROATIA

Osijek•

YUGOSLAVIA

•Timişoara

Sibiu•

Karlovac

Central Europe
5th edition – January 2003
First published – January 1995

Published by
Lonely Planet Publications Pty Ltd ABN. 36 005 607 983
90 Maribyrnong St, Footscray, Victoria 3011, Australia

Lonely Planet Offices
Australia Locked Bag 1, Footscray, Victoria 3011
USA 150 Linden St, Oakland, CA 94607
UK 10a Spring Place, London NW5 3BH
France 1 rue du Dahomey, 75011 Paris

Photographs
Many of the images in this guide are available for licensing from
Lonely Planet Images.
ⓦ www.lonelyplanetimages.com

Front cover photograph
Colourful gabled houses along the old town square, Jelenia Góra,
Poland (Krzysztof Dydyński)

ISBN 1 74059 285 9

Printed by The Bookmaker International Ltd
Printed in China

**Although the authors
and Lonely Planet try
to make the informa-
tion as accurate as
possible, we accept
no responsibility for
any loss, injury or
inconvenience sus-
tained by anyone
using this book.**

Contents – Text

2 Contents – Text

GERMANY 185

HUNGARY 347

LIECHTENSTEIN 425

Contents – Maps

Contents – Maps

SLOVENIA

SWITZERLAND

The Authors

Susie Ashworth
Susie updated the Switzerland and Liechtenstein chapters. Years spent in the sleepy Blue Mountains of Australia in her teens inspired her to hit the road. She caught her first glimpse of the stunning Swiss Alps during her obligatory year-long backpacking trip in the late 1980s, where she gained an addiction for Lindt chocolate that remains a problem to this day. Since then, she's done odd jobs in London, written headlines and corrected spelling for magazines in Sydney and travelled rural Oz with her life packed into a camper trailer. Susie lives in Melbourne with her partner and two cats.

Chris Baty
Chris updated the Germany chapter – his first authoring assignment for Lonely Planet. His deep admiration for the German people began in 1992, when a study abroad program took him deep into the maw of a Northern European winter. Heeding the example of the savvy natives, Chris soon discovered that beer and chocolate, in sufficient quantities, can sate the body's need for actual sunlight. He hasn't been the same since. Chris lives in Oakland, California where he supplements his vast travel writing fortune with other equally questionable part-time occupations: music journalism and novel writing.

Neal Bedford
Neal updated the Danube Bend, Transdanubia, Lake Balaton, and Great Plains sections of the Hungary chapter. Born in Papakura, New Zealand, Neal gave up an exciting career in accounting for the mundane life of a traveller. Travel led him through a number of countries and jobs, ranging from an au pair in Vienna to fruit picker in Israel. Deciding to give his life some direction, he landed the lucrative job of packing books in Lonely Planet's London office. One thing led to another and he managed to cross over into the mystic world of authoring. He now resides in Vienna.

Andrew Bender (not shown)
Andrew updated the Germany chapter. Yet another LP author with an MBA, Andy worked with companies in Japan and the US but leapt to write full time after selling his first travel article. His writing has since appeared in Travel & Leisure, Fortune, In Style and the Los Angeles Times. He also reviews restaurants (hence no photo, but trust us, he's cute) and edits the Kyoto Diary, a journal of Japanese culture. Other LP titles include Germany (2002) and Norway (2002). At home in Los Angeles, he rollerblades at the beach, eats Asian food and schemes over ways to spoil his nephews, Ethan and Matthew.

Yvonne Byron
Yvonne updated the Getting There & Away chapter. After a quiet up-bringing in rural Australia, Yvonne has travelled widely and lived in places as diverse as Dhaka, Oxford, Vancouver and Jakarta. After starting work as a defence analyst she has since been a pre-school teacher, university researcher and is now an editor with Lonely Planet. She has also co-authored or co-edited a number books on the relationship between people and forests. At Lonely Planet, Yvonne has been involved in the production of many guides, including 1st editions of the Trans-Siberian Railway and Cyprus. She now spends most weekends bushwalking in Victoria.

Steve Fallon

Steve updated the introductory, Budapest and Northern Hungary sections of the Hungary chapter. A native of Boston, he graduated from Georgetown University with a degree in languages and then taught at the University of Silesia near Katowice in Poland. After working for several years for an American daily newspaper and earning a master's degree in journalism, he travelled to Hong Kong, where he lived for over a dozen years, working for a variety of publications and running a travel bookshop. Steve lived in Budapest for 2½ years before moving to London in 1994. He has written or contributed to more than two dozen Lonely Planet titles, including the Lonely Planet Journeys title *Home with Alice: A Journey in Gaelic Ireland*.

Paul Greenway

Paul updated the Poland, Ukraine and Bulgaria chapters. Gratefully plucked from the blandness and security of the Australian Public Service, Paul has now worked on over 20 Lonely Planet titles, including *Jordan, Bulgaria and Botswana,* as well as various guides for India, Indonesia, Africa and the Middle East. During the rare times that he's not travelling – or writing, reading and dreaming about it – Paul relaxes to (and pretends he can play) heavy rock, eats and breathes Australian Rules Football, and will go to any lengths to avoid settling down.

Sarah Johnstone

Sarah updated the Austria chapter. She's not really keen on author biographies, but the publishers insist. A freelance journalist raised in Queensland but based in London, she has previously worked for Reuters, Virgin Atlantic's in-flight magazine, *Hot Air, and Business Traveller,* among others. Her writing has also appeared in the *Times,* the *Independent on Sunday* and the Face. A great big coward, somehow Sarah still occasionally finds herself in places like Soweto or Libya (before the UN embargo was lifted – oops). A serial hugger of central heating systems the world over, she managed to find the Austrian outdoors a bit chilly, too.

Matt Lane

Matt updated the Germany chapter. Born in England, he grew up in country Australia where he started what was to be a checkered non-career in journalism. Three newspaper jobs, a stint in television, some freelancing and travel, and one-third of a graphic design degree later, he wound up at Lonely Planet. This is his third LP job, having also worked on the most recent editions of *Australia* and *Queensland*. He lives in northeast Victoria, Australia, with his wife.

Alex 'Pooky' Leviton

Alex updated the Slovenia chapter. Possibly Lonely Planet's shortest author ever at 4'9", Alex felt right at home in tiny Slovenia. She was raised in Los Angeles, but quickly escaped to the far reaches of Humboldt County. After college, she got a job at an alternative science/conspiracy theory magazine. This experience led her to leave the country, repeatedly. Alex has visited 46 countries on six continents. She worked on Slovenia while in her last semester at UC Berkeley's Graduate School of Journalism, and is currently a freelance writer and editor based in North Carolina and San Francisco.

Craig MacKenzie

Craig worked on the Introduction and Facts for the Visitor chapter. Born in Kinlochleven in the Scottish West Highlands, his parents told him he was on a two-week holiday back in 1963 when he arrived in Melbourne, Australia, as an unwitting migrant. He's still in Melbourne having spent over 15 years with the Fairfax media group as a sports journalist and subeditor with freelance stints on SBS radio and TV. Seeking a haven for industrial misfits he joined Lonely Planet as a book editor in June 1996. He's balding, fat, smokes long panatellas and drinks pints of Guinness.

Rachel Suddart

Rachel updated the Getting Around chapter. Originally from the Lake District (UK) and a graduate of Manchester University she spent several years trying to work out how to combine her love for writing with her incurable wanderlust. In 2000 she had her first taste of authorship when she took part in a BBC documentary. After getting her foot stuck firmly in the door she took on a full-time role in Lonely Planet's London office, which is where you'll find her now (probably singing along to some dodgy rock music). She has contributed to several LP titles.

Neil Wilson

Neil updated the Slovakia and Czech Republic chapters. After working as a petroleum geologist in Australia and the North Sea and doing geological research at Oxford University, Neil gave up the rock business for the more precarious life of a freelance writer and photographer. Since 1988 he has travelled in five continents and written around 35 travel and walking guidebooks for various publishers. He has worked on Lonely Planet's *Georgia, Armenia & Azerbaijan, Czech & Slovak Republics, Slovenia, Scotland* and *Edinburgh* guides. Although he was born in Glasgow, in the west of Scotland, Neil defected to the east at the age of 18 and has lived in Edinburgh ever since.

FROM THE AUTHORS

Neal Bedford Longest and loudest thanks go to Steve Fallon, for asking me to jump aboard the Hungary Express, for all his worldly advice and for the friendship and beer. Special thanks goes to Zsuzsa Gaspar for the brief Hungarian lessons, the critical praise of any Hungarian wines I smuggled home and for looking after the plant. A heartfelt thanks to all the Tourinform staff that helped me in so many ways, and thankfully spoke English and/or German. Also köszönöm szépen to the Hungarian folk I met along the way that made my trip all that more fun.

Yvonne Byron I'd like to thank Leonie Mugavin at Lonely Planet in Melbourne and Rachel Suddart, formerly in the London office, for their assistance in navigating my way around the abundance of websites and other valuable sources providing information on how to actually get to Europe.

Steve Fallon Special thanks to Bea Szirti and to Erzsébet Tszai, who helped with the research of the Budapest and transport chapters. Tourinform remains the most authoritative and knowledgable source of information on Hungary and things Hungarian; köszönöm szépen to Ágnes Padányi in Budapest and staff elsewhere in Magyarország. Dr Zsuzsa Medgyes of M&G Marketing in Budapest came forward with all those wonderful little details again. Many thanks. I am indebted to Michael Kovrig and to András Cseh for their hospitality in Budapest and Eger; Ildikó Nagy Moran was as welcoming and helpful as always. Once again, this book is dedicated to Michael Rothschild, with love and gratitude.

Paul Greenway In Poland, thanks to Piotr Kaminski; and to Marcin Ğawrysz for showing me around Biağowiecťa and to his girlfriend Marta Kaminski for the grand tour of Warsaw. Also thanks to Tomasz Jĺdrzejewski for a drunken tour of Olsztyn.
    And apologies if I have misspelt anyone's name.

Alex Leviton This chapter would not have been possible without unending support from several incredibly wonderful and generous people, including my host Tanja Pajevic, my travelling partner and translator Freddy Wyss, and the helpful Ljubljana tourist board team of Tatjana Radović and Petra Čuk. I'd also like to thank Tadeja Urbas, John Whaley, Jerry Wagner, Dave Barnes, Tim Steyskal, Sarah Isakson, Rok Krančnik, Brigita Mark, Miha Rott, Franci at the Ljubljana bus station, the tourist offices in Maribor, Ptuj, and Bled, and Lonely Planet Slovenian pioneer Steve Fallon, for paving the way.

Rachel Suddart Thanks to the MTA staff (especially Adriana Cacciottolo in London), Philip Fenech (President of the GRTU's Hospitality and Leisure Division), Jacqui Roberts, Neil Wilson for his help and advice, Paul Gowen from the RAC for 'behind-the-wheel' knowledge, Mark Waters from the CTC for all things bicycle related, the UK IT team for all their patience and expertise, and Tom Hall for never getting sick of hearing 'Can I just run something past you...'. Thanks to Megan Hitchin for her tireless enthusiasm (and for saving me from being a billy-no-mates in the bars and restaurants), my Mum and Dad for their love and support and Paul for sending that all-important email. Thanks also to all the travellers that I met out on the road and those that took the time to write to our offices. Cheers to one and all.

Neil Wilson Mockrat děkuji to the helpful staff at Prague Information Service, to Carol Downie for help with shops and restaurants, and to Richard Nebeský and Tomáš Harabíš for conversations over a cold pivo or six. Also, thanks to the editorial and cartographic staff at Lonely Planet.

Susie Ashworth First and foremost I would like to thank Gordon for his unwavering support and encouragement every step of the way. Thanks to Markus Hoffmann and Julie for their hospitality and guided tour of Basel, Russell and Marg Huntington in Zürich for their time and energy, Markus Leuthard and Doris Stüker for fantastic local tips and advice, and Terry Carter and Lara Dunstan for spot-on foodie suggestions. Back in Oz, Gabrielle, Ronnie and Yvonne offered some excellent pretrip insights, while Kieran Grogan and Craig MacKenzie at LP were particularly helpful and patient. Finally, thanks to my parents, John and Lil, for taking charge in our absence.

Chris Baty Thanks to Heike Neumann in Volksdorf for her unfailing kindness, hospitality, and bottomless pots of strong coffee. A danke as well to old friends Anke and Philipp Bergman in Düsseldorf who were there to help me over the wall, and to Katja Bode, Queen of Göttingen. Much gratitude to Frau Schick in the Frankfurt tourist office, and Frau Mertens in the Kiel tourist office. And a final note of gratitude to the purveyors of milk chocolate and Apfeltaschen throughout Germany; your selfless dedication to the confectionary arts is an inspiration to us all.

Andrew Bender Thanks first to German tourism representatives in Los Angeles, Helmut Helas and Kristina von Sachs of the GNTO, and Kirsten Schmidt of Berlin Tourismus Marketing, for the warm welcome even before my departure. That spirit continued courtesy of Natascha Kompatzki and Britta Grigull in Berlin, Brigit Wachs and staff in Stralsund, Sabine Weigand in Rostock, Christine Lambrecht in Dessau, Stephan Schellhass in Lutherstadt Wittenberg, Annett Morche in Leipzig and Christoph Münch and Christine Ross in Dresden. Chris Baty and Matt Lane were a pleasure to work with, Andrea Schulte-Peevers came through in a pinch, and thanks finally to Chris Wyness for the opportunity.

Sarah Johnstone Thanks to friends and family who helped in various ways, especially Helle, Richard, Alex, Lindsay, Marusa and Luka, Annette, Lisa, Ros, Beth and Brian. Thanks, too, to Andrea and Rhys for the Heuriger experience. (We made it in the end!) I owe a huge debt to various bods in Austrian tourist offices, including Helga Percht in Salzburg, Friedrich Kraft in Innsbruck, Heinrich Wagner and Rebecca in St Anton am Arlberg and Barbara Gigler, at the Austrian National Tourist Office in London.

Matt Lane My first big thanks goes to Paul, my best man, and he knows why. On the road, I had invaluable help from many tourist offices, most notably Vera and the crew in Munich, Karin in Stuttgart, Renate in Erfurt, Kerstin in Weimar, the girls in Regensburg and Andrea in Heidelberg. Thanks to numerous travellers who helped along the way, and all the hostel and hotel staff who made the job easier. Special thanks to my drinking partners in Heidelberg and Munich for keeping me sane. Lastly, thanks to my wife, Simone, who patiently waited for me despite being a newlywed.

Craig MacKenzie I'm particularly grateful to Emma Sangster who provided invaluable assistance during a difficult period for her. Thanks also to Chris Adlam (Automobile Association), David Burnett, Yvonne Byron, Emma Cafferty (YHA England & Wales), Brigitte Ellemor, Paul Guy (HI Northern Ireland), Bibiana Jaramillo, Hilary Rogers, and Joyce Turton (HI Canada).

This Book

Many people have had a hand in the making of this book, over the years they have included: Ryan Ver Berkmoes, Krzystof Dydyński, Steve Fallon, Anthony Haywood, Mark Honan, Rosemary Klaskin, Clem Lindenmayer, Jon Murray, Richard Nebeský, David Peevers, Andrea Schulte-Peevers, David Stanley and Greg Videon.

Central Europe is part of Lonely Planet's Europe series, which includes *Eastern Europe*, *Mediterranean Europe*, *Western Europe*, *Scandinavian Europe* and *Europe on a shoestring*. Lonely Planet also publishes phrasebooks to these regions.

FROM THE PUBLISHER

The coordinating designer of this title was Indra Kilfoyle. Nominal coordinating editor was Michael Day. They were ably assisted by Yvonne Byron, Csanad Csutoros, Hunor Csutoros, James Ellis, Karen Fry, Jocelyn Harwood, Nancy Ianni, Valentina Kremenchutskaya, Sally Morgan, Jacqueline Nguyen, Adrian Persoglia, Cherry Prior, Anastasia Safioleas, Ann Seward, Nick Stebbing, Linda Suttie, Julia Taylor and Helen Yeates. Also helping out were Kerryn Burgess, David Burnett, Bruce Evans, Liz Filluel, Huw Fowles, Quentin Frayne, Mark Germanchis, Mark Griffiths, Kieran Grogan, David Kemp, Emma Koch, Adriana Mammarella, Daniel New, Robert Reid, Tim Ryder, Ray Thomson, Chris Wyness, Isabelle Young and the good people in Lonely Planet Images.

ACKNOWLEDGMENTS

Grateful acknowledgment is made for reproduction permission:
Mountain High Maps ® Copyright © 1993 Digital Wisdom, Inc.

THANKS

Many thanks to the travellers who used the last edition and wrote to us with helpful hints, advice and interesting anecdotes. Your names appear in the back of this book.

Foreword

ABOUT LONELY PLANET GUIDEBOOKS

The story begins with a classic travel adventure: Tony and Maureen Wheeler's 1972 journey across Europe and Asia to Australia. There was no useful information about the overland trail then, so Tony and Maureen published the first Lonely Planet guidebook to meet a growing need.

From a kitchen table, Lonely Planet has grown to become the largest independent travel publisher in the world, with offices in Melbourne (Australia), Oakland (USA), London (UK) and Paris (France).

Today Lonely Planet guidebooks cover the globe. There is an ever-growing list of books and information in a variety of media. Some things haven't changed. The main aim is still to make it possible for adventurous travellers to get out there – to explore and better understand the world.

At Lonely Planet we believe travellers can make a positive contribution to the countries they visit – if they respect their host communities and spend their money wisely. Since 1986 a percentage of the income from each book has been donated to aid projects and human rights campaigns, and, more recently, to wildlife conservation.

> Although inclusion in a guidebook usually implies a recommendation we cannot list every good place. Exclusion does not necessarily imply criticism. In fact there are a number of reasons why we might exclude a place – sometimes it is simply inappropriate to encourage an influx of travellers.

UPDATES & READER FEEDBACK

Things change – prices go up, schedules change, good places go bad and bad places go bankrupt. Nothing stays the same. So, if you find things better or worse, recently opened or long-since closed, please tell us and help make the next edition even more accurate and useful.

Lonely Planet thoroughly updates each guidebook as often as possible – usually every two years, although for some destinations the gap can be longer. Between editions, up-to-date information is available in our free, quarterly *Planet Talk* newsletter and monthly email bulletin *Comet*. The *Scoop* section of our website covers news and current affairs relevant to travellers. Lastly, the *Thorn Tree* bulletin board and *Postcards* section carry unverified, but fascinating, reports from travellers.

Tell us about it! We genuinely value your feedback. A well-travelled team at Lonely Planet reads and acknowledges every email and letter we receive and ensures that every morsel of information finds its way to the relevant authors, editors and cartographers.

Everyone who writes to us will find their name listed in the next edition of the appropriate guidebook, and will receive the latest issue of *Comet* or *Planet Talk*. The very best contributions will be rewarded with a free guidebook.

We may edit, reproduce and incorporate your comments in Lonely Planet products such as guidebooks, websites and digital products, so let us know if you don't want your comments reproduced or your name acknowledged.

How to contact Lonely Planet:
Online: e talk2us@lonelyplanet.com.au, w www.lonelyplanet.com
Australia: Locked Bag 1, Footscray, Victoria 3011
UK: 10a Spring Place, London NW5 3BH
USA: 150 Linden St, Oakland, CA 94607

Introduction

Central Europe is the very heart of the European continent. This enticing region encompasses the nations of Austria, the Czech Republic, Germany, Hungary, Liechtenstein, Poland, Slovakia, Slovenia and Switzerland. Its boundaries reach from the Baltic Sea in the north to the Adriatic in the south, and from the western Alps to the vast plains of Poland in the east and the Carpathian Mountains to the southeast.

Central Europe has been the source of much of what we know as Western culture, not just in music and literature (Mozart, Beethoven, Dvořák, Liszt, Chopin, Goethe, Kafka etc) but in so many other disciplines: think of the works of Freud and Jung, of Marx and Engels. The region's cities – Prague, Vienna, Berlin, Budapest – have, at various times, been important centres of European culture, and their museums, theatres, concert halls and historical sites remain world class.

But central Europe boasts more than cultural wealth and history – it is also a region of startling beauty with some of the best hiking, skiing and water sports in all of Europe. Natural wonders range from the soaring Alps and the High Tatra Mountains to the Baltic and Adriatic coastlines. The Karst region of Slovenia and the Jungfrau region of Switzerland are awe-inspiring. And bisecting it all is the mighty Danube River.

If visiting central Europe's multitude of sites becomes overwhelming, it's time to relax and let the food, wine and beer of this fascinating region take over. There's an abundance of places here where it's simply fun to be: clubs in Berlin, beer halls in Prague, cafés in Vienna and Budapest.

As the 21st century gets into full stride, the political ideologies that once divided central Europe are but faded memories. Most of the eastern countries in central Europe are expected to be in the first wave of former communist countries to be admitted into the European Union.

This guide to central Europe covers this diverse collection of countries, offering an insight into their history, people and culture, as well as providing the practical information that will help you make the most of your time and money. It takes you through central Europe from predeparture preparations to packing your bag for the return journey home. There's information on how to get there and how to get around once you've arrived, as well as extensive details on what to see, when to see it and how much it all costs.

The thousands of recommendations on places to stay range from Swiss camping sites, independent German hostels and Polish mountain refuges to Hungary's excellent *fizetővendég szolgálat* (paying guest accommodation service), cheap hotels in Prague and farmstays in Slovenia. Cafés, restaurants and bars are covered in equally exhaustive detail, with suggestions from the cheapest of cheap eats to the ideal place for that long-awaited splurge. Indeed, this is a book for all budgets.

Central Europe is the very essence of Europe and there's lots waiting to be enjoyed. All the details you need for your journey are here in this newly updated edition of *Central Europe* – all you have to do is go, so don't linger a second longer.

Facts for the Visitor

HIGHLIGHTS
The Top 10

There is so much to see in central Europe that compiling a list of the top 10 highlights is next to impossible. Nevertheless, we have compiled this list. You may agree with some entries while some omissions may raise your hackles – it's OK, we've got broad shoulders:

1. Prague ✓
2. The Alps
3. Budapest ✓
4. Czech beer
5. Berlin
6. The High Tatra Mountains in Poland and Slovakia
7. Kraków's old town ✓
8. Munich
9. Vienna's wine taverns
10. Zamość, Poland

Other nominations include Salzburg's baroque centre, a night at the Vienna Opera House, the Jungfrau region of Switzerland, the Słowiński National Park in Poland and the Karst region of Slovenia.

PLANNING

There are those who say that central Europe is so well developed you don't have to plan a thing before your trip – everything can be arranged on the spot. As any experienced traveller knows, the problems you thought about at home often turn out to be irrelevant or will sort themselves out once you're on the move.

This is fine if you've decided to blow the massive inheritance sitting in your bank account, but if your financial status is somewhat more modest, a bit of prior knowledge and careful planning can make your hard-earned travel budget stretch further. You'll also want to make sure that the things you plan to see and do will be possible when you are be travelling.

When to Go

Summer lasts roughly from June to September. Unfortunately, you won't be the only tourist in central Europe during summer – most Europeans take their holidays in August (and usually for the entire month). Prices can be high, accommodation fully booked and the sights packed. You'll find much better deals and fewer people in the shoulder seasons either side of summer. In April and May, for instance, flowers are in bloom and the weather can be surprisingly mild. September and even October can be summer-like in parts of central Europe.

On the other hand, if you're keen on winter sports, resorts in the Alps, High Tatra Mountains and Julian Alps generally begin operating in early December and move into full swing after the New Year, closing down again when the snows begin to melt in March or even April.

The Climate and When to Go sections under Facts for the Visitor in the individual country chapters explain what to expect and when to expect it, and the climate charts in country chapters will help you compare the weather in different destinations. As a rule, spring and autumn in central Europe tend to be wetter and windier than summer and winter, and the extremes between summer and winter can be great.

When summer and winter are mentioned throughout this book we generally mean high and low tourist seasons, ie, for summer read roughly May to September and for winter read October to April.

What Kind of Trip?

Travelling Companions If you decide to travel with others, keep in mind that travel can put relationships to the test like few other experiences can. Make sure you agree on itineraries and routines beforehand and try to remain flexible about everything – even in the heat of an August afternoon in Vienna. Travelling with someone else also has financial benefits, as single rooms are more expensive per person than a double in most countries.

If travel is a good way of testing established friendships, it's also a great way of making new ones. Hostels and camping grounds are good places to meet fellow travellers, so even if you're travelling alone, you need never be lonely.

The Getting Around chapter has information on organised tours.

Maps

Good maps are easy to come by once you're in Europe, but you might want to buy a few beforehand to plan your route. The maps in this book will help you get an idea of where you might want to go and will be a useful first reference when you arrive in a city. Proper road maps are essential if you're driving or cycling.

For some European cities (eg, Berlin, Budapest and Prague) Lonely Planet now has detailed city maps. You can't go wrong with Michelin maps either and, because of their soft covers, they fold up easily so you can stick them in your pocket. Some people prefer the maps meticulously produced by Freytag & Berndt, Kümmerly + Frey and Hallwag. As a rule, maps published by European automobile associations (the AA in Britain, the ADAC and AvD in Germany etc) are excellent and sometimes free if membership of your local association gives you reciprocal rights. Some of the best city maps are produced by Falk; RV Verlag's EuroCity series is another good bet. Tourist offices are often another good source for maps, which are usually free and fairly basic.

What to Bring

It's very easy to find almost anything you need in central Europe, and since you'll probably buy things as you travel, it's better to start with too little rather than too much.

A backpack is still the most popular method of carrying gear as it is convenient, especially for walking. Travelpacks, a combination backpack/shoulder bag, are very popular. The backpack straps zip away inside the pack when they are not needed, so you almost have the best of both worlds. Backpacks or travelpacks can be made reasonably theft-proof with small padlocks. Another alternative is a large, soft zip bag with a wide shoulder strap so it can be carried with relative ease. Forget suitcases unless you are travelling in style, but if you do take one, make sure it has wheels to allow you to drag it along behind you.

As for clothing, the climate will have a bearing on what you take along. Remember that insulation works on the principle of trapped air, so several layers of thin clothing are warmer than a single thick one (and will be easier to dry). You'll also be much more flexible if the weather suddenly turns warm.

Just be prepared for rain at any time of year. Bearing in mind that you can buy virtually anything on the spot, a minimum packing list could include:

- underwear, socks and swimming gear
- a pair of jeans and maybe a pair of shorts or skirt
- a few T-shirts and shirts
- a warm sweater
- a solid pair of walking shoes
- sandals or thongs for showers
- a coat or jacket
- a raincoat, waterproof jacket or umbrella
- a medical kit and sewing kit
- a padlock
- a Swiss Army knife
- soap and towel
- toothpaste, toothbrush and other toiletries

RESPONSIBLE TOURISM

As a visitor, you have a responsibility to the local people and to the environment. For guidelines on how to avoid offending the people you meet, read the following Appearances & Conduct section. When it comes to the environment, the key rules are to preserve natural resources and to leave the countryside as you find it. Those Alpine flowers look much better on the mountainside than squashed in your pocket (many species are protected anyway).

Wherever you are, littering is irresponsible and offensive. Mountain areas have fragile ecosystems, so stick to prepared paths whenever possible, and always carry your rubbish away with you. Don't use detergents or toothpaste (even if they are biodegradable) in or near watercourses. If you just gotta go when you're out in the wilderness, bury human waste in holes at least 15cm deep and at least 100m from any watercourse.

Recycling is an important issue, especially in Austria, Germany and Switzerland, and you will be encouraged to follow suit. Traffic congestion on the roads is a major problem, and visitors will do themselves and residents a favour if they forgo driving and use public transport.

Appearances & Conduct

Central Europeans are very tolerant of eccentric fashions and behaviour, especially in big cities such as Berlin. But although dress standards are fairly informal in Austria, Switzerland, Germany and Slovenia, your

Central Europe World Heritage List

Unesco's list of 'cultural and natural treasures of the world's heritage' includes the following places in central Europe:

AUSTRIA
Graz's historic centre
Hallstatt-Dachstein (Salzkam-
   mergut) cultural landscape
Palaces and gardens of
   Schönbrunn near Vienna
Semmering railway
Salzburg's historic city
   centre
The Wachau (between Melk
   and Krems) cultural landscape
Vienna's historic centre

CZECH REPUBLIC
Český Krumlov's historic
   centre
Holašovice historical village
Komeríz Castle and gardens
Kutná Hora Church of St
   Barbara and medieval silver
   town.
Lednice-Valtice
Litomyšyl Castle
Prague's historic centre
Telč's old city
Pilgrimage Church of St John
   Nepomuk at Zelena Hora

GERMANY
Aachen Cathedral
Bamberg
Berlin's Museuminsel
   (Museum Island)
Augustusburg and Falkenlust
   Castles at Brühl
Cologne Cathedral
Garden kingdom of Dessau-
   Wörlitz
Luther memorials in Eisleben
   and Wittenberg

Zollverein coal mine
   industrial complex in Essen
Goslar and mines of
   Rammelsberg
Cathedral and St Michael's
   Church at Hildesheim
Abbey and Altenmünster of
   Lorsch
Lübeck
Maulbronn Monastery
   complex
Messel fossil site
The palaces and parks of
   Potsdam and Berlin
Quedlinburg's Collegiate
   Church, castle and old town
Speyer Cathedral
Monastic island of Reichenau
Trier's Roman monuments,
   cathedral and Liebfrauen
   Church
Völklingen ironworks
Wartburg Castle
Classical Weimar
The Bauhaus sites in Weimar
   and Dessau
Wies' pilgrimage church
Würzburg's Residence and
   Court Gardens

HUNGARY
Budapest's Castle District and
   the banks of the Danube
Karst caves at Aggtelek
   (shared with Slovakia)
Hollókő (traditional village)
Hortobágy National Park
Pannonhalma Benedictine
   Abbey
Pécs' Early Christian Cemetery

POLAND
Auschwitz concentration camp
Białowieża Forest
Churches of Peace in Jaworki
   and Świdnica
Mannerist architecture of
   Kalwaria Zebrzydowska
   pilgrimage site
Kraków's historic centre
Castle of the Teutonic Order
   in Malbork
Medieval town of Toruń
Warsaw's old city
Wieliczka salt mines near
   Kraków
Zamość's old city

SLOVAKIA
Banská Štiavnica medieval
   mining centre
Bardejov Town Conservation
   Reserve
Slovakian Karst and Aggtelek
   Caves (shared with Hungary)
Spišský Hrad
Vlkolinec folk village near
   Ružomberok

SLOVENIA
Škocjan Caves

SWITZERLAND
The three castles, defensive
   wall and ramparts of
   Bellinzona
The old city section of Bern
Jungrau-Aletsch-Bietschhorn
Müstair's Convent of
   St John
St Gall Convent

clothes may well have some bearing on how you're treated in Poland, the Czech Republic, Slovakia and Hungary.

By all means dress casually, but keep your clothes clean, and ensure sufficient body cover (trousers or knee-length dress) if your sightseeing plans include churches, monasteries, synagogues or mosques. Apart from the lederhosen (leather shorts with H-shaped braces/suspenders) seen at cultural events and beer festivals in Germany, wearing shorts away from the beach or camping ground is not common among men in central European countries. Some nightclubs and fancy restaurants may refuse entry to people wearing jeans, a tracksuit or sneakers (trainers); men should consider packing a tie, just in case.

While nude bathing is usually limited to certain beaches, topless sunbathing is very common throughout central Europe even in city parks.

You'll soon notice that central Europeans are very heavily into shaking hands when they greet one another. Try to get into the habit of doing so with virtually everyone you meet; it's an important ritual. It's also customary to greet the proprietor when entering a small shop, café or quiet bar, and to say goodbye when you leave. This is particularly true in Germany, Austria, the Czech Republic, Slovakia and Hungary.

VISAS & DOCUMENTS
Passport

Your most important travel document is your passport, which should remain valid until well after you return home. If it's just about to expire, renew it before you go. Having this done by your embassy in Vienna or Warsaw, for example, can be very inconvenient. Some countries insist that your passport remain valid for a specified period – usually three months beyond the date of your departure from that country.

Applying for or renewing a passport can take anything from an hour to several months, so don't leave it until the last minute. Bureaucratic wheels usually turn faster if you do everything in person rather than relying on the post or agents, but check first what you need to take with you: photos of a certain size, birth certificate, population register extract, signed statements, exact payment in cash etc.

Australian citizens can apply at a post office or the passport office in their state capital; Britons can pick up application forms from major post offices, and the passport is issued by the regional passport office; Canadians can apply at regional passport offices; New Zealanders can apply at any district office of the Department of Internal Affairs; US citizens must apply in person (but may usually renew by mail) at a US Passport Agency office or at some courthouses and post offices.

Once you start travelling, carry your passport at all times and guard it carefully (see Copies later in this section for advice about carrying copies of your passport and other important documents). Camping grounds and hotels sometimes insist that you hand over your passport for the duration of your stay, which is very inconvenient, but a driving licence or Camping Card International usually solves the problem.

Citizens of the European Union (EU) and those from certain other European countries (eg, Switzerland) don't need a valid passport to travel to another EU country or even some non-EU countries; a national identity card is sufficient. But if you want to exercise this option, check with your travel agency or the embassies of the countries you plan to visit.

Note that the Czech Republic, Hungary, Poland, Slovakia and Slovenia may become EU members within the next few years, but the first wave of countries probably won't be admitted before 2004 at the earliest.

Visas

A visa is a stamp in your passport or on a separate piece of paper permitting you to enter the country in question and stay for a specified period of time. Often you can get the visa at the border or at the airport on arrival, but not always – check first with the embassies or consulates of the countries you plan to visit – and seldom on trains.

There's a wide variety of visas, including tourist, transit and business visas. Transit visas are usually cheaper than tourist or business visas, but they only allow a very short stay (one or two days) and are often difficult to extend. Most readers of this book, however, will have very little to do with visas. As long as you have a valid passport, you'll be able to visit most European countries for up to three (sometimes even six) months, provided you have some sort of onward or return ticket and/or 'sufficient means of support' (ie, money).

In line with the Schengen Agreement there are no passport controls at the borders between Austria, Belgium, Denmark, Finland, France, Germany, Greece, Iceland, Italy, Luxembourg, Netherlands, Norway, Portugal, Spain and Sweden; an identity card should suffice, but it's always safest to carry your passport. Britain, Ireland, Liechtenstein and Switzerland are not full members of Schengen.

Border procedures between EU and non-EU countries can still be fairly thorough, though citizens of Australia, Canada, Israel,

Japan, New Zealand and the USA do not need visas for tourist visits to any Schengen country.

All non-EU citizens visiting a Schengen country and intending to stay for longer than three days or to visit another Schengen country are supposed to obtain an official entry stamp in their passport either at the point of entry or from the local police within 72 hours. But this is very loosely enforced. In general registering at a hotel will be sufficient.

For those who do require visas, it's important to remember that these will have a 'use-by' date, and you'll be refused entry after that period has elapsed. It may not be checked when entering these countries overland, but major problems can arise if it is requested during your stay or on departure and you can't produce it.

Visa requirements can change, and you should always check with the individual embassies or a reputable travel agency before travelling. It's generally easier to get your visas as you go along, rather than arranging them all beforehand. You should carry spare passport photos (you may need from one to four every time you apply for a visa).

Travel Insurance

A travel insurance policy to cover theft, loss and medical problems is a good idea. The policies handled by STA Travel and other student travel organisations are usually good value. Some policies offer lower and higher medical expense options; the higher ones are chiefly for countries such as the USA that have extremely high medical costs. There is a wide variety of policies available so check the small print.

Some policies specifically exclude 'dangerous activities', which can include scuba diving, motorcycling and even trekking. A locally acquired motorcycle licence is not valid under some policies.

You may prefer a policy that pays doctors or hospitals directly rather than you having to pay on the spot and claim later. If you do have to claim later make sure you keep all documentation. Some policies ask you to call back (reverse charges) to a centre in your home country where an immediate assessment of your problem is made.

Check that the policy covers ambulances and an emergency flight home.

EU nationals can obtain free emergency treatment on presentation of an E111 form, validated in their home country. Note, however, that this form does not provide health cover in Czech Republic, Hungary, Poland, Slovakia, Slovenia and Switzerland.

Driving Licence & Permits

Many non-European driving licences are valid in Europe, but it's still a good idea to bring along an International Driving Permit (IDP), which can make life much simpler, especially when you are hiring cars and motorcycles. Basically a multilingual translation of the vehicle class and personal details noted on your local driving licence, an IDP is not valid unless accompanied by your original licence. An IDP can be obtained for a small fee from your local automobile association – bring along a passport photo and a valid licence.

Camping Card International

The Camping Card International (CCI) is a camping ground ID that can be used instead of a passport when checking in and includes third-party insurance. Many camping grounds offer a small discount (usually 5% to 10%) if you sign in with one. CCIs are issued by automobile associations, camping federations and sometimes on the spot at camping grounds. In the UK, the AA and RAC issues them to members for UK£6.50. The CCI is also useful as it can sometimes serve as a guarantee so that you don't have to leave your passport at reception.

Hostel Cards

A hostelling card is useful, if not always mandatory, for those staying at hostels. Some hostels in central Europe don't require that you be a hostelling association member, but they often charge less if you have a card. Many hostels will issue one on the spot or after a few stays, although this might cost a bit more than getting it in your home country. See Hostels under Accommodation later in this chapter.

Student & Youth Cards

The most useful of these is the International Student Identity Card (ISIC), a plastic ID-style card with your photograph, which provides discounts on many forms of transport (including airlines and local public transport), cheap or free admission to museums and sights, and inexpensive meals in some student cafeterias and restaurants. If you're aged under 26 but not a student, you can apply for an International Youth Travel Card (IYTC, formerly GO25) issued by the Federation of International Youth Travel Organisations (FIYTO) or the Euro<26 card. Both go under different names in different countries and give much the same discounts and benefits as an ISIC. All these cards are issued by student unions, hostelling organisations or youth-oriented travel agencies.

Seniors Cards

Many attractions offer reduced-price admission for people over 60 or 65 (sometimes as low as 55 for women). Make sure you bring proof of age. For a fee of around €20, European residents aged 60 and over can get a Railplus Card as an add-on to their national rail senior pass. It entitles the holder to train fare reductions of around 25%.

International Health Certificate

You'll need this yellow booklet only if you're coming to the region from certain parts of Asia, Africa and South America, where diseases such as yellow fever are prevalent. See Immunisations under Health later in this chapter for more information on jabs.

Copies

The hassles created by losing your passport can be considerably reduced if you have a record of its number and issue date or, even better, photocopies of the relevant data pages. A photocopy of your birth certificate can also be useful.

Also note the serial numbers of your travellers cheques (cross them off as you cash them) and take photocopies of your credit cards, airline ticket and other travel documents. Keep all this emergency material separate from your passport, cheques and cash, and leave extra copies with someone you can rely on back home. Add some emergency money (eg, US$50 to US$100 in cash) to this separate stash as well. If you do lose your passport, notify the police immediately to get a statement, and contact your nearest consulate.

There is another option for storing details of your vital travel documents before you leave – Lonely Planet's free online Travel Vault, a method that can be safer than carrying photocopies. It's the best option if you travel in a country with easy Internet access. Your password-protected travel vault is accessible online at any time. You can create your own travel vault at **W** www.ekno.lonelyplanet.com.

EMBASSIES & CONSULATES

See the individual country chapters for the addresses of embassies and consulates.

It's important to realise what your embassy can and cannot do to help you if you get into trouble while abroad. Generally speaking, it won't be much help in emergencies if the trouble you're in is remotely your own fault. Remember that you are bound by the laws of the country you are travelling in.

In genuine emergencies you might get some assistance, but only if other channels have been exhausted. For example, if you need to get home urgently, a free ticket home is exceedingly unlikely – the embassy would expect you to have insurance. If you have all your money and documents stolen, it might assist with getting a new passport, but a loan for onward travel is almost always out of the question.

MONEY
Exchanging Money

Dealing with money has never been easier in central Europe – all the national currencies are now 100% fully convertible and exchanged abroad. However, outside Europe, not all banks would routinely handle currencies such as the Polish złoty or the Slovenian tolar, so you might find it more convenient to sort out the Eastern currencies after you arrive in central Europe and before you depart. See under Money in the individual country chapters for more details.

In 2002, the EU's 12 Eurozone countries adopted a single currency called the euro (see the boxed text 'The Euro').

Most airports, central train stations, some fancy hotels and many border posts have banking facilities that operate outside working hours; some of them are open on a 24-hour, 7-day-a-week basis. Post offices in central Europe often perform banking tasks, tend to have longer opening hours and outnumber banks in remote places. Be aware, though, that while they always exchange cash, they might not be prepared to change travellers cheques unless they're denominated in the local currency.

The best exchange rates are usually at banks. *Bureaux de change* often – but not always by any means – offer worse rates or charge higher commissions. Hotels are almost always the worst places to change money. American Express and Thomas Cook offices usually do not charge commissions for changing their own cheques, but they may offer a less favourable exchange rate than banks. ATMs (automatic teller machines) are a handy resource, and are as ubiquitous as drunks on a Saturday night in Warsaw.

Cash Nothing beats cash for convenience ...or risk. If you lose it, it's gone forever and few travel insurers will come to your rescue. Those that will, usually limit the amount to somewhere around UK£200/US$300. For tips on carrying your money safely, see Theft under Dangers & Annoyances later in this chapter. It is still a good idea, though, to bring some local currency in cash, if only to tide you over until you get to an exchange facility or find an ATM. The equivalent of US$50 to US$100 should usually be enough. Some extra cash in an easily exchanged currency (eg, US dollars) is also a good idea.

Travellers Cheques & Eurocheques
The main idea of carrying travellers cheques rather than cash is the protection they offer from theft, although they are losing their popularity as more travellers – including those on tight budgets – deposit their money in their bank at home and withdraw it through ATMs as they go along.

American Express, Visa and Thomas Cook cheques are widely accepted and have efficient replacement policies. If you're going to remote places, it's worth sticking to American Express since small local banks may not always accept other brands.

When you change cheques, don't look only at the exchange rate; ask about fees and commissions as well. There may be a per-cheque service fee, a flat transaction fee, or a percentage of the total amount irrespective of the number of cheques. Privately owned exchange offices in Poland and Slovenia, for example, change cash at excellent rates without commission. Not only are their rates sometimes higher than those offered by the banks for travellers cheques, but they also

The Euro

The European Central Bank's highly anticipated roll-out of new euro coins and banknotes took place on 1 January 2002 in all 12 participating Eurozone countries – Austria, Belgium, Finland, France, Germany, Greece, Ireland, Italy, Luxembourg, the Netherlands, Portugal and Spain.

The euro has the same value in all EU member countries. There are seven euro notes (five, 10, 20, 50, 100, 200 and 500 euros) and eight euro coins (one and two euros, then one, two, five, 10, 20 and 50 cents). One side is standard for all euro coins and the other side bears the national emblem of participating countries.

So, if you stumble across some Deutschmarks or Austrian Schillings on your travels, you're staring at museum pieces, albeit that old currencies can still be exchanged at central banks.

Treat the euro as you would any major world currency. Just as you'd exchange say, US dollars, for euros in the Eurozone, you'll find yourself exchanging euros for a local currency outside the Eurozone. And think of its portability and usability throughout much of Europe.

Rates of exchange of the euro and foreign currencies against local currencies are given in the appropriate country chapters.

country	unit		euro
Australia	A$1	=	€0.55
Canada	C$1	=	€0.64
Japan	¥100	=	€0.82
New Zealand	NZ$1	=	€0.49
South Africa	R1	=	€0.10
UK	UK£1	=	€1.58
USA	US$1	=	€1.01

stay open much longer hours, sometimes 24 hours a day.

Guaranteed personal cheques are another way of carrying money or obtaining cash. Eurocheques, which are available if you have a European bank account, are guaranteed up to a certain limit. When you cash them (eg, at post offices), you will be asked to show your Eurocheque card bearing your signature and registration number, and perhaps a passport or ID card. Your Eurocheque card should be kept separately from the cheques. Many hotels and merchants refuse to accept Eurocheques because of the relatively large commissions applied.

ATMs & Credit Cards If you're not familiar with the options, ask your bank to explain the workings and relative merits of credit, credit/debit, debit, charge and cash cards.

A major advantage of credit cards is that they allow you to pay for expensive items such as airline tickets without having to carry great wads of cash around. They also allow you to withdraw cash at selected banks or from the many ATMs that are linked up internationally. However, if an ATM in Europe swallows a card that was issued outside Europe, it can be a major headache. Also, some credit cards aren't hooked up to ATM networks unless you specifically ask your bank to do this.

Cash cards, which you use at home to withdraw money directly from your bank account or savings account, can be used throughout Europe at ATMs linked to international networks such as Cirrus and Maestro.

Credit and credit/debit cards such as Visa and MasterCard are widely accepted. MasterCard is linked to Europe's extensive Eurocard system. However, these cards often have a credit limit that is too low to cover major expenses such as long-term car rental or airline tickets, and can be difficult to replace if lost abroad. Also when you get a cash advance against your Visa or MasterCard credit card account, your issuer charges a transaction fee and/or finance charge. With some issuers, the fees can reach as high as US$10 *plus* interest per transaction so it's best to check with your card issuer before leaving home and compare rates.

Charge cards such as American Express and Diners Club have offices in the major cities of most countries that will replace a lost card within 24 hours. However, charge cards are not widely accepted off the beaten track.

If you want to rely heavily on bits of plastic, go for two different cards – an American Express or Diners Club, for instance, along with a Visa or MasterCard. Better still is a combination of credit or cash card and travellers cheques so you have something to fall back on if an ATM swallows your card or the banks in the area are closed.

A word of warning: fraudulent shopkeepers have been known to quickly make several charge slip imprints with your credit card when you're not looking, and then simply copy your signature from the authorised slip. Try not to let your card out of sight, and always check your statements upon your return.

International Transfers Telegraphic transfers are not very expensive but, despite their name, they can be quite slow. Be sure to specify the name of the bank and the name and address of the branch where you'd like to pick it up.

Having money wired through American Express or MoneyGram, used by Thomas Cook, is faster and fairly straightforward. For American Express transfers you don't need to be a cardholder and it takes less than a day. You should know the sender's full name, the exact amount and the reference number when you're picking up the cash. With a passport or other ID you'll be given the amount in US dollars or local currency. The sender pays the service fee (eg, US$20 for $100, US$40 for $500, US$60 for $1000 etc).

Costs
This book provides a range of prices to suit every budget. See the Facts for the Visitor sections in the individual country chapters for specific information regarding travelling expenses.

Tipping & Bargaining
In central Europe, tipping is less prevalent than in North America, although it's common to round up restaurant bills. Hungary is the most tip-conscious place in the region. See the individual country chapters for more details.

Some bargaining goes on in the markets, but the best you should hope for is a 20% reduction in the initial asking price.

Taxes & Refunds
A kind of sales tax called value-added tax (VAT) applies in some form or other to most goods and services in central European countries. The rate is usually around the 20% mark, although often there's a much lower rate for accommodation and meals. In the Czech Republic, for example, the rates are 22% and 5% respectively. Switzerland has

the highest prices yet lowest VAT rates (7.5% or 3.5%) in the region.

Visitors can usually claim back the VAT on purchases that are being taken out of the country. Remember, that those actually *residing* in one EU country are not entitled to a refund on VAT paid on goods bought in another EU country. Thus an American citizen living in London is not entitled to a VAT rebate on items bought in Berlin while an EU passport holder residing in New York is.

The procedure for making the claim is fairly straightforward, although it may vary somewhat from country to country (it's more complicated in Hungary) and there are minimum purchase amounts imposed. First of all make sure the shop offers duty-free sales (often identified with a sign reading 'Tax-Free for Tourists'). When making your purchase, ask the shop attendant for a VAT refund voucher (sometimes called a Tax-Free Shopping Cheque) filled in with the correct amount and the date. This can either be refunded directly at international airports on departure or stamped at ferry ports or border crossings and mailed back for a refund. If you buy something in an EU country, you can't claim back the VAT until you finally leave the EU; hence, if you're going to Germany after Austria, you claim the VAT for your Austrian purchases once you leave Germany.

CUSTOMS

Throughout much of central Europe, the usual allowances on tobacco (eg, 200 cigarettes), alcohol (2L of wine, 1L of spirits) and perfume (50g) apply to duty-free goods purchased at the airport. For the past few years, however, duty-free goods are no longer sold to those travelling from one EU country to another.

In theory there's no limit on duty-paid items purchased in normal shops for personal use (ie, your perfume buying spree won't be in vain). In practice, however, customs officials will regard you suspiciously if you exceed the following quantities: 800 cigarettes, 200 cigars, or 1kg of loose tobacco; 10L of spirits (more than 22% alcohol by volume), 20L of fortified wine or aperitif, 90L of wine or 110L of beer.

POST & COMMUNICATIONS
Post

From major centres in central Europe, airmail typically takes about five days to North Amer-

ica and a week to Australasian destinations. Postage costs vary from country to country; so does post office efficiency – it ranges from not very reliable (Poland) to ultra-efficient (Switzerland).

You can collect mail from poste restante sections at major post offices. Ask people writing to you to print your name clearly and underline your surname. When collecting mail, your passport may be required for identification and you may have to pay a small fee. If an expected letter is not awaiting you, ask to check under your given name; letters commonly get misfiled, especially in Hungary where the surname always comes first. Post offices usually hold mail for about a month, but sometimes less (in Germany, for instance, they only hold mail for a fortnight). Unless the sender specifies otherwise, mail will always be sent to the city's main post office.

You can also have mail (but not parcels) sent to you at American Express offices as long as you have an American Express card or are carrying American Express travellers cheques. When you buy the cheques, ask for a booklet listing all the American Express offices worldwide.

Telephone

You can ring abroad from almost any phone box in central Europe nowadays. Public telephones accepting stored value phonecards, available from post offices, telephone centres, newsstands or retail outlets, are virtually the norm now; in some countries, coin-operated phones are difficult to find. The card solves the problem of finding the correct coins for calls (or lots of correct coins for international calls) and come in various denominations. Deregulation of the telephone industry has meant some private companies offer discounted phone calls on their own prepaid phonecards.

There's a wide range of local and international phonecards. Lonely Planet's ekno global communication service provides low-cost international calls, a range of innovative messaging services, an online travel vault where you can securely store all your important documents, free email and travel information, all in one easy service. You can join online at W www.ekno.lonelyplanet.com, where you can also find the best local access numbers to connect to the 24-hour customer service centre to join or find out more. Once you have joined always check the ekno website for the latest access numbers for each country and updates on new features. For local calls you're usually better off with a local phonecard.

Without a phonecard, you can often ring from a booth inside a post office or telephone centre and settle your bill at the counter. Reverse-charge (collect) calls are often possible, but not always. From many countries, however, the Country Direct system lets you phone home by billing the long-distance carrier you use at home. The numbers can often be dialled from public phones without even inserting a phonecard.

Area codes for individual cities are provided in the country chapters. For country codes, see Appendix – Telephones at the end of the book.

Fax

You can send faxes, telegrams and telexes from most main post offices in central Europe.

Email & Internet Access

The major international Internet service providers (ISPs) such as **AOL** (W *www.aol.com*), **CompuServe** (W *www.compuserve.com*) and **AT&T** (W *www.att.com*) have dial-in nodes throughout Europe; it's best to download a list of the dial-in numbers before you leave home. If you access your Internet email account at home through a smaller ISP or your office or school network, your best option is either to open an account with a global ISP, like those already mentioned, or to rely on Internet cafés and other public access points to collect your mail.

If you do intend to rely on Internet cafés, you'll need to carry three pieces of information with you so you can access your Internet mail account: your incoming (POP or IMAP) mail server name, your account name, and your password. Your ISP or network supervisor will give you these. Armed with this information, you should be able to access your Internet mail account from any Internet-connected machine in the world, provided it runs some kind of email software (remember that Netscape and Internet Explorer both have mail modules). Most ISPs also enable you to receive your emails through their websites, which only requires you to remember your account name and password. It pays to

become familiar with the process for doing this before you leave home.

You'll find Internet cafés throughout Europe: check the country chapters in this book for details, or see W www.netcafeguide.com for an up-to-date list. You may also find public Net access in post offices, libraries, hostels, hotels, universities and so on.

DIGITAL RESOURCES

The Internet is a rich resource for travellers. You can research your trip, hunt down bargain air fares, book hotels, check on weather conditions or chat with locals and other travellers about the best places to visit (or avoid!).

The following websites offer useful general information about central Europe, its cities, transport systems, currencies etc.

Airline Information What airlines fly where, when and for how much.
  W www.travelocity.com

Airline Tickets Name the price you're willing to pay and if an airline has an empty seat for which it would rather get something than nothing, US-based Priceline lets you know.
  W www.priceline.com

Currency Conversions Exchange rates of hundreds of currencies worldwide.
  W www.xe.net/ucc

Lonely Planet There's no better place to start your Web explorations than the Lonely Planet website. Here you'll find succinct summaries on travelling to most places on earth, postcards from other travellers and the Thorn Tree bulletin board, where you can ask questions before you go or dispense advice when you get back. You can also find travel news and updates to many of our most popular guidebooks, and the subWWWay section links you to the most useful travel resources elsewhere on the Web.
  W www.lonelyplanet.com

Tourist Offices Lists tourist offices at home and around the world for most countries.
  W www.towd.com

Train Information Train fares and schedules on the most popular routes in Europe, including information on rail and youth passes.
  W www.raileurope.com

NEWSPAPERS & MAGAZINES

In larger towns and cities you can buy the *International Herald Tribune* or *USA Today* on the day of publication. Other English-language newspapers widely available include the *Guardian*, the *Financial Times* and the *Times*.

Magazines such as *Newsweek*, *Time* and the *Economist* are also readily available. For a local slant on international coverage and to learn lots more about the country you're in, pick up one of the English-language newspapers available weekly or fortnightly in the eastern half of central Europe, such as the Czech Republic's *Prague Post*, the *Budapest Sun* in Hungary and the *Slovak Spectator* in Slovakia.

RADIO & TV

You can pick up a mixture of the BBC World Service and BBC for Europe on medium wave at 648kHz AM and on short wave at 1296kHz, 6195kHz, 9410kHz, 12095kHz (a good daytime frequency) 15485kHz and 17640kHz, depending on the time of day.

The Voice of America (VOA) can usually be found at various times of the day on 7170kHz, 9530kHz, 9690kHz, 9760kHz, 11825kHz, 15165kHz, 15205kHz, 15335kHz and 15580kHz. There are also numerous English-language broadcasts (or even BBC World Service and VOA rebroadcasts) on local AM and FM radio stations.

Cable and satellite TV have spread across Europe with much more gusto than radio. Many hotels and pensions (even at the budget level) subscribe to satellite channels such as Sky News, CNN, BBC Prime, BBC World and Eurosport.

VIDEO SYSTEMS

If you want to record or buy videotapes to play back home, you won't get the picture if the image registration systems are different. Like Australia and the UK, central Europe generally uses PAL, which is incompatible with the North American and Japanese NTSC system.

PHOTOGRAPHY & VIDEO

Where you'll be travelling and the weather will dictate what film to take or buy locally. In sunny weather, slower film such as 100 ASA is best. In places such as northern Poland or Germany, where winter skies can often be overcast, you might do better with high-speed film (200 or 400 ASA), even though the image is grainier.

Lonely Planet's *Travel Photography* by Richard I'Anson will help you capture the pictures you've always wanted.

Film and camera equipment is available everywhere in central Europe, but shops in the larger cities and towns have a wider selection. Avoid buying film at tourist sites in Europe, such as the Castle District in Budapest or by the Charles Bridge in Prague. It may have been stored badly or reached its sell-by date. It certainly will be more expensive.

Properly used, a video camera can give a fascinating record of your holiday. Unlike still photography, video 'flows' so, for example, you can shoot scenes of countryside rolling past the train window. Make sure you keep the batteries charged and have the necessary charger, plugs and transformer for the country you are visiting. In most countries, it is possible to obtain video cartridges easily in large towns and cities, but make sure you buy the correct format. It is usually worth buying at least a few cartridges duty-free at the start of your trip.

TIME

All nine countries covered in this book are on Central European Time, ie, GMT/UTC plus one hour. When daylight-saving time is in force from the last Sunday in March to the last Sunday in October, Central European Time is GMT/UTC plus two hours.

ELECTRICITY
Voltages & Cycles

All the countries of central Europe run on 220V, 50Hz AC. Check the voltage and cycle (usually 50Hz) used in your home country. Most appliances that are set up for 220V will handle 240V quite happily without modifications (and vice versa); the same goes for 110V and 125V combinations. It's always preferable to adjust your appliance to the exact voltage if you can (some modern battery chargers and radios will do this automatically). Don't mix 110/125V with 220/240V without a transformer, which will be built in if the appliance can be adjusted.

Several countries outside Europe (the USA and Canada, for instance) have 60Hz AC, which will affect the speed of electric motors even after the voltage has been adjusted, so CD and tape players (where motor speed is all-important) will be useless. But appliances such as electric razors, hair dryers, irons and radios will work fine.

Plugs & Sockets

Plugs in central Europe are the standard round two-pin variety, sometimes called the 'europlug'. Many plugs and some sockets don't have provision for earth, since most local home appliances are double insulated. When provided, earth usually consists of two contact points along the edge, although Switzerland is an exception – it uses a third round pin in such a way that the standard two-pin plug still fits the sockets (well, most of the time).

If your plugs are of a different design, you'll need an adapter. They're available in all their many permutations throughout central Europe.

WEIGHTS & MEASURES

The metric system is used throughout central Europe – there's a conversion table at the back of this book. In Germany, cheese and other food items are often sold per *Pfund*, which means 500g. As elsewhere in continental Europe, decimals are indicated with commas and thousands with points.

HEALTH

Travel health depends on your predeparture preparations, your daily health care while travelling and how you handle any medical problem that does develop.

Predeparture Planning

Immunisations Before you leave, find out from your doctor, a travel health centre or an organisation such as the US-based **Centers for Disease Control and Prevention** (W *www.cdc.gov*) what the current rec-

ommendations are for travel to your destination. Remember to leave enough time so that you can get any vaccinations you need – six weeks before you travel is ideal. Discuss your requirements with your doctor, but generally it's a good idea to make sure your tetanus, diphtheria and polio vaccinations are up to date before travelling. Other vaccinations that may be recommended for travel to your destination include typhoid, hepatitis A, hepatitis B, rabies and tick-borne encephalitis.

All vaccinations should be recorded on an International Health Certificate (see that section under Visas & Documents earlier in this chapter).

Health Insurance Make sure that you have adequate health insurance. See Travel Insurance under Visas & Documents earlier in this chapter.

Travel Health Guides *Travel with Children* from Lonely Planet includes advice on travel health for younger children.

There are also a number of excellent travel health sites on the Internet. The World Health Organization at W www.who.int and the US Centers for Disease Control and Prevention at W www.cdc.gov both have useful sites, while the Lonely Planet website at W www.lonelyplanet.com/weblinks/wlheal.htm has a number of excellent links.

Other Preparations Make sure you're healthy before you start travelling. If you are

Travellers Thrombosis

Sitting inactive for long periods of time on any form of transport (bus, train or plane), especially if in cramped conditions, can give you swollen feet and ankles, and may increase the possibility of deep vein thrombosis (DVT).

DVT is when a clot forms in the deep veins of your legs. DVT may be symptomless or you may get an uncomfortable ache and swelling of your calf. What makes DVT a concern is that in a minority of people, a small piece of the clot can break off and travel to the lungs to cause a pulmonary embolism, a very serious medical condition.

To help prevent DVT during long-haul travel, you should move around as much as possible and while you are sitting you should flex your calf muscles and wriggle your toes every half-hour. It's also a good idea to drink plenty of water or juices during the journey to prevent dehydration, and, for the same reason, avoid drinking lots of alcohol or drinks containing caffeine. In addition, you may want to consider wearing support stockings if you have had leg swelling in the past or you are over 40.

If you are prone to blood clotting or you are pregnant, you will need to discuss preventive measures with your doctor before you leave.

going on a long trip make sure your teeth are OK. If you wear glasses, take a spare pair and your prescription.

If you require a particular medication take an adequate supply, as it may not be available locally. Take part of the packaging showing the generic name, rather than the brand, which will make getting replacements easier. It's a good idea to have a legible prescription or letter from your doctor to show that you legally use the medication.

Basic Rules

Food Take great care with fish or shellfish (for instance, cooked mussels that haven't opened properly can be dangerous) and avoid undercooked meat. In general, places that are packed with either travellers or locals (or both) should be fine. Always be wary of an empty budget restaurant.

Picking mushrooms is a favourite pastime in some parts of central Europe as autumn approaches, but make sure that you don't eat any mushrooms that haven't been positively identified as safe. Many cities and towns set up inspection tables at markets or at entrances to national parks to separate the good from the deadly.

Water Tap water is almost always safe to drink in Europe, but bottled water is advisable in the Czech Republic, Hungary, Poland, Slovakia and Slovenia. Be wary of water taken directly from rivers or lakes unless you can be sure that there are no people or cattle upstream. Run-off from fertilised fields is also a concern.

If you are planning extended hikes where you have to rely on water from rivers or streams, you will need to know about water purification. The simplest way of purifying water is to boil it thoroughly. Vigorous boiling should be satisfactory, although at high altitude water boils at a lower temperature, so germs are less likely to be killed. Boil it for longer in this situation.

Consider purchasing a water filter for a long trip. They're a bit labour intensive but they save on money (and plastic bottles). Alternatively, iodine is effective and is available in tablet form. Follow the directions carefully and remember that too much iodine can be harmful. Chlorine tablets will kill many pathogens, but not some parasites such as Giardia lamblia and amoebic cysts.

Medical Problems & Treatment

Local pharmacies or neighbourhood medical centres are good places to visit if you have a small medical problem and can explain what the problem is. Hospital casualty wards will help if it's more serious. Major hospitals and emergency numbers are mentioned in the various country chapters of this book and indicated on maps where possible. Tourist offices and hotels can put you on to a doctor or dentist, and your embassy or consulate will probably know one who speaks your language.

Environmental Hazards

Altitude Sickness This can occur above 3000m. Headache, vomiting, dizziness, extreme faintness, and difficulty in breathing and sleeping are all signs to heed. Treat mild symptoms with rest and simple painkillers. If mild symptoms persist or get worse, descend to a lower altitude and seek medical advice.

Heat Exhaustion & Prickly Heat Dehydration and salt deficiency can cause heat exhaustion and can lead to severe heatstroke. Take some time to acclimatise to high temperatures, drink sufficient liquids such as tea and drinks rich in mineral salts (eg, clear soups, and fruit and vegetable juices) and do not do anything too physically demanding.

Salt deficiency is characterised by fatigue, lethargy, headaches, giddiness and muscle cramps; salt tablets may help, but adding extra salt on your food is better.

Prickly heat is an itchy rash caused by excessive perspiration trapped under the skin. It usually strikes people who have just arrived in a hot climate. Keeping cool, showering often, drying the skin and using a mild talcum or prickly heat powder, wearing loose cotton clothing, or resorting to air-conditioning may help.

Sunburn You can get sunburn surprisingly quickly, even through cloud cover. Use a sunscreen, hat, and barrier cream for your nose and lips. Calamine lotion or a sting-relief spray are good for mild sunburn. Protect your eyes with good quality sunglasses, particularly if you will be near water, sand or snow.

Heatstroke This serious, occasionally fatal, condition can occur if the body's heat-regulating mechanism breaks down and the body temperature rises to dangerous levels.

Long, continuous periods of exposure to high temperatures and insufficient fluids can leave you vulnerable to heatstroke.

The symptoms are feeling unwell, not sweating very much (or at all) and a high body temperature (39°C to 41°C or 102°F to 106°F). Where sweating has ceased the skin becomes flushed and red. Severe, throbbing headaches and lack of coordination will also occur, and the sufferer may be confused or aggressive. If untreated, severe cases will eventually become delirious or convulse. Hospitalisation is essential, but in the interim get the victim out of the sun, remove their clothing, cover them with a wet sheet or towel and then fan continually. Give fluids if they are conscious.

Hypothermia Be prepared for cold, wet or windy conditions even if you're just out walking or hitching.

Hypothermia occurs when the body loses heat faster than it can produce it and the core temperature of the body falls. It is surprisingly easy to progress from very cold to dangerously cold due to a combination of wind, wet clothing, fatigue and hunger, even if the air temperature is above freezing. It is best to dress in layers; silk, wool and some of the new artificial fibres are all good insulating materials. A hat is also important, as a lot of heat is lost through the head. A strong, waterproof outer layer (and a 'space' blanket for emergencies) are essential. Carry basic supplies, including food containing simple sugars to generate heat quickly and fluid to drink.

Symptoms of hypothermia are exhaustion, numb skin (particularly toes and fingers), shivering, slurred speech, irrational or violent behaviour, lethargy, stumbling, dizzy spells, muscle cramps and violent bursts of energy. Irrationality may take the form of sufferers claiming they are warm and trying to take off their clothes.

To treat mild hypothermia, first get the person out of the wind and/or rain, remove their clothing if it's wet and replace it with dry, warm clothing. Give them hot liquids – not alcohol – and some high-kilojoule (calorie), easily digestible food. Do not rub victims; instead allow them to slowly warm themselves. This should be enough to treat the early stages of hypothermia. The early recognition and treatment of mild hypothermia

is the only way to prevent severe hypothermia, which is a critical condition.

Infectious Diseases

Diarrhoea Simple things like a change of water, food or climate can all cause a mild bout of diarrhoea, but a few rushed toilet trips with no other symptoms is not indicative of a major problem.

Dehydration is the main danger with any diarrhoea, particularly in children or the elderly, as dehydration can occur quite quickly. Under all circumstances fluid replacement (at least equal to the volume being lost) is the most important thing to remember. Weak black tea with a little sugar, soda water or soft drinks allowed to go flat and diluted 50% with clean water are all good. With severe diarrhoea a rehydrating solution is preferable to replace minerals and salts lost. Commercially available oral rehydration salts (ORS) are very useful; add them to boiled or bottled water. In an emergency you can make up a solution of six teaspoons of sugar and half a teaspoon of salt to a litre of boiled or bottled water. Keep drinking small amounts often. Stick to a bland diet as you recover.

Over-the-counter diarrhoea remedies such as loperamide or diphenoxylate (sold under many different brand names) can be used to bring relief from the symptoms, although they do not actually cure the problem. Only use these drugs if you do not have access to toilets, eg, if you *must* travel. Note that these drugs are not recommended for children under 12 years.

In certain situations antibiotics may be required: severe diarrhoea, diarrhoea with blood or mucus (dysentery), any diarrhoea with fever, profuse watery diarrhoea, persistent diarrhoea not improving after 48 hours and severe diarrhoea. These suggest a more serious cause of diarrhoea and in these situations over-the-counter diarrhoea remedies should be avoided.

Fungal Infections These types of infections occur more commonly in hot weather and are usually found on the scalp, between the toes (athlete's foot) or fingers, in the groin and on the body (ringworm). You get ringworm (which is a fungal infection, not a worm) from infected animals or other people. Moisture encourages these infections.

To prevent fungal infections wear loose, comfortable clothes, avoid artificial fibres, wash frequently and dry carefully. If you do get an infection, wash the infected area at least daily with a disinfectant or medicated soap and water, and rinse and dry well. Apply an antifungal cream or powder such as tolnaftate. Try to expose the infected area to air or sunlight as much as possible and wash all towels and underwear in hot water, change them often and let them dry in the sun.

Hepatitis This is a general term for inflammation of the liver. It's a common disease worldwide. The symptoms include fever, chills, headache, fatigue, feelings of weakness and aches and pains, followed by loss of appetite, nausea, vomiting, abdominal pain, dark urine, light-coloured faeces, and jaundiced (yellow) skin and yellowing of the whites of the eyes. People who have had hepatitis should avoid alcohol for some time after the illness, as the liver needs time to recover.

Hepatitis A is transmitted by contaminated food and drinking water. You should seek medical advice, but there's not much you can do apart from resting, drinking lots of fluids, eating lightly and avoiding fatty foods. Hepatitis E is transmitted in the same way as hepatitis A; it can be particularly serious in pregnant women.

Hepatitis B is spread through contact with infected blood, blood products or body fluids, such as sexual contact, unsterilised needles and blood transfusions, or contact with blood via small breaks in the skin. Other risk situations include having a shave, tattoo, or having your body pierced with contaminated equipment. The symptoms of hepatitis B may be more severe than type A and the disease may lead to long-term problems such as chronic liver damage, liver cancer or a long-term carrier state. Hepatitis C and D are spread in the same way as hepatitis B and can also lead to long-term complications.

HIV & AIDS The Human Immunodeficiency Virus (HIV), can develop into Acquired Immune Deficiency Syndrome (AIDS), which is a fatal disease. HIV is a major problem in many countries. Any exposure to blood, blood products or body fluids may put the individual at risk. The disease is often transmitted through sexual contact or dirty needles – vaccinations, acupuncture, tattooing and body piercing can be potentially as dangerous as intravenous drug use. HIV/AIDS can also be spread through infected blood transfusions; blood used for transfusions in European hospitals is screened for HIV and should be safe.

HIV testing is required for foreigners staying more than 180 days in Bavaria in Germany (foreign tests are not accepted). HIV testing also is required in Hungary (for anyone staying over one year, and all intending immigrants – some employers may require workers to be tested) and Slovakia (for applicants for long-term or permanent residency visas).

Sexually Transmitted Infections HIV/AIDS and hepatitis B can be transmitted through sexual contact – see the relevant sections earlier for more details. Other STIs include gonorrhoea, herpes and syphilis; sores, blisters or rashes around the genitals, and discharges or pain when urinating are common symptoms. In some STIs, such as wart virus or chlamydia, symptoms may be less marked or not observed at all, especially in women. Chlamydia infection can cause infertility in men and women before any symptoms have been noticed. Syphilis symptoms eventually disappear completely but the disease continues and can cause severe problems in later years. While abstinence from sexual contact is the only 100% effective prevention, using condoms is also effective.

Cuts, Bites & Stings
Bedbugs & Lice Bedbugs live in various places, but particularly in dirty mattresses and bedding, evidenced by spots of blood on bedclothes or on the wall. Look for these signs in hostels, where bedbugs can be a problem in places (eg, in the Czech Republic). Bedbugs leave itchy bites in neat rows. Calamine lotion or a sting-relief spray may help.

All lice cause itching and discomfort. They make themselves at home in your hair (head lice), your clothing (body lice) or in your pubic hair (crabs). You catch lice through direct contact with infected people or by sharing combs, clothing and the like. Powder or shampoo treatment will kill the lice, and infected clothing should then be washed in very hot, soapy water and left in the sun to dry.

Jellyfish Stings Avoid contact with jellyfish, which have stinging tentacles – seek local advice. Stings from jellyfish in Europe can be very painful but are not dangerous. Dousing in vinegar will deactivate any stingers which have not 'fired'. Calamine lotion, antihistamines and analgesics may reduce the reaction and relieve the pain.

Ticks You should always check all over your body if you have been walking through a potentially tick-infested area as ticks can cause skin infections and other more serious diseases. If a tick is found attached, press down around the tick's head with tweezers, grab the head and gently pull upwards. Avoid pulling the rear of the body as this may squeeze the tick's gut contents through the attached mouth parts and into the skin, increasing the risk of infection and disease. Smearing chemicals on the tick will not make it let go and is not recommended.

Snakes To minimise your chances of being bitten always wear boots, socks and long trousers when walking through undergrowth where snakes may be present. Don't put your hands into holes and crevices, and be careful when collecting firewood.

Snake bites do not cause instantaneous death and antivenenes are usually available. Immediately wrap the bitten limb tightly, as you would for a sprained ankle, and then attach a splint to immobilise it. Keep the victim very still and seek medical help, if possible with the dead snake for identification. Don't attempt to catch the snake if there is a possibility of being bitten again. Tourniquets and sucking out the poison are now comprehensively discredited.

Women's Health

Antibiotic use, synthetic underwear, sweating and contraceptive pills can lead to fungal vaginal infections when travelling in hot climates. Fungal infections, characterised by a rash, itch and discharge, can be treated with a highly diluted vinegar or lemon-juice douche, or with yogurt. Antifungal pessaries or vaginal cream are the usual treatment. Maintaining good personal hygiene, and wearing loose-fitting clothes and cotton underwear will help to prevent these infections.

Sexually transmitted infections are a major cause of gynaecological problems. Symptoms include an odorous discharge, painful intercourse and sometimes a burning sensation when urinating. Male sexual partners must also be treated. Medical attention should be sought. Remember, in addition to these diseases HIV or hepatitis B may also be acquired during exposure. Besides abstinence, the best thing is to practise safer sex using condoms.

Less Common Diseases

The following diseases pose a small risk to travellers, and so are only mentioned in passing. Seek medical advice if you think you may have any of these diseases.

Diphtheria Cases of diphtheria have been reported from Poland. It mainly affects children and causes a cold-like illness which is associated with a severe sore throat. A thick white membrane forms at the back of the throat which can suffocate you, but what makes this a really nasty disease is that the diphtheria bug produces a very powerful poison which can cause paralysis and affect the heart. Vaccination against this serious disease is very effective.

Rabies The only central European country that is rabies-free is Switzerland. Many animals can be infected (eg, dogs, cats, bats and monkeys) and it is their saliva which is infectious. Any bite, scratch or even lick from an animal should be cleaned immediately and thoroughly. Scrub with soap and running water, and then apply alcohol or iodine solution. Medical advice should be sought immediately as to the possibility of rabies in the region. A course of injections may then be required in order to prevent the onset of symptoms and death.

Lyme Disease This is a tick-transmitted infection which may be acquired in Europe. The illness usually begins with a spreading rash at the site of the tick bite and is accompanied by fever, headache, extreme fatigue, aching joints and muscles and mild neck stiffness. If untreated, these symptoms usually resolve over several weeks but over subsequent weeks or months disorders of the nervous system, heart and joints may develop. Treatment works best early in the illness. If you suspect you may have Lyme disease, seek medical attention.

Tick-borne Encephalitis Ticks can carry encephalitis, a virus-borne cerebral inflammation. Tick-borne encephalitis can occur in most forest and rural areas of Europe. Symptoms include blotches around the bite, which is sometimes pale in the middle. Headache, stiffness and other flu-like symptoms, as well as extreme tiredness, appearing a week or two after the bite, can progress to more serious problems. Medical help must be sought.

Typhoid This fever is a dangerous gut infection caused by contaminated water and food. Medical help must be sought. In its early stages sufferers may feel they have a bad cold or flu on the way, as early symptoms are a headache, body aches and a fever which rises a little each day until it is around 40°C (104°F) or more. The victim's pulse is often slow relative to the degree of fever present – unlike a normal fever where the pulse increases. There may also be vomiting, abdominal pain, diarrhoea or constipation. In the second week the high fever and slow pulse continue and a few pink spots may appear on the body; trembling, delirium, weakness, weight loss and dehydration may occur. Complications such as pneumonia, perforated bowel or meningitis may occur.

WOMEN TRAVELLERS

Frustrating though it may be, women travellers continue to face more challenging situations when travelling than men do. If you are a women traveller, especially a solo woman, you may find it helpful to understand the status of local women to better understand the responses you illicit from locals. Hopes of travelling inconspicuously, spending time alone and absorbing the surroundings are often thwarted by men who assume a lone woman desires company, or who seemingly find it impossible to avert their penetrating gaze. Bear in mind that most of this behaviour, which can come across as threatening, is more often than not harmless. Don't let it deter you! The more women that travel, alone or in pairs or groups, the less attention women will attract and, in time, the more freedom women will feel to gallivant across the globe, *sans* beau in tow.

Despite feminism's grip on many European countries, women remain underrepresented in positions of power, in both governmental and corporate spheres. Despite the exciting progress to elevate the status of women in recent years, women's leadership at the upper echelons of institutions still leaves a lot to be desired, and in many areas, you may notice the glut of women in low-paid, menial jobs. As is the case worldwide, women remain overrepresented among the illiterate and unemployed.

Women travellers will find central Europe relatively enlightened, and shouldn't often have to invent husbands that will be joining them soon or muscle-bound boyfriends that will be back any minute. If you do find yourself in an uncomfortable situation or area, jump in a taxi if you possibly can (and worry about the cost later), or pipe up and make a racket.

GAY & LESBIAN TRAVELLERS

Central Europe lists contact addresses and gay and lesbian venues in the individual country chapters; look in the Facts for the Visitor and Entertainment sections.

The *Spartacus International Gay Guide* (Bruno Gmünder, US$39.95) is a good male-only international directory of gay entertainment venues in Europe and elsewhere. It's best when used in conjunction with listings in local gay papers, usually distributed for free at gay bars and clubs. For lesbians, *Women's Travel in Your Pocket* (Ferrari Publications, US$15.95) is a good international guide.

DISABLED TRAVELLERS

If you have a physical disability, get in touch with your national support organisation (preferably the 'travel officer' if there is one) and ask about the countries you plan to visit. They often have complete libraries devoted to travel, and they can put you in touch with travel agencies who specialise in tours for the disabled.

The British-based **Royal Association for Disability & Rehabilitation** *(Radar; ☎ 020-7250 3222; 12 City Forum, 250 City Rd, London EC1V 8AF)* is a helpful association with a number of publications for the disabled on sale. An excellent organisation is the **Holiday Care Service** *(☎ 01293-774535, fax 784647; 2nd floor, Imperial Buildings, Victoria Rd, Horley, Surrey, RH6 7PZ)*. This charity has information sheets on all the countries in this book, except Slovakia and Slovenia; send a stamped self-addressed envelope for details. A good resource in the

USA is **Mobility International** (☎ 541-343 1284, fax 343 6812; Ⓦ www.miusa.org; PO Box 10767, Eugene, Oregon, USA 97440).

SENIOR TRAVELLERS

Senior citizens are entitled to many discounts in Europe on things such as public transport and museum admission fees, provided they show proof of their age. In some cases seniors might need a special pass. The minimum qualifying age is generally 60 or 65 for men, and 60 for women.

In your home country, a lower age may already entitle you to all sorts of interesting travel packages and discounts (eg, on car hire) through organisations and travel agencies that cater for senior travellers. Start hunting at your local senior citizens advice bureau. European residents over 60 are eligible for the Railplus Card; see Cheap Tickets under Trains in the Getting Around chapter for details.

TRAVEL WITH CHILDREN

Successful travel with young children requires planning and effort. Don't try to overdo things; even for adults, packing too much into the time available can cause problems. And make sure the activities include the kids as well – balance that day at Vienna's Museum of Fine Arts with a day at the Prater amusement park. Include children in the trip planning; if they have helped to work out where you'll be going, they will be more interested when they get there. Lonely Planet's *Travel with Children* by Cathy Lanigan (with a foreword by Maureen Wheeler) is an excellent source of information.

In central Europe most car-rental firms have children's safety seats for hire at a nominal cost, but it's essential that you book them in advance. The same goes for highchairs and cots (cribs); they're standard in many restaurants and hotels but numbers are limited. The choice of baby food, infant formulas, soy and cow's milk, disposable nappies (diapers) and the like can be as great in the supermarkets of most central European countries as it is back home, but the opening hours may be quite different. Run out of nappies at 5pm on Saturday in Innsbruck and you're facing a very long and messy weekend.

DANGERS & ANNOYANCES

On the whole, you should experience few problems travelling in central Europe – even alone – as the region is well developed and relatively safe. You're less likely to become a victim if you look purposeful, keep alert and exercise common sense.

Whatever you do, don't leave friends and relatives back home worrying about how to get in touch with you in case of an emergency. Work out a list of places where they can contact you. Better still, phone home now and then, or email.

Theft

Theft is definitely a problem in central Europe – the threat comes both from local thieves and your fellow travellers.

The most important things to guard are your passport, tickets and money – in that order. It's always best to carry these next to your skin or in a sturdy leather pouch on your belt. Train-station lockers or luggage-storage counters are useful places to store your luggage (but not valuables) while you get your bearings in a new town. Be very suspicious about people who offer to help you operate your locker. Carry your own padlock for hostel lockers.

You can lessen the risks further by being careful of snatch thieves. Cameras or shoulder bags are great for these people, who sometimes operate from motorbikes or scooters and expertly slash the strap before you have a chance to react. A small daypack is better, but watch your rear. Be very careful at cafés and bars; loop the strap of your bag around your leg while seated.

Pickpockets are most active in dense crowds, especially in busy train stations and on buses and metros during peak hours. A common ploy in the Budapest and Prague metros has been for a group of well-dressed young people to surround you, chattering away while one of the group zips through your pockets or purse.

Be careful even in hotels; don't leave valuables lying around in your room. Parked cars containing luggage or other bags are prime targets for petty criminals in most cities, and cars with foreign number plates and/or rental agency stickers in particular. While driving in cities be careful of snatch thieves when you pull up at the lights – keep doors locked and windows rolled up high.

In case of theft or loss, always report the incident to the police and ask for a statement, or your travel insurance company won't pay out.

Violence

Although it's unlikely that travellers will encounter violence in central Europe, skinheads and neo-Nazis have singled out resident blacks and Asians as scapegoats for their own problems, and foreigners have been attacked in eastern Germany, Hungary and the Czech Republic. Especially avoid the rundown areas of east Berlin and Pest. These people can be extremely dangerous.

Drugs

Always treat drugs with a great deal of caution. There are a lot of drugs available in the region, sometimes quite openly, but that doesn't mean it's legal. The continual fighting in the former Yugoslavia in the 1990s forced drug traders to seek alternative routes from Asia to Western Europe, sometimes crossing through Hungary, Slovakia, the Czech Republic and Poland. These countries, desperately seeking integration into the 'new' Europe, do not look lightly upon drug abuse. Even a little hashish can cause a great deal of trouble in certain parts of the region.

ACTIVITIES

Central Europe offers countless opportunities to indulge in more active pursuits than sightseeing. The varied geography and climate supports the full range of outdoor pursuits: windsurfing, skiing, fishing, hiking and mountaineering, boating, cycling, horse riding and taking to the waters. For more local information, see entries under the individual country chapters. You can also visit the website at W www.budgettravel.com.

Cycling

Along with hiking, cycling is the best way to really get close to the scenery and the people, keeping yourself fit in the process. It's also a good way to get around many cities and towns and to see remote corners of a country you wouldn't ordinarily get to.

The hills and mountains of central Europe can be heavy going, but this is offset by the dense concentration of things to see. Physical fitness is *not* a major prerequisite for cycling on the plains of eastern Hungary – they're flatter than pancakes – but the wind might slow you down.

Popular areas for cycling holidays in central Europe include the upper reaches of the Danube in southern Germany and Austria, a circuit of Lake Constance, anywhere in the Alps (for those fit enough), the Danube Bend in Hungary and most of eastern Slovakia. The Karst region of Slovenia is a wonderful place for a cycling tour.

If you are arriving from outside central Europe, you can often bring your own bicycle along on the plane for a surprisingly reasonable fee. Alternatively, this book lists places where you can hire one (make sure it has plenty of gears if you plan anything serious).

See Bicycle in the Getting Around chapter for more information on bicycle touring and rentals.

Skiing

During winter, numerous visitors flock to hundreds of mountain resorts for downhill skiing and snowboarding. The skiing season generally lasts from early December to late March, but at higher altitudes it may extend a few weeks either way – on some glaciers you can ski virtually year-round. Snow conditions can vary greatly from one year to another and from region to region, but February tends to be the best (and busiest) month.

Skiing can be expensive because of the costs of ski lifts, accommodation and the inevitable aprés-ski drinking sessions. Equipment hire (or even purchase), on the other hand, can be relatively cheap – though not in Switzerland. The hassle of transporting your own skis may not be worth it.

Ski resorts in the Swiss Alps offer great skiing and facilities but are also the most expensive. Expect high prices, too, in the German Alps, though Germany has cheaper (but far less spectacular) options in the Black Forest and Harz Mountains. Austria is generally slightly cheaper than Switzerland. In any of these countries, a skiing holiday could work out twice as expensive as a summer holiday of the same length.

By far the cheapest skiing in central Europe is to be found in the High Tatras of Poland and Slovakia, but the facilities can't compare with those on offer elsewhere in the region. And don't expect empty slopes or trails; Poles, Czechs and Slovaks are avid skiers. Perhaps the best choice in the region are the Julian Alps in Slovenia, which are easily accessible and cheap, with excellent facilities.

Cross-country is also popular in some areas, and (for a bit extra effort) costs less than downhill because you don't rely as much on ski lifts.

Hiking

Keen hikers can spend a lifetime exploring central Europe's many exciting trails. Probably the most spectacular are to be found in the Alps, which are crisscrossed with well-marked trails (some with distance and duration indicators), and food and accommodation are available along the way in season. The equally sensational High Tatras are less developed, which can add to the experience, as you often rely on remote mountain villages for rest and sustenance. Hiking areas that are less well known include the Bieszczady Mountains in Poland, Germany's Harz Mountains, the Julian Alps in Slovenia and the Zemplén Hills in Hungary.

National hiking and mountaineering clubs and organisations are superb sources of information. See the individual country chapters for details. The **Ramblers' Association** (☎ 020-7339 8500; ⓦ www.ramblers.org .uk) is a London charity that promotes long-distance walking in the UK and can provide contact details for equivalent organisations in Europe. If you're interested in a structured walking holiday, see Organised Tours in the Getting Around chapter.

Every country in central Europe has its share of national parks and other interesting areas that may qualify as a trekker's paradise, depending on your preferences. Guided treks are often available for those who aren't sure about their physical abilities or who simply don't know the lay of the land. Read the Hiking information in the individual country chapters in this book and take your pick: guided or unguided; short-haul or long-haul.

Mountaineering

There is no shortage of vertical challenges in the Alps and other mountain ranges. Where there is skiing, there is often climbing, too. However, mountaineering is not for the uninitiated and you should never climb on your own, or without being properly equipped and attired.

The various national hiking clubs (see the country chapters) can offer mountaineering information, or in well-established climbing regions (such as Grindelwald and Zermatt in Switzerland) you will find a mountain guides office in the resort.

Windsurfing

There are many water sports on offer in central Europe, not least swimming and fishing. Windsurfing is also very popular, especially in Germany. Wetsuits enable the keener windsurfers to continue their sport throughout the colder months. It's easy to rent sailboards in many tourist centres, and courses are usually on offer for beginners.

Boating

Although much of central Europe is landlocked, there's no shortage of boating options. You can row on a peaceful Alpine lake, join a Danube River cruise from Amsterdam to Vienna (see the Getting Around chapter for details), go sailing on the Baltic or Adriatic coasts or on Lake Balaton in Hungary, kayak the lakes of Poland's Masuria region or canoe the Sooa River in Slovenia – the possibilities are endless. The country chapters have more details.

Horse Riding

Although horse riding is available throughout central Europe, the sport is best organised (and cheapest) in Hungary, whose people, they say, 'were created by God to sit on horseback'. The best centres are on the Great Plain, though you'll also find schools in Transdanubia and in the north. Horse riding is also very popular (and affordable) in Slovenia and Poland.

Thermal Baths

There are hundreds of thermal baths in central Europe which are open to the public. The most affordable ones are in Hungary, the Czech Republic and Slovenia – these are heavily patronised by Germans and Austrians trying to prolong their lives or just having a soak, even though they have plenty of spas available in their home countries. Among the best are the thermal lake at Hévíz, the Turkish baths of Budapest and the spa town of Harkány in Hungary; the attractive *fin-de-siécle* spas of Karlovy Vary (Karlsbad) and Mariánské Lázně (Marienbad) in the Czech Republic; and Dolenjske Toplice and Rogaška Slatina in Slovenia.

COURSES

Apart from learning new physical skills by doing something like having skiing lessons in Austria or horse riding in Hungary, you can enrich your mind with a variety of classroom-based courses in central Europe. Language courses are often available to foreigners through universities or private schools, and are justifiably popular since the best way to learn a language is in the country where it's spoken. But you can also take courses in art, literature, architecture, alternative medicine, alternative energy, drama, music, cooking, photography, organic farming – name it, and chances are that there will be a course somewhere that suits you.

The individual country chapters in this book give pointers on where to start looking. In general, the best sources of information are the cultural institutes maintained by many European countries around the world; failing that, try their national tourist offices or embassies. Student-exchange organisations, student travel agencies, and organisations such as the YMCA/YWCA and Hostelling International (HI) can also put you on the right track. Ask about special holiday packages that include a course.

WORK

An EU citizen is allowed to work in any other EU country, although after three months they will probably need to apply for a residency permit. The EU currently includes only Germany and Austria in central Europe, although additional countries could join in 2004. Switzerland has signed bilateral agreements with the EU that will improve employment prospects for EU citizens.

Other country/nationality combinations require special work permits that can be almost impossible to arrange, especially for temporary work. That doesn't prevent enterprising travellers from topping up their funds occasionally by working in the hotel or restaurant trades or teaching a little English, and they don't always have to do this illegally either. Working is less of an option in the eastern countries of central Europe, where unemployment is higher and wages are lower.

Your national student-exchange organisation may be able to arrange temporary work permits to several countries through special programmes. For more information on working as a foreigner, see Work in the Facts for the Visitor sections of the individual country chapters.

If you have a parent or grandparent who was born in an EU country, you may have certain rights you don't know about. Get in touch with that country's embassy and ask about dual citizenship and work permits – if you go for citizenship, also ask about any obligations, such as military service and residency. Ireland is particularly easy-going about granting citizenship to people with an Irish parent or grandparent, and with an Irish passport, the EU is your oyster. Be aware that your home country may not recognise dual citizenship.

If you do find a temporary job, the pay may be less than that offered to local people. The one big exception is teaching English, but these jobs are hard to come by – at least officially – and the market is saturated in places such as Prague and Budapest. Other typical tourist jobs, including washing dishes or clearing snow at Alpine resorts, often come with board and lodging. The salary is little more than pocket money (one exception is Switzerland), but you'll have a good time partying with other travellers.

If you play an instrument or have other artistic talents, you could try working the streets. As every Peruvian pipe player (and his fifth cousin) knows, busking is fairly common in major central European cities such as Berlin, Budapest and Ljubljana, but it may be illegal in some parts of Switzerland and Austria. It is illegal in Germany, where it has been more or less tolerated in the past, but crackdowns are not unknown. Most other countries require municipal permits that can be hard to obtain. Talk to other street artists before you start.

Selling goods on the street is generally frowned upon and can be tantamount to vagrancy apart from at flea markets. It's also a hard way to make money if you're not selling something special. Most countries require permits for this sort of thing. You can try your luck at the markets in some towns of Hungary, Poland, the Czech Republic and Slovenia, but you'll be competing with fresh arrivals from the east and south – not all of them legal – who know the game a lot better than you do.

There are several references and websites that publicise specific positions in central Europe. **Transitions Abroad** (**w** *www.transabroad.com*) publishes *Work Abroad: The Complete Guide to Finding a Job Overseas* and the *Alternative Travel Directory: The Complete Guide to Work, Study and Travel*

Overseas as well as a colour magazine, *Transitions Abroad*. Its website lists paid positions and volunteer and service programmes. **Action Without Borders** (W *www.idealist.org*) and **GoAbroad.com** (W *www.goabroad.com*) list hundreds of jobs and volunteer opportunities.

Work Your Way Around the World by Susan Griffith gives good, practical advice on a wide range of issues. Its publisher, **Vacation Work** (W *www.vacationwork.co.uk*), has many other useful titles, including the *Directory of Summer Jobs Abroad* and *Teaching English Abroad*.

Volunteer Work

Organising a volunteer work placement is a great way to gain a deeper insight into local culture. If you're staying with a family, or working alongside local colleagues, you will probably learn much more about life here than you would if you were travelling through the country.

In some instances volunteers are paid a living allowance, sometimes they work for their keep and other programmes require the volunteer to pay.

There are several Internet sites that can help you search for volunteer work opportunities in central Europe. As well as the websites mentioned earlier, **WorkingAbroad** (W *www.workingabroad.com*) has a good website for researching possibilities and applying for positions.

The **International Willing Workers On Organic Farms Association** (WWOOF; W *www.wwoof.org*) has organisations throughout central Europe. If you join a WWOOF organisation, you can arrange to live and work on a host's organic farm.

ACCOMMODATION

As in the rest of Europe, the cheapest places to stay in central Europe are camping grounds, followed by hostels and student dormitories. Cheap hotels are not as widespread in Switzerland, and to a lesser extent in Germany and Austria, but guesthouses, pensions and private rooms often represent good value. Self-contained apartments and cottages are worth considering with a group, especially if you plan to stay in one place for a while.

See the Facts for the Visitor sections in the country chapters for an overview of local accommodation options. During peak holiday periods, accommodation can be hard to find, and unless you're camping, it's advisable to book ahead. Even camping grounds can fill up, particularly popular ones near large towns or cities.

Reservations

Cheap hotels in popular destinations (such as Munich, Prague and Budapest) fill up quickly, especially the well-run ones in desirable or central neighbourhoods. It's a good idea to make reservations several weeks ahead, at least for the first night or two. An international phone call or quick email to reserve a room (followed, if necessary, by written confirmation and/or a deposit) is less of a hassle than wasting your first day in a city looking for a place to stay.

If you arrive in a country by air and without a reservation, there is often an airport accommodation-booking desk, although it rarely covers the lower strata of hotels. Tourist offices often have extensive accommodation lists, and the more helpful ones will go out of their way to find you something suitable. In most countries the fee for this service is very low, and if accommodation is tight, it can save you a lot of running around. This is also an easy way to get around any language problems. Agencies offering private rooms can be good value. Staying with a local family doesn't always mean that you'll lack privacy, but you'll probably have less freedom than in a hotel.

Sometimes people will come up to you on the street offering a private room or a hostel bed. This can be good or it can be bad; it is impossible to generalise. Just make sure it is not way out in a dingy suburb somewhere and that you negotiate a clear price. As always, be careful when someone offers to carry your luggage: they might carry it away altogether!

Camping

Camping is immensely popular in central Europe (especially among Germans and the Dutch) and provides the cheapest accommodation. There is usually a charge per tent or camper van, per person and per vehicle. National tourist offices should have booklets or brochures listing camping grounds all over their country. See Visas & Documents earlier in this chapter for information on the Camping Card International.

In large cities, most camping grounds will be some distance from the centre. For this reason, camping is most popular with people who have their own transport. If you're on foot, the money you save by camping can quickly be eaten up by the bus or train fares spent on commuting to and from a town centre. Unless the camping ground rents out bungalows or small cabins on site (very common in central Europe), you'll also need a tent, sleeping bag, cooking equipment and other bits and pieces, all of which are easier to cart around if you have a vehicle.

Camping other than in designated camping grounds is illegal without permission from the local authorities (the police or local council office) or from the owner of the land. However, don't be shy about asking landowners – you may be pleasantly surprised by the response.

In some countries, such as Austria and Germany, freelance camping (camping 'wild' or 'rough') is illegal on all but private land, and in Hungary and Slovenia it's illegal altogether. This doesn't prevent hikers from occasionally pitching their tent for the night, and they usually get away with it if they keep a low profile (don't make noise, build a fire or leave rubbish). At worst, they are woken up by the police and asked to move on.

Hostels

Hostels offer the cheapest (secure) roof over your head in central Europe, and you don't have to be a youngster to use them. Most hostels are part of the national Youth Hostel Association (YHA), which is affiliated with what was formerly called the IYHF (International Youth Hostel Federation) and has been renamed Hostelling International (HI) to attract a wider clientele and move away from the emphasis on 'youth'. The situation remains slightly confused, however. Some countries, such as the USA and Canada, immediately adopted the new name, but many European countries will take a few years to change their logos. In practice it makes no difference: IYHF and HI are the same thing and the domestic YHA almost always belongs to the parent group.

Technically, you're supposed to be a YHA or HI member to use affiliated hostels, but you can often stay by paying an extra charge and this will usually be set against future membership. Stay enough nights as a non-member and you're automatically a member. In Bavaria, in Germany, the strict maximum age for anyone, except group leaders or parents accompanying a child, is 26, although most countries don't adhere to an age limit.

To join the HI, ask at any hostel or contact your local or national hostelling office. The offices in English-speaking countries are in the following list. Otherwise, check the individual country chapters for addresses. The HI website at W www.iyhf.org has links to all the websites of the various country associations.

Australia Australian Youth Hostels Association (☎ 02-9261 1111, fax 9261 1969, e yha@ yhansw.org.au) 422 Kent St, Sydney, NSW 2000

Canada Hostelling International Canada (☎ 613-237 7884, fax 237 7868, e info@hihostels. ca) 205 Catherine St, Suite 400, Ottawa, Ont K2P 1C3

England & Wales Youth Hostels Association (☎ 01629-592600, fax 592702, e customer services@yha.org.uk) Trevelyan House, Dimple Rd, Matlock, Derbyshire DE4 3YH

Ireland An Óige (Irish Youth Hostel Association; ☎ 01-830 4555, fax 830 5808, e mailbox@ anoige.ie) 61 Mountjoy St, Dublin 7

New Zealand Youth Hostels Association of New Zealand (☎ 03-379 9970, fax 365 4476, e info@yha.org.nz) PO Box 436, Level 3, 193 Cashel St, Christchurch

Northern Ireland Hostelling International Northern Ireland (☎ 028-9031 5435, fax 9043 9699, e info@hini.org.uk) 22–32 Donegall Rd, Belfast BT12 5JN

Scotland Scottish Youth Hostels Association (☎ 01786-891400, fax 891333, e info@syha .org.uk), 7 Glebe Crescent, Stirling FK8 2JA

South Africa Hostelling International South Africa (☎ 021-424 2511, fax 424 4119, e info@hisa.org.za) PO Box 4402, St George's House, 73 St George's Mall, Cape Town 8001

USA Hostelling International/American Youth Hostels (☎ 202-783 6161, fax 783 6171, e hiayhserv@hiayh.org) 733 15th St NW, Suite 840, Washington DC 20005

At a hostel, you get a bed for the night plus use of communal facilities, which may include a kitchen where you can prepare your own meals. You are usually required to have a sleeping sheet – simply using your sleeping bag is not permitted. If you don't have your own approved sleeping sheet, you can usually hire or buy one, or in some places they're included in the overnight price. Hostels vary widely in character and quality, but the growing number of travellers and the increased competition from other forms of accommodation, particularly private 'backpacker hostels' (such as those in Germany or the Czech Republic), have prompted many hostels to improve their facilities and cut back on rules and regulations. Increasingly, hostels are open all day, curfews are disappearing and 'wardens' with sergeant-major mentalities are an endangered species. In some places you'll even find hostels with single and double rooms. Everywhere the trend has been towards smaller dormitories with just four to six beds.

There are many hostel guides available that have listings, including HI's *Europe* (UK £8.50). Some hostels accept reservations by phone or fax but usually not during peak periods; they'll often book the next hostel you're heading to for a small fee. You can also book hostels through national hostel offices. Popular hostels can be heavily booked in summer and limits may even be placed on how many nights you can stay.

University Accommodation

Some universities rent out student accommodation to tourists in July and August. This is quite popular in Poland, Slovakia, the Czech Republic, Hungary and Slovenia; see Places to Stay in those chapters for more details. Accommodation will sometimes be in single rooms (more commonly in doubles or triples) and cooking facilities may be available. Inquire at the college or university, at student information services or at local tourist offices.

Private Rooms, Guesthouses & Hotels

There's a huge range of accommodation above the hostel level. In Hungary and to a lesser degree in the other countries of central Europe, the real bargain in this field is a room in a private home or apartment. In some areas every other house will have a *szoba kiadó* or *Zimmer frei* (rooms for rent) sign out the front. In other countries, similar private accommodation goes under the name of pension, guesthouse, *Gasthaus* and so on. Although the majority are simple affairs, there are more expensive ones where you will find attached bathrooms and other luxuries.

Farmhouse stays are very popular in Slovenia and an excellent way to experience rural life and meet local people. Hay hotels are a unique form of accommodation in Germany.

Above this level are hotels, which at the very bottom of the bracket may be no more expensive than private rooms or guesthouses, while at the other extreme they extend to luxury five-star hotels with price tags to match. You'll often find hotels clustered around the bus and train station areas – always good places to start hunting.

Check your hotel room and the bathroom before you agree to take it, and make sure you know what it's going to cost (eg, if taxes are extra). Ask about breakfast – sometimes it's included, but other times there's an extra yet obligatory charge for it. If the sheets don't look clean, ask to have them changed right away. Check where the fire exits are.

If you think a hotel room is too expensive, ask if they have anything cheaper. In the eastern half of central Europe, hotel owners may be open to a little bargaining if times are slack, particularly in autumn and winter. If you're with a group or plan to stay for a reasonable length of time, it's always worth trying to negotiate a special rate. High-class hotels often have cheaper deals at weekends.

FOOD

Sampling the local food is one of the most enjoyable aspects of travel. Central European cuisine, although often a heavy and stodgy one of goulash, sausages, dumplings, groats and schnitzel, comes into its own in soups, game, the use of forest products (eg, mushrooms and wild berries) and truly extravagant pastries. The Facts for the Visitor sections in the individual country chapters contain details of local cuisines, and the Places to Eat sections list many suggestions.

Restaurant types and prices vary enormously in central Europe. The cheapest place for a decent meal is the self-service cafeteria – often called *buffet* or some variation of the word – still found in Poland, the Czech Republic, Slovakia and, to a lesser extent, Hungary and Slovenia. Elsewhere, department-store restaurants are a good bet. Meals at an official student *mensa* (university restaurant) are very cheap, but the food tends to be bland, and it's not always clear whether you'll be allowed in if you're not a local student. Kiosks often sell cheap snacks that can be as much a part of the national cuisine as fancy dishes.

Self-catering can be a cheap and wholesome way of eating. Even if you don't cook, a lunch on a park bench (or on a mountain top!) with a fresh loaf of bread, some local cheese and salami and a tomato or two, washed down with a bottle of local wine, can be a recurring highlight of your trip.

If you have dietary restrictions – you're a vegetarian or you keep kosher, for example – tourist organisations may be able to advise you or provide lists of suitable restaurants. Some vegetarian and kosher restaurants are listed in this book.

Vegetarians won't starve. Vegetarianism has taken off in central Europe (a part of the world that has traditionally been *very* big on meat), although not everywhere to the same extent. Many restaurants have one or two vegetarian dishes, such as deep-fried mushroom caps, pasta dishes with cheese, vegetable dumplings, or Greek-style 'peasant' salads. Others might prepare special dishes on request as long as you approach them about this in advance.

DRINKS

If you like beer, you'll probably already know all about the liquid pleasures available in Germany and the Czech Republic – experiencing their beer halls is almost a cultural necessity. Yet beer is a treat in most of the countries in this region. Even Poland, formerly a country where the choice was vodka or vodka (albeit with interesting flavoured varieties), has some decent home-brewed beers. Wine – both red and white – is also pretty good, with most countries producing their own vintages. For more detail on local specialities, such as Hungarian *pálinka* (a strong brandy), turn to the country chapters.

Getting There & Away

In these days of strong competition among airlines, there are many opportunities to find cheap tickets to a variety of European cities that provide a gateway for your central European travel.

Some travellers still arrive or depart overland; the options are Africa, the Middle East and Asia, and the Commonwealth of Independent States region. The Trans-Siberian, Trans-Mongolian and Trans-Manchurian express trains carry travellers to and from Europe through Russia, Central Asia and China. See the Land section later in this chapter for more information.

Forget shipping – unless by 'shipping' you mean the ferry services operating in the English Channel, the Baltic Sea between central Europe and Scandinavia or those linking southern Europe and North Africa. Only a handful of ships still carry passengers across the Atlantic; they don't sail often and are very expensive, even compared with full-fare air tickets. The days of ocean liners as modes of transport are well and truly over, but if you're still keen, see the Sea section at the end of this chapter for details.

You can find useful websites with information on travel planning and ticket prices under the Digital Resources section of the Facts for the Visitor chapter of this book.

AIR
Buying Tickets

With a bit of research – ringing around travel agencies, checking Internet sites, perusing the travel ads in newspapers – you can often get yourself a good travel deal. Start early as some of the cheapest tickets need to be bought well in advance and popular flights can sell out.

Generally, there is nothing to be gained by buying a ticket direct from the airline. Discounted tickets are released to selected travel agencies and specialist discount agencies, and these are usually the cheapest deals going. One exception to this rule is the expanding number of no-frills carriers, which mostly only sell direct to travellers. Unlike the full-service airlines, no-frills carriers often make one-way tickets available at around half the return fare, meaning that it is much easier to put together an open-jaw

---

> ### Warning
>
> The information in this chapter is particularly vulnerable to change: Prices for international travel are volatile, routes are introduced and cancelled, schedules change, special deals come and go, and rules and visa requirements are amended. Airlines and governments seem to take a perverse pleasure in making price structures and regulations as complicated as possible. You should check directly with the airline or a travel agent to make sure you understand how a fare (and ticket you may buy) works. In addition, the travel industry is highly competitive and there are many lurks and perks. The upshot of this is that you should get opinions, quotes and advice from as many airlines and travel agents as possible before you part with your hard-earned cash. The details given in this chapter should be regarded as pointers and are not a substitute for your own careful, up-to-date research.

ticket (flying to one place but leaving from another).

The other exception is booking on the Internet. Many airlines, full-service and no-frills, offer some excellent fares to Net surfers. They may sell seats by auction or simply cut prices to reflect the reduced cost of electronic selling. Many travel agencies around the world have websites, which can make the Internet a quick and easy way to compare prices. There's also an increasing number of online agencies that operate only on the Internet. Online ticket sales work well if you are doing a simple one-way or return trip on specified dates. However, online superfast fare generators are no substitute for a travel agent who knows all about special deals, has strategies for avoiding layovers and can offer advice on everything from which airline has the best vegetarian food to the best travel insurance to bundle with your ticket.

You may find the cheapest flights are advertised by obscure agencies. Most such firms are honest and solvent, but there are some rogue fly-by-night outfits around. Paying by credit card generally offers protection, as most card issuers provide refunds if you can prove you didn't get what you paid for. Similar protection can be obtained by buying a ticket from a bonded agency, such as one covered by the Air Travel Organisers' Licensing (ATOL) scheme in the UK. Agencies who accept only cash should hand over the tickets straight away and not tell you to 'come back tomorrow'. After you've made a booking or paid your deposit, call the airline and confirm that the booking was made. It's generally not advisable to send money (even cheques) through the post unless the agency is very well established – some travellers have reported being ripped off by fly-by-night mail-order ticket agencies.

If you purchase a ticket and later want to make changes to your route or get a refund, you need to contact the original travel agency. Airlines issue refunds only to the purchaser of a ticket – usually the travel agency who bought the ticket on your behalf. Many travellers change their routes halfway through their trips, so think carefully before you buy a ticket which is not easily refunded. Don't bother buying half-used tickets from other travellers, no matter how low the price. You won't be able to board the flight unless the name on the ticket matches the one on your passport.

You may decide to pay more than the rock-bottom fare by opting for the safety of a better-known travel agency. Firms such as STA Travel, with offices worldwide, are long-standing companies that offer good prices to most destinations.

Round-the-World (RTW) tickets are a useful option for long-haul travellers. Usually the tickets are valid for between 90 days and a year. Make sure you understand what restrictions apply – there'll be a limit to how many stops (or kilometres/miles) you are permitted, and you won't be able to backtrack. Prices start at about UK£720, A$2250 or US$1450, depending on the number of stops, the route and the season. For short-term travel, cheaper fares are available by travelling mid-week, staying away at least one Saturday night or taking advantage of short-lived promotional fares.

Student & Youth Fares

Full-time students and people under 26 years (under 30 in some countries) have access to better deals than other travellers. The better deals may not always be cheaper fares but can include more flexibility in changing flights and/or routes. You have to show a document proving your date of birth or a valid International Student Identity Card (ISIC) or an International Youth Travel Card (IYTC) when buying your ticket and boarding the plane. See W www.istc.org for more information.

Courier Flights

Another option if you're after cheap fares is a courier flight, where an air-freight company uses your checked luggage allowance to send its parcels. The drawbacks are that your stay in Europe may be limited to one or two weeks, your luggage is usually restricted to hand luggage, and there is unlikely to be more than one courier ticket available for any given flight. Courier flights are occasionally advertised in newspapers, or check the telephone book for air-freight companies. You may even have to go to the air-freight company to get an answer – the companies aren't always keen to give out information over the phone.

You can find out more about courier flights from the **International Association of Air Travel Couriers** (W *www.courier.org in the USA*, W *www.aircourier.co.uk in the UK*). Joining the association costs US$45 or UK£32, but this does not guarantee a flight. **Travel Unlimited** (*PO Box 1058, Allston, MA 02134, USA*) is a US-based monthly travel newsletter that publishes many courier flight deals from destinations worldwide.

Travellers with Special Needs

If they are warned early enough, airlines can often make special arrangements for travellers, such as wheelchair assistance at airports or vegetarian meals on the flight. Children under two years fly for 10% of the standard fare (or free on some airlines) as long as they do not occupy a seat. They also don't get a baggage allowance. 'Skycots', baby food and nappies (diapers) should be provided by the airline if requested in advance. Children aged between two and 12 can usually occupy a seat for around two-thirds of the full fare, and do get a baggage allowance.

The disability-friendly website W www .everybody.co.uk has an airline directory that provides information on the facilities offered by various airlines.

The USA

The flight options across the north Atlantic, the world's busiest long-haul air corridor, are bewildering. The *New York Times*, *LA Times*, *Chicago Tribune* and *San Francisco Chronicle* all have weekly travel sections in which you'll find any number of ads for consolidators (discount travel agencies). San Francisco is the ticket consolidator capital of America, although some good deals can be found in Los Angeles, New York and other big cities. **Priceline** (W *www.priceline.com*) is a 'name-your-price' auction service on the Web.

STA (☎ *800 781 4040;* W *www.statravel.com*) has offices in major cities nationwide. You should be able to fly from New York to London and back for around US$450 in the low season (September to May) and US$750 in the high season; even lower promotional or restricted validity flights are sometimes on offer. Equivalent fares from the west coast are US$100 to US$300 higher. Directly into Budapest, prices start at about US$550 return in the low season.

On a stand-by basis, one-way fares can work out to be remarkably cheap. New York-based **Airhitch** (☎ *212-864 2000;* W *www.airhitch.org*) specialises in this sort of thing and can get you between Europe and the east coast/Midwest/west coast for as little as US$165/199/233 each way, plus taxes and a processing fee.

An interesting alternative to the boring New York to London flight is offered by **Icelandair** (☎ *800 223 5500;* W *www.icelandair.com*), which flies from northeastern USA to several European cities. You can include a three-night stopover in Iceland's capital, Reykjavík – a great way to spend a few days in a country that's otherwise hard to get to. New York to Frankfurt costs about US$860 return.

Travelling as a courier, a New York to London return ticket can be bought for as little as US$300 in the low season. You may also be able to fly one-way. See Courier Flights earlier in this chapter.

Canada

Canadian discount air-ticket sellers are also known as consolidators and their air fares tend to be about 10% higher than those sold in the USA. **Travel CUTS** (☎ *800 667 2887;* W *www.travelcuts.com*) is Canada's national student travel agency and has offices in all major cities. The *Globe & Mail*, *Toronto Star* and *Vancouver Sun* newspapers all carry travel agency ads offering discounted fares. Airhitch (see The USA section, previous) has stand-by fares to/from Toronto, Montreal and Vancouver.

The UK

If you are looking for a cheap way into or out of central Europe, London is Europe's major centre for discounted fares. You should be able to fly from London to any of the following cities and back for between UK£100 and UK£165: Berlin, Budapest, Frankfurt, Geneva, Munich, Prague, Vienna, Warsaw and Zürich. Flying is more convenient and probably cheaper than the equivalent journey by bus or train.

The no-frills airlines, **Ryanair** (W *www.ryanair.co.uk*), **easyJet** (W *www.easyjet.com*) and **Go** (W *www.go-fly.com*), have cheap flights into Germany, Switzerland, the Czech Republic and Slovakia in central Europe. Otherwise you could take one of these carriers to a more westerly city such as Paris and travel on from there.

Courier flights are a possibility, although European Union (EU) integration and electronic communications mean there's increasingly less call for couriers. See that section earlier for more information.

For students and travellers under 26, a popular travel agency is **STA Travel** (☎ *020-7361 6161;* W *www.statravel.co.uk*) with branches in London and across the country. STA sells tickets to all travellers but caters especially to young people and students. Other recommended travel agencies include **Trailfinders** (☎ *020-7938 1234;* W *www.trailfinders.co.uk; 215 Kensington High St, London W8*), which also has branches in Manchester, Glasgow and other British cities; **Bridge the World** (☎ *020-7734 7447;* W *www.b-t-w.co.uk; 4 Regent Place, London W1*); and **Flightbookers** (☎ *020-7757 2000;* W *www.ebookers.com; 34-42 Woburn Place, London WC1*).

Charter flights can work out as a cheaper alternative to scheduled flights, especially if you do not qualify for the under-26 and student discounts. See a travel agency for possibilities.

Advertisements for many travel agencies appear in the travel pages of the weekend broadsheets, in *Time Out*, the *Evening Standard* and in the free magazine *TNT*.

The Rest of Europe

Although London is the travel discount capital of Europe, there are several other cities in the region where you'll find a wide range of good deals. STA Travel has offices throughout Europe where cheap tickets can be purchased and STA-issued tickets can be altered (usually for a fee). Check out its website for locations and contact details. **Nouvelles Frontières** (W *www.nouvelles-frontieres .com)* also has branches throughout the world.

France has a network of student travel agencies that can supply discount tickets to travellers of all ages. **OTU Voyages** (☎ *0820 817 817;* W *www.otu.fr)* and **Voyageurs du Monde** (☎ *01 42 86 16 00;* W *www.vdm .com)* have branches throughout the country and offer some of the best services and deals. **CTS Viaggi** (☎ *840 501 150;* W *www.cts.it)* is a student and youth specialist in Italy. In Spain recommended agencies include **Usit Unlimited** (☎ *902 25 25 75;* W *www.unlim ited.es)* and **Barcelo Viajes** (☎ *902 116 226;* W *www.barceloviajes.es).*

Scheduled flights between Paris and Warsaw start at about €345 return and at around €300 on the Barcelona to Warsaw route.

Australia

STA (☎ *131 776;* W *www.statravel.com.au)* and **Flight Centre** (☎ *131 600;* W *www .flightcentre.com.au)* are major dealers in cheap air fares. **Student Uni Travel** (☎ *02-9232 7300;* W *sut.com.au)* specialises in the youth/backpacker market. Saturday's travel sections in the *Sydney Morning Herald* and Melbourne's *The Age* have many ads offering cheap fares to Europe. With Australia's large and well-organised ethnic populations, it pays to check special deals in the ethnic press.

Thai Airways International, Malaysia Airways, Qantas Airways and Singapore Airlines flights to Europe start from about A$1500 (low season) up to A$2500. All have frequent promotional fares so it pays to check daily newspapers. Flights from Perth are a couple of hundred dollars cheaper than from east-coast cities.

Another option for travellers to get to Britain between November and February is to hook up with a returning charter flight. These low-season, one-way fares do have restrictions, but may work out to be considerably cheaper. Ask your travel agent for details.

New Zealand

As in Australia, STA and Flight Centre are popular travel agencies in New Zealand. **Student Uni Travel** (☎ *09-379 4224;* W *www .sut.co.nz)* has offices in Auckland, Christchurch and Hamilton. Also check the *New Zealand Herald* for ads. The cheapest fares to Europe are routed through Asia; a discounted return ticket to Europe from Auckland starts at around NZ$2100. A RTW ticket is about NZ$2850.

Africa

Nairobi and Johannesburg are probably the best places in East and South Africa to buy tickets to Europe. One of the best agencies in Nairobi is **Flight Centre** (☎ *02-210 024; 2nd floor, Lakhamshi House, Biashara St).* A return Nairobi to Zürich flight on Emirates Airlines starts as low as US$600, although with a limited period of validity. In Johannesburg **STA Travel** (☎ *011-447 5414;* e *rosebank@statravel.co.za; Mutual Square, Rosebank)* and **Rennies Travel** (☎ *011-833 1441;* W *www.renniestravel.co.za, Unitas Bldg, 42 Marshall St)* are recommended. A return flight to Berlin will cost from R7000.

Several West African countries such as Burkina Faso, Gambia and Morocco offer cheap charter flights to France, from where you can continue to central Europe.

Asia

Hong Kong, Singapore and Bangkok are the discount air-fare capitals of Asia, but ask the advice of other travellers before handing over any money for tickets in these cities. In Singapore **STA** (☎ *737 7188;* W *www.statravel .com.sg; 35a Cuppage Rd, Cuppage Terrace)* offers competitive fares. In Hong Kong try **Phoenix Services** (☎ *2722 7378; Rm B, 6th floor, Milton mansion, 96 Nathan Rd, Tsim Sha Tsui).*

In India, cheap tickets can be bought from the bucket shops around Connaught Place in Delhi. Check with other travellers about the most trustworthy ones.

LAND
Bus

International bus travel tends to take second place to going by train. The bus has the edge in terms of cost, but is generally slower and less comfortable. Europe's biggest network of international buses is provided by a group of companies operating under the name **Eurolines** (W *www.eurolines.co.uk*). The website has a complete list of representatives in Europe. These offices may also be able to advise you on other bus companies and deals.

Eurolines also offers passes. Compared with rail passes, they're cheaper but not as extensive or as flexible. The Eurolines pass covers 31 European cities including Berlin, Budapest, Cologne, Frankfurt, Hamburg, Kraków, Munich, Prague, Vienna, Warsaw and Zürich in central Europe. The cost is UK£229 for 30 days (UK£186 for those under 26 or over 60) or UK£267 for 60 days (UK£205). The passes are cheaper in the low season (mid-September to the end of May).

On ordinary return trips, youths under 26 and seniors over 60 pay around 10% less and there are also off-peak and promotional discounts. The adult/youth fares from London in the high season are UK£119/107 to Budapest, UK£87/79 to Prague and UK£79/75 to Warsaw. Return tickets are valid for six months.

Busabout (☎ *020-7950 1661;* W *www .busabout.com*) operates buses that complete set circuits around Europe, stopping at major cities. You get unlimited travel per sector, and can 'hop on, hop off' at any scheduled stop, then resume with a later bus. Buses are often oversubscribed, so prebook each sector to avoid being stranded. Departures are every two days from April to October. The circuits cover all countries in continental Western Europe, including the western part of central Europe (not Poland, Hungary, Slovakia or Slovenia).

Busabout's Consecutive Pass allows unlimited travel within the given time period. For two/three weeks the cost is UK£179/249 for adults or UK£159/219 for students and those under 26. Passes are also available for one, two or three months, or for the whole season from April to September (adult/concession UK£699/629). The Flexipass allows you to select travel days within the given time period. Six days in one month costs UK£169/149, while 20 days in three months is UK£479/429. Starting your trip before mid-May will also get you a reduced rate.

See the individual country chapters for more information about long-distance buses.

Train

The *Thomas Cook European Timetable* is the trainophile's bible, giving a complete listing of schedules, supplements and reservations information. It is updated monthly and is available from any outlet of **Thomas Cook** (☎ *800 367 7984 in USA*).

The UK The Channel Tunnel allows for a land link between Britain and France, from where you can continue into central Europe. The **Eurostar** (☎ *020-7928 5163 in the UK, 08 36 35 35 39 in France;* W *www.eu rostar.com*) passenger train service travels between London and Paris (three hours) and London and Brussels (2¾ hours). The **Eurotunnel** (☎ *08705-353 535 in the UK, 03 21 00 61 00 in France;* W *www.eurotunnel .com*) vehicle service travels between terminals in Folkestone and Calais. This train carries cars, motorcycles and bicycles with their passengers and riders. Prices for both train and vehicle service vary, depending on the time of year, the days of travel and how far ahead you book.

The Rest of Europe To get to individual countries in central Europe see the Getting There & Away sections of those chapters. However, rail passes are another alternative for reaching some of these countries from other parts of Europe. See the Getting Around chapter for details of passes that include central European countries.

Africa & the Mediterranean Morocco and most of Turkey lie outside Europe, but the rail systems of both countries are still covered by Inter-Rail (Zone F & Zone G respectively). Most of Europe's rail routes pass through central Europe, although coming from Morocco you'll probably have to change trains in France. For details of rail passes see the Getting Around chapter.

Asia It *is* possible to get to central Europe by rail from central and eastern Asia, although count on spending at least eight days doing it. You can choose from four different routes to Moscow. They are the Trans-Siberian (from Vladivostok), the Trans-Mongolian (from Beijing) and the Trans-Manchurian (from Beijing via Harbin), which all use the same tracks across Siberia but have different routes east of Lake Baikal. There is also the

Trans-Kazakhstan, which runs between Moscow and Urumqi in northwestern China. Prices vary enormously, depending on where you buy the ticket and what is included. Information is also available from the **Russian National Tourist Office** (W *www.interknowledge.com/Russia*). Lonely Planet's *Trans-Siberian Railway* is a comprehensive guide to the route with details of costs, travel agencies who specialise in the trip and highlights. *The Big Red Train Ride* by Eric Newby is a good choice as reading material to take along for the ride.

There are countless travel options between Moscow and the rest of Europe. Most people will opt for the train, usually to/from Berlin, Helsinki, Munich, Budapest or Vienna.

Car & Motorcycle

Driving in Europe is pretty straightforward, and usually pleasurable. For detailed information, turn to the Getting Around chapter. If you're coming from northern Europe and want to save most of your driving until you reach central Europe, consider putting your vehicle on a motorail train, run by the national railways. There are different routes through France (see W www.frenchmotorail.com) and Germany (see W www.bahn.de).

Travelling by private transport beyond Europe requires plenty of paperwork and other preparations. You'll need to do your own research – a detailed description is beyond the scope of this book. Check with your local automobile association as a start.

Overland Trails

The overland trail to/from Asia through Iran is still possible but, at the time of writing, unsettled conditions in Afghanistan, southern Pakistan and northwestern India make this route inadvisable without careful assessment of the situation. Check with your own foreign office before making a decision.

Discounting the complicated Middle East route, going to/from Africa involves a Mediterranean ferry crossing (see the following Sea section). Due to unrest in Africa, the most feasible overland routes through the continent have all but closed down.

SEA
Channel Ferries

Several ferry companies compete on all the main ferry routes, and the resulting service is comprehensive but complicated. The same ferry company can have different prices for the same route, depending upon the time of day or year, the validity of the ticket or, if you're driving, the length of your vehicle. It is worth planning (and booking) ahead where possible as there may be special reductions on off-peak crossings and advance-purchase tickets. Most ferry companies adjust prices according to the level of demand (so-called 'fluid' or 'dynamic' pricing) so it may pay to be flexible with your travel dates. Vehicle tickets usually include the driver and passengers.

P&O Stena Line (W *www.posl.com*) is one of the largest ferry companies in the world. It services British, Irish and some Scandinavian routes. **P&O Portsmouth** (W *www.poportsmouth.com*) and **Brittany Ferries** (W *www.Brittany-ferries.com*) sail direct between England and northern Spain. The shortest cross-Channel routes (Dover to Calais, and Folkestone to Boulogne) are also the busiest, although there is now great competition from the Channel Tunnel. The French line **Seafrance** (W *www.seafrance.com*) also operates across the Channel. You can book ferry tickets online (often at a discount). Catamarans operated by **Hoverspeed** (☎ 08 705-240 241 in the UK; W *www.hoverspeed.co.uk*) are quicker than ferries – Dover to Calais takes about an hour – yet prices are competitive.

Rail-pass holders are entitled to discounts or free travel on some lines, and most ferry companies give discounts to drivers with disabilities. Food on ferries is often expensive (and lousy), so it's worth bringing your own when possible. It's also worth knowing that if you take your vehicle on board, you're usually denied access to it during the voyage.

Baltic & North Sea Ferries

Central Europe can be reached from the north, west and east by ferry via the North or Baltic Seas. **DFDS Seaways** (W *www.dfdsseaways.com*) has direct services between Harwich in the UK and Hamburg at least three times a week, and a slew of other seacraft transport cars and people between Germany and Scandinavia. Daily scheduled services by **Stena Line** (W *www.stenaline.com*) from Kiel travel to Gothenburg in Sweden (14 hours) and **Colorline** (W *www.colorline.de*) goes all the way to Oslo in Norway (19½ hours). There are also ferries to

Denmark, Sweden and/or Finland from the eastern German ports of Rostock, Travemünde and, on Rügen Island, Sassnitz.

Poland also has a ferry service – year-round for the most part – to and from Scandinavia. Routings include Gdynia to Karlskrona and Świnoujście to Copenhagen. See Getting There & Away in the Germany and Poland chapters for more details.

Mediterranean Ferries

There are many ferries across the Mediterranean between Africa and Europe. The ferry you take will depend on your travels in Africa, but options include: Spain to Morocco, Italy to Tunisia, France to Morocco, and France to Tunisia. There are also ferries between Greece and Israel via Cyprus. Boats are often filled to capacity in summer, especially to and from Tunisia, so book well in advance if you're taking a vehicle across. Companies operating on these routes include **Ferrimaroc** (W *www.ferrimaroc.com*) and **SNCM** (W *www.sncm.fr*).

Passenger Ships & Freighters

Regular, long-distance passenger ships disappeared with the advent of cheap air travel, leaving a small number of luxury cruise ships. **Cunard** (W *www.cunard.com*) has the *Queen Elizabeth 2*, which sails between New York and Southampton about 20 times a year; the trip takes six nights. Special deals are as low as US$999 for the crossing including a one-way economy air fare.

A more adventurous alternative is as a paying passenger on a freighter. Freighters are far more numerous than cruise ships and there are many more routes from which to choose. With a bit of homework, you'll be able to sail between Europe and just about anywhere else in the world, with stopovers at exotic ports.

Passenger freighters typically carry five to 12 passengers (more than 12 would require a doctor on board) and, although less luxurious than dedicated cruise ships, you'll get a real taste of life at sea. Schedules tend to be flexible and costs are about $150 a day; vehicles can often be included for an additional fee. Get an idea of what's available at the website W *www.freighter-travel.com*.

DEPARTURE TAX

Some countries in central Europe charge you a fee for the privilege of leaving from their airports. Some also charge port fees when you are leaving by ship. Such fees are often included in the ticket price, but it pays to check this when purchasing your ticket. If not, you will have to have the fee ready when you leave – usually in local currency. Details are given in the relevant country chapters.

Getting Around

Travel within most of the European Union (EU), whether by air, rail or car, has been made easier following the Schengen Agreement. This abolished border controls between signatory countries. In central Europe the only two Schengen countries that are also EU members are Germany and Austria. Getting around the rest of the region does not provide too much of a problem, however, thanks to a comprehensive transport network and good relations between neighbouring countries. Ensure that you have a valid passport and check visa requirements with the appropriate authorities.

AIR

Air travel is best viewed as a means to get you to the starting point of your itinerary rather than as your main means of travel. It lacks the flexibility of ground transport and tends to be expensive for short trips. Occasionally, you will find low fares and special deals. In order to secure the best price, shop around and be prepared to be flexible with travel dates.

BUS

Buses provide a viable alternative to the rail network in most central European countries. Generally they tend to complement the rail system rather than duplicate it, although in some countries – notably Hungary, the Czech Republic and Slovakia – you will almost always have a choice.

Eurolines (see the Bus section in the Getting There & Away chapter for details about passes) has representatives within central Europe. They include:

Deutsche-Touring (☎ 069-230 735) Mannheimerstrasse 4, Frankfurt am Main 60329
Eurolines Austria (☎ 01-712 04 53) Autobusbahnhof Wien-Mitte, Landstrasser Hauptstrasse, 1030 Vienna
Eurolines Czech Republic (☎ 2 24 21 34 20) Opletalova 37, Prague 1
Eurolines Poland (☎ 022-870 59 40) Centrum Rezerwacj, Grochowsja 207, Warsaw
Volanbusz (☎ 1-117 2562) 1st floor, Erzsebet Ter Bus Station, Budapest

In general, buses are slightly cheaper and slower than trains in western central Europe

and a bit more expensive or the same price in eastern central Europe. Buses are best used for shorter hops such as getting around cities and reaching remote rural villages. They are often the only option in mountainous regions (eg, in Austria and Slovenia) where trains fear to tread (or roll). The other good thing about buses is that advance reservations are rarely necessary. Many city buses operate on a pay-in-advance system (where you punch your own ticket after boarding) and offer some good-value day and weekly passes. See the individual country chapters and city sections for more details.

TRAIN

Trains are a popular way to get around in central Europe: they are good meeting places, generally comfortable, frequent and run on time. In some countries, such as those in the eastern half of central Europe, fares are partly subsidised; in others, some sort of rail pass will make travel more affordable. Supplements and reservation costs are not covered by passes, and pass-holders must always carry their passport on the train for identification purposes.

If you plan to travel extensively by train, it might be worth getting hold of the *Thomas Cook European Timetable*, which gives a complete listing of train schedules and indicates where supplements apply or where reservations are necessary. It is updated monthly and is available from **Thomas Cook** (W *www.thomascook.com*) outlets in the UK, and from **Forsyth Travel Library** (☎ 800-367 7984; W *www.forsyth.com*) in the USA. Check out the websites. In Australia, look for it in one of the bigger bookstores, which can order in copies if they don't have any in stock.

If you are planning to do a lot of train travel in one or a handful of countries – Hungary, the Czech Republic and Slovakia, for instance – it might be worthwhile getting hold of the national timetable(s) published by the state railroad(s). The *European Planning & Rail Guide* is an informative annual magazine, primarily geared towards North American travellers. To get a copy, call the toll-free US number ☎ 877-441 2387, or visit the website at W www.budgeteuropetravel.com. It's free within the USA; send US$3 if you want it posted anywhere else.

The central European cities of Munich, Vienna and Berlin are important hubs for international rail connections. See the relevant city sections for details.

Note that European trains sometimes split en route in order to service two different destinations, so even if you know you're on the right train, make sure you're in the correct carriage, too.

Express Trains

Fast trains or ones that make few stops are identified by the symbols EC (EuroCity) or IC (InterCity). The German ICE is an even faster train. Supplements can apply on fast trains, and it's a good idea (sometimes obligatory) to make seat reservations at peak times and on certain lines.

Overnight Trains

Overnight trains will usually offer a choice of couchette or sleeper if you don't fancy sleeping in your seat with somebody else's elbow in your ear. Again, reservations are advisable as sleeping options are allocated on a first-come, first-served basis.

Couchette bunks are comfortable enough, if lacking a bit in privacy. There are four per compartment in 1st class or six in 2nd class. A bunk costs around UK£10 (in addition to the ticket price) for most international trains, irrespective of the length of the journey.

Sleepers are the most comfortable option, offering beds for one or two passengers in 1st class, and two or three passengers in 2nd class. Charges vary depending upon the journey, but they are significantly more expensive than couchettes. Most long-distance trains have a dining (buffet) car or an attendant who wheels a snack trolley through carriages. If possible, buy your food before travelling as on-board prices tend to be high.

Security

You should be safe travelling on most trains in central Europe but be security conscious nonetheless. Keep an eye on your luggage at all times (especially when stopping at stations) and lock compartment doors at night.

Rail Passes

Shop around, as pass prices can vary between different outlets. Once purchased, take care

of your pass, as it cannot be replaced or refunded if lost or stolen. European passes get reductions on *Eurostar* through the Channel Tunnel and on ferries on certain routes. In the USA, **Rail Europe** (☎ 800 438 7245; W *www.raileurope.com*) sells all sorts of rail passes. See the website.

Eurail These passes can be bought only by residents of non-European countries, and are supposed to be purchased before arriving in Europe. Eurail passes *can* be purchased within Europe, as long as your passport proves you've been there for less than six months, but the outlets where you can do this are limited and the passes will be more expensive than getting them outside of Europe. In London, **Rail Europe** (☎ 0870 584 8848; 179 Piccadilly; W *www.raileurope.co.uk*) is one such outlet. If you've lived in Europe for more than six months, you are eligible for an Inter-Rail pass, which is a better buy.

Eurail passes are valid for unlimited travel on national railways and some private lines but the only countries in central Europe covered by Eurail are Austria, Germany, Hungary and Switzerland (including Liechtenstein). The passes do *not* cover Poland, the Czech Republic, Slovenia or Slovakia, so they are not ideal for tours of this region. If you are also travelling in other parts of Europe, this pass would be worthwhile.

Eurail passes offer reasonable value to people aged under 26. A Youthpass gives unlimited 2nd-class travel within a choice of five validity periods: 15/21 days which costs UK£325/415 or one/two/three months for UK£525/740/925. The Youth Flexipass, also for 2nd class, is valid for a specified number of days within a two-month period: 10 days for UK£390 or 15 days for UK£510. Overnight journeys commencing after 7pm count as the following day's travel. The traveller must fill out in ink the relevant box in the calendar on the pass before starting a day's travel.

For travellers aged over 26, the equivalent passes provide 1st-class travel. A standard Eurail pass costs UK£470/605 for 15/21 days or UK£750/1065/1320 for one/two/three months. The Flexipass costs UK£545/730 for 10/15 days within two months.

Two to five people travelling together can get a 'saver' version of either pass, saving about 15%. Eurail passes for children are also available.

Europass Also for non-Europeans, the Europass gives unlimited travel on freely chosen days within a two-month period. Youth (aged under 26) and adult (solo, or two to five sharing) versions are available. Purchasing requirements and sales outlets are as for Eurail passes. They are cheaper than Eurail passes but only cover Germany and Switzerland in central Europe. The youth/adult price for the minimum five travel days is UK£190/295; it costs UK£430/615 for a maximum 15 days. Certain 'associate countries' (including Austria and Hungary) can be added on to the basic pass. Prices vary.

Inter-Rail These passes are available to European residents of more than six months' standing (passport identification is required). Terms and conditions vary slightly from country to country, but in the country of origin there is only a discount of around 50% on normal fares.

The Inter-Rail pass is split into zones covering most of Europe. A number of central European countries are covered. Zone C includes Germany, Switzerland and Austria; zone D is the Czech Republic, Slovakia, Poland, Hungary and Croatia; and zone G includes Turkey and Slovenia.

The normal Inter-Rail pass is for people under 26, although travellers over 26 can get the Inter-Rail 26+ version. The price for any one zone is UK£139 (UK£209 for 26+) for 22 days. Multizone passes are valid for one month: two zones cost UK£189 (UK£265), three zones UK£209 (UK£299) and the all-zone global pass is UK£249 (UK£355).

Euro Domino There is a Euro Domino pass for each of the countries covered in the Inter-Rail pass, and they're worth considering if you're homing in on a particular region. They're sold in Europe to European residents. Adults (travelling 1st or 2nd class) and youths under 26 can opt for three to eight days' free travel within one month. Examples of adult/youth prices for eight days in 2nd class are UK£52/39 for Slovenia and UK£167/125 for Germany.

European East Pass This is sold in North America and Australia and is valid in Austria,

Hungary, Poland, the Czech Republic and Slovakia. In the USA, **Rail Europe** (☎ 800 257 2887; W www.raileurope.com) charges US$220 for five days' 1st-class travel within one month; extra rail days (five maximum) cost $25 each.

National Rail Passes If you intend to travel extensively within one country, check which national rail passes are available; most countries in central Europe have them. These can sometimes save you a lot of money; see the Getting Around sections in the individual country chapters for details. Plan ahead if you intend to take this option – some passes can only be purchased prior to arrival in the country concerned. Some national flexipasses, similar to the Domino passes mentioned earlier, are only available to non-Europeans.

Cheap Tickets

European rail passes are only worth buying if you plan to do a reasonable amount of inter-country travelling within a short space of time. Plan your itinerary carefully. Don't overdo the overnight travelling. Although it can work out to be a great way of saving time and money you don't want to be too tired to enjoy the next day of sightseeing.

When weighing up options, consider the cost of other cheap ticket deals, including advance purchase reductions, one-off promotions or special circular-route tickets. Normal international tickets are valid for two months, and you can make as many stops as you like en route; make your intentions known when purchasing, and inform the train conductor how far you're going before they punch your ticket.

In some of the eastern countries of central Europe, tickets to and from the countries of the former Soviet bloc are still heavily discounted – in Hungary reductions are 30% to 70% on regular prices. In Germany, there are special deals for train travel on the weekends. See the individual country chapters for details.

For a small fee, European residents can buy a Railplus Card, entitling the holder to a 25% discount on international train journeys. In most countries it is sold only to people over 60 who hold a valid seniors card (eg, a British Senior Card in the UK). However, some national rail networks may make the Railplus Card available also to young people or other travellers. The Railplus card costs UK£12 and lasts for one year.

CAR & MOTORCYCLE

Travelling with your own vehicle allows increased flexibility and the option to get off the beaten track. Unfortunately, cars can be inconvenient in city centres when you have to negotiate strange one-way systems or find somewhere to park in a confusing concrete jungle.

Paperwork & Preparations

Proof of ownership of a private vehicle should always be carried (a Vehicle Registration Document for British-registered cars) when touring Europe. An EU driving licence is acceptable for driving throughout central Europe, and generally North American and Australian ones are too. To be on the safe side – or if you have any other type of licence – you should obtain an International Driving Permit (IDP) from your motoring organisation (see Visas & Documents in the Facts for the Visitor chapter). Always check what type of licence is required in your chosen destination prior to departure.

Third-party motor insurance is compulsory in Europe. Most UK motor insurance policies automatically provide this for EU countries. Get your insurer to issue a Green Card (which may cost extra), an internationally recognised proof of insurance, and check that it lists all the countries you intend to visit. You'll need this in the event of an accident outside the country where the vehicle is insured. The European Accident Statement (known as as the 'Constat Amiable' in France) is available from your insurance company and is copied so that each party at an accident can record identical information for insurance purposes. The Association of British Insurers can give more information. Never sign statements you can't read or understand – insist on a translation and sign that only if it's acceptable. For non-EU countries make sure you check the requirements with your insurer. For further advice and information contact the **Association of British Insurers** (☎ 020-7600 3333; **W** www.abi.org.uk) or check their website.

Taking out a European motoring assistance policy, such as the **AA** (☎ 0870 550 0600) Five Star Service or the **RAC** (☎ 0800 550 055; **W** www.rac.co.uk) European Motoring Assistance, is a good investment. Expect to pay about UK£50 for 14 days' cover with a 10% discount for association members. Non-Europeans might find it cheaper to arrange international coverage with their national motoring organisation before leaving home. Ask your motoring organisation for details about free services offered by affiliated organisations around Europe.

Every vehicle travelling across an international border should display a sticker showing its country of registration. It is compulsory to carry a warning triangle almost everywhere in Europe, which must be displayed in the event of a breakdown. Recommended accessories are a spare bulb kit and a fire extinguisher. A first-aid kit is recommended everywhere and is compulsory in several central European countries, including Austria, Czech Republic, Slovakia and Switzerland. In the UK, contact the RAC or the AA for more information.

Road Rules

Motoring organisations can supply members with country-by-country information about motoring regulations, or they may produce motoring guidebooks for general sale. The RAC provides comprehensive destination-specific notes offering a summary of national road rules and regulations. Contact them by telephone or check their website.

Across central Europe, driving is on the right. Vehicles brought over from the UK or Ireland should have their headlights adjusted to avoid blinding oncoming traffic at night (a simple solution on older headlight lenses is to cover up a triangular section of the lens with tape). This is particularly necessary in Hungary, where by law headlights must be illuminated at all times – day and night – outside built-up areas. Priority is usually given to traffic approaching from the right.

Take care with speed limits, as they vary from country to country. You may be surprised at the apparent disregard of traffic regulations in some places (particularly in Hungary, where driving in general can be a nightmare), but as a visitor it's always best to be cautious. Many driving infringements are subject to an on-the-spot fine in central Europe. Always ask for a receipt.

Central Europeans are particularly strict with drink-driving laws. In most countries, the blood-alcohol concentration (BAC) limit when driving is 0.05% (it's 0.08% in some Western European countries). In Hungary, the Czech Republic and Slovakia the BAC is *zero* per cent, and in Poland it's just 0.02%. You will be breathalysed and fined heavily if the result is positive. In the event of an accident in some of these countries, the drinking party is automatically regarded as guilty and can face imprisonment. See the introductory Getting Around sections in the country chapters for more details on traffic laws.

Roads

Conditions and types of roads vary considerably across central Europe, but it is possible to make some generalisations. The fastest routes are four- or six-lane dual carriageways (motorway, *Autobahn*, *autópálya*, *avtocesta* etc). These roads are great in terms of speed and comfort but driving can be quite dull with little or no interesting scenery. Some motorways and tunnels incur tolls. There's usually an alternative route you can take if you don't want to pay. Austria, the Czech Republic, Slovakia and Switzerland levy a general tax on vehicles using their motorways (see the country chapters for details). Motorways and other primary routes are in good to fair condition, depending on the country.

Road surfaces on minor routes are not so reliable in some countries (eg, the Czech Republic, Slovakia and Poland), although normally they will be more than adequate, and standards are improving. Some back roads are narrow and winding, progress is slow and horse-drawn vehicles, cyclists and pedestrians may be encountered at any time. To compensate, you can expect much better scenery and plenty of interesting villages along the way.

Rental

The big firms will give you reliable service and a good standard of vehicle. Usually you will have the option of returning the car to a different outlet at the end of the rental period. Prebook for the lowest rates – if you walk into an office and ask for a car on the spot, you will pay over the odds, even allowing for special weekend deals. Fly-drive combinations and other programmes are worth looking into. You should be able to make advance reservations online. Check out the websites:

Hertz (**W** www.hertz.com)
Avis (**W** www.avis.com)
Budget (**W** www.budget.com)
Europcar (**W** www.europcar.com)

Brokers can cut hire costs. **Holiday Autos** (**☎** 0870 400 4477 in the UK; **W** www.holidayautos.com • Kemwel Holiday Autos; **☎** 877-820 0668 in the US) has low rates and offices or representatives in over 20 countries. See the website. In the UK a competitor with even lower prices is **Autos Abroad** (**☎** 020-7287 6000; **W** www.autosabroad .co.uk).

If you want to rent a car and haven't prebooked, look for national or local firms, which can often undercut the big companies. Nevertheless, you need to be wary of dodgy deals where they take your money and point you towards some clapped-out wreck.

No matter where you rent, it is imperative to understand exactly what is included in your rental agreement (collision waiver, unlimited mileage etc). Make sure you are covered by an adequate insurance policy. Ask in advance if you can drive a rented car across borders, such as from Germany (where hire prices are low) to Austria (where they're high). Some rental companies do not allow you to drive their cars into certain countries in the eastern corners of central Europe (such as Poland), where car theft is a big problem.

The minimum rental age is usually 21 or even 23, and you'll probably need a credit card. Note that prices at airport rental offices are usually higher than at branches in the city centre.

Motorcycle and moped rental is not very common in most of central Europe, but occasionally bicycle shops and service stations by lakes and along the coasts may oblige. See individual country chapters for details.

Purchase

Britain is probably the best place to buy. Second-hand prices are good and, whether buying privately or from a dealer, the absence of language difficulties (if your first language is English) will help you establish exactly what you are getting and what guarantees you can expect in the event of a breakdown.

Bear in mind that you will be getting a car with the steering wheel on the right in Britain. If you want left-hand drive and can afford to buy new, prices are usually reasonable in Germany. Paperwork can be tricky wherever you buy, and many countries have compulsory roadworthy checks on older vehicles. Do not even consider buying a used car in Poland, Hungary, the Czech Republic or Slovakia. The paperwork is complicated, the after-sale care is nonexistent and the quality of vehicle is generally poor.

Camper Van

A popular way to tour Europe is for three or four people to band together to buy or rent a camper van. London is the usual embarkation point. Look at the advertisements in London's free magazine *TNT* if you wish to form or join a group. *TNT* is also a good source for purchasing a van, as is the *Loot* newspaper.

Some second-hand dealers offer a 'buy-back' scheme for when you return from the Continent, but we've received warnings that some dealers don't fully honour their refund commitments. Anyway, buying and re-selling privately should be more advantageous if you have the time. A reader recommended **Down Under Insurance** (☎ 020-7402 9211; W *www.downunderinsurance.co.uk*) for European cover. Check the website.

Camper vans usually feature a fixed high-top or elevating roof and two to five bunk beds. Apart from the essential camping gas cooker, professional conversions may include a sink, fridge and built-in cupboards. Prices and facilities vary considerably and it's certainly worth getting advice from a mechanic to see if you are being offered a fair price. Getting a mechanical check (from UK£35) is also a good idea. Once on the road you should be able to keep budgets lower than backpackers using trains, but don't forget to set some money aside for emergency repairs.

The main advantage of going by camper van is flexibility. Transport, accommodation and storage are all taken care of in one small unit. Unfortunately the self-contained factor can also prove to be one of the downsides. Conditions can get very cramped, tempers can become easily frayed and your romantic, hippy-style trail may dissolve into the camper van trip from hell. Other disadvantages include having to leave your gear inside when you are exploring. Invest in good locks and try to keep the inside tidy with your belongings stored away at all times.

Motorcycle Touring

Most of central Europe is made for motorcycle touring, with good-quality winding roads and an active motorcycling scene. In places where the roads aren't so good, the stunning scenery more than makes up for the substandard surfaces. You'll need to kill your speed but if you pay adequate attention to the roads you shouldn't incur any damages to you or your bike. Bear in mind that the weather is not always reliable so make sure your wet weather gear is up to scratch.

The wearing of crash helmets for rider and passenger is compulsory everywhere in central Europe. Austria, Germany and Hungary require that motorcyclists also use headlights during the day; in other countries it's recommended.

On ferries, motorcyclists can sometimes be squeezed in without a reservation although booking ahead is certainly advisable during peak travelling periods. In some countries parking motorcycles on pavements (sidewalks) is illegal, but the police may turn a blind eye so long as the vehicle doesn't obstruct pedestrians. Take note of local customs.

If you are thinking of touring Europe on a motorcycle try contacting the **British Motorcyclists Federation** (☎ 0116-254 8818) for help and advice. An excellent source of information for those interested in more adventurous biking activities can be found at W www.horizonsunlimited.com.

Fuel

Fuel prices can vary enormously from country to country (although it's always more expensive than in North America or Australia) and may bear little relation to the general cost of living there; expensive Switzerland is fairly cheap when it comes to fuel, for example, while the opposite is true in inexpensive Hungary. Savings can be made if you fill up in the right place – for example, in Poland, before heading for Germany, in Slovenia before Italy, or Romania before anywhere. Motoring organisations such as the RAC can give more details.

Unleaded petrol is now widely available throughout central Europe (but maybe not at the odd station on back roads in the eastern countries). Diesel is usually much cheaper in central Europe, although the difference is only marginal in Switzerland.

TAXI

Taxis in countries such as Germany, Austria, Switzerland and Liechtenstein are an expensive luxury and best avoided. They are metered and rates are high (watch your savings ebb away), plus there may be supplements for luggage, the time of day, the day of the week, the location where you boarded, extra people in the cab etc. Good bus, rail and metro (subway) networks make the taking of taxis all but unnecessary, but if you need one in a hurry, they can usually be found idling near train stations.

In Poland, the Czech Republic, Slovakia, Slovenia and Hungary, lower fares make taxis more viable, but scams and rip-offs (eg, in the Czech Republic and to some extent Hungary) can make taking a cab an unpleasant, expensive and even dangerous experience.

Don't underestimate the local knowledge that can be gleaned from taxi drivers. They can often tell you about the liveliest places in town and know all about events happening during your stay.

BICYCLE

A tour of central Europe by bike may seem like a daunting prospect but help is at hand. The **Cyclists' Touring Club** (CTC; ☎ 0870 873 0060; W www.ctc.org.uk; Cotterell House, 69 Meadrow, Godalming, Surrey GU7 3HS) is based in the UK and offers its members an information service on all matters associated with cycling (including cycling conditions, detailed routes, itineraries and maps). If they are not able to answer your questions the chances are they will know someone who can. Membership costs UK£27 for adults, UK£10 for those aged under 25 and UK£16.50 for those over 65.

The key to a successful trip is to travel light. What you carry should be largely determined by your destination and type of trip. Even for the shortest and most basic trip it's worth carrying the tools necessary for repairing a puncture. Other things you might want to consider packing are spare brake and gear cables, spanners, Allen keys, spare spokes of the correct length and strong adhesive tape. Before you set off ensure that you are competent at carrying out basic repairs. There's no point in weighing yourself down with equipment that you haven't got a clue how to use. Always check over your bike thoroughly each morning and again at night when the day's touring is over. Take a good lock and always use it when you leave your bike unattended.

The wearing of helmets is not compulsory but is certainly advised. A seasoned cyclist can average about 80km a day but this depends on the terrain and how much weight you are carrying. Don't overdo it – there's no point in burning yourself out during the initial stages.

For more information on cycling, see Activities in the earlier Facts for the Visitor chapter and in the individual country chapters.

Rental

It's easy to hire bikes in the western half of central Europe on a half-day, daily or weekly basis, and sometimes it's possible to return the machine at a different point so you don't have to double back. It's more difficult to rent bikes in the eastern countries, especially in Hungary; your best bets are camping grounds, resort hotels in season and occasionally bike repair shops. See the country chapters for more details.

Purchase

For major cycling tours, it's best to have a bike you're familiar with, so consider bringing your own (see the following section) rather than buying on arrival. There are plenty of places to buy in central Europe (shops selling new and second-hand bicycles or you can check local papers for private vendors), but you'll need a specialist bicycle shop for a machine capable of withstanding European touring. Germany has many suitable places. Prices are relatively high (certainly higher than in North America), but non-Europeans should be able to claim back VAT on the purchase. CTC can provide members with a leaflet on purchasing.

Transporting a Bicycle

If you want to bring your own bicycle to central Europe, you should be able to take it along with you on the plane relatively easily. You can either take it apart and pack everything in a bike bag or box, or simply wheel it to the check-in desk, where it should be treated as a piece of luggage. You may have to remove the pedals and turn the handlebars sideways so that it takes up less space in the aircraft's hold; check all this with the airline well in advance, preferably before you pay for your ticket. If your bicycle and other luggage exceed your weight allowance, ask about alternatives or you may suddenly find yourself being charged a fortune for excess baggage.

Within Europe, bikes can usually be transported as luggage on slower trains, subject to a small supplementary fee. Fast trains can rarely accommodate bikes: they might need to be sent as registered luggage and may end up on a different train to you.

HITCHING

Hitching is never entirely safe in any country in the world, and we don't recommend it. Travellers who decide to hitch should understand that they are taking a small but potentially serious risk. People who do choose to hitch will be safer if they travel in pairs and let someone know where they plan to go.

Hitching can be the most rewarding and frustrating way of getting around. Rewarding, because you get to meet and interact with local people and are forced into unplanned detours that may yield unexpected highlights off the beaten track. Frustrating, because you may get stuck on the side of the road to nowhere with nowhere (or nowhere cheap) to stay. Then it begins to rain…

That said, hitchers can end up making good time, but obviously your plans need to be flexible in case a trick of the light makes you appear invisible to passing motorists. A man and woman travelling together is probably the best combination. Two or more men must expect some delays; two women together will make good time and should be relatively safe. A woman hitching on her own is taking a big risk.

Don't try to hitch from city centres: take public transport to suburban exit routes. Hitching is usually illegal on motorways (freeways) – stand on the slip roads, or approach drivers at petrol stations and truck stops. Look presentable and cheerful and make a cardboard sign indicating your intended destination in the local language. Never hitch where drivers can't stop in good time or without causing an obstruction. At dusk, give up and think about finding somewhere to stay. If your itinerary includes a ferry crossing, it might be worth trying to score a ride before the ferry rather than after, since vehicle tickets sometimes include all passengers free of charge.

Hitching conditions vary from country to country in central Europe. They are good in the Czech Republic, Germany, Slovenia and Austria, and only so-so in Hungary and Switzerland. Hitchhiking is a way of life in Slovakia and Poland so expect competition

(and don't be surprised if a Polish driver asks you for some payment).

It's sometimes possible to arrange a lift in advance: scan student notice boards in colleges and hostels or contact car-sharing agencies. Such agencies, for whose services you pay a fee, are particularly popular in Germany (where they're called *Mitfahrzentralen*) and Poland: there's also a service in Budapest called Kenguru that matches up drivers and riders. See the relevant country chapters.

Travellers considering hitching as a way of getting around central Europe may find the following websites useful. For general facts, destination-based information and rideshare options visit W www.bugeurope.com. The useful W www.hitchhikers.org connects hitchhikers and drivers worldwide.

BOAT

Some of central Europe's lakes and rivers are serviced by steamers and ferries; as you'd expect, schedules are more extensive in the summer months. Rail-pass holders are entitled to some discounts. In most cases, extended boat trips should be considered as relaxing and scenic excursions; viewed merely as a functional means of transport, they can be grotesquely expensive.

It's possible to take leisurely river cruises, but you'll need a boatload of cash. Since the early 1990s the Danube has been connected to the Rhine by the Main-Danube Canal in Germany. The *Viking Europe* does 13-day cruises along this route, from Vienna to Amsterdam between May and September. In Britain, bookings can be made through **Noble Caledonia** (☎ 020-7752 0000; W *www .noble-caledonia.co.uk*). In the USA, you can book through **Uniworld** (☎ 800 360 9550; W *www.cruiseuniworld.com*).

Getting out on the water in Hungary for the day is cheap and easy: local river ferries link Budapest with the picturesque towns of the Danube Bend to the north, and ferries serve all of the built-up areas on Lake Balaton. See the Hungary chapter for details.

ORGANISED TOURS

A package tour of central Europe is worth considering if your time is very limited or you have a special interest such as canoeing, bird-watching, cycling or rock climbing. Tailor-made tours abound; see your travel agent or look at the small ads in newspaper travel pages. Specialists include **Ramblers Holidays** *(☎ 01707-331133;* W *www.ramblessholidays.co.uk)* in Britain for hiking trips and **CBT Tours** *(☎ 800-736 2453;* W *www.cbttours.com)* in the USA for bicycle trips.

New Millennium Holidays *(☎ 0870 240 3217; Icon House, 209 Yardley Rd, Birmingham, B27 6LZ, England;* W *www.newmillennium-holidays.com)* runs inexpensive bus or air tours year-round from the UK to central and Eastern Europe. Another British company is **Regent Holidays** *(☎ 0117-921 1711;* W *www.regent-holidays.co.uk; 15 John St, Bristol BS1 2HR).* It runs tours in Hungary, the Czech Republic and Poland.

Young revellers can party on Europe-wide bus tours. Contiki and Top Deck offer camping or hotel-based bus tours for the 18-to-35 age group. The duration of Contiki's tours are five to 46 days. **Contiki** *(☎ 020-8290 6777;* W *www.contiki.com)* and **Top Deck** *(☎ 020-*7370 4555;* W *www.topdecktravel.co.uk)* have London offices, as well as offices or representatives in Europe, North America, Australasia and South Africa. Check the websites.

For people aged over 50, **Saga Holidays** *(☎ 0800 300 500 in the UK; Saga Building, Middelburg Square, Folkestone, Kent CT20 1AZ, UK • ☎ 617-262 2262 in USA; 222 Berkeley St, Boston, MA 02116, USA)* offers holidays ranging from cheap coach tours to luxury cruises (and it also has cheap travel insurance).

National tourist offices in most countries offer organised trips to points of interest. These may range from one-hour city tours to several-day circular excursions. They often work out more expensive than going it alone, but are sometimes worth it if you are pressed for time. A short city tour will give you a quick overview of the place and can be a good way to begin your visit.

Austria

What a difference a century makes, huh? Under the rule of the mighty Habsburgs, Austria (Österreich) began the 1900s as the dominant political force in central Europe. Today that era of empire, or *Kaiserzeit*, is but a memory; after one of the biggest downsizings in history, the modern state has long reconciled itself to being a minor player in European affairs.

In the world of tourism, however, Austria remains a superpower, hanging out the *'Zimmer frei'* (rooms vacant) sign year-round. Its Schwarzenegger-sized Alps invite sports fans up for a spot of skiing, snowboarding or hiking. Its baroque architecture and Art Deco paintings woo culture vultures. And its homegrown strains of Mozart and Strauss serenade visitors, to gently win them over.

Facts about Austria

HISTORY

In its early years, the land that became Austria was invaded by successive tribes and armies using the Danube Valley as a conduit to new lands – Celts, Romans, Vandals, Visigoths, Huns, Avars and Slavs all came and went. In 803, Charlemagne established a territory in the Danube basin known as the Ostmark, and the area became Christianised and predominantly Germanic. The Ostmark was undermined by invading Magyars but was re-established by Otto I in 955. In 962, Pope John XII crowned Otto as Holy Roman Emperor of the German princes.

A period of growth and prosperity followed under the reign of the Babenbergs, and the territory became a duchy in 1156. Influence in what is now Lower Austria expanded and Styria also came under central control in 1192. The last Babenberg died in 1246 without an heir. The duchy's future was uncertain until, in 1278, it fell into the hands of the Habsburgs, who ruled Austria until WWI.

The Habsburg Dynasty

Austrian territory gradually expanded under the Habsburgs. Carinthia (Kärnten) and Carniola were annexed in 1335, followed by Tirol in 1363. However, the family preferred to extend its territory without force. Much of Vorarlberg, for example, was purchased from

At a Glance

- **Vienna** – magnificent imperial architecture, famous festivals, world-class cuisine and atmospheric wine taverns
- **Graz** – Unesco World Heritage Site, lively university town with excellent art museums, the gateway to the Styrian wine routes
- **Salzburg** – Mozart's one-time stomping grounds, a breathtaking baroque centre and easy access to the Salzkammergut lakes and mountains
- **Innsbruck** – alpine settings, winter sports, vibrant nightlife
- **Hohe Tauern National Park** – Krimml Falls, magical Grossglockner Road amid Austria's highest peaks

Capital	Vienna
Population	8.1 million
Official Language	German
Currency	euro
Time	GMT/UTC+0100
Country Phone Code	☎ 43

bankrupt lords, while significant gains were achieved through marriage. Intermarriage was extremely effective, although it did have a genetic side-effect; a distended lower jaw became an increasingly visible family trait, albeit discreetly ignored in official portraits.

In 1477, Emperor Maximilian 1 gained control of Burgundy and the Netherlands by marrying Maria of Burgundy. His eldest son, Philip, was wed to the Infanta of Spain in 1496. In 1516, Philip's son became Charles I of Spain, a title granting control of vast overseas territories. Three years later, he also became Charles V of the Holy Roman Empire.

These acquisitions were too diverse for one person to rule effectively, so Charles handed over the Austrian territories to his younger brother Ferdinand in 1521. Ferdinand, the first Habsburg to live in Vienna, also ruled Hungary and Bohemia. In 1556, Charles abdicated as emperor and Ferdinand I was crowned in his place. Charles' remaining territory was inherited by his son, Philip II, thereby splitting the Habsburg dynasty into two distinct lines – the Spanish and Austrian.

In 1571, when the emperor granted religious freedom, most Austrians turned to Protestantism. Five years later, new emperor Rudolf II embraced the Counter-Reformation and many people reverted to Catholicism – not always without coercion. The attempt to impose Catholicism on Protestant areas of Europe led to the devastating Thirty Years' War. Peace was finally achieved in 1648 with the Treaty of Westphalia, signalling the end of the push for Catholic control over Europe. But there were other threats. In 1683, as they had once before in 1529, Turkish troops advanced as west as Vienna. Their siege of the city lasted two months before it was repelled.

In 1740, Maria Theresa ascended the throne, despite being ineligible to do so as a woman. Her rule lasted 40 years, and is generally acknowledged as the era in which Austria developed as a modern state. She centralised control, established a civil service, reformed the army and the economy, and introduced a public education system. Progress was halted when Napoleon defeated Austria at Austerlitz in 1805 and forced the abolition of the title of Holy Roman Emperor.

European conflict dragged on until the settlement at the Congress of Vienna in 1814–15, which was dominated by the Austrian foreign minister, Metternich. Austria was left with control of the German Confederation, however, it suffered internal upheaval during the 1848 revolutions and eventual defeat in the 1866 Austro-Prussian War.

Defeat led to exclusion from Bismarck's new German empire and the formation of the dual monarchy of Austria-Hungary in 1867 under Emperor Franz Josef. The dual monarchy established a common defence, foreign and economic policy, but retained two separate parliaments.

Another period of prosperity followed and Vienna, in particular, flourished. The situation changed in 1914 when the emperor's nephew, Archduke Franz Ferdinand, was assassinated in Sarajevo on 28 June. A month later, Austria-Hungary declared war on Serbia and WWI began.

Post-Habsburgs

Franz Josef died in 1916, in the middle of the war. His successor abdicated at its conclusion in 1918 and the Republic of Austria was created on 12 November. In 1919, the new, reduced state was forced to recognise the independent states of Czechoslovakia, Poland, Hungary and Yugoslavia, which, along with Transylvania (now in Romania), had previously been under Habsburg control. Losing so much land caused severe economic difficulties and political and social unrest.

More problems ensued during the rise of National Socialism in Germany during the 1930s. The Nazis tried to start a civil war in Austria and succeeded in killing Chancellor Dolfuss in 1934. Hitler manipulated the new chancellor to increase the power of the National Socialists in Austria, and was so successful that German troops met little resistance when they invaded Austria in 1938 and brought it into the German Reich. A national referendum that April supported the *Anschluss* (annexation).

Austria was bombed heavily in WWII, and in 1945 the victorious Allies restored it to its 1937 frontiers. Allied troops from the USA, UK, Soviet Union and France remained in the country and divided it into four zones. Vienna, in the Soviet zone, was also divided into four zones. Fortunately, free movement between zones allowed Vienna to escape the fate that eventually befell Berlin, though the period of occupation was generally a tough time. The ratification of the Austrian State Treaty and the withdrawal of the occupying powers were not completed until 1955, when Austria proclaimed its neutrality.

Since WWII, Austria has worked hard to overcome economic difficulties. It established a free-trade treaty with the EU (then known as the EC) in 1972, and applied for membership

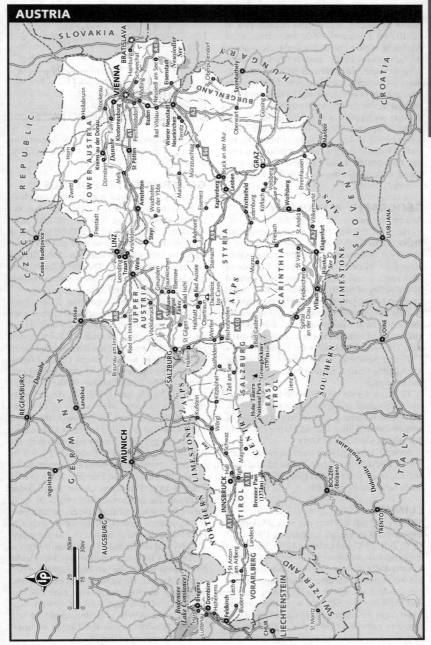

in 1989. In a 1994 referendum, 66.4% voted in favour of joining, and Austria became part of the EU on 1 January 1995. Since then, most Austrians have been rather ambivalent about the advantages of EU membership. EU relations worsened in 1999 and 2000 when sanctions were temporarily imposed on Austria after members of the far-right Freedom Party entered a new coalition government.

After such political woes, the country again made world headlines in November 2000 when the Gletscherbahn railway in the ski resort of Kaprun caught fire in a mountain tunnel. One hundred and fifty-five people were killed, making this the worst alpine disaster in history.

GEOGRAPHY & ECOLOGY

Austria occupies an area of 83,855 sq km, extending for 560km from west to east, and 280km from north to south. Two-thirds of the country is mountainous, with three chains running west to east. The Northern Limestone Alps reach nearly 3000m. These are separated by the valley of the River Inn from the Central (or High) Alps, which have the tallest peaks in Austria. Most mountains in this region are above 3000m and many ridges are topped with glaciers, which makes north-south travel difficult. The Grossglockner is the highest peak at 3797m. Elsewhere, the Southern Limestone Alps partly form a natural border with Italy and Slovenia.

The most fertile land is in the Danube Valley. Cultivation is intensive and 90% of Austria's food is home-grown. North of Linz is an area of forested land; the only other relatively flat area is southeast of Graz.

Austria is highly environmentally conscious. Recycling is legally enforced, and flora and fauna are protected in Hohe Tauern, Europe's largest national park.

CLIMATE

Average rainfall is 71cm per year. Maximum temperatures in Vienna are January 1°C, April 15°C, July 25°C and October 14°C. Minimum temperatures are lower by about 10°C (summer) to 4°C (winter). Salzburg and Innsbruck can be as hot as Vienna, but a couple of degrees colder on winter nights. Some people find the *Föhn* – a hot, dry wind that sweeps down from the mountains in early spring and autumn – rather uncomfortable. That's not all. Folk wisdom holds the *Föhn* responsible for

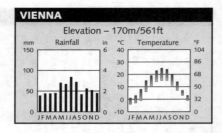

anything from restless farm animals and poor exam performances to increased car accidents or suicides.

GOVERNMENT & POLITICS

As head of the federal government, the chancellor is the central political figure – a role occupied by Wolfgang Schüssel at least until elections scheduled for late 2003. The head of state is the president, who is elected separately by voters for six years and formally appoints the chancellor. Thomas Klestil, well into his second term as president, has been a particularly active and high-profile player.

Austria is divided into nine federal provinces *(Bundesländer)*, each one with its own head of government *(Landeshauptmann)* and provincial assembly *(Landtag)*. Each assembly has a degree of local autonomy and elects representatives to the Federal Council *(Bundesrat)*, the upper house of the national parliament. The lower house is the National Council *(Nationalrat)*, which is elected every four years by voters over the age of 18.

In 1999, after decades in power, the Social Democrats (SPÖ) failed to win a viable electoral majority. Their former coalition partners, the right-wing People's Party (ÖVP), led by Schüssel, eventually formed a government instead with the far-right Freedom Party (FPÖ). The Freedom Party was led by Jörg Haider, notorious for making several pro-Nazi statements during his political career. International condemnation prompted Haider to resign as FPÖ leader, but he remained its dominant personality and continued to court controversy.

Austria's love-hate relationship with Haider hints that at least some pro-Nazi sentiment persists in Austria. Previously, the country faced international embarrassment over the 1986 appointment of President Kurt Waldheim, who served in a WWII unit implicated in war crimes. Waldheim was the United Nations' General Secretary in the 1970s.

ECONOMY

Austria's economy is reasonably strong (unemployment under 6%, inflation under 8%), despite few natural resources. Deposits of oil and natural gas are supplemented by hydroelectric power and imported coal. Agriculture and forestry employ 5% of the population.

The economy is bolstered by a large contingent of foreign workers, particularly from Eastern Europe. Austria generally has a trade deficit, which is usually offset by income from tourism. Its main exports are machinery, metallurgical products and textiles.

The country's wide-ranging welfare services, including free education and health care (for locals), generous pensions and housing, are being threatened by proposed Government cutbacks. Privatisation has bitten into Austria's nationalised industries.

POPULATION & PEOPLE

Austria has a population of about 8.1 million. Vienna is the most populous city with 1.6 million people, followed by Graz (245,000), Linz (208,000), Salzburg (145,000), and Innsbruck (111,000). On average, there are 96 inhabitants per sq km. Native Austrians are mostly of Germanic origin.

ARTS

Austria is renowned for its musical heritage. European composers were drawn to the country by the Habsburgs' generous patronage during the 18th and 19th centuries. The various classical music forms – symphony, concerto, sonata, opera and operetta – were developed and explored in Austria by the era's most eminent exponents. Haydn, Mozart, Beethoven, Brahms and Schubert all made Vienna their home during this period. The waltz also originated in the city in the 19th century and the genre was perfected by Johann Strauss senior and junior.

Musical innovation continued in the 20th century with Arnold Schönberg. Today, Austrian orchestras have a global reputation, and important music festivals are held annually in Vienna, Salzburg and Graz.

Architecture is another important tradition. The Gothic style was popular, before architect Fischer von Erlach developed a distinct Austrian baroque style from the Italian model in the 17th century. (The Church of St Charles in Vienna is one example.) In the late 19th century, the Austrian Secessionist movement embraced Art Nouveau (Jugendstil). But architects Otto Wagner, creator of the Post Office Savings Bank, and Adolf Loos moved progressively away from ornamentation to functionalism.

Secessionist painter Gustav Klimt and the expressionists Egon Schiele and Oskar Kokoschka also emerged in the early 20th century. By that time, elaborate Art Nouveau household objects from the Vienna Workshops (Wiener Werkstätte) had overtaken the more traditional Biedermeier style of furniture design of 100 years before.

SOCIETY & CONDUCT

Traditional costumes are still worn in rural areas of Tirol, but you're more likely to see them during celebrations. Traditional attire for men is shorts with wide braces, and jackets without collars or lapels. The best-known form of dress for women is the Dirndl: pleated skirt, apron, and a white, pleated corsage with full sleeves.

Many festivals act out ancient traditions, such as welcoming the spring with painted masks and bells.

The departure of herders and cattle to high alpine pastures in early summer and their return in autumn are the cause of much jollity in village life.

It is customary to greet people, even shop assistants, with the salute 'Grüss Gott', and to say 'Auf Wiedersehen' before leaving. Upon being introduced to someone, shake hands.

RELIGION

Roman Catholicism is embraced by 80% of the population; many of the remainder are Protestants, concentrated in both Burgenland and Carinthia, or nondenominational. Religion plays an important part in many Austrians' lives.

LANGUAGE

About 98% of Austrians speak German, although there are Croatian- and Slovenian-speaking pockets in the southeastern provinces of Burgenland and Carinthia respectively.

English is widely understood in cities. In smaller towns, hotel and railway staff usually know some English, but don't bank on it.

Knowledge of some German is appreciated. See the Language chapter at the back of the book for pronunciation guidelines and useful words and phrases.

Facts for the Visitor

HIGHLIGHTS

With its rich history, musical heritage and architectural jewels housing myriad art treasures, Vienna is usually the top of most travellers' list. Picture-book Salzburg, with its mementos of Mozart and stunning skyline, usually comes next. Innsbruck and particularly Graz, a new European Culture Capital, are vibrant provincial capitals with plenty to explore. To ski or snowboard, head to one of the many resorts concentrated in Tirol, such as Kitzbühel or St Anton am Arlberg.

SUGGESTED ITINERARIES

Depending on the length of your stay, you might want to see and do the following:

Two days
Vienna – see the central sights, visit the opera and sample a few *Heurigen* (wine taverns).

One week
Spend four days in Vienna, including a Danube cruise; two days in Salzburg; and one day visiting the Salzkammergut lakes.

Two weeks
Spend five days in Vienna, three days in Salzburg (with a day trip to the Werfen ice caves), two days at the Salzkammergut lakes, two days in Innsbruck and two days in Graz.

One month
Visit the same places as the two-week scenario at a more leisurely pace and adding an alpine resort. If the time of year permits, travel south through the Hohe Tauern National Park and over the Grossglockner, stopping in Lienz en route to Graz and Klagenfurt.

PLANNING

When to Go

Summer sightseeing and winter sports make Austria a year-round destination, though alpine resorts are pretty dead between seasons, ie, May, June and November. The summer high season is July and August. Christmas to late February is the winter high season in the ski resorts, though Christmas and New Year are also peak times elsewhere.

Maps

Freytag & Berndt of Vienna publishes good maps in varying scales. Its 1:100,000 series and 1:50,000 blue series are popular with hikers. Extremely detailed maps are produced by the Austrian Alpine Club. Bikeline maps are good for cyclists.

What to Bring

Pack warm clothing for nights at high altitude. A series of thinner layers is better than bulky, thick woollens.

TOURIST OFFICES

Local Tourist Offices

Local tourist offices (usually called *Kurverein*, *Verkehrsamt* or *Tourismusverband*) are efficient and helpful, and can be found in all towns and villages of touristic interest. Beware that local tourist office hours change from one year to the next, so the hours that we list may have changed by the time you arrive. Most offices have a room-finding service, often without commission. Maps are always available and usually free. Each region has a provincial tourist board.

Tourist Offices Abroad

Austrian National Tourist Office (ANTO) branches abroad include:

Australia (☎ 02-9299 3621, fax 9299 3808,
  ⓔ info@antosyd.org.au) 1st floor,
  36 Carrington St, Sydney, NSW 2000
UK (☎ 020-7629 0461, fax 7499 6038,
  ⓔ info@anto.co.uk) 14 Cork St, London
  W1S 3NS
USA (☎ 212-944 6880, fax 730 4568,
  ⓔ info@oewnyc.com) PO Box 1142, New
  York, NY 10108-1142

Some offices aren't open to personal callers, so phone first. There are also tourist offices located in Budapest, Dublin, Milan, Munich, Paris, Tokyo, and Zürich. New Zealanders can get information from the Austrian consulate in Wellington (see Embassies & Consulates later in this section).

Flood Damage

At the time of writing Austria was facing an estimated clean-up bill of around €2 billion following the floods that hit the northern part of the country in the summer of 2002, although the consequences of the flood damage for travellers do not appear to be as serious as in the neighbouring Czech Republic and Germany.

VISAS & DOCUMENTS
Visas are not required for EU, US, Canadian, Australian or New Zealand citizens. Visitors may stay a maximum of three months (six months for Japanese). There are no time limits for EU and Swiss nationals, but they should register with the police before taking up residency. Most African and Arab nationals require a visa.

EMBASSIES & CONSULATES
Austrian Embassies & Consulates
Diplomatic representation abroad includes:

Australia (☎ 02-6295 1533, fax 6239 6751, ⓦ www.austriaemb.org.au) 12 Talbot St, Forrest, Canberra, ACT 2603
Canada (☎ 613-789 1444, fax 789 3431, ⓔ embassy@austro.org) 445 Wilbrod St, Ottawa, ON K1N 6M7
New Zealand (☎ 04-499 6393, fax 499 6392) Austrian Consulate, Level 2, Willbank House, 587 Willis St, Wellington – does not issue visas or passports; contact the Australian office for these services
UK (☎ 020-7235 3731, fax 7235 8025, ⓦ www.austria.org.uk) 18 Belgrave Mews West, London SW1X 8HU
USA (☎ 202-895 6700, fax 895 6750, ⓔ obwascon@sysnet.net) 3524 International Court NW, Washington, DC 20008

Embassies & Consulates in Austria
The following foreign embassies are in Vienna. All these countries have a consulate in Vienna too, but not necessarily at the same address. Check the telephone book for more detailed listings of embassies (*Botschaften*) or consulates (*Konsulate*).

Australia (☎ 01-506 74 04), Mattiellistrasse 2–4
Canada (☎ 01-531 38-3000) 01, Laurenzerberg 2
Czech Republic (☎ 01-894 37 41) 14, Penzingerstrasse 11–13
Germany (☎ 01-711 54-0) 03, Metternichgasse 3
Hungary (☎ 01-537 80-300) 01, Bankgasse 4–6
Italy (☎ 01-712 51 21-0) 03, Rennweg 27
New Zealand The embassy (☎ 030 20 62 10) is in Berlin, Germany; Vienna has only an honorary consul (☎ 01-318 85 05)
Slovakia (☎ 01-318 90 55) 19, Armbrustergasse 24
Switzerland (☎ 01-795 05-0) 03, Prinz Eugen Strasse 7
UK (☎ 01-716 13-0) 03, Jaurèsgasse 12
USA (☎ 01-313 39-0) 09, Boltzmanngasse 16

Foreign consulates in other cities include:

Germany (☎ 0662-84 15 91-0) Bürgerspitalplatz 1-II, Salzburg
Italy (☎ 0512-58 13 33) Conradstrasse 9, Innsbruck; (☎ 0662-87 83 01) Bergstrasse 22, Salzburg
Switzerland (☎ 0662-62 25 30), Alpenstrasse 85, Salzburg
UK (☎ 0662-84 81 33) Alter Markt 4, Salzburg; (☎ 0512-58 83 20) Kaiserjägerstrasse 1/1, Innsbruck
USA (☎ 0662-84 87 76), Alter Markt 1, Salzburg

CUSTOMS
Duty-free shopping has been abolished within the EU, so there are no set limits on goods purchased within the EU for personal use. People aged 17 or over can bring in 200 cigarettes (or 50 cigars or 250g of tobacco), 2L of wine and 1L of spirits from non-EU countries.

MONEY
In 2002, Austria switched from the Austrian Schilling to the euro, with a minimum of fuss. See the boxed text 'The Euro' in the introductory Facts for the Visitor chapter.

Both Visa and MasterCard credit cards are more widely accepted than American Express (AmEx) and Diners Club, though some places accept no cards at all.

If you're coming from outside the euro zone, beware that exchange rates and commission charges can vary between banks, and it pays to shop around. Changing cash usually attracts lower commission rates, but always check first. Some private exchange offices charge as much as 10% commission on transactions. AmEx offices don't have the best rates, but their commission charges are low (for Austria) – from about €1.85 for cash and €3.65 for travellers cheques; no commission applies on AmEx's own travellers cheques. The post office charges 1% (€2.20 minimum) for cash but doesn't change cheques. Train stations charge about €3 for cash and €4.70 minimum for cheques. Banks typically charge €7 to €8. Avoid changing a lot of low-value cheques because commission costs will be higher.

The most efficient way to manage your money in Austria is with the ATM withdrawal/debit card you use at home to access your bank account. If it has a Cirrus or Plus sign on it – and most today have – the card will work in many of the Bankomat machines (ATMs) around Austria. The small fee for making overseas transactions is much lower than the interest you'd be charged for a cash advance on your credit card.

Sending funds electronically is quick and efficient using Western Union or AmEx – and there's no fee at the receiving end.

Costs

Expenses are average for Western Europe, and prices are highest in big cities and ski resorts. Budget travellers can get by on €40 a day, after rail-card costs; double this if you want to avoid self-catering or staying in hostels. The *minimum* you can expect to pay per person is €10/22 for a hostel/hotel and €3.50/5.80 for a lunch/dinner, excluding drinks.

Tipping & Bargaining

In restaurants, it is customary to round off the bill so that it includes an approximate 10% tip and pay it directly to the server. (Sadly, Austrian waiters are not particularly renowned for friendly or speedy service.) Taxi drivers will expect tips of 10%. Prices are fixed, so bargaining for goods is not generally an option.

Taxes & Refunds

Value-added tax, or VAT (*Mehrwertsteuer* or *MwSt*), is charged at 10% (eg, travel, food and museum entry) and 20% (drinks and luxury goods). Prices are always displayed inclusive of all taxes.

For purchases over €75, non-EU residents can reclaim the MwSt (though one-third will be absorbed in charges), either upon leaving the EU or afterwards. Ensure the shop has the forms that need to be filled out at the time of purchase. Present the documentation to customs on departure for checking and stamping. The airports at Vienna, Salzburg, Innsbruck, Linz and Graz have counters for instant refunds, as do some land crossings, but you can only claim your refunds here if you're not going to another EU country. You can also reclaim by post.

POST & COMMUNICATIONS
Post

Post office hours vary: typical hours in smaller towns are 8am to noon and 2pm to 6pm Monday to Friday (money exchange to 5pm), and 8am to 11am Saturday, but a few main post offices in big cities are open daily till late, or even 24 hours. Stamps are also available in tobacco (*Tabak*) shops.

Postcards and standard letters (up to 20g) cost €0.51 both within Austria and to Europe. Standard letters to other destinations cost €1.09.

Poste restante is *Postlagernde Sendungen* in German. Mail can be sent care of any post office and is held for a month (address it to 'Postamt', followed by the postcode); a passport must be shown to collect mail. AmEx will also hold mail for 30 days for customers who have its charge card.

Telephone & Fax

Call charges dropped after telecommunications liberalisation in 1998, and it now costs €0.12 a minute to call anywhere in Austria, be it next door or across the country.

The minimum tariff in phone boxes is €0.20, but as some now take only phonecards (*Telefon-Wertkarte*) it's often more convenient to buy one of those. In 2002, these were streamlined into just two denominations – €3.63 and €7.27 – but this seems likely to change in subsequent years.

International direct dialling is nearly always possible. To call collect, you have to dial a freephone number; ask directory assistance on ☎ 118200. Calls to Germany, Switzerland and Italy are €0.50 per minute, to the rest of Europe and the USA €0.67. The national and international cheap rate applies from 6pm to 8am, and on weekends; rates drop greatly for national calls, but only marginally for international calls.

Of course, telephones in hotels cost much more than public pay phones. Cut-price telephone call centres in cities offer the best rates.

Email & Internet Access

There is public Internet access in most towns; see the individual city sections. Terminals in coffee houses and bars tend to be more expensive than dedicated Internet cafés, and it's always worth keeping an eye out for cheaper online facilities in public libraries. The **Bignet chain** (ⓦ *www.bignet.at; see individual city sections*) has reliable well-equipped outlets in Vienna, Salzburg and Linz. Many post offices now also offer Internet access, although you need to buy a prepaid card before using these 'surf points'. The same card works at Bignet outlets.

Phone Quirks

Don't worry if a telephone number you're given has only four digits, as many as nine or somewhere in between. The Austrian system often adds direct-dial (DW) extensions to the main number – after a hyphen. Thus, say ☎ 12 345 is a main number, ☎ 12 345-67 will be an extension, which could be a phone or fax. Mostly, a -0 gives you the switchboard operator. In this chapter, where an organisation's phone and fax numbers are based on the same main number the fax is only marked by a hyphen and extension number. In these cases, you send a fax by dialling the main number, dropping the phone extension (if there is one, ie, any digits following a hyphen) and adding the fax extension.

DIGITAL RESOURCES

Most Austrian businesses have email addresses and websites. The **Austrian National Tourist Office website** (W *www.austria-tourism.at*) is an excellent starting point; the **Austrian Press & Information Service** (W *www.austria.org*) offers weekly news and visa details. Another useful website for travellers is the **Austrian Railways** (*Österreiche Bundesbahnen* or *ÖBB*; W *www.oebb.at*) home pages, which have details of train times and fares. Budget travellers might also find quite useful the listing of university canteens, or *mensas*, at W www.mensen.at.

BOOKS

Lonely Planet has guides to both *Austria* and *Vienna*, and Western/Central Europe phrasebooks. *The Xenophobe's Guide to the Austrians* by Louis James is both informative and amusing, while Graham Greene's evocative spy story *The Third Man*, John Irving's *Setting Free the Bears* and Arthur Schnitzler's *Dream Story* are all set in Austria. The last is a lot easier to fathom than its Stanley Kubrick movie adaptation *Eyes Wide Shut*.

NEWSPAPERS & MAGAZINES

English-language newspapers and magazines (*The Times, International Herald Tribune, Newsweek*) are available for €2.20 to €3.80.

RADIO & TV

FM4 is a news and music station, mostly in English, with hourly news until 7pm. It's on 103.8FM in Vienna. Austria has only two (terrestrial) national TV channels (ORF 1 and 2), and a national cable channel (ATV). Many hotels have multilingual cable TV.

PHOTOGRAPHY & VIDEO

The Niedermeyer chain is one of the cheapest stores for buying film; a roll of Kodak Farbwelt 100 print film with 36 exposures costs €3.69, Elite Chrome slide film €4.99 (without mounting and processing). Austria uses the PAL video system.

TIME

Austrian time is GMT/UTC plus one hour. Clocks go forward one hour on the last Saturday night in March and back again on the last Saturday night in October.

LAUNDRY

Look out for *Wäscherei* for self-service or service washes. Expect to pay around €7 to wash and dry a load. Many hostels have cheaper laundry facilities.

TOILETS

There is no shortage of public toilets, however, some cubicles may have a charge of €0.35 to €0.50.

WOMEN TRAVELLERS

Women should experience no special problems. Physical violations and verbal harassment are less common than in many other countries. Vienna has a **Rape Crisis Hotline** (☎ 01-717 19).

GAY & LESBIAN TRAVELLERS

Public attitudes to homosexuality are less tolerant than in most other Western European countries, except perhaps in Vienna. A good information centre in Vienna is **Rosa Lila** (☎ 01-586 8150; 06, Linke Wienziele 102). The age of consent for gay men is 18; for everyone else it's 14. Vienna has a Pride march, the Rainbow Parade, on the last Saturday in June.

SENIOR TRAVELLERS

With proof of age, senior travellers are entitled to many public transport and sightseeing discounts. The official qualifying age in Austria is 65 for men and 60 for women, however, some attractions do offer discounts for those aged 62 and over. Vienna-based

AUSTRIA

Seniorenbüro der Stadt Wien (☎ 01-4000-8580; 08, Schlesingerplatz 2; open 8am-3.30pm Mon-Fri) can give advice.

DISABLED TRAVELLERS

Many sights and venues have wheelchair ramps.

Local tourist offices usually have good information on facilities for the disabled; the Vienna office, for example, has a free 90-page booklet.

Car drivers have free, unlimited parking in blue zones with the international disabled sticker.

DANGERS & ANNOYANCES

You always need to beware of theft, even in a relatively orderly country like Austria. Pickpockets particularly work in Vienna's two main train stations and pedestrian centre, and there has been some trouble with unlicensed people offering rooms at the Westbahnhof in Vienna.

Some anti-foreigner feeling exists. It tends to be directed at East European, Turkish and African immigrants, but if you're a tourist who comes from one of those places, or look like you do, you could be in for some unnecessary questioning by police.

Take care in the mountains; helicopter rescue is expensive unless you are covered by insurance (assuming they find you in the first place).

BUSINESS HOURS

Shops are usually open at 8am (except Sunday), and close between 6pm and 7.30pm on weekdays, and 1pm to 5pm on Saturday. They sometimes close for up to two hours at noon, except in big cities.

Some shops in train stations have extended hours. Banking hours can vary but are commonly 9am to 12.30pm and 1.30pm to 3pm Monday to Friday, with late (5.30pm) closing on Thursday.

Emergency Services

The emergency number for the police is ☎ 133, for an ambulance ☎ 144, for a doctor (after hours) ☎ 141, in the case of fire ☎ 122, and if you require an alpine rescue ☎ 140. For emergency vehicle breakdown assistance phone ☎ 120 or ☎ 123.

PUBLIC HOLIDAYS & SPECIAL EVENTS

Public holidays are 1 and 6 January, Easter Monday, 1 May, Ascension Day, Whit Monday, Corpus Christi, 15 August, 26 October, 1 November, and 8, 25 and 26 December.

Numerous local events take place throughout the year, so it's worth checking with the tourist office. ANTO compiles an updated list of annual and one-off events. Vienna and Salzburg have almost continuous music festivals (see their Special Events headings). Linz has the Bruckner Festival in September.

There are trade fairs in Vienna, Innsbruck and Graz in September. Religious holidays provide an opportunity to stage colourful processions. Look out for Fasching (Shrovetide carnival) in early February, maypoles on 1 May, midsummer night's celebrations on 21 June, the autumn cattle roundup at the end of October, much flag-waving on national day on 26 October and St Nicholas Day parades on 5 and 6 December.

ACTIVITIES
Skiing & Snowboarding

Austria has world-renowned skiing and snowboarding areas, particularly in the Vorarlberg and Tirol regions. There are plenty of winter sports in Salzburg province, Upper Austria and Carinthia, where prices can be lower. Equipment can always be hired at resorts.

Generally, you need a complete or partial day pass to ride on ski lifts, although coupons for individual rides are sometimes available. For one day, count on spending €20 to €38 for a ski pass. Rental generally starts at €15 for downhill equipment and €11 for cross-country rental; rates drop for multiple days. The skiing season starts in December and lasts well into April at higher altitude resorts. Year-round skiing is possible at the Stubai Glacier near Innsbruck.

Hiking & Mountaineering

Walking and climbing are popular with visitors and Austrians alike. Mountain paths are marked with direction indicators, and most tourist offices have maps of hiking routes. There are 10 long-distance national hiking routes, and three European routes pass through Austria. Options include the northern alpine route from Lake Constance to Vienna, via Dachstein, or the central route from Feldkirch to Hainburger Pforte, via Hohe Tauern.

Mountaineering should not be undertaken without proper equipment or experience. Tirol province has many mountain guides and mountaineering schools; these are listed in the *Walking Guide Tirol*, free from the ANTO and the Tirol regional tourist office (see Information under Innsbruck later in this chapter). The **Austrian Alpine Club** (*Österreichischer Alpenverein*, ÖAV; ☎ *0512-58 78 28, fax 58 88 42;* W *www.alpenverein-ibk.at; Wilhelm Greil Strasse 15, A-6010 Innsbruck)* has touring programmes, and also maintains a list of alpine huts. These are situated between 900m and 2700m in hill-walking regions; they're inexpensive and often have meals or cooking facilities. Members of the club take priority but anyone can stay. It's a good idea to book huts. The Austrian Alpine Club can give you the phone numbers to book specific huts, and some are also listed on its website.

Spa Resorts

There are spa resorts throughout the country, identifiable by the prefix *Bad* (Bath), eg, Bad Ischl. While perfect for the self-indulgent pampering which stressed-out city-dwellers nowadays so often crave, they also promise more traditional healing cures for respiratory, circulatory and other ailments.

WORK

EU nationals can work in Austria without a permit. Everyone else must obtain a work permit and (except for seasonal work) a residency permit in advance.

In ski resorts, there are often jobs going with unsociable hours – clearing snow, cleaning chalets or working in restaurants and ski-equipment shops. Employers face big fines if they're caught employing workers illegally.

ACCOMMODATION

Reservations are recommended in July and August and at the peak times of Christmas and Easter. Reservations are binding on either side and compensation may be claimed if you do not take a reserved room or if a reserved room is unavailable.

A cheap and widely available option is to take a room in a private house (€12 to €22 per person). Look out for the ubiquitous *Zimmer frei* (rooms vacant) signs. See Hiking & Mountaineering under Activities earlier in this chapter for information on alpine huts. Tourist offices can supply lists of all types of accommodation, and often make reservations. Accommodation sometimes costs more for a single night's stay. Prices are lower out of season. Assume breakfast is included in prices listed in this chapter, unless otherwise stated.

In many resorts (rarely in towns) a guest card is issued to people who stay overnight, which offers useful discounts. Check with the tourist office if you're not offered one at your resort accommodation.

Guest cards can be funded by a resort tax of around €1 to €1.50 per night, which is added to the accommodation tariff. Prices quoted for accommodation in this book generally include this tax.

Camping

There are more than 400 camping grounds, but most close in the winter. They charge around €2.60 to €5.80 per person, plus about €3 for a tent and €3 for a car.

Free camping in camper vans is OK (in tents it's illegal), except in urban and protected rural areas. Just don't set up equipment outside the van. Contact the **Austrian Camping Club** (*Österreichischer Camping Club;* ☎ *01-711 99-1272; Schubertring 1-3, A-1010 Vienna).*

Hostels

In Austria there is an excellent network of HI-affiliated hostels (*Jugendherbergen*). Membership cards are always required, except in a few private hostels. Nonmembers pay a surcharge of about €3 per night for a guest card; after six nights, the guest card counts as a full membership card. Some hostels will accept reservations by telephone, and some are part of the worldwide computer reservations system. Hostel prices are around €10 to €18. Austria has two hostel associations: **Österreichischer Jugendherbergsverband** (☎ *01-533 53 53, fax 535 08 61;* e *backpacker -austria@or.at;* W *www.oejhv.or.at; 01, Schottenring 28, A-1010 Vienna)* and **Österreichischer Jugendherbergswerk** (☎ *01-533 18 33, fax -85;* W *www.oejhw.or.at; 01, Helferstorferstrasse 4, Vienna).*

Hotels & Pensions

With very few exceptions, rooms are clean and adequately appointed. Expect to pay from €25/45 for a single/double. In low-budget accommodation, a room with a private shower may mean a room with a shower cubicle rather than a proper en suite bathroom. Prices in the major cities (particularly in Vienna) are significantly higher than in the untouristed rural areas. A small country inn (*Gasthaus* or *Gasthof*) or a guesthouse (*Pension*) tends to be much more intimate than a hotel. Self-catering chalets or apartments are common in ski resorts.

FOOD

The main meal is at midday. Most restaurants have a set meal of the day (*Tagesteller* or *Tagesmenu*), which provides the best value for money. The cheapest deal is in university restaurants (*mensas*); these are only listed if they are open to all. Wine taverns are fairly cheap eateries, and Asian restaurants and pizzerias are plentiful. For a stand-up snack, head for a sausage (*Wurst*) stall or *Würstel Stand*.

Hearty soups often include dumplings (*Knödel*) or pasta. *Wiener Schnitzel*, a veal or pork cutlet coated in breadcrumbs, is Austria's best-known dish, but *Chicken Huhn* is also popular. Paprika is used to flavour several dishes, including *Gulasch* (beef stew). Look out for regional dishes such as *Tiroler Bauernschmaus*, a selection of meats served with sauerkraut, potatoes and dumplings. Austrians eat lots of meat, although it's increasingly easier for vegetarians to find things to eat.

Famous desserts include *Strudel* (baked dough filled with a variety of fruits) and *Salzburger Nockerl* (an egg, flour and sugar pudding). Pancakes are also popular.

DRINKS

Eastern Austria specialises in producing white wines. Heuriger wine is the year's new vintage. It's avidly consumed, even in autumn while still semi-fermented (called *Sturm*). Austria is famous for its lager beer; some well-known brands include Gösser, Schwechater, Stiegl and Zipfer. Also try *Weizenbier* (wheat beer). Beer is usually served by the 0.5L or 0.3L; in eastern Austria, these are respectively called a *Krügerl* and a *Seidel*.

Leading historian Simon Schama has wryly observed that when it was under attack in 1683, Austria managed to 'resist the Turkish siege but (was) defenceless against the coffee bean'. There are competing stories as to exactly how Austrians developed a taste for their enemy's beverage – from spies infiltrating the Turkish army to sacks of beans abandoned outside Vienna's gates. But the fact is even today locals love to linger over a cup in coffee houses (*Kaffeehäuse* or *Café Konditoreien*). Drinks come in more than a dozen variations, but the *Grosser Brauner* and, in Vienna, the milky, foamy *Melange* are probably the most popular.

ENTERTAINMENT

Late-night bars, clubs and music venues proliferate in Vienna, Graz, Innsbruck and Salzburg and there is plenty of convivial (and sometimes rowdy) après ski in many winter resorts.

In cinemas (cheaper on Monday) some films are dubbed, but look for OF, meaning *Original Fassung* (original-language production), or OmU, meaning *Original mit Untertiteln* (original language with subtitles).

The main season for opera, theatre and concerts is September to June. Cheap, standing-room tickets are often available shortly before performances begin.

SHOPPING

Confectionery and local crafts such as textiles, pottery, painted glassware, woodcarving and wrought-iron work make popular souvenirs.

Getting There & Away

AIR

The airports at Vienna, Linz, Graz, Salzburg, Innsbruck and Klagenfurt all receive international flights. Vienna is the busiest airport, with several daily, nonstop flights to major transport hubs such as Amsterdam, Berlin, Frankfurt, London, Paris and Zürich.

LAND

Bus

Buses depart from London's Victoria Station five days a week (daily in summer), arriving in Vienna 22 hours later (adult and student UK£65/99 one way/return, senior UK£59/89). See the Vienna Getting There & Away section later in this chapter for services to Eastern Europe. The website for Eurolines in Austria is W www.eurolines.at.

Train

Austria has excellent rail connections. Vienna is its main hub (see its Getting There & Away section for details); Salzburg has at least hourly trains to Munich with onward connections north. Express services to Italy go via Innsbruck or Villach; trains to Slovenia are routed through Graz.

Reserving 2nd-class train seats in Austria costs €3.60; in 1st class it's free. Supplements sometimes apply on international trains.

Car & Motorcycle

There are many entry points from the Czech Republic, Hungary, Slovakia, Slovenia, and Switzerland; main border crossings are open 24 hours. There are no border controls to/from Germany and Italy.

Austria levies fees for its entire motorway network and tourists not only need to choose between a 10-day pass (€7.60/4.30 for cars/motorcycles), a two-month pass (€21.80/10.90) or a yearly pass (€72.60/29), they must also clearly display the toll label *(Vignette)* on their vehicle. Passes are available at borders, on freeways or from service stations. Without one, you will face an on-the-spot fine of up to €220 or, if you don't pay up immediately, an enormous €2180 fine. For details, see w www .vignette.at.

RIVER

Steamers and hydrofoils operate along the Danube in the summer. See the Vienna and The Danube Valley sections later in this chapter for details.

DEPARTURE TAX

There is no departure tax to pay at the airport, as all taxes are included in the ticket price.

Getting Around

AIR

There are several flights a day from Vienna to Graz, Klagenfurt, Innsbruck, Salzburg and Linz. The main national carrier is Austrian Airlines; its subsidiary, Tyrolean Airlines, has nonstop flights between most domestic airports. Schedules change half-yearly.

BUS

Yellow or orange/red buses are operated by the post office or Austrian Railways; either way, they're called *Bundesbus*. Sometimes, buses duplicate rail routes, but generally they operate in the more inaccessible mountainous regions. They are clean, efficient and run on time. Advance reservations are possible, but sometimes you can only buy tickets from the drivers. The fares are comparable to the train fares. For national information call **Bundesbus** (☎ 01-711 01).

TRAIN

Trains are efficient and frequent. The state network covers the whole country, and is supplemented by a few private lines. Eurail and Inter-Rail passes are valid on the former; inquire about the latter. Despite what it says on your pass, Austrian Railways does not charge a supplement for national travel on faster EC (Eurocity) and IC (Intercity) trains. 'We're not in Germany here, you know,' one conductor reassured us. Many stations have information centres where staff speak English. Tickets can be purchased on the train, but they cost about €3 extra. In this chapter, fares quoted are for 2nd class.

Trains are relatively expensive and Austria has withdrawn most of its rail passes. You could consider buying a Euro Domino Pass (see the introductory Getting Around chapter earlier in this book) – the Austrian version costs UK£68/108 for three/eight days. The Vorteilscard (under 26/over 26/senior €18.17/93.75/25.44; valid one year) reduces fares by 50%. If you're not under 26 or a senior, it's only worth buying if you stay a while. For

---

Bahn-storming

Austria is embarking on a major renovation of its train stations in 2003–04. It shouldn't cause any disruption to services, but be aware that facilities in and around stations, such as bus stops, banks and tourist information desks, might be shifted. Twenty stations will be affected. Work will be under way in 2003 on stations in: Baden, Feldkirch, Graz, Klagenfurt, Krems an der Donau, Leoben, Linz, Wels, Wien Mitte and Wiener Neustadt. In 2004, renovation begins in Attnang Puchheim, Bruck an der Mur, St Pölten and Salzburg. Wien Nord (Praterstern), Wien Südbahnhof, Wien Westbahnhof, Wien Heiligenstadt and Wien Hütteldorf will also receive a makeover then.

AUSTRIA

under-26s and seniors, however, if offers great savings even for short stays. Even without a VORTEILScard, reduced fares are sometimes available for those aged under 26; wave your passport and ask.

Stations are called *Bahnhof* (train station) or *Hauptbahnhof* (main train station). Single/return tickets for journeys over 100km are valid for three days/one month and you can break your journey, however, tell the conductor first.

Some provinces have zonal day passes, (valid for trains and buses), which may save money compared with buying ordinary tickets. Nationwide train information can be obtained by dialling ☎ 05-1717 (local rate).

CAR & MOTORCYCLE

Visitors require an international driver's licence. Traffic drives on the right. Roads are generally good, but care is needed on difficult mountain routes. In addition to the absolutely vital motorway tax (see Car & Motorcycle in the Getting There & Away section earlier in this chapter), there are hefty toll charges for some mountain tunnels. The tourist office has details of the few roads and passes closed in winter.

Give way to vehicles from the right. On mountain roads, Bundesbuses always have priority; otherwise, priority lies with uphill traffic.

Drive in low gear on steep downhill stretches. There's a steep on-the-spot fine for drink-driving (over 0.05% blood alcohol content) and your licence may be confiscated. The usual speed limits are 50km/h in towns, 130km/h on motorways and 100km/h on other roads. Snow chains are highly recommended in winter.

Many city streets have restricted parking (called blue zones), normally limiting parking during shopping hours. Parking is unrestricted on unmarked streets.

Cars can be transported by train; Vienna is linked by a daily motorail service to Feldkirch, Innsbruck, Salzburg and Villach.

Motorcyclists must have their headlights on during the day and crash helmets are compulsory for both them and their passengers.

Contact the **Austrian Automobile Club** (*Österreichischer Automobil, Motorrad und Touring Club, ÖAMTC;* ☎ *01-711 99-0; Schubertring 1-3, A-1010 Vienna*).

For emergency vehicle breakdown assistance phone ☎ 120 or ☎ 123.

Rental

Hertz, Avis, Budget and Europcar have offices in major cities. With all the usual caveats about it being cheaper to book ahead and on weekends, you should expect to pay between €30 and €60 a day to rent from a multinational. Local rental agencies may be cheaper; tourist offices should have details. The minimum age for renting small cars is 19, or 25 for larger 'prestige' cars. Many contracts forbid customers to take cars outside Austria.

BICYCLE

Bicycles can no longer be hired from train stations, and at the time of writing private operators were only beginning to step into the breach. Some hostels rent bikes, but if you get stuck ask the tourist office. You can expect to pay anything from €6 a day in smaller cities to a hefty €30 in Vienna. Cycling is popular even though sometimes strenuous on steep minor roads. You can always take your bike on slow trains (€2.95/6.55/19.65 for a daily/weekly/monthly ticket); on fast trains you might have to send your bike as registered luggage (€10.20).

HITCHING

Lonely Planet doesn't recommend hitching, as it is never entirely safe. Additionally, in Austria, it's illegal for minors under 16 to hitch in Burgenland, Upper Austria, Styria and Vorarlberg, or for anyone to hitch on motorways. Otherwise, trucks are usually your best bet, particularly when stopped at border posts or truck parking stops *(Autohof)*. Show your destination on a sign and stay clear of the route from Salzburg to Munich; it's been named one of Europe's most difficult spots to get a lift. Austria has only one *Mitfahrzentrale* hitching agency – see Hitching under Getting There & Away in the Vienna section later for details.

BOAT

The only services along the Danube are scenic pleasure cruises, but these can be a good way of getting from A to B if you have the time, money and inclination. The larger Salzkammergut lakes have ferry services.

LOCAL TRANSPORT

Buses, trams and underground railways are efficient and reliable. Most towns have an integrated system and offer good-value daily or

24-hour tickets (€2.90 to €4.30), which are available in advance from dispensers or Tabak shops. Even single tickets can sometimes only be purchased prior to boarding buses/trams. On-the-spot fines apply to those caught travelling without tickets, though some locals are prepared to take the risk.

Taxis are metered. If you need one, look around train stations and large hotels.

For a rundown on mountain transport, see the introductory Getting Around section in the Switzerland chapter later in this book.

ORGANISED TOURS

These vary from two-hour walks in city centres to all-inclusive packages at ski resorts. Inquire at tourist offices.

Vienna

☎ 01 • pop 1.6 million

Vienna, the capital of Austria, is so like an eccentric grandmother that it's hard not to feel affection for her. Her home is full of the treasures of a full and colourful life, from Habsburg riches to the outpourings of Art Nouveau artists such as Gustav Klimt. She has nostalgic memories of famous old companions, including Johann Strauss, who created the waltz, and Sigmund Freud, the father of psychoanalysis – all of which make her a great storyteller. And even if her grumpy manners, and her continual smoking and wearing fur, make you want to shout at her occasionally, Vienna (Wien) has made progress in the last decade in shaking off a deeply ingrained conservatism. Since Austria's central European neighbours were released from communism in the early 1990s, this frontline Cold War city has opened up a bit to the world.

Orientation

Many historic sights are in the old city, the *Innere Stadt*. This is encircled by the Danube Canal (Donaukanal) to the northeast and a series of broad boulevards called the Ring or Ringstrasse. Most attractions in the centre are within walking distance of each other. St Stephen's Cathedral, right in the heart of the city, is the principal landmark.

When reading addresses, remember the number of a building within a street *follows* the street name. Any number *before* the street name denotes the district, of which there are

23. District 1 (the Innere Stadt) is the central region, mostly within the Ring. Generally, the higher the district number, the further it is from the city centre. The middle two digits of postcodes refer to the district, hence places with a postcode 1010 are in district 1, and 1230 means district 23.

The main train stations are Franz Josefs Bahnhof to the north, Westbahnhof to the west and Südbahnhof to the south; transferring between them is easy. Most hotels and pensions are in the centre and to the west.

Information

Tourist Offices The **main tourist office** (☎ 24 555, fax -666; **e** info@info.wien.at; **w** www.info.wien.at; 01, Am Albertinaplatz; open 9am-7pm daily) can provide information, including an excellent city map, and same-day hotel bookings (€2.90). Postal inquiries should be simply addressed to the Vienna Tourist Board, A-1025 Wien.

Information and room reservations (€3.50 to €4 commission) are also available in Westbahnhof and Südbahnhof (6.30am or 7am until 9pm or 10pm daily). There is also an **information and hotel reservation counter** (open 8am-11pm Mon-Fri, 9am-7pm Sat & Sun) in the arrival hall of the airport.

The **Austria Information Office** (☎ 587 20 00; fax 588 66-20; **e** oeinfo@oewwien.via.at; 04, Margaretenstrasse 1; open 10am-5pm Mon-Wed & Fri, 10am-6pm Thur) also has information. **Jugend-Info Wien** (☎ 17 99; 01, Babenbergerstrasse 1; open noon-7pm Mon-Sat), a youth information centre, can get tickets for varied events at reduced rates for those aged between 14 and 26. Its phone number is not accessible from outside Austria. Information on municipal facilities is available in the **Rathaus** (Town Hall; ☎ 525 50).

For sports, however, contact the **Sportamt** (☎ 4000-84111; Ernst-Happel-Stadion, 02, Meiereistrasse 7).

Tourist offices and hotels sell the Vienna Card (€15.25), providing admission discounts and a free 72-hour travel pass.

Money Banks are open from 8am or 9am to 3pm Monday to Wednesday and Friday, and to 5.30pm on Thursday; smaller branches close from 12.30pm to 1.30pm. Numerous Bankomat ATMs allow cash withdrawals. Train stations have extended hours for exchanging money.

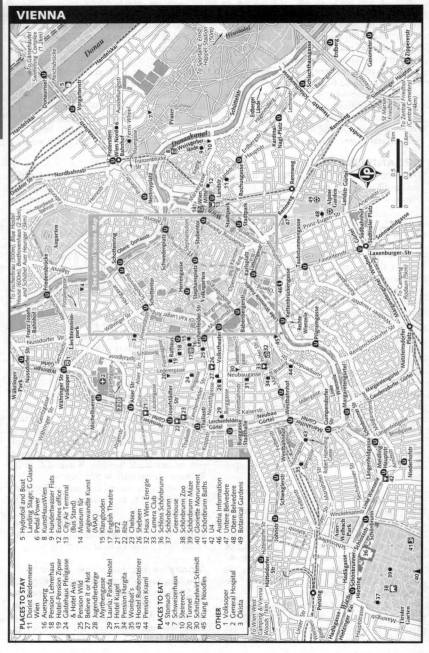

VIENNA

Post & Communications The main post office *(Hauptpost 1010; 01, Fleischmarkt 19; open 24hr)* is close to the Danube Canal. There are also post offices open long hours daily at Südbahnhof, Franz Josefs Bahnhof and Westbahnhof.

Email & Internet Access For a listing of public Internet centres, go to Jugend-Info Wien (see under Tourist Offices earlier in this section). Some places are free, like **Haus Wien Energie** *(☎ 58 20 00; 06, Mariahilfer Strasse 63; open shop hours)*. The most central Internet cafés are a branch of **Bignet** *(Kärntner Strasse 61; open daily)*, which charges €1.45 for 10 minutes' Net access and **Surfland Internetcafe** *(Krugerstrasse 10; open daily)*, where the initial charge is €1.40 then it's €0.08 a minute afterwards. Most hostels have Internet access.

Travel Agencies Handily located in the middle of Kärntnerstrasse is **American Express** *(☎ 515 40, fax -777; 01, Kärntner Strasse 21-23; open 9am-5.30pm Mon-Fri, 9am-noon Sat)*. The **Österreichisches Komitee für Internationalen Studienaustausch** *(ÖKISTA; ☎ 401 48-0, fax -2290; e info@ oekista.co.at; 09, Garnisongasse 7; open 9am-5.30pm Mon-Fri)* is a specialist in student and budget fares, linked to STA Travel. Around town you'll find other **branches** *(☎ 401 48-0; 09, Türkenstrasse 6 • ☎ 502 43-0; 04, Karlsgasse 3)*.

Bookshops The **British Bookshop** *(☎ 512 19 45; 01, Weihburggasse 24-6)* has the most English-language titles. **Shakespeare & Co Booksellers** *(☎ 535 50 53; 01, Sterngasse 2)* has new and second-hand books. **Freytag & Berndt** *(☎ 533 85 85; 01, Kohlmarkt 9)* stocks a vast selection of maps. **Reisebuchladen** *(☎ 317 33 84; 09, Kolingasse 6)* has many Lonely Planet guides.

Medical & Emergency Services For medical attention, try the **Allgemeines Krankenhaus** *(general hospital; ☎ 404 00; 09, Währinger Gürtel 18-20)*. For out-of-hours dental treatment call ☎ 512 20 78.

Things to See & Do

Walking is the best way to see the centre. Architectural riches confront you at nearly every corner, testimony to the power and wealth of the Habsburg dynasty. Ostentatious public buildings and statues line both sides of the Ring, so doing a circuit of this boulevard by tram (or foot or bicycle) is strongly recommended. The stand-out buildings include the neo-Gothic Rathaus, the Greek Revival-style Parlament (in particular the Athena statue), the 19th-century Burgtheater and the baroque Karlskirche (St Charles' Church). Carefully tended gardens and parks intersperse the stonework.

Walk north up the pedestrian-only Kärntner Strasse, a thoroughfare of plush shops, trees, café tables and street entertainers. It leads directly to Stephansplatz and the prime landmark of **Stephansdom** (St Stephen's Cathedral).

The latticework spire of this 13th-century Gothic masterpiece rises high above the city. Take the lift up the **north tower** *(admission €3.50)* or the stairs up the higher **south tower** *(admission €2.50)* for a view that's only slightly impeded by building work on the cathedral.

Some of the internal organs of the Habsburgs reside in the **Katakomben** *(catacombs; admission €3; open daily)*, which are also in Stephansdom. Others are located in the **Augustinerkirche** *(01, Augustinerstrasse 3)*. You will find the flower-strewn coffin of the celebrated Empress Elisabeth ('Sissi'), alongside that of her husband, the penultimate emperor, Franz Josef, in the morbid but compelling **Kaisergruft** *(01, Neuer Markt/Tegetthofstrasse; admission €3.60)*.

From Stephansplatz, turn west down Graben, which is dominated by the knobbly outline of the **Plague Column**. If you turn right into Tuchlaubenstrasse and left into Schulterstrasse, you'll come to the concrete **Jewish memorial** for Holocaust victims. If you turn left from Graben into Kohlmarkt and walk down, you'll reach the St Michael's Gateway of the **Hofburg** (Imperial Palace).

The Hofburg has been periodically enlarged since the 13th century, resulting in a mix of architectural styles. The Spanish Riding School office is to the left within the entrance dome (see Entertainment later in this chapter). Opposite are the **Kaiserappartements** *(adult/ senior & student under 26 €6.90/5.40; open daily)*. Walk into the large courtyard, and take a left into the small Swiss Courtyard. Here you'll find the **Burgkapelle** (Royal Chapel; see Vienna Boys' Choir under Entertainment,

AUSTRIA

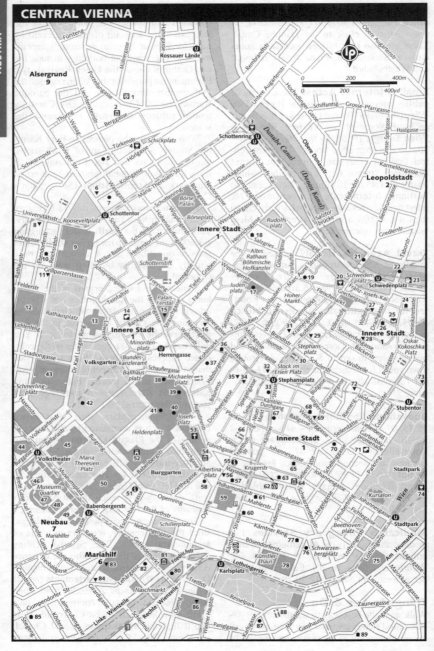

CENTRAL VIENNA

CENTRAL VIENNA

PLACES TO STAY	83	Ra'mien	43	Parlament
10 Pension Residenz	84	Café Sperl	44	Volkstheater
18 Schweizer Pension Solderer	86	Technical University Mensa	45	Naturhistoriches Museum
24 Pension Dr Geissler			46	Museum of Modern Art
26 Hotel Post		OTHER		(MUMOK, Stiftung
36 Pension Nossek	1	International Theatre		Ludwig Wien)
57 Hotel Sacher & Café	2	Sigmund Freud Museum	47	Kunsthalle
60 Hotel Bristol;	3	Flex	48	Leopold Museum
Korso Restaurant	4	Billy's Bones	49	ZOOM Children's
61 Hotel-Pension Suzanne	5	Ökista		Museum
63 Hotel zur Wiener Staatsoper	7	Reisebuchladen	50	Musuem of Fine Arts
65 Music Academy & Mensa		(Bookshop & Tourguide)	51	Jugend-Info Wien
68 Hotel Kaiserin Elisabeth	9	University	52	Hofburg
77 Hotel Imperial	12	Rathaus (City Hall)	53	Augustinerkirche
85 Kolping-Gästehaus	13	Burgtheater (National	54	Albertina
89 Hotel im Palais		Theatre)	55	Main Tourist Office
chwarzenberg	14	Hungarian Embassy	58	State Ticket Office
	17	Jewish Memorial	59	Staatsoper (State Opera)
PLACES TO EAT	19	Shakespeare & Co	62	Surfland Internetcafe
6 Café Stein		Booksellers	64	Haus der Musik
8 University Mensa & Café	20	Krah Krah	66	Kaisergruft
11 Café Einstein	21	Marienbrücke	67	American Express
15 Café Central	22	Schwedenbrücke	70	British Bookshop
16 Esterházykeller	23	Danube Canal	71	US Consulate
27 Griechenbeisl		Tour Landing Stage	74	Meierei im Stadtpark
28 Restaurant Bauer	25	Main Post Office	75	Konzerthaus;
29 Pizza Bizi	30	Stephansdom		Akademietheater
31 Wrenkh		(St Stephen's Cathedral)	76	Austrian Airlines
32 DO & CO	33	Österreichische Werkstätten	78	Musikverein
34 Trzesniewski	37	Freytag & Berndt	79	Bignet
35 Café Hawelka	38	Kaiserappartements	80	DDSG Blue Danube
56 Café Mozart	39	Spanish Riding School	81	Secession Building
69 Immervoll	40	Schatzkammer	82	Wiener Festwochen
72 Gulaschmuseum	41	Burgkapelle	87	ÖKISTA
73 Café Prückl	42	Volksgarten	88	Karlskirche

later in this section), and the **Schatzkammer** *(Imperial Treasury; adult/senior & student under 27 €7/5; open Wed-Mon).* The latter contains treasures and relics spanning 1000 years, including the crown jewels. Allow an hour or more to get round.

Schloss Schönbrunn The Habsburgs' summer palace was the sumptuous 1440-room **Schloss Schönbrunn** *(☎ 811 13-0; 13, Schönbrunner Schlossstrasse 47; U-Bahn No 4; self-guided 22-/40-room tour €7.50/9.80, students €6.90/7.99; open 8.30am-5pm daily Apr-Oct, 8.30am-4.30pm Nov-Mar).* Today, it's a world-renowned tourist attraction; so much so, that sometimes in summer it's too crowded to fully appreciate. Inside the palace of this mini-Versailles, you'll traipse through progressively more luxurious apartments, the most impressive being the **Audience Rooms**. It's worth noting that these are only included in the 40-room grand tour.

Other points of interest within the grounds include the formal gardens and fountains, the **maze** *(adult/concession €2.10/1.45),* the **Palmenhaus** *(greenhouse; adult/concession €3.30/2.20)* and the **Gloriette Monument** *(adult/concession €2.10/1.45),* whose roof offers a wonderful view over the palace grounds and beyond. There is even a **Tiergarten** *(zoo; adult/concession €9/6).*

Two combined tickets in the summer (€14/17.20) provide good value if you're interested in several features. And the Schönbrunn public swimming baths have now been reopened after extensive renovation (see Watersports under Activities later in this section).

Schloss Belvedere This palace *(combined admission adult/student €7.50/5; open 10am-6pm Tues-Sun)* consists of two main buildings housing the **Österreichische Galerie** *(Austrian Gallery; ☎ 795 57-261).* One building is the **Obere Belvedere** *(Upper Belvedere;*

03, Prinz Eugen Strasse 27), where you'll find instantly recognisable works, such as Gustav Klimt's *The Kiss*, accompanied by other late-19th-/early-20th-century Austrian works. The other is **Untere (Lower) Belvedere** (03, Rennweg 6A) which contains a baroque museum. The buildings sit at opposite ends of a manicured garden.

Kunsthistorisches Museum A huge range of the art amassed by the Habsburgs is showcased at the **Museum of Fine Arts** (☎ 525 24-0; w www.khm.at; 01, Maria Theresien-Platz; adult/concession €8.70/6.50; open 10am-6pm Tues-Sun, 10am-10pm Thur). The collection includes works by Rubens, van Dyck, Holbein and Caravaggio. Paintings by Peter Brueghel the Elder, including *Hunters in the Snow*, also feature. There is an entire wing full of ornaments, clocks and glassware, in which you'll see Cellini's stunning salt-cellar. If you can stay the distance, a collection of Greek, Roman and Egyptian antiquities also awaits.

Secession Building This extremely popular Art Nouveau 'temple of art' (☎ 587 53 07; Friedrichstrasse 12; adult/student €5.09/2.91; open 10am-6pm Tues-Sun, to 10pm Thur) was built in 1898 and bears an intricate golden dome that the Viennese say looks like a 'golden cabbage'. And it does. Inside, the highlight is the 34m-long *Beethoven Frieze* by Klimt.

KunstHausWien Hey, where did the floor go? This fairytale gallery (☎ 712 04 91-0; 03, Untere Weissgerberstrasse 13; adult/concession €8/6 for entry to Hundertwasser collection, or €14/11 with temporary exhibitions, half-price Mon; open 10am-7pm daily) certainly sweeps you off your feet with its uneven surfaces, irregular corners and coloured ceramics. Designed by Friedensreich Hundertwasser in order to house his art, it's vaguely reminiscent of Anton Gaudi's buildings in Barcelona and a leading example of organic architecture well before the Guggenheim Museum in Bilbao, Spain, came along. Down the road there's a block of residential flats by Hundertwasser, on the corner of Löwengasse and Kegelgasse.

Museums Quarter The **Leopold Museum** (☎ 525 70-0; 07, Museumsplatz 1; adult/concession €9/5.50; open 11am-7pm Wed-Mon, to 9pm Fri) is the highest-profile spot in Vienna's new Museumsquartier, containing as it does the world's largest collection of Egon Schiele paintings. However, the complex also includes the new main home of the **Museum of Modern Art** (MUMOK, Stiftung Ludwig Wien; ☎ 525 00; adult/concession €6.50/5; open 9am-6pm Tues-Sun, to 9pm Thur), the **City Art Gallery** (Kunsthalle; ☎ 521 89-33; adult/concession €8/6.50; open 10am-7pm daily, to 10pm Thur) and the **Zoom Children's museum** (☎ 522 67 48; adult/child €4.50/3.50; open 9am-4pm Mon-Fri, 11am-5pm Sat & Sun). A combined ticket to all (€25) can be bought from the ticket office in the complex.

Other Museums It doesn't begin to do justice to the **Haus der Musik** (House of Music; ☎ 516 48-51; w www.haus-der-musik.at; Seilerstätte 30; adult/student & senior €8.50/6.50; open 10am-10pm daily) to list its myriad features.

Its interactive electronic displays allow you to create 'brain operas' through your movement and touch, to virtually conduct the Vienna Philharmonic Orchestra, to make your own CD and listen to snatches of sound from Broadway to the moon. Blah, blah, blah. More simply put, after a deceptively slow start, this amazing museum tickles your eardrums and blows your mind.

With your neurons still buzzing, a good next stop is the **Sigmund Freud Museum** (☎ 319 1596; 09, Bergasse 19; admission €4.36; open 9am-6pm July-Sept, otherwise to 5pm). It's more a memorial to Freud himself than an explication of his psychoanalytical theories, though.

The **Albertina** (☎ 534 83; w www.albert ina.at) is reopening in mid-March 2003 after a lengthy refurbishment, which means Albrecht Dürer's *Hare*, among others, will be on display again. The **Museum für angewandte Kunst** (MAK; ☎ 711 36-0; 01, Stubenring 5; adult/concession €2.20/1.10 permanent exhibition, €6.60/3.30 temporary exhibitions, free Sat; open Tues-Sun) displays Art Deco objects from the Wiener Werkstatte and 20th-century architectural models.

Some former homes of the great composers, including one of Mozart's, are also open to the public; ask at the tourist office.

Cemeteries Beethoven, Schubert, Brahms and Schönberg have memorial tombs in the

Zentralfriedhof *(Central Cemetery; 11, Simmeringer Hauptstrasse 232-244)*, about 4km south of the centre. Mozart also has a monument here, but he is actually buried in the **St Marxer Friedhof** *(Cemetery of St Mark; 03, Leberstrasse 6-8)*. Initially unmarked, his grave now has a poignant memorial.

Naschmarkt This **market** *(06, Linke Wienzeile; open 6am-6pm Mon-Sat)* consists primarily of fruit, vegetable and meat stalls, but there are a few stalls selling clothing and curios as well. There is also an atmospheric **flea market** *(open Sat)*. Snack bars provide cheap, hot food, especially kebabs.

Prater If you're a fan of the film *The Third Man*, you might look forward to riding the **Riesenrad** *(giant wheel; €4.36)* in this amusement park as a great way to relive a classic cinema moment. Truth be told, you'll be too busy jostling for space to recall the immortal speech actor Orson Welles made in one of the gondolas. So, give in – just enjoy the view as the Ferris wheel languidly takes you 65m aloft. More hardened adrenalin junkies will prefer the Prater's faster-spinning rides.

Activities

Hiking To the west of the city, the rolling hills and marked trails of the Vienna Woods are perfect for walkers; the *Wander bares Wien* leaflet, available from the Sportamt, outlines hiking routes and how to reach them. The Lower Austria Information office has a free map of routes further from the city.

Watersports You can swim, sail, boat and windsurf in the stretches of water known as the Old Danube, northeast of the Donaustadt island and the New Donau, which runs parallel to and just north of the Donaukanal (Danube Canal). There are stretches of river bank with unrestricted access. Alternatively, go to much-loved **Schönbrunn baths** *(full day/afternoon including locker €9.50/6.50; open May-Sept)*. Or try the swimming complex **Gänsehäufel** *(full day/afternoon including locker €8.50/6.50; open May-Sept)*.

Organised Tours

Several companies offer tours of the city and surrounding areas, either by coach, foot (try the Third Man Tour, which visits spots featured in the famous film, including the underground sewers) or bicycle; contact **Pedal Power** *(☎ 729 72 34; 02, Ausstellungsstrasse 3)*. **Reisebuchladen** *(☎ 317 33 84; 09, Kolingasse 6)* gives an interesting tour of 'alternative' Vienna (€24). Boat operators conduct tours of the Danube Canal; the tourist office has details. See also The Danube Valley section later in this chapter.

Special Events

The Vienna Festival, from mid-May to mid-June, has a wide-ranging programme of the arts. Contact the **Wiener Festwochen** *(☎ 589 22-22, fax -49;* **w** *www.festwochen.or.at; Lehárgasse 11, A-1060 Vienna; open Jan–mid-June)* for details.

Vienna's Summer of Music runs from mid-July to mid-September; contact **KlangBoden** *(☎ 4000-8410; 01, Stadiongasse 9)*. Reduced student tickets go on sale at the venue 10 minutes before the performance.

At the end of June, look out for free rock, jazz and folk concerts in the Donauinselfest. The free open-air Opera Film Festival on Rathausplatz runs throughout July and August.

Vienna's traditional Christmas market *(Christkindlmarkt)* takes place in front of the city hall between mid-November and 24 December. Other seasonal events include New Year concerts and gala balls (January and February), the Vienna Spring Marathon (April/May) and the Schubert Festival (November). The tourist office does not sell tickets, but has details.

Places to Stay – Budget

Vienna can be a budget traveller's nightmare. Cheaper places are often full, especially in summer. Reserve beforehand, or at least phone before turning up.

Tourist offices (see under Information earlier this section) list private rooms and offer a useful *Camping* pamphlet. They will also book rooms.

Camping To get to the **Wien West** *(☎ 914 23 14; 14, Hüttelbergstrasse 80; site per adult/tent/car €5/3/2; open all year)*, take U4 or the S-Bahn to Hütteldorf, then bus No 148 or 152. **Camping Rodaun** *(☎ 888 41 54; 23, An der Au 2; site per adult/tent/car €5.45/4.36/1.09; open late Mar–mid-Nov)* is another option. Take S1 or S2 to Liesing then bus No 60A.

Hostels Undoubtedly, the Viennese des-res (most desirable residence) of the savvy backpacker is **Wombat's** (☎ 897 23 36, fax 897 25 77; e wombats@chello.at; 15, Grangasse 6; dorm beds/doubles €14/18). This hostel's clean, modern dorms and doubles have won it favourable word-of-mouth from all quarters, and it's been adding extra rooms.

Nearby is **Hostel Ruthensteiner** (☎ 893 42 02, fax 893 27 96; e info@hostel.ruthen steiner.com; 15, Robert Hamerling Gasse 24; beds in large/small dorms €11.50/13, triples/ doubles €19/20, key deposit €10). It's an older building, but it has a nice garden and is still very lively. There are small extra charges for sheets, credit card payments and breakfast.

Moving towards the centre, in an area of cheap restaurants and second-hand clothes shops, you'll find **Jugendherberge Myrthengasse** (☎ 523 63 16, fax 523 58 49; e hos tel@chello.at; 07, Myrthengasse 7; beds in 4–6-bed dorms/doubles €15/17 including breakfast & sheets). It's based in two buildings, with reception in the main one. Although the desk is staffed 24 hours a day, check-in is limited to between 11am and 4pm.

The dorms can feel a bit claustrophobic in both **Believe It or Not** (☎ 526 46 58; 07, Apartment 14, Myrthengasse 10; dorm beds €12.50) and **Panda Hostel** (☎ 522 53 53; 07, 3rd floor, Kaiserstrasse 77; dorm beds €12). However, both of these private hostels offer kitchen facilities, if no breakfast, and are friendly places. Panda is linked to **Lauria** (see Hotels & Pensions later in this section).

There are also two large HI hostels out in the suburbs: to get to **Brigittenau** (☎ 332 82 94, fax 330 83 79; e jgh1200wien@chello.at; 20, Friedrich Engels Platz 24; beds in dorms without/with shower €15/16) take the U6 to Handelskai and then bus 11A one stop to Friedrich Engels Platz; and for **Hütteldorf-Hacking** (☎ 877 02 63, fax -2; e jgh@wigast .com; 13, Schlossberggasse 8; dorm beds from €13.90) take the U4 to Hütteldorf and leave the station by the Habikgasse exit.

Student Residences These are available to tourists from 1 July to 30 September while students are on holiday. The cheapest, and one of the nicest, is the **Blue Hostel House** (☎ 369 55 85-0, fax -12; 19, Peter Jordan Strasse 29; singles/doubles with shared facilities €16/ 26.20). It's not that near to the centre, though. Other Studentenheime to consider include:

Gästehaus Pfeilgasse & Hotel Avis (☎ 401 74, fax 401 76-20; 08, Pfeilgasse 4-6; singles/ doubles/triples with shared facilities €21/38/ 51, with bathroom €46/62/81) and **Music Academy** (☎ 514 84-7700, fax -7799; e jag ersberger@mdw.ac.at; 01, Johannesgasse 8; singles/doubles with shared facilities €33/58, with private bathroom €36/70). If you want to book a room contact this last one by fax or email, rather than phone.

Auersperg (☎ 406 25 40, fax 406 25 49-13; 09, Auerspergstrasse 9; singles/doubles with shared facilities €28/46, with private bathroom €38/64) is one of several establishments that can be booked through **Albertina Hotels** (☎ 512 74 93, fax 512 1968; w www.albertina-hotels.at).

Hotels & Pensions A great place for young couples or small groups of travellers is **Lauria** (☎ 522 25 55; e lauria.apartments@chello.at; 07, 3rd floor, Kaiserstrasse 77; twins/doubles €35/40, with shower €60, triples €45-60, with shower €70, quads without/with shower €70/80, 4-person apartments €105, first night supplement €5). Its rooms are comfortable and personable, there's a kitchen and you get your own key.

Pension Lehrerhaus (☎ 404 23 58-100, fax -69; 08, Lange Gasse 20; singles/doubles without shower & toilet €27/49, with facilities €34/57, surcharge for single-night stays €1.50) was designed to accommodate visiting teachers, but now offers excellent value to all travellers with its basic but clean rooms. Breakfast is not included in the tariff.

Kolping-Gästehaus (☎ 587 56 31, fax 586 36 3; e reservierung@wien-zentral.kolping .at; 06, Gumpendorfer Strasse 39; singles without shower & toilet €22; singles/doubles with facilities from €52/65) is a student residence, rather than one for teachers, so there's an institutional feel to its rooms, but they're comfortable and conveniently located all the same.

Pension Hargita (☎ 526 19 28, fax 526 04 92; e pension@hargita.at; 07, Andreasgasse 1; singles/doubles without bathroom 31/45, with bathroom €35/65) surely must be the cleanest and most charming in Vienna for the price. The owner's warm manner, pastel-coloured rooms and spruced-up entrance hall will make you forgive the absence of a lift. If you can get a room, that is. Book ahead; breakfast is available on request.

Family-run and traditionally decorated **Pension Kraml** (☎ 587 85 88, fax 586 75 73; e pension.kraml@chello.at; 06, Brauergasse 5; singles/doubles without bathroom €26/48, with bathroom €43/65) is another sound choice. The breakfast here is generous.

Friendly **Hotel Kugel** (☎ 523 33 55, fax -5; 07, Siebensterngasse 43; singles/doubles without shower & toilet €33/45, with facilities from €42/64; no credit cards) is near tram tracks, but you don't hear much noise inside. The four-poster beds in some of its more up-market rooms make it popular with American tourists, but it offers good bargains as well.

Proud to call itself 'gay-friendly, everyone-friendly', **Pension Wild** (☎ 406 51 74, fax 402 21 68; 08, Langegasse 10; singles €37-65, doubles €45-90) has been doing some renovation of late. So it now has luxury rooms, as well as its traditionally cheaper accommodation, with showers and toilets outside the rooms. By the way, 'Wild' is the family name, not a description.

Places to Stay – Mid-Range

Schweizer Pension Solderer (☎ 533 81 56, fax 535 64 69; e schweizer.pension@chello .at; 01, Heinrichsgasse 2; singles/doubles from €36/56, with shower & toilet €60/80) is a cosy hotel in the northern part of the city centre. **Hotel Post** (☎ 515 83-0, fax -808; 01, Fleischmarkt 24; singles/doubles without bathroom €42/68, with bathroom €72/111) is right in the heart of things. With its parquet flooring in the rooms, long carpeted hallways and decorative cast-iron lift, it feels like a grand old 19th-century boarding house. The rooms without bathrooms are a fantastic bargain.

Don't be deterred by the slow lift to nearby **Pension Dr Geissler** (☎ 533 28 03, fax 533 26 35; 01 Postgasse 14; singles/doubles without private facilities from €39/50, with private facilities from €65/88). Inside, it's been renovated in a pleasantly baroque style.

Baroque is also the style favoured by **Hotel-Pension Suzanne** (☎ 513 25-07, fax -00; e info@pension-suzanne.at; 01, Walfischgasse 4; singles/twins/doubles €69/87/99) and **Pension Nossek** (☎ 533 70 41-0, fax 535 36 46; 01, Graben 17; singles €43-65, doubles €98-120; no credit cards). Both are right in the centre, close to the madding crowds.

A little further out, close to the university, you'll find **Pension Residenz** (☎ 406 47 86-0, fax -50; e vienna@pension-residenz.co.at; 01, Ebendorferstrasse 10; singles/doubles €58/87). Also traditionally decorated, with white, light-coloured fittings, it's a pleasant place to stay.

Hotel-Pension Zipser (☎ 404 54-0, fax 408 52 66-13; e zipser@netway.at; 08, Lange Gasse 49; singles/doubles from €67/101) has elegant contemporary furnishings and some rooms have balconies facing a garden.

Hotel zur Wiener Staatsoper (☎ 513 12 74, fax -15; e office@zurwienerstaatsoper .at; 01, Krugerstrasse 11; singles/doubles from €76/109) is famous for its appealing facade. Its rooms are small, but its prices great for such a central location.

Places to Stay – Top End

If anything, Vienna has a glut of four- and five-star hotels. Every major chain is here, from Best Western, Hilton and InterContinental to Marriott and Radisson SAS.

Even the city's most recognisable names now belong to groups, including the **Hotel Sacher** (☎ 514 56-0, fax -810; 01, Philharmoniker Strasse 4; singles/doubles from €200/298), **Hotel Bristol** (☎ 515 16-0, fax -550; 01, Kärntner Ring 1; singles/doubles both from €335) and **Hotel Imperial** (☎ 501 10-0; fax -410; 01, Kärntner Ring 16; singles/doubles from €406/486).

Slightly kinder on the wallet is the pleasant and central **Kaiserin Elisabeth** (☎ 515 26, fax -7; e info@kaiserinelisabeth.at; 01, Weihburggasse 13; singles €73-113, doubles €193). Delightful **Dorint Biedermeier Wien** (☎ 71 671-0, fax -716; 03, Landstrasser Hauptstrasse 28; singles/doubles from €129/159) is memorably located in a mews with shops and restaurants.

One of Vienna's most exclusive addresses is **Hotel im Palais Schwarzenberg** (☎ 798 4515, fax 798 4714; 03, Schwarzenbergplatz 9; singles/doubles from €233/262).

Places to Eat

You can buy groceries outside normal shopping hours at the train stations; prices are considerably higher except in a **Billa supermarket** (Franz Josefs Bahnhof; open 7am-7.30pm daily). Westbahnhof has a large shop in the main hall, which is open 5.30am to 11pm daily; and Südbahnhof has a few tiny kiosks open daily till late. There is another **Billa supermarket** (open 7.30am-10pm daily) in the airport.

Würstel stands are scattered around the city and provide a quick snack of sausage and bread for around €2.50.

Vienna's best known dish, the Wiener Schnitzel, is available everywhere; goulash is also common. Vienna is renowned for its excellent pastries and desserts, which are very effective at transferring the bulk from your moneybelt to your waistline.

Places to Eat – Budget The best deal is in the various student cafeterias (mensas). They're usually only open for weekday lunches between 11am and 2pm. Meals are €3.20 to €4.80, often with a reduction for students. **University Mensa** (01, Universitätsstrasse 7) has an adjoining **café** (open 8am-6pm Mon-Fri). **Technical University Mensa** (04, Resselgasse 7-9) is also convenient. **Music Academy Mensa** (01, Johannesgasse 8) is the only one inside the Ring.

Tunnel (08, Florianigasse 39; breakfast €2.50, lunch specials €4, pizzas €5-7, other mains €4-10; open daily) is also a student haunt. The food is satisfying, although you might have to wait a while for it to arrive.

There are several cheap places in the centre to fuel up. **Trzesniewski** (01, Dorotheergasse 1; open sandwiches €0.73 each; open Mon-Sat) is the most traditional, albeit not for those with a phobia about egg, onions or fish, one of which is on every tiny open sandwich for sale. While you eat standing up and wash your food down with a beer, you can make believe that you're one of the Austrian Emperor's minions on the way home from a hard day at the factory.

Pizza Bizi (01, Rotenturmstrasse 4; pizzas €5.70; open daily) is rather less quaint – a fact that hardly registers with the multilingual crowd who flock here for the prices and convenience. The restaurant is self-service.

Gulaschmuseum (01, Schulerstrasse 20; vegie & meat dishes from €6, lunch menu €6.18; open daily) serves every type of goulash you can imagine, and quite a few you can't – including the actually rather celebrated chocolate goulash for dessert.

Visiting **Café Einstein** (01, Rathausplatz 4; schnitzels from €4.20, other meat & vegie mains from €5.50; open daily) is a smart move. By the university, it has some of the cheapest Wiener Schnitzels in town. For a more authentic Viennese atmosphere, venture into **Schnitzelwirt Schmidt** (07, Neubaugasse

52; schnitzels from €5.10; open Mon-Sat). Perhaps it's having to carry such huge portions to the tables that makes the waiters here so temperamental.

The Rabelaisian adventures continue in the Prater park, where **Schweizerhaus** (02, Strasse des Ersten Mai 116; open daily Mar-Oct) serves Hintere Schweinsstelze (roasted pork hocks). Mustard or horseradish are recommended accompaniments to these massive chunks of meat on the bone.

Relaxed Asian noodle bar **Ra'mien** (06, Gumperndorferstrasse 9; mains from €6.80; open Tues-Sun) provides a change with refreshing, if not particularly spicy soups, noodles and other, meat and vegetarian, dishes. Those who arrive alone may be seated at one of the long communal benches. **Kiang Noodles** (06 Joanelligasse 3) is another, more upmarket noodle bar. It's a chain, but this is one of the most conveniently located.

Places to Eat – Mid-Range & Top-End
Its name means 'always full' and **Immervoll** (☎ 513 522 88; 01 Weihburggasse 17; mains from €6.90; open daily) pretty well is. Customers can't resist its pleasant environment and dishes including gnocchi and Wiener Schnitzel.

Wrenkh (☎ 533 15 26; 01, Bauernmarkt 10; lunch menus €11.04; open daily) is a classy vegetarian restaurant, featuring some lip-smacking Mediterranean, Austrian and Asian dishes – from risotto to tofu.

Once a real insider's tip, **Stomach** (☎ 310 20 99; 9 Seegasse 26; mains from €10, open Wed-Sat) is now such a favourite that it pays to book ahead. Delicious Styrian and Italian cuisine is served in its rustic room and pleasant garden. Fantastic.

Much more touristy is **Griechenbeisl** (01, Fleischmarkt 11; mains from €12; open daily). However, this interlocking collection of rooms is atmospheric and full of history.

The busy **DO & CO** (☎ 535 39 69; 01, Haas Haus, Stephansplatz 12; mains from €13; open daily) has great food and views. One half serves Asian dishes, the other international cuisine. Book ahead.

The long-standing gourmet temple **Steirereck** (☎ 713 31 68; 08, Rasumofskygasse 2; mains around €24; open Mon-Fri) has had some competition in recent years. When Viennese go out for a grand meal, they might just as easily choose **Restaurant Bauer** (☎ 512 98

71; 01, Sonnenfelsgasse 17; mains from €18; open Mon-Fri) or **Korso** *(☎ 515 16-546; 01, Mahlerstrasse 2; mains from €28.50; open Sun-Fri)* at Hotel Bristol.

Coffee Houses 'Vienna's coffee houses are full of people who want to be alone...without feeling lonely,' wrote the local 19th-century author Alfred Polgar. Sometimes today it's hard to get that sense of personal space when the city's most famous cafés are brimming over with other curious visitors.

A good Viennese café provides somewhere to relax, people-watch and catch up on international newspapers. Sadly, you don't really find that in the hectic **Hotel Sacher Café** *(01, Philharmonikerstrasse 4)* or **Café Mozart** *(01 Albertinaplatz 2)*.

Russian revolutionary Leon Trotsky might also spin in his grave to see how commercial his former chess haunt now feels. But the high moulded ceilings and palms in **Café Central** *(01, Herrengasse 14; open Mon-Sat)* go a long way to offsetting the touristy aura.

Inside the slightly worn, 1950s-style **Café Prückl** *(01, Stubenring 24; open daily)*, you get the feeling that you're surrounded by more locals – whether they be trendy students or refined old ladies.

One of the most charmingly unspoilt of Vienna's coffee houses is the **Café Sperl** *(06, Gumpendorfer Strasse 11; open daily, except Sun in July & Aug)*. Original architectural features, a dishevelled pile of papers, billiards tables and a cast of interesting characters can make you reluctant to finish your coffee.

Café Hawelka *(01, Dorotheergasse 6; open Wed-Mon)* is smoky, crowded, noisy, with nicotine-stained walls – which is precisely why its many regulars love it.

It's not strictly a coffee house and other Internet cafés have overtaken its Web facilities, but **Café Stein** *(09, Währinger Strasse 6; open Mon-Sat)* is still a regular fixture on the Vienna scene – for trendy students and arty types.

Across the city, full-sized coffees cost roughly €2.80 to €3.50 – but then the custom is to take one's time.

Entertainment

From the sweet strains of Mozart, to the smoky dub lounge of celebrity DJ duos Kruder & Dorfmeister or Pulsinger & Tunakan, Vienna prefers to take its entertainment sitting down. (It's no coincidence this city has

spawned a band called the Sofa Surfers.) There are still plenty of chances to drink and dance the night away, though, as you'll find by flipping through listings magazines *City* (€1) and *Falter* (€2.05). The tourist office has copies of *Vienna Scene* and produces monthly events listings.

The state ticket office, **Bundestheater-verkassen** *(☎ 514 44-7880; 01, Goethegasse 1)*, sells tickets without commission for the Staatsoper, Volksoper, Burgtheater and Akademietheater. For other places, try **Wien Ticket** *(☎ 588 85)* in the hut by the Oper; it charges little or no commission for cash sales.

Cheap standing-room *(Stehplatz)* tickets are often the best deal (see the following sections for details). By contrast, concert tickets touted on the streets by numerous be-wigged Mozart wannabes are truly overpriced.

Cinema & Theatre Check local papers for listings. All cinema seats are cheaper (€5.40 rather than €8.30) on Monday. There are performances in English at the **English Theatre** *(☎ 402 82 84; w www.englishtheatre.at; 08, Josefsgasse 12)* and the **International Theatre** *(☎ 319 62 72; 09, Porzellangasse 8)*. If you understand German, try either the **Burgtheater** *(☎ 514 44-4145; 01, Dr Karl Lueger Ring 2)* or the **Akademietheater** *(☎ 514 44; 01 Lisztstrasse 1)*.

Classical Music In a city that Beethoven, Brahms, Haydn, Mozart and Schubert once called home and where even today buskers often have classical training, it's a pity not to visit the opera or orchestra.

Performances at the **Staatsoper** *(State Opera; ☎ 514 44-2960; 01, Opernring 2; seats €5.10-179, standing room €3.65)*, are lavish, formal affairs, where people dress up. The **Volksoper** *(People's Opera; ☎ 514 44-3670; 09 Währinger Strasse 78; tickets €3.65-72, standing room €1.50-20.64)* puts on more modern or niche performances and is a little more relaxed in atmosphere. At both these venues, standing-room tickets go on sale an hour before each performance, and you may need to queue three hours before that for major productions. An hour before the curtain goes up, unsold tickets also go on sale at cheap prices (from €3.65) to students under 27 (home university ID plus ISIC card necessary).

The **Musikverein** *(☎ 505 18 90; 01, Bösendorferstrasse 12; seats from €15-110,* standing room €5-7) is the opulent and acoustically perfect (unofficial) home of the world-class Vienna Philharmonic Orchestra. Here, standing tickets can be bought three weeks in advance at the box office.

There are no performances in July and August. Ask the tourist office for details of free concerts at the Rathaus or in churches.

Vienna Boys' Choir Never mind Johnny-come-lately global chart-toppers like NSync or Boyzone, the Vienna Boys' Choir *(Wiener Sängerknaben)* is *the* original boy band. The choir performs at the **Burgkapelle** *(music chapel; ☎ 533 99 27; e hofmusikkapelle@ asn-wien.ac.at; inside the Hofburg; seats €5.10-27.65, standing room free, tickets available Fri & 8.15am Sun; performances 9.15am Sun, except July–mid-Sept).* Formed in 1498, the choir has been around longer than ex-Take That singer Robbie Williams, had more hit records than the short-lived Bros and looks more angelic than golden-haired Hanson. True, the individual members are a trifle younger than most teen stars, but their concerts are routinely sold out and there's often a crush of fans to meet them afterwards. These classical singers have even recently recorded a cover version of a Metallica song. Whatever next? Perhaps a guest performance by Ozzy Osbourne.

The choir also performs regularly in the **Konzerthaus** *(03, Lotheringerstrasse 20; 3.30pm Fri in May, June, Sept & Oct).*

Spanish Riding School The famous Lipizzaner stallions strut their stuff in the Spanish Riding School *(fax 535 01 86; e tickets@ srs.at; seats €33-145, standing room €22-25)* behind the Hofburg. Performances are sold out months in advance, so write to the Spanische Reitschule, Michaelerplatz 1, A-1010 Wien, or ask in the office about cancellations (unclaimed tickets are sold 45 minutes before performances); there's no phone. Deal directly with the school to avoid the hefty 20% to 30% commission charged by travel agents.

You need to be pretty keen on horses to pay the prices asked, although a few of the tricks, such as a stallion bounding along on its hind legs like a demented kangaroo, do stick in the mind. Tickets to watch the horses train can be bought the same day (€14.50). Training is from 10am to noon, Tuesday to Saturday, from mid-February to mid-December except in July and August when the stallions go on holiday. These sessions are only intermittently interesting, and if you try around 11am you can usually get in fairly quickly. Watching the weekly final rehearsal (€20; Friday or Saturday) is also an option.

Nightclubs & Bars The area around Ruprechtsplatz, Seitenstettengasse and Rabensteig in the Innere Stadt has been dubbed the 'Bermuda Triangle' for the way drinkers disappear into its numerous pubs and clubs, but you'd have to seriously overindulge to become lost in the small *Bermudadreieck*. Venues here are lively and inexpensive, but not particularly atmospheric.

Krah Krah *(01, Rabensteig 8)* has 50 different brands of beer and is open 11am until late.

Other good places for a beer are the shady garden at **Fischerbräu** *(Billrothstrasse 17)* or smoky Irish pub **Billy's Bones** *(Schickplatz 4)*. **Shebeen** *(Lerchenfelderstrasse 45-47)* is a popular evening spot for travellers and expats alike.

If you head for the U-Bahn arches near the Gürtel you'll find a good choice of bars. **Chelsea** *(08, Lechenfelder Gürtel 29-31)* has DJs, occasional indie bands, and English football via satellite. **Rhiz** *(No 37-38)* is a comfy hang-out, favouring modern electronic music, while **B72** *(No 72)*, is slightly more posey. It features varied bands and DJs.

Laidback **Camera Club** *(07, Neubaugasse 2)*, still aspires to being an Amsterdam coffee shop rather than a Viennese disco, but it's not quite as popular as it once was.

More serious clubbing goes on in the young and lively **Flex** *(near Schottenring U-bahn & Donaukanal)* by the water, and in **Volksgarten** *(01, Burgring 1)*, which is three linked venues: a café with DJs and a garden, a disco with theme evenings, and a more formal 'Walzer Dancing' place. **Meierei im Stadtpark** *(Heumarkt 3)* is another favourite for catching up on Vienna's DJ scene. When the weekend crush there gets too much, you can always cool off in the surrounding park.

U4 *(12, Schönbrunner Strasse 222)* is one of Vienna's longest-standing discos. Each night has a different theme. Sunday is 1960s and '70s music; Thursday is gay night.

Heurigen Wine taverns or *Heurigen* sell 'new' wine produced on the premises, a concession first granted by Emperor Joseph II;

traditionally they can be identified by a green wreath or branch hanging over the door. Outside tables are common and there's a selection from inexpensive hot and cold buffet counters.

Heurigen usually have a relaxed atmosphere, which becomes increasingly lively as the evening progresses. The more touristy taverns feature traditional live music; native Viennese, however, tend to prefer a music-free environment. Opening times are approximately 4pm to 11pm, and wine costs around €2.50 a *Viertel* (0.25L).

Heurigen are concentrated in the wine-growing suburbs to the north, south and west of the city. Taverns are so close together that it is best to pick a region and just explore.

The Heurigen areas of Nussdorf and Heiligenstadt are near each other at the terminus of tram D. In 1817, Beethoven lived in the **Beethovenhaus** *(19, Pfarrplatz 3, Heiligenstadt)*. Down the road (bus No 38A from Heiligenstadt or tram 38 from the Ring) is Grinzing, an area favoured by tour groups (count the tour buses lined up outside in the evening). There are several Heurigen in a row where Cobenzlgasse and Sandgasse meet. Alternatively, catch bus 38A east to Ambrüstergasse and follow Kahlenberger Strasse to **Schübel Auer** *(19 Kahlenberger Strasse; open Mon-Sat)*, which has a great food buffet and atmosphere.

Stammersdorf (tram No 31) and Strebersdorf (tram No 32) are cheaper, quieter regions. At **Esterházykeller** *(01, Haarhof 1; open from 11am daily, closed Sat & Sun evenings)* you can get an approximate taste of the Heurigen experience without leaving the centre.

Shopping

Waltzing along the shopaholic's mecca of Kärntner Strasse, a good place to stop is the **Österreiche Werkstätten** *(Kärntner Strasse 6)*, for Art Deco-type jewellery and household objects in the Viennese tradition. Other local specialities include lamps, handmade dolls, wrought-iron and leather goods. Some prices include VAT, which can be claimed back (see Taxes & Refunds under Money in the Facts for the Visitor section earlier in this chapter).

Getting There & Away

Air Regular nonstop flights link Vienna to Linz, Salzburg, Innsbruck, Klagenfurt and Graz. There are daily nonstop flights to all major European destinations. Check with

Austrian Airlines *(☎ 1789; city office: 01, Kärntner Ring 18)*.

Bus Since the central bus station at Wien Mitte was closed in 2000, departures are split between different locations. Buses to Budapest (€28, 3½ hours) leave opposite the offices of **Eurolines** *(☎ 7102 0453; ⓦ www.eurolines .at; 03, Invalidenstrasse 5-7; open daily)*. Eurolines buses to Prague depart twice daily from 01, Rathausplatz 5 (€23.30, five hours). Meanwhile, the ÖBB services to Bratislava (€10.90, 1½ hours) leave from Südtirolerplatz near Südbahnhof. Call ☎ 93000-34305 for details of these.

Train Schedules are subject to change, and not all destinations are exclusively serviced by one station, so check with train information centres in stations or call ☎ 05-1717.

International trains leave from either Westbahnhof or Südbahnhof. Westbahnhof has trains to Western and northern Europe and western Austria. Services head to Salzburg roughly every hour; some continue to Munich and terminate in Paris (14½ hours total). To Zürich, there are two day trains (€77.80, nine hours) and one night train (same fare, plus charge for fold-down seat/couchette). Eight trains a day go to Budapest (€32.80, 3½ hours).

Südbahnhof has trains to Italy (eg, Rome, via Venice and Florence), Slovakia, the Czech Republic, Hungary and Poland, and southern Austria. Five trains a day go to Bratislava (€13.80, 1½ hours) and four to Prague (€36, five hours), with two of those continuing to Berlin (10 hours in total).

Wien-Mitte Bahnhof handles local trains only and Franz Josefs Bahnhof has local and regional trains.

Car & Motorcycle The Gürtel is an outer ring road which joins up with the A22 on the north bank of the Danube and the A23 southeast of town. All the main road routes intersect with this system, including the A1 from Linz and Salzburg, and the A2 from Graz.

Hitching Hitchhikers and drivers are linked through **Rot-Weiss-Rot Mitfahrzentrale** *(☎ 408 22 10; ⓔ office@mfz.at)*. There's no physical office, however, you can phone 24 hours a day, seven days a week. Some examples of the fares for hitchers are Salzburg

€18.20, Innsbruck €25.45, Frankfurt €36.35 and Munich €25.45.

Boat Fast hydrofoils travel eastwards in the summer to Bratislava and Budapest, once per day. To Bratislava (Wednesday to Sunday, 1½ hours) costs €19/29 one way/return. To Budapest (at least daily, 5½ hours) costs €65/89. Bookings can be made through **DDSG Blue Danube** (☎ 588 80-0, fax -440; **w** www .ddsg-blue-danube.at; 01, Friedrichstrasse 7) or **G Glaser** (☎/fax 726 08 20; **w** www.mem bers.aon.at/danube; 02, Handelskai 265).

Heading west, a series of boats ply the Danube between Krems and Passau (in Germany), though services originating in Vienna are very infrequent. More operators are listed in The Danube Valley section later in this chapter.

Getting Around

To/From the Airport
Some 19km from the city centre is **Wien Schwechat airport** (☎ 7007-2233). There are buses every 20 or 30 minutes, 24 hours a day, between the airport and the city air terminal at the Hotel Hilton (€5.80). Buses also run every 30 or 60 minutes from Westbahnhof and Südbahnhof between 3.30am and midnight. By 2003, the reconstructed S-Bahn (S7 line) to the airport might be running again from Wien Mitte, instead of Sudbahnhof. However, it's best to check before setting out for the station (☎ 93000-2300). Taxis should cost €25 to €30. **C&K Airport Service** (☎ 1731) does the trip for a €21 fixed fare.

Public Transport
Vienna has a comprehensive and unified public transport network. Flat-fare tickets are valid for trains, trams, buses, the underground (U-Bahn) and suburban (S-Bahn) trains.

All advance-purchase tickets must be validated in the machines before use. Routes are outlined in the free tourist office map. Single tickets cost €1.60 via machines on buses/trams. Otherwise they cost €1.30 each from ticket machines in U-Bahn stations; it's the same rate in multiples of four/five from ticket offices, machines or Tabak shops. You may change lines on the same trip.

Children under six always travel free; those under 16 go free on Sunday, public holidays and during Vienna school holidays (photo ID necessary).

Daily passes (*Stunden-Netzkarte*) cost €4.30 (valid 24 hours from first use) or €10.90 (valid 72 hours). Validate the ticket in the machine at the beginning of your first journey. An eight-day multiple-user pass (8-Tage-Karte) costs €21.80; validate the ticket once per day per person. Weekly tickets, valid Monday to Sunday, cost €11.20.

Ticket inspections are not very frequent, but fare dodgers who are caught pay an on-the-spot fine of €40.70, plus the fare. Austrian and European rail passes are valid on the S-Bahn only. Public transport finishes around midnight, but there's also a comprehensive night bus service. They run every 30 minutes nightly, around the Ring and to the suburbs, and tickets are €1 (day tickets/passes not valid).

Car & Motorcycle
Parking is a problem in the city centre and the Viennese are impatient drivers. Using public transport is therefore preferable while sightseeing. Blue parking zones allow a maximum stop of 1½ or two hours from 9am to 8pm (to 7pm in the Innere Stadt) on weekdays.

Parking vouchers (€0.40 per 30 minutes) for these times can be purchased in Tabak shops and banks. The cheapest parking garage in the centre is situated at Museumsplatz and the cost is €2 per hour, €12 for 24 hours).

Taxi
They are metered for city journeys: €2 or €2.10 flag fall, plus €1.09 or €1.38 per kilometre – the higher rate is on Sunday and at night. There is a €2 surcharge (€2.10 at night) for phoning a radio taxi.

Bicycle
With bikes no longer available from train stations, the best thing is to ask your hostel or hotel for small local operators. **Pedal Power** (☎ 729 72 34; 02, Ausstellungsstrasse 3; 1st-day/half-day rental €27/17) is the city's dominant operator, although its prices are rather steep. *Tips für Radfahrer* is available from the tourist office and shows circular bike tours.

Fiacres
Before hiring one of these horse-drawn carriages (*Fiakers*) by the Stephansdom, it's worth asking yourself whether these are pony traps or tourist traps.

Sure, they're kind of cute, but at €65 for a 40-minute ride... well, you do the maths.

The Danube Valley

The strategic importance of the Danube (Donau) Valley as an east-west corridor meant that control of the area was hotly contested throughout history. As a result, there are hundreds of castles and fortified abbeys throughout the region.

The 36km Wachau section of the Danube, between Krems and Melk, is the river's most picturesque stretch, with wine-growing villages, forested slopes and vineyards at every bend.

Several companies operate boats along the Danube, generally from early April to late October. **DDSG Blue Danube** (☎ 01-588 80-0, fax -440; w www.ddsg-blue-danube.at; 01, Friedrichstrasse 7, Vienna) has three departures daily (one daily in April and October) passing through the Wachau. From Melk to Krems (1¾ hours, downstream) or from Krems to Melk (three hours, upstream) costs €15.50/20.50 one way/return; shorter journeys between Melk and Spitz cost €9/12 one way/return. **Brandner** (☎ 07433-25 90-21; e schiffahrt@brander.at) offers the same trips at the same prices.

Ardagger (☎ 07479-64 64-0; e dsa@pgv .at) connects Linz and Krems three times a week in each direction during the summer. **Donauschiffahrt Wurm & Köck** (☎ 0732-78 36 07; w www.donauschiffahrt.com; Untere Donaulände 1, Linz) has twice daily services between Linz and Passau in Germany (six hours), which stop in the Wachau.

G Glaser (☎/fax 01-726 08 20; w www .members.aon.at/danube; 02, Handelskai 265, Vienna) sails between Passau and Budapest, stopping at Krems and Melk en route. Most operators carry bicycles free of charge.

The route by road is also scenic. Hwy 3 links Vienna and Linz and stays close to the north bank of the Danube much of the way. There is a cycle track along the south bank from Vienna to Krems, and along both sides of the river from Krems to Linz.

St Pölten is the state capital of Lower Austria, but contact the Lower Austria Information Office mentioned in the Vienna section earlier for region-wide information.

If you stay in the Wachau, be sure to get the guest card. The benefits include free entry to Melk's open-air swimming pool during the summer.

KREMS AN DER DONAU
☎ 02732 • pop 23,000

The historic town of Krems sits on the Danube's north bank, surrounded by terraced vineyards. It consists of three linked areas: Krems, the smaller town of Stein, and the connecting suburb of Und. That's why locals joke that 'Krems und Stein sind drei Städte' (Krems and Stein are three towns). To best appreciate the surroundings, stroll in and around the cobbled, pedestrian-only main thoroughfare of Landstrasse, noting the baroque houses and adjoining courtyards, gothic churches and ancient city walls.

You'll find the **tourist office** (☎ 826 76; e austropa.krems@netway.at; Undstrasse 6) in the **Kloster Und**, where there are also wine tastings. **Net-Café** (Untere Landstrasse 35) offers Internet access, while bike rental is available from **Hentschl** (☎ 822 83; Wienerstrasse 129).

One of the highlights is the **Weinstadt Museum** (☎ 80 15 67; Körnermarkt 14; adult/ concession €3.60/2.50; open 10am-6pm Tues-Sun Mar-Nov). In a former medieval Dominican monastery, it houses some captivatingly ancient animal sculptures.

Places to Stay & Eat
Budget options include **ÖAMTC Camping Krems** (☎ 844 55; Wiedengasse 7; €3.65/ 2.20-4.36/3.65 per person/tent/car), near the boat station, as well as the HI **Jugendherberge** (☎ 834 52; Ringstrasse 77; dorm beds from €12.20). Both are open April to October.

Gästehaus Einzinger (☎ 823 16, fax -6; Steiner Landstrasse 82, Krems-Stein; singles/ doubles €36/48) has atmospheric, individually designed rooms around a leafy courtyard. The stairs are rather precarious, but the decoration is sweet.

Gästehaus Weingut Hutter (☎ 820 06; e hutter-krems@yline.com; Weinzierlbergstrasse 10, Krems; singles/doubles from €31/ 56) is one of the nicest 'Winzers', where you stay with a wine-growing family in the hills above the town.

You'll find places to eat and a supermarket along Obere and Untere Landstrasse. The tourist office has the opening times of local Heurigen.

Getting There & Away
The boat station (Schiffsstation) is a 20-minute walk west from the train station along

Donaulände. Between three and five buses leave daily from outside the train station to Melk (€5.80, 65 minutes). Trains to Vienna (€10.40, one hour) arrive at Franz Josefs Bahnhof.

DÜRNSTEIN
☎ 02711 • pop 1000

Dürnstein, west by road or rail from Krems, is where English king Richard I (the Lionheart) was imprisoned in 1192. His unscheduled stopover on the way home from the Crusades came courtesy of Austrian Archduke Leopold V, whom he had insulted. A trip today to the ruins of the **Künringerburg** castle hints that the kidnapped English monarch, at least potentially, had wonderful views of the Danube.

For more about Dürnstein, contact the **Rathaus** (☎ 219, fax 442; e duernstein@net way.at; Hauptstrasse) or the makeshift **tourist office** (☎ 200; in the train station car park; open Apr-Oct).

MELK
☎ 02752 • pop 6500

Featured in both the epic medieval German poem *Nibelungenlied* and Umberto Eco's best-selling novel *The Name of the Rose*, Melk's impressive Benedictine monastery endures as a major Wachau landmark.

Orientation & Information

The train station is some 300m from the town centre. Walking straight ahead from the train station exit, along Bahnhofstrasse you immediately come to the **post office** (Postamt 3390; open 8am-noon, 2pm-6pm Mon-Fri & 8am-10am Sat), where money exchange is available. Turn right here into Abt Karl Strasse if you're going to the HI hostel. Otherwise, carry straight on. The quickest way to the central Rathausplatz is through the small Bahngasse path (right of the cow's head mural at the bottom of the hill), rather than veering left into Hauptplatz.

Turn right from Bahngasse into Rathausplatz, and right again at the end, following the signs to the **tourist office** (☎ 523 07-410, fax -490; e melk@smaragd.at; Babenbergerstrasse 1; open 9am-noon & 2pm-6pm Mon-Fri & 10am-2pm Sat Apr-Oct; 9am-7pm Mon-Sat & 10am-2pm Sun July & Aug; closed Nov-Mar). Internet access is available at **Teletechnik Wepper** (Wienerstrasse 3).

Things to See & Do

On a hill overlooking the town is the ornate golden abbey **Stift Melk** (☎ 555-232; w www .stiftmelk.at; adult/senior/student under 27 from €5.09/4.72/2.54, guided tours €1.45 extra; open 9am-5pm daily Apr-Nov, to 6pm May-Sept, open for guided tours only Nov-Mar). Once a noble abode, then home to monks since the 11th century, the current building was erected in the 18th century after a devastating fire. Consequently, it's an elaborate example of baroque architecture, most often lauded for its imposing marble hall and beautiful library, but just as unforgettable for the curved terrace connecting these two rooms. You can easily imagine past abbots pausing to take in the views of the Danube and feeling like lord of all they surveyed. (The film *The Name of the Rose* was shot elsewhere.)

Explanatory booklets are available in various languages for €3.50, or phone ahead if you want a tour in English, which works out cheaper.

Places to Stay & Eat

Camping Melk (sites per adult/tent/car €2.60/2.60/1.90; open Mar-Oct) is on the west bank of the canal that joins the Danube. Reception is in restaurant **Melker Fährhaus** (☎ 532 91; Kolomaniau 3; dishes from €5.75; open daily Mar-Oct).

The HI **Jugendherberge** (☎ 526 81, fax 542 57; Abt Karl Strasse 42; dorm beds €11.90, under-19s €9.90; open Apr-Nov, reception closed 10am-5pm) levies a €0.80 surcharge for single-night stays. During the day you can reserve a bed and leave your bags.

Gasthof Weisses Lamm (☎ 540 85; Linzer Strasse 7; from €20 per person) has basic, but reasonably pleasant rooms. On the premises is **Pizzeria Venezia** (open daily), with many tasty pizzas starting at €5.80. **Gasthof Goldener Stern** (☎ 522 14, fax -4; Sterngasse 17; singles/doubles €25/42 without shower & toilet, from €32/54 with private facilities) has been recently renovated, but has retained some cheaper rooms. Even when the adjoining restaurant is shut on Tuesday and Wednesday, the hotel desk is open.

Restaurant **Pasta e Pizza** (Jakob Prandtauerstrasse 4; pizzas from €6) is tucked away from the main tourist trail.

There is a **Spar supermarket** (Rathausplatz 9) for self-caterers.

Getting There & Away

Boats leave from the canal by Pionierstrasse, 400m behind the monastery. Trains to Vienna Westbahnhof (€12, 60 to 70 minutes) are direct or via St Pölten.

LINZ

☎ 0732 • pop 208,000

Poor Linz. Essentially industrial by nature, it discovered years ago that its small old-town centre couldn't compete with Vienna or Salzburg. Its biggest claims to 'fame' were having been Adolf Hitler's favourite town and having a type of cake – Linzer Torte – named after it. So the city decided to carve out a niche for itself in contemporary culture and technology.

Orientation & Information

Most of the town is on the south bank of the Danube. The **tourist office** (☎ 7070-1777, fax 700 11; Hauptplatz 1; open 8am-7pm Mon-Fri, 10am-7pm Sat & Sun, to 6pm Nov-Apr) has a free room-finding service and sells the Linz Museums Card (10 museums for €7.27) and the Linz Card (10 museums, sightseeing tour, restaurant voucher, multiple discounts for €20). It's on the main square, which is reached from the train station via tram No 3 outside.

If you prefer to walk, turn right (northeast) out of the station, then left (north-northwest) at the far side of the park and continue along Landstrasse for 10 minutes.

The large **post office** (Postamt 4020; open 7am-10pm Mon-Fri, 9am-6pm Sat, 9am-1pm Sun) is to the left of the train station exit.

The **provincial tourist office** (☎ 77 12 64, fax 60 02 20; e info@upperaustria.or.at; Schillerstrasse 50; open 9am-noon & 1pm-4.30pm Mon-Thur, 9am-noon Fri) has information on Salzkammergut.

You can surf the Internet at **Bignet** (Promenade 3), while the **Lilo** suburban train station (☎ 65 43 76; Coulinstrasse 30) has bike rental. A **Creditanstalt** bank on Hauptplatz changes money.

Things to See & Do

Suspended from the ceiling of the **Ars Electronica Center** (☎ 72 72-0; Hauptstrasse 2; adult/student €6/3; open 10am-6pm Wed-Sun), and wearing a virtual reality headset, you get an idea of what it's like to fly, as well as having a glimpse of the future. This art and technology centre on the Danube's north bank offers several simulated experiences, including the world's only public 'Cave', a virtual environment where you can travel through space and time. More prosaically, free Internet access is included.

The **Neue Galerie** (☎ 7070 3600; Blütenstrasse 15; adult/student from €5/3; open 10am-6pm Mon-Fri, to 10pm Thur, 10am-1pm Sat) continues the shock-of-the-new theme, with temporary exhibitions ranging from Keith Haring to modern local artists.

The remarkable stained-glass windows depicting the history of the town in the neo-Gothic **Neuer Dom** (New Cathedral; entrances on Hafnerstrasse & Herrenstrasse) have been supplemented by modern designs, too.

For more traditional sightseeing, stroll around the large, baroque **Hauptplatz** or head to the **Schlossmuseum** (castle museum; ☎ 77 44 19; Tummelplatz 10; adult/concession €4/2.20; open Tues-Sun).

Looking like something out of a Western movie, the **Pöstlingbergbahn** (funicular railway; €3.20 return) wends its way to the ornate church and children's grotto railway atop the Pöstlingberg hill.

Tickets for classic music performances during autumn's **Bruckner Festival** (☎ 77 52 30; Brucknerhaus Kasse, Untere Donaulände, A-4010 Linz) should be booked early. The Pflasterspektakel performing arts street festival is in summer.

Places to Stay

Camping is southeast of town at **Pichlinger See** (☎ 30 53 14; Wiener Bundesstrasse 937; adult/tent & car €4/9.08; open Apr-Oct).

There are three HI hostels in Linz. The pick of them really is the **Jugendgästehaus** (☎ 66 44 34, fax -75; Stanglhofweg 3; dorm beds €14.39, singles/doubles €19.48/26.74) on bus routes 17, 19 and 27. Dorms are rather cramped in the **Jugendherberge** (☎ 78 27 20, fax 78 17 894; e zentral@jutel.at; Kapuzinerstrasse 14; dorm beds for over/under 19 €12/15; closed around Nov-Mar). The **Landesjugendherberge** (☎ 73 70 78, fax -15; Blütenstrasse 19-23; dorm beds for over/under 19 €9.08/10.90, plus small heating charge Nov-April) caters primarily for school groups and entry is, peculiarly, through a multistorey car park. Each hostel closes its reception at intermittent times, so phone ahead.

AUSTRIA

Recently renovated **Wilder Mann** (*☎/fax 65 60 78;* e *wilder-mann@aon.at; Goethestrasse 14; singles/doubles without shower & toilet €26.20/46.60, with bathroom €31.30/ 53.80)* offers good value in a city that's otherwise pretty short of budget accommodation options.

The mid-priced rooms at **Goldener Anker** (*☎/fax 77 10 88; Hofgasse 5; singles/doubles from €42/70)* are also quite comfortable and convenient.

Hotel Wolfinger (*☎ 77 32 91-0, fax -55; Hauptplatz 19; singles/doubles without shower €40/60, with bathroom €79/110)* is a wonderful former cloister renovated in a baroque style. Sadly, it has a very limited number of cheaper rooms.

Places to Eat

There's a **Billa** supermarket *(Landstrasse 44)*, heading towards town from the train station, as well as many Würstel stands.

Mangolds *(Hauptplatz 3; salads from €1.13 per 100g; open Mon-Sat)* offers self-serve vegie food. The **Josef Stadtbräu** *(Landstrasse 49; weekday lunches €6.90)* is a popular evening haunt for its beer and beer garden, but it also attracts midday diners. Chinese food is found at **Lotos** *(Landstrasse 11; lunch €5.01),* and Mexican at **Los Caballeros** *(Landstrasse 32; lunch €6.40).*

Etagen Bieserl *(Domgasse 8; mains from €6.70)* is a lively, friendly place to partake of homy Austrian lunches and dinners. Just try not to spoil your appetite beforehand by sampling too much Linzer Torte, a heavy nutty-tasting sponge filled with strawberry jam, at **Café Glockenspiel** *(Hauptplatz 18)!*

Stiegelbräu zum Klosterhof *(Landstrasse 30; most mains from €11; open daily)* has a huge beer garden, but also a fine gastronomical reputation and seems popular for business lunches and tourist outings alike.

Getting There & Around

Linz is approximately halfway between Salzburg and Vienna on the main road and rail routes. Trains to Salzburg (€16.50) and Vienna (€21.80) both take between 1¼ and two hours.

Trains leave approximately every hour. City transport tickets are bought before you board: €0.70 per journey or €2.90 for a day card. Some of the bus services stop early in the evening.

The South

The two main southern states, Styria (Steiermark) and Carinthia (Kärnten) retain elements of Italian, Slovenian and Hungarian culture, with which they have historical connections.

GRAZ
☎ 0316 • pop 245,000

Graz hopes its reign as European City of Culture in 2003 will bring it the same lasting success as previous incumbents such as Helsinki, Reykjavík and, er, Bergen in Norway. A new art gallery resembling a mutant human organ in design should at least focus some attention on the much-underrated Styrian capital.

Orientation

Austria's second largest city is dominated by its Schlossberg, or castle hill, which looms over the medieval town centre. The River Mur cuts a north-south path west of the hill, dividing the old centre from the main train station. Tram Nos 3, 6 and 14 run from the station to the central Hauptplatz. Several streets radiate from this square, including café-lined Sporgasse and the main pedestrian thoroughfare, Herrengasse, which leads to Jakominiplatz, a major transport hub.

Information

At the train station, there is a basic **tourist information desk** *(open 8.30am-5.30pm Mon-Fri).* More detailed information is available from the **main tourist office** (*☎ 80 75-0, fax -15;* e *info@graztourismus.at; Herrengasse 16; open 9am-6pm Mon-Fri, 9am-3pm Sat, 10am-3pm Sun Oct-May, 1-2hr later in Jun-Sept).* Send mail at the **main post office** *(Hauptpostamt 8010; Neutorgasse 46; open 7.30am-8pm Mon-Fri, 8am-noon Sat).*

Bicycle (*☎ 82 13 57-0; Kaiser-Franz-Josef Kai 56)* can rent you a set of two wheels. **Café Zentral** *(Andreas Hofer Platz)* has Internet access.

Things to See & Do

The tourist office organises guided walks of the city (from €7.50), daily in summer and on Saturday in winter. However, most visitors head straight for the **Schlossberg** to enjoy the views and see the remnants of the city's fortress. These include a **bell tower**, **bastion** and **garrison museum** and the charming

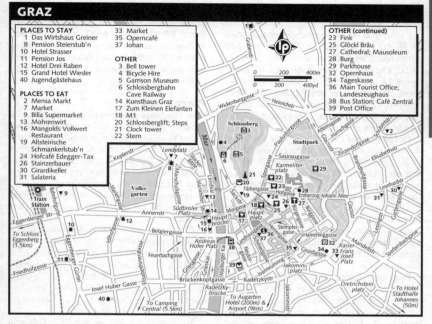

GRAZ

PLACES TO STAY
1 Das Wirtshaus Greiner
8 Pension Steierstub'n
10 Hotel Strasser
11 Pension Jos
12 Hotel Drei Raben
15 Grand Hotel Wiesler
40 Jugendgästehaus

PLACES TO EAT
2 Mensa Markt
7 Market
9 Billa Supermarket
13 Mohrenwirt
16 Mangolds Vollwert Restaurant
19 Altsteirische Schmankerlstub'n
24 Hofcafé Edegger-Tax
28 Stainzerbauer
30 Girardikeller
31 Salateria

33 Market
35 Operncafé
37 Johan

OTHER
3 Bell tower
4 Bicycle Hire
5 Garrison Museum
6 Schlossbergbahn Cave Railway
14 Kunsthaus Graz
17 Zum Kleinen Elefanten
18 M1
20 Schlossberglift; Steps
21 Clock tower
22 Stern

OTHER (continued)
23 Fink
25 Glöckl Bräu
27 Cathedral; Mausoleum
28 Burg
29 Parkhouse
32 Opernhaus
34 Tageskasse
36 Main Tourist Office; Landeszeughaus
38 Bus Station; Café Zentral
39 Post Office

---

clock tower – with its minute and hour hands reversed – which is the emblem of Graz. There are three main ways to ascend: the glass **Schlossberglift** hewn through the hill, the **Schlossbergbahn** funicular railway, and the 260 steps near the lift. Gates are sometimes locked at the top of other paths.

The old town below the hill is a Unesco World Heritage Site. Among its highlights are the **cathedral** (cnr Hofgasse & Bürgergasse) and the **Burg** complex of the Styrian parliament across from it on Hofgasse. Left of the door marked 'Stiege III', there's a **double-winding staircase** as good as any perspective-defying drawing by MC Escher.

The **Mausoleum** of Ferdinand II, behind the cathedral, will be closed for restoration until mid-2003. After that, the tourist office will have admission details.

The **Landeszeughaus** (Armoury; ☎ 82 87 96; Herrengasse 16; adult/student €4.30/60; open 9am-5pm Tues-Sun Mar-Oct, 10am-3pm Tues-Sun Nov & Dec) is lined with row upon deadly row of armour and weapons and explains Graz's history in resisting invasions by Ottoman Turks. Undeniably, these 32,000 pieces represent an important social legacy,

but being in their company is a rather chilling experience.

Schloss Eggenberg (☎ 58 32 64-0; Eggenberger Allee 90; tram No 1; adult/senior or student €5.45/4.30; open Tues-Sun Apr-Oct), an opulent residence 4km west of the centre, harks back to the city's 17th-century past while the bizarre, bubble-shaped **Kunsthaus Graz** (Südtiroler Platz) is shaping up to be part of its future. The opening is scheduled for September 2003, but some local politicians may try to enforce a more conventional design until the last moment possible.

Graz already has many funky street sculptures. Several temporary installations, including an artificial island in the River Mur, will join them for the cultural capital celebrations. Contact **Graz 2003** (☎ 2003; ⓦ www.graz03.at) for information.

Places to Stay

Graz is the nearest city to the Austrian Grand Prix circuit at Spielberg, so some hotels will inevitably fill up when that event is on (in May).

Camping Central (☎ 378 51 02, fax 69 78 24; Martinhofstrasse 3; bus No 32 from Jakominiplatz; single tent site with 1/2 people

€13/20; open Apr-Nov) is 5.5km southwest of the centre.

Closer in is the HI **Jugendgästehaus** (☎ 71 48 76, fax -88; Idlhofgasse 74; beds in 4-bed dorms/doubles with shower & toilet €17/ 21.50, cheaper dorms without private facilities €14 on request, €2.50 surcharge for single-night stays; reception open 7am-10pm Mon-Fri, 7am-10am & 5pm-10pm Sat, Sun & holidays). Right from the cartoon motifs on its facade, it sets a friendly tone.

Hotel Strasser (☎ 71 39 77, fax 71 68 56; e hotel@clicking.at; Eggenberger Gürtel 11; singles/doubles without shower €25.50/42, with shower €32/53) has spacious, well-kept rooms that make it a pleasant surprise for a cheap hotel close to the train station.

The same applies for nearby **Pension Jos** (☎ 71 05 05, fax 71 04 06; Friedhofgasse 14; singles/doubles from €29/51). Rooms come with their own, admittedly small, bathrooms. There's a bell by the driveway to attract attention on arrival.

Pension Steierstub'n (☎/fax 71 68 55; Lendplatz 8; singles/doubles €35/62) seems luxurious for the price, and the pumpkin seeds, rather than chocolates, on the pillow are a nice local touch. But avoid being home around 5pm, when the oompah musicians next door crank it up for an hour or so.

Das Wirtshaus Greiner (☎ 68 50 90, fax -4; e das.wirtshaus.greiner@eunet.at; Grabenstrasse 64; singles/doubles from €40/72) emits a refined air with its white walls and polished floorboards. The restaurant/reception closes at weekends, so phone ahead at those times.

Hotel Stadthalle Johannes (☎/fax 83 77 66; Münzgrabenstrasse 48; singles/doubles from €43/64) has older Italianate decor, but it's been well looked after. A convenient location, a tram stop outside and a nearby sister hotel to accommodate extra guests, add to its appeal.

At **Hotel Drei Raben** (☎ 71 26 86, fax 71 59 59-6; e dreiraben@vivat.at; Annenstrasse 43; singles/doubles from €59/93) you also get value for money. This friendly, modern hotel has satellite TV in all rooms.

The inside of **Augarten** (☎ 208 00-0, fax -80; Schönaugasse 53; singles/doubles from €110/150) aims for a *Wallpaper** magazine style. Expensive modern furnishings in clean lines, with artwork to match, make this a sought-after address.

However, the accolade of being Graz's grande dame of hotels goes to the **Grand Hotel Wiesler** (☎ 70 66-0, fax -76; e wiesler@weitzer.com; Grieskai 4; singles/doubles from €159/209). Its sumptuous Art Deco features include a tiled mural created by a student of Gustav Klimt.

Places to Eat

The Annenpassage shopping centre opposite the train station has a **Billa supermarket**, but if you're self-catering don't miss the **farmers markets** (Kaiser-Franz-Josef Platz; open Mon-Sat • Lendplatz; open Sat). Lendplatz market is reported to operate on weekdays also, but this didn't happen during our visit. It specialises in local produce, including many varieties of apples, fresh fruit juices and schnapps.

Cheap eats are available all around the university, especially at the **Mensa Markt** (Schubertstrasse 2-4; menus for €3.56, €3.85 & €4.29) as well as the cellar bar **Girardikeller** (Leonhardstrasse 28; pizzas, lasagnes, Spätzle all €4; open 5pm-2am Tues-Fri, 6pm-2am Sat, plus 4am-9am 'breakfast club' Fri, Sat & Sun).

Vegetarian lunches are served at **Salateria** (Leonhardstrasse 18; mains from €3.30; open 11am-2pm Mon-Fri), and at other times at **Mangolds Vollwert Restaurant** (Griesgasse 11; salad from €1.05 per 100g; open 11am-8pm Mon-Fri, 11am-4pm Sat).

Thanks to its salads in pumpkinseed oil, fish specialities and *Pfand'l* grilled pan dishes, Styrian cuisine feels healthier than other regional Austrian cooking. Good places to sample it include the low-key inn **Mohrenwirt** (Mariahilfer Strasse 16; mains from €5; open Sat-Wed), the rustic **Altsteirische Schmankerlstub'n** (Sackstrasse 10; mains from €9; open daily) and the high-quality **Stainzerbauer** (Bürgergasse 4; mains from €12; closed Sun).

Iohan (☎ 82 13 12; Landhausgasse 1; mains from €13; open Tues-Sat for dinner) is the city's classiest restaurant. It's located in the former cold storage room of the city hall.

When looking for a typical Austrian coffee house, **Hofcafé Edegger-Tax** (Hofgasse 8; open Mon-Fri, Sat morning) might tempt with its stunning sculptured wood facade, but **Operncafé** (Opernring 22; open daily) is more atmospheric inside.

Entertainment

Many favourite nightspots double as restaurants, among them **Stern** (Sporgasse 38), which draws a wide crowd, and the more exclusive **Fink** (Freiheitsplatz 2). **Zum Kleinen Elefanten** (Neu Weltgasse 3) is a relaxed café that also hosts a wide range of live bands.

Graz, like Vienna, has an area of bars known as the Bermudadreieck. This one is located between Sporgasse, Färbergasse and Stempfergasse, where you'll find venues ranging from the humble **Glöckl Bräu** (Glockenspielplatz 2-3) to the third-floor **M1** (Färbergasse 1), favoured by the beautiful people. M1 is more relaxed by day, when it's pleasant just to have a drink on its rooftop terrace.

If the weather's warm, you also want to head for **Parkhouse** (Stadtpark 2). This island of bonhomie in the city park is a great place to meet locals, and at night, with music pumping out at the trees, there's a special vibe.

Graz hosts classical and other musical events throughout the year. The **Tageskasse** (☎ 8000; Kaiser Josef Platz 10) sells tickets without commission for the **Opernhaus** (opera). Cheap student deals, last-minute returns as well as standing-room tickets are all available.

Getting There & Away

Low-cost Ryanair flies from London Stansted daily; check **w** www.ryanair.com for prices. Direct IC trains to Vienna's Südbahnhof depart every two hours (€24.70, 2¾ hours). Trains depart every two hours to Salzburg (€33.40, 4¼ hours), either direct or changing at Bischofshofen. Two daily direct trains depart for Ljubljana (€32.70, four hours), and every hour or two to Budapest via Szentgotthard and Szombathely (€41, 6½ hours). Trains to Klagenfurt (€26.10, three hours) go via Bruck an der Mur. The bus station is at Andreas Hofer Platz. The A2 autobahn from Vienna to Klagenfurt passes a few kilometres south of the city.

Getting Around

Public transport tickets cover the Schlossbergbahn (castle-hill railway) that runs from Sackstrasse up the Schlossberg and bus No 631 to/from the airport. Tickets cost €1.45 each (€11.63 for a strip of 10). The 24-hour/weekly passes cost €3.05/7.27. If you're driving, blue parking zones allow a three-hour stop (€0.50 for 30 minutes) during specified times.

AROUND GRAZ

The stud farm that produces the Lipizzaner stallions which perform in Vienna is about 40km west of Graz at **Piber** (adult/senior/student €10/8/5; open Easter-end Oct). Get basic details from the Graz tourist office. It's also possible to make a day trip from Graz to **Bärnbach**, where there's a remarkable parish church created by Hundertwasser and other artists.

KLAGENFURT

☎ 0463 • pop 87,000

The capital of Carinthia (Kärnten), Klagenfurt seems rather unassuming to be the seat of power of Austria's most controversial politician in recent years. Jörg Haider was first elected provincial governor here in 1989, but the tourist industry revolves around the nearby lake and theme park of tiny famous buildings instead.

Orientation & Information

The heart of the city is Neuer Platz (New Square), which is 1km north of the main train station; walk straight down Bahnhofstrasse and turn left into Paradiesergasse to get there. Across the square, in the Rathaus, you'll find the **tourist office** (☎ 53 72 23, fax 53 72 95; **e** tourismus@klagenfurt.at; open 8am-8pm Mon-Fri, 10am-5pm Sat, Sun & holidays May-Sept, 8am-6.30pm Mon-Fri, 10am-3pm Sat & Sun otherwise). The **main post office** (Postamt 9010; Dr Hermann Gasse) is one block west of Neuer Platz. Bikes can be hired from **Verein Zweirad Impulse** (☎ 51 63 10), which has several rental points around town. Internet access is available at **Gates Cafebar** (Waagplatz 7).

Things to See & Do

The **Neuer Platz** (New Square) is dominated by the town emblem, the Dragon Fountain. At the west end of the pedestrianised **Alter Platz** (Old Square) is the 16th-century **Landhaus**, with a striking **Hall of Arms** (Wappensaal; adult/student €2/1; open Sat & Sun Apr-Sept). Paintings of 655 coats of arms cover the walls, while the trompe l'oeil ceiling creates the illusion of a balcony above them.

The **Wörther See**, 4km west of the centre, is one of the region's warmer lakes, thanks to subterranean thermal springs. You can swim or go boating in summer. Steamers also embark on circular tours; get details from **STW**

AUSTRIA

(☎ 211 55; e schifffahrt@stw.at). Neighbouring Europa Park has various attractions, including the touristy **Minimundus** (☎ 211 94-0; Villacher Strasse 241; adult/senior & student/child €10/8.50/4.50; open daily Apr-Oct), which displays more than 150 models of famous international buildings on a 1:25 scale.

Places to Stay

Choose **Camping Strandbad** (☎ 211 69, fax -93) in Europa Park and you'll be close to many major attractions in summer.

The modern HI **Jugendherberge** (☎ 23 00 20, fax -20; Neckheimgasse 6; beds in 4-bed dorms €16.30, doubles €19.93; reception open 7am-11am, 5pm-10pm) is also near the university and Europa Park and offers Internet access. Bus 12 is the closest stop.

Back in town, **Pension Klepp** (☎ 322 78; Platzgasse 4; singles/doubles €22/36.50 without breakfast) is a good, cheap option.

Hotel Liebetegger (☎ 569 35, fax -6; Völkermarkter Strasse 8; singles/doubles €32/51 without breakfast) is classier and more recently renovated.

Places to Eat

The **University Mensa** (Universitätsstrasse 90; mains from €4.10; open 11am-2.30pm Mon-Fri) is by Europa Park, while back in the centre, the stalls in the **Benediktinerplatz market** serve hot meals for only about €4.

Gasthaus Pirker (cnr Adlergasse & Lidmanskygasse; mains from €5.80) has cheap Austrian food, while **Zum Augustin** (Pfarrhofgasse 2; mains from €7.20) impresses just as much with its tasty regional food as it does with its range of beers. Hip **Pankraz** (8 de Mai Strasse 16; sandwiches €3.50) is mainly a café, but does sell snacks. It attracts a wide range of people from students and Goths to yuppies.

Getting There & Around

Ryanair flies from London daily. Trains to Graz depart every one to two hours (€33.40, three hours). Trains to western Austria, Italy and Germany go via Villach, 40 minutes away.

Bus drivers sell single tickets (€1.60), while a strip of 10 costs €12 from ticket machines. Passes for 24 hours cost €3.30, for a week €13. For the Europa Park vicinity, take bus No 10, 11, 12, 20, 21 or 22 from Heiligengeistplatz in the centre. To the airport, take bus No 42 or a taxi (about €15).

Salzburg

☎ 0662 • pop 145,000

Salzburg certainly has chocolate-box appeal (literally, in fact, when it comes to the rows of Mozartkugeln confectionery named after its most famous son). From its quaint old town nestled below the medieval Hohensalzburg Fortress to its baroque palace and manicured gardens, the city presents one picture-postcard vista after another.

If that and Mozart weren't enough to explain why it's Austria's second biggest tourist destination after Vienna, there's also the Von Trapp family story, which was partly filmed here. Yup, them thar' hills are alive to The Sound of Music.

Orientation

The city centre is split by the River Salzach. The old part of town (mostly pedestrianised) is on the left (south) bank, with the Hohensalzburg Fortress on the hill above. Most attractions are this side of the river, as is the fashionable shopping street of Getreidegasse. On the right (north) bank is the new town and business centre, where you'll find most of the cheaper hotels.

Information

Tourist Offices The **main tourist office** (☎ 889 87-330, hotel reservations ☎ 889 87-314, fax -32; Mozartplatz 5; open 9am-6pm daily May-Oct, to 7pm in Dec, July & Aug, 9am-6pm Mon-Sat otherwise) will book rooms, at €2.20 commission for up to two people or €4 for three people or more. There is a **provincial information section** (☎ 66 88 0; open 9am-6pm Mon-Fri, 9am-3.30pm Sat) in the same building as the main tourist office.

The information office at the train station on platform 2a is also open throughout the year; the Mitte (central) office at Münchner Bundesstrasse 1 and that in the south at Park & Ride Parkplatz, Alpensiedlung Süd, Alpenstrasse, are open from Easter to November; the office in the north, at Autobahnstation Kasern, is open from June to September.

Tourist offices and hotels sell the Salzburg Card, which provides free museum entry and public transport, and gives various reductions. The price is €18/26/32 for 24/48/72 hours (students get a 10% discount).

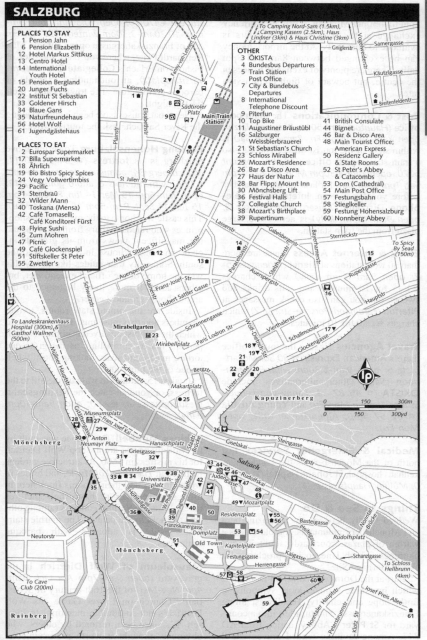

SALZBURG

PLACES TO STAY
1 Pension Jahn
6 Pension Elizabeth
12 Hotel Markus Sittikus
13 Centro Hotel
14 International
   Youth Hotel
15 Pension Bergland
20 Junger Fuchs
22 Institut St Sebastian
33 Goldener Hirsch
34 Blaue Gans
35 Naturfreundehaus
56 Hotel Wolf
61 Jugendgästehaus

PLACES TO EAT
2 Eurospar Supermarket
17 Billa Supermarket
18 Ährlich
19 Bio Bistro Spicy Spices
24 Vegy Vollwertimbiss
29 Pacific
31 Sternbräu
32 Wilder Mann
40 Toskana (Mensa)
42 Café Tomaselli;
   Café Konditorei Fürst
43 Flying Sushi
45 Zum Mohren
47 Picnic
49 Café Glockenspiel
51 Stiftskeller St Peter
55 Zwettler's

OTHER
3 ÖKISTA
4 Bundesbus Departures
5 Train Station
   Post Office
7 City & Bundesbus
   Departures
8 International
   Telephone Discount
9 Piterfun
10 Top Bike
11 Augustiner Bräustübl
16 Salzburger
   Weissbierbrauerei
21 St Sebastian's Church
23 Schloss Mirabell
25 Mozart's Residence
26 Bar & Disco Area
27 Haus der Natur
28 Bar Flipp; Mount Inn
30 Mönchsberg Lift
36 Festival Halls
37 Collegiate Church
38 Mozart's Birthplace
39 Rupertinum
41 British Consulate
44 Bignet
46 Bar & Disco Area
48 Main Tourist Office;
   American Express
50 Residenz Gallery
   & State Rooms
52 St Peter's Abbey
   & Catacombs
53 Dom (Cathedral)
54 Main Post Office
57 Festungsbahn
58 Stieglkeller
59 Festung Hohensalzburg
60 Nonnberg Abbey

Money Banks are open 8am to noon and 2pm to 4.30pm Monday to Friday. Currency exchange at the train station counters is available to 8pm daily. At the airport, money can be exchanged between 8am and 8pm daily. There are plenty of exchange offices in the centre, but beware of high commission rates.

Post & Communications The **main post office** (Hauptpostamt 5010; Residenzplatz 9; open 7am-7pm Mon-Fri, 8am-10am Sat) is within sight of the tourist office. There's also a train station **post office** (Bahnhofspostamt 5020; open 7am-8.30pm Mon-Fri, 8am-2pm Sat, 1pm-6pm Sun) for last-minute dispatches before you leave town. **International Telephone Discount** (Kaiserschützenstrasse 8; open 9am-11pm daily) is across the large plaza from the train station.

Email & Internet Access There are more than 30 workstations at **Bignet** (Judengasse 5-7; open 9am-10pm daily) which charges €1.45 for 10 minutes and sells drinks and sweets, but you can also check messages at **Piterfun** (Ferdinand-Porsche-Strasse 7) which charges €1.80 for 10 minutes.

Travel Agencies Next to the tourist office there's **American Express** (☎ 80 80; Mozartplatz 5; open 9am-5.30pm Mon-Fri, 9am-noon Sat). Other alternatives include **ÖKISTA** (☎ 45 87 33; Fanny-von-Lehnert Strasse 1; open Mon-Fri) and **Young Austria** (☎ 62 57 58-0; Alpenstrasse 108a; open Mon-Fri).

Medical & Emergency Services Just north of the Mönchsberg is the Landeskrankenhaus hospital, **St Johanns-Spital** (☎ 44 82-0; Müllner Hauptstrasse 48).

Things to See & Do

Wedged tightly between the Kapuzinerberg and Mönchsberg mountains, the old city is a warren of plazas, courtyards, fountains and churches, which Unesco has proclaimed a World Heritage Site.

Start at the **Dom** (cathedral) on Domplatz, which has three bronze doors symbolising faith, hope and charity. Head west along Franziskanergasse, and turn left into a courtyard for **St Peter's Abbey**, dating from AD 847. Among lovingly tended graves you'll find the entrance to the **catacombs** (adult/student €1/0.70; open 10.30am-5pm summer, 10.30am-3.30pm winter). The western end of Franziskanergasse opens out into Max Reinhardt Platz, where you'll see the back of Fisher von Erlach's **Collegiate Church** (Universitätsplatz), an outstanding example of baroque architecture. The town is at its prettiest at night.

New boat cruises have been launched along the River Salzach. Ask the tourist office.

Festung Hohensalzburg Towering above Salzburg is its **fortress** (☎ 84 24 30-11; Mönchsberg 34; admission to grounds only €3.56, with interiors & audio guide €7.12; open 9am-6pm 15 Mar-14 Jun, 8.30am-7pm 15 Jun-14 Sept, 9am-5pm 15 Sept-14 Mar). This castle was home to the many archbishop-princes who ruled Salzburg from AD 798, and the magnificent views from its grounds include an isolated house in a big field to the south. Some city tour guides like to say this was the home of the official executioner, but others admit it more likely belonged to the archbishop's groundskeeper.

Inside are the ornate state rooms, torture chambers and two museums. The opulence in which the archbishops lived is impressive, but perhaps not as compelling as the grotesque torture masks and scary-looking chastity belt in one of the museums.

It takes 15 minutes to walk up the hill to the fortress, or you can catch the **Festungsbahn** (Festungsgasse 4; €2.80; open 9am-10pm daily).

Schloss Mirabell This palace was built by the worldly prince-archbishop Wolf Dietrich for his mistress in 1606. Its attractive gardens featured in The Sound of Music, and brides in white dresses and their grooms flock here in droves in summer to have their pictures taken. 'Musical Spring' concerts (among others) are held in the palace. The marble staircase inside is adorned with baroque sculptures.

Mausoleum of Wolf Dietrich In the graveyard (open 9am-7pm Apr-Oct, 9am-4pm Nov-Mar) of the 16th-century St Sebastian's Church on Linzer Gasse sits Wolf Dietrich's not-so-humble memorial to himself. It's since been restored by others, who obviously thought it worth preserving the amusingly bombastic epitaphs here. Both Mozart's father and widow are buried in the graveyard.

Museums It's supremely ironic that although Mozart found Salzburg stifling and couldn't wait to leave, his life here is one of the city's major tourist drawcards. People flock to Mozart's **Geburtshaus** (Birthplace; ☎ 84 43 13; Getreidegasse 9; adults/students & seniors €5.50/4.50; open 9am-6pm daily, to 7pm July & Aug) and his **Wohnhaus** (Residence; ☎ 87 42 27-40; Makartplatz 8; admission & hours as for Geburtshaus) to see musical instruments, sheet music, letters, family paintings and other memorabilia of the composer's early years. A combined ticket to both houses is €9 (students and seniors €7). The Wohnhaus is more extensive, and houses the **Mozart Sound and Film Museum** (admission free).

In the **Residenz** (☎ 80 42-2690; Residenzplatz 1; €7.25/5.50 adult/student), you can visit the archbishops' baroque state rooms and a gallery housing good 16th- and 17th-century Dutch and Flemish paintings. The **Rupertinum** (☎ 80 42 23 36; Wiener Philharmoniker Gasse 9; adult/student €7/4.36; open 10am-5pm Tues-Sun) contains contemporary art.

The **Haus der Natur** (Museum of Natural History; ☎ 84 26 53 Museumsplatz 5; adult/senior/student under 27 €4.50/4/2.50; open 9am-5pm daily) is a surprise hit in a city normally preoccupied with music and the baroque. Schoolchildren and adults flock to see rooms full of crystals, watch the moon diorama, watch sharks being fed and generally learn about the animal world.

Organised Tours
One-hour walking tours (€8) of the old city leave from the main tourist office. Other tours of Salzburg mostly leave from Mirabellplatz, including regular Sound of Music tours.

This tour is enduringly popular with the English-speaking visitors, even if there's a certain tackiness about it.

It lasts three to four hours, costs around €29 and takes in sights in the city, including a passing wave at the **Nonnberg Abbey** that featured in the movie, as well as some in neighbouring Salzkammergut.

Some visitors find the proceedings quite dull. Yet, if you go with a group with the right tongue-in-cheek enthusiasm, it can be brilliant fun. Consider yourself blessed if you find

yourself among manic Julie Andrews impersonators flouncing in the fields, screeching 'the hills are alive', or with loutish youths who skip about chanting 'I am 16 going on 17'. Unfortunately, there's no longer access to the summer house where this last song was performed, as, according to one reader:

The gazebo is now locked. No tourists can leap from bench to bench as a result of an 85-year-old fan imitating Liesel and falling – breaking a hip.
J Smethurst

Special Events
The **Salzburg International Festival** (ⓦ www .salzburgfestival.at) takes place from late July to the end of August, and includes music ranging from Mozart (of course!) to contemporary. Several events take place each day in different locations. Prices range from €12 to €340. The cheapest tickets are for standing-room, which can usually be booked beforehand. Most things sell out months in advance. Write for information as early as October to: **Kartenbüro der Salzburger Festspiele** (Postfach 140, A-5010 Salzburg). Try checking closer to the event for cancellations – inquire at the **ticket office** (☎ 80 45, fax -401; Herbert von Karajan Platz 11; open 9.30am-7pm, until the last daily performance during the festival), behind the horse fountain. Other important music festivals are at Easter and Whit Sunday.

Places to Stay
Ask for the tourist office's hotel brochure, which gives prices for hotels, pensions, hostels and camping grounds. Accommodation is at a premium during festivals.

Camping Just north of the A1 Nord exit is **Camping Kasern** (☎/fax 45 05 76; ⓔ camp ingkasern@aon.at; Carl Zuckmayer Strasse 4; sites per adult/car/tent €4.50/3/3; open Apr-Oct). **Camping Nord-Sam** (☎/fax 66 04 94; Samstrasse 22a; sites per adult/car & tent €5.50/8; open Easter & May-Sept) is slightly closer to town.

Private Rooms The tourist office's list of private rooms and apartments doesn't include the Kasern area, as this is just north of the city limits. But this area, up the hill from the Salzburg-Maria Plain mainline train station (warning – not the Maria-Plain station on the local train network), has the best bargains.

Haus Lindner (*π 45 66 81;* e *info@haus -lindner.at; Panoramaweg 5; €15 per person in double & triple rooms*) is one of the most popular. Its comfortable rooms and its homy atmosphere make it feel like you're staying with friends. Although breakfast is provided, there are kitchen facilities, too.

Another good option among the forest of 'Zimmer frei' (rooms vacant) signs is neighbouring **Haus Christine** (*π 45 67 73; Panoramaweg 3; €14-15 per person*).

Hostels If you're travelling to party, head for the sociable **International Youth Hotel** (*YoHo; π 87 96 49, fax 87 88 10;* e *office@yoho.at;* w *www.yoho.at; Paracelsusstrasse 9; 8-bed dorms/4-bed dorms/doubles €14/16/19, including 1 free shower a day; open all day*). There's a bar with loud music and cheap beer, the staff are mostly young, native English-speakers, outings are organised and *The Sound of Music* is screened daily. This place accepts phone reservations no earlier than one day in advance, although you can book ahead on the Internet. There are separate charges for extra showers (€1), lockers (€0.50 to €1) and breakfast (€3).

The large HI **Jugendgästehaus** (*π 84 26 70-0, fax 84 11 01;* e *jgh.salzburg@jgh.at; Josef Preis Allee 18; 8-bed dorms/4-bed dorms/doubles from €13.34/17.44/21.80, surcharge for single-night stays €2.50; check-in from 11am, although reception closed intermittently during the day*) is probably the most comfortable hostel. It has free lockers, a bar and a small kitchen. Daily *Sound of Music* tours are the cheapest in town at €25.45 for anybody who shows up by 8.45am or 1.30pm. The film is also shown daily.

To reach **Institut St Sebastian** (*π 87 13 86, fax -85;* e *office@st-sebastian-salzburg.at; Linzer Gasse 41; dorm beds without/with sheets €14.50/16.70, singles/doubles without shower & toilet €26/38.50, with facilities €30.50/52.30*), you turn through the gate marked 'Feuerwache Bruderhof'. This hostel has a roof terrace and kitchens, but the sound of church bells is loud in some rooms.

The **Naturfreundehaus** (*π/fax 84 17 29; Mönchsberg 19; dorm beds €12.50-13.50, showers €0.80; 1am curfew, open mid-April to mid-Oct*) compensates for its fairly ordinary dorm rooms with priceless views over the city. High on the Mönchsberg hill, this hostel is reached via the Mönchsberg lift

(€2.40 return) from A Neumayr Platz or by climbing the stairs from Toscanini Hof, behind the Festival Halls. There's also a café. Sometimes, its too cold to open the unheated rooms, so phone ahead.

Hotels & Pensions – Budget Centrally located **Junger Fuchs** (*π 87 54 96; Linzer Gasse 54; singles/doubles/triples €25.50/33.50/44 without breakfast*) remains a solid, if unremarkable, budget choice. Its cramped stairwell opens out into reasonably sized rooms with wooden floorboards.

Rooms at **Pension Jahn** (*π 87 14 05, fax 87 55 35; Elisabethenstrasse 31; singles/doubles from €31/43, doubles with private shower €64*) are also fairly spartan, but clean. And the pension is handy for the train station.

Gasthof Wallner (*π 84 50 23, fax -3; Aiglhofstrasse 15; singles/doubles €26/42, singles/doubles/quads with private bathroom €40/60/85*) hardly seems like it's in Salzburg, as it lies on the opposite side of the Mönchsberg from the old town. However, it's only a 10-minute ride from the centre on bus No 29 from Hanuschplatz. The reception faces a main road, but the pleasant, airy rooms are in a separate building set back from the street.

Pension Elisabeth (*π/fax 87 16 64; Vogelweiderstrasse 52; singles/doubles €33/39, singles/doubles with bathroom €42/64*) has been nicely renovated in recent years, making it Salzburg's top budget choice. It's near the Breitenfelderstrasse stop of bus No 15, which heads for town every 15 minutes.

Hotels & Pensions – Mid-Range & Top End For an option that really does possess the personal atmosphere it boasts of, try **Pension Bergland** (*π 87 23 18, fax -8;* e *pkuhn@ berglandhotel.at; Rupertgasse 15; singles/doubles €50/80*). Small, family-run, with individual touches in each folksy room, it's a 15-minute walk from the old town.

The friendly staff at **Centro Hotel** (*π 88 22 21, fax -55;* e *centro-hotel@Salzburg.co.at; Auerspergstrasse 24; singles/doubles €66/104*) are happy to show you to the lift or free overnight parking. This is a fairly new hotel and its modern rooms are spotless, if a trifle bland. The hotel caters for many youth groups.

Hotel Markus Sittikus (*π 87 11 21-0, fax -58; Markus Sittikus Strasse 20; singles/doubles €73/110*) is more formal, possibly due to its location near the Salzburg Congress Centre.

CHRISTIAN ASLUND

St Anton am Arlberg, Austria – a mecca for international skiers

PATRICK HORTON

Johann Strauss, Vienna, Austria

DIANA MAYFIELD

The sleek lines of Haas-Haus contrast with the Gothic Stephansdom (St Stephen's Cathedral), Vienna

CHRIS MELLOR

After a long day of exploring Innsbruck, enjoy a coffee at an outdoor *Café Konditorei*

Prague Castle lights the night sky over Malá Strana (the Small Quarter) and the Vltava River

Live rock performances at Lucerna Music Bar are just one part of Prague's vibrant nightlife

Night lights around the neo-Renaissance National Theatre, Prague

With all mod cons, however, it's a very pleasant place to stay.

Being housed in medieval buildings, many hotels in the historic city centre have rather musty and gloomy interiors. **Hotel Wolf** (☎ 84 34 53-0, fax 84 24 23-4; e office@hotelwolf .com; Kaigasse 7; singles/doubles from €68/ 98) manages to avoid that, while retaining the essential character of its 500-year-old abode. It's an ideal mix of quaint bedrooms and tasteful bathrooms.

Blaue Gans (☎ 84 24 91, fax -9; e office@ blauegans.at; Getreidegasse 41-43; singles/ doubles from €115/119) also offers modern luxury (just think blond-wood furniture and frosted-glass bathroom doors) in a historic setting.

If you prefer baroque decor, **Goldener Hirsch** (☎ 80 84-0, fax 84 33 49; Getreidegasse 37; singles/doubles from €129/165) is one of the best places in town.

Places to Eat

There's a **fruit and vegetable market** at Mirabellplatz on Thursday morning. On Universitätsplatz and Kapitelplatz there are **market stalls** and **fast-food stands**. There's a **Billa supermarket** (Schallmooser Hauptstrasse) and a **Eurospar supermarket** (open 8am-7pm Mon-Fri, 7.30am-5pm Sat) situated by the train station.

Places to Eat – Budget The most convenient university mensa is **Toskana** (Sigmund Haffner Gasse 11), where lunches are served from 11.30am to 2pm on weekdays, and cost from €2.50 for students, €3.50 for others.

Sushi and salads are available from **Flying Sushi** (Rudolfskai 8; boxes to eat-in or takeaway from €5.80).

For vegetarian nourishment on weekdays, try **Vegy Vollwertimbiss** (Schwarzstrasse 21; salads from €3, lunch menu €7.20; open 11am-5pm), or the holistic **Bio Bistro Spicy Spices** (☎ 87 07 12; Wolf-Dietrich-Strasse 1; mains €5, salads €3). At weekends, you can walk 15 minutes to the latter's sister restaurant **Spicy by Sead** (Schallmooser Hauptstrasse 48), which offers much the same deal.

Picnic (Judengasse 15; sandwiches from €4.72, pasta from €5.67; open daily May-Sept, otherwise closed on Tues) seems an enduringly popular joint. It serves cheap snacks, including 'big sandwiches' so big you can't get your mouth around them.

Wilder Mann (in the passageway off Getreidegasse 20; mains €5-7.90; open Mon-Fri), serves traditional Austrian food in a friendly, bustling environment. Tables, both inside and out, are often so packed it's almost impossible not to get chatting with fellow diners.

Stadtalm (Mönchsberg 19c; mains from €6.80; open daily mid-Apr–mid-Oct) is a great place to tuck into a well-priced meal while you admire the view.

For coffee houses, try **Café Tomaselli**, **Café Konditorei Fürst** (both on Alter Markt) or **Café Glockenspiel** (Mozartplatz 2).

Places to Eat – Mid-Range & Top End Just off Mozartplatz, **Zwettler's** (Kaigasse 3; mains €6.50-10.50; open Mon-Sat for dinner) serves up Italo-Austrian cuisine, from Wiener Schnitzel, Styrian chicken breast and beef goulash to spinach gnocchi. Its Salzburger Nockerl (soufflé) is renowned.

Ährlich (Wolf Dietrich Strasse 7; mains €9.50-16.30; open Mon-Sat) has given local cuisine a healthy twist, and serves vegetarian as well as meat-based mains.

However, for a complete antidote to feeling weighed down by stodgy fare, sample the sharp, fresh tastes of Thai restaurant **Pacific** (☎ 84 22 88; Franz Josef Kai 13; noodle dishes from €7, curries from €11; open Mon-Sat evenings).

Two huge dining complexes, with a series of different rooms, hark back to a different era, although both are a bit touristy. **Sternbräu** (between Getreidegasse 36 & Griesgasse 23; mains from €5.60; open daily) serves Austrian food, such as Tafelspitsz, and fish when in season. The adjoining courtyard features a self-service summer buffet and a pizzeria. **Stiftskeller St Peter** (☎ 84 12 68-34; St Peter Bezirk I/4; mains from €10; open daily) is more upmarket. It offers healthy options like asparagus or cottage cheese, smoked salmon and wasabi, but determinedly old-fashioned dishes are also on the menu. Even if you don't eat in the complex's baroque main salon, have a quick look inside.

Cellar restaurant **Zum Mohren** (☎ 484 23 87; Judengasse 9; mains from €12; open Mon-Sat) offers traditional food in a reasonably formal environment.

Entertainment

When you enter **Augustiner Bräustübl** (Augustinergasse 4-6; open 3pm-11pm Mon-Fri,

2.30pm-11pm Sat & Sun) you hear the contented hum of the crowd well before you descend the steps into the beer halls or garden. The brew produced by local monks – served in litre (€5) or half-litre (€2.50) ceramic mugs – is doing a good job as a social lubricant. Other convivial beer halls include **Stieglkeller** *(Festungsgasse 10; open 10am-10pm daily Apr-Oct)*, which has a garden overlooking the town, and **Salzburger Weissbierbrauerei** *(cnr Rupertgasse & Virgilgasse)*.

There's a lively stretch of bars, clubs and discos near the Hotel Altstadt on Rudolfskai, including **Irish pubs** with live music. Directly across the river, there's also a little scene along Steingasse. However, things in both these strips generally quieten down soon after midnight. Real night owls need to head to **Bar Flip** *(Gstättengasse 17)*, or **Mount Inn** *(Gstättengasse 21)*, establishments which both keep humming until 4am.

The legendary **Cave Club** *(☎ 84 00 26;* W *www.cave-club.at; Leopoldskronstrasse 26)* is still pumping out hard-core techno. Phone ahead or check the website to see what's on.

Shopping

The obvious souvenir is confectionery, particularly *Mozartkugeln*. These chocolate-coated combinations of nougat and marzipan cost around €0.45 per piece (cheaper in supermarkets), available individually or in presentation packs.

Getting There & Away

Air The airport *(☎ 85 80)* handles regular scheduled flights to Amsterdam, Brussels, Frankfurt, London, Paris and Zürich. Contact **Austrian Airlines** *(☎ 85 45 11-0)* there or go online to no-frills **Ryanair** *(W www.ryanair.com)*, which has two flights a day (three on Saturday) from London.

Bus Bundesbuses to Kitzbühel (€12 one way, 2¼ hours, at least three times daily) and other ski resorts depart from the train station post office. Those to the Salzkammergut region now leave from just to the left of the main station exit. Destinations include Bad Ischl (€7.40, 1¾ hours), Mondsee (€4.50, 50 minutes), St Gilgen (€4.50, 50 minutes) and St Wolfgang (€6.70, 1½ hours). There are timetable boards at each departure point and a bus information office

in the train station. Alternatively, call ☎ 4660-333 for information.

Train Fast trains leave for Vienna (€33.40, 3¼ hours) via Linz every hour. The express service to Klagenfurt (€26.10, three hours) goes via Villach. The quickest way to Innsbruck (two hours) is by the 'corridor' train through Germany via Kufstein; trains depart at least every two hours and the fare is €27.60. There are trains every 30 to 60 minutes to Munich (€21.60, two hours).

Car & Motorcycle Three autobahns converge on Salzburg and form a loop round the city: the A1 from Linz, Vienna and the east; the A8/E52 from Munich and the west; and the A10/E55 from Villach and the south. Heading south to Carinthia on the A10, there are two tunnels through the mountains; the combined toll is €10 (€7 for motorcycles).

Getting Around

To/From the Airport Salzburg airport is 4km directly west of the city centre. Bus No 77 goes there from the main train station. A taxi costs about €12.

Bus Bus drivers sell single bus tickets for €1.60. Other tickets must be bought from the automatic machines at major stops, Tabak shops or tourist offices. Day passes are €2.90 and weeklies cost €9. Prices are 50% less for children aged six to 15 years; those under six travel free.

Car & Motorcycle Don't drive in the city centre. Parking places are scarce and much of the old town is pedestrianised. The largest central park is the Altstadt Garage under the Mönchsberg. Attended car parks cost €1.40 to €2.40 an hour. On streets with automatic ticket machines (blue zones), a three-hour maximum applies (€3, or €0.50 for 30 minutes) during specified times – usually shopping hours.

Other Transport Flag fall in a taxi is €2.40 (€3.20 at night), plus about €1.10 per kilometre inside the city or €1.60 per kilometre outside the city. To book a taxi, call ☎ 87 44 00. **Top Bike** *(☎ 0676 476 72 59)* rents bikes from the Intertreff Café just outside the train station and from the main city bridge. A pony-and-trap *(fiaker)* ride for up to four passengers costs €30.50 for 25 minutes.

AROUND SALZBURG

Hellbrunn

Four kilometres south of Salzburg's old-town centre is the popular **Schloss Hellbrunn** (☎ 82 03 72-0; Fürstenweg 37; adult/student €7.50/5.50; open 9am-4.30pm, April & Oct, to 5.30pm in May, June & Sept, to 10pm in July & Aug). Built in the 17th century by bishop Markus Sittikus, Wolf Dietrich's nephew, this castle is mainly known for its ingenious trick fountains and water-powered figures. When the tour guides set them off, expect to get wet! Admission includes a tour of the **baroque palace**. Other parts of the garden (without fountains) are open year-round and free to visit.

The **Hellbrunn Zoo** (adult/student €6.50/4.70; open 8.30am-6.60pm daily in summer, 8.30am-4.30pm daily in winter) is as naturalistic and open-plan as possible.

Getting There & Away City bus No 55 runs to the palace every half-hour from Salzburg Hauptbahnhof, via Rudolfskai in the old town (Salzburg tickets are valid).

Hallein

☎ 06245 • pop 20,000

Hallein's prime attraction is the **salt mine** (Salzbergwerk; ☎ 825 85 15; open 9am-5pm daily Apr-Oct, 11am-3pm Nov-Mar) at Bad Dürrnberg, situated on the hill above. Much of Salzburg's past prosperity was dependent upon salt mines, and this one is the easiest to visit from the city. Some people rave about the experience, while others find the one-hour tour disappointing and overpriced (adults/student €15.50/9.30). Careering down the wooden slides in the caves is fun, and you get a brief raft trip on the salt lake, but there's little else to see. Overalls are supplied. The salt-mine tours in the Salzkammergut are cheaper – see the Salzkammergut section later in this chapter.

The Hallein **tourist office** (☎ 853 94; e info-tg@eunet.at; Mauttorpromenade; open 9am-6pm Mon-Thur, 9am-8pm Fri-Sat, 10am-3pm Sun July–mid-Sept, otherwise 10am-6pm Mon-Thur, 10am-8pm Fri) is on the narrow island adjoining the Stadtbrücke.

Getting There & Away Hallein is 30 minutes or less from Salzburg by bus or train (€3). Since the cable-car service was discontinued, the only way to reach Bad Dürrnberg is with a car or by taking the bus (€1.60) from outside

the station. You could also hike to the mine, though it's a steep 40-minute climb – at the church with the bare concrete tower, turn left along Ferchl Strasse, and follow the sign pointing to the right after the yellow Volksschule building.

Werfen

☎ 06468 • pop 3000

Werfen is a rewarding day trip from Salzburg. The **Hohenwerfen Fortress** (adult/student €9/7.50; open daily Apr-Nov) stands on the hill above the village. Originally built in 1077, the present building dates from the 16th century. Admission includes an exhibition, a guided tour of the interior and a dramatic falconry show, where birds of prey swoop low over the heads of the crowd. The walk up from the village takes 20 minutes.

The **Eisriesenwelt Höhle** (Giant Ice Caves; ☎ 5646; adult/student & senior €7.20/6.50 without cable car; open 1 May-26 Oct) in the mountains are the largest accessible ice caves in the world. The vast, natural ice formations inside are elaborate and beautiful. Take warm clothes because it gets cold inside and the tour lasts 75 minutes. Some elderly visitors find the going too arduous. The cable-car fare is often included in the quoted price.

Both attractions can be visited in one day if you start early (tour the caves first, and be at the castle by 3pm for the falconry show). The **tourist office** (☎ 5388; e info@werfen.at; Markt 24; open 9am-5pm Mon-Fri mid-Aug–mid-July, 9am-7pm Mon-Fri & 5pm-7pm Sat mid-July–mid-Aug) is in the village main street.

Getting There & Around Werfen (and Hallein) can be reached from Salzburg by Hwy 10. By train (€6) it takes 50 minutes. The village is a five-minute walk from Werfen station. Getting to the caves is more complicated, though scenic. A minibus service (€5.50 return) from the station operates along the steep, 6km road to the car park, which is as far as cars can go. A 15-minute walk then brings you to the cable car (€8.80/8 return adult/concession) from which it is a further 15-minute walk to the caves. Allow four hours return from the station, or three hours from the car park (peak-season queues may add an hour). The whole route can be hiked, but it's a very hard four-hour ascent, rising 1100m above the village.

AUSTRIA

Salzkammergut

Salzkammergut, named after its salt mines, is a picturesque holiday region of mountains and lakes east of Salzburg. The main season is summer, when hiking and water sports – or simply relaxing – are popular pursuits. In winter, some hiking paths stay open and there's downhill or cross-country skiing. The Salzkammergut Lammertal ski region includes 80 cable cars and lifts, serving 145km of ski runs; the general ski pass costs €51 for a minimum two days. You can also get one-day passes for individual resorts.

Orientation & Information

Bad Ischl is the geographical centre of Salzkammergut. The largest lake is Attersee, situated to the north. Most of the lakes south of Bad Ischl are much smaller, the largest there being Hallstätter See. West of Bad Ischl is the Wolfgangsee.

Because the area straddles several of Austria's federal provinces, various details are available from provincial tourist offices in Salzburg and Linz (see individual city sections). Once within the region, a central point of information is **Salzkammergut Touristik** (☎ 06132-240 00-0; e office@salzkammergut.co.at; Götzstrasse 12, Bad Ischl; open 9am-8pm daily). Staff are helpful, but because it's a private agency they might try to sell you holiday packages.

The area is dotted with hostels and affordable hotels. Rooms in private homes often come with a surcharge for single-night stays (€3 to €4), but are still usually the best deals. Tourist offices can supply accommodation lists and generally make free bookings. Some lodgings close in winter. Resorts have a holiday/guest card (Gästekarte) offering discounts in the whole region; ask for this if it is not offered. Your hotel, hostel or camping ground must stamp the card for it to be valid.

If you plan to stay a while, buy the Salzkammergut Card for €4.90. It's valid between May and October for the duration of your visit and provides a 25% discount on sights, ferries, cable cars and some Bundesbuses.

Getting Around

The major rail routes bypass the heart of Salzkammergut, but regional trains cross the area in a north-south direction. You get on this route from Attnang Puchheim on the Salzburg-Linz line. The track from here connects Gmunden, Traunkirchen, Ebensee, Bad Ischl, Hallstatt and Obertraun. When you're travelling from a small unstaffed station (unbesetzter Bahnhof), you buy your ticket on the train; no surcharge applies. After Obertraun, the railway continues east via Bad Aussee before connecting with the main Bischofshofen-Graz line at Stainach Irdning. Attersee can also be reached via Vöcklamarkt, the next stop on the Salzburg–Linz line before Attnang Puchheim.

Regular Bundesbuses connect the region's towns and villages, though less frequently on weekends. Timetables are displayed at stops, and tickets can be bought from the driver.

Passenger boats ply the waters of the Attersee, Traunsee, Mondsee, Hallstätter See and Wolfgangsee.

To reach Salzkammergut from Salzburg by car or motorcycle, take the A1 or Hwy 158.

BAD ISCHL

☎ 06132 • pop 13,000

WWI – or what became WWI – was declared in Bad Ischl. It's an unlikely birthplace for such brutality, given that it's a spa resort devoted to rather more relaxing and healthier pursuits (and now a genteel retirees' paradise to boot). However, in the 19th and early 20th centuries, it was fashionable for Austria's power-brokers to 'take the cure' in the town's salty waters. Emperor Franz Josef was enjoying his annual summer holiday here in 1914 when difficulties with Serbia demanded his urgent attention.

Orientation & Information

The town centre rests within a bend of the River Traun. If you turn left into the main road as you come out of the train station, you will see the **tourist office** (Kurdirektion; ☎ 277 57-0, fax -77; e office@badischl.at; Bahnhofstrasse 6; open 8am-6pm Mon-Fri, 9am-3pm Sat, 10am-1pm Sun July-Sept, 8am-5pm Mon-Fri, 8am-noon Sat Oct-June) almost immediately. A telephone lobby in its doorway can be used to make free hotel bookings after hours. The **post office** (Postamt 4820), along the road at Aübockplatz, changes money (cash only). Salzkammergut Touristik (see the introductory Salzkammergut Orientation & Information section earlier) offers bike rentals and Internet access.

SALZKAMMERGUT

Things to See & Do

The **Kaiservilla** (☎ 232 41; Kaiserpark; tours €9.50; open daily May–mid-Oct) was Franz Josef's summer residence and shows he loved little better than huntin', shootin' and fishin'; it's decorated with an obscene number of animal trophies. The villa can be visited only by guided tour (in German but with written English translations), during which you'll pick up little gems like the fact that Franz Josef was conceived in Bad Ischl after his mother, Princess Sophie, took a treatment to cure her infertility in 1828. There are several 40-minute tours daily during the main season, but one is also offered every Wednesday from January to April.

The teahouse of Franz Josef's wife, Elisabeth, is now a **photo museum** (entry €1.50).

Free *Kurkonzerte* (spa concerts) are held regularly during summer; the tourist office has venues and times. An operetta festival takes place in July and August; for details and advance reservations, call ☎ 238 39.

Bad Ischl has downhill skiing from **Mt Katrin** (a winter day-pass costs €18) and various cross-country skiing routes. In summer, the Mt Katrin cable car costs €12 return. The **salt mine** (Salzbergwerk) is south of town; tours cost €10.90, are conducted daily from May to late September and receive mixed reviews.

The tourist office has information on health treatments in the resort.

Places to Stay & Eat

In the town centre behind Kreuzplatz is the HI **Jugendgästehaus** (☎ 265 77, fax -75; Am

Rechensteg 5; dorm beds €12.50, singles/ doubles €25.44/36.34, plus €1-1.50 spa tax depending on the season; reception open 8am-1pm & 5pm-7pm).

Otherwise, the cheapest deal is the immaculate **Haus Rothauer** *(☎ 236 28; Kaltenbachstrasse 12; singles €20, doubles with shower €48).* **Haus Baumgartner** *(☎ 241 66, fax 222 08; Maxquellgasse 26; rooms €20-27 per person)* is less modern, but its leafy location by the river makes it equally appealing. **Goldener Ochs** *(☎ 235 29-0, fax -50; Grazer Strasse 4; singles/doubles from €41/74)* is amazing value for the luxury it offers.

Umeko *(Rettenbachweg 1; mains from €6.50; open daily)* is a delightful fusion of tasty Asian cuisine and Austrian farmhouse decor, high on a hill above the river. At lunchtime (except Sunday) you can eat your fill from the €5.80 buffet. Laidback **Blauen Enzian** *(Wirerstrasse 2; dishes €8-14; closed Sun)* offers a variety of pasta, salads, regional and seasonal dishes. **Café Zauner** on the Esplanade by the river (there's also a branch at Pfarrgasse 2) is a great place to sit in summer.

There's a **Konsum supermarket** behind the Trinkhalle.

Getting There & Away

Bundesbuses leave in front of the train station. They run hourly to Salzburg (€7.40) via St Gilgen between 5am and approximately 8pm. To St Wolfgang (€3), you generally need to change at Strobl (although you can buy one ticket straight through). Buses go to Hallstatt every couple of hours (€3.60, 50 minutes), arriving in the village itself. Some services continue to Obertraun.

Trains depart roughly hourly. It costs €2.80 to Hallstatt station, to which you must add the €1.80 cost of the boat to the village (see the Hallstatt Getting There & Away section later). The train fare to Salzburg (two hours), via Attnang Puchheim, is €15.50.

HALLSTATT
☎ 06134 • pop 1150

There's evidence of human settlement at Hallstatt as long as 4500 years ago – and who wouldn't want to move into such a breathtaking location as early as possible? The village, now a designated Unesco World Heritage Site, perches on a steep mountainside, beside a placid lake. Mining salt in the peak above was the main activity for thousands of years.

Today, tourism is the major money-spinner. Fortunately, the crowds of day-trippers during the summer only stay a few hours, then calm returns.

Orientation & Information

Seestrasse is the main street. Turn left from the ferry to reach the **tourist office** *(☎ 8208, fax 8352; e hallstatt-info@eunet.at; Seestrasse 169; open 9am-noon, 1pm-5pm Mon-Fri year-round, 10am-5pm Sat May-Oct, 10am-2pm Sun July-Aug).* The **post office** *(Postamt 4830)* is around the corner, and changes money.

Things to See & Do

Above the village are the **Salzbergwerk** *(saltworks; ☎ 8400; admission €14; open 9am-4pm daily late Apr-26 Oct, to 3.30pm from mid-Sept).* Riding the funicular up adds €5.50 to the salt mine ticket, or costs €7.50 return if you just want to get up the mountain. However, there are two scenic hiking trails you could take instead. Hallstatt is rich with archaeological interest. Near the mine, 2000 graves were discovered, dating from 1000 to 500 BC. Don't miss the macabre **Beinhaus** *(Bone House; admission €1)* near the village parish church; it contains rows of decorated skulls from the 15th century and later. Around the lake at Obertraun are the **Dachstein Rieseneishöhle** *(Giant Ice Caves; admission €8, with Mammoth Cave €12.30; open early May–mid-Oct).* These include a reportedly spectacular giant stone (rather than ice) cave with sheer walls meeting in an arched ceiling called the Mammoth Cave. A cable car provides easy access.

Places to Stay & Eat

Some private rooms are only available during the busiest months of July and August; others require a minimum three-night stay. Ask at the tourist office, which will telephone around without charge.

For camping there's **Campingplatz Höll** *(☎ 8322; Lahn 201; sites per adult/tent/car €5.80/3.70/2.90; open Apr-Oct).* Tax is extra. There are two hostels: the HI **Jugendherberge** *(☎ 8212; Salzbergstrasse 50; dorm beds without/with sheets €9.30/12.60; open around May-Oct, check-in 5pm-6pm),* which is usually full with groups in July and August, and the **TVN Naturfreunde Herberge** *(☎/fax 8318; Kirchenweg 36; dorm beds without/*

with sheets €10/12.50). At both the hostels breakfast is available for €2.50.

Friendly and charming **Tauchergasthof Hallberg** (☎ 8709, fax 828 65; Seestrasse 113; per person €35-60) is near the tourist office, and the hub of the lake's scuba diving community.

Hallstatt's steep pavements certainly help you work up an appetite. Good restaurants include **Bräu Gasthof** (Seestrasse 120; dishes from €7.40; open daily 1 May-26 Oct) for typical Austrian food in an old-fashioned atmosphere, **Gasthof Weisses Lamm** (Morton-weg 166; mains from €7.50) which has some healthier options, and **Grüner Anger** (Lahn 10; mains from €7) near the HI hostel.

Nearby, **Obertraun** is another possible base: there's a **youth hostel** (☎ 06131-360; Winkl 26) and restaurants with affordable rooms. Ask the local **tourist office** (☎ 06131-351; e tourismus@obertraun.or.at).

Getting There & Away

There are some six buses a day to/from Obertraun and Bad Ischl. Until the 'Parkterrasse' stop downtown reopens, you can only alight in one place in Hallstatt – at 'Lahn', just south of the road tunnel. Beware, as services finish very early and the last guaranteed departure from Bad Ischl is 4.10pm. There are at least nine train services a day from Bad Ischl (€2.80, 50 minutes). The station is across the lake from the village, but the ferry captain waits for trains to arrive before making the short crossing (€1.80). Though trains run later, the last ferry departs the train station at 6.44pm (leaving Hallstatt at 6.10pm). Parking in the village is free if you have a guest card, though car access is restricted in the summer.

WOLFGANGSEE

You can swim or go boating on this lake, climb the mountain above it or just sit on the shore, gazing at the scenery. However, its proximity to Salzburg means the Wolfgangsee can become crowded in summer.

Orientation & Information

The lake is dominated by the Schafberg on the northern shore. Next to it is the resort of St Wolfgang. On the main street by the entrance to the road tunnel you'll find the **tourist office** (☎ 06138-2239-0; e info@stwolfgang .at; open 9am-noon Mon-Sat & 2pm-5pm Mon, Tues, Thur & Fri Sept-June, 8am-8pm Mon-Sat, noon-6pm Sun July & Aug). St Gilgen, on the western shore, provides easy access to Salzburg, 29km away. Its **tourist office** (☎ 06227-2348; e info@stgilgen .co.at; Mozartplatz 1; open 9am-noon Mon-Fri & 2pm-5pm Mon, Tues, Thur & Fri Sept-June, 8.30am-7pm Mon-Sat, 9am-noon Sun July & Aug) is in the Rathaus.

Things to See & Do

St Wolfgang's 14th-century **Pilgrimage Church** (open 9am-6pm daily), still attracts pilgrims. Today they're mainly interested in seeing the winged high altar, created by Michael Pacher between 1471 and 1481. Its eight large painted panels depict scenes from the life of Christ, and while the four outermost paintings once remained folded inwards much of the time, they now seem to be always open. For those churchgoers who find that one altar is not enough, there's an additional baroque double altar in the middle of the nave.

Another major attraction is the **Schafberg** (1783m). Some people like to climb mountains because they're there; others of us prefer the less strenuous train ride to the top. The first group will love the four-hour hike to the peak. The rest need to get there between early May and the end of October, when the Schafberg cog-wheel railway operates. It runs approximately hourly during the day and costs €12.70 to the top and €20.90 return. There is also a stop halfway up.

Hot-air ballooning and paragliding are also popular (ask at the tourist office) and **St Gilgen** offers good views and some pleasant swimming spots.

Places to Stay & Eat

Camping Appesbach (☎ 06138-2206; Au 99; sites per adult €5, tent & car €6; open Easter-Oct) is on the lakefront, 1km from St Wolfgang heading towards Strobl.

St Gilgen has a good HI **Jugendgästehaus** (☎ 06227-2365; Mondseestrasse 7; dorm beds/twin rooms/doubles €12.35/14.53/ 18.16; check-in 5pm-7pm), where some of the rooms have a lake view.

Both St Wolfgang and St Gilgen have numerous pensions, private rooms and holiday apartments. Most start at about €18 per person, although a few cheaper deals are available. The tourist offices have listings or will phone around for you without charge.

In St Wolfgang, the chalet-style **Gästehaus Raudaschl** (☎ 06138-2329; Pilgerstrasse 4; singles/doubles from €30/56) is lively and friendly.

Rooms in smaller **Pension Ellmauer** (☎/fax 06138-2388; Markt 183; singles/doubles €33/54) are of a much higher standard and have lake views.

In St Gilgen, you could try **Pension Pichler** (☎ 06227-7113; Helenenstrasse 8; rooms per person €21-28) across the highway from the centre of town, for a welcoming, cheap option.

Alternatively, you could try **Haus Schernthaner** (☎ 06227-2402, fax -2; e garni-schern taner@aon.at; Schwarzenbrunnerstrasse 4; singles/doubles €36.50/64) which is both pleasant and central.

There are many places to eat in both towns, from cheap snack joints to quaint touristy restaurants. Just follow your nose.

Getting There & Away

A ferry operates from Strobl to St Gilgen, stopping at various points en route, including St Wolfgang. Services are from late April to 26 October, but are more frequent from early July to early September. The journey from St Wolfgang to St Gilgen takes 45 to 50 minutes (€4.30), with boats sailing during the high season approximately twice an hour between 8am and 8pm.

Buses from St Wolfgang to St Gilgen and Salzburg go via Strobl on the east side of the lake. St Gilgen is 50 minutes from Salzburg by bus, with hourly departures till at least 8.30pm. The fare is €4.50.

NORTHERN SALZKAMMERGUT

West of Attersee is **Mondsee**, a lake whose warm water makes it a favourite swimming spot. Mondsee village has an attractive church that was used in the wedding scenes of *The Sound of Music*.

East of Attersee is Traunsee and its three main resorts: Gmunden, Traunkirchen and Ebensee. Gmunden is famous for its twin castles linked by a causeway on the lake, and the manufacture of ceramics.

Buses go east from Gmunden to Grünau (or take the train from Wels). This out-of-the-way destination has a good backpacker hostel, **The Tree House** (☎ 07616-8499; e treehouseho tel@hotmail.com; Schindlbachstrasse 525; dorm beds/doubles €13.80/16.44).

Tirol

Hooray for Tirolliwood! Its wonderful mountain scenery makes Tirol (sometimes spelled Tyrol) an ideal playground for hikers and mountaineers and its glitzy ski resorts add glamour. The province is divided in two: East Tirol has been isolated from the main part of the state ever since prosperous South Tirol was ceded to Italy at the end of WWI.

Train and bus journeys within Tirol are cheaper using VVT tickets, which can only be bought within Tirol (from train stations etc). These tickets can be combined with city passes. The system is quite complicated; the **IVB Kundenbüro** (☎ 0512-53 07-103; Stainerstrasse 2, Innsbruck) can give information.

INNSBRUCK

☎ 0512 • pop 111,000

As a two-time host to the winter Olympics – in 1964 and 1976 – Innsbruck could be easily mistaken for a sports-mad destination with little else to offer than skiing, snowboarding and a landmark ski-jump. How wrong that would be. An important trading post since the 12th century, the city also boasts the cultural legacy of being home to one branch of the Habsburgs. Emperor Maximilian erected the golden roof in the old town.

Orientation

Innsbruck lies in the valley of the River Inn, scenically squeezed between the northern chain of the Alps and the Tuxer mountain range to the south. The town centre is very compact, with the Hauptbahnhof only a 10-minute walk from the pedestrian-only, old town centre (Altstadt). The main street in the Altstadt is Herzog Friedrich Strasse.

Information

Tourist Offices The **main tourist office** (☎ 53 56-36, fax -41; e info@innsbruck .tvb.co.at; Burggraben 3; open 9am-6pm Mon-Sun) books hotel rooms (€3 commission) and sells ski passes and public transport tickets. Ask for the free tear-off map sheet, rather than buying one.

There are hotel **reservation centres** (open 9am-8pm daily, to 9.15pm in July, Aug & around Christmas) located in the main train station and at motorway exits near the city. The **youth waiting room** (Jugendwarteraum;

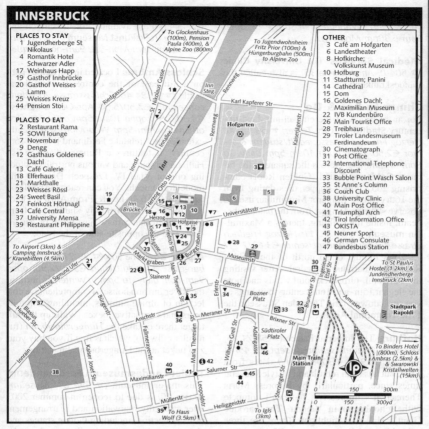

INNSBRUCK

PLACES TO STAY
1 Jugendherberge St Nikolaus
4 Romantik Hotel Schwarzer Adler
17 Weinhaus Happ
19 Gasthof Innbrücke
20 Gasthof Weisses Lamm
25 Weisses Kreuz
44 Pension Stoi

PLACES TO EAT
2 Restaurant Rama
5 SOWI lounge
7 Novembar
9 Dengg
12 Gasthaus Goldenes Dachl
13 Café Galerie
18 Elferhaus
21 Markthalle
23 Weisses Rössl
24 Sweet Basil
27 Feinkost Hörtnagl
34 Café Central
37 University Mensa
39 Restaurant Philippine

OTHER
3 Café am Hofgarten
6 Landestheater
8 Hofkirche; Volkskunst Museum
10 Hofburg
11 Stadtturm; Panini
14 Cathedral
15 Dom
16 Goldenes Dachl; Maximilian Museum
22 IVB Kundenbüro
26 Main Tourist Office
28 Treibhaus
29 Tiroler Landesmuseum Ferdinandeum
30 Cinematograph
31 Post Office
32 International Telephone Discount
33 Bubble Point Wasch Salon
35 St Anne's Column
36 Couch Club
40 University Clinic
41 Triumphal Arch
42 Tirol Information Office
43 ÖKISTA
45 Neuner Sport
46 German Consulate
47 Bundesbus Station

open mid-Sept–mid-July) in the train station also offers useful information.

The **Tirol Information office** (☎ 72 72, fax -7; e tirol.info@tirolwerbung.at; Maria Theresien Strasse 55; open 8am-6pm Mon-Fri) also has information.

Ask your hotel for the complementary 'Club Innsbruck' membership card. It provides various discounts and benefits, such as free guided mountain hikes between June and September. The Innsbruck Card, available at the main tourist office, gives free entry to museums and free use of public transport. It costs €18.89/23.98/29.07 for 24/48/72 hours.

Money There are various exchange bureaus around town (compare rates and commission) as well as Bankomats. The tourist office also exchanges money, however, it charges a hefty commission.

Post & Communications The **main post office** (Hauptpostamt 6010; Maximilianstrasse 2; open 7am-11pm Mon-Fri, 7am-9pm Sat, 8am-9pm Sun) is yet another place for changing cash. There's also a **train station post office** (Brunecker Strasse 1-3; open 7am-7pm Mon-Fri).

Email & Internet Access Owned by someone who's obviously seen the film *My Beautiful Laundrette* a few times, the fabulous, neon-coloured **Bubble Point Wasch Salon** (Brixner Strasse 1) allows you to read your email cheaply while doing your laundry. Internet access costs €1 for 10 minutes.

Travel Agencies Agencies include ÖKISTA (☎ 58 89 97; *Wilhelm Greil Strasse 17; open 9am-5.30pm Mon-Fri*).

Medical Services The **University Clinic** (☎ 504-0; *Anichstrasse 35*) is also called the Landeskrankenhaus.

Things to See & Do

For an overview of the city, climb the 14th-century **Stadtturm** (*City Tower; ☎ 56 15 00; Herzog Friedrich Strasse; adult/student & senior €2.50/2.00; open 10am-5pm daily, to 8pm in summer*). Across the square is the famous **Goldenes Dachl** (Golden Roof) comprising 2657 gilded copper tiles dating from the 16th century. Emperor Maximilian used to observe street performers from the balcony beneath. Inside the building, there's a Maximilian **museum** (☎ 58 11 11; *Herzog Friedrich Strasse 15; adult/student/senior €3.63/2.91/1.45*). A minute or so north of the Golden Roof is the baroque cathedral. After visiting the cathedral, turn back southwards and note the elegant 15th- and 16th-century buildings as you stroll down Maria Theresien Strasse to the 1767 **Triumphal Arch**.

Hofburg The Imperial Palace (☎ 58 71 86; *Rennweg 1; adult/senior/student €5.45/4/3.63; open 9am-4.30pm daily*) dates from 1397, but has been rebuilt and restyled several times since, particularly by Empress Maria Theresa. It's impressive, but can't compete with Schönbrunn in Vienna. The baroque Giant's Hall is a highlight. There are three guided tours daily in German (€2.18). Alternatively, for a do-it-yourself tour, buy the explanatory booklet in English (€1.81).

Hofkirche Diagonally across Universitätsstrasse from the palace is the Imperial Church (☎ 58 43 02; *Universitätsstrasse 2; adult/student under 27 €2.20/1.45, admission free Sun & holidays; visits 9am-5pm Mon-Sat, before 8am, noon-3pm & after 5pm Sun*). Major restoration means the empty sarcophagus of Maximilian I will be under wraps until autumn 2003 or later. Although you're now forbidden to touch the 28 giant statues of Habsburgs lining either side of the cask, these thankfully aren't being refurbished; it would be a shame to erase the traces of numerous inquisitive hands, which have polished parts of the dull bronze, including Kaiser Rudolf's

codpiece! Combined tickets (adult/student €5.45/4.00) are available for the church and adjoining **Volkskunst Museum** (*Folk Art Museum; 9am-5pm Mon-Sat, 9am-noon Sun*).

Schloss Ambras Located in a spacious park on a hill east of the centre, this medieval castle (☎ 34 84 46; *Schlossstrasse 20; adult/concession €7.50/5.50 Apr-Oct, otherwise €4.30/2.90; open 10am-5pm daily Apr-Oct, otherwise 2pm-5pm Wed-Mon*) was greatly extended by Archduke Ferdinand II in the 16th century. It features a Renaissance Spanish Hall, an armoury and various portraits including one of Vlad IV Tzespech Dracul – the model for Dracula. You can reach the castle on tram No 3 or 6, or bus K. From April to October, there's also an hourly shuttle bus from Maria Theresien Strasse, just north of Anichstrasse on the opposite side of the road.

Alpine Zoo The zoo (☎ 29 23 23; *Weiherburggasse 37; adult/child €5.80/2.90; open 9am-6pm daily, to 5pm in winter*) is north of the River Inn and houses a comprehensive collection of alpine animals, including amorous bears and combative ibexes. Walk up the hill to get there or take the *Hungerburgbahn* (funicular railway), which is free if you buy your zoo ticket at the Hungerburgbahn station.

Tiroler Landesmuseum Ferdinandeum This major museum (☎ 594 89; *Museumstrasse 15*) is due to reopen in summer 2003 after a lengthy renovation and rearrangement of its collection, including Gothic statues and altarpieces. Phone for details, or ask at the tourist office.

Swarovski Kristallwelten The Crystal Worlds (☎ 05224 51080; e *scs.visitors-centre@swarovski.com; Kristallweltenstrasse 1; admission €5.45; open 9am-6pm daily*) is a series of caverns featuring the famous Swarovski crystals. Greats like Salvador Dali, Andy Warhol and Keith Haring designed some of the displays, which are all very sparkly. The centre in Wattens is best reached by Bundesbus (€6.20 return, 30 minutes), which leaves from the train station.

Skiing

The ski region around Innsbruck has been totally refurbished, with the long-awaited reopening of the Mutters area, and new chair lifts and cable cars connecting previously separate runs. A one-day ski pass is €20 to €26, depending on the area, and there are several versions of multiday tickets available. Downhill equipment rental starts at €15. With 'Club Innsbruck', ski buses are free.

You can ski or snowboard all year at the popular **Stubai Glacier**. A one-day pass costs €35. Catch the white IVB Stubaltalbahn bus, departing roughly hourly from the bus station, or ask the tourist office about the free ski bus in winter. The journey there takes 80 minutes and the last bus back is usually at 5.30pm. Several places offer complete packages to the glacier, which compare favourably with going it alone. The tourist office package for €46.51 includes transport, passes and equipment rental. In winter, if you take the free ski bus, there's a cheaper €41.42 package.

Places to Stay

Camping West of the town centre, **Camping Innsbruck Kranebitten** (*☎/fax 28 41 80; Kranebitter Allee 214; sites per adult/tent/car €5.55/3/3; open year-round*) has a restaurant on site.

Private Rooms The tourist office has lists of private rooms in Innsbruck and Igls ranging from €15 per person. Igls is south of town; get there by tram No 6 or bus J. Further afield is **Haus Wolf** (*☎ 54 86 73; Dorfstrasse 48, Mutters; dorm beds €14*). Rooms have one to three beds, and rates include a big breakfast. Take the Stubaitalbahn tram from in front of the train station to Birchfeld (€1.82, 30 minutes). Trams depart every 50 minutes till 10.30pm.

Hostels None of Innsbruck's hostels is particularly convenient, but **Jugendherberge St Nikolaus** (*☎ 28 65 15, fax -14; e innsbruck@ hostelnikolaus.at; Innstrasse 95; dorm beds from €13, plus €0.80 surcharge for first night, doubles €18.20; check-in 5pm-10pm*) is probably the best located. It has a bar and restaurant and is a sociable place. There's more privacy, but, more of a draught too, in the hostel's sister **Glockenhaus pension** (*Weiherburggasse 3; singles/doubles €29/ 43.60*) up the hill.

The **Jugendherberge Innsbruck** (*☎ 34 61 79, fax -12; Reichenauerstrasse 147; dorm beds 1st night/additional nights €12.05/ 9.50; curfew 11pm, closed 10am-3pm summer, 10am-5pm rest of year*) is a huge, Soviet-

style concrete monstrosity that's more pleasant inside than out. Rates are €0.50 less if you're aged under 18. It has a kitchen and washing machines and is reached by bus O from Museumstrasse.

Two extra hostels to try in summer are **St Paulus Hostel** (*☎ 34 42 91; Reichenauerstrasse 72; open mid-June–early Sept*) and **Jugendwohnheim Fritz Prior** (*☎ 58 58 14, fax -4; Rennweg 17b; open July, Aug & New Year*). Both have similar prices to the above hostels, with check-in from 5pm.

Hotels & Pensions A pleasant choice is **Pension Paula** (*☎ 29 22 62, fax 29 30 17; e office@pensionpaula.at; Weiherburggasse 15; singles/doubles without shower & toilet €26/44, with facilities €33/53*) which has been made even more pleasant as it has been renovating its bathrooms. Guests aren't deterred by the uphill walk (with great views), so book ahead.

Two other cheapish options are situated on the northern bank of the River Inn: **Gasthof Innbrücke** (*☎ 28 19 34, fax 27 84 10; e inn bruecke@magnet.at; Innstrasse 1; singles/ doubles without shower & toilet €25.50/ 43.60, with facilities €32.70/58.20*) and the **Gasthof Weisses Lamm** (*☎ 831 56; Mariahilfstrasse 12; singles/doubles €33/55*).

If you stay at **Pension Stoi** (*☎ 58 54 34, fax 872 82; Salurner Strasse 7; singles/doubles without shower & toilet €29/47, with facilities €34/54*) you'll need to breakfast elsewhere but that's a small price to pay for such decent, centrally located rooms. Coming from the train station, turn left after the Neuner Sport shop.

Binders (*☎ 334 36-0, fax 334 39-99; Dr Glatz Strasse 20; singles without shower & toilet €36/49, with facilities from €43/64*) is for those whose taste for modern comfort and style exceeds their budget. Even those rooms without shower and toilet feel luxurious and the breakfast room and other public spaces are just nice to be in, too.

Two hotels in the old town stand out. **Weisses Kreuz** (*☎ 594 79, fax -90; e hotel .weisses.kreuz@eunet.at; Herzog Friedrich Strasse 31; singles from €35, singles/doubles with shower & toilet from €59/89*), once played host to Mozart and resonates with history. Across the street, **Weinhaus Happ** (*☎ 58 29 80, fax -11; e office@weinhaus-happ.at; Herzog Friedrich Strasse 14; singles/doubles* *from €51/88)* has some rooms with views of the Golden Roof.

Innsbruck's most opulent accommodation is the **Romantik Hotel Schwarzer Adler** *(☎ 58 71 09, fax 56 16 97; e romantikhotel-inns bruck@netway.at; Kaiserjägerstrasse 2; singles/ doubles from €98/140).* Its rooms are individually styled and its over-the-top suites include one fitted by Versace and another with Swarovski crystals.

Places to Eat

A group of international restaurants has diffused Innsbruck's focus on Tirolean cuisine. Whether you think that's a good thing or not depends on how much you crave a break from calorific regional specialities.

For groceries and fresh produce, there is the supermarket **Feinkost Hörtnagl** *(Burggraben)* or a large indoor food market by the river in **Markthalle** *(Herzog Siegmund Ufer; open Mon-Fri & Sat morning).*

You enjoy great views of the Alps lunching at **University Mensa** *(Herzog Siegmund Ufer 15; mains from €4.60; open 11am-1.30pm Mon-Thur, 11am-2pm Fri & Sat).* Another mensa option is the **SOWI lounge** *(Universitätsstrasse 15; mains from €3; open 8am-5pm Mon-Thur, 10am-3pm Fri).*

The first floor of self-service restaurant **Panini** *(cnr of Hofgasse & Herzog Friedrich Strasse; meals from €3.60),* next door to the Stadtturm, overlooks the Golden Roof, so it's a great viewpoint if you can get into it in summer.

Nearby **Elferhaus** *(Herzog Friedrich Strasse 11; daily menus €6.35 & €8.70)* has sausages, burgers and other fare to accompany its vast range of beers.

Nonmeat eaters will find solace at vegie **Restaurant Philippine** *(☎ 58 91 57; Müllerstrasse 9; daily menus €6.80 & €7.80; open 11.30am-2pm, 6.30pm-8pm Mon-Sat).*

The ever-popular **Restaurant Rama** *(Innstrasse 81; Indian meals around €8; open Tues-Sun),* also known as Shashi's, provides vegetarian options, as well as meat, curries and pizzas.

Italian-influenced **Sweet Basil** *(Herzog Friedrich Strasse 31; mains from €9.80)* is one of a new breed of trendy restaurants. Another is **Dengg** *(Riesengasse 11-13; light dishes €4.50, mains from €13),* serving everything from Italian focaccia, Thai coconut curry soup and international fish and meat dishes.

Novembar *(Universitätstrasse 1; small meals from €6.60, mains from €12.40)* is one of Innsbruck's 'in' haunts. Overlooking the square in front of the Hofburg, it attracts a wide range of customers, from students to suits.

Of course, old-school Austrian eateries survive. **Gasthaus Goldenes Dachl** *(Hofgasse 1; open daily)* offers Tirolean specialities such as *Bauerngröstl,* a pork, bacon, potato and egg concoction which is served with salad (€9.65). **Weisses Rössl** *(Kiebachgasse 8; daily menu €6.90; open Mon-Sat)* is another favourite for regional food.

The traditional **Café Central** *(Gilmstrasse 5; specials from €7.30; open daily)* is a great place to hang out, snacking and reading the English newspapers. The actual coffee can be dire, though. For a delicious café latte, make tracks instead for **Café Galerie** *(Pfarrgasse 6)* near the cathedral.

Entertainment

The tourist office sells tickets for 'Tirolean evenings' (€30 for alpine music, folk dancing, yodelling and one drink), classical concerts, and performances in the **Landestheater** *(Rennweg 2).* Commission is usually charged.

If these don't appeal, 'eyebk' as local hipsters call it, has a pretty good bar and club scene. Firstly, Elferhaus, Sweet Basil, Novembar, Café Galerie (see Places to Eat earlier) all double as very popular bars. **Dom** *(Pfarrgasse 3)* is another. Hopefully, **Café im Hofgarten** *(Rennweg 6A)* will still be running its student nights on Tuesday. With a student card that shows you're over 20, they've been letting you have six drinks for €10 after 8pm. Although the official address is Rennweg it is actually some distance away in the Hofgarten.

Additionally, under the railway arches along Ingenieur Etzel Strasse, there is a row of late-night bars (mostly opening after midnight). Walk along and take your pick. Then, there's the hip **Couch Club** *(Anichstrasse 7; open Thur-Sat)* and the arty, community-minded **Treibhaus** *(☎ 58 68 74; Angerzellgasse 8),* which hosts live music, short-film festivals and the like and has a play area for kids. On Sunday, there's a 'jazz breakfast' from 10.30am and 'five o'clock tea'.

Cinematograph *(☎ 57 85 00; Museumstrasse 31)* is a good place to catch independent films in their original language.

Getting There & Away

Air Tyrolean Airways flies daily to Amsterdam, Frankfurt, Paris, Vienna and Zürich.

Bus Bundesbuses leave from the south end of the main train station, which has been undergoing refurbishment. Meanwhile, bus tickets and information have been available from, you guessed it, the north end of the station.

Train Fast trains depart seven times a day for Bregenz (2¾ hours) and every two hours to Salzburg (two hours). Regular express trains head north to Munich (via Kufstein; two hours) and south to Verona (3½ hours). Connections are hourly to Kitzbühel (€13.30 1¼ hours). On many trains to Lienz, people travelling on Austrian passes must pay a surcharge for travelling through Italy. On the 6.56am, 1.56pm and 5.53pm 'corridor' services, this is not the case, but otherwise the situation can vary, so it's best to ask before boarding. Alternatively, call ☎ 05-1717, available 24 hours.

Car & Motorcycle The A12 and the parallel Hwy 171 are the main roads to the west and east. Hwy 177, to the west of Innsbruck, heads north to Germany and Munich. The A13 motorway is a toll road (€7.99) southwards through the Brenner Pass to Italy; it includes the impressive Europabrücke (Europe Bridge) several kilometres south of the city. Toll-free Hwy 182 follows the same route, passing under the bridge.

Getting Around

The airport is 4km west of the centre. To get there, take bus F, which leaves from opposite the main train station half-hourly (hourly on Saturday afternoon and Sunday) and passes through Maria Theresien Strasse.

Single tickets, including to the airport, cost €1.60. A 24-hour pass is €3.20 and a weekly €10.10.

Private transport is a real hassle in the city centre. Most central streets are blue zones with maximum parking of 1½ hours; the charge is €0.50 per 30 minutes (tickets from pavement dispensers). Parking garages (eg, under the Altstadt) are €10 and upwards per day.

Taxis cost €3.80 for the first 1.3km, then €1.31 per kilometre. A taxi to the airport costs around €10. Bike rental is available from **Neuner Sport** (☎ 56 15 01; *Salurner Strasse 5*).

KITZBÜHEL

☎ 05356 • pop 8200

Kitzbühel is a fashionable and prosperous winter resort, offering excellent skiing.

Orientation & Information

From the main train station to the town centre is 1km. You emerge from the train station onto Bahnhofstrasse and walk straight ahead, then turn left onto Josef Pirchl Strasse; take the right fork (no entry for cars), which is still Josef Pirchl Strasse, and continue past the post office (Postamt 6370).

The **tourist office** (☎ 62155-0, fax 62307; e *info@kitzbuehel.com; Hinterstadt 18; open daily high season, Mon-Fri & Sat morning low season*) is in the centre.

The staff are not always that helpful, but ask about the guest card, which offers various discounts. There is Internet access at **Kitz Video** (*Schlossergasse 10*).

Activities

Skiing In winter, there is good intermediate skiing on Kitzbüheler Horn to the north and Hahnenkamm to the south. A one-day general ski pass costs €32, though some pensions/hotels can offer 'Ski Hit' reductions before mid-December or after mid-March. The cost of a day's ski rental is around €11/9 for downhill/cross-country. The professional Hahnenkamm downhill ski race takes place in mid to late January.

Hiking Dozens of summer hiking trails surround the town; the tourist office gives free maps and free guided hikes. Get a head start to the heights with the three-day cable-car pass for €32.70.

There is an alpine flower garden (free) on the slopes of the Kitzbüheler Horn (toll-road for drivers). The scenic Schwarzsee lake is a fine location for summer swimming.

Places to Stay & Eat

Rates often rise by €2 to €4 for stays of one or two nights. Prices are higher at Christmas and Easter, in July and August (the summer high season), but they peak during the winter high season, which are the prices quoted here. Quite a few private rooms and apartments are available.

Alternatively, you can pitch your tent at **Campingplatz Schwarzsee** (☎ 628 06; *Reither Strasse 24; open year-round*) by the lake.

AUSTRIA

Now that Jugendhotel Kaiser no longer takes backpackers or other individual travellers, the closest place to stay to the train station is **Pension Hörl** (*☎/fax 631 44; Josef Pirchl Strasse 60; singles/doubles without shower €18/36, with shower €20/40*). It's cheap, friendly and a lot more comfortable than its jumble-sale decor first suggests.

Renovated **Pension Schmidinger** (*☎/fax 631 34; Ehrenbachgasse 3; €32 per person*) offers bright, comfortable rooms. So does conveniently located **Pension Mühlbergerhof** (*☎ 62835, fax 644 88; Schwarzseestrasse 6; from €33 per person per night*). The owners here serve breakfast with produce from their farm.

On Bichlstrasse there's a **Billa supermarket** (*open daily high season*), while grocery store **Asia Markt** (*Josef Pirchl Strasse 16; meals from €4.50; open Mon-Sat*) serves light, weekday lunches and early evening meals.

A trip to Kitzbühel isn't complete without visiting **Huberbräu Stüberl** (*Vorderstadt 18; mains from €6.45; open daily*), where diners and drinkers congregate around the Austrian food and beers. The Tex-Mex place **La Fonda** (*Hinterstadt 13; mains around €6-7; open evenings*) is similarly popular. The Anglophile **Hölzl** (*Jochbergerstrasse 4; open daily*) is mainly a bar, but also lays on pork sandwiches (€4). It's particularly busy with tour groups on Saturday in winter.

Pricier **Zinnkrug** (*Untere Gänsbachgasse 12*) is known for its pork spare ribs (€15.60).

Getting There & Away

Direct trains to Innsbruck (€3.30, one to two hours, depending on the service) only leave Kitzbühel every two hours or so, but there are hourly services to Wörgl, where you can change for Innsbruck. Trains to Salzburg (€19.60, two hours) leave roughly hourly. Slower trains stop at Kitzbühel-Hahnenkamm, which is closer to the centre than the main Kitzbühel stop.

Getting to Lienz by public transport is awkward. The train is slow and the bus is infrequent (€9.96, two hours). There are four bus departures Monday to Friday and two each on Saturday and Sunday.

Heading south to Lienz, you pass through some marvellous scenery. Hwy 108 (the Felber Tauern Tunnel) and Hwy 107 (the Grossglockner mountain road, closed in winter) both have toll sections.

KUFSTEIN
☎ 05372 • pop 15,000

A 13th-century **fortress** (*☎ 602 350; admission €8/4.50 July & Aug; €7/4 Easter-July & Sept-mid-Nov*) dominates Kufstein town centre. Inside is a wide-ranging but not over-large **Heimat Museum**, and a massive 'Heroes Organ' (recital at noon, and at 5pm in summer, which is audible all over town). There is a lift to the fortress, which is included in the entry price.

A free city bus goes to the nearby **Hechtsee** lake in summer.

Information

The **tourist office** (*☎ 62207; e kufstein@net way.at; Unterer Stadtplatz 8; open Mon-Fri year-round, Sat morning in summer*) is in the centre of town, across the River Inn and three minutes' walk from the train station. It makes room reservations without charge.

Places to Stay & Eat

Should you decide to stay overnight, ask for the guest card. There is a **camping ground** (*☎ 622 29-55; Salurner Strasse 36*) by the river. A few blocks southeast of the castle is **Pension Striede** (*☎ 623 16, fax -33; Mitterndorfer Strasse 20; rooms per person €23/46*), with hospital-like rooms with shower and toilet. There are several affordable places to eat on Stadtplatz, and a **supermarket**.

Getting There & Away

Kufstein is on the main Innsbruck-Salzburg 'corridor' train route. To reach Kitzbühel (€6.90, one hour), change at Wörgl; the easiest road route is also via Wörgl.

LIENZ
☎ 04852 • pop 13,000

Many travellers view the capital of East Tirol principally as a handy stopover on the way to Italy, but it's also a good base for skiing or hiking. That's thanks to the jagged Dolomite mountain range, which crowds the southern skyline.

Orientation & Information

The town centre is within the junction of the Rivers Isel and Drau. To reach pivotal Hauptplatz from the train station, cross the road (or take the 'Zur Stadt' exit) and follow the street past the post office (Postamt 9900). Staff at the **tourist office** (*☎ 652 65, fax -2;*

(e) *lienz@netway.at; Europaplatz 1; open 8am-6pm Mon-Fri, 9am-noon Sat, also Sun summer & winter high seasons)* will find rooms free of charge, or you can use the hotel board (free telephone) outside. **Probike** *(☎ 735 76; Amlacherstrasse 1a)* rents bicycles; to get on the Internet visit **Net-Planet/ Odin's** *(Schweizergasse 3)*.

Things to See & Do
Schloss Bruck *(adult/senior/student €7/5/4; open 10am-6pm daily May-Nov)* displays the powerful, if sometimes dour, paintings of local artist Albin Egger (1868–1926), as well as some folk art.

There is downhill skiing on the nearby **Zettersfeld** and **Hochstein** peaks; a one-day ski pass covering both is €26. However, the area around Lienz is more renowned for its cross-country skiing; the town fills up for the annual **Dolomitenlauf** cross-country skiing race in mid-January.

In summer, hiking is good in the mountains. The cable cars are closed during the off-season (April, May, October and November).

Places to Stay
Just south of the town, **Camping Falken** *(☎ 640 22; Eichholz 7; open mid-Dec–Oct)* is the best place in Austria to wash your clothes. At least, that's according to the quirky newspaper article on its laundrette wall, which praises the view while you wait.

Most of the private rooms around the town don't have quite the same close-up of the Dolomite range but are great value nonetheless. Some allow a single night's stay, like the **Haus Egger** *(☎ 720 98; Alleestrasse 33; rooms per person €14)* or the **Gästehaus Masnata** *(☎ 655 36; Drahtzuggasse 4; apartments around €19-20 per person)*.

Gästehaus Gretl *(☎ 621 06; Schweizergasse 32; singles/doubles €23/46)* has been recently renovated, adding TVs to the rooms. There is courtyard parking, but the guesthouse is closed between seasons.

The atmospheric, spacious **Altstadthotel Eck** *(☎ 647 85, fax -3; (e) altstadthotel.eck@ utanet.at; Hauptplatz 20; singles/doubles from €55/110)* provides all the comfort you'd expect from one of the town's leading hotels.

Places to Eat
There are **ADEG supermarkets** on Hauptplatz and Tiroler Platz. **Imbissstube** *(Albin Egger*

Strasse 5) offers mouth-watering rotisserie chicken sprinkled with spices. A *Hendl* (half-chicken) with a roll is just €3.

Pick Nick Ossi *(Europaplatz 2; snacks from €2.91)* has a range of salads, pizzas and other fast food. **Vinothek** *(Zwergergasse 4; mains from €6.80)* is a popular place, with many Italian-style dishes.

There are lots of places to try regional dishes, such as **Adlerstüberl** *(Andrä Kranz Gasse 5; meals from €7.80)*, which has daily specials. **Goldener Fisch** *(Kärntner Strasse 9; menus for €8.10 & €10.80)* is also good.

Getting There & Away
Except for the 'corridor' route to Innsbruck (see the Innsbruck Getting There & Away section earlier in this chapter), trains to the rest of Austria connect via Spittal Millstättersee to the east. Trains to Salzburg (€24.70) take at least three hours. Villach, between Spittal and Klagenfurt, is a main junction for rail routes to the south. To head south by car, you must first divert west or east along Hwy 100.

Hohe Tauern National Park

Flora and fauna are protected in this 1786 sq km hiking paradise that straddles Tirol, Salzburg and Carinthia.

It contains **Grossglockner** (3797m), Austria's highest mountain, which towers over the 10km-long Pasterze Glacier. The best viewing point is **Franz Josefs Höhe**, reached from Lienz by Bundesbus. The bus runs from mid-June to late September and the return fare is covered by a zonal day pass for Carinthia (available in Lienz; €10.20), plus a €2.67 toll for the park. For longer stays, you should ask about the seven-day Bundesbus pass for the park (€22.60).

The route north (Hwy 107, the Grossglockner Hochalpenstrasse) is breathtakingly scenic. Along the way you pass Heiligenblut (buses year-round from Lienz), where there's a HI **Jugendherberge** *(☎ 04824-2259; Hof 36; open mid-Dec–mid-Oct)*. By car, you can reach Franz Josefs Höhe from May to November, but the daily toll for using the road is €25.44 for cars and €16.71 for motorcycles. An eight-day pass is €33.43 and €22.53 respectively. There are places to stay overnight.

AUSTRIA

Cyclists and hikers pay nothing to enter the park.

Farther west, Felbertauernstrasse also goes north-south through the park. For the tunnel section, there's a toll of €10 for cars and €8 for motorcycles. At the northern end of the park, turn west along Hwy 165 to reach **Krimml Falls**. These triple-level falls make a great spectacle. It takes 1½ hours to walk to the top, where there's an equally good view looking back down the valley.

Vorarlberg

The small state of Vorarlberg trickles down from the Alps to the shores of Lake Constance (Bodensee) and provides a convenient gateway to Germany, Liechtenstein and Switzerland. To travel the province you can buy VVV tickets, similar to VVT tickets (see the Tirol introduction earlier in this chapter).

BREGENZ
☎ 05574 • pop 27,500

With its face to the waters of Lake Constance and its disproportionate number of expensive clothes stores, Bregenz feels more like a posh seaside village than the provincial capital it is. The town is busiest during its annual music festival.

Orientation & Information
Bregenz is on Lake Constance's eastern shore. Turn left at the main train station exit and take Bahnhofstrasse to the centre (five minutes). Among the first things you'll see is the **tourist office** (☎ 4959-0, fax -59; e tourismus@bre genz.at; Bahnhofstrasse 14; open 9am-noon Mon-Sat & 1pm-5pm Mon-Fri, to 7pm daily during the Bregenz Festival).

The **post office** (Postamt 6900; Seestrasse; open 8am-7pm Mon-Fri, to 2pm Sat) is a few minutes further on. The tourist office provides free Internet access, while after-hours Web surfers should head for **S'Logo** (Kirchstrasse 47; open 5pm-midnight daily). Bundesbuses leave from outside the train station.

Things to See & Do
The **Bregenz Festival** runs for four weeks in July and August, when operas and classical works are performed from a floating stage on the lake's edge. If you want tickets contact the **Kartenbüro** (☎ 407-6, fax -400; w www

.bregenzerfestspiele.com; Postfach 311, A-6901) about nine months beforehand.

Even when the last diva has trilled the festival's closing note, there's spectacular sightseeing from the **Pfänder** mountain. A **cable car** (adults/seniors return €9.50/8.60; 9am-7pm daily; closed 2 weeks in Nov) carries you up and back.

Bregenz has several landmark buildings in wildly different styles, from the baroque **St Martin's Tower** in the old town to its – love it or loathe it – shimmering modern block of an art gallery, the **Kunsthaus**.

Places to Stay & Eat
The least expensive site is **Camping Lamm** (☎ 717 01; Mehrerauerstrasse 51; adult/tent/car €3.27/3.27/2.54; open May–mid-Oct), 1.5km west of the station. The HI **Jugend-gästehaus Bregenz** (☎ 42867, fax -88; e jgh .bregenz@jgh.at; Mehrerauerstrasse 5; dorm beds from €15-17, doubles or singles available off-peak for €5-7 extra; open year-round) is near the skateboard park. To get to this hostel from the train station, get on the walkway above the platforms, then head for the 'Zum See' exit, not the 'Kassenhalle' (ticket office) exit, and continue past the casino.

Private singles/doubles start at €18/22; ask at the tourist office, which has a room-booking service (€3).

Two budget options in the centre are **Pension Gunz** (☎/fax 436 57; Anton Schneider Strasse 38; singles/doubles without shower €29/46, with shower from €31/52; reception open Wed-Mon) and **Pension Sonne** (☎ 425 72, fax -4; e office@bbn.at; Kaiserstrasse 8; singles/doubles without shower & toilet €35/66, with facilities €40/78; closed winter). For a once-in-a-lifetime experience, stay at **Gäste-haus am Tannenbauch** (☎ 441 74; Im Gehren 1; €22-37 per person; open May-Oct). The ornate breakfast room, decorated with family memorabilia, is fit for a Habsburg – which you wouldn't realise from the house's reasonably humble exterior.

Trek through the first-floor clothes department in the GWL centre on Römerstrasse into **Leutbühel** (Römerstrasse 2; lunches from €6.30; open Mon-Sat) for salads and sausage dishes. Or tuck into Greek food at **Poseidon** (Kornmarktstrasse 2; most lunch dishes from €8.30; open daily).

Gösserbräu (Anton Schneider Strasse 1; dishes €6-9; open Tues-Sun) serves up local cuisine that's hearty rather than stodgy; its vegetarian mushroom goulash with dumplings is delicious. **Goldener Hirschen** *(Kirchstrasse 8; dishes €6.40-17.80; open Wed-Mon)* is another popular choice for Austrian food.

Getting There & Away
Trains to Munich (€44.60, 2½ hours) go via Lindau. There are also regular departures to St Gallen and Zürich. Trains to Innsbruck (€23.20, 2¾ hours) depart every two hours. Feldkirch is on the same route (€11.80, 30 minutes).

Boat services operate from late May to late October, with a reduced schedule from early March. For information, call ☎ 428 68. Bregenz to Constance by boat (via Friedrichshafen) takes about 3½ hours and there are about seven departures a day. Special boat passes offer discounts.

FELDKIRCH
☎ 05522 • pop 29,000
Granted its town charter in 1218, Feldkirch retains many medieval buildings, including the **Schattenburg** castle and **museum** *(adult/student €2/1; open Tues-Sun Dec-Oct)*. The musical **Feldkirch Festival** *(☎ 05576-720 91, fax 754 50;* **w** *www.feldkirchfestival.at)* takes place in May to June. The town nests in the Liechtenstein border region, not an immediately obvious location for a **Tibetan monastery**, but one exists. Ask at the tourist office for information about hikes to the monks' **Peace Stupa** monument.

Information
Feldkirch tourist office *(☎ 734 67, fax 798 67;* **e** *tourismus@feldkirch.at; Herrengasse 12; open 9am-6pm Mon-Fri, 9am-noon Sat; closed lunchtime in winter)* reserves rooms free of charge.

Places to Stay & Eat
The HI **Jugendherberge** *(☎ 731 81, fax 793 99; Reichsstrasse 111; beds in dorms/doubles from €10.80/14.50, €2 heating charge in winter; reception open 8am-10pm; hostel closed 2 weeks early Dec)* truly is one of Austria's most memorable, situated in a refurbished medieval infirmary with exposed timber and historic features.

Private rooms and budget pensions are scarce, but you can try **Haus Greiner** *(☎ 811 48; Rundblick 8; €20 per person per night)* or **Gasthof Engel** *(☎/fax 720 56; Liechtensteiner Strasse, Tisis; singles/doubles with hall shower €28/46)*. Both are on the bus route to Liechtenstein, but Gasthof Engel's reception is closed Monday and Tuesday. In the centre, **Gasthof Lingg** *(☎ 720 62, fax -6; Kreuzgasse 10; singles/doubles €60/65)* is good value for those travelling in pairs.

For meat eaters, the best daytime deal is at delicatessen **Metzgerei Spieler** *(Johanitergasse 6; menu €4.72)*; for an Austrian dinner, you could try **Johanniterhof** *(Marktgasse 1; menus €8.30)*.

Some vegie options are available at **Dogana** *(Neustadt 20; sandwiches from €3.40, menus €8.40)*, which is a trendy but relaxed place to hang out.

Getting There & Away
Two buses an hour (one per hour on weekends) depart for Liechtenstein from outside the train station. Travelling to Liechtenstein's capital, Vaduz (€3.60, 40 minutes), often requires a change in Schaans.

From Schaans, you can catch a train to Buchs and onward to major Swiss destinations, including Zürich.

ARLBERG REGION
The Arlberg region, shared by Vorarlberg and neighbouring Tirol, has some of the best skiing in Austria. Summer is less busy, when many bars are closed.

St Anton am Arlberg is the largest resort, where you're as likely to hear a cheery antipodean 'G'day' or Scandinavian *'God dag'* as you are to hear an Austrian *'Grüss' Di'*. There are good medium-to-advanced runs here, as well as nursery slopes on Gampen and Kapall. The **tourist office** *(☎ 05446-226 90;* **e** *st.anton@netway.at)* on the main street, has details. Head diagonally left from the train station to find it.

Lech, a more upmarket resort, is a favourite with royalty and film stars. Runs are predominantly medium to advanced. For details, contact the **Lech tourist office** *(☎ 05583-2161-0;* **e** *lech-info@lech.at)*.

A ski pass valid for 83 ski lifts in Lech, Zürs, Stuben, St Anton and St Christoph costs €37 for one day and €171 for six (reductions for children and seniors). Rental starts at €15 for both downhill and cross-country skis and poles.

AUSTRIA

Places to Stay & Eat

Accommodation is mainly in a bewildering number of small B&Bs. The tourist office has brochures. Alternatively, try the accommodation board with free telephones outside its office. Many budget places (prices from €26 per person in winter high season) are booked months or even years in advance.

Central **Haus Wannali** (☎ 05446-2350; *Arlberg Strasse 509; per person €37*) has a friendly atmosphere and entertaining regulars, but the views are also worth the ski-bus ride and walk to the new **Pension Strolz Christian** (☎ 05446-301 19, fax -4; *Ing Gomperz Strasse 606; per person €38*). When the hunger pangs hit, there is a **Spar supermarket** on the main street and good pizzas at **Pomodoro**. At night, there is certainly a whiff of testosterone in the St Anton air. By

about 6pm, people are often bawling rock standards from the door of **Piccadilly**, while it takes slightly longer for things to get going in **Kandahar**, which also serves Indian food. **Krazy Kanguruh** is a popular bar on the slopes.

Getting There & Away

St Anton is on the main railway route between Bregenz and Innsbruck, less than 1½ hours from both. St Anton is close to the eastern entrance of the Arlberg Tunnel, the toll road connecting Vorarlberg and Tirol. The tunnel toll is €9.45/7.25 for cars/motorcycles. You can avoid the toll by taking the B197, but no vehicles with trailers are allowed on this winding road. There is a choice of about 3/12 buses a day in summer/winter to Lech (€3.42, 40 minutes) from St Anton.

Czech Republic

Deep in the heart of Europe lie the ancient lands of Bohemia and Moravia, which together make up the Czech Republic. It's one of Europe's most historic countries, full of fairytale castles, chateaux, manors and museums. The medieval cores of several dozen towns have been carefully preserved and there's so much to see that you could spend several months exploring.

The Czech Republic is doubly inviting for its cultured, generally friendly people and excellent facilities; the transportation network is both cheap and efficient. Although 90% of English-speaking visitors limit themselves to Prague, the clever few who escape the hordes and high prices in the capital soon experience just how helpful the Czech people can be. Almost everywhere outside Prague and Český Krumlov still feels off the beaten tourist track.

Facts about the Czech Republic

HISTORY

In antiquity the Bohemian Basin was inhabited by a Celtic tribe called the Boii, who gave their name to the land of Bohemia. Germanic tribes conquered the Celts in the 4th century AD, and between the 5th and 10th centuries the Western Slavs settled here. From 830 to 907, the Slavic tribes were united in the Great Moravian Empire. They adopted Christianity after the arrival in 863 of the Thessalonian missionaries Cyril and Methodius, who created the first Slavic (Cyrillic) alphabet.

In 995 the Czech lands were united under the native Přemysl dynasty as the principality of Bohemia. The Czech state became a kingdom in the 12th century and reached its peak under Přemysl Otakar II (1253–78). The rule of the Přemysls ended in 1306 and, in 1310, John of Luxembourg came to the Bohemian throne through marriage and annexed the kingdom to the German Empire. His son, Charles IV, became king of the Germans in 1346 and Holy Roman Emperor in 1355. Inclusion in this empire led to a blossoming of trade and culture. The capital, Prague, was made an archbishopric in 1344, and in 1348 Charles University was founded.

Prague Maps Prague p136
Prague Castle p140
Central Prague pp142-3

In 1415, the Protestant religious reformer Jan Hus, rector of Charles University, was burnt at the stake in Constance. His ideas inspired the religious and nationalist Hussite movement, which swept Bohemia betweeen 1419 and 1434.

After the defeat of the Hussites, the Jagiello dynasty ruled until 1526 when the Austrian Habsburg dynasty ascended the Bohemian throne. Thus Bohemia, strongly affected by the Protestant Reformation, was subject to the

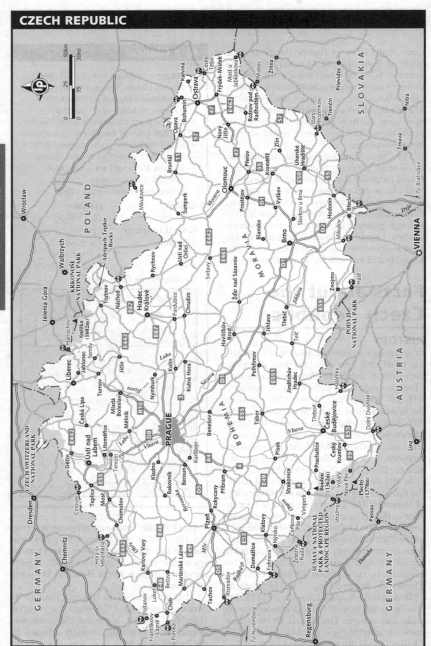

CZECH REPUBLIC

Catholic Counter-Reformation backed by the Habsburgs. The Thirty Years' War (1618–48), which devastated Central Europe, began in Prague, and the defeat of the uprising of the Czech Estates at the Battle of White Mountain in 1620 marked the start of a long period of forced re-Catholicisation, Germanisation and oppression of Czech language and culture.

The Czechs began to rediscover their linguistic and cultural roots at the start of the 19th century during the so-called National Revival. Despite defeat of the 1848 democratic revolution, the Industrial Revolution took firm hold here and a middle class emerged.

After WWI, during which Czech and Slovak nationalists strove for a common state, the Czechoslovak Republic was created on 28 October 1918. The first president was Tomáš Garrigue Masaryk. Three-quarters of the Austro-Hungarian empire's industrial power fell within Czechoslovakia, as did three million Germans, mostly in the border areas of Bohemia and Moravia (the *pohraniči*, known in German as the Sudetenland).

After annexing Austria in the Anschluss of March 1938, Hitler turned his attention to Czechoslovakia. Under the infamous Munich Pact of September 1938, Britain and France agreed not to oppose the annexation of the Sudetenland by Nazi Germany, and in March 1939 the Germans went onto occupy the rest of the country (calling it the Protectorate of Bohemia and Moravia). Slovakia became a fascist puppet state.

On 29 May 1942 the Nazi Reichs-Protector, Reinhard 'Hangman' Heydrich, was assassinated by Czechoslovak resistance fighters who had been parachuted in from London. In the reprisals, the Nazis razed the village of Lidice, 25km northwest of Prague, shot all the males and deported all the females and children to concentration camps. At the end of WWII, West Bohemia was liberated by US troops, and the rest of the country by the Soviet army.

Post-WWII

After the liberation of the regional capital of Košice (eastern Slovakia), a National Front was formed, which was covertly controlled by the Czechoslovak Communist Party and fully backed by the Soviets. This body laid out a blueprint for the takeover of the country. In the Constituent National Assembly elections of May 1946, the Communists won 36% of the vote and the Social Democrats 15.6%, and together they formed a National Front majority. The Communist Party chairman Klement Gottwald became prime minister.

A power struggle developed between the communist and democratic forces. In early 1948, the Social Democrats withdrew from the coalition in protest against the antidemocratic activities of the communists. The result was the communist-staged and Soviet-backed 'February coup d'etat'. The new communist-led government set up the dictatorship of the proletariat and, in July, Gottwald also became the country's president.

The whole industrial sector was nationalised and the government's economic policies nearly bankrupted the country. The 1950s were years of harsh repression when thousands of noncommunists fled the country. Many people were imprisoned, and hundreds were executed or died in labour camps, often for little more than a belief in democracy or religion. A series of Stalinist purges was organised by the Communist Party, during which many people, including top members of the party itself, were executed.

In April 1968, the new first secretary of the Communist Party, Alexander Dubček, introduced liberalising reforms to create 'socialism with a human face' – referred to as the 'Prague Spring'. Censorship ended, political prisoners were released and decentralisation of the economy began. Dubček refused to bow to pressure from Moscow to withdraw the reforms, resulting in the occupation of Czechoslovakia by 200,000 Soviet and Warsaw Pact soldiers on the night of 20 August 1968, when Soviet tanks rumbled through the streets of Prague. The Czechs and Slovaks met the invaders with passive resistance.

Renewed dictatorship saw the expulsion of around 14,000 Communist Party functionaries and 500,000 party members lost their jobs. Many educated professionals were made street cleaners and manual labourers. Dissidents were routinely imprisoned.

In 1977 the trial of the rock group The Plastic People of the Universe inspired the formation of the human-rights group Charter 77. (The communists saw the musicians as a threat to the status quo, while others viewed the trial as part of a pervasive assault on human rights.) Made up of a small group of Prague intellectuals, including the playwright/philosopher Václav Havel, Charter 77 functioned as an underground opposition throughout the 1980s.

By 1989, Gorbachev's *perestroika* was sending shock waves through the region and the fall of the Berlin Wall on 9 November raised expectations of change in Czechoslovakia. On 17 November, an officially sanctioned student march in Prague in memory of students executed by the Nazis in 1939 was smashed by police. Daily demonstrations ensued, and protests widened, with a general strike on 27 November, culminating in the resignation of the Communist Party's Politburo. The 'Velvet Revolution' was over.

Civic Forum (Občanské Forum), an umbrella organisation of opponents of the regime formed in the wake of the 17 November violence, was led by Havel, Prague's best-known 'dissident' and ex-political prisoner. Havel took over as the country's interim president, by popular demand, and in the free elections of June 1990, Civic Forum and its counterpart in Slovakia, Society Against Violence, were successful. The Communist Party won 47 seats in the 300-seat federal parliament.

Velvet Divorce

With the strong central authority provided by the communists gone, old antagonisms between Slovakia and Prague re-emerged. The federal parliament tried to stabilise matters by approving a constitutional amendment in December 1990, which gave each of the Czech and Slovak Republics full federal status within the Czech and Slovak Federated Republic (ČSFR), as Czechoslovakia was now known. But these moves failed to satisfy Slovak nationalists. Meanwhile Civic Forum had split into two factions, the centrist Civic Movement, and the Civic Democratic Party (ODS). In Slovakia several separatist parties emerged.

The ODS instigated a purge of former communist officials and alleged secret-police informers in 1991, a process known as *lustrace*. However, the communists who had committed many crimes, including the torture and murder of many innocent people, have not been brought to trial.

The June 1992 elections sealed the fate of Czechoslovakia. Václav Klaus' ODS took 48 seats in the 150-seat federal parliament, while 24 seats went to the Movement for a Democratic Slovakia (HZDS), a left-leaning Slovak nationalist party led by Vladimír Mečiar.

The incompatibility of Klaus and Mečiar soon became apparent, with Klaus pushing for shock-therapy economic reform and Mečiar

for state intervention to save key industries in Slovakia. In August 1992, Klaus and Mečiar agreed that the Czechoslovak federation would cease to exist at midnight on 31 December 1992. The peaceful 'velvet divorce' was over.

In January 1993, the Czech parliament elected Václav Havel president for a five-year term, and re-elected him by a margin of one vote in 1998. Prime Minister Klaus staked his political future on the success of rapid economic reforms, but by 1996 the economy was slowing down. Among other major problems were corruption, an ineffective judiciary and a lack of openness in business, all contributing to hesitant foreign investment.

As the 21st century begins, the Czech Republic stands on the threshold of the EU, and in 2004 is expected to join, along with Poland, Hungary and Slovenia.

GEOGRAPHY

The Czech Republic is a landlocked country of 78,864 sq km squeezed between Germany, Austria, Slovakia and Poland. The Bohemian Massif forms the broad, rounded ranges of the Czech Republic with the Šumava Mountains along the Bavarian border, the Ore Mountains (Krušné hory) along the eastern German border and the Krakonos Mountains (Krkonoše) along the Polish border east of Liberec. The Czech Republic's highest peak, Sněžka (1602m), is in the Krkonoše. In between these ranges are rolling plains mixed with forests and farm land. The forests – mainly spruce, oak and beech – still cover one-third of the country. Dwarf pine is common near the tree line and above that (1400m) there is little but grasses, shrubs and lichens.

The Czech Republic has been called 'the roof of Europe' because no rivers or streams flow into the country. The three main rivers in the country – Morava, Vltava (Moldau) and Labe (Elbe) – all flow out into bordering Slovakia and Germany.

CLIMATE

The Czech climate is temperate, with cool and humid winters, warm summers and clearly defined spring and autumn seasons. Prague has average daily temperatures above 14°C from May to September, above 8°C in April and October, and below freezing point in December and January. In winter dense fog (or smog) can set in anywhere.

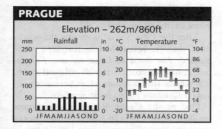

PRAGUE

Elevation – 262m/860ft

ECOLOGY & ENVIRONMENT

The forests of northern Bohemia and Moravia have been devastated by acid rain created by the burning of poor-quality brown coal at factories and thermal power stations. These industries spew sulphur dioxide, nitrogen dioxide and carbon monoxide into the atmosphere, creating one of Europe's most serious environmental disaster areas. The most affected region is the eastern Ore Mountains where the most trees are dead. In recent years sulphur dioxide levels in Prague have declined, while carbon monoxide pollution from cars and trucks has increased. There are two nuclear power-generating stations – the ageing Soviet reactor at Dukovany (between Znojmo and Brno), and the controversial Temelin reactor in South Bohemia, which came online in 2001 despite strong protest from Austria and environmental groups.

The most common types of wildlife in the mountains are wildcats, marmots, otters, marten and mink. Occasionally a bear makes an appearance in northeastern Moravia. In the woods and fields there are plenty of pheasants, partridges, deer, ducks and wild geese. Eagles, vultures, osprey, storks, bustards, grouse and lynx are rarer.

GOVERNMENT & POLITICS

The present constitution was passed by parliament in 1992. The country is a parliamentary democracy headed by President Havel who faces election by parliament every five years. Real power lies with the prime minister and the cabinet, and parliament can override the president's veto on most issues by a simple majority. There are two chambers in the parliament – the House of Representatives and the Senate – whose members are elected by Czech citizens every four and six years respectively.

The largest party is the left-of-centre Social Democrats (ČSSD) led by Vladimir Spidal, the current prime minister. Until 2002, the conservative opposition Civic Democratic Party (ODS) was led by Václav Klaus, prime minister from 1992 to 1997 and a pivotal character in economic reform; a poor performance in the June 2002 elections led to his decision not to stand in the 2003 presidential elections.

The Czech Communist Party of Bohemia & Moravia (KSČM) is one of the few communist parties left in the world that still adheres to Marxist-Stalinist doctrine; it has a solid core of mostly elderly followers.

The Social Democrats (ČSSD) remained the largest party at the June 2002 elections with an increased share of the vote (30.2% and 70 seats), led by its new leader and prime minister, Vladimir Spidl. Second was the right-wing Civic Democratic Party (ODS) with 24.5% and 58 seats. The Communist Party (KSČM) moved to third place (18.5% and 41 seats) and the Christian Democrat Coalition (Koalice; 14.3%, 31 seats) slipped to fourth. The turnout, however, was only 58%.

The traditional lands of the Czech Republic, Bohemia and Moravia, are divided into 14 administrative *kraje* (regions), consisting of Prague and nine regions in Bohemia, and four regions in Moravia. These are further subdivided into 76 *okresy* (districts).

ECONOMY

Bohemia and Moravia have specialised in light industry since the Industrial Revolution. Under communist rule, industry and agriculture were nationalised and heavy industry was introduced along Stalinist lines. Steel and machinery production are the main forms of heavy industry. Other important products include armaments, vehicles, cement, ceramics, plastics, cotton and beer.

Privatisation was carried out in three stages after the fall of communism. The first was the restitution of property to the original owners. Then, about 30,000 small retail outlets and service facilities were auctioned off. The third and most difficult stage of privatising 1500 medium- and large-sized companies is almost complete. Some companies were auctioned off and the majority were privatised by a voucher scheme – this, and other aspects of privatisation, have been dogged by corruption. In April 1993, the Prague stock market opened, and trading began in June of that year.

Agriculture is a small part of the Czech economy, employing about 2.9% of a workforce that is about one-third less productive

CZECH REPUBLIC

than its EU counterparts. Most of the land has been returned to its previous owners or privatised, however many people formed their own cooperatives based on old government cooperatives. Major crops are sugar-beet, wheat, potatoes, corn, barley and hops, while cattle, pigs and chickens are the preferred livestock.

In 1998 the Czech economy, considered for years one of the best in the former Eastern Bloc, suffered a slump and has had budget deficits ever since. The unemployment rate stood at 9.5% in 2000, but had fallen to 8.8% by May 2002. Continuing problems include a drop in foreign investment, increasing public and government debt, and the lack of strong laws in the business sphere. The average monthly wage in May 2002 was approximately US$500 (16,219 Kč).

POPULATION & PEOPLE

The Czech Republic is fairly homogeneous; 95% of the people are Czech and 3% Slovak. A small Polish minority lives in the borderlands near Ostrava. After WWII three million Sudeten Germans were evicted from the country, and today only about 150,000 of this group remain.

The principal cities and their populations are: Prague (1,197,000), Brno (379,200), Ostrava (327,000), Plzeň (173,000) and Olomouc (106,000).

ARTS

Czech culture has a long and distinguished history. Charles University, the oldest in Central Europe, was founded in 1348, about the time that the Gothic architect Petr Parléř was directing the construction of St Vitus Cathedral, Karlův most (Charles Bridge) and other illustrious works.

In the early 17th century, the Thirty Years' War forced the educational reformer Jan Ámos Comenius (1592–1670) to flee Moravia. While in exile, Comenius (Komenský in Czech) produced a series of textbooks that were to be used throughout Europe for two centuries. *The Visible World in Pictures,* featuring woodcuts made at Nuremberg, was the forerunner of today's illustrated school book.

Literature

Another literary genius, Franz Kafka (1883–1924), wrote in German but was, nevertheless, a son of Prague. He was born and lived there most of his life, haunted by the city he both

hated and needed. His novel *The Trial* (1925) gives an insight into his world.

After the 1968 Soviet invasion, the works of Czech novelist Milan Kundera were banned. *The Book of Laughter and Forgetting* combines eroticism with political satire, for which the communist government revoked Kundera's Czech citizenship.

One of the Czech Republic's foremost resident writers is Ivan Klíma, whose works were also banned from 1970 to 1989. Klíma's novels such as *Love and Garbage* (1986) tackle the human dimension behind the contradictions of contemporary Czech life.

Perhaps one of the best 20th-century Czech novelists is Bohumil Hrabal (1914–97; see Books in Facts for the Visitor), while by far the most brilliant plays are by the current president Václav Havel – among the most popular are *Audience* and *Largo Desolato*.

Music

During the 17th century, when Bohemia and Moravia came under Austrian domination and German was the official language, Czech culture survived in folk music. Moravian folk orchestras are built around the *cymbalum,* a copper-stringed dulcimer of Middle Eastern origin that stands on four legs and is played by striking the strings with two mallets.

Bohemia's pre-eminent baroque composer was Jan Dismas Zelenka (1679–1745) who spent some of his life in Dresden, where he was a composer to the Saxon court. The symbolism and subtle expression of Zelenka's last masses are unique expressions of his introverted, restrained character.

The works of the Czech Republic's foremost composers, Bedřich Smetana (1824–84) and Antonín Dvořák (1841–1904), express nostalgia, melancholy and joy. In his operas, Bedřich Smetana used popular songs displaying the innate peasant wisdom of the people to capture the nationalist sentiments of his time. His symphonic cycle *Má Vlast* (My Country) is a musical history of the country. Antonín Dvořák attracted world attention to Czech music through his use of native folk materials in works such as *Slavonic Dances* (1878).

Leoš Janáček (1854–1928) shared Dvořák's intense interest in folk music and created an original national style by combining the scales and melodies of folksongs with the inflections of the Czech language. One of his best known works is *Jenůfa* (1904).

Dance

Bohemia's greatest contribution to dance floors is the polka, a lively folk dance in which couples rapidly circle the floor in three-four time with three quick steps and a hop. Since its appearance in Paris in 1843, the polka has been popular worldwide. Smetana used it in his opera *The Bartered Bride* (1866). In some of Moravia's villages whirling couples dance the *vrtěná*, while the *hošije* and *verbuňk* are vigorous male solo dances.

SOCIETY & CONDUCT

The best way to see traditional Bohemian and Moravian folk customs, dress, song, dance, music and food is at any weekend folk festival held in villages around the country from spring to autumn (see Public Holidays & Special Events in the Facts for the Visitor section).

When it comes to attending classical music concerts, opera and traditional theatre, Czechs are quite conservative and dress formally. Foreign visitors are expected to dress the same. Contemporary dress is fine for other venues.

It is customary to say 'good day' *(dobrý den)* when entering a shop, café or quiet bar, and 'goodbye' *(na shledanou)* when leaving. If you are invited to a Czech home bring fresh flowers and when entering someone's home remember to remove your shoes, unless you're told not to bother. On public transport, young people readily give up their seats to the elderly, the sick, pregnant women or women carrying children.

RELIGION

Most Czechs are Catholic (40%), but church attendance is extremely low. Various Protestant sects makeup a small percentage of the population, while the Jewish community (1% of the population in 1918) today is only a few thousand. Religious tolerance is well established and the Catholic Church makes little attempt to involve itself in politics.

LANGUAGE

German is understood by many Czechs and is useful in most parts of the country, while in the capital you can get by with English. Under the communists everybody learned Russian at school but this has now been replaced by English.

Czech seems an outlandish language to native English-speakers, who must abandon linguistic habits to learn it. Its peculiarity is a lack of vowels, with many words containing nothing that we could identify as a vowel. One famous tongue twister goes *strč prst skrz krk* which means 'stick your finger through your neck' and is pronounced just as it's spelt!

An English-Czech phrasebook will prove invaluable, so consider Lonely Planet's *Czech phrasebook* or *Eastern Europe phrasebook*. Some useful Czech words that are frequently used in this chapter are: *most* (bridge), *nábřeží* (embankment), *nám* or *náměstí* (square), *nádraží* (station), *ostrov* (island), *třída* (avenue) and *ulice* (street). To open and close doors you will find the signs *sem* (pull) and *tam* (push). See the Language chapter at the back of the book for pronunciation guidelines and more useful words and phrases.

Facts for the Visitor

HIGHLIGHTS

The Czech Republic boasts many historic towns. The most authentic and picturesque include Prague, Litoměřice, Český Krumlov, Kutná Hora and Telč. There are magnificent castles at Karlštejn, Konopiště and Český Krumlov.

Some of the best museums are in Prague, where the Jewish Museum in the former Prague ghetto is easily the largest of its kind in Central Europe. Prague Castle is packed with art treasures, notably the collection of the National Gallery in the Šternberg Palace at the entrance of the castle. The Brewery Museum in Plzeň highlights one of the country's noblest contributions to humanity.

The Šumava National Park is a beautiful wooded mountain region great for hiking, cycling and cross-country skiing, while the Adršpach-Teplice Rocks have some of the country's most spectacular scenery.

SUGGESTED ITINERARIES

Depending on the length of your stay, you might want to see and do the following things in the Czech Republic:

Two days
Visit Prague
One week
Visit Prague, Český Krumlov, Litoměřice and Kutná Hora
Two weeks
Visit the places listed above, plus Adršpach-Teplice, Šumava and Telč

CZECH REPUBLIC

2002 Floods

In the summer of 2002 the Czech Republic, along with neighbouring Austria and Germany, suffered its worst floods in over a century. The country is facing an estimated clean-up bill of around €3 billion. Prague was severely affected with the famous Charles Bridge being threatened at one stage and the Jewish section of town badly damaged.

Visitors to Prague and the other affected regions may find some attractions limited by repair work into 2003. The former concentration camp at Terezín in North Bohemia also suffered severely, and may not be fully repaired until 2006. Check with tourist information offices for the latest situation.

PLANNING
When to Go
The weather is best in summer, but July and August as well as Christmas-New Year and Easter are very busy, so it's better to visit in May, June and September. Winter also has its charms. During the Prague Spring festival (in May), accommodation in Prague can be tight.

Maps
The Austrian publisher Freytag & Berndt publishes a good map of the Czech Republic. The best Czech road maps and city plans are the GeoClub series by SHOCart. Klub Cých Turistů produces excellent 1:50,000 hiking maps that cover the entire country.

TOURIST OFFICES
Local Tourist Offices
The municipal Prague Information Service (PIS) staff are very knowledgable about attractions, eateries and entertainment in the capital. There's also a network of municipal information centres (městské informační centrum/středisko) in all major tourist areas.

The travel agency Čedok, oriented towards the mid-range market, has offices around the country, which you can consult about exchanging money, accommodation, travel and sightseeing arrangements.

Within the Czech Republic there are several youth travel bureaus including CKM (Cestovní kancelář mládeže) in Prague. Former CKM offices in Plzeň, České Budějovice and Brno are now independently owned but still offer information on budget travel and ac-

commodation. GTS International is another agency that provides information on money-saving deals and also sells ISIC, ITIC, IYTC and Euro<26 cards.

Tourist Offices Abroad
The Czech Tourist Authority (ČCCR) offices abroad provide information about the whole of the Czech Republic, but do not book any hotels or transportation.

Canada (☎ 416-363 9928, fax 363 0239,
  e ctacanada@iprimus.ca) Czech Airlines
  Office, 401 Bay St, Suite 1510, Toronto,
  Ontario M5H 2Y4
France (☎ 01 53 73 00 32, fax 01 53 73 00 33,
  e bohmova@czech.cz) rue Bonaparte 19,
  75006 Paris
Germany (☎/fax 030-204 4770, e tourinfo@
  czech-tourist.de) Karl Liebknecht Strasse 34,
  10178 Berlin
UK (☎ 020-7291 9925, fax 7436 8300,
  e ctainfo@czechcentre.org.uk) 95 Great
  Portland St, London W1W 7NY
USA (☎ 212-288 0830, fax 288 0971,
  e travelczech@pop.net) 1109-1111 Madison
  Ave, New York, NY 10028

VISAS & DOCUMENTS
Everyone needs a passport valid until at least 90 days after your date of entry. Citizens of EU countries, Switzerland, the USA, Japan and New Zealand can stay for up to 90 days without a visa; for UK citizens the limit is 180 days. At the time of research, citizens of Australia, Canada and South Africa need a visa (even if you are only passing through by train or bus), which you should obtain in advance at a consulate in your own country. Visas are not available at border crossings or Prague's Ruzyně airport; you'll be refused entry if you need a visa and arrive without one.

Tourist visas valid for up to 90 days are readily available at Czech consulates for about US$24/88 for single/multiple entry. A five-day transit visa costs US$24/35 for single/double entry; it cannot be changed to a tourist visa upon arrival. You can use your visa at any time within six months of the date of issue.

Czech visa regulations change frequently, so check the latest situation on the Czech Ministry of Foreign Affairs website at w www .mzv.cz. If your country is *not* on the Visa Waiver list, then you *will* need a visa.

Arriving visitors are occasionally asked to show that they have the equivalent of at least 1100 Kč (US$30) for every day that they are intending to stay, or a credit card. You may also be asked to produce evidence of travel health insurance.

All foreign visitors must register with the Czech immigration police within three days of arrival; this is strictly enforced with a fine of 400 Kč. Hotels, hostels and camping grounds will automatically register you when you check in; otherwise – if you are staying with friends, for example – you will need to register yourself at a foreigners police office.

You can extend your stay in the country only once, for a fee of 1000 Kč, at foreigners police stations inside the Czech Republic.

EMBASSIES & CONSULATES
Czech Embassies & Consulates
The Czech Republic has diplomatic representation in the following countries:

Australia *Consulate:* (☎ 02-9371 0860) 169 Military Rd, Dover Heights, Sydney NSW 2030
Canada (☎ 613-562 3875) 251 Cooper St, Ottawa, Ontario K2P 0G2
France (☎ 01 40 65 13 01) 15 ave Charles Floquet, 75343 Paris Cedex 07
Germany (☎ 030-22 63 80) Wilhelmstrasse 44, 10117 Berlin
Ireland (☎ 031-668 1135) 57 Northumberland Rd, Ballsbridge, Dublin 4
Netherlands (☎ 070-346 9712) Paleisstraat 4, 2514 JA The Hague
New Zealand Contact the Czech consulate in Sydney
UK (☎ 020-7243 1115) 26 Kensington Palace Gardens, London W8 4QY
USA (☎ 202-274 9100) 3900 Spring of Freedom St NW, Washington, DC 20008

Embassies & Consulates in the Czech Republic
Most embassies and consulates are open at least 9am to noon Monday to Friday.

Australia (☎ 251 01 83 50) Klimentská 10, Prague 1 – this is an honorary consulate for emergency help only (eg, a stolen passport); otherwise contact the Australian embassy in Vienna
Austria (☎ 257 09 05 11) Viktora Huga 10, Prague 5
Canada (☎ 272 10 18 00) Mickiewiczova 6, Prague 6
France (☎ 251 17 17 11) Velkopřerovské nám 2, Prague 2
Germany (☎ 257 11 31 11) Vlašská 19, Prague 1
Ireland (☎ 257 53 00 61) Tržiště 13, Prague 1
Netherlands (☎ 224 31 21 90) Gotthardská 6/27, Prague 6

New Zealand (☎ 222 51 46 72) Dykova 19, Prague 10 – this is an honorary consulate that provides assistance (eg, a stolen passport) by appointment only; otherwise the nearest NZ embassy is in Berlin
Poland (☎ 224 22 87 22) Václavské nám 49, Prague 1
Slovakia (☎ 233 32 54 43) Pod Hradbami 1, Prague 6
UK (☎ 257 40 21 11) Thunovská 14, Prague 1
USA (☎ 257 53 06 63) Tržiště 15, Prague 1

CUSTOMS
Customs officers can be strict about antiques and will confiscate goods that are even slightly suspect. If you have any doubt about what you are taking out, talk to curatorial staff at the **National Museum** *(☎ 224 49 71 11; Václavské náměstí)* for coins, at the **National Gallery** *(☎ 224 30 11 11; Dukelských hrdinů 47)* for paintings and sculptures and at the **Museum of Decorative Arts** *(☎ 251 09 31 11; 17.listopadu 2)* for antiques. All these offices are in Prague.

There is no limit to the amount of Czech or foreign currency that can be taken in or out of the country, but amounts exceeding 350,000 Kč must be declared.

MONEY
Currency
The Czech crown or Koruna česká (Kč) is divided into 100 hellers or haléřů (h). Banknotes come in denominations of 20, 50, 100, 200, 500, 1000, 2000 and 5000 Kč; coins are of 10, 20 and 50 h and one, two, five, 10, 20 and 50 Kč. Keep a few 2 Kč, 10 Kč and 20 Kč coins handy for use in public toilets, telephones and tram-ticket machines.

Exchange Rates
Conversion rates for major currencies at the time of publication were:

country	unit		Czech crown
Australia	A$1	=	16.74 Kč
Canada	C$1	=	19.68 Kč
Euro Zone	€1	=	30.56 Kč
Japan	¥100	=	25.85 Kč
NZ	NZ$1	=	14.48 Kč
UK	UK£1	=	48.38 Kč
USA	US$1	=	30.94 Kč

For up-to-date exchange rates go to **W** www .xe.net/ucc/full.shtml.

CZECH REPUBLIC

Exchanging Money

There is no longer a black market in currency exchange; anyone who offers to change money in the street is a thief.

Remember when comparing exchange rates that you are interested in the 'buy' rate (they will be buying currency or travellers cheques from you).

Cash The main banks – Komerční banka, Česká spořitelna, ČSOB and Živnostenská banka – are the best places to change cash, charging 2% commission with a 50 Kč minimum (but always check, as commissions can vary from branch to branch). They will also provide a cash advance on Visa or Master-Card without commission. Most banks are open at least 8am to 4pm weekdays; in smaller towns they may close for lunch between noon and 1pm.

Hotels charge about 5% to 8% commission at poorer rates while Čedok travel agencies and post offices charge 2% at similar rates to the banks.

Many private-exchange offices, especially in Prague, charge exorbitant commissions (*výlohy*) of up to 10%. Some of these advertise higher rates and 0% commission but don't mention their sky-high 'handling fee', or charge no commission but have very poor exchange rates – if in doubt, ask first.

Travellers Cheques Banks charge 2% with a 50 Kč minimum for changing travellers cheques. American Express and Thomas Cook offices change their own-brand cheques without commission, but charge 2% or 3% for other brands, 3% or 4% for credit-card cash advances and 5% for changing cash.

ATMs There is a good network of ATMs, or *bankomaty,* throughout the country. Most accept Visa, Plus, Visa electron, MasterCard, Cirrus, Maestro, Euro and EC cards.

Credit Cards You'll find that credit cards are widely accepted in mid-range and top-end hotels and restaurants. You can use a card to get a cash advance in a bank or to withdraw money from ATMs. Your own bank may charge a fee of about US$3 and possibly a 1% commission for using an ATM, but this is still more favourable (if you take out large amounts) than the commissions and exchange rates charged on travellers cheques.

You can report any lost MasterCard/Euro cards on ☎ 261 35 46 50 and lost Visa cards on ☎ 224 12 53 53.

Costs

Food, transport and admission fees are fairly cheap, but accommodation in hotels is fairly expensive, at least in Prague. If you want to save money you'll have to spend a little more time looking for cheap pensions, hostels or camping grounds, and eat in pubs or stand-up cafeterias. You might be able to get away with US$15 a day in summer. Staying in private rooms or better pensions, eating at cheap restaurants and using public transport, you can count on US$25 to US$30. Get out of the capital and your costs will drop dramatically.

A disappointing side of the Czech concept of a 'free-market economy' is the official two-tier price system in which foreigners can pay up to double the local price for some hotel rooms, airline and bus tickets, and museum and concert tickets. In Prague most tickets are snapped up by scalpers and travel agencies who resell them to foreigners at several times the original price. Sometimes simply questioning the price difference results in an 'error correction'; if not, you either pay the higher price or go elsewhere. When you do get something for the local price (eg, beer or domestic train tickets), you'll find that it is inexpensive. Students usually get 50% off at museums, galleries, theatres, fairs, etc.

Tipping

Tipping in restaurants is optional but if there is no service charge and service is good you should certainly round up the bill to the next 10 Kč or 20 Kč (up to 10%). The same applies to tipping taxi drivers. If your driver is honest and turns on the meter then you should round up the fare at the end of your journey.

Taxes & Refunds

Value-added tax (VAT, or DPH in Czech) is 5% on food, hotel rooms and restaurant meals, but 22% on luxury items (including alcohol). This tax is included in the sticker price and not added at the cash register.

You can claim VAT refunds for purchases worth more than 1000 Kč made in shops displaying the 'Tax-Free Shopping' sticker. They will give you a VAT Refund Form, which you must present to customs for validation when you leave the country. You can then claim a refund from a collecting agency within three months of the purchase date.

POST & COMMUNICATIONS
Post
Main post offices are open 7am or 8am to 5pm or 7pm Monday to Friday, and until noon on Saturday.

Postcards and letters up to 20g cost 9 Kč to other European countries and 14 Kč to the USA and Canada. A 2kg parcel by airmail costs 348 Kč to other European countries and 691 Kč to North America.

In principle, anything can be posted internationally from any major post office. In practice, some postal employees still suffer from communist-era anxieties about 'regulations', and may send you off to the customs post office (usually open 8am to 3pm) to send anything over 2kg. Don't send parcels containing anything valuable by ordinary mail; for fast, secure delivery, use the more expensive Express Mail Service (EMS) or a courier service such as DHL.

General delivery mail can be addressed to Poste Restante, Pošta 1, in most major cities. For Prague, also include: Jindřišská 14, 11000 Praha 1, Czech Republic.

American Express card-holders can receive mail addressed c/o American Express, Václavské nám 56, 11000 Praha 1, Czech Republic; letters are held for 30 days, but parcels and registered mail are not accepted.

Telephone
Český Telecom has replaced its antiquated telephone network with a modern digital system. Beginning 22 September 2002 all Czech phone numbers will have nine-digits, without an initial zero and without a separate area code – you will have to dial all nine digits for any call, local or long distance. For example, all Prague numbers (former area code 02) will change from 02-xx xx xx xx to 2 xx xx xx xx, and you will have to the dial the '2' even if you are calling from within Prague. Czech mobile numbers will also drop the initial zero.

Local calls cost 4 Kč for two minutes at peak rate (7am to 7pm weekdays) using a coin-phone, 3.20 Kč with a cardphone; phonecards costing 175/320 Kč for 50/100 units are sold at newsstands and post offices.

You can make international telephone calls at main post offices or directly from cardphone booths. The international access code

is ☎ 00. Three-minute direct-dial international calls at peak rate cost around 35 Kč to Germany; 42 Kč to the UK, France, Australia, the USA and Canada; and 63 Kč to New Zealand and Japan.

The Country Direct service is available in the Czech Republic (get a full list of countries and numbers from any telephone office or directory). Use the following numbers to make a charge-card or reverse-charge call to your home country:

Australia Direct	☎ 00420 06101
Canada Direct	☎ 00420 00151
Canada (AT&T)	☎ 00420 00152
France Direct	☎ 00420 03301
Deutschland Direct	☎ 00420 04949
Netherlands	☎ 00420 03101
UK Direct (BT)	☎ 00420 04401
USA (AT&T)	☎ 00420 00101
USA (MCI)	☎ 00420 00112
USA (Sprint)	☎ 00420 87187

See also 'Appendix – Telephones' at the back of this book.

Fax & Telegram
Telegrams can be sent from most post offices, while faxes can be sent from certain major post offices and hotel business centres. You can dictate telegrams on ☎ 0127.

Email & Internet Access
There are Internet cafés in most towns and cities; see the relevant sections for details. The usual charge is about 1 Kč to 2 Kč per minute.

DIGITAL RESOURCES
Websites at W www.prague-info.cz, W www.czechsite.com and W www.ceskenoviny.cz/news are packed with useful information and lots of links. The Czech Press Agency (ČTK) has a website at W www.ctknews.com and W www.europeaninternet.com/czech also has Czech news and current affairs.

BOOKS
Lonely Planet's guides to *Czech & Slovak Republics* and *Prague* both have extensive information on travelling in the Czech Republic, while LP's *Czech phrasebook* is a good introduction to the language.

The Coasts of Bohemia by Derek Sayer is a very readable exploration of the ironies of Czech history from the 18th century to 1968.

The collection of essays entitled *Václav Havel, or Living in Truth* (1986), edited by Jan Vladislav, includes Havel's famous 1978 piece 'The power of the powerless'. Havel describes the conformity of those who simply accepted the 'post-totalitarian system' as 'living within the lie'. In contrast, the dissidents endured many difficulties but earned respect by 'living within the truth'. *The Reluctant President: A Political Life of Václav Havel*, by Michael Simmons, also portrays this captivating figure well.

In a classic Czech novel *The Good Soldier Švejk*, Jaroslav Hašek (1883–1923) satirises the pettiness of government and military service. A Prague dog-catcher is drafted into the Austrian army before WWI, and by carrying out stupid orders to the letter he succeeds in completely disrupting military life.

Probably the best Czech novelist of the 20th century is Bohumil Hrabal (1914–97). One of his finest works is *The Little Town Where Time Stood Still*, a novel set in a small town, which shows in a humorous way how the close-knit community interacts.

NEWSPAPERS & MAGAZINES

The *Prague Post* at **w** www.praguepost.cz is a good weekly newspaper founded by a group of US expats in October 1991. It has a 'Calendar' section with entertainment listings and practical visitor information. There are also several business papers, including the *Prague Business Journal* and the glossy *Prague Tribune*. Major European and US newspapers and magazines are on sale at newsstands in Prague and other tourist hot spots.

RADIO & TV

Between Czech programmes, the BBC World Service broadcasts news and other programmes in English hourly, throughout the day from 5am to midnight weekdays and from 8am on weekends. Tune into 101.1FM in Prague, 101.3FM in Brno and 98.6FM in Plzeň.

On TV, Euronews in English is on channel ČT 2 on some days at either noon or 1am. Cable and satellite TV has most of the English-language European stations.

TIME

The Czech Republic is on GMT/UTC plus one hour. On the last weekend in March the clocks go forward an hour. On the last weekend in October they're turned back an hour.

LAUNDRY

There are self-service laundrettes in Prague and Český Krumlov; anywhere else you will have to rely on laundries or dry cleaners (*prádelna or čistírna*) that can take up to a week to wash clothes. Some top-end hotels have an expensive overnight laundry service.

TOILETS

Public toilets usually charge 2 Kč to 5 Kč, but as there are only a few around you may have to resort to using the facilities in restaurants or pubs; in tourist areas some of these also charge 5 Kč. Toilets might be marked *záchody* or *WC,* while men's may be marked *páni* or *muži* and women's *dámy* or *ženy.*

The handful of public toilets in central Prague are mainly in metro stations.

HEALTH

Tap water is safe to drink, but many people prefer bottled water. The most popular brand is Dobra Voda ('Good Water') – blue bottle-caps for still, red for sparkling.

Thermal Baths

There are hundreds of curative mineral springs and dozens of health spas in the Czech Republic that use mineral waters, mud or peat. Most famous are the spas of West Bohemia – these include Karlovy Vary, Františkovy Lázně and Mariánské Lázně.

Unfortunately, the spas are reserved for the medical treatment of patients. Yet all have colonnades where you can join in the 'drinking cure', a social ritual that involves imbibing liberal quantities of warm spring water and then parading up and down to stimulate circulation. Admission is free but you need to bring your own cup or buy a special *lázeňský pohárek* (sap cup).

For medical treatment at a spa you must book in advance through a booking agency (see the Karlovy Vary section), a Čedok office, a Czech Tourist Authority office abroad or the **Czech Spas Association** (**☎** 354 54 22 25, fax 354 54 23 56; **e** mip@mip.cz). The recommended stay is 21 days, although you can book for as few as three days. Daily prices begin at US$38 per person in the cheapest category during winter (October to April) and US$50 during summer. The price includes medical examination and care, spa curative treatment, room and board, and the spa tax. The clientele tends to be elderly.

WOMEN TRAVELLERS

Sexual violence has been on the rise in the Czech Republic but is still much lower than in the West. Nonetheless, solo female travellers should avoid deserted and unlit areas, especially at night. Women may experience cat calls and whistling.

GAY & LESBIAN TRAVELLERS

The bimonthly gay guide and contact magazine *Amigo* has a few pages in English, and a useful English-language website at w www .amigo.cz/indexe.htm. Gay Guide.Net Prague at w www.gayguide.net/Europe/Czech/Prague is another useful source of information.

Czechs are generally not accustomed to seeing homosexuals showing affection for each other in public, but their reaction will most likely be just a surprised look.

DISABLED TRAVELLERS

Facilities for disabled people are receiving some attention. Ramps for wheelchair users in Prague are becoming more common, especially at more expensive hotels, major street crossings, McDonald's and KFC entrances and toilets. Transport is a major problem as most buses and trams have no wheelchair access. In Prague, the Hlavní nádraží and Holešovice trains stations, and 23 metro stations, have lifts (that don't always work); bus Nos 1 and 3 are wheelchair accessible on weekdays only.

Elsewhere, only Plzeň's train station has a self-operating lift, while those at Brno, České Budějovice and Karlovy Vary have easy street and ramp access. For wheelchair assistance you need to inform the stationmaster 30 minutes before the train's departure.

The Stavovské Theatre (and several other theatres) in Prague has wheelchair access and is equipped for the hearing-impaired. Most pedestrian crossings with lights in city centres give off a steady ticking noise which speeds up when the light is green, signalling that it is OK to cross the street.

For more information, get in contact with the **Prague Wheelchair Users Organisation** (*Pražská organizace vozíčkářů;* ☎ 224 82 72 10; e *pov@gts.cz; Benediktská 6, Josefov*). It can organise a guide and transporta at about half the cost of a taxi, and has an online database of barrier-free places in Prague. Also visit w www.pov.cz; the site is currently in Czech only, but an English translation is planned.

Emergency Services

The telephone number for all emergency services is ☎ 112. For state police dial ☎ 158 and for local police ☎ 156.

For the fire brigade ring ☎ 150 and for the ambulance call ☎ 155.

Assistance for car breakdowns is available through ☎ 1230 and ☎ 1240.

All numbers are valid nationwide.

DANGERS & ANNOYANCES

Violent crime is low compared with the West, but theft and pickpocketing are a real problem in Prague's tourist zone (see that section for more details). Prague's international Ruzyně airport is also a haven for thieves. Another problem is the increasing number of robberies on international trains passing through the country. The victims are usually sleeping passengers, some of whom are gassed to sleep in their compartments and then relieved of their valuables. Groups of skinheads occasionally abuse and assault darker-skinned people.

Confusingly, buildings on some streets have two sets of numbers. The blue number is the actual street number while the red number is the old building-registration number. The streets themselves are sometimes poorly labelled.

BUSINESS HOURS

From Monday to Friday, shops open at around 8.30am (bakeries and some grocery stores at 7am) and close at 5pm or 6pm, though major department stores stay open until at least 8pm. Outside Prague, almost everything closes on Saturday afternoon and all day Sunday. Many department stores, some grocery stores and tourist-oriented shops (especially those in the centre of Prague) remain open on weekends until around 5pm. Most of the restaurants are open every day, but in the smaller towns it can be difficult to find a restaurant open on Sunday evening.

Most museums are closed on Monday and the day following a public holiday, but some are open seven days a week, especially in summer. Many gardens, castles and historic sites are closed from November to March and open on weekends only in April and October. In winter, before making a long trip out to an attraction in the countryside, be sure to check that it's open. At any sight where a guided

CZECH REPUBLIC

tour is required the ticket office closes an hour or so before the official closing time, depending on the length of the tour.

PUBLIC HOLIDAYS & SPECIAL EVENTS

Public holidays are New Year's Day (1 January), Easter Monday (March/April), Labour Day (1 May), Liberation Day (8 May), Cyril and Methodius Day (5 July), Jan Hus Day (6 July), Czech Statehood Day (28 September), Republic Day (28 October), Struggle for Freedom and Democracy Day (17 November) and Christmas (24 to 26 December). On Christmas and New Year's Eves many restaurants and bars will either be rented out for private parties or closed.

Major festivals include the Prague Spring International Music Festival during the second half of May (most performances are sold out well in advance). Karlovy Vary holds an International Film Festival in July and the Dvořák Autumn Music Festival in September. Brno has an Easter Festival of Spiritual Music, as well as the International Moravian Music Festival in September.

Moravian folk-art traditions culminate in late June at the Strážnice Folk Festival. In mid-August the Chod Festival at Domažlice affords you a chance to enjoy the folk songs and dances of South and West Bohemia. Medieval festivals are held in Český Krumlov (June) and Tábor (September).

ACTIVITIES
Hiking

There are good hiking possibilities in the forests around Karlovy Vary and in the Moravian karst area, north of Brno. The Šumava hills in the southern part of Bohemia offers some of the best hiking in the country, while the Adršpach-Teplice Rocks in East Bohemia has the most spectacular scenery.

Cycling

The whole country is ideal for cycling and cycle-touring. For information on bicycle rentals and suggested trips, see Prague and Český Krumlov later in this chapter.

Canoeing

A number of rivers are good for canoeing, including the Otava. In summer, it is possible to transport canoes on trains. For canoeing possibilities, see the Český Krumlov section.

COURSES

The **Information-Advisory Centre of Charles University** (*IPC*; ☎ 224 49 18 96, 222 23 24 52, fax 222 23 22 52; e ipc@ruk.cuni.cz; Školská 13a, Prague 1), provides information about the university and its courses, and sells ISIC, IYTC and Euro<26 cards.

The **Institute of Linguistics & Professional Training** (*Ústav jazykové a odborné přípravy, UJOP;* ☎ 224 99 04 17/12, fax 224 99 04 40; e ujop@ruk.cuni.cz; Vratislavova 10, Prague 2), at the Charles University, runs four-week Czech-language courses for foreigners in July and August. The application deadline is mid-June. No prior knowledge of the Czech language is required, and the course fee is US$590, not including accommodation. You can also opt for individual lessons (45 minutes) at US$16 each. The university's website w www.cuni.cz/cuni/ujop/czech.htm has information.

WORK

Unless you speak Czech or have a job with an English-speaking company the most likely work is English teaching or assisting in one of the backpacker hostels in Prague or Český Krumlov. It's easier to find a teaching job in provincial towns and your living costs will be much lower. In Prague, look in the Czech advertising paper *Annonce*, the *Prague Post*, and around the expat cafés. Also try the **American Embassy Information Resource Center** (*IRC;* ☎ 224 23 10 85; Hybernská 7a, Nové Město) and the **British Council** (☎ 221 91 11 11; Národní 10, Nové Město).

To obtain work legally you need a working visa and residency permit, for which you must apply at a Czech embassy or consulate before entering the country. Your employer will need to obtain the permits. These visas can take some months to process.

The **Klub mladých cestovatelů** (*KMC, Young Travellers Club;* ☎/fax 222 22 03 47; w www.kmc.cz; Karolíny Světlé 30, Prague 1) organises international work camps from June to August renovating historic buildings, maintaining national parks and teaching children English etc. Contracts are for a minimum of three weeks with no pay, but room and board are provided. The registration fee, if you book ahead through a volunteer or Hostelling International organisation in your home country, is US$50 to US$100 (some are free). There's a list of upcoming camps on the KMC website.

Astronomical clock, Old Town Hall, Prague

RICHARD NEBESKÝ

Water Chateau gardens, Telč, Czech Republic

BRUCE YUAN-YUE BI

Medieval Český Krumlov, Czech Republic

MARTIN MOOS

Typical red-brick facades on the historic old market square, Wismar, Germany

DAVID PEEVERS

Colour and strength, Fischmarkt district, Hamburg

Café life on Marienplatz, Munich, Germany

The ultra-modern Jewish Museum, Berlin

Unesco-listed Wartburg castle, Eisenach

Boats for hire, Friedrichshafen harbour, Germany

ACCOMMODATION
Camping
At around 50 Kč to 100 Kč per person, pitching your own tent is definitely the cheapest form of accommodation. There are several hundred camping grounds in the Czech Republic, most of which are open from May to September only. The grounds are often accessible by public transport, but there's usually no hot water. Most have a small snack bar where beer is sold and many have small cabins for rent that are cheaper than a hotel room. Camping on public land is prohibited. Camping Gaz and Coleman gas canisters are widely available, as is Coleman fuel (technický benzín) and methylated spirits (líh).

Hostels
The Hostelling International (HI) handbook lists an impressive network of associate hostels across the Czech Republic. In July and August many student dormitories become temporary hostels, while a number in Prague have been converted into all year, Western-style hostels. In central Prague, some normal schools also turn into temporary hostels during summer. Český Krumlov is the only place, apart from Prague, with a solid network of backpacker hostels.

Hostelling is controlled by **Klub mladých cestovatelů** (KMC, Young Travellers Club; ☎/fax 222 22 03 47; ⓦ www.kmc.cz; Karolíny Světlé 30, Prague 1). It's usually best to book ahead. You can book hostels in Prague and Brno from anywhere in the world via the computerised international booking network (IBN) that is linked to the HI booking service. A HI membership card is not usually required to stay at hostels, although it will usually get you a reduced rate. An ISIC, ITIC, IYTC or Euro<26 card may also get you a discount. A dorm bed costs around 300 Kč to 400 Kč.

Another category of hostel not connected with HI is tourist hostels (Turistické ubytovny), which provide very basic and cheap (200 Kč to 300 Kč) dormitory accommodation without the standards and controls associated with HI hostels. Ask about tourist hostels at information, CKM or GTS international offices and watch out for the letters 'TU' on accommodation lists published in languages other than English.

Private Rooms & Pensions
Private rooms (look for signs reading 'privát' or 'Zimmer frei') are usually available in the tourist towns, and many tourist information offices can book them for you; expect to pay from 250 Kč to 500 Kč per person outside Prague. Some have a three-night minimum-stay requirement.

In Prague, many private travel agencies offer private rooms, and the service is available daily and during evenings. This is the easiest way to find accommodation in Prague if you don't mind paying at least 500 Kč per person per night.

The are many small pensions (occasionally glorified private rooms), especially on the outskirts of Prague and in South Bohemia, and these offer a more personalised service at lower rates than the hotels.

Hotels
Hotels in Prague and Brno are expensive, whereas those in smaller towns are usually much cheaper. Czechs pay less than half as much as foreigners at some hotels.

Hotels are rated with stars, with four- and five-star hotels being luxury per single/double. Two-star hotels usually offer reasonable comfort for about 500/700 Kč for a single/double with shared bathroom, or 600/1000 Kč with private facilities (these prices are about 50% higher in Prague).

FOOD
The cheapest places to eat are self-service restaurants (jídelna or samoobsluha). Sometimes they have tasty dishes like barbecued chicken or hot German sausage – handy for a quick lunch. Train stations in large cities often have cheap restaurants or buffets/bistros but the best-value meals are in busy beer halls. If the place is crowded with locals, is noisy and looks chaotic, chances are it will have great lunch specials at low prices. As a general rule, a restaurant calling itself restaurace is usually cheaper than a 'restaurant'. Also, with the exception of Prague, the food in most restaurants is the same no matter what the price. Your pork and dumplings will taste the same in a hospoda (pub) or vinárna (wine bar) for 60 Kč as in a four-star hotel for 180 Kč.

Lunches are generally bigger and cheaper than dinners in the less expensive places. Dinner is eaten early and latecomers may have little to choose from.

In Czech the word for menu is jídelní lístek. Menus are mostly in Czech, except in touristy areas where they are also in German and/or English. Anything that comes with *knedlíky* (dumplings) will be a hearty local meal. Some Prague restaurants are notorious for overcharging foreigners (see Places to Eat in the Prague section).

Most beer halls have a system of marking everything you eat or drink on a small piece of paper that is left on your table. Waiters in all Czech restaurants, including the expensive ones, whisk away empty plates from under your nose before you manage to swallow your last dumpling.

There are great little *cukrárna* (pastry shops) throughout the country. These offer cakes, pastries and puddings as good as anything you'll find in neighbouring Austria at a fraction of the price.

Local Specialities
Czech cuisine is strong on sauces and gravies and weak on fresh vegetables. *Pražská šunka* (smoked Prague ham) is often eaten as a starter with Znojmo gherkins, followed by a thick soup, such as *bramborová polévka* (potato soup) or *zeleninová polévka* (vegetable soup). *Dršťková polévka* (tripe soup) is a treat not to be missed.

The Czechs love meat dishes with sauerkraut and/or *knedlíky*, dumplings made with *bramborové* (potato) or *houskové* (bread). Unfortunately, many of the bread dumplings are pre-made in factories and pale in comparison to home-made ones. In inexpensive pubs or restaurants bread dumplings taste fine, but the potato ones are usually tasteless and stodgy. However, in most expensive restaurants the potato dumplings are reasonably good.

Kapr (carp) from Bohemia's fish ponds is served fried or baked. Prague has a good range of vegetarian restaurants; elsewhere, *bezmasá* (vegie) dishes are limited to pizzas, *smažený sýr* (fried cheese) and *knedlíky s vejci* (scrambled eggs with dumplings). *Ovocné knedlíky* (Czech fruit dumplings), with whole fruit, are served as a dessert with cottage cheese or crushed poppy seeds and melted butter.

DRINKS
The Czech Republic is a beer drinker's paradise – where else could you get two or three 500mL glasses of top-quality Pilsner for under a dollar? One of the first words of Czech you'll learn is *pivo* (beer); alcohol-free beer (yuck!) is *nealkoholické pivo*. The Czechs serve their draught beer with a high head of foam.

Bohemian beer is probably the best in the world – the most famous brands are Budvar (the original Budweiser) and Plzeňský Prazdroj (Pilsner Urquell in German, the original Pilsner). The South Moravia and Mělník regions produce reasonable white wines (*bílé víno*), but Czech red wines (*červené víno*) are not great.

Special treats include Becherovka (an exquisite bittersweet Czech liqueur), *zubrovka* (vodka with herb extracts) and *slivovice* (plum brandy). *Grog* is rum with hot water and sugar. *Limonáda* often refers to any soft drink, not just lemonade.

ENTERTAINMENT
Theatres and concert-hall admission prices are still well below those in Western Europe and most performances are first rate.

In Prague, most of the best theatre tickets are snapped up by scalpers and travel agencies who demand higher prices (these are still inexpensive), but in other towns such as Karlovy Vary, Plzeň, České Budějovice and Brno you can see top performances at minimal expense. Most theatres are closed in summer.

Outside Prague, the nightlife is rather limited, although after 9pm there's usually a band playing in the bar of the best hotel in town and on weekends a club will be pumping somewhere, so just ask. You often have to contend with overbearing door attendants and contemptuous waiters.

Cinema is always cheap and films are usually shown in the original language with local subtitles.

SPECTATOR SPORTS
European handball is the national sport but the most popular is *fotbal* (soccer). Outstanding soccer teams include SK Slavia Praha and AC Sparta Praha.

Ice hockey is followed with even more passion as the Czech national team is world class. Among the best ice hockey teams are HC Petra Vsetín (a South Moravian team) and HC Sparta Praha (a Prague city club).

Tennis is also popular, as is cross-country ski racing in winter.

SHOPPING
Good buys for the avid shopper include china, Bohemian crystal, costume jewellery, folk ceramics, lace, embroidery, wooden toys, shoes, colour-photography books, classical

CDs and souvenirs. Garnet, ruby and amber jewellery is a speciality in Bohemia.

Getting There & Away

AIR

The national air carrier, **Czech Airlines** (ČSA; ☎ 220 10 46 20; V celnici 5; metro Náměstí Republiky), has direct flights to Prague from many European cities, including Sofia, Zagreb, Budapest, Rīga, Bucharest, Moscow, Bratislava, Ljubljana and Kyiv, and also from Beirut, Cairo, Dubai, İstanbul, Larnaca, Malta, Montreal, New York, Tel Aviv and Toronto. Return fares to Prague offered by ČSA include €342 from Paris, €252 from Frankfurt and UK£95 from London Stansted. Return fares from Prague include 1990 Kč to Bratislava, 9400 Kč to Budapest, 10,700 Kč to Sofia and 11,100 Kč to Kyiv.

The British airline **Go** (in Prague ☎ 296 33 33 33) has direct flights to Prague from London Stansted, Bristol and East Midlands, with one-way fares from as little as UK£45. **KLM** (in Prague ☎ 233 09 09 33) is also a good bet for low-cost flights to Prague via Amsterdam.

Flights from New York to Prague with Austrian Airlines or SAS start at around US$500.

LAND

Bus

Most of the international buses are operated by **Eurolines-Sodeli CZ** (☎ 224 23 93 18; Ⓦ www.eurolines.cz; Senovážné nám 6, Prague 1) and **Bohemia Euroexpress International** (☎ 224 21 86 80; Ⓦ www.bei.cz; Florenc Bus Station, Křižíkova 4-6, Prague 8). Prague's main international bus station is Florenc (Autobusové nádraží Florenc), 600m northwest of the main train station, but some buses use stands at Holešovice train station or Želivského metro station – make sure you know where your bus departs from. It's easier to buy a bus ticket from a travel agency such as GTS (see the Prague section) than to struggle with the queues and grumpy salespeople at Florenc bus station.

The peak season for bus travel is from mid-June to the end of September, when there are daily Eurolines buses to Prague from London (UK£61/95 single/return, 23 hours), Paris (€68/122, 15 hours), Frankfurt (€44/69, 9½

hours), Vienna (€24/47, 4¾ hours) and Amsterdam (€73/130, 15 to 19 hours). Two buses a week link Kraków in Poland with Brno (80/130 zł, 6½ hours). Outside peak season daily services fall to two or three a week.

There are several buses daily to Bratislava from Prague (300 Kč one-way, 4¾ hours) and Brno (250 Kč, 1¾ hours), five a week from Prague to Budapest (1100 Kč, 7¼ hours) and three a week from Prague to Warsaw (550 Kč, 10½ hours) via Wrocław (350 Kč, five hours).

Kingscourt Express company (☎ 224 23 45 83; Ⓦ www.kce.cz; Havelská 8, Prague 1) runs four buses a week (six in summer) from Brno to London calling at Prague and Plzeň (1850/2900 Kč one way/return from all three Czech cities, 20 hours from Prague). **Capital Express** (☎ 020-7243 0488; Ⓦ www.capital express.cz; 57 Princedale Rd, Holland Park, London W11 4NP) has daily buses (twice daily in summer) from London to Plzeň, Prague (UK£40/60, 21 hours), Brno (UK£43/65, 24 hours), Olomouc and Ostrava.

Train

Train travel is the easiest and the most comfortable way to get from Western Europe to the Czech Republic, but it's expensive compared to the bus, and even budget airlines. Keep in mind that domestic Czech train fares are cheaper than what you might pay for the Czech section of a ticket to or from Western Europe. You can save a bit by buying a ticket that terminates at a border town, then continuing with a cheaper, Czech-bought ticket.

In the capital, international trains arrive at Prague's central station (Praha hlavní nádraží, or Praha hl. n.), Holešovice (Praha Hol.), Smíchov (Praha Smv.) or Masarykovo (Praha Mas.) stations. Make sure you know which station your train will arrive at or depart from.

Prague and Brno are on the main line used by daily express trains from Berlin and Dresden to Bratislava and Budapest, and from Hamburg and Berlin to Vienna. Trains from Frankfurt and Munich pass through Nuremberg, Cheb and Plzeň on the way to Prague. Local railcars shuttle between Cheb and Schirnding (15 minutes) in Germany several times a day. There are also daily express trains between Prague and Warsaw, Poland, via Wrocław or Katowice.

If you're planning to travel between Prague and Budapest check whether you need a Slovak transit visa (the train goes via Bratislava).

Sample one-way fares to Prague include €130 from Paris (15 hours); UK£95 from London (25 to 30 hours); €42 from Salzburg (eight hours); €122 from Amsterdam (12½ hours); €46 from Berlin (five hours); and €85 from Frankfurt (7½ hours).

One-way train fares from Prague include 400 Kč to Bratislava; 750 Kč to Vienna; 1150 Kč to Budapest; 750 Kč to Kraków; and 890 Kč to Warsaw.

You can buy tickets in advance from Czech Railways (ČD) ticket offices, ČD travel agencies or other travel agencies. International tickets are valid for two months with unlimited stopovers. Inter-Rail (Zone D) passes are valid in the Czech Republic, but Eurail passes are not. For travel within the Czech Republic only, the Czech Flexipass is available (from US$48 to US$78 for three to eight days' travel in a 15-day period).

Seat reservations are compulsory on all the international trains. First-class sleepers and 2nd-class couchettes are available on overnight services.

Car & Motorcycle

Motorists can enter the country at one of the many border crossings marked on most road maps (see the Czech Republic map for all major 24-hour crossings). Foreign driving licences are valid for up to 90 days; strictly speaking, licences that do not include a photo ID need an International Driving Permit as well, although this rule is rarely enforced.

A vehicle must be equipped with a first-aid kit, a red-and-white warning triangle and a nationality sticker on the rear; the use of seat belts is compulsory. Drinking and driving is strictly forbidden – the legal blood alcohol level is zero. Police can hit you with on-the-spot fines of up to 2000 Kč for speeding and other traffic offences (be sure to insist on a receipt).

You will need to buy a motorway tax coupon (nálepka), costing 100/200/800 Kč for 10 days/one month/one year for vehicles under 3.5 tonnes, in order to use Czech motorways; failure to display one risks a 5000 Kč fine. They are on sale at border crossings, petrol stations and post offices.

DEPARTURE TAX

The airport departure tax on international flights leaving the Czech Republic is included in the ticket price.

Getting Around

AIR

ČSA has flights between Brno and Prague but it is much cheaper, and almost as fast, to take the bus or the train.

BUS

Within the Czech Republic buses are often faster, cheaper and more convenient than the train, and by European standards both are cheap. Long-distance companies include the national carrier ČSAD, Čebus and Bohemia Euroexpress, and there are several buses a day from Prague to Brno (140 Kč, 2½ hours), Plzeň (60 Kč, 1½ hours), Karlovy Vary (100 Kč, 2¼ hours) and Český Krumlov (120 Kč, three hours). You sometimes have to pay a small additional charge for checked luggage.

A mass of complex footnotes often makes posted bus timetables difficult to read. Two crossed hammers means the bus only runs on weekdays; 'jede' means 'runs', 'nejede' means 'doesn't run', 'denně' means 'daily', 'so' and 'ne' mean 'Saturday' and 'Sunday'. As most buses leave in the morning, it's best to get an early start. Many buses don't operate on weekends, when trains are more reliable. Buses sometimes leave a few minutes early, so it's best to get to the station at least 15 minutes before the official departure time.

Bus ticketing at main stations such as Prague and Karlovy Vary is computerised, so you can often book a seat ahead and be sure of a comfortable trip. Way stations are rarely computerised and you must line up and pay the driver. Reservations can only be made at the bus' point of departure; at peak periods you may have to stand part of the way if you don't have a reservation.

TRAIN

Czech Railways (České dráhy, or ČD) provides efficient train services to almost every part of the country. However, some remote places are difficult or impossible to get to by train. One-way, 2nd-class fares cost around 64/120/224/424 Kč for 50/100/200/400km; 1st-class fares are 50% more expensive.

Some trains operate only on certain days, but the footnotes on the posted timetables are incomprehensible unless you speak Czech or have a timetable booklet (Jízdní řád) in English. The clerks at information counters very seldom speak English (even in the major stations), so to find out a departure time, try writing down your destination and the date you wish to travel, then point to your watch and pray. Alternatively, go to an Internet café and check train (and bus) timetables in English on [w] www.vlak.cz. All train ticket offices in the Czech Republic are computerised and will give you a print-out in English with information about your train.

Departures *(odjezdy)* notice boards in train stations are usually yellow, while the arrivals *(příjezdy)* boards are white. Both these and the posted timetables indicate the category and platform number *(č. nástupiště)* for each train. Categories include:

SC (SuperCity) – a few top-quality services with 1st-class coaches only; supplementary charge of 1000 Kč, reservations compulsory

EC (EuroCity) – fast, comfortable international trains, stopping at main stations only with 1st- and 2nd-class coaches; supplementary charge of 60 Kč, reservations recommended

IC (InterCity) – long-distance and international trains with 1st- and 2nd-class coaches; supplement of 40 Kč, reservations recommended

Ex (express) – as for IC, but no supplementary charge

R *(rychlík)* – the main domestic network of fast trains with 1st- and 2nd-class coaches and sleeper services; no supplement except for sleepers; express and *rychlík* trains are usually marked in red on timetables

Sp *(spěšný)* – slower and cheaper than *rychlík* trains; 2nd class only

Os *(osobní)* – slow trains using older rolling stock that stop in every one-horse town; 2nd class only

Only SC, IC, EC and express trains include a dining carriage *(restaurační vůz)*.

If there is a notice over the timetable or a footnote with the Slovakian *'Náhradní autobusová doprava'*, it means that a bus that is departing from outside the train station is replacing the train service.

A letter 'R' after the train name means that reservations are available; an 'R' inside a box or circle means that they are compulsory. Reservations are not available on *osobní* trains. In major cities, you usually have to make seat reservations *(místenka* or *rezervace míst)* for domestic travel at a separate counter, so make sure you're standing in the right queue. Reservations costs only 20 Kč, and are recommended whenever possible.

Domestic train tickets for distances of more than 50km are valid for 24 hours, but for distances under 50km only until 6am the next day. Note that domestic return *(zpáteční)* tickets (about 10% more expensive than singles) are only valid for 48 hours from the time of purchase. International train tickets are valid for two months with unlimited stopovers. If you have to purchase a ticket or pay a supplement on the train for any reason, you'll have to pay a fine if you do not tell the conductor *before* you're asked for your ticket.

Always check to see if your train is an SC, IC or EC and pay the surcharge in the station when buying your ticket. Staff at some ticket counters will happily sell you an invalid ticket and you'll have no recourse later.

In many stations, complete timetables for all services are posted on notice boards. Look at the map first and find the route number you want, then look for the table with the corresponding number. If you're going to be in the Czech Republic for any length of time, it's a good idea to purchase the national timetable from a train station information office.

One way to save on hotel bills while getting around is by using overnight trains. Sleepers *(lůžko* – more like a bed with sheets included) and couchettes *(lehátko* – narrower than a sleeper with only a blanket) are available on overnight trains. Book at least one day before departure at a train station ticket counter. On departure day, sleepers and couchettes can only be bought from the conductor, when available. Sleepers cost 518/222 Kč per person in a single/double compartment in 1st class and 148 Kč in 2nd class (double only), while couchettes are 134/89 Kč in a four/six-person compartment. All these charges are on top of the cost of the regular train ticket.

Annoyances

Some Czech train conductors try to intimidate foreigners by pretending there's something wrong with their ticket, usually in the hope that the confused tourists will give them some money to get rid of them. Always insure that you have the right ticket for your train and don't pay any 'fine', 'supplement' or 'reservation fee' unless you first get a written receipt *(doklad)*. When you arrive at your destination, take your ticket and the receipt to an information office and politely ask for an explanation.

Conductors have also been known to take passengers' tickets claiming they will return them later. The only circumstance in which a conductor has the right to hold your ticket is when you board a train where you've reserved a couchette or sleeper, in which case the attendant will keep your ticket overnight so you don't have to be woken up for ticket controls. Don't forget to ask for your ticket back.

Several travellers have reported having problems with the lockers at the train and bus stations. Always remember to set the combination dial on the *inside* of the door *before* you close the locker; you then enter the same combination (write it down!) on the outside dial to open the locker.

CAR & MOTORCYCLE

Take care – there is a lot of dangerous driving on Czech roads. There are plenty of petrol stations, many open 24/7. Leaded petrol is available as *special* (91 octane) and *super* (96 octane), unleaded as *natural* (95 octane) or *natural plus* (98 octane); the Czech for diesel is *nafta* or just *diesel*. LPG gas *(autoplyn)* is available in every major town but at very few outlets. Natural 95 costs around 24.50 Kč a litre, diesel 22.30 Kč.

Road Rules

Speed limits are 30km/h or 50km/h in built-up areas, 90km/h on open roads and 130km/h on motorways; motorbikes are limited to 80km/h. At level crossings over railway lines the speed limit is 30km/h. Beware of speed traps, as the police are empowered to levy on-the-spot fines of up to 2000 Kč and foreigners are the preferred targets. You need a motorway tax coupon (see Car & Motorcycle in the Getting There & Away section of this chapter) to use the motorways; this is included with most rental cars.

Driving and parking in Prague are a nightmare so it's best to leave your vehicle somewhere safe and then use public transport. Unmetered parking in the historic centre of Prague is only allowed if you have a permit. Car theft by organised gangs is routine, with expensive Western cars disappearing across the country's borders within hours.

Rental

The major international car-rental chains including A-Rent-Car/Thrifty, Avis, Budget, Europcar and Hertz; all have outlets in the Czech Republic. A-Rent-Car is the cheapest, charging 1684/9666 Kč daily/weekly for a

Škoda Felicia including unlimited mileage, Collision Damage Waiver and tax. There's a 395 Kč surcharge to pick up your car from the airport; delivery to hotels in central Prague is free. Other major companies are up to 100% more expensive; Prague-based Dvorak Rent A Car has lower rates (from 1560/8400 Kč) but in Prague and Brno only. Most major companies allow one-way rentals to their other locations in the country at no extra cost.

Small local companies are much cheaper – from 680 Kč a day all inclusive – but are less likely to have English-speaking staff. See Getting Around in the Prague section.

BICYCLE

The Czech Republic offers some good opportunities for cycle touring. Cyclists should be careful, though, as minor roads are often very narrow and pot-holed, and in the towns cobblestones and tram tracks can be a dangerous combination, especially when it has been raining. Theft is a problem, especially in Prague and other large cities, so a good long chain and lock are essential.

It's fairly easy to transport your bike on Czech trains. First purchase your train ticket and then take it with your bicycle to the railway luggage office. There you fill out a card, which will be attached to your bike; on the card you should write your name, address, departure station and destination. You will be given a receipt that should include all the accessories that your bicycle has, such as lights and dynamo. You are not allowed to leave any luggage on the bicycle, and it is advisable to take off the pump and water bottles.

The cost of transporting a bicycle is 40 Kč to 60 Kč depending on the length of the journey. You can also transport bicycles on most buses if they are not too crowded and if the bus driver is willing.

HITCHING

The Czech Republic is no safer than other European countries when it comes to hitching; many hitchhikers are assaulted or raped, and each year a few are killed. Despite these dangers many Czechs, including young women, still choose to hitch.

LOCAL TRANSPORT

City buses and trams operate from around 4.30am to midnight daily. In Prague, buses and trains on some main routes operate every

40 minutes all night long. Tickets – sold at bus and train stations, newsstands and vending machines – must be validated using the time-stamping machines found on buses and trams and at the entrance to metro stations; failure to do so can result in a fine. Tickets are hard to find at night, on weekends and out in the residential areas, so carry a good supply. The yellow-ticket vending machines at Prague metro stations and some bus and tram stops sell tickets that can be used on all forms of public transport in Prague.

Taxi

Taxis have meters – just make sure the meter is switched on. Many Prague taxi drivers are highly experienced at overcharging tourists. See the Prague section for more details.

Prague

pop 1,197,000

Prague (Praha in Czech) has a magical feel about it, like a history lesson come to life. As you walk among the baroque palaces or across the Karlův most (Charles Bridge), with Smetana's Vltava flowing below and pointed towers all around, you'll feel as if history has stopped back in the 18th century. Goethe called Prague the prettiest gem in the stone crown of the world. The city is on the Unesco World Heritage list.

Prague enjoyed two architectural golden ages: a Gothic period under Holy Roman Emperor Charles IV, and a baroque period during the Habsburg Counter-Reformation. In the 18th century Czech culture was suppressed, so it's not surprising that Prague's two greatest baroque architects, Christopher and Kilian Dientzenhofer, were German.

Today Prague is the seat of government and the centre of much of the country's intellectual and cultural life. Unlike Warsaw, Budapest and Berlin, which were both major battlefields during WWII, Prague escaped almost unscathed, and after the war lack of modernisation prevented haphazard development. Since 1989, however, central Prague has been swamped by capitalism as the street vendors, cafés and restaurants take over pavements, streets and parks.

The way you feel about Prague's current tourist glut may depend on where you're coming from. If you're arriving from London,

Paris or Rome it may all seem quite normal, but if you've been elsewhere in Eastern Europe for a while, you'll be in for a bit of a shock. As you're being jostled by all the hawkers and hordes of tourists, you may begin to feel that Prague has become a tacky tourist trap, but try to overcome that feeling and enjoy this great European art centre for all it has to offer and all its beauty.

Remember, if you're in Prague on a Monday, many museums and galleries will be closed. However, the Jewish Quarter, the Mozart Museum, the National Museum, the Strahov Library, St Vitus Cathedral and many attractions in Prague Castle, the Old Town Hall and most sights in Vyšehrad citadel will still be open.

Orientation

Almost exactly midway between Berlin and Vienna, Prague nestles in a picturesque bend of the Vltava (Moldau) river, its seven hills topped by castles and churches. The Vltava swings through the centre of the city like a question mark, separating Malá Strana (Little Quarter) on the west bank from Staré Město (Old Town), the early Gothic city centre, on the east. North of Malá Strana is Hradčany, the medieval castle district, while Nové Město (New Town) is a late-Gothic extension of Staré Město to the east and south. Only in 1784 did these four royal towns unite within a single system of fortifications.

Prague Castle, visible from almost everywhere in the city, overlooks Malá Strana, while the twin Gothic spires of Týn Church dominates the wide, open space of Staroměstské nám, the old town square. The long broad avenue of Václavské nám (Wenceslas Square), Prague's Champs Elysées, stretches southeast from Staré Město towards the National Museum and the main train station. At its northwestern end is Na příkopě, a busy, pedestrian shopping street where most of the information offices are found.

Maps Our maps of Prague are for initial orientation only – for serious navigation you'll need a detailed street map. Lonely Planet's plastic-coasted *Prague City Map* is good value; other good maps include SHOCart's GeoClub *Praha – plán města* (1:15,000) and VKÚ's *Praha – mapa města* (1:10,000). PIS has a free *Welcome to the Czech Republic* pamphlet with a map of the city centre.

CZECH REPUBLIC

CZECH REPUBLIC

PRAGUE

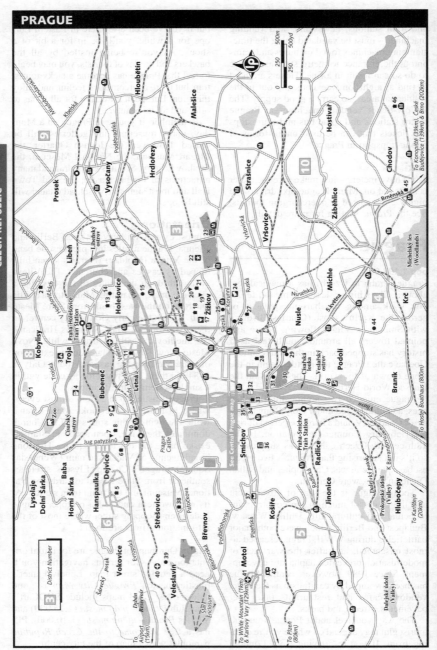

PRAGUE

PLACES TO STAY		
2	Hotel Apollo	
3	Camp Dana Troja	
5	Hotel Praha	
6	Welcome Hostel Dejvice & Accommodation Service	
8	Hostel Orlík	
11	Hotel Belvedere	
13	Sir Toby's Hostel	
16	Hostel Elf	
18	Clown & Bard Hostel	
21	Hotel Golden City Garni	
27	Penzion Máchova	
28	Hostel U Melounu	
33	Admirál Botel	
34	Hotel Balkán	
38	Hotel Markéta	
42	USK Caravan Camp	

45	AV Pension Praha	
46	Hotel Business	
PLACES TO EAT		
7	Pizzeria Grosseto	
19	Mailsi	
20	U radnice	
35	Hospoda U Starého lva	
OTHER		
1	Botanic Gardens	
4	Zoo Boat Landing	
9	Dutch Embassy	
10	Laundry Kings	
12	American Medical Center	
14	Secco Car Rental	
15	Bohemia Express Bus Company Office	
17	Palác Akropolis	

22	Foreigners Police	
23	Želivského Bus Station (Eurolines) & Metro Station	
24	New Zealand Consulate	
25	CKM Travel Centre	
26	Prague Laundromat	
29	Congress Centre	
30	Vyšehrad Complex	
31	Institute of Linguistics & Professional Training	
32	PPS Riverboat Terminal	
36	Mozart Museum	
37	Customs Post Office	
40	West Car Praha Car Rental	
41	Canadian Medical Centre	
41	Na Homolce Hospital	
43	Swimming Pool	
44	ÚAMK	

CZECH REPUBLIC

Information

Tourist Offices The municipal **Prague Information Service** (*Pražská informační služba, PIS;* ☎ 12444; ⓦ *www.prague-info.cz; open 9am-7pm Mon-Fri, 9am-5pm Sat & Sun Apr-Oct; 9am-6pm Mon-Fri, 9am-3pm Sat Nov-Mar)* has branches: at Na příkopě 20; in the Old Town Hall on Staroměstské nám (open to 6pm Saturday and Sunday in summer); at Malá Strana Bridge Tower (open 10am to 6pm daily from April to October only); and in the Praha-hlavní nádraží train station, next to the metro entrance.

The monthly *Culture in Prague* booklet in English is an invaluable guide to action in the city. All the PIS offices offer Ticketpro concert tickets and AVE accommodation services, while the Old Town Hall branch arranges guides and sells city tours (a three-hour tour is 500 Kč per person for two or more people).

For motoring matters, contact **Autoklub Bohemia Assistance** (*ABA;* ☎ 222 24 12 57; *Opletalova 29),* opposite the main train station, or **ÚAMK** (☎ 261 10 43 33; *Na Strži 6).*

Publications The English-language *Prague Post* (50 Kč, weekly) is a good source of information on what's happening in Prague; check out the website at ⓦ www.praguepost .cz. The irreverent *Prague Pill* (free, fortnightly) covers club culture and politics. *Think* (free, monthly) is a glossy magazine in Czech and English that covers art, music, fashion and subculture, along with good restaurant and bar reviews.

Money You can change American Express or Thomas Cook travellers cheques without commission at their respective city offices. **American Express** (*AmEx;* ☎ 222 80 02 37; *Václavské nám 56; open 9am-7pm daily)* changes non-AmEx travellers cheques for 2% commission. **Thomas Cook** (☎ 221 10 53 71; *Národní 28; open 9am-7pm Mon-Fri, 9am-6pm Sat, 10am-6pm Sun)* also changes Visa travellers cheques without commission. Both have poorer exchange rates than local banks.

Major banks are the best places for changing cash. Convenient branches include:

Česká spořitelna (Václavské nám 16) open 8am to 5pm Monday to Friday
ČSOB (Na příkopě 14) open 8am to 5pm Monday to Friday
Komerční banka (Václavské nám 42) open 8am to 5pm Monday to Friday
Živnostenská banka (Na příkopě 20) open 8am to 4.30pm Monday to Friday

Be on your guard against the exorbitant commission charged by private exchange offices in Prague such as Chequepoint and Change. Many charge from 4% to 12% commission (with a 95 Kč minimum), or advertise 0% commission but give a much poorer exchange rate and/or add on a hefty 'handling charge'.

Post & Communications To use the **main post office** (*Jindřišská 14; metro Můstek; open 7am-8pm daily),* take a ticket from one of the automated machines just outside the main hall (press button No 1 for stamps and parcels, No 4 for EMS). Wait until your number *(lístek číslo)* comes up on the electronic boards inside; these tell you which window to go to for service *(přepážka)*.

You can pick up poste-restante mail at window No 1 and buy phonecards at window No 28. Parcels weighing up to 2kg, as well as international and EMS parcels are sent from window Nos 7 to 10. (Note that these services close at 1pm on Saturday and all day Sunday.)

There's a telegraph and 24-hour telephone centre to the left of the right-hand post office entrance.

To reach the **customs post office** *(Pobočka Celního Úřadu; Plzeňská 139; open 7am-3pm Mon-Fri, to 6pm Wed)*, take the metro to Anděl, then go for three stops west on tram No 4, 7 or 9.

Email & Internet Access The centre of Prague is overflowing with Internet cafés. The cheapest places are **Bohemia Bagel** *(☎ 224 81 25 60; Masná 2, Staré Město • ☎ 257 31 06 94; Újezd 16, Malá Strana; both open 7am-midnight Mon-Fri, 8am-midnight Sat & Sun)* and **The Globe** (see Bookshops, later in this section), which both charge 1 Kč a minute with no minimum. The Globe also has network sockets where you can connect your own laptop (also 1 Kč a minute; cables provided, 50 Kč deposit).

Other convenient city-centre Internet cafés (with 10- or 15-minute minimum charges) include **Internet Cafe Prague** *(☎ 606 38 68 17; Liliová 18; open 9am-11pm Mon-Fri, 10am-11pm Sat & Sun)*, charging 120 Kč an hour; **Internet Nescafe Live** *(☎ 221 63 71 68; Rathova Pasaž, Na příkopě 23; open 9am-10pm Mon-Fri, 10am-8pm Sat & Sun)* where rates are 102 Kč an hour; and **Internet Kafe** *(☎ 220 10 81 47; Batalion Bar, 28.října 3; open 24hr)*, where it's just 80 Kč per hour.

Travel Agencies The CKM Travel Centre *(☎ 222 72 15 95; e ckmprg@login.cz; Mánesova 77, Vinohrady; metro Jiřího z Poděbrad; open 10am-6pm Mon-Thur, 10am-4pm Fri)* makes reservations for accommodation and books air and bus tickets, with discounts for those aged under 26 (it also sells youth cards). A similar agency for the younger traveller is **GTS International** *(☎ 222 21 12 04; e gts.smecky@gtsint.cz; Ve Smečkách 33; open 8am-6pm Mon-Fri, 11am-3pm Sat)*, which also sells train tickets and youth cards.

People aged under 26 can also purchase discounted train and bus tickets to Western Europe or book accommodation in Prague at **Wasteels** *(☎ 224 61 74 54; e wasteels@iol .cz; open 7.30am-8pm Mon-Fri, 8am-3pm Sat)* in Praha-hlavní nádraží train station.

Čedok *(☎ 224 19 71 21; Na příkopě 18; open 9am-6pm Mon-Fri, 10am-3pm Sat)* sells international air, train and bus tickets. **Bohemiatour** *(☎ 231 39 17; Zlatnická 7; open 8.30am-7pm Mon-Fri)* also sells international bus tickets to many European cities. **Eurolines-Sodeli CZ** *(☎ 24 23 93 18; Senovážné nám 6; open 8am-6pm Mon-Fri)* is the agency for Eurolines.

At the main train station, the **Czech Railways Travel Agency** *(CKČD; ☎ 224 21 79 48; Praha-hlavní nádraží, Wilsonova 80; open 8am-6pm daily)* sells air, train and bus tickets to points all over Western Europe, and also has cheap youth air fares.

Bookshops One of the city's best-stocked English-language bookshops is **Big Ben** *(Malá Štupartská 5; open 9am-6.30pm Mon-Fri, 10am-5pm Sat & Sun)*. Nearby **Anagram** *(Týn 4; open 10am-8pm Mon-Sat, 10am-6pm Sun)* is also good, and has a broad range of second-hand books as well.

Na můstku *(Na příkopě 3; open to 8am-7pm Mon-Fri, 9.30am-6pm Sat & Sun)* sells city maps, guides and souvenir books. **Kiwi** *(Jungmannova 23; open 9am-6.30pm Mon-Fri, 9am-2pm Sat)* has an excellent range of maps and Lonely Planet guidebooks. Famous expat hang-out **The Globe** *(Pštrossova 6; open 10am-midnight daily)* is a cosy English-language bookshop, bar and Internet café.

Laundry Most self-service laundrettes charge around 140 Kč to wash and dry a 6kg load of laundry. There's a convenient **Laundryland** *(Na příkopě 12; open 9am-8pm Mon-Fri, 9am-7pm Sat, 11am-7pm Sun)* on the 1st floor of Černá Růže shopping centre, above the Panská entrance.

Other self-service laundrettes in the city include: **Astera** *(Jindřišská 5)* off Valavské nám; **Laundryland** *(Londýnská 71)* and **Prague Laundromat** *(Korunní 14)* near nám Míru; and the **Laundry Kings** *(Dejvická 16)* in Dejvice.

Medical Services Emergency medical aid for foreigners is available at **Na Homolce Hospital** *(☎ 257 27 11 11, after hours ☎ 257*

27 25 27; 5th floor, Foreign Pavilion, Roentgenova 2), with some of the best facilities in the country. Staff speak English, German, French and Spanish, but there are no English speakers on the after-hours telephone number. Take bus No 167 from Anděl metro station and get off at the sixth stop.

District clinics have after-hours emergency services (from 7pm to 7am, and 24 hours on weekends and holidays). The **Polyclinic at Národní** (☎ 222 07 51 20; *Národní 9; metro Národní Třída*) has staff who speak English, French and German. Expect to pay around 800 Kč to 1200 Kč for an initial consultation.

There are several private centres that have English and German-speaking staff providing emergency medical and dental care. An initial consultation will cost US$50 to US$200; you can pay by cash or credit card. Reputable establishments include the **American Medical Center** (*24hr* ☎ 220 80 77 56; *Janovského 48, Prague 7; metro Vltavská*) and the **Canadian Medical Centre** (☎ 235 36 01 33, *after hours* ☎ 60321 23 20; *Veleslavínská 1; tram No 20 or 26 west from metro Dejvická*).

There are several 24-hour pharmacies (*lékárna*) in the city centre, including the **Praha lékárna** (☎ 224 94 69 82; *Palackého 5*) and **Lékárna U sv Ludmily** (☎ 222 51 33 96; *Belgická 37; metro Náměstí Míru*). For emergency service after hours, ring the bell (usually a red button with a sign saying *'zvonek léka'* or *'první pomoc'*).

Police Official police reports for stolen belongings (needed for insurance claims) can only be obtained at the main police station in the district in which the theft occurred. This process can take a couple of hours and the officer on duty will probably have to call an interpreter. In central Prague the **police station** (☎ 261 45 17 60; *Jungmannovo nám 9*) can arrange for an interpreter. Unless you can speak Czech, forget about telephoning any other police station as English is rarely spoken.

Dangers & Annoyances The crime rate is low by Western standards but theft is rife. Pickpockets regularly work the crowds at the astronomical clock on the Old Town Hall, at Prague Castle, Karlův most (Charles Bridge), the entrance to the Old Jewish Cemetery, Václavské nám, Na příkopě and on the central metro and tram lines, especially tourists getting on or off crowded tram Nos 9 and 22.

We've also had reports of bogus police who approach tourists and ask to see their money, claiming that they are looking for counterfeit notes. They then run off with substantial amounts of cash. If in doubt, ask the 'policeman' to go with you to the nearest police station; a genuine cop will happily do so.

Being ripped off by taxi drivers is another hazard. Most taxi drivers are honest, but a large minority who operate from tourist areas greatly overcharge their customers (even Czechs). Try not to take a taxi from Václavské nám, Národní and other tourist areas. It is better to phone for a taxi (see Getting Around later in this section) or walk a couple of streets into the suburbs before hailing one.

Be aware that the park outside the main train station is a hang-out for drunks and questionable characters and should be avoided late at night.

Hradčany

Prague's finest churches and museums are in Hradčany, the wonderful castle district stretching along a hill top west of the river. During weekends and summer, Prague Castle is packed with sightseers. Early morning is a good time to visit, and evening is even better (although all the museums will be closed). Unless otherwise indicated, museums and galleries are closed on Monday; concession prices are for children under 16 and students.

The easiest way to get to this area is by metro to Malostranská, then tram No 22 up the hill to the back of Hradčany as far as the fourth stop, Památník Písemnictví. From here Pohořelec and Loretánská slope down to the castle gate.

A passage at Pohořelec 8 leads up to the **Strahov Library** (*adult/concession 50/30 Kč; open 9am-noon & 1pm-5pm daily*), the largest monastic library in the country, built in 1679. The Philosophy Hall features beautifully carved shelves and a gorgeous frescoed ceiling. Look out for the books on tree-growing bound in the bark of the trees they describe. The lane east of the monastery leads to a terrace with a good view over the city.

Nearby on Loretánská nám is the splendid **Černín Palace** (1687), now the Ministry of Foreign Affairs. The exuberantly baroque **Loreta** (*adult/concession 80/60 Kč; open 9.15am-12.15pm & 1pm-4.30pm daily*), opposite the palace, is a convent with a fabulous treasure of diamonds, pearls and gold, and a

CZECH REPUBLIC

1631 replica of the Santa Casa in the Italian town of Loreto, itself said to be the replica of the Virgin Mary's house in Nazareth, carried to Italy by angels in the 13th century. The convent gets very crowded with tourists.

Loretánská soon opens onto Hradčanské nám, with the main gate to Prague Castle at its eastern end. On the square at No 2 is the imposing Renaissance **Schwarzenberg Palace** (1563) with its sgraffito decoration. Just across the square at No 15 is the 18th-century Šternberg Palace, the main branch of the **National Gallery** *(adult/concession 60/30 Kč; open 10am-6pm)*. This houses the country's main collection of 14th- to 18th-century European paintings, including Cranachs and Goyas.

Prague Castle

Founded in the 9th century, Prague Castle *(☎ 224 37 33 68; adult/concession 220/110 Kč; buildings open 9am-5pm daily Apr-Oct, 9am-4pm Nov-March; grounds open 5am-midnight daily Apr-Oct, 6am-11pm Nov-Mar)* was rebuilt and extended many times. Always the centre of political power, it's still the official residence of the president. The full-price ticket (valid for one day) allows entry to St Vitus Cathedral, the Old Royal Palace, Basilica of St George, Powder Gate (Mihulka), Golden Lane and Dalibor Tower. Guided tours in English cost 400 Kč for up to five people. Cheaper tickets are available for

more limited sightseeing. Note that cameras and videos cannot be used inside the buildings without official permission.

Matthias Gate leads from the first courtyard under an arch dated 1614 to the second courtyard and the **Chapel of the Holy Cross** (with the castle ticket and information office). On the north side of this courtyard is the **Prague Castle Gallery** *(adult/concession 100/50 Kč; open 10am-6pm daily)*, with a good collection of European baroque paintings.

The third courtyard is dominated by **St Vitus Cathedral**, a glorious French Gothic structure begun in 1344 by order of Emperor Charles IV and finally completed in 1929. Its stained-glass windows, frescoes and tombstones (including that of its founder inside the crypt) merit careful attention. The 14th-century chapel on the cathedral's southern side with the black imperial eagle on the door contains the **tomb of St Wenceslas**, the Czech's patron saint and the 'Good King Wenceslas' of the Christmas carol. Wenceslas' zeal in spreading Christianity and his submission to the German King Henry I led to his murder by his brother, Boleslav I. Alarmed by reports of miracles at Wenceslas' grave, Boleslav had the remains re-interred in St Vitus Cathedral in 932, and the saint's tomb soon became a great pilgrimage site. The small door beside the chapel windows leads to a chamber where the Bohemian crown jewels are kept (not open to

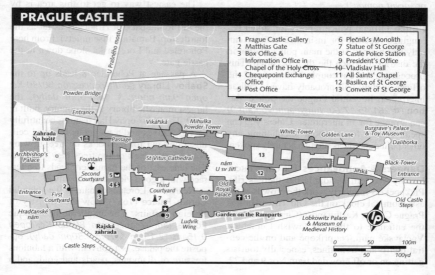

PRAGUE CASTLE

1 Prague Castle Gallery
2 Matthias Gate
3 Box Office & Information Office in Chapel of the Holy Cross
4 Chequepoint Exchange Office
5 Post Office
6 Plečník's Monolith
7 Statue of St George
8 Castle Police Station
9 President's Office
10 Vladislav Hall
11 All Saints' Chapel
12 Basilica of St George
13 Convent of St George

the public). You can climb the 287 steps of the cathedral's **Great Tower** (open 9am-4.15pm daily Apr-Oct).

On the southern side of the cathedral is the entrance to the **Old Royal Palace** with the huge and elegantly vaulted Vladislav Hall, built between 1486 and 1502. A ramp up to one side allowed mounted horsemen to ride into the hall for indoor jousts. On 23 May 1618 two Catholic councillors were thrown from the window of an adjacent chamber by irate Protestant nobles, the so-called 'Defenestration of Prague' that touched off the Thirty Years' War.

As you leave the palace, the **Basilica of St George** (1142), Prague's finest Romanesque church, is right in front of you. Next to the church, in the **Convent of St George** (adult/ concession 50/20 Kč; open 10am-6pm), you'll find the National Gallery's collection of Czech art from the 16th to 18th centuries.

Beyond the basilica, follow the crowd into **Golden Lane**, a 16th-century tradesmen's quarter of tiny houses built into the castle walls. Franz Kafka, who was born in Prague in 1883, lived and wrote in the tiny house at No 22 from 1916 to 1917.

On the right, just before the gate leading out of the castle, is **Lobkowitz Palace** (adult/ concession 40/20 Kč; open 9am-5pm), which houses a museum of Czech history with replicas of the crown jewels. From the eastern end of the castle, the Old Castle Steps lead back down towards Malostranská metro station. Alternatively, you can turn sharp right and then wander back through the lovely **Castle Gardens** (admission free; open 10am-6pm daily Apr-Oct).

Malá Strana

Malá Strana (The Small Quarter), sheltered beneath the protective walls of Prague Castle, was built in the 17th and 18th centuries by victorious Catholic clerics and nobles on the foundations of the Renaissance palaces of their Protestant predecessors.

From Malostranská metro station, follow Valdštejnská around to Valdštejnské nám, past many impressive buildings, notably the **Wallenstein Palace** (1630), now home to the Senate of the Czech Republic, which fills the entire eastern side of the square.

Albrecht Wallenstein, a famous figure in the Thirty Years' War, started out on the Protestant side then went over to the Catholics

and built this palace with the expropriated wealth of his former colleagues. In 1634 the Habsburg Emperor Ferdinand II learned that Wallenstein was about to switch sides again and had him assassinated at Cheb. The **palace gardens** (admission free; open 10am-6pm daily Mar-Sept) are through a gate at Letenská 10, a block to the east.

Continue south on Tomášská and round the corner to Letenská to reach **St Thomas Church**, a splendid baroque edifice built in 1731. Beyond nearby Malostranské nám is the formerly Jesuit **St Nicholas Church** (admission 45 Kč; open 9am-6pm daily Apr-Oct, 9am-4pm daily Nov-Mar), built in 1755, one of the greatest baroque buildings in Prague, its dome visible from afar.

Once you have had a wander around the square, follow the tram tracks south along Karmelitská. At No 9 is the **Church of Our Lady Victorious** (1613), with the venerated wax figure of the Holy Infant of Prague (1628). Originally erected by Lutherans, the church was taken over by the Carmelite Order following the Catholic victory at the Battle of White Mountain (1620).

Backtrack a little and take narrow Prokopská east towards the river. You'll soon reach a beautiful square surrounded by fine baroque palaces. Bear left on Lázeňská towards the massive stone towers of the **Church of Our Lady Below the Chain**. To the left of the church, Lázeňská leads to Mostecká.

Turn right to reach **Charles Bridge** (Karlův most). This enchanting structure, which was built in 1357 and graced by 30 statues dating from the 18th century, was the only bridge in Prague until 1841. Take a leisurely stroll across it, but first climb the **Malá Strana bridge tower** (admission 30 Kč; open 9am-6pm Tues-Sun, 11am-5pm Mon) on the Malá Strana side for a great bird's-eye view of the city. In the middle of the bridge is a bronze statue (1683) of St John Nepomuk, a priest who was thrown to his death from the bridge in 1393 for refusing to reveal the queen's confessions to King Wenceslas IV. The bridge's atmosphere is best appreciated at dawn, before the crowds arrive.

Staré Město

On the Staré Město side of Charles Bridge is the 17th-century **Klementinum**, once a Jesuit college but now the State Library, the largest historic building in the city after the Prague

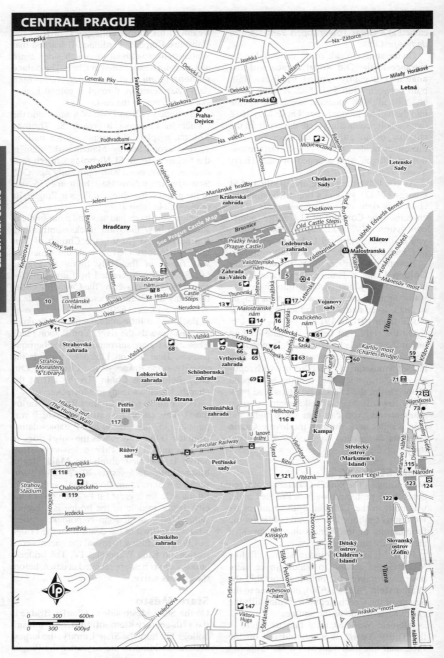

CENTRAL PRAGUE

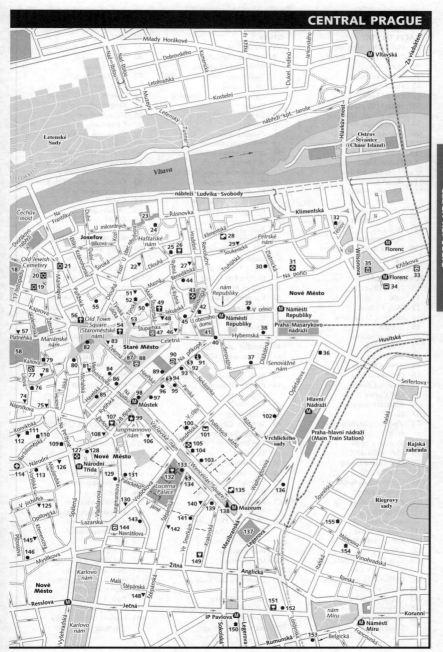

CENTRAL PRAGUE

CZECH REPUBLIC

CENTRAL PRAGUE

PLACES TO STAY
24 Hotel Casa Marcello
25 Travellers Hostel Dlouhá
32 Hôtel Opera
36 Hostel Jednota
42 Hotel Paříž
52 Hostel Týn
61 Hotel U tří pštroů
76 Dům U krále Jiřího
79 Hotel Clementin
104 Grand Hotel Evropa
109 Pension U medvídků
110 Unitas Pension;
    Cloister Inn
111 Hotel Cloister Inn
116 Hostel Sokol
118 Welcome Hostel
    Strahov
119 Hostel SPUS Strahov
150 Pension Březina
154 Stop City
    Accommodation
155 Mary's Accommodation
    Agency

PLACES TO EAT
3 Pálffy Palác
11 Sate
12 Malý Buddha
13 Hostinec U kocoura
15 Jo's Bar
22 Orange Moon
27 U Benedikta
29 U Góvindy
46 Pivnice Radegast
48 Le Saint-Jacques
51 Bohemia Bagel
53 Ebel Coffee House;
    Anagram Bookshop
57 Lotos
64 Vinárna U Maltézských
    rytířů
74 Vinárna v zátiší
75 Klub architektů
78 Ebel Coffee House
81 Country Life
83 Staroměstská restaurace
106 Dobrá Čajovna
108 Káva.Káva.Káva
112 Restaurace U
    Ampezonů
115 Kavárna Slávia
121 Bohemia Bagel
125 Kmotra
126 Café Louvre; Reduta Jazz
    Club; Rock Café
130 Buffalo Bill's Bar & Grille
140 Pizzeria Václavka
142 Titanic Steak House
145 U Fleků
148 Jihočeská restaurace u
    Šumavy

OTHER
1 Slovak Embassy
2 Canadian Embassy
4 Wallenstein Gardens
5 Wallenstein Palace
6 UK Embassy
7 National Gallery; Šternberg
    Palace
8 Schwarzenberg Palace
9 Loreta
10 Černín Palace
14 St Nicholas Church
16 Malostranská beseda
17 St Thomas Church
18 Rudolfinum (Concert Hall)
19 Pinkas Synagogue
20 Klaus Synagogue
21 Staronová Synagogue
23 Convent of St Agnes
26 Roxy
28 Australian Consulate
30 Bohemiatour
31 Bílá Labuť Department
    Store
33 Karlin Theatre of Music
34 Florenc Bus Station
35 City of Prague Museum
37 Eurolines-Sodeli CZ
38 American Embassy
    Information Rescource
    Center
39 Czech Airlines (ČSA)
40 Powder Gate
41 Obecni dům; FOK Box
    Office
43 Kotva Department Store
44 Prague Wheelchair Users
    Organisation
45 City Bike
47 Black Theatre of Jiří Srnec
49 St James Church
50 Big Ben Bookshop
54 Týn Church
55 Ticketpro
56 St Nicholas Church
58 Klementinum
59 Prague Venice Boat Trips
60 PPS Kampa Landing
62 Malá Strana Bridge
    Tower
63 Church of Our Lady
    Below the Chain
65 U malého Glena
66 Irish Embassy
67 US Embassy
68 German Embassy
69 Church of Our Lady
    Victorious
70 French Embassy
71 Smetana Museum; Karlovy
    lázně
72 Na zábradlí Theatre

73 KMC
77 Internet Café Prague
80 Bohemia Ticket
    International
82 Old Town Hall; PIS;
    Pragotour
84 Tupesy
85 Kingscourt Express
86 Ticketcentrum
87 Carolinum
88 Stavovské Theatre
89 Sklo
90 Internet Nescafe Live
91 Prague Information Service
92 Živnostenská banka
93 Čedok; Bohemia Ticket
    International
94 ČSOB
95 Laundryland
96 Moser
97 Bontonland
98 Na Můstku Bookshop
99 Police Station
100 Astera Laundrette
101 Main Post Office
102 Autoklub Bohemia
    Assistance
103 Alimex ČR Car Rental
105 Krone Department Store
107 Batalion; Internet Kafe
113 British Council
114 Polyclinic at Národní
117 Petřín Tower
120 Klub 007 Strahov
122 Boat Rental
123 National Theatre
124 Laterna Magika
127 Tesco Department Store
128 Thomas Cook
129 Kiwi
131 Praha Lékárna (24-Hour
    Pharmacy)
132 Lucerna Music Bar
133 Ticketpro Agency
    (Melantrich)
134 Komerční banka
135 Polish Consulate
136 State Opera
137 National Museum
138 St Wencelaus Statue
139 American Express
141 GTS International
143 IPC
144 Divadlo Minor
146 The Globe Bookshop
147 Austrian Embassy
149 AghaRTA Jazz Centrum
151 Club Radost FX;
    Radost Café
152 Laundryland
153 Lékárna U sv Ludmily
    (24-Hour Pharmacy)

Castle. Just south of Charles bridge is the **Smetana Museum** (adult/concession 50/20 Kč; open 10am-noon & 12.30pm-5pm Wed-Mon), in a former waterworks building beside the river. The view from the terrace in front of the museum is one of the best in Prague.

Beside the Klementinum, narrow and crowded Karlova leads east towards Staroměstské nám, Prague's old town square and still the heart of the city. Below the clock tower of the **Old Town Hall** (admission 30 Kč) is a Gothic astronomical clock (1410) that entertains the crowds with its parade of Apostles and bell-ringing skeleton every hour on the hour. Climb up the **tower** (admission 30 Kč; open 9am-6pm Tues-Sun, 11am-5pm Mon) for an outstanding view.

At the centre of Staroměstské nám is the **Jan Hus Monument**, erected in 1915 on the 500th anniversary of the religious reformer's death by fire at the stake. On one side of the square is the baroque wedding cake structure of **St Nicholas Church**, designed by Kilian Dientzenhofer in the 1730s. More striking are the twin Gothic steeples of **Týn Church** (1365); the tomb of the 16th-century Danish astronomer Tycho Brahe is in front of the main altar.

Leaving the square near the astronomical clock, head southeast along Železná to the **Carolinum**, the oldest remaining part of the Charles University, and the neoclassical **Stavovské Theatre** (1783), where the premiere of Mozart's *Don Giovanni* took place on 29 October 1787 with the maestro himself conducting. Return to the square and then follow Celetná east to the Gothic Powder Gate and Prague's unrivalled Art Nouveau masterpiece, the **Obecní Dům** (Municipal House; 1912).

Tucked away in the northern part of Staré Město's narrow streets is one of Prague's oldest Gothic structures, the magnificent **Convent of St Agnes** (adult/concession 100/50 Kč; open 10am-6pm) housing the National Gallery's collection of Czech and Central European medieval art.

Josefov

Josefov – the area north and northwest of Staroměstské nám, bordered by Kaprova, Dlouhá and Kozí streets – was once the city's Jewish Quarter. It retains a fascinating variety of monuments, all now part of the **Prague Jewish Museum** (adult/concession 500/340 Kč; open 9am-5.30pm Sun-Fri) complex.

Men must cover their heads to enter the synagogues; bring a cap of your own or buy a paper cap at the entrance.

The collections of the Prague Jewish Museum have a remarkable origin. In 1942 the Nazis brought the objects here from 153 Jewish communities in Bohemia and Moravia for a planned 'museum of an extinct race' to be opened once their extermination programme was completed. The combined ticket allows entry to all the sights; alternatively, the 200/140 Kč adult/concession ticket gets you into the Staronová Synagogue only, and the 300/200 Kč ticket gives access to all the others.

The early Gothic **Staronová Synagogue** (1270) is one of the oldest in Europe; opposite is the pink Jewish town hall with its picturesque 16th-century clock tower. The **Klaus Synagogue** (1694), west along crowded U starého hřbitova, houses an exhibition on Jewish customs and traditions. The walls of the **Pinkas Synagogue**, a block south on Široká, bear the names of 77,297 Czech Jews – including Franz Kafka's three sisters – and the names of the camps where they perished. The synagogue is likely to be closed until winter 2003 as a result of the 2002 floods.

The **Old Jewish Cemetery** (entered from the Pinkas Synagogue), with its 12,000 tombstones, is the most evocative corner of the Josefov area. The oldest grave is dated 1439. By 1787 when the cemetery stopped being used, it had become so crowded that burials were carried out one on top of the other, up to 12 layers deep!

Nové Město

If Staroměstské nám and Charles Bridge are the heart of tourist Prague, the fashionable boulevard of **Václavské nám** (Wenceslas Square) is the city's focus for local residents, its majestic Art Nouveau facades rising above a bustle of shoppers, trams and taxis. At its upper end stands an **equestrian statue** of the 10th-century king Václav I, or St Wenceslas, patron saint of Bohemia. In the 20th century, this broad avenue was often the scene of public protests – on 16 January 1969, a Czech student named Jan Palach publicly burned himself to death in protest against the Soviet invasion, and in 1989 demonstrators again gathered at this spot. Just below the statue is a simple memorial with photos and flowers dedicated to those who resisted the communists.

Looming over the southeastern end of Václavské nám is the **National Museum** (adult/concession 80/40 Kč; open 10am-6pm May-Oct, 9am-5pm Nov-Apr), with some ho-hum collections covering prehistory, mineralogy and stuffed animals. The captions on the exhibits are in Czech only and the grand interior of this neo-Renaissance museum building (1890) is more interesting than the displays.

Vyšehrad

Take the metro to Vyšehrad station where the concrete **Congress Centre** (1981) rises above a deep ravine crossed by the Nuselský Bridge. Pass to the north of the centre and along Na Bučance to the gates of the 17th-century **Vyšehrad Citadel**, built on a crag above the Vltava, and once the seat of the 11th-century Přemysl princes of Bohemia. You pass the Romanesque **Rotunda of St Martin** before reaching the twin towers of **SS Peter and Paul Church**, founded in the 11th century but rebuilt in neo-Gothic style between 1885 and 1903. **Slavín Cemetery**, beside the church, contains the graves of many distinguished Czechs, including the composers Smetana and Dvořák. The view of the Vltava Valley from the citadel battlements along the southern side of the Vyšehrad ridge is superb.

Other Museums

The **Mozart Museum** (Mozartova 169; adult/concession 90/50 Kč; open 9.30am-6pm daily Apr-Oct, 9.30am-5pm Nov-Mar) in Vila Bertrámka, is where Mozart finished composing Don Giovanni in 1787. To get there take metro Anděl, then head west on Plzeňská three blocks and left on Mozartova. Czech film maker Miloš Forman's Oscar-winning movie Amadeus, about the life of Mozart, was shot mostly in Prague.

The **City of Prague Museum** (Na Poříčí 52; adult/concession 30/15 Kč; open 9am-6pm Tues-Sun), in a grand, neo-Renaissance building near Florenc metro station, contains maps and photos of the city's monuments, plus interesting artefacts to put them in perspective, such as the original Mánes calendar wheel from the Old Town Hall clock tower. The museum's crowning glory is a huge scale model of Prague made in 1834. Don't miss it!

Petřín Hill

On a hot summer afternoon you can escape the tourist throngs via the **funicular railway**

from Újezd up to the rose gardens of **Petřínské sady**. You can climb the iron **Petřín Tower** (adult/concession 40/30 Kč; open 10am-7pm daily Apr-Oct), built in 1891 in imitation of the Eiffel Tower, for one of the best views of Prague. A stairway behind the tower leads down into a series of picturesque lanes and back to Malostranské nám.

Organised Tours

Pragotur (☎ 224 48 25 62; Old Town Hall, Staroměstské nám) in the PIS office arranges personal guides fluent in all major European languages. **City Walks** (☎ 608 200 912, 222 24 45 31; w www.praguewalkingtours.com) offers guided walks for 300 Kč to 450 Kč per person and **Prague Walks** (☎ 261 21 46 03; w www.praguewalks.com) charges 300 Kč per person. The walks last from 75 minutes to four hours with themes ranging from 'Mysterious Prague' to Prague pubs to the Velvet Revolution. Most walks begin at the astronomical clock in the Old Town Hall square.

Pragotur and various private companies operating from kiosks along Na příkopě offer three-hour city bus tours for 560 Kč per person. These are fine if your time is very short, but the castle and other major sights get so crowded that you can't enjoy the tour or even hear your guide.

Boat Trips From May to early September **Prague Passenger Shipping** (PPS; ☎ 224 93 00 17; Rašínovo nábr; metro Karlovo Náměstí) runs all-day cruises upriver to Slapy (250 Kč return, 9½ hours), departing at 9am Friday to Sunday. The riverboat terminal is on the right bank of the Vltava between Jiráskův most and Palackého most.

Shorter trips downriver to the zoo (Troja landing; 60 Kč return, 1¼ hours each way) depart three or four times daily between May and August, and Saturday and Sunday only in April, September and October. Allow 15 minutes to walk from the zoo to the landing. From the Kampa landing next to Charles Bridge there are 50-minute cruises (200 Kč) hourly from 11am to 8pm between March and December.

Prague Venice (☎ 603 819 947; Křížovnické nám 3 • Čertovka, Kampa Island, Malá Strana) operates 30-minute cruises (270 Kč per person including drink) in small boats under the hidden arches of Charles Bridge, and along the Čertovka mill stream in Kampa.

The cruises run between 10.30am and 11pm daily in July and August and 10.30am to 8pm daily between March and June.

You can cruise the Vltava under your own steam in a rowing boat or pedalo rented from one of several places along the river.

Places to Stay

Prague is an extremely popular destination; if you're thinking of visiting during Christmas, Easter or May to September then bookings are strongly recommended, especially if you want to stay in or near the centre. Prices quoted are for 'high season', generally May, June, September and October; however, even these rates can increase by up to 15% on certain dates, notably during Christmas to New Year, Easter, and on weekends in May (during the Prague Spring festival). Some hotels (but not all) have slightly lower rates in July and August. November to March is low season, with the cheapest rates.

Accommodation Agencies

There are dozens of agencies that will help you find a place to stay – some of which are better than others. Even if you turn up in peak period without a booking, these places should be able to find you a bed.

Look at the **TravelGuide website** (W *www.travelguide.cz*), which has a database of almost 400 hostels, pensions and hotels, and a straighforward online booking system.

The long-established **AVE** (☎ *224 22 32 26, reservations ☎ 251 55 10 11, fax 224 22 34 63;* W *www.avetravel.cz*) has convenient booking offices at Praha-hlavní nádraží and Praha-Holešovice train stations, at Ruzyně airport and in PIS offices (see Tourist Offices, earlier in this section); the branch at Praha-hlavní nádraží is open 6am to 11pm daily. However, a few readers have reported problems using its reservation service.

Mary's Travel & Tourist Service (☎ *222 25 35 10, ☎/fax 222 25 22 15;* W *www.marys.cz; Italska 31, Prague 2*) offers a range of hostels, pensions, hotels and apartments, and has been recommended by travellers.

Stop City Accommodation (☎ *222 52 12 33, ☎/fax 222 52 12 52;* W *www.stopcity.com; Vinohradská 24, Prague 2; open 11am-8pm daily*), about six blocks away from the Praha-hlavní nádraží train station, has a large selection of private rooms and apartments available, with rates from €20 per person.

Welcome Accommodation Service (☎ *224 32 02 02, fax 224 32 34 89;* W *www.bed.cz; Zikova 13, Prague 6*) is in a student hostel in Dejvice – go in the main entrance, turn left, and it's the second door on the left; or just say 'Hostel?' to the lady at reception. It has rooms in student dormitories, hostels and hotels.

You can also rent a private room unofficially from householders who will approach you at the train and bus stations. They'll ask from about 300 Kč to 800 Kč per person, depending on the location. Check the location on a map before accepting – many places are way out in the suburbs.

Camping There are several camping grounds within reasonably easy reach of Prague's city centre. Most charge 75 Kč to 110 Kč for a small tent, plus a similar amount per person and also for a car.

The **USK Caravan Camp** (☎ *257 21 49 91; Plzeňská 279, Motol, Prague 5; tent sites 85 Kč plus per person 100 Kč; open year-round*), just west of Smíchov, is Prague's most convenient camping ground. Take tram No 7, 9 or 10 from the Anděl metro to the Hotel Golf stop (10 minutes).

There are half-a-dozen camping grounds clustered together in Troja, in the north of the city, including **Camp Dana Troja** (☎/fax *283 85 04 82;* E *campdana@volny.cz; Trojská 129, Troja, Prague 71; tent sites 75 Kč plus per person 115 Kč; open year-round*). Take tram No 5 from the Hlavní nádraží stop outside the main train station to the Trojská stop (20 minutes), then walk west along Trojská.

Hostels The central **Hostel Sokol** (☎ *257 00 73 97;* E *hostel@sokol-cos.cz; 3rd floor, Tyršův dům, Nostícova 2, Prague; dorm beds/doubles 270/1200 Kč*) in Malá Strana gets good reports from travellers. Take the metro to Malostranská and then tram No 12, 22 or 23 two stops south.

On the opposite side of the river to the Sokol in Staré Město is **Travellers Hostel Dlouhá** (*Roxy;* ☎ *224 82 66 62;* E *hostel@travellers.cz; Dlouhá 33, Prague 1; dorm beds/singles/doubles 370/1120/1240 Kč*), with basic but clean accommodation and a 24-hour service that also includes lockers and Internet access. There are five other Travellers Hostels in central Prague, with cheaper dorm beds (220 Kč to 300 Kč) available from mid-June to August only.

Another good central place is **Hostel Týn** (☎ 222 73 45 90; e info@itastour.cz; *Týnská 19; dorm beds 370 Kč*), only a few minutes' walk from Staroměestské nám.

The popular **Clown & Bard Hostel** (☎ 222 71 64 53; e reservations@clownandbard .com; *Bořivojova 102, Prague 3; metro Jiřího z Poděbrad; dorm beds/doubles 250/900 Kč*) is in the heart of Žižkov's pub district. It's a party place, so don't come here seeking peace and quiet.

Also located in Žižkov, the friendly **Hostel Elf** (☎ 222 54 09 63; e info@hostelelf.com; *Husitská 11, Prague 3; dorm beds/doubles 260/840 Kč*) is recommended by readers.

The attractive **Hostel U Melounu** (☎/fax 224 91 83 22; e info@hostelumelounu.cz; *Ke Karlovu 7, Prague 2; dorm beds 380 Kč*) is in a historic building in a quiet back street, a ten-minute walk south of metro IP Pavlova.

Across the river in the Holešice area is the fairly new **Sir Toby's Hostel** (☎ 283 87 06 35; e info@sirtobys.com; *Dělnická 24, Prague 7; dorm beds/doubles 325/1150 Kč*), where the rooms include private shower and toilet, in a nicely refurbished apartment building.

Another popular place is the excellent **Hostel Boathaus** (☎ 402 10 76; *V náklích 1A, Prague 4; dorm beds 290 Kč*), with a peaceful riverside setting about 3km south of the city centre. To get there from Václavské nám take tram No 3 at Jindřišská in the direction of Modřany to the Černý kůň stop (20 minutes) and follow the hostel signs to the river.

Student Residences Many of the student residences (*koleje*) in Prague rent accommodation to tourists (students or not) year-round. As well as dormitory beds, they offer good-value single, double and triple rooms, often with four rooms sharing a small lounge, toilet, bathroom and cooking facilities.

The central **Hostel Jednota** (☎ 224 21 17 73, ☎/fax 224 81 82 00; *Opletalova 38, Prague 1; singles/doubles/triples/quads 550/ 680/1020/1240 Kč*) is only five minutes' walk from Praha-hlavní nádraží train station. You can arrange a bed through the **Alfa Tourist Service** (☎/fax 224 23 00 37; e info@ alfatourist.cz), which is based at the same address. It also offers accommodation at several other hostels and hotels in Prague.

There is plenty of accommodation at the student dormitory complex opposite the Strahov stadium west of the centre. Bus Nos 143,

149 and 217 run directly there from Dejvická metro station. As you get off the bus you'll see 11 huge blocks of flats. Although the capacity is enormous, the whole complex does occasionally get booked out by groups. The blocks of flats operate as separate hostels in July and August, while in the off season only five will be open at minimum capacity. Noisy nightclubs operate from 7pm to midnight downstairs in block Nos 7 and 11, and until 4am at No 1.

The main providers of year-round accommodation in the complex are **Hostel SPUS Strahov** (☎/fax 283 88 25 72; e reception@ spushostels.cz; *Chaloupeckého, Block 4, Prague 6; dorm beds/singles/quads 250/ 480/1160 Kč*), and the **Welcome Hostel Strahov** (☎ 224 32 02 02, fax 224 32 34 89; e welcome@bed.cz; *Vaníčkova, Block 3; dorm beds/singles/doubles 150/350/480 Kč*). Both of these hostels offer 10% discount to ISIC card-holders.

There's another concentration of student dorms in the suburb of Dejvice, only five minutes' walk from the Dejvická metro station, which includes **Hostel Orlík** (☎ 224 31 12 40; e praguehotel@atlas.cz; *Terronská 6, Prague 6; singles/doubles/triples 550/860/ 1250Kč; open July-Aug*), and **Welcome Hostel Dejvice** (☎ 224 32 02 02, fax 224 32 34 89; e welcome@bed.cz; *Zikova 13, Prague 6; singles/doubles 400/540 Kč*).

Pensions An interesting place to stay is **Unitas Pension** (☎ 224 21 10 20, fax 224 21 08 00; e unitas@cloisterinn.com; *Bartolomějská 9, Prague 1; metro Národní třída; singles/ doubles 1100/1400 Kč*) in Staré Město. This former convent has cramped rooms that were once used as prison cells (President Havel did time in one of them), with shared bathrooms and a generous breakfast included.

South of IP Pavlova metro station is **Pension Březina** (☎ 296 18 88 88, fax 224 26 67 77; e info@brezina.cz; *Legerova 41, Prague 2; economy singles/doubles 900/1100 Kč, luxury 1800/2000 Kč*). The economy rooms have shared bathrooms; luxury ones have private facilities, air-con and Ethernet sockets for your laptop (free use of Internet). Rooms facing the street can be pretty noisy.

Southeast of the centre and a five-minute walk east of Chodov metro station is the superb **AV Pension Praha** (☎ 272 95 17 26, fax 267 91 26 95; e votava@pension-praha.cz;

Malebná 75, Prague 4; singles/doubles with bath 1200/1630 Kč). It has just eight rooms.

The **Penzion Máchova** (☎ *222 51 01 07, fax 222 51 17 77;* e *machova@motylek.cz; Máchova 11, Prague 2; singles/doubles/ triples 850/1400/1800 Kč)* is in a quiet neighbourhood five minutes' walk south of metro Náměstí Míru.

Hotels – Budget There are no cheap hotels in central Prague; to get a double for under 2500 Kč you'll have to settle for the burbs.

The recently modernised **Hotel Golden City Garni** (☎ *222 71 10 08, fax 222 71 60 08;* e *hotel@goldencity.cz; Táboritská 3, Prague 3; singles/doubles/triples 1650/2450/ 2700 Kč),* in the suburb of Žižkov, is three stops east of the main train station on tram No 5, 9 or 26, has friendly and helpful staff and is excellent value.

Hotel Balkán (☎ *257 32 21 50;* e *balkan@ mbox.dkm.cz; třída Svornosti 28, Prague 4; singles/doubles/triples 2000/2400/2700 Kč),* just south of the centre and two blocks from Anděl metro station, is a good deal. The hotel also has a decent restaurant.

Hotel Apollo (☎ *688 06 28, fax 688 45 70; Kubišova 23, Prague 8; singles/doubles/ triples 1800/2300/2700 Kč)* is a bland, modern place in a quiet housing estate north of the centre, 15 minutes from the centre on tram No 5, 14 or 17.

Modern **Hotel Markéta** (☎ *220 51 83 16, fax 220 51 32 83;* e *marketa@motylek.com; Na Petynce 45, Prague 6; singles/doubles/ triples 1850/2500/3100 Kč)* is in the suburb of Střešovice, about 10 minutes' walk west of Hradčany. From Hradčanská metro station take bus No 108 or 174 for three stops west to Kajetánka.

If a 20-minute metro ride doesn't deter you, consider the soulless but affordable **Hotel Business** (☎ *267 99 51 50, fax 267 99 51 33;* e *business3@motylek.com; Kupeckého 842, Prague 4; singles/doubles 980/1560 Kč, with bath 1140/1710 Kč).* When you come out of Háje metro station, it's the tallest building you can see. It has very basic rooms sharing a toilet and shower between two, or renovated rooms with private bathrooms.

Hotels – Mid-Range There are several interesting hotels in Staré Město, including the appealing **Dům U krále Jiřího** (☎ *222 22 09 25, fax 222 22 17 07;* e *krak.jiri@telecom.cz;*

Liliová 10, Prague 1; singles/doubles 1800/ 3100 Kč). The attic rooms with exposed wooden beams are especially attractive.

Not far from here is the small **Pension U medvídků** (☎ *24 21 19 16, fax 24 22 09 30;* e *pension@umedvidku.cz; Na Perštýně 7, Prague 1; singles/doubles 2300/3500 Kč),* another historic building with appealing rooms.

Fancy retiring to a convent? About a block west is the **Cloister Inn** (☎ *224 21 10 20, fax 224 21 08 00;* e *cloister@cloister-inn.cz; Konviktská 14, Prague 1; singles/doubles/ triples 3400/3800/4750 Kč),* a comfortably refurbished convent with private parking and free Internet access.

The extravagant Art Nouveau facade of the **Grand Hotel Evropa** (☎ *224 22 81 17, fax 224 22 45 44; Václavské nám 25, Prague 1; metro Můstek; singles/doubles/triples 1600/2600/3100 Kč, with bathroom 3000/ 4000/5000 Kč)* conceals a musty warren of run-down rooms that appear to have barely been touched since the 1950s. It still has a certain charm though, and considering its location is reasonable value.

The luxurious neo-Renaissance **Hotel Opera** (☎ *222 31 56 09, fax 222 32 14 77;* e *reception@hotel-opera.cz; Těš nov 13, Prague 1; metro Florenc; singles/doubles 3550/4200 Kč)* is just 10 minutes' walk east of the Old Town.

Pleasant **Hotel Belvedere** (☎ *220 10 61 11, fax 233 37 23 68;* e *prague@belvedere-hotel .com; Milady Horákové 19, Prague 7; singles/ doubles 2130/2850 Kč),* north of the centre, has posh four-star rooms at reasonable rates. Take westbound tram No 1 or 25 two stops from Vltavská metro station.

Admirál Botel (☎ *257 32 13 02, fax 257 31 95 16;* e *info@admiral-botel.cz; Hořejš í nábřeží 57, Prague 5; metro Anděl; singles/ doubles 2710/2840 Kč, triple/quad suites 4520/4910 Kč),* about four blocks from Anděl metro station, offers an unusual alternative for a bed. It's a huge luxury riverboat permanently moored on the Vltava River with 82 double cabins and five suites.

Hotels – Top End The pretty little **Hotel Clementin** (☎ *222 22 17 98, fax 222 22 17 68;* e *hotel@clementin.cz; Seminárš ká 4, Prague 1; singles/doubles 4250/5250 Kč)* – probably the narrowest hotel in Prague – has nine cosy rooms on a narrow street just off the tourist thoroughfare of Karlova.

On the other side of Staré Město is **Hotel Casa Marcello** (☎ 222 31 02 60, fax 222 31 33 23; e booking@casa-marcello.cz; Řásnovka 783, Prague 1; doubles 7500 Kč), a former aristocratic residence with stylishly furnished rooms and a pleasant courtyard where you can enjoy a drink or a snack. Prices can fall to almost half the advertised rack rate in July, August and winter.

South of here is the sumptuous Art Nouveau **Hotel Paříž** (☎ 222 19 51 95, fax 224 22 54 75; e booking@hotel-pariz.cz; U obecního domu 1, Prague 1; singles/doubles 9500/9800 Kč), a great place for a splurge. Facilities include a sauna and fitness room.

Hotel U tří pštrosů (☎ 257 53 24 10, fax 257 53 32 17; e info@utripstrosu.cz; Dražického nám 12, Prague 1; singles/doubles 5900/7900 Kč) is a grand old merchant's house at the foot of the Malá Strana tower on Charles Bridge, filled with interesting historical details. The rooms may be expensive, but it does have an unbeatable location and some splendid views.

Hotel Praha (☎ 224 34 11 11, fax 224 32 12 18; e reserv@htlpraha.cz; Sušická 20, Prague 6; singles/doubles 5900/6840 Kč) in Dejvice is a luxury complex with stunning views over the city that was built for the Communist Party apparatchiks in 1981. Tom Cruise stayed here during the filming of *Mission Impossible* in 1995.

Places to Eat

Tourism has had a heavy impact on the Prague restaurant scene. Cheaper restaurants have almost disappeared from the historical centre, while most of the restaurants in the Old Town, the castle district and along Václavské nám are now more expensive.

If you're on a tight budget it might be worth walking a few streets away from the tourist centres or taking the metro a few stops out of the centre and eating near there. Žižkov and Smíchov have plenty of inexpensive places.

Be aware that the serving staff in some Prague restaurants in the tourist centre shamelessly overcharge foreigners. Some restaurants in touristy areas have two menus, one in Czech and the other in German, English and French with higher prices. Insist on a menu with prices; if the waiter refuses to show you one listing specific prices, just get up and walk out. Don't be intimidated by the language barrier.

A good idea is to have a glance at the price of the beer on the menu, as this varies a lot and can cancel your savings on lower meal prices. If the drink prices aren't listed expect them to be sky high. At lunchtime the waiter may bring you the more expensive dinner menu.

Even if you do check the menu prices, the waiter may claim you were served a larger portion or may bring you a different, cheaper dish but still charge the higher price. Extras such as a side salad and bread and butter sometimes incur an added charge, so if you are served something you didn't order and don't want, send it back. Many of the tourist restaurants add about a 20 Kč cover charge (*couvert*) to the bill.

Hradčany & Malá Strana

Five minutes' walk west of the castle is **Sate** (Pohořelec 3; mains 90-110 Kč; open 11am-10pm daily), which serves up some tasty Indonesian and Malaysian dishes.

There are many tourist places on and near Malostranské nám, including popular expat hang-out **Jo's Bar** (mains 100-150 Kč; open 11am-2am daily) at No 7, with Mexican food and burgers. Nearby is **Hostinec U kocoura** (cnr Nerudova & Zámecká; mains 70-100 Kč; open 11am-11pm daily) with inexpensive Bohemian beer snacks and pub grub.

Cosy and romantic **Vinárna U Maltézských rytířů** (Prokopská 10; mains 200-400 Kč; open 11am-11pm daily) offers top-notch food and professional service.

The elegant **Pálffy Palác** (Valdštejnská 14; mains 475-525 Kč; open 11am-midnight daily) is a Prague institution serving fish and meat dishes with mouth-watering sauces.

Informal **Bohemia Bagel** (Újezd 18, Malá Strana • Masná 2, Staré Město; mains 50-100 Kč; open 7am-midnight daily) is a great place to eat, and is one of the few places that offers early morning breakfast.

Staroměstské Nám & Around

The **Staroměstská restaurace** (Staroměstské nám 19; mains 75-245 Kč; open 10am-11pm daily) has good Czech food and beer, and is easily the best of the restaurants on the square.

Behind Týn Church is an excellent French restaurant with pleasant service, **Le Saint-Jacques** (Jakubská 4; mains 400-800 Kč; open noon-3pm & 6pm-midnight Mon-Fri, 6pm-midnight Sat). **Pivnice Radegast** (Templová 2; mains 55-110 Kč; open 11am-12.30am *daily)*, off Celetná, has good cheap Czech food; try the tasty *guláš* (goulash).

Five minutes' walk from the square is the **Orange Moon** *(Rámová 5; mains 150-220 Kč; open 11.30am-11.30pm daily)*, with excellent Thai, Burmese and Indian dishes. Nearby is **U Benedikta** *(Benediktská 11; mains 60-180 Kč; open 11am-11pm daily)*, another good Czech place.

There are a few good places around Betlémské nám. The popular, subterranean **Klub architektů** *(Betlémské nám 5; mains 100-220 Kč; open 11.30am-11pm daily)* serves tasty and inventive dishes, including vegetarian ones. Nearby is the top-notch **Vinárna v zátiší** *(Liliová 1; mains 500-900 Kč; open noon-3pm & 5.30pm-11pm daily)*, offering Czech cuisine with a gourmet twist.

Václavské Nám & Around In a courtyard through a passage on Václavské nám 48 is the decent **Pizzeria Václavka** *(mains 65-120 Kč; open 11am-11pm daily)* with good inexpensive pizzas, pastas and salads.

Southwest of the square sample the Tex-Mex cuisine at **Buffalo Bill's Bar & Grille** *(Vodičkova 9; mains 180-280 Kč; open noon-midnight daily)*, or try the excellent steaks and salads at **Titanic Steak House** *(Štěpánská 22; mains 90-190 Kč; open 11am-11pm Mon-Sat, 3pm-11pm Sun)*.

A little bit farther away from the square is **Jihočeská restaurace u Šumavy** *(Štěpánská 3; mains 95-155 Kč; open 10am-11pm Mon-Fri, 11am-11pm Sat & Sun)*, serving delicious, inexpensive South Bohemian dishes.

Národní Třída & Around The elegant **Café Louvre** *(Národní 22; breakfast 70-120 Kč; open 8am-11pm Mon-Fri, 9am-11pm Sat & Sun)* serves excellent breakfasts; it's also open for lunch and dinner but prices are higher. **Kmotra** *(V jirchářích 12; mains 100-180 Kč; open 11am-1am daily)* prepares mouth-watering pizzas in a wood-fired oven.

On the Staré Město side of the avenue is the inexpensive **Restaurace U Ampezonů** *(Konviktská 11; mains 70-100 Kč; open 11am-11pm daily)*, whose solid Bohemian fare – such as roast chicken with potato dumplings – is good value.

U Fleků *(Křemencova 11)* is a German-style beer hall and garden where you can sit at long communal tables and drink the excellent dark ale brewed in-house. It's a Prague institution

but also a tourist trap; while the beer is good, the food is overpriced and forgettable.

Around Town A good Czech restaurant – with a sauna! – is **U radnice** *(Havlíčkovo nám 7, Žižkov, Prague 3; mains 50-85 Kč; open 11am-11pm Mon-Fri, 11am-10pm Sat & Sun)*. Book ahead for the sauna. Nearby is **Mailsi** *(Lipanská 1; mains 150-300 Kč; open noon-11pm daily)*, a great little Pakistani restaurant.

Pizzeria Grosseto *(Jugoslávsch patyzánů 8, Dejvice, Prague 6; mains 70-125 Kč; open 11.30am-11pm daily)* is a friendly place with excellent pizzas.

On the west bank of the river in Smíchov is **Hospoda U Starého lva** *(Lidická 13; mains 60-75 Kč; open 11am-11pm daily)*, yet another reliable place for Czech pub grub.

Vegetarian In a passage south of Staroměstské nám, **Country Life** *(Melantrichova 15; mains 75-150 Kč; open 9am-8.30pm Mon-Fri)* has inexpensive salad sandwiches, pizzas, goulash and other vegetarian dishes. **Lotos** *(Platnéřská 13; mains 70-150 Kč; noon-10pm daily)*, just north of the Klementinum, does gourmet vegie food with many dishes modelled on Bohemian cuisine.

Cafeteria-style **U Góvindy** *(Soukenická 27; open 11am-5.30pm Mon-Sat)* in the northern part of Nové Město is run by Hare Krishnas; a donation of at least 50 Kč gets you a hearty meal.

The best vegie food in Prague is served at **Radost Café** *(Belehradska 120; mains 110-230 Kč; open 11am-5am daily)*, in the Club Radost FX (see Entertainment) where the menu ranges from Mexican to Italian to Thai.

Cafés Art Deco **Kavárna Slávia** *(Národní 1; open 8am-midnight Mon-Fri, 9am-midnight Sat & Sun)* is a classic but pricey Prague institution. A bit farther east on Národní is **Káva.Káva.Káva** *(open 7am-10pm daily)* in the Platýz courtyard at No 37, where you can indulge in huge cappuccinos along with carrot cake and other goodies. **Ebel Coffee House** *(Týn 2 • Řetězová 9; both open 9am-10pm daily)* offers superb coffee only a few minutes' walk from Staroměstské nám.

Prague also has several excellent oriental tearooms *(čajovny)* including **Dobra Čajovna** *(open 10am-11pm Mon-Sat, 2pm-11pm Sun)* in a passage at Václavské nám 14, and **Malý**

CZECH REPUBLIC

Buddha *(Úvoz 46; open 1pm-10.30pm Tues-Sun)* in Hradčany.

Self-Catering The Tesco, Kotva, Krone and Bílá Labuť department stores all have **supermarkets** in their basements. In the suburbs, the **Delvita** chain of supermarkets offers low prices and a wide selection of groceries.

Entertainment

Prague offers an amazing range of entertainment. While it has long been one of Europe's centres of classical music and jazz, it is now known for its rock and post-rock scenes as well. In such a vibrant city, it is quite possible that some places listed here will have changed by the time you arrive. For the most up-to-date information, refer to the *Prague Post, The Prague Pill, Culture in Prague* and the *Do města – Downtown* freesheet, and keep an eye on posters and bulletin boards.

For classical music, opera, ballet, theatre and some rock concerts – even the most 'sold-out' *(vyprodáno)* events – you can often find a ticket or two on sale at the box office 30 minutes or so before concert time. In addition, there are plenty of ticket agencies around Prague that will sell the same tickets at a high commission. Touts also sell tickets at the door, but avoid them unless you have no other option. Although some expensive tickets are set aside for foreigners, non-Czechs normally pay the same price as Czechs at the box office. Tickets can cost as little as 30 Kč for standing room only to over 900 Kč for the best seats in the house; the average price is about 500 Kč.

Cinema is good – films are usually screened in their original language with Czech subtitles – and tickets cost between 60 Kč and 130 Kč. The *Prague Post* lists what's on.

Ticket Agencies One of the largest ticket agencies is **Ticketpro** *(☎ 296 32 99 99, fax 296 32 88 88; ⓦ www.ticketpro.cz; Salvátorská 10, Prague 1; open 9am-12.30pm & 1pm-5.15pm Mon-Fri)*, with branches in PIS offices (see Information earlier) and many other spots around Prague, including **Ticketcentrum** *(Rytířská 31; open 8.30am-8.30pm daily)*. Some music stores and other outlets also act as its agents – look for the Ticketpro sticker. The best place to buy your tickets for rock concerts is at Ticketpro's Melantrich outlet in the Rokoko passage at Václavské nám 38.

Other agencies include **Bohemia Ticket International** *(☎ 224 22 78 32, fax 221 61 21 26; ⓦ www.ticketsbti.cz; Malé nám 13; open 9am-5pm Mon-Fri, 9am-2pm Sat • Na příkopě 16; open 10am-7pm Mon-Fri, 10am-5pm Sat, 10am-3pm Sun)*, American Express and Čedok (see Information, earlier).

Classical concert tickets are also available from the **FOK Box Office** *(☎ 222 00 23 36, fax 222 32 25 01; U obecního domu 2, Prague 1; open 10am-6pm Mon-Fri)*.

Most agencies charge similar prices for the following shows: the Laterna Magika (690 Kč), opera (230 Kč to 950 Kč), the National Theatre (600 Kč to 950 Kč) and the National Marionette Theatre (490 Kč).

Classical Music Prague's main concert venues include the Dvořák Hall in the neo-Renaissance **Rudolfinum** *(nám Jana Palacha; metro Staroměstská)*, and the Smetana Hall in the city's wonderful Art Nouveau **Obecní dům** *(nám Republiky 5)*. The latter always plays host to the opening concert of the Prague Spring festival.

Lots of organ concerts and recitals for tourists are performed in old churches and in historic buildings, but unfortunately many are of poor quality. You'll see stacks of fliers advertising these in every tourist office and travel agency around Prague. Seat prices begin at around 350 Kč, and the programmes change from week to week.

Jazz There are dozens of jazz clubs. The **Reduta Jazz Club** *(Národní 20; metro Národní Třída; cover charge 200 Kč; open 9pm-3am daily)* was founded in 1958 and is one of the oldest in Europe. You can hear live jazz every night at the unpretentious **AghaRTA jazz centrum** *(Krakovská 5; metro Muzeum; open 9pm-midnight daily)* and in the cosy basement at **U malého Glena** *(Karmelitská 23; metro Malostranská; music 9pm-2am daily)*.

Rock & Clubs Adjacent to the Reduta Jazz Club is the **Rock Café** *(Národní 20; open 10am-1am Mon-Fri, 8pm-3am Sat)*; wear black clothing if you can. **Batalion** *(28.října 3; open 24hr)* offers local rock, folk, jazz or blues bands downstairs, while DJs spin discs late at night or when there are no bands playing. **Lucerna Music Bar** *(Vodičkova 36; open 8pm-3am daily)*, inside the Lucerna passage, has live rock bands performing most nights.

Klub 007 Strahov (*Block 7, Chaloupeck-ého 7, Prague 6; open 8pm-1am daily*) has underground rock, punk, reggae bands or DJs playing nightly. Another place which has inexpensive beer and is popular with students is **Malostranská beseda** (*Malostranské nám 21; metro Malostranská; open 11am-1am daily*), where jazz, folk, country and rock can be heard nightly from 8.30pm.

Prague's prime club venue is **Radost FX** (**w** *www.radostfx.cz; Bělehradská 120, Prague 2; metro IP Pavlova*), with famous local and European guest DJs. The **Karlovy lázně** (*Novotného lávka, Prague 1*) complex, near the Smetana Museum, has a nightclub playing anything from 1960s hits to the latest techno on each of its three floors, while the basement hosts live bands.

Alternative Venues The **Roxy** (*Dlouhá 33, Prague 1; open 5pm-1am daily*) is a decrepit place with surprising longevity as an experimental venue – mostly avant-garde drama, dance and music.

One place with a difference is the **Palác Akropolis** (*Kubelíkova 27, Žižkov; metro Jiř-ího z Poděbrad*), where local bands perform. On some nights there are plays, films or other cultural shows.

Theatres Opera, ballet and classical drama (in Czech) are performed regularly at the neo-Renaissance **National Theatre** (*Národní 2; metro Národní Třída*). Next door is the modern **Laterna Magika** (*Národní 4*), established in 1983, which offers a widely imitated combination of theatre, dance and film.

Opera and ballet are also presented at the neo-Renaissance **State Opera** (*Wilsonova; metro Muzeum*). The neoclassical **Stavovské Theatre** (*Ovocný trh 1; metro Můstek*) also presents opera. Headphones providing simultaneous translation into English are available for some of its Czech plays.

For operettas and old-fashioned musicals in Czech go to the **Karlín Theatre of Music** (*Křižíkova 10; metro Florenc*), near Florenc bus station. Because it's a little out of the way and not as famous as some other venues, tickets are often available; it is highly recommended. The ticket office is open 10am to 1pm and 2pm to 6pm Monday to Saturday.

Several theatres around town stage 'black theatre' or 'magic theatre' performances combining mime, film, dance and music. **Black** **Theatre of Jiří Srnec** (*Celetná 17, Nové Město; tickets from 370 Kč*) is one such place.

Plays by Václav Havel are often staged (in Czech) at **Na zábradlí Theatre** (*Anenské nám 5; metro Staroměstská*).

Puppet Theatres Children's theatre **Div-adlo Minor** (*Vodičkova 6, Prague 1; metro Národní Třída*) has a fun mix of puppets and pantomime. Performances are at 9.30am, 3pm or 7pm Monday to Saturday and you can usually get a ticket at the door before the show.

What's Free

The National Museum is free on the first Monday of each month, and the City of Prague Museum is free on the first Thursday. All the galleries run by the City of Prague are free on the first Tuesday of the month.

Staroměstské nám and Karlův most are magical nocturnal attractions, and often have jazz bands busking for pennies. In the evening you can stroll along Na příkopě, where buskers play for the throng, or Václavské nám, where fast-food stands, cinemas and night bars stay open till late.

Shopping

You'll find many interesting shops along Karlova and Celetná, between Staroměstské nám and nám Republiky. One of the branches of **Česká lidová řemesla**, whose main shop is at Melantrichova 17, sells traditional Czech handicrafts. There are several good antique and bric-a-brac shops along Týnská and Týnská ulička, near Staroměstské nám.

For Bohemian crystal check the **Sklo** (*Václavské nám 28*) glass shop in the Alfa Cinema Arcade, or for the best-quality glass at premium prices there is **Moser** (*Na příkopě 17*). Ceramics with unusual Czech folk designs are worth checking out at **Tupesy** (*Havelská 21*). For all types of music **Bontonland** has the most choices – there is a major outlet at Václavské nám 1-3.

Getting There & Away

Air There are daily flights from Prague to Bratislava (from around 3000 Kč return) on **Czech Airlines** (*ČSA; ☎ 220 10 46 20; V celnici 5; metro Náměstí Republiky*).

Bus The **Florenc bus station** (*Florenc ÚAN; Křižíkova 4; metro Florenc*) is the departure point for buses that are travelling to Karlovy

Vary (110 Kč, 2½ hours), Brno (140 Kč, 2½ hours) and most other towns in the Czech Republic. Seven express buses a day go from Florenc to Bratislava (300 Kč). They take 4½ hours, compared to 5½ hours by train. Reservations are recommended on all these services.

The left-luggage room at Florenc station is upstairs above the information office (open 5am to 11pm daily).

Train Prague has four main train stations. International trains between Berlin and Budapest often stop at **Praha-Holešovice station** (metro Nádraží Holešovice) on the northern side of the city. Other important trains terminate at **Praha-hlavní nádraží** (metro Hlavní Nádraží) or **Praha-Masarykovo nádraží** (metro Náměstí Republiky), both of which are close to the city centre. Some local trains to the southwest depart from **Praha-Smíchov station** (metro Smíchovské Nádraží).

Praha-hlavní nádraží handles trains to České Budějovice (16 Kč, 2½ hours), Cheb via Plzeň (154 Kč, 3½ hours), Karlovy Vary (138 Kč, four hours), Košice (640 Kč, 10 hours), Kutná Hora (60 Kč, one hour), Plzeň (126 Kč, 1½ hours) and Tábor (80 Kč, 1½ hours). Trains to Brno (242 Kč, three hours) and Bratislava (400 Kč, 5½ hours) may leave from either Praha-hlavní nádraží, Praha-Holešovice or Masarykovo nádraží. Karlštejn (28 Kč, 35 minutes) trains depart from Hlavní nádraží and Smíchov.

This can be confusing, so study the timetables carefully to find out from which station you'll depart, then confirm the time and station at the information counter.

Praha-hlavní nádraží is Prague's largest train station with several exchange offices and accommodation services on levels 2 and 3, and a tourist information booth on level 2. The various snack stands on levels 2 and 3 are nothing special, but on level 4 is the pleasant Fantova kavárna, in a lovely Art Nouveau hall. Be extremely careful in and around the train station, as there are many thieves preying on unsuspecting foreigners.

The 24-hour left-luggage office (note its three half-hour breaks) is on level 1, so drop your bags off upon arrival and stroll into town to look for a room or a meal (you pay the fee – 15 Kč or 30 Kč per item per day depending on size – when you pick your bags up).

International tickets, domestic and international couchettes and seat reservations are sold on level 2 at the even-numbered windows from 10 to 24 to the right of the stairs leading to level 3. Domestic tickets are sold at the odd-numbered windows from 1 to 23 to the left of the stairs.

At Praha-Holešovice, windows marked ARES 1 and 2 are for booking international tickets and couchettes.

See the Getting There & Away and Getting Around sections earlier in this chapter introduction for more information.

Getting Around

To/From the Airport Prague's Ruzyně airport is 17km west of the city centre. City bus No 119 runs between the airport and Dejvická metro station (12 Kč, 20 minutes) daily from 5am to midnight. Buy tickets at the DPP desk in the airport (open 7am to 10pm daily), or from the vending machine at the bus stop (coins only).

Čedaz (☎ 220 11 42 96, 224 28 10 05; open 5.30am-9.30pm daily) has minibuses which depart every 30 minutes from nám Republiky, across from the Kotva department store (metro: Náměstí Republiky), and pick up passengers about 30 minutes later at Dejvická metro station on Evropská. Buy your ticket (90 Kč per person) from the driver. From the airport, they will take you to any address in central Prague (360 Kč for up to four people). To book a return trip to the airport, call at least two hours before your planned departure time.

Airport Cars taxi service, whose prices are regulated by the airport administration, charge 650 Kč (20% discount for return trip) into the centre of Prague (a regular taxi fare from central Prague should be about 450 Kč). Drivers accept Visa credit cards. If you take a regular taxi from the airport, there's a very good chance you will be ripped off, but going to the airport you should be safe taking a taxi with a reputable taxi company.

There's a 24-hour left-luggage office (40 Kč per day) in the terminal.

Public Transport All public transport is operated by **Dopravní podnik Praha** (DP; ☎ 22 62 37 77; ⓦ www.dp-praha.cz), which has information offices at Ruzyně airport and in five metro stations: Muzeum and Můstek (open 7am to 9pm daily), and Karlovo Náměstí, Nádraží Holešovice and Černý Most (open 7am to 6pm). Here you can get tickets, directions, a multilingual system map, a map

LITOMĚŘICE
pop 25,100
Litoměřice and was founded by German colonists in the 13th century, beneath the site of a 9th-century Slavic hill-top fortress. Five hundred years later, under Ferdinand III, the town's new status as a royal seat and bishopric brought it more prosperity. Today, the old town centre has many picturesque baroque buildings and churches, some of which were designed by the 18th-century architect Ottavio Broggio, who was born in the town.

Orientation & Information
The old centre is just across the road to the west of the adjacent train and bus stations, past the best-preserved parts of the 14th-century town walls. Walk down Dlouhá to the central square, Mírové nám.

The **information centre** (☎ 416 73 24 40; e info@mulitom.cz; Mírové nám 15; open 8am-6pm Mon-Sat, 9.30am-4pm Sun May-Sept; 8am-4pm Mon-Fri, 8am-11am Sat Oct-Apr) is in the distinctive House at the Chalice, the present town hall. The **Komerční banka** (Mírové nám 37) cashes travellers cheques and has an ATM. The **post and telephone office** is on Osvobození, two blocks north of Mírové nám.

Things to See
Dominating the broad and beautiful main square is the Gothic-turned-baroque **All Saints Church**. Across the street is the **Old Town Hall** with a small town museum, while the thin slice of pink baroque wedding cake at the uphill end of the square is the **House of Ottavio Broggio**. Compare it to the plain Gothic house at No 16, the oldest on the square, now the **Museum and Gallery of Litoměřice** (open 9am-noon & 1pm-6pm Tues-Sun Apr-Sept, to 5pm Oct-Mar) with a collection of religious art from St Stephen Cathedral. The green copper artichoke sprouting from the roof of the new town hall is actually a chalice, the traditional symbol of the Hussite church.

West of the square is another house where Broggio also left his touch, the excellent **North Bohemia Fine Arts Gallery** (Michalská 7; open 9am-noon & 1pm-6pm Tues-Sun) with its priceless panels from the Litoměřice Altarpiece.

Grassy, tree-lined, Domské nám on Cathedral Hill, southwest of the main square, is the town's historical centre. Pretty **St Wenceslas Church**, a true baroque gem, is just off the square at Domská. On top of Cathedral Hill is the town's oldest church, **St Stephen Cathedral**, dating from the 11th century.

Places to Stay
Autocamp Slavoj (☎ 416 73 44 81; open May-Sept), on Střelecký ostrov just south of the train and bus stations, has cheap bungalows as well as tent sites.

The best bargain in town is **Penzion U pavouka** (☎ 416 73 44 09; Pekařská 7; doubles 550 Kč), where the price includes breakfast. The new **Pension U svatého Václava** (☎ 416 73 75 00; Svatováclavská 12; singles/doubles 600/1000 Kč) is a bit more posh.

The top place in town, **Hotel Salva Guarda** (☎ 73 25 06, fax 73 27 98; Mírové nám 12; singles/doubles 920/1400 Kč), is in the historic House at the Black Eagle, where cosy rooms come with bathroom and TV.

Places to Eat
There's a **pekárna-potraviny** (bakery & grocery; open 7am-7pm Mon-Fri, 7am-noon Sat, 8am-noon Sun) at the top end of the square.

There is pleasant **café** (open 8am-10pm daily) in the arcade beneath the Old Town Hall. **Radniční sklípek** (Mírové nám 21; mains 85-125 Kč; open 10am-11pm daily) is a good cellar pub and restaurant serving cheap Czech grub.

Getting There & Away
There are no direct trains from Prague to Litoměřice, but there are hourly buses (61 Kč, one hour).

AROUND LITOMĚŘICE
Terezín
The huge 18th-century fortress town of Terezín is better known to history as Theriesenstadt – a notorious WWII concentration camp. It's only 3km south of Litoměřice and makes a deeply moving day trip.

Hourly buses from Litoměřice will drop you off at the main square, nám Československé armády, in the Main Fortress, where the **Museum of the Ghetto** (combined ticket to all museums 160 Kč; open 8am-6pm daily Apr-Sept, 8am-4.30pm Oct-Mar) documents daily life in the town in WWII. The Lesser Fortress is a 10-minute walk east across the Ohře River, where you can take a grimly fascinating self-guided tour through the prison barracks, isolation cells, workshops, morgues, execution grounds and former mass graves. During the floods of summer 2002, Terezín suffered severely, with buildings damaged and much original furniture destroyed. It is still partly open to visitors, but may not be fully repaired until 2006.

West Bohemia

Cheb and Plzeň are the western gateways to the Czech Republic. All trains from western Germany pass this way and the stately imperial spa of Karlovy Vary is nearby.

KARLOVY VARY
pop 53,900

Karlovy Vary (which means 'Charles' Hot Springs') is the largest and oldest of the Czech Republic's many spas. A local tradition says Emperor Charles IV discovered the springs by chance while hunting a stag. In 1358, he built a hunting lodge here and gave the town his name. From the 19th century, celebrities such as Beethoven, Bismarck, Brahms, Chopin, Franz Josef I, Goethe, Metternich, Paganini, Liszt, Peter the Great, Schiller, Tolstoy, Karl Marx and Yuri Gagarin came here to take the waters, and the busts of a few of them grace the promenades. Ludvík Moser began making glassware at Karlovy Vary in 1857 and today Bohemian crystal is prized around the world.

Karlovy Vary's 12 hot springs contain the various minerals used in the treatment of metabolic disorders and diseases of the digestive tract. The locally produced Becherovka herbal liqueur is known as the 13th spring.

Karlovy Vary still retains a 19th-century atmosphere despite being crowded with tourists. Elegant colonnades and boulevards complement the many peaceful walks in surrounding parkland. The picturesque river valley winds between wooded hills, yet the spa offers all the facilities of a medium-sized town.

Orientation

Karlovy Vary has two train stations. Express trains from Prague and Cheb use Karlovy Vary-horní nádraží, across the Ohře, just north of the city. Local trains stop at Karlovy Vary Dolní nádraží, which is beside the main ČSAD bus station. The Tržnice city bus station is in front of the market (*Městská tržnice*), three blocks east of Karlovy Vary Dolní nádraží.

TG Masaryka, the pedestrian mall in Karlovy Vary's city centre, runs east to the Teplá River. Upstream is the heart of the spa area.

If you decide to walk from town to Karlovy Vary-horní nádraží, you'll see a huge, pale pinkish-brown building directly in front of you as you cross the bridge leading to Sokolovska. Go around to the left behind this building and then straight ahead until you see a signposted way on the left which leads through a tunnel and straight up to the station.

Both train stations have left-luggage rooms; the one at Karlovy Vary-horní nádraží is open 24 hours a day.

Maps One of the best city maps is SHOCart/ GeoClub's *Karlovy Vary* (1:12,000) available from Infocentrum and bookshops.

Information

The main information office is **Infocentrum** (☎ 353 22 40 97; ⓔ *infocentrum@email.cz; Lázeňská 1; open 8am-6pm Mon-Fri, 10am-4pm Sat & Sun*), which has brochures and maps, including the monthly *Promenáda* magazine full of all the latest information on Karlovy Vary. It can arrange spa treatment for visitors from 2500 Kč per person a day including room and board.

Money You'll find an exchange counter and an ATM at **Česká spořitelna** (*TG Masaryka 14*). **Incentives CZ** (☎ 353 22 60 27; *Vřídelní 51; open 10am-6pm Mon-Fri, 10am-4pm Sat*) is an American Express representative and has an exchange office.

Post & Communications The **main post office** (*TG Masaryka 1; open 7.30am-7pm Mon-Fri, 7am-1pm Sat, 7am-noon Sun*) includes a telephone centre; there's also a branch post office on Vřídelní. You can check email at the **Internet Café** (*open 10am-10pm daily*) in the Hotel Thermal for a minimum charge of 40 Kč or 80 Kč an hour.

Medical & Emergency Services There's a 24-hour **medical centre** (*lekárská pohotovost; ☎ 353 22 46 79; Krymská 2a*) near the Dolní nádraží train station; nearby **Aesculap** (*nám Dr M Horákové 8*) is a pharmacy. To get to the **Foreigners Police** (☎ 353 50 32 00; *Závodu míru 16; open 8am-5pm Mon & Wed*), take bus No 3 from Tržnice bus station and get off at the fifth stop.

KARLOVY VARY

PLACES TO STAY
6 W-Privat
  Accommodation
  Agency
10 Hotel Kavalerie
21 Pension Kosmos
25 Hotel Kolonáda
39 Hotel Embassy
42 Grandhotel Pupp

PLACES TO EAT
1 Městská tržnice
  (Market)
9 Parlament
12 Trumf Bakery

14 Bistro Pupík
17 VgR Vegetarian
  Restaurant
18 P & P Pizzeria
37 Café Elefant
45 Café

OTHER
2 ČSAD Long-Distance
  Bus Station
3 24-Hour Medical Centre
4 Aesculap Pharmacy
5 ČSAD Agency
7 Propaganda Music Club
8 Čedok Travel Agency

11 MHD Office (Public
  Transport Information)
13 Tržnice City Bus Station
15 Česká spořitelna
16 Kino Čas
19 Poštovní Bridge
20 Post & Telephone Office
22 Hotel Thermal; Internet
  Café
23 Open-Air Thermal Pool
24 Sadová Kolonáda
26 Church of SS Peter & Paul
27 Karl Marx Monument
28 Mlýnská Kolonáda &
  Bandstand

29 Infocentrum
30 Golden Key Museum
31 Incentives CZ
32 Branch Post Office
33 Zámecká Tower
34 House of the Three Moors
35 Vřídelní Kolonáda
36 Church of Mary
  Magdalene
38 Divadlo Vítězslava
  Nezvala
40 Karlovy Vary Museum
41 Lázně I (Spa No 1)
43 Diana Funicular Railway
44 Diana Tower

CZECH REPUBLIC

CZECH REPUBLIC

Things to See

As you follow the riverside promenade south, you'll pass the towering concrete **Hotel Thermal and Spa** (1976) and the neoclassical **Mlýnská Kolonáda** (1881), designed by Josef Zítek. The **Golden Key Museum** (*Lázeňská 3; admission 20 Kč; open 9am-noon & 1pm-5pm Wed-Sun*) is next, with paintings of the spa from the early 20th century. On a nearby hill is the old **Zámecká tower** (1608) on the site of Charles IV's 1358 hunting lodge; today it's a restaurant. Down the hill from the tower is the **House of the Three Moors** (*Dagmar House; Tržiště 25*), where Goethe stayed during his many visits to Karlovy Vary.

Opposite this building is a bridge which leads to the pulsing heart of Karlovy Vary, the **Vřídelní Kolonáda**. A modern glass enclosure houses the Vřídlo or Sprudel (geyser), where spring water at 72.2°C spurts 12m into the air. Throngs of Czech tourists, little porcelain spa cups (*lázeňský pohárek*) in hand, pace up and down the neighbouring colonnade, taking the drinking cure (you're free to try it too, as long as you have your own cup).

Overlooking the Vřídelní Kolonáda is the baroque **Church of Mary Magdalene** (1736) designed by Kilian Dientzenhofer. Continue southwest along the river past the **Divadlo Vítězslava Nezvala** theatre (1886) to the **Karlovy Vary Museum** (*Nová Louka 23; admission 30 Kč; open 9am-noon & 1pm-5pm Wed-Sun*), which has displays on local and natural history.

Beyond the park past the museum is the beautifully restored **Lázně I** (Spa No 1; 1895). Cross the bridge beside it and return north along the promenade on the far bank, past the **Grandhotel Pupp**, a former meeting place of the European aristocracy.

Just beyond the hotel you'll see Mariánská, a narrow alley on the left leading to the bottom station of the **Diana Funicular Railway** (*one way/return 25/40 Kč; open 9am-6pm daily*), which climbs the 166m to the **Diana Tower** every 15 minutes. There are great views from the top, and pleasant walks back down through the forest. A café adjoins the Diana Tower.

Activities

Relax after your sightseeing with a swim in the large **open-air thermal pool** (*bazén; admission 30 Kč an hour; open 8am-8.30pm Mon-Sat, 9am-9.30pm Sun*) on the cliff top overlooking the Hotel Thermal.

The pool is closed every third Monday. There's also a **sauna** (*10am-9.30pm daily*), a solarium and a fitness club.

Special Events

Cultural events include the Jazz Festival in May, the Dvořák Singing Contest in June, the International Film Festival (**w** www.kviff .com) in July, the Dvořák Autumn Festival and Tourfilm (International Festival of Films about Tourism) in September.

Places to Stay

Camp Březový Háj (**☎** 353 22 26 65, **☎** 602 120 477; **e** info@brezovy-haj.cz; *Staromlýnská, Březová; tent sites 90 Kč; bungalow beds 150 Kč; open May-Sept*) is in the Teplá valley 3km southwest of town. There are hourly buses (weekdays only) from the Tržnice bus station to Brežova (20 minutes).

On weekends Karlovy Vary fills up with German visitors and accommodation can be tight. **Čedok** (**☎** 353 22 33 35; *Dr Bechera 21; open 9am-6pm Mon-Fri, 9am-noon Sat*) travel agency and **W-Privat Accommodation Agency** (**☎**/fax 353 22 77 68; *nám Republiky 5; open 8.30am-5pm Mon-Fri, 9.30am-1pm Sat*) can organise private rooms from 350 Kč per person.

A 15 Kč per person spa tax is added to regular hotel rates. The hostel-style **Penzión Hestia** (**☎** 353 22 59 85, fax 353 22 04 82; *Stará Kysibelská 45; beds 350 Kč*) is a half-hour walk east of the centre, or you can take bus No 6 from Tržnice bus station. It has clean rooms, with shared facilities.

There are a number of reasonable pensions along Zahradní, such as **Pension Kosmos** (**☎**/fax 353 22 31 68; *singles/doubles from 450/720 Kč*) at No 39.

The two-star **Hotel Kavalerie** (**☎** 353 22 96 13, fax 353 23 61 71; **e** kavalerie@volny .cz; *TG Masaryka 43; singles/doubles 950/1350 Kč*) is probably the best-value hotel in the town centre.

Hotel Embassy (**☎** 353 22 11 61, fax 353 22 31 46; **e** embassy@mbox.vol.cz; *Nová Louka 21; singles/doubles 2020/2980 Kč*) is a good mid-range place with elegant 19th-century-style decor.

The attractive **Hotel Kolonáda** (**☎** 353 34 55 55, fax 353 34 78 18; **e** reception@ kolonada.cz; *IP Pavlova 8; singles/doubles 3355/5810 Kč*), in the heart of the spa area, is even more luxurious.

Karlovy Vary's premier address is the opulent five-star **Grandhotel Pupp** (☎ 353 10 91 11, fax 353 22 40 32; e pupp@pupp.cz; Mírové nám 2; singles/doubles US$180/220), an imposing 112-room hotel founded in 1701. Its annexe, the **Parkhotel Pupp**, has slightly less expensive rooms.

Places to Eat
P & P Pizzeria (IP Pavlova 13; mains 75-90 Kč; open 10am-10pm Mon-Sat, 10am-8pm Sun) is just across Poštovní Bridge. In a back court around the corner is the good **VgR Vegetarian Restaurant** (IP Pavlova 23; open 11am-10pm daily).

Parlament (cnr TG Masaryka & Zeyerova; mains 65-85 Kč; open 9am-10pm Mon-Sat) is a good inexpensive place serving pork sauerkraut and dumplings and other Czech dishes.

The upmarket **Café Elefant** (Stará Louka 30) is perhaps Karlovy Vary's most popular and elegant café.

There's a good, cheap **bufet** inside the entrance to the market, which itself is a large supermarket. **Trumf** (Zeyerova 17) is a good cake shop and bakery. **Bistro Pupík** (Horova 2), next to the Tržnice city bus station, has cheap beer on tap.

Entertainment
Karlovy Vary's main theatre is the **Divadlo Vítězslava Nezvala** (Divadlo nám). From mid-May and mid-September concerts are held in Vřídelní Kolonáda Tuesday to Sunday.

Propaganda Music Club (Jaltská 7) has occasional live bands or DJs spinning rock/pop music nightly. Seeing a movie at the **Kino Čas** (TG Masaryka 3) is another option.

Getting There & Away
Bus There are direct trains to Prague, but it's faster and easier to take one of the five daily buses (110 Kč, 2½ hours). For Cheb, the bus (50 Kč, one hour) is also slightly faster than the train. The only way to get directly to Plzeň (1½ hours, 84km) and České Budějovice (four hours, 220km) is by bus. Seats on express buses should be reserved in advance at the **ČSAD agency** (☎ 353 22 36 62; nám Republiky 7; open 6am-6pm Mon-Fri, 7am-noon Sat) at the Dolní nádraží train station.

Train There are several direct trains daily from Karlovy Vary to Prague (168 Kč, 4½ hours). Hourly local trains connect Cheb (48

Kč, one hour) to Karlovy Vary. Heading west from Karlovy Vary to Nuremberg, Germany, and beyond, you'll have to change at Cheb.

Getting Around
You can buy local bus tickets (8 Kč) at the MHD office on Zeyerova and from automatic ticket machines. Bus No 11 runs hourly from Karlovy Vary-horní nádraží to the Tržnice city bus station at the market, then over the hills to Divadlo nám and the Vřídelní Kolonáda. Bus No 2 runs between Tržnice and Grandhotel Pupp (Lázně I) every half-hour or so from 6am to 11pm daily.

You can rent mountain bikes for 60/320 Kč per hour/day from Incentives CZ (see Money, earlier in this section).

AROUND KARLOVY VARY
Loket
If you have an afternoon free, take a ČSAD bus for Sokolov and get off 8km southwest of Karlovy Vary at Loket (20 Kč, 20 minutes). There's an impressive 13th-century **castle** (English guided tours 100 Kč; open 9am-4.30pm daily Apr-Oct, 9am-3.30pm Nov-Mar) on the hill in the town centre. A museum in the castle is dedicated to the china made in Loket since 1815. On the facade of Hotel Bílý Kůň, in Loket's picturesque town square, is a plaque commemorating Goethe's seven visits.

You can walk back to Karlovy Vary from Loket in three hours. Follow the scenic trail (blue waymarks) along the left bank of the Ohře to the **Svatošské Rocks**. Here, cross the river on a footbridge and follow the road to Doubí where you can catch Karlovy Vary city bus No 6 the rest of the way into town.

CHEB
pop 33,000
This medieval town (known as Eger in German) on the Ohře River, near the western tip of the Czech Republic, is an easy day trip on the train from Karlovy Vary. Only a few kilometres from the Bavarian border, Cheb retains a strong German flavour.

Orientation & Information
The train station and left-luggage office are at the southeastern end of třída Svobody.

The **Tourist Infocentrum** (☎ 354 42 27 05; e infocentrum.cheb@email.cz; nám krále Jiřího z Poděbrad 33; open 9am-5pm Mon-Fri, 9am-noon Sat) sells maps, guidebooks and theatre and concert tickets, and can organise guides.

Česká spořitelna (cnr třída Svobody & Májová) has an exchange counter and an ATM. There's also a 24-hour ATM farther along třída Svobody towards nám krále Jiřího z Poděbrad.

The main post office is beside the train station. There's a telephone centre on nám krále Jiřího z Poděbrad at No 38.

The **24-hour pharmacy** (nám krále Jiřího z Poděbrad 6) has a red button to press in case of an emergency that happens outside normal business hours.

Things to See
Only a just few minutes' walk along třída Svobody from the ugly train-station area is the picturesque town square, nám krále Jiřího z Poděbrad, surrounded by burgher houses with red-tiled roofs. In the middle is the **Špalíček**, a cluster of 16th-century Gothic houses, which were once Jewish shops. Behind these is the **Cheb Museum** (admission 50 Kč; open 9am-12.30pm & 1pm-5pm Tues-Sun Mar-Dec), which has an excellent historical exhibition. The Thirty Years' War military commander Duke Albrecht Wallenstein was murdered in this building in 1634 and the museum devotes a room to him. Also on the square is the baroque, formerly new town hall (1728), now the **Museum of Fine Arts** (admission 20 Kč; open same hours as Cheb Museum) with changing art exhibits.

Behind Cheb Museum is **St Nicholas Church**, a massive Gothic structure with a sculpture-filled interior. Notice the portal (1270) and Romanesque features, such as the twin towers. West is **Cheb Castle** (admission 30 Kč; open 9am-6pm Tues-Sun June-Aug, 9am-5pm Tues-Sun May & Sept, 9am-4pm Tues-Sun Apr & Oct), erected in the 12th century by Friedrich I Barbarossa, leader of the Eastern Crusades. The Black Tower dates from 1222 but the exterior fortifications were built in the 17th century. In the castle is a 12th-century chapel, a rare sight in the Czech Republic.

Places to Stay
The nearest camping ground is **Autokempink Dřenice** (☎ 354 43 15 91; tent sites 190 Kč, plus per person 30 Kč; open May–mid-Sept) on Jesenice Lake, 5km east of Cheb. It also has bungalows for 170 Kč per person.

There are several pensions around town including the homely **Pension U kata** (☎ 354 42 34 65; Židovská 17; singles/doubles 350/700 Kč). The nearby **Hostel Židovská ulice** (☎ 354 42 34 01; Židovská 11; quads 1050 Kč) has basic accommodation in four-bed rooms; if available, a single costs 400 Kč.

The handful of hotels in Cheb includes just two in the city centre. The **Hotel Slávie** (☎/fax 354 43 32 16; třída Svobody 75) was undergoing renovation at the time of writing. **Hotel Hvězda** (☎ 354 42 25 49, fax 354 42 25 46; nám krále Jiřího z Poděbrad 4; singles/doubles 900/1500 Kč) on the main square is the most expensive place in town, although the rooms are still pretty basic.

Places to Eat
The Prior department store on třída Svobody has a basement **supermarket** and there is a small open-air **market** on Obrněné brigády. There are a couple of tourist restaurants around nám krále Jiřího z Poděbrad; the best bet is **Kavárna Špalíček** (mains 90-150 Kč; open 9am-10pm daily) at No 499. The food is good, but the modern decor (and purple furniture) destroys any historical ambience.

Getting There & Away
Most trains arriving in the Czech Republic from Nuremberg and Leipzig stop here, and there are express trains to and from Stuttgart (six hours, 342km), Frankfurt am Main (five hours, 389km) and Dortmund (eight hours, 728km) daily. There are plenty of trains to Cheb from Prague (194 Kč, 3½ hours) via Plzeň (120 Kč, 1½ hours).

A railcar covers the 13km from Cheb to Schirnding, Germany (15 minutes, 13km), every two hours daily. To board an international train, enter through the door marked zoll-douane (customs) to one side of the main station entrance at least an hour before departure. If you miss the train to Schirnding you could take city bus No 5 to Pomezí (15 minutes), which is near the border 8km west of Cheb, and then cross into Germany on foot. The bus to Pomezí leaves from stand No 9 at the train station every hour or so.

PLZEŇ
pop 173,000
The city of Plzeň (Pilsen), midway between Prague and Nuremberg, is the capital of West Bohemia. At the confluence of four rivers,

this town was once an active medieval trading centre. An ironworks was founded here in 1859, which Emil Škoda purchased 10 years later. The Škoda Engineering Works became a producer of high-quality armaments and was subject to heavy bombing at the end of WWII. The rebuilt Škoda Works now produces machinery and locomotives.

Beer has been brewed in Plzeň for 700 years and the town is famous as the original home of Pilsner. The only original Pilsner trademark is Pilsner Urquell (in German; Plzeňský Prazdroj in Czech). Connoisseurs of the brewer's art will not regret the pilgrimage.

Orientation

The main train station, Plzeň-hlavní nádraží, is on the eastern side of town. The central bus station is west of the centre on Husova, opposite the Škoda Works. Between these is the old town, which is centred on nám Republiky.

Tram No 2 goes from the train station to the centre of town and on to the bus station. The left-luggage office at the bus station is open 8am to 8pm Monday to Friday; the office at the train station is open 24 hours.

Information

The **city information centre** (☎ 377 03 27 50; ⓔ *infocenter@mmp.plzen-city.cz; open 9am-6pm daily Apr-Sept, 10am-5pm Mon-Fri, 10am-3.30pm Sat & Sun Oct-Mar*) is on the main square at nám Republiky 41.

Komerční banka (*Zbrojnická 4*) has an exchange desk, and there's a 24-hour ATM at the ČSOB on Americká.

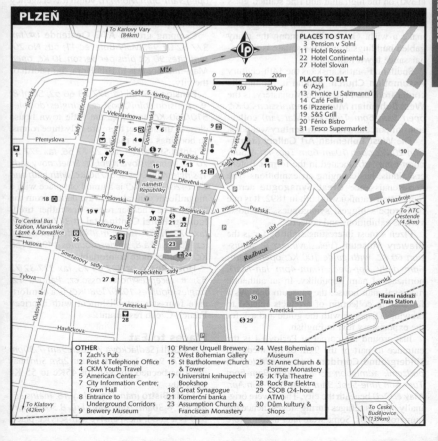

PLZEŇ

PLACES TO STAY
3 Pension v Solní
11 Hotel Rosso
22 Hotel Continental
27 Hotel Slovan

PLACES TO EAT
6 Azyl
13 Pivnice U Salzmannů
14 Café Fellini
16 Pizzerie
19 S&S Grill
20 Fénix Bistro
31 Tesco Supermarket

OTHER
1 Zach's Pub
2 Post & Telephone Office
4 CKM Youth Travel
5 American Center
7 City Information Centre; Town Hall
8 Entrance to Underground Corridors
9 Brewery Museum
10 Pilsner Urquell Brewery
12 West Bohemian Gallery
15 St Bartholomew Church & Tower
17 Universitní knihupectví Bookshop
18 Great Synagogue
21 Komerční banka
23 Assumption Church & Franciscan Monastery
24 West Bohemian Museum
25 St Anne Church & Former Monastery
26 JK Tyla Theatre
28 Rock Bar Elektra
29 ČSOB (24-hour ATM)
30 Dům kultury & Shops

CZECH REPUBLIC

There's a telephone centre in the **main post office** *(Solní 20; open 7am-7pm Mon-Fri, 8am-1pm Sat, 8am-noon Sun)*, and you can check email at the **American Center** *(☎ 377 23 77 22; Dominikánská 9; open 8am-6pm Mon-Fri)* for 30 Kč per half hour.

Universitní knihkupectví *(cnr Sedláčkova & Solní)* sells maps and a small collection of English books.

Things to See

Gothic **St Bartholomew Church** *(admission 20 Kč; open 10am-4pm Wed-Sat, noon-7pm Sun Apr-Dec)* in the middle of nám Republiky has the highest **tower** *(admission 20 Kč; open 10am-6pm daily)* in Bohemia at 102m; the view from the top is superb. Inside the soaring 13th-century structure are a Gothic Madonna (1390) on the high altar and fine stained-glass windows. On the back of the outer side of the church is an iron grille. Touch the angel and make a wish. Outstanding among the many gabled buildings around the square is the Renaissance **town hall** (1558).

South on Františkánská is the 14th-century **Assumption Church**. Behind it, around the corner from the Franciscan Monastery, is the **West Bohemian Museum** *(admission 20 Kč; open 9am-5pm Tues-Sun Mar-Jan)* collections of porcelain and 17th-century weapons.

The **West Bohemian Art Gallery** *(admission 20 Kč; open 10am-6pm Tues-Fri & Sun, noon-6pm Sat)*, located in the former Butchers' Stalls, has changing art exhibitions. The neo-Renaissance **Great Synagogue** across Sady Pětatřicátníků was built in 1892. It is one of Europe's biggest synagogues, and hosts various exhibitions and concerts.

Plzeň's most interesting sight by far is the **Brewery Museum** *(Veleslavínova 6; admission 60 Kč, with guide 100 Kč; open 10am-6pm daily Apr-Dec, 10am-4pm Jan-Mar)*, northeast of nám Republiky. In an authentic medieval malt house, the museum displays a fascinating collection of artefacts related to brewing. Dispense with the guide and ask for the explanatory text in English.

Just around the corner at Perlová 4 is the entrance to part of the 9km of the medieval **Underground Corridors** *(Plzeňské historické podzemí; admission 35 Kč; open 9am-5pm Tues-Sun June-Sept, 9am-5pm Wed-Sun Apr, May & Oct)* beneath the city. These were originally built as refuges during sieges, hence the numerous wells. Some were later used to store kegs of maturing beer. To enter you must wait for a group of at least five people to gather, then follow a tour (if there is no English-speaking guide ask for the text in English).

The very famous **Pilsner Urquell Brewery** *(☎ 377 06 11 11; tour 100 Kč; open 8am-4pm Mon-Fri, 8am-1pm Sat & Sun)* is only a 10-minute walk east along Pražská over the river. The twin-arched gate dated 1842–92, which appears on every genuine Pilsner label, is here. A one-hour tour of the brewing room and fermentation cellar is offered to individuals at 12.30pm on weekdays only. The rest of the day is reserved for organised groups.

Places to Stay

The **CKM** *(☎ 377 23 63 93, fax 377 23 69 09; ℮ ckm-plzen@volny.cz; Dominikánská 1; open 9am-5pm Mon-Fri)* youth travel agency can book hostels in summer (from 200 Kč per person), pensions and hotels.

Camping ground **ATC Oestende** *(☎/fax 377 52 01 94; Malý Bolevec 41; bus No 20; tent sites 90 Kč plus per person 30 Kč; open May–mid-Sept)* is in Bílá Hora, 5km north of the city.

Pension v Solní *(☎ 377 23 66 52; Solní 8; ℮ pension.solni@post.cz; singles/doubles 510/850 Kč)* is a pleasant little town house close to the square; there are only three rooms, so bookings are a must.

Hotel Slovan *(☎ 377 22 72 56, fax 377 22 70 12; ℮ hotelslovan@iol.cz; Smetanovy sady 1; singles/doubles 500/750 Kč, with bath and TV 1420/2040 Kč)* is a grand old place with a magnificent central stairway, dating from the 1890s. The cheaper rooms are rather tired-looking. **Hotel Continental** *(☎ 377 23 52 92, fax 377 22 17 46; ℮ mail@hotelcontinental.cz; Zbrojnická 8; singles/doubles 1490/2150 Kč)* is rather more comfortable.

Hotel Rosso *(☎ 722 64 73, fax 377 32 72 53; ℮ recepce@hotel-rosso.cz; Pallova 12; singles/doubles 1080/1980Kč)* is a comfortable four-star establishment with a pricey French-Czech restaurant.

Places to Eat

S & S Grill *(Sedláčkova 7; open 9am-7.30pm Mon-Fri, 9am-3pm Sat, 10am-2pm Sun)* has great barbecued chicken for 45Kč to 55 Kč per 100g.

Fénix Bistro *(nám Republiky 18; mains 35-80 Kč; 8.30am-7pm Mon-Fri, 8.30am-3pm Sat)* is a good, inexpensive self-service place.

You can get decent, inexpensive pizzas at **Pizzerie** *(Solní 9; pizzas 52-62 Kč; open 10am-10pm Mon-Fri, 11am-11pm Sat, 11.30am-10pm Sun)*. Not far from the square is **Pivnice U Salzmannů** *(Pražská 8; mains 80-180 Kč; open 11am-11pm Mon-Sat, 11am-10pm Sun)*, a Plzeň institution known for its good-quality food and fine beer.

Café Fellini *(open 8am-midnight daily)* is the only place on the main square with decent coffee. **Azyl** *(Veleslavínova 17; open 8am-11pm Mon-Thur, 8am-1am Fri, 4pm-1am Sat, 4pm-10pm Sun)* is a cool café-bar and art gallery.

There is a **supermarket** *(open 7am-7pm Mon-Wed, 7am-8pm Thur & Fri, 8am-6pm Sat & Sun)* in Tesco, near the train station.

Entertainment
For entertainment, try **JK Tyla Theatre** or the ultramodern **Dům kultury** beside the river. There are also interesting tours of the backstage area, dressing rooms and below the stage of the Tyla Theatre, in Czech only, during July and August (20 Kč).

You can listen to local and foreign rock bands (till 11.30pm) or dance to pop tunes (till 5am) at **Rock Bar Elektra** *(Americká 24)*. **Zach's Pub** *(Palackého nám 2; open 11am-1am daily)* serves Guinness and English beers.

Getting There & Away
All international trains from Munich and Nuremberg to Prague stop at Plzeň. There are fast trains from here to České Budějovice (100 Kč, two hours) and Cheb (120 Kč, 1½ hours).

If you're heading for Karlovy Vary, take a bus (80 Kč, 1¾ hours). Buses also travel to Prague (60 Kč, 1½ hours) and České Budějovice (96 Kč, 2¾ hours).

South Bohemia

South Bohemia has many quaint little towns with a Bavarian or Austrian flavour mixed with local folk baroque buildings, enhanced by some 5000 carp ponds, many of them dating from the Middle Ages. In the Šumava hills, southwest of Prachatice, is the peak of Boubín (1362m) with its primeval forest of spruce, pine and beech trees. The Vltava River has its source among these hills.

After WWI, the southern part of South Bohemia was transferred to Czechoslovakia, even though over half of its population was German; after WWII all German residents were expelled.

ČESKÉ BUDĚJOVICE
pop 98,900
České Budějovice (Budweis), the regional capital of South Bohemia, is a charming medieval city halfway between Plzeň and Vienna. Here the Vltava River meets the Malše and flows north to Prague. Founded in 1265, České Budějovice imported salt and wine from Austria and was a Catholic stronghold in the 15th century. Nearby silver mines made the town rich in the 16th century. After a fire in 1641 much of the town was rebuilt in the baroque style. In 1832, the first horse-drawn railway on the Continent arrived at České Budějovice from Linz. The city is famous as the original home of Budvar (Budweiser) beer.

The town is a good base for day trips to many local attractions, including picturesque little Bohemian towns such as Jindřichův Hradec, Písek, Prachatice, Tábor and Třeboň.

Orientation
It's a 10-minute walk west down Lannova třída, then Kanovnická, from the adjacent bus and train stations to nám Přemysla Otakara II, the main square. The left-luggage office at the bus station is open 7am to 7pm weekdays, to 2pm Saturday. The one at the train station is open 2.30am to 11pm daily.

Information
The helpful **city information centre** *(☎/fax 386 35 94 80;* [e] *infocb@c-budejovice.cz; nám Přemysla Otakara II 1; open 8.30am-8pm Mon-Fri, 9am-5pm Sat, 10am-4pm Sun June-Sept; 9am-5pm Mon-Fri, 9am-4pm Sun Oct-May)* sells maps and can arrange guides, theatre tickets and accommodation.

Also selling maps and tickets is the commercial **Tourist Information and Map Centre** *(☎/fax 386 35 25 89;* [e] *mapcentrum@ mbox.vol.cz; nám Přemysla Otakara II 28; open 7.45am-6pm Mon-Fri, 8.45am-4pm Sat, 1pm-4pm Sun)*. It can also arrange tour guides and book accommodation.

Motorists can go to **Jihočeský autoklub** *(☎ 635 65 66; Žižkova třída 13)* for help.

The **Raiffeisen Bank** *(open 8.30am-5pm Mon-Thur, 8.30am-4.30pm Fri)* on the main square changes travellers cheques and has an ATM.

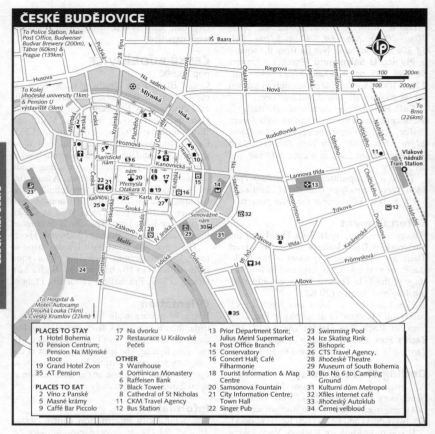

ČESKÉ BUDĚJOVICE

PLACES TO STAY
1 Hotel Bohemia
10 Pension Centrum;
  Pension Na Mlýnské
  stoce
19 Grand Hotel Zvon
35 AT Pension

PLACES TO EAT
2 Víno z Panské
5 Masné krámy
9 Caffé Bar Piccolo

17 Na dvorku
27 Restaurace U Královské
  Pečeti

OTHER
3 Warehouse
4 Dominican Monastery
6 Raiffeisen Bank
7 Black Tower
8 Cathedral of St Nicholas
11 CKM Travel Agency
12 Bus Station

13 Prior Department Store;
  Julius Meinl Supermarket
14 Post Office Branch
15 Conservatory
16 Concert Hall; Café
  Filharmonie
18 Tourist Information & Map
  Centre
20 Samsonova Fountain
21 City Information Centre;
  Town Hall
22 Singer Pub

23 Swimming Pool
24 Ice Skating Rink
25 Bishopric
26 CTS Travel Agency
28 Jihočeské Theatre
29 Museum of South Bohemia
30 Bus No 6 to Camping
  Ground
31 Kulturní dům Metropol
32 Xfiles internet café
33 Jihočeský Autoklub
34 Černej velbloud

The 24-hour **main post office** (*Pražská 69*) is north of the centre; there's a more convenient **branch post office** (*open 7am-7pm Mon-Fri, 8am-noon Sat*) on Senovážné nám. You can surf the Internet at **Xfiles internet café** (*Senovážné nám; open 10am-10pm Mon-Fri, 4pm-10pm Sat & Sun*) opposite the post office for 1 Kč a minute.

There's a **24-hour pharmacy** (☎ *387 87 31 03*) at the **hospital** (☎ *387 87 11 11; B Němcové 54*).

The **police station** (☎ *387 31 36 88; at Pražská 5*) is in the northern part of town.

Things to See

Nám Přemysla Otakara II, a vast, open square surrounded by 18th-century arcades, is one of the largest of its kind in Europe. At

its centre is the **Samsonova Fountain** (1727), and on the western side stands the baroque **town hall** (1731). On the hour a tune is played from its tower. The allegorical figures of the cardinal virtues – Justice, Wisdom, Courage and Prudence – on the town hall balustrade, stand above four bronze dragon gargoyles. Looming above the opposite corner of the square is the 72m-tall **Black Tower** (*admission 15 Kč; open 10am-6pm daily July & Aug, 10am-6pm Tues-Sun Apr-June, Sept & Oct*), dating from 1553, which has great views from the gallery. Beside it is the **Cathedral of St Nicholas**.

The streets around the square, especially Česká, are lined with old burgher houses. West near the river is the former **Dominican monastery** (1265) with another tall tower and a splendid pulpit. You enter the church from the Gothic cloister. Beside the church is a medieval warehouse where salt was stored before it was carried in barges down the Vltava to Prague. South along the riverside behind the warehouse are the remaining sections of the 16th-century walls. The **Museum of South Bohemia** (*admission 20 Kč; open 9am-12.30pm & 1pm-5pm Tues-Sun*) is just south of the old town.

The **Budweiser Budvar Brewery** (☎ 387 70 53 41; cnr Pražská & K Světlé; bus No 2; open 9am-5pm daily) is involved in a long-standing legal tussle with the US brewer Anheuser-Busch over the brand name 'Budweiser', which has been used by both breweries since the 19th century. However, there's no contest as to which beer is superior; one taste of Budvar and you'll be an instant convert. Tour groups need 10 or more people, except for the 2pm tour which is open to individual travellers. A one-hour tour in English costs 70/100 Kč on weekdays/weekends. If you miss the tour, the brewery's **beer hall** is open 10am to 10pm daily. The brewery is in an industrial area several kilometres north of the centre and lacks the picturesque appearance of the Urquell Brewery in Plzeň.

Places to Stay

Accommodation can be tight during the regular trade fairs held here throughout the year. Check with the tourist information centre before turning up without a booking.

Camping A 20-minute walk southwest of town (or take bus No 6 from opposite Kulturní dům Metropol to the fourth stop) is **Motel-Autocamp Dlouhá Louka** (☎ 387 21 06 01, fax 387 21 05 95; Stromovka 8; tent sites 50 Kč plus per person 50 Kč; open May-Sept). Bungalows with double rooms are available all year for 1080 Kč.

Hostels The **CKM** (☎ 386 35 12 70; Lannova třída 63; open 9am-5pm Mon-Thur, 9am-3.30pm Fri) youth travel agency and both tourist information offices can arrange dorm accommodation from 120 Kč per person. **Kolej jihočeské university** (☎ 387 77 42 01; Studentská 13-19; doubles 240 Kč), west of the centre, has beds available between July and September.

The closest thing to a travellers hostel is **Pension U výstaviště** (☎ 387 24 01 48; U výzstaviště 17; beds 240 Kč). This place is 30 minutes from the city centre on bus No 1 from outside the bus station to the fifth stop (U parku); the pension is about 100m up the street (Čajkovského) on the right.

Private Rooms Both tourist information offices offer private rooms from around 300 Kč per person. Another good place with similarly priced rooms is **CTS Travel Agency** (☎ 386 35 39 68; nám Přemysla Otakara II 38; open 7.30am-7pm Mon-Thur).

Pensions The small private pensions around town are a better deal than the hotels, but the quality varies. **Pension Centrum** (☎ 386 35 20 30; Mlýnská stoka 6; doubles 850 Kč), just off Kanovnická, has been recommended by readers. Its neighbour **Pension Na Mlýnské stoce** (☎/fax 386 35 34 75; ☏ penzion.garni@mybox.cz; Mlýnska stoka 7; singles 600-800 Kč, doubles 800-950 Kč) has also generated good feedback.

AT Pension (☎ 387 31 25 29; Dukelská 15; singles/doubles 650/980 Kč) has similar accommodation and is in a quiet street south of the centre.

Hotels The **Hotel Bohemia** (☎/fax 386 36 06 91; ☏ hotel-bohemia@volny.cz; Hradební 20; singles/doubles 1290/1690 Kč) on a quiet side street has comfy rooms and a cellar wine bar with plenty of character.

The finest hotel in České Budějovice is the **Grand Hotel Zvon** (☎ 387 31 13 84, fax 387 31 13 85; ☏ ghz@hotel-zvon.cz; nám Přemysla Otakara II 28; singles/doubles from 1780/2580 Kč).

Places to Eat

Try the local carp, which is on the menu of many restaurants.

Masné krámy (mains 40-60 Kč; open 10am-11pm daily) beer hall in the old meat market (1560), on the corner of Hroznová and 5.května, has been a local institution for centuries. Today it's a bit touristy but still worth a look. **Na dvorku** (Kněžská 11; mains 40-60 Kč; open 9.30am-10pm Mon-Fri, 10am-10pm Sat, 10am-3pm Sun) has a more genuine beer hall atmosphere.

Víno z Panské (Panská 14; restaurant open 5pm-1am Mon-Sat) is a good wine bar that serves vegetarian and chicken dishes. Its wine is served straight from the barrel.

CZECH REPUBLIC

In a higher price bracket is the **Restaurace U Královské Pečeti** (Karla IV 8) in the Hotel Malý Pivovar, serving excellent South Bohemian and Moravian food.

Café filharmonie (cnr Kněžská & Karla IV; open 9am-10pm Mon-Sat), in the concert hall foyer, is the town's most elegant café; but the best coffee is at friendly little **Caffé Bar Piccolo** (Mlýnská stoka 9; open 7.30am-7pm Mon-Thur, 7.30am-10pm Fri & Sat).

The Prior department store has a big **Julius Meinl supermarket** (Lannova třída; open 8am-7pm Mon-Fri, 8am-1pm Sat).

Entertainment
Regular classical music concerts are staged by the Chamber Philharmonic Orchestra of South Bohemia at the **Concert Hall** (Kněžská 6) in the Church of St Anne, and also at the **Conservatory** (Kanovnická 22).

The **Jihočeské Theatre**, by the river on Dr Stejskala, usually presents plays in Czech, but operas, operettas and concerts are also performed here.

Singer Pub (Česká 55; open 11am-11pm daily) is a lively Irish-type pub. Rock bands often play at **Černej velbloud** (U tří lvů 4; open 6pm-1am Mon-Fri, 6pm-3am Sat).

Getting There & Away
There are fast trains from České Budějovice to Plzeň (100 Kč, two hours), Tábor (55 Kč, one hour) and Prague (126 Kč, 2½ hours). You can connect with trains between Prague and Vienna at České Velenice, 50km southeast of České Budějovice. For shorter trips you're probably better off travelling by bus. The bus to Brno (182 Kč, four hours) travels via Telč (86 Kč, two hours). Twice a week there's a bus to Linz, Austria (2¼ hours, 125km).

AROUND ČESKÉ BUDĚJOVICE
Hluboká nad Vltavou
One side trip not to miss is the neo-Gothic Tudor palace of Hluboká nad Vltavou (open 9am-5pm daily July & Aug, 9am-5pm Tues-Sun June, 9am-4.30pm Tues-Sun Apr, May, Sept & Oct), 10km north, which is easily accessible by bus. The 13th-century castle was rebuilt by the Schwarzenberg family between 1841 and 1871 in the style of Windsor Castle. The palace's 144 rooms remained in use right up to WWII. To visit, you must join a guided tour, which costs 130/60 Kč with an English- or Czech-speaking guide.

The surrounding park is open throughout the year, as is the **Alšova jihočeská galerie** (admission 30 Kč), an exceptional collection of Gothic paintings and sculptures housed in a former riding school. The **information centre** (☎ 387 96 61 64; Masarykova 35), opposite the church, can help with accommodation.

ČESKÝ KRUMLOV
pop 14,600
Český Krumlov, a small medieval town 25km south of České Budějovice, is one of the most picturesque – and touristy – towns in Europe, its appearance almost unchanged since the 18th century. Built on a looping bend in the Vltava River, it has become a haven for Austrian tourists and backpackers. Its sprawling chateau occupies a ridge above the west bank of the river, while the old town centre sits on the tongue of land inside the loop on the east bank. To the southwest are the Šumava Hills, which separate Bohemia from both Austria and Bavaria.

Český Krumlov's Gothic border castle, rebuilt as a huge Renaissance chateau by 16th-century Italian architects, is second only to Prague Castle in size and splendour. The Renaissance lords of Rožmberk, whose seat this was, possessed the largest landed estate in Bohemia. In 1992 the town was added to Unesco's World Heritage List.

Orientation
Arriving by bus from České Budějovice, get off at the Český Krumlov Špičák bus stop, the first in town. The road on the bridge above this stop runs south to the Budějovická Gate, which leads directly into the old town.

The train station is 1.5km north of the old town centre. Bus Nos 1, 2 and 3 go from the station to the Špičák bus stop.

Information
The Český Krumlov **Infocentrum** (☎ 380 70 46 22, fax 380 70 46 19; ⓔ infocentrum@ ckrf.ckrumlov.cz; nám Svornosti 2; open 9am-8pm daily July & Aug, 9am-7pm daily June & Sept, 9am-6pm daily Apr, May & Oct, 9am-5pm daily Nov-Mar; closed noon-1pm Sat, Sun & holidays) is able to provide information about the town and region. It arranges accommodation, books tickets for concerts and the festivals, sells maps and guides, and organises tour guides. You can check email here for 10 Kč per 10 minutes.

ČESKÝ KRUMLOV

PLACES TO STAY
4 Hostel 99
6 Pension Ve Věži
23 Travellers' Hostel
25 Hotel Dvořák
33 Pension Myší Díra;
   Maleček Boat Rental
34 Hotel Růže
41 Krumlov House
42 U vodníka

PLACES TO EAT
14 Potraviny (Grocery)
24 Cikánská jizba

26 Dobrá Čajovna
27 Laibon
30 Restaurace Maštal
32 Krčma Barbakán
37 Hospoda Na louži

OTHER
1 24-Hour Pharmacy
   & Polyclinic
2 Špičák Bus Stop
3 Budějovická Gate
5 Post Office &
   Telephone Centre
7 Bus Station

8 Brewery
9 Minorite Monastery
10 Church of Božího
   Těla
11 Convent of the
   Poor Clares
12 Pension Lobo
13 Café Internet
15 Red Gate
16 Bear Pit
17 Round Tower
18 First Courtyard
19 Chateau Ticket Office

20 Castle
21 Chateau Theatre
22 Former Riding School
28 Raffeisen Bank
29 Infocentrum, Town
   Hall & Police
31 Regional Museum
35 Church of St Vitus
36 Plague Column
38 Vltava Travel
   Agency; Pension
   Vltava
39 U hada
40 M-club

To Train Station
(300m)

To Zlatá Koruna (6km) &
České Budějovice (22km)

CZECH REPUBLIC

0   100   200m
0   100   200yd

To Horní Planá
(29km)

TG Masaryka

Pod kamenem

Špičák

Věžní

Chvalšinská silnice

Jelení Zahrada

Polečnice

Pivovarská

Latrán

Klášterní

Nové – město

Castle Steps

Latrán

Most Na Plášti

Na ostrově

Weir

Zámecká zahrada
(Castle Gardens)

Dlouhá

Lázebnický Bridge

Vltava

Parkán

Vnitřní Město
(Inner Town)

Kaplická

Široká

Panská

Radniční

Masná

Horní

Rybářská

Soukenická

nám Svornosti

náměstí
Na louži

Roosevettova

Tavírna

Dlouhá

Kostelní

Kájovská

Dělní

Linecká

Městské sady

To Nové Spolí
Camp Site (1.5km),
Lake Lipno (24km)

The **Raiffeisen Bank** *(open 8.30am-4.30pm Mon-Fri)* on nám Svornosti changes travellers cheques and has an ATM.

The telephone centre is in the **post office** *(Latrán 81; 7am-6pm Mon-Fri, 7am-11am Sat)*. **Café Internet** *(open 8am-10pm daily June-Sept, 9am-8pm Oct-May)* in the Unios Tourist Service office in the first courtyard of the Chateau charges 1.50 Kč per minute.

Pension Lobo *(Latrán 73)* has a self-service laundrette.

There is a police station in nám Svornosti and a 24-hour pharmacy and polyclinic on TG Masaryka north of the centre.

Things to See

Two blocks south of the **Budějovická Gate** (1598) is the **Red Gate**, the main entrance to **Český Krumlov Chateau** *(open 9am-noon & 1pm-6pm daily July & Aug, 9am-noon & 1pm-5pm Apr, May, Sept & Oct)*. The chateau is said to be haunted by a white lady who appears from time to time to forecast doom.

You enter the first courtyard via a bridge across a bear pit. This is the oldest part of the chateau complex with its colourfully frescoed **round tower** *(admission 30 Kč)*, which looks like a space rocket designed by Hans Christian Andersen; there are great views from the top. The nearby ticket office sells tickets for three different tours of the chateau – Tour I (the Renaissance Rooms), Tour II (the Schwarzenberg Gallery) and the Theatre Tour (the chateau's stunning rococo theatre). Tours I and II in English/Czech are 140/70 Kč each, while the theatre tour costs 170/100 Kč. But you are free to wander through the courtyards and grounds without buying a ticket.

A path through the second and third courtyards leads across a bridge with a spectacular view to the baroque part of the castle. Beyond this a ramp to the right leads to the former **riding school**, now a restaurant. Cherubs above the door offer the head and boots of a vanquished Turk. From here the Italian-style chateau **gardens**, with the **'Bellarie' summer pavilion** and a modern revolving open-air theatre, stretch away to the southwest.

Nám Svornosti, the old town square across the river, is overlooked by the plain Gothic **town hall** and a baroque **plague column** (1716), and ringed by some pleasant outdoor cafés. Above the square is the striking Gothic **Church of St Vitus** (1439), and nearby is the **Regional Museum** *(admission 20 Kč; open* 10am-5pm Tues-Sun)*, with a surprisingly interesting collection housed in the old Jesuit seminary (1652). The scale model of Český Krumlov as it was in 1800 is a highlight.

Activities

In summer you can rent boats from **Maleček** (☎ 337 71 25 08; [e] lode@malecek.cz; Rooseveltova 28) at Pension Myší Díra. Prices range from 250 Kč for a half-hour splash through the town in a two-seater canoe, to 1650 Kč for a four-hour trip from Český Krumlov to Zlatá Koruna in a six-person raft. Longer trips are possible from Lake Lipno and Vyšší Brod down to Český Budějovice, at 380/980 Kč a day for a two/six-person raft.

The **Vltava Travel Agency** (☎ 71 19 78; Kájovská 62) can also organise boat trips, and rents kayaks, inflatable rafts, catamarans and bicycles; it also organises horse riding.

It's a pleasant two-hour bicycle ride southwest to Lake Lipno, involving a long, slow climb and a short drop to the lake, and a great downhill run on the way back. There are plenty of places to eat in Horní Planá. If the weather turns bad you can take your bike back to Český Krumlov from Horní Planá by train (seven a day).

Special Events

Infocentrum sells tickets to major festivals, including the Chamber Music Festival in late June and early July. The Pětilisté růže (Five-Petalled Rose) Festival in mid-June features two days of street performances, parades and medieval games.

Places to Stay

Camping On the east bank of the Vltava River, **Nové Spolí camp site** *(no ☎; U Vlaštovičníku, Nové Spolí; tent sites per person 30 Kč, plus per car 30 Kč; open June-Aug)* is about 2km south of town. The facilities are basic but the management is friendly and the location idyllic. Take bus No 3 from the train or bus station to the Spolí mat. šk. stop (eight a day on weekdays); otherwise it's a half-hour walk from the old town.

Hostels There are lots of backpacker hostels in town. The **Travellers' Hostel** (☎/fax 337 71 13 45; [e] krumlov@travellers.cz; Soukenická 43; dorm beds 250 Kč), operated by the Prague Travellers Hostel chain, has a lively bar and is popular with the party crowd.

Hostel 99 (☎ 377 71 28 12; ℮ hostel99@
hotmail.com; Věžní 99; dorm beds 250 Kč,
doubles 600 Kč) is another good place with a
cool sun terrace to hang out on.

Right next to the river, **U vodníka** (☎ 377
71 19 35; ℮ zukowski3@hotmail.com; Po-
vodě 55; doubles 600 Kč) is a much more
peaceful spot, down a cobbled lane off Rooseveltova. It has three double rooms, cooking
facilities, a small English library and a nice
garden. Nearby **Krumlov House** (Rooseveltova 68; dorm beds 250 Kč, doubles 800 Kč),
at the top of the hill, is under the same management, with accommodation in dorms or in
a suite with two double rooms. It has a potter's
wheel, darkroom and a washing machine.

Private Rooms & Pensions The Infocentrum has private rooms from 400 Kč per person with breakfast. You may also be offered
a private room by someone on the street. This
is fine, but check the location before you
agree to anything.

There are plenty of small pensions around
the town, with new ones appearing all the
time. In the same location as Vltava Travel
Agency, the **Pension Vltava** (☎ 377 71 19 78;
℮ ckvltava@ckvltava.cz; Kájovská 62; singles/
doubles 850/1200 Kč) is good.

In a great location overlooking the river,
Pension Myší Díra (☎ 337 71 28 53, fax 337
71 19 00; ℮ pension@ceskykrumlov-info.cz;
Rooseveltova 28; singles/doubles 1390/
1480) has bright, beautiful rooms with lots of
pale wood. Rates fall by 40% in winter

For character, you can't beat **Pension Ve
Věži** (☎/fax 337 71 17 42, ☎ 607 915 160;
℮ info@reality-kolar.cz; Pivovarská 28; dou-
bles/triples/quads 1200/1500/1800 Kč), set
in a fairy-tale medieval round tower. There
are only four rooms, so book well ahead.

Hotels Also overlooking the river, **Hotel
Dvořák** (☎ 377 71 10 20, fax 377 71 10 24;
℮ dvorak@ckmbox.vol.cz; Radniční 101;
singles/doubles 2800/3500 Kč) is good for a
splurge. The top place in town is the five-star
Hotel Růže (☎ 377 77 21 00, fax 377 71 31
46; ℮ info@hotelruze.cz; Horní 154; singles/
doubles 4000/4900 Kč), in a former Jesuit
college building dating from 1588.

Places to Eat
Cikánská jizba (Dlouhá 31; mains 65-85 Kč;
open 3pm-11pm Mon-Thur, 3pm-midnight

Fri & Sat) is a very popular and inexpensive
pub serving Czech food.

Restaurace Maštal (nám Svornosti 2;
mains 80-150 Kč; open 10.30am-10pm daily)
has a mixed menu that includes a few good
vegetarian dishes.

Laibon (Parkán 105; mains 55-95 Kč; open
noon-2pm & 6pm-10pm daily) is an excellent
vegetarian restaurant with an attractive terrace beside the river.

You can enjoy good Czech food at the traditional **Hospoda Na louži** (Kájovaská 66;
mains 60-100 Kč; open 9am-11pm daily) and
the Gothic cellar tavern of **Krčma Barbakán**
(Horní 26; mains 95-195 Kč; open 11am-
midnight daily mid-Apr–Oct, 3pm-midnight
Nov–mid-Apr). The latter has a superb terrace
perched high above the river.

Dobrá Čajovna (open 1pm-10pm daily)
tearoom opposite the bottom of the castle
steps on Latrán has a wide range of teas.

There's a **potraviny** (grocery; open 7am-
6pm Mon-Fri, 7am-noon Sat, 9am-3pm Sun)
on Latrán, opposite the chateau entrance.

Entertainment
M-Club (cnr Rybářská & Plešivecké schody;
4pm-2am daily) offers pounding rock music
and a pool table.

Just a few doors west, on the same side of
Rybářská, is **U hada** (open 7pm-3am Mon-
Thur, 7pm-4am Fri & Sat, 7pm-2am Sun), a
hang-out for the rap/techno crowd.

Getting There & Away
The best way to get to Český Krumlov is by
bus, with a fast service from České Budějovice (26 Kč, 45 minutes). Trains are slower
(32 Kč, one hour) and the station is several
kilometres north of town (although it's an
easy downhill walk into town).

AROUND ČESKÝ KRUMLOV
Zlatá Koruna
Above the Vltava in the small village of Zlatá
Koruna is one of the country's best-preserved
Gothic Cistercian monasteries, founded in
1263 by Přemysl Otakar II. The monastery
cathedral is clearly a Gothic building despite
its baroque facelift.

The monastery complex also houses the
Museum of South Bohemian Literature (ad-
mission 55 Kč; open 9am-noon & 1pm-4pm
Tues-Sun Apr-Oct). Trains here from Český
Krumlov are much more frequent than buses.

ŠUMAVA

The Šumava is a range of thickly wooded hills stretching for 125km along the border with Austria and Germany; the highest summit is Plechý (1378m), west of Horní Planá. The range is popular for hiking, cycling and cross-country skiing. You can hike the length of the national park, from Nová Pec, at the northern tip of Lake Lipno, up to Nýrsko, southwest of Klatovy.

Maps

The best hiking map is Klub Českých turistů's *Šumava* (1:50,000) and for cyclists there is SHOCart's *Šumava Trojmezí velká cykloturistická* (1:75,000) map.

National Park Walks

The **Povydří trail** along the Vydra (Otter) River is one of the most popular walks in the park. It is an easy 7km trail along a deep, forested river valley between Čeňkova Pila and Antýgl. The walk takes approximately two hours, with the Vydra itself running alongside between huge rounded boulders. There are about five buses a day running between Sušice and Modrava, stopping at Čeňkova Pila and Antýgl. Most of these places have plenty of accommodation.

Around the peak of **Boubín** (1362m), the 46-hectare *prales* (virgin forest) is the only part of the Šumava forest that is regarded as completely untouched. The trailhead is 2km northeast of the zastávka Zátoň train stop (not Zátoň town train station) at Kaplice, where there is a car park and a basic camping ground. From here it's an easy 2.5km to U pralesa Lake on a blue and green marked trail. To reach the top of Boubín peak, remain on the blue trail; it's a further 7.5km to the top. To return follow the trail southwest to complete the loop. The complete loop should take about five hours.

Getting There & Away

Šumava can be approached along three roads: road 169 via Sušice, road 4 via Strakonice and Vimperk, or road 141 via Prachatice and Volary. Regular buses and trains cover these routes. Up to eight trains a day run between the scenic route of Volary and Strakonice, stopping at Lenora, zastávka Zátoň and Horní Vltavice; the first two stops are several kilometres from their respective towns (Kubova Huť and Vimperk).

TÁBOR

pop 36,800

The Hussites – 'God's warriors' – founded Tábor in 1420 as a military bastion standing in defiance of Catholic Europe. The town was organised according to the precept that 'nothing is mine and nothing is yours, because the community is owned equally by everyone'. New arrivals threw all their worldly possessions into large casks at the marketplace and joined in communal work. This nonconformism helped to give the word 'Bohemian' its present-day connotations.

Planned as a bulwark against Catholics in České Budějovice and farther south, Tábor is a warren of narrow zigzag streets with protruding houses that were intended to disorient enemy attackers. Below ground, 14km of catacombs provided a refuge for the defenders. This friendly old town, 100km south of Prague, is well worth a brief stop.

Orientation & Information

From the train station walk west through the park past the bus station. Go west down třída 9.května, the main shopping street, till you reach a major intersection. Žižkovo nám, the old town square, is straight ahead on Palackého třída, 15 minutes' walk from the stations.

The municipal **Infocentrum** (☎ 381 48 62 30; e infocentrum@mu.tabor.cz; Žižkovo nám 2; open 8.30am-7pm Mon-Fri, 9am-1pm Sat, 1pm-5pm Sun May-Sept, 9am-4pm Mon-Fri Oct-Apr) is very helpful and informative. It sells maps and will organise your accommodation and guided tours.

Česká spořitelna (třída 9.května 10) changes travellers cheques and has an ATM. The **post office**, icluding the telephone centre, is in the pink building on the opposite side of Žižkovo nám from the museum. The **Internetový klub Euro** (Farského 17; open 9am-8pm Mon-Thur, 9am-6pm Fri, 1pm-6pm Sat) has Internet access at 60 Kč per hour.

Things to See

Unless otherwise stated, all museums are open from 8.30am to 5pm daily from April and October, and weekdays only during the rest of the year.

A statue of the Hussite commander Jan Žižka graces Žižkovo nám. Žižka's military successes were due to the novel use of peasant wagons (you can see one in the Hussite museum) against crusading Catholic knights.

CZECH REPUBLIC

BRNO

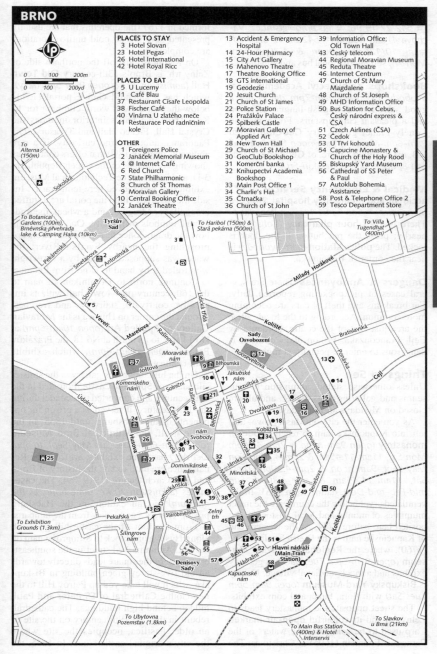

PLACES TO STAY
3 Hotel Slovan
23 Hotel Pegas
26 Hotel International
42 Hotel Royal Ricc

PLACES TO EAT
5 U Lucerny
11 Café Blau
37 Restaurant Císaře Leopolda
38 Fischer Café
40 Vinárna U zlatého meče
41 Restaurace Pod radničním kole

OTHER
1 Foreigners Police
2 Janáček Memorial Museum
4 @ Internet Café
6 Red Church
7 State Philharmonic
8 Church of St Thomas
9 Moravian Gallery
10 Central Booking Office
12 Janáček Theatre
13 Accident & Emergency Hospital
14 24-Hour Pharmacy
15 City Art Gallery
16 Mahenovo Theatre
17 Theatre Booking Office
18 GTS international
19 Geodezie
20 Jesuit Church
21 Church of St James
22 Police Station
24 Pražákův Palace
25 Špilberk Castle
27 Moravian Gallery of Applied Art
28 New Town Hall
29 Church of St Michael
30 GeoClub Bookshop
31 Komerční banka
32 Knihupectví Academia Bookshop
33 Main Post Office 1
34 Charlie's Hat
35 Čtrnačka
36 Church of St John
39 Information Office; Old Town Hall
43 Český telecom
44 Regional Moravian Museum
45 Reduta Theatre
46 Internet Centrum
47 Church of St Mary Magdalene
48 Church of St Joseph
49 MHD Information Office
50 Bus Station for Čebus, Český národní express & ČSA
51 Czech Airlines (ČSA)
52 Čedok
53 U Tří kohoutů
54 Capucine Monastery & Church of the Holy Rood
55 Biskupský Yard Museum
56 Cathedral of SS Peter & Paul
57 Autoklub Bohemia Assistance
58 Post & Telephone Office 2
59 Tesco Department Store

The youth travel agency **GTS International** (☎ 542 22 19 96; e gts.brno@gtsint.cz; Vachova 4) and **Čedok** (☎ 542 32 12 67; Nádražní 10/12; 9am-noon & 1.30pm-5pm Mon-Fri) sell international bus and tain tickets.

Bookshops Knihupectvi **Academia** (nám Svobody 13; open 9am-7pm daily) has a good selection of English-language fiction and a pleasant café upstairs. For maps and Lonely Planet guides, try **GeoClub** (open 9am-6pm Mon-Fri, 9am-noon Sat) in Pasaž KB, off the main square, or **Geodezie** (Vachova 8; open 9am-6pm Mon-Fri).

Medical & Emergency Services Brno's accident and emergency hospital (Urazova nemocnice; ☎ 545 53 81 11) is at Ponávka 6. There is a **24-hour pharmacy** (Koliště 47) nearby; press the red button if the door is locked. The **police station** (nám Svobody) is near the corner of Běhounská.

Dangers & Annoyances There are several cases of pickpocketing reported daily. Car break-ins and theft of cars are becoming more common. According to the local police the area just east of the centre, bordered by Cejl, Francouzská, Příkop and Ponávka, is dangerous to enter, especially at night.

Things to See

Unless otherwise stated, admission to museums and galleries costs 40 Kč, and all are closed on Mondays and Tuesdays.

As you enter the city on Masarykova, turn left into Kapučínské nám to reach **Capuchin monastery** (open 9am-noon & 2pm-4.30pm Mon-Sat, 11am-11.45am & 2pm-4.30pm Sun May-Sept; 9am-noon & 2pm-4.30pm Tues-Sat, 11am-11.45am & 2pm-4.30pm Sun mid-Feb–mid-Dec), dating from 1651. In the ventilated crypt below the church are the intact mummies of monks and local aristocrats deposited here before 1784. At the western end of Kapučínské nám is the Dietrichstein Palace (1760), where the **Regional Moravian Museum** (open 9am-5pm Tues-Sat) has geology exhibits and a mock medieval village. Nearby is **Biskupský Yard Museum** (open 9am-5pm Tues-Sat) with flora, fauna and coin exhibits.

The street opposite the monastery leads to Zelný trh and its colourful **open-air market**. Carp used to be sold from the waters of the Parnassus Fountain (1695) at Christmas. The nearby **Reduta Theatre** is where Mozart performed in 1767 (the operettas that are usually presented here are on hold until restorations are completed).

On Radnická, just off the northern side of Zelný trh, is Brno's 13th-century **Old Town Hall** (admission 20 Kč; open 9am-5pm daily), which has a splendid Gothic portal (1511) below the tower (well worth climbing for 10 Kč). The town hall's interior includes the Crystal Hall, Fresco Hall and Treasury. The Panorama, another Brno curiosity, is a rare apparatus made in 1890 that offers continuous showings of images of the Czech Republic in 3-D, and is part of the Technological Museum exhibit that was moved here temporarily. Inside the passage behind the portal are a stuffed crocodile, or 'dragon', and a wheel, the traditional symbols of the city. One legend tells how the dragon once terrorised wayfarers approaching the nearby Svratka River; the wheel was supposedly made by a cartwright who rolled it by hand to Brno from Lednice.

Continue north to Dominikánské nám to the 16th-century **new town hall** with its impressive courtyard, stairways and frescoes. Around the corner on Husova is the **Moravian Gallery of Applied Art** (open 10am-6pm) at No 14 and, to its north at No 18, the **Pražákův Palace** (open 10am-6pm), which exhibits 20th-century Czech art.

On the hill above this gallery is the sinister silhouette of **Špilberk Castle**. Founded in the 13th century and converted to a citadel during the 17th century, it served as a prison for opponents of the Habsburgs until 1855. In the castle itself, the **Municipal Brno Museum** (open 9am-6pm Tues-Sun May-Sept, to 5pm Oct-Apr) has three exhibits: art from the Renaissance era until today; the history of Brno; and Brno architecture (1919–39). The **casemates** (admission 20 Kč; same hours as the museum) has an exhibit on the Habsburg prison. There's a good view from the ramparts.

From the foot of the castle hill go south along Husova one block to Šilingrovo nám on the left. An unmarked street in the southeastern corner of the square leads directly towards an old five-storey green building in Biskupská, which will take you up Petrov Hill to the neo-Gothic **Cathedral of SS Peter and Paul**, hidden behind high buildings. The cathedral, rebuilt in the late 19th century on the site of an older basilica, occupies the site where the city's original castle stood. In 1645, the

Swedish general Torstensson who was besieging Brno declared that he would leave if his troops hadn't captured the city by noon. At 11am the Swedes were about to scale the walls when the cathedral bell keeper suddenly rang noon. True to his word, the general broke off the attack; since that day the cathedral bells have always rung noon at 11am.

From Petrov Hill descend Petrská into Zelný trh and continue on Orlí to Minoritská and the **Church of St John** (rebuilt in 1733) which has fine altarpieces, an organ and painted ceilings. Nám Svobody – the city's broad main square – has a striking plague column (1680). North of the square is the parish church, **St James** (1473), with a soaring nave in the purest Gothic style. The **Church of St Thomas** and the former Augustinian monastery, which is now the **Moravian Gallery** (open 10am-6pm), are just north again on Moravské nám.

Also worth seeing is the **City Art Gallery** (Dům umění; Malinovského nám 2; admission 30 Kč; open 10am-6pm Tues-Sun), next to the Mahenovo Theatre east of the centre. Excellent art exhibitions are often staged here.

Other good museums are the **Janáček Memorial Museum** (Smetanova 14; open 8am-noon & 1pm-4pm Mon-Fri), which is a house-museum dedicated to the composer, and the **Mendelianum**, which records the work of Gregor Mendel (at the time of research the Mendelianum was closed and searching for new premises). The functionalist **Vila Tugendhat** (Černopolní 45; admission 80 Kč; open 10am-6pm), is a shrine for fans of modern architecture.

Language Courses
If you'd like to learn Czech, contact either **Lingua centrum** (☎ 543 23 44 34; Křenova 52), or **U tří kohoutů** (☎ 542 32 13 09; Masarykova 32). Rates begin at about 200 Kč per hour.

Special Events
The annual Brno Motorcycle Grand Prix is held at the end of August.

Places to Stay
Brno hosts international trade fairs all year round and accommodation is a problem during the main ones in February, March, April, August, September and October. Before you arrive, check carefully that your visit does not coincide with one of these three- or four-day fairs – as hotels fill, rates can almost double and all public facilities are very overcrowded.

Camping The attractive **Camping Hana** (☎/fax 549 42 03 31; e camping.hana@ quick.cz; Veverská bítýška; tent sites 40-60 Kč plus per person 80 Kč, car 60 Kč; open May-Sept) is at the northwestern end of Brněnska přehrada lake, about 10km northwest of the city centre. From the train station take tram No 4 eastbound to the third stop (Česká), then tram No 3 or 11 to the Přistavistě stop, then bus 103 to Veverská bítýška. In summer you can also take a boat along the lake from Přistavistě.

Hostels Both **Čedok** and **GTS International** (see Information, earlier) can arrange accommodation in student dormitories during July and August.

South of the centre, the HI-listed **Hotel Interservis** (☎ 545 23 42 32; Lomená; beds from 225 Kč) rents beds in double rooms. Take tram No 12 eastbound from the train station to the end of the line, go through the underpass and continue south on the main road, then turn left along Pompova. The hostel is the tall block of flats rising behind the houses on the right.

Ubytovna Pozemstav (☎ 543 21 47 63, fax 543 21 53 08; e hotel.brno@brn.czn.cz; Horní 19; singles/doubles 200/300 Kč) is a similar distance southwest of the centre. Take tram No 2 westbound from the train station to the Celní stop. Walk on about 100m, turn right on Celní and then take the second left on Horní; the hostel is near Hotel Brno at the end of the street.

Private Rooms From 550 Kč per person a night **Čedok** can arrange private rooms. Most are far from the centre but can easily be reached on public transport. **Infocentrum** also has private rooms from 350 Kč.

Hotels On a quiet street right in the centre of town is **Hotel Pegas** (☎ 542 21 01 04, fax 542 21 43 14; Jakubská 4; singles/doubles 1200/1700 Kč). Rooms are bright and clean and come with bath and breakfast.

Hotel Slovan (☎ 541 32 12 07, fax 541 21 11 37; e hotel@hotelslovan.cz; Lidická 23; singles/doubles 1200/1800 Kč) is a pleasant-enough business hotel just north of the centre.

One of the top hotels is the baroque **Hotel Royal Ricc** (☎ *542 21 92 62, fax 542 21 92 65;* e *hotelroyalricc@brn.inecnet.cz; Starobrněnská 10; singles/doubles 2500/2800 Kč*), with smallish luxury historical rooms. Another is the Best Western **Hotel International** (☎ *42 12 28 11, fax 42 21 08 43;* e *sales@ hotelinternational.cz; Husova 16; singles/ doubles 2490/2990 Kč*) near the castle.

Places to Eat

The touristy **Pivnice Pegas** (*Jakubská 4; mains 60-100 Kč; open 9am-midnight daily*) is an attractive place with an extensive menu in English. The food is reasonable, and it brews its own beer on the premises.

An inexpensive and pleasant place to order a bottle of local wine with your meal is **Vinárna U zlatého meče** (*Mečová 3; mains 60-110 Kč; open 11am-10pm Mon-Thur, 11am-2am Fri & Sat, 11am-4pm Sun*). Nearby **Restaurace Pod radničním kole** (*Mečová 5; mains 80-150 Kč; open 11am-midnight daily*) is a red-brick cellar with good Moravian food and plenty of charming atmosphere.

Restaurant Císaře Leopolda (*Orlí 3; mains 85-125 Kč; open 11am-11pm Mon-Thur, 11am-midnight Fri & Sat, noon-10pm Sun*) serves hearty Italian dishes. The popular **U Lucerny** (*Slovákova 2; mains 90-150 Kč; open 11am-midnight daily*) is another excellent Italian restaurant with a garden out back in summer.

Haribol (*Lužanecká 4; mains 50-90 Kč; open 11am-4pm Mon-Fri*) is a vegetarian restaurant with some Indian dishes.

For good coffee, you can try the small and intimate **Café Blau** (*Běhounská 18*), or the stylish **Fischer Café** (*cnr Masarykovo & Orlí*).

There's a good **supermarket** in the basement of Tesco behind the train station on the way to the bus station.

Entertainment

Brno's theatres are excellent (although they close in midsummer). The tickets aren't cornered by scalpers and profiteers as they are in Prague, but you are expected to dress up a bit.

Opera, operettas and ballet are performed at the modern **Janáček Theatre** (*Janáčkovo divadlo; Sady Osvobození*), named after the composer Leoš Janáček, who spent much of his life in Brno.

The neobaroque **Mahenovo Theatre** (Mahenovo divadlo), a beautifully decorated old-style theatre in an 1882 building designed by the famous Viennese theatrical architects Fellner and Hellmer, presents classical drama in Czech and operettas.

The **Brno State Philharmonic** (*Státní filharmonie Brno, SFB; Komenského nám 8*), in Besední dům (the entrance is from Husova), has regular concerts. Tickets can be bought from **SFB** in Besední dům.

For tickets to the Janáček and Mahenovo theatres, go to the small **booking office** (*předprodej;* ☎ *542 32 12 85; Dvořákova 11; open 8am-5.30pm Mon-Fri, 9am-noon Sat*) behind the Mahenovo Theatre.

The **Central Booking Office** (*Centrální předprodej; Běhounská 17*) sells tickets to classical, rock and folk concerts at a variety of venues.

Bars & Clubs

Popular **Charlie's Hat** (*Kobližná 12; open 11am-4am*) is a cellar bar with many rooms and a small dance floor where DJs spin anything from heavy rock to dance music. Nearby restaurant and bar **Čtrnáčka** (*Jánská 14; open 11am-11pm Mon-Sat*) is hugely popular with students.

North of the city centre is **Stará pekárna** (*Štefánikova 8; open 5pm-1am daily*), with live bands playing a variety of styles, including jazz, funk and rock on most nights.

Alterna (*Kounicova 48, block B; open 7pm-12.30am daily*) is an alternative *klub* where you can enjoy some live rock, punk, jazz and other alternative entertainment. From Česká take trolleybus No 134 or 136 three stops north.

Getting There & Away

Bus The bus to Vienna–Mitte Bahnhof (350 Kč, 2½ hours) departs from platform No 20 at the main bus station twice a day. There are also buses to Prague (140 Kč, 2½ hours). For shorter trips such as Telč (86 Kč, two hours) buses are faster and more efficient than trains.

Train All trains running between Budapest and Berlin stop at Brno. If you're going to or from Vienna, change trains at Břeclav. To get to or from Košice, change trains at Přerov. There are also frequent direct trains between Brno and Bratislava (two hours, 141km) and Prague (242 Kč, 2¾ hours).

Three overnight trains with couchettes and sleepers travel between Brno and Košice. Reserve international tickets, couchettes or sleepers at windows to the right of the main entrance in the train station.

Getting Around

You can buy public transport tickets from shops, vending machines and the **MHD Information Office** (*Novobranská 18; open 6am-6pm Mon-Fri, 8am-3.30pm Sat & Sun*). Tickets valid for 10/40/60 minutes cost 7/12/15 Kč, 24-hour tickets are 48 Kč and seven-day tickets are 165 Kč.

AROUND BRNO
Slavkov u Brna

Slavkov u Brna, 21km east of Brno, is better known to history by its Austrian name – Austerlitz. On 2 December 1805, the famous 'Battle of the Three Emperors' took place in the open, rolling countryside between Brno and Slavkov u Brna, where Napoleon Bonaparte's French army defeated the combined forces of Emperor Franz I (Austria) and Tsar Alexander I (Russia). The battle was decided at **Pracký kopec**, a hill 12km west of Slavkov, marked by a monumental chapel (1912) and a small museum. After the battle Napoleon spent four days concluding an armistice at Slavkov's baroque **chateau** (*Slavkov Zámek; open 9am-6pm daily July & Aug; 9am-5pm May, June & Sept; 9am-4pm Apr, Oct & Nov; closed Mon Apr, May & Sept-Nov*), where you can visit the ornate rooms and gallery (route A), or the Napoleonic exhibit (route B). Tours in Czech/English cost 45 Kč/80 Kč.

Slavkov u Brna is easily accessible by bus or train from Brno, but Pracký kopec is difficult to reach by public transport. You can get a bus from Brno's bus station to Prace (nine a day – ask to get off at Náves stop), from where it is a 1.6km walk south to the top of the hill. On weekends it is better to catch one of the more frequent Brno–Slavkov trains (14km, 10 a day), getting off at Potovice and walking the 3.5km southeast through Prace.

Moravian Karst

The limestone plateau of the Moravský kras (Moravian Karst), 20km north of Brno, is riddled with caves and canyons carved by the Punkva River.

The **Ústřední informační služba** of Moravský kras (☎ *516 41 35 75; Skalní Mlýn*) provides information and books accommodation and tickets for the caves.

The Caves A tour of the famous **Punkevní Cave** (*admission 80 Kč; open 8.20am-3.50pm daily Apr-Sept; 8.40am-2pm Mon-Fri, 8.20am-3.40pm Sat & Sun Oct; 8.40am-2pm daily Nov-Mar*) takes 75 minutes, and involves a 1km walk through caverns draped with stalactites and stalagmites to the bottom of the Macocha Abyss, where you board a small boat for a 400m ride along an underground river and out of the cave.

Kateřinská Cave (*admission 40 Kč*) has similar opening hours to Punkevní, except that it's closed from November to January. On weekends and in midsummer, all the tickets will usually have been sold two hours or more before the tours are due to commence, so be sure to arrive early. A shuttle 'train' covers the 2km road between the car park and the cave entrance (40 Kč), or you can walk there in 30 minutes.

From Punkevní it's a 15-minute hike, or an easy gondola ride (50 Kč return, 70 Kč for a combined ticket with the train), to the top of the 139m-deep Macocha Abyss. Other caves in the area include Balčárka and Sloupsko-Šošuvské (both have similar hours to Kateřinská – contact the information service). Traces of prehistoric humans have been found in the caves.

Places to Stay & Eat Near the Macocha Abyss is the hostel and restaurant **Chata Macocha** (*dorm beds 210 Kč*); book at Hotel Skalní Mlýn. The pricier **Hotel Skalní Mlýn** (☎ *516 41 81 13, fax 516 41 81 14;* e *smk@smk.cz; singles/doubles from 990/1290 Kč*) is beside the car park in Skalní Mlýn.

Getting There & Away From Brno, take one of the frequent trains to Blansko (24 Kč, 30 minutes). From the nearby bus station, there are buses to Skalní Mlýn at 7.40am, 9.15am and 11.40am, returning at 3.25pm and 5.10pm (May to September); the rest of the year there is only the 7.40am bus there and the 3.25pm bus back. Check times at the Brno tourist office before setting off. You can also hike an 8km trail from Blansko to Skalní Mlýn (two hours).

Germany

Few countries in Western Europe have such a fascinating and complicated past as Germany, and much of this history is easily explored by visitors today. It is also a country of sheer beauty, where outdoor activity is a way of life, and there is a huge variety of museums, architecture from many historical periods and a heavy emphasis on cultural pursuits. Infrastructure is well organised, there is plenty of accommodation, and the frothy beer, heady wine and hearty food are superb.

Germany's reunification in 1990 was the beginning of yet another intriguing chapter, more than a decade old yet hardly forgotten. Though some cultural, social and economic differences of the formerly separate Germanys still exist, visitors will find that they both have their – significant – charms.

Facts about Germany

HISTORY
Events in Germany have often dominated Europe's history. But for many centuries Germany was a patchwork of semi-independent principalities and city-states, preoccupied with internal quarrels and at the mercy of foreign conquerors. In the 18th and 19th centuries, these squabbling territories gradually came under the control of Prussia, a state created by the rulers of Brandenburg. Germany only became a nation-state in 1871 and, despite the momentous events that have occurred since, many Germans still retain a strong regional identity.

Ancient & Medieval History
Germany west of the Rhine and south of the Main was part of the Roman Empire, but Roman legions never managed to subdue the warrior tribes beyond. As the Roman Empire crumbled, these tribes spread out over much of Europe, establishing small kingdoms. The Frankish conqueror Charlemagne, from his court in Aachen, forged a huge empire that covered most of Christian Western Europe, but it broke up after his death in AD 814.

The eastern branch of Charlemagne's empire developed in AD 962 into the Holy

Roman Empire, organised under Otto I (Otto the Great). It included much of present-day Germany, Austria, Switzerland and Benelux. The term 'Holy Roman' was coined in an effort to assume some of the authority of the defunct Roman Empire.

The house of Habsburg, ruling from Vienna, took control of the shrinking empire in the 13th century, which became little more than a conglomerate of German-speaking states run by local rulers who paid mere lip service to the Habsburg emperor. A semblance

of unity in northern Germany was maintained by the Hanseatic League, a federation of German and Baltic city-states with Lübeck as its centre. The League began to form in the mid-12th century and dissolved in 1669.

The Reformation

Things would never be the same in Europe after Martin Luther, a scholar from the monastery in Erfurt, nailed his *95 Theses* to the church door in Wittenberg in 1517. Luther opposed the Catholic Church's system involving the selling of so-called 'indulgences', which absolved sinners from temporal punishment. In 1521 he was condemned by the Church and went into hiding in Wartburg Castle in Eisenach. There he translated the Bible from the Greek version into an everyday form of German. This Bible was printed on presses developed by Gutenberg in Mainz and was then read widely to the masses.

Luther's efforts at reforming the Church gained widespread support from merchants, wealthy townsfolk and, crucially, several ambitious German princes. This protest against the established Church began the Protestant movement and the Reformation. The Peace of Augsburg in 1555 declared that the religion of a state would be determined by its ruler.

Meanwhile the established Church, often called the 'Roman' Catholic Church, began a campaign known as the Counter-Reformation to stem the spread of Protestantism.

Thirty Years' War

The tensions between Protestant and Catholic states across Europe led to the catastrophic Thirty Years' War (1618–48). Germany became the battlefield for the great powers of Europe, losing more than one-third of its population and many of its towns and cities. It took the country centuries to recover.

The Peace of Westphalia in 1648 established the rights of both faiths in Germany but also sealed the country's political division. The German-speaking states remained a patchwork of independent principalities within the loose framework of the Holy Roman Empire, but were weakened further by the loss of important territories.

Prussia Unites Germany

During the 18th century the Kingdom of Prussia, with its capital in Berlin, became one of Europe's strongest powers. Thanks to the organisational talents of Friedrich Wilhelm I (the Soldier King) and his son Friedrich II (Frederick the Great), it expanded eastwards at the expense of Poland, Lithuania and Russia.

In the early 19th century, the fragmented German states proved easy pickings for Napoleon. The Austrian emperor, Francis II, relinquished his crown as Holy Roman Emperor in 1806 following his defeat at Austerlitz. But the French never quite managed to subdue Prussia, which became the centre of German resistance. After his disastrous foray into Russia, Prussia led the war that put an end to Napoleon's German aspirations in a decisive battle at Leipzig in 1813.

In 1815 the Congress of Vienna again redrew the map of Europe. The Holy Roman Empire was replaced with a German Confederation of 35 states; it had a parliament in Frankfurt and was led by the Austrian chancellor Klemens von Metternich. The Confederation was shaken by liberal revolutions in Europe in 1830 and 1848, but the Austrian monarchy continued to dominate a divided Germany.

The well-oiled Prussian civil and military machine eventually smashed this arrangement. In 1866, Otto von Bismarck (the Iron Chancellor) took Prussia to war against Austria, and rapidly annexed northern Germany. Another successful war in 1870–71 resulted in Prussia defeating France and seizing Alsace and Lorraine. The Catholic, anti-Prussian states in southern Germany were forced to negotiate with Bismarck, who had achieved his dream of German unity. The Prussian king, Wilhelm I, became *Kaiser* (German emperor).

WWI & the Rise of Hitler

Wilhelm II dismissed Bismarck in 1890, however, Germany's rapid growth overtaxed the Kaiser's political talents and led to mounting tensions with England, Russia and France. When war broke out in 1914, Germany's only ally was a weakened Austria-Hungary.

Gruelling trench warfare on two fronts sapped the nation's resources, and by late 1918 Germany sued for peace. The Kaiser abdicated and escaped to Holland. Anger on the home front, which had been mounting during the fighting and deprivation, exploded when the troops returned home. A full-scale socialist uprising, based in Berlin and led by the Spartacus League, was put down, and its leaders, Karl Liebknecht and Rosa Luxemburg, were murdered. A new republic, which became known as the Weimar Republic, was proclaimed.

The Treaty of Versailles in 1919 chopped huge areas off Germany and imposed heavy reparation payments. These were impossible to meet, and when France and Belgium occupied the Rhineland to ensure continued payments, the subsequent hyperinflation and miserable economic conditions provided fertile ground for political extremists. One of these was Adolf Hitler.

Led by Hitler, an Austrian drifter and German army veteran, the National (or Nazi) Socialist German Workers' Party staged an abortive coup in Munich in 1923. This landed Hitler in prison for nine months, during which time he wrote *Mein Kampf.*

From 1929 the worldwide economic depression hit Germany particularly hard, leading to massive unemployment, strikes and demonstrations. The Communist Party under Ernst Thälmann gained strength, but wealthy industrialists began to support the Nazis and police turned a blind eye to Nazi street thugs.

The Nazis increased their strength in general elections and in 1933 replaced the Social Democrats as the largest party in the Reichstag (parliament), with about one-third of the seats. Hitler was appointed chancellor and one year later assumed absolute control as *Führer* (leader) of what he called the Third Reich (the 'third empire'; the previous two being the Holy Roman Empire and Wilhelm I's German Empire).

WWII & the Division of Germany

From 1935 Germany began to re-arm and build its way out of depression with strategic public works such as the autobahns. Hitler reoccupied the Rhineland in 1936, and in 1938 annexed Austria and, following a compromise agreement with Britain and France, parts of Czechoslovakia.

All of this took place against a backdrop of growing racism at home. The Nuremburg Laws of 1935 deprived non-Aryans – mostly Jews and Roma (Gypsies) – of German citizenship and many other rights. On 9 November 1938, the horror escalated into the *Reichspogromnacht* (often called *Kristallnacht* or the 'night of broken glass'), in which synagogues and Jewish cemeteries, property and businesses across Germany were desecrated, burnt or demolished.

In September 1939, after signing a pact that allowed both Stalin and himself a free hand in the east of Europe, Hitler attacked Poland, which led to war with Britain and France. Germany quickly invaded large parts of Europe, but after 1942 began to suffer increasingly heavy losses. Massive bombing reduced Germany's centres to rubble, and the country lost 10% of its population. Meanwhile, Nazi racism was creating unprecedented horrors. 'Concentration camps' were intended to rid Europe of people considered undesirable according to Nazi doctrine, with the resulting extermination of some six million Jews and one million more Roma, communists, homosexuals and others in what has come to be known as 'the Holocaust,' history's first 'assembly-line' genocide. Germany accepted unconditional surrender in May 1945, soon after Hitler's suicide.

At conferences in Yalta and Potsdam, the Allies (the Soviet Union, the USA, the UK and France) redrew the borders of Germany, making it around 25% smaller than it had already become after the Treaty of Versailles 26 years earlier. Some 6.5 million ethnic Germans migrated or were expelled to Germany from Eastern Europe, where they had lived for centuries. Germany was divided into four occupation zones, and Berlin was occupied jointly by the four victorious powers.

In the Soviet zone of the country, the communist Socialist Unity Party (SED) won the 1946 elections and began a rapid nationalisation of industry. In June 1948 the Soviet Union stopped all land traffic between Germany's western zones and Berlin. This forced the Western allies to mount a military operation known as the Berlin Airlift, which brought food and other supplies to West Berlin by plane until the Soviets lifted the blockade in May 1949.

In September 1949 the Federal Republic of Germany (FRG) was created out of the three western zones; in response the German Democratic Republic (GDR) was founded in the Soviet zone the following month, with (East) Berlin as its capital.

From Division to Unity

As the West's bulwark against communism, the FRG received massive injections of US capital, and experienced rapid economic development (the *Wirtschaftswunder,* or 'economic miracle') under the leadership of Konrad Adenauer. At the same time the

GDR had to pay US$10 billion in war reparations to the Soviet Union and rebuild itself from scratch.

A better life in the west increasingly attracted skilled workers away from the miserable economic conditions in the east. As these were people the GDR could ill afford to lose, in 1961 it built a wall around West Berlin and sealed its border with the FRG. As the Cold War intensified, TV and radio stations in both Germanys beamed programmes heavy with propaganda to the other side.

Coinciding with a change to the more flexible leadership of Erich Honecker in the east, the *Ostpolitik* of FRG chancellor Willy Brandt allowed an easier political relationship between the two Germanys. In 1971 the four occupying powers formally accepted the division of Berlin. Many Western countries, but not West Germany itself, then officially recognised the GDR.

Honecker's policies produced higher living standards in the GDR, yet East Germany barely managed to achieve a level of prosperity half that of the FRG. After Mikhail Gorbachev came to power in the Soviet Union in March 1985, the East German communists gradually lost Soviet backing.

Events in 1989 rapidly overtook the East German government, which resisted pressure to introduce reforms. When Hungary relaxed its border controls in May 1989, East Germans began crossing to the west. Tighter travel controls introduced by the Politburo resulted in would-be defectors taking refuge in the FRG's embassy in Prague. Meanwhile, mass demonstrations in Leipzig spread to other cities of the GDR and Honecker was replaced by his security chief, Egon Krenz, who introduced cosmetic reforms. Then suddenly on 9 November 1989, a Politburo decision to allow direct travel to the west was mistakenly interpreted as the immediate opening of all GDR borders with West Germany. That same night thousands of people streamed into the west past stunned border guards. Millions more followed in the next few days, and dismantling of the Berlin Wall began soon thereafter.

The trend at first was to reform the GDR but, in East German elections held in early 1990, citizens voted clearly in favour of the Christian Democratic Union (CDU), thus paving the way for fast-track reunification. The wartime Allies signed the Two-Plus-Four Treaty which ended the postwar system of occupation zones, and a Unification Treaty was drawn up to integrate East Germany into the Federal Republic of Germany, which came about on 3 October 1990. All-German elections were held on 2 December that year and, in the midst of national euphoria, the CDU-led coalition, which strongly favoured reunification, soundly defeated the Social Democrat opposition, earning the CDU's leader, Helmut Kohl, the moniker of 'unification chancellor'.

The Land in the Middle

In 1998, a coalition of Social Democrats, led by Gerhard Schröder, and Bündnis 90/the Green party took political office from Kohl and the CDU. Schröder and the SDP-Greens coalition narrowly retained office in the 2002 election, although the close result foreshadowed a period of instability.

At reunification, it was said that it would take 10 years to bring the two Germanys to parity, but now it's generally considered that another 10 years will be needed. Unemployment in some eastern states hovers above 20%, there have been occasionally violent attacks on foreigners, and the German 'economic miracle' seems to be losing steam.

Still, Germany, the 'land in the middle', is more confident than it was under division and more democratic, and it has assumed a more assertive role in world affairs, strongly bound to the European Union (EU) but also focusing attention on the East.

GEOGRAPHY

Germany covers 356,866 sq km and can be divided from north to south into several geographical regions.

The Northern Lowlands are a broad expanse of flat, low-lying land that sweeps across the northern third of the country from the Netherlands into Poland. The landscape is characterised by moist heaths interspersed with pastures and farmland.

The complex Central Uplands region divides northern Germany from the south. Extending from the deep schisms of the Rhineland massifs to the Black Forest, the Bavarian Forest, the Ore Mountains and the Harz Mountains, these low mountain ranges are Germany's heartland. The Rhine and Main Rivers, important waterways for inland shipping, cut through the southwest of this region. With large deposits of coal as well as favourable transport conditions, this was one of the first regions in Germany to undergo industrialisation.

The Alpine Foothills, wedged between the Danube and the Alps, are typified by subalpine plateau and rolling hills, and by moors in eastern regions around the Danube.

Germany's Alps lie entirely within Bavaria and stretch from the large, glacially formed Lake Constance in the west to Berchtesgaden in Germany's southeastern corner. Though lower than the mountains to their south, many summits are well above 2000m, rising dramatically from the Alpine Foothills to the 2966m Zugspitze, Germany's highest mountain.

CLIMATE

German weather can be variable, so it's best to be prepared for many conditions throughout the year. That said, the most reliable weather is from May to October, coinciding with the standard tourist season (except for skiing). The shoulder periods (late March to May and September to October) can bring fewer tourists and surprisingly pleasant weather.

Eastern Germany lies in a transition zone between the temperate maritime climate of Western Europe and the rougher continental climate of Eastern Europe – continental and Atlantic air masses meet here. The mean daily temperature in Berlin is 11°C, the average range of temperatures varying from -1°C in January to 18°C in July. The average annual precipitation is 585mm and there is no special rainy season. Camping season is from May to September.

ECOLOGY & ENVIRONMENT

Germans are fiercely protective of their natural surroundings. Households and businesses participate enthusiastically in waste-recycling programmes. A refund system applies to a wide range of glass bottles and jars, while containers for waste paper and glass can be found in each neighbourhood. Though acid rain is a problem, German forests have lost little of their wonderful fairy-tale charm, whereas in eastern Germany regions around the Oder River and in parts of Mecklenburg and Western Pomerania have retained an intact central European ecosystem.

Energy

Clashes between the police and antinuclear demonstrators in Germany in the 1980s were the most violent and bloody in Europe since the 1968 Paris student riots: armed anarchists,

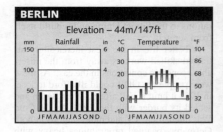

armed police, and committed ordinary Germans were caught between revolutionary intent and a state of siege. In Germany, it was all about shutting down nuclear reactors and preventing new ones being built. Times have changed. Germany still generates about one-third of its energy from its 19 atomic plants, but a deal has been struck with the powerful energy lobby to close the plants over the next three decades. In the meantime, nuclear waste remains a sticky, unresolved issue.

FLORA & FAUNA

Few species of flora and fauna are unique to Germany. Unique, however, is the importance Germans place on their forests, the prettiest of which are mixed-species deciduous forests planted with beech, oak, maple and birch. You'll find that many cities even have their own city forest (*Stadtwald*). Alpine regions bloom in spring with orchids, cyclamen, gentians, edelweiss, and more; and the heather blossom on the Lüneburg Heath, north of Hanover, is stunning in August.

Apart from human beings, common mammals include deer, wild pigs, rabbits, foxes and hares. The chances of seeing any of these in summer are fairly good, especially in eastern Germany. The wild pig population is particularly thriving; some pigs even wander occasionally into the suburbs of Berlin! On the coasts you will find seals and, throughout Germany, falcons, hawks, storks and migratory geese are a common sight.

Berchtesgaden (in the Bavarian Alps), the Wattenmeer parks in Schleswig-Holstein, Lower Saxony and Hamburg, and the Unteres Odertal, which is a joint German-Polish endeavour, are highlights among Germany's dozen or so national parks.

GOVERNMENT & POLITICS

Germany has a very decentralised governmental structure – a federal system based

GERMANY

upon regional states. Reunification resulted in eastern Germany's six original (pre-1952) states of Berlin, Brandenburg, Mecklenburg-Vorpommern (Mecklenburg-Western Pomerania), Sachsen (Saxony), Sachsen-Anhalt (Saxony-Anhalt) and Thüringen (Thuringia) all being re-established. In the context of the Federal Republic of Germany they are called *Bundesländer* (federal states).

The Bundesländer in western Germany are Schleswig-Holstein, Hamburg, Niedersachsen (Lower Saxony), Bremen, Nordrhein-Westfalen (North Rhine-Westphalia), Hessen (Hesse), Rheinland-Pfalz (the Rhineland-Palatinate), Saarland, Baden-Württemberg and Bayern (Bavaria). Germans commonly refer to the eastern states as the *neue Bundesländer* (new states) and to the western states as the *alte Bundesländer* (old states).

The Bundesländer have a large degree of autonomy in internal affairs and exert influence on the central government through the *Bundesrat* (upper house). The *Bundestag* (lower house) is elected by direct universal suffrage with proportional representation, although a party must have at least 5% of the vote to gain a seat. In September 1999 the Bundestag resumed sitting in Berlin's restored Reichstag building, transferring the seat of government from Bonn.

Germany's two major parties are the Christian Democrats (CDU, or CSU in Bavaria) and the Social Democrats (SPD). The Free Democrats (FDP), a small but influential liberal party, often holds the balance of power. The Democratic Socialists (PDS), the former East German SED, is a strong force in eastern Germany, whereas the popularity and fortunes of Bündnis 90/the Green party have been mixed in recent years.

ECONOMY

The Marshall Plan helped to produce West Germany's *Wirtschaftswunder* (economic miracle), which in the 1950s and 1960s turned the FRG into the world's third-largest economy. Trade unions and industrial corporations developed a unique economic contract which involves employees in company decisions. Important industries include electrical manufacturing, precision and optical instruments, chemicals and vehicle manufacturing, and environmental technology.

East Germany's recovery was even more remarkable given the wartime destruction, postwar looting by the USSR, loss of skilled labour, and isolation from Western markets. The GDR was by any measure an important industrial nation, with major metallurgical, electrical, chemical and engineering industries. As a result of reunification, many industries were privatised, but others were closed down, causing unemployment and hardship in some regions. Those most affected were women and older workers.

Eastern Germany now has a modern infrastructure, but little is being invested there, and it has been losing population since reunification. About 15 million people currently live in the eastern states. However, with the decline of traditional heavy industries in the region, tourism has become important; the region is also well-placed geographically to gain from restructured Eastern European markets or an expanded EU.

Unemployment remains a major problem throughout Germany, especially in the eastern regions where some 17.5% of the work force is unemployed. The national figure is around 9.5%.

Germany, though slow at first to adapt to the 'new economy' of the 1990s, now has thriving IT, online and telecommunications industries.

Economic growth is slow in comparison to most other European countries, particularly in eastern Germany.

When Germany switched its currency from the hallowed Deutschmark to the forward-thinking euro in 2002, there was supposed to be an even conversion of prices; but many business owners used the opportunity to raise prices, causing a low-level stir.

POPULATION & PEOPLE

Germany has a population of around 82.5 million, making it the most populous in Europe after Russia. Germany's main native minority is the tiny group of Slavonic Sorbs in the eastern states of Saxony and Brandenburg. In political and economic terms, Germany is Europe's most decentralised nation, but considerable variation in population density exists. The Ruhr district in the northern Rhineland has Germany's densest concentration of people and industry, while Mecklenburg-Western Pomerania in the northeastern corner is relatively sparsely settled. About one-third of the population lives in 84 cities, each with more than 100,000 people.

A strong immigrant tradition in Germany dates back to around 1700, when some 30% of Berlin's population consisted of Huguenots who had fled religious oppression in France. Another large wave of immigrants moved to the Ruhr region from Poland in the late 19th century. In effect, immigration compensates for the extremely low birth rate among the established German population.

More than seven million foreigners now live in Germany. Most hail from Turkey, Italy, Greece and the former Yugoslavia, and have arrived as 'guest workers' in the FRG since the early 1960s to work in lower-paid jobs. In 1999 archaic immigration laws dating back to 1913 were changed to make it easier for residents without German ancestry to gain citizenship. This now takes about seven years. Eastern Germany has fewer resident foreigners, though some of the roughly 200,000 workers who arrived in the GDR during the 1980s from 'fraternal socialist' countries remain.

ARTS

Germany's meticulously creative population has made major contributions to international culture. Germans take their *Kultur* so seriously that visitors sometimes wonder how on earth they manage to actually enjoy it. The answer may lie in a German musician's proverb: 'True bliss is absolute concentration'.

Architecture, Painting & Literature

The scope of German art is such that it could be the focus of an entire visit. The arts first blossomed during the Romanesque period (800–1200), of which examples can be found at the Germanisches Nationalmuseum in Nuremberg, Trier Cathedral, the churches of Cologne, the chapel of Charlemagne's palace in Aachen, and the Stiftskirche in Gernrode.

The Gothic style (1200–1500) is best viewed at Freiburg's Münster cathedral, Meissen Cathedral, Cologne's Dom and the Marienkirche in Lübeck. Artists from the Cologne school of painters and sculptor Peter Vischer and his sons produced both Gothic sculpture and innovative paintings featuring rudimentary landscapes. One famous panel painting is a work by Meister Bertram (c. 1340), in Hamburg's Kunsthalle.

The Renaissance came late to Germany but flourished once it took hold. The draughtsman Albrecht Dürer of Nuremberg (1471–1528) was one of the world's finest portraitists, as was the prolific Lucas Cranach the Elder (1472–1553) who worked in Wittenberg (now Lutherstadt Wittenberg) for more than 45 years.

The baroque period brought great sculpture, including works by Andreas Schlüter in Berlin. Balthasar Neumann's superb Residenz in Würzburg and the magnificent cathedral in Passau are the foremost examples of baroque architecture.

The Enlightenment During the 18th century, the Saxon court at Weimar attracted some of the major cultural figures of Europe. Among them was Johann Wolfgang von Goethe (1749–1832), the poet, dramatist, painter, scientist, philosopher and perhaps the last European to achieve the Renaissance ideal of excellence in many fields. His greatest work, the drama *Faust*, is a masterful epic of all that went before him, as the archetypal human strives for meaning and knowledge.

Goethe's close friend, Friedrich Schiller (1759–1805), was a poet, dramatist and novelist. His most famous work is the dramatic cycle *Wallenstein*, based on the life of a treacherous general of the Thirty Years' War who plotted to make himself arbiter of the empire. Schiller's other great play, *William Tell*, dealt with the right of the oppressed to rise against tyranny. There are large museums in Weimar dedicated to both Schiller and Goethe.

The 19th & Early 20th Centuries Berlin too produced remarkable individuals, such as Alexander von Humboldt (1769–1859), an advanced thinker in environmentalism through his studies of the relationship of plants and animals to their physical surroundings. His contemporary, the philosopher Georg Wilhelm Friedrich Hegel (1770–1831), created an all-embracing classical philosophy that is still influential today. The neoclassical period in Germany was led by Karl Friedrich Schinkel and the Munich neoclassical school. The romantic period is best exemplified by the paintings of Caspar David Friedrich and Otto Runge.

Art Nouveau also made important contributions to German architecture. Expressionism followed, with great names like Paul Klee and the Russian-born painter Vasili Kandinsky. In 1919, Walter Gropius founded the Bauhaus movement in an attempt to meld theoretical concerns of architecture with the practical problems faced by artists and craftspeople. The Bauhaus flourished in Dessau, but with the arrival of the Nazis, Gropius left for Harvard University.

In the 1920s, Berlin was the theatrical capital of Germany; one of its most famous practitioners was the poet and playwright Bertold Brecht (1898–1956). Brecht introduced Marxist concepts into his plays, and his work was distinguished by the simplicity of its moral parables, its language and its sharp characterisation. Brecht revolutionised the theatre by detaching the audience from what was happening on stage, enabling them to observe the content without being distracted by the form. In 1933 Brecht fled the Nazis and lived in various countries, eventually accepting the directorship of the Berliner Ensemble in East Berlin, where his work has been performed ever since.

One of Brecht's contemporaries was Kurt Weill (A Threepenny Opera), associated with Dessau and Berlin before fleeing the Nazis for New York.

Easily Germany's most famous performer of the 20th century was Marlene Dietrich (1901–1992). The Berlin-born femme fatale started as a silent film star, later moved to Hollywood and refused to return to Germany after Hitler's rise to power. She became an icon for her androgynous getups and erotic overtones, represented by her signature song 'Falling in Love Again', and led a reclusive later life in Paris.

WWII & Beyond During the Third Reich, the arts were devoted mainly to propaganda, with grandiose projects and realist art extolling the virtues of German nationhood. The best-known Nazi-era director was Leni Riefenstahl (1902-). Her Triumph of the Will (1934) won some of filmmaking's highest honours but later rendered her unemployable due to its status as Nazi propaganda. Albert Speer was Hitler's favourite architect, known for pompous neoclassical buildings.

Max Ernst, resident in France and the USA, was an exponent of dada and surrealism who developed the technique of collage.

Postwar literature in both Germanys was influenced by the politically focused Gruppe 47. It included writers such as Günter Grass, winner of the 1999 Nobel Prize for Literature, whose modern classic, Die Blechtrommel (The Tin Drum), humorously follows German history through the eyes of a young boy who refuses to grow. Christa Wolf, an East German novelist and Gruppe 47 writer, won high esteem in both Germanys. Her 1963 story Der geteilte Himmel (Divided Heaven) tells of a young woman whose fiance abandons her for life in the West.

Patrick Süskind's Das Parfum (The Perfume) is the extraordinary tale of a psychotic 18th-century perfume-maker with an obsessive genius. Helden wie wir (Heroes Like Us) by Thomas Brussig, an eastern German, tells the story of a man whose penis brings about the collapse of the Berlin Wall.

Music

Few countries can claim the impressive musical heritage of Germany. A partial list of household names includes Johann Sebastian Bach, Georg Friedrich Händel, Ludwig van Beethoven, Richard Wagner, Richard Strauss, Felix Mendelssohn-Bartholdy, Robert Schumann, Johannes Brahms and Gustav Mahler.

Johann Sebastian Bach (1685–1750) was born at Eisenach into a prominent family of musicians. During his time as court organist at Weimar and city musical director at Leipzig, Bach produced some 200 cantatas, as well as masses, oratorios, passions and other elaborate music for the Lutheran service, as well as sonatas, concertos, preludes and fugues for secular use.

Georg Friedrich Händel (1685–1759) left his native Halle for Hamburg at 18. He composed numerous operas and oratorios, including his masterpiece Messiah (1742). The birthplaces of both Händel and Bach are now large museums.

In 1843, Robert Schumann (1810–56) opened a music school at Leipzig in collaboration with composer Felix Mendelssohn-Bartholdy (1809–47), director of Leipzig's famous Gewandhaus Orchestra. Works by Richard Wagner (1813–83) represent a milestone in European classical music, and no composer since Wagner's time could ignore his attempts to balance all operatic forms to produce a 'total work of art'.

These musical traditions continue to thrive: the Dresden Opera and Leipzig Orchestra are known around the world, and musical performances are hosted almost daily in every major theatre in the country.

Germany has also made a significant contribution to the contemporary music scene, with Kraftwerk creating the first 'techno' sounds, and through internationally renowned Nina Hagen, Nena, the Scorpions, Die Toten Hosen and Fury in the Slaughterhouse.

You can hear jazz, folk, techno, house and other sounds in clubs in major cities. The Studio for Electronic Music in Cologne and Hamburg's Mojo club are two innovative venues. Traditional German oompah music is still popular with some locals and tourists, while Schlager music, with its treacly lyrics, confounds foreigners with its popularity.

SOCIETY & CONDUCT

The unflattering image of Germans as overly disciplined and humourless is a stereotype. On the whole, you'll find Germans relaxed, personable and interested in enjoying life.

Tradition plays a surprisingly strong role despite, or perhaps because of, the country's modern industrial achievements. Hunters still wear green, many Bavarian women don the *Dirndl* (skirt and blouse), while some menfolk sport the typical Bavarian *Lederhosen* (leather shorts), a *Loden* (short jacket) and felt hat. In contrast, you might hear young Germans dismiss this sort of thing as *typisch deutsch* (typically German), a phrase that usually has negative connotations.

While Germans are generally not prudish or awkwardly polite, formal manners remain important. When making a phone call to anywhere in Germany, you'll find people more helpful if you first introduce yourself by name. Germans sometimes shake hands when greeting or leaving. Hugging and cheek kissing is common between males and females who know one another.

The Holocaust and WWII, while by no means taboo topics, should be discussed with tact and understanding in Germany. In western Germany these themes have been dealt with openly for decades – less so in eastern Germany until reunification – but Germans sometimes feel their country's pre and postwar contributions are under-emphasised against its relatively short period under the Nazis. Germans take great offence at the presumption that fascist ideas are somehow part of or even compatible with their national culture.

RELIGION

Most Germans belong to a church, and there are almost equal numbers of Catholics and Protestants; roughly speaking, the Catholics predominate in the south, Protestants in the north and east. Most citizens pay contributions to their church, which the government collects along with their taxes, but in practice few Germans regularly attend church services.

Despite their bitter historical rivalry, conflict between Catholics and Protestants in Germany is not an issue. In eastern Germany, the Protestant Church, which claims support among the overwhelming majority of the population there, played a major role in the overthrow of German communism by providing a gathering place for antigovernment protesters. Active church membership, however, remains lower than in western Germany.

In 1933 some 530,000 Jews lived in Germany. Today that number is around 50,000, with the largest communities in Berlin, Frankfurt and Munich. Their population is growing with the recent influx of Russian Jews. There are also more than 1.7 million Muslims, most of them Turks.

LANGUAGE

It might come as a surprise to learn that German is a close relative of English. English, German and Dutch are all known as West Germanic languages. This means that you already know lots of German words – *Arm, Finger, Gold* – and you'll be able to figure out many of the others, such as *Mutter* (mother), *trinken* (drink), *gut* (good). A primary reason why English and German have grown apart is that when the Normans invaded England in 1066 they brought in many non-Germanic words. For this reason, English has many synonyms, usually with the everyday word being German, and the more literary or specialised one coming from French, eg, 'start' and 'green' as opposed to 'commence' and 'verdant'.

German is spoken throughout Germany and Austria and in much of Switzerland. It is also useful in Eastern Europe, especially with older people. Although you will hear different regional dialects, the official language, *Hochdeutsch*, is universally understood. English is widely understood by young or educated Germans, but as soon as you try to meet ordinary people or move out of the big cities, especially in eastern Germany, the situation is rather different. Your efforts to speak the local language will be appreciated and will make your trip much more enjoyable.

Words that you'll often encounter on maps and throughout this chapter include: *Altstadt* (old city), *Bahnhof* (train station), *Brücke* (bridge), *Hauptbahnhof* (main train station), *Markt* (market, often the central square in old towns), *Platz* (square), *Rathaus* (town hall) and *Strasse* (street). German nouns are always written with a capital letter.

See the Language chapter at the back of the book for pronunciation guidelines and useful words and phrases.

Facts for the Visitor

HIGHLIGHTS
Museums & Galleries

Germany is a museum-lover's dream. Munich features the huge Deutsches Museum, and Frankfurt's Museumsufer (Museum Embankment) has enough museums for any addict. Berlin's Kulturforum and Museumsinsel (Museum Island, still being rebuilt) are home to some astounding works. Dresden's Zwinger and Albertinum are among its chief art museums, while cultural treasures are centred at Nuremberg's Germanisches Nationalmuseum.

Castles

Germany has castles of all periods and styles. If you're into castles, make sure to hit Heidelberg Meissen, Neuschwanstein, Burg Rheinfels on the Rhine River, Burg Eltz on the Moselle, the medieval Königstein and Wartburg Castles, Renaissance Wittenberg Castle, baroque Schloss Moritzburg and the romantic Wernigerode Castle.

Historic Towns

Time stands still in parts of Germany, and some of the best towns in which to find this flavour are Wismar, Goslar and Regensburg. Meissen and Quedlinburg have a fairy-tale air, Weimar has a special place in German culture, and Lübeck is one of Europe's true gems. The *Altstadt* (old district) of many large cities also imparts this historic feel.

Roads & Rivers

Germany has many scenic theme roads, such as those in the Black Forest and the Fairy-Tale Road between Hanau and Bremen. The best way to explore them is by car. Check with local or regional tourist offices for maps and highlights of the route.

Important rivers such as the Rhine, Danube, Moselle and Elbe are well-serviced by boats in summer, and the Rhine and Moselle Rivers are especially suited to combined wine quaffing and cruising.

SUGGESTED ITINERARIES

Depending on the length of your stay, you might want to see and do the following things:

Two days
Depending on where you enter the country, try to spend your days in either Berlin or Munich.
One week
Divide your time between Berlin and Munich, and throw in a visit to Dresden or Bamberg.
Two weeks
Berlin (including Potsdam), Dresden or Bamberg, Munich, Freiburg and the Rhine or Moselle Valley.
One month
Berlin (including Potsdam), Dresden or Bamberg, Meissen, the Harz Mountains, the Rhine or Moselle Valley, Munich, the Alps, Lake Constance, Freiburg or Lübeck.
Two months
As for one month, plus Weimar, Regensburg, Passau, the Romantic Road, Cologne, and the North Frisian Islands.

PLANNING
When to Go

Unless frolicking in winter snow is your thing, Germany is best visited from April to October – July and August tend to have the most visitors. If you don't mind slushy, bitterly cold and bleak weather, a winter visit does have its charms; large cities and the Baltic coast can be blessedly free of tourists. Central Uplands regions, like the Harz Mountains and Black Forest, are good places to hike and relax year-round, especially at the higher altitudes. Bring good winter gear and rain jackets.

Flood Damage

At the time of writing Germany was facing an estimated clean-up bill of around €15 billion following the floods that hit the southern and eastern parts of the country in the summer of 2002. What effect the flood damage will have on travellers is not yet clear; however, visitors to affected regions – particularly the Dresden area – would be well advised to check on the latest situation.

GERMANY

TOURIST OFFICES

German tourist offices are efficient, a mine of information and have useful free maps.

Local Tourist Offices

Before your trip, consult the **German National Tourist Office** (*Deutsche Zentrale für Tourismus, DZT;* ☎ 069-97 46 40, fax 75 19 03; ⓔ *info@d-z-t.com;* ⓦ *www.visits-to-Germany .com; Beethovenstrasse 69, 60325 Frankfurt/ Main).* For local information, you can go to the *Verkehrsamt* (tourist office) or *Kurverwaltung* (resort administration), listed for each town.

Tourist Offices Abroad

German National Tourist Office representatives abroad include:

Australia & New Zealand (☎ 02-9267 8148, fax 9267 9035, ⓔ gnto@germany.org.au) PO Box A 980, Sydney, NSW 1235

Canada (☎ 416-968 1570, fax 968 1986, ⓔ gnto@aol.com) 175 Bloor St East, North Tower, 6th floor, Toronto, Ont M4W 3R8

South Africa (☎ 011-643 1615, fax 484 2750) c/o Lufthansa German Airlines, PO Box 10883, Johannesburg 2000

UK (☎ 020-7317 0908, fax 7495 6129) PO Box 2695, London W1A 3TN

USA (☎ 212-661 7200, fax 661 7174, ⓔ gntony@aol.com) 122 East 42nd St, 52nd floor, New York, NY 10168-0072

Other offices are in Amsterdam, Brussels, Copenhagen, Helsinki, Hong Kong, Madrid, Milan, Moscow, Oslo, Paris, São Paulo, Stockholm, Tel Aviv, Tokyo, Vienna and Zürich.

VISAS & DOCUMENTS

Americans, Australians, Britons, Canadians, Israelis, Japanese, New Zealanders and Singaporeans require only a valid passport (no visa) to enter Germany. Citizens of the EU and some other Western European countries can enter on an official identity card. Three months is the usual limit of stay; less for citizens of some developing countries. See Work later in this section for information on work permits.

EMBASSIES & CONSULATES
German Embassies & Consulates

Diplomatic representation abroad includes:

Australia (☎ 02-6270 1911, fax 6270 1951) 119 Empire Circuit, Yarralumla, ACT 2600

Canada (☎ 613-232 1101, fax 594 9330) 1 Waverley St, Ottawa, Ont K2P 0T8

Ireland (☎ 01-269 3011, fax 269 3946) 31 Trimleston Ave, Booterstown, Dublin

New Zealand (☎ 04-473 6063, fax 473 6069) 90-92 Hobson St, Wellington

UK (☎ 020-7824 1300, fax 7824 1435) 23 Belgrave Square, London SW1X 8PZ

USA (☎ 202-298 4000, fax 298 4249) 4645 Reservoir Rd, NW Washington, DC 20007-1998

Embassies & Consulates in Germany

The area code for Berlin is ☎ 030.

Australia (☎ 880 08 80, fax 880 08 80 351) Friedrichstrasse 200, 10117 Berlin

Canada (☎ 20 31 20, fax 20 31 25 90) Friedrichstrasse 95, 10117 Berlin

Ireland (☎ 22 07 20, fax 22 07 22 99) Friedrichstrasse 200, 10117 Berlin

New Zealand (☎ 20 62 10, fax 20 62 11 14) Friedrichstrasse 60, 10117 Berlin

South Africa (☎ 82 52 711, fax 82 66 543) Friedrichstrasse 60, 10117 Berlin

UK (☎ 20 45 70) Wilhelmstrasse 70-71, 10117 Berlin

USA (☎ 238 51 74, fax 238 62 90 1) Neustädtische Kirchstrasse 4-5, 10117 Berlin

CUSTOMS

Most items needed for personal use during a visit are duty free. In Germany, usual allowances apply to duty-free and duty-paid items if you're coming from a non-EU country.

MONEY

The easiest places to change cash in Germany are banks or foreign exchange counters at airports and train stations, particularly those of the Reisebank. Main banks in larger cities generally have money-changing machines for after-hours use, though they don't often give good rates. The Reisebank charges a flat €2.50 to change cash. Some local Sparkasse banks have good rates and low charges.

There are ATMs virtually everywhere in Germany; most accept Visa, MasterCard, American Express (AmEx), Eurocard, and bankcards linked to the Plus and Cirrus networks. Typically, withdrawals over the counter against cards at major banks cost a flat €5 per transaction. Check other fees and the availability of services with your bank before you leave home.

Travellers cheques can be cashed at any bank and the most widely accepted are AmEx,

Thomas Cook and Barclays. A percentage commission (usually a minimum of €5) is charged by most banks on any travellers cheque, even those issued in euros. The Reisebank charges 1% or a minimum of €5 (€2.50 on amounts less than €50) and €3.75 for AmEx. Note that AmEx does not charge commission on its own cheques.

Credit cards are especially useful for emergencies, although they are often not accepted by hotels in the budget category and restaurants outside major cities. Cards most widely accepted for payment for goods and services are Eurocard (linked to Access and MasterCard), Visa and AmEx.

Having money sent to Germany is straightforward, albeit expensive. For emergencies, both Reisebank (Western Union) and Thomas Cook (MoneyGram) offer ready and fast international cash transfers through agent banks, but commissions are costly.

Currency
In 2002, Germany switched from its beloved Deutschmark (DM) to the euro, with a minimum of trauma. See the boxed text 'The Euro' in the earlier Facts for the Visitor chapter.

Costs
A tight budget can easily blow out in Germany. You can minimise costs by staying in hostels or private rooms, eating midday restaurant specials or by self-catering, and by limiting museum visits to days when they are free. Students pay the concession price mentioned in this chapter; the price for children is usually the same or marginally lower (often depending on age). Campers can expect to pay around €7.50 per night, less if there are two of you. Add another €10 for self-catering expenses and a beer or two from the supermarket, and your food, drinks and accommodation costs will be around €17.50 per day. If travelling on a rail pass, but allowing for public transport costs and occasional expenses like toiletries, €22.50 per day should be sufficient. Local public transit passes for tourists often offer discounts to museums and attractions.

Tipping & Bargaining
Apart from restaurants and taxis, tipping is not widespread in Germany. In restaurants, rather than leave money on the table, tip when you pay by stating a rounded-up figure or saying *es stimmt so* (that's the right amount). A tip of 10% is generally more than sufficient. Bargaining is usual only at flea markets.

Taxes & Refunds
Most German goods and services include a value-added tax (VAT, or *Mehrwertsteuer*) of 16% (7% for books and anything else involving copyright). Non-EU residents leaving the EU can have this tax refunded for any goods (not services) they buy.

At Frankfurt airport you should have your luggage labelled at the check-in and then take it to customs in area B6 of terminal 1, level 0.

POST & COMMUNICATIONS
Post
Standard post office hours are 8am to 6pm weekdays and to noon on Saturday. Many train station post offices stay open later or offer limited services outside these hours.

Postal Rates Postcard rates are €0.51 within Europe, €1.02 to North America and Australasia; a 200g letter to anywhere in Europe costs €0.56 and a 50g letter is €1.53. Aerograms to North America and Australia cost €1.02, and 20g letters by air to North America and Australasia cost €1.53. Surface-mail parcels of up to 2kg to Europe/elsewhere cost €7.67/9.71; the airmail cost is €11.71/20.40.

Receiving Mail Mail can be sent *Postlagernde* (poste restante) to the main post office in any city. There's no fee for collection, but German post offices will only hold mail for two weeks.

Telephone
Most pay phones in Germany accept only phonecards, available for €6 and €25 at post offices and some news kiosks, tourist offices and banks. One call unit costs a little more than €0.06 from a private telephone and €0.10 from a public phone. Calling from a private phone is most expensive between 9am and 6pm, when a unit lasts 90 seconds for a city call, 45 seconds for a regional call (up to 50km) and 30 seconds for a Deutschland call (more than 50km) during the peak period. From telephone boxes city calls cost €0.10 per minute. Calls to anywhere else in Germany from a phone box cost €0.20 per minute. Note that calls made to mobile (cell) phones (prefix generally ☎ 016 or 017) cost €0.54 per minute.

To ring abroad from Germany, dial ☎ 00 followed by the country code, area code and number. A three-minute call to the USA from a public phone in Germany at peak time costs €2.70, but you can reduce most international costs substantially by using prepaid private telephone cards.

The country code for Germany is ☎ 49.

Home direct services whereby you reach the operator direct for a reverse charge (collect) call from Germany are only possible to some countries. The prefix is ☎ 0800 followed by the home direct number. For the USA dial ☎ 888 225 5388 (AT&T) or ☎ 888 00 13 (Sprint). For Canada, dial ☎ 080 10 14; Australia, ☎ 080 00 61 (Telstra); and for Britain dial ☎ 080 00 44.

For directory assistance within Germany call ☎ 11833 (☎ 11837 in English); both cost €1 for the first minute and €0.49 after that. International information is ☎ 11834 (€1.48/ first minute, €0.97 after that).

Fax

Most main post offices and main train stations have public fax-phones that operate with a phone card. The regular cost of the call, plus €1 service charge, will be deducted from your card on connection.

Sending a telegram, though still possible, is costly and slow and has few advantages over using a telephone or fax.

Email & Internet Access

Internet cafés, where you can buy online time and send email, exist in most large cities. Locations change frequently, so check at tourist offices.

The price in an Internet café is anything from around €3 to €10 per hour. If you wish to plug in your own laptop, you'll need a telephone plug adapter. Major Internet service providers have dial-in nodes in Germany. Because these usually vary from town to town, it's best to download a list from your provider before setting out.

DIGITAL RESOURCES

For up-to-date information about Germany on the Net, try the German Information Centre website at Ⓦ www.germany-info.org. Most of the information there is in English. The website Ⓦ www.visits-to-germany.com is targeted at tourists, while individual cities and regions also have websites.

BOOKS

For a more detailed guide to the country, pick up a copy of Lonely Planet's *Germany*. Lonely Planet also publishes *Bavaria*, and *Berlin* and *Munich* city guides.

The German literary tradition is strong and there are many works that provide excellent background to the German experience. Mark Twain's *A Tramp Abroad* is recommended for his comical observations on German life. For a more modern analysis of the German character and the issues facing Germany, dip into the Penguin paperback *Germany and the Germans* by John Ardagh.

NEWSPAPERS & MAGAZINES

Major British newspapers, the *International Herald Tribune* and *USA Today* are available from news kiosks at major train stations or throughout large cities, as are international editions of *Time*, *Newsweek* and the *Economist*. In smaller towns the choice may be limited.

The most widely read newspapers in Germany are *Die Welt*, *Bild*, *Frankfurter Allgemeine*, Munich's *Süddeutsche Zeitung* and the green-leaning *Die Tageszeitung (Taz)*. Germany's most popular magazines are *Der Spiegel*, *Focus* and *Stern*. *Die Zeit* is a weekly publication about culture and the arts.

RADIO & TV

Germany's two national TV channels are the government-funded ARD and ZDF. They are augmented by a plethora of regional and cable channels. You can catch English-language news and sports programmes (Sky News, CNN and BBC World depending on the region) on cable or satellite TV in many midrange hotels and pensions.

The BBC World Service (on varying AM wavelengths depending on the region) and the Armed Forces Network (AM 873 around Frankfurt) broadcast in English.

LAUNDRY

You'll find a coin-operated *Münzwäscherei* (laundry) in most cities. Average costs are €3.50 per wash, €0.50 for optional spinning, plus €0.50 per 15 minutes for drying. Some camping grounds and a few hostels also have laundry facilities.

If you're staying in a private room, the host may take care of your washing for a reasonable fee. Most major hotels provide laundering services at fairly steep charges.

GERMANY

TOILETS

Finding a public toilet when you need one is usually not a problem in Germany, but it may cost anything from €0.25 to €1 for the convenience. All train stations and large public transit stations have toilets, and at some main stations you can even shower for around €1 to €5. The level of hygiene is usually very high, although some train stations and otherwise nice pubs can be surprisingly grotty. Public toilets also exist in larger parks, pedestrian malls and inner-city shopping areas, where ultra-modern self-cleaning pay toilets (with wide automatic doorways that allow easy wheelchair access) are increasingly being installed. Restaurant and pub owners rarely mind passers-by using their toilet in cases of emergency if you ask first.

WOMEN TRAVELLERS

Women should not encounter particular difficulties while travelling in Germany. Most larger cities have women-only cultural organisations. If you are a victim of harassment or violence, get in touch with **Frauenhaus München** (☎ 089-354 83 11, 24hr service ☎ 089-35 48 30) in Munich, and **LARA – Krisen und Beratungszentrum für vergewaltigte Frauen** (Crisis and Counselling Centre for Raped Women; ☎ 030-216 88 88) in Berlin.

GAY & LESBIAN TRAVELLERS

Germans are generally fairly tolerant of homosexuality, but gays (who call themselves Schwule) and lesbians (Lesben) still don't enjoy quite the same social acceptance as in some other northern European countries. Most progressive are the large cities, particularly Berlin and Frankfurt, where the sight of homosexual couples holding hands is not unusual, although kissing in public is less common. The age of consent is 18 years. Larger cities have many gay and lesbian bars as well as other meeting places for homosexuals. Berlin Pride festival is held in June. Other Pride festivals are held in June in Bielefeld, Bochum, Hamburg, Mannheim and Wurzburg, and in July in Cologne.

DISABLED TRAVELLERS

Germany caters reasonably well to the needs of disabled travellers, with access ramps for wheelchairs and/or lifts in most public buildings, including toilets, train stations, museums, theatres and cinemas. Assistance is usually

---

Emergency Services

The emergency number for the police is ☎ 110 and the fire brigade/ambulance is ☎ 112. See Car & Motorcycle in the introductory Getting Around section later in this chapter for information regarding roadside assistance in the event of breakdown.

---

required when boarding any means of public transport in Germany. On Deutsche Bahn (DB) distance services, you can arrange this when buying your ticket.

DANGERS & ANNOYANCES

Although the usual cautions should be taken, theft and other crimes against travellers are relatively rare in Germany. In the event of problems, the police are helpful and efficient.

Africans, Asians and southern Europeans may encounter racial prejudice, especially in eastern Germany where they have been singled out as convenient scapegoats for economic hardship. However, the animosity is usually directed against the immigrants, not tourists.

LEGAL MATTERS

Police in Germany are well trained and usually treat tourists with respect. You are required by law to prove your identity if asked by the police, so always carry your passport, or an identity card if you're an EU citizen.

BUSINESS HOURS

By law, shops in Germany may open from 6am to 8pm on weekdays and until 4pm on Saturday. In practice, however, only department stores and some supermarkets and fashion shops stay open until 8pm; most open at 8am or 9am. Bakeries are open 7am to 6pm on weekdays, until 1pm on Saturday, and some open for the allowable maximum of three hours on Sunday.

Banking hours are generally 8.30am to 1pm and 2.30pm to 4pm weekdays, but many banks remain open all day, and until 5.30pm on Thursday. Government offices close for the weekend at 1pm or 3pm on Friday. Museums are generally closed on Monday; opening hours vary greatly, although many art museums are open later one evening per week.

Restaurants usually open 11am to midnight (the kitchen often closes at 10pm), with varying *Ruhetage* or closing days. Many restaurants close during the day from 3pm to 6pm. All shops and banks are closed on public holidays.

PUBLIC HOLIDAYS & SPECIAL EVENTS

Germany has many holidays, some of which vary from state to state. Public holidays include New Year's Day; Good Friday to Easter Monday; 1 May (Labour Day); Ascension Day (40 days after Easter); Whit/Pentecost Sunday & Monday (May or June); Corpus Christi (10 days after Pentecost); 3 October (Day of German Unity); 1 November (All Saints' Day); 18 November (Day of Prayer and Repentance); and usually Christmas Eve to the day after Christmas.

There are many festivals, fairs and cultural events throughout the year. The famous and worthwhile ones include:

January
Carnival season (Shrovetide, known as 'Fasching')
Many carnival events begin in large cities, most notably Cologne, Munich, Düsseldorf and Mainz; the partying peaks just before Ash Wednesday.

February
International Toy Fair Held in Nuremberg.
International Film Festival Held in Berlin.

March
Frankfurt Music Fair and **Frankfurt Jazz Fair**
Thuringian Bach Festival
Spring Fairs Held throughout Germany.

April
Stuttgart Jazz Festival
Munich Ballet Days
Mannheim May Fair
Walpurgisnacht Festivals Held the night before May Day in the Harz Mountains.

May
International Mime Festival Held in Stuttgart.
Red Wine Festival Held in Rüdesheim.
Dresden International Dixieland Jazz Festival
Dresden Music Festival Held in last week of May into first week of June.

June
Moselle Wine Week Held in Cochem.
Händel Festival Held in Halle.
Sailing regatta Held in Kiel.
Munich Film Festival
International Theatre Festival Held in Freiburg.

July
Folk festivals Held throughout Germany.
Berlin Love Parade
Munich Opera Festival
Richard Wagner Festival Held in Bayreuth.
German-American Folk Festival Held in Berlin.
Kulmbach Beer Festival
International Music Seminar Held in Weimar.

August
Heidelberg Castle Festival
Wine festivals Held throughout the Rhineland area.

September-October
Oktoberfest Held in Munich.
Berlin Festival of Music & Drama

October
Frankfurt Book Fair
Bremen Freimarkt
Gewandhaus Festival Held in Leipzig.
Berlin Jazzfest

November
St Martin's Festival Held throughout Rhineland and Bavaria.

December
Christmas fairs Held throughout Germany, most famously in Munich, Nuremberg, Berlin, Essen and Heidelberg.

ACTIVITIES

Germany, with its rugged Alps, picturesque uplands and fairy-tale forests, is ideal for hiking and mountaineering. Well-marked trails crisscross the country, especially popular areas like the Black Forest, the Harz Mountains, the so-called Saxon Switzerland area and the Thuringian Forest. The Bavarian Alps offer the most inspiring scenery, however, and are the centre of mountaineering in Germany. Good sources of information on hiking and mountaineering are: **Verband Deutscher Gebirgs-und Wandervereine** *(Federation of German Hiking Clubs;* ☎ *0561-93 87 30, fax 938 73 10; Wilhelmshöher Allee 157-159, 34121 Kassel)*; and **Deutscher Alpenverein** *(German Alpine Club;* ☎ *089-14 00 30, fax 140 03 98; Von-Kahr-Strasse 2-4, 80997 Munich)*.

The Bavarian Alps are the most extensive area for winter sports. Cross-country skiing is also good in the Black Forest and Harz Mountains. Ski equipment starts at around €12 per day, and daily ski-lift passes start at around €13. Local tourist offices are the best sources of information.

Cyclists will often find marked cycling routes, and eastern Germany has much to offer cyclists in the way of lightly travelled back roads, especially in the flat and less-populated north. There's also an extensive cycling trail along the Elbe River. Islands like Amrum and Rügen are also good for cycling. For more details and tips, see Cycling in the Getting Around section later in this chapter.

Railway enthusiasts will be excited by the wide range of excursions on old steam trains organised by the Deutsche Bahn and local services. Ask for the free booklet *Nostalgiereisen* at any large train station in Germany. Historic steam trains ply a 132km integrated narrow-gauge network year-round in the eastern Harz. For more information, see Wernigerode in the Saxony-Anhalt section.

WORK

Germany currently offers limited employment prospects for anyone except computer programmers and software specialists, who can apply for so-called Green Cards, which will allow you to work and live in Germany for a restricted period. EU citizens may work in Germany (with an *EU-Aufenthaltserlaubnis* residency permit), and special conditions apply for citizens of Australia, Canada, Israel, Japan, New Zealand, Switzerland and the USA.

Employment offices *(Arbeitsamt)* have an excellent data bank (SIS) of vacancies, or try major newspapers. Private language-teaching is another option. Street artists and hawkers are widespread in the cities, though these activities are often associated with begging. Numerous approved agencies can help you find work as an au pair.

An organisation that arranges unpaid cooperative work is the **Christlicher Friedensdienst** (☎ 069-45 90 72, fax 46 12 13; e yap -cfd@t-online.de; *Rendeler Strasse 9-11, 60385 Frankfurt/Main)*.

ACCOMMODATION

Accommodation in Germany is well organised, though some cities are short on budget hotels; private rooms are one option in such situations. Accommodation usually includes breakfast. Look for signs saying *Zimmer frei* (rooms available) or *Fremdenzimmer* (tourist rooms) in house or shop windows of many towns. If you're after a hotel or especially a private room, head straight for the tourist office and use the room-finding service *(Zimmervermittlung)*, which is free or typically €3. Staff will usually go out of their way to find something in your price range, although telephone bookings are not always available. **TIBS** (☎ 0761-88 58 10, fax 885 81 19; e email@TIBS.de) handles accommodation bookings throughout Germany.

In official resorts and spas, displayed prices usually don't include *Kurtaxe* (resort tax) levies. Tourist offices can also help with farm stays.

Camping

Germany has more than 2000 organised camping grounds. Most are open from April to September, but several hundred stay open throughout the year. Facilities range from primitive to over-equipped. In eastern Germany camping grounds often rent out small bungalows. For camping on private property, permission from the landowner is required. The best overall source of information is the **Deutscher Camping Club** (☎ 089-380 14 20, fax 33 47 37; *Mandlstrasse 28, 80802 Munich)*. Local tourist information sources can also help.

Hostels

The **Deutsches Jugendherbergswerk** (DJH; ☎ 05231-740 10, fax 74 01 49), or write to: DJH Service GmbH, 32754 Detmold, coordinates all affiliated Hostelling International (HI) hostels in Germany. Almost all hostels in Germany are open all year. Guests must be members of a HI-affiliated organisation, or join the DJH when checking in. The annual fee is €10/17.50 for juniors/seniors, which refers to visitors below/above 26 years old, with hostel cards.

A dorm bed in a DJH hostel ranges from around €12 to €20 for juniors to €15 to €23 for seniors. Camping at a hostel (where permitted) is generally half price. If you don't have a hostel-approved sleeping sheet, it usually costs from €2.50 to €3.50 to hire one (some hostels insist you hire one anyway). Breakfast is always included in the overnight price. Lunch or an evening meal will cost between €3 and €4.50.

Theoretically, visitors aged under 27 get preference, but in practice prior booking or arrival determines who gets rooms, not age. In Bavaria, though, the strict maximum age for anyone, except group leaders or parents accompanying a child, is 26. Check-in hours vary, but you usually must be out by 9am. You don't need to do chores at the hostels and there are few rules. Most hostels have a curfew, which may be as early as 10pm in small towns. The curfew is rarely before 11pm in large cities; several have no curfew.

DJH's *Jugendgästehäuser* (youth guesthouses) offer some better facilities, freer hours and two- to four-bed dorm rooms from €12.50 to €22.50 per person, which includes sleeping sheet.

Pensions & Guesthouses

Pensions offer the basics of hotel comfort without asking hotel prices. Many of these are private homes with several rooms to rent, often a bit out of the centre of town. Private facilities may or may not be included. Some proprietors are a little sensitive about who they take in and others are nervous about telephone bookings – you may have to give a time of arrival and stick to it (many visitors have lost rooms by turning up late).

Hotels

Cheap hotel rooms are a bit hard to find during summer, but there is usually not much seasonal price variation except in luxury and resort hotels.

The cheapest hotels have only rooms with shared toilets (and showers) in the corridor. Average budget prices are €30 for a single and €45 for a double (without bathroom). Rates almost always include breakfast. This section lists prices for single/double rooms, but many lodgings have larger, less-expensive dorm-style rooms.

Expensive hotels provide few advantages for their upmarket prices. Some city hotels offer weekend packages, while spa towns are nice places to splurge on luxury hotels and healthy pursuits.

Rentals

Renting an apartment for a week or more is a popular form of holiday accommodation in Germany.

Look in newspaper classifieds for *Ferienwohnungen* (sometimes abbreviated to *FeWo*) or *Ferien-Apartments*, or particularly if you want shared accommodation somewhere in an urban centre contact the local *Mitwohnzentrale* (accommodation-finding service). Rates vary widely, but are lower than hotels and decrease dramatically with the length of stay.

FOOD

Germans are hearty eaters and this is truly a meat-and-potatoes kind of country, although vegetarians will usually find suitable restaurants or fast-food places. Restaurants always display their menus outside with prices, but watch for daily or lunch specials chalked onto blackboards. Beware of early closing hours, and of the *Ruhetag* (rest day) at some establishments. Lunch is the main meal of the day; getting a main meal in the evening is never a problem, but you may find that the dish or menu of the day only applies to lunch.

A German breakfast in a pension or hotel is solid and filling. Germans at home might eat their heaviest meal at noon and then have lighter evening fare (*Abendbrot* or *Abendessen*, consisting of cheeses and bread).

Students can eat cheaply (well or badly, depending on the town) at university *Mensa* cafeterias if they can show international student ID. This is not always checked.

Cafés & Bars

Much of the German daily and social life revolves around these institutions, which often serve meals and alcohol as well as coffee. Some attract a young or student crowd, stay open until late and are great places to meet people.

Snacks

If you're on a low budget, you can get a feed at stand-up food stalls (*Schnellimbiss* or *Imbiss*). The food is usually quite reasonable and filling, ranging from döner kebabs (Turkish sandwiches of grilled meat) to Chinese stir-fries and traditional German sausages with beer.

Main Dishes

Wurst (sausage), in its hundreds of forms, is by far the most universal main dish. Regional favourites include *Bratwurst* (spiced sausage), *Weisswurst* (veal sausage) and *Blutwurst* (blood sausage). Other popular main dishes include *Rippenspeer* (spare ribs), *Rotwurst* (black pudding), *gegrilltes Fleisch* or *Rostbrätl* (grilled meat), *Putenbrust* (turkey breast) and many forms of *Schnitzel* (breaded pork or veal cutlet). Many restaurants serve at least one fish dish; vegetarian dishes may be harder to find.

Potatoes feature prominently in German meals, either *Bratkartoffeln* (fried), *Kartoffelpüree* (mashed), grated and then Swiss *Rösti* (fried), or as *Pommes Frites* (french fries); a Thuringian speciality is *Klösse*, a ball of mashed and raw potato which is then cooked into a dumpling. A similar Bavarian version is the *Knödel*. In Baden-Württemberg, potatoes are often replaced by *Spätzle*, a local noodle variety.

Mid-priced Italian, Turkish, Greek and Chinese restaurants can be found in every town.

Desserts

Germans are keen on rich desserts. Popular choices are the *Schwarzwälder Kirschtorte* (Black Forest cherry cake), one worthwhile tourist trap, as well as endless varieties of *Apfeltasche* (apple pastry). In the north you're likely to find berry *mus*, a sort of compote. Desserts and pastries are also often enjoyed during another German tradition, the 4pm coffee break.

Self-Catering

It's very easy and relatively cheap to put together picnic meals in any town. Simply head for the local market or supermarket and stock up on breads, sandwich meats, cheeses, wine and beer. Supermarkets such as Penny Markt, Kaiser's, Aldi, Rewe and Plus are cheap and have quite a good range.

DRINKS

Buying beverages in restaurants is expensive. Make a point of buying your drinks in supermarkets if your budget is tight.

Nonalcoholic Drinks

The most popular choices are mineral water and soft drinks, coffee and fruit or black tea. Bottled water almost always comes bubbly *(mit Kohlensäure)* – order *ohne Kohlensäure* if you're bothered by bubbles. Nonalcoholic beers are popular; Löwenbräu makes a nonalcoholic beer that is frequently served on tap in Bavaria.

Alcoholic Drinks

Beer is the national beverage and it's one cultural phenomenon that must be adequately explored. The beer is excellent and relatively cheap. Each region and brewery has its own distinctive taste and body.

Beer-drinking in Germany has its own vocabulary. *Vollbier* is 4% alcohol by volume, *Export* is 5% and *Bockbier* is 6%. *Helles Bier* is light, while *dunkles Bier* is dark. Export is

similar to, but much better than, typical international brews, while the *Pils* is more bitter. *Alt* is darker and more full-bodied. A speciality is *Weizenbier*, which is made with wheat instead of barley malt and served in a tall, 500ml glass with a slice of lemon.

Eastern Germany's best beers hail from Saxony, especially *Radeberger Pils* from near Dresden and *Wernesgrüner* from the Erzgebirge on the Czech border. *Berliner Weisse* is a foaming, low-alcohol wheat beer mixed with woodruff or raspberry syrup. The breweries of Cologne produce *Kölsch*; in Bamberg *Schlenkerla Rauchbier* is smoked to a dark-red colour.

German wines are exported around the world, and for good reason. They are inexpensive and typically white, light and intensely fruity. Wines are usually served in glasses or tiny carafes holding 200ml or 250ml. A *Weinschorle* or *Spritzer* is white wine mixed with mineral water. Wines don't have to be drunk with meals. The Rhine and Moselle Valleys are the classic wine-growing regions. The *Ebbelwei* of Hesse is a strong apple wine with an earthy flavour, and the Saale-Unstrut region around Naumburg in Saxony-Anhalt is famous for tart wines and Rotkäppchen *Sekt* (sparkling wine).

ENTERTAINMENT

The standard of theatre performances, concerts and operas is among the highest in Europe. Berlin is unrivalled when it comes to concerts and theatre and Dresden is famed for its opera.

Tickets can usually be purchased at short notice from tourist offices and directly from box offices.

Pubs & Beer Halls

The variety of pubs in Germany is enormous, ranging from vaulted-cellar bars through to theme pubs, Irish pubs, historic student pubs and clubs offering music or performances. Beer gardens are especially common in the south. It is worth experiencing the raucous atmosphere of a traditional Bavarian beer hall at least once during a visit to Germany.

Nightclubs

Germany's large cities throb with club and disco sounds. Berlin is a world techno capital, but you'll find a variety of lively clubs in most major cities. Posters around clubs, universities and cafés or city listing guides are good information sources.

GERMANY

Cinemas

Germans are avid movie-goers, but foreign films are usually dubbed into German. Original soundtrack versions (identifiable by letter-codes OF, OV or OmU with subtitles) are mostly limited to university towns and bigger cities such as Berlin, Munich, Hamburg and Frankfurt.

SPECTATOR SPORTS

Soccer is by far Germany's most popular sport, and the country will host the 2006 World Cup. Tickets to first-division games, usually played from Friday to Sunday, can be purchased at grounds and outlets. National knockout and European matches are mostly played during the week. The national team made the 2002 World Cup final, only to lose to Brazil. The popularity of tennis has been boosted by the past achievements of Boris Becker and Steffi Graf, and motor racing is a national passion, due in no small part to Michael Schumacher. Exciting winter sports events are held annually in Oberstdorf and Garmisch-Partenkirchen.

SHOPPING

Products made in Germany are rarely cheap, but higher prices generally mean high quality. Worthwhile products include optical lenses, fine crystal glassware (particularly from the Bavarian Forest), fine porcelain (particularly from Meissen) and therapeutic footwear such as the sandals and shoes made by Birkenstock. Excellent art reproductions, books and posters are sold in some museums and speciality shops. Germany's fine regional wines give you a real taste of the country. More predictable souvenirs include colourful heraldic emblems, cuckoo clocks from the Black Forest, Bavarian wooden carvings and traditional Bavarian clothing. Some open-air streetsellers in Berlin offer GDR-era memorabilia, though sometimes of questionable authenticity.

Getting There & Away

AIR

The main arrival and departure points in Germany are Frankfurt, Munich, Düsseldorf and Berlin. Frankfurt is Europe's busiest airport after London's Heathrow. Flights are generally priced competitively among all major airlines, but **Lufthansa** (W *www.lufthansa.com*) offers the most flexibility.

Flights to Frankfurt are usually cheaper than to other German cities. Regular flights from Western Europe to Germany tend to be more expensive than the train or bus. Airline deregulation within Europe has encouraged cheap, no-frills deals, especially between London and Frankfurt, Berlin or Düsseldorf. Ryanair and Buzz are cheap options.

From North America, Lufthansa, United Airlines, Air Canada, Delta Airlines and Singapore Airlines have the most frequent flights. You can often get the best fare by flying another European carrier and changing planes for Germany at their home-country hub. The German charter company LTU makes regular scheduled international flights between North America and Düsseldorf, but these fill up quickly.

Asian carriers offer the cheapest – but often the most indirect – flights from Australia and New Zealand. Qantas and Lufthansa both fly via Asian hubs such as Singapore and Bangkok and continue on to Germany.

Lufthansa has many flights to the Eastern European nations, but the region's national carriers are cheaper.

LAND
Bus

If you're already in Europe, it's generally cheaper to get to/from Germany by bus than it is by train or plane, but you trade price for speed. Return fares are noticeably cheaper than two one-way fares.

Eurolines is a consortium of national bus companies operating routes throughout the continent. Some sample one-way fares and travel times for routes include:

London–Frankfurt	€72	14¼ hours
Amsterdam–Frankfurt	€36	6 hours
Paris–Hamburg	€55	12½ hours
Paris–Cologne	€34	7¼ hours
Prague–Berlin	€35	6½ hours
Barcelona–Frankfurt	€85	20 hours

Eurolines has a youth fare for those aged under 26 that saves around 10%. Tickets can be bought in Germany at most train stations. For detailed information (but not bookings), contact **Deutsche-Touring GmbH** (☎ *069-79 03 50, fax 790 32 19; Am Römerhof 17, 60486 Frankfurt/Main*).

Train

Another good way to get to Germany from elsewhere in Europe is by train. It's a lot more comfortable (albeit more expensive) than the bus.

Long-distance trains between major German cities and other countries are called Euro-City (EC) trains. The main German hubs with the best connections to/from major European cities are Hamburg (Scandinavia); Cologne (France, Belgium and the Netherlands, with Eurostar connections from Brussels or Paris going on to London); Munich (southern and southeastern Europe); and Berlin (Eastern Europe). Frankfurt-am-Main has the widest range of, but not always the quickest, international connections.

Generally the longer international routes are served by at least one day train and often a night train as well. Many night trains only carry sleeping cars, but a bunk is more comfortable than sitting up in a compartment and only adds from €21/14 to the cost of a 2nd-class ticket in four-/six-berth compartments.

Car & Motorcycle

Germany is served by an excellent highway system. If you're coming from the UK, the quickest option is the Channel Tunnel. Ferries take longer but are cheaper. Choices include hovercraft from Dover, Folkestone or Ramsgate to Calais in France. You can be in Germany three hours after the ferry docks.

Within Europe, autobahns and highways become jammed on weekends in summer and before and after holidays. This is especially true where border checks are still carried out, such as going to/from the Czech Republic and Poland.

You must have third-party insurance to enter Germany with a car or motorcycle.

Hitching & Ride Services

Lonely Planet does not recommend hitching, but should you decide to try it you may encounter delays getting to Germany via the main highways as hitching is becoming less popular both for riders and drivers.

Aside from hitching, the cheapest way to get to Germany from elsewhere in Europe is as a paying passenger in a private car. Leaving Germany, or travelling within the country, such rides are arranged by *Mitfahrzentrale* (ride sharing agencies) in many German cities. You pay a reservation fee to the agency and a share of petrol and costs to the driver. Local tourist offices can direct you to local agencies, or call the city area code and ☎ 194 40 in large German cities. Agencies for major cities are listed in the Getting There & Away sections for each city.

BOAT

If you're heading to or from the UK or Scandinavia, the port options are Hamburg, Lübeck, Rostock, Sassnitz, and Kiel. The Hamburg–Harwich service operates at least three times a week. The Puttgarden–Rodbyhavn ferry is popular with those heading to Copenhagen (see the Hamburg Getting There & Away section for details). In eastern Germany, there are five ferries in each direction daily all year between Trelleborg (Sweden) and Sassnitz near Stralsund (see the Rügen Island section).

There are daily services between Kiel and Gothenburg (Sweden) and Oslo. A ferry between Travemünde (near Lübeck) and Trelleborg (Sweden) runs one to four times daily. Ferries also run several times a week between the Danish island of Bornholm and Sassnitz. Car-ferry service is also good from Gedser (Denmark) to Rostock. Finnjet-Silja runs fast ferries several times a week on the Rostock–Tallin–Helsinki route (23 hours) from June to September. Finnlines has daily sailings from Lübeck to Helsinki. See the Kiel, Rostock, Stralsund and Rügen Island Getting There & Away sections for more details.

DEPARTURE TAX

All security, airport and departure taxes are included in ticket prices. Be aware that some companies in Germany will advertise a flight *excluding* these charges, so check the fine print carefully. There is no departure tax if you depart by sea or land.

Getting Around

AIR

There are lots of flights within the country, but costs can be prohibitive compared to other modes of transport. Lufthansa has the most frequent air services within Germany. Deregulation has brought some competition. **Lufthansa** and **Deutsche BA** (☎ 01805-35 93 32) regularly offer special fares, mostly from around €35 to €105 for the longest routes.

It is also well worth checking with a travel agency for other savers including youth (under 27) fares.

BUS

The bus network in Germany functions primarily in support of the train network, going places where trains don't. Bus stations or stops are usually near the train station in any town. Schedule and route information is usually posted. Consider buses when you want to cut across two train lines and avoid long train rides to and from a transfer point. A good example of this is in the Alps, where the best way to follow the peaks is by bus.

In the Getting There & Away section for each city and town we note any bus services that are useful for reaching other places described in this chapter. **Deutsche Bahn** agencies have information on certain key regional services, otherwise check with tourist offices.

Eurolines operates within Germany as Deutsche-Touring GmbH, a subsidiary of the German Federal Railways (Deutsche Bahn). Eurolines services include the Romantic and Castle Roads buses in southern Germany, as well as organised bus tours of Germany lasting a week or more. See the Frankfurt and Romantic Road sections for details, or contact **Deutsche-Touring GmbH** (☎ 069-79 03 50, fax 790 32 19), in Frankfurt/Main.

TRAIN

Operated almost entirely by the **Deutsche Bahn** (DB), the German train system is arguably the best in Europe.

The trains run on an interval system that means from the busiest to the quietest routes, you can count on service every one or two hours. The schedules are integrated throughout the country so that connections between trains are time-saving and tight, often only five minutes. Of course the obverse of this is that when a train is late (a not uncommon occurrence, especially during busy travel periods) connections are missed and you can find yourself stuck waiting for the next train. If you have to be somewhere at a specified time, put some slack in your itinerary so you won't miss a connection and be really stranded.

Types of Trains

There is rarely ever a need to buy a 1st-class ticket on German trains; 2nd class is usually quite comfortable. German trains fall into specific classifications; supplements (Zuschlag) for faster trains are built into fares:

ICE
The InterCityExpress trains run at speeds up to 280km/h when they use special high-speed tracks. The trains are very comfortable and feature restaurant cars. Main routes link Hamburg to Munich, Cologne to Berlin, Frankfurt to Berlin, Frankfurt to Munich and Frankfurt to Basel, Switzerland.

IC/EC
Called InterCity or EuroCity, these are the premier conventional trains of DB. When trains are crowded, the open-seating coaches are much more comfortable than the older carriages with compartments.

IR
Called InterRegio, these are fast trains that cover secondary routes and usually run at intervals of two hours. For journeys of more than two hours you can usually get to your destination faster by transferring from an IR train to an IC or ICE.

RE
RegionalExpress trains are local trains that make limited stops. They are fairly fast and run at one- or two-hourly intervals.

SE
StadtExpress trains are found in metropolitan areas. They make few stops in urban areas and all stops in rural areas.

RB
RegionalBahn are the slowest DB trains, not missing a single cow town or junction of roads so sit back and enjoy the view.

S-Bahn
These DB-operated trains run frequent services in larger urban areas and sometimes run in tunnels under the city centre. Not to be confused with U-Bahns, which are run by local authorities who don't honour rail passes.

EN, ICN, D
These are night trains, although an occasional D may be an extra daytime train.

Tickets & Reservations

Nearly every DB station offers the option of purchasing tickets with credit cards at ticket machines for longer haul trains; these usually have English-language options, but when in doubt consult at the ticket window. It is always better to buy your ticket before boarding, since buying a ticket or Zuschlag from a conductor carries a penalty (€1.50 to €4.50). If you're really stuck you can *technically* use a credit card to buy a ticket on the train, but you're likely to get a better response, say, if you ask the conductor to launder your dirty clothes. Ticket agents, on the other hand, cheerfully accept credit cards, as do most machines.

On some trains there are no conductors at all, and roving teams of inspectors enforce compliance. If you are caught travelling without a ticket the fine is €30 and they accept *no* excuses.

During peak travel periods, a seat reservation (€2.50) on a long-distance train can mean the difference between squatting near the toilet or relaxing in your own seat. Express reservations can be made at the last minute. If a crowded train is sold out or you don't have a reservation, try the end carriages. Most waiting passengers mill about the middle of platforms like flocks of sheep.

Fares

Standard DB ticket prices are distance-based. You will usually be sold a ticket for the shortest distance to your destination, so if for example you wish to travel from Munich to Frankfurt via Nuremberg (a slightly more expensive route than via Stuttgart), say so when you buy your ticket.

Sample fares for one-way, 2nd-class ICE travel include: Hamburg to Munich €137.80; Frankfurt to Berlin €106.40; and Frankfurt to Munich €75.60. Tickets are good for four days from the day you tell the agent your journey will begin and you can make unlimited stopovers along your route during that time (if you break your journey, it's wise to inform the conductor).

There are hosts of special fares that allow you to beat the high cost of regular tickets. The following are the most popular special train fares offered by DB (all fares are for 2nd class):

BahnCard
A €140/280 card (2nd/1st class) that entitles the owner to half-price travel on all trains (except S-Bahn). It's only worthwhile for extended visits to Germany.

Guten Abend
Literally 'Good Evening' tickets. They are valid for unlimited travel between 7pm and 3am the next day and cost €30 (€36 for ICE). They can offer significant reductions in price. For instance, you can take the 7.15pm ICE from Hamburg to Munich, arriving at 1.26am, for €36 instead of the usual €137.80.

Länder Tickets
Good within individual German states, for up to five people travelling together, or one or both parents and all their children. Tickets cost €21, and are valid in 2nd class, weekdays from 9am on the first day until 3pm the next day. Other conditions vary by state.

Schönes Wochenende
These cheerful 'Good Weekend' tickets allow unlimited use of trains on a Saturday or Sunday between midnight and 3am the next day, for up to five people travelling together, or one or both parents and all their children for €21. The catch is that they are only good on RE, SE, RB and S-Bahns, so a money-saving trip from Cologne to Dresden can be a 12-hour ordeal of frequent train-changing or an adventure, depending on your outlook. They are best suited to weekend day trips from urban areas.

In addition, ask about various 'Sparpreis' schemes that offer big savings on return tickets if one leg of the journey is on a weekend or a weekend falls between the forward and return trip.

Most ticket agents are quite willing to help you find the cheapest options for your intended trip. For schedule and fare information (available in English), you can call ☎ 01805-99 66 33 from anywhere in Germany (€0.13 per minute).

Rail Passes

Travel agencies outside Germany sell German Rail Passes valid for unlimited travel on all DB trains for a given number of days within a 30-day period. Sample prices per person (in US$), good for 2nd-class travel, are for adults/two adults together/individuals under 26 for five days $202/151.50/156 and for 10 days $316/237/216. There also are 1st-class adult passes available.

The passes also include some ships but not seat reservations. Eurail and Inter-Rail passes are also valid in Germany.

Stations

Almost all train stations have lockers (from €1 depending on size). The few exceptions are noted in the Getting There & Away section for each city or town. Larger stations have DB Service Points counters that offer schedule information and are open long hours. Many have local maps that will help you find the tourist office.

Disabled passengers who need assistance must notify DB in advance of their needs. Train station platforms and the trains themselves are often not easily accessible.

GERMANY

CAR & MOTORCYCLE

German roads are excellent, and motorised transport can be a great way to tour the country. Prices for fuel vary from €1.04 to €1.08 per litre for unleaded regular. Avoid buying fuel at the more expensive autobahn filling stations.

The autobahn system of motorways runs throughout Germany. Road signs (and most motoring maps) indicate national autobahn routes in blue with an 'A' number, while international routes have green signs with an 'E' number. Though efficient, the autobahns are often busy, and resemble life in the fast lane. Tourists often have trouble coping with the very high speeds and the dangers involved in overtaking – don't underestimate the time it takes for a car in the rear-view mirror to close in at 180km/h. Secondary roads (usually designated with a 'B' number) are easier on the nerves and much more scenic, but can be slow going. Most are just two lanes, and you're bound to get stuck behind a lorry, camping caravan or farm vehicle. Hone your passing skills.

Cars are impractical in urban areas. Vending machines on many streets sell parking vouchers which must be displayed clearly behind the windscreen. Leaving your car in a central *Parkhaus* (car park) costs roughly €10 per day or €1.25 per hour.

To find passengers willing to pay their share of fuel costs, drivers should contact the local Mitfahrzentrale (see Hitching & Ride Services in the earlier Getting There & Away section). Germany's main motoring organisation is the Munich-based **Allgemeiner Deutscher Automobil Club** (ADAC; ☎ 089-767 60, fax 76 76 28 01); it has offices in all major cities. Call the **ADAC road patrol** (☎ 0180-222 22 22) if your car breaks down.

Road Rules

Road rules are easy to understand and standard international signs are in use. The usual speed limits are 50km/h in built-up areas (in effect as soon as you see the yellow name board of the town) and 100km/h on the open road. The speed on autobahns is unlimited, though there's an advisory speed of 130km/h; exceptions are clearly signposted. The blood-alcohol limit for drivers is 0.05%. Obey the road rules carefully: the German police are very efficient and issue heavy on-the-spot fines; cameras are in widespread use and notices are sent to the car's registration address wherever that may be. If it's a rental company, they will bill your credit card.

Rental

Germany's four main rental companies are **Avis** (☎ 0180-555 77), **Europcar** (☎ 0180-580 00), **Hertz** (☎ 0180-533 35 35) and **Sixt** (☎ 0180-526 02 50). There are numerous smaller local rental companies – **AutoEurope** (☎ 800-822 19 80) offers some great deals – and there's a new DB Reisebüro car rental programme. For weekend deals, expect to pay €100 to €130 including collision damage waiver. You usually must be at least 21 years of age to hire a car.

Deals that include rental cars with train passes or airline tickets can be excellent value. Check with your travel agent.

Purchase

Due to the costs, paperwork and insurance hassles involved, buying a car in Germany tends to be an unwise option.

BICYCLE

Radwandern (bicycle touring) is very popular in Germany. In urban areas the pavement is often divided into separate sections for pedestrians and cyclists – be warned that these divisions are taken very seriously. Even outside towns and cities there are often separate cycling routes. Favoured routes include the Rhine, Moselle, Elbe and Danube Rivers and the Lake Constance area. Of course, cycling is strictly *verboten* (forbidden) on the autobahns. Hostel-to-hostel biking is an easy way to go, and route guides are often sold at local DJH hostels. There are well-equipped cycling shops in almost every town, and a fairly active market for used touring bikes.

Simple three-gear bicycles can be hired from around €8/32 per day/week, and more robust mountain bikes from €10/48. Rental shops in many cities are noted in the Getting Around sections of the city and town listings. The DB publishes *Bahn&Bike*, an excellent annual handbook covering bike rental and repair shops, routes, maps and other resources.

A separate ticket must be purchased whenever you carry your bike on most trains (generally €3 to €6). Most trains (excluding ICEs) have a 2nd-class carriage at one end with a bicycle compartment.

The central office of Germany's main cycling organisation is **Allgemeiner Deutscher**

Fahrrad Club (ADFC; ☎ 0421-34 62 90, fax 346 29 50; e kontakt@adfc.de) in Bremen.

See also Activities in the earlier Facts for the Visitor section.

HITCHING

Lonely Planet does not recommend *Trampen* (hitching), and it's not absolutely not allowed on autobahns. Mitfahrzentrale ride-share services (see Hitching & Ride Services in the earlier Getting There & Away section) is a cheap, more reliable and safer option.

BOAT

Boats are most likely to be used for basic transport when travelling to or between the Frisian Islands, though tours along the Rhine and Moselle Rivers are also popular. In summer there are frequent services on Lake Constance but, except for the Constance to Meersburg and the Friedrichshafen to Romanshorn car ferries, these boats are really more tourist craft than a transport option. From April to October, excursion boats ply lakes and rivers throughout Germany and on a nice day can be a lovely way to see the country.

LOCAL TRANSPORT

Local transport is excellent within big cities and small towns, and is generally based on buses, Strassenbahn (trams), S-Bahn and/or U-Bahn (underground train system). The systems integrate all forms of transit; fares are determined by the zones or the time travelled, or sometimes both. Multiticket strips or day passes are generally available and offer better value than single-ride tickets. In some cities, tourist offices sell one- to three-day transit passes that also include discounts to attractions. See the individual city and town Getting Around entries in this chapter for details.

Make certain that you have a ticket when boarding – on buses and some trams, you can buy tickets when you board. In some cases you will have to validate it in a little time-stamp machine on the platform or once aboard. Ticket inspections are frequent (especially at night and on holidays) and the fine is a non-negotiable €30 payable on the spot. If you can't pay, the inspector will take your passport until you can.

Bus & Tram

Cities and towns operate their own services that can include buses, trolleybuses and/or trams. Bus drivers usually sell single-trip tickets as a service to forgetful passengers, but these are more expensive than tickets bought in advance. Large cities often have a limited night-bus system operating from about 1am to 4am, when everything else has shut down.

Underground

Larger cities such as Berlin, Hamburg, Munich and Frankfurt have underground metro systems known as the U-Bahn. They have the same ticketing and validation requirements as the local buses and/or trams.

Train

Most large cities have a system of S-Bahn suburban trains. In places like Berlin, Hamburg, Munich and Frankfurt, they also serve the city centre. Tickets on these lines are integrated with other forms of local transport; however train pass-holders can ride S-Bahns (and only S-Bahns!) for free since they are operated by DB.

Taxi

Taxis are expensive and only really needed late, late at night. In fact, given traffic, they can actually take longer than public transport. For fast service, look up 'TaxiRuf' in the local telephone directory to find the nearest taxi rank. Taxis are metered and cost up to €2.30 flag fall and €1.30 per kilometre; higher night tariffs apply.

ORGANISED TOURS

Local tourist offices offer various tour options, from short city sightseeing trips to multiday adventure, spa-bath and wine-tasting packages. Apart from city tours, other good sources for organised tours in and around Germany are Deutsche-Touring and DB.

There are scores of international and national tour operators with specific options. Your travel agent should have some details. Many airlines also offer tour packages with their tickets.

Berlin

☎ 030 • pop 3.45 million

Berlin, Germany's largest city, has more to offer visitors than almost any city in Europe: bustling pubs, peerless cultural life, a worldly-wise, tolerant attitude and an indomitable

GERMANY

spirit. No other city has been split by a brutal, impenetrable, 162km wall (torn down in 1990), and no other city has reintegrated so completely or quickly – the construction still continues. Some eastern neighbourhoods near the wall are now centres of artistic and cultural activity, although a few outlying areas, with their grim communist-era high-rise housing, remain as bleak as ever.

The centre of 19th-century Prussian military and industrial might, this great city reached maturity in the 1920s, only to be bombed into rubble in WWII. After hibernating for decades after the war, Berlin is now reassuming its role as the heart of Germany. With hundreds of construction cranes dotting the city, the changes are breathtaking and it is an exciting time to visit Berlin, once again the nation's capital and one of Europe's most dynamic cities.

HISTORY

The first recorded settlement in present-day Berlin was named Cölln (1237) around the Spree River, south of the present-day Museumsinsel (Museum Island), although Spandau to the west, the junction of the Spree and the ponded Havel Rivers, is considered to be older. Medieval Berlin developed on the bank of the Spree around Nikolaikirche and spread northeast towards today's Alexanderplatz. In 1432, Berlin and Cölln, which were linked by the Mühlendamm, merged.

In the 1440s, Elector Friedrich II of Brandenburg established the rule of the Hohenzollern dynasty, which was to last until Kaiser Wilhelm II's escape from Potsdam in 1918. Berlin's importance increased in 1470 when the elector moved his residence here from Brandenburg and built a palace near the present Marx-Engels-Platz.

During the Thirty Years' War, Berlin's population was decimated, but in the mid-17th century the city was reborn stronger than before under the so-called Great Elector Friedrich Wilhelm. His vision was the basis of Prussian power and he sponsored Huguenot refugees seeking princely tolerance.

The Great Elector's son, Friedrich I, the first Prussian king, made fast-growing Berlin his capital, and his daughter-in-law Sophie Charlotte encouraged the development of the arts and sciences and presided over a lively, intellectual court. Friedrich II sought greatness through building and was known for his

political and military savvy. All this led to the city being nicknamed *Spreeathen* (Athens-on-Spree).

The Enlightenment arrived with some authority in the form of the playwright Gotthold Ephraim Lessing, and thinker and publisher Friedrich Nicolai; both helped make Berlin a truly international city.

The 19th century began on a low note with the French occupation of 1806–13, and in 1848 a bourgeois democratic revolution was suppressed, somewhat stifling the political development that had been set in motion by the Enlightenment. The population doubled between 1850 and 1870 as the Industrial Revolution, spurred on by companies such as Siemens and Borsig, took hold. In 1871 Bismarck united Germany under Kaiser Wilhelm I. By 1900, Berlin's population was almost two million.

Before WWI Berlin had become an industrial giant, but the war and its aftermath led to revolt throughout Germany. On 9 November 1918 Philipp Scheidemann, leader of the Social Democrats, proclaimed the German Republic from a balcony of the *Reichstag* (parliament) and hours later Karl Liebknecht proclaimed a free Socialist republic from a balcony of the Berliner Schloss. In January 1919 the Berlin Spartacists, Liebknecht and Rosa Luxemburg, were murdered by remnants of the old imperial army, which entered the city and brought the Revolution to a bloody end.

On the eve of the Nazi takeover, the Communist Party under Ernst Thälmann was the strongest single party in 'Red Berlin', having polled 31% of the votes in 1932. Berlin was heavily bombed by the Allies in WWII and, during the 'Battle of Berlin' from August 1943 to March 1944, British bombers hammered the city every night. Most of the buildings you see today along Unter den Linden were reconstructed from the ruins. The Soviets shelled Berlin from the east, and after the last terrible battle, buried 18,000 of their own troops.

In August 1945, the Potsdam Conference sealed the fate of the city by finalising plans for each of the victorious powers – the USA, Britain, France and the Soviet Union – to occupy a separate zone. In June 1948 the city was split in two when the three Western Allies introduced a western German currency and established a separate administration in their sectors. The Soviets then blockaded West Berlin, but an airlift by the Western Allies kept the

city stocked with food and supplies. In October 1949 East Berlin became the capital of the GDR. The construction of the Berlin Wall in August 1961 prevented the drain of skilled labour (between 1945 and 1961 four million East Germans were lured westwards by higher wages and political freedom).

When Hungary breached the Iron Curtain in May 1989, the GDR government was back where it had been in 1961, but this time without Soviet backing. On 9 November 1989 the Wall opened and by 1 July 1990, when the Bundesrepublik's currency was adopted in the GDR, the Wall was being hacked to pieces. The Unification Treaty between the two Germanys designated Berlin the official capital of Germany, and in June 1991 the Bundestag voted to move the seat of government from Bonn to Berlin over the following decade at a cost of €10 billion. A huge consortium of public and private organisations was charged with constructing the heart of a metropolis from scratch.

Finally, in 1999, the federal government moved back to Berlin, with a newly refurbished Reichstag just one of the city's great symbols.

ORIENTATION

Berlin sits in the middle of the region known from medieval times as the Mark and is surrounded by the *Bundesland* (federal state) of Brandenburg. Roughly one-third of the city's municipal area is made up of parks, forests, lakes and rivers. There are more trees here than in Paris and more bridges than in Venice. Much of the natural beauty of rolling hills and quiet shorelines is in the southeast and southwest of the city.

The Spree River winds across the city for more than 30km, from Grosser Müggelsee in the east to Spandau in the west. North and south of Spandau the Havel River widens into a series of lakes from Tegel to Potsdam. A network of canals links the waterways to each other and to the Oder River to the east, and there are beautiful walks along some of them.

Berlin has 23 *Bezirken* (independent administrative districts), although most travellers will end up visiting only the eight 'core' ones. They are (clockwise from the west): Charlottenburg, Tiergarten, Mitte, Prenzlauer Berg, Friedrichshain, Kreuzberg, Schöneberg and Wilmersdorf.

The Wall once ran east of Brandenburger Tor (Brandenburg Gate), and now the gate is a symbol of city unity. From here Unter den Linden, the fashionable avenue of aristocratic old Berlin, and its continuation, Karl-Liebknecht-Strasse, extend eastwards to Alexanderplatz, once the heart of socialist Germany. En route are some of Berlin's finest museums, on Museumsinsel (Museum Island) in the Spree, and the monstrous Fernsehturm (TV Tower, probably Berlin's most useful landmark). The cultural centre is around Friedrichstrasse, which crosses Unter den Linden. South of here, in areas once occupied by the Wall, the former Checkpoint Charlie is now almost lost amid new construction. Some startling new buildings have been built around Potsdamer Platz, which before the war had been the busiest intersection in Europe. A few sections of the Wall have been preserved for public view, but otherwise it is virtually impossible to tell where the historic barrier once stood.

To the west, near Zoo station, you will find the ruin and the modern annexes of Kaiser-Wilhelm-Gedächtnis-Kirche, the shattered memorial church on Breitscheidplatz. A branch of the tourist office and hundreds of shops are situated in the faded Europa-Center at the end of the square farthest from the station. The Kurfürstendamm (known colloquially as the 'Ku'damm') runs 3.5km southwest from Breitscheidplatz. To the northeast, between Breitscheidplatz and the Brandenburger Tor, is Tiergarten, a district named after the vast city park which was once a royal hunting domain. Nearby is another Brobdingnagian work site around the Lehrter Bahnhof, where the Spree has actually been rerouted to allow a vast underground tunnel to create a new central train station in 2007. Just north of the Hackescher Markt Bahnhof stretches the ancient neighbourhood of the Scheunenviertel (barn district). This was a centre of Jewish life before the war and is now home to stylish businesses and residents.

In central Berlin, street numbers usually run sequentially up one side of the street and down the other (important exceptions are Martin-Luther-Strasse in Schöneberg, and Unter den Linden). Number guides appear on most corner street signs. Be aware, too, that a continuous street may change names several times and that on some streets (Pariser Strasse, Knesebeckstrasse) numbering sequences continue after interruptions for squares or plazas.

INFORMATION
Tourist Offices

The main office of **Berlin Tourismus Mar-keting** (☎ 0190-01 31 16 for information, ☎ 25 00 25 for hotel & event reservations both from inside Germany, ☎ 1805-75 40 40 from outside Germany, fax 25 00 24 24; e hotel-reservation@t-online.de; Budapester Strasse 45; open 8.30am-8.30pm Mon-Sat, 10am-6.30pm Sun) is located at the Europa-Center. This office also handles hotel reservations. There are other branches situated in the southern wing of the Brandenburger Tor (open 9.30am-6pm daily) and at the base of the Fernsehturm (TV Tower) at Alexanderplatz (open 10am-6pm daily). The website is w www.berlin-tourism.de.

The tourist office sells the Berlin-Potsdam Welcome Card (€18), which entitles you to unlimited transport for three days and discounted admission to major museums, shows, attractions, sightseeing tours and boat cruises in both Berlin and Potsdam.

It is also available at hotels and public transport ticket offices.

EurAide (open 8am-noon & 1pm-4pm Mon-Sat), which is located in Zoo station, is an English-language service offering train advice and reservations.

Money

With offices at two locations, **AmEx** (Bayreuther Strasse 37 • Friedrichstrasse 172) cashes its own travellers cheques without charging commission. The Friedrichstrasse office is across from Galeries Lafayette department store. There is an exchange office of **Thomas Cook** (Friedrichstrasse 56, Mitte).

Reisebank (Hardenbergplatz 1; open 7.30am-10pm daily) has an exchange office outside Zoo station. If you show a EurAide coupon you'll pay less commission. There is another branch inside Ostbahnhof.

Post & Communications

The **main post office** (open 8am-midnight Mon-Sat, 10am-midnight Sun) is in Joachimstalerstrasse, one block south of Zoo station. The poste restante service is here; letters should be clearly marked 'Hauptpostlagernd' and addressed to you at 10612 Berlin.

Note that mail will only be held for a two-week period. There are dozens of post offices throughout Berlin with more-restricted opening hours.

Email & Internet Access

With hundreds of terminals for your surfing pleasure, try **Easy Everything** (☎ 88 70 79 70; Kurfürstendamm 224). You could also try the rather smoky **Alpha Café** (☎ 447 90 67; Dunckerstrasse 72, Prenzlauer Berg); take S8 or S10 to Prenzlauer Allee.

Travel Agencies

Travel agencies offering cheap flights advertise in the Reisen (travel) classified section (Kleinanzeigen) of the city magazines Zitty and Tip. One of the better discount operators is **Alternativ Tours** (☎ 881 20 89; Wilmersdorfer Strasse 94, Wilmersdorf; U7 to Adenauerplatz), which specialises in a range of unpublished, discounted fares to anywhere in the world.

The following agencies are generally open between 9am and 6pm weekdays and until 1pm Saturday. The most convenient **Atlas Reisewelt branch** (☎ 247 57 60; Alexanderplatz 9) is inside the Kaufhof department store; it's a big chain with several offices around Berlin. **STA Travel** (☎ 28 59 82 64; Gleimstrasse 28, Prenzlauer Berg • ☎ 311 09 50, Goethestrasse 73, Charlottenburg • ☎ 310 00 40; Hardenbergstrasse 9, Charlottenburg) specialises in travel for young people and issues ISIC cards, provided you have proper and recognisable student and personal ID.

Newspapers & Magazines

The bimonthly English-German Berlin Kalender (€1.75) has mainstream listings and is available at newsstands, hotels and tourist offices. The magazines Zitty (€2.30) and Tip (€2.50) offer comprehensive listings (in German only) of all current events, including concerts, theatre, clubs, gallery exhibits, readings, movies etc. Also look for the free 030 (in pubs and cafés), which has the latest club and rave news (in German).

Bookshops

Books in Berlin (☎ 313 12 33; Goethestrasse 69, Charlottenburg) has a good selection of English and American literature. Large German bookshops with decent English-language sections include the vast **Hugendubel** (☎ 21 40 60; Tauentzienstrasse 13, Charlottenburg). **Kiepert** (☎ 31 18 80; Hardenbergstrasse 4-5, Charlottenburg) has many departments, from guidebooks to foreign-language dictionaries. **Europa Presse Center** at ground level in the

Europa-Center has a big range of international papers and magazines.

Laundry

The Schnell & Sauber chain has various **laundrette branches** (*Uhlandstrasse 53 & Leibnizstrasse 72, Charlottenburg • Torstrasse 115, Mitte • Mehringdamm 32, Kreuzberg*); the Kreuzberg branch is situated just outside the Mehringdamm U-Bahn station. Hours are generally from 6am to 11pm, and to wash and dry a load costs about €5.

Medical & Emergency Services

For 24-hour medical aid, advice and referrals, call the **Kassenärztliche Bereitschaftsdienst** (*Public Physicians' Emergency Service;* ☎ 31 00 31). If you need a **pharmacy** after hours, dial ☎ 118 80. For information on where you can find an emergency **dentist** (*Zahnarzt*), dial ☎ 89 00 43 33.

The general emergency number for a **doctor** (*Notarzt*) or **fire brigade** (*Feuerwehr*) throughout Berlin is ☎ 112.

Call ☎ 110 for police emergencies only. Otherwise, there are police stations all over the city, including the upstairs **City Wache** (*Joachimstaler Strasse 15*), south of Ku'damm and near Zoo station. In eastern Berlin, there's a station at Otto-Braun-Strasse 27, northeast of Alexanderplatz.

Police headquarters and the municipal **lost-and-found office** (☎ 69 95; *Platz der Luftbrücke 6*) are beside Tempelhof airport. If you've lost something on public transport, contact the **BVG** (☎ 25 62 30 40; *Potsdamer Strasse 182, Schöneberg*).

Dangers & Annoyances

Berlin is generally safe and tolerant. Walking alone at night on city streets shouldn't be considered a risk, bearing in mind the caveat that there is always safety in numbers in any urban environment. You may want to avoid the area along the Spree south of the Ostbahnhof, until recently the haunt of punks, urban drifters and druggies, although the neighbourhood is rapidly gentrifying. Also use the usual cautions against robberies in the Zoo station area. Some travellers may be put off by graffiti, sometimes found even in upscale neighbourhoods.

THINGS TO SEE & DO

Among Berlin's 170 museums, the **State museums** (denoted in this section by 'SMB')

are among the highlights. Unless otherwise noted, the SMB museums are closed on Monday, admission is by day-pass (€6/3 adult/concession), valid for all SMB museums on that day, and is free the first Sunday of each month. Serious museumgoers may invest in the Drei-Tages-Touristenkarte (€10/5), offering free entry to more than 50 museums during three consecutive days (ask at tourist offices).

Around Alexanderplatz

Soaring above Berlin is the restored 368m **Fernsehturm** (*TV Tower;* ☎ 242 33 33; *Panoramastrasse 1A; adult/concession €6/3; open 10am-1am daily*) built in 1969. If it's a clear day and the queue isn't too long, it's worth paying the fee to go up the tower or have a drink at the 207m-level Telecafé, which revolves twice an hour. The best thing about the view from the tower is that it is the one place in the city where you can't see it.

On the opposite side of the elevated train station from the tower is **Alexanderplatz** (or, affectionately, 'Alex'), the square named after Tsar Alexander I who visited Berlin in 1805. The area was redesigned several times in the late 1920s but little was ever actually built because of the Depression. It was bombed in WWII and completely reconstructed in the 1960s. The **World Time Clock** (1969) is nearby in case you want to check the time before making a telephone call home.

Museumsinsel

Berlin's famed Museum Island is a scene of heavy construction as its grand buildings are restored. West of the Fernsehturm, on an island between two arms of the Spree River, is the GDR's **Palace of the Republic** (1976), which occupies the site of the bombed baroque Berliner Schloss that was demolished in 1950. During the communist era, the Volkskammer (People's Chamber) used to meet in this monstrosity which faces Marx-Engels-Platz. In 1990 it was discovered that asbestos had been used in the construction and its future has been up in the air ever since.

On the southern side is the former **Staatsrat** (Council of State; 1964) building, with a portal from the old city palace incorporated in the facade. Immediately east are the **Neue Marstall** (New Royal Stables), built at the end of the 19th century, which house the State Archives.

North of Marx-Engels-Platz looms the great neo-Renaissance **Berliner Dom** (1904), the former court church of the Hohenzollern family. The 1930 SMB **Pergamonmuseum** (☎ 20 90 55 55; *Am Kupfergraben*) is a feast of classical Greek, Babylonian, Roman, Islamic and Oriental antiquity. The world-renowned Ishtar Gate from Babylon (580 BC), the reconstructed Pergamon Altar from Asia Minor (160 BC) and the Market Gate from Greek Miletus (Asia Minor, 2nd century AD) are among the beautiful Middle Eastern artefacts. The SMB **Alte Nationalgalerie** (*Old National Gallery;* ☎ 20 90 58 01; *Bodestrasse 1-3*) houses classical sculpture, and paintings by European masters in dozens of tiny galleries. Inside the stairwell is a massive frieze of the great German philosophers, thinkers, writers and patrons. The imposing edifice beside it is Karl Friedrich Schinkel's 1829 neoclassical SMB **Altes Museum** (☎ 20 90 52 01; *Am Lustgarten*), with its famed rotunda area featuring statues of the Greek divinities, a permanent antiquities display plus special exhibitions. The Museumsinsel's two remaining museums are undergoing badly needed facelifts; the **Bodemuseum** (1904) is closed until mid-2004, and the **Neues Museum** (1855) until 2005.

Nikolaiviertel

The rebuilt 13th-century **Nikolaikirche** stands amid the forced charms of the Nikolaiviertel (Nikolai quarter), conceived and executed under the GDR's Berlin restoration programme. Another medieval church is **Marienkirche** (*Karl-Liebknecht-Strasse*), which stands across the square from the monumental **Rotes Rathaus** (or Red Town Hall, named for its appearance, not its politics), a neo-Renaissance structure from 1860, which has been proudly restored and is once again the centre of Berlin's municipal government. Across Grunerstrasse, the remains of the bombed-out shell of the late 13th-century **Franciscan Abbey** mark the position of the former Spandauer Tor and the earliest town wall.

Märkisches Ufer

Several interesting sights can be covered from the Märkisches Museum U-Bahn station. The collections of the **Märkisches Museum** (☎ 30 86 60; *Am Köllnischen Park 5; adult/ concession €4/2, free Wed; open Tues-Sun*) cover Berlin's history, art and culture. The

brown bears housed in a pit in the park behind the main museum are the official mascots of the city.

Unter den Linden

A stroll west of Museumsinsel along Unter den Linden takes in the greatest surviving monuments of the former Prussian capital. The **Deutsches Historisches Museum** in a former armoury (Zeughaus; 1706) should have reopened after a renovation by the time you read this, with a collection on German history from AD 900 to the present, under a new glass roof by architect IM Pei.

Opposite the museum is the beautiful colonnaded **Kronprinzenpalais** (*Crown Princes' Palace;* ☎ 20 30 40; *admission free; open Thur-Tues*) dating from 1732. Next to the museum is Schinkel's **Neue Wache** (*admission free; open daily*), an 1818 memorial to the victims of fascism and despotism, which harbours Käthe Kollwitz's sculpture *Mother and Her Dead Son.* **Humboldt Universität** (1753), the next building situated to the west, was originally a palace of the brother of King Friedrich II of Prussia and was converted to a university in 1810. Take note of the restored equestrian **statue of Friedrich II** in the avenue. Beside this is the enormous **Staatsbibliothek** (State Library; 1914).

Across the street from the university, beside the **Alte Königliche Bibliothek** (Old Royal Library; 1780) with its curving baroque facade, is Wenzeslaus von Knobelsdorff's **Staatsoper** (State Opera; 1743). The square between them, **Bebelplatz**, was the site of the Nazis' first book-burning on 10 May 1933. A poignant, below-ground memorial marks the spot. South of here is the Catholic **St Hedwig Kirche** (1783), partly modelled on Rome's Pantheon.

Just south is Gendarmenmarkt, an elegant square containing a trio of magnificent buildings. The **Deutscher Dom** (*German Cathedral;* ☎ 22 73 04 31; *admission free; open Tues-Sun*) at the southern end of the square boasts a museum with an excellent exhibit on German history from 1800 to the present. The **Französischer Dom** (French Cathedral) contains the **Hugenottenmuseum** (*Huguenot Museum;* ☎ 229 17 60; *adult/concession €1.50/1; open Tues-Sun*), which covers the French Protestant contribution to Berlin life. The statuesque **Konzerthaus** (Concert Hall) completes the picture.

GERMANY

GERMANY

BERLIN – MITTE & PRENZLAUER BERG

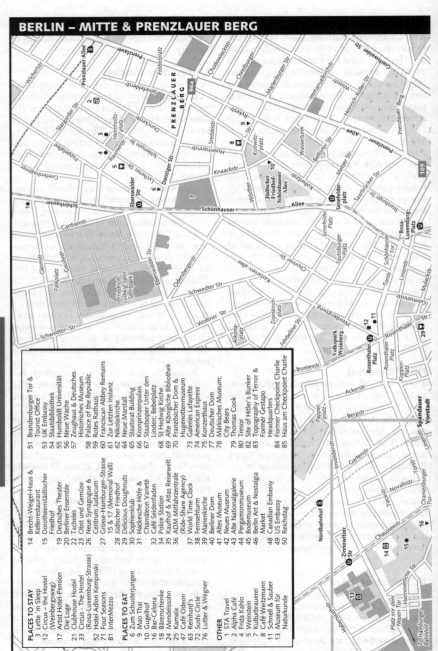

PLACES TO STAY
3 Lette 'm Sleep
12 Circus – the Hostel (Weinbergsweg)
17 Artist Hotel-Pension Die Loge
21 Clubhouse Hostel
33 Circus – The Hostel (Rosa-Luxemburg-Strasse)
52 Hotel Adlon Kempinski
71 Four Seasons
81 InterMezzo

PLACES TO EAT
6 Zum Schusterjungen
9 Mao Thai
10 Gugelhof
16 Bar-Celona
24 Bärenschenke
25 Kamala
47 Café Odeon
63 Reinhard's
72 Sushi Circle
76 Lutter & Wegner

OTHER
1 STA Travel
2 Alpha Café
4 Frida Kahlo
5 Weinstein
8 Kulturbrauerei
11 Café Weitzmann
13 Museum für Naturkunde

14 Brecht-Weigel-Haus & Kellerrestaurant
15 Dorotheenstädtischer Friedhof
19 Deutsches Theater
20 Berliner Ensemble
22 Tacheles
23 Obst und Gemüse
26 Neue Synagogue & Centrum Judaicum
27 Grosse-Hamburger-Strasse
28 Jüdischer Friedhof
29 Delicious Doughnuts
30 Sophienklub
31 Hackesche Höfe & Chamäleon Varieté
32 Café Seidenfaden
34 Police Station
35 Kaufhof & Atlas Reisewelt
36 ADM Mitfahrzentrale (Ride-Share Agency)
37 World Time Clock
38 Fernsehturm
39 Marienkirche
40 Berliner Dom
41 Altes Museum
42 Neues Museum
43 Alte Nationalgalerie
44 Pergamonmuseum
45 Bodemuseum
46 Berlin Art & Nostalgia Market
48 Canadian Embassy
49 US Embassy
50 Reichstag

51 Brandenburger Tor & Tourist Office
53 UK Embassy
54 Staatsbibliothek
55 Humboldt Universität
57 Zeughaus & Deutsches Historisches Museum
58 Palace of the Republic
59 Rotes Rathaus
60 Franciscan Abbey Remains
61 Zur Letzten Instanz
62 Nikolaikirche
64 Neue Marstall
65 Staatsrat Building
66 Kronprinzenpalais
67 Staatsoper Unter den Linden; Bebelplatz
68 St Hedwig Kirche
69 Alte Königliche Bibliothek
70 Französicher Dom & Hugenottenmuseum
73 Galeries Lafayette
74 American Express
75 Konzerthaus
77 Deutscher Dom
78 Märkisches Museum; City Bears
79 Thomas Cook
80 Tresor
82 Site of Hitler's Bunker
83 Topography of Terror & Former Gestapo Headquarters
84 Former Checkpoint Charlie
85 Haus am Checkpoint Charlie

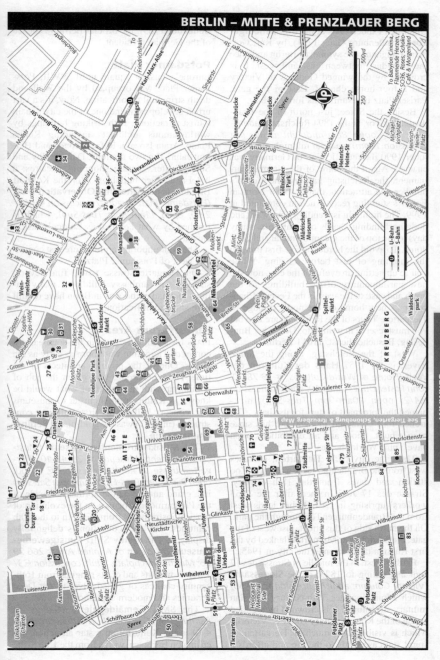

BERLIN – MITTE & PRENZLAUER BERG

Tiergarten

Unter den Linden ends at the **Brandenburger Tor** (Brandenburg Gate; 1791), by Karl Gotthard Langhans, the symbol of Berlin and once the boundary between east and west. It is crowned by the winged Goddess of Victory and a four-horse chariot. East of the gate, Pariser Platz is resuming its former glory.

Beside the Spree, just north of the Brandenburger Tor, is the 1894 **Reichstag** (admission free; open 8am-midnight daily, last admission 10pm) where at midnight on 2 October 1990 the reunification of Germany was enacted. Again the home of the German parliament, the Reichstag has become Berlin's number one attraction, thanks to Sir Norman Foster's stunning reconstruction completed in 1999. The highlight is wending your way (and dodging blinding shards of light on a sunny day) to the top of the gleaming metal and glass dome. To avoid the hordes, arrive first thing in the morning or just before closing. While you're up getting an eyeful of the city, note the new parliamentary office buildings to the north and east; to the west is the Federal Chancellery's new home on the northern edge of Tiergarten. Tours of the Reichstag are free but you must reserve in writing to: Deutscher Bundestag, Besucherdienst, 11011 Berlin.

West of the Reichstag, along the Spree River, is the 1957 **Haus der Kulturen der Welt** (House of World Cultures; ☎ 39 78 70; John Foster Dulles-Allee 10; adult/concession €4/2; open 10am-9pm Tues-Sun), nicknamed the 'pregnant oyster' for its shape. The arched roof collapsed in 1980 but has since been rebuilt. Photo and art exhibitions often have Third World themes.

The huge city park, **Tiergarten**, stretches west from the Brandenburger Tor towards Zoo station and dates from the 18th century. Strasse des 17 Juni (named after the 1953 workers' uprising in East Berlin) leads west from the Brandenburger Tor through the park. On the north side of this street, just west of the gate, is a **Soviet War Memorial** flanked by the first Russian tanks to enter the city in 1945.

Farther west, in the middle of Strasse des 17 Juni and dating to 1873, is the **Siegessäule** (Victory Column; adult/concession €1/0.50) which commemorates 19th-century Prussian military adventures. It is crowned by a gilded statue of the Roman victory goddess, Victoria, which is visible from much of Tiergarten. A spiral staircase leads to the top and affords a worthwhile view. Just northeast is **Schloss Bellevue** (1785), the official Berlin residence of the German president.

Potsdamer Platz

Europe's busiest square until WWII, Potsdamer Platz was occupied by the Wall and death strip until reunification. Now, it's a vast urban development and one of the city's main tourist attractions, with striking buildings by world-famous architects including Renzo Piano, Arata Isozaki, Rafael Moneo and Helmut Jahn. The two sections, DaimlerCity and Sony Center, feature shopping, theatres, a hotel and office buildings. Atop the Kollhoff Building is the **Panorama Observation Deck** (Potsdamer Platz 1; adult/concession €3.50/ 2.50; open 11am-8pm Tues-Sun), which is reached by what is billed as Europe's fastest elevator.

The contemporary architecture fest continues west of Potsdamer Platz.

On Tiergartenstrasse you'll find several striking new embassy buildings; many nations that had embassies in Bonn have rebuilt here since reunification.

Kulturforum Area

Plans for a cultural centre in the southeastern corner of Tiergarten were born as early as the 1950s. One of the premier architects of the time, Hans Scharoun, was given the job of coming up with the design of what would be known as Kulturforum, a cluster of museums and concert halls. The first building constructed (in 1961) was the gold-plated **Berliner Philharmonie**.

The **Musikinstrumenten-Museum** (Musical Instruments Museum; ☎ 25 48 10; Tiergartenstrasse 1; adult/concession €3/1.50; open 9am-5pm Tues-Fri, 10am-5pm Sat-Sun) in a grand annexe on the northeastern side of the Philharmonie, focuses on the evolution of musical instruments from the 16th to the 20th centuries. The rich collection is delightfully displayed. The nearby SMB **Kunstgewerbemuseum** (Museum of Applied Art; ☎ 266 29 25; Matthäiskirchplatz; adult/concession €3/ 1.50) shows arts and crafts ranging from 16th-century chalices of gilded silver to Art Deco ceramics and modern appliances.

The SMB **Gemäldegalerie** (Gallery of Paintings; ☎ 20 90 55 55; Matthäiskirchplatz 4-6) is the Kulturforum's star attraction, focusing on European works from the 13th to the

18th centuries; its 1200-plus collection includes works by Dürer, Rembrandt, Botticelli and Goya.

To the southeast, looking a bit forlorn amid the modern museums, there's the 1846 **St Matthäus Kirche** (☎ 262 12 02; Matthäiskirchplatz 12; open noon-6pm Tues-Sun). The **bell tower** (admission €1) offers panoramic views. Continue on to the squat SMB **Neue Nationalgalerie** (New National Gallery; ☎ 266 26 51; Potsdamer Strasse 50) for a collection of 19th- and 20th-century paintings and sculptures by Picasso, Klee, Miró and many German expressionists.

Several blocks west, the **Bauhaus Archiv/ Museum für Gestaltung** (Bauhaus Archive/ Museum of Design; ☎ 254 00 20; Klingelhöferstrasse 14; adult/concession €4/2; open 10am-5pm Wed-Mon) is dedicated to artists of the Bauhaus school, who developed the tenets of modern architecture and design. The building is designed by Bauhaus founder Walter Gropius.

Around Oranienburger Tor

Known as the Scheunenviertel, this neighbourhood is one of Berlin's most vibrant. The **Brecht-Weigel Gedenkstätte** (Brecht-Wegel-Haus; ☎ 283 05 70 44; Chausseestrasse 125; adult/concession €3/1.50; open daily, ring for hours & tour info) is where the socialist playwright Bertolt Brecht and his wife Helene Weigel lived from 1948 until his death in 1956. Behind is **Dorotheenstädtischer Friedhof** with tombs of the illustrious, such as philosopher Georg Friedrich Hegel, poet Johannes Becher, and Brecht and Weigel. There are two adjacent cemeteries here; you want the one closer to Brecht's house.

Nearby, the 1810 **Museum für Naturkunde** (Natural History Museum; ☎ 20 93 85 91; Invalidenstrasse 43; adult/concession €2.50/ 1.25; open 9.30am-5pm Tues-Sun) has an impressive dinosaur collection. To the west is the SMB **Hamburger Bahnhof** (☎ 39 78 34 12; Invalidenstrasse 50), a former train station cleverly converted into a top contemporary gallery. Lofty ceilings and streams of natural light make the collection, including works by Warhol, Lichtenstein and Rauschenberg, even more appealing.

If you travel east along Oranienburger Strasse you'll come across the rambling, crumbling **Tacheles** alternative art, culture and entertainment centre. Made famous by post-Wende squatters who gave the former department store a new lease of life, it's run by a self-governed, nonprofit organisation and boasts galleries, a theatre and studios. Not surprisingly, it's under threat from developers but was given a reprieve, supposedly until around 2010.

Don't miss the magnificent **Neue Synagogue**. Built in the Moorish-Byzantine style in 1866, it was desecrated by the Nazis and later destroyed by WWII bombing. It is no longer a functioning synagogue these days, but instead houses the **Centrum Judaicum** (☎ 88 02 83 16; Oranienburger Strasse 28-30; adult/ concession €3/2; open 10am-6pm Sun-Thur, 10am-2pm Fri) with permanent and special exhibitions on Jewish life in Berlin. You may climb the dome for an additional €1.50/1, but it is closed from November to March.

Another legacy of the area's Jewish culture is the **Jüdischer Friedhof** (Jewish Cemetery; Grosse-Hamburger-Strasse). Although some 10,000 people are buried here including Moses Mendelssohn, the revered Enlightenment philosopher, few tombstones survived Nazi destruction in 1942. Across the street, plaques climbing the walls of the courtyard between Grosse-Hamburger-Strasse 15 and 17 identify the buildings' prewar residents; the simplicity is wrenching.

The district's big drawcard is the **Hackesche Höfe** (1907), once owned by a Jewish businessman. This Art Nouveau cluster of buildings with eight interconnected courtyards is filled with galleries, shops, theatres and cafés.

Kreuzberg

Parallel to a section of the Wall is the site of the former SS-Gestapo headquarters, where the open-air **Topography of Terror** (☎ 25 48 67 03; Niederkirchnerstrasse 8; admission free; open 10am-6pm daily in summer, until dusk in winter) exhibition documents Nazi crimes.

Almost nothing remains at the site of the famous **Checkpoint Charlie**, a major crossing between east and west during the Cold War. However, the history of the Wall is commemorated nearby in the **Haus am Checkpoint Charlie** (☎ 253 72 50; Friedrichstrasse 43-45; adult/concession €7/4; open 9am-8pm daily), a fascinating private museum of escape memorabilia and photos.

The longest surviving stretch of the **Berlin Wall** is just west of the Warschauer Strasse terminus of the U1. This 300m section was

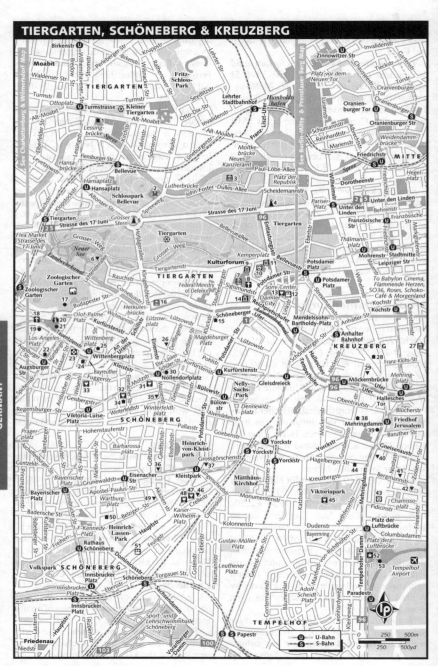

TIERGARTEN, SCHÖNEBERG & KREUZBERG

TIERGARTEN, SCHÖNEBERG & KREUZBERG

PLACES TO STAY		42	Barcomi's	18	Kaiser-Wilhelm-Gedächt-
1	Hotel Tiergarten	46	Pasodoble		niskirche (Memorial Church)
15	Jugendherberge Berlin	49	Don Antonio	19	Hugendubel Bookshop
	International			20	Tourist Office
22	Pension Fischer	**OTHER**		21	Europa-Center
24	Comfort Hotel Auberge	2	Schloss Bellevue	23	KaDeWe Department Store
28	Hotel am Anhalter Bahnhof	3	Haus der Kulturen	25	American Express
34	Hotel Gunia		der Welt	27	Jüdisches Museum
38	Pension Kreuzberg	4	Soviet War Memorial	30	Mann-O-Meter
44	Hotel Transit	5	Siegessäule	31	KitKat Club
50	Studentenhotel Meininger 10	7	Gemäldegalerie	32	Tom's Bar; Hafen
		8	St Matthäus Kirche	33	Connection Disco
PLACES TO EAT		9	Kunstgewerbemuseum	39	Schnell & Sauber
6	Café am Neuen See	10	Berliner Philharmonie	43	Friends of Italian Opera
26	Café Einstein	11	Musikinstrumenten-Museum	45	Golgatha
29	Grossbeerenkeller	12	Cinestar	47	Leuchtturm
35	Tim's Canadian Deli	13	Blu Discothek	48	Café Mirell
36	Ousies Taverna	14	Neue Nationalgalerie	51	Odeon Cinema
37	Tuk-Tuk	16	Bauhaus Archiv/Museum für	52	Police Headquarters
40	Seerose		Gestaltung	53	Municipal Lost & Found
41	Knofi	17	Aquarium		Office

turned over to artists who created the **East Side Gallery**, a permanent open-air art gallery along the side facing Mühlenstrasse.

Be careful when you visit this area as it can be a bit seedy, however, it is improving with gentrification.

Even before it opened in 2001, the zinc-clad shell of the Daniel Libeskind-designed **Jüdisches Museum** (Jewish Museum; ☎ 25 99 33 00; Lindenstrasse 9-14; adult/concession €5.50/2.75; open 10am-8pm daily, except Jewish high holidays & Christmas eve) drew thousands of visitors. Now its collection covers 1000 years of Jewish history in Germany in a manner that's both admiring and wistful.

Kurfürstendamm

Once the commercial heart of West Berlin, the 'Ku'damm' is showing a touch of age as creative and commercial energies are focused elsewhere in town. The area around Zoo station can become a stultifying tourist ghetto in summer.

The stark ruins of the **Kaiser-Wilhelm-Gedächtniskirche** (1895) in Breitscheidplatz, engulfed in roaring commercialism, are a world-famous landmark. A British bombing on 22 November 1943 left only the broken west tower standing.

South of Zoo station is the **Erotik-Museum** (☎ 866 06 66; Joachimstalerstrasse 4; adult/concession €5/4; open 9am-midnight daily) a surprisingly highbrow creation of Beate Uhse, the German porno and sex toy queen.

On the other side of Gedächtniskirche rises the **Europa-Center** (1965), a shopping and restaurant complex that's still bustling when other shops are closed. Situated northeast of the Europa-Center is the elephant gate of Germany's oldest **Zoo and Aquarium** (☎ 25 40 10; Budapester Strasse 34; each section adult/concession €7/6, combined ticket €11/8; zoo open 9am-6.30pm or dusk, aquarium open 9am-6pm daily). It is more than 150 years old and contains around 1400 species.

Charlottenburg

Completed in 1699 as a summer residence for Queen Sophie Charlotte, the **Schloss Charlottenburg** (☎ 0331-969 42 02; Luisenplatz; day card adult/concession €7.50/5), is a truly exquisite baroque palace (U-Bahn to Sophie-Charlotte-Platz, then a 15-minute walk north along Schlossstrasse; or take bus No 145 from Zoo station to the door). The palace was bombed in 1943 but has been completely rebuilt. Before the entrance is an equestrian statue of the Great Elector (1620–88), Sophie Charlotte's father-in-law. Along the Spree River behind the palace are extensive French and English **gardens** (admission free).

In the central building below the dome are the former royal living quarters. The winter chambers of Friedrich II, upstairs in the new wing (1746) to the east, are highlights, as well as the **Schinkel Pavilion**, the neoclassical **Mausoleum** and the rococo **Belvedere pavilion**. Huge crowds are often waiting for the

GERMANY

guided tour of the palace and it may be difficult to get a ticket, especially on weekends and holidays in summer. If you can't get into the main palace, content yourself with the facades and gardens. A day card is good for all the tours and attractions.

Across the street at the beginning of Schlossstrasse is the SMB **Ägyptisches Museum** (*Egyptian Museum;* ☎ 34 35 73 11; *Schlossstrasse 70*). The highlight here is the 14th-century BC bust of Queen Nefertiti. Across the road from the museum is the SMB **Sammlung Berggruen** (☎ 32 69 58 15; *Schlossstrasse 1*), which is showing a collection called 'Picasso and His Time', on loan until 2006. As well as many Picasso paintings, drawings and sculptures, you'll be treated to the works of Cézanne, Van Gogh, Gauguin, Braque and Klee.

Olympic Stadium
Built by Hitler for the 1936 Olympic Games in which African-American runner Jesse Owens won four gold medals, this 85,000-seat stadium (☎ 301 11 00; *Olympischer Platz 3; adult/concession €2.50/1, guided tours €5 per person*) is situated southwest of Schloss Charlottenburg. One of the best examples of Nazi-era neoclassical architecture, it's still very much in use – the finals of the 2006 World Cup will be played here. Renovations for the occasion will continue until 2004. Take the U2 to Olympia-Stadion Ost, then it's a 10-minute walk along Olympische Strasse to Olympischer Platz.

Zehlendorf
A mere shadow of their former selves, the **Dahlem Museums** in southwest Berlin (U1 to Dahlem-Dorf, then walk five minutes south on Iltisstrasse) all can be entered at Lansstrasse 8 and each costs €3/1.50 per adult/concession. The SMB **Ethnologisches Museum** (*Museum of Ethnology;* ☎ 830 14 38) takes you back to the early cultures from around the world. You'll also find the SMB **Museum für Ostasiatische Kunst** (*Museum of East Asian Art;* ☎ 830 13 82) and SMB **Museum für Indisches Kunst** (*Museum of Indian Art;* ☎ 830 13 61).

Treptower Park
The city's largest **Soviet Monument** (*open daily*) is a 1949 grave site built to the heroic style and scale favoured by Stalin – some 5000

Soviet soldiers are buried here. It's a remarkable place, although somewhat faded since its days as a top attraction in East Berlin. The Treptower Park S-Bahn station is served by several lines.

ORGANISED TOURS
Guide yourself for the price of a bus ticket (€2.10) on bus No 100, which passes 18 major sights as it makes its way from Zoo station to Michelangelostrasse in Prenzlauer Berg via Alexanderplatz, providing you with a great overview and cheap orientation to Berlin. The BVG even puts out a special brochure describing the route.

Walking Tours
Among the best walking tours we've ever taken are those by **Berlin Walks** (☎ 301 91 94; W *www.berlinwalks.com*), which take between three and four hours and cost €10/7.50 for those over/under 26 (and Berlin-Potsdam Welcome Card holders). The Discover Berlin tour covers the heart of the city and runs twice daily from April to October (once daily the rest of the year). It also offers tours of Third Reich sites and Berlin's Jewish heritage. The walks leave from outside the main entrance of Zoo station at the top of the taxi rank.

Insider Tours (☎ 692 31 49; W *www.insidertour.com*) has 3½-hour walking tours of the major sites in the city twice daily from April to October (once daily from November to March). The walks (€12/9) leave from in front of the Reisebank at Zoo station. It also has four-hour bike tours (€20/17, including bikes).

Readers have also written in praise of the knowledge and breadth of **Brewer's Best of Berlin Walking Tour** (☎ 70 13 10 37; W *www.brewersberlin.com*). Tours meet opposite the Neue Synagoge in Oranienburger Strasse. The four-hour Classic Berlin tour takes in important sights, while the Total Berlin tour may last 10 hours. Both cost €10.

Cruises
One of the best ways to see Berlin's historic past is by boat. **Reederei Bruno Winkler** (☎ 349 95 95) runs a variety of tours on the Spree. The most popular is a three-hour cruise (€13) that leaves several times a day from mid-March to October. It departs from the Schlossbrücke across the Spree just east of Schloss Charlottenburg.

GERMANY

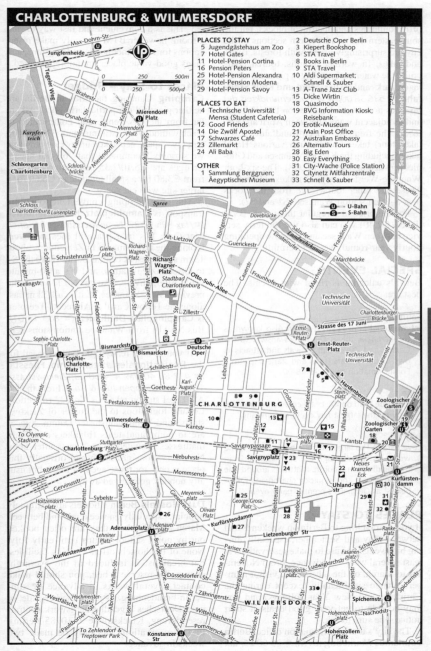

CHARLOTTENBURG & WILMERSDORF

PLACES TO STAY
5 Jugendgästehaus am Zoo
7 Hotel Gates
11 Hotel-Pension Cortina
16 Pension Peters
25 Hotel-Pension Alexandra
27 Hotel-Pension Modena
29 Hotel-Pension Savoy

PLACES TO EAT
4 Technische Universität Mensa (Student Cafeteria)
12 Good Friends
14 Die Zwölf Apostel
17 Schwarzes Café
23 Zillemarkt
24 Ali Baba

OTHER
1 Sammlung Berggruen; Ägyptisches Museum

2 Deutsche Oper Berlin
3 Kiepert Bookshop
6 STA Travel
8 Books in Berlin
9 STA Travel
10 Aldi Supermarket; Schnell & Sauber
13 A-Trane Jazz Club
15 Dicke Wirtin
18 Quasimodo
19 BVG Information Kiosk; Reisebank
20 Erotik-Museum
21 Main Post Office
22 Australian Embassy
26 Alternativ Tours
28 Big Eden
30 Easy Everything
31 City-Wache (Police Station)
32 Citynetz Mitfahrzentrale
33 Schnell & Sauber

U — U-Bahn
S — S-Bahn

GERMANY

Central Berlin may be crowded with roads, office buildings and apartment blocks, but the southeastern and southwestern sections of the city are surprisingly green, with forests, rivers and lakes. In warmer months, tourist boats cruise the waterways, calling at picturesque villages, parks and castles. **Stern und Kreis Schiffahrt** (☎ 536 36 00; ⊛ www.sternundkreis.de) operates a number of cruises on the Wannsee and its adjacent waters between April and October. The frequent 7-Seen-Rundfahrt (seven lakes tour) takes you through various Havel lakes (including the Kleiner Wannsee and Glieniecker) lasting two hours (€8). The six-hour Wannsee-Werder tour (€13) takes in Potsdam. These and other tours leave from the docks near S-Bahn station Wannsee (S1 and S7).

For the price of a regular three-zone BVG ticket (€2.40) you can also use the ferry service between Wannsee and Kladow operating hourly year-round, weather permitting.

SPECIAL EVENTS
Berlin's calendar is filled with events. The best are:

February
International Film Festival Berlin Also known as the Berlinale, this is Germany's answer to the Cannes and Venice film festivals and attracts its own stable of stars (few) and starlets (plenty). For information call ☎ 25 48 90.

June
Berlin Pride Held on the last weekend in June, this is by far the largest gay event in Germany.

July
Love Parade The largest techno party in the world wends its way through the streets of Berlin in the middle of the month. It attracts around one million people and is quickly challenging Oktoberfest as Germany's premier party event.

PLACES TO STAY
If you're travelling to Berlin on weekends and between May and September, especially during big events, be sure to make reservations at least several weeks in advance. From November to March, on the other hand, visitor numbers plunge significantly (except during the Christmas and New Year holidays) and you may be able to get very good deals at short notice – be sure to ask.

The city's tourist information office, **Berlin Tourismus Marketing** (BTM; ☎ 25 00 25, fax 25 00 24 24), handles hotel reservations for €3. This is a convenient and fast way to find a room; however BTM can only make reservations for its partner hotels and pensions, and many good-value places are not represented.

Places to Stay – Budget
Camping Camping facilities in Berlin are neither plentiful nor particularly good. All are far from the city centre and complicated to reach without your own transport. They fill up quickly – space gets taken up by caravans – so we strongly recommend that you call ahead. Charges are €5.10/2.35 per adult/child, plus from €3.80 for a small tent site to €6.60 for a larger site with car space.

The only camping convenient to public transport is **Campingplatz Kohlhasenbrück** (☎/fax 805 17 37; Neue Kreisstrasse 36; open Mar-Oct). It's in a peaceful location overlooking the Griebnitzsee in Zehlendorf, about 15km southwest of central Berlin. Take the S7 to Griebnitzsee station, and it's a 10-minute walk. Alternatively, take bus No 118 from the previous stop, Wannsee. If it's full, 2km east along the Teltow Canal at Albrechts-Teerofen is **Campingplatz Dreilinden** (☎ 805 12 01). Bus No 118 from Wannsee station stops here as well.

If you're on a really tight budget, head for the **Internationales Jugendcamp Fliesstal** (☎ 433 86 40, fax 434 50 63; Ziekowstrasse 161; beds €5; open July & Aug). From the U6 Alt-Tegel station take bus No 222 (direction: Lübars) four stops to the corner of Ziekowstrasse and Waidmannsluster Damm. Spaces are in communal tents (blankets and foam mattresses provided); check-in is after 5pm. No reservations are taken and officially this place is only for those aged 14 to 27, but usually nobody gets turned away.

DJH Hostels Berlin's hostels are extremely popular, especially on weekends and between March and October; they are often booked out by noisy school groups until early July. None of the hostels offers cooking facilities, but breakfast is included in the overnight charge. To reserve a bed, you should contact several weeks in advance (⊛ djh-berlin-brandenburgzr@jugendherberge.de, or post: Deutsches Jugendherbergswerk Zentralreservierung, Kluckstrasse 3, 10785 Berlin). Phone reservations can only be made two weeks in advance.

The only DJH hostel within the city centre is the institutional, 364-bed **Jugendherberge Berlin International** (☎ 261 10 98, fax 265 03 83; Kluckstrasse 3; dorm beds juniors/seniors €18.50/22.60, doubles €23/27.10). It's in Schöneberg, near the Landwehrkanal (U1 to Kurfürstenstrasse). Double rooms and the less-expensive dorm rooms are available.

Jugendherberge am Wannsee (☎ 803 20 34, fax 803 59 08; Badeweg 1; beds juniors/ seniors €18/22.10), on the corner of Kronprinzessinnenweg, is pleasantly located on Grosser Wannsee, the lake southwest of the city on the way to Potsdam. The hostel is a 10-minute walk from Nikolassee S-Bahn station (S1 and S7) via the footbridge; turn left at Kronprinzessinnenweg.

Jugendherberge Ernst Reuter (☎ 404 16 10, fax 404 59 72; Hermsdorfer Damm 48-50; beds juniors/seniors €14.40/18) is in the far northwest of Berlin. Take the U6 to Alt-Tegel, then bus No 125 right to the door.

Independent Hostels & Guesthouses

The non-DJH hostels listed following don't have curfews. Rooms do not have private facilities, and breakfast costs extra unless indicated. Some give discounts to students with ID.

In Charlottenburg, **Jugendgästehaus am Zoo** (☎ 312 94 10, fax 312 54 30; Hardenbergstrasse 9a; dorm beds €18, singles/ doubles €25/44) is just three blocks from Zoo station and has handsome, wooded communal spaces. Add €3 if you're over 27.

In Mitte, **Circus – The Hostel** (☎ 28 39 14 33, fax 28 39 14 84; e info@circus-berlin.de; Rosa-Luxemburg-Strasse 39 & Weinbergsweg 1a; dorm beds/singles/doubles/triples €14/ 30/46/60) has two hugely popular, well-run hostels. The newer Weinbergsweg location has a café and bar. You'll find similarly helpful and friendly staff at the **Clubhouse Hostel** (☎ 28 09 79 79, 28 09 79 77; e info@club house-berlin.de; Kalkscheune 4-5; dorm beds/ doubles/triples from €14/45/60), near Friedrichstrasse and Tacheles.

In the heart of Prenzlauer Berg's nightlife and across from a park is **Lette 'm Sleep** (☎ 44 73 36 23, fax 44 73 36 25; e info@ backpackers.de; Lettestrasse 7; dorm beds €15-19 with linen €3 extra, doubles €48 including linen). Doubles have kitchenettes.

Two moderately priced hotels close to Mehringdamm station in Kreuzberg (U6 or U7) have dorm accommodation. Friendly **Pension Kreuzberg** (☎ 251 13 62, fax 251 06 38; Grossbeerenstrasse 64; dorm beds/ singles/doubles €22.50/40/52) has plain rooms and garden views at the back. **Hotel Transit** (☎ 789 04 70, fax 78 90 47 77, e info@hotel-transit.de; Hagelberger Strasse 53-54; dorm beds/singles/doubles €19/ 52/60, including breakfast) is in a former factory teeming with character and, occasionally, school groups. Most rooms have shower but no private toilet.

Hotels In Charlottenburg, there's the **Hotel-Pension Cortina** (☎ 313 90 59, fax 312 73 96; Kantstrasse 140; singles/doubles from €31/50 with shared toilet) with plenty of basic rooms, some with shower. Mitte's **Artist Hotel-Pension Die Loge** (☎/fax 280 75 13; e die-loge@t-online.de; Friedrichstrasse 115; singles/doubles from €40/60) has far more personality than your average hotel, a clientele including actors and artists, and a great deal on rooms with shared bath.

New **InterMezzo** (☎ 22 48 90 96, fax 22 48 90 97; w www.hotelintermezzo.de; Gertrud-Kolmar-Strasse 5; singles/doubles €40/67) is a spotless place between Brandenburger Tor and Potsdamer Platz, exclusively for women (and their children). Most rooms have shower but no toilet. Gay men might try **Hotel Gunia** (☎ 218 59 40, fax 218 59 44; e info@hotel gunia.de; Eisenacher Strasse 10; singles without bath €45, singles/doubles with bath €50/70), offering simple but well-kept rooms near Nollendorfplatz, right in the heart of the gay district.

Readers have written to recommend cheery **Pension Peters** (☎ 312 22 78, fax 312 35 19; e penspeters@aol.com; Kantstrasse 146; singles/doubles from €58/78) for service above the call. Rooms without toilet cost less.

Places to Stay – Mid-Range

In Kreuzberg, **Hotel am Anhalter Bahnhof** (☎ 251 03 42, fax 251 48 97; e hotel-aab@ t-online.de; Stresemannstrasse 36; singles/ doubles from €45/70 without facilities, €65/90 with facilities) has simple, reasonably priced digs. Schöneberg's **Pension Fischer** (☎ 21 91 55 66, fax 21 01 96 14; e hotelpensionfischer@t-online.de; Nürnberger Strasse 24a; singles/doubles from €60/70) has only recently been handsomely renovated.

GERMANY

In Charlottenburg is **Hotel-Pension Modena** (☎ 885 70 10, fax 881 52 94; *Wielandstrasse 26; singles without bath €41, singles/ doubles with bath from €65/95)* in an atmospheric old building. Attractive **Hotel-Pension Alexandra** (☎ 885 77 80, fax 88 57 78 18; e *mail@alexandra-berlin.de; Wielandstrasse 32; singles/doubles €72/82)* has quiet, simple rooms, some with full facilities. The **Hotel-Pension Savoy** (☎ 88 47 16 10, fax 882 37 46, e *info@hotel-pension-savoy.de; Meinekestrasse 4; singles €62-73, doubles €90-109)* is in a beautiful building featuring a muralled, church-like entrance and an antique lift.

Hotel Tiergarten (☎ 39 98 96, fax 39 98 97 35; e *hotel.tiergarten@t-online.de; Alt-Moabit 89; singles/doubles from €77/92)* is a contemporary business-style hotel in a bourgeois 19th-century house. For Internet junkies, *every* room at Charlottenburg's **Hotel Gates** (☎ 31 10 60, fax 312 20 60; e *info@hotel -gates.com; singles/doubles from €95/120)* has its own computer terminal. It's in a historic house with contemporary renovations.

Comfort Hotel Auberge (☎ 235 00 20, fax 23 50 02 99; e *hotel-auberge@t-online.de; Bayreuther Strasse 10; singles/doubles from €104/132)*, in an interesting old building in Schöneberg, is a good place with large rooms, or mini-singles for €79.

Places to Stay – Top End

Those holding generous expense accounts might head for **Hotel Adlon Kempinski** (☎ 226 10, toll-free 00800-42 63 13 55, fax 22 61 22 22; *Unter den Linden 77; singles/ doubles from €260/310)*, which offers front-row vistas of Brandenburger Tor. This replica of the famous historic hotel reopened to great fanfare in mid-1997 after a hiatus of more than half a century. It has lavish rooms, but rates do *not* include the €27 breakfast buffet.

On fashionable Gendarmenmarkt, the **Four Seasons Berlin** (☎ 203 38, toll-free 00800-64 88 64 88, fax 203 61 66; w *www.fourseasons .com; Charlottenstrasse 49; singles/doubles from €280/315)* pampers guests with large, luxurious rooms, sauna and fitness centre.

PLACES TO EAT

Berliners love eating out and have literally thousands of restaurants and cafés to choose from. There's no need to travel far, since every neighbourhood has its own cluster of eateries running the gamut of cuisines and price categories. The blocks around Savignyplatz in Charlottenburg, Prenzlauer Berg's Kollwitzplatz, and south of Winterfeldtplatz in Schöneberg are great places to browse for good restaurants with character.

German

In Charlottenburg is the Art Nouveau **Zillemarkt** (☎ 881 70 40; *Bleibtreustrasse 48a; mains €8-12.50)*, serving huge portions at fair prices. In Mitte, you can eat like a playwright at the **Kellerrestaurant** (☎ 282 38 43; *Chausseestrasse 125; mains €6-15.50)* in Brecht-Weigel-Haus, which serves up Helene Weigel's Austrian-influenced recipes, or slum like a beer-slogger at **Bärenschenke** (☎ 282 90 78; *Friedrichstrasse 124; mains €3-10)*, with a long bar and local specialities. The rustic **Grossbeerenkeller** (☎ 742 39 30; *Grossbeerenstrasse 90; mains €7-14.20)* serves delicious artery-cloggers in Kreuzberg. For hearty home-style basics, head for the corner **Zum Schusterjungen** (☎ 442 76 54; *Danziger Strasse 9; mains €4.50-9)* in Prenzlauer Berg. At the top of the spectrum, there's Gendarmenmarkt's **Lutter & Wegner** (☎ 20 29 54 10; *Charlottenstrasse 56; mains €16-21)*, one of Berlin's oldest restaurants and possibly its fanciest.

Asian

Near Savignyplatz in Charlottenburg, the Chinese **Good Friends** (☎ 313 26 59; *Kantstrasse 30; most dishes €6.80-23.50)* is short on decor but big on popularity. In Mitte, **Sushi Circle** (☎ 20 38 79 60; *Französische Strasse 48)* has all-you-can-eat conveyor-belt sushi for €14.90 on weekday evenings.

Tuk-Tuk (☎ 781 15 88; *Grossgörschenstrasse 2; mains €8.50-17.50)* in Schöneberg feels like an intimate bamboo den in Jakarta. For Thai specialities, **Mao Thai** (☎ 441 92 61; *Wörtherstrasse 30; mains €10-19)* in Prenzlauer Berg is pricey but delightful; its less-expensive sister restaurant, which is situated in Mitte, is the rather pleasant cellar **Kamala** (☎ 283 27 97; *Oranienburger Strasse 69; mains around €8.20)*.

French

The atmospheric **Gugelhof** (☎ 442 92 29; *Kollwitzplatz cnr Knaackstrasse 37; mains €8-13.40)* serves Alsatian specialities overlooking the square and has a nice wine list. Franco-German **Reinhard's** (☎ 242 52 95;

Poststrasse 28; mains €9-20.50) is an island of sophistication situated in the touristy Niko-laiviertel area.

Italian

Readers have recommended the atmospheric **Die Zwölf Apostel** *(12 Apostles; ☎ 312 14 33; Bleibtreustrasse 49; mains €7.50-11; open 24hr)*, which serves light meals, pastas, *insalate* and large, brick-oven pizzas named for Matthew, Thomas et al. Busy **Ali Baba** *(☎ 881 13 50; Bleibtreustrasse 45; mains €3-10.50)* is nearby and, situated in Schöne-berg, there's **Don Antonio** *(☎ 78 71 56 00; Akazienstrasse 24; mains €3-12.60)*; both serve individual pizzas starting at €3 in a cosy atmosphere.

Mediterranean

Highly recommended is the Greek **Ousies Taverna** *(☎ 216 79 57; Grunewaldstrasse 16; mains €4.90/14.60)* in Schöneberg, where the atmosphere is as boisterous as the waiters. In Kreuzberg, **Knofi** *(☎ 694 58 07; Berg-mannstrasse 98)* is a takeaway shop with lav-ish displays of Greek, Italian and Turkish specialities.

North American

Never mind that we've always associated delis with New York; **Tim's Canadian Deli** *(☎ 21 75 69 60; Maassenstrasse 14; dishes €3-19.50)* in Schöneberg has great bagels for breakfast (from €0.80), sandwiches, burgers and steaks for later in the day, and a diverse crowd all day.

Spanish

Bar-Celona *(☎ 282 91 53; Hannoversche Strasse 2; tapas €2.50-9, mains €11-18.50)* is a friendly, well-regarded tapas bar near Brecht-Weigel Haus. On a pretty block in Schöneberg, **Pasodoble** *(☎ 784 52 44; Crelle-strasse 39; tapas €1.80-7, mains €7-12.20)* offers tapas, tortillas, paellas and some Mexi-can specialities.

Vegetarian

Homy **Seerose** *(☎ 69 81 59 27; Mehring-damm 47; mains €4.20-6.20)* in Kreuzberg (U6 or U7 to Mehringdamm) has takeaway or eat-in choices. Most Asian restaurants will make vegetarian dishes too, including several Indian places on Goltzstrasse, south of Win-terfeldtplatz in Schöneberg.

Cafés

The number and variety of cafés in Berlin is astonishing. They're wonderful places to relax over a cup of coffee and some cake, while ploughing through a newspaper or chatting with friends. Many of these places also honour the great Berlin tradition of serving breakfast all day, and some serve more-elaborate meals.

The elegant **Café Einstein** *(☎ 261 50 96; Kurfürstenstrasse 58; mains €5-21.50)* is a Viennese-style coffee house in a rambling villa. The more rock-and-roll **Schwarzes Café** *(☎ 313 80 38; Kantstrasse 148; dishes €4.50-9; open 24hr)* in Charlottenburg is not far from Zoo station. Footpath benches at **Mendels-sohn** *(☎ 281 78 59; Oranienburger Strasse 39; mains €7-13.20)* are pleasant places to slurp *Milchkaffee* and to people-watch on a sunny morning. Mains include steaks and salads. **Barcomi's** *(☎ 694 81 38; Bergmannstrasse 21; baked goods from around €1)* in Kreuzberg is a hole-in-the-wall loved by locals for coffee and bagels.

Beneath the S-Bahn near Museumsinsel, **Café Odéon** *(☎ 208 26 00; Georgenstrasse, S-Bahn arch 192; dishes €1.80-6.90)* serves light meals like quiche lorraine and vegetable lasagne. The walls are plastered with old-time, enamelled advertising signs. Balmy summer nights are the best time to be at the **Café am Neuen See** *(☎ 254 49 30; Lichtensteinallee 1; dishes €3-11.50)*, in Tiergarten park. Service in the beer garden is pretty slow, but that just gives you more time for people-watching and enjoying the view over the lake.

Student Cafeterias

Anyone, student or not, may eat at the 1st-floor **Technische Universität Mensa** *(Hard-enbergstrasse 34; 3-course lunch €3-5 for students, add about €2 for nonstudents; open 11am-2.30pm)*, three blocks from Zoo station. The **Humboldt Universität Mensa** *(Unter den Linden 6)* in Mitte has the same hours, and similar prices, and can be found by entering the main portal, then taking the first door on your left, turning right at the end of the corri-dor and following your nose.

Snacks & Fast Food

Berlin is paradise for snackers on the go, with Turkish (your best bet), *Wurst*, Greek, Italian, Chinese – you name it – available at *Imbiss* (snack) stands throughout the city. The good areas to look are along Budapester Strasse in

Tiergarten, the eastern end of Kantstrasse near Zoo station, on Wittenbergplatz in Schöneberg, on Alexanderplatz in Mitte and around Schlesisches Tor station in the Kreuzberg district.

Self-Catering

To prepare your own food, there are the discount Aldi, Lidl or Penny Markt **supermarket** chains, which have outlets throughout Berlin. There are also **farmers' markets** around town, the most famous (though not necessarily cheapest) of which is held on Wednesday and Saturday on Schöneberg's Winterfeldtplatz. Snootier self-caterers should not miss the food floor of **KaDeWe** (see Shopping later in this section).

ENTERTAINMENT

Berliners take culture and fun seriously. The options are almost daunting and are always changing, so don't be surprised if the places we list are a bit different by the time you get to them. Put your faith in word-of-mouth tips for the most up-to-date, cutting-edge scenes.

For fancy, fairly upmarket venues, go to Savignyplatz and side streets like Bleibtreustrasse and northern Grolmannstrasse in Charlottenburg.

Kreuzberg – around Mehringdamm, Gneisenaustrasse and Bergmannstrasse – is alternative albeit with some trendy touches, while Kreuzberg along Oranienstrasse and Wiener Strasse has a grungy and slightly edgy feel. Around Winterfeldtplatz in Schöneberg, you will find few tourists and plenty of the 30-something brigade with alternative lifestyles and young families.

In the eastern districts, the nightlife is far more earthy and experimental. New bars and restaurants open, bringing previously dull streets to life, seemingly overnight. The most dynamic scenes are in Prenzlauer Berg and Friedrichshain, where the feel is energetic and slightly gritty. More established are the nightclubs and cafés/pubs in Mitte along Oranienburger Strasse, Rosenthaler Platz, Hackescher Markt and adjacent streets in the Scheunenviertel area.

Pubs & Bars

Gentrifying Kreuzberg is **Morgenland** (☎ 611 31 83; Skalitzer Strasse 35), which is good for long conversations at oddly shaped designer tables. A longtime hang-out is **Flammende Herzen** (Flaming Hearts; ☎ 615 71 02; Oranienstrasse 170), which is dark, knick-knack-filled and, occasionally, gay.

Plenty of popular cafés/pubs with outdoor tables during the warm weather are clustered around Kollwitz-Platz and Helmholtz-Platz in Prenzlauer Berg, including the contemporary **Café Weitzmann** (Husemannstrasse 2), the Mexican-themed **Frida Kahlo** (☎ 445 70 16; Lychener Strasse 37) and the cosy wine bar **Weinstein** (☎ 441 18 42; Lychener Strasse 33). Dark and retro, **Astro** (☎ 29 66 16 15; Simon-Dach-Strasse 40) is a bar in a relatively gritty section of Friedrichshain that's developing into party central. In Schöneberg are lots of interesting pubs and cafés around Akazienstrasse and on lovely Crellestrasse, including the inexpensive, tropical **Café Mirell** (☎ 782 04 57; Crellestrasse 46) and the **Leuchtturm** (Lighthouse; Crellestrasse 41), which features walls plastered in kitsch oil paintings. **Obst und Gemüse** (☎ 282 96 47; Oranienburger Strasse 49) in Mitte is a hip and popular bar.

Berliner Kneipen

Typical Berlin pubs have their own tradition of hospitality: good food (sometimes rustic daily dishes or stews), beer, humour and *Schlagfertigkeit* (quick-wittedness). In Charlottenburg, **Dicke Wirtin** (☎ 314 49 52; Carmerstrasse 9) is an earthy place and sports bar off Savignyplatz. Historic **Zur letzten Instanz** (The Final Authority; ☎ 242 55 28; Waisenstrasse 14) in Mitte claims traditions dating back to the 1600s and is next to a chunk of medieval town wall.

Beer Gardens

As soon as the last winter storms have blown away, pallid Berliners reacquaint themselves with the sun. The open-air **Golgatha** (☎ 785 24 53; Viktoriapark) in Kreuzberg is an institution (enter off Katzbachstrasse). In the southwestern district of Zehlendorf is **Loretta am Wannsee** (☎ 803 51 56; Kronprinzessinenweg 260), a huge garden with seating for more than 1000 (S-bahn to Wannsee).

Clubs

Berlin has a reputation for unbridled and very late nightlife. Not much starts before 11pm at the earliest, though there's a growing trend for 'after-work' clubs and raves, so those hip, hard-working, hard-clubbing types don't have to kiss their partying lifestyle goodbye. Cover charges (when they apply) range from €2.50 to €10 and usually don't include a drink.

Berlin *is* techno music and you'll be hard pressed to find a nightclub that plays anything else. One of the oldest techno temples is Mitte's **Tresor** (☎ 609 37 02; *Leipziger Strasse 126a*), housed inside the actual money vault of a former department store. It also has a summer beer garden.

Also very popular is **Delicious Doughnuts** (☎ 28 09 92 74; *Rosenthaler Strasse 9*), an acid jazz club in Mitte. **SO 36** (☎ 61 40 13 07; *Oranienstrasse 190*) in Kreuzberg is one of Berlin's longest-running techno nightclubs with theme nights including punk and gay and lesbian. In Friedrichshain, **Matrix** (☎ 29 49 10 47; *Warschauer Platz 18*) has several dance floors situated beneath U-Bahn arches; it attracts young techno-ravers.

Technoed-out? At Mitte's **Sophienklub** (☎ 282 45 52; *Sophienstrasse 6*), you'll hear Brazilian, house, reggae, but *no* techno. The hot-spot on busy Potsdamer Platz is **Blu** (☎ 25 59 30 30; *Marlene-Dietrich-Platz 4*), with three floors of dancing, plus city views.

A great example of Berlin's wilder side is the **KitKat Club** (*Bessemerstrasse 2-14*) in Tempelhof-Schöneberg. On Friday and Saturday nights you only get in wearing your 'sexual fantasy outfit' (meaning erotic or basically no clothes!), and women choose who's admitted.

The nightclubs around the Ku'damm are generally avoided by most Berliners. Places tend to be packed with tourists, especially German high-school kids, who usually disappear with the last U-Bahn train. Typical is **Big Eden** (☎ 882 61 20; *Kurfürstendamm 202*).

Gay & Lesbian

Pardon our presumption, but if you're reading this, you probably don't need to be told that Berlin is about the gayest city in Europe. *Anything* goes, and we can just scratch the surface; for more specialised listings, consult the gay and lesbian freebie *Siegessäule* or the strictly gay *Sergej* magazine, or contact **Mann-O-Meter** (☎ 216 80 08; *Bülowstrasse 106*) in Schöneberg.

Hafen (☎ 214 11 18; *Motzstrasse 19*), near Nollendorfplatz, is full of gay yuppies fortifying themselves before they move next door to the legendary **Tom's Bar** (☎ 213 45 70; *Motzstrasse 19*), with its famous dark and active cellar. The multiroomed **Connection**

(☎ 218 14 32; *Fuggerstrasse 33*) is the biggest and arguably the busiest gay nightclub in the city.

Interesting places in Kreuzberg include the over-the-top, kitschy **Roses** (☎ 615 75 70; *Oranienstrasse 187*), as well as the **Schoko-Café** (☎ 615 15 61; *Mariannenstrasse 6*), which is a convivial meeting place for lesbians. Alcohol-free **Café Seidenfaden** (☎ 283 27 83; *Dircksenstrasse 47*) is a pleasant lesbian café near Häckische Höfe.

Jazz

The **A-Trane** (☎ 313 25 50; *Bleibtreustrasse 1; admission €5-10*) in Charlottenburg, is still *the* place in Berlin for jazz. There is a cover charge but on some nights (usually Tuesday and Wednesday) admission is free. **Quasimodo** (☎ 312 80 86; *Kantstrasse 12a*) has live jazz, blues or rock acts in the basement every night. The stylish café on the ground floor is a good place for a preshow drink.

Classical Music

The **Berliner Philharmonie** (☎ 25 48 81 32; *Herbert-von-Karajan Strasse 1*) is famous for its supreme acoustics. All seats are excellent, so just take the cheapest. The lavish **Konzerthaus** (☎ 25 00 25; *Gendarmenmarkt*) in Mitte is home to the renowned Berlin Symphony Orchestra.

Cinemas

Films cost as much as €9, and foreign films are usually dubbed into German. If the film is shown in the original language with German subtitles, it will say 'OmU' on the advertisement. If the film is screened in the original language without German subtitles, it will say 'OF' or 'OV'.

Cinemas with frequent original-language showings include the new **Cinestar** (☎ 26 06 62 60; *Potsdamer Strasse 4*) at Potsdamer Platz, the **Odeon** (☎ 78 70 40 19; *Hauptstrasse 116*) – take the U4 to Innsbrucker Platz or S1, S45 or S46 to Schöneberg – and the **The Babylon** (☎ 61 60 91 93; *Dresdner Strasse 126*) in Kreuzberg.

Theatre

Berlin has around 150 theatres, so there should be something for everybody. In the former eastern section, they cluster around Friedrichstrasse; in the western part they're concentrated along Ku'damm. The historic

Deutsches Theater *(☎ 25 00 25; Schumann-strasse 13a)* offers both classic and modern productions. Situated nearby, the **Berliner Ensemble** *(☎ 282 31 60; Bertolt-Brecht-Platz 1)* performs works by Brecht and other 20th-century Europeans. **Friends of Italian Opera** *(☎ 691 12 11; Fidicinstrasse 40)* in Kreuzberg is Berlin's only regular English-language theatre venue.

Opera

The **Staatsoper Unter den Linden** *(☎ 20 35 34 55; Unter den Linden 5-7)* in Mitte, hosts lavish productions with international talent in an exquisite building dating from 1743.

The **Deutsche Oper Berlin** *(☎ 343 84 01; Bismarckstrasse 35, Charlottenburg)* has classical works of mostly Italian and French composers, plus contemporary works.

Cabaret

A number of venues are trying to revive the lively and lavish variety shows of 1920s Berlin. Programmes include dancers, singers, jugglers, acrobats and other entertainers, who each perform a short piece. Expect to pay at least €12. Don't confuse cabaret with *Kabarett*, political and satirical revues.

Chamäleon Varieté *(☎ 282 71 18; Rosenthalerstrasse 40-41)* in the Hackesche Höfe in Mitte, has a variety show which includes comedy and slapstick, juggling acts, singing and more.

Cultural Centres

The hottest venue in Prenzl'berg is the **Kulturbrauerei** *(Culture Brewery; ☎ 441 92 69; Knaackstrasse 97)*, a renovated 8000 sq metre space where artists from around the world work. It attracts people from all walks of life with galleries, cinemas and events as diverse as post-Love Parade raves and poetry readings.

SHOPPING

Berlin's decentralised character is reflected in the fact that it doesn't have a clearly defined shopping artery like London's Oxford Street or New York's Fifth Avenue. Rather, the numerous shopping areas are in various neighbourhoods, many of which have a local speciality and 'feel'. For art galleries and *haute couture*, for instance, you should head for posh Charlottenburg, while multiethnic Kreuzberg is known for its eclectic second-hand and junk stores.

The closest Berlin gets to an international shopping strip is the area along Kurfürstendamm and its extension, Tauentzienstrasse. The star of this area is **KaDeWe** *(Tauentzienstrasse 21)*. This is truly one of Europe's grand department stores, the Harrods of Germany. Every year, about 30 million shopping fetishists have a field day on its top floors. The gourmet food halls located on the 6th floor are extraordinary.

The Wilmersdorfer Strasse stop of the U7 will put you in the thick of pedestrian streets filled with affordable shops and department stores patronised by real Berliners. Much more upmarket is the chic indoor shopping complex outside the U6 Französische Strasse in Mitte. Anchored by **Galeries Lafayette**, a branch of the famous Parisian department store, it is connected by an underground tunnel to smallish malls filled with international designer boutiques.

Markets

The **Berlin Art and Nostalgia Market** *(open 8am-5pm Sat & Sun)* is held at the northeastern end of Museumsinsel. The selection here is heavy on collectibles, books, ethnic crafts and possibly authentic GDR memorabilia. From U/S-Bahn station Friedrichstrasse, walk east along Georgenstrasse for about 10 minutes.

GETTING THERE & AWAY
Air

There are few direct flights to Berlin from overseas and, depending on the airline you use, you're likely to fly first into another European city like Frankfurt, Amsterdam, Paris or London and catch a connecting flight from there.

For now, Berlin has three airports. **Tegel** (TXL) primarily serves destinations within Germany and Europe, while **Schönefeld** (SXF) mostly operates international flights to/from Europe, Asia, Africa and Central America. Eventually, Tegel will close, leaving a revamped and expanded Schönefeld as Berlin's airport hub. Close-in **Berlin-Tempelhof** (THF) became famous as the landing hub for Allied airlifts during the Berlin blockade of 1948–49. However, as Schönefeld expands, Tempelhof's future is, shall we say, up in the air.

Bus

Berlin is well connected to the rest of Europe by long-distance bus. Most buses arrive at and depart from the **Zentraler Omnibusbahnhof**

(ZOB; ☎ 302 53 61; Masurenalee 4-6) in Charlottenburg, opposite the stately Funkturm radio tower (U2 to Kaiserdamm or S45 to Witzleben). Tickets are available from many travel agencies in Berlin or at the bus station.

Train

ICE and IC trains have hourly services to every major city in Germany. There are night trains to the capitals of most major central European countries.

That said, until the opening of the huge new, centralised Lehrter Bahnhof (scheduled for 2007; the current station is just for local trains), visitors may find train services to and from Berlin confusing.

Zoo station is the principal station for long-distance travellers going to/from the west. It has scores of lockers (from €1) and a large Reisezentrum (reservation and information office). Ostbahnhof (the former main station) is gaining importance as the train system is revised, while Lichtenberg station in the east generally handles trains to/from the old east and countries beyond, as well as night trains.

Many trains serving Zoo station also stop at Ostbahnhof (the former main train station) and may also stop at Friedrichstrasse and Alexanderplatz. Check your schedules carefully and be aware that you may need to switch stations, usually easily done via S-Bahn. The S5 and S7 travel directly between Zoo and Lichtenberg (35 to 45 minutes); several additional lines serve the rest.

Conventional train tickets to and from Berlin are valid for all trains on the S-Bahn, which means that you can use your train ticket to ride the S-Bahn to/from your train station.

Hitching

Lonely Planet does not encourage hitching for all the obvious reasons. Having said that, if you do want to hitch a ride, it's best to head to one of the service areas on the city autobahns. If your destination is Leipzig, Nuremberg, Munich and beyond, make your way to the Dreilinden service area on the A115. Take the U1 to Krumme Lanke, then bus No 211 to Quantzstrasse, then walk down to the rest area. For Dresden, take the S9 or the S45 to Altglienicke and position yourself near the autobahn on-ramp. Those headed to Hamburg or Rostock should go to the former border checkpoint Stolpe by catching the U6 to Alt-Tegel and then bus No 224 to Stolpe.

Mitfahrzentralen (ride-share agencies) organise lifts and charge a fixed amount payable to the driver, plus commission ranging from €6 for short distances to €10.50 for longer trips (including outside Germany). Some sample fares (including commission) are Leipzig €13.50, Hanover €17, Frankfurt/Main, Munich or Cologne €28.50. **ADM Mitfahrzentrale** *(☎ 194 40)* has two branches: at Zoo station on the Vinetastrasse platform of the U2 *(open 9am-8pm Mon-Fri & 10am-6pm Sat & Sun)*, and in the Alexanderplatz U-Bahn station as you cross from U2 to U8 *(open 10am-6pm Mon-Fri, 11am-4pm Sat & Sun)*. Another agency is **Citynetz** *(☎ 194 44; Joachimstalerstrasse 17)*.

GETTING AROUND

Ongoing construction in central Berlin has the expected effect on traffic flow. Gridlock, mysteriously rerouted roads and sudden dead ends that weren't there yesterday are among the obstacles you'll have to navigate when driving through the core districts.

However, Berlin's public transport system is excellent, so use it. Roughly one billion passengers each year ride the huge network of U-Bahn and S-Bahn trains, buses, trams and ferries which extends pretty much into every corner of Berlin and the surrounding areas.

To/From the Airport

Tegel airport is connected by bus No 109 to Zoo station (€2.10), a route that travels via Kurfürstendamm and Luisenplatz.

JetExpress Bus TXL (€3.10) goes via Unter den Linden, Potsdamer Platz and the Reichstag. The trip between the airport and the western centre takes around 30 minutes. A taxi between Tegel and Zoo station costs about €19.

Schönefeld airport is easily reached in 30 minutes by **Airport Express** trains leaving from Zoo station every 30 minutes. The train also stops at the rest of the stations along the central train line including Friedrichstrasse and Ostbahnhof. The station is about 300m from the terminal and is connected by a free shuttle bus. A taxi to Zoo station costs between €25 and €35.

Close-in Tempelhof airport is reached by the U6 (Platz der Luftbrücke) and by bus No 119 from Kurfürstendamm via Kreuzberg. A taxi to/from Zoo station will cost about €16.

GERMANY

Public Transport

Berlin's public transport system offers services provided by **Berliner Verkehrsbetriebe** (BVG; ☎ 194 49), which operates the U-Bahn, buses, trams and ferries; and the **Deutsche Bahn** (DB; ☎ 01805-99 66 33, call cost €0.12 per min) which runs the S-Bahn and regional RE, SE and RB trains (rail pass-holders can use the DB trains for free). Since the system is jointly operated, one type of ticket is valid on all forms of transport (with the few exceptions noted following). BVG has information kiosks at major entry points, which also sell tickets and passes. For information on S-Bahn, RE and RB connections, visit the Reisezentrum office inside Zoo station.

Greater Berlin is divided into three tariff zones: A, B and C. Tickets are valid in at least two zones (AB or BC), or in all three zones. Unless you're venturing to Potsdam or the very outer suburbs, you'll only need the AB ticket. Taking a bicycle in specially marked carriages of the S-Bahn or U-Bahn costs €1.25 (free if you hold a monthly ticket). On the U-Bahn, bikes are allowed only between 9am and 2pm and from 5.30pm to closing time on weekdays (any time on weekends). The following types of tickets and passes are available:

Ganzstrecke (Entire Route System) – This ticket (€2.40) also allows unlimited travel for two hours, but in all three zones (ABC). It's also valid on RE, SE and RB trains.

Kurzstrecke (Short Trip) – This ticket (€1.20) allows you to travel any three stops by U-Bahn or S-Bahn or six stops by bus or tram.

Langstrecke (Long Trip) – With this ticket (€2.10) you can travel on all forms of public transport (except RE, SE and RB trains) for two hours within two of the three zones (AB or BC) with unlimited transfers.

Tageskarte (Day Pass) – This ticket gives you unlimited travel until 3am the following day and costs only €6.10 (zones AB or BC) or €6.30 (zones ABC).

Bus drivers sell single and day tickets, but tickets for U/S-Bahn trains and other multiple day tickets must be purchased in advance.

Most types of tickets are available from vending machines (which feature instructions in English) in U/S-Bahn stations. Tickets must be stamped (validated) in a red or yellow machine (Entwerter) at the platform entrances to U/S-Bahn stations, at bus stops before boarding, or as you enter the bus or tram. If you're using a timed ticket like the Langstrecke, validate it just as your train or bus arrives to ensure full value. If you're caught without a ticket (or with an unvalidated one), there's a €30 on-the-spot fine.

The most efficient way to travel around Berlin is by U/S-Bahn. A network of some 30 tram lines crisscross the entire eastern half of Berlin. There's also bus service throughout the city, but if you need to travel across town in a hurry, don't take the bus! Traffic congestion can slow your journey. Bus and tram stops are marked with a large 'H' and the name of the stop.

Services operate from 4am until just after midnight, but most S-Bahns continue to operate hourly between midnight and 4am on Saturday and Sunday. Some 70 bus lines operate between 1am and about 4am (Nachtbus), when regular service resumes. Buses leave from the major nightlife areas like Zoo station, Hackescher Markt in Mitte and Nollendorfplatz in Schöneberg, and cover the entire Berlin area, including the outer districts. Normal fares apply.

Car & Motorcycle

You'll soon want to ditch your wheels in Berlin. Garage parking is expensive (about €1 to €1.50 per hour), but it'll often be your only choice if you want to be near the main shopping areas or attractions. Free street parking, while impossible to find in these central areas, is usually available in residential streets, especially in the eastern districts. If you're staying at a hotel, keep in mind that most don't have their own garages.

Taxi

Taxi stands with call columns are located beside all main train stations and throughout the city. Basic fare flag fall is €2.50; then it's €1.53 per kilometre for the first 7km and €1.02 thereafter; short trips (less than 2km) cost €3. If you order a taxi by phone (☎ 194 10, 21 01 01, 21 02 02), flag fall goes up to €3.

Bicycle

Fahrradstation is the largest bike-rental agency with branches all over the city, including at the **left-luggage office** (☎ 29 74 93 19) in Zoo station. Bikes cost from €10 a day with a €50 deposit.

Brandenburg

The state of Brandenburg surrounds the city-state of Berlin and is a flat region of lakes, marshes, rivers and canals. In 1618, the electors of Brandenburg acquired the eastern Baltic duchy of Prussia, eventually merging the two states into a powerful union called the Kingdom of Prussia. By 1871, this kingdom brought all the German states under its control, leading to the establishment of the German Empire.

Many Berliners will warn you about the 'Wild East', advising you not to stray too far afield in what they consider to be a backward and sometimes violent region. But Brandenburgers, ever *korrekt* in the Prussian style, sniff and say that's what they'd expect from a bunch of loud-mouthed and brash upstarts like the Berliners. However, there are still occasional violent attacks against African and Asian foreigners in some small Brandenburg towns. In 1996 the dichotomy was set in stone when a referendum to merge Brandenburg with the city-state of Berlin failed at the polls.

POTSDAM
☎ 0331 • pop 130,500

Potsdam, on the Havel River just beyond the southwestern tip of Greater Berlin, is the capital of Brandenburg state. During the mid-18th century Friedrich II (Frederick the Great, 1740–86) built many of those marvellous palaces in Sanssouci Park, to which visitors flock today.

In April 1945, British bombers attacked Potsdam, devastating much of the historic centre including the City Palace on Alter Markt. However, parts of downtown have been pleasantly restored, and most of the palaces in the park escaped undamaged. The Allies chose Schloss Cecilienhof for the Potsdam Conference of August 1945, which set the stage for the division of Berlin and Germany into occupation zones.

Only 24km from central Berlin and easily accessible by S-Bahn, Potsdam is an ideal day trip.

Orientation & Information
Potsdam's main train station and last stop for the S-Bahn from Berlin is Potsdam Hauptbahnhof. From here, it is about a 3km walk over the Lange Brücke (long bridge) and through the town centre to the gates of Sanssouci Park; two other stations are closer to Sanssouci but not as conveniently reached. You can also take a bus or tram (see Getting Around later in this section).

The town centre provides an interesting mix of newly restored buildings exuding charm, bad GDR-era architecture, and some old classics that have been mouldering away for decades.

Potsdam-Information (☎ 27 55 80, fax 27 55 99; Friedrich-Ebert-Strasse 5; open 9am-7pm Mon-Fri, 9am-4pm Sat & Sun Apr-Oct, 10am-6pm Mon-Fri, 10am-2pm Sat & Sun Nov-Mar) is situated beside the Alter Markt. **Sanssouci-Information** (☎ 969 42 02; An der Historischen Mühle; ⓦ www.spsg.de), near the old windmill northwest of Schloss Sanssouci, has details on the palaces in the park and is usually open the same hours as the Schloss.

The Berlin-Potsdam Welcome Card (€18) gets you here on public transport and offers discounts to some attractions.

Sanssouci Park
This large park (admission free; open dawn-dusk daily) contains palaces and outbuildings which all keep separate hours and charge separate admission prices. A ticket valid for two consecutive days offers admission to all the park sites (Premium Tageskarte) including the tour of Schloss Sanssouci. It costs €15 and must be purchased at Schloss Sanssouci. A two-day ticket to all the other park sites (Tageskarte) is sold for €12 at other venues. Note that some sites have different days of closure.

Covering the entire circuit of sites means walking several kilometres. Begin your tour of the park with Georg Wenzeslaus von Knobelsdorff's **Schloss Sanssouci** (adult/concession €8/5; tours depart 9am-5pm Tues-Sun Apr–mid-Oct & 9am-4pm Tues-Sun Nov-May), the celebrated 1747 rococo palace with glorious interiors. You have to take the guided tour (around 40 minutes), so arrive early and avoid weekends and holidays, or you may not get in. They're usually sold out by 2.30pm, even in the shoulder seasons. Tours are in German, but guides have text in English.

The late-baroque **Neues Palais** (1769), the summer residence of the royal family, is one of the most imposing buildings in the park

GERMANY

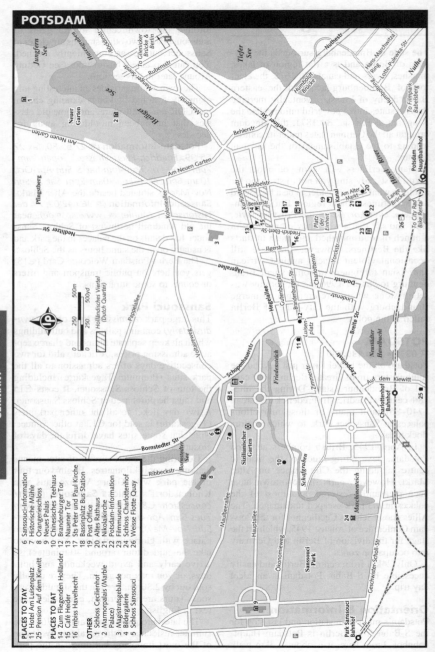

POTSDAM

PLACES TO STAY
11 Hotel Am Luisenplatz
25 Pension Auf dem Kiewitt

PLACES TO EAT
14 Zum Fliegenden Holländer
16 Café Heider
16 Imbiss Havelhecht

OTHER
1 Schloss Cecilienhof
2 Marmorpalais (Marble Palace)
3 Magistratsgebäude
4 Bildergalerie
5 Schloss Sanssouci
6 Sanssouci-Information
7 Historische Mühle
8 Orangerieschloss
9 Neues Palais
10 Chinesisches Teehaus
12 Brandenburger Tor
13 Nauener Tor
17 Sts Peter und Paul Kirche
18 Bassinplatz Bus Station
19 Post Office
20 Altes Rathaus
21 Nikolaikirche
22 Potsdam-Information
23 Filmmuseum
24 Schloss Charlottenhof
26 Weisse Flotte Quay

Holländisches Viertel (Dutch Quarter)

and the one to see if your time is limited. It keeps the same hours as the Schloss but closes on Friday instead of Monday.

The following sites are closed on Monday and 15 October to 15 May. The **Bildergalerie** (1764) contains an extensive collection of 17th-century paintings. The Renaissance-style **Orangerieschloss** (1864) was built as a guesthouse for foreign royalty. Although it's the largest palace on the grounds, it is not the most interesting. The **Schloss Charlottenhof** (1826) is a must and can be visited on a 30-minute German-language tour. However, the exterior is more interesting than the interior.

Take some time to wander around the royal grounds and use up some film on the **Chinesisches Teehaus** (1757).

Altstadt

From the baroque **Brandenburger Tor** (1770) on Luisenplatz at the western end of the old town, pedestrian Brandenburger Strasse runs east to **Sts Peter und Paul Kirche** (Sts Peter and Paul Church; 1868). Northwest of here there's the 1755 **Nauener Tor** (Nauen Gate; Friedrich-Ebert-Strasse), another monumental arch. North of the church, the **Holländisches Viertel** (Dutch Quarter) features some 134 gabled red-brick houses built for Dutch workers in the 1730s.

Southeast of central Platz der Einheit is the great neoclassical dome of Schinkel's **Nikolaikirche** (1850) on Alter Markt. On the eastern side of the square is Potsdam's 1753 **Altes Rathaus** (Old Town Hall; adult/concession €2/1; open 10am-6pm Tues-Sun), which now contains several art galleries.

West of the Alter Markt and housed in the **Marstall**, the former royal stables designed by Knobelsdorff in 1746, is the **Filmmuseum** (☎ 271 81 12; Breite Strasse; adult/concession €2/1; open 10am-6pm daily). It contains exhibits on the history of the UFA and DEFA movie studios in nearby Babelsberg and some excellent footage from Nazi-era and postwar communist propaganda films.

Neuer Garten, the winding lakeside park on the west bank of the Heiliger See, northeast of the city centre, is home to **Schloss Cecilienhof** (admission €2; open daily), an English-style country manor. This was the site of the 1945 Potsdam Conference. The park is also home to the lovely **Marmorpalais** (Marble Palace; 1792).

Filmpark Babelsberg

This theme park (August-Bebel-Strasse; adult/concession/child €15/14/9; open 10am-6pm Mar-Oct) is on the site of the UFA Studios, Germany's one-time response to Hollywood, east of the city centre (enter from Grossbeerenstrasse). This is where silent movie epics such as Fritz Lang's Metropolis were made, along with some early Greta Garbo films. For a look behind the scenes you can take the commercial, and expensive, tour.

Cruises

Weisse Flotte (☎ 275 92 10) operates boats on the Havel River and the lakes around Potsdam, departing regularly from April to early October from the dock below the Hotel Mercure near Lange Brücke. There are frequent boats to Wannsee (€9.50 return).

Places to Stay & Eat

Potsdam's proximity to Berlin and the dearth of cheap accommodation make staying overnight an unappealing option. However, should you end up here for the night, **Pension Auf dem Kiewitt** (☎ 90 36 78, fax 967 87 55; Auf dem Kiewitt 8; singles/doubles €48/69) is kindly despite the GDR high-rises surrounding it. **Hotel am Luisenplatz** (☎ 97 19 00, fax 971 90 19; e info@hotel-luisenplatz.de; singles/doubles from €79/109) is just west of the centre and run by a friendly Dutchman.

For breakfast, lunch or dinner try the classic **Café Heider** (☎ 270 55 96; Friedrich-Ebert-Strasse 29; dishes €4.80-9.80), a lively meeting and eating place adjacent to Nauener Tor. In the Dutch Quarter, **Zum Fliegenden Holländer** (☎ 27 50 30; Benkertstrasse 5; mains €8-15.50) has German cooking and reasonable lunch specials.

Brandenburger Strasse has several nice cafés, shops and snack shops (we like **Imbiss Havelhecht** at No 25 for fishy snacks); there's also good people-watching.

Getting There & Away

Potsdam Hauptbahnhof is just southeast of the town centre across the Havel River. Two other stations, Charlottenhof and Sanssouci, are closer to Sanssouci Park but are not served by the Regional Express (RE) or S-Bahn Nos 3 and 7, which is how most people get here from Berlin.

Potsdam Hauptbahnhof is also served by ICE and IC trains linking Berlin with points west, so you can stop off on your way to or from the big metropolis.

Getting Around

Bus No 695 goes past Schloss Sanssouci, the Orangerieschloss and the Neues Palais, from the south exit of Potsdam Hauptbahnhof. Change to bus No 692 to Schloss Cecilienhof. To reach Schloss Charlottenhof and the Neues Palais, take bus No 606; tram No 610 is also good for the former.

City Rad (☎ 620 06 06) rents bikes from the shopping centre beneath Potsdam Hauptbahnhof, from €13 per day.

SACHSENHAUSEN CONCENTRATION CAMP

In 1936 the Nazis opened a 'model' concentration camp near the town of Oranienburg, about 35km north of Berlin. By 1945 about 220,000 men from 22 countries had passed through the gates of Sachsenhausen labelled, as at Auschwitz in southwestern Poland, *Arbeit Macht Frei* (Work Makes Free); about 100,000 died here. After the war, the Soviets and the communist leaders of the GDR used the camp for *their* undesirables.

Plan on spending at least two hours at Sachsenhausen (☎ 03301-20 02 00; admission free; open 8.30am-6pm daily Apr-Sept, 8.30am-4.30pm daily Oct-Mar), which is quite easily reached from Berlin. Among the many museums and monuments within the triangular-shaped, walled grounds are **Barracks 38 and 39**. Rebuilt after an arson attack by neo-Nazis in 1992, they contain excellent displays of the camp's history. At the front gate you may rent a chilling audio guide in English (€2.50), and an **information office** sells maps, brochures and books, including several useful English-language guides.

From Berlin take the S1 to Oranienburg (€2.40, 40 minutes). The camp is an easy 2km northeast of the station. Follow Stralsunder Strasse north and turn east (right) onto Bernauer Strasse. After about 600m turn left at Strasse der Einheit and then right on Strasse der Nationen to the camp entrance.

Saxony

The Free State of Saxony (Sachsen) is the most densely populated and industrialised region in eastern Germany. Germanic Saxon tribes originally occupied large parts of north-western Germany, but in the 10th century they expanded southeastwards into the territory of the pagan Slavs.

The medieval history of the various Saxon duchies and dynasties is complex, but in the 13th century the Duke of Saxony at Wittenberg obtained the right to participate in the election of Holy Roman emperors. Involvement in Poland weakened Saxony in the 18th century, and ill-fated alliances, first with Napoleon and then with Austria, led to the ascendancy of Prussia over Saxony in the 19th century.

In the south, Saxony is separated from Czech Bohemia by the Erzgebirge, eastern Germany's highest mountain range. The Elbe River cuts northwest from the Czech border through a picturesque area known as 'Saxon Switzerland' towards the capital, Dresden. Leipzig, a great educational and commercial centre on the Weisse Elster River, rivals Dresden in historic associations. Quaint little towns like Görlitz and Meissen punctuate this colourful, accessible corner of Germany.

DRESDEN

☎ 0351 • pop 463,000

In the 18th century the Saxon capital Dresden was famous throughout Europe as 'the Florence of the north'. During the reigns of Augustus the Strong (r. 1694–1733) and his son Augustus III (r. 1733–63), Italian artists, musicians, actors and master craftsmen, particularly from Venice, flocked to the Dresden court. The Italian painter Canaletto depicted the rich architecture of the time in many paintings which now hang in Dresden's Alte Meister Gallery, alongside countless masterpieces purchased for Augustus III with income from the silver mines of Saxony.

In February 1945 much of Dresden was devastated by Anglo-American fire-bombing raids. At least 35,000 people died at a time when the city was jammed with refugees and the war was almost over. This horrific attack is the basis for the book *Slaughterhouse Five* by Kurt Vonnegut, who was a POW in Dresden at the time. Quite a number of Dresden's great baroque buildings have been restored, but the city's former architectural masterpiece, the Frauenkirche, is still in the midst of a laborious and enormously expensive reconstruction.

The Elbe River cuts a curving course between the low, rolling hills. In spite of modern rebuilding in concrete and steel, this city

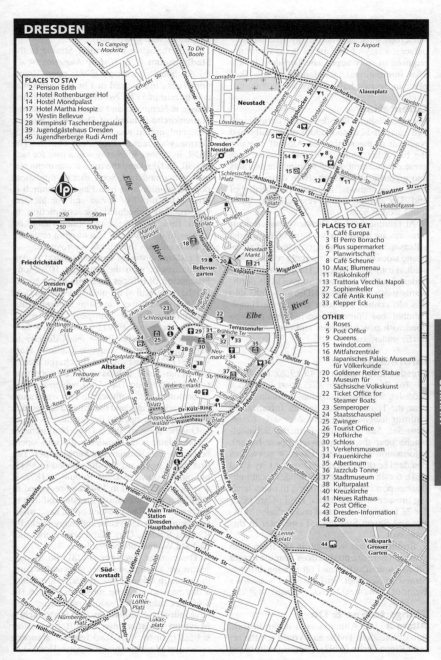

DRESDEN

PLACES TO STAY
2 Pension Edith
12 Hotel Rothenburger Hof
14 Hostel Mondpalast
17 Hotel Martha Hospiz
19 Westin Bellevue
28 Kempinski Taschenbergpalais
39 Jugendgästehaus Dresden
45 Jugendherberge Rudi Arndt

PLACES TO EAT
1 Café Europa
3 El Perro Borracho
6 Plus supermarket
7 Planwirtschaft
8 Café Scheune
10 Max; Blumenau
11 Raskolnikoff
13 Trattoria Vecchia Napoli
27 Sophienkeller
32 Café Antik Kunst
33 Klepper Eck

OTHER
4 Roses
5 Post Office
9 Queens
15 twindot.com
16 Mitfahrzentrale
18 Japanisches Palais; Museum
      für Völkerkunde
20 Goldener Reiter Statue
21 Museum für
      Sächsische Volkskunst
22 Ticket Office for
      Steamer Boats
23 Semperoper
24 Staatsschauspiel
25 Zwinger
26 Tourist Office
29 Hofkirche
30 Schloss
31 Verkehrsmuseum
34 Frauenkirche
35 Albertinum
36 Jazzclub Tonne
37 Stadtmuseum
38 Kulturpalast
40 Kreuzkirche
41 Neues Rathaus
42 Post Office
43 Dresden-Information
44 Zoo

GERMANY

invariably wins visitors' affections. With its numerous museums and many fine baroque palaces, a stay of two nights is the minimum required to fully appreciate Dresden. Its annual International Dixieland Festival takes place in the first half of May.

Orientation

For most visitors, Dresden can be divided into two parts: the Altstadt south of the Elbe and Neustadt to the north. The Altstadt contains the big-ticket tourist sites, while there is a greater concentration of lodging, restaurants and nightlife in Neustadt. Both districts have large train stations, Dresden Hauptbahnhof and Dresden-Neustadt respectively; most trains stop at both.

At present most of Dresden's priceless art treasures are housed in two large buildings, the Albertinum and the Zwinger, which are at opposite sides of Dresden's largely restored Altstadt. From the Dresden Hauptbahnhof, the pedestrian mall of Prager Strasse leads northwards past some classic GDR monoliths into this old centre. The area around the Hauptbahnhof and Prager Stasse is being redeveloped with new high-rises and pedestrian and traffic underpasses.

Information

Dresden-Information *(☎ 49 19 20, fax 49 19 21 16; Prager Strasse 10; open 9am-7pm Mon-Fri, 9am-4pm Sat)* has its main office near the Hauptbahnhof and an **information counter** *(open 10am-6pm Mon-Fri, 10am-4pm Sat, Sun & holidays)* in the Schinkelwache near the Semperoper (opera house). Information is also available at w www.dresden.de. The offices sell the Dresden-City-Card (€16 for 48 hours) which includes local public transport and free admission to many leading museums. The Dresden-Regio-Card (€25 for 72 hours) does all that and includes Meissen and Saxon Switzerland (see later in this section).

Reisebank has a branch in the main train station. There are **post offices** near the Prager Strasse tourist office and on Köningsbrücker Strasse in Neustadt. Surf the net at Neustadt's **twindot.com** *(☎ 802 06 02; Alaunstrasse 19).*

Things to See & Do

Altstadt The Altmarkt area is the historic hub of Dresden. To the east you'll see the rebuilt **Kreuzkirche** (1792), famous for its boys'

choir, and in the distance the 1912 **Neues Rathaus** (New Town Hall).

Cross the wide Wilsdruffer Strasse to the **Stadtmuseum** *(City History Museum; ☎ 49 86 60; adult/concession €2/1; open 10am-6pm Tues-Sun)* located in a building that was constructed in 1776. Northwest up Landhausstrasse is Neumarkt and the site of the ruined **Frauenkirche** (Church of Our Lady) built in 1738 and, until it was badly bombed in 1945, Germany's greatest Protestant church. The GDR, in a move many say was a ruse for lack of will, had declared the ruins a war memorial to remain untouched. Soon after reunification, popular opinion was heard and the church is now in the midst of a vast and complex reconstruction scheduled for completion in 2006. Ruse or not, the remaining rubble on display to the southeast is a moving reminder of the bombings that all but destroyed it.

Leading northwest from Neumarkt is Augustusstrasse, with the stunning 102m-long **Procession of Princes** porcelain mural covering the outer wall of the old royal stables. Here you'll also find the interesting **Verkehrsmuseum** *(Museum of Transport; ☎ 864 40; adult/concession €2/1; open 10am-5pm Tues-Sun).* Augustusstrasse leads directly to Schlossplatz and the baroque Catholic **Hofkirche** (1755). Just south of the church there's the Renaissance **Schloss** *(adult/concession €2.60/1.50; open Tues-Sun),* which is being reconstructed as a museum. The restoration work is advancing, and the tower and a palace exhibit are now open to the public.

On the western side of the Hofkirche is Theaterplatz, with Dresden's glorious opera house, the neo-Renaissance **Semperoper**. The first opera house on the site opened in 1841, but burned down in 1869. Rebuilt in 1878, it was again destroyed in 1945 and reopened in 1985 after the communists invested millions in the restoration. The Dresden opera has a tradition going back 350 years, and many works by Richard Strauss, Carl Maria von Weber and Richard Wagner premiered here.

The baroque **Zwinger** (1728) and its museums are among Dresden's stars and occupy the southern side of Theaterplatz. You can buy a day pass to all these museums for €6.10/3.60 per adult/concession, otherwise they have individual admissions. The **Historisches Museum** *(Rüstkammer; adult/concession €1.50/1; open Tues-Sun)* features a superb collection of ceremonial weapons. Housed in opposite corners of the complex with separate entrances are the **Mathematisch-Physikaler Salon** (*adult/concession €1.50/1; open Fri-Wed*) displaying scientific instruments and timepieces, the **Museum für Tierkunde** (*Zoological Museum; adult/concession €3/1.50; open Wed-Mon*), with natural history exhibits, and the **Porcelain Collection**, which should have reopened by the time you read this.

East of the Augustusbrücke is the **Brülsche Terrasse**, a pleasant elevated riverside promenade with the overwrought moniker 'the Balcony of Europe'. At the eastern end is the **Albertinum** (1885). Here you will find the **Gemäldegalerie Alte Meister** (*open Tues-Sun*), which boasts Raphael's *Sistine Madonna*, **Gemäldegalerie Neue Meister** (*open Wed-Mon*), with renowned 19th- and 20th-century paintings, and the **Grünes Gewölbe** (*Green Vault; open Wed-Mon*), hosting a collection of jewel-studded precious objects. Eventually the Grünes Gewölbe will be relocated to its original site in the Schloss. You can visit all three with a combined ticket (adult/concession €4.50/2.50).

Southeast of the Altstadt is the Grosser Garten, enchanting in summer and home to a fine **zoo** (☎ 471 80 60; *Tiergartenstrasse 1; adult/concession €5/3; open daily*) with more than 400 species. In the garden's northwestern corner are the **Botanical Gardens** (*admission free*). The hothouse is especially lovely during a freezing Dresden winter. And for a glimpse of Dresden's newest architectural marvel, check out the glass-enclosed **VW factory**, opened 2001, north of the zoo at Lennéstrasse and Stübelallee.

Neustadt This is an old part of Dresden largely untouched by wartime bombings. After unification it became the centre of the city's alternative scene and is now the centre of Dresden's nightlife.

The **Goldener Reiter** statue (1736; under repair during our visit) of Augustus the Strong stands at the northern end of the Augustusbrücke, leading to Hauptstrasse, a (largely GDR-era) pedestrian mall. At the mall's northern end, on Albertplatz, there's an evocative marble monument to the poet Schiller. Just west is Königstrasse, lined with genteel renovated buildings and high-end shops. Other museums near the Goldener Reiter include the **Museum für Sächsische Volkskunst** (*Museum of Saxon Folk Art; Grosse Meissner Strasse 1; adult/concession €1.50/1; open Tues-Sun*), and the **Japanisches Palais** (1737), with the famous **Museum für Völkerkunde** (*Ethnological Museum; ☎ 81 44 50; Palaisplatz; adult/concession €2/1; open Sat-Thur*).

Neustadt is also where you'll find Dresden's greatest variety of dining and nightlife, mostly northeast of Albertplatz.

Elbe River Excursions

From March through November, **Sächsische Dampfschifffahrts GmbH** (☎ 86 60 90), which prides itself on having the world's oldest and largest fleet of paddle-wheel steamers, has frequent excursions on the Elbe River. A one-hour tour costs €10/5 per adult/child. You can also use the boats to reach Pillnitz Palace (€8.50/13 one way/return, 1¾ hours) and even as far as lovely Meissen (€10.50/15 one way/return, two hours). Schedules vary and you may need to book, so check with the ticket office, in a small glass building on the waterfront just east of Augustusbrücke.

Places to Stay

The **tourist office** (☎ 49 19 22 22 for bookings) can arrange **private rooms** for a €3 fee.

Camping The closest place to pitch your tent is **Camping Mockritz** (☎ 471 52 50; *open Mar-Dec*), 5km south of the city. Take the frequent Mockritz bus from behind the Dresden train station. It has bungalows, but like the camping ground they're often full in summer.

Hostels In a former Communist Party training centre, **Jugendgästehaus Dresden** (☎ 49 26 20, fax 492 62 99; *Maternistrasse 22; dorm beds juniors/seniors without bath €17.50/21, with bath €19.70/23.20*) is a 15-minute walk northwest of the Hauptbahnhof (or take tram No 7, 9, 10 or 26 to the corner of Ammonstrasse and Freiberger Strasse). The non-DJH **Jugendherberge Rudi Arndt** (☎ 471 06 67, fax 472 89 59; *Hübnerstrasse 11; beds juniors/seniors €16.80/19.50*) is a 10-minute walk south of the Hauptbahnhof in a residential neighbourhood.

In Neustadt are two hostels enjoyed by readers; their prices exclude breakfast. **Hostel Mondpalast Dresden** (☎/fax 804 60 61; e *mondpalast@t-online.de; Katherinenstrasse 11-13; dorm beds €13, singles/doubles*

€23/34) is in the centre of Neustadt's nightlife. **Die Boofe** (☎ 801 33 61, fax 801 33 62; e info@boofe.com; Hechtstrasse 10; beds from €14.50 per person) had just moved to a new location north of Neustadt station. It has a sauna and was installing a courtyard garden during our visit.

Hotels Average hotel rates in Dresden are among the highest in Germany, with few genuine budget places near the centre. Pickings south of the Elbe are especially slim.

Pension Edith (☎/fax 802 83 42; Priesnitzstrasse 63; singles/doubles €41/61), in a quiet backstreet, has rooms with private shower; it only has a few, so you need to book well ahead. **Hotel Rothenburger Hof** (☎ 88 12 60, fax 812 62 22; e kontakt@dresden -hotel.de; Rothenburger Strasse 15-17; singles/doubles from €64/85) is clean and bright and boasts a good restaurant. **Hotel Martha Hospiz** (☎ 817 60, fax 817 62 22, e marthahospiz.dresden@t-online.de; Nieritzstrasse 11; singles/doubles from €72/102) is cosy, well-kept and a few minutes' walk from Neustadt's high-end Königstrasse.

The **Westin Bellevue** (☎ 805 17 33, fax 805 17 49, e hotelinfo@westin-bellevue.de; Grosse Meissner Strasse 15; rooms from €102, excluding breakfast) has nice business-standard accommodation and awesome Altstadt views from rooms facing the Elbe. King of the hill is the **Kempinski Taschenberg-palais** (☎ 491 20, fax 491 28 12, e reserva tion@kempinski-dresden.de; Taschenberg 3; singles/doubles from €250/280, excluding breakfast), next to the Schloss, with palaistial rooms, spa and fitness facilities and crisp service.

Places to Eat

Head straight to Neustadt for food and fun – few of Altstadt's culinary options match its archi-cultural wonders.

Raskolnikoff (Böhmische Strasse 34; mains €3-12) serves dishes from the four corners of central Europe. Alaunstrasse has loads of Italian places including comfortable **Trattoria Vecchia Napoli** (☎ 802 90 55; Alaunstrasse 33; mains €4.50-14.90), where wood-oven baked pizzas and enticing pastas demand to be washed down with red wine.

You'll also find many late-night restaurant-bars nearby. Some long-standing favourites include the **Planwirtschaft** (☎ 801 31 87;

Louisenstrasse 20; mains €6.50-12.50), with a beer cellar and some Saxon dishes; **Café Scheune** (☎ 802 66 19; Alaunstrasse 36; mains €6.30-10) with a rock-and-roll setting and popular Indian food; and the **Café Europa** (☎ 804 48 10; Königsbrücker Strasse 68; mains €4-18.20; open 24hr). **El Perro Borracho** (☎ 803 67 23; Alaunstrasse 70; dishes €2.80-10.20) serves tapas and other Spanish fare in an avant-garde courtyard.

You really don't need help in choosing a place near Altstadt's Brühlsche Terrace as long as you're happy with high prices, marginal food and excellent people-watching. **Café Antik Kunst** (☎ 498 98 36; Terrassengasse) is an exception; sit amid antique art and furniture and drink good coffee. On the next corner, **Klepper Eck** (☎ 496 51 23; Münzgasse 10; mains €6.50-18.80) is well-regarded for Saxon cooking. Otherwise in Altstadt, hotels offer your best restaurant options, or families might enjoy **Sophienkeller** (☎ 49 72 60; Taschenberg 3; mains €9-16.50), a theme restaurant decorated like an 18th-century fair.

Popular Neustadt cafés include **Max** (☎ 563 59 96; Louisenstrasse 65) and **Blumenau** (☎ 802 65 02; Louisenstrasse 67) next door. You'll find several fast-food options on Prager Strasse and around the transit hub at Postplatz; there are several supermarkets in Neustadt, including a **Plus** at Königsbrückerstrasse south of Louisenstrasse.

Entertainment

Sax (€1.25) is a comprehensive German-language listings guide available at newsstands throughout the city.

Dresden is synonymous with opera performances at the **Semperoper**. Dresden's two other great theatres are the **Staatsschauspiel** (☎ 491 35 55), also near the Zwinger, and the **Staatsoperette** (☎ 207 99 29; Pirnaer Landstrasse 131) in Leuben in the far east of the city. Tickets for all three theatres can be bought from Dresden-Information, or an hour before each performance at the appropriate theatre's box office. Tickets for the Semperoper usually sell out well in advance. Many theatres close from mid-July to the end of August.

A variety of musical events are presented in the austere **Kulturpalast** (☎ 486 60; Schlossstrasse 2). **Jazzclub Tonne** (☎ 802 60 17; Königstrasse 15; admission €6-10) has live jazz five nights per week.

For a drink, the choices in the café-laden blocks around Alaunstrasse and Louisenstrasse are many and change frequently (see also Places to Eat earlier). Gay visitors might start at the cocktail bar **Roses** (☎ 802 42 64; Jordanstrasse 10) or amid a young-ish crowd at the club **Queens** (☎ 803 16 50; Görlitzerstrasse 3). Gegenpol magazine has gay and lesbian listings.

Getting There & Around

Dresden airport is 9km from the city centre. A new S-Bahn line connects both main stations with the airport (€1.50, 15 minutes from Neustadt, 20 minutes from Hauptbahnhof). From either station you have easy access to local transport.

Hourly trains link Dresden to the Berlin-Ostbahnhof (€30.60, two hours) and Leipzig (ICE: €24, 1¼ hours; IR: €16.80, 1¾ hours), where you can connect to major cities all over Germany. IR trains running every two hours to Hanover (€54.40, 4½ hours) allow more connection possibilities. There's a **Mitfahrzentrale** (☎ 194 40; Dr.-Friedrich-Wolfsstrasse 2) across from Neustadt station.

For travel on Dresden's local transit, a single-trip ticket is €1.50, a day ticket is €4 and a weekly ticket is €13. Regional day tickets cost €8.

AROUND DRESDEN
Schloss Pillnitz

From 1765 to 1918, Schloss Pillnitz was the summer residence of the kings and queens of Saxony. The most romantic way to get to this palace, on the Elbe about 10km southeast of Dresden, is on one of Dresden's old steamers. Otherwise, take tram No 9 or 14 to the end of the line, then walk a few blocks down to the riverside and cross the Elbe on the small ferry, which operates year-round. Bus No 83 also gets you almost to the palace. There's a museum (☎ 261 32 60; adult/concession €1.50/1; open 9.30am-5.30pm Tues-Sun May–mid-Oct), but the gardens (which stay open until 8pm) and the palace exterior with its Oriental motifs are far more interesting than anything inside.

Schloss Moritzburg

This palace (☎ 035207-87 30; adult/concession €4.10/2.60; open 10am-4pm daily) rises impressively from its lake 14km northwest of Dresden. Erected as a hunting lodge for the Duke of Saxony in 1546, Moritzburg was completely remodelled in baroque style in 1730 and has an impressive interior. You can catch a bus or train from Dresden-Hauptbahnhof.

Meissen
☎ 03521 • pop 32,000

Just 27km northwest of Dresden, Meissen is a perfectly preserved old German town and the centre of a rich wine-growing region. Augustus the Strong of Saxony created Europe's first porcelain factory at the Albrechtsburg palace in 1710. Meissen straddles the Elbe, with the old town on the western bank and the train station on the eastern bank. The train-pedestrian bridge behind the station is the quickest way across (and presents a picture-postcard view). From the bridge, continue up Obergasse then bear right through Hahnemannsplatz and Rossplatz to Markt, the town's central square.

There you'll find **Meissen-Information** (☎ 03521-419 40, fax 41 94 19; Markt 3; open 10am-6pm Mon-Fri, 10am-4pm Sat & Sun Apr-Oct, 10am-5pm Mon-Fri, 10am-3pm Sat Nov-Mar). Also on Markt are the restored **Rathaus** (1472) and the 15th-century **Frauenkirche** (☎ 45 38 32; open 10am-noon, 1pm-5pm daily May-Oct). The church's 1549 **tower** (adult/concession €1/0.50), with a porcelain carillon that chimes every quarter-hour, is well worth climbing for fine views of the Altstadt; pick up the key in the church or from the adjacent Pfarrbüro (parish office).

Various steeply stepped lanes lead up to **Albrechtsburg** (☎ 45 24 90; adult/concession €2/1.50; open daily). Its towering medieval Dom with its altarpiece by Lucas Cranach the Elder, is visible from afar. Beside the cathedral is the remarkable 15th-century Albrechtsburg **castle** (adult/concession €3.50/2.50; open daily 1 Feb-9 Jan). Constructed with an ingenious system of internal arches, it was the first palace-style castle built in Germany.

Meissen has long been famous for its china-ware, with its trademark blue crossed-swords insignia. The **porcelain factory** (☎ 46 87 00; Talstrasse 9; open daily) is now 1km southwest of town. There are often long queues for the workshop demonstrations (admission €3), but you can view the fascinating porcelain collection in the **museum** (adult/concession €4.50/4) at your leisure.

Campingplatz Waldbad (☎ 035243-360 12; adult/child/car €4/3/5) is in Niederau, 8km from Meissen. The **Pension Burkhardt**

(☎ 45 81 98, fax 45 81 97; Neugasse 29; singles/doubles from €25/50) has attractive rooms with full facilities. Hotel-restaurant **Burgkeller** (☎ 414 00, fax 414 04; e burgkell er@meissen-hotels.com; Domplatz; singles/ doubles from €60/100) offers unparalleled city views from atop Albrechtsburg. At **Gold-ener Löwe** (☎ 441 10; Heinrichsplatz 6; mains €6.75-15.25) you can sit on the square and people-watch. Around the Markt are grocers, bakers, eiscafés and butchers selling snacks.

Half-hourly S-Bahns travel to Meissen from both Dresden train stations (€4.40, 40 minutes), but it's far nicer, between May and September, to travel by steamer (see Cruises in the earlier Dresden section).

Sächsische Schweiz
'Saxon Switzerland' is only a quick jaunt from Dresden, near the Czech border, but feels continents away. This national park's central attraction, **Bastei**, has breathtaking outcrops that recall New Mexico, towering 305m above the Elbe River and connected by a series of footbridges.

Berghotel Bastei (☎ 035024-77 90, fax 77 94 81; w www.bastei-berghotel.de; singles/ doubles €44/82) is surprisingly pleasant for a former GDR holiday lodge. In the nearby town of Lohmen, the **tourist office** (☎ 03501-58 10 24, fax 58 10 25; Basteistrasse 79) can help book private rooms from about €15 per person, or try in the poky little spa town of Bad Schandau at its **tourist office** (☎ 035022-900 31, fax 900 34; e info@bad-schandau.de).

LEIPZIG
☎ 0341 • pop 437,000
Since the discovery of rich silver mines in the nearby Erzgebirge (Ore Mountains) in the 16th century, Leipzig has enjoyed almost continual prosperity. Today Leipzig is a major business and transport centre, and the second-largest city in eastern Germany. It has a strong cultural tradition and offers plenty for book and music lovers, particularly Bach, as well as pub-crawlers.

Since medieval times Leipzig has hosted annual trade fairs, and during the communist era these provided an important exchange window between East and West. After unification, the city built a new ultramodern fairground. Leipzig, never as heavily bombed as nearby Dresden, has undergone a restoration and construction boom that has brought new life to

many fine old buildings. Still, you might find these structures adjacent to crumbling prewar grand dames and GDR era monstrosities.

Orientation
With 26 platforms, the imposing Leipzig train station (1915) is Europe's largest. It has been lavishly renovated and houses many shops and restaurants. To reach the city centre, cross Willy-Brandt-Platz; the central Markt square is just a couple of blocks southwest. Ring roads surround the centre, more or less where the city walls once stood.

Information
Leipzig-Information (☎ 710 42 60, fax 710 42 71; w www.leipzig.de; Richard-Wagner-Strasse 1; open 9am-7pm Mon-Fri, 9am-4pm Sat, 9am-2pm Sun) is directly opposite the train station. You can buy the Leipzig Card here (one/three days €9.90/21) for unlimited local transport and discounts at attractions and some restaurants.

There is a **Reisebank** at the Hauptbahnhof. There's also a main **post office** (Augustus-platz 1). Sip coffee and watch your dirty clothes spin at the laundrette-café **Maga Pon** (Gottschedstrasse 3). You can surf the Internet at **Le Bit** (☎ 998 20 20; Friedrich-List-Platz), east of the Hauptbahnhof, for €3 per hour.

Things to See & Do
The Renaissance **Altes Rathaus** (1556) on Markt is one of Germany's most beautiful town halls. Behind it is the **Alte Börse** (1687), with a monument to Goethe (1903) in front. The former Leipzig University law student called the town a 'little Paris' in his drama Faust. **Nikolaikirche** (☎ 960 52 70; Niko-laikirchhof 3), between Markt and Augustus-platz, dates back to 1165. It has a truly remarkable interior and was the local meeting point of the 'Gentle Revolution' that helped overthrow the Communist regime.

Just southwest of Markt is the 13th-century **Thomaskirche** (☎ 960 28 55; Thomaskirchhof 18), with Bach's tomb in front of the altar. Bach worked in Leipzig from 1723 until his death in 1750, and the St Thomas Boys' Choir, which he once led, is still going strong. Opposite the church is the **Bach Museum** (☎ 964 41 33; Thomaskirchhof 16; adult/concession €3/2; open 10am-5pm daily).

To the south, **Neues Rathaus**, with its impressive 108m tower, was completed in 1905

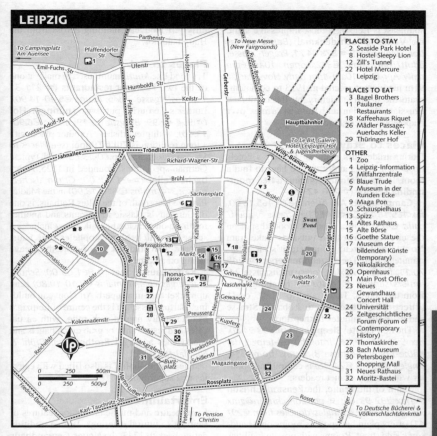

LEIPZIG

PLACES TO STAY
2 Seaside Park Hotel
8 Hostel Sleepy Lion
12 Zill's Tunnel
22 Hotel Mercure Leipzig

PLACES TO EAT
3 Bagel Brothers
11 Paulaner Restaurants
18 Kaffeehaus Riquet
26 Mädler Passage; Auerbachs Keller
29 Thüringer Hof

OTHER
1 Zoo
4 Leipzig-Information
5 Mitfahrzentrale
6 Blaue Trude
7 Museum in der Runden Ecke
9 Maga Pon
10 Schauspielhaus
13 Spizz
14 Altes Rathaus
15 Alte Börse
16 Goethe Statue
17 Museum der bildenden Künste (temporary)
19 Nikolaikirche
20 Opernhaus
21 Main Post Office
23 Neues Gewandhaus Concert Hall
24 Universität
25 Zeitgeschichtliches Forum (Forum of Contemporary History)
27 Thomaskirche
28 Bach Museum
30 Petersbogen Shopping Mall
31 Neues Rathaus
32 Moritz-Bastei

GERMANY

although its origins date back to the 16th century. North along Dittrichring is the former East German *Stasi* (secret police) headquarters, diagonally opposite the Schauspielhaus. Now it houses the **Museum in der Runden Ecke** (☎ 961 24 43; admission free; open 10am-6pm daily), outlining Stasi methods of investigation and intimidation – some appalling, some worthy of Inspector Clouseau. A new museum, **Zeitgeschichtliches Forum** (Forum of Contemporary History; ☎ 222 00; Grimmaishce Strasse 6; admission free; open 9am-6pm Tues-Fri, 10am-6pm Sat & Sun), gives a history of the GDR that's both fact-filled and wrenching.

Across the street are the temporary quarters of the best of Leipzig's fine museums, **Museum der bildenden Künste** (Museum of Fine Arts; ☎ 21 69 90; Grimmaische Strasse 1-7; adult/concession €2.50/1.25), until a new building is completed, scheduled for late 2003. It has an excellent collection of old masters.

Wide Augustusplatz, three blocks east of Markt, is ex-socialist Leipzig, with the squat **universität** (university; 1975) and space-age **Neues Gewandhaus** concert hall (1983) juxtaposed with the functional **Opernhaus** (opera house; 1960). Leipzig's dazzling **Neue Messe** (trade fairgrounds) are 5km north of the train station (take tram No 16).

Leipzig has long been a publishing and library centre, and the **Deutsche Bücherei** (German Library; ☎ 227 13 24; Deutscher Platz 1; admission free; open 9am-4pm Mon-Sat), houses millions of books (including most titles published in German since 1913) as well as a

book and printing museum. Farther to the southeast is Leipzig's most impressive sight, the **Völkerschlachtdenkmal** (*Battle of Nations Monument*; ☎ 878 04 71; *Prager Strasse; adult/concession €3/2; open 10am-6pm daily Apr-Oct, 10am-4pm daily Nov-Mar*), a 91m monument erected in 1913 to commemorate the decisive victory by the combined Prussian, Austrian and Russian armies over Napoleon's forces here in 1813.

Places to Stay

During trade fairs many of Leipzig's hotels raise their prices and it can be hard to find a room. Leipzig-Information runs a free **room-finding service** (☎ 710 42 55).

Campingplatz Am Auensee (☎ 465 16 00, fax 465 16 17; *Gustav-Esche-Strasse 5; adult/child €4/3*) is in a pleasant wooded spot on the city's northwestern outskirts (take tram No 11 to Wahren; from here it's an eight-minute walk). The **Jugendherberge** (☎ 245 70 11, fax 245 70 12; *Volksgartenstrasse 24; juniors/seniors €14.30/17*) is about 3km from the centre. Take tram No 17, 27 or 31 (direction: Schönefeld) to Löbauer Strasse and walk five minutes farther north.

The new **Hostel Sleepy Lion** (☎ 993 94 80, fax 993 94 82; e *info@hostel-leipzig.de; Käthe-Kollwitz-Strasse 3; dorms from €14, singles/doubles €24/36*) is central and popular with Lonely Planet readers.

South of the centre, the **Pension Christin** (☎/fax 232 93 66; e *pension-christin@gmx.de; Kochstrasse 4; singles/doubles from €29/41*) offers plain but spotless rooms on a handsome side street. Rooms with private facilities cost more. Take tram No 10 or 11 to Kochstrasse. **Zill's Tunnel** (☎ 960 20 78, fax 960 19 69; e *info@zillstunnel.de; Barfussgasschen 9; doubles from €67*) is a real find; a couple of lovely rooms with private facilities above Leipzig's pub district.

Stay amid what's often called Leipzig's second best art collection at **Galerie Hotel Leipziger Hof** (☎ 697 40, fax 697 41 50; *Hedwigstrasse 1-3; singles/doubles from €55/65*), about 1.2km east of the centre. Or sleep like a politburo member at the GDR-era **Hotel Mercure Leipzig** (☎ 214 60, fax 960 49 16; e *mercure_leipzig@t-online.de; Augustusplatz 5-6; singles/doubles from €61/77*), with large rooms. The **Seaside Park Hotel** (☎ 985 20, fax 98 57 50; e *seaside-hotels@regionett.de; Richard-Wagner-Strasse 7; singles/doubles from €78/93*) occupies a nifty Art Nouveau building across from the Hauptbahnhof.

Places to Eat

Try food like *Mutti* (mum) used to make at one of the two **Paulaner restaurants** (☎ 211 31 15; *Klostergasse 3 & 5; mains €5.40-14.90*). Luther's favourite pub was **Thüringer Hof** (☎ 994 49 99; *Burgstrasse 19; mains €6.90-13.15*), with great dishes. Another place with a long tradition is **Zill's Tunnel** (see *Places to Stay* earlier; *mains €6.60-13.60*), with typical German specialities. Founded in 1525, **Auerbachs Keller** (☎ 21 61 00; *Grimmaischerstrasse 3-4; mains €7.10-18.90*) in the Mädler Passage just south of the Altes Rathaus, is one of Germany's classic restaurants and another for those on the Goethe trail. *Faust* includes a scene in which Mephistopheles and Faust carouse with students here before they leave riding on a barrel.

Kaffeehaus Riquet (☎ 961 00 00; *Schuhmachergässchen 1; mains €7.10-10.80*) is an upmarket café in a superb Art Nouveau building. Barfussgässchen is the centre of Leipzig's exaggeratedly named **pub mile**, with casual cafés and restaurants, or grab quick bagels and sandwiches at **Bagel Brothers** (*cnr Brühl & Nikolaistrasse*).

The Hauptbahnhof is also filled with eateries and supermarkets.

Entertainment

Live theatre and music are major features of Leipzig's cultural offerings. With a tradition dating back to 1743, the **Neues Gewandhaus** (☎ 127 02 80; *Augustusplatz 8*) has Europe's longest established civic orchestra; one of its conductors was the noted composer Felix Mendelssohn-Bartholdy. Leipzig's modern **Opernhaus** is just across the square. The **Schauspielhaus** (☎ 126 81 68; *Bosestrasse 1*), a few blocks west of Markt, mixes classic theatre with modern works.

Moritz-Bastei (☎ 70 25 90; *Universitätsstrasse 9*), spread over three underground floors, has live music or disco most nights, but in summer it really comes into its own as a cultural venue. **Spizz** (☎ 960 80 43; *Markt 9*) is a trendy café by day and slick drinking and dancing venue by night. Both of these clubs have music ranging from rock to jazz. **Blaue Trude** (☎ 212 66 79; *Katharinenstrasse 17*) is Leipzig's current gay club.

Getting There & Away

Leipzig is linked by fast and frequent trains to all major German cities, including Dresden (€24, 1¼ hours), Berlin (€33.40, 1¾ hours) and Munich (€76, five hours). Major car rental agencies are at the Hauptbahnhof. Ride sharers can visit the **Mitfahrzentrale** (☎ 194 40; Goethestrasse 7-10).

Getting Around

Trams are the main form of public transport in Leipzig, with the most important lines running via Willy-Brandt-Platz in front of the Hauptbahnhof. A 15-minute ticket in the inner city is €1 while a one-hour ticket on the whole system is €1.30. Strip tickets valid for four rides are €4/4.90 for short/long trips. Day tickets are €4.

GÖRLITZ

☎ 03581 • pop 63,000

Situated 100km east of Dresden on the Neisse River, Görlitz emerged from WWII with its beautiful old town undamaged. The town was split in two, however, under the Potsdam Treaty, which used the Neisse as the boundary between Germany and Poland. The Polish part of Görlitz was renamed Zgorzelec. The town is an important border stop between the two countries.

Görlitz's Renaissance and baroque architecture is better preserved than that of any city its size in Saxony. Of particular interest are the **Rathaus** (1537), the **Peterskirche** (1497) and the 16th-century **Dreifaltigkeitskirche** on Obermarkt. The **tourist office** (☎ 475 70, fax 47 57 27; Obermarkt 29; open 9am-6.30pm Mon-Fri, 10am-4pm Sat, 10am-1pm Sun) has a free room-finding service.

The **DJH hostel** (☎ 40 65 10, fax 66 17 75; e jugendherbergegoerlitz@t-online.de; Goethestrasse 17; juniors/seniors €12.50/15) is south of the station. **Gästehaus Lisakowski** (☎ 40 05 39, fax 31 30 19; Landeskronstrasse 23; singles/doubles €23/46) offers simple rooms near the train station and is a 10-minute walk from the centre. **Hotel Tuchmacher** (☎ 473 10, fax 47 31 79; w www.tuchmacher .de; Peterstrasse 8; singles/doubles from €79/ 105) is a delightful, top-end place in the old town. **Zum Flyns** (☎ 40 06 97; Langenstrasse 1; mains €6.50-14.50) serves local specialities amid vaulted ceilings and tiny nooks. There are a number of fast-food options in the Strassburg Passage shopping centre.

Frequent trains run to/from Dresden (€14.80, 1½ hours). There are a few nonstop trains daily to/from Berlin (€30, three hours). Not surprisingly, Görlitz is an important stop to/from Poland.

Thuringia

The state of Thuringia (Thüringen) occupies a basin cutting into the heart of Germany between the Harz Mountains and the hilly Thuringian Forest. The Germanic Thuringians were conquered by the Franks in AD 531 and converted to Christianity by St Boniface in the 8th century. The Duke of Saxony seized the area in AD 908 and for the next 1000 years the region belonged to one German principality or another. Only in 1920 was Thuringia reconstituted as a state with something approaching its original borders. Under the communists it was again split into separate districts, but since 1990 it has been a single unit once again.

ERFURT

☎ 0361 • pop 215,000

This trading and university centre, founded as a bishop's residence by St Boniface in AD 742, is the lively capital of Thuringia. Erfurt was only slightly damaged during WWII and boasts numerous burgher town houses, churches and monasteries gracing the surprisingly well-preserved medieval quarter. Mindless graffiti has unfortunately become an all-too-common sight in the city; nonetheless this is a charming and often fascinating destination.

In April 2002 Erfurt became the unlikely focus of worldwide grief when a disgruntled former student shot dead 16 people and himself at a local high school.

Orientation & Information

Bahnhofstrasse leads north from the train station to Anger, a large square in the heart of the city. Continue straight ahead, following tram tracks along Schlösserstrasse to Fischmarkt. The friendly and efficient **tourist office** (☎ 664 00; Benediktsplatz 1; e service@erfurt -tourist-info.de; open 10am-7pm Mon-Fri, 10am-4pm Sat & Sun Apr-Dec, 10am-6pm Mon-Fri, 10am-4pm Sat & Sun Jan-Mar) is just east of Fischmarkt and the Rathaus. It sells the three-day Erfurt Card (€14), which allows unlimited use of public transport and entry to museums.

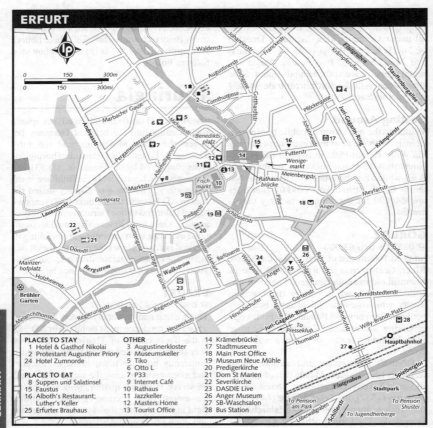

ERFURT

PLACES TO STAY	OTHER	14 Krämerbrücke
1 Hotel & Gasthof Nikolai	3 Augustinerkloster	17 Stadtmuseum
2 Protestant Augustiner Priory	4 Museumskeller	18 Main Post Office
24 Hotel Zumnorde	5 Tiko	19 Museum Neue Mühle
	6 Otto L	20 Predigerkirche
PLACES TO EAT	7 P33	21 Dom St Marien
8 Suppen und Salatinsel	9 Internet Café	22 Severikirche
15 Faustus	10 Rathaus	23 DASDIE Live
16 Alboth's Restaurant;	11 Jazzkeller	26 Anger Museum
Luther's Keller	12 Masters Home	27 SB-Waschsalon
25 Erfurter Brauhaus	13 Tourist Office	28 Bus Station

There's a **Reisebank** at Erfurt's Hauptbahnhof, and the main **post office** is on Anger. The laundrette **SB-Waschsalon** (*Bahnhofstrasse 22*) is conveniently located below the rail bridge. The **Internet Café** (*Fischmarkt 5*) charges €4 per hour.

Things to See & Do

The numerous interesting backstreets and laneways in Erfurt's surprisingly large Altstadt make this a fascinating place to explore on foot. Pick up the tourist office's *A Tour of the Historical City* booklet (€1.50), which has a map and good descriptions of numbered sights.

Don't miss the 13th-century Gothic **Dom St Marien** and **Severikirche**, which stand together on a hillock dominating the central square of Domplatz. The wooden stools (1350) and stained glass (1410) in the choir, and figures on the portals, make the cathedral one of the richest medieval churches in Germany.

Around Fischmarkt you will find numerous historical buildings. The eastbound street beside the town hall leads to the medieval restored **Krämerbrücke** (1325), which is lined on each side with timber-framed shops. This is the only such bridge north of the Alps. Further north, on the same side of the River Gera, is **Augustinerkloster** (☎ 576 60; *Augustinerstrasse 10; adult/concession €3.50/2.50; open 9am-noon, 2pm-5pm Mon-Sat, from 11am Sun Apr-Oct & 10am-noon, 2pm-4pm Mon-Sat, from 11am Sun Nov-Mar*), a late-medieval monastery that was home to Luther early in the 16th century.

Although Erfurt's main attraction is its magnificent Altstadt buildings, it also has some interesting museums. The **Anger Museum** (☎ 562 33 11; Anger 18; adult/concession €1.50/0.75; open 10am-6pm Tues-Sun) has regional medieval art, frescoes and faience; the **Stadtmuseum** (☎ 562 48 88; Johannesstrasse 169; adult/concession €1.50/0.75; open 10am-6pm Tues-Sun) focuses mainly on Erfurt's Stone Age and medieval history; whereas the **Museum Neue Mühle** (☎ 646 10 59; Schlösserstrasse 25a; adult/concession €1.50/0.75; open 10am-6pm Tues-Sun) is an old streamside millhouse (the last of some 60 water mills that Erfurt once had) with working machinery dating from the early 1880s.

Places to Stay

Erfurt's **Jugendherberge** (☎ 562 67 05, fax 562 67 06; e jh-erfurt@djh-thueringen.de; Hochheimer Strasse 12; juniors/seniors €15/18) is southwest of the centre. Take tram No 5 from Erfurt train station to Steigerstrasse, then it's a five-minute walk.

The tourist office arranges private accommodation from around €20/40 for doubles/singles (plus a booking fee of 10%).

Pension Schuster (☎ 373 50 52; Rubenstrasse 11; rooms €40 with bathroom) has sunny, spotless rooms just a 10-minute walk from the train station. Stay among the nuns at the historic **Protestant Augustiner Priory** (☎ 57 66 00, fax 576 60 99; e AK-efurt@ augustinerkloster.de; Augustinerstrasse 10; singles/doubles €40/70), which offers fully renovated but simple lodgings. Nearby, the **Hotel & Gasthof Nikolai** (☎ 59 81 70, fax 59 81 71 20; e info@hotel-nikolai-erfurt .com; Augustinerstrasse 30; singles/doubles from €65/84) has charming rooms with varnished furniture.

Top of the scale is **Hotel Zumnorde** (☎ 568 00, fax 568 04 00; e info@hotel-zummnorde .de; Anger 50-51; singles/doubles with bathroom €98/118) with large and comfortable rooms.

Places to Eat

Erfurt has a lively restaurant and eatery scene. **Suppen und Salatinsel** (Marktstrasse 45; dishes €2-7) is a simple place that serves up soups, vegetarian fare and German goodies like Bratwurst. **Erfurter Brauhaus** (☎ 562 58 27; Anger 21; mains €5-10) is a microbrewery that serves its own beer, and has a good

selection of regional specialities. **Faustus** (☎ 540 09 54; Wenigemarkt 5; mains €7-17), at the foot of the Krämerbrücke, adds an international flavour to its mostly German menu.

Descend into the middle ages at **Luther Keller** (☎ 568 82 05; Futterstrasse 15-16; mains €8-12) where there's cheap, traditional food, lusty wenches and tankards of frothy brew. Sharing this address is **Alboth's Restaurant** (☎ 568 82 07; mains €10-24), which is the total opposite – refined, intimate and expensive.

Entertainment

There are several small bars like **Otto L** (Pergamentergasse 30) and **Tiko** (Michaelistrasse 35) huddled throughout the Andreasviertel, northwest of Fischmarkt. The focus here is **P33** (Pergamentergasse 33), a popular live music venue that attracts a student crowd. **Masters Home** (Michaelistrasse 48) is a stylish bar with a lively mixed clientele, while nearby the **Jazzkeller** (Fischmarkt 12-13) makes Thursday night its own with live jazz from 8.30pm. Try **Museumskeller** (Juri-Gargarin-Ring 140a) for rock music, **DASDIE Live** (Marstallstrasse 12) for Kabarett and variety, and for Latin and blues venture out to **Presseklub** (Dalbersweg 1). The tourist office sells the monthly Erfurt Magazine (€0.50), which outlines entertainment happenings in the city.

Getting There & Away

Every two hours a direct IR train connects Frankfurt (€37, 2½ hours) and Erfurt. The same train goes to/from Berlin (€49, 3½ hours) and to/from Weimar (€4, 15 minutes) and Eisenach (€15.20, 27 minutes). Cheaper but slower regional trains also run to/from Weimar and Eisenach. ICE trains go to/from Leipzig (€23.60, 1¾ hours) every two hours.

WEIMAR
☎ 03643 • pop 62,000

Not a monumental city nor a medieval one, Weimar appeals to more refined tastes. As a repository of German humanistic traditions it is unrivalled. Many famous people lived and worked in Weimar, including Lucas Cranach the Elder, Johann Sebastian Bach, Friedrich Schiller, Johann Wolfgang von Goethe, Franz Liszt, Walter Gropius, Wassily Kandinsky, and Paul Klee. From 1919 to 1925 it was the focal point of the Bauhaus movement, which laid the foundations of modern architecture, and today

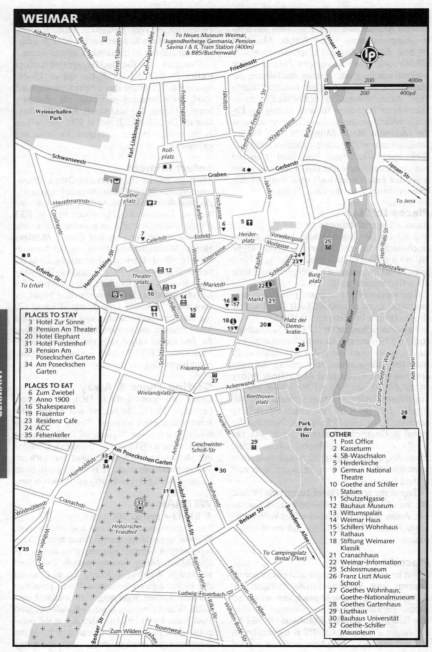

WEIMAR

To Neues Museum Weimar,
Jugendherberge Germania, Pension
Savina I & II, Train Station (400m)
& B85/Buchenwald

To Jena

To Erfurt

To Campingplatz
Ilmtal (7km)

PLACES TO STAY
3 Hotel Zur Sonne
8 Pension Am Theater
20 Hotel Elephant
31 Hotel Furstenhof
33 Pension Am
   Poseckschen Garten
34 Am Poseckschen
   Garten

PLACES TO EAT
6 Zum Zwiebel
7 Anno 1900
16 Shakespeares
19 Frauentor
23 Residenz Cafe
24 ACC
35 Felsenkeller

OTHER
1 Post Office
2 Kasseturm
4 SB-Waschsalon
5 Herderkirche
9 German National
   Theatre
10 Goethe and Schiller
   Statues
11 SchutzeNgasse
12 Bauhaus Museum
13 Wittumspalais
14 Weimar Haus
15 Schillers Wohnhaus
17 Rathaus
18 Stiftung Weimarer
   Klassik
21 Cranachhaus
22 Weimar-Information
25 Schlossmuseum
26 Franz Liszt Music
   School
27 Goethes Wohnhaus;
   Goethe-Nationalmuseum
28 Goethes Gartenhaus
29 Liszthaus
30 Bauhaus Universität
32 Goethe-Schiller
   Mausoleum

Weimarhallen
Park

Historischer
Friedhof

Park
an der
Ilm

Ilm River

is a centre for architecture, music and media studies. Weimar's rich contribution to the continent's cultural life was recognised in 1999 when it was named European City of Culture.

Weimar is also known as the place where the German republican constitution was drafted after WWI (hence, the 1919–33 Weimar Republic). The ruins of the Buchenwald concentration camp, near Weimar, are haunting evidence of the terrors of the Nazi regime (see the Around Weimar section later).

Orientation & Information

The centre of town is just west of the Ilm River and a 20-minute walk south of the Hauptbahnhof. Buses run fairly frequently between the station and Goetheplatz, from where it's a short walk east along small streets to Herderplatz or Markt.

The tourist office **Weimar-Information** (☎ 240 00; e tourist-info@weimar.de; Markt 10; open 9.30am-6pm Mon-Fri, 9.30am-4pm Sat, 9.30am-3pm Sun Apr-Oct, 10am-6pm Mon-Fri, 10am-2pm Sat & Sun Nov-Mar) is very helpful. There is a smaller **tourist office** (☎ 24 00 45; open 10am-8pm daily) inside the Hauptbahnhof. Both offices sell the three-day Weimar Card (€10), providing entry to most of Weimar's museums, unlimited travel on city buses and other benefits.

Most of Weimar's museums and many cultural activities are managed by a trust foundation, the **Stiftung Weimarer Klassik** (☎ 54 51 02; Frauentorstrasse 4; e info@weimar -klassik.de).

There's a central **post office** (cnr Heinrich-Heine-Strasse & Schwanseestrasse). Unfortunately, at present there's no public Internet access in Weimar, but for laundry services head to Graben 47.

Things to See & Do

Except where otherwise noted, attractions are closed on Monday.

A good place to begin your visit is on Herderplatz. The **Herderkirche** (1500) has an altarpiece (1555) by Lucas Cranach the Elder, who died before he could finish it. His son, Lucas Cranach the Younger, completed the work and included a portrait of his father (to the right of the crucifix, between John the Baptist and Martin Luther).

A block east of Herderplatz towards the Ilm River is Weimar's main art museum, the **Schlossmuseum** (☎ 54 60; Burgplatz 4; adult/concession €4/2.50; open 10am-6pm Tues-Sun Apr-Oct, 10am-4.30pm Tues-Sun Nov-Mar). The large collection, with masterpieces by Cranach, Dürer and others, occupies three floors of this castle, formerly the residence of the Elector of the Duchy of Saxony-Weimar. North of the centre, the **Neues Museum Weimar** (☎ 54 60; Weimarplatz; adult/concession €3/2; open 10am-6pm Tues-Sun Apr-Oct, 10am-4.30pm Tues-Sun Nov-Mar) houses, among other pieces, one of Germany's most important private collections of contemporary art.

Platz der Demokratie, with the renowned music school founded in 1872 by Franz Liszt, is south of the Schlossmuseum. This square spills into Markt, where you'll find the neo-Gothic **Rathaus** (1841), and the **Cranachhaus**, in which Lucas Cranach the Elder spent his last two years before his death in 1553. West of Markt via some narrow lanes is Theaterplatz, with **Goethe and Schiller statues** (1857), and the **German National Theatre**, where the constitution of the Weimar Republic was drafted in 1919. Opposite the theatre on this same square is the **Bauhaus Museum** (☎ 54 51 02; Theaterplatz; adult/concession €3/2; open 10am-6pm Tues-Sun Apr-Oct, 10am-4.30pm Tues-Sun Nov-Mar), which documents the evolution of this influential artistic and architectural movement. Nearby, **Weimar Haus** (☎ 90 18 90; Schillerstrasse 16-18; adult/concession €6.50/5.50; open 10am-8pm daily Apr-Sept, 10am-6pm daily Oct-Mar) offers a modern multimedia take on 5000 years of history.

Houses & Tombs From Theaterplatz, the elegant Schillerstrasse curves its way around to **Schillers Wohnhaus** (☎ 54 51 02; Schillerstrasse 12; adult/concession €3.50/2.50; open 9am-6pm Wed-Mon Apr-Oct, 9am-4pm Wed-Mon Nov-Mar). Schiller lived in Weimar from 1799 to 1805. Goethe, his contemporary, spent the years 1775 to 1832 here. **Goethes Wohnhaus** (☎ 54 51 02; Frauenplan 1; adult/concession €6/4.50; open 9am-6pm Tues-Sun Apr-Oct, 9am-4pm Tues-Sun Nov-Mar), where the immortal work Faust was written, is nearby. Attached to the house is the **Goethe-Nationalmuseum** (☎ 54 51 02; Frauenplan 1; adult/concession €2.50/2; open 9am-6pm Tues-Sun Apr-Oct, 9am-4pm Tues-Sun Nov-Mar) with exhibits on Schiller, Goethe and their life and times.

GERMANY

The **Liszthaus** (☎ 54 51 02; Marienstrasse 17; adult/concession €2/1.50; open 9am-1pm, 2pm-6pm Tues-Sun Apr-Oct, 10am-1pm, 2pm-4pm Tues-Sun Nov-Mar) is by the edge of Park an der Ilm. Liszt resided in Weimar during 1848 and from 1869 to 1886, and here he wrote his *Hungarian Rhapsody* and *Faust Symphony*. In the yellow complex across the road from the Liszthaus, Walter Gropius laid the groundwork for modern architecture. The buildings themselves, erected by the famous architect Henry van de Velde between 1904 and 1911, now house Weimar's **Bauhaus Universität**.

The tombs of Goethe and Schiller lie side by side in a neoclassical crypt in the **Historischer Friedhof** (Historical Cemetery), two blocks west of the Liszthaus.

Parks & Palaces Weimar boasts three large parks, each replete with monuments, museums and attractions. The most accessible is **Park an der Ilm**, running along the eastern side of Weimar and containing **Goethes Gartenhaus** (☎ 54 51 02; Park an der Ilm; adult/concession €2.50/2; open 9am-6pm Tues-Sun Apr-Oct, 10am-4pm Tues-Sun Nov-Mar). Goethe himself landscaped the park.

On Theaterplatz you'll find the **Wittumspalais** (Widow's Palace; ☎ 54 51 02; adult/concession €3.50/2; open 9am-6pm Tues-Sun Apr-Oct, 10am-4pm Tues-Sun Nov-Mar), the former residence of Duchess Anna Amalia who, after acquiring it in 1774, held meetings of the round table with court personalities, literary figures, scholars and artists, making the baroque palace the focus of intellectual life in Weimar.

Places to Stay

For a flat fee of €2.50 the tourist office arranges private rooms (from about €20 per person).

Camping The closest camping ground is **Campingplatz Ilmtal** (☎ 802 64; Oettern; person/vehicle/site €3/5/2; open Apr-Nov), at Oettern in the scenic Ilm Valley, 7km southeast of Weimar.

Hostels Weimar has four DJH hostels, but the most central are **Jugendherberge Germania** (☎ 85 04 90, fax 85 04 91; e jh-germania@djh-thueringen.de; Carl-August-Allee 13) in the street running south (downhill) from the station, and **Am Poseckschen Garten** (☎ 85 07 92, fax 85 07 93; e jh-posgarten@djh-thueringen.de; Humboldtstrasse 17) near the Historischer Friedhof. Both charge €15/18 for juniors/seniors.

Pensions & Hotels Cheapest of the pensions is **Am Poseckschen Garten** (☎ 51 12 39; e koenig-weimar@t-online.de; Am Poseckschen Garten 1; singles/doubles €18/34), which has reasonable rooms. **Pension Savina II** (☎ 866 90, fax 86 69 11; e savina@pension-savina.de; Meyerstrasse 60; singles/doubles with shower & toilet €40/70) is a comfortable option near the train station. Its sister **Savina I** (☎ 866 90, fax 86 69 11; e savina@pension-savina.de; Rembrandtweg 13; singles/doubles with shared facilities €34/52) is more basic. **Pension Am Theater** (☎ 889 40, fax 88 94 32; Erfurterstrasse 10; singles/doubles with bathroom €45/65) is about the friendliest accommodation you'll find anywhere. And the rooms aren't bad either.

The tastefully restored **Hotel Furstenhof** (☎ 83 32 31, fax 83 32 32; e furstenhofweimar@t-online.de; Rudolf-Breitscheid-Strasse 2; singles/doubles from €52/80) has small and comfortable rooms. The **Hotel Zur Sonne** (☎ 80 04 10, fax 86 29 32; Rollplatz 2; singles/doubles from €51/77) offers good value for money in a central location.

At historic **Hotel Elephant** (☎ 80 20, fax 80 26 10; e elephant.weimar@arabellasheraton.com; Markt 19; singles/doubles from €179/205) a night of luxury awaits, followed by an exorbitant €18 breakfast.

Places to Eat

ACC (☎ 85 11 61; Burgplatz 2; mains €6-10) is an alternative little place with an interesting menu and a palatable price range. Next door, **Residenz Cafe** (☎ 594 08; Grüner Markt 4; dishes €4-15) is a bit glitzier; it serves Thuringian specialities like *Braeti* (pig's neck steak in beer and mustard) and vegetarian dishes.

In a restored late 19th-century winter garden, **Anno 1900** (☎ 90 35 71; Geleitstrasse 12a; mains €6-11) pulls a good crowd with its well-priced pastas, steaks, fish and vegetarian. Everything is in its place at **Frauentor** (☎ 51 13 22; Schillerstrasse 2; mains €8-17), a simple and intimate place with an international menu. **Zum Zwiebel** (☎ 50 23 75; Teichgasse 6; mains €6-13) serves hearty regional dishes, while classy **Shakespeares** (☎ 90 12 85; Windischenstrasse 4-6; mains €13-16) has acclaimed gourmet cuisine and hosts live performances in its Othello Theatre.

Southwest of the centre, the ever-popular **Felsenkeller** (☎ 85 03 66; Humboldstrasse 37; mains €6-13) has brewed its own Felsenbräu since 1889, and serves it liberally with cheap, traditional German food.

Entertainment

The **German National Theatre** (☎ 75 53 34; Theaterplatz) is the main stage for Weimar's cultural activities, including Goethe's theatrical works. Tickets for it and other events can be bought at the tourist office.

The **Kasseturm** (Goetheplatz 1), a beer cellar in a round tower, has live music, disco or cabaret most nights. The **SchutzeNgasse** (Schutzengasse 2) is a relaxed bar that packs in the student crowd.

Getting There & Away

There are frequent direct IR trains to Berlin-Zoo (€38.40, three hours) via Naumburg and Halle, and to Frankfurt/Main (€40, three hours) via Erfurt and Eisenach. ICE trains go to Dresden (€37, two hours) and Leipzig (€21.20, one hour).

AROUND WEIMAR
Buchenwald

The **Buchenwald museum and concentration camp** (☎ 43 02 00; Ettersburg Hill; admission free; open 9.45am-6pm Tues-Sun May-Sept, 9.45am-5pm Tues-Sun Oct-Apr) is 10km north of Weimar. You first pass the memorial with mass graves of some of the 56,500 WWII victims from 18 nations, including German antifascists, Jews, and Soviet and Polish prisoners of war. The concentration camp and museum is 1km beyond the memorial. Many prominent German communists and Social Democrats, Ernst Thälmann and Rudolf Breitscheid among them, were murdered here. On 11 April 1945, as US troops approached, the prisoners rebelled at 3.15pm (the clock tower above the entrance still shows that time), overcame the SS guards and liberated themselves.

After the war the Soviet victors turned the tables by establishing Special Camp No 2, in which thousands of (alleged) anticommunists and former Nazis were worked to death.

Last entry is 45 minutes before closing. Bus No 6 runs via Goetheplatz and Weimar train station to Buchenwald roughly every 40 minutes.

EISENACH
☎ 03691 • pop 44,000

The birthplace of Johann Sebastian Bach, Eisenach is a small picturesque city on the edge of the Thuringian Forest. Its main attraction is the Wartburg castle, from where the landgraves (German counts) ruled medieval Thuringia. Luther went into hiding here under the assumed name of Junker Jörg after being excommunicated and put under a papal ban.

Information

Eisenach-Information (☎ 194 33; Markt 2; e tourist-info@eisenach-tourist.de; open 10am-6pm Mon, 9am-6pm Tues-Fri, 10am-2pm Sat & Sun) is friendly and well-organised. Its three-day Classic-Card (€14) provides free admission to the castle, most museums and use of public transport.

Wartburg

Superb **Wartburg** (☎ 770 73; tour adult/concession €6/3; open 8.30am-5pm Mar-Oct, 9am-3.30pm Nov-Feb), on a forested hill overlooking Eisenach, is world famous, with a Unesco World Heritage Site designation to prove it. Luther translated the New Testament from Greek into German while in hiding here (1521–22), thus making an enormous contribution to the development of the written German language. You can only visit the castle's interior with a guided tour (most of the tours are in German), which includes the museum, Luther's study room and the amazing Romanesque great hall; arrive early to avoid the crowds. Guided tours in English are only possible by prior reservation (at least two weeks beforehand in summer) through **Wartburg-Information** (☎ 770 73; Am Schlossberg 2). A free English-language leaflet set out in the sequence of the tour is available.

Between April and October there's a shuttle bus running up to the castle; it leaves from the terminal in front of the train station roughly every hour (€1.60 return). Alternatively, you can walk the 2km.

Places to Stay & Eat

The nearest camping ground is the **Campingplatz Altenberger See** (☎ 21 56 37, fax 21 56 07; Neubau 24; site/person €3/4), 7km south of town in Wilhelmsthal. **Jugendherberge**

Artur Becker (☎ 74 32 59, fax 74 32 60; e jh-eisenach@djh-thueringen.de; Mariental 24; juniors/seniors €14/17) is in the valley below Wartburg. Take bus No 3 to Liliengrund.

Eisenach-Information has an extensive list of hotels and private rooms from €15, and offers free reservations. Gasthof Storchenturm (☎ 73 32 63, fax 73 32 65; Georgenstrasse 43; beds €18 per person, groups of 4 or more €15.50) has bare, clean rooms with facilities. Pension Mahret (☎ 74 27 44, fax 750 33; e pension.mahret@t-online.de; Neustadt 30; singles/doubles €35/52) offers pleasant self-contained apartments near the town centre.

The 18th-century Thüringer Hof (☎ 280, fax 28 19 00; e eisenach@steigenberger.de; Karlsplatz 11; singles/doubles with breakfast €92/107) provides plush rooms with attractive town views.

In a cave-like cellar, Brunnenkeller (☎ 21 23 58; Markt 13; dishes €6-8) has a cosy feel and cheap Thuringian specialities. Kartoffelhaus (Sophienstrasse 44) offers all things potato for around €8.

Getting There & Away

Use the frequent RB/RE services to Erfurt (€8.10, 50 minutes) and Weimar (€10.70, 70 minutes) rather than the IC as they are far cheaper and take only a few minutes longer. IR services run direct to Frankfurt/Main (€29) and ICE to Berlin-Zoo (€56.60).

Saxony-Anhalt

The state of Saxony-Anhalt (Sachsen-Anhalt) comprises the former East German districts of Magdeburg and Halle. Originally part of the duchy of Saxony, medieval Anhalt was split into smaller units by the sons of various princes. In 1863 Leopold IV of Anhalt-Dessau united the three existing duchies, and in 1871 his realm was made a state of the German Reich. Today, it is Germany's poorest state, with unemployment hovering at more than 20%.

The mighty Elbe flows northwest across Saxony-Anhalt, past Lutherstadt-Wittenberg, Dessau and Magdeburg on its way to the North Sea at Hamburg. Halle and Naumburg are on the Saale River south of Magdeburg.

The Harz Mountains fill the southwestern corner of Saxony-Anhalt and spread right across Lower Saxony to Goslar (see the Harz

Mountains map in the Lower Saxony section). Historical Harz towns like Quedlinburg and Wernigerode are highly recommended, and Dessau and Lutherstadt-Wittenberg are gaining visitors for lovers of the Bauhaus and Luther; the state's two largest cities, Halle and Magdeburg, are of limited interest.

MAGDEBURG
☎ 0391 • pop 250,000

Magdeburg, on the Elbe River, is situated at a strategic crossing of transport routes from Thuringia to the Baltic and Western Europe to Berlin. It was severely damaged by wartime bombing and became an unfortunate example of GDR post-war reconstruction; recent building has helped it regain some charm. The main reason for visiting Magdeburg, the capital of Saxony-Anhalt, is for its splendid churches and Gothic cathedral.

Orientation & Information

From the broad square in front of the train station, take Ernst-Reuter-Allee east towards the Elbe. After two large blocks, turn left (north) into Breiter Weg to Alter Markt. Tourist Information Magdeburg (☎ 540 49 01, fax 540 49 10; e info@magdeburg-tourist.de; Julius-Bremer-Strasse 10; open 10am-6pm Mon-Fri, 10am-1pm Sat) is just north of Alter Markt, though there was talk that it might move.

Things to See & Do

The centre of the old town is Alter Markt, with a copy of the bronze Magdeburger Reiter (Magdeburg Rider; 1240) said to be Otto the Great, in front of the high-Renaissance Rathaus (1698). Just east there's the Johanniskirche (☎ 540 21 26; Johannisbergstrasse 1; admission €1; open 10am-8pm Tues-Sun May-Sept, 10am-4pm Tues-Sun Oct-Apr); destroyed in the war, it was proudly reconstructed in 1999. To the south, Magdeburg's oldest building, the 12th-century Romanesque convent Kloster Unser Lieben Frauen, is now a museum (☎ 540 61 64; Regierungstrasse 4-6; adult/concession €2/1; open 10am-5pm Tues-Sun); you can enter the cloister and church for free. A little farther south is the soaring Gothic Dom (cathedral; ☎ 543 24 14; Am Dom 1; open 10am-4pm Mon-Sat, 11.30am-4pm Sun), said to be the oldest on German soil. The cathedral, the second tallest in Germany after Cologne, has evocative and moody cloisters.

Places to Stay & Eat

The simple but pleasant **Campingplatz Barleber See** (☎/fax 50 32 44; adult/child/car €1.50/1/1.70) is 8km north of town at a lake. Take tram No 10 to the last stop. The DJH **Jugendgästehaus Magdeburg** (☎ 53 21 01, fax 53 21 02; e JH-Magdeburg@sjh-sachsen-anhalt.de; Leiterstrasse 10; beds juniors/seniors €18/20.70) is a little austere but very central. You can book private rooms from around €20 through Tourist Information Magdeburg. **Hotel Stadtfeld** (☎ 50 77 60, fax 506 66 99; Maxim-Gorki-Strasse 31/37; singles/doubles from €40/50) is a good mid-priced option above an apartment building. **Geheimer Rat** (☎ 738 02, fax 738 05 99; e geheimer-rat@t-online.de; Goethestrasse 38; singles/doubles from €72/85) is a very professional operation, on a park-like street west of the centre.

Zum Paulaner (☎ 543 88 13; Einsteinstrasse 13; mains €8.50-13.50) serves hearty Bavarian chow and beer in a rather elegant quarter of town. Down the block, **Athen** (☎ 544 09 66; Schleinufer 14; mains €5.30-13.50) is a popular Greek place with reasonable plate dinners. You'll find plenty of **fast-food** options in the Allee Center off Ernst-Reuter-Allee.

Getting There & Away

There are frequent regional trains operating to/from Berlin-Zoo (€20.40, 1½ hours) and trains to Leipzig (€17.20, 1½ hours), Hanover (€23.80, 1½ hours) and Quedlinburg (€10.70, 1¼ hours). Change trains in Halberstadt if heading for Wernigerode (€12.40, 1¼ hours).

QUEDLINBURG

☎ 03946 • pop 26,000

One of Germany's true gems, Quedlinburg dates back more than 1000 years. It once exercised considerable power in German affairs through a collegiate foundation for widows and daughters of the nobility. Almost all buildings in the centre are half-timbered, street after cobbled street of them, earning Quedlinburg the honour of being a Unesco World Heritage Site.

Orientation & Information

The centre of the old town is a 10-minute walk from the train station down Bahnhofstrasse. There is a **Quedlinburg-Information** (☎ 90 56 24, fax 90 56 29; e q.t.m@t-online.de; Markt 2; open 9am-7pm Mon-Fri, 10am-3pm Sat & Sun Apr-Oct, 9.30am-6pm Mon-Fri, 10am-4pm Sat Nov-Mar).

Things to See & Do

The Renaissance **Rathaus** (1615) on Markt has its own Roland statue (1426), however, the real focal point for visitors is the hill just southwest with the old castle district, known as **Schlossberg**. The area features the 1129 Romanesque **Church of St Servatii** (Dom; ☎ 70 99 00; Am Dom; adult/concession €3/2; open 10am-6pm Tues-Fri, 10am-4pm Sat, noon-6pm Sun May-Oct & 10am-4pm Mon-Sat, noon-4pm Sun Nov-Apr), with a 10th-century crypt and priceless reliquaries and early Bibles. In 1938 SS meetings were held in the Dom – a 'Germanic solemn shrine'. On a more contemporary note, try visiting **Lyonel-Feininger-Galerie** (☎ 22 38; Finkenherd 5a; adult/concession €6/3; open 10am-6pm Tues-Sun Apr-Oct, 10am-5pm Tues-Sun Nov-Mar) where you can view brilliant works by this Bauhaus artist who fled the Nazis and settled in America.

For hiking, take a bus or train 10km southwest to Thale, the starting point for hikes along the lovely Bode Valley in the Harz Mountains. From here it's just a short walk to Hexentanzplatz, the site of a raucous celebration during *Walpurgisnacht* every 30 April, believed in German folklore to be the night of a witches' sabbath. Also worthwhile is a visit to Gernrode and its delightful **Church of St Cyriakus**, just 8km south of Quedlinburg.

Places to Stay & Eat

Hotel and private rooms can be booked free of charge through Quedlinburg-Information. The central **Familie Klindt** (☎ 70 29 11; Hohe Strasse 19; without/with breakfast €12/16 per person) is a great deal, with comfy rooms. **Hotel am Dippeplatz** (☎ 77 14 11, fax 77 14 47; Breite Strasse 16; singles/doubles from €49/59) is bright and clean. **Hotel Theophano** (☎ 963 00, fax 96 30 36; e theophano@t-online.de; Markt 13/14; singles/doubles from €62/93) is top of the range, a gracious 350-year-old building with an up-market restaurant.

Kartoffelhaus No 1 (☎ 70 83 34; Breite Strasse 37; mains €5.10-11.60) serves filling meals and snacks for all budgets. Enter off Klink. **Brauhaus Lüdde** (☎ 70 52 06; Blasiistrasse 14; dishes €8.50-14.50) has hearty pub food and brews its own pilsener, *Altbier*, and the sweetish low-alcohol *Pubarschknall*.

Getting There & Away

You can change trains in Magdeburg (€10.70, 1¼ hours) for long-distance routes. To Wernigerode (€6.60, one hour), trains connect via Halberstadt.

WERNIGERODE
☎ 03943 • pop 35,000

Wernigerode is flanked by the foothills of the Harz Mountains. A romantic ducal castle rises above the old town, which contains some 1000 half-timbered houses from five centuries in various states of repair. Summer throngs of tourists have brought cash that has all but erased any trace of the old GDR. The century-old steam-powered, narrow-gauge Harzquerbahn runs a gorgeous 60km route south through the Harz Mountains to Nordhausen and also to Brocken, the highest mountain in northern Germany (1142m).

Orientation & Information

From the Bahnhofsplatz, Rudolf-Breitscheid-Strasse leads southeast to Breite Strasse, which runs southwest to Markt, the old town centre. The **tourist office** (*☎ 194 33, fax 63 20 40; Nicolaiplatz 1; open 9am-7pm Mon-Fri May-Sept, 9am-6pm Mon-Fri Nov-Apr, 10am-3pm Sat & Sun year-round)* is near Markt.

Things to See & Do

It's nice to wander along the streets of the medieval old town centre. The **Rathaus** (1277) on Markt, with its pair of pointed black-slate towers, is a focal point. From here it's just a short climb to the neo-Gothic **castle**. First built in the 12th century, the castle has been renovated and enlarged over the centuries and got its current fairy-tale facade from Count Otto of Stolberg-Wernigerode in the 19th century. The castle's **museum** (*adult/concession €4/3.50; open 10am-6pm daily May-Oct, 10am-4pm Tues-Fri, 10am-6pm Sat & Sun Nov-Apr)* has a nice chapel and hall.

Activities

There are plenty of short walks and day hikes nearby. The beautiful deciduous forest behind the castle is highly recommended. The more serious might tackle the 30km route (marked by blue crosses) from Mühlental southeast of

the town centre to Elbingerode, Königshütte, with its 18th-century wooden church, and the remains of medieval Trageburg castle at Trautenstein. The tourist office can make suggestions and you'll need a good topographic map for some of them.

Wernigerode is the major northern terminus for steam train services throughout the Harz Mountains and Hochharz National Park. For information contact **Harzer Schmalspurbahnen** (*☎ 55 80; Marktstrasse 3)*.

Services to Brocken from Wernigerode cost €14/22 one way/return (1¾ hours), and those to Nordhausen-Nord €8/14 (three hours). There is a three-day steam-train pass for €35/17.50 (adult/child) and a one-week pass for €70/35.

Places to Stay & Eat

Wernigerode has a new DJH **Jugendherberge** (*☎ 60 61 76, fax 60 61 77; e JH-Wernigerode@djh-sachsen-anhalt.de; Am Eichberg 5; juniors/seniors €15/17.70)* with a disco and sauna. It's a 35-minute walk from the centre.

Rooms booked through the tourist office's free room-finding service cost around €25. The central **Hotel zur Tanne** (*☎ 63 25 54, fax 67 37 35; Breite Strasse 57-59; singles/doubles from €41/49)* has basic rooms. **Pension Schweizer Hof** (*☎/fax 63 20 98; Salzbergstrasse 13; singles/doubles from €35/50)* is quiet and away from the centre, catering to hikers. **Gothisches Haus** (*☎ 67 50, fax 67 55 37; e gothisches-haus@tc-hotels.de; Marktplatz 2; singles/doubles from €82/98)* on the Markt, is the place to splurge. It also has a ritzy restaurant.

Altwernigerode Kartoffelhaus (*☎ 94 92 90; Marktstrasse 14; dishes €2.50/14.50)* serves well-priced traditional and potato dishes. **Restaurant Am Nicolaiplatz** (*☎ 63 23 28; Breite Strasse 17; mains €6.90-13.50)* is a local favourite for regional specialities. There are lots of cafés around the Markt.

Getting There & Away

There are frequent trains to Goslar (€6.60, 40 minutes), Hanover (€18.60, two hours) and Halle (€16, 1¼ hours). Change trains in Halberstadt for Magdeburg (€12.40, 1¼ hours), from where you can catch longer-distance trains. See also the Getting Around section under Western Harz Mountains in Lower Saxony.

DESSAU
☎ 0340 • pop 87,000

The Bauhaus school – a cradle of contemporary design – was born in Weimar but became synonymous with Dessau when Walter Gropius moved the school here in 1925. The school languished under the Nazis and GDR, but recent renovations of key Bauhaus sites have put this ancient ducal city on tourist maps. These Bauhaus buildings can be seen in a few hours, but many visitors spend the night between days cycling along the Elbe, or in the adjacent Dessau-Wörlitz Garden Realm.

Orientation & Information
Dessau's well-equipped tourist office (☎ 204 22 42; ⓦ www.dessau.de; Zerbsterstrasse 4) is in the Rathaus, a 10-minute walk southeast of the Hauptbahnhof via Antoinettenstrasse, crossing Kavalierstrasse and a pedestrian district. Bauhaus sites begin about a five-minute walk west of the Hauptbahnhof.

Things to See & Do
The **Bauhausgebäude** (Bauhaus Building; ☎ 650 82 51; Gropiusallee 38; open 10am-6pm Tues-Sun) is a touchstone of modern architecture, with three glass and concrete sections, galleries and a 'form follows function' interior. It was being renovated as we went to print, but open to visitors. The **Meisterhäuser** (Masters' Houses; Ebertallee; open 10am-6pm Tues-Sun mid-Feb–Oct, 10am-5pm Nov–mid-Feb) are three restored homes that Gropius built for important Bauhaus teachers including Lyonel Feininger, Wassily Kandinsky and Paul Klee. You can see their studio and living spaces; the interior of the Kandinsky/Klee Haus is painted some 170 colours, while the Feiningerhaus is home to the Kurt-Weill-Zentrum, dedicated to the life of this noted Dessau-born theatrical composer (A Threepenny Opera, the song Mack the Knife).

A combination card for all these sites costs €7.50/5.50 (adult/concesion); it's €4/3 for the Bauhausgebäude or the Meisterhäuser alone.

Ask at the tourist office for detailed information on the lovely, green Dessau-Wörlitz Garden Realm, including the fairytale Schloss Wörlitz (1769–73).

Places to Stay & Eat
The **Jugendherberge** (☎/fax 61 94 52; Waldkaterweg 11; juniors/seniors €11.50/14.20) is in a wooded spot situated 3km west of the Hauptbahnhof.

Hotel-Pension an den 7 Säulen (☎ 61 96 30, fax 61 96 22; Ebertallee 66; singles/doubles from €41/62) is well-kept, across from the Masters' Houses and popular with cyclists. The swish, Bauhaus-influenced **Hotel Fürst Leopold** (☎ 251 50, fax 251 51 77; ⓔ reservierung@hotel-fuerst-leopold.de; Friedensplatz; singles/doubles from €100/130) is a one-minute walk from the Hauptbahnhof and overlooks a park. Ask about the weekend deals.

Rub elbows with Bauhaus students at the fun **Cafe im Bauhaus** (☎ 650 84 44; Gropiusallee 38; dishes €2.60-8). **Kornhaus** (☎ 640 41 41; Kornhausstrasse 146; mains €6.90-8.40) combines the best of Bauhaus design with modern German cooking; its terrace is great for coffee and cake overlooking the Elbe. **Zum Alten Dessauer** (☎ 220 59 09; Lange Gasse 16; mains €7.40-14.80) is a friendly brewery-pub in the city centre.

Getting There & Away
Dessau is easily reached by fast train from Berlin (€16.80, 1¾ hours), Leipzig, Magdeburg and Halle (all €8.10, 40 minutes), and Lutherstadt Wittenberg (€5.50, 30 minutes). There's a Dessau exit from the A9 autobahn.

LUTHERSTADT WITTENBERG
☎ 03491 • pop 53,000

Wittenberg is where Luther did most of his work, including launching the Protestant Reformation in 1517, which changed the face of Europe. Ever quotable, Luther hurled vitriol at the corrupt church in Rome, even calling the Vatican a 'gigantic, bloodsucking worm'. The town's a must for anyone interested in the great man; it can be seen in a day from Berlin but is worth a longer look.

Orientation & Information
Hauptbahnhof Lutherstadt Wittenberg is a 15-minute walk from the tourist office, through the city centre. Go under the tracks and on to Collegienstrasse.

Wittenberg-Information (☎ 49 86 10, fax 49 86 11; ⓔ wb_info@wittenberg.de; Schlossplatz 2; open 9am-6pm Mon-Sat, 11am-4pm Sun Mar-Oct, 10am-4pm Mon-Sat, 11am-3pm Sun Nov-Feb) is very well organised and offers an excellent audio guide to the town (€5).

GERMANY

Things to See & Do

The **Lutherhaus** (☎ 420 30; Collegienstrasse 54; adult/concession €5/3) is a Reformation museum inside Lutherhalle, a former monastery. It contains an original room furnished by Luther in 1535. He stayed here in 1508 while teaching at Wittenberg University and made the building his home for the rest of his life after returning in 1511.

The large altarpiece in **Stadtkirche St Marien** (☎ 40 44 15; Jüdenstrasse 35; admission free; open 9am-5pm Mon-Sat, 11.30am-5pm Sun May-Oct, 10am-4pm Mon-Sat, 11.30am-4pm Sun Nov-Apr) was created jointly by Renaissance painter Lucas Cranach the Elder and his son in 1547. It shows Luther, his friend and supporter Melanchthon and other Reformation figures, as well as Cranach the Elder himself, in Biblical contexts. Luther preached in this church and was married here; the town recalls the nuptials in a festival each June. The **Luthereiche** (Luther's Oak; cnr Lutherstrasse & Am Bahnhof) is the site where Luther burnt the papers that threatened his excommunication.

Imposing monuments to both Luther and Melanchthon stand in front of the impressive **Altes Rathaus** (1535) on Markt. Also on Markt, the **Cranachhaus** is where painter Louis Cranach the Elder lived and worked; there's also the **Galerie im Cranachhaus** (☎ 420 19 17; Markt 4; adult/concession €2/1; open 10am-5pm Thur, 10am-6pm Tues, Wed & Fri, 1pm-5pm Sat & Sun).

At the western end of town is the **Schloss** (1499) with its huge, rebuilt church onto the door Luther allegedly nailed his 95 Theses on 31 October 1517. His tombstone is below the pulpit, and Melanchthon's is opposite.

Places to Stay & Eat

Camping ground **Bergwitzsee** (☎ 034921-282 28; e info@Bergwitzsee.de; adult/child/car €2.50/1/2) is some 11km south of town on Lake Bergwitz. There are hourly trains. The often-mobbed **Jugendherberge** (☎ 40 32 55, fax 40 94 22; e Jugendherberge@wittenberg.de; Schloss; beds juniors/seniors €12/14.70) is situated upstairs in the Schloss (sheets €3.50).

Wittenberg-Information finds private rooms from €25 per person. The **Hotel-Garni Am Schwanenteich** (☎ 41 10 34, fax 40 28 07; Töpferstrasse 1; singles/doubles from €31/59) is central and has charming staff. For a

room with a brew **Im Beyerhof** (☎ 43 31 30, fax 43 31 31; Markt 6; singles/doubles €50/70) has comfy accommodation located above a brewery. For a stylish upmarket option try the **Best Western Stadtpalais** (☎ 42 50, fax 42 51 00; e info@stadtpalais.bestwestern.de; Collegienstrasse 56-57; singles/doubles from €86/107).

Most of the town's food options face Collegienstrasse. One block north, **Schlossfreiheit** (☎ 40 29 80; Coswigerstrasse 24; mains €6.25-10.50) serves theme dishes including Lutherschmaus, duck in a peppery sultana sauce.

Getting There & Away

Wittenberg is on the main train line between Berlin (€23.60, one hour) and Leipzig (€15.80, 30 minutes) and has direct trains to/from Dessau (€5.50, 30 minutes) and Halle (€9, one hour). Be sure you buy tickets to 'Lutherstadt Wittenberg', as there is another town, Wittenberge, in eastern Germany.

HALLE

☎ 0345 • pop 262,000

The former state capital and largest city in Saxony-Anhalt, Halle was the centre of the GDR chemical industry – with all that implies. But it also has a 500-year-old university, a nice old castle and some other cultural attractions worth a visit.

Orientation & Information

To walk to the city centre from the Hauptbahnhof, head through the underpass and down pedestrian Leipziger Strasse, past the 15th-century Leipziger Turm to Markt, Halle's central square. **Halle Tourist** (☎ 47 23 30, fax 472 33 33; open 10am-6pm Mon-Fri, 10am-2pm Sat) is in the elevated gallery built around the 1506 Roter Turm on the Markt.

Things to See & Do

The Markt has a statue (1859) of the great composer Georg Friedrich Händel, born in Halle in 1685. The four tall towers of the 1529 **Marktkirche** (☎ 517 08 94; An der Marienkirche 1; admission free; open 10am-noon, 3pm-5pm Mon-Sat, 3pm-5pm Wed, 11am-noon Sun) loom above the square; you can climb one for a view of the city. Don't miss the exquisitely decorated Gothic interior.

The **Händelhaus** (☎ 50 09 00; Grosse Nikolai Strasse 5-6; adult/concession €2.60/1.80;

open daily) was the composer's birthplace and now houses a major collection of musical instruments. Nearby is the imposing 15th-century **Schloss Moritzburg** (☎ 212 55 90; Friedemann-Bach-Platz 5; adult/concession €4/2, free Tues; open 11am-8.30pm Tues, 10am-6pm Wed-Sun), a former residence of the archbishops of Magdeburg and now a museum of 19th- and 20th-century art, including GDR art and some impressive German expressionist works. Fans of the Fab Four will appreciate the Continent's only **Beatles Museum** (☎ 290 39 00; Alter Markt 12; adult/child €3/2; open 10am-6pm Wed-Sun, closed September); it's also a great example of historic warehouse architecture. If you're walking from the Hauptbahnhof, note the graffiti art in the underpass. It's legal, encouraged and sometimes pretty skillful, though that does not explain the graffiti throughout much of the rest of the city. Also note the goofy GDR workers' monument, **Die Fäuste** (The Fists; Riebeck Platz), looking like a pulled tooth.

Places to Stay & Eat
The municipal **Am Nordbad Campingplatz** (☎ 523 40 85; Am Nordbad 12; site/person/car €1/4/2; open early May-late Sept) is near the Saale River; take tram No 2 or 3 to Am Nordbad. **Jugendherberge** (☎ 202 47 16, fax 202 51 72; e jh-halle@djh-sachsen-anhalt .de; August-Bebel-Strasse 48a; beds juniors/seniors €13.50/16.20) is central.

The tourist office can find private rooms from €15.50 per person. **Pension Am Alten Markt** (☎ 521 14 11, fax 523 29 56; Schmeerstrasse 3; singles/doubles €48/65) is small but very central; rooms have shower and toilet. **Hotel Dorint Charlottenhof** (☎ 292 30, fax 232 31 00; w www.dorint.de/halle; Dorotheenstrasse 12; singles/doubles from €105/110) has the cure for the post-GDR blues with modern rooms in a shopping complex.

Drei Kaiser (☎ 203 28 68; Bergstrasse 1; mains €7.50-15.90) near Schloss Mortizburg, has a genteel atmosphere and fine German and international cuisine. There are cheap eats throughout town and some handsome pubs on Sternstrasse.

Getting There & Away
Several trains per hour go to/from Leipzig (€7, 30 minutes). Direct IR trains go to/from Berlin-Zoo (€24.60, two hours).

NAUMBURG
☎ 03445 • pop 32,000
Naumburg is one of those pretty little medieval towns for which Germany is so famous. It is strategically located inbetween Halle/Leipzig and Weimar, in the very scenic Saale-Unstrut wine country. It can be hurriedly seen in a two-hour break between trains but really deserves a day.

Orientation & Information
The main train station (Naumburg/Saale) is 1.5km northwest of the old town. Out of the station take Markgrafenweg to Rossbacher Strasse, then turn left and walk to Bauernweg, which heads up the hill. From here, follow the curving road to the cathedral. Markt, the central square, is a five-minute walk from the cathedral along the pedestrian quarter. Alternatively, bus Nos 1 and 2 run frequently from the train station to Markt or to the nearby Theaterplatz.

Naumburg's helpful **tourist office** (☎ 20 16 14, fax 26 60 47; e stadt.naumburg@t-online .de; Markt 6; open 9am-6pm Mon-Fri, 9am-4pm Sat all year, also 10am-1pm Sun Apr-Oct) offers the excellent A Walk Through Town brochure (free).

Things to See & Do
In the ancient western quarter of town stands the magnificent late-Romanesque/early-Gothic **Dom Sts Peter and Paul** (☎ 23 01 10; Domplatz 16-17; adult/concession/student €4/3/2; open 9am-6pm Mon-Sat, noon-6pm Sun Apr-Sept, shorter hours Oct-Mar) filled with art treasures such as the famous 13th-century statues of Uta and Ekkehard in the west choir. Don't miss the 1972 bronze handrails on the stairs to the east choir. Naumburg's picturesque **Rathaus** (1528) and the Gothic **Stadtkirche St Wenzel** (☎ 30 84 01; Topfmarkt; admission free; open 10am-noon & 2pm-5pm Apr-Oct, hours vary Nov-Mar), built between 1218 and 1523, rise above Markt. Friedrich Nietzsche enthusiasts will want to make a pilgrimage to **Nietzsche-Haus** (☎ 20 16 38; Weingarten 18; adult/concession €1.50/1; open 2pm-5pm Tues-Fri, 10am-4pm Sat & Sun), the existentialist's one-time home.

Naumburg is an ideal base for **hiking, cycling, kayaking** and **winery touring** throughout the Saale-Unstrut region. The tourist office has information.

GERMANY

Places to Stay & Eat

Campingplatz Blütengrund (*☎ 20 27 11, fax 20 05 71; adult/child/car €4/1.50/2*), 1.5km northeast of Naumburg, is at the confluence of the Saale and Unstrut Rivers and has a popular swimming facility. The rather institutional **Jugendherberge** (*☎ 70 34 22, fax 77 95 60; e JH-Naumburg@djh-sachsen-anhalt.de; Am Tennisplatz 9; juniors/seniors €16.50/18.70*) is up a hill 1.5km south of the town centre. Subtract €3 if you bring your own linen.

The tourist office organises private rooms; expect to pay around €15 per person for somewhere central. The friendly **Zur Alten Schmiede** (*☎ 243 60, fax 24 33 66; e Hotel _Zur_Alten_Schmiede@t-online.de; Lindenring 36-37; singles/doubles from €44/57*) is just outside the Altstadt, while **Hotel Stadt Aachen** (*☎ 24 70, fax 24 71 30; e Hotel-Stadt-Aachen@t-online.de; Markt 11; singles/doubles €50/70*) is Naumburg's central, establishment choice.

Both of these hotels have top-notch restaurants. **Alt Naumburg** (*☎ 20 42 95; Marienplatz 13; mains €4.90/12.40*) is a relaxing place for a beer or coffee and cake on the square.

Getting There & Away

Frequent IR trains stop at Naumburg to/from Frankfurt (€45.60, 3½ hours), Berlin (€32.60, 2½ hours), Leipzig (€12.40, 45 minutes) and Weimar (€6.60, 30 minutes).

Mecklenburg-Western Pomerania

The state of Mecklenburg-Western Pomerania (Mecklenburg-Vorpommern) is a low-lying, postglacial region of lakes, meadows, forests and Baltic Sea (Ostsee) beaches, stretching across northern Germany from Schleswig-Holstein to Poland. Most of the state is historic Mecklenburg; only the island of Rügen and the area from Stralsund to the Polish border traditionally belong to Western Pomerania, or Vorpommern.

In 1160 the Duke of Saxony, Heinrich (Henry the Lion), Christianised the region and made the local Polish princes his vassals. Germanisation gradually reduced the Slavonic element, and in 1348 the dukes of Mecklenburg became princes of the Holy Roman Empire.

Sweden entered the scene during the Thirty Years' War (1618–48). In 1867 the whole region joined the North German Confederation and, in 1871, the German Reich.

Offshore islands like Poel and Hiddensee are largely untouched, while others, including Rügen, are popular resorts. Just keep in mind the very short swimming season (July and August usually).

SCHWERIN
☎ 0385 • pop 105,000

Surrounded by lakes, Schwerin is one of eastern Germany's most genteel and picturesque towns. The town gets its name from a Slavic castle known as Zaurin (animal pasture) on the site of the present Schloss. This former seat of the Grand Duchy of Mecklenburg – now the capital of Mecklenburg-Western Pomerania – is an interesting mix of renovated 16th- and 17th-century half-timbered houses and 19th-century architecture.

Orientation & Information

Down the hill east of the Hauptbahnhof there's the Pfaffenteich, the rectangular lake whose southern end is at the beginning of Schwerin's main street, Mecklenburgstrasse. Markt is southeast of here. Farther southeast, around Alter Garten on Schweriner See, are the monumental Marstall (the former royal stables), the Schloss (ducal castle), and museums, parks, tour boats and other treats. Marienplatz, the major shopping and transit centre, is about a five-minute walk to the west.

Schwerin-Information (*☎ 592 52 13, fax 55 50 94; e stadtmarketing-schwerin@t-online.de; Am Markt 10; open 9am-6pm Mon-Fri, 10am-4pm Sat, 10am-2pm Sun*) sells the Schwerin-Ticket, covering local transport and discounted admissions for €6/4 per adult/child (€8/5 for two days).

Things to See & Do

Above the **Markt** rises the tall 14th-century Gothic **Dom** (*☎ 56 50 14; Am Dom 1; adult/concession €1/0.50; open 11am-5pm Mon-Sat, noon-5pm Sun May-Oct, shorter hours Nov-Apr*); you can climb the 219 steps up the 19th-century **church tower** (*an additional €1*) for the view. The cathedral is a wonderful example of north German red and glazed-black brick architecture.

Southeast of Alter Garten, over a causeway, there's the neo-Gothic **Schloss** (*☎ 56 57 38;*

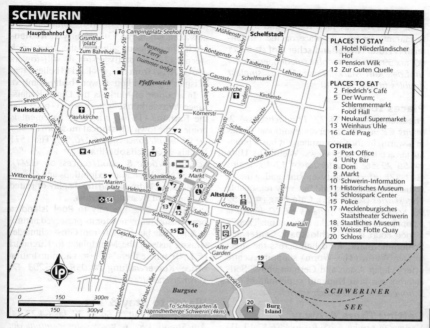

SCHWERIN

PLACES TO STAY
1 Hotel Niederländischer Hof
6 Pension Wilk
12 Zur Guten Quelle

PLACES TO EAT
2 Friedrich's Café
5 Der Wurm; Schlemmermarkt Food Hall
7 Neukauf Supermarket
13 Weinhaus Uhle
16 Café Prag

OTHER
3 Post Office
4 Unity Bar
8 Dom
9 Markt
10 Schwerin-Information
11 Historisches Museum
14 Schlosspark Center
15 Police
17 Mecklenburgisches Staatstheater Schwerin
18 Staatliches Museum
19 Weisse Flotte Quay
20 Schloss

Lennéstrasse 1; adult/concession €4/2.50; open 10am-6pm Wed-Sun Apr-Oct, 10am-5pm Wed-Sun Nov-Mar), with superb interiors and lake country views. It's connected to the **Schlossgarten** by another causeway. On the city side of Alter Garten is the **Staatliches Museum** (☎ 595 80; *Alter Garten 3; adult/concession €3/2; open 10am-8pm Tues, 10am-6pm Wed-Sun Apr-Oct, 10am-5pm Tues-Sun Nov-Mar)*, with an excellent collection of works by old Dutch masters.

The dramatic cream-coloured building next to the museum is the **Mecklenburgisches Staatstheater Schwerin** (State Theatre). There is also a **Historisches Museum** (☎ 59 38 10; *Grosser Moor 38; adult/concession €1.50/1; open 10am-6pm Tues-Sun)*.

Town **markets** are held on Schlachtermarkt, behind the Rathaus, from Tuesday to Saturday. At No 3, on the same square, stands the building that housed a synagogue until Nazi atrocities of 1938.

Cruises

From May to September, excursion boats operate every 30 minutes on the Schweriner See. They depart from the **Weisse Flotte** (☎ 55 77 70) quay near the Staatliches Museum, and 1½-hour cruises cost €9.50. There is a reduced schedule in March, April and early October.

Places to Stay

There's a nifty computerised accommodation system in front of the Hauptbahnhof. You'll find lists and locations of hotels and pensions with available rooms, and a free phone for calling the place of your choice.

Campingplatz Seehof (☎ 51 25 40, fax 581 41 70; ⓔ info@fereinparkseehof.de; *2-person sites €17.50)* is 10km north of Schwerin on the western shore of Schweriner See (take bus No 8 from the train station). It gets crowded in summer. **Jugendherberge Schwerin** (☎ 326 00 06, fax 326 03 03; *Waldschulweg 3; beds juniors/seniors €14.30/17)* is lakeside, about 4km south of the city centre (take bus No 14 from Marienplatz).

Schwerin-Information can book private rooms from about €25 per person. Tiny, central **Pension Wilk** (☎ 550 70 24; *Buschstrasse 13; €18 per person)* has basic rooms without private facilities (breakfast €5 extra). The following include breakfast and private facilities. Historic **Zur Guten Quelle** (☎ 56 59 85, fax

500 76 02; Schusterstrasse 12; singles/doubles from €51/70) has nice rooms and a good restaurant. An upscale place on the Pfaffenteich is **Hotel Niederländischer Hof** (☎ 59 11 00, fax 591 10 99; e hotel@niederlaendischer -hof.de; Karl-Marx-Strasse 12-13; singles/ doubles from €90/118).

Places to Eat

Friedrich's (☎ 55 54 73; Friedrichstrasse 2; mains €8.90-12.50) serves traditional dishes in a warm, historic atmosphere; it has a popular terrace and water views. **Weinhaus Uhle** (☎ 56 29 56; Schusterstrasse 13-15; mains €11-17) offers quality cuisine and wine in stylish surroundings, and has very reasonable Tageskartes (set menus). **Café Prag** (☎ 56 59 00; Schlossstrasse 17; mains €6.10-10.40) is a popular coffee and cake destination. There's a food court in the **Schlosspark Center** and **Schlemmermarkt food hall** across the street in Der Wurm (The Worm) shopping centre offers cheap Asian and German chow. Self-caterers can visit **Neukauf supermarket** (cnr Schmiedestrasse & Buschstrasse).

Getting There & Away

Various fast trains serve Rostock (€12.40, 1¼ hours), Stralsund (€22.40, 2½ hours) and Hamburg (€17.60, 1¼ hours). Frequent trains go to/from Wismar (€5.50, 30 minutes). Most travel to/from Berlin (€33.40, two hours) requires a change at Wittenberge or Ludwigslust.

WISMAR
☎ 03841 • pop 47,500

Wismar, about halfway between Rostock and Lübeck, became a Hanseatic trading town in the 13th century. For centuries Wismar belonged to Sweden, and traces of Scandinavian rule can still be seen (and heard). It's less hectic than Rostock or Stralsund and is a pretty little town worth seeing for its historic centre and crumbling architectural gems.

Information

Wismar-Information (☎ 194 33, fax 251 30 91; e touristinfo@wismar.de; Am Markt 11; open 9am-6pm daily) is very helpful.

Things to See & Do

Of the three great red-brick churches that once climbed above the rooftops, it was only **St Nikolai** (donation €1) that survived the Anglo-American bombing raids during WWII intact. The massive red shell of **St Georgenkirche** is under long-term restoration. Cars now park where the 13th-century **St Marienkirche** once stood, although the great brick steeple (1339), partly restored, still towers above. Apart from this, it's hard to believe that Wismar's gabled houses were badly bombed.

In a corner of Markt is the Dutch Renaissance **Wasserkunst** waterworks (1602) and the **Rathaus** (1819), where its basement is home to the town's **historical museum** (☎ 251 30 96; adult/concession €1/0.50). The 1571 Renaissance **Schabbellhaus** (☎ 28 23 50; Schweinsbrücke 8; adult/concession €2/1), near St Nikolai, has art exhibitions and special displays, including a horrific display of rotted teeth yanked by a local dentist.

Wismar is the gateway to **Poel Island**, a beach resort renowned for its preserved natural beauty. Take bus No 430 from Grossschmiedestrasse, just off the Marktplatz, to Kirchdorf (€1.90), where there's a resort administration office, **Kurverwaltung** (☎ 038 425-203 47; Wismarsche Strasse 2).

Places to Stay & Eat

Ostsee-Camping (☎ 64 23 77, fax 64 23 74; Am Strand 19c; w www.ostee-camping.de; tent site with adult/child/car €4/2.50/6 in summer, less rest of year) is by the beach in Zierow, 9km northwest of Wismar. Among its other charms, it has a beer garden. Take route B105 or bus No 401. The **Jugendherberge** (☎ 326 80, fax 32 68 68; Juri-Gagarin-Ring 30a; e jh-wismar@t-online.de; beds juniors/ seniors €16/19) is a 15-minute walk from the centre in Friedenshof or can be reached with bus D from the main train station.

Wismar-Information arranges private rooms from €13 per person. The central, charming **Pension Chez Fasan** (☎ 21 34 25, fax 20 22 85; Bademutterstrasse 19; beds €21 per person) offers good value (breakfast €4 extra).

New Orleans Hotel (☎ 268 60, fax 26 86 10; Runde Grube 3; singles/doubles from €49/72) is a modern hotel and restaurant on the waterfront with nice sized rooms with facilities; some with harbour views. **Steigenberger Hotel Stadt Hamburg** (☎ 23 90, fax 23 92 39; e info@steigenberger-wismar.de; Am Markt 24; singles/doubles from €82/ 104) has pleasant rooms in a beautifully renovated building on the Markt.

A string of restaurants and bars line the car-free quarter near Alter Hafen. **Brauhaus am**

Lohberg (☎ 25 02 38; Am Lohberg; mains €3-16.50) brews its own beer and serves traditional dishes in a historic building. **To'n Zägenkrog** (☎ 28 27 16; Ziegenmarkt 10; mains €4-11.50) is filled with maritime mementoes and serves excellent fish dishes. In town, you'll find Mecklenburg specialities at **Zum Weinberg** (☎ 28 35 30; Hinter dem Rathaus 3; mains €5.30-15), while **Alter Schwede** (☎ 28 35 52; Alter Markt 18; mains €7-15) is an upmarket option located in Wismar's oldest burgher house.

Busy town **markets** (Am Markt) are held on Tuesday, Thursday and Saturday. On Saturday, a lively fish market takes place at the Alter Hafen fishing harbour.

Getting There & Away

Regional trains run to/from Rostock every hour (€8.10, 1¼ hours) and regularly to/from Schwerin (€5.50, 30 minutes). Connect in Bad Kleinen for trains to Lübeck (€10.70, 1¼ hours).

ROSTOCK & WARNEMÜNDE

☎ 0381 • pop 210,000

Rostock, the largest city in lightly populated northeastern Germany, is a major Baltic port and ship-building centre. In the 14th and 15th centuries Rostock was an important Hanseatic city trading with Rīga, Bergen and Bruges. Rostock University, founded in 1419, was the first in northern Europe.

The years after reunification were difficult in Rostock – unemployment soared and neo-Nazis engaged in attacks on foreign workers, bringing national and worldwide condemnation. Now, however, the city centre along Kröpeliner Strasse and the former dock area on the Warnow River have been redeveloped into pleasant pedestrian quarters. Rostock hosts the **IGA** (International Garden Show; w www.iga.de) from April to October 2003, cause for more, er, sprucing up.

Rostock's chief suburb is the beach resort and fishing village of Warnemünde, 12km north. In winter this popular getaway offers a picturesque alternative as a place to stay, while on warm days it is jammed with Berlin's fun-seekers. The IGA site is between central Rostock and Warnemünde.

Orientation & Information

Rostock-Information (☎ 194 33, 381 22 22, fax 381 26 01; e touristinfo@rostock.de; Neuer Markt 3-8; open 10am-6pm Mon-Fri, 10am-4pm Sat & Sun May-Sept, closed weekends Oct-Apr) is about 1.5km from the Hauptbahnhof (tram No 11 or 12). The tourist office sells the 48-hour Rostock Card (€8), which entitles holders to a free walking tour (in German), various reductions for sights and performances, and free public transport (including the S-Bahn to/from Warnemünde). Rostock's **post office** is in the same building. Web information on Rostock is available at w www.rostock.de.

Things to See & Do

Rostock's splendid 13th-century **Marienkirche** (☎ 45 33 25; Am Ziegenmarkt; adult/concession €1/0.50; open 10am-5pm Mon-Sat, 11.15am-5pm Sun), survived WWII unscathed. This huge brick edifice contains a functioning astronomical clock (1472), a Gothic bronze baptismal font (1290), a Renaissance pulpit (1574) and a baroque organ (1770). For a bird's-eye view of town, visit the **Petrikirche** (☎ 211 01; Alter Markt; open 10am-5pm daily Apr-Oct, 10am-4pm Mon-Fri Nov-Mar) and scale the stairs or take the lift up the tower (€2).

Kröpeliner Strasse, a broad pedestrian mall lined with 15th- and 16th-century burgher houses, runs west from the **Rathaus** on Neuer Markt to the 14th-century **Kröpeliner Tor** (☎ 45 41 77; Kröpeliner Strasse; adult/concession €3/1; open 10am-6pm Wed-Sun), near a stretch of old city wall. Halfway along, off the southwestern corner of Universitätsplatz, is the **Kloster 'Zum Heiligen Kreuz' Museum** (☎ 20 35 90; Klosterhof; adult/concession €2/1; open 10am-6pm Tues-Sun) situated in an old convent (1270).

The city will permanently move its interesting **Schifffahrtsmuseum** (shipping museum) to the IGA site.

At Warnemünde's north end, a broad, sandy beach stretches west from the **lighthouse** (1898). It's chock-a-block with bathers on hot summer days, and its promenade makes for a nice stroll.

Places to Stay

Both Rostock-Information and Warnemünde-Information can book private rooms from €15 per person, plus a €2.50 fee. After hours, you can call ☎ 194 14 for a recorded message (in German only) about vacant hotel rooms.

GERMANY

The new **Jugendherberge** (☎ 54 81 70, fax 548 17 23; Parkstrasse 47, Warnemünde; e jh-warnemuende@t-online.de; juniors/seniors €19.30/23.30) is a two-minute walk to the beach and sporting activities.

The small **City-Pension** (☎ 459 07 04, fax 25 22 60; Krönkenhagen 3; singles/doubles from €44/67) is central, quiet and homy with rooms with facilities, near the Warnow River. **Courtyard by Marriott** (☎ 497 00, fax 497 07 00; Schwaansche Strasse 6; w www.court yard.com; rooms from €80) offers plenty of comfort off Universitätsplatz. The upmarket **Steigenberger Hotel Sonne** (☎ 497 30, fax 497 33 51; e info@hotel-sonne-rostock.de; singles/doubles from €99/127) is Rostock's premier downtown hotel, with a contemporary gabled facade.

In Warnemünde finding good, cheap accommodation is easy in winter, and it makes a wonderful alternative to Rostock. In summer, however, rooms in Warnemünde are as scarce as hen's teeth.

Places to Eat

Kölsch-& Altbierhaus (☎ 490 38 62; Wokrenter Strasse 36; dinner mains €5-14) has a good pub atmosphere – lunches and pub selections are cheaper. Down the hill, **Zur Kogge** (☎ 493 44 93; Wokrenter Strasse 27; mains €7.65-14.30) is a seafood place with a seafaring feel, plus some meat and veg selections. If you're looking to explore Rostock's Swedish heritage, **Tre Kronor** (☎ 490 42 60; Lange Strasse 11; mains €7.50-15.80) serves salmon, reindeer and elk. **Fast food** is available in the Rostocker Hof shopping centre, off Universitätsplatz.

In Warnemünde, along Alter Strom, the picturesque fishing harbour, stallholders sell the daily catch – fresh, smoked or in bread rolls...it's delicious! There are also loads of fish restaurants. A couple of blocks to the west, **Salsalitos** (☎ 519 35 65; Am Leuchtturm 9; mains €7.50-15) pulls a young crowd in the evenings for expensive Mexican.

Getting There & Away

There are hourly trains from Wismar (€8.10, 1¼ hours), and frequent trains to/from Berlin-Zoo (€33.40, 2¾ hours), Stralsund (€10.70, one hour), Schwerin (€12.40, 1¼ hours) and Hamburg (€28, 2¼ hours).

Vehicle-passenger ferries cross to Trelleborg (Sweden) and Gedser (Denmark) from Rostock Seaport (bus No 19 or 20). **Scandlines** (☎ 01805-722 63 54 637, call cost €0.12 per min; w www.scandlines.de) has services daily between Rostock and Trelleborg for €14 to €19 per passenger (5¾ hours). Trips to Gedser cost €5 to €8 per person and take up to two hours. **TT-Line** (☎ 040-360 14 42, fax 360 14 07; w www.TTLine.de) departs from Rostock for Trelleborg several times daily using fast and slow boats. The crossing takes three to six hours and costs average €40; costs vary by season and boat.

Getting Around

Tageskarte (day tickets) cost €3.15. For two zones (covering Rostock and Warnemünde), single rides cost €1.70, or €0.90 within either zone. The double-decker S-Bahn north to Warnemünde departs from Rostock Hauptbahnhof every 15 minutes during the day, every 30 minutes in the evenings, and hourly from midnight to dawn.

STRALSUND

☎ 03831 • pop 61,500

Stralsund, an enjoyable city on the Baltic Sea north of Berlin, is almost completely surrounded by lakes and the sea, which once contributed to its defence. It was a Hanseatic city in the Middle Ages and later formed part of the Duchy of Pommern-Wolgast. From 1648 to 1815 it was under Swedish control. Today it's an attractive, historic town with fine museums and buildings, pleasant walks and a restful, uncluttered waterfront. The island of Rügen is just across the sound, the Strelasund, and in summer the ferry to Hiddensee Island leaves from here.

Orientation & Information

Stralsund's Altstadt is compact and easily walkable. It's connected by causeways to its surrounds; the main train station is across the Tribseer Damm causeway to the west, with Rügen to the east. Neuer Markt is the southwestern hub, and the bus station is a few blocks south, past the Marienkirche. You'll find the **post office** (Neuer Markt) opposite the Marienkirche.

Stralsund Tourismuszentrale (☎ 246 90; Alter Markt 9; e info@stralsund-tourismus .de; open 9am-7pm Mon-Fri, 9am-2pm Sat, 10am-2pm Sun May-Sept & 9am-5pm Mon-Fri, 10am-2pm Sat Oct-Apr) is near the northern focus of the old town. Here you can pick

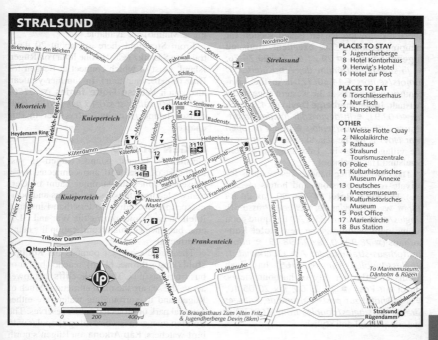

STRALSUND

PLACES TO STAY
5 Jugendherberge
8 Hotel Kontorhaus
9 Herwig's Hotel
16 Hotel zur Post

PLACES TO EAT
6 Torschliesserhaus
7 Nur Fisch
12 Hansekeller

OTHER
1 Weisse Flotte Quay
2 Nikolaikirche
3 Rathaus
4 Stralsund
Tourismuszentrale
10 Police
11 Kulturhistorisches
Museum Annexe
13 Deutsches
Meeresmuseum
14 Kulturhistorisches
Museum
15 Post Office
17 Marienkirche
18 Bus Station

up a pamphlet guide to the city's Gothic architecture (€0.50).

Things to See & Do

On Alter Markt is the medieval **Rathaus**, where you can stroll through the vaulted and pillared structures and around to the impressive **Nikolaikirche** (☎ 29 71 99). The 14th-century **Marienkirche** (☎ 29 35 29; *Neuer Markt; open 10am-noon Mon-Sat, 2pm-4pm Sat, 11.30am-noon Sun*) is a massive red-brick edifice typical of north German Gothic architecture.

You can climb the 350 steps of the **tower** (*admission €2*), on a daunting network of steep ladders, for a sweeping view of Stralsund. Ask at the tourist office about **organ recitals** and chamber music at these churches, especially in summer.

There are two excellent museums on Mönchstrasse. **Deutsches Meeresmuseum** (*German Oceanographic Museum; ☎ 265 00; Katharinenberg 14-20; adult/concession €4.50/3; open 9am-6pm daily July & Aug, 10am-5pm Sept-June*), is an oceanic complex and aquarium in a 13th-century convent church. Some aquariums contain tropical fish

and coral, while others display creatures of the Baltic and North Seas.

The **Kulturhistorisches Museum** (*Cultural History Museum; ☎ 287 90; Mönchstrasse 25-27; adult/concession €3/1.50; open 10am-5pm Tues-Sun*) has a large collection housed in the cloister of an old convent (and an annexe for local history at Böttcherstrasse 23; one ticket admits you to both). It's affiliated with the **Marinemuseum** (*Naval Museum; ☎ 29 73 27; Sternschanze 10; adult/concession €3/1.50; open Tues-Sun*), on the island of Dänholm, off the B96 towards Rügen, covering the colourful history of Baltic seafaring, with some cool equipment in the yard.

Many fine buildings have been restored on the showpiece **Mühlenstrasse** near Alter Markt. The old harbour is close by and you can stroll along the sea wall, then west along the waterfront park for a great view of Stralsund's skyline.

Cruises

There are short crossings to Altefähr (on Rügen; adult/child €1.50/0.75 one way) as well as one-hour harbour cruises from May to October (€5/3).

GERMANY

Places to Stay

See the following Rügen Island section for camping grounds. The excellent Stralsund **Jugendherberge** (☎ 29 21 60, fax 29 76 76; e jh-stralsund@t-online.de; Am Kütertor 1; juniors/seniors €14.30/17) is in the 17th-century waterworks at the western edge of the Altstadt. **Jugendherberge Devin** (☎ 49 02 89, fax 40 02 91; e jh-devin@djh-mv.de; Strandstrasse 219; juniors/seniors €14.30/17; open Mar-Nov) is by the sea, 8km east of town in the village of Devin. Take bus No 3 from Stralsund Hauptbahnhof.

The tourist office handles reservations for private rooms, pensions and hotels (€2.50 fee). **Herwig's Hotel** (☎ 266 80, fax 26 68 23; w www.herwigs.de; Heilgeiststrasse 50; singles/doubles from €50/70) has quite good rooms with facilities. The new **Hotel Kontorhaus** (☎ 28 90 00, fax 28 98 09; e info@kontorhaus-stralsund.de; Am Querkanal 1; singles/doubles from €55/65) has flash rooms and flashier city or harbour views. **Hotel zur Post** (☎ 20 05 00, fax 20 05 10; e info@hotel-zur-post-stralsund.de; Tribseer Strasse 22; singles/doubles from €60/75) is historic, central and stylish.

Places to Eat

Torschliesserhaus (☎ 29 30 32; Am Kütertor; mains €7.40-14.90) is a cosy pub in the old gatekeeper's house next to the youth hostel. Less-expensive pub grub is available. **Nur Fisch** (☎ 28 85 95; Heilgeiststrasse 92; mains €7.20-19.50) is a daytime bistro specialising in its namesake. The **Hansekeller** (☎ 70 38 40; Mönchstrasse 48; mains €7-12.30) serves hearty regional dishes in a vaulted cellar. The brewhouse **Zum Alten Fritz** (☎ 25 55 00; Greifswalder Chausee 84-85; mains €7.20-15.10) is worth the trek out of town (take bus No 3 from the main train station), with good beer and some tasty and well-priced dishes. There's also a selection of *imbisse* (snack stands) around Apollonienmarkt.

Getting There & Away

Frequent IR trains operate to/from Rostock (€10.70, 50 minutes), Berlin (€35, three hours), Schwerin (€22.40, two hours) and Hamburg (€38.20, 3¼ hours).

International trains between Berlin and Stockholm or Oslo use the car ferry connecting Sassnitz Mukran harbour on Rügen Island with Trelleborg and Malmö (Sweden). Two or three daily connections to Stockholm (changing at Malmö) are available.

From Stralsund there are about 20 daily trains to Sassnitz (€8.10, one hour) on Rügen Island, most of which connect at Bergen for Binz (€8.10, one hour). In summer you can also catch **Weisse Flotte ferries** (☎ 0180-321 21 50, call cost €0.18 per min) to Hiddensee Island (see that entry later in this chapter).

RÜGEN ISLAND

Germany's largest island, Rügen is just northeast of Stralsund and connected by a causeway. Once the summer haunt of Germany's leading thinkers, politicoes and businesspeople (including no less than Einstein), it fell on hard times during the War and GDR eras, but since German reunification it's being resurrected.

The island's highest point is the **Königsstuhl** (king's throne, 117m), reached by car or bus from Sassnitz. The **chalk cliffs** that tower above the sea are the main attraction. Much of Rügen and its surrounding waters are either national park or protected nature reserves. The **Bodden** inlet area is a bird refuge popular with bird-watchers. **Kap Arkona**, on Rügen's north shore, is famous for rugged cliffs and two lighthouses.

The main resort area is in eastern Rügen, around the towns of Binz, Sellin and Göhren. A lovely hike from Binz to Sellin skirts the cliffs above the sea through beech and pine forest and offers great coastal views. Another destination is **Jagdschloss Granitz** (1834), also surrounded by lush forest, and Prora, up the coast from Binz, is the site of a 2km-long workers' retreat built by Hitler before the war, now housing several museums.

Tourismus Verband Rügen (☎ 03838-807 70; Am Markt 4) in Bergen, the administrative centre, publishes a huge booklet listing all accommodation on the island and other useful information. Otherwise, Rügen has dozens of tourist offices, both municipal and private. We've found **Tourismusgesellschaft Binz** (☎ 038393-134 60; e tourismusag@binz.de; Hauptstrasse 1, Binz) to be especially helpful.

Places to Stay & Eat

Rügen has 21 **camping grounds** – the largest concentration of them is at Göhren. Also popular are **Fereinwohnungen**, longer-term apartment rentals.

Rügen's **Jugendherberge** (☎ 038393-325 97, fax 325 96; e jugendherberge-binz@t-on line.de; Strandpromenade 35; beds juniors/ seniors €18.30/22.30) is across from the beach in Binz.

Binz is also the island's top resort, with lodgings known for their distinctive *Bäder-arkitektur* (spa architecture) of whitewashed wooden balconies. The **Hotel Villa Neander** (☎ 038393-42 90, fax 529 99; e glasner@ binz.de; Hauptstrasse 16; rooms from €41 per person) has warm rooms and friendly owners. **Deutsche Flagge** (☎ 038393-460, fax 462 99; Schillerstrasse 9; singles/doubles €55/80) has comfortable accommodation.

Fischmarkt (☎ 038393-38 14 43; Strand-promenade 41, Binz; mains €12-17.50) has an upscale atmosphere and fish fondue. At **Lohme** (☎ 038302-9221; Dorfstrasse 35, Lohme), on the island's north side, you can dine on regional specialities while watching the sun set over Kap Arkona.

Getting There & Away
Local trains run almost hourly from 8am to 9pm between Stralsund and Sassnitz (€8.10, one hour) or Binz via Bergen (€8.10, one hour). A historic and fun narrow-gauge train links Putbus to Göhren via Binz.

Fares for Baltic ferries vary with the season. **Scandlines** (☎ 01805-722 63 54 637, call cost €0.12 per min; w www.scand lines.de) runs five passenger-vehicle ferries daily from Sassnitz Mukran ferry terminal, 5km south of town, to/from Trelleborg (Swe-den; €10 to €15 one way). Cars are €83 to €104, including all passengers. Scandlines also has at least two services weekly to/from Ronne on Bornholm (€12 to €17, daily in summer) in Denmark.

To reach the ferries by train, make sure the train goes to Sassnitz Mukran station. Other-wise, you can either catch a bus or walk from Sassnitz.

HIDDENSEE ISLAND
Hiddensee is a narrow 17km-long island off Rügen's west coast, north of Stralsund. No cars are allowed on Hiddensee and there are no camping grounds or hostels. The **tourist office** (☎ 038300-642 26; e insel.information@ t-online.de; Norderende 162; open 7am-5pm Mon-Fri year-round, 10am-noon Sat May-Sept) in Vitte, has accommodation informa-tion and a free booking service.

Weisse-Flotte Ferries (☎ 0180-321 21 50, call cost €0.18 per min) runs frequent services from Schaprode on Rügen's west coast to Hiddensee (€6.50/11.50 one way/return to Neuendorf, €8/13.50 to Kloster and Vitte). Buses link Schaprode to Bergen, which is on the main Rügen train line. Summer ferries also link Hiddensee with Stralsund (€8/14.50).

Bavaria

For many visitors to Germany, Bavaria (Bay-ern) is a microcosm of the whole country. Here you will find fulfilled the German stereotypes of *Lederhosen*, beer halls, oom-pah bands and romantic castles.

Bavaria was ruled for centuries as a duchy under the line founded by Otto I of Wittels-bach, and eventually graduated to the status of kingdom in 1806. The region suffered amid numerous power struggles between Prussia and Austria and was finally brought into the German Empire in 1871 by Bismarck. The last king of Bavaria was Ludwig II (1845–86), who earned the epithet the 'mad king' due to his obsession for building fantastic fairy-tale castles at enormous expense. He was found drowned in Starnberger See in suspicious cir-cumstances and left no heirs.

Bavaria draws visitors all year. If you only have time for one part of Germany after Berlin, this is it. Munich, the capital, is the heart and soul. The Bavarian Alps, Nurem-berg and the medieval towns on the Roman-tic Road are other important attractions.

MUNICH
☎ 089 • pop 1.3 million
Munich (München) is the Bavarian mother lode. But this beer-quaffing, sausage-eating city can be as cosmopolitan as anywhere in Europe. Munich residents have figured out how to enjoy life and are perfectly happy to show outsiders, as a visit to a beer hall will confirm. There's much more to Munich, how-ever, than beer. Decide on one of the many fine museums and take a leisurely look.

Munich has been the capital of Bavaria since 1503, but really achieved prominence under the guiding hand of Ludwig I in the 19th century. It has endured many turbulent times, but the 20th century was particularly rough. The city almost starved during WWI, the Nazis got their start here in the 1920s and

WWII brought bombing and more than 6000 civilian deaths. Today it is the centre of Germany's burgeoning high-tech industries and boasts lower unemployment than many other regions.

Orientation

The main train station is just west of the centre. Although there is extensive public transport, old-town Munich is enjoyable for walking. From the station, head east along Bayerstrasse, through Karlsplatz, and then along Neuhauser Strasse and Kaufingerstrasse to Marienplatz, the hub of Munich.

North of Marienplatz are the Residenz (the former royal palace), Schwabing (the famous student section) and the parklands of the Englischer Garten. East of Marienplatz is the Platzl quarter for beer houses and restaurants, as well as Maximilianstrasse, a fashionable street that is ideal for simply strolling and window-shopping.

Information

Tourist Offices The main branch of the tourist office (☎ 23 33 03 00; e tourismus@ ems.muenchen-tourist.de; Hauptbahnhof; open 8am-8pm Mon-Sat, 10am-6pm Sun) is at the main train station, to the right as you exit via the eastern entrance. Its room-finding service is free and you must apply in person; call ☎ 23 33 03 00 or write to: Fremdenverkehrsamt München, D-80313 München. There's another **branch** (Marienplatz; open 10am-8pm Mon-Fri, 10am-4pm Sat) beneath the Neues Rathaus. Both offices sell the Munich Welcome Card (€15.50), which allows three days unlimited travel on public transport, plus discounts for many museums, galleries and other attractions.

EurAide (☎ 59 38 89; e euraide@compu serve.com; Hauptbahnhof; open 7.45am-12.45pm & 2pm-4pm daily May-Oct, 8am-noon & 1pm-4pm Sat & Sun Nov-Mar), near platform 11 at the main train station, is an excellent source of information in English. The office gives advice on local and European train travel, and its room-finding service (€4 per booking) is at least as skilful as the tourist office's.

Yet another useful office is the **Jugend-informationszentrum** (Youth Information Centre; ☎ 51 41 06 60; Paul-Heyse-Strasse 22; open noon-6pm Mon-Fri, to 8pm Thur). It has a wide range of information for young people as well as an extensive library of periodicals and cheap Internet access.

The excellent Young People's Guide (€0.50) is available from information offices. The English-language monthly Munich Found (€3) is also useful (find it at English bookstores, cafés and restaurants) as is the annual Visitors' Guide (free), which is published by the same organisation and available at the tourist offices. There is a useful website at w www.munich-tourist.de.

Money Reisebank has two offices at the main train station; if you show a EurAide newsletter, The Inside Track, your commission will be 50% cheaper. You can also use **AmEx** (Promenadeplatz 6) and **Thomas Cook** (Kaiserstrasse 45, Schwabing).

Post & Communications Munich's main **post office** (Bahnhofplatz 1) is open from 8am to 8pm weekdays and until noon Saturday. The poste restante address is: Hauptpostlagernd (Poste Restante), Bahnhofplatz 1, 80074 München.

Sharing the post office building is **easy-Everything** (Bahnhofplatz 1; open 24hr), part of a chain of Internet cafés. It costs €2 for 80 minutes online, has hundreds of terminals and is normally packed with cyber surfers.

At **Savic Internet Point** (☎ 55 02 89 88; Schillerstrasse 17), you can download, print files and burn CDs. It costs €3 an hour.

Travel Agencies In the main train station there's **ABR Reisebüro** (☎ 120 40).

Bookshops The best travel bookshop in town is **Geobuch** (Rosental 6), opposite Viktualienmarkt. The widest cultural book range is available at **Hugendubel** (Marienplatz), with a good selection of Lonely Planet guides and tons of English-language offerings. **Anglia English Bookshop** (Schellingstrasse 3) is overflowing with English titles.

Laundry Close to the Hauptbahnhof is **City SB-Waschcenter** (Paul-Heyse-Strasse 21; open 7am-11pm daily) where loads cost €4.

Medical & Emergency Services Medical help is available at the **Home Medical Service** (☎ 55 17 71, 724 20 01). For **ambulances** call ☎ 112. There is an English-speaking **pharmacy** at the main train station, as well as a

police station (*emergency number* ☎ *110*) on the Arnulfstrasse side.

Dangers & Annoyances Munich residents love to stroll in the evening, so walking around the city centre feels pretty safe. The usual precautions apply in regard to staggering drunks from the beer halls, and you need to be wary of pickpockets around the touristy areas, near the Hauptbahnhof, and during major festivals like Oktoberfest and the *Christkindlmarkt* (Christmas Market). A common trick is to steal your gear if you strip off in the Englischer Garten (don't let that stop you, just watch your stuff!)

Things to See & Do

Except where otherwise noted, museums and galleries are closed on Monday.

The pivotal **Marienplatz** is a good starting point. Dominating the square is the towering neo-Gothic **Neues Rathaus** (*Marienplatz*), with its incessantly photographed **Glockenspiel** (carillon) which performs at 11am and noon (also at 5pm from May to October), bringing the square to an expectant standstill. Two important churches are on this square: **Peterskirche** and, behind the Altes Rathaus, the **Heiliggeistkirche**. Head west along shopping street Kaufingerstrasse to the late-Gothic **Frauenkirche** (*Church of Our Lady;* ☎ *42 34 57; Frauenplatz; tower adult/concession* €3/ 1.50), the landmark church of Munich. Go inside and join the hordes wandering in stupefied awe at the grandeur of the place, or climb the tower for majestic views of Munich. Continue west to the large, grey **Michaelskirche** (☎ *609 02 24; Kaufingerstrasse*), Germany's grandest Renaissance church.

Farther west is the **Richard Strauss Fountain** and then the medieval **Karlstor**, an old city gate. Double back towards Marienplatz and turn right onto Eisenmannstrasse, which becomes Kreuzstrasse and converges with Herzog-Wilhelm-Strasse at the medieval gate of **Sendlinger Tor**. Go down the left side of the shopping street Sendlinger Strasse to the **Asamkirche** (*Sendlinger Strasse 34*), a remarkable church designed by brothers Cosmas Damian and Egid Quirin Asam. It shows a rare unity of style, with scarcely a single unembellished surface.

Continue along Sendlinger Strasse and turn right on Hermann-Sack-Strasse to reach the **Stadtmuseum** (☎ *233; St-Jakobs-Platz 1;*

adult/concession €2.50/1.50; *open 10am-6pm Tues-Sun*), where the outstanding exhibits cover beer brewing, fashion, musical instruments, photography and puppets.

Palaces The huge **Residenz** (*Max-Joseph-Platz 3*) housed Bavarian rulers from 1385 to 1918 and features more than 500 years of architectural history. Apart from the palace itself, the **Residenzmuseum** (☎ *29 06 71; enter from Max-Joseph-Platz 3; adult/concession* €4/2; *open 9am-6pm Tues-Sun, 9am-8pm Thur*) has an extraordinary array of 100 rooms containing the Wittelsbach house's belongings, while in the same building, the **Schatzkammer** (☎ *29 06 71; enter from Max-Joseph-Platz 3; adult/concession* €4/2; *open 9am-6pm Tues-Sun, 9am-8pm Thur*) exhibits a ridiculous quantity of jewels, crowns and ornate gold.

If this doesn't satisfy your passion for palaces, visit **Schloss Nymphenburg** (☎ *17 90 80; adult/concession* €3.60/2.60, *museum & gallery* €7.70/6.15; *open 9am-6pm Tues-Sun, 9am-8pm Thur*) northwest of the city centre via tram No 17 from the main train station. This was the royal family's equally impressive summer home. The surrounding park is worth a long, regal stroll.

Deutsches Museum A vast science and technology museum (☎ *217 91; Theresienhöhe 14a; adult/concession* €6/4, *planetarium* €1.50 *extra; open 9am-5pm Tues-Sun*), this is like a combination of Disneyland and the Smithsonian Institution all under one huge roof that covers 13km of corridors on eight floors. You can explore anything from the depths of coal mines to the stars, but it's definitely too large to see everything so pursue specific interests. It can be reached via the S-Bahn to Isartor or tram No 18 to Deutsches Museum.

Other Museums The **Glyptothek** (☎ *28 61 00; Königsplatz 3; adult/concession* €3/1.75; *open 10am-5pm Tues-Sun, 10am-8pm Thur*) and **Antikensammlungen** (☎ *59 83 59; Königsplatz 1; adult/concession* €3/1.75; *open 10am-5pm Tues-Sun, 10am-8pm Wed*) have some of Germany's best antiquities. To visit both is €5.

Bayerisches Nationalmuseum (☎ *211 24 01; Prinzregentenstrasse 3; adult/concession* €3.10/1.80; *open 9.30am-5pm Tues-Sun*) houses an impressive collection of Bavarian and southern German artefacts.

GERMANY

CENTRAL MUNICH (MÜNCHEN)

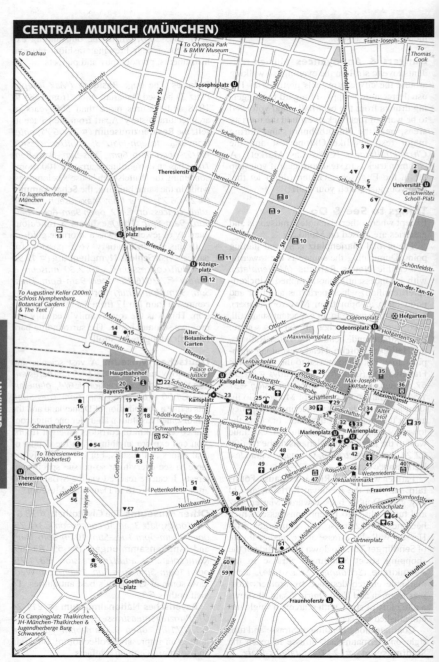

GERMANY

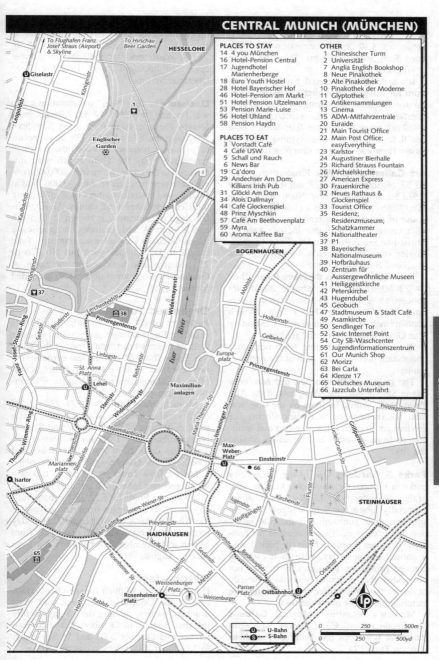

CENTRAL MUNICH (MÜNCHEN)

PLACES TO STAY
14 4 you München
16 Hotel-Pension Central
17 Jugendhotel
    Marienherberge
18 Euro Youth Hostel
28 Hotel Bayerischer Hof
46 Hotel-Pension am Markt
51 Hotel Pension Utzelmann
53 Pension Marie-Luise
56 Hotel Uhland
58 Pension Haydn

PLACES TO EAT
3 Vorstadt Café
4 Café USW
5 Schall und Rauch
6 News Bar
19 Ca'doro
29 Andechser Am Dom;
    Killians Irish Pub
31 Glöckl Am Dom
34 Alois Dallmayr
44 Café Glockenspiel
48 Prinz Myschkin
57 Café Am Beethovenplatz
59 Myra
60 Aroma Kaffee Bar

OTHER
1 Chinesischer Turm
2 Universität
7 Anglia English Bookshop
8 Neue Pinakothek
9 Alte Pinakothek
10 Pinakothek der Moderne
11 Glyptothek
12 Antikensammlungen
13 Cinema
15 ADM-Mitfahrzentrale
20 Euraide
21 Main Tourist Office
22 Main Post Office;
    easyEverything
23 Karlstor
24 Augustiner Bierhalle
25 Richard Strauss Fountain
26 Michaelskirche
27 American Express
30 Frauenkirche
32 Neues Rathaus &
    Glockenspiel
33 Tourist Office
35 Residenz;
    Residenzmuseum;
    Schatzkammer
36 Nationaltheater
37 P1
38 Bayerisches
    Nationalmuseum
39 Hofbräuhaus
40 Zentrum für
    Aussergewöhnliche Museen
41 Heiliggeistkirche
42 Peterskirche
43 Hugendubel
45 Geobuch
47 Stadtmuseum & Stadt Café
49 Asamkirche
50 Sendlinger Tor
52 Savic Internet Point
54 City SB-Waschcenter
55 Jugendinformationszentrum
61 Our Munich Shop
62 Morizz
63 Bei Carla
64 Klenze 17
65 Deutsches Museum
66 Jazzclub Unterfahrt

GERMANY

U-Bahn
S-Bahn

0   250   500m
0   250   500yd

North of the city, auto-fetishists can thrill to the **BMW Museum** (☎ 38 22 33 07; *Petuelring 130; adult/concession €2.75/2; open 9am-5pm Tues-Sun*). Take the U3 to Olympiazentrum.

It's a delightfully mixed bag at the **Zentrum für Aussergewöhnliche Museen** (*Centre for Unusual Museums;* ☎ 290 41 21; *Westenriederstrasse 26; adult/concession €4/2.50; open 10am-6pm Tues-Sun*), where you'll find displays on everything from the Easter Bunny to Austrian Empress Elisabeth.

Art Galleries The **Alte Pinakothek** (☎ 23 80 52 16; *Barer Strasse 27; adult/concession €5/3.50, free Sun; open 10am-5pm Tues-Sun, 10am-10pm Thur*) is a veritable treasure house of European masters from the 14th to 18th centuries. Highlights include Dürer's Christ-like *Self Portrait* and his *Four Apostles*, Rogier van der Weyden's *Adoration of the Magi* and Botticelli's *Pietà*.

Immediately north is the **Neue Pinakothek** (☎ 23 80 51 95; *Barer Strasse 29; adult/concession €5/3.50, free Sun; open 10am-5pm Wed-Sun, 10am-10pm Thur*), which contains mainly 19th-century works, including Van Gogh's *Sunflowers*, and sculpture.

A combined card costing €8/5 per adult/concession gets you into both of the previous listings.

The huge new **Pinakothek der Moderne** (*Barer Strasse 40*), one block east of the Alte Pinakothek, should be open by the time you read this. It brings together four collections of modern art, graphic art, applied art and architecture from galleries and museums around the city.

Parks & Gardens One of the largest city parks in Europe, the Englischer Garten, west of the city centre, is a great place for strolling, especially along the Schwabinger Bach. In summer, nude sunbathing is the rule rather than the exception. It's not unusual for hundreds of naked people to be in the park during a normal business day, with their clothing stacked primly on the grass. If they're not doing this, they're probably drinking merrily at one of the park's three **beer gardens** (see Entertainment later in this section).

Munich's beautiful **Botanical Gardens** (*adult/concession €3/2; open 9am-6pm daily*) are two stops past Schloss Nymphenburg on Tram 17.

Olympiaturm If you like heights, then go up the lift of the 290m Olympiaturm (tower) situated in the Olympia Park complex (☎ 67 24 14; *adult/concession €2.80/1.70; tower open 9am-midnight daily*). Take the U3 to Olympiazentrum.

Dachau The first Nazi concentration camp was Dachau (☎ 08131-17 41; *Alte-Roemer-Strasse 75; admission free; open 9am-5pm Tues-Sun*), built in March 1933. Jews, political prisoners, homosexuals and others deemed 'undesirable' by the Third Reich were imprisoned in the camp. More than 200,000 people were sent here; more than 30,000 died at Dachau and countless others died after being transferred to other death camps. An English-language documentary is shown at 11.30am and 3.30pm. A visit includes camp relics, a memorial and a very sobering museum. Take the S2 to Dachau and then bus No 726 or 724 (Sunday and holidays) to the camp. A Gesamtnetz (total area) ticket (€9) is needed for the trip.

Organised Tours

Radius (☎ 55 02 93 74; *Arnulfstrasse 3*) runs excellent English-language tours: a two-hour walk of the city heart, and a tour of the Third Reich sites (both €9). Tours leave from its office near track 30 at the Hauptbahnhof. It also offers five-hour trips to Dachau for €18, including transport.

Munich Walk Tours (☎ 0171-274 02 04) offers similar options at similar prices, plus a royal castle tour of the Residenz and Schloss Nymphenburg for €18/16 for over/under 26s. Tours run daily from April to October and meet under the Glockenspiel on Marienplatz.

Mike's Bike Tours (☎ 25 54 39 87) runs highly recommended (and leisurely) city cycling tours in English (€22/33 for half-/full-day tours). Tours depart from the archway at the Altes Rathaus on Marienplatz. Half-day tours (four hours) run at least once daily from March to November; all-day tours run from June to August.

Oktoberfest

Hordes come to Munich for the Oktoberfest, one of the Continent's biggest, and most drunken, parties, running the 15 days before the first Sunday in October (that's 20 September to 5 October 2003 and 18 September to 3 October 2004). Reserve accommodation well ahead and go early in the day so you can grab a seat in one of the hangar-sized beer 'tents'. The action takes place at the Theresienwiese grounds, about a 10-minute walk southwest of the main train station. While there is no entrance fee, those €6 1L steins of beer add up fast.

Places to Stay

Munich can be jammed with tourists year-round. Without reservations you may have to throw yourself at the mercy of the tourist office or EurAide room-finding services (see Tourist Offices under Information earlier).

Camping The most central camping ground is **Campingplatz Thalkirchen** (☎ 723 17 07, fax 724 31 77; Zentralländstrasse 49; tent/person €3.60/4.40, heated cabin €10.50 per person), southwest of the city centre. Take the U3 to Thalkirchen and then bus No 57 (about 20 minutes). This place is closed from November to mid-March.

Youth Hostels Munich's youth hostels that are DJH and HI affiliated do not accept guests over age 26, except group leaders or parents accompanying a child.

The **Jugendherberge München** (☎ 13 11 56, fax 167 87 45; e jhmuenchen@djh-bayern.de; Wendl-Dietrich-Strasse 20; dorm beds €19.20) is northwest of the centre (U1 to Rotkreuzplatz). It lacks atmosphere, but has plenty of beds. Also fairly close is the modern **JH München-Thalkirchen** (☎ 723 65 50, fax 724 25 67; e jhmuenchen-thalkirchen@djh.de; Miesingstrasse 4; dorm beds €19.20). Take the U3 to Thalkirchen, then follow the signs. Cheaper is the **Jugendherberge Burg Schwaneck** (☎ 74 48 66 70, fax 74 48 66 80; e info@jugendherberge-burgschwaneck.de; Burgweg 4-6; dorm beds €15.50), in a superb old castle; take the S7 to Pullach, then it's a 10-minute walk.

The Tent (☎ 141 43 00, fax 17 50 90; e see-you@the-tent.com; In den Kirschen 30; bed in main tent €9, camp site €5.50) is a fun and cheap summer option. This mass camp is open from June to September, and has a beer garden and no curfew. Take Tram 17 to the Botanic Gardens then follow the signs.

Other Hostels Close to the Hauptbahnhof, the **Euro Youth Hotel** (☎ 59 90 88 11, fax 59 90 88 22; e info@euro-youth-hotel.de; Senefelderstrasse 5; dorm beds €17.50, singles/doubles without bathroom €45/72) is a backpacker favourite, though the bathrooms could use a scrub. There are wool-fibre pillows and cotton sheets at ecologically correct **4 you München** (☎ 55 21 60, fax 55 21 66 66; e info@the4you.de; Hirtenstrasse 18; dorm beds under/over 27s €16.50/17.50, singles/doubles with breakfast €43.50/68.50). This has a hostel section downstairs and a guesthouse upstairs.

Women under 26 can try the pleasant **Jugendhotel Marienherberge** (☎ 55 58 05, fax 55 02 82 60; e invia-marienherberge@t-online.de; Goethestrasse 9; dorm beds €17, singles/doubles €25/40).

Hotels There are plenty of fairly cheap, if scruffy, places near the station. One of the better deals is tidy **Hotel Pension Central** (☎ 543 98 46, fax 543 98 47; e pensioncentral@t-online.de; Bayerstrasse 55; singles/doubles with breakfast €34/40). Similar but more worn is **Pension Marie Luise** (☎ 55 25 56 60, fax 55 45 56 66; e comfort-hotel-andi@t-online.de; Landwehrstrasse 35; singles/doubles €30/45), but you don't get breakfast.

Close to the Goetheplatz U-Bahn station, **Pension Haydn** (☎ 53 11 19, fax 54 40 48 27; Haydnstrasse 9; singles/doubles from €35/50) is a pleasant surprise. Beneath the shabby facade it's spotless, friendly and cheap.

There's an old-fashioned feel at **Hotel Pension Utzelmann** (☎ 59 48 89, fax 59 62 28; Pettenkoferstrasse 6; singles/doubles with breakfast €33/53) in an attractive building in a quiet street. Near the Viktualienmarkt, **Hotel-Pension am Markt** (☎ 22 50 14, fax 22 40 17; e hotel-am-markt.muenchen@t-online.de; Heiliggeistrasse 6; singles/doubles with breakfast from €38/68) has a pleasant feel and lovely rooms.

One of the classier (and friendlier) hotels in town is **Hotel Uhland** (☎ 54 33 50, fax 54 33 52 50; e hotel_uhland@compuserve.com; Uhlandstrasse 1; singles/doubles from €64/77), near the Oktoberfest site. Behind a beautiful neo-Renaissance facade you'll find all the mod cons and an inspirational breakfast buffet.

Hotel Bayerischer Hof (☎ 212 00, fax 212 09 06; e info@bayerischerhof.de; Promenadeplatz 2-6; singles/doubles from €182/232) is all marble, gold leaf and bustling efficiency, and won't leave you much change from a week's pay.

GERMANY

Places to Eat

At **Viktualienmarkt**, just south of Marienplatz, you can put together a picnic feast to take to the Englischer Garten. More prosperous picnickers might prefer the legendary **Alois Dallmayr** *(Dienerstrasse 14)*, one of the world's greatest (and priciest) delicatessens, with an amazing range of exotic foods imported from every corner of the earth.

Student card-holders can fill up for around €2 in any of the university **Mensas** *(Leopoldstrasse 13 • Arcistrasse 17 • Helene-Mayer-Ring 9)*. If your sightseeing timetable is tight, you can pick up some cheap Italian from the window at the **Ca'Doro** *(Bayerstrasse 31; pizza pieces €1.90)*.

South of the Hauptbahnhof, the **Café Am Beethovenplatz** *(Goethenstrasse 51; dishes €7-10)* is a casual hang-out with no airs and graces. It also serves great, affordable food.

For hearty Bavarian chow at its best, slip behind the Frauenkirche to **Andechser Am Dom** *(☎ 29 84 81; Weinstrasse 7; mains €9-14)*. If that's packed (probable), try nearby **Glöckl Am Dom** *(☎ 291 94 50; Frauenplatz 9; mains €5-13)*, a medieval Bratwurst house where they serve up your sausages and sauerkraut on pewter plates.

The sprawling **Ratskeller** *(☎ 219 98 90; Marienplatz 8; mains €11-19)*, in the cellar beneath the Neues Rathaus, has an extensive menu with dishes like Scottish salmon and hickory-smoked trout. South of Sendlinger Tor, **Myra** *(☎ 26 01 83 84; Pestalozzistrasse 32; mains €10-19)* has a menu of meat, seafood, vegetarian dishes infused with a Turkish tang, and an awe-inspiring cocktail list.

The stylish **Prinz Myschkin** *(☎ 26 55 96; Hackenstrasse 2; mains €9-13)* provides a spirited cosmopolitan vegetarian menu, and a tasty selection of pizza and pasta.

Cafés Most of Munich's café culture centres on Schwabing, the university haunt. Here you'll find plenty of snug little spots filled with laid-back laureates and lively lingo.

For the ultimately cool hang-out, head to unpretentious **Schall und Rauch** *(Schellingstrasse 22)*, where ciggies are smoked and the problems solved over coffee. To chill out even more, grab your book and join the mellow gang around the corner at **Café USW** *(Turkenstrasse 55)*.

Nearby, **Vorstadt Café** *(Turkenstrasse 83)* is busy and trendy, while at the modern **News**

Bar *(Amalienstrasse 54)*, an entire wall is dedicated to the latest magazines and newspapers (some in English).

In the Altstadt, a window seat at **Café Glockenspiel** *(Marienplatz 28)* is a much-sought, if ambitious, goal – here you can view the café's namesake at eye level. **Stadt Café** *(St-Jakobsplatz 1)*, at the Stadtmuseum, has funky decor and an intellectual crowd, while south of Sendlinger Tor, cramming 30 people into a shoebox isn't easy, so the coffee must be good at the tiny **Aroma Kaffee Bar** *(Pestalozzistrasse 24)*.

Entertainment

Beer Halls & Beer Gardens Beer drinking is an integral part of Munich's entertainment scene. Germans drink an average of 130L of the amber liquid each per year, while Munich residents manage to drink much more than this!

Several breweries run their own beer halls, so try at least one large, frothy, 1L mug (called a *Mass*) of beer before heading off to another hall. Most famous is the enormous **Hofbräuhaus** *(Am Platzl 9)*. A tourist trap it may be, but it's still a rollicking good time – singing, drinking and general merriment is encouraged. Less prominent but no less enjoyable is the **Augustiner Bierhalle** *(Neuhauser Strasse 27)*, an authentic example of an old-style Munich beer hall, filled with laughter, smoke and clinking glasses.

On a summer day there's nothing better than sitting and sipping among the greenery at one of Munich's beer gardens. In the Englischer Garten is the classic **Chinesischer Turm** beer garden, although the nearby **Hirschau** beer garden on the banks of Kleinhesseloher See is less crowded. The **Augustiner Keller** *(Arnulfstrasse 52)*, five minutes from the Hauptbahnhof, has a large and leafy beer garden. Its beer hall is a fine place when the weather keeps you indoors.

Pubs & Clubs Munich has no shortage of lively pubs and clubs. The *Young People's Guide* (see the earlier Information section) keeps abreast of the hot spots to party. **Klenze 17** *(Klenzestrasse 17)* has a great crowd and an extensive whisky selection, while in a cellar behind the Frauenkirche, **Killians Irish Pub** *(Frauenplatz 11)* is a cosy, casual drinking hole. If you can get past the goons at the door, **P1** *(Prinzregentenstrasse 1)* is a classy club with a high celebrity quotient. In northern Schwabing, **Skyline** (Leopoldstrasse 82) plays hip-hop on the top floor of the Hertie department store.

Performing Arts, Cinemas & Jazz Munich is one of the cultural capitals of Germany; the publications listed in the earlier Information section can guide you to the best events. The **Nationaltheater** (☎ 21 85 19 20; Max-Joseph-Platz 2) is the home of the Bavarian State Opera and the site of many cultural events (particularly during the opera festival in July). You can buy tickets at the box office or book by telephone.

You can catch films in English at **Cinema** (☎ 55 52 55; Nymphenburger Strasse 31).

Munich's hot jazz scene is led by **Jazzclub Unterfahrt** (☎ 448 27 94; Kirchenstrasse 42-44), near the Max-Weber-Platz U-Bahn station. It has live music every night from 7.30pm, and open jam sessions on Sunday night.

Gay & Lesbian Much of Munich's gay and lesbian nightlife is in the area just south of Sendlinger Tor, especially around Gärtnerplatz. Our Munich is a monthly guide to gay and lesbian life, and is available at **Our Munich Shop** (☎ 26 01 85 03; Müllerstrasse 36). Resembling a Paris bar, **Morizz** (Klenzestrasse 43) is a popular haunt for gay men, serving food and cocktails and cranking up later in the night. **Bei Carla** (Buttermelcherstrasse 9) is an exclusively lesbian bar-café with a friendly atmosphere and lots of regulars.

Shopping

Christkindlmarkt (Marienplatz) in December is large and well stocked but often expensive, so buy a warm drink and just wander around. A huge flea market, the **Auer Dult** (Mariahilfplatz), has great buys and takes place during the last weeks of April, July and October.

Getting There & Away

Air Munich is second in importance only to Frankfurt for international and national connections. Flights will take you to all major destinations worldwide. Main German cities are serviced by at least half a dozen flights daily.

Train Train services to/from Munich are excellent. There are rapid connections at least every two hours to all major cities in Germany, as well as frequent EC trains to other

European cities such as Innsbruck (two hours), Vienna (five hours), Prague (six hours), Zürich (4¼ hours), Verona (5½ hours) and Paris (eight hours).

High-speed ICE services from Munich include Frankfurt (€75.60, 3½ hours), Hamburg (€127, six hours) and Berlin (€142.40, 6½ hours).

Bus Munich is linked to the Romantic Road by the Deutsche-Touring (also known as the Europabus) Munich-Frankfurt service (see Getting Around in the following Romantic Road section). Inquire at **Deutsche-Touring** (☎ 545 87 00, fax 54 58 70 21; e service@ deutsche-touring.com), near platform 26 of the main train station, about its international services to destinations such as Prague and Budapest. Buses stop along the northern side of the train station.

Car & Motorcycle Munich has autobahns radiating outwards on all sides. Take the A9 to Nuremberg, the A92 to Passau, the A8 east to Salzburg, the A95 to Garmisch-Partenkirchen and the A8 west to Ulm or Stuttgart. The main rental companies have counters together on the second level of the main train station. For arranged rides, the **ADM-Mitfahrzentrale** (☎ 194 40; Lämmerstrasse 6) is near the main train station. Destinations and sample charges (including booking fees) include: Berlin €32, Frankfurt €25 and Hamburg €39.

Getting Around

To/From the Airport Munich's gleaming Flughafen Franz Josef Strauss is connected by the S8 and the S1 to Marienplatz and the main train station (€8). The service takes 40 minutes and runs every 20 minutes from 4am until around 12.30am.

The airport bus also runs at 20-minute intervals from Arnulfstrasse on the north side of the main train station (€9, 45 minutes) between 6.50am and 7.50pm. Forget taxis (at least €50!).

Public Transport Getting around is easy on Munich's excellent public transport network (MVV). The system is zone-based, and most places of interest to tourists (except Dachau and the airport) are within the 'blue' inner zone (Innenraum). MVV tickets are valid for the S-Bahn, U-Bahn, trams and buses, but must be validated before use. The U-Bahn stops operating around 12.30am on weekdays and 1.30am on weekends, but there are some later buses and S-Bahns. Rail passes are valid only on the S-Bahn.

Kurzstrecke (short rides) cost €1 and are good for no more than four stops on buses and trams and two stops on the U and S-Bahns. Longer trips cost €2. It's cheaper to buy a strip-card of 10 tickets *(Mehrfahrtenkarte)* for €9 and stamp one strip per adult on short rides, two strips for longer rides in the inner zone. *Tageskarte* (day passes) for the inner zone cost €4.50, while three-day tickets cost €11, or €15 for two adults.

Taxi Taxis are expensive (€2.50 flag fall, plus €1.30 per kilometre) and not much more convenient than public transport. For a radio-dispatched taxi dial ☎ 216 10.

Car & Motorcycle It's not worth driving in the city centre – many streets are pedestrian only. The tourist office has a map that shows city parking places (€1.50 or more per hour).

Bicycle Pedal power is popular in relatively flat Munich. **Radius Bike Rental** (☎ 59 61 13) rents out two-wheelers from €14/43 per day/ week.

AUGSBURG
☎ 0821 • pop 262,000

Originally established by the Romans, Augsburg later became a centre of Luther's Reformation and is now a lively provincial city crisscrossed by small streams. For some it will be a day trip from Munich, for others it's an ideal base (especially during Oktoberfest) or a gateway to the Romantic Road.

Augsburg's tourist offices are at Bahnhofstrasse 7 (☎ 502 07 22), open 9am to 6pm weekdays; and at Rathausplatz (☎ 502 07 35), open 9am to 6pm weekdays and 10am to 4pm Saturday (to 1pm Sunday). Both keep slightly shorter hours in winter.

Things to See & Do
The onion-shaped towers of the modest, 16th-century **St Maria Stern Kloster** in Elias-Holl-Platz started a fashion that spread throughout southern Germany. More impressive are those on the **Rathaus**, the adjacent **Perlachturm** and the soaring tower of **St Ulrich und Afra Basilika** (on Ulrichsplatz near the southern edge of the old town). **Dom Mariae Heimsuchung**, on

Hoher Weg north of Rathausplatz, is more conventionally styled. One of Luther's more colourful anti-papal documents was posted here after he was run out of town in 1518. Dramatist Bertolt Brecht's family home was on the stream and is now the **Bertolt-Brecht-Gedänkstätte** (☎ 324 27 79; Am Rain 7; adult/concession €1.50/1; open 10am-4pm Wed-Sun), a museum dedicated to Brecht and the work of young artists.

Places to Stay & Eat
Campingplatz Augusta (☎ 70 75 75, fax 70 58 83; e info@campingplatz-augusta.de; Mülhaserstrasse 54b; tent/car/person €3/3/4) is 7km northeast of the centre (bus No 23 to the terminus then a 2km walk). Augsburg's seedy **DJH Hostel** (☎ 339 09, fax 15 11 49; e jugendherberge@kvaugsburg-stadt.bvk .de; Beim Pfaffenkeller 3; dorm beds from €12.30), just east of St Mary's Cathedral, needs a serious spruce-up, but its beds are cheap.

Jakoberhof (☎ 51 00 30, fax 15 08 44; Jakobstrasse 39-41; singles/doubles €25/32.50) is a simple place with a good Bavarian restaurant downstairs. Modern **Dom Hotel** (☎ 34 39 03, fax 34 39 32 00; e info@dom hotel-augsburg.de; Frauentorstrasse 8; singles/doubles €63/73 with breakfast) has attractive rooms, a pool and a sauna.

Der Andechser (☎ 349 79 90; Johannisgasse 4; mains €5-12) is cosy, affordable and serves hearty German fare. Tucked in behind the Rathaus is **Die Ecke** (☎ 51 06 00; Elias-Holl-Platz 2; mains €18-26), one of Augsburg's best (and most expensive) restaurants.

Getting There & Away
Trains between Munich and Augsburg are frequent (€9, 40 minutes). Regular ICE/IC trains also serve Ulm (€12.40, 50 minutes), Stuttgart (€33.80, 1½ hours) and Nuremberg (€19.20, 1½ hours). Connections to/from Regensburg take two hours via Ingolstadt. The Deutsche-Touring Romantic Road bus stops at the train station.

ROMANTIC ROAD
Originally conceived as a way of promoting tourism in western Bavaria, the popular Romantic Road (Romantische Strasse) links a series of picturesque Bavarian towns and cities.

The road runs north-south through western Bavaria, from Würzburg to Füssen near the

Austrian border, passing through Rothenburg ob der Tauber, Dinkelsbühl and Augsburg. The main places for information about the Romantic Road are the tourist offices in Würzburg and Augsburg.

Locals get their cut of the Romantic Road hordes through, among other things, scores of good-value private accommodation offerings. Look for the 'Zimmer Frei' signs and expect to pay around €15 to €25 per person. Tourist offices are efficient at finding accommodation in almost any price range. DJH hostels listed in this section only accept people aged under 27.

Getting There & Away

In the north of the Romantic Road route, Würzburg is well-served by trains. To start at the southern end, take the hourly RE train from Munich to Füssen (€18.20, two hours). Rothenburg is linked by train to Würzburg, Nuremberg and Munich via Steinach. To reach Dinkelsbühl, take a train to Ansbach and from there a frequent bus onwards. Nördlingen has train connections to Stuttgart and Munich.

There are four daily buses between Füssen and Garmisch-Partenkirchen (€7; all stop at Hohenschwangau and Oberammergau), as well as several connections between Füssen and Oberstdorf (€8.10; via Pfronten). Deutsche-Touring runs a daily 'Castle Road' coach service in each direction between Mannheim and Rothenburg via Heidelberg (€29, 5½ hours).

Getting Around

It is possible to do this route using train connections, local buses or by car (just follow the brown 'Romantische Strasse' signs), but most train pass-holders prefer to take the Deutsche-Touring (also known as Europabus) bus. From April to October Deutsche-Touring runs one coach daily in each direction between Frankfurt and Munich (12 hours), and another in either direction between Dinkelsbühl and Füssen (4½ hours). The bus makes short stops in some towns, but it's both silly and mind-numbing to do the whole trip in one go, since you can break the journey at any point and continue the next day (reserve a seat for the next day as you disembark).

The full fare from Frankfurt to Füssen is €74 (change buses at Rothenburg). Eurail and German Rail passes are valid and Inter-Rail pass-holders receive a 50% discount, as do those over 60, while those under 26 save 10%.

Tickets are available for short segments and reservations are only necessary on summer weekends. Bike transport is €6 for up to 12 stops. For detailed information and reservations, you should contact **Deutsche-Touring GmbH** (☎ 069-79 03 50, fax 790 32 19; e ser vice@deutsche-touring.com; Am Römerhof 17, 60486 Frankfurt/Main).

With its gentle gradients and ever-changing scenery, the Romantic Road makes a good bike trip. **Radl-Tours** (☎ 09341-53 95) offers nine-day cycling packages from Würzburg to Dinkelsbühl from €398.

Rothenburg ob der Tauber
☎ 09861 • pop 12,000

Visit Rothenburg and it's soon obvious why this charmingly preserved medieval town is continually under siege from tourists. Granted 'free imperial city' status in 1274, it's an enchanting place of twisting cobbled lanes and strikingly pretty architecture enclosed by towered stone walls. The town's museums only open in the afternoon from November to March. There's a **tourist office** (☎ 404 92; e info@rothenburg.de; Markt 1; open 9am-6pm, with a 1hr break at noon Mon-Fri, 10am-3pm Sat May-Oct & 9am-5pm Mon-Fri, 10am-1pm Sat Nov-Apr).

Things to See The **Rathaus on Markt** was commenced in Gothic style in the 14th century but completed in Renaissance style. The **tower** (€1) gives a majestic view over the town and the Tauber Valley. According to legend, the town was saved during the Thirty Years' War when the mayor won a challenge by the Imperial general Tilly and downed more than 3L of wine at a gulp. The **Meistertrunk** scene is re-enacted by the clock figures on the tourist office building (eight times daily in summer).

The **Puppen und Spielzeugmuseum** (Doll and Toy Museum; ☎ 73 30; Hofbronnengasse 13; adult/concession €4/2.50; open 9.30am-6pm Mar-Dec, 11am-5pm Jan & Feb) is the largest private doll and toy collection in Germany. The **Reichsstadt Museum** (☎ 93 90 43; Klosterhof 5; adult/concession €3/1.50; open 10am-5pm Apr-Oct, 1pm-4pm Nov-Mar), in the former convent, features the superb Rothenburger Passion in 12 panels (by Martinus Schwarz, 1494) and the Judaica room, with a collection of gravestones with Hebrew inscriptions. Get a gruesome glimpse of the past at the **Krimminalmuseum** (☎ 53 59; Burggasse

GERMANY

3-5; adult/concession €3.20/1.70; open 10am-5pm Apr-Oct, 1pm-4pm Nov-Mar), which houses all manner of devices with which to torture and shame medieval miscreants.

Places to Stay & Eat Camping options are 1km to 2km or two north of the town walls at Detwang, west of the road on the river. There are signs to **Tauber-Romantik** (☎ 61 91, fax 868 99; Detwang 39; tent/person €4/3.75), open from Easter to late October. Rothenburg's jammed **Youth Hostel** (☎ 941 60, fax 94 16 20; e jhrothenburg@djh.bayern.de; Mülacker 1; dorm beds €15.10) is housed in two enormous renovated old buildings in the south of the old town.

Das Lädle (☎/fax 61 30; e das-laedle-pension-hess@t-online.de; Spitalgasse 18; singles/doubles €22/40 with breakfast) is a good budget option, with casual, comfortable rooms in a central location.

There are bright, spotless lodgings at **Gasthof Butz** (☎ 22 01; e gasthofbutz@rothenburg.com; Kapellenplatz 4; singles/doubles €37/73). **Reichs Küchenmeister** (☎ 97 00, fax 869 65; e hotel@reichskuechenmeister.com; Kirchplatz 8-10; singles/doubles from €57/67) is a quality top-end choice, with a popular restaurant downstairs (mains €8 to €21).

Vine-covered and impossibly cosy, **Altfrankische Weinstube** (☎ 64 04; Klosterhof 7; mains €6-13) is justifiably popular, with a varied and well-priced menu and fantastic atmosphere.

Resist the temptation to try a Schneeball, a crumbly ball of bland dough with the taste and consistency of chalk – surely one of Europe's worst 'local specialities'.

Dinkelsbühl
☎ 09581 • pop 11,500

South of Rothenburg, Dinkelsbühl is another walled town of cobbled streets. It celebrates the **Kinderzeche** (Children's Festival) in mid-July, commemorating a legend from the Thirty Years' War that the town's children successfully begged the invading Swedish troops to leave Dinkelsbühl unharmed. The hour-long walk around the town's **walls** and its almost 30 **towers** is the scenic highlight. There's a **tourist office** (☎ 902 40; e touristik.service@dinkelsbuehl.de; Marktplatz 1; open 9am-6pm Mon-Fri, 10am-4pm Sat, 10am-1pm Sun; closed 1pm-2pm Sat).

DCC-Campingplatz Romantische Strasse (☎ 78 17, fax 78 48; Kobeltsmühle 2; tent/person €6/4) is open all year. Dinkelsbühl's **Youth Hostel** (☎ 95 09, fax 48 74; e ballheimer@t-online.de; Koppengasse 10; dorm beds €11.20) is super cheap. The **Fränkischer Hof** (☎ 579 00, fax 57 90 99; Nördlinger Strasse 10; singles/doubles from €34/57) is a good budget option. The ornate facade of **Deutsches Haus** (☎ 60 59, fax 98 51 79 11; Weinmarkt 3; singles/doubles from €75/115) is one of the town's attractions. The hotel features a cosy restaurant serving Franconian dishes for around €12.

Nördlingen
☎ 09081 • pop 20,000

Nördlingen is encircled by its original 14th-century walls and lies within the basin of the **Ries**, a huge crater created by a meteor more than 15 million years ago. The crater is one of the largest in existence (25km in diameter) and the **Rieskrater Museum** (☎ 273 82 20; Eugene-Shoemaker-Platz 1; adult/concession €3/1.50; open 10am-noon & 1.30pm-4.30pm Tues-Sun) gives details. For a bird's-eye view of the town, climb the tower of **St Georg Kirche**. You'll find the **tourist office** (☎ 43 80; e verkersamt@noerdlingen.de; Marktplatz 2) very helpful. The **Youth Hostel** (☎/fax 27 18 16; Kaiserwiese 1; dorm beds €11.25) is a signposted 10-minute walk from the centre. **Altreuter Garni** (☎ 43 19, fax 97 97; Markt 11; singles/doubles with bath & toilet €38/52) has simple, pleasant rooms.

Füssen
☎ 08362 • pop 14,000

Just short of the Austrian border, Füssen has a monastery, a castle and splendid baroque architecture, but it is primarily visited for the two castles in nearby Schwangau associated with King Ludwig II. There's a **tourist office** (☎ 938 50; e tourismus@fuessen.de; Kaiser-Maximillian-Platz 1; open 8.30am-6pm Mon-Fri, 10am-noon Sat).

Neuschwanstein & Hohenschwangau Castles The castles provide a fascinating glimpse into the king's state of mind (or lack thereof). Hohenschwangau (☎ 811 27; adult/concession €7/6, combination €13/11; open 9am-6pm daily, 9am-8pm Thur Apr-Oct, 10am-4pm daily Oct-Apr) is where Ludwig lived as a child, but more interesting is the adjacent Neuschwanstein (☎ 810 35; *same hours & prices as Hohenschwangau*), his own creation (albeit with the help of a theatrical designer). Although it was unfinished when he died in 1886, there is plenty of evidence of Ludwig's twin obsessions: swans and Wagnerian operas. The sugary pastiche of architectural styles reputedly inspired Disney's Fantasyland castle. There's a great view of Neuschwanstein from the Marienbrücke (bridge) over a waterfall and gorge just above the castle. From here you can hike the Tegelberg for even better vistas.

Take the bus from Füssen train station (€2.80 return), share a taxi (☎ 77 00; €8.50) or walk the 5km. The only way to enter the castles is with a 35-minute guided tour, which can be purchased from the ticket centre at Alpseestrasse 12, near Hohenschwangau. Go early to avoid the massive crowds.

Places to Stay & Eat The Youth Hostel (☎ 77 54, fax 27 70; e *jhfuessen@djh-bayern .de; Mariahilferstrasse 5; dorm beds €13.30*) is a signposted 10-minute walk from the train station.

A pavillion near the tourist office has a computerised list of vacant rooms in town; the cheapest are private rooms at around €12 per person. Hotel Filser (☎ 912 50, fax 91 25 73; *Saulingerstrasse 3; singles/doubles €49/86*) is a quiet, comfortable place with clean rooms, a good restaurant downstairs (mains €7 to €15) and a health spa in the basement. Central Sonne Café (*Reichenstrasse 37; dishes €3-15*) has great baguettes, salads and schnitzels. There are light bites at the cosy Downtown Bistro-Café (*Hinteregasse 29; dishes €3-5*).

WÜRZBURG
☎ 0931 • pop 130,000
Surrounded by forests and vineyards, the charming city of Würzburg straddles the upper Main River. Rebuilt after bombings late in the war, Würzburg is a centre of art, beautiful architecture and delicate wines.

The **tourist office** (☎ 37 23 98; e *touris mus@wuerzburg.de; Oberer Markt*), in the rococo masterpiece Haus zum Falken, is open 10am to 6pm weekdays and to 2pm weekends (closed Sunday November to April). In the same building, the Stadtbücherei (☎ 37 34 38) provides 10 minutes of Internet access for €0.50.

Things to See & Do
The magnificent, sprawling **Residenz** (☎ 35 51 70; *Balthasar-Neumann-Promenade; adult/ concession €4/3; open 9am-6pm daily, 9am-8pm Thur Apr-Oct, 10am-4pm Oct-Mar*), a baroque masterpiece by Neumann, took a generation to build and is well worth the admission. The open **Hofgarten** at the back is a favourite spot. The **Dom St Kilian** interior and the adjacent **Neumünster** in the old town continue the baroque themes of the Residenz.

Neumann's fortified **Alter Kranen** (old crane), which serviced a dock on the riverbank south of Friedensbrücke, is now the **Haus des Frankenweins** (☎ 390 11 11; *Kranenkai 1*), where you can taste Franconian wines (for around €3 per glass).

The fortress **Marienberg**, across the river on the hill, is reached by crossing the 15th-century stone **Alte Mainbrücke** (bridge) from the city and walking up Tellstiege, a small alley. It encloses the **Fürstenbau Museum** (☎ 438 38; *adult/concession €3/1.50; open 9am-6pm Tues-Sun Apr-Oct, 10am-4pm Tues-Sun Oct-Mar*) featuring the episcopal apartments, and the regional **Mainfränkisches Museum** (☎ 430 16; *adult/concession €3/ 1.50; open 10am-6pm Tues-Sun Apr-Sept, 10am-4pm Tues-Sun Oct-Mar*). See both on a combined card (€4). For a dizzy thrill, look down the well in the courtyard. For a simple thrill, wander the walls enjoying the panoramic views.

Places to Stay & Eat
Kanu-Club (☎ 725 36; *Mergentheimer Strasse 13b; tent/person €3.50 each*) is a camping ground on the west bank of the Main; take tram No 3 or 5 to Jugendbühlweg. **Jugendgästehaus Würzburg** (☎ 425 90, fax 41 68 62; e *jhwuerzburg@djh-bayern.de; Burkarderstrasse 44; dorm beds €17.70*) is below the fortress (tram No 3 or 5 from the train station).

Simple and friendly **Pension Spehnkuch** (☎ 547 52, fax 547 60; e *spehnkuch@ web.de; Röntgenring 7; singles/doubles/ triples from €29/52/75*) has spotless rooms and welcoming hosts. **Hotel Alter Kranen** (☎ 351 80, fax 500 10; e *mail@hotel-alter -kranen.de; Kärrnergasse 11; singles/doubles €60/80*) offers lovely lodgings overlooking the river and fort. Breakfast is included. For a treat, try **Schloss Steinburg** (☎ 970 20, fax 971 21; e *hotel@steinburg.com; Auf dem*

GERMANY

Steinburg; singles/doubles from €80/120) in a gorgeous castle with majestic town views.

Just south of the Friedensbrücke, **Pane e Vino** (Dreikronenstrasse 2; dishes €6-15) is a sunny lunch spot with views of vine-covered hills. It serves up fresh pastas for around €8. Insanely popular **Bürgerspital** (☎ 35 28 80; Theaterstrasse 19; mains €5-18) is in a labyrinthine former medieval hospice; the atmosphere, food and the local wines are all first class.

Getting There & Away
Würzburg is two hours by frequent RE trains from Frankfurt (€19.20) and one hour from Nuremberg (€14.40). It's a major stop-off for the ICE trains on the Hamburg-Munich line. It is also on the Deutsche-Touring Romantic Road bus route (2½ hours to/from Rothenburg by bus). The main bus station is next to the train station off Röntgenring.

BAMBERG
☎ 0951 • pop 70,000
Tucked away from the main routes in northern Bavaria, Bamberg is practically a byword for magnificence – an untouched monument to the Holy Roman Emperor Heinrich II (who conceived it), to its prince-bishops and clergy and to its patriciate and townsfolk. It is a fun and beautiful town recognised by Unesco as a World Heritage Site.

The **tourist office** (☎ 87 11 61; e info@bamberg.de; Geyerswörthstrasse 3) is situated on an island in the Regnitz River. It's open 9am to 6pm weekdays and 9am to 3pm Saturday (plus 10am to 2pm Sunday from May to October).

Things to See & Do
Bamberg's main appeal is its fine buildings; their sheer number, their jumble of styles and the ambience this helps create. Most attractions are spread either side of the Regnitz River, but the colourful **Altes Rathaus** is actually in it, precariously perched on its own islet. The princely and ecclesiastical district is centred on Domplatz, where the Romanesque and Gothic **cathedral**, housing the statue of the chivalric king-knight, the *Bamberger Reiter*, is the biggest attraction. Above Domplatz is the former Benedictine monastery of St Michael, at the top of Michaelsberg. The **Kirche St Michael** is a must-see for its baroque art and the herbal compendium painted on its ceiling.

The garden terraces afford another marvellous overview of the city's splendour. There is also the **Fränkisches Brauereimuseum** (☎ 530 16; Michaelsberg 10f; adult/concession €2/1.50; open 1pm-5pm Wed-Sun Apr-Oct), which shows how the monks brewed their robust *Benediktiner Dunkel* beer.

Places to Stay & Eat
You can camp at **Campingplatz Insel** (☎ 563 20, fax 563 21; e campinginsel@web.de; Am Campingplatz 1; tent/person €6/3.50). **Jugendherberge Wolfsschlucht** (☎ 560 02, fax 552 11; e jh-bamberg@stadt.bamberg .de; Oberer Leinritt 70; dorm beds €14.60) is on the river's west bank, and is closed from mid-December to mid-January; take bus No 18 to Rodelbahn, walk northeast to the riverbank, then turn left.

Gasthof Fässla (☎ 265 16, fax 20 19 89; e kaspar_schultz@t-online.de; Hallstadter Strasse 174; singles/doubles €34/52) offers a drinker's dream – a bed in a brewery. The rooms are large, clean and comfy. The quaint **Barock Hotel** (☎ 540 31, fax 540 21; Vorderer Bach 4; singles/doubles with bathroom from €57/80), near the Dom, offers lovely rooms in a quiet spot. **Wirsthaus zum Schlenkerla** (Dominikanerstrasse 6; mains €7-12) has been brewing its extraordinary *Rauchbier* since 1678. The dark-red concoction with a smoky flavour accompanies a menu of Franconian specialities. Nearby, the **Fränkischer Gästhaus** (Obere Sandstrasse 1; mains €5-15) serves hearty mains and excellent Bratwurst on outdoor tables.

Getting There & Away
There are hourly RE and RB trains to/from both Würzburg (€14) and Nuremberg (€9), taking one hour. Bamberg is also served by ICE trains running between Munich (€45.20, 2½ hours) and Berlin (€68.80, 4½ hours) every two hours.

NUREMBERG
☎ 0911 • pop 500,000
Nuremberg (Nürnberg) is the largest city of the Franconia region of northern Bavaria. Though the flood of tourists to this historical town never seems to cease – especially during its world-famous Christmas market – it's still worth the trip. Nuremberg played a major role during the Nazi years and during the war crimes trials afterwards. The city was rebuilt

NUREMBERG (NÜRNBERG)

PLACES TO STAY
1 Jugendherberge Nürnberg
7 Hotel Agneshof
15 Pension Sonne
19 Lette'm Sleep

PLACES TO EAT
5 Alstadthof Brewery
6 Kaiserburg
9 Bratwursthäusle
13 Café Am Trödelmarkt
18 Mount Lavinia

OTHER
2 Kaiserburg
3 Tiergärtnertor
4 Albrecht-Dürer-Haus
8 St Sebalduskirche
10 Laundrette
11 Main Tourist Office
12 Pfarrkirche Unsere Liebe Frau
14 St Lorenzkirche
16 Citypoint Shopping Centre & Supermarket
17 M@x Internet-Café
20 Germanisches Nationalmuseum
21 Neues Museum
22 Handwerkerhof
23 Tourist Office
24 Bus Station
25 Main Post Office

after Allied bombs reduced it to rubble on 2 January 1945.

Orientation & Information

The main train station is just outside the city walls of the old town. The main artery, the mostly pedestrian Königstrasse, takes you through the old town and its major squares. The main **tourist office** (☎ 233 61 32; ⓔ tourismus@nuernberg.de; Königstrasse 93; open 9am-7pm Mon-Sat) is near the train station. A smaller **branch** (☎ 233 61 35; Hauptmarkt 18; open 9am-6pm Mon-Sat, 10am-4pm Sun May-Sept) operates on the city's main square. Both offices sell the two-day Kultour Ticket (€14.50), available to visitors staying one night. It provides free public transport, and entry to most museums and attractions.

The main **post office** (Bahnhofplatz 1) is by the station and a **Reisebank** operates inside the station. There's a central **laundrette** (Fünferplatz 2). **M@x Internet-Cafe** (☎ 23 23 84; Färberstrasse 11) offers one hour of surfing for €2.50.

Things to See & Do

The spectacular **Germanisches Nationalmuseum** (☎ 133 10; Kartäusergasse 1; adult/concession €4/3, free 6pm-9pm Wed; open 10am-5pm Tues-Sun, 10am-9pm Wed) is the most important general museum of German culture. It displays works by German painters and sculptors, an archaeological collection, arms and armour, musical and scientific instruments and toys. Close by, the sleek and harmonious **Neues Museum** (☎ 24 02 00;

Luitpoldstrasse 5; adult/concession €3.50/
2.50; open 10am-8pm Tues-Fri, 10am-6pm
Sat & Sun) contains a superb collection of contemporary art and design.

The scenic **Altstadt** is easily covered on
foot. The **Handwerkerhof**, a re-creation of the
crafts quarter of old Nuremberg, is walled in
opposite the main train station. It's about as
quaint (read 'over-priced') as they can possibly make it. On Lorenzer Platz there's the **St
Lorenzkirche**, noted for the 15th-century tab-
ernacle that climbs like a vine up a pillar to the
vaulted ceiling.

To the north is the bustling **Hauptmarkt**,
where the most famous Christkindlesmarkt in
Germany is held from the Friday before Advent to Christmas Eve. The church here is the
ornate **Pfarrkirche Unsere Liebe Frau**; the
clock's figures go strolling at noon. Near the
Rathaus is **St Sebalduskirche**, Nuremberg's
oldest church (dating from the 13th century),
with the shrine of St Sebaldus.

It's not a bad climb up Burgstrasse to the
enormous **Kaiserburg complex** (☎ 22 57 26;
Burg 13; adult/concession €5/4; open 9am-
6pm daily Apr-Sept, 10am-4pm Oct-Mar) for
a good view of the city. You can visit the
palace complex, chapel, well, tower and museum on the one ticket. The walls spread west
to the tunnel-gate of **Tiergärtnertor**, where
you can stroll behind the castle to the gardens.
Nearby is the renovated **Albrecht-Dürer-Haus**
(☎ 231 25 68; Albrecht-Dürer-Strasse 39;
adult/concession €4/2; open 10am-5pm
Tues-Sun, 10am-8pm Thur), where Dürer,
Germany's renowned Renaissance draughtsman, lived from 1509 to 1528.

Nuremberg's role during the Third Reich is
well known. The Nazis chose this city as their
propaganda centre and for mass rallies, which
were held at **Luitpoldhain**, a (never completed) sports complex of megalomaniac pro-
portions. After the war, the Allies deliberately
chose Nuremberg as the site for the trials of
Nazi war criminals. A new museum called
Dokumentationzentrum (☎ 231 56 66; Bay-
ernstrasse 110; adult/concession €5/2.50;
open 9am-6pm Mon-Fri, 10am-6pm Sat &
Sun) opened in 2002 in the north wing of the
massive Congress Hall. The upper level
houses a permanent exhibition, Fascination
and Terror, dealing with the causes, relationships and consequences of the Nazi regime,
and its links with Nuremberg. Take tram No 9
to Luitpoldhain.

Places to Stay

Knaus-Campingpark 'Am Dutzendteich'
(☎ 981 27 17, fax 981 27 18; Hans-Kalb-
Strasse 56; site/person €4.50/5) is southeast
of the centre (U1 to Messezentrum), and is
open all year.

In the historic Kaiserstallung next to the
castle, **Jugendherberge Nürnberg** (☎ 230 93
60, fax 23 09 36 11; e jhnuernberg@djh
-bayern.de; Burg 2; dorm beds with linen
€17.70) has more character than most. Another good and central backpacker option is
Lette'm Sleep (☎ 99 28 128, fax 99 28 130;
Frauentormauer 42; dorm beds €13, doubles
from €22), which offers a choice of dormitory accommodation or double rooms.

Family-run **Pension Vater Jahn** (☎ 44 45
07, fax 43 15 236; Jahnstrasse 13; singles/
doubles from €25/39) is no-frills and friendly,
offering clean rooms with shared facilities.
Pension Sonne (☎ 22 71 66; Königstrasse 45;
singles/doubles with breakfast €30/50) has
bright, cheery rooms up a steep flight of stairs.

Sunny **Hotel Agneshof** (☎ 21 44 40, fax 21
44 41 44; e info@agneshof-nuernberg.de;
Agnesgasse 10; singles/doubles from €90/
105) has welcoming rooms with an extra
touch of comfort. Breakfast is included.

Places to Eat

Don't leave Nuremberg without trying its famous Bratwurstl (small grilled sausages). The
best place is the **Bratwursthäusle** (☎ 22 76 95;
Rathausplatz 2; 10 for €8.30), where they're
flame-grilled, scrumptious, and served with
Meerrettich (horseradish) and Kartoffelsalat
(potato salad).

Kaiserburg (☎ 22 12 16; Obere Krämers-
gasse 20; mains €8-17) is steeped in medieval
ambience and has a Franconian/international
menu.

Nearby, there's the sprawling **Alstadthof**
(☎ 22 43 27; Bergstrasse 19; light meals €6-
9), a brewery, café, theatre and bar all thrown
together.

On an island in the Pegnitz River, **Café Am
Trödelmarkt** (☎ 20 88 77; Trödelmarkt 42;
salads & light snacks €5-10) is in a plum position, with views of the water, the ducks, the
houses and the three bridges. **Mount Lavinia**
(☎ 22 70 09; Jakobsplatz 22; mains €12-16)
is a superb little Ceylon-Thai restaurant decorated with grass matting and stencilled cloth.
It serves up delicious spicy concoctions to
make you sweat.

Getting There & Around

IC trains run hourly to/from Frankfurt (€37.20, 2¼ hours) and Munich (€38, 1½ hours). IR trains run every two hours to Stuttgart (€28, two hours) and ICE trains every two hours to Berlin Ostbahhof (€78.20, five hours). Several daily EC trains travel to Vienna (seven hours) and Prague (5½ hours). Buses to regional destinations leave from the station just east of the main train station.

Tickets on the bus, tram and U-Bahn system cost €1.35/1.75 for each short/long ride in the central zone. A day pass is €3.50.

REGENSBURG

☎ 0941 • pop 143,000

On the Danube River, Regensburg has relics of all periods, yet lacks the packaged feel of some other German cities. It escaped the carpet bombing, and here, as nowhere else in Germany, you enter the misty ages between the Roman and the Carolingian.

From the main train station, you walk up Maximillianstrasse for 10 minutes to reach the centre. There's a tourist office (☎ 507 44 10; e tourismus@info.regensburg.baynet.de; open 8.30am-6pm Mon-Fri, 9am-4pm Sat, 9.30am-4pm Sun) in the Altes Rathaus. Surf City (Speichergasse 1) charges €3 for 30 minutes on the Internet.

Things to See

Dominating the skyline are the twin spires of the Gothic Dom St Peter (☎ 597 10 02; Domplatz; admission free; tours in German adult/concession €2.50/1.50; tours 10am, 11am, 2pm Mon-Fri, noon, 2pm Sun May-Nov, 11am Mon-Fri, noon Sun low season) built during the 14th and 15th centuries from unusual green limestone. It has striking original stained-glass windows above the choir on the eastern side. The Altes Rathaus was progressively extended from medieval to baroque times and remained the seat of the Reichstag for almost 150 years. Guided tours in English (€2.50; 3pm Mon-Sat May-Sept) are available through the tourist office. The Roman wall, with its Porta Praetoria arch, follows Unter den Schwibbögen onto Dr-Martin-Luther-Strasse.

Lavish Schloss Thurn und Taxis (☎ 504 81 33; Emmeramsplatz 6; adult/concession for all three €10/8.50; open 11am-5pm Mon-Fri, 10am-5pm Sat & Sun Apr-Oct, 10am-5pm Sat & Sun Nov-Mar) is near the train station and is divided into three separate sections: the castle proper (Schloss), the monastery (Kreuzgang) and the royal stables (Marstall). Nearby is St Emmeram Basilika (Emmeramplatz 3; admission free), a baroque masterpiece containing untouched Carolingian and episcopal graves and relics.

Places to Stay & Eat

Campers can head to Azur-Camping (☎ 27 00 25, fax 29 94 32; Weinweg 40; site/person €5.50/4.50). Bus No 6 from the train station goes to the entrance.

The Youth Hostel (☎ 574 02, fax 524 11; e jhregensburg@djh-bayern.de; Wöhrdstrasse 60; dorm beds €16.60) can be reached on bus No 3 to the Eisstadion stop.

Central Hotel Am Peterstor (☎ 545 45, fax 545 42; Fröliche-Türken-Strasse 12; singles/doubles €40/50) is good value, with clean, basic rooms. The attractive Bischofshof Hotel (☎ 584 60, fax 584 61 46; e info@hotel-bischofshof.de; Krauterermarkt 3; singles/doubles from €67/119) has pleasant rooms, some overlooking a pretty courtyard. On warm nights and sunny days, the courtyard accommodates the hotel's quality restaurant.

Wok House (☎ 56 73 34; Obermünsterplatz 2; mains €6-8) is an above-average Asian place, while by far the best spot for a snack of Bratwurstl in bread is the Historische Wurstküche (Thundorferstrasse; €6), on the banks of the roaring Danube.

Getting There & Away

Regensburg is on the train line between Nuremberg (€19, one hour) and Austria and there are EC/IC trains in both directions every two hours, as well as RB/RE trains to Munich (€19.20, 1½ hours). EC/IC services run every two hours to Passau (€20.20, one hour). Regensburg is a major stop on the Danube bike route.

PASSAU

☎ 0851 • pop 51,000

As it exits Germany for Austria, the Danube River flows through the lovely baroque town of Passau, where it is joined by the Inn and Ilz Rivers. Passau is not only at a confluence of inland waterways, but also forms the hub of long-distance cycling routes.

The main tourist office (☎ 95 59 80; e tourist-info@passau.de; Rathausplatz 3; open 8.30am-6pm Mon-Fri, 9.30am-3pm Sat

GERMANY

& Sun Easter–mid-Oct, 8.30am-5pm Mon-Thur, 8.30am-4pm Fri mid-Oct–Easter) is in the Altstadt. The **regional tourist centre** (same contact details; Bahnhofstrasse 36), virtually opposite the train station, is useful for information about bicycle and boat travel along the Danube.

Things to See & Do

You'll notice that the Italian-baroque essence has not doused the medieval feel as you wander through the narrow lanes, tunnels and archways of the old town and monastic district to Ortspitze, where the rivers meet. The 13th-century **Veste Oberhaus** (☎ 49 33 50; Oberhaus 125; adult/concession €4/2.50; open 9am-5pm Mon-Fri, 10am-6pm Sat & Sun, closed Nov-Mar) has a museum and views over the city from the castle tower. Imposing cathedral **Dom St Stephan** (Domplatz; concerts adult/concession €3/1, evening €5/3), built between 1680 and 1890, houses the world's largest church organ (17,774 pipes). From May to October there are acoustically stunning daily half-hour concerts at noon and at 7.30pm Thursday. The glockenspiel in the colourful **Rathaus** chimes several times daily and wall markings show historical flood levels.

Places to Stay & Eat

There's camping at **Zeltplatz Ilzstadt** (☎ 414 57; Halser Strasse 34; person €5), over the Ilz River bridge on bus No 1, 2, 3 or 4. Passau's **Youth Hostel** (☎ 49 37 80, fax 49 37 820; e jhpassau@djh-bayern.de; Veste Oberhaus 125; dorm beds juniors only €14.10) is situated in the castle across the Danube. Take bus No 1, 2 or 4.

In the shape of a supine sleeper, modern **Rotel Inn** (☎ 951 60, fax 95 16 100; e info@ rotel.de; singles/doubles €25/30) is on the river near the train station. **Pension Rössner** (☎ 931 350, fax 931 3595; e info@pension -roessner.de; Braugasse 19; singles with bathroom from €35/50) is ideally situated in the Altstadt. It has basic, clean rooms. Nestled beneath the castle, **Hotel Schloss Ort** (☎ 340 72, fax 318 17; e info@schlosshotel-passau.de; Im Ort 11; singles/doubles from €49/78) has lovely timber-floored rooms with four-poster beds. Its downstairs restaurant has a cosy open fire and a shiny suit of armour.

For cheap eats, there's a large **marketplace** (Ludwigstrasse 16), complete with fruit stalls, meat and fish stands. **Zum König** (☎ 93 10 60;

Rindermarkt 2; mains €8-13) is a cosy spot with a varied international menu, including some Balkan specialities.

Getting There & Away

RE and RB trains run direct to/from Munich (€27, two hours), Regensburg (€16.60, one hour) and EC trains to Nuremberg (€34.40, two hours). EC trains also serve Austria, including Linz (2¼ hours) and Vienna (three hours). From May through October **Wurm + Köck** (☎ 92 92 92; Höllgasse 26), sails down the Danube to Linz (€21, five hours) twice daily.

BAVARIAN ALPS

While not quite as high as their sister summits farther south in Austria, the Bavarian Alps (Bayerische Alpen) rise so abruptly from the rolling hills of southern Bavaria that their appearance seems all the more dramatic. Stretching westward from Germany's southeastern corner to the Allgäu region near Lake Constance, the Alps take in most of the mountainous country fringing the southern border with Austria.

Activities

The Bavarian Alps are extraordinarily well organised for outdoor pursuits, with skiing, snowboarding and hiking being the most popular. The ski season usually runs from mid-December to April. Ski gear is available for hire in all the resorts, with the lowest daily/weekly rates including skis, boots and stocks at around €12/48 (downhill), €7/32 (cross-country) and €16/57 (snowboard). Five-day skiing courses start at around €100.

During the warmer months, the activities include hiking, canoeing, rafting, biking and paragliding.

Accommodation

Most of the resorts have plenty of reasonably priced guesthouses and private rooms, though it's still a good idea to reserve accommodation. Tourist offices can help you find a room; otherwise look out for 'Zimmer Frei' signs. In most resorts a local tax (or Kurtaxe, usually an extra €1.80 per night) is levied, although this usually gives free local transport and other deals. Be warned that rates can be higher in July and August, and that hotel and pension owners may not be keen to let rooms for short stays.

Getting Around

While the public transport network is very good, the mountain geography means there are few direct routes between main centres; sometimes a short cut via Austria is quicker (such as between Füssen and Oberstdorf). Road rather than rail routes are often more practical. For those driving, the German Alpine Road (Deutsche Alpenstrasse) is a scenic way to go, though obviously much slower than the autobahns and highways that fan out across southern Bavaria.

Regional RVO bus passes giving free travel on the network between Füssen, Garmisch and Mittenwald are excellent value (☎ 089-55 16 40); the day pass is €7 and a pass for five days' travel within one month costs €22.50.

Berchtesgaden

☎ 08652 • pop 8200

Berchtesgaden is perhaps the most romantically scenic place in the Bavarian Alps. To reach the centre from the train station, cross the footbridge and walk uphill up Bahnhofstrasse. The helpful tourist office (☎ 96 70; e info@berchtesgaden.de; Königsseer Strasse 2) is just across the river from the train station at Königsseer Strasse 2. It's open 8am to 6pm weekdays and 8am to 5pm Saturday (plus 9am to 3pm Sunday from mid-June to September). Outside these months, it's open 8am to 5pm weekdays and 9am to noon Saturday.

Things to See & Do A tour of the Salzbergwerk (☎ 600 20; Bergwerkstrasse 83; adult/concession €12/6.50; open 9am-5pm May–mid-Oct; 12.30pm-3.30pm Mon-Sat mid-Oct–Apr) combines history with a carnival (rides and games to amuse you). Visitors descend into the salt mine for a 1½-hour tour.

Nearby **Obersalzberg** is a deceptively innocent-looking place with a creepy legacy as the second seat of government for the Third Reich. Hitler, Himmler, Goebbels and the rest of the Nazi hierarchy all maintained homes here. The Dokumentation Obersalzberg museum (☎ 94 79 60; Salzbergstrasse 41; adult/concession €2.50/1.50; open 9am-5pm Tues-Sun May-Nov, 10am-3pm Tues-Sun Nov-May) documents the evil bunch's time in the area (don't miss the photo of the fun-loving Führer relaxing in Lederhosen), as well as the horrors their policies produced, through photos, audio and film. Ask for the free brochure in English (the explanatory captions and audio are in German). The admission fee also gets you into the eerie Hitler's bunker. Catch bus No 9538 (€3.70 return) from the Nazi-constructed Berchtesgaden train station to Obersalzberg-Hintereck. Take the first major street on the right after alighting from the bus and follow it for five minutes.

Kehlstein (☎ 29 69; admission €12; buses run 7.40am-4.25pm; open May-Oct) is a spectacular meeting house built for, but seldom used by, Hitler. Despite its reputation as the 'Eagle's Nest', it's a popular destination. The views are stunning and the history is bracing. Entry includes transport on special buses which link the summit with Hintereck/Obersalzberg as well as the 120m lift through solid rock to the peak. Alternatively you can make the steep ascent or descent on foot in two to three hours.

The best way to see Obersalzberg and Kehlstein is with Eagle's Nest Tours (☎ 649 71; €35), which has English-language tours lasting four hours and covering the entire history of the area during WWII.

You can forget the horrors of war at the Königssee, a beautiful alpine lake situated 5km south of Berchtesgaden (and linked by hourly buses in summer). There are frequent boat tours across the lake to the quaint chapel at St Bartholomä (€10.50), or all the way to Obersee (€13.50).

The wilds of Berchtesgaden National Park unquestionably offer some of the best hiking in Germany. A good introduction to the area is a 2km path up from St Bartholomä beside the Königssee to the Watzmann-Ostwand, a massive 2000m-high rock face where scores of ambitious mountaineers have died.

Berchtesgaden has five major skiing resorts, and you can buy five-day lift passes that cover them all (€98). Rossfeld is the cheapest for day passes (€13), while Götschen, with a permanent half-pipe, is the destination for snowboarders (€20 per day).

Places to Stay & Eat Of the five camping grounds in the Berchtesgaden area, the nicest are up at Königssee: **Grafenlehen** (☎ 41 40; site/person €5.11/4.35) and **Mühleiten** (☎ 45 84; site/person €5.11/4.35). The pleasant **Youth Hostel** (☎ 943 70, fax 94 37 37; e jhberchtesgaden@djh-bayern.de; Gebirgsjägerstrasse 52; dorm beds €13.10) is closed in November and December. Take bus No 9539 to Jugendherberge.

GERMANY

Lovely **Hotel Watzmann** (☎ 20 55, fax 51 74; Franziskanerplatz 2; singles/doubles from €28/50) is decorated in traditional upper-Bavarian style, and has comfortable rooms and an excellent outdoor terrace with top food (mains €9 to €11).

You'll get a warm welcome at **Hotel Floriani** (☎ 660 11, fax 634 53; Königsseer Strasse 37; singles/doubles from €33/56), which has cheerful, vista-flooded rooms. If you have an itch for schnitzel, head to **Alt Berchtesgaden** (☎ 45 19; Bahnhofstrasse 3; schnitzel €4.99), with 15 varieties to choose from.

Getting There & Away Both RB and RE trains run to Munich and cost €24.80.

Garmisch-Partenkirchen
☎ 08821 • pop 27,000

The combined towns of Garmisch and Partenkirchen were merged by Hitler for the 1936 Winter Olympics. Munich residents' favourite getaway spot, this often-snooty, year-round resort is also a big draw for skiers, snowboarders, hikers and mountaineers.

The huge **ski stadium** outside town hosted the Olympics. From the pedestrian Am Kurpark, walk up Klammstrasse, cross the tracks and veer left on the first path to reach the stadium and enjoy the spectacular views. The **tourist office** (☎ 18 07 00; e tourist-info@ garmisch-partenkirchen.de; Richard Strauss Platz 2; open 8am-6pm Mon-Sat, 10am-noon Sun) is in the centre of town.

About 20km north of Garmisch is over-touristed **Oberammergau**. The town becomes a focus of world attention every 10 years when many of the local populace perform day-long Passion plays. The next series of performances, which date back to the 17th century, will be held in 2010.

An excellent short hike from Garmisch is to the **Partnachklamm gorge**, via a winding path above a stream and underneath the waterfalls. You take the Graseck cable car and follow the signs.

An excursion to the **Zugspitze** summit, Germany's highest peak (2963m), is the most popular outing from Garmisch. There are various ways up, including a return trip by rack-railway (just west of the main train station), summit cable car and Eibsee cable car for €42, or you can scale it in two days. For detailed information concerning guided hiking

or mountaineering courses, check with **Bergsteigerschule Zugspitze** (☎ 589 99; Am Gudiberg 7, Garmisch).

Garmisch is bounded by four separate ski areas – **Zugspitze plateau** (the highest), **Alpspitze/Hausberg** (the largest), **Eckbauer** (the cheapest) and **Wank** (the most evocative, despite its name). Day ski passes range from €16 for Eckbauer to €33 for Zugspitze. The Happy Ski Card covers all four areas and is valid for a minimum of three days (€77). A web of cross-country ski trails runs along the main valleys.

Flori Wörndle (☎ 583 00) has ski-hire outlets at the Alpspitze and Hausbergbahn lifts. For detailed skiing information and instruction (downhill), contact the **Skischule Garmisch-Partenkirchen** (☎ 49 31; Am Hausberg 4), or (cross-country) the **Skilanglaufschule** (☎ 15 16; Olympia-Skistadion).

Places to Stay & Eat The closest camping ground, **Zugspitze** (☎ 31 80, fax 94 75 94; Greisener Strasse 4, Grainau; tent/ person/vehicle €3/5/3) is along highway B24. Take the blue-and-white bus (outside the train station and left across the street) towards Eibsee.

The **Youth Hostel** (☎ 29 80, fax 585 36; e jhgarmisch@djh-bayern.de; Jochstrasse 10; dorm beds €15.10), situated in the suburb of Burgrain, is closed from mid-November to Christmas. From the train station take bus No 3 or 4 to the Burgrain stop.

Sunny **Gästehaus Becherer** (☎ 547 57, fax 73 07 17; Hollentalstrasse 4; singles/doubles with bathroom & breakfast €29/46) offers a warm welcome and spotless comfort. Near the train station, **Hotel Schell** (☎ 95 750, fax 95 7540; e hotel-schell@hotel-schell.de; Partnachauenstrasse 3; singles/doubles from €23/ 46) is another good option. Neither will mind if you only stay one night.

Quality **Hotel Zugspitze** (☎ 90 10, fax 90 13 33; e info@hotel-zugspitze.de; Klammstrasse 19; singles from €72/97) has a lovely feel, and cosy timber-lined rooms.

Café Mukkefuck (☎ 73 440; Zugspitzstrasse 3; meals €6-12) has a double-take name, an outdoor courtyard and a tasty array of light meals. Work up your hunger with the hour's climb to **St Martin Am Grasberg** (☎ 49 70; Am Grasberg; mains €7-15), an eatery perched in the mountains northwest of the centre that boasts spectacular views.

Getting There & Away Garmisch is serviced from Munich by hourly trains (€14, 1½ hours). Trains from Garmisch to Innsbruck (1½ hours) pass through Mittenwald (€3.10, 20 minutes). RVO bus No 1084, from in front of the train station, links Garmisch with Füssen (€7, two hours) four times daily via Oberammergau. There is a daily bus to Oberstdorf (€16).

Mittenwald
☎ 08823 • pop 8500

Mittenwald is a less-hectic alternative to the nearby Garmisch-Partenkirchen. The **tourist office** (☎ 339 81; e kurvewaltung@mitten wald.de; Dammkarstrasse 3) is open 8am to noon and 1pm to 5pm weekdays, and 10am to noon on weekends.

Popular local hikes with cable-car access go to Wank (1780m), Mt Karwendel (2384m) and Wettersteinspitze (2297m). The Karwendel ski area has the longest run (7km) in Germany. Combined day ski passes covering the Karwendel and nearby Kranzberg ski areas cost €24. For ski hire and instruction, you should contact **Erste Skischule** (☎ 35 82; Bahnhofsplatz).

The closest camping ground is **Am Isarhorn** (☎ 52 16, fax 80 91; e camping@mitt enwald.de; Isarhorn 4; site/adult/car €4/ 4.50/6.70), 3km north of town off the B2 highway. The **Youth Hostel** (☎ 17 01, fax 29 07; e jhmittenwald@djh-bayern.de; Buck-elwiesen 7; beds €13.10) is in a beautiful, isolated spot, some 4km outside Mittenwald. There's no bus service and the walk takes about one hour.

Gästehaus Sonnenheim (☎ 82 47, fax 25 28; e sonnenheim@mittenwald.de; Damm-karstrasse 5; singles/doubles with bathroom & breakfast from €41.50/78) has classy rooms lined with honey-coloured timber. **Die Alpenrose** (☎ 92 700, fax 37 20; e alpen-rose.mittenwald@t-online.de; Obermarkt 1; basic singles €28, singles/doubles from €44/ 85) offers cramped but otherwise comfortable lodgings. There's a cosy restaurant downstairs with filling fare (mains €8 to €10) and live Bavarian music. **Hochland Restaurant-Café** (Albert-Schott-Strasse 5; mains €8-17) has an eat-on-the-street courtyard, and fresh fish and steak dishes.

For information on getting to/from Mitten-wald, see the earlier Garmisch-Partenkirchen entry.

Oberstdorf
☎ 08322 • pop 10,400

Over in the western part of the Bavarian Alps, Oberstdorf is a car-free resort. Like Garmisch, it is surrounded by towering peaks and offers superb hiking.

The main **tourist office** (☎ 70 00; e info@ oberstdorf.de; Marktplatz 7) is open from 8.30am to 6pm weekdays and 9.30am to noon Saturday. There's another office near the train station (☎ 70 02 17; Bahnhofplatz 3); both offer a convenient room-finding service.

For an exhilarating day **hike**, ride the Nebelhorn cable car to the upper station then walk down via the Gaisalpseen, two lovely alpine lakes. In-the-know skiers value Oberst-dorf for its friendliness, its lower prices and generally uncrowded pistes. The village is surrounded by several ski areas: the **Nebelhorn**, **Fellhorn/Kanzelwand** and **Söllereck**. Combined daily/weekly ski passes that include all three areas (plus the adjoining Kleinwalsertal lifts on the Austrian side) cost €30/160. For ski hire and tuition, try the Neue Skischule, which has convenient outlets at the valley stations of the Nebelhorn (☎ 27 37) and Söllereck (☎ 51 54) lifts.

Oberstdorf's barren **camping ground** (☎ 65 25, fax 80 97 60; e camping-oberstdorf@ t-online.de; Rubingerstrasse 16; tent/person/ car €2.60-4.60/4.60-5.10/2.60) is 2km north of the station beside the train line, and open all year. The **Youth Hostel** (☎ 22 25, fax 804 46; e jhoberstdorf@djh-bayern.de; Kornau 8; beds €14.10), sits on the outskirts of town near the Söllereck chairlift; take the Kleinwalsertal bus to the Reute stop.

Gästehaus Geiger (☎ 98 84 70, fax 804 98, e gabi_geiger@t-online.de; Am Frohmarkt 5; singles with breakfast €25/50) is small and friendly, with pleasant rooms. For the more indulgent, **Hotel Traube** (☎ 46 48, fax 31 68; e hotel-traube@hotel-traube.de; Haupt-strasse 6; singles/doubles from €66.50/122) has delightful rooms with four-poster beds and a large Bavarian-style restaurant downstairs (mains €10 to €20). **Paulaner Bräu** (☎ 96 760; Kirchstrasse 1; meals €7.50) has a similar menu, but is simpler and cheaper.

There are hourly RB trains to/from Immenstadt where you connect to Lindau (€13.50, two hours) and Munich (€24, 2½ hours; IR train). Direct RE trains to/from Ulm run hourly (€17.80, 1¾ hours). On weekdays, several bus connections to Füssen go via Pfronten (€8.10).

GERMANY

Baden-Württemberg

Baden-Württemberg is one of Germany's main tourist regions. With recreational centres such as the Black Forest and Lake Constance, medieval towns like Heidelberg and the health spa of Baden-Baden, it's one of the most varied parts of Germany.

The prosperous modern state of Baden-Württemberg was created in 1951 out of three smaller regions: Baden, Württemberg and Hohenzollern. Baden was first unified and made a grand duchy by Napoleon, who was also responsible for making Württemberg a kingdom in 1806. Both areas, in conjunction with Bavaria and 16 other states, formed the Confederation of the Rhine under French protection. Baden and Württemberg both sided with Austria against Prussia in 1866, but were ultimately drafted into the German Empire in 1871.

STUTTGART
☎ 0711 • pop 590,000

Stuttgart enjoys the status of being Baden-Württemberg's state capital and the hub of its industries. At the forefront of Germany's economic recovery from the ravages of WWII, Stuttgart started life less auspiciously in AD 950 as a horse stud farm. About 80% of the city centre was destroyed in the war, but there are still some fine historical buildings left, along with huge expanses of parkland, vine-covered hills and an air of relaxed prosperity.

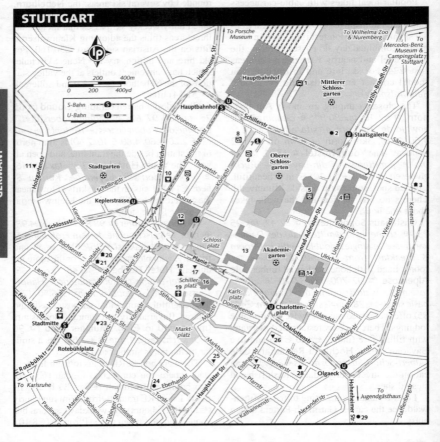

Information

The **tourist office** (☎ 22 280; e info@
stuttgart-tourist.de; Königstrasse 1a; open
9.30am-8.30pm Mon-Fri, 9.30am-6pm Sat,
10.30am-6pm Sun Mar-Oct, same hours
Nov-Apr except 1pm-6pm Sun) is opposite
the main train station and on the main pedestrian strip. Room reservations can be made
here for no fee. The office sells the three-day
StuttCard (€14), which allows free public
transport and free entry to some museums.

There's a main **post office** (Bolzstrasse 3).
You'll find a **Reisebank** at the main train station, and there's a convenient (if expensive)
laundry (Hohenheimer Strasse 33). **Surf Inn**
(Königstrasse 6), situated on the top floor of
the Kaufhof department store, charges €1.50
for 30 minutes on the Internet. **Cyberb@r**
(Königstrasse 27-29) in the Karstadt building
opposite, charges €2.50. **Netbox** (Lauten-
schlager Strasse 21) is free.

Things to See & Do

The tower at the main train station sports the
three-pointed star of the Mercedes-Benz.
It's also an excellent vantage point for the
sprawling city and surrounding hills, and is
reached via a lift (elevator; free; open 10am-
10pm Tues-Sun).

Stretching southwest from the Neckar River
to the city centre is the **Schlossgarten**, an
extensive strip of parkland divided into three
sections (Unterer, Mittlerer and Oberer), complete with ponds, swans, street entertainers and
modern sculptures. At their northern edge the
gardens take in the **Wilhelma** zoo and botanical gardens (☎ 540 20; Neckarstrasse;
adult/concession €9/4.50; open 8.15am-
6pm May-Aug, 8.15am-5.30pm Apr & Sept,
8.15am-5pm Mar & Oct, 8.15am-4pm Nov-
Feb). At their southern end they encompass the

sprawling baroque **Neues Schloss** and the Renaissance **Altes Schloss**, which houses a **regional museum** (☎ 279 34 00; Schillerplatz 6;
adult/concession €2.60/1.50; open 10am-
5pm Wed-Sun, 10am-1pm Tues).

Next to the Altes Schloss is the city's oldest
square, Schillerplatz, with its monument to the
poet **Schiller** and the 12th-century **Stiftkirche**.
Adjoining the park you'll find the **Staatsga-
lerie** (☎ 212 40 50; Konrad-Adenauer-Strasse
30; adult/concession €4.50/2.50; open
10am-6pm daily, 10am-9pm Thur) housing an
excellent collection from the Middle Ages to
the present.

Next door there's the **Haus der Geschichte**
(House of History; ☎ 212 39 50; Urbansplatz
2; admission €3), which opened in late 2002.
This ia an eye-catching post-modern museum
which covers the past 200 years of the Baden-
Württemburg area in film, photography, documents and multimedia.

In the Mittlerer Schlossgarten, is the **Carl
Zeiss Planetarium** (shows from 10am & 3pm
Tues-Fri, plus 8pm Wed & Fri, 2pm, 4pm &
6pm Sat & Sun; adult/concession €5/3).

Motor Museums The motor car was first
developed by Gottlieb Daimler and Carl
Benz at the end of the 19th century. The impressive **Mercedes-Benz Museum** (☎ 172
25 78; Mercedesstrasse 137; admission free;
open 9am-5pm Tues-Sun) is in the suburb of
Bad-Cannstatt; take S-Bahn No 1 to Neckar-
stadion. Mercedes-Benz also runs free weekday tours of its Sindelfingen plant, but you
must reserve a spot in advance (☎ 07031-907
04 03; children under 6 not allowed). For
even faster cars, cruise over to the **Porsche
Museum** (☎ 911 56 85; Porschestrasse 42;
admission free; open 9am-4pm Mon-Fri,
9am-5pm Sat & Sun); take S-Bahn No 6 to

STUTTGART

PLACES TO STAY		26	Zur Kiste	9	Netbox
3	DJH Youth Hostel	27	Bovie	10	Palast de Republic
20	Museumstube			12	Main Post Office
21	Gasthof Alte Mira	**OTHER**		13	Neues Schloss
28	Der Zauberlehrling	1	Bus Station	14	Haus der
		2	Carl Zeiss		Geschichte
PLACES TO EAT			Planetarium	16	Altes Schloss
11	University Mensa	4	Staatsgalerie	18	Schiller Statue
15	Markthalle	5	Staatstheater	19	Stiftkirche
17	Alte Kanzlei	6	Cyberb@r; Karstadt	22	Bar Code
23	Calwer Eck Bräu	7	Tourist Office	24	Hans-im-Glück Platz
25	iden	8	Surf Inn; Kaufhof	29	Laundrette

GERMANY

Neuwirtshaus. Sadly, neither place offers free samples.

Places to Stay

You can camp at **Campingplatz Stuttgart** (☎ 55 66 96, fax 55 74 54; e info@camping platz-stuttgart.de; Mercedesstrasse 40; site/ person €4.10/4.60), beside the river and 500m from the Bad Cannstatt S-Bahn station. It's a steep climb to the **DJH Hostel** (☎ 24 15 83, fax 236 10 41; e info@jugendherberge -stuttgart.de; Haussmannstrasse 27; juniors/ seniors €13.35/16.05), which is a signposted 15-minute walk from the train station.

You might prefer the spacious, bright non-DJH **Jugengästehaus** (☎ 24 11 32, fax 236 11 10; e JGH.Stuttgart@internationaler -bund.de; Richard-Wagner-Strasse 2; singles/ doubles/triples €21/36/48). Take the U15 to Bubenbad.

Gasthof Alte Mira (☎ 222 95 02, fax 222 95 03 29; e altemira@web.de; Büchenstrasse 24; singles/doubles from €31/52) offers clean, simple rooms with shared facilities. Around the corner, **Museumstube** (☎/fax 29 68 10; Hospitalstrasse 9; singles/doubles €32/50) offers similar lodgings.

For a splurge, don't go anywhere but **Der Zauberlehrling** (☎ 237 77 70, fax 237 77 75; e contact@zauberlehrling.de; Rosenstrasse 38; singles/doubles without breakfast from €117/200). This innovative place has nine distinctly different thematic rooms that marry ultra-contemporary design with tasteful old-fashioned touches.

Places to Eat

Pack a picnic at the **Markthalle** (Dorotheen-strasse 4; open 7am-6.30pm Mon-Fri, 7am-4pm Sat), an excellent Art Nouveau-style market that's jam-packed with fresh fare. Alternatively, fill up for around €2.50 at the university **Mensa** (Holzgartenstrasse 11), which has a downstairs cafeteria for the un-educated masses. Vegetarians (and those who have overdosed on German sausages) can try **iden** (Eberhardtsrasse 1), which serves cheap, self-serve salad (€1.50), 100g of vegetarian lasagne (€1.50) and soup (€2.50).

Alte Kanzlei (☎ 29 44 57; Schillerplatz 5b; dishes €6-10) is excellent for a sunny lunch, with pastas, wraps and salads.

Stuttgart is a great place to sample Swabian specialities such as Spätzle (like doughy pasta) and Maultaschen (similar to ravioli).

The best spot is cosy **Zur Kiste** (☎ 24 40 02; Kanalstrasse 2; mains €8-15) in the Bohnen-viertel (Bean Quarter). This is Stuttgart's old-est restaurant and its delicious menu really packs 'em in. Two blocks down **Bovie** (☎ 23 37 78; Eslinger Strasse 8; €9-16) is friendly and casual, and provides an inspiring inter-national selection with Swabian influences. **Calwer Eck Bräu** (☎ 22 24 94 40; Calwer-strasse 31; mains €9-12) brews its own beer, and serves top-notch regional fare.

Entertainment

Lift Stuttgart is a comprehensive guide to local entertainment and events (€1).

Home of the famous Stuttgart Ballet, the **Staatstheater** (☎ 20 20 90; Oberer Schloss-garten 6) holds regular symphony, ballet and opera performances.

The grandly-named **Palast de Republic** (Friedrichstrasse 27), is a tiny bar that pulls a huge crowd of laid-back footpath drinkers. There are several funky drinking holes around Hans-im-Glück-Platz, a small square that's often packed with party-goers. Nearby, **Bar Code** (Theodore-Heuss-Strasse 30) is a cool modern bar with a young crowd. For leafy fun, there's a **beer garden** in the Mit-tlerer Schlossgarten, northeast of the main train station.

Getting There & Around

Stuttgart's international airport is south of the city and is served by S2 and S3 trains (30 min-utes from the main train station). There are frequent train departures for all major German and many international cities. ICE trains run to Frankfurt (€45.20, 1½ hours), Berlin (€127.00, 5½ hours) and Munich (€44.60, two hours). Regional and long-distance buses leave from the station next to the main train station.

One-way fares on Stuttgart's public trans-port network are €1.10/5.30 for short/long trips. A four-ride strip ticket costs €5.80 and a central zone day pass is €4.70.

AROUND STUTTGART
Tübingen
☎ 07071 • pop 8000

This gentle, picturesque university town is a perfect place to spend a day wandering wind-ing alleys and enjoying the views of half-timbered houses and old stone walls. On **Marktplatz**, the centre of town, is the 1435

Rathaus with its ornate baroque facade and astronomical clock. The nearby late-Gothic **Stiftkirche** *(Am Holz-markt)* houses the tombs of the Württemberg dukes and has excellent medieval stained-glass windows. From the heights of the Renaissance **Schloss Hohentübingen** *(Burgsteig 11)*, now part of the university, there are fine views over the steep, red-tiled rooftops of the old town. The **tourist office** *(☎ 913 60; e mail@tuebingen-info.de; An der Neckarbrücke; open 9am-7pm Mon-Fri, 9am-5pm Sat all year & 2pm-5pm Sun May-Sept)* is beside the bridge.

The **DJH hostel** *(☎ 230 02, fax 250 61; Gartenstrasse 22/2; juniors/seniors €14.90/ 17.60)* has a delightful location by the river. Attractive **Hotel Am Schloss** *(☎ 929 40, fax 92 94 10; e info@hotelamschloss.de; Burgsteige 18; singles/doubles with breakfast €51/76)* has simple and pleasant rooms. Its restaurant, *Maultaschen*, is a local institution. **Al Dente Spaghetteria** *(☎ 251 57; Clinicumsgasse 20; dishes €6-10)* serves superb pasta in a sunny little nook.

There are regular RE trains between Tübingen and Stuttgart (€9; one hour).

HEIDELBERG
☎ 06221 • 140,000

The French destroyed Heidelberg in 1693; they may have been the last visitors to dislike this charming town on the Neckar River. Its magnificent castle and medieval town are irresistible drawcards for most travellers in Germany. Mark Twain began his European travels here and recounted his comical observations in *A Tramp Abroad*. Britain's JMW Turner loved Heidelberg and it inspired him to produce some of his finest landscape paintings.

Heidelberg's sizable student population (attending the oldest university in the country) makes it a lively city. But be warned; this place is chock-a-block with tourists during July and August, so try to avoid coming then or you might start to empathise with the French...

Orientation & Information
Heidelberg's captivating old town starts to reveal itself about a 15-minute walk west of the main train station, along the Kurfürsten-Anlage. Hauptstrasse is the pedestrian way leading eastwards through the heart of the Altstadt from Bismarckplatz via Marktplatz to Karlstor.

The main **tourist office** *(☎ 194 33; e cvb@ heidelberg.de; Willy-Brandt-Platz 1; open 9am-7pm Mon-Sat all year plus 10am-6pm Sun Apr-Nov)* is outside the train station. There are smaller, independent offices at the funicular train station near the castle and on Neckarmünzplatz that keep reduced hours. The €12 Heidelberg Card offers unlimited public transport and free admission to many sights.

There's a post office branch to the right as you leave the train station – the main office is on Sophienstrasse near the Altstadt. You'll find a **Reisebank** in the train station. **Office Shop GmbH** *(Plock 85)* charges €1.30 for 15 minutes on the Internet. **Waschsalon Wojtala** *(Kettergasse 17)* is a convenient, if expensive, laundry, charging €8 to wash and dry. **Schnell & Sauber Waschcenter** *(Poststrasse 44)* charges €3.50 per wash.

Things to See & Do
Heidelberg's imposing **Schloss** *(☎ 53 84 14; admission free to grounds, adult/concession €2/1 to castle; open 8am-5.30pm daily)* is one of Germany's finest examples of grand Gothic-Renaissance architecture. The building's half-ruined state actually adds to its romantic appeal. Seen from anywhere in the Altstadt, this striking red-sandstone castle dominates the hillside. The entry fee covers the castle, the **Grosses Fass** (Great Vat), an enormous 18th-century keg capable of holding 221,726L, and **Deutsches Apothekenmuseum** (German Pharmaceutical Museum).

You can take the funicular railway to the castle from lower Kornmarkt station *(adult/ concession €3/2 return)*, or enjoy an invigorating 10-minute walk up steep, stone-laid lanes. The funicular continues up to the **Königstuhl**, where there's a TV and lookout tower *(adult/concession €5.10/3.60 return, including a castle stop)*.

Dominating Universitätsplatz are the 18th-century **Alte Universität** and the **Neue Universität**. Nearby there's the **Studentenkarzer** *(student jail; ☎ 54 21 63; Augustinergasse 2; adult/concession €2.50/2; open 10am-noon & 2pm-5pm Tues-Sat Apr-Oct, 10am-2pm Tues-Fri Nov-Mar)*. From 1778 to 1914 this jail was used for uproarious students. Sentences (usually two to 10 days) were earned for heinous crimes such as drinking, singing and womanising (no word as to whether 'manising' was *verboten*). The **Marstall** is the

GERMANY

GERMANY

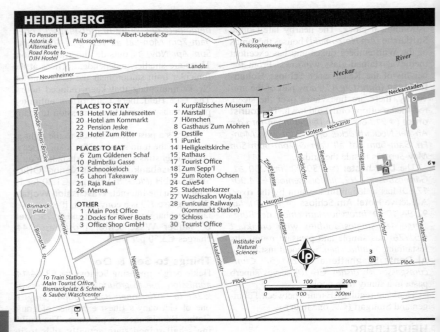

HEIDELBERG

PLACES TO STAY
13 Hotel Vier Jahreszeiten
20 Hotel am Kornmarkt
22 Pension Jeske
23 Hotel Zum Ritter

PLACES TO EAT
6 Zum Güldenen Schaf
10 Palmbräu Gasse
12 Schnookeloch
16 Lahori Takeaway
21 Raja Rani
26 Mensa

OTHER
1 Main Post Office
2 Docks for River Boats
3 Office Shop GmbH
4 Kurpfälzisches Museum
5 Marstall
7 Hörnchen
8 Gasthaus Zum Mohren
9 Destille
11 iPunkt
14 Heiligkeitskirche
15 Rathaus
17 Tourist Office
18 Zum Sepp'l
19 Zum Roten Ochsen
24 Cave54
25 Studentenkarzer
27 Waschsalon Wojtala
28 Funicular Railway
    (Kornmarkt Station)
29 Schloss
30 Tourist Office

former arsenal, now a student mensa. The **Kurpfälzisches Museum** (Palatinate Museum; ☎ 58 34 02; Hauptstrasse 97; adult/concession €2.50/1.50; open 10am-5pm Tues-Sun, 10am-9pm Wed) contains paintings, sculptures and the jawbone of the 600,000-year-old Heidelberg Man.

A stroll along the **Philosophenweg**, north of the Neckar River, gives a welcome respite from Heidelberg's tourist hordes.

Places to Stay

Finding any accommodation in Heidelberg's high season can be difficult. Arrive early in the day or book ahead.

Camping Haide (☎ 21 11, fax 71 959; Ziegelhäuser Landstrasse, Haide; site/person €3/4.60) is in a pretty spot on the river. Take bus No 35 to Orthopädische Klinik. The local **DJH hostel** (☎ 41 20 66, fax 40 25 59; e jh-heidelberg@t-online.de; Tiergartenstrasse 5; juniors/seniors €13.35/16.05) is across the river from the train station. From the station or Bismarckplatz, take bus No 33 towards Ziegelhausen.

Labyrinthine backpacker favourite **Pension Jeske** (☎ 237 33, fax 65 91 23; Mittelbadgasse 2; dorm beds €20, doubles from €50) has new owners, beds and bathrooms, but is still the cheapest in the Altstadt. Quaint, friendly **Pension Astoria** (☎ 40 29 29; Rahmengasse 30; singles/doubles from €40/65) has comfy rooms with character. It's north of the river, across Theodor-Heuss-Brücke.

Amiable **Hotel am Kornmarkt** (☎ 243 25, fax 282 18; Kornmarkt 7; singles/doubles without bathroom €50/98) has pleasant, spacious rooms and a superb breakfast buffet. There are newly renovated lodgings at **Hotel Vier Jahreszeiten** (☎ 241 64, fax 16 31 10; e info@4-jahreszeiten.de; Haspelgasse 2; singles/doubles from €80/100), where the great Goethe himself reputedly once slumbered.

The ornate **Hotel Zum Ritter** (☎ 13 50, fax 13 52 30; e info@ritter-heidelberg.de; Hauptstrasse 178; singles/doubles €92/155) is close to the cathedral, and provides grand accommodation.

Places to Eat

The **Mensa** (Univsersitätsplatz; meals for students/guests €2/3) has budget feeds whether you're the studious type or not. There are two decent, cheap Indian takeaways in the

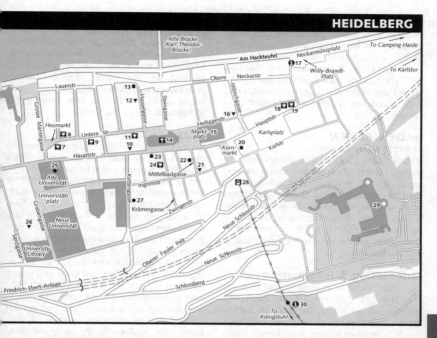

HEIDELBERG

Altstadt: **Raja Rani** *(Mittelbadgasse 5)* and **Lahori** *(Heiliggeistrasse 9a)*. Both sell curries, tandoori and other spicy favourites from around €3.

You can grab a feed at many student pubs (see Entertainment later) for around €8. In a dimly-lit stone tunnel adorned with blackened wood and heavy chains, medieval **Palmbräu Gasse** *(☎ 285 36; Hauptstrasse 185; mains €8-16)* wins hands down for atmosphere, service and food. Dialect for 'mosquito hole', **Schnookeloch** *(☎ 13 80 80; Haspelgasse 8; mains €7-20)* defies its name, with an inviting and insect-free atmosphere and a good German/Italian menu. **Zum Güldenen Schaf** *(☎ 208 79; Hauptstrasse 115; lunch €7-17, dinner €14-23)* is pricey, however, the spread is great.

Entertainment

This being a university town, you won't have to go far to find a happening backstreet bar. Tiny **Hörnchen** *(Heumarkt)* is the perfect place to start an evening out; it's laid-back, intimate and friendly. In contrast, nearby **Gasthaus Zum Mohren** *(Untere Strasse 5-7)* is loud, proud and crowded – watch for presumptuous,

tip-hungry bar staff. At the **Destille** *(Untere Strasse 16)*, there's an eclectic mix of loud chat, louder music and board games. Also popular is modern **iPunkt** *(Untere Strasse 30)*. Heidelberg's famous historic student pubs **Zum Roten Oschen** *(Hauptstrasse 213)* and **Zum Sepp'l** *(Hauptstrasse 217)* don't get much more than a tourist trade these days.

For live jazz and blues, head to **Cave54** *(Krämergasse 2)*, an underground stone cellar that oozes character, and once hosted Louis Armstrong. It's big on Thursday, Friday and Saturday.

Getting There & Around

Heidelberg is on the Castle Road route from Mannheim to Nuremberg. From mid-May until the end of September Deutsche-Touring has a daily coach service, with one bus in either direction between Heidelberg and Rothenburg ob der Tauber (€29, five hours); contact **Deutsche-Touring GmbH** *(☎ 089-59 38 89, fax 550 39 65;* e *service@deutsche -touring.com; Am Römerhof 17, 60486 Frankfurt/Main)*.

There are hourly ICE/IC trains which operate to/from Frankfurt (€22.80, one hour),

Stuttgart (€19.60, 40 minutes) and Munich (€53.40, three hours). Mannheim, 12 minutes to the west by frequent trains, has connections to cities throughout Germany.

Bismarckplatz is the main local transport hub. The bus and tram system in and around Heidelberg is extensive and efficient. One-way tickets are €1.80 and a 24-hour pass costs €5.90.

BADEN-BADEN
☎ 07221 • pop 50,000

Baden-Baden's natural hot springs have attracted visitors since Roman times, but this small city only really became fashionable in the 19th century when the likes of Victor Hugo came to bathe in and imbibe its therapeutic waters. Today Baden-Baden is Germany's premier (and ritziest) health spa and offers many other salubrious activities in a friendly and relaxed atmosphere.

Orientation & Information

The train station is 7km northwest of town. Bus Nos 201, 205 and 216 run frequently to/from Leopoldsplatz, the heart of Baden-Baden. From here, Sophienstrasse leads eastwards to the more historic part of town. North of Sophienstrasse are the baths, the Stiftskirche and the Neues Schloss. Across the river to the west you will find the Trinkhalle (pump room) and the tourist office, and past Goetheplatz both the Kurhaus and Spielhalle (casino).

The tourist office (☎ 27 52 00; e info@ baden-baden.com; Kaiserallee 3; open 10am-5pm Mon-Sat, 2pm-5pm Sun) is in the Trinkhalle; collect some information and sample the local drop. There is a spa *Kurtaxe* (visitors' tax) of €2.50, entitling you to a *Kurkarte* from your hotel that brings various discounts. The tax doesn't apply to those staying at the hostel.

Things to See & Do

The ancient **Römische Badruinen** (*Roman Bath Ruins; Römerplatz 1; admission free*) are worth a quick look, but for a real taste of Baden-Baden head for the ornate and grand **Trinkhalle** (*Kaiserallee 3*). You can have a free drink of the spa water piped in hot from the ground. Next door is the 1820s **Kurhaus**, which houses the opulent **casino** (☎ 210 60; *Kaiserallee 1; guided tours adult/child €4/2; tours 9.30am-noon daily*) where Dostoyevsky

was inspired to write *The Gambler*. Call ahead to arrange a tour in English.

The **Merkur Cable Car** (*€4; open 10am-10pm daily*) takes you up to the 660m summit, where there are fine views and numerous walking trails (bus No 204 or 205 from Leopoldplatz takes you to the cable-car station). A good hiking-driving tour is to the wine-growing area of **Rebland**, 6km to the west.

Spas

On either side of Römerplatz are the two places where you can take the waters. Don't leave town without a visit to one or both.

The 19th-century **Friedrichsbad** (☎ 27 59 20; *Römerplatz 1; bathing programme €21; open 9am-10pm Mon-Sat, noon-8pm Sun*) is decadently Roman in style and provides a muscle-melting Roman-Irish bathing programme. Your three hours of humid bliss comprises 16 steps of hot and cold baths, saunas, steam rooms and showers that leave you feeling scrubbed, sparkling and loose as a goose. An extra €8 gets you a soap-and-brush massage covering almost every nook and cranny. No clothing is allowed inside, and several bathing sections are mixed on most days, so leave your modesty at the reception desk. Modern **Caracalla-Therme** (☎ 27 59 40; *Römerplatz 11; €11 for 2hr; open 8am-10pm*) is a vast complex of outdoor and indoor pools, hot and cold-water grottoes and many more delights. You must wear a bathing costume and bring your own towel.

Places to Stay & Eat

The closest camping ground is **Campingplatz Adam** (☎ 07223-231 94; *Campingplatzstrasse 1, Bühl-Oberbruch; tent/person €8/6.50*) about 12km outside town.

Baden-Baden's **DJH hostel** (☎ 522 23, fax 600 12; e info@jugend herberge-baden-bad en.de; Hardbergstrasse 34; juniors/seniors €13.35/16.05) is situated 3km northwest of the centre; take bus No 201 to Grosse Dollenstrasse then walk for 10 minutes.

The tourist office has a free room reservation service.

Central **Hotel Zur Altstadt** (☎ 30 22 80, fax 302 28 28; *Baldreitstrasse 1; singles/doubles with bathroom from €34/64*) is a good deal, with rooms that are both pleasant and ample.

Lovely **Holland Hotel Sophienpark** (☎ 35 60, fax 35 61 21; e info@holland-hotel-so phienpark.de; Sophienstrasse 14; singles/

doubles from €110/165) has its own park, and bright and sunny rooms with a touch of luxury.

For a light bite, head to **Leo's** (*☎ 380 81; Luisenstrasse 8; meals €8)*, a trendy spot with outdoor tables as well as tasty, well-presented dishes. Ambient **Rathausglöckl** (*☎ 906 10; Steinstrasse 7; mains €8-17)* serves excellent regional fare in a historic setting.

Getting There & Away

Baden-Baden is on the busy Mannheim-Basel train line. Fast trains in either direction stop every two hours. Frequent local trains serve both Karlsruhe and Offenburg, from where you can make connections to much of Germany.

BLACK FOREST

Home of the cuckoo clock, the Black Forest (Schwarzwald) gets its name from the dark canopy of evergreens. The fictional Hansel and Gretel encountered their wicked witch in these parts, but modern-day hazards are more likely to include packs of tourists piling out of buses. However, a 20-minute walk from even the most crowded spots will put you in quiet countryside dotted with huge traditional farmhouses and patrolled by amiable dairy cows.

Orientation & Information

The Black Forest is east of the Rhine between Karlsruhe and Basel. It's roughly triangular in shape, about 160km long and 50km wide. Baden-Baden, Freudenstadt, Titisee and Freiburg act as convenient information posts for Black Forest excursions. Even smaller towns in the area generally have tourist offices.

Freudenstadt is a good place for information on the northern section. Its **tourist office** (*☎ 07441-86 40;* e *touristinfo@freudenstadt .de; open 9am-6pm Mon-Fri, 10am-2pm Sat & Sun Mar-Nov, 10am-5pm Mon-Fri, 10am-1pm Sat & Sun Dec-Feb)* is on Am Marktplatz. Titisee's **tourist office** (*☎ 07651-980 40;* e *touristinfo@titisee.de; Strandbadstrasse 4; open 8am-noon & 1.30pm-5.30pm Mon-Fri all year, 10am-noon Sat & Sun May-Oct)*, situated inside the Kurhaus, also covers the southern Black Forest. The Feldberg **tourist office** (*☎ 07655-80 19;* e *tourist-info@ feldbergschwarzwald.de; Kirchgasse 1; open 8am-5.30pm Mon-Fri all year & Sat Jun-Sept, Sun July-Aug)* also supplies ski information.

Things to See

Enjoying the natural countryside will be the main focus, although you can take a plunge in a lake or down a ski slope, or lose yourself in shops full of cuckoo clocks.

Roughly halfway between Baden-Baden and Freudenstadt – along the Schwarzwald-Hochstrasse (Black Forest Highway) – the first major tourist sight is the **Mummelsee**, south of the Hornisgrinde peak. It's a small and deep lake steeped in folklore (legend says an evil sea king inhabits the depths).

Farther south, **Freudenstadt** is mainly used as a base for excursions into the countryside, however the central marketplace, the largest in Germany, is worth a look.

The area between Freudenstadt and Freiburg is cuckoo-clock country, a name that takes on new meaning when you see the prices people are willing to pay. A few popular stops are **Schramberg**, **Triberg** and **Furtwangen**. In Furtwangen, visit the **Deutsches Uhrenmuseum** (*German Clock Museum; ☎ 07723-92 01 17; Gerwigstrasse 11; adult/concession €3/2.50; open 9am-6pm daily, 10am-6pm Nov-Mar)* for a look at the traditional Black Forest skill of clock-making.

Titisee boasts its namesake natural lake where you can take a soothing **cruise** (*€4; 25min)* or rent a boat in summer. The engines are all electric to preserve the lake's serenity.

Activities

Summer With more than 7000km of marked trails, the possibilities are, almost literally, endless. Hiking maps are everywhere and any tourist office can set you off on anything from easy one-hour jaunts to multiday treks. Three classic long-distance **hiking trails** run south from the northern Black Forest city of Pforzheim as far as the Swiss Rhine: the 280km Westweg to Basel; the 230km Mittelweg to Waldhut-Tiengen; and the 240km Ostweg to Schaffhausen.

The southern Black Forest, especially the area around the 1493m Feldberg summit, offers some of the best hiking; small towns like Todtmoos or Bonndorf serve as useful bases for those wanting to get off the more heavily trodden trails. The 10km **Wutachschlucht** (Wutach Gorge) outside Bonndorf is justifiably famous. You can also try windsurfing, boating or swimming on the highland lakes, though some may find the water a bit cool. Titisee boasts several beaches.

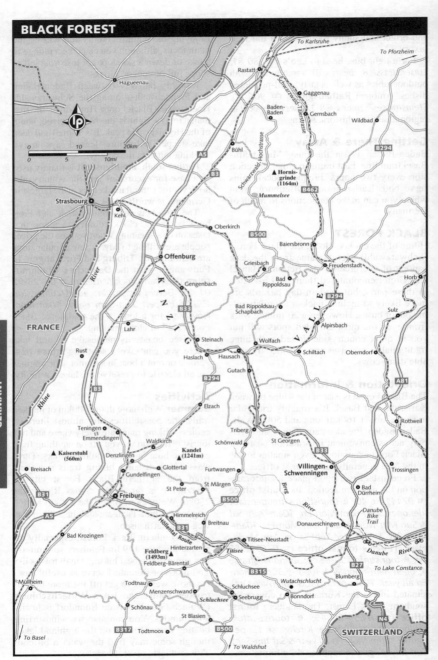

BLACK FOREST

To Karlsruhe

To Pforzheim

Hagueenau

Rastatt

Schwarzwald-Talstrasse

Gaggenau

Baden-Baden

Gernsbach

Wildbad

B294

Bühl

Schwarzwald-Hochstrasse

Hornis-
grinde
(1164m)

B462

Mummelsee

Strasbourg

Kehl

Oberkirch

B500

Baiersbronn

Offenburg

Griesbach

Bad
Rippoldsau

Freudenstadt

Horb

K I N Z I G

Gengenbach

Bad Rippoldsau-
Schapbach

B294

Sulz

FRANCE

Lahr

Rust

Steinach

Wolfach

V A L L E Y

Alpirsbach

Schiltach

Oberndorf

River Rhine

Haslach

Hausach

Gutach

B294

Elzach

A81

Rottweil

Teningen

Emmendingen

Waldkirch

Triberg

Schönwald

St Georgen

B33

Kaiserstuhl
(560m)

Denzlingen

Kandel
(1241m)

Furtwangen

Villingen-
Schwenningen

Trossingen

Breisach

Glottertal

Gundelfingen

St Märgen

St Peter

Breg River

Bad
Dürrheim

Freiburg

B500

B31

Himmelreich

Breitnau

Donaueschingen

Danube
Bike
Trail

B31

Höllental
Route

Danube River

Bad Krozingen

Feldberg
(1493m)

Hinterzarten

Titisee-Neustadt

Titisee

B27

To Lake Constance

Feldberg-Bärental

Müllheim

B315

Wutachschlucht

Blumberg

Todtnau

Menzenschwand

Schluchsee

Seebrugg

Bonndorf

N4

Schönau

Schluchsee

St Blasien

B500

SWITZERLAND

Todtmoos

Schönau

B317

Todtmoos

To Basel

To Waldshut

0   10   20km
0   5   10mi

GERMANY

Winter The Black Forest ski season runs from late December to March. While there is some good downhill skiing, the Black Forest is more suited to cross-country skiing. The Titisee area is the main centre for winter sports, with uncrowded downhill runs at **Feldberg** (day passes €20; rental equipment available) and numerous graded cross-country trails. In midwinter, ice skating is also possible on the Titisee and the Schluchsee. For winter sports information, check with the Feldberg or Titisee tourist offices.

Places to Stay

Away from the major towns you can find scores of simple guesthouses where the rates are cheap and the welcome warm. The Black Forest is also good for longer stays, with holiday apartments and private rooms available in almost every town.

Camping It's only natural that a forest would have plenty of excellent camping. Facilities include **Campingplatz Wolfsgrund** (☎ 07656-573; site/person €5-6/4.25-4.75) on the Schluchsee and **Terrassencamping Sandbank** (☎ 07651-82 43, fax 82 86; Seerundweg; site/person €5-6.50/3.25-4.25), one of four camping grounds on the Titisee.

Hostels The DJH net is extensive in the southern Black Forest but limited in the north. Some convenient hostels are in: **Freudenstadt** (☎ 07441-77 20; e info@jugendher berge-freudenstadt.de; Eugen-Nägele-Strasse 69); **Triberg** (☎ 07722-41 10; e info@ju gendherberge-triberg.de; Rohrbacher Strasse 3); and **Zuflucht** (☎ 07804-611; e info@ju gendherberge-zuflucht.de; Schwarzwaldhoch strasse). All of them charge €13.35/16.05 for juniors/seniors.

Hotels & Pensions Lodges may outnumber cows (but not cuckoo clocks) in the Black Forest and there are some good deals for basic rooms. Tourist offices can also direct you to private rooms from about €16 per person.

In Freudenstadt there's **Gasthof Pension Traube** (☎ 07441-91 74 50, fax 853 28; Markt 41; singles/doubles €30/57), with simple rooms.

Triberg's attractive **Hotel Pfaff** (☎ 07722-44 79, fax 78 97; e hotel-pfaff-triberg@t-on line.de; Hauptstrasse 85; singles/doubles with bathroom €38/66) offers comfortable

lodgings near the waterfall. At Titisee, **Hotel Sonneneck** (☎ 07651-82 46, fax 881 74; Parkstrasse 2; singles/doubles €44/88) provides spacious comfort as well as an excellent restaurant downstairs. In neighbouring Neustadt, **Hotel Adler-Post** (☎ 07651-50 66, fax 37 29; Hauptstrasse 16; singles/doubles from €49/83) has charming rooms furnished in period style; the price includes use of the luxurious indoor pool, sauna and solarium.

Berggasthof Wasmer (☎ 07676-230, fax 430; An der Wiesenquelle 1; singles/doubles from €23/46) in Feldberg offers small, comfortable timber-lined rooms.

Places to Eat

Regional specialities include *Schwarzwälder schinken* (ham), which is smoked and served in a variety of ways. Rivalling those ubiquitous clocks in fame (but not price), *Schwarz wälderkirschtorte* (Black Forest cake) is a chocolate and cherry concoction. Restaurants are often expensive, therefore a picnic in the woods makes both fiscal and scenic sense. Most hotels and guesthouses have restaurants serving traditional hearty German fare.

Getting There & Away

The Mannheim to Basel train line has numerous branches that serve the Black Forest. Trains for Freudenstadt and the north leave from Karlsruhe. Triberg is on the busy line linking Offenburg and Constance. Titisee has frequent services from Freiburg with some trains continuing to Feldberg and others to Neustadt, where there are connections to Donaueschingen.

Getting Around

The rail network is extensive and where trains don't go, buses do. However travel times can be slow and service infrequent, so check the schedules at bus stops, which are usually located outside train stations, or consult with the tourist offices. There's a variety of group and multiday deals valid on trains and buses and sold from ticket machines at the stations.

To reach Feldberg, take one of the frequent buses from the train stations in Titisee or Bärental.

Drivers will enjoy flexibility in an area that really rewards it. The main tourist road is the Schwarzwald-Hochstrasse (B500), which runs from Baden-Baden to Freudenstadt and from Triberg to Waldshut. Other thematic roads

GERMANY

with maps provided by tourist offices include Schwarzwald-Bäderstrasse (spa town route), Schwarzwald-Panoramastrasse (panoramic view route) and Badische Weinstrasse (wine route).

FREIBURG
☎ 0761 • pop 200,500

The gateway to the southern Black Forest, Freiburg im Breisgau is a fun place, thanks to the city's large and thriving university community. Ruled for centuries by the Austrian Habsburgs, Freiburg has retained many traditional features, although major reconstruction was necessary following severe bombing damage during WWII. The monumental 13th-century cathedral is the city's key landmark but the real attractions are the vibrant cafés, bars and street-life, plus the local wines. The best times for tasting are early July for the four days of *Weinfest* (Wine Festival), or early August for the nine days of *Weinkost* (loosely meaning 'wine as food').

Orientation & Information

The city centre is a convenient 10-minute walk from the train station. Walk east along Eisenbahnstrasse to the tourist office, then continue through the bustling pedestrian zone to Münsterplatz, dominated by the red stone cathedral.

The **tourist office** (☎ 388 18 80; e *tourist ik@fwt-online.de; Rotteckring 14; open 9.30am-8pm Mon-Fri, 9.30am-5pm Sat, 10am-noon Sun May-Oct & 9.30am-6pm Mon-Fri, 9.30am-2pm Sat, 10am-noon Sun Nov-Apr*) has piles of information on the Black Forest.

The main post office is at Eisenbahnstrasse 58–62, while Volksbank Freiburg is opposite the train station. The **PingWing Internet Center** (*Niemensstrasse 3*) is pretty central and charges €1.20 per 15 minutes. **Wash & Tours** (*Salzstrasse 22; wash €3*) is a combined laundry and Internet café.

Things to See & Do

The major sight in Freiburg is the 700-year-old **Münster** (*Cathedral; Münsterplatz; steeple adult/child €1.30/0.80; open 9.30am-5pm Mon-Sat, 1pm-5pm Sun Easter-Oct & 10am-4pm Tues-Sat, 1pm-5pm Sun Nov-Easter*), a classic example of both high and late-Gothic architecture which looms over Münsterplatz,

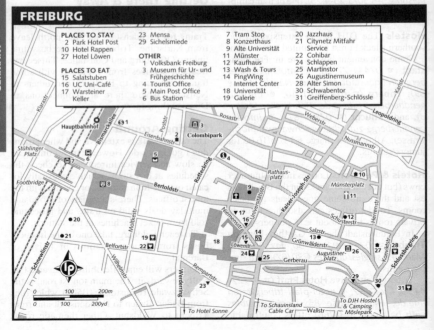

FREIBURG

PLACES TO STAY
2 Park Hotel Post
10 Hotel Rappen
27 Hotel Löwen

PLACES TO EAT
15 Salatstuben
16 UC Uni-Café
17 Warsteiner Keller
23 Mensa
29 Sichelsmiede

OTHER
1 Volksbank Freiburg
3 Museum für Ur- und Frühgeschichte
4 Tourist Office
5 Main Post Office
6 Bus Station
7 Tram Stop
8 Konzerthaus
9 Alte Universität
11 Münster
12 Kaufhaus
13 Wash & Tours
14 PingWing Internet Center
18 Universität
19 Galerie
20 Jazzhaus
21 Citynetz Mitfahr Service
22 Cohibar
24 Schlappen
25 Martinstor
26 Augustinermuseum
28 Alter Simon
30 Schwabentor
31 Greiffenberg-Schlössle

Freiburg's market square. Check out the stone and wood carvings, the stained-glass windows and the western porch. Ascend the tower to the stunning pierced spire for great views of Freiburg and, on a clear day, the Kaiserstuhl and the Vosges. South of the Münster stands the picturesque **Kaufhaus**, the 16th-century merchants' hall.

The bustling **university quarter** is northwest of the Martinstor (one of the old city gates).

Freiburg's main museum, the **Augustinermuseum** (☎ 201 25 31; Salzstrasse 32; adult/concession €2/1; open 10am-5pm Tues-Sun) has a fine collection of medieval art. The **Museum für Ur- und Frühgeschichte** (Museum of Pre- & Early History; ☎ 201 25 71; Rotteckring 5; admission free; open 10am-5pm Tues-Sun) is in Columbipark; it has, among other things, lots of pots.

The popular trip by cable car to the 1286m **Schauinsland** peak is a quick way to reach the Black Forest highlands (one way/return €6.60/10.20, concession €3.60/5.60; open 9am-5pm daily). Numerous easy and well-marked trails make the Schauinsland area ideal for day walks. From Freiburg take tram No 4 south to Günterstal and then bus No 21 to Talstation. The five-hour hike from Schauinsland to the Untermünstertal offers some of the best views with the fewest people; return to Freiburg via the train to Staufen and then take the bus.

Places to Stay

Pleasant **Camping Möslepark** (☎ 729 38, fax 775 78; e campingfreizeit@aol.com; Waldseestrasse 77; tent/person €2.10-2.60/5) is open all year. Take tram No 1 to Stadthalle (direction: Littenweiler), turn right under the road, go over the train tracks and follow the bike path. The modern **DJH Hostel** (☎ 675 65, fax 603 67; e jh-freiburg@t-online.de; Karthäuserstrasse 151; juniors/seniors €14.90/17.60) isn't very convenient. Take tram No 1 to Römerhof (direction: Littenweiler) then follow the signs down Fritz-Geiges-Strasse.

A 10-minute walk south of the centre, friendly **Hotel Sonne** (☎ 40 30 48, fax 409 88 56; Basler Strasse 58; singles/doubles €35/52) has decent, simple rooms and a magnificent breakfast buffet. **Hotel Löwen** (☎ 331 61, fax 362 38; Herrenstrasse 47; singles/doubles €35/80) offers clean, basic rooms in a busy part of the Altstadt.

Charming **Hotel Rappen** (☎ 313 53, fax 38 22 52; e rappen@t-online.de; Münsterplatz 13; singles/doubles from €55/70) has lovely rooms with close-up views of the Münster. **Park Hotel Post** (☎ 38 54 80, fax 316 80; e park-hotel-post-freiburg@t-online.de; Eisenbahnstrasse 35-37; singles/doubles €89/114) is an attractive option, with harmoniously hued rooms near Columbipark.

Places to Eat

Being a university town, Freiburg virtually guarantees cheap eats and boasts a lively restaurant scene. University-subsidised **Mensas** (Rempartstrasse 18 • Hebelstrasse 9a) have salad buffets and other filling fodder. You may be asked to show student ID.

Most of the student bars serve good, cheap meals for between €3 and €8 (see Entertainment later). **UC Uni-Café** (☎ 38 33 55; Niemensstrasse 7; meals €3-7) is a popular hang-out that serves light bites on its highly-visible outdoor terrace. **Warsteiner Keller** (☎ 329 29; Niemensstrasse 13; meals €7.50) is a bar/café that oozes atmosphere, and has an excellent range of cheap chow. At the self-serve **Salatstuben** (Löwenstrasse 1; 100g salad €1.20, hot meal €4.10) there's a great range of cheap vegetarian dishes.

For something more substantial, try the cosy **Sichelschmiede** (☎ 350 37; Insel 1; mains around €12), in the eastern Altstadt.

Entertainment

The Freiburg **Konzerthaus** (☎ 388 85 52; Konrad-Adenauer-Platz 1) hosts an impressive range of orchestral performances, while nearby the **Jazzhaus** (☎ 34 973; Schnewlinstrasse 1) has live jazz every night, and hosts many touring acts. Admission starts at €6, depending on who's playing.

Schlappen (Lowenstrasse 2) is where it happens with the student crowd on most nights. It's a large, sprawling bar with a lively vibe, a budget menu and late closing. **Galerie** (Milchstrasse 7) is an intimate watering hole with a nice courtyard and cheap Spanish eats. Mellow and candlelit **Cohibar** (Milchstrasse 9) is a nearby cocktail bar that doesn't close till 3am on weekends. **Alter Simon** (Konviktstrasse 43) has a laid-back feel, and provides a good stopover on your way back from the **Greiffenberg-Schlössle** (Schlossbergring 3), a hilltop beer garden with stunning views over the town.

GERMANY

Getting There & Around

Freiburg is situated on the Mannheim-Basel train corridor and is served by numerous ICE and EC trains in both directions. The trains to Titisee leave every 30 minutes (€9). The regional bus station is next to Track 1. For ridesharing information contact the **Citynetz Mitfahr-Service** (☎ 194 44; *Belfortstrasse 55*).

Single rides on the efficient local bus and tram system cost €1.75. A 24-hour pass costs €4.60. Trams depart from the bridge over the train tracks.

DANUBE RIVER

The Danube (Donau), one of Europe's great rivers, rises in the Black Forest. In Austria, Hungary and Romania it is a mighty, almost intimidating, waterway, but in Germany it's narrower and more tranquil, making it ideal for hiking and biking tours. In fact, Donaueschingen is the gateway to the **Donauradwanderweg** (Danube Bike Trail), a beautiful and level trail that stretches 583km east through cities that include Ulm and Regensburg, to Passau on the Austrian border. From there you can continue on to Vienna and beyond.

The booklet *Donauradwanderführer* provides maps and descriptions of the German route and is available from bookshops and tourist offices for €10.

To exploit its location at the source of the Danube, **Donaueschingen** boasts the Donauquelle (Danube Source) monument in the park of the Fürstenberg Schloss. However, the river really begins 1km east where two tributaries – the Brigach and the Breg – meet at a site dominated by a charmless highway bridge.

Donaueschingen's **tourist office** (☎ 0771-85 72 21; *Karlstrasse 58; open 9am-6pm Mon-Fri, 10am-noon Sat Apr-Oct, 9am-5pm Mon-Fri Nov-Mar*) provides heaps of information on Danube cycling. **Josef Rothweiler** (☎ 0771-131 48; *Max-Egan-Strasse 11*) rents bikes from €6.50 per day. Trains runs to/from Offenburg (€13.50), Constance (€12.40) and Neustadt (€5.50) in the Black Forest.

ULM

☎ 0731 • pop 165,000

A city well worth a visit, Ulm is famous for its Münster tower, the highest cathedral spire in Europe. It's also the birthplace of Albert Einstein. It was a trading city in the 12th century and barges with local goods floated down the Danube as far as the Black Sea.

Greater Ulm is actually two cities in two *Länder* (states), a situation that dates back to Napoleon's influence on the region: he decreed that the middle of the river would divide Baden-Württemberg and Bavaria.

On the southern side of the Danube, the Bavarian city of Neu Ulm is bland and modern. On the other side is Ulm, with the main attractions. Ulm is a hub for frequent fast trains to Lindau, Munich, Stuttgart and the north.

Orientation & Information

Ulm's **tourist office** (☎ 161 28 30; e info@ tourismus.ulm.de; *Münsterplatz; open 9am-6pm Mon-Fri, 9am-1pm Sat all year, plus 10.30am-2.30pm Sun May-Oct*) is very helpful. **Albert's Café** (*Kornhausplatz 5*) offers free Internet access.

Things to See & Do

The main reason for coming to Ulm is to see the huge **Münster** (*Cathedral; Münsterplatz; steeple climb adult/concession €3/2; open 9am-5pm Sept-May, longer hours June-Aug*) famous for its 161m-high steeple, the tallest in the world. Though begun in 1377, it took more than 500 years for the entire structure to be completed. Climbing to the third gallery via the 768 spiralling steps yields great views and a dizzy head. A stained-glass window above the entrance recalls the Holocaust.

Schwörmontag (Oath Monday), held on the second-last Monday in July, has been going on since 1397. After the mayor makes an oath, at the **Schwörhaus** (Oath House), the populace moves down to **Fischerviertel**, a charming old quarter built around streams flowing into the Danube, for a raucous procession of rafts and barges. Later, all-night parties take place on the town's streets and squares. The next day is a local holiday as everybody sleeps it off.

Places to Stay & Eat

The **DJH hostel** (☎ 38 44 55, fax 38 45 11; e jh-ulm@t-online.de; *Grimmelfinger Weg 45; juniors/seniors €13.35/16.05*) can be reached by taking the S1 to Ehinger Tor, then bus No 4 or 8 to Schulzentrum; from here is a five-minute walk. Over in Neu-Ulm is the **Rose** (☎ 778 03, fax 977 17 68; e u.hil pert@t-online.de; *Kasernstrasse 42a; singles/ doubles €22/44*) with tidy, spacious rooms and friendly hosts. Near the Münster, **Hotel Bäumle** (☎ 622 87, fax 602 26 04; *Kohlgasse 6; singles/doubles from €30/45*) is terrific value, with lovely timber-lined rooms, and a snug **downstairs restaurant** *(mains €7-14)* with regional fare. In a charmingly crooked historic half-timbered building, there's **Hotel Schiefes Haus** *(☎ 96 79 30, fax 967 93 33; Schwörhausgasse 6; singles/doubles €100/ 130)* which offers pleasant rooms. **Drei Kannen** *(☎ 677 17; Hafenbad 31; mains €4-11)* brews its own dark beer and serves hearty German tucker in its sunny courtyard.

LAKE CONSTANCE

Lake Constance (Bodensee) is a perfect cure for travellers stranded in landlocked southern Germany. Often jokingly called the 'Swabian Ocean', this giant bulge in the sinewy course of the Rhine offers a choice of water sports, relaxation or cultural pursuits. The lake itself adds special atmosphere to the many historic towns around its periphery, which can be explored by boat or bicycle and on foot.

The lake's southern side belongs to Switzerland and Austria, where the snow-capped mountain tops provide a perfect backdrop when viewed from the northern (German) shore. The German side of Lake Constance features three often-crowded tourist centres in Constance, Meersburg and the island of Lindau. It's essentially a summer area, when it abounds with liquid joy, and is too often foggy, or at best hazy, in winter.

Cycling

A 270km international bike track circumnavigates Lake Constance through Germany, Austria and Switzerland, tracing the often steep shoreline beside vineyards and pebble beaches. The route is well signposted, but you may want one of the many widely sold cycling maps. The tourist booklet *Rad Urlaub am Bodensee* lists routes, rental places and a wealth of other information for the region.

In Constance, **Velotours** *(☎ 07531-982 80; Fritz-Arnold-Strasse 2b; bike rental €11/ 52 daily/weekly)* rents out bikes and organises cycling tours.

Accommodation

The lake's popularity pushes up accommodation prices; fortunately excellent hostel and camping facilities exist around the lake. During summer the hostels roar with mobs, so call ahead.

See tourist offices for apartments and private rooms away from the tourist mobs (and often set among vineyards overlooking the lake).

Getting There & Around

Constance has train connections every one to two hours to Offenburg (€25.40) and Stuttgart (€34). Meersburg is easily reached by bus No 7395 from Friedrichshafen (€6.40, every 30 minutes), or by **Weisse Flotte** *(☎ 07531-28 13 98)* boats from Constance (€3.40, several times daily in season). The Constance to Meersburg **car ferry** *(☎ 07531-80 36 66; person/bicycle/car €1.40/0.75/4.65)* runs every 15 minutes all year from the northeastern Constance suburb of Staad. Lindau has trains to/from Ulm (€17.80), Munich (€28) and Bregenz (€2.10), where you can connect to the rest of Austria.

Trains link Lindau, Friedrichshafen and Constance, and buses fill in the gaps. By car, the B31 hugs the northern shore of Lake Constance, but it can get rather busy. The most enjoyable, albeit slowest, way to get around is on the Weisse Flotte boats which, from Easter to late October, call several times a day at the larger towns along both sides of the lake; there are discounts for rail pass-holders. The **Erlebniskarte** *(3/7/14 days €47/60/87)* is a handy pass that allows free boat travel and free access to a host of activities around the lake. The seven-day **Bodensee-Pass** *(€30)* gives half-price fares on all boats, buses, trains and mountain cableways on and around Lake Constance (including its Austrian and Swiss shores).

CONSTANCE
☎ 07531 • pop 76,000

The town of Constance (Konstanz) achieved historical significance in 1414 when the Council of Constance convened to try to heal huge rifts in the Church. The consequent burning at the stake of the religious reformer Jan Hus as a heretic, and the scattering of his ashes over the lake, failed to block the impetus of the Reformation.

In the west, Constance straddles the Swiss border, a good fortune that spared it from Allied bombing in WWII. The **tourist office** *(☎ 13 30 30; e info@ti.konstanz.de; Bahnhofplatz 13; open 9am-6.30pm Mon-Fri, 9am-4pm Sat, 10am-1pm Sun Apr-Oct, 9.30am-12.30pm & 2pm-6pm Mon-Fri Nov-Mar)* is 150m to the right from the train station exit.

GERMANY

Things to See & Do

The city's most visible feature is the Gothic spire of the cathedral, added only in 1856 to a church that was started in 1052, which gives excellent views over the old town. Visit the old **Niederburg** quarter or relax in the parklands of the **Stadtgarten**. If you have time, head across to **Mainau Island** (☎ 30 30; adult/concession €10/5; open 7am-8pm mid-Mar–Nov, 9am-6pm Nov–mid-Mar), with its baroque castle set among vast and gorgeous gardens that include a butterfly house. Take bus No 4 or a Weisse Flotte boat from the harbour behind the station. Five public beaches are open from May to September, including the Strandbad Horn with shrub-enclosed nude bathing. Take bus No 5 or walk for 20 scenic minutes around the shore.

Places to Stay & Eat

Campingplatz Bruderhofer (☎ 313 88, fax 313 92; Fohrenbülweg 50; person €3.50) is a lovely spot to camp. Take bus No 1 to the auto ferry terminal, then walk south along the shore for 10 minutes. Stay in a converted water tower at the **DJH Hostel** (☎ 322 60, fax 311 63; e jh-konstanz@t-online.de; Zur Allmannshöhe 16; juniors/seniors €14.90/17.60). Take bus No 1 or 4 from the station to the Jugendherberge stop.

Central **Pension Gretel** (☎ 45 58 25, fax 99 12 54; e rezeption@hotel-gretel.de; Zollernstrasse 6-8; singles/doubles from €36/64) has basic but decent rooms. **Hotel Barbarossa** (☎ 12 89 90, fax 12 89 97 00; e wiedermann@barbarossa-hotel.com; Obermarkt 8-12; singles/doubles from €38/85) is a charming old place with period furniture and creaky floors. There's also a **restaurant** (mains €10-19) downstairs with local specialities.

Latinos (☎ 173 99; Am Fischmarkt; all-you-can-eat €7.80) serves an eclectic mix of Mexican food, sushi and barbecue spare ribs. The **Restaurant Elefanten** (☎ 221 64; Salmannsweilergasse 34; mains €10-21) offers a cosy dining room, an international menu and elephant-sized serves.

MEERSBURG
☎ 07532 • pop 5200

Across the lake from Constance, enchanting Meersburg boasts winding cobblestone streets, vine-patterned hills and a sunny lakeside promenade. Its helpful **tourist office** (☎ 43 11 10; e info@meersburg.de; Kirchstrasse 4; open 9am-6.30pm Mon-Fri, 10am-2pm Sat May-Sept, 9am-noon & 2pm-4.30pm Mon-Fri Oct-Apr) is in the Altstadt.

Steigstrasse is lined with delightful half-timbered houses, each boasting a gift shop. The 11th-century **Altes Schloss** (☎ 800 00; adult/concession €5.50/4; open 9am-6.30pm daily May-Oct, 10am-6pm Nov-Apr) is the oldest structurally intact castle in Germany. Baroque **Neues Schloss** (☎ 41 40 71; adult/concession €4/3; open 10am-1pm & 2pm-6pm daily) houses the town's art collection.

Meersburg is a good base for watery pursuits and is popular with windsurfers. **Rudi Thum's** (☎ 73 11) at the yacht harbour, rents out equipment and offers sailing courses.

With no DJH hostel or handy camping grounds, cheap accommodation is hard to find. Not far from the town centre, brand-new **Pension Schönblick** (☎ 97 50, fax 16 57; Von Lassberg-Strasse 8; singles/doubles from €45/85) offers large rooms with contemporary stylings. The historic **Hotel Weinstube Löwen** (☎ 430 40, fax 43 04 10; e info@hotel-loewen-meersburg.de; Marktplatz 2; singles/doubles from €67/105) has pretty rooms with views of the cobbled streets.

There's no shortage of gastronomic options on the promenade, with dozens of cafés and restaurants jostling for attention; meals average about €11. You can eat cheap soups, pastas and pizzas at **Schlossplatz Café** (Schlossplatz 11; dishes around €6), or try the expensive international spread at historic **Winzerstube Zum Becher** (☎ 075 32; Hollgasse 4; mains from €12).

LINDAU
☎ 08382 • pop 26,000

Most of the German part of Lake Constance lies within Baden-Württemberg, but Lindau in the east is just inside Bavaria, near the Austrian border. The **tourist office** (☎ 26 00 30; e info@lindau-tourismus.de; Ludwigstrasse 68; open 9am-6pm Mon-Fri all year, plus 10am-2pm Sat Apr-Oct) is directly opposite the train station.

Connected to the nearby lakeshore by bridges, key sights of this oh-so-charming island town are muralled **Altes Rathaus** (Reichsplatz), the **city theatre** (Barfüsser-platz) and the harbour's **Seepromenade**, with its Bavarian Lion monument and lighthouse. When the haze clears, the Alps provide a stunning backdrop for a zillion photos.

Lindau's water isn't as crowded as the land. **Windsurf-Schule Kreitmeir** (☎ 233 30; *Strandbad Eichwald*) has a windsurfing school and equipment rental. For boat rental contact **Grahneis** (☎ 55 14).

Pleasant **Park Camping Lindau am See** (☎ 722 36; e *info@park-camping.de; Fraunhoferstrasse 20; tent/person €2.50/5.50*) is on the foreshore 3km southeast of Lindau. The rather posh **DJH Hostel** (☎ 96 71, fax 96 71 50; e *jhlindau@djh-bayern.de; Herbergsweg 11; dorm beds €17.20*) is only open to under 27s. For both, take bus No 1 or 2 to the bus station, then bus No 3.

On the island, family-run **Pension Noris** (☎ 36 45, fax 10 42; *Brettermarkt 13; singles/doubles from €30/62*) is basic and clean. **Alte Post** (☎ 934 60, fax 93 46 46; e *info@alte-post-lindau.de; Fischergasse 3; singles/doubles from €44/67*) has beautifully maintained rooms and a Bavarian/Austrian restaurant (mains €7 to €17). Five-star **Bayerischer Hof** (☎ 91 50, fax 91 55 91; e *bayerischerhof-lindau@t-online.de; Seepromenade; singles/doubles from €103/135*) has the best views in town. **Gasthaus zum Sünfzen** (*Maximilianstrasse 1; dishes from €7*) is a popular island institution.

FRIEDRICHSHAFEN
☎ 07541 • pop 56,400
Friedrichshafen, the largest and most 'central' city on the lake's northern shore, has its **tourist office** (☎ 300 10; *Bahnhofplatz 2*) near the Stadtbahnhof train station. Count Zeppelin built his first explodable cigar-shaped airships here. This is commemorated in the town's **Zeppelin Museum** (☎ 380 10; *Seestrasse 22; adult/concession €6.50/3; open 10am-6pm Tues-Sun all year, 10am-5pm Nov-Mar*). The **DJH hostel** (☎ 724 04, fax 749 86; e *jh-fried richschafen@t-online.de; Lindauer Strasse 3; juniors/seniors €14.90/17.60*) is a 15-minute walk from the harbour.

Rhineland-Palatinate

Rhineland-Palatinate (Rheinland-Pfalz) has a rugged topography characterised by thinly populated mountain ranges and forests cut by deep river valleys. Created after WWII from parts of the former Rhineland and Rhenish Palatinate regions, its turbulent history resulted in the area being settled by the Romans and later hotly contested by the French and a variety of German states. The state capital is Mainz.

This land of wine and great natural beauty reaches its apex in the enchanted Moselle Valley towns like Cochem, and along the heavily touristed Rhine, where verdant hillside vineyards twine around the foundations of noble castles and looming medieval fortresses.

THE MOSELLE VALLEY
Exploring the vineyards and wineries of the Moselle (Mosel) Valley is an ideal way to get a taste of German culture and people – and, of course, the wonderful wines. Take the time to slow down and do some sipping. (But don't take it too slow as most wineries close from November to March.)

The Moselle is bursting at the seams with historical sites and picturesque towns built along the river below steep rocky cliffs planted with vineyards (they say locals are born with one leg shorter than the other so that they can easily work the vines). It's one of the country's most romantically scenic regions, with stunning views rewarding the intrepid hikers who brave the hilly trails. Tourist offices sell good maps showing trails and paths, and usually have tips on short hikes.

There are camping grounds, hostels and rooms with classic views all along the Moselle Valley. Many wine-makers also have their own small pensions and, as usual, local tourist offices operate well-organised room-finding services. In May, on summer weekends or during the local wine harvest (mid-September to mid-October), accommodation is hard to find.

Getting There & Away
The most scenic section of the Moselle Valley runs 195km northeast from Trier to Koblenz; it's most practical to begin your Moselle Valley trip from either of these two hubs. If you have private transport and are coming from the north, however, you might head up the Ahr Valley and cut through the scenic Eifel Mountain area between the A61 and A48.

Getting Around
It is not possible to travel the length of the Moselle River via rail. Local and fast trains run every hour between Trier and Koblenz (€16, 1½ hours), but the only riverside stretch

GERMANY

of this line is between Cochem and Koblenz. Apart from this run – and the scenic Mosel-weinbahn line taking tourists between Bullay and Traben-Trarbach (€2.50, 20 minutes) – travellers must use buses, ferries, bicycles, or cars to travel between Moselle towns.

Moselbahn (☎ 0651-14 77 50) runs eight buses on weekdays (fewer on weekends) between Trier and Bullay (three hours each way). It's a very scenic route, following the river's winding course and passing through numerous quaint villages along the way. Buses leave from outside the train stations in Trier, Traben-Trarbach and Bullay. Frequent buses operate between Kues (Alter Bahnhof) and the Wittlich main train station (€3.60, 30 minutes one way), and connect with trains to Koblenz and Trier.

A great way to explore the Moselle in the high season is by boat. Just make sure you have enough time to relax and enjoy the languorous pace; getting from Koblenz to Trier using scheduled ferry services takes two days. Between early May and mid-October, **Köln-Düsseldorfer (KD) Line** (☎ 0221-208 8318) ferries sail daily between Koblenz and Cochem (€20.20 one way, 4½ hours), and the **Gebrüder Kolb Line** (☎ 02673-15 15) runs boats upriver from Cochem to Trier and back via Traben-Trarbach and Bernkastel. Various smaller ferry companies also operate on the Moselle. Eurail and German Rail passes are valid for all normal KD Line services, and travel on your birthday is free. There are numerous other possible excursions, ranging from short return cruises to multiday wine-tasting packages.

The Moselle is a popular area among cyclists, and for much of the river's course there's a separate 'Moselroute' bike track. **Touren-Rad** (☎ 0261-911 60 16; Hohenzollernstrasse 127), six blocks from the main train station in Koblenz, rents quality mountain and touring bicycles from €6 to €10 per day. It has a deal with the rental shop at Trier's main **train station** (☎ 0651-14 88 56), so you can pick up or return bikes at either. In Bernkastel, **Fun-Bike Team** (☎ 06531-940 24; Schanzstrasse 22) rents standard bikes from €8 per day.

Koblenz
☎ 0261 • pop 109,000
While not to be compared with Trier or Cochem, Koblenz is a nice enough place to spend around half a day or so. The **tourist office**

(☎ 30 38 80; e info@koblenz-touristik.de; Bahnhofsplatz) is in front of the Hauptbahnhof.

Things to See The Deutsches Eck is a park at the sharp confluence of the Rhine and Moselle Rivers dedicated to German unity. Immediately across the Rhine is the impressive **Festung Ehrenbreitstein fortress** (☎ 974 24 45; adult/concession €1.10/0.50), which houses both the DJH hostel and the rather staid **Landesmuseum** (☎ 970 30; adult/concession €2/1.50).

South of Koblenz, at the head of the beautiful Eltz Valley, **Burg Eltz** (☎ 02672-95 05 00; open daily Apr-Nov) is not to be missed. Towering over the surrounding hills, this superb medieval castle has frescoes, paintings, furniture and ornately decorated rooms. Burg Eltz is best reached by train to Moselkern, from where it's a 50-minute walk up through the forest. Alternatively, you can drive via Münster-Maifeld to the nearby car park. Entry is allowed only with regular guided tours (adult/concession €5/3), but the **Schatzkammer** (treasure chamber; adult/concession €2/1) can be visited without one.

Places to Stay & Eat The camping ground **Rhein Mosel** (☎/fax 827 19; open Apr–mid-Oct), is on Schartwiesenweg at the confluence of the Moselle and Rhine Rivers opposite the Deutsches Eck. The daytime passenger ferry across the Moselle puts the camping ground within a five-minute walk of town.

Koblenz has a wonderful **DJH hostel** (☎ 97 28 70; e jh-koblenz@djh-info.de; dorm beds €14.20-17.50) housed in the old Ehrenbreitstein fortress, but it's advisable to book ahead in summer. From the main train station take bus No 7, 8 or 9; there's also a chairlift (€4/6 up/return) from Ehrenbreitstein station by the river. **Hotel Jahn van Werth** (☎ 365 00, fax 365 06; van Werth Strasse 9; singles/doubles €23/44, with bath €41/62) offers good value and basic rooms.

Altenhof and the area around Münzplatz in the Altstadt offer many good eating options. **Café Miljöö** (☎ 142 37; Gemüsegasse 8-10) does light dishes in a pleasant café atmosphere till late.

Cochem
☎ 02671 • pop 5300
This pretty picture-postcard German town has narrow alleyways and one of the most

beautiful castles in the region. It's also a good base for hikes into the hills. The staff are very helpful in Cochem's **tourist office** (☎ *600 40;* e *verkehrsamt.Cochem@lcoc .de; Endertplatz)* next to the Moselbrücke bridge.

Things to See For a great view, head up to the **Pinnerkreuz** with the chairlift on Endertstrasse (€4). The stunning **Reichsburg Castle** (☎ *255; open 9am-5pm daily mid-Mar–mid-Nov)* is just a 15-minute walk up the hill from town. There are regular daily tours (adult/ concession €3/1.60) and English translation sheets are available.

Cochem's **HH Hieronimi** (☎ *221; Stadionstrasse 1-3),* just across the river is a friendly, family-run winery that offers tours for €5, including two tastings, a bottle of its own wine and a souvenir glass. Also in Cochem there's **Weingut Rademacher** (☎ *41 64; Pinnerstrasse 10),* diagonally behind the train station, where you can tour its winery and cellar (an old WWII bunker) for €5/6.80 with four/six wine tastings.

Places to Stay & Eat Lodging options in Cochem are copious. The riverside **Campingplatz Am Freizeitszentrum** (☎ *44 09; Stadionstrasse; tent/person/car €4/4/6.50)* is downstream from the northern bridge; it's open from eight days before Easter to the end of October. Cochem's **DJH hostel** (☎ *86 33;* e *jh-cochem@djh-info.de; Klottener Strasse 9; dorm beds €16.10-21.20)* was closed for renovation at the time of our visit; they expect to open again in April 2003. The large **Hotel Noss** (☎ *36 12, fax 53 66; Moselpromenade 17; singles/doubles €44/86)* is on the waterfront and has quite good rooms with shower and toilet.

A cheap fast-food choice is **Kochlöffel** (Am Markt 10), where you can eat well for less than €5 (chicken halves €2.50). **Zom Stüffje** (☎ *72 60; Oberbachstrasse 14; mains €8-18)* is a traditional eating house.

Bernkastel-Kues
☎ 06531 • pop 7500
The twin town of Bernkastel-Kues is at the heart of the middle Moselle region. On the right bank, Bernkastel has a charming **Markt**, a romantic ensemble of half-timbered houses with beautifully decorated gables. For a primer on the local vino, try Bernkastel's **Weingut Dr**

Willkomm (☎ *80 54; Gestade 1).* Located in a lovely old arched cellar, the winery also distils its own brandy. For a more thorough course, head across the river to Kues' **Vinothek** (☎ *41 41; Cusanusstrasse 2; admission €1.50, admission with tastings €9),* where €9 entitles you to taste as much or as little of the 130 wines and sparkling wines from the Moselle-Saar-Ruwer growing region as you wish. The **tourist office** (☎ *40 23; Am Gestade 6)* is on the Bernkastel side.

The **Campingplatz Kueser Werth** (☎ *82 00; Am Hafen 2)* has pleasant tent sites by the river. The **DJH hostel** (☎ *23 95;* e *jh-bernkas tel-kues@djh-info.de; Jugendherbergsstrasse 1; dorm beds €12.30)* is near the castle. **Hotel Bären** (☎ *95 04 40, fax 950 44 46; singles/ doubles €38/88)* has first-rate, modern rooms, some with river views.

Traben-Trarbach
☎ 06541 • pop 5800
Full of fanciful Art Nouveau villas, the smart double town of Traben-Trarbach is a welcome relief from the 'romantic-half-timbered-town' circuit. Pick up a map at the **tourist office** (☎ *839 80;* e *info@traben-trarbach.de; Bahnstrasse 22),* a five-minute walk south of Traben's train station.

For camping, there's the **Rissbach** (☎ *31 11; Rissbacher Strasse 170; open Apr–mid-Oct).* The **DJH hostel** (☎ *92 78;* e *jh-traben -trarbach@djh-info.de; Hirtenpfad 6; dorm beds €14.60-17.90)* has small and modern dorms.

The **Central-Hotel** (☎ *62 38; Bahnstrasse 43; singles/doubles €33/60)* is clean, friendly and provides a good breakfast and rooms with toilet and shower.

Unusual and popular with the locals, the restaurant **Alte Zunftscheune** (☎ *97 37; Neue Rathausstrasse)* serves steak with horseradish sauce, salad and fried potato for €14.

TRIER
☎ 0651 • pop 100,000
Trier is touted as Germany's oldest town. Although settlement of the site dates back to 400 BC, Trier itself was founded in 15 BC as Augusta Treverorum, the capital of Gaul, and was second in importance only to Rome in the Western Roman Empire. You'll find more Roman ruins here than anywhere else north of the Alps. There's a university too, and the city is quite lively.

GERMANY

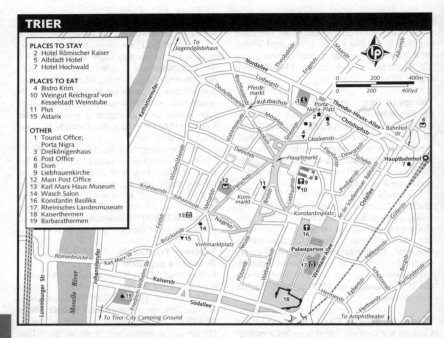

TRIER

PLACES TO STAY
2 Hotel Römischer Kaiser
5 Altstadt Hotel
7 Hotel Hochwald

PLACES TO EAT
4 Bistro Krim
10 Weingut Reichsgraf von
    Kesselstadt Weinstube
11 Plus
15 Astarix

OTHER
1 Tourist Office;
   Porta Nigra
3 Dreikönigenhaus
6 Post Office
8 Dom
9 Liebfrauenkirche
12 Main Post Office
13 Karl Marx Haus Museum
14 Wasch Salon
16 Konstantin Basilika
17 Rheinisches Landesmuseum
18 Kaiserthermen
19 Barbarathermen

Orientation & Information

From the main train station head west along Bahnhofstrasse and Theodor-Heuss-Allee to the Porta Nigra, where you'll find Trier's **tourist office** (☎ 97 80 80; e info@tit.de; open 9am-6pm Mon-Sat, 10am-3pm Sun Apr-Oct, 10am-5pm Mon-Sat Nov-Mar). It has a free and efficient room-finding service. Ask here about daily guided **city walking tours** in English (€6), and the three-day Trier-Card (€9), a combined ticket for the city's main sights, museums and public transport. From Porta Nigra, walk along Simeonstrasse's pedestrian zone to Hauptmarkt, the heart of the old city. Most of the sights are within this area of roughly one sq km. There's a convenient and cheap **Wasch Salon laundrette** (Brücken-strasse 19-21). The **main post office** is near the station.

Things to See

The town's chief landmark is the **Porta Nigra** (adult/concession €2.10/1.60; open 9am-6pm daily Apr-Sept, till 9am-5pm Oct-Mar), the imposing city gate on the northern edge of the town centre, which dates back to the 2nd century. The interesting **Rheinisches Landesmuseum** (Weimarer Allee 1; admission €5.50; open 9.30am-5pm Tues-Fri, 10.30am-5pm Sat & Sun) has works of art dating from Paleolithic, Roman and modern times.

Trier's massive Romanesque **Dom** shares a 1600-year history with the nearby and equally impressive **Konstantin Basilika**. Also worth visiting are the ancient **Amphitheater**, the **Kaiserthermen** and **Barbarathermen** (Roman baths). The early-Gothic **Dreikönigenhaus** (Simeonstrasse 19) was built around 1230 as a protective tower; the original entrance was on the second level, accessible only by way of a retractable rope ladder.

History buffs and nostalgic socialists can visit the **Karl Marx Haus Museum** (☎ 97 06 80; Brückenstrasse 10; adult/concession €2/1; open daily), in the house where a star was born (but don't expect to view anything particularly revolutionary).

Places to Stay

The municipal camping ground **Trier-City** (☎ 869 21; Luxemburger Strasse 81; tent/person/car €4/6/4; open Apr-Oct) is nicely positioned beside the Moselle River. The **DJH**

Jugendgästehaus (☎ 14 66 20; e jh-trier@ djh-info.de; An der Jugendherberge 4; dorm beds/doubles/singles €16/21/29 per person) is also down by the riverside.

Hotel Hochwald (☎ 758 03, fax 743 54; Bahnhofplatz 5; singles €26, singles/doubles with bath €36/60) is opposite the train station and has austere but clean rooms. **Altstadt Hotel** (☎ 480 41, fax 412 93; Am Porta-Nigra-Platz; singles/doubles from €66/96) in the centre, has spacious rooms. **Hotel Römischer Kaiser** (☎ 977 00, fax 97 70 99; Am Porta-Nigra-Platz 6; singles/doubles from €67/98) is across the road and offers even better rooms.

Places to Eat

Trier is a great place to sample some Franco-German cooking. The bustling **Bistro Krim** (☎ 739 43; Glockenstrasse 7) offers generous Mediterranean-inspired dishes at affordable prices. There are also several set menus such as its two-course 'Mediterranean' menu for €14.80. **Astarix** (☎ 722 39; Karl-Marx-Strasse 11) is a favourite student hang-out back in an arcade that serves large salads and main dishes for under €6 (open till late). The weinstube of the **Weingut Reichsgraf von Kesselstadt** (☎ 411 78; Liebfrauenstrasse 10; mains from €7) offers a limited menu and superlative wines in a casual outdoor setting beside the Liebfrauenkirche.

Plus (Brotstrasse 23) is a central supermarket. The narrow Judengasse, near Markt, has several bars and cafés for tipples and nibbles, whereas a slicker crowd gravitates towards a cluster of bars on Viehmarktplatz.

Getting There & Away

Trier has hourly local and fast trains to Saarbrücken (€12.40, 1½ hours) and Koblenz (€15.60, 1½ hours), as well as services to Luxembourg (€7.40, 45 minutes) and Metz (in France; €18.20, 2½ hours). For information on river ferries, see Getting There & Away in the previous Moselle Valley section.

RHINE VALLEY – KOBLENZ TO MAINZ

A trip along the Rhine is on the itinerary of most travellers. The section between Mainz and Koblenz offers the best scenery, especially the narrow tract downriver from Rüdesheim. Spring and autumn are the best times to visit; in summer it's over-run and in winter most towns go into hibernation. For information on Koblenz, see the previous Moselle Valley section.

Activities

The Koblenz-to-Mainz section of the Rhine Valley is great for wine tasting, with Bacharach, 45km south of Koblenz, being one of the top choices for sipping. For tastings in other towns, ask for recommendations at the tourist offices or just follow your nose.

Though the trails here may be a bit more crowded with day-trippers than those along the Moselle, hiking along the Rhine is also excellent. The slopes and trails around Bacharach are justly famous.

Getting There & Away

Koblenz and Mainz are the best starting points. The Rhine Valley is also easily accessible from Frankfurt on a long day trip, but that won't do justice to the region.

Getting Around

Each mode of transport on the Rhine has its own advantages and all are equally enjoyable. Try combining several of them by going on foot one day, cycling the next, and then taking a boat for a view from the river. The **Köln-Düsseldorfer (KD) Line** (☎ 0221-208 83 18) earns its bread and butter on the Rhine, with many slow and fast boats daily between Koblenz and Mainz. The most scenic stretch is between Koblenz and Rüdesheim; the journey takes about four hours downstream, about 5½ hours upstream (€23.20). See Getting Around in the previous Moselle Valley section for information about concessions. Boats stop at many riverside towns along the way.

Train services operate on both sides of the Rhine River, but are more convenient on the left bank. You can travel nonstop on IC/EC trains or travel by regional RB or SE services.

Touring the Rhine Valley by car is also ideal. The route between Koblenz and Mainz is short enough for a car to be rented and returned to either city. There are no bridge crossings between Koblenz and Rüdesheim, but there are several ferry crossings.

Mainz

☎ 06131 • pop 183,000

A 30-minute train ride from Frankfurt, Mainz has an attractive old town. Though it can't compare to the compact beauty of the nearby

GERMANY

towns along the Rhine, Mainz impresses with its massive **Domstrasse** (*cathedral; admission free; open daily*) and the **St Stephanskirche** (*Weissgasse 12; admission free; open daily*), with stained-glass windows by Marc Chagall. Mainz's museums include the **Gutenberg Museum** (☎ 26 40; *Liebfrauenplatz 5; adult/ concession €3/1.30; open Tues-Sun*), which contains two precious copies of the first printed Bible. For more information on attractions in Mainz, visit the **tourist office** (☎ 28 62 10; e tourist@info-mainz.de; *Brücken-turm am Rathaus*). **C@fé Enterprise** (*Bilhild-isstrasse 2*), on Münsterplatz in Mainz, has Internet facilities.

If you are staying overnight, try the **Jugendgästehaus** (☎ 853 32; e jh-mainz@ djh-info.de; *Otto-Brunfels-Schneise 4; beds €16.10-21.20*); take bus No 62, 63 or 92 towards Weisenau. The **Hotel Stadt Coblenz** (☎ 22 76 02, fax 22 33 07; *Rheinstrasse 499; singles/doubles without bath €42/55, with bath €52/68*) has hostel-quality rooms (ask for one away from the street).

The **Augustiner Keller** (☎ 22 26 62; *Augustinerstrasse 26; mains €6-14*) serves tasty Alsatian-style pizzas in a homy, old-fashioned setting.

St Goar/St Goarhausen
☎ 06741 • pop 3500
Where the slopes along the Rhine aren't covered with vines, you can bet they built a castle. One of the most impressive is **Burg Rheinfels** (☎ 383; *adult/concession €4/2; open 9am-5pm daily Apr-Oct, 10am-4pm Sat & Sun in good weather Nov-Mar*) in St Goar. An absolute must-see, the labyrinthine ruins reflect the greed and ambition of Count Dieter V of Katzenelnbogen, who built the castle in 1245 to help levy tolls on passing ships. You will need a torch (flashlight) to explore the more removed of the castle's spooky corridors. Across the river, just south of St Goarshausen, is the Rhine's most famous sight, the **Loreley Cliff**. Legend has it that a maiden sang sailors to their deaths against its base. It's worth the trek to the top of the Loreley for the view, but try to get up there early in the morning before the hordes ascend.

For camping, **Campingplatz Loreleyblick** (☎ 20 66; *tent sites €2.20, plus €3 per person; open Mar-Oct*) is on the banks of the Rhine, opposite the legendary rock. St Goar's

Jugendherberge (☎ 388; e jh-st-goar@djh -info.de; *Bismarckweg 17; dorm beds €11.80*) is right below the castle. More restful accommodation can be found at **Knab's Mühlen-schänke** (☎ 16 98, fax 16 78; *Gründelbachtal 73; singles/doubles €25/48*) about 1.5km north of St Goar. You can sip the house wine here in a rural atmosphere. The **Schlosshotel Rheinfels** (☎ 80 20, fax 80 28 02; *singles/ doubles from €85/128*) in the castle is the top address in town, with rooms and a fine restaurant with prices to match.

Bacharach
☎ 06743 • pop 2400
The town of Bacharach hides its not inconsiderable charms behind a time-worn wall and is therefore easily bypassed.

Walk beneath one of its thick arched gateways, however, and you'll find yourself in a beautifully preserved medieval village. Drop by the **tourist office** (☎ 91 93 03; *Oberstrasse 45; open 9am-5pm Mon-Fri, 10am-4pm Sat Apr-Oct*) for information on Bacharach's sights and lodging.

The **Sonnenstrand** (☎ 17 52; *tent/person/ car €3/4.20/5.50; open Apr–mid-Oct*) offers riverside camping just 500m south of the centre. Bacharach's **Jugendherberge** (☎ 12 66; e jh-bacharach@djh-info.de; *dorm beds €14.20-17.50*) is a legendary facility housed in the Burg Stahleck castle. In town, **Irmgaard Orth** (☎ 15 53; *Spurgasse 2; singles/doubles €18/34*) offers good budget rooms.

Kurpfälzische Münze (☎ 13 75; *Oberstrasse 72; dishes €7-20*) serves traditional dishes, including game. **Zum Grünen Baum** (☎ 12 08; *Oberstrasse 63; mains from €7*) is wonderful place to sample the region's abundance of top-notch wines.

Rüdesheim
☎ 06722 • pop 10,360
Rolling drunk on tourism, this town is worth a visit only if you are studying mass tourism at its worst, or seeking out the bucolic paths in the hills above. Avoid eating anywhere in Rüdesheim's Drosselgasse, an oversold row of touristy shops and restaurants. Instead, get some perspective on the area by taking the **Weinlehrpfad** walking route from above the touristy main drag. It leads through vineyard slopes to the **Brömserburg**, an old riverside castle that houses an interesting **wine museum** (*adult/concession €3/2*).

The **Jugendherberge** (☎ 27 11; e *ruede sheim@djh-hessen.de; Am Kreuzberg; dorm beds juniors/seniors €12/14.70)* is about a 30-minute walk from the train station. The large **Parkhotel Deutscher Hof** (☎ 30 16, fax 17 17; e *info@parkhotel-ruedesheim.de; Rhein-strasse 21-23; singles/doubles €50/74)* is nicely situated along the river.

Saarland

In the late 19th century, Saarland's coal mines and steel mills fuelled the burgeoning German economy. Since WWII, however, the steady economic decline of coal and steel has made Saarland the poorest region in western Germany. Though distinctly German since the early Middle Ages, Saarland was ruled by France for several periods during its turbulent history. Reoccupied by the French after WWII, it only joined the Federal Republic of Germany in 1957, after the population rejected French efforts to turn it into an independent state.

SAARBRÜCKEN
☎ 0681 • pop 185,000
Saarbrücken, capital of Saarland, has an interesting mixed French and German feel. While lacking in major tourist sights, this city is a matter-of-fact place where people go about their daily business and where tourists are treated as individuals. It's also an easy base for day trips to some of the beautiful little towns nearby, such as Ottweiler, Saarburg, Mettlach and St Wendel.

Orientation & Information
The main train station is in the northwestern corner of the old town, which stretches out on both sides of the Saar River. The **tourist office** (☎ 93 80 90; *Reichsstrasse 1; open 9am-6pm Mon-Fri, 10am-12.30pm & 1pm-6pm Sat)* is directly in front of the station.

The **Reisebank** in the main train station is open daily. There's also a **post office** here and another in the city centre at Dudweilerstrasse 17. There is a laundry **Waschhaus** (*Nauwie-serstrasse 22; open 8am-10pm daily).*

Things to See & Do
Start your visit by strolling along the lanes around lively **St Johanner Markt** in the central pedestrian zone. A flea market is held here every second Saturday from April to

November. Not far away beside the Saar River are the **Saarländische Staatstheater** (*Schillerplatz 1),* a neoclassical structure built by the Nazis, and the two buildings of the **Saarland-Museum** (*Bismarckstrasse 11-19 • Karlstrasse 1; adult/concession €1.50/1; open Tues-Sun).* The modern gallery on Bismarckstrasse is the more interesting of the two, displaying pieces by Picasso, Otto Dix, and other renowned 20th-century artists. The best bet for contemporary art is the **Stadt-galerie Saarbrücken** (☎ 93 68 30; *St Johanner Markt 24; admission free),* a playful, fascinating gallery dedicated to cutting-edge works.

Cross the 1549 **Alte Brücke** (Old Bridge) to the **Schloss Saarbrücken**, the former palace on Schlossplatz designed by King Wilhelm Friedrich's court architect, Friedrich Joachim Stengel, in the 18th century. A 1989 facelift by Gottfried Böhm gives the building a distinctly sinister, Darth Vader-ish appearance.

There are several museums located around Schlossplatz; the most interesting being the **Abenteuer Museum** (*Adventure Museum; adult/concession €3/2; open 9am-1pm Tues & Wed, 3pm-7pm Thur & Fri),* with a hotchpotch of weird souvenirs and photos collected since 1950 by solo adventurer extraordinaire, Heinz Rox-Schulz.

The nearby **Ludwigsplatz**, a baroque square that is also the work of Stengel, is dominated by the Lutheran **Ludwigskirche**. It is often closed, but you can peer through the glass doorway.

Places to Stay & Eat
The **Campingplatz Saarbrücken** (☎ 517 80; *Am Spicherer Berg; tent sites €6, plus €4 per person)* is on the French border, south of the city; take bus No 42 to Spicherer Weg from where it's a five-minute walk. The excellent **Jugendherberge** (☎ 330 40, fax 37 49 11; *Meerwiesertalweg 31; dorm beds/twins €16.10-21.20 per person)* is a 30-minute walk northeast of the train station. Or take bus No 49 or 69 to Prinzenweiher. Beds are in four-person dorms, or two-person rooms.

Hotel zur Klause (☎ 92 69 60, fax 926 96 50; *Deutschherrnstrasse 72; singles/doubles €36/62)* is one of the cheapest in the city. **Hotel Stadt Hamburg** (☎ 330 53, fax 37 43 30; *Bahnhofstrasse 71-73; singles/doubles €49/78)* has clean rooms. **Hotel im Fuchs** (☎ 93 65 50, fax 936 55 36; *Kappenstrasse 12;*

singles/doubles €57/81) has nice rooms with facilities.

In Saarbrücken's eateries, your taste buds get to visit France while enjoying hearty German servings. **Gasthaus Zum Stiefel** (☎ 93 54 50; Am Stiefel 2; restaurant mains from €9) is in an old brewery just off St Johanner Markt. It has an upmarket restaurant at the front specialising in fine meat and fish dishes. The pub out the back (enter from Froschengasse) has house beers on tap and serves less expensive food. Also try some of the other bistros and fast-food places along Froschengasse.

You'll find many restaurants and student pubs along the streets running off Max-Ophüls-Platz. The **Café Kostbar** (Nauwieserstrasse 19), situated in an attractive backstreet courtyard, has well-priced set menus from €6.50. **Tomate 2** (Schlossstrasse 2; dishes €7-14) is a Mediterranean-style bistro across the river, near Schlossplatz.

Getting There & Away

There are frequent trains to the connecting cities of Mannheim (€18.60, 2¼ hours), Koblenz (€28, 2½ hours), Mainz (€23.40, two hours) and Frankfurt (€30.80, 2½ hours), as well as services across the border to Metz.

Hesse

The Hessians, a Frankish tribe, were among the first to convert to Lutheranism in the early 16th century. Apart from a brief period of unity in that same century under Philip the Magnanimous, Hesse (Hessen) remained a motley collection of principalities and, later, of Prussian administrative districts until proclaimed a state in 1945. Its main cities are Frankfurt, Kassel and the capital, Wiesbaden.

As well as being a transport hub, the very un-German city of Frankfurt can also be used as a base to explore some of the smaller towns in Hesse. The beautiful Taunus and Spessart regions offer quiet village life and hours of scenic walks.

FRANKFURT/MAIN
☎ 069 • pop 650,000
They call it 'Bankfurt', 'Mainhattan' and much more. It's on the Main (pronounced 'mine') River, and is generally referred to as Frankfurt-am-Main, or Frankfurt/Main, since there is another large city called Frankfurt

(Frankfurt an der Oder) which is near the Polish border.

Frankfurt/Main is the financial and geographical centre of western Germany, as well as the host of important trade fairs. Thanks to generous funding in the 1980s and early 1990s, Frankfurt also has some excellent museums.

It is Germany's most important transport hub for air, train and road connections so you'll probably end up here at some point. Don't be surprised if you find this cosmopolitan melting pot much more interesting than you had expected.

Orientation

The airport is 11 minutes by train southwest of the city centre. The Hauptbahnhof is on the western side of the city, but within walking distance of the old city centre.

The safest route to the city centre through the sleazy train station area is along Kaiserstrasse. This leads to Kaiserplatz and then to a large square called An der Hauptwache. The area between the former lockup (Hauptwache), and the Römerberg, in the tiny vestige of Frankfurt's original old city, is the centre of Frankfurt. The Main River flows just south of the Altstadt, with several bridges leading to one of the city's livelier areas, Sachsenhausen. Its northeastern corner, behind the youth hostel (see Places to Stay later in this section), is known as Alt-Sachsenhausen and is full of quaint old houses and narrow alleyways.

Information

Tourist Offices Frankfurt's most convenient **tourist office** (☎ 21 23 88 00; open 8am-5pm Mon-Fri, 9am-6pm Sat, Sun & holidays) is in the main hall of the train station. For its efficient room-finding service there's a charge of €2.50.

In the centre of the city, the **Römer tourist office** (☎ 21 23 88 00; Römerberg 27; open 9.30am-5.30pm Mon-Fri, 10am-4pm Sat & Sun) occupies the northwest corner of the Römerberg square. Another conveniently located branch is the **CityInfo Zeil** (☎ 21 23 88 00; cnr Zeil & Stiftstrasse; open 10am-6pm Mon-Fri, 10am-4pm Sat & Sun), where you can reserve rooms and pick up city maps and brochures.

The head office of the **German National Tourist Office** (☎ 974 64, fax 75 19 03; w www.deutschland-tourismus.de; Beethovenstrasse 69), is a good place to contact if you're still planning your trip to Germany; it has brochures on all areas of the country.

One- and two-day Frankfurt cards (€7.50/ 11) give 50% reductions on admission to all of the city's important museums, the airport terraces, the zoo and Palmengarten, as well as unlimited travel on public transport.

Money The main train station has a branch of the **Reisebank** *(open 6.30am-10pm daily)*, near the southern exit at the head of platform No 1. There are banks and numerous ATMs at the airport, including a **Reisebank** *(Terminal 1, arrival hall B; open 6am-11pm daily)*.

AmEx and **Thomas Cook** are situated opposite each other on Kaiserstrasse at Nos 10 and 11 respectively.

Post & Communications The **main post office** *(Zeil 90)* is on the ground floor of the Karstadt department store (standard shop hours). Inside the Hauptbahnhof there is a **post office** *(open 7am-7.30pm Mon-Fri, 8am-4pm Sat)*. The airport **post office** *(open 7am-9pm daily)* is in the waiting lounge, departure hall B.

Email & Internet Access Directly across from the train station, **Telebistro** *(☎ 61 99 11 87; Poststrasse 2)* charges €2.10 for 30 minutes online.

Bookshops Between the Hauptwache and Rathenauplatz, **Hugendubel** *(Beibergasse)* stocks Lonely Planet guides and has a café downstairs. The **British Bookshop** *(Börsenstrasse 17)* provides a wide range of English-language fiction and nonfiction.

Laundry The Waschcenter chain in Frankfurt has a **laundrette** *(Wallstrasse 8)* in Sachsenhausen. In Bockenheim, the **SB-Waschcenter** *(Grosse Seestrasse 46)* is another option.

Medical Services The **Uni-Klinik** *(☎ 630 10; Theodor Stern Kai; open 24hr)* is in Sachsenhausen. For medical queries, contact the 24-hour **doctor** service on ☎ 192 92.

Dangers & Annoyances The area around the main train station is a base for Frankfurt's sex and illegal drug trades. Frequent police patrols of the station and the surrounding Bahnhofsviertel keep things under control, but it's advisable to exercise 'big city' sense.

Things to See & Do

About 80% of the old city was wiped off the map by two Allied bombing raids in March 1944, and postwar reconstruction was subject to the demands of the new age. Rebuilding efforts were more thoughtful, however, in the **Römerberg**, the old central area of Frankfurt west of the cathedral, where restored 14th- and 15th-century buildings provide a glimpse of the beautiful city this once was. The old town hall, or **Römer**, is in the northwestern corner of Römerberg and consists of three 15th-century houses topped with Frankfurt's trademark stepped gables.

East of Römerberg, behind the Historischer Garten (Historical Garden), which has the remains of Roman and Carolingian foundations, is the **Dom**, the coronation site of Holy Roman emperors from 1562 to 1792. It's dominated by the elegant 15th-century Gothic **tower** (completed in the 1860s) – one of the few structures left standing after the 1944 raids. The small **Wahlkapelle** (Voting Chapel) on the cathedral's southern side is where the seven electors of the Holy Roman Empire chose the emperor from 1356 onwards; the adjoining **choir** has beautiful wooden stalls.

Anyone with an interest in German literature should visit **Goethe Haus** *(☎ 13 88 00; Grosser Hirschgraben 23-25; adult/concession €5/3; open 9am-6pm Mon-Fri Apr-Sept, 9am-4pm Mon-Fri Oct-Mar, 10am-4pm Sat & Sun all year)*. Johann Wolfgang von Goethe was born in this house in 1749.

A little bit farther afield, there's the botanical **Palmengarten** *(Siesmayerstrasse; adult/ concession €3.50/1.50)* as well as the creative **Frankfurt Zoo** *(Alfred-Brehm-Platz 16; adult/ concession €5.50/2.50)*, both good places to unwind. It is also a nice 40-minute walk east along the south bank of the Main River to the **lock** in Offenbach – just before it there's a good beer garden.

There's a great **flea market** along Museumsufer between 8am and 2pm every Saturday.

Museums Most of Frankfurt's museums are closed on Monday and offer free entry on Wednesday. Unless otherwise indicated, the ones below are open 10am to 5pm Tuesday to Sunday (to 8pm Wednesday).

The **Museum für Moderne Kunst** *(☎ 21 23 04 47; Domstrasse 10; adult/concession €5/ 2.50)* north of the cathedral, features works of modern art by Joseph Beuys, Claes Oldenburg

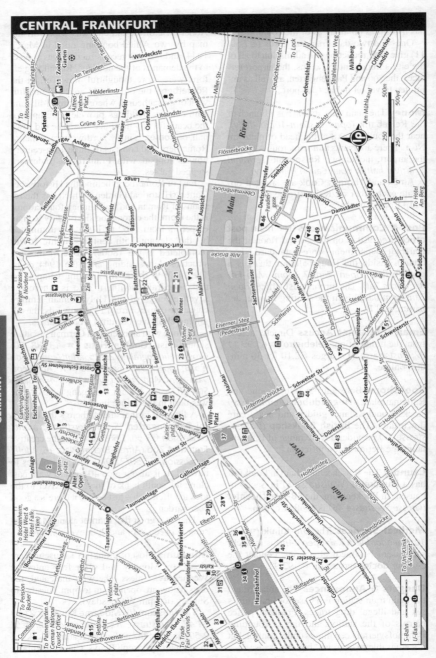

CENTRAL FRANKFURT

CENTRAL FRANKFURT

PLACES TO STAY
1 Hotel-Pension Gölz; Hotel Beethoven
12 Hotel Am Zoo
15 Hotel-Pension Bruns
19 Hotel-Garni Diplomat
27 Steinberger Frankfurter Hof
30 Hotel Carlton; Concorde Hotel
32 Hotel Glockshuber
33 Hotel Topas
35 Hotel Münchner Hof
36 Hotel Eden
40 Hotel Wiesbaden
41 Hotel Tourist
46 Haus der Jugend

PLACES TO EAT
3 Blaubart Gewölbekeller
18 Kleinmarkthalle
20 Metropol
28 India Curry House
39 Ginger Brasserie
48 Fichte-Kränzi
50 HL Supermarket
51 Zum Gemalten Haus

OTHER
2 Alte Oper (Old Opera House)
4 British Bookshop
5 Turm-Palast Cinema
6 The Cave
7 Sinkkasten
8 CityInfo Zeil
9 Main Post Office; Karstadt Department Store
10 Zum Schwejk
11 Zoo
13 Hugendubel
14 Jazzkeller
16 American Express
17 U60311
21 Dom
22 Museum für Moderne Kunst
23 Römer Tourist Office
24 Cooky's
25 Goethe Haus
26 Thomas Cook
29 English Theater
31 Telebistro
34 Tourist Office
37 Städtische Bühnen/ Frankfurter Oper
38 Jüdisches Museum
42 ADM-Mitfahrzentrale
43 Städtisches Kunstinstitut
44 Deutsches Filmmuseum
45 Museum für Angewandte Kunst
47 Waschcenter
49 Stereo Bar

and many others. Also on the north bank there's the **Jüdisches Museum** *(Jewish Museum;* ☎ *21 23 50 00; adult/concession €2.60/1.30, free Sat).*

Numerous museums line the south bank of the Main River along the so-called **Museumsufer** *(Museum Embankment).* Pick of the crop is the **Städelsches Kunstinstitut** *(*☎ *605 09 80; Schaumainkai 63; adult/concession €6/5; open to 8pm Thur),* with a world-class collection of paintings by artists from the Renaissance to the 20th century, including Botticelli, Dürer, Van Eyck, Rubens, Rembrandt, Vermeer, Cézanne and Renoir. Other highlights include the **Deutsches Filmmuseum** *(*☎ *21 23 88 30; Schaumainkai 41; adult/concession €2.50/1.30; open 2pm-8pm Sat);* and the fascinating, design-oriented **Museum für Angewandte Kunst** *(Museum of Applied Arts;* ☎ *21 23 40 37; Schaumainkai 17; admission €5).*

Places to Stay

Camping The most recommended camping ground is **Campingplatz Heddernheim** *(*☎ *57 03 32; An der Sandelmühle 35; tent sites €3.50, plus €5.20/4.50 per person/car; open year-round)* in the Heddernheim district northwest of the city centre. It's a 15-minute ride on the U1, U2 or U3 from the Hauptwache U-Bahn station – get off at Heddernheim.

Hostels The big, bustling and crowded **Haus der Jugend** *(*☎ *610 01 50, fax 61 00 15 99; Deutschherrnufer 12; beds under/over 20*

years €14.50/18; curfew 2am) is within walking distance of the city centre and Sachsenhausen's nightspots. From the train station take bus No 46 to Frankensteinerplatz, or take S-Bahn No 2, 3, 4, 5 or 6 to Lokalbahnhof, then walk north for 10 minutes. Check-in begins at 1pm (postcode for bookings: 60594 Frankfurt/Main).

Hotels & Pensions In this city, 'cheap' can mean paying more than €60 for a spartan double room. During the many busy trade fairs even that price is unrealistic, with scarce rooms commanding a 50% to 200% premium.

Predictably, most of Frankfurt's budget accommodation is in the sleazy Bahnhofsviertel which surrounds the station. **Hotel Eden** *(*☎ *25 19 14, fax 25 23 37; Münchener Strasse 42; singles/doubles €45/60)* has fairly reasonable rooms with toilet and shower. **Hotel Münchner Hof** *(*☎ *23 00 66, fax 23 44 28; Münchener Strasse 46; singles/doubles €49/65)* has fairly good basic offerings with toilet and shower. **Hotel Carlton** *(*☎ *23 20 93, fax 23 36 73; Karlstrasse 11; singles/doubles €57/73)* and the neighbouring **Concorde Hotel** *(*☎ *242 42 20, fax 24 24 22 88; Karlstrasse 9; singles/ doubles €50/65)* both have rooms with facilities. **Hotel Tourist** *(*☎ *23 30 95/96/97, fax 23 69 86; Baseler Strasse 23-25; singles/doubles €55/75)* is similar. **Hotel Wiesbaden** *(*☎ *23 23 47, fax 25 28 45; Baseler Strasse 52; singles/doubles from €65/75)* is one of the better options in the area.

GERMANY

Hotel Glockshuber (☎ 74 26 28, fax 74 26 29; Mainzer Landstrasse 120; singles/doubles from €35/60), north of the main train station, is another pleasant option. **Hotel Topas** (☎ 23 08 52, fax 238 05 82 60; Niddastrasse 88; singles/doubles €64.50/68) has quite nice rooms with bathroom.

Sachsenhausen has few budget places. **Hotel Am Berg** (☎ 61 20 21, fax 61 51 09; Grethenweg 23; singles/doubles without bath from €33/55, doubles with bath from €70), in the quiet backstreets a few minutes' walk southeast from Südbahnhof, has rooms with and without bathroom, and several more expensive choices.

Some of the best pensions are in Frankfurt's posh Westend. **Pension Backer** (☎ 74 79 92, fax 74 79 00; Mendelssohnstrasse 92; singles/doubles €25/40) has basic rooms. **Hotel-Pension Bruns** (☎ 74 88 96, fax 74 88 46; singles/doubles without bath €40/50, with bath €50/65) at No 42 has simple rooms in a spacious house. The pleasant **Hotel-Pension Gölz** (☎ 74 67 35, fax 74 61 42; e info@hotel-goelz.de; Beethovenstrasse 44; singles/doubles with bath €45/70) has basic rooms.

The **Hotel Beethoven** (☎ 74 60 91, fax 74 84 66; e mail@hotelbeethoven.de; Beethovenstrasse 44; singles/doubles with bath €70/145) has newly renovated rooms.

In Bockenheim, **Hotel West** (☎ 247 90 20, fax 707 53 09; Gräfstrasse 81; singles/doubles €60/80) has quite good rooms with facilities. **Hotel Falk** (☎ 70 80 94, fax 70 80 17; Falkstrasse 38a; singles/doubles €89/109), in a quiet but still central neighbourhood, is one notch higher.

East of Konstablerwache there's the friendly **Hotel-Garni Diplomat** (☎ 430 40 40, fax 430 40 22; Ostendstrasse 24-26; singles/doubles €50/70) which has passable rooms a short walk from the Ostend S-Bahn station. The **Hotel am Zoo** (☎ 94 99 30, fax 94 99 31 99; e Hotel-am-Zoo@t-online.de; Alfred-Brehm-Platz 6; singles/doubles €72/106) is a reasonable option.

The quality **Steigenberger Frankfurter Hof** (☎ 215 02, fax 21 59 00; e frankfurter-hot@steigenberger.de; Am Kaiserplatz; singles/doubles Mon-Fri €335/385, Sat & Sun €160/210) has rates during the week that exclude breakfast, however, it's a far better bet on the weekend when there are special rates that include breakfast.

Places to Eat

The area around the main train station has lots of ethnic eating options. Baseler Strasse in particular has a Middle Eastern tone. **India Curry House** (Weserstrasse 17; mains from €5) has savoury kormas and curries. The pan-Asian **Ginger Brasserie** (Windmühlstrasse 14; mains €10-17) has everything Eastern on the menu from Sichuan to sushi, tandoori to Thai.

Known to the locals as Fressgass (Munch-Alley), the Kalbächer Gasse and Grosse Bockenheimer Strasse area, between Opernplatz and Börsenstrasse, has some medium-priced restaurants and fast-food places with outdoor tables in summer. **Blaubart Gewölbekeller** (Kaiserhofstrasse 18; mains from €6) serves well-priced hearty dishes in a beer cellar atmosphere. It's also a lively place to drink until late. The **Kleinmarkthalle** off Hasengasse, is a great produce market with loads of fruit, vegetables, meats and hot food. **Metropol** (Weckmarkt 13-15; mains from €7.20), near the Dom, serves up well-priced and filling salads, casseroles and the like until late, but the service is notoriously slow.

Apple-wine taverns are a Frankfurt eating and drinking tradition. They serve Ebbelwoi (Frankfurt dialect for Apfelwein), an alcoholic apple cider, along with local specialities like Handkäse mit Musik (literally, 'hand-cheese with music'). This is a round cheese soaked in oil and vinegar and topped with onions; your bowel supplies the music. Some good Ebbelwoi are situated in Alt-Sachsenhausen – the area directly behind the DJH hostel – which bulges with eateries and pubs. The **Fichte-Kränzi** (Wallstrasse 5; mains around €8) is highly recommended for its friendly atmosphere and well-priced food. It also serves beer. **Zum Gemalten Haus** (Schweizer Strasse 67; mains from €7) is a lively place full of paintings of old Frankfurt. The **Zur Sonne** (☎ 45 93 96; Berger Strasse 312; open from 4pm daily), in Bornheim, is authentic and has a gorgeous yard for summer tippling. Take the U-4 to Bornheim-Mitte.

Wallstrasse and the surrounding streets in Alt-Sachsenhausen also have lots of ethnic mid-priced restaurants.

Another good place for ravenous hunters and gatherers is the cosmopolitan Berger Strasse and Nordend areas north of the Zeil. **Eckhaus** (Bornheimer Landstrasse 45; meals from €6) is a relaxed restaurant and bar that serves well-priced salads and main dishes in the evening. For both of these, take the U-4 to Merianplatz. **Strandcafé** *(Koselstrasse 46; dishes under €13)* serves delicious felafel and salads and other Middle Eastern dishes in a pleasant atmosphere; take the U-5 to Musterschule. **Grössenwahn** *(☎ 59 93 56; Lenau-Strasse 97)* is a truly wonderful upmarket pub where, if you choose carefully, you can eat for less than €15. Take the U-5 to Glauburgstrasse. Follow Lenaustrasse north until you think you've reached the end – and keep going north.

In Bockenheim, **Stattcafé** *(Grempstrasse 21; dishes from €6)* offers vegetarian and meat dishes, as well as good coffee and cakes. **Pielok** *(Jordanstrasse 3; mains around €7)* looks like your grandmother had a hand in the decorations; it's cosy and the food is traditional, filling and very popular with students.

Fresh produce **markets** are held 8am to 6pm on Thursday and Friday at Bockenheimer Warte and Südbahnhof respectively. There is a **supermarket** in the basement of Karstadt on Zeil. An **HL supermarket** is situated in the basement of Woolworths on Schweizer Strasse in Sachsenhausen.

Entertainment

Ballet, opera and theatre are strong features of Frankfurt's entertainment scene. For information and bookings, ring **Städtische Bühnen** *(☎ 134 04 00; Willy-Brandt-Platz)*, or the **Karstadt concert and theatre-booking service** *(☎ 29 48 48; Zeil 90; commission charged)*. *Journal Frankfurt* *(€1.50)* and *Fritz* have good listings in German of what's on in town.

The **Turm-Palast** *(☎ 28 17 87; Am Eschenheimer Turm)* is a multiscreen cinema showing films in English. English-language plays and musicals are staged every evening (except Monday) by the **English Theater** *(☎ 24 23 16 20; Kaiserstrasse 52)*.

Frankfurt also has a couple of very good jazz venues. **Blues & Beyond** *(☎ 46 99 09 87; Berger Strasse 159)* is a small venue for blues and jazz bands; the **Jazzkeller** *(☎ 28 85 37; Kleine Bockenheimer Strasse 18a)* gets top acts. **Sinkkasten** *(☎ 28 03 85; Brönnerstrasse 5)* has a mix of acoustic shows and 1980s-themed dance nights. **Mousonturm** *(☎ 40 58 95 20; Waldschmidtstrasse 4)*, in a converted soap factory in Bornheim, offers arty rock, dance performances and politically oriented cabaret.

The Cave *(Brönnerstrasse 11)* is a club that spins goth and features occasional live concerts; **U60311** *(Rossmarkt)* has techno and house music; **Cooky's** *(Am Salzhaus 4)* stays open until the wee hours, delivering a winning combination of hip-hop and house nights and live indie bands; **Stereo Bar** *(Abtgässchen 7)*, in Sachsenhausen, has a 1970s feel. A popular gay bar is **Zum Schwejk** *(Schäffergasse 20)*, while **Harvey's** *(Friedberger Platz)*, a restaurant and bar, is a favoured meeting place for Frankfurt's gay and lesbian yuppies.

Getting There & Away

Air Germany's largest airport is **Flughafen Frankfurt/Main** *(☎ 69 01)*, with the highest freight and second-highest passenger turnover in Europe. This high-tech town has two terminals linked by an elevated railway. Departure and arrival halls A, B and C are in Terminal 1, with Lufthansa flights handled in hall A; halls D and E are in the new Terminal 2. The airport train station has two sections: platforms 1 to 3 (below Terminal 1, hall B) handle regional and S-Bahn connections, whereas IR, IC and ICE connections are in the long-distance train station. Signs point the way. Hourly IC or EC trains go to Cologne *(€33.80, two hours)* and Nuremberg *(€38.80, 2½ hours)* and ICEs run to/from Hamburg on weekdays *(€100, four hours)*.

Bus Long-distance buses leave from the southern side of the main train station, where there's a **Deutsche Touring/Eurolines office** *(☎ 79 03 50; Mannheimer Strasse 4)* that handles bookings. It handles most European destinations; the most interesting possibility is the Romantic Road bus (see the Bavaria section earlier in this chapter). Also see the introductory Getting There & Away section.

Train The Hauptbahnhof handles more departures and arrivals than any other station in Germany. For rail information, call ☎ 01805-99 66 33. The **DB Lounge** *(open 6am-11pm daily)* above the information office is a comfortable retreat for anyone with a valid train ticket.

Car Frankfurt features the famed Frankfurter Kreuz, the biggest autobahn intersection in the country. All main car rental companies have offices in the main hall of the train station and at the airport.

The **ADM-Mitfahrzentrale** (☎ 194 40; Baselerplatz), is a three-minute walk south of the train station. A sample of fares (including fees) is: Berlin €29, Hamburg €28, Cologne €14, Dresden €27 and Munich €22.

Getting Around

To/From the Airport The S-Bahn's S8/S9 train runs every 15 minutes between the airport and Frankfurt Hauptbahnhof (11 minutes), usually continuing via Hauptwache and Konstablerwache to Offenbach; a fixed fare of €5.90 applies. Taxis (about €25 and taking 30 minutes without traffic jams) or the frequent airport bus No 61 (from Südbahnhof; €3.10) take longer.

Public Transport Frankfurt's excellent transport network (RMV) integrates all bus, tram, S-Bahn and U-Bahn lines. Single or day tickets can be purchased from automatic machines (press the flag button for explanations in English) at almost any stop. Press *Einzelfahrt Frankfurt* for destinations in zone 50, which takes in most of Frankfurt (a plane symbol indicates the button for the airport). Peak period short-trip tickets (*Kurzstrecken*) cost €1.05, single tickets cost €1.60 and a *Tageskarte* (24-hour ticket) is €4.35 without a trip to the airport and €6.65 with an airport trip.

Car Traffic flows smoothly in Frankfurt, but the extensive system of one-way streets can be extremely frustrating. You might want to park your vehicle in an outlying area or one of the many car parks and proceed on foot or by public transport.

Taxi They are slow compared with public transport and expensive at €2.05 flag fall plus a minimum of €1.48 per kilometre. There are numerous taxi ranks throughout the city, or you can book a cab (☎ 23 00 01, 25 00 01, 54 50 11).

MARBURG
☎ 06421 • pop 77,000
Situated 90km north of Frankfurt, Marburg is known for its charming Altstadt with the splendid **Elizabethkirche** and **Philipps-Universität**, Europe's very first Protestant university, which was founded in 1527. Wander up to the museum in the **castle**, from where there are nice views of the old town.

Places to Stay & Eat
Marburg's **DJH hostel** (☎ 234 61; e marburg@djh-hessen.de; Jahnstrasse 1; juniors/seniors €16.50/19.20) is about a 10-minute walk upstream along the river from Rudolfsplatz in the Altstadt. For other budget accommodation drop in at the **tourist office** (☎ 99 12 23; e mtm@marburg.de; Pilgrimstein 26); it has a free room-finding service. The **Barfuss** (☎ 253 49; Barfüsserstrasse 33) is a very lively eatery with moderately priced food.

North Rhine-Westphalia

The North Rhine-Westphalia (Nordrhein-Westfalen) region was formed in 1946 from a hotchpotch of principalities and bishoprics, most of which had belonged to Prussia since the early 19th century. One-quarter of Germany's population lives here. The Rhine-Ruhr industrial area is Germany's economic powerhouse and one of the most densely populated conurbations in the world. Though the area is dominated by bleak industrial centres connected by a maze of train lines and autobahns, some of the cities are steeped in history and their attractions warrant an extensive visit.

COLOGNE
☎ 0221 • pop 1 million
Located at a major crossroads of European trade routes, Cologne (Köln) was an important city even in Roman times. It was then known as Colonia Agrippinensis, the capital of the province of Germania, and had no fewer than 300,000 inhabitants. In later years it remained one of northern Europe's main cities (the largest in Germany until the 19th century), and it is still the centre of the German Roman Catholic church. Almost completely destroyed in WWII, it was quickly rebuilt and many of its old churches and monuments have been meticulously restored.

It's worth making the effort to visit this lively, relaxed city, especially for its famous cathedral, interesting museums and vibrant nightlife.

Orientation
Situated on the Rhine River, the skyline of Cologne is dominated by the cathedral. The pedestrianised Hohe Strasse runs straight

through the middle of the old town from north to south and is Cologne's main shopping street. The main train station is just north of the cathedral. The main bus station is just behind the train station, on Breslauer Platz.

Maps The DB Service Point has useful free maps of the central area and the tourist office sells an excellent map (€2) with a street key.

Information
Tourist Offices The helpful **tourist office** (☎ 22 12 33 45; e *koelntourismus@stadt -koeln.de; Unter Fettenhennen 19; open 8am-9pm Mon-Sat, 9.30am-7pm Sun & holidays May-Oct, 8am-9pm Mon-Sat, 9.30am-7pm Sun & holidays Nov-Apr)* is opposite the cathedral's main entrance. Browse through the guide booklets before deciding which one to buy. *Monatsvorschau*, the monthly what's-on booklet, is a good investment at €1.20. The room-finding service (€3) is a bargain when the city is busy with trade fairs, however, note that you cannot book by telephone.

Money There is a **Reisebank** *(open 8am-10pm daily)* situated at the train station. There is an office of **AmEx** *(Burgmauer 14)* and a **Thomas Cook** *(Burgmauer 4)* near the tourist office.

Post & Communications The **post office** *(open 6am-10pm Mon-Sat, 7am-10pm Sun)* is in Ludwig im Bahnhof bookshop near track 6 inside the main train station.

Email & Internet Access At **Future Point** (☎ 206 72 51; *Richmodstrasse 13; open 8am-1am Mon-Sat, 10am-1am Sun)*, the charge is €1.50 per 30 minutes online.

Bookshops Inside the main train station, **Ludwig im Bahnhof** stocks the international press and also has Lonely Planet titles.

Laundry There is an **Eko-Express Waschsalon** *(cnr Händelstrasse & Richard-Wagner-Strasse; open Mon-Sat)*.

Medical & Emergency Services The **police** are on ☎ 110; for **fire and ambulance** call ☎ 112. An on-call **doctor** can be contacted on ☎ 192 92.

Things to See
Cologne has a large town centre and the cathedral (Dom) is its heart, soul and tourist draw. Combined with the excellent museums next door, plan to spend at least one full day inside and around the Dom.

Dom Head first to the southern side of the Dom *(open 7am-7.30pm daily)* for an overall view. The structure's sheer size, with spires rising to 157m, is overwhelming. Building began in 1248 in the French Gothic style. The huge project was stopped in 1560 but started again in 1842, in the style originally planned, as a symbol of Prussia's drive for unification. It was finally finished in 1880. Miraculously, it survived WWII's heavy night bombing intact.

When you reach the transept you'll be overwhelmed by the sheer size and magnificence of it all. The five **stained-glass windows** along the north aisle depict the lives of the Virgin and St Peter. Behind the high altar you can see the **Magi's Shrine** (c. 1150–1210), believed to contain the remains of the Three Wise Men, which was brought to Cologne from Milan in the 12th century. On the south side, in a chapel off the ambulatory, is the 15th-century **Adoration of the Magi altarpiece**. Guided tours in English are held at 10.30am and 2.30pm Monday to Saturday (at 2.30pm only on Sunday) and cost €4/2 per adult/concession; meet inside the main portal. Tours in German are more frequent and cost €3/2.

For a fitness fix, climb 509 steps up the Dom's south tower to view the stupendous **steeples** *(adult/concession €2/1; open 9am-5pm daily Mar-Sept, 9am-4pm Oct-Feb)*, which towered over all of Europe until the Eiffel Tower was erected. Look at the 24-tonne **Peter Bell**, the largest working bell in the world, on your way up. At the end of your climb, the view from the vantage point, 98.25m up, is absolutely stunning; on a clear day you can see all the way to the Siebengebirge Mountains beyond Bonn. The cathedral **treasury** *(adult/concession €4/2; open 10am-6pm daily)* has a small but valuable collection of reliquaries. Cologne's archbishops are interred in the crypt.

Other Churches Many other churches are worth a look, particularly Romanesque ones that have been restored since WWII bombing. The most handsome from the outside is **Gross St Martin**, near Fischmarkt, while the most

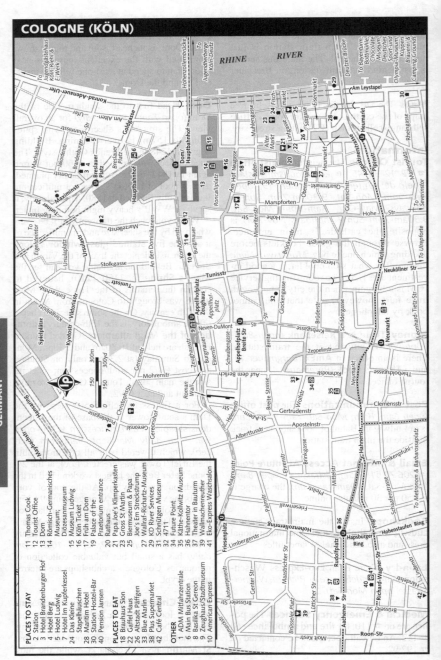

COLOGNE (KÖLN)

PLACES TO STAY
2 Station
3 Hotel Brandenburger Hof
4 Hotel Berg
5 Hotel Ludwig
7 Hotel Im Kupferkessel
24 Das Kleine Stapelhäuschen
28 Maritim Hotel
30 Station Hostel+Bar
40 Pension Jansen

PLACES TO EAT
18 Brauhaus Sion
22 Gaffel Haus
26 Altstadt Päffgen
33 Joe's Em Streckstrump
38 Blue Marlin
41 Café Central

11 Thomas Cook
12 Tourist Office
13 Dom
14 Römisch-Germanisches Museum; Diözesanmuseum
15 Museum Ludwig
16 Köln Ticket
17 Früh am Dom
19 Palace of the Praetorium entrance
20 Rathaus
21 Papa Joe's Klimperkasten
23 Gross St Martin
25 Biermuseum & Papa
27 Wallraf-Richartz-Museum
29 KD River Services
31 Schnütgen Museum
32 4711
34 Future Point
35 Käthe-Kollwitz Museum
36 Hahnentor
37 Theater in Bauturm
39 Wallmachenreuther
41 Eko-Express Waschsalon

OTHER
1 ADM Mitfahrzentrale
6 Main Bus Station
8 Basilika St Gereon
9 Zeughaus/Stadtmuseum
10 American Express

stunning interior is that of the **Basilika St Gereon** (*Christophstrasse*), with its incredible four-storey **decagon** (*open 9am-12.30pm & 1.30pm-6pm Mon-Fri, Sat morning & Sun afternoon*); enter from Gereonkloster.

Museums Next to the cathedral there's the **Römisch-Germanisches Museum** (*Roman Germanic Museum; Roncalliplatz 4; adult/concession €4/2; open 10am-5pm Tues-Sun*), which displays artefacts from all aspects of the Roman settlement in the Rhine Valley. The highlights are the giant Poblicius grave monument and the Dionysos mosaic around which the museum was built.

The **Wallraf-Richartz-Museum** (*Martinstrasse 39; adult/concession €6.60/4.10; open 10am-6pm Wed-Fri, 10am-8pm Tues, 11am-6pm Sat & Sun*) has a fantastic collection that includes paintings by Rubens, Rembrandt and Monet. The **Museum Ludwig** (*Bischofsgartenstrasse 1; adult/concession €7.70/4.10; open 10am-6pm Wed-Fri, 10am-8pm Tues, 11am-6pm Sat & Sun*) uses natural light to brilliant effect, displaying prime pieces from Kirchner, Kandinsky and Max Ernst, as well as pop-art works by Rauschenberg and Andy Warhol. The building also houses a unique photography collection from the former Agfa Museum in Leverkusen.

The former church of St Cecilia houses the **Schnütgen Museum** (*Cäcilienstrasse 29; adult/concession €2.50/1.25; open 10am-5pm Tues-Fri, 11am-5pm Sat & Sun*), an overwhelming display of church riches, including many religious artefacts as well as early ivory carvings. At the **Diözesanmuseum** (*Roncalliplatz; admission free; open Fri-Wed*) you can see religious treasures.

The multimedia **Deutsches Sport- und Olympia-Museum** (*Rheinaufen 1; adult/concession €4/2; open 10am-6pm Tues-Fri, 11am-7pm Sat & Sun*) is a great place to find out all about the history of sport from ancient times to the present day.

Other museums worth visiting are **Käthe Kollwitz Museum** (*Neumarkt 18-24; adult/concession €2.50/1*), with some fine sculpture and graphics by this acclaimed socialist artist; the **Zeughaus** (*Zeughausstrasse*), restored as the **Stadtmuseum** (*adult/concession €3.60/2*), with a model of Cologne and a good armoury collection; and the **Chocolate Museum** (*Rheinauhafen 1a; adult/concession €5.50/3*), on the river in the Rheinauhafen

near the Altstadt, where you will learn everything about the history of making chocolate – as if you cared beyond the taste (all closed Monday).

Activities
Guided Tours
The summer daily **city tour** in English lasts two hours; the bus departs from the tourist office at 10am, 12.30pm and 3pm (at 11am and 2pm from November to March). The cost is a steep €14. You can also make day trips to nearby cities with **KD River Cruises** (see Getting There & Away later in this section). A trip down the Rhine to Bonn is €10.40 and to Koblenz it's €32.80 one way.

Historical Walks
You can give yourself a free tour of ancient and medieval Cologne by walking around its restored monuments with a free city-sights map from the tourist office. If you walk west from the Dom along Komödienstrasse over Tunisstrasse, you'll reach the Zeughaus museum, the Burgmauer side of which was built along the line of the **Roman wall**.

Continue west until you find a complete section of the north wall, which leads to a corner tower standing among buildings on the street corner at St-Apern-Strasse. One block south of here is another tower ruin near Helenenstrasse.

You can also take a lift down and walk through the **Roman sewer** to view the remains of the **palace of the Praetorium** (*adult/concession €1.50/0.75; open Tues-Sun*) under the medieval town hall (the entry is located on Kleine Budengasse). The **Rathaus** (*open 7.30am-4.15pm Mon-Thur, 7.30am-12.15pm Fri*) is open for viewing; the facades, foyer and tower have been restored.

The city's medieval towers and gates complement its Romanesque churches. The Bayenturm on the Rhine bank at the eastern end of Severinswall was completely rebuilt, but along the street to the west the vine-bedecked Bottmühle and the mighty main south gate of Severinstor have more of the original basalt and tuff stones.

To the northwest along Sachsenring is the vaulted Ulrepforte tower-gate and a section of wall with two more towers.

North of the city centre is the gate of Eigelsteintor on Eigelstein, suspended from which is a boat from the MS *Schiff Cöln*, which sank off Heligoland in 1914. The main west gate, Hahnentor, is at Rudolfplatz.

Special Events
Try to visit Cologne during the wild and crazy period of the Cologne Carnival (Karneval), rivalled only by Munich's Oktoberfest. People dress in creative costumes, clown suits, as popular personalities and whatever else their alcohol-numbed brains may invent. The streets explode with activity on the Thursday before the seventh Sunday before Easter. On Friday and Saturday evening the streets pep up, Sunday is like Thursday and on Monday (*Rosenmontag*) there are formal and informal parades, and much spontaneous singing and celebrating.

Places to Stay
Cheap accommodation in Cologne is not plentiful, but there are a couple of good pensions around the city, and you should be able to get private rooms unless there's a trade fair on.

Camping The most convenient camping ground is **Campingplatz der Stadt Köln** (☎ 83 19 66; *tent sites €4, plus €4 per person; open Easter–mid-Oct)* on Weidenweg in Poll, 5km southeast of the city centre. Take U16 to Marienburg and cross the Rodenkirchener bridge. **Campingplatz Berger** (☎ 39 22 11; *Uferstrasse 71; tent sites €4.50/6 per person/ car; open all year)* is 7km southeast of the city in Rodenkirchen. Take the U16 to Heinrich-Lübke-Ufer and from there bus No 130.

Hostels Cologne has two DJH hostels. The bustling **Jugendherberge Köln-Deutz** (☎ 81 47 11; e jh-koeln-deutz@djh-rheinland.de; *Siegesstrasse 5a; dorm beds juniors/seniors €17/19.50)* in Deutz is a 15-minute walk east from the main train station over the Hohenzollernbrücke, or three minutes from Bahnhof Köln-Deutz (sometimes called the Messe-Osthallen. The more pleasant **Jugendgästehaus Köln-Riehl** (☎ 76 70 81; e jh-koeln-riehl@djh-rheinland.de; *An der Schanz 14; rooms €21-34 per person)* is north of the city and has one- to six-bed rooms. Take the U15 or U16 to Boltensternstrasse. The backpackers hostel **Station** (☎ 912 53 01, fax 912 53 03; e station@hostel-cologne.de; *Marzellenstrasse 44-48; dorm beds €14, singles €25)* is an easy walk from the main train station.

Station Hostel+Bar (☎ 221 23 02 47; e station2@hotel-cologne.de; *Rheingasse 34-6; dorm beds €16.50, singles €25)*, the hostel's other branch, is closer to Cologne's pubs.

Hotels & Pensions Accommodation prices in Cologne increase by at least 20% when fairs are on. If you have private transport, inquire about parking – a night in a car park will set you back €15 or more (and not all of them operate 24 hours). The tourist office has a room-finding service that can help with hotel rooms in the lower price range.

Pension Jansen (☎/fax 25 18 75; *Richard-Wagner-Strasse 18; singles/doubles from €31/62)* provides basic rooms and is convenient to the restaurant quarter of town. **Hotel Im Kupferkessel** (☎ 13 53 38, fax 12 51 21; *Probsteigasse 6; singles/doubles from €26/ 49)* has recently remodelled rooms just a 15-minute walk west of the train station.

A lot of other budget and mid-range hotels cluster in the streets just north of the main train station. **Hotel Brandenburger Hof** (☎ 12 28 89, fax 13 53 04; *Brandenburger Strasse 2; singles/doubles without bath from €27/48, with bath €50/75)* has basic rooms. **Hotel Berg** (☎ 12 11 24, fax 139 00 11; e hotel@ hotel-berg.com; *Brandenburger Strasse 6; singles/doubles without bath from €41/49, with bath €62/72)* has fairly good rooms and offers Internet access. **Hotel Ludwig** (☎ 16 05 40, fax 16 05 44 44; e hotel@hotelludwig .com; *Brandenburger Strasse 22-24; singles/ doubles €70/110)* is a fairly good option in the mid-price range, with decent rooms; some have a view to the Dom and there are also weekend deals.

Das Kleine Stapelhäuschen (☎ 257 77 77, fax 257 42 32; e stapelhaeuschen@compu serve.com; *Fischmarkt 1-3; singles/doubles from €38.50/64, with bath €51/90)*, in the middle of the Altstadt, has pleasant rooms. Catering largely to a trade fair and business clientele is the **Maritim Hotel** (☎ 202 70, fax 202 78 26; e info.kol@maritim.de; *Heumarkt 20; singles/doubles from €145/169)*.

Places to Eat
Cologne's beer halls serve cheap and filling (though often bland) meals to go with their home brew (see Beer Halls under Entertainment later).

Brauhaus Sion (*Unter Taschenmacher 9)* is a big beer hall, packed most nights and for good reason: you'll eat your fill for well under €15, including a couple of beers. **Altstadt Päffgen** (*Heumarkt 62; dishes around €8*) at the northern end of the Heumarkt is more up-market but authentic. The **Gaffel Haus** (*Alter Markt 20-22*) is another nice place to eat and sample the local concoction. The **Blue Marlin** (*Wolfsstrasse 4*) does delicious sushi from €8 for eight pieces or from €1.10 a piece.

The Belgisches Viertel (Belgian Quarter) around and west of Hahnentor is packed with restaurants of all descriptions. You'll find a couple of moderately priced Asian eating houses on Händelstrasse.

Café Central (*Jülicher Strasse 1*), on the corner of Händelstrasse, is open till late and has an adjoining restaurant called **o.T.** (*mains €6.50-9.50*); the café itself does breakfast and light dishes.

To put together a picnic, visit a **market**; the biggest is held on Tuesday and Friday at the Aposteln-Kloster near Neumarkt. The supermarket **Plus** (*Aachener Strasse 64*) is in the Belgisches Viertel.

Entertainment

Evenings and weekends in the Altstadt are like miniature carnivals, with bustling crowds and lots to do.

Papa Joe's Klimperkasten (*Alter Markt 50*) is a lively jazz pub with a wonderful pianola. **Papa Joe's Em Streckstrump** (*Buttermarkt 37*) is more intimate. **Metronom** (☎ 21 34 65; *Weyerstrasse 59*), near the Kwartier Latäng (Latin Quarter), is Cologne's most respected evening bar for jazz enthusiasts, with live performances mainly weekdays.

Wallmachenreuther (*Brüsseler Platz 9*) is an off-beat bar in the Belgisches Viertel that also serves food. The gay scene also centres on the Belgisches Viertel.

E-Werk (☎ 96 27 90; *Schanzenstrasse 37*), in a converted power station in Mülheim, is Cologne's usual venue for rock concerts. It turns into a huge techno club on Friday and Saturday nights.

Köln Ticket (☎ 28 02 80; *Roncalliplatz*), next to the Römisch-Germanisches Museum, has tickets and information on classical music and theatre performances in town. **Theater im Bauturm** (☎ 52 42 42; *Aachener Strasse 24*) is one of Cologne's more innovative theatres.

Beer Halls As in Munich, beer in Cologne reigns supreme. There are more than 20 local breweries, all producing a variety called *Kölsch*, which is relatively light and slightly bitter. The breweries run their own beer halls and serve their wares in skinny glasses holding a mere 200ml, but you'll soon agree it's a very satisfying way to drink the stuff. See Places to Eat earlier for other suggestions. **Früh am Dom** (*Am Hof 12-14*) is famous for its own-brew beer; the **Biermuseum** (*Buttermarkt 39*) – beside Papa Joe's – has 18 varieties on tap. **Küppers Brauerei** (☎ 934 78 10; *Alteburger Strasse 157*) is in Bayenthal, south of the city (take the U16 to Bayenthalgürtel). It has a nice beer garden and there's also a beer museum which you can visit if you call ahead.

Shopping

A good Cologne souvenir might be a small bottle of *eau de Cologne*, which is still produced in its namesake city. The most famous brand is called 4711, after the house number where it was invented. There's still a **perfumery and gift shop** (*cnr Glockengasse & Schwertnergasse*) by that name. Try to catch the Glockenspiel, with characters from Prussian lore parading above the store hourly from 9am to 9pm.

Getting There & Away

Air Cologne/Bonn airport has many connections within Europe and to the rest of the world. For detailed flight information phone ☎ 02203-40 40 01/02.

Bus Deutsche Touring's **Eurolines** (☎ 13 52 52) offers overnight trips to Paris (€34, 6½ hours). The office is at the main train station at the Breslauer Platz exit.

Train There are frequent services operating to both nearby Bonn (€7, 18 minutes) and Düsseldorf (€8.10, 20 minutes) as well as to Aachen (€10.70, one hour). Frequent direct IC/EC (€47.80, 3¼ hours) and ICE (€53.40, 2¾ hours) trains go to Hanover. There are ICE links with Frankfurt/Main (€39, 2¼ hours) and Berlin (€97.60, 4½ hours). The Thalys high-speed train connects Paris and Cologne via Aachen and Brussels (€74.60/67.10 weekdays/weekends, four hours, seven times daily), with only a small discount for rail pass-holders!

Car The city is on a main north-south autobahn route and is easily accessible for drivers and hitchhikers. The **ADM Mitfahrzentrale** (☎ 194 40; *Maximinen Strasse 2*) is near the train station.

Boat An enjoyable way to travel to/from Cologne is by boat. **KD River Cruises** (☎ 208 83 18; *Frankenwerft 1*) has its headquarters in the city, and has services all along the Rhine.

Getting Around
To/From the Airport
Bus No 170 runs between Cologne/Bonn airport and the main bus station every 15 minutes from 5.30am to 11.20pm daily (€4.80, 20 minutes).

Public Transport Cologne offers a convenient and extensive mix of buses, trams and local trains – trams go underground in the inner city, and trains handle destinations up to 50km around Cologne. Ticketing and tariff structures are complicated. The best ticket option is the one-day pass: €5.15 if you're staying near the city (one or two zones); €8.25 for most of the Cologne area (four zones); and €11.50 including Bonn (seven zones). Single city trips cost €1.20 and 1½-hour two-zone tickets are €1.90.

Taxi To order a taxi call ☎ 194 10 or ☎ 28 82.

AROUND COLOGNE
Bonn
☎ 0228 • pop 293,000
This friendly, relaxed city on the Rhine south of Cologne became West Germany's temporary capital in 1949 and is mainly an administrative centre now that the seat of government and embassies are in Berlin. Settled in Roman times, Bonn was the seat of the electors of Cologne in the 18th century, and some of their baroque architecture survived the ravages of WWII and the postwar demand for modern government buildings. Organise a day trip out here and to the nearby spa town of Bad Godesberg. Classical music buffs can pay homage to Bonn's most famous son – Ludwig van Beethoven.

The **tourist office** (☎ 77 50 00, 194 33, fax 77 50 77, e *bonninformation@bonn.de; open 9am-6.30pm Mon-Fri, 9am-4pm Sat, 10am-2pm Sun*) is behind the Karstadt department store in Windeckstrasse, a three-minute walk along Poststrasse from the Hauptbahnhof.

Bonn is a city that lives and breathes Beethoven. You can visit the **Beethoven-Haus** (☎ 981 75; *Bonngasse 20; adult/concession €4/3; open 10am-6pm Mon-Sat Apr-Oct, 10am-5pm Mon-Sat Nov-Mar, 11am to 4pm Sunday all year*), where the composer was born in 1770. The house contains much memorabilia concerning his life and music, including his last piano, specially made with an amplified sounding board to accommodate his deafness. The annual Beethoven Festival takes place in September/October.

The **Münsterbasilika** (*Münsterplatz*) has a splendid interior and honours Sts Cassius and Florentius, two martyred Roman officers who became the patron saints of Bonn.

Bonn also boasts several interesting museums. The **Frauenmuseum** (☎ 69 13 44; *Im Krausfeld 10; adult/concession €8/5; open 2pm-6pm Tues-Sat, 11am-6pm Sun*) promotes and exhibits art created by women in an environment that combines history, mythology and contemporary artistic expressions. Take bus No 625, 626, 627 or 635 to Kaiser-Karl-Ring.

The **Haus der Geschichte der Bundesrepublik Deutschland** (*FRG History Museum; ☎ 916 50; Willy-Brandt-Allee 14; admission free; open 9am-7pm Tues-Sun*) covers the history of Germany from 1945; it is part of the **Museumsmeile**, a row of four museums that also includes the **Museum Alexander Koenig** (☎ 912 20; *Willy-Brandt-Allee 160*), a natural history museum; the **Kunstmuseum** (☎ 77 62 60; *Friedrich-Ebert-Allee 2*) with its collection of 20th-century art; and exhibitions at the **Kunst- und Ausstellungshalle der Bundesrepublik Deutschland** (☎ 917 12 00; *Friedrich-Ebert-Allee 2*).

There are frequent trains to Cologne in the north and to Koblenz (€15.40, 30 minutes) in the south. See the earlier Cologne Activities section for river cruises to/from Bonn. The Bonn transit system is linked with Cologne's and a one-way train ride between the two cities costs only €7 (see the earlier Cologne Getting Around section for passes covering both).

DÜSSELDORF
☎ 0211 • pop 571,000
Though not particularly strong in historical sights, this elegant and wealthy capital of North Rhine-Westphalia is, however, an important centre for fashion and commerce, and a charming example of big-city living along the Rhine River.

The massive Romanesque Dom (cathedral) in Trier, Germany

Cologne Carnival revellers

Once the boundary between East and West, Berlin's Brandenburg Gate is now the symbol of city unity

Surreal architecture of Caligari Hall, part of the Filmpark Babelsberg theme park, Potsdam, Germany

Looking out, Goslar, **Germany**

Contrasting styles at Goetheplatz, Frankfurt-am-Main

Lake Balaton in Hungary is one of Europe's largest freshwater lakes and a favourite with sailors

Buda's Castle Hill with Matthias Church and Fishermen's Bastion, from across the Danube, Budapest

Information

The **tourist office** (☎ 17 20 20; e tourist@ duesseldorf.de; open 8am-8pm Mon-Sat, 4pm-8pm Sun) is opposite the main exit of the train station towards the northern end of Konrad-Adenauer-Platz. The **main post office** is across the street. The **Reisebank** (open to 10pm Mon-Fri, until 9pm Sat & Sun) is in the train station's main hall. There's a convenient **SB Waschsalon laundry** (Charlottenstrasse 87).

Email & Internet Access Internet Café World (Worringer Platz 21), three blocks north of the train station, charges €2 for 30 minutes online.

Things to See & Do

To catch a glimpse of Düsseldorf's swish lifestyle, head for the famed Königsallee, or 'Kö', with its stylish (and pricey) boutiques and arcades. Stroll north along the Kö to the **Hofgarten**, a large park in the city centre.

The city has several interesting museums. These include the **Kunstmuseum Düsseldorf** (☎ 899 24 60; adult/concession €4/2; open 10am-6pm Tues-Sun) at Ehrenhof north of the Oberkasseler Brücke, with a comprehensive European collection, and the incorporated **Glasmuseum Hentrich** (open 10am-6pm Tues-Sun). The quite expansive modern art collection in the **Kunstsammlung Nordrhein-Westfalen** is displayed in two different galleries: **K20** (☎ 838 11 30; Grabbeplatz 5; adult/concession €6.50/4.50; open 10am-6pm Tues-Fri, 11am-6pm Sat & Sun) features works by 20th-century masters; **K21** (☎ 838 16 00; Ständehausstrasse 1; adult concession €6.50/4.50) specialises in art from 1990 onwards. A combined ticket to both costs €10/8.

The **Goethe-Museum Düsseldorf** (☎ 899 62 62; Jacobistrasse 2; adult/concession €2/1; open 11am-5pm Tues-Fri & Sun, 1pm-5pm Sat) in Schloss Jägerhof, pays tribute to the life and work of one of Europe's great men of letters. The large collection includes books, first drafts, letters, medals and more. Any German-literature buff will also want to visit **Heinrich-Heine-Institut** (Bilker Strasse 12-14; adult/concession €2/1; open 11am-5pm Tues-Fri & Sun, 1pm-5pm Sat), which documents this Düsseldorfer's career, or his house at Bolkerstrasse 53, now a literary pub.

On Marktplatz, the restored **Rathaus** looks out onto the **statue of Prince Elector Johann Wilhelm**, known in local speech as 'Jan Wellem'. He lies buried in the ornate early-baroque **St Andreas Kirche** (cnr Kay-und-Lore-Lorentz-Platz & Andreasstrasse), now in the care of a Dominican monastery. Another church worth visiting is the 13th-century **St Lambertus Basilika** (Stiftsplatz).

Nearby, the reconstructed **Schlossturm** of the long-destroyed Residenz stands on Burgplatz as a forlorn reminder of the Palatine elector's glory. In summer, the town's youth congregate on the steps below the tower. From here the pedestrian-only **Rheinuferpromenade** provides perfect strolling along the river. **Schloss Benrath** (☎ 899 72 71; open daily), a late-baroque pleasure palace with a park, located 12km south of the city, makes for a lovely excursion. Take tram No 701 from Jan-Wellem-Platz.

Places to Stay

There are two camping grounds relatively close to the city. **Campingplatz Nord Unterbacher See** (☎ 899 20 38; tent sites €5.50, plus €3.25/4 per person/car; open 4 Apr-27 Sept) is at Kleiner Torfbruch in Düsseldorf-Unterbach (take S-Bahn No 7 to Eller, and then bus No 735 to Seeweg). **Camping Oberlörick** (☎ 59 14 01; tent sites €4, plus €3/4.50 per person/car; open all year) is at Lutticherstrasse, just beside the Rhine in Düsseldorf-Lörick (U-Bahn No 70, 74 or 76 to Löricker Strasse, and then bus No 833 to Strandbad Lörick). The trek to the Altstadt is particularly inconvenient from either camping ground.

The **Jugendgästehaus** (☎ 55 73 10, fax 57 25 13; e jgh-duesseldorf@t-online.de; Düsseldorfer Strasse 1; dorm beds €20.20) is in posh Oberkassel across the Rhine from the Altstadt. It also has some private rooms. Take U-Bahn No 70, 74, 75, 76, or 77 from the main train station to Luegplatz. From there it's a short walk.

Düsseldorf frequently hosts trade shows that inflate its already high hotel and pension prices. The tourist office can help with finding big discounts offered by many of the comfortable business hotels on weekends and when no fair is in town. It levies €4 for bookings made on the day of check-in, otherwise it's €5.

Hotel Komet (☎ 17 87 90, fax 178 79 50; e info@hotelkomet.de; Bismarckstrasse 93; singles/doubles €33/44) provides reasonable

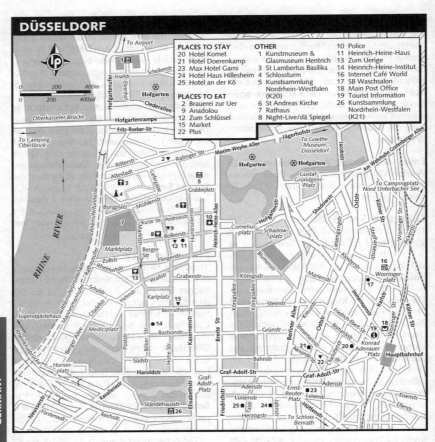

DÜSSELDORF

PLACES TO STAY	OTHER	10 Police
20 Hotel Komet	1 Kunstmuseum &	11 Heinrich-Heine-Haus
21 Hotel Doerenkamp	Glasmuseum Hentrich	13 Zum Uerige
23 Max Hotel Garni	3 St Lambertus Basilika	14 Heinrich-Heine-Institut
24 Hotel Haus Hillesheim	4 Schlossturm	16 Internet Café World
25 Hotel an der Kö	5 Kunstsammlung	17 SB Waschsalon
	Nordrhein-Westfalen	18 Main Post Office
PLACES TO EAT	(K20)	19 Tourist Information
2 Brauerei zur Uer	6 St Andreas Kirche	26 Kunstsammlung
9 Anadolou	7 Rathaus	Nordrhein-Westfalen
12 Zum Schlüssel	8 Night-Live/dä Spiegel	(K21)
15 Market		
22 Plus		

rooms including bathroom. The **Hotel Haus Hillesheim** (☎ 38 68 60, fax 386 86 33; e rezeption@hotel-hillesheim.de; Jahnstrasse 19; singles/doubles without bath €40/55, with bath €60/70) is a good value option. **Hotel Doerenkamp** (☎ 32 80 11, fax 13 45 82; Stresemannstrasse 25; singles/doubles €60/80) has fine rooms with facilities (ask for a quiet one), and pet rabbits to thrill the kids.

Hotel an der Kö (☎ 37 10 48, fax 37 08 35; Talstrasse 9; singles/doubles €78/87) has nice bright rooms with all facilities. **Max Hotel Garni** (☎ 38 68 00, fax 386 80 22; e info@max-hotelgarni.de; Aderstrasse 65; singles/doubles €115/140) has colourful, unique rooms with toilet and shower. Call before arriving.

Places to Eat
Brauerei zur Uer (Ratinger Strasse 16) is a rustic place to fill up for less than €10. Ratinger Strasse is also home to a couple of other pub-style places where you can eat and drink. **Zum Schlüssel** (Bolkerstrasse 43-47; dishes €5-11) is popular for beer, but also has good food. **Anadolou** (Mertensgasse 10; mains from €4) serves delicious Anatolian sit-down and take-away food including vegetarian dishes.

You can replenish supplies at the supermarket **Plus** (Stresemannstrasse 31), near Hotel Doerenkamp. A fresh produce **market** (open Mon-Sat) is held on Karlplatz.

Entertainment
Besides walking and museum-hopping, one of the best things to do in Düsseldorf is (surprise!)

drink beer. There are lots of bars (for drinking and eating) in the Altstadt, affectionately referred to as the 'longest bar in the world'. On evenings and weekends, the best places overflow onto the pedestrian-only streets. Favoured streets include Bolkerstrasse, Kurze Strasse, and Andreasstrasse as well as the surrounding side streets.

The beverage of choice is Alt beer, a dark and semisweet brew typical of Düsseldorf. Try Gatzweilers Alt in **Zum Schlüssel** (see Places to Eat earlier). Spartan **Zum Uerige** (*Berger Strasse*) is the only place where you can buy Uerige Alt beer. It's €1.40 per 250ml glass, and the beer flows so quickly that the waiters just carry around trays and give you a glass when you're ready (and sometimes even when you're not!). **Night-Live** (*Bolkerstrasse 22*) has live bands; it's upstairs from the **dä Spiegel**, itself a popular bar.

Getting There & Away

Düsseldorf's Lohausen airport (S-Bahn trains run every 20 minutes between the airport and the main train station) is busy with many national and international flights. Düsseldorf is part of a dense S-Bahn and train network in the Rhine-Ruhr region and there are regular IC/EC services to/from Hamburg (€63.20, 3¾ hours), ICE services to Hanover (€48.80, 2¾ hours) and Frankfurt (€47.20, 2½ hours), and trains to Cologne (€6.60, 30 minutes) and most other major German cities.

Getting Around

As Düsseldorf is very spread out, it's easiest to get around by public transport. Buy your ticket from one of the orange machines at stops, although bus drivers will sell singles, and validate it before boarding. A short-trip ticket up to 1.5km (destinations are listed on the machines) costs €2. A single ticket for zone A, which includes all of Düsseldorf proper, is €3.30. Better value is the 24-hour *Tages-Ticket* for €12, valid for up to five people in zone A.

AACHEN

☎ 0241 • pop 244,000

Aachen was famous in Roman times for its thermal springs. The great Frankish conqueror Charlemagne was so impressed by their revitalising qualities that he settled here and made it the capital of his kingdom in AD 794. Ever since, Aachen has held special significance

among the icons of German nationhood. It is now an industrial and commercial centre and is home to the country's largest technical university.

Orientation

Aachen's compact old centre is contained within two ring roads that roughly follow the old city walls. The inner ring road, or Graben-ring, changes names – most ending in 'graben' – and encloses the old city proper. To get to the tourist office from the Hauptbahnhof, turn left on leaving the main entrance, cross Römerstrasse, follow Bahnhofstrasse north and then go left along Theaterstrasse to Kapuzinergraben. Pick up an excellent free city map from the DB Service Point counter in the train station.

Information

The efficient **tourist office** (☎ 180 29 60/1; *e mail@aachen-tourist.de; Kapuzinergraben; open 9am-6pm Mon-Fri, 9am-2pm Sat, 10am-2pm Sun*) is at Atrium Elisenbrunnen. The **Sparkasse bank** (*Lagerhausstrasse 12; open 8.30am-4.30pm Mon-Wed, 8.30am-5.30pm Thur, 8.30am-4pm Fri*) is one block west of the train station. Three blocks northwest from there is the **main post office** (*An den Frauenbrüdern 1*). The bus station is at the northeastern edge of Grabenring on the corner of Kurhausstrasse and Peterstrasse.

Email & Internet Access Surf until late at **The Web** (*Kleinmarschierstrasse 74-76*), where 30 minutes of Internet time costs €2.

Things to See & Do

Dom Aachen's drawing card is its cathedral Dom (*Kaiserdom or Münster; open 7am-7pm daily*). The cathedral's subtle grandeur, its historical significance and interior serenity make a visit almost obligatory – it's a Unesco World Heritage Site. No fewer than 30 Holy Roman emperors were crowned here from 936 to 1531.

The heart of the cathedral is a Byzantine-inspired **octagon**, built on Roman foundations, which was the largest vaulted structure north of the Alps when consecrated as Charlemagne's court chapel in AD 805. He lies buried here in the golden **shrine**, and the cathedral became a site of pilgrimage after his death, not least for its religious relics. The Gothic **choir** was added in 1414; its massive stained-glass windows are impressive even though some date from after WWII. The octagon received its **folded dome** after the city fire of 1656 destroyed the original tent roof. The **western tower** dates from the 19th century.

Worth noting is the huge brass **chandelier**, which was added to the octagon by Emperor Friedrich Barbarossa in 1165; the **high altar** with its 11th-century gold-plated Pala d'Oro (altar front) depicting scenes of the Passion; and the gilded copper ambo, or **pulpit**, donated by Henry II. Unless you join up with a German-language tour (€2), you'll only catch a glimpse of Charlemagne's white-marble **throne** on the upper gallery of the octagon on the western side, where the nobles sat.

The entrance to the **Domschatzkammer** (*cathedral treasury; adult/concession €2.50/ 2; open 10am-1pm Mon, 10am-6pm Tues, Wed & Fri-Sun, 10am-9pm Thur*), with one of the richest collections of religious art north of the Alps, is on nearby Klostergasse. The entrance fee includes a pamphlet.

Other Attractions North of the cathedral, the 14th-century **Rathaus** (*adult/concession €1.50/0.75; open 10am-5pm Mon-Fri, 10am-1pm & 2pm-5pm Sat & Sun*) overlooks Markt, a lively gathering place in summer, with its fountain statue of Charlemagne. The eastern tower of the Rathaus, the Granusturm, was once part of Charlemagne's palace. History buffs will be thrilled by the grand Empire Hall upstairs, where Holy Roman emperors enjoyed their coronation feasts.

Foremost among Aachen's worthwhile museums is the **Ludwig Forum for International Art** (*☎ 180 70; Jülicherstrasse 97-109; adult/ concession €3/1.50; open 10am-4pm Tues & Thur, 10am-7.30pm Wed & Fri, 11am-4.30pm Sat & Sun*) with works by Warhol, Lichtenstein, Baselitz and others.

Thermal Baths Aachen was known for its thermal springs as early as Roman times, and the 8th-century Franks called the town 'Ahha', which is supposed to mean water. A visit to the city-owned **Carolus Thermen** (*☎ 18 27 40; Passstrasse 79*) costs €8 for two hours (€15 with the sauna), or €14 for up to five hours of splashy activity (€24 with sauna). It's in the city garden, northeast of the centre.

Places to Stay

The nearest camping ground is **Hoeve de Gastmolen** (*☎ 0031-433 06 57 55; tent sites,*

including 1 car, €7, plus €2.50 per person*) in the Dutch town of Vaals, about 6km outside Aachen at Lemierserberg 23. Take bus No 15 or 65 and get off at the 'Heuvel' stop.

The DJH **Jugendgästehaus** (*☎ 71 10 10; Maria-Theresia-Allee 260; dorm beds €20.50, singles/doubles €33.80/38.80*) is 4km southwest of the train station on a hill overlooking the city. Take bus No 2 to Ronheide, or bus No 12 to the closer Colynshof at the foot of the hill.

Hotels & Pensions The tourist office can arrange private rooms (in person only) from €13.50 to €64, but ask for something within walking distance of the city centre. To arrange a room in advance, call Aachen's room reservation line weekdays on ☎ 180 29 50/1.

Hotel Marx (*☎ 375 41, fax 267 05; e info@hotel-marx.de; Hubertusstrasse 33-35; singles/doubles €34/62, with bath from €49/67*) offers good cheap rooms but you'll have to perform your ablutions acrobatically in the basin. The central **Hotel Drei Könige** (*☎ 483 93, fax 361 52; Büchel 5; singles/ doubles €35/55, with shower & toilet €60/ 75*) has a few rather basic rooms. **Hotel am Marschiertor** (*☎ 319 41, fax 319 44; e hotel .marschiertor@t-online.de; Wallstrasse 1-7; singles/doubles from €62/75*), near the train station, has nice rooms (breakfast €8.50 extra). The historic hotel **Dorint Select Quellenhof** (*☎ 913 20, fax 913 21 00; e info .aahque@dorint.com; Monheimsallee 52; singles/doubles €170/195*) near the city park, charges an extra €19 for breakfast.

Places to Eat

Being a university town, Aachen is full of spirited cafés, restaurants and pubs, especially along Pontstrasse, referred to by locals as the 'Quartier Latin'. **Café Kittel** (*Pontstrasse 39; mains around €6*) is a cosy hang-out with a lively garden area. It serves reasonably priced light meals, including vegetarian dishes. **Gaststätte Labyrinth** (*Pontstrasse 156-158; dishes €7-11*) is a rambling beer-hall type place that lives up to its name and serves good, filling meals.

Alt Aachener Kaffeestuben (*Büchel 18*) is a coffee house (where wine also is served) with old-world charm that does a traditional lunchtime dish for €7. **Plus** (*Bahnhofstrasse 18*) is a fairly centrally situated supermarket for self-caterers.

Entertainment

The best source of information on bars, clubs and restaurants in Aachen and the Maas-Rhine region is the free *Euroview* guide in English – the tourist office keeps copies. **Domkeller** *(Hof 1)* has been a student pub since the 1950s and usually features jazz or blues on Monday. **B9** *(Blondelstrasse 9)* is one club that attracts a young crowd. The style changes nightly. **Club Voltaire** *(Friedrichstrasse 9)* attracts an older, mixed crowd. The **City Theatre** *(☎ 478 42 44; Theaterplatz)* has concerts and opera most nights; **Aachen Ticket** *(☎ 180 29 65)* in the tourist office has information and sells tickets.

Getting There & Away

Aachen is well served by road and rail. There are fast trains almost every hour to Cologne (€10, 43 minutes) and Liège (€9.90, 40 minutes). The high-speed Thalys passes through seven times daily on its way to Brussels and Paris. There's also a frequent bus service to Maastricht (€5, 55 minutes).

Getting Around

Aachen's points of interest are clustered around the city centre, which is covered easily on foot. Those arriving with private transport can park their cars in one of the many car parks. City bus tickets bought from the driver cost €1.20. A 24-hour Familienkarte und Gruppenkarte is valid for up to five people and costs €4.85. You can buy it on buses and from machines and outlets.

Bremen

The federal state of Bremen covers only the 404 sq km comprising the two cities of Bremen (the state capital) and Bremerhaven. In medieval times Bremen was Europe's northernmost archbishopric. The city was ruled by the Church until joining the Hanseatic League in the 14th century. Controlled by the French from 1810 to 1813, Bremen went on to join the German Confederation in 1815. In 1871 the city was made a state of the German Empire. In 1949 Bremen was officially declared a state of the Federal Republic of Germany.

BREMEN

☎ 0421 • pop 550,000

Bremen is, after Hamburg, the most important harbour in Germany, even though the open sea lies 113km to the north. Its Hanseatic past and congenial Altstadt area around Am Markt and Domsheide make it an enjoyable place to explore on foot, and Bremen's vibrant student population ensures the fun continues long after dark.

Orientation & Information

The heart of the city is Am Markt, but its soul is the port. The **tourist office** *(☎ 30 80 00; e btz@bremen-tourism.de; open 9.30am-6.30pm Mon-Wed, 9.30am-8pm Thur & Fri, 9.30am-4pm Sat & Sun)* is before the main train station. There is also a booth at the Rathaus opposite the smaller of the main Altstadt churches, Unser Lieben Frauen Kirche. **City walks** (English explanations provided) leave at 2pm daily from the tourist office at the station (€6). A Bremen tourist card (from €8.50 for two days) offers unlimited public transport and substantial discounts on city sights.

There's a **Reisebank** inside the train station. The **main post office** is also on Domsheide and there's another one near the train station. For more information visit the city's website at W www.bremen-tourism.de.

Things to See & Do

Around Am Markt don't miss the splendid and ornate **Rathaus**, the cathedral **St-Petri-Dom**, which has a tower **lookout** *(admission €1; open Easter-Oct)* and **museum** *(adult/concession €1.50/1)* For general gawking and climbing, the Dom, lookout, and museum are open 10am to 5pm Monday to Friday, 10am to 2pm Saturday and 2pm to 5pm Sunday. The lookout, though is only open half the year. There's also the large statue of **Roland**, Bremen's sentimental protector, which was erected in 1404.

Walk down **Böttcherstrasse**, a must-see recreation of a medieval alley, complete with tall brick houses, shops, galleries, restaurants and three **museums** *(adult/concession combined ticket €6/3; open 11pm-6pm Tues-Sun)*. The **Paula Modersohn-Becker Museum**, at No 8, has works by its namesake contemporary painter, and varied exhibits of the **Bernhard Hoetger Collection**; Hoetger's striking sculptures grace much of the Böttcherstrasse. The **Museum im Roselius-Haus** is at No 6, with a collection of paintings and applied arts from the 12th through to the 19th centuries. The **Glockenspiel**, active in summer hourly from

GERMANY

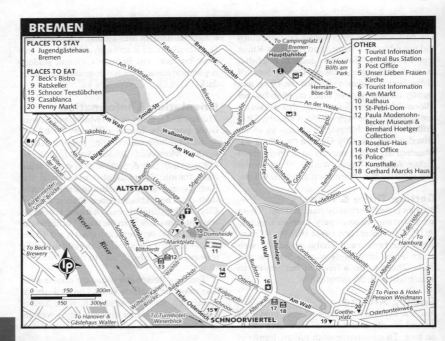

BREMEN

PLACES TO STAY
4 Jugendgästehaus Bremen

PLACES TO EAT
7 Beck's Bistro
9 Ratskeller
15 Schnoor Teestübchen
19 Casablanca
20 Penny Markt

OTHER
1 Tourist Information
2 Central Bus Station
3 Post Office
5 Unser Lieben Frauen Kirche
6 Tourist Information
8 Am Markt
10 Rathaus
11 St-Petri-Dom
12 Paula Modersohn-Becker Museum & Bernhard Hoetger Collection
13 Roselius-Haus
14 Post Office
16 Police
17 Kunsthalle
18 Gerhard Marcks Haus

noon to 6pm (in winter at noon, 3pm and 6pm), plays an extended tune between rooftops and an adjacent panel swivels to reveal a rotating cast of fearless explorers, from Leif Erikson to Charles Lindbergh.

The nearby **Schnoorviertel** area features fishing cottages that are now a tourist attraction, with shops, cafés and tiny lanes.

An excellent walk around the Altstadt is along the **Wallanlagen**, peaceful parks stretching along the old city walls and moat. Backing onto the parkland is Bremen's **Kunsthalle** (*adult/concession €5/2.50; open 10am-5pm Wed-Sun, 10am-9pm Tues*) art gallery. **Gerhard Marcks Haus** (*adult/concession €3.50/2.50; open 10am-6pm Tues-Sun*) contains a good collection which spans the breadth of sculpting history, including works by the museum's namesake. Both museums are closed on Monday.

Beck's Brewery Tours of Beck's Brewery (☎ 50 94 55 55; Am Deich 18-19) are available (take tram No 1 or 5 from the train station to Westerstrasse). German-language tours are run hourly from 10am to 5pm Tuesday to Saturday, to 3pm Sunday, and tours in English are

at 1.30pm on the same days. Tours cost €3 and include a tasting.

One good reference around which to frame a Bremen trip is the **Fairy-Tale Road** between Hanau, the birthplace of the Brothers Grimm, and Bremen (see Fairy-Tale Road in the Lower Saxony section later in this chapter).

Places to Stay
The closest camping ground is **Campingplatz Bremen** (☎ 21 20 02; Am Stadtwaldsee 1; tent sites €4, plus €4/2 per person/car). Take tram No 6 from the train station to the Klagenfurter Strasse stop.

Jugendgästehaus Bremen (☎ 17 13 69, fax 17 11 02; Kalkstrasse 6; beds juniors/seniors €17/19.70) is across the river from Beck's Brewery. Take tram No 3 or 5 from the train station to Am Brill.

The friendly **Hotel Garni Gästehaus Walter** (☎ 55 80 27, fax 55 80 29; Buntentorsteinweg 86-88; singles/doubles from €25/40) has pleasant rooms, some with shower and toilet. Take tram No 4 or 5 from the main train station. **Hotel-Pension Weidmann** (☎ 498 44 55; Am Schwarzen Meer 35; singles/doubles €21/41) provides basic accommodation. Take tram No 2 from Domsheide or No 10 from the station. The Art Nouveau **Hotel Bölts am Park** (☎ 34 61 10, fax 34 12 27; Slevogtstrasse 23; singles/doubles from €35/75) has very nice rooms with facilities. You get a pretty nifty view at the **Turmhotel Weserblick** (☎ 94 94 10, fax 949 41 10; Osterdeich 53; singles/doubles €67/82).

Places to Eat

A prowl around Ostertorsteinweg (near Am Dobben) will offer all sorts of gastronomic possibilities. **Casablanca** (Ostertorsteinweg 59; mains €5-12) is known for its breakfasts; it also has cheap pastas and soups. **Piano** (Fehrfeld 64), just east of Am Dobben, serves huge Mediterranean-inspired salads and tasty baked casseroles for around €5.50 to €7.50.

The long courtyard of Auf den Höfen, north of Ostertorsteinweg, has several restaurants and bars and serves as one of the epicentres of Bremen's nightlife. **Zum Hofheurigen** serves schnitzel to an older crowd for around €10. **Savarin** serves good casseroles by candlelight for around €6; **2Raum Lounge** is an achingly hip, minimalist bar/restaurant that offers a limited menu starting at €6.50.

On Markt, **Beck's Bistro** (Markt 9; lunch specials around €8) has traditional dishes à la carte, and lunch specials. **Schnoor Teestübchen** (Wüstestätte 1; lunch dishes around €6) specialises in tea and cakes, but it also serves vegetarian soups and quiche in a low-ceilinged, hobbit-like setting. Bremen's **Ratskeller** has 650 varieties of wine but no Beck's beer.

The **Penny Markt** (Ostertorsteinweg) is one convenient supermarket.

Getting There & Away

There are frequent regional and IC trains servicing Hamburg (€16.80, one hour). There are hourly IC trains to Cologne (€46.60, three hours). A couple of ICE trains run direct to Frankfurt (€88.40, 3½ hours) and Munich (€124, six hours) daily. Change trains in Hanover for Berlin (€135, 3½ hours). For Amsterdam (€54, four hours), you change in Osnabrück.

Getting Around

To get to Am Markt follow the tram route from directly in front of the train station. The tourist office stocks good public transport maps. Short trips on buses and trams cost €1.85, a four-trip transferable ticket is €5.60 and a day pass is €4.50.

Lower Saxony

Lower Saxony (Niedersachsen) has much to offer, and it's a quick train ride or autobahn drive from the tourist centres down south. The scenic Harz Mountains, the old student town of Göttingen, and the picturesque towns along the Fairy-Tale Road are the most popular tourist attractions. British occupation forces created the federal state of Lower Saxony during 1946, when the states of Braunschweig (Brunswick), Schaumburg-Lippe and Oldenburg were amalgamated with the Prussian province of Hanover.

HANOVER
☎ 0511 • pop 523,000

Hanover (Hannover), the capital of Lower Saxony, has close links with the English-speaking world. In 1714, the eldest son of Electress Sophie of Hannover, a granddaughter of James I of England and VI of Scotland, ascended the British throne as King George I. This Anglo-German union lasted through several generations until 1837. Savaged by heavy bombing in 1943, Hanover was rebuilt into a prosperous city known throughout Europe for its trade fairs.

Information

The **tourist office** (☎ 16 84 97 11; Ernst-August-Platz 2; open 9am-6pm Mon-Fri, 9am-2pm Sat) is next to the main post office and near the main train station. The Hannover-Card, which entitles you to unlimited public transport and discount admission to museums and other attractions, costs €8 for one day or €12 for three days.

Things to See & Do

One way to pick out most city sights on foot is to follow the numbered attractions with the help of the Red Thread Guide (€2) from the tourist office. The chief attractions are the glorious parks of the **Herrenhäuser Gärten** (☎ 16 84 77 43; open from 9am all year, closing coincides with sunset), especially the baroque **Grosser Garten** and the **Berggarten** (admission €3; open to 8pm in summer), with its newly installed rainforest exhibit, the

GERMANY

Regenwald Haus (*adult/concession €9/6*). The gardens also include two museums: **Fürstenhaus** (*adult/concession €3.30/1.50; open Tues-Sun*) shows how royalty lived in the 1700s; and the **Wilhelm-Busch-Museum** (*adult/concession €4.50/2.50; open Tues-Sun*) of caricature and satirical art contains the work of Wilhelm Busch and others. To reach the gardens, take tram No 4 or 5.

Sprengel Museum (*☎ 16 84 38 75; Kurt-Schwitters-Platz; adult/concession €3.50/1.80; open Tues-Sun, to 8pm Tues*) exhibits contemporary works, the highlights being Picasso and Max Beckmann. **Niedersächsisches Landesmuseum** (*☎ 980 75; Willy-Brandt-Allee 5; adult/concession €3/1.50; open Tues-Sun*) has displays of natural history and European paintings.

At Am Markt in the old town is the 14th-century **Marktkirche**. Apart from its truncated tower, it is characteristic of the northern red-brick Gothic style; the original stained-glass windows are particularly beautiful. The **Altes Rathaus** – across the marketplace – was built in various sections over a century. Around **Burgstrasse** some of the half-timbered town houses remain, as well as the **Ballhof** (*Ballhofstrasse*), originally built for badminton-type games of the 17th century, but nowadays offering theatrical plays.

On Breite Strasse near the corner of Osterstrasse, the ruin of the **Aegidienkirche** – smashed in 1943 – is an eloquent memorial; the peace bell inside is a gift from one of Hanover's sister-cities, Hiroshima.

Places to Stay
The tourist office only offers a private room-finding service during trade fairs but will arrange a hotel room year-round for €6.50. The **Jugendherberge** (*☎ 131 76 74, fax 185 55; Ferdinand-Wilhelm-Fricke-Weg 1; dorm beds juniors/seniors €13.50/16*) is 3km out of town. Take the U3 or U7 from Hauptbahnhof to Fischerhof, then cross the river on the Lodemannbrücke bridge and turn right.

Hotel Flora (*☎ 38 39 10, fax 383 91 91; Heinrichstrasse 36; singles/doubles from €36/62, with bath €46/72*) provides pleasant rooms. **Hotel Gildehof** (*☎ 36 36 80, fax 30 66 44; Joachimstrasse 6; singles/doubles €41/65, with bath €57/75*) has clean rooms, some with bathroom. The restaurant downstairs serves well-priced traditional dishes. **Hotel am Thielenplatz** (*☎ 32 76 91, fax 32 51 88;*

e hotel.am.thielenplatz@t-online.de; Thielenplatz 2; singles/doubles from €45/68) is centrally located. The **Hotel Alpha** (*☎ 34 15 35; Friesenstrasse 19; singles/doubles €79/99*) offers rooms with all facilities. **Congress Hotel am Stadtpark** (*☎ 280 50, fax 81 46 52; e info@congress-hotel-hannover.de; Clausewitzstrasse 6; singles/doubles from €96/166*) gets congress and trade fair visitors.

Places to Eat
The Altstadt area behind Marktkirche has plenty of well-priced restaurants offering German cuisine. The food hall **Markthalle** (*cnr Karmarschstrasse & Leinestrasse*) is a gourmand's paradise – it roughly keeps normal shop hours and has lots of budget ethnic food stalls, some vegetarian offerings and fresh produce. The Hanover institution **Brauhaus Ernst August** (*Schmiedestrasse 13a; mains €5-17*) brews its own Hannöversch beer and also serves German dishes. Thai restaurant **Sawaddi** (*☎ 34 43 67; Königstrasse 7; mains about €11*) is behind the train station; its all-you-can-eat lunch buffet is good value.

Getting There & Away
Hanover's spruced-up train station is a major hub. ICE trains to/from Hamburg (€34.40, 1½ hours), Munich (€110, 4½ hours), Frankfurt (€72, 2½ hours) and Cologne (€53.40, 2¾ hours) leave hourly, and every two hours to Berlin-Zoo (€51.80, 1¾ hours). A web of regional services fills in the gaps locally.

Getting Around
The city centre is fairly compact and can be easily covered on foot. Single journeys on the combined tram/U-Bahn system for one zone cost €1 and day passes cost €3.10. The S5 connects the airport with the fairgrounds via the main train station in 25 minutes. For the Messe, the U8 also runs to Messe Nord from the main train station.

AROUND HANOVER
Hildesheim
☎ 05121 • pop 103,000
When a 1945 bombing raid destroyed the city centre of Hildesheim, the town responded in then-typical fashion – it replaced many of the damaged age-old buildings with modern, 'German Post-War Hideous' concrete structures. What makes Hildesheim worth a day trip, though, is what happened next – a town

movement forced the city's leaders to tear down the ugly new buildings and painstakingly reconstruct the town's historic heart according to the original plans (at fantastic expense). As a result, Hildesheim boasts two Unesco World Heritage Sites and some of the most authentic (if not authentically old) examples of Gothic and late Gothic architecture in Germany.

The **tourist office** (☎ 179 80; e tourist -info@hildesheim.com; Rathausstrasse 18-20) is 750m south of the train station. Stop by and pick up a copy of *Hildesheimer Rosenroute* (€1), a guide to the city's buildings and their history.

The town's jewel is the **Hildesheimer Dom** (*Domhof; admission free*), which contains the priceless **Bernward bronze doors** and the elegant **Column of Christ**, both dating back to the early 1000s. In the cathedral's cloister blooms the **Thousand-Year-Old Rosebush** (*adult/concession €0.50/0.30*), alleged to be the same one that Ludwig the Pious hung his gear on in AD 815. Other reconstructed churches of note include the Romanesque **St Michaeliskirche** (*Michaelisplatz; admission free*) and the Gothic **St Andreaskirche** (*Andreasplatz; admission free*). If you're looking for a way to work off the calories from that lunchtime schnitzel, you can climb the 364 steps of the St Andreaskirche's **tower** (*adult/concession €1.50/1*) for a breathtaking view over the city.

The **Roemer- Und Pelizaeusmusuem** (*Am Steine 1-2; adult/concession €6/5; open 9am-6pm daily*) has one of Europe's best collections of Egyptian art and artefacts.

The picturesque Lappenberg neighbourhood south of the city centre is an ideal place for a stroll. The former **Jewish Quarter** is the oldest area of the town, and is home to a moving **memorial** (*Gelber Stern*) to the synagogue that was burned down here on Kristallnacht in 1938.

There are frequent trains to Hanover (€5.50, 30 minutes), as well as ICE trains to Göttingen (€11.60, 25 minutes).

FAIRY-TALE ROAD

The Fairy-Tale Road (Märchenstrasse), so called because of the number of legends and fairy tales that sprang from this region, is well worth a day or two. The route begins at Hanau and runs to Kassel and Göttingen, passes near Hanover and ends in Bremen.

The stretch between Hanover and Göttingen is the most historical section of the route. Among the most interesting towns here are Hamelin (Hameln) of Pied Piper fame, Bodenwerder where the great adventurer Baron von Münchhausen made his home, and the surprising town of Bad Karlshafen.

Information

Every town, village and hamlet along the Fairy-Tale Road has an information office of some sort. The **Fremdenverkehrsverband Weserbergland-Mittelweser E.V.** (☎ 930 00, fax 93 00 33; Deisterallee 1) in Hamelin is the best place to obtain brochures on activities and sights all along the middle Weser. Weserdampfschiffahrt GmbH ferries is in the same building.

In Hamelin there is a **tourist office** (☎ 95 78 23; Deisterallee 1); in Bodenwerder there is a **tourist office** (☎ 405 41; Weserstrasse 3); and in Bad Karlshafen it is in the **Kurverwaltung** (☎ 99 99 24) by the 'harbour'.

The telephone area codes are Hamelin ☎ 05151, Bodenwerder ☎ 05533 and Bad Karlshafen ☎ 05672.

Things to See

Hamelin Among the most interesting sights is the **Rattenfängerhaus** (*Rat Catcher's, aka Pied Piper's, House; Osterstrasse*), the old town's main street, built at the beginning of the 17th century. On the Bungelosenstrasse side is an inscription that tells how, in 1284, 130 children of Hamelin were led past this site and out of town by a piper wearing multicoloured clothes, never to be seen again. Also have a look at the Rattenfänger **Glockenspiel** at the Weser Renaissance **Hochzeitshaus** at the Markt end of Osterstrasse (daily at 1.05pm, 3.35pm and 5.35pm). More of the story is at the museum in the ornate **Leisthaus** (*adult/concession €3/1.50; open Tues-Sun*).

For the other beauties of Hamelin – restored 16th- to 18th-century half-timbered houses with inscribed dedications – stroll through the southeastern quarter of the old town, around the Alte Marktstrasse and Grossehofstrasse areas or Kupferschmiedestrasse.

Bodenwerder The **Rathaus** (*Münchhausenplatz 1*) is said to be the house in which the legendary Baron von Münchhausen was born. The baron became known for telling outrageous tales, the most famous of which was how he rode through the air on a cannonball. This very cannonball is in a room dedicated to the baron in the Rathaus. Also interesting is the statue of the baron, riding half a horse, in the garden outside the Rathaus. This was, of course, another of his stories.

There is a rather pleasant **walking track** along the Weser River in both directions from Bodenwerder.

Bad Karlshafen After passing through the towns like Hamelin and Bodenwerder, the last thing you expect is this whitewashed, meticulously planned, baroque village. Originally the city was planned with an impressive harbour and a canal connecting the Weser River with the Rhine in the hope of diverting trade away from Hanover and Münden in the north. The plans were laid by a local earl with help from Huguenot refugees. The earl's death in 1730 prevented completion of the project, but even today his incomplete masterpiece and the influence of the Huguenots is too beautiful to miss.

Places to Stay & Eat

In Hamelin the camping ground **Fährhaus an der Weser** (☎ 611 67; tent sites €6, plus €4 per person) is on Uferstrasse, across the Weser River from the old town and a 10-minute walk north. Also in Hamelin, there's the **DJH hostel** (☎ 34 25; Fischbeckerstrasse 33; dorm beds juniors/seniors €12.30/15); in Bodenwerder the **DJH hostel** (☎ 05533-26 85; Richard-Schirrmann-Weg; dorm beds juniors/seniors €12.30/15); and in Bad Karlshafen the hostel is **Hermann Wenning** (☎ 338, fax 83 61; Winnefelderstrasse 7; dorm beds juniors/seniors €13.50/16.20).

Hotel Altstadtwiege (☎ 05151-278 54; Neue Marktstrasse 10; singles/doubles from €33/75) is in Hamelin. **Hotel-Garni Christinenhof** (☎ 950 80, fax 436 11; Alte Marktstrasse 18, Hamelin; singles/doubles from €66/95) offers stylish rooms. The **Gaststätte Rattenfängerhaus** in the Rat Catcher's House, serves main courses averaging €12.

Getting Around

The easiest way to follow the Fairy-Tale Road is by car. There are frequent regional trains operating between Hanover and Hamelin (€8.10, 45 minutes). From Hamelin's train station, direct bus No 520 follows the Weser River to Holzminden via Bodenwerder

several times daily. Bus No 221 from Holzminden (board at Hafendamm) runs to Höxter bus station, which connects with bus No 220 to Bad Karlshafen, from where trains go to Göttingen.

GÖTTINGEN
☎ 0551 • pop 130,000

This leafy university town is an ideal stopover on your way north or south; it's on the direct train line between Munich and Hamburg. Though small, Göttingen is lively, mostly because of its large student population. A legion of notables, including Otto von Bismarck and the Brothers Grimm, studied and worked here, and the university has produced more than 40 Nobel Prize winners.

Information

The **main tourist office** (☎ 49 98 00; e tourismus@goettingen.de; Markt 9; open 9.30am-6pm Mon-Fri, 10am-4pm Sat & Sun in summer, 9.30am-1pm & 2pm-6pm Mon-Fri, 10am-1pm Sat in winter) is in the old Rathaus. There's a **post office** just to the left (north) and another in the Altstadt at Groner Strasse 15–17. There is a **Waschcenter laundry** (Ritterplan 4). Check your email at **Computerwerk** (Düsterestrasse 20), where 30 minutes of Internet time costs €2.

Things to See

The tourist office sells the excellent brochure *Göttingen Komplett* for €2.50. At Markt, don't miss the **Great Hall** in the Rathaus where colourful frescoes cover every centimetre of wall space. Just outside, students and a colourful assortment of harmless punk rockers mill about the **Gänseliesel** fountain, the town's symbol. The bronze beauty has a reputation as 'the most kissed girl in the world' because every student who obtains a doctor's degree must then plant a kiss on her cheek.

The 15th-century **Junkernschänke** (Barfüsserstrasse 5), with its colourful carved facade, is the most stunning of the town's half-timbered buildings. A walk on top of the old **town wall** along Bürgerstrasse takes you past **Bismarckhäuschen** (admission free; open 10am-1pm Tues, 3pm-5pm Wed, Thur & Sat), a modest building where the Iron Chancellor lived in 1833 during his wild student days, and the pretty **Botanical Gardens**.

Places to Stay

Camping am Hohen Hagen (☎ 05502-21 47; tent sites €3, plus €5 per person; open all year) is about 10km west of town in Dransfeld (bus No 120). To reach the **Jugendherberge** (☎ 576 22, fax 438 87; Habichtsweg 2; dorm beds juniors/seniors €14.80/20.70) from the train station main entrance take bus No 6 to the Jugendherberge stop.

The friendly **Hotel Garni Gräfin von Holtzenorff** (☎ 639 87, fax 63 29 85; Ernst-Ruhstrat-Strasse 4; singles/doubles €26/45, with bath €45/65) has basic rooms. Take bus No 13 to Florenz-Sartorius-Strasse. **Berliner Hof** (☎ 38 33 20, fax 383 32 32; e info@ berlinerhof.de; Weender Landstrasse 43; singles/doubles €36/52) is located directly across from the university. The **Hotel Kasseler Hof** (☎ 720 81, 770 34 29; Rosdorfer Weg 26; singles/doubles from €34/67, with bath €52/85), on the edge of the old town, has simple rooms. **Hotel Central** (☎ 571 57, fax 571 05; Jüdenstrasse 12; singles without bath from €40, singles/doubles with bath €52/80) is conveniently situated in the middle of town.

Places to Eat

Nikolaistrasse and Goethe Allee offer loads of takeaway options. The **Mensa Am Turm** (Gosslerstrasse 12b), just east of campus, is the most pleasant of the dirt-cheap student cafeterias in town; lunches cost €4 or less. There's another more convenient Mensa on Wilhelmsplatz. **Salamanca** (Gartenstrasse 21b; mains €5-10; open from 6pm Mon-Fri, from 1pm Sat & Sun) offers tasty, well-priced food in a prototypical leftist 20-something café. **Diwan** (Rote Strasse 11) is a good Turkish restaurant in the mid-price range. **La Hacienda** (☎ 531 13 39; Weender Landstrasse 23) serves delicious Mexican food and drinks in a lively atmosphere. Make sure you reserve ahead for dinner on weekends.

Plus (cnr Prinzenstrasse & Stumpfebiel) is a convenient supermarket.

Entertainment

Göttingen's bars and clubs give this small university town a lively, big-city atmosphere. **Apex** (Burgstrasse 46) is a nice place for a nibble and drink. The **Irish Pub** (Mühlenstrasse 4) offers a few dishes and has live music. The salsa, hip-hop, and funk dance nights at the **Blue Note** (Wilhelmsplatz 3) are popular with students and nonstudents alike; **Tangente** (☎ 463 76; Goetheallee 8a) gets an older student crowd. The **Sechs Million Dollar Club** (Neustadt 1) has a cool and retro feel and stiff cocktails. Tiny **Elektroosho** (Weender Strasse 38), Göttingen's hippest dance club, specialises in house music. Things don't get started there until late.

Getting There & Away

Hourly ICE trains pass through on their way to/from Hanover (€26.20, 30 minutes), Berlin (€62.60, 2¼ hours), Hamburg (€53, two hours), Frankfurt (€48.20, two hours) and Munich (€92.60, 4½ hours). Direct RB trains depart every two hours from Göttingen for Goslar in the Harz Mountains (€12.40, 1¼ hours).

GOSLAR

☎ 05321 • pop 48,000

Goslar is a centre for Harz Mountains tourism, but this 1000-year-old city with its beautifully preserved half-timbered buildings has plenty of charm in its own right. The town and the nearby Rammelsberg Mine is listed as a World Heritage Site by Unesco.

Information

The **tourist office** (☎ 780 60; e goslarinfo@ t-online.de; Markt 7; open 9.15am-6pm Mon-Fri, 9.30am-4pm Sat, 9.30am-2pm Sun May-Oct, 9.15am-5pm Mon-Fri, 9.30am-2pm Sat Nov-Apr) can help when the area's accommodation is packed. For information on the Harz Mountains go to **Harzer Verkehrsverband** (☎ 340 40, fax 34 04 66; e info@harzinfo.de; Marktstrasse 45; open 8am-4pm Mon-Thur, 8am-1pm Fri).

Things to See & Do

The **Marktplatz** has several photogenic houses. The one opposite the Gothic **Rathaus** has a chiming clock depicting four scenes from the history of mining in the area. It struts its stuff at 9am, noon, 3pm and 6pm. The **market fountain** dates from the 13th century and is crowned by an eagle.

Usually jammed with tour-bus visitors, the **Kaiserpfalz** (Kaiserbleek 6; adult/concession €4.50/2.50; open daily) is a reconstructed Romanesque 11th-century palace. Just below there's the restored **Domvorhalle** which displays the 11th-century 'Kaiserstuhl' throne, used by German emperors. At the **Rammelsberger Bergbaumuseum** (adult/concession

€8.50/5.50; open 9am-6pm daily), about 1km south of the town centre on Rammelsberger Strasse, you can delve into the 1000-year mining history of the area and descend into the shafts on a variety of tours.

Places to Stay

The pretty **Jugendherberge** (☎ 222 40, fax 413 76; Rammelsberger Strasse 25; dorm beds juniors/seniors €15.40/18.10) is situated behind the Kaiserpfalz (take bus No 803 to Theresienhof from the train station). It is often full of high-school students.

Another option is **Hotel und Campingplatz Sennhütte** (☎ 225 02; Clausthaler Strasse 28; tent sites €2.50, plus €3.30/2 per person/car, singles/doubles from €20/40; open Fri-Wed), 3km south on Route B241. Take bus No 830 from the train station to Sennhütte. There are also several clean, simple rooms with nice views and you'll find lots of trails nearby.

The tourist office can help with room bookings, especially on busy weekends and in summer. **Gästehaus Schmitz** (☎ 234 45, fax 30 60 39; Kornstrasse 1; singles/doubles €30/40, apartments from €30) offers the best value with bright, cheerful rooms. **Gästehaus Verhoeven** (☎ 238 12; Hoher Weg 12; singles/doubles from €32/50, with bath €42/58) has clean and simple rooms. The upmarket **Hotel Kaiserworth** (☎ 70 90, fax 70 93 45; ☎hotel@kaiserworth.de; Markt 3; singles/doubles from €49/99) is in a magnificent 500-year-old building.

Places to Eat

The **Altdeutsches Kartoffelhaus** (Breite Strasse) in the Kaiserpassage shopping arcade offers generous portions of potato dishes for between €4 and €11. **Brauhaus Wolperting-er** (Marstallstrasse 1; mains €5-15) is a restaurant with whimsical decor. **Didgeridoo** (Hoher Weg 13; mains €7-10) specialises in well-priced kangaroo burgers and barbecue meals (and has some good Australian wines). **Restaurant Aubergine** (☎ 421 36; Marktstrasse 4; mains €18-36) has delicious Mediterranean cuisine.

Getting There & Away

Goslar is regularly connected by train to Göttingen (€12.40, 1¼ hours), Hanover (€12.40, one hour) and Wernigerode (€5.50, 30 minutes). For information on getting to/from the eastern Harz region, see Getting Around in the following Western Harz Mountains section and the Getting There & Away sections under Quedlinburg and Wernigerode earlier in this chapter.

WESTERN HARZ MOUNTAINS

Known mostly to Germans and Scandinavians, the Harz Mountains (Harzgebirge) don't have the dramatic peaks and valleys of the Alps, but they offer a great four-seasons sports getaway without some of the Alpine tackiness and tourism. Silver, lead and copper mines in the area have been largely exhausted, and many can now be visited.

Orientation & Information

Pick up the booklet Der Harz (€3), available at any tourist office in the Harz and at many hotels. For weather reports and winter snow information (in German), contact the **Harzer Verkehrsverband** (☎ 05325-340 40) in Goslar.

The **Goslar tourist office** has information on the Harz Mountains. Hahnenklee has a **tourist office** (☎ 05325-510 40; Kurhausweg 7); in Bad Harzburg there is a **tourist office** (☎ 05322-753 30; Herzog-Wilhelm-Strasse 86); and in Clausthal-Zellerfeld there is a **tourist office** (☎ 05323-810 24; Bahnhof-strasse 5a).

Things to See

Hahnenklee is proud of its Norwegian-style **'stave' church**, but most remarkable is Clausthal-Zellerfeld's 17th-century wooden church **Zum Heiligen Geist** (Hindenburg-platz), built to accommodate more than 2000 worshippers! Nearby, the technical university's **mineral collection** (Römerstrasse 2a; admission €1.50) is one of the largest in Germany.

For a fine view, take the **Bergbahn** car up to the castle ruins above Bad Harzburg (€2/3 one way/return, less with resort card). The embarkation point is 2km uphill from the train station, so you can promenade among German wealth and ambition and check the array of furs and other luxury goods flaunted in this health resort.

Activities

Despite 500km of groomed **hiking trails**, the beauty of the National Park Harz hasn't suffered. Maps and information are abundant, and most of the hikes are less than 10km. Trails through wildly romantic Okertal (just outside

Goslar), and the 15km to Hahnenklee from Goslar, are especially picturesque. From the cable-car station in Bad Harzburg, paths lead to Sennhütte (1.3km), Molkenhaus (3km) and to the scenic Rabenklippe (7km) overlooking the Ecker Valley. All have restaurants; a blackboard inside the cable-car station indicates the ones that are open. From Bad Harzburg you can also pick up the medieval Kaiserweg route, which joins the Goetheweg to Torfhaus (11km) and the Brocken (7km from Torfhaus).

Cycling is popular in summer among those seeking a hilly challenge, and in winter the Harz Mountains offers excellent conditions for **cross-country skiing**. Snow enthusiasts will find **downhill skiing** conditions average, but slopes can be quite good in Hahnenklee, St Andreasberg and Braunlage. Rental equipment is easy to find. Both downhill and cross-country gear start at about €15 a day. Tourist offices in most towns keep a list of places that hire bikes and ski equipment.

The Harz Mountains also has a healthy number of spa towns where **spa activities** are offered. Most spa towns have indoor swimming facilities and all have *Kurzentren* (spa centres) that offer massages and other physical therapies to soothe an aching body after an all-too-brisk hike, ride or ski through hilly terrain.

Places to Stay

Many of the 30 or so camping grounds in the Harz Mountains are open all year – pick up the free *Der Harz Camping* brochure at local tourist offices. There is no shortage of budget rooms in hotels and pensions. Tourist offices in each town have useful listings and can help with bookings. For extended stays ask about apartments or holiday homes, which become good deals when staying a week or more. In spa resorts you will pay about a €2 *Kurtaxe* (resort tax) per day on hotel accommodation (less in hostels and at camping grounds).

Hahnenklee Around 2km north of Hahnenklee there's the **Campingplatz am Kreuzeck** (☎ 05325-25 70; tent sites €5.50, plus €3.50 per person). To get there, take bus No 830 from Goslar or Hahnenklee. The **Jugendherberge** (☎ 05325-22 56, fax 35 24; Hahnenkleer Strasse 11; juniors/seniors €12.30/15) is near the Bockswiese bus stop (same bus) on the road from Goslar.

Bad Harzburg Between Goslar and Bad Harzburg, on the L501 (bus No 810 or 871 to Campingplatz stop) is **Harz-Camp Göttingerode** (☎ 05322-812 15; Kreisstrasse 66; tent sites €5, plus €4.40 per person). Rustic youth hostel **Braunschweiger Haus** (☎ 05322-45 82, fax 18 67; Waldstrasse 5; juniors/seniors €16/20) has one-, two-, and three-bed rooms. Take bus No 873 from the train station to the Lärchenweg stop.

Clausthal-Zellerfeld Around 1km west of Zellerfeld there's **Campingplatz Waldweben** (☎ 05323-817 12; Spiegeltaler Strasse 31; tent sites €4.80, plus €3.50 per person). The **Jugendherberge** (☎ 05323-842 93, fax 838 27; Altenauer Strasse 55; juniors/seniors €12.30/15) is in the forest about 2km from town; take bus No 831 to the Jugendherberge stop. The hostel is usually closed on the first weekend of the month from mid-September to mid-May.

Getting Around

Frequent regional trains link Goslar with Wernigerode. Four direct trains depart daily for Göttingen via Bad Harzburg. Bus No 877 shuttles several times daily between Bad Harzburg and Wernigerode (just under one hour; €3). It stops on the far side of Am Bahnhofsplatz at Bad Harzburg train station and next to the main station in Wernigerode.

Bus No 861 runs between Goslar and Altenau, while Nos 830 and 831 connect Goslar with Clausthal-Zellerfeld (No 830 via Hahnenklee on alternating hours).

Hamburg

☎ 040 • pop 1.7 million

The first recorded settlement on the present site of Hamburg was the moated fortress of Hammaburg, built in the first half of the 9th century. The city that developed around it became the northernmost archbishopric in Europe, to facilitate the conversion of the northern peoples.

The city was burned down many times, but in the 13th century it became the Hanseatic League's gateway to the North Sea and was second in importance and influence only to Lübeck. With the decline of the Hanseatic League in the 16th century, Lübeck faded into insignificance but Hamburg continued to thrive.

Hamburg strode confidently into the 20th century but WWI stopped all trade and most of Hamburg's merchant shipping fleet (almost 1500 ships) was forfeited to the Allies as reparation payment. In WWII, more than half of Hamburg's residential areas and port facilities were demolished and 55,000 people killed in the Allied air raids that spawned such horrific firestorms.

Today this is a sprawling port city and a separate state of Germany, with a stylish shopping district, numerous waterways (with more bridges than Venice), and even a beach (in Blankenese, which is one of Germany's most exclusive suburbs).

Orientation

The Hauptbahnhof is very central, near Aussenalster lake and fairly close to most of the sights. These are south of Aussenalster and north of the Elbe River, which runs all the way from the Czech Republic to Hamburg before flowing into the North Sea. The city centre features the Rathaus and the beautiful Hauptkirche St Michaelis. The port is west of the city centre, facing the Elbe.

Information

The small **tourist office** (☎ 30 05 12 00; e info@hamburg-tourism.de; open 7am-11pm daily) is in the main train station and offers limited brochures and a room-finding service (€4). It has great hours and friendly staff. There's also a **tourist office** (open 8am-8pm Mon-Sat, 8am-7pm Sun Apr-Sept, 10am-5.30pm daily Oct-Mar) at St Pauli harbour, between piers 4 and 5. View its official website at w www.hamburg-tourism.de.

Both tourist offices stock the Hamburg Card, which offers unlimited public transport and free or slightly discounted admission to many attractions, museums and cruises. The 'day card' is valid on the day of purchase and costs €6.80 (single) or €12.70 (groups of up to five people). The 'multiday card' is valid on the day of purchase and the following two days (€14/22.50). An even better deal is the Power Pass, which gives steep discounts to anyone under 30 for a mere €6.70 (extendable for an extra €3 per day).

Money There is a **Reisebank** (open 7.30am-10pm daily) above the Kirchenallee exit of the main train station, and others at Altona train station (open Mon-Sat) and in terminal 4 at the airport (open 6am-10pm daily).

Post & Communications There's a small **post office** (open 8am-8pm Mon-Fri, 9am-6pm Sat, 10am-6pm Sun) with a poste-restante service (four weeks for international mail) near the Kirchenallee exit of the train station. There is a main **post office** (cnr Dammtorstrasse & Stephansplatz) close to the Stephansplatz U-Bahn stop.

Email & Internet Access On the 3rd floor of the Karstadt department store, **Cyberb@r** (Mönchebergstrasse 16) charges €1.50 for 30 minutes online.

Newspapers & Magazines For cultural events and lifestyle information, look for the weekly magazines Szene (€2.50) and Oxmox (€1.50), and the monthly Prinz (€1).

Bookshops There are guidebooks in English at **Dr Götze Land & Karte** (Alstertor 14-18) which claims to be the biggest specialist map and travel bookshop in Europe. The branch of **Thalia Bücher** (Grosse Bleichen 19) has a large selection of English-language books and some guidebooks. Second-hand books can be bought at the **English Bookstore** (Stresemannstrasse 169; S-Bahn to Holstenstrasse).

Laundry The Schnell & Sauber chain has a **laundrette** (Nobistor 34) in St Pauli, and another outlet at Neuer Pferdemarkt 27 (U3 to Feldstrasse).

Medical & Emergency Services For an **ambulance** call ☎ 112. A **medical** emergency service is available on ☎ 22 80 22. For urgent **dental** treatment call ☎ 33 11 55. The **police** emergency number is ☎ 110; there is one station in St Georg at Steindamm 82 and another in St Pauli at Spielbudenplatz 31, on the corner of Davidstrasse.

Dangers & Annoyances Overall, Hamburg is a very safe city, but you should take special care in the seedy drug and prostitution area near the Hauptbahnhof.

Things to See & Do

Altstadt Much of Hamburg's old city centre was lost in WWII, but it's still worth a walking tour. The area is laced with wonderful canals (called 'fleets') running from the Alster lakes to the Elbe.

The Altstadt is centred on Rathausmarkt, where the large **Rathaus** and the huge clock tower overlook the lively square. This is one of the most interesting city halls in Germany, and the 35-minute tour is worthwhile at €1/0.50 per adult/concession. It's in English hourly from 10.15am to 3.15pm Monday to Thursday, to 1.15pm Friday to Sunday. The building has 647 rooms – six more than Buckingham Palace.

It is a moving experience to visit the remaining tower of the devastated **St-Nikolai-Kirche**, now an antiwar memorial, nearby on Ost-West-Strasse. From there, walk a few blocks west to the baroque **Hauptkirche St Michaelis** and take the lift up the **tower** (adult/concession €2.50/1.25; open 10am-6pm daily Apr-Oct, 10am-5pm Nov-Mar), enter through portal No 3, for a great view of the city and the port. Inside, the beautiful interiors and the crypt (a donation of €1.25 is requested) are open for viewing.

Port After exploring the Altstadt, stroll down to one of the busiest ports in the world. It boasts the world's largest carpet warehouse complex, while the Free Port Warehouses stockpile goods from all continents.

The **port cruises** are touristy but still worthwhile. There are many options; for details see Organised Tours later in this section.

If you're in the port area early on a Sunday (5am to 10am, October to March from 7am), head for **Fischmarkt** (Fish Market) in St Pauli, right on the Elbe. Hamburg's oldest market (established 1703) is popular with locals and tourists alike and everything under the sun is sold here. Cap your morning with a visit to the live music session at the **Fischauktionshalle** (Fish Auction Hall; Grosse Elbstrasse 9).

Reeperbahn Among Hamburg's biggest tourist attractions is the famous Reeperbahn red-light district. It is 600m long and is the heart of the St Pauli entertainment district, which includes shows, bars, cabarets, clubs, theatres and a casino. In recent years, the Reeperbahn sex establishments have been gradually moving over for popular restaurants and bars, with a dwindling number of peep shows and sex shops plying a 'traditional' trade.

If you go to one of these haunts, make sure you understand costs beforehand. Ask for the price list if it's not posted by the entrance. Entry is sometimes free or €2 to €5, but there will likely be a minumum purchase of €25 or more – enough for a campari and soda in some places. On **Grosse Freiheit**, Safari is one of the more famous clubs. Notorious **Herbertstrasse** is where prostitutes pose in windows offering their wares. It is fenced off at each end and men under 18 and women are not allowed in. Ironically, hustling is much more aggressive on the surrounding regular streets.

Other Attractions Hamburg's **Kunsthalle** (Glockengiesserwall) has old masters and a large collection of German paintings from both the 19th and 20th centuries. Contemporary art is housed next door in the modern **Galerie der Gegenwart** (adult/concession for both museums €7.50/5; both open 10am-6pm Tues-Sun, 10am-9pm Thur). The waxworks museum **Panoptikum** (Spielbudenplatz 3; adult/concession €4/2.50; open 11am-9pm Mon-Fri, 11am-midnight Sat, 10am-9pm Sun early Feb–mid-Jan) is kitschy fun; don't miss the gruesomely realistic syphilitic hands in the 'medical history' wing.

Harry's Hamburger Hafen Basar (Bernhard-Nocht-Strasse 89-91; admission €2.50) is a fascinating 'shop'. It's the life's work of Harry, a bearded character known to seamen all over the world, who for decades bought trinkets and souvenirs from sailors and others. Now run by Harry's daughter, the shop has a wealth of curiosities and the entry fee is refunded with a €5 purchase. The **Erotic Art Museum** (Nobistor 10a; adult/concession €8/5; open 10am-midnight Sun-Thur, 10am-1am Fri & Sat) contains some 1800 paintings, drawings and sculptures by artists from Delacroix to Picasso.

The viewing deck of Hamburg's **TV Tower** (Lagerstrasse 2-8) was closed indefinitely for renovations at the time of our visit, but you can still bungee jump off the 130m-high platform (€99), Germany's tallest jump. Call ☎ 089-60 60 89 23 for bookings. From the free fall, you'll see the adjacent sprawling gardens of **Planten un Blomen**, a gorgeous landscaped city park with a large Japanese garden.

Organised Tours

Basic city sightseeing **bus tours** in English operate at least twice daily from April to October,

HAMBURG

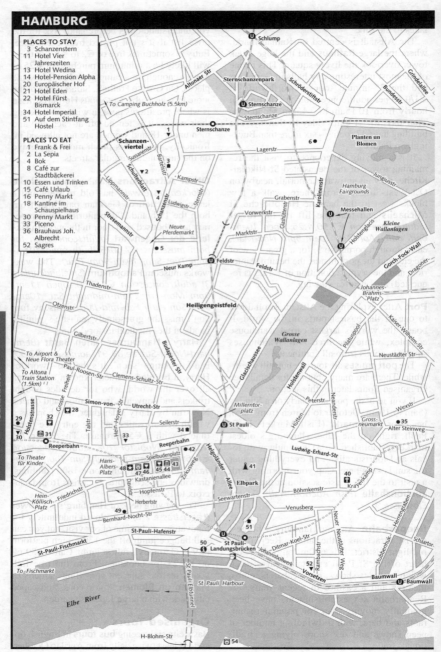

PLACES TO STAY
3 Schanzenstern
11 Hotel Vier
    Jahreszeiten
13 Hotel Wedina
14 Hotel-Pension Alpha
20 Europäischer Hof
21 Hotel Eden
22 Hotel Fürst
    Bismarck
34 Hotel Imperial
51 Auf dem Stintfang
    Hostel

PLACES TO EAT
1 Frank & Frei
2 La Sepia
4 Bok
8 Café zur
    Stadtbäckerei
10 Essen und Trinken
15 Café Urlaub
16 Penny Markt
18 Kantine im
    Schauspielhaus
30 Penny Markt
33 Piceno
36 Brauhaus Joh.
    Albrecht
52 Sagres

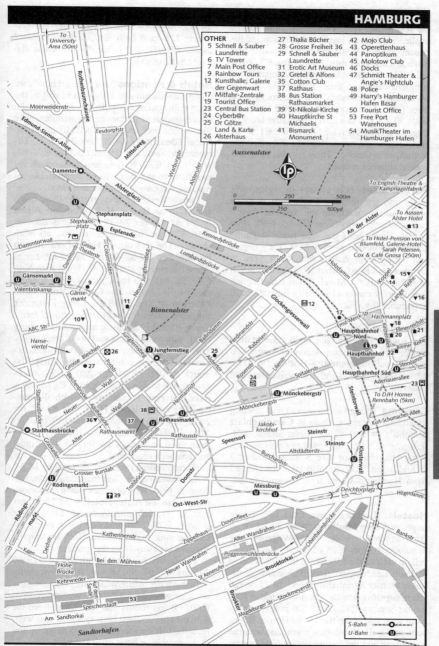

OTHER
5 Schnell & Sauber Laundrette
6 TV Tower
7 Main Post Office
9 Rainbow Tours
12 Kunsthalle; Galerie der Gegenwart
17 Mitfahr-Zentrale
19 Tourist Office
23 Central Bus Station
24 Cyberb@r
25 Dr Götze Land & Karte
26 Alsterhaus
27 Thalia Bücher
28 Grosse Freiheit 36
29 Schnell & Sauber Laundrette
31 Erotic Art Museum
32 Gretel & Alfons
35 Cotton Club
37 Rathaus
38 Bus Station Rathausmarket
39 St-Nikolai-Kirche
40 Hauptkirche St Michaelis
41 Bismarck Monument
42 Mojo Club
43 Operettenhaus
44 Panoptikum
45 Molotow Club
46 Docks
47 Schmidt Theater & Angie's Nightclub
48 Police
49 Harry's Hamburger Hafen Basar
50 Tourist Office
53 Free Port Warehouses
54 MusikTheater im Hamburger Hafen

GERMANY

and every 30 minutes from 9.30am to 4.45pm the rest of the year. They leave from Kirchenallee next to the main train station (adult/ concession €12/6.50) and last 1¾ hours; you can add a harbour cruise for an extra €7. Two-hour 'Fleet' (inner canal) **cruises** depart from Jungfernstieg three times daily (€14/7). The 50-minute Alster lakes tour departs at least three times daily from Jungfernstieg and costs €9/4.50. Or you can cover the Alster lakes in stages with boats leaving hourly; it's €1.50 for each stop or €7 return. Both of these operate from April to October. There are also canal and special summer cruises.

Port Cruises Port cruises in sightseeing boats and the unusual **Barkassen** wooden boats built to navigate the Speicherstadt's canals (adult/concession €8.50/4.50; 1hr) operate throughout the year from St Pauli-Landungsbrücken, piers 1 to 9. They depart half-hourly from 9am to 6pm from April to October, and hourly from 10.30am to 3.30pm from November to March. Tours with English commentary run at 11am daily from April to September from pier 1.

Places to Stay

The tourist office at the main train station charges €4 for accommodation bookings. You can also call the **Hamburg-Hotline** (☎ 30 05 13 00; 8am-8pm daily) for availability and reservations.

Camping Though inconvenient and catering mainly for caravans, there is **Campingplatz Buchholz** (☎ 540 45 32; Kieler Strasse 374; tent sites €7-10, plus €4/4 per person/car). From Hauptbahnhof take S-Bahn No 2 or 3 to Stellingen. You can also take bus No 183 from Hamburg-Altona train station towards Schnelsen.

Hostels Hamburg's two DJH hostels are large. **Auf dem Stintfang** (☎ 31 34 88; e jh -stintfang@t-online.de; Alfred-Wegener-Weg 5; juniors/seniors €15.25/19.25) has an excellent view of the Elbe. Take the U/S-Bahn to St Pauli-Landungsbrücken. The youth guesthouse **Horner Rennbahn** (☎ 651 16 71; e jgh -hamburg@t-online.de; Rennbahnstrasse 100; juniors/seniors €16.75/19.50) is less convenient to reach. Take the U3 to Horner Rennbahn and walk 10 minutes north past both the racecourse and the leisure centre. The private

hostel **Schanzenstern** (☎ 439 84 41, fax 439 34 13; e info@schanzenstern.de; Bartelsstrasse 12; dorm beds €17, singles/doubles/ triples €35/50/60) is ideally located in the lively Schanzenviertel.

Hotels & Pensions Many budget hotels are along Steindamm and a few blocks east of the main train station along Bremer Reihe, but the concentration of junkies and prostitutes make the streets feel unsafe, especially at night. **Hotel Eden** (☎ 24 84 80, fax 24 15 21; Ellmenreichstrasse 20; singles/doubles €41/62, with bath €72/103) is just far enough removed from the sleaze to be comfortable; its renovated rooms are simple and clean.

Lange Reihe is less grubby than other streets in St Georg. **Hotel-Pension Alpha** (☎ 24 53 65, fax 24 37 94; singles/doubles €36/62) has bare-bones rooms, all with shower. The welcoming **Hotel-Pension von Blumfeld** (☎ 24 58 60, fax 24 32 82; Lange Reihe 54; singles/doubles €31/46, with bath €41/56) has nice basic rooms and a friendly parrot called Jakob. The **Galerie-Hotel Sarah Petersen** (☎/fax 24 98 26; Lange Reihe 50; singles/doubles from €45/65, with all facilities €70/85) is a classic art-scene Hamburg hotel, with rooms decorated in different styles. The most expensive rooms have video, fax and other useful comforts. **Hotel Fürst Bismarck** (☎ 280 10 91, fax 280 10 96; Kirchenallee 49; singles/doubles from €61/100) is more conventional with rooms with all facilities. The **Europäischer Hof** (☎ 24 82 48, fax 24 82 47 99; Kirchenallee 45; singles/doubles from €103/133) has rooms directly across from the train station; ask for one that's quiet and has been renovated.

Hotel Wedina (☎ 24 30 11, fax 280 38 94; e info@wedina.de; Gurlittstrasse 23; singles/ doubles €90/105) provides quality, spacious rooms. **Aussen Alster Hotel** (☎ 24 15 57, fax 280 32 31; Schmilinskystrasse 11; singles/ doubles €79/128), just one block north, offers the same high standard. Both are in quiet streets a bit away from the grunge.

The family-run **Hotel Imperial** (☎ 319 60 21, fax 31 56 85; e info@hotel-imperial -hamburg.de; Millerntorplatz 3-5; singles/ doubles weekdays €50/77, weekends from €60/85) has rooms that face away from the Reeperbahn, and are both spacious and well-furnished. It's an excellent mid-range option in the throbbing heart of St Pauli.

Hotel Vier Jahreszeiten (☎ 349 40, fax 34 94 26 00; e vier-jahreszeiten@hvj.de; Neuer Jungfernstieg 9-14; singles/doubles from €175/225) is Hamburg's premier address for big spenders.

Places to Eat
Hauptbahnhof Area Kantine im Schauspielhaus (Kirchenallee; lunches €6) downstairs in the Deutsches Schauspielhaus, is one of the best kept secrets in this part of town, with plain but filling lunches. The student **Café Urlaub** (Lange Reihe 63; dishes around €7; open until 2am), which is open from breakfast until late, is a good eating and drinking option. Here you can find good salads and pasta dishes. **Cafe Gnosa** (Lange Reihe 93; mains from €6.20) is especially popular among gays and lesbians. It has good lunch specials, wonderful home-made cakes, and is nice for an evening meal or drink. The upmarket bistro **Cox** (☎ 24 94 22; Lange Reihe 68; mains around €16), with its stylish, Continental decor and friendly staff, is a great place to spend an hour or three.

Gänsemarkt & Around You'll find a wide choice around Gänsemarkt and Jungfernstieg near the Binnenalster lake. **Essen und Trinken** (Gänsemarkt 21) is a food hall in an arcade where you can choose from Asian, Mediterranean and German cuisine at budget prices. **Café zur Stadtbäckerei** is a bakery which also supplies shoppers and workers with warm drinks and filling, tasty snacks. **Brauhaus Joh. Albrecht** (Adolfsbrücke 7; dishes less than €10) is a bustling microbrewery with a few canal-side tables.

Schanzenviertel The lively Schanzenviertel neighbourhood lies west of the TV Tower and north of St Pauli (take the U-Bahn or S-Bahn to Sternschanze) and is shared by students and immigrants. Lots of cosy cafés and restaurants string along Schanzenstrasse and Susannenstrasse; **Frank and Frei** on the corner of the two, is a student hang-out offering a small menu. **La Sepia** (Schulterblatt 36; dishes around €13) provides terrific seafood in a Mediterranean atmosphere, at times with live music. The main outpost of **Bok** (Schanzenstrasse 27; mains around €8) draws a young crowd with an array of Thai, Korean and Japanese dishes. A delicious 18-piece Bento II sushi platter costs €32.

St Pauli/Port Area There is a cluster of good Portuguese and Spanish restaurants situated along Ditmar-Koel-Strasse and Reimarus-Strasse near St Pauli Landungsbrücken. **Sagres** (Vorsetzen 52; mains €10) specialises in fresh-off-the-boat fish dishes and is always packed. Just off the Reeperbahn, **Piceno** (Hein-Hoyer-Strasse 8) is good for Italian fare at reasonable prices in a cosy, relaxed atmosphere.

Self-Catering Head for one of the **Penny Markt** budget groceries. There's one on Baumeisterstrasse, one on the corner of Lange Reihe and Schmilinskystrasse to the east of the main train station, and one near the corner of Königstrasse and Holstenstrasse at the western end of the Reeperbahn. Really good fresh fare is offered at Grossneumarkt on market days (Wednesday and Saturday).

Entertainment
The jazz scene in Hamburg is hot. Hip **Mojo Club** (☎ 43 52 32; www.mojo.de; Reeperbahn 1) should absolutely not be missed by aficionados of jazz or avante garde music, or by anyone else for that matter who has more than a passing interest in music. The **Cotton Club** (☎ 34 38 78; Alter Steinweg 10) has more traditional jazz flavours. Get there before 8.30pm if you've reserved seats.

The **English Theatre** (☎ 227 70 89; Lerchenfeld 14) is good for a language fix; **Theater für Kinder** (☎ 38 25 38; Max-Brauer-Allee 76) in Altona is great for kids – its language is more international. The small cinema **Abaton** (☎ 41 32 03 20; Allende-Platz 3) screens English-language films.

Hamburg has an excellent alternative and experimental theatre scene. **Kampnagelfabrik** (☎ 27 09 49 49; Jarrestrasse 20-24) is a good place to start. Take bus No 172 or 173 from U-Bahn station Mundsburg. **Schmidt Theater** (☎ 31 77 88 99; Spielbudenplatz 27) is much loved for its wild variety shows and a casual atmosphere.

Musicals are big in Hamburg. Catch them at the **Neue Flora Theater** (cnr Alsenstrasse & Stresemannstrasse; S-Bahn to Holstenstrasse) and **MusikTheater im Hamburger Hafen** (Norderelbstrasse 6; shuttle service from Pier 1 of St Pauli Landungsbrücken), which was showing The Lion King on our visit. Tickets, which start at around €26, can be reserved at the tourist offices or on the hotline ☎ 30 05 13 00.

GERMANY

For central theatre or concert bookings, go to the **Theaterkasse** (☎ 35 35 55) in the basement of the Alsterhaus shopping complex on Grosse Bleichen.

Not surprisingly, St Pauli is the flash point for nightclubs. **Angie's Nightclub** (☎ 31 77 88 16; Spielbudenplatz 27-28) is a classy, sweaty local favourite for dancing to live music. For indie oddities, cool 1960s London soul and dub music, head to the **Molotow Club** (☎ 31 08 45; Spielbudenplatz 5). **Docks** (☎ 31 78 83 11; Spielbudenplatz 19) sometimes has live bands; as does the hip **Grosse Freiheit 36** (Grosse Freiheit 36). At **Gretel & Alfons** across the street, you can have a drink where the Beatles once quaffed.

Getting There & Away

Air Hamburg's **international airport** (☎ 50 75 25 57) in Fuhlsbüttel has frequent flights to domestic destinations as well as cities in Scandinavia and elsewhere in Europe.

Bus International destinations that aren't served directly by train from Hamburg, such as Amsterdam (€44.50, 6½ hours) and London (€61.50, 17½ hours), are served by Eurolines buses.

A good option for getting to London is **Rainbow Tours** (☎ 32 09 33 09, fax 32 09 30 99; Gänsemarkt 45), which offers return trips without an overnight stay from €55 – a cheap way to get to London, even if you don't use the return portion of the ticket. The central bus station is southeast of the main train station on Adenauerallee.

Train Hamburg's Hauptbahnhof is one of the busiest in Germany, although it does not handle all the through traffic. There are frequent RE/RB trains to Lübeck (€9, 45 minutes) and Kiel (€15.20, 1¼ hours), various services to Hanover (€26.50, 1½ hours) and Bremen (€16, 1¼ hours), as well as ICE trains to Berlin (€51.40, 2½ hours) and Frankfurt/Main (€98.20, 3½ hours). Almost hourly trains depart for Copenhagen (4½ hours). There are overnight services to Munich, Vienna and Paris as well as Zurich via Basel. Hamburg-Altona station is quieter but has a monopoly on some services to the north. Carefully read the timetables when booking to/from Hamburg stations or you could finish up at the wrong station at the wrong time. Hamburg-Harburg handles some regional services (for

instance to/from Cuxhaven, the main port for Heligoland).

Car & Motorcycle The autobahns of the A1 (Bremen-Lübeck) and A7 (Hanover-Kiel) cross south of the Elbe River. Hamburg's only **Mitfahr-Zentrale** (☎ 194 40; Ernst-Merck-Strasse 8) is near the train station. Sample one-way prices are Cologne €24, Frankfurt/Main €28, Amsterdam €33 and Berlin €17.

Ferry Hamburg is 20 hours by car ferry from the English port of Harwich. **DFDS Seaways** (☎ 389 03 71, fax 38 90 31 20) runs services at least three times a week in either direction. The Fischereihafen terminal is at Van-der-Smissen-Strasse 4, about 1km west of the Fischmarkt (S1 to Königstrasse, or bus No 383 to/from Altona station). It is open 10am to 4.30pm weekdays, just before departure at weekends (exchange money before you reach the terminal or on board). The one-way passenger fare to Harwich ranges from €35 to €319, depending on the season, the day of the week and cabin comforts. A car costs an extra €25 to €128 and a bicycle will cost €2.

Scandlines (☎ 01805-72 26 35 46 37; W www.scandlines.com) operates a busy car and passenger ferry from the German harbour town of Puttgarden to Rodby in Denmark, which leaves every half-hour 24 hours a day and takes 45 minutes. The cost is €60 each way for a car including up to five people all year. A bicycle costs €7, including one person. A single passenger pays €3 (€6 mid-June to August) each way. If you're travelling by train, the cost of the ferry is included in your ticket.

Getting Around

To/From the Airport A taxi from the main train station costs around €30 (one easy number to use is ☎ 21 12 11). A better airport option is to take the U1 from the main train station to Ohlsdorf and from there the No 110 express bus (€2.20). Airport buses (€4.25) make the 25-minute trip to the airport from the train station every 25 minutes between 5am and 9.20pm.

Public transport buses, the U-Bahn and the S-Bahn operate in Hamburg. A day pass for travel after 9am in most of Hamburg is €4.25 (€6.85 if you include the surrounding area) and there are various family passes. Single journeys cost €1.40 for the city tariff area, €2.20 for the city and surrounding area, and

€3.60 within the outer tariff area. Children pay a basic €0.80. For the Schnellbus or 1st-class S-Bahn the day supplements are €1.05. A three-day travel-only pass is €12.25, and weekly cards range from €12.50 to €26.30 depending on your status and the distance you want to travel (check the diagrams with the oval-shaped zones marked in yellow). From midnight to dawn the night-bus network takes over from the trains, converging on the main metropolitan bus station at Rathausmarkt. For transport options with a Hamburg Card see the earlier Information section.

Hamburg's bicycle tracks are extensive and reach almost to the centre of the city.

Schleswig-Holstein

Schleswig-Holstein is Germany's northernmost state and borders Denmark at the southern end of the Jutland Peninsula. Among the many attractions here are the North Frisian Islands and the historical city of Lübeck.

Schleswig and Holstein began breaking away from Denmark with the help of Sweden in the mid-17th century, a process which took until 1773.

When Holstein joined the German Confederation in 1815, Denmark attempted to lure Schleswig back to the motherland.

Three wars were fought over the region between Germany and Denmark: the first in 1848–50; a second in 1864; and a third in 1866, when Bismarck annexed it to unify Germany. Under the Treaty of Versailles in 1919, North Schleswig was given to Denmark. Finally, in 1946, the British military government formed the state of Schleswig-Holstein from the Prussian province of the same name.

LÜBECK
☎ 0451 • pop 215,000
Medieval Lübeck was known as the Queen of the Hanseatic League, as it was the capital of this association of towns that ruled trade on the Baltic Sea from the 12th to the 16th centuries. This beautiful city, with its red-stone buildings, is a highlight of the region and well worth taking the time to explore.

Orientation & Information
Lübeck's old town is set on an island ringed by the canalised Trave River, a 15-minute walk east from the main train station. To get there,

just take Konrad-Adenauer-Strasse across the pretty Puppenbrücke (Doll Bridge) to Holstentor, the city's western gateway. Then follow Holstenstrasse east from An der Untertrave to Kohlmarkt, from where Breite Strasse leads north to Markt and the historic Rathaus.

Lübeck-Information (*☎/fax 122 54 19; Breite Strasse 62; open 9.30am-6pm Mon-Fri, 10am-2pm Sat & Sun*) is near the Rathaus. Both city tourist offices run a room-finding service. The private **room-finding office** (*☎ 86 46 75, fax 86 30 24*) at the train station charges €3 (free if reserved by phone). See w www.Luebeck-info.de.

The Lübeck Happy Day Card entitles you to unlimited travel and discounts on cruises, museums, cinema and other attractions. It costs €5 for 24 hours and €10 for three days and is available at tourist offices, hotels, youth hostels and museums.

The **central post office** (*Königstrasse 46*) is across from the Katarinenkirche. For Internet access, visit **PC & Internet Café** (*Am der Untertrave 103*) near the Holstentor. There's a police station situated near the youth hostel at Mengstrasse 20.

Things to See & Do
The landmark **Holstentor** (*☎ 122 41 29; adult/concession €5/3; open Tues-Sun*), a fortified gate with huge twin towers, serves as the city's symbol as well as its museum, but for a literary kick, visit the recently refurbished **Buddenbrookhaus** (*Mengstrasse 4; adult/concession €4.10/2.60; open daily*), the family house where Thomas Mann was born and which he made famous in his novel *Buddenbrooks*. The literary works and philosophical rivalry of the brothers Thomas and Heinrich are commemorated here. The must-see **Marienkirche** (*Markt*) contains a stark reminder of WWII; a bombing raid brought the church bells crashing to the stone floor and the townspeople have left the bell fragments in place, with a small sign saying: 'A protest against war and violence'. Also on Markt is the imposing **Rathaus** which covers two full sides of the square. It can be toured with a guide – three times on weekdays – for €2.60/1.50 per adult/concession.

Lübeck's **Marionettentheater** (*Puppet Theatre; ☎ 700 60; cnr Am Kolk & Kleine Petersgrube; open Tues-Sun*) is a must. Usually there is a daily afternoon performance for children (3pm) and an evening performance for adults only on Saturday, however, the schedule varies. Afternoon seats cost €4 and evening seats €8 to €11 depending on the play. It's best to book ahead. **Museum für Puppentheater** (☎ 786 26; Am Kolk 14; adult/student/child €3/ 2.50/1.50; open 10am-6pm daily), a survey of all types of dolls and puppetry, is just around the corner from the theatre.

The tower lift at the partly restored **Petrikirche** (adult/concession €2/1.20; open 9am-7pm daily May-Oct, closed Jan & Feb) affords a superb view over the Altstadt. It is usually open the listed hours above and shorter hours in other months.

Places to Stay

The nearest camping ground is **Campingplatz Schönböcken** (☎ 89 30 90; Steinrader Damm 12; tent site/person/car €3.50/4.50/1; open Apr-Oct) in a western suburb of Lübeck. The tourist office can help with information on camping grounds in the nearby coastal resort of Travemünde.

Lübeck has two DJH hostels. The **Jugendgästehaus Lübeck** (☎ 702 03 99; Mengstrasse 33; dorm beds juniors/seniors €17.40/20.10, singles/twins €25.60 per person) is clean, comfortable and well situated in the middle of the old town, a 15-minute walk from the train station. The **Jugendherberge 'Vor dem Burgtor'** (☎ 334 33, fax 345 40; Am Gertrudenkirchhof 4; juniors/seniors €15.40/ 18.10) is a little outside the old town. Take bus No 1, 3, 11, 12 or 31 to Gustav-Radbruch-Platz. The YMCA's centrally located **Sleep-Inn** (☎ 719 20, fax 789 97; Grosse Petersgrube 11; dorm beds €10, doubles €30, apartments €32 per person; open mid-Jan–mid-Dec) charges €4 extra for breakfast and €4.50 extra for sheets.

The **Hotel Stadt Lübeck** (☎ 838 83, fax 86 32 21; Am Bahnhof 21; singles/doubles €43/ 63) is just outside the main train station. Fairly good rooms come with shower and toilet. The **Klassik Altstadt Hotel** (☎ 720 83, fax 737 78; [e] info@klassik-hotel.de; Fischergrube 52; singles/doubles €44/105, suites €123) is convenient and pleasant. The **Mövenpick Hotel** (☎ 150 40, fax 150 41 11; Willy-Brandt-Allee 1-3; singles €95-165, doubles €115-185) is opposite the Holstentor.

Places to Eat

The best eating and drinking options are in the area directly east of the Rathaus. The fun

Tipasa (Schlumacherstrasse 12-14; mains from €4.40) serves everything from tandoori to tacos. It's also a great place to eat and drink in the evening. **Hieronymus** (☎ 706 30 17; Fleischhauerstrasse 81; mains €4.50-19.40) is a relaxed and rambling restaurant which is spread over three floors of a 15th-century building. Most dishes on the creative menu are quite filling. The lunch specials are good value. The **Schiffergesellschaft** (Breite Strasse 2; mains from €14.80) has a unique maritime atmosphere.

Save room for a dessert or a snack of marzipan, which was invented in Lübeck (local legend has it that the town ran out of flour during a long siege and resorted to grinding almonds to make bread). **JG Niederegger** (Breite Strasse 89), a shop and café directly opposite the Rathaus, is Lübeck's mecca of marzipan. The supermarket **Sky** (Sandstrasse 24) is conveniently located near Kohlmarkt.

Getting There & Away

Lübeck is close to Hamburg, with at least one train every hour (€9, 45 minutes). There are also frequent services to Kiel (€12.40, 1¼ hours) and Schwerin (€10.70, 1¼ hours). Trains to/from Copenhagen also stop here.

The central bus station is next to the main train station. Services to/from Wismar stop here, as well as Autokraft buses to/from Hamburg, Schwerin, Kiel, Rostock and Berlin.

Getting Around

Frequent double-decker buses run to Travemünde (€3.50, 45 minutes) from the central bus station. City buses also leave from here; a single journey costs €1.35.

KIEL

☎ 0431 • pop 246,000

Kiel, the capital of Schleswig-Holstein, was seriously damaged by Allied bombing during WWII, but is now a vibrant and modern city. At the end of a modest firth, it has long been one of Germany's most important Baltic Sea harbours and was the host of Olympic sailing events in 1936 and 1972.

Orientation & Information

Kiel's main street is Holstenstrasse, a colourful pedestrian street near the fjord. It runs north-south from the Nikolaikirche to Sophienhof, a large indoor shopping mall connected to the main train station by an overpass.

The **tourist office** (☎ 67 91 00; e info@kiel
-tourist.de; Andreas-Gayk-Strasse 31; open
9am-6.30pm Mon-Fri all year, 9am-1pm Sat
Oct-Apr, 9am-4.30pm Sat May-Sept) is a
northern extension of Sophienblatt and just
five minutes by foot from the main train station. **Cyber Treff** (Bergstrasse 17) is a good
place to surf the Web until late. See w www
.kiel-tourist.de.

Things to See & Do
Kiel's most famous attraction is the **Kieler
Woche** (Kiel Week) in the last full week in
June, a festival revolving around a series of
yachting regattas attended by more than 4000
of the world's sailing elite and half a million
spectators. Even if you're not into sailing, the
atmosphere is electric – just make sure you
book a room in advance if you want to be in
on the fun.

To experience Kiel's love for the sea in a
less energetic fashion, take a ferry ride to the
village of **Laboe** at the mouth of the firth. Ferries leave hourly from Bahnhofbrücke pier behind the train station. They take around one
hour to reach Laboe, hopping back and forth
across the firth along the way. In Laboe, you
can visit the **U995**, a wartime U-boat, on the
beach, which is now a **technical museum**
(adult/concession €2.10/1.50; open daily).
Nearby is the **Marine-Ehrenmal** (Naval Memorial; adult/concession €2.80/1.80; open
daily) with a navigation museum.

Kiel is also the point at which the shipping
canal from the North Sea enters the Baltic Sea.
Some 60,000 ships pass through the canal
every year, and the **locks** (Schleusen; ☎ 360
30; adult/concession €1.50/1) at Holtenau,
6km north of the city centre, are worth a visit.
There's an admission fee to the viewing platform; tours of the locks are at 9am, 11am, 1pm
and 3pm daily (adult/concession €2.30/1.50).

The open-air **Schleswig-Holstein Freilichtmuseum** (☎ 65 96 60; adult/concession
€4.50/2.50; open 9am-6pm daily Apr-Oct,
11am-4pm Sun Nov-Mar) in nearby Molfsee
(take Autokraftbus No 501) is also worth seeing. More than 60 historical houses typical of
the region have been relocated here, giving
you a thorough introduction to the northern
way of life.

Places to Stay
Kiel's **Campingplatz Falckenstein** (☎ 39 20
78; Palisadenweg 171; tent sites €4.90-7.50,
plus €4.35/1.90 per person/car; open Apr-
Oct) is in the northern suburb of Friedrich-
sort. The **Jugenherberge** (☎ 73 14 88, fax 73
57 23; Johannesstrasse 1; juniors/seniors
€14.90/16.90) is in the suburb of Gaarden.
You can walk across the pretty drawbridge
behind the train station, or take the Laboe ferry
to Gaarden, from where it's a 10-minute walk;
or take bus No 11 from the main train station
to Kieler Strasse.

The tourist office charges €2.50 for accommodation bookings and stocks an excellent free brochure listing private rooms and
apartments.

The **Hotel Runge** (☎ 733 33 96, 73 19 92;
Elisabethstrasse 16; singles/doubles €34/56,
with shower & toilet €46/61) in Gaarden is
one of the area's cheapest options. Take bus
No 11 or 12 to Augustern from the main train
station. The central **Hotel Schweriner Hof**
(☎ 614 16, fax 67 41 34; Königsweg 13;
singles €36, singles/doubles with shower &
toilet €57/77) provides good rooms. **Muhl's
Hotel** (☎ 997 90, fax 997 91 79; Lange Reihe
5; singles/doubles €57/77) is central and has
nice rooms with facilities. The **Steigenberger
Hotel Conti-Hansa** (☎ 511 50, fax 511 54 44;
Schlossgarten 7; singles/doubles €135/160)
has standard rooms.

Places to Eat
The **Ratskeller** (Fleethörn 9; mains €8.40-
17.90) in the Rathaus serves typical German
cuisine with an emphasis on fish.

The **Klosterbrauerei** (Alter Markt 9; lunch
specials €7.40) is a private brewery with
good beer, well-priced food and a great atmosphere. You'll find lots of cheap takeaway
options in the Turkish quarter around the hostel in Gaarden. **Ça va** (Holtenauer Strasse
107; dishes from €5.50) is a popular gay
café-bar that does light dishes in the evening
(open late).

Getting There & Away
There are regional buses to/from Lübeck,
Schleswig and Puttgarden from the bus station
on Auguste-Viktoria-Strasse, just north of the
main train station. Numerous RE trains run
every day between Kiel and Hamburg-Altona
or Hamburg Hauptbahnhof (€15.20, 1¼
hours). The trains to Lübeck leave every hour
(€12.40, 1¼ hours). For ride-sharing, you
should contact **ADM Mitfahrzentrale** (☎ 194
40; Sophienblatt 52a).

The daily Kiel-Gothenburg ferry (13½ hours) leaves from Schwedenkai and is run by **Stena Line** (☎ *0431-90 99;* **w** *www.stena line.de).* One-way passenger prices go from €38 to €74 depending on the season.

Color Line ferries (☎ *730 03 00;* **w** *www .colorline.com)* run direct to/from Kiel and Oslo daily (19½ hours). Noncabin space is only available from mid-June to mid-August (€64/72 during the week/weekend). Otherwise, basic double cabins cost from €84 to €116 per person depending on the season. There are 50% off-peak student concessions. Ferries depart from the Norwegenkai across the fjord in Gaarden (use the footbridge).

Getting Around
City buses leave from Sophienblatt, in front of the train station. To get to the North-Baltic Sea Canal and the locks, take bus No 11 to Wik; the locks are about a five-minute walk from the terminus.

NORTH FRISIAN ISLANDS
Sylt ☎ 04651 • pop 21,600
Amrum ☎ 04682 • pop 2100
The Frisian Islands reward those who make the trek with sand dunes, sea, pure air and, every so often, sunshine. Friesland covers an area stretching from the northern Netherlands along the coast up into Denmark. North Friesland (Nordfriesland) is the western coastal area of Schleswig-Holstein up to and into Denmark. The sea area forms the National Park of Wattenmeer, and the shifting dunes, particularly on the islands of Amrum, Föhr and Langeness, are sensitive and cannot be disturbed; paths and boardwalks are provided for strolling. The most popular of the North Frisian Islands is the glamorous resort of Sylt, which gets very crowded from June to August; the neighbouring islands of Föhr and Amrum are far more relaxed and less touristy.

Orientation & Information
The excellent **tourist office** (☎ *99 88; open 9am-6pm Mon-Fri, 9am-4.30pm Sat all year, 9am-2pm Sun June-Sept)* is inside Westerland's train station on Sylt and can help with information and accommodation. **Sylt Marketing** (☎ *820 20, fax 82 02 22; Stephanstrasse 6),* near the Westerland Rathaus, and **Sylt Tourismus Zentrale** (☎ *60 26, fax 281 80; Keitumer Landstrasse 10b)* just outside of town in Tinnum, are other useful sources of information. On Amrum, the friendly **tourist office** (☎ *940 30)* is at the harbour car park. The spa administrations **Kurverwaltungen** at the various resorts are also useful sources of information.

All communities charge visitors a so-called *Kurtaxe,* a resort tax of about €3 a day, depending on the town and the season. Paying the tax gets you a *Kurkarte* which you need on Sylt even just to get onto the beach. Day passes are available from kiosks at beach entrances, but if you're spending more than one night, your hotel can obtain a pass for you for the length of your stay (not included in the room rate).

Things to See
Nature is the prime attraction on the North Frisian Islands; the different moods of the rough North Sea and the placid Wattenmeer lend the region its unique character. Beautiful dunes stretch out for kilometres, red and white cliffs border wide beaches, and bird lovers will be amply rewarded. The reed-roofed *Friesenhäuser* is typical of the region. But, of course, civilisation has also taken hold here, especially in Westerland on Sylt. After WWII, the German jet-set invaded the island, which explains the abundance of luxury homes, cars and expensive restaurants, particularly around Kampen.

On Amrum, you'll find signs of traditional Frisian life around the village of **Nebel**. The **lighthouse** (*adult/concession €2/0.50; open 8.30am-12.30pm Mon-Fri Apr-Oct, 8.30am-12.30pm Wed Nov-Mar),* the tallest in northern Germany at 63m, affords a spectacular view of the dunes from the southwest of the island and over to the islands of Sylt, Föhr and Langeness.

Activities
In Westerland, a visit to the indoor water park and health spa **Sylter Welle** (☎ *99 82 42; open 10am-9pm or 10pm daily)* is fun, especially when it's too cold for the beach. It includes saunas, solariums, a wave pool and a slide (€8.70, €12.80 with sauna; no time limit). For a real thrill, though, visit one of Sylt's **beach saunas** – the tourist office can point you in the right direction.

Heiko's Reitwiese (☎ *56 00)* in Westerland on Sylt, and **Reiterhof Jensen** (☎ *20 30)* on Amrum offer **horse riding**. One of several excellent **hikes** on Amrum (8km return) is from

Norddorf along the beach to the tranquil Odde nature reserve. The tourist office can help with information on guided hikes in summer across the Watt to Föhr. The flat terrain of the islands is also suited to **cycling**. On Amrum, the tourist office keeps a list of rental places. In Westerland on Sylt, **Fahrrad am Bahnhof** (☎ 58 03) is conveniently situated at the train station (€5 per day).

Places to Stay

Low-budget accommodation is hard to find on the islands, but the tourist offices can help with private rooms from €20 per person. Another option may be to rent an apartment, which can cost as little as €45 in the low season and around €85 in the high season. Unless it's a particularly slow time proprietors may be reluctant to rent for fewer than three days.

Sylt It has seven camping grounds. **Campingplatz Kampen** (☎ 420 86; Möwenweg 4; tent/person/car sites €4.50/3.50/1.50; open Easter-Oct) is set beautifully amid dunes near the small town of Kampen. In Hörnum, there's the **Jugendherberge** (☎ 88 02 94, fax 88 13 92; Friesenplatz 2) in the south of the island. There's also a **Jugendherberge** (☎ 87 03 97, fax 87 10 39) in List. Both charge €13.30/16 for juniors/seniors and neither is very central, but bus services bring you close.

Hotel Garni Diana (☎ 988 60, fax 98 86 86; Elisabethstrasse 19; singles/doubles €41/72, with bath €46/87) has basic rooms near the beach. The delightful **Landhaus Nielsen** (☎ 986 90, fax 98 69 60; Bastianstrasse 5; doubles €65/75) has lower winter prices.

Amrum At the northern edge of Wittdün is **Campingplatz Schade** (☎ 22 54; tent sites €4, plus €5 per person). The **Jugendherberge** (☎ 20 10, fax 17 47; Mittelstrasse 1; beds juniors/seniors €13.30/16) has 218 beds but it's best to book ahead, even in the low season. The historic **Hotel Ual Öömrang** (☎ 836, fax 14 32; Bräätlun 4; singles/doubles €51/102; open Mar-Dec) has a sauna.

Places to Eat

Sylt Picnics are a fine option on the islands. On Westerland, pick up groceries and fresh-baked bread at **Spar** (Sandstrasse 24) near the Sylter Welle. **Toni's Restaurant** (Norderstrasse 3; dishes from €5.80-12.80) serves good, inexpensive fare; it also has a pleasant

garden. **Blum's** (Neue Strasse 4; mains from €8) has soup from €4.35, main dishes and some of the freshest fish in town. The **Alte Friesenstube** (☎ 12 28; Gaadt 4) is in a cosy 17th-century building. It specialises in northern German and Frisian cooking but you can expect to pay around €35 per person for a three-course meal with wine. Kampen's **Kupferkanne** (☎ 410 109) in Stapelhooger Wai is a beautiful stop during a bike tour. You'll end up paying €8 for a giant cup of coffee and a slice of cake with cream, but the view of the Wattenmeer is free.

List's harbour sports a number of colourful kiosks. **Gosch** prides itself on being Germany's northernmost fish kiosk, and is an institution well known beyond Sylt.

Amrum Amrum has only a few restaurants and many of them close in the low season. The **Hotel Ual Öömrang** (dishes around €14) serves filling traditional dishes. The **Haus Burg**, built on an old Viking hill-fort above the eastern beach at Norddorf, has a teahouse atmosphere and home-made cakes.

Note that restaurants can close as early as 7pm in the low season.

Getting There & Away

Sylt Sylt is connected to the mainland by a scenic train-only causeway right through the Wattenmeer. Around seven trains leave from Hamburg-Hauptbahnhof daily for Westerland (€33, 3¼ hours). If you are travelling by car, you must load it onto a train in the town of Niebüll near the Danish border. There are about 26 crossings in both directions every day and no reservations can be made. The cost per car is a shocking €77 return, but that includes all passengers.

Amrum To get to Amrum and the island of Föhr, you must board a ferry in Dagebüll Hafen. To get there, take the Sylt-bound train from Hamburg-Altona and change in Niebüll. In summer, there are also some through trains. A day-return from Dagebüll costs €17.50, which allows you to visit both islands. If you stay overnight, return tickets cost €18.20 (bicycle €4). The trip to Amrum takes around two hours, stopping at Föhr on the way.

There are daily flights between Westerland airport and Hamburg, Munich and Berlin, and several flights weekly from other German cities.

GERMANY

Getting Around

Sylt's two north-south bus lines run every 20 to 30 minutes, and three other frequent lines cover the rest of the island. There are seven price zones, costing from €1.30 to €5.60. Some buses have bicycle hangers. On Amrum, a bus runs from the ferry terminal in Wittdün to Norddorf and back every 30 to 60 minutes, depending on the season. The slow, fun inter-island options are the day-return cruises to Föhr (Wyk) and Amrum (Wittdün) from the harbour at Hörnum on Sylt. Day-return cruises through shallow banks that attract both seals and sea birds are offered by **Adler-Schiffe** (☎ 04651-836 10 28 in Westerland; €18.50). Bicycles are an extra €5. WDR ferries also run on day-return trips in the summer from Wittdün on Amrum to Föhr (€6.70/3.40 per adult/concession) and the two nearby islands of Hallig Hooge and Nordmarsch-Langeness (€8.70/4.40 per adult/concession).

HELIGOLAND
☎ 04725 • pop 1650

Not technically part of the Frisian Islands, Heligoland (Helgoland) is 70km out to sea and is a popular day trip from the islands. Oddly, Heligoland is economically not part of the EU and therefore it remains a duty-free port.

Because of the North Sea's strong currents and unpredictable weather, however, the passage will be most enjoyed by people with iron stomachs.

From April through September, **WDR ferries** (☎ 01805-08 01 40) sail from Hörnum on Sylt at least twice weekly and from Amrum and Dagebüll (all €26 to €42.50 day return).

Seasick crowds flock like lemmings to this unlikely chunk of red rock sticking out of the sea. It was used as a submarine base in WWII, and it's still possible to tour the strong bunkers and underground tunnels. The island was heavily bombed and all of the houses are new. Take a walk along Lung Wai ('long way'), filled with duty-free shops, and then up the stairway of 180 steps to Oberland for what view there is.

There's also a scenic trail around the island. Small boats run from Heligoland to neighbouring **Düne**, a tiny island filled with beaches and nudists.

Hungary

Hungary is just the place to kick off an Eastern or Central European trip. Just a short hop from Vienna, the land of Franz Liszt and Béla Bartók, Gypsy music, the romantic Danube River and piquant paprika continues to entice and enchant visitors. The allure of Budapest, once an imperial city, is apparent on arrival, but other cities such as Pécs, the sunny heart of the south, and Eger, the wine capital of the north, have much to offer travellers, as does the beautiful countryside.

In Hungary you'll find much of the glamour and excitement of Western Europe – at half the cost.

Facts about Hungary

HISTORY
Early Settlements & the Middle Ages

The Celts occupied the Carpathian Basin in the 3rd century BC but were conquered by the Romans just before the Christian era. Until the early 5th century AD, all of today's Hungary west of the Danube (Transdanubia) was in the Roman province of Pannonia. The Roman legion stationed at Aquincum, in what is now Óbuda, guarded the northeastern frontier of the empire. The Romans brought writing, planted the first vineyards in Hungary and built baths near the region's thermal waters.

The Romans were forced to abandon Pannonia in 451 by the Huns, whose short-lived empire had been established by Attila. The Huns were followed by the Goths, Longobards and the Avars, a powerful Turkic people who were subdued by Charlemagne in 796.

Exactly a century later, seven Magyar tribes swept in from the area between the Dnieper and lower Danube Rivers above the Black Sea and occupied the Danube Basin. The Magyars terrorised much of Europe with raids reaching as far as Spain, northern Germany and southern Italy until they were stopped at the Battle of Augsburg in 955 and subsequently converted to Christianity. Hungary's first king and its patron saint, Stephen (István), was crowned on Christmas Day in 1000, which marked the foundation of the Hungarian state. After the

At a Glance

- **Budapest** – romantic and cosmopolitan; Buda's medieval Castle Hill; Pest's leafy boulevards
- **Visegrád** – poetic Danube town with a Royal Palace and mighty Citadel
- **Fertőd** – beautiful Esterházy Palace, home to classical music performances in summer
- **Lake Balaton** – warm, sandy beaches; superb yachting; rejuvenating thermal baths

Capital	Budapest
Population	10.2 million
Official Language	Hungarian
Currency	1 forint (Ft) = 100 fillér
Time	GMT/UTC+0100
Country Phone Code	☎ 36

Budapest Maps
Budapest pp370-1
Central Pest p374
The Castle District pp376-7

Mongols sacked Hungary in 1241–42, killing an estimated one-third of its population of two million, many cities were fortified.

Medieval Hungary was a powerful state that included Transylvania (now in Romania), Slovakia and Croatia. The so-called Golden Bull, a kind of Magna Carta limiting some of the king's powers in favour of the nobility, was signed at Székesfehérvár in 1222, and universities were founded in Pécs in 1367 and in Óbuda in 1389.

HUNGARY

In 1456 at Nándorfehérvár (today's Belgrade), Hungarians under János Hunyadi (r. 1445–56) stopped the Ottoman Turkish advance through Hungary to Vienna; under Hunyadi's son, Matthias Corvinus (1458–90), Hungary experienced a brief flowering of Renaissance culture. Then in 1514 what had started as a crusade by peasants turned into a revolt against landowners. The peasants were eventually suppressed, with tens of thousands massacred and their leader, György Dózsa, burned alive on a red-hot iron throne.

Turkish Occupation & Habsburg Rule

Hungary was seriously weakened by the revolt, and the Turks defeated the Hungarian army at Mohács in 1526. Buda Castle was seized in 1541 and Hungary divided in three. The central part, including Buda, was in Turkish hands while Transdanubia and present-day Slovakia were under the Austrian House of Habsburg, aided by Hungarian nobility based in Pozsony (Bratislava). The principality of Transylvania, east of the Tisza, prospered as a vassal state of the Ottoman Empire.

After the Turks were expelled from Buda in 1686, Habsburg domination of Hungary began. From 1703 to 1711 Ferenc Rákóczi II, prince of Transylvania, led an unsuccessful war of independence but united Hungarians against the Austrians for the first time.

Hungary never fully recovered from these disasters and from the 18th century had to be rebuilt from the ground up. Under the 'enlightened absolutism' of the Habsburg monarchs Maria Theresa (r. 1740–80) and her son Joseph II (r. 1780–90), the country made great steps forward economically and culturally.

The revolution of 1848, led by the lawyer Lajos Kossuth and poet Sándor Petőfi, demanded freedom for serfs and independence. Although it was put down a year later, the uprising shook the oligarchy. In 1865 Austria was defeated by Prussia and the next year a compromise was struck, creating the Dual Monarchy of Austria (the empire) and Hungary (the kingdom). This 'Age of Dualism' continued until 1918 and spurred economic, cultural and intellectual rebirth in Hungary.

Trianon & WWII

After WWI and the collapse of the Habsburg Empire in November 1918, Hungary was proclaimed a republic. However, the 1920 Trianon Treaty stripped the country of more than two-thirds of its territory.

In August 1919, a brutal communist government led by Béla Kun was overthrown after five months in power. In March of the next year, Admiral Miklós Horthy established a repressive rightist regime that attacked Jews and communists, imprisoning and executing many and forcing still more to flee the country.

Horthy immediately embarked on a 'white terror' – every bit as brutal as the red one of Béla Kun – that attacked communists and Jews for their roles in supporting the Republic of Councils. As the regime was consolidated over the next decade, it showed itself to be extremely rightist and conservative, advocating the status quo and 'traditional values' – family, state, religion. Though the country had the remnants of a parliamentary system, Horthy was all-powerful, and very few reforms were enacted. On the contrary, the lot of the working class and the peasantry worsened.

In 1941 Hungary's ambition to recover its lost territories drew the nation into war on the side of Nazi Germany. When Horthy tried to negotiate a separate peace with the Allies in 1944, the Germans occupied Hungary and brought the fascist Arrow Cross Party to power. The Arrow Cross then began deporting hundreds of thousands of Jews to Auschwitz.

In December 1944 a provisional government was established at Debrecen, and by early April 1945 all of Hungary had been liberated by the Soviet army.

The Communist Era

In 1947 the communists assumed complete control of the government and began nationalising industry and dividing up large estates among the peasantry.

On 23 October 1956 student demonstrators demanding the withdrawal of Soviet troops were fired upon. The next day Imre Nagy, the reformist minister of agriculture, was named prime minister. On 28 October Nagy's government offered amnesty to all those involved in the violence and promised to abolish the ÁVH (known as ÁVO until 1949), the hated secret police. But the fighting intensified, with some Hungarian military units joining rebels. Soviet troops, who had become involved in the conflict, began a slow withdrawal.

On 31 October hundreds of political prisoners were released, and widespread reprisals began against ÁVH agents. On 1 November

HUNGARY

Nagy announced that Hungary would leave the Warsaw Pact and assume neutral status. At this, the Soviet forces began to redeploy and on 4 November tanks moved into Budapest, crushing the uprising. When the fighting ended on 11 November, some 25,000 people were dead. Then the reprisals began: an estimated 20,000 people were arrested; 2000 were executed, including Nagy; and another 250,000 fled to Austria.

After the revolt, the Hungarian Socialist Workers' Party was reorganised, and János Kádár, proclaiming a new social unity, named party president and premier. After 1968 Hungary abandoned strict central economic control in favour of a limited market system.

In June 1987 Károly Grósz took over as premier and in May 1988, after Kádár's forced retirement, became party secretary general. Under Grósz and other reformers, Hungary began moving towards full democracy.

The Republic of Hungary

At their party congress in February 1989 the communists agreed to give up their monopoly on power, the Republic of Hungary was proclaimed in October, and democratic elections were scheduled for March 1990. Though they had changed their name and now advocated a free-market economy, the communists could not shake the stigma of four decades of autocratic rule, and the elections were won by the centrist Hungarian Democratic Forum (MDF), which advocated a gradual transition towards capitalism. Hungary had changed political systems with scarcely a murmur, and the last Soviet troops left the country in June 1991.

In coalition with two smaller parties, the MDF oversaw the painful transition to a full market economy, which resulted in declining living standards for most people. In 1991 most state subsidies were removed, leading to a severe recession. Beggars and homeless people appeared on the streets, and free education and health-care programmes were cut.

Disillusionment with this ugly side of capitalism brought the Hungarian Socialist Party (MSZP) to power in the 1994 elections. This in no way implied a return to the past, and party leader Gyula Horn was quick to point out that it was the socialists who had initiated the reform process in the first place.

In the elections of 1998, the once left-wing Alliance of Young Democrats (Fidesz) moved significantly to the right and then added the

extension 'MPP' (Hungarian Civic Party) to its name in order to attract the support of the burgeoning middle class. It won government by forming a coalition with the MDF and the agrarian conservative Independent Smallholders Party (FKgP). Fidesz-MPP's youthful leader, Viktor Orbán, became prime minister.

Despite the astonishing economic growth and other gains made by the coalition government, the electorate grew increasingly hostile to Fidesz-MPP's – and Orbán's – strongly nationalistic rhetoric and arrogance. In April 2002 the largest turnout of voters in Hungarian history unseated the government and returned the MSZP, allied with the Alliance of Free Democrats (SZDSZ), to power under Prime Minister Péter Medgyessy, a free-market advocate who had served as the finance minister in the Horn government.

Hungary became a fully fledged member of NATO in 1999 and hopes to join the European Union (EU) by 2004.

GEOGRAPHY

Hungary occupies the Carpathian Basin in the very centre of Eastern Europe. It covers just over 93,000 sq km and shares borders with Austria, Slovakia, Ukraine, Romania, Yugoslavia, Croatia and Slovenia.

The longest rivers are the Tisza (597km in Hungary) and the Danube (417km), which divide the country into three parts. The country has well over 1000 lakes (of which the largest is Lake Balaton at 596 sq km) and is riddled with thermal springs.

The Danube separates the Great Plain (Nagyalföld, or *puszta*) in the east and Transdanubia (Dunántúl) in the west. Hungary's 'mountains' to the north are merely hills, with the highest peak being Kékes (1014m) in the Mátra Range.

CLIMATE

Hungary has a temperate Continental climate with Mediterranean and Atlantic influences. Winters are cold, cloudy and damp or windy, and summers are warm – sometimes very hot. March, April and November are the wettest months. The number of hours of sunshine averages 2209 a year – among the highest in Europe. From late April to the end of September, you can expect the sun to shine for about 10 hours a day. August is the hottest month (average temperature 23.9°C) and January the coldest (-0.7°C).

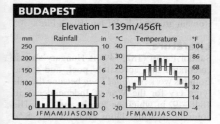

ECOLOGY & ENVIRONMENT

Pollution is a large and costly problem. Low-grade coal that fuels some industry and heats some homes creates sulphur dioxide and acid rain. Nitrogen oxides emitted by cars on the highways and in city centres cause severe air pollution. The over-use of nitrate fertilisers in agriculture has caused the ground water beneath the plains to become contaminated with phosphates and has even threatened Lake Balaton. But there has been marked improvement in air and water quality in recent years as Hungary attempts to conform to EU environmental standards. Between 1990 and 1997, for example, sulphur dioxide emissions fell by one-third while levels of nitrogen oxide decreased by one-fifth over the same period.

The most serious environmental disaster in recent years occurred in January 2000, when cyanide from a gold mine in Baia Mare in Romania emptied into the Tisza River, poisoning the water and killing fish and other animals and plant life for hundreds of kilometres downstream. Environmentalists now say the heavy-metal contamination will affect the food chain for years and the regeneration of the flora and fauna of the Tisza could take decades. The Szentendre-based Regional Environmental Center for Central and Eastern Europe is developing a common ecosystem strategy for the five nations sharing the Tisza.

FLORA & FAUNA

Hungary is home to over 2000 flowering plant species, many of which are not normally found at this latitude. There are a lot of common European animals (deer, wild hare, boar, otter) as well as some rarer species (wild cat, lake bat, Pannonian lizard), but three-quarters of the country's 450 vertebrates are birds, especially waterfowl.

There are 10 national parks in Hungary, including three on the Great Plain and two in the hilly north.

GOVERNMENT & POLITICS

Hungary's 1989 constitution provides for a parliamentary system of government. The unicameral assembly consists of 386 members chosen for four years in a complex, two-round system that balances direct ('first past the post') and proportional representation. The head of state, the president, is elected by the house for five years. The prime minister is head of government.

The main political parties are: the rightist Fidesz-MPP (Alliance of Young Democrats-Hungarian Civic Party); the conservative MDF (Hungarian Democratic Forum); the agrarian conservative FKgP (Independent Smallholders Party); the socialist MSZP (Hungarian Socialist Party); the liberal SZDSZ (Alliance of Free Democrats); and the xenophobic and ultra-nationalist MIÉP (Hungarian Justice and Life Party).

ECONOMY

With the strongest economy in Eastern and Central Europe, Hungary's painful restructuring appears to be over. The spiralling inflation and unemployment levels of the early to mid-1990s have finally settled, with figures now approaching those in the West. As long as economic targets are met and administrative reform continued, Hungary should be one of the first countries admitted to the EU when it expands its membership, possibly by 2004.

Behind the economic surge are European, Asian and North American companies that have invested more than US$20 billion over the past decade, mainly because wages and operational costs are relatively low. Hungary's workforce is also considered flexible, skilled and highly educated.

Still, it's not all rosy. Wages growth lags behind inflation and the country's poorer areas – the northeast and southeast, in particular, are yet to feel the boom that has buoyed Budapest and the western counties.

POPULATION & PEOPLE

Neither a Slavic nor a Germanic people, the Ugric Hungarians were the last major ethnic group to arrive in Europe during the period of the Great Migrations. Some 10.2 million Hungarians live within the national borders, and another five million Hungarians and their descendants are abroad. The estimated 1.65 million Hungarians in Transylvania (now Romania) constitute the largest ethnic minority in Europe, and there are another 600,000 in Slovakia, 350,000 in Yugoslavia, 180,000 in Ukraine and 35,000 in Austria. Hungarian immigrants to the USA, Canada, Australia and Israel add up to more than half a million.

Ethnic Magyars make up some 97.7% of the population. Minorities include Germans (0.3%), Slovaks (0.1%), Croatians (0.1%) and Romanians (0.1%). The number of Roma is officially put at 1.4% of the population (or 132,600 people) though some sources place it as high as 3%.

ARTS

While the Renaissance flourished briefly in the late 15th century, rump Hungary was isolated from the mainstream of European culture during Turkish rule. Then came domination by the Habsburgs, Nazi Germany and the Soviet Union. It's not surprising that the works of Hungarian writers and artists have tended to reflect the struggle against oppression.

Music

Franz (or Ferenc) Liszt (1811–86) described himself as 'part Gypsy', and some of his works, notably *Hungarian Rhapsodies*, echo Romani music. Ferenc Erkel (1810–93) is the father of Hungarian opera, and two of his works – the stirringly nationalist *Bánk Bán* and *László Hunyadi* – are standards at the Hungarian State Opera House in Budapest.

Béla Bartók (1881–1945) and Zoltán Kodály (1882–1967) made the first systematic study of Hungarian folk music, travelling and recording throughout the linguistic region in 1906. Both integrated some of their findings into their compositions.

Hungarian folk musicians play violins, zithers, hurdy-gurdies, bagpipes and lutes on a five-tone diatonic scale. There are lots of different performers – watch out especially for Muzsikás and the incomparable Marta Sebestyén. Anyone playing the haunting music of the Csángó, pockets of Hungarians living in eastern Transylvania and Moldavia, is a good bet.

Gypsy music, as it is known and played in Hungarian restaurants from Budapest to Boston, is urban schmaltz and based on recruiting tunes played during the Rákóczi independence war. At least two fiddles, a bass and a cymbalom (a curious stringed instrument played with sticks) are *de rigueur*. Real Romani music usually doesn't employ instruments but is sung a cappella. One of the best modern Romani groups is Kalyi Jag (Black Fire).

Literature

Sándor Petőfi (1823–49) is Hungary's most celebrated and accessible poet, and a line from his work *National Song* became the rallying cry for the War of Independence in 1848–49, in which he fought and died. His comrade-in-arms, János Arany (1817–82), wrote epic poetry *(Toldi Trilogy)* and ballads. Another friend, the prolific novelist and playwright Mór Jókai (1825–1904), gave expression to heroism and honesty in such wonderful works as *The Man with the Golden Touch* and *Black Diamonds*.

Hungary's finest 20th-century lyric poet, Endre Ady (1877–1919), attacked narrow materialism, provoking a storm of indignation from right-wing nationalists. The work of the poet Attila József (1905–37) expresses the alienation felt by individuals in the modern age. The novels of Zsigmond Móricz (1879–1942) examine the harsh reality of peasant life in Hungary.

Three important contemporary writers are György Konrád (1933–), Péter Nádas (1942–) and Péter Esterházy (1950–), whose works now appear in English translation.

Painting

Favourite painters from the 19th century include realist Mihály Munkácsy (1844–1900), the so-called painter of the *puszta*; Tivadar Kosztka Csontváry (1853–1919), who has been compared with Van Gogh, and József Rippl-Rónai (1861–1927), the key exponent of Secessionist art in Hungary. Győző Vásárhelyi (1908–97), who changed his name to Victor Vasarely when he emigrated to Paris in 1930, is considered the 'Father of Op Art'.

SOCIETY & CONDUCT

In general Hungarians are not uninhibited like the extroverted Romanians or the sentimental Slavs. They are a reserved, somewhat formal people. Forget about the impassioned, devil-may-care Gypsy-fiddling stereotype – it does not exist. The overall mood is one of *honfibú*, literally 'patriotic sorrow' but really a penchant for the blues, with a sufficient amount of hope to keep most people going. Family is very important in Hungarian society. If you're invited to someone's home, bring a bunch of flowers and/or a bottle of good local wine.

The Royal Palace in Budapest houses a number of important art and history museums

A medieval shepherd in Parliament, Budapest

Dining al fresco on Király utca in Pécs, Hungary

Group water aerobics at Harkány's spa, Hungary

Climb the hills around Vaduz, Liechtenstein, for a closer look at Vaduz Castle and the mountains

The Chopin monument in Łazienki Park, Warsaw, watches over open-air concerts in summer

Snows on the Tatra Mountains in southern Poland feed a chain of picturesque mountain lakes

RELIGION

Of those Hungarians declaring religious affiliation, about 68% are Roman Catholic, 21% Reformed (Calvinist) Protestant and nearly 6% Evangelical (Lutheran) Protestant. There are also small Greek Catholic and Orthodox congregations. Hungary's Jews number about 100,000, down from a prewar population of nearly 10 times that size.

LANGUAGE

Hungarians speak Magyar, a member of the Ugric group of the Uralic family of languages that is related very, very distantly to Finnish, Estonian and about a dozen other very minor languages in Russia and western Siberia. Hungarian is not an Indo-European language, so you'll recognise very few words.

Many older Hungarians, particularly in the western part of the country, can understand German and more and more young people, particularly in Budapest, speak some English. Any travel-related business will have at least one staff member who can speak English.

Some useful words to learn are: *utca* or *utcája* (street), *út* or *útja* (road), *tér* or *tere* (square), *körút* (boulevard), *sétány* (promenade) and *híd* (bridge).

Hungarians always put surnames before given names. To avoid confusion, all Hungarian names in this chapter are written in the Western manner – Christian name first – including the names of museums and theatres if they are translated into English. For example, Budapest's Arany János színház is Hungarian, but it's the János Arany Theatre in English. Addresses are always written in Hungarian: Kossuth Lajos utca, Arany János tér etc.

See the Language chapter at the back of the book for pronunciation guidelines and more useful words and phrases in Hungarian. Lonely Planet's *Eastern Europe phrasebook* contains a chapter on the language.

Facts for the Visitor

HIGHLIGHTS
Historic Towns

Many historic towns, including Eger, Győr and Veszprém, were rebuilt in the baroque style during the 18th century. Sopron and Kőszeg are among the few towns in Hungary with a strong medieval flavour. The greatest monuments of the Turkish period are in Pécs.

Budapest has wonderful examples of all architectural styles but especially Secessionist (Art Nouveau).

Castles & Palaces

Hungary's most famous castles are those that resisted the Turkish onslaught in Eger, Kőszeg and Siklós. Though in ruins, the citadel at Visegrád evokes the power of medieval Hungary. Esterházy Palace at Fertőd and the Festetics Palace at Keszthely are among the finest in the land.

Museums & Galleries

The following museums and galleries are among the best: the Christian Museum (Gothic paintings) in Esztergom, the Imre Patkó Collection in Győr (Asian and African art), the Storno House Collection (Romanesque and Gothic furnishings) in Sopron, the Zsolnay Porcelain Museum (Art Nouveau porcelain) and the Vasarely Museum in Pécs (op art), the Ferenc Móra Museum in Szeged (Avar finds and a mock yurt), and the Museum of Applied Arts (Art Nouveau furnishings) and Museum of Fine Arts (foreign art) in Budapest.

SUGGESTED ITINERARIES

Depending on the length of your stay, you could see and do the following:

Two days
Visit Budapest

One week
Visit Budapest, the Danube Bend and one or two of the following places: Sopron, Pécs, Eger, Kecskemét or Szeged

Two weeks
Visit Budapest, Győr, Sopron, the northern shore of Lake Balaton, Pécs, Szeged and Eger

PLANNING
When to Go

Every season has its attractions. Though it can be pretty wet in April and even May, spring is excellent as the weather is usually mild and the crowds of tourists have not yet arrived. Summer is warm, sunny and unusually long, but the resorts are crowded. If you avoid Lake Balaton, you'll do OK. Budapest comes to a grinding halt in August. Autumn is beautiful, particularly in the hills around Budapest and in the north. In Transdanubia and on the Great Plain this is harvest and vintage time. Avoid winter; apart from being cold and often bleak, winter sees museums

HUNGARY

and other tourist sights closed or their hours sharply curtailed.

Maps

In this small country you could easily get by with the *Road Map Hungary*, available free from branches of the Hungarian National Tourist Office (HNTO) abroad and from Tourinform offices in Hungary.

The Hungarian map-making company **Cartographia** (w *www.cartographia.hu*) publishes a useful 1:450,000 scale sheet map (800Ft) and its *Magyarország autóatlasza* (Road Atlas of Hungary) is indispensable if you plan to do a lot of travelling in the countryside by car. It comes in two sizes and scales – 1:360,000 (1600Ft) and 1:250,000 (2000Ft). The smaller scale atlas has thumbnail plans of virtually every community in the land, while the larger one has 23 city maps.

Discount Cards

Those planning extensive travel in Hungary might consider the **Hungary Card** (☎ *1-266 3741;* w *www.hungarycard.hu)*, which gives 50% discounts on all return train fares, some bus and boat travel, and some museums and attractions; up to 25% off selected accommodation; and 20% off the price of the Budapest Card (see Information in the Budapest section). The card, available at Tourinform and Volánbusz offices, larger train stations, some newsagents and petrol stations throughout Hungary, costs 6888Ft and is valid for a year.

What to Bring

A swimsuit for use in the mixed-sex thermal spas and pools is a good idea as are sandals or thongs (flip flops). If you plan to stay in hostels, pack a towel and a plastic soap container. Bedclothes are usually provided, though you might want to bring your own sheet bag and padlock for storage cupboards.

TOURIST OFFICES
Local Tourist Offices

The Hungarian National Tourist Office (HNTO) has a chain of 120 Tourinform information bureaus across the country, and these are the best places to ask general any questions and pick up brochures. The main **Tourinform office** (☎ *1-438 8080, fax 318 9059;* w *www.hungarytourism.hu;* V *Vigadó utca 6)* in Budapest is open 24 hours a day, seven days a week.

If your query is about private accommodation, flights or international train travel, you may have to ask a commercial travel agency; most towns have at least a couple. The oldest, Ibusz, is arguably the best for private accommodation. Others include Cooptourist and Vista. The Express travel agency, with branches in many cities, issues student, youth, teacher and hostel cards (1600Ft) and sells discounted Billet International de Jeunesse (BIJ) train tickets and cheap airfares. Some local Express offices can tell you about university accommodation as well.

Tourist Offices Abroad

The HNTO has offices in some 19 countries, including the following:

Austria (☎ 01-585 20 1213, fax 585 20 1214,
   e htvienna@hungarytourism.hu) Opernring
   5/2, A-1010 Vienna
Czech Republic (☎ 02-2109 0135, fax 2109
   0139, e htpragaue@hungarytourism.hu)
   Rumunská 22, 22537 Prague 2
France (☎ 01 53 70 67 17, fax 01 47 04 83 57,
   e htparis@hungarytourism.hu) 140 ave
   Victor Hugo, 75116 Paris
Germany (☎ 030-243 146 0, fax 243 146 13,
   e htberlin@hungarytourism.hu) Karl
   Liebknecht Strasse 34, D-10178 Berlin
Netherlands (☎ 070-320 9092, fax 327 2833,
   e htdenhaga@hungarytourism.hu) Laan van
   Nieuw Oost Indie 271, 2593 BS The Hague
UK (☎/fax 020-7823 1032, fax 7823 1459,
   e htlondon@hungarytourism.hu) 46 Eaton
   Place, London SW1X 8AL
USA (☎ 212-355 0240, fax 207 4103,
   e htnewyork@hungarytourism.hu) 33rd floor,
   150 East 58th St, New York, NY 10155-3398

In countries without an HNTO office, contact Malév Hungarian Airlines, which has offices or associated agencies in some 40 countries worldwide.

VISAS & DOCUMENTS

Everyone needs a valid passport or, for citizens of certain European countries, a national identification card, to enter Hungary. Citizens of virtually all European countries, the USA, Canada, Israel, Japan and New Zealand do not require visas to visit Hungary for stays of up to 90 days. UK citizens do not need a visa for a stay of up to six months. Nationals of Australia and now South Africa (among others) require visas. Check current visa requirements at a consulate, any HNTO or Malév office or on the website of the **Foreign Ministry** (W *www.kum.hu*) as these can change without notice.

Visas are issued at Hungarian consulates or missions, most international highway border crossings, Ferihegy airport and the International Ferry Pier in Budapest. Visas are never issued on trains and rarely on buses. Be sure to retain the separate entry and exit forms issued with the visa stamped in your passport.

Single-entry tourist visas are issued at Hungarian missions in the applicant's country of residence upon receipt of the equivalent of US$40 and three photos (US$65 at a mission outside the country of residence or at the border). A double-entry tourist visa costs US$75/100, and you must have five photos. A multiple-entry visa is US$180/200. Express service (10 minutes as opposed to overnight) costs US$15 extra. Single- and double-entry visas are valid for six months prior to use. Multiple entries are good for a year.

Be sure to get a tourist rather than a transit visa; the latter – available for single (US$38/50), double (US$65/90) and also multiple (US$150/180) entries – is only good for a stay of 48 hours each time, you must enter and leave through different border crossings and already hold a visa (if required) for the next country you visit.

Tourist visas can only be extended (3000Ft) in emergencies (eg, medical reasons) and must be done at the central police station (*rendőrkapitányság*) of any city or town 15 days before the original one expires. It's no longer an option to go to a neighbouring country like Austria or Slovakia and then re-enter; as of January 2002, tourist visas now allow visitors to stay for 90 days within a six-month period only.

EMBASSIES & CONSULATES
Hungarian Embassies & Consulates

Hungarian embassies around the world include the following:

Australia (☎ 02-6282 2555) 17 Beale Crescent, Deakin, ACT 2600
Consulate: (☎ 02-9328 7859) Suite 405, Edgecliff Centre, 203-233 New South Head Rd, Edgecliff, NSW 2027
Austria (☎ 01-537 80 300) 1 Bankgasse 4–6, 1010 Vienna
Canada (☎ 613-230 9614) 299 Waverley St, Ottawa, Ontario K2P 0V9

Consulate: (☎ 416-923 8981) Suite 1115, 121 Bloor St East, Toronto, Ontario M4W 3M5
Croatia (☎ 01-489 0900) Krlezin gvozd 11/a, 10000 Zagreb
Germany (☎ 030-203 100) Unter den Linden 76, 10117 Berlin
Consulate: (☎ 089-911 032) Vollmannstrasse 2, 81927 Munich
Ireland (☎ 01-661 2902) 2 Fitzwilliam Place, Dublin 2
Romania (☎ 01-311 0062) Strada Jean-Louis Calderon 63–65, Bucharest 70202
Slovakia (☎ 02-544 30541) ul Sedlárska 3, 81425 Bratislava
Slovenia (☎ 01-512 1882) Konrada Babnika ulica 5, 1210 Ljubljana-Sentvid
South Africa (☎ 012-430 3030) 959 Arcadia St, Hatfield, 0083 Pretoria
UK (☎ 020-7235 5218) 35 Eaton Place, London SW1X 8BY
Consulate: (☎ 020-7235 2664) 35/b Eaton Place, London SW1X 8BY
Ukraine (☎ 044-212 4134) ul Rejtarszkaja 33, Kyiv 01034
USA (☎ 202-362 6730) 3910 Shoemaker St NW, Washington, DC 20008
Consulate: (☎ 212-752 0661) 223 East 52nd St, New York, NY 10022
Consulate: (☎ 310-473 9344) Suite 410, 11766 Wilshire Blvd, Los Angeles, CA 90025
Yugoslavia (☎ 011-444 0472) ul Ivana Milutinovica 74, Belgrade 11000

Embassies & Consulates in Hungary

Countries with representation in Budapest (phone code ☎ 1) include the following (hours indicate when consular or chancellery services are available):

Australia (☎ 457 9777) XII Királyhágó tér 8–9 (open 9am–noon Mon-Fri)
Austria (☎ 352 9613) VI Benczúr utca 16 (open 9am–11am Mon-Fri)
Canada (☎ 392 3360) XII Budakeszi út 32 (open 8.30am–11am & 2pm-3.30pm Mon-Thur)
Croatia (☎ 354 1315) VI Munkácsy Mihály utca 15 (open 1pm-3pm Mon, Tues, Thur & Fri)
Germany (☎ 488 3500) I Úri utca 64-66 (open 9am–noon Mon-Fri)
Ireland (☎ 302 9600) V Szabadság tér 7–9 (open 9.30am-12.30pm & 2.30pm-4.30pm Mon-Fri)
Romania (☎ 352 0271) XIV Thököly út 72 (open 8.30am–noon Mon-Fri)
Slovakia (☎ 460 9010) XIV Stefánia út 22–24 (open 8am–noon Mon-Fri)
Slovenia (☎ 438 5600) II Cseppkő utca 68 (open 9am–noon Mon-Fri)
South Africa (☎ 392 0999) II Gárdonyi Géza út 17 (open 9am-12.30pm Mon-Fri)

UK (☎ 266 2888) V Harmincad utca 6 (open 9.30am-12.30pm & 2.30pm-4.30pm Mon-Fri)
Ukraine (☎ 355 2443) XII Nógrádi utca 8 (open 9am-noon Mon-Wed & Fri by appointment only)
USA (☎ 475 4400) V Szabadság tér 12 (open 8.15am-5pm Mon-Fri)
Yugoslavia (☎ 322 9838) VI Dózsa György út 92/b (open 9am-1pm Mon-Fri)

CUSTOMS

You can bring the usual personal effects, 200 cigarettes, 1L of wine or champagne and 1L of spirits. You are not supposed to export valuable antiques without a special permit; this should be available from the place of purchase. You must declare the import/export of any amount of cash exceeding the sum of 1,000,000Ft.

MONEY
Currency

The unit of currency is the Hungarian forint (Ft). Coins come in denominations of one, two, five, 10, 20, 50 and 100Ft, and notes are denominated 200, 500, 1000, 2000, 5000, 10,000 and 20,000Ft.

Exchange Rates

Exchange rates at the time of going to press were:

country	unit		forint
Australia	A$1	=	139Ft
Canada	C$1	=	163Ft
Euro Zone	€1	=	245Ft
Japan	¥100	=	206Ft
New Zealand	NZ$1	=	120Ft
UK	UK£1	=	378Ft
USA	US$1	=	247Ft

Exchanging Money

You'll find automated teller machines (ATMs) accepting most credit and cash cards throughout the country; all banks mentioned in this chapter have them unless indicated otherwise. It's always prudent to carry a little foreign cash, preferably euros or US dollars, and perhaps some travellers cheques (eg, American Express, Visa or Thomas Cook).

Banks and bureaux de change generally don't take a commission, but exchange rates vary tremendously; private agencies are always the most expensive. The national savings bank, Országos Takarékpenztár (OTP), has branches everywhere and offers some of the best rates; Ibusz is also a good bet. Many banks, including K&H and Postabank (at post offices nationwide), give cash advances on most credit cards.

The use of credit cards is gaining ground, especially Visa, MasterCard and American Express. You'll be able to use them at upmarket restaurants, shops, hotels, car-rental firms, travel agencies and petrol stations but not museums, supermarkets or train and bus stations.

Money can be wired to Hungary through American Express – you don't need to be an Amex card-holder but the sender does. The procedure takes less than 30 minutes. You should know the sender's full name, the exact amount and the reference number when you're picking up the cash. You'll be given the amount in US dollars travellers cheques or forint. The sender pays the service fee (about US$50 for US$1000 sent).

Security

Overall, Hungary is a very safe country but pickpocketing can be a problem, especially in Budapest (see the Dangers & Annoyances section). Always put your wallet in your front pocket, hold your purse close to your body and keep your backpack or baggage in sight. And watch out for tricks. The usual method on the street is for someone to distract you by running into you and then apologising profusely – as an accomplice takes off with the goods. We have received amny reports of unscrupulous waiters and shop assistants making high-tech duplicates of credit- or debit-card information with a machine. If your card leaves your possession for a considerable length of time, think about having it cancelled.

Costs

Prices may have risen over the past few years, but Hungary remains a bargain destination for Western travellers. If you stay in private rooms, eat at medium-priced restaurants and travel on public transport, you should get by on US$30 a day without scrimping. Those staying at hostels, dormitories or camping grounds and eating at food stalls or self-catering will cut costs substantially.

Because of the changing value of the forint, many hotels quote their rates in euros, as does the national rail company. In such cases, we have followed suit.

Tipping

Hungarians routinely give tips of about 10% to waiters, hairdressers, taxi drivers and even doctors, dentists and petrol station attendants manning the pumps. In restaurants, do this on payment of the bill; leaving money on the table is considered rude in Hungary. If you were less than impressed with the service, don't feel obliged to leave a gratuity. Some upmarket places add a 10% service charge to the bill, which makes tipping unnecessary.

Taxes & Refunds

ÁFA, a value-added tax of 11% to 25%, covers the purchase of all new goods. It's usually included in the quoted price but not always, so it pays to check. Visitors can claim refunds for total purchases of more than 50,000Ft on one receipt as long as they take the goods out of the country within 90 days. The ÁFA receipts (available from the shops where you made the purchases) should be stamped by customs at the border, and the claim has to be made within 183 days of exporting the goods.

Budapest-based **Global Refund Hungary** (*☎/fax 1-468 2965, fax 468 2966; ☒ www.globalrefund.com; XIV Zászlós utca 54*) can help you with refunds for a fee.

POST & COMMUNICATIONS
Post

Letters/postcards sent within Hungary and to neighbouring countries cost 38/30Ft. Airmail letters within Europe cost 150/240Ft for up to 20/50g and 160/260Ft for the rest of the world. Postcards cost 100Ft and 110Ft respectively.

Mail addressed to poste restante in any town or city will go to the main post office (*főposta*), which is listed under Information in the destination sections. When collecting poste-restante mail, look for the sign '*postán maradó küldemények*'. Don't forget identification and write your full name on a piece of paper; otherwise the clerk might look under your first name.

If you hold an American Express credit card or are carrying their travellers cheques, you can have your mail sent to **American Express** (*Deák Ferenc utca 10, 1052 Budapest*), where it will be held for one month.

Telephone

You can make domestic and international calls from public telephones. They work with both coins and phonecards, though the latter are now more common. Phonecards (800Ft or 1800Ft) are available from post offices, newsagents, hotels and petrol stations. Telephone boxes with a black and white arrow and red target on the door and the word '*Visszahívható*' display a telephone number, so you can be phoned back.

All localities in Hungary have a two-digit area code, except for Budapest, which has '1'. Local codes appear under the destination headings in this chapter.

To make a local call, pick up the receiver and listen for the continuous dial tone, then dial the phone number. For an intercity call within Hungary, dial ☎ 06 and wait for the second, more musical, tone. Then dial the area code and phone number. You must *always* dial ☎ 06 when ringing a mobile telephone, whose area codes are ☎ 06-20 (Pannon), ☎ 06-30 and ☎ 06-60 (Westel), and ☎ 06-70 (Vodafone).

The procedure for making an international call is the same except that you dial ☎ 00, followed by the country code, the area code and then the number. International phone charges from a phone box are: 131Ft per minute to neighbouring countries and 136Ft to Europe, North America, Australia and New Zealand.

Useful phone numbers include domestic (☎ 198) and international operator/directory inquiries (☎ 199).

Fax

You can send faxes from most main post offices and Internet cafés for 150/500Ft per page within/outside Hungary.

Email & Internet Access

Internet cafés have sprouted in Budapest (see that section) like mushrooms after rain and all the capital's year-round hostels offer access. Public Internet connections in the provinces are harder to find, though most major towns now have a Matáv Pont outlet, which usually has at least a couple of terminals available (300/500Ft for 30/60 minutes).

DIGITAL RESOURCES

Tourinform's informative website ☒ www.hungarytourism.hu should be your initial portal of call. For information on hotels, try ☒ www.hotelshungary.com, ☒ www.hotelsinfo.hu or ☒ www.szallasinfo.hu. Check out ☒ www.youthhostels.hu for hostel accommodation and also ☒ www.camping.hu for camping grounds in Hungary.

HUNGARY

The website ⓦ www.budapestinfo.hu is the best overall site for information about Budapest, and Budapest Week Online, at ⓦ www.budapestweek.com, has events, music and movie listings. Budapest Sun Online, found at ⓦ www.budapestsun.com, is similar but with a focus on local news, interviews and features. For national news, visit the website at ⓦ www.insidehungary.com.

BOOKS

An excellent overall guidebook is Lonely Planet's *Hungary*, while the *Budapest* guide takes an in-depth look at the capital.

An Illustrated History of Hungary by István Lázár is an easy introduction to the nation's past, but more serious students will pick up a copy of Miklós Molnár's *A Concise History of Hungary*.

Budapest: A Cultural Guide by Michael Jacobs is a history-cum-walking guide that sometimes borders on the academic. Imre Móra's *Budapest Then & Now*, now in its second edition, is a collection of essays that has some esoteric bits of information relating to the capital.

NEWSPAPERS & MAGAZINES

Budapest has two English-language weeklies: the fluffy *Budapest Sun* (298Ft), with a useful 'Style' arts and entertainment supplement, and the *Budapest Business Journal* (550Ft). *The Hungarian Spectator* (100Ft), an unsuccessful mix of the two, appears twice a month.

A number of Western English-language newspapers, including the *International Herald Tribune*, are available on the day of publication in Budapest and in certain other large western Hungary cities. Many more, mainly British, French and German, are sold a day late. International news magazines are also widely available.

RADIO & TV

With the sale of the state-owned TV2, Magyar Televízió (MTV) controls only one TV channel (M1). There are also the public channels M2 and Duna TV and a host of cable and satellite ones (such as RTL Klub and Magyar ATV) broadcasting everything from game and talk shows to Pokemon, all in – or dubbed into – Hungarian. Most larger hotels and pensions have satellite TV, mainly German, but sometimes Sky News, CNN, Eurosport and BBC News.

Hungarian Radio has three stations, named after Lajos Kossuth (jazz, news; 98.6AM), Sándor Petőfi (1960s to 80s music, news; 94.8FM) and Béla Bartók (classical music, news; 105.3FM). Est.fm (98.6FM) is a popular alternative music station while Radio © (88.8FM) is super for Romani music as well as jazz, Latino and North African sounds. Budapest Rádió is on 88.1 FM and 91.9FM.

PHOTOGRAPHY & VIDEO

Major brands of film are readily available and one-hour processing places are common in Budapest and larger cities and towns.

Film prices vary but basically 24 exposures of 100 ASA Kodacolor II, Agfa or Fujifilm costs 1000Ft, and 36 exposures is 1290Ft. Ektachrome 100 costs 1790Ft for 36 exposures. Developing print film is 1099Ft a roll; for the prints themselves, you choose the size and pay accordingly (eg, 10cm x 15cm prints cost 89Ft each). Slide film costs 1100Ft to process. Videotape such as TDK EHG 30/45 minutes costs 990/1310Ft.

TIME

Time is GMT plus one hour. Clocks are advanced at 2am on the last Sunday in March and set back at the same time on the last Sunday in October. In Hungarian, 'half eight' means 7.30 and not 8.30.

LAUNDRY

Most hostels and camping grounds have some sort of laundry facilities; expect to pay about 1000Ft per good-sized load. Commercial laundries often take days to do your wash and are never cheap. Self-service laundries are virtually nonexistent.

TOILETS

Public toilets, which always levy a user's fee (usually 50Ft), are invariably staffed by an old *néné* (auntie), who continuously mops the floor, hands out sheets of Grade AAA sandpaper and has seen it all before.

Public toilets (*WC* or *toalett*) are signposted *női* or *nők* for women and *férfi* or *férfiak* for men.

WOMEN TRAVELLERS

Hungarian men can be very sexist in their thinking, but women do not suffer any particular form of harassment (though domestic violence and rape get little media coverage).

For assistance and/or information ring the **Women's Line** (*Nővonal*; ☎ 06-80 505 101) or **Women for Women against Violence** (*NANE*; ☎ 1-267 4900), which operates from 6pm to 10pm daily.

GAY & LESBIAN TRAVELLERS

For up-to-date information on venues, events, parties etc, pick up the pamphlet *Na végre!* (At Last!) at gay venues in Budapest or contact the group directly (**e** navegre@hotmail.com). The websites **w** www.pride.hu, **w** www.gayguide.net/europe/hungary/budapest, **w** english.gay.hu and **w** masprogram.freeweb.hu are good sources of information.

For one-to-one contact, ring either the **Gay Switchboard** (☎ 06-30 932 3334, 1-351 2015; *open 4pm-8pm Mon-Fri*) or **Háttér Gay & Lesbian Association** (☎ 1-329 3380; *open 6pm-11pm daily*).

DISABLED TRAVELLERS

Most of Hungary has a long way to go before it becomes accessible to the disabled. Wheelchair ramps, toilets fitted for the disabled and inward opening doors are virtually nonexistent, though audible traffic signals for the blind are becoming increasingly commonplace and the higher-denominated forint notes have markings in Braille.

For more information, contact the **Hungarian Disabled Association** (*MEOSZ*; ☎ 1-388 5529, 388 2387; **e** meosz@matavnet.hu; *San Marco utca 76, Budapest 1035; open 8am-4pm Mon-Fri*).

DANGERS & ANNOYANCES

Hungary is not a violent or dangerous society, but crime has increased fourfold from a communist-era base of virtually nil over the past 15 years. Racially motivated attacks against Roma, Africans and Arabs are not unknown, but violence is very seldom directed against travellers in the country.

As a traveller you are most vulnerable to pickpockets and taxi louts (see Getting Around in the Budapest section) and possibly car thieves.

BUSINESS HOURS

With some rare exceptions, the opening hours (*nyitvatartás*) of any concern to the ordinary traveller are posted on the front door of establishements; *nyitva* means 'open' and *zárva* is 'closed'.

Emergency Services

In the event of an emergency anywhere in Hungary, phone the central emergency number on ☎ 112 (English spoken).

For police call ☎ 107, for fire ☎ 105 and for ambulance ☎ 104. The English-language crime hotline is ☎ 1-438 8000.

Car assistance (24 hours) is available by calling ☎ 188.

Grocery stores and supermarkets open from about 7am to 6pm or 7pm on weekdays, and department stores 10am to 6pm. Most shops stay open until 8pm on Thursday; on Saturday they usually close at 1pm. Main post offices are open 8am to 6pm weekdays, and to noon or 1pm Saturday. Banking hours vary but are usually 8am to about 4pm Monday to Thursday and to 1pm on Friday. With few exceptions, museums are open 10am to 6pm Tuesday to Sunday from April to October and to 4pm on the same days the rest of the year.

Most places have a 'nonstop' convenience store, which opens late (but not always 24 hours), and many of the hyper-supermarkets open on Sunday.

PUBLIC HOLIDAYS & SPECIAL EVENTS

Hungary's 10 public holidays are: New Year's Day (1 January), 1848 Revolution Day (15 March), Easter Monday (March/April), International Labour Day (1 May), Whit Monday (May/June), St Stephen's Day (20 August), 1956 Remembrance Day (23 October), All Saints' Day (1 November) and Christmas and Boxing Days (25 and 26 December).

The best annual events include: the Budapest Spring Festival (March); the Balaton Festival based in Keszthely (May); the Hungarian Dance Festival in Győr (late June); Sopron Festival Weeks (late June to mid-July); Győr Summer Cultural Festival (late June to late July); Hortobágy International Equestrian Days (July); Szeged Open-Air Festival (July); Kőszeg Castle Theatre Festival (mid- to late July); Pepsi Sziget Music Festival on Óbudai hajógyár-sziget (Óbuda Shipbuilding Island) in Budapest (late July to early August); Hungaroring Formula-1 races at Mogyoród, 24km northeast of Budapest (mid-August); and the Budapest Autumn Festival (mid-October to early November).

HUNGARY

ACTIVITIES
Thermal Baths
More than 100 thermal baths are open to the public. The thermal lake at Hévíz is Hungary's most impressive. Public thermal pools at Budapest, Eger, Győr and Harkány are also covered in this chapter.

Water Sports
The main places for water sports in Hungary are Lake Balaton (Keszthely, Balatonszabadi, Balatonvilágos and Balatonaliga) and Lake Velence. Qualified sailors can rent yachts on Balaton; motorboats are banned.

Many canoe and kayak trips are available. Following the Danube from Rajka in the northwest to Mohács in the southwest (386km) or the Tisza River from Tiszabecs on the border with Ukraine southward to Szeged (570km) are popular runs, but there are less congested waterways and shorter trips, such as the Rába River from Szentgotthárd north to Győr (205km).

The HNTO publishes a brochure titled *Water Tourism: 3500km of Waterways*, which introduces what's available on Hungary's rivers, streams and canals, and offers practical information.

Cycling
Hungary now counts 2500km of dedicated bicycle lanes around the country, with more on the way. In addition there are thousands of kilometres of roads with light traffic and dikes suitable for cycling. The HNTO produces the useful *Cycling in Hungary* brochure, with 12 recommended routes with maps, as well as a 60-page insert crammed with all sorts of practical information.

Cartographia produces a series of 1:100,000 regional Tourist Maps (*Turistatérkép*; 650Ft), with cycling routes marked and explanatory notes in English. Another possibility is the 1:250,000-scale *Cycling around Hungary* (*Kerékpártúrák Magyarországon*; 2600Ft), with 100 tours outlined and places of interest and service centres listed in English.

For information and advice in Budapest, contact the helpful **Hungarian Bicycle Touring Association** (*MKTSZ*; ☎ 1-311 2467; e mktsz@dpg.hu; VI Bajcsy-Zsilinszky út 31). Also in the capital, the enthusiastic **Friends of Nature Bicycle Touring Association** (*TTE*; ☎ 1-316 5867; II Bem rakpart 51) can help organise bike tours and supply guides.

Hiking
You can enjoy good hiking in the forests around Visegrád, Esztergom, Badacsony, Kőszeg and Budapest. North of Eger are the Bükk Hills and south of Kecskemét the Bugac Puszta, both with marked trails. Cartographia publishes three dozen hiking maps (average scales 1:40,000 and 1:50,000; 650/1600Ft folded/spiral-bound) to the hills, forests, rivers and lakes of Hungary. Most are available from its outlet in Budapest (see Orientation in the Budapest section).

The HNTO produces the free *The Beauty of Nature: 11,000 kms of Marked Rambling Paths*, with ideas for treks and walks around the country and an insert with practical information and tips.

Horse Riding
The Magyars say they were 'created by God to sit on horseback' and that still holds true today. But it's risky to show up at a riding centre without a booking, particularly in the high season. Book through a local tourist office or the **Hungarian Equestrian Tourism Association** (*MLTSZ*; ☎ 1-456 0444, fax 456 0445; W www.equi.hu; IX Ráday utca 8) in Budapest. Also in the capital, **Pegazus Tours** (☎ 1-317 1644, fax 266 2827; e orycsilla@ pegazus.hu; V Ferenciek tere 5) organises riding tours.

The HNTO produces a useful 64-page brochure called *Riding in Hungary* with both general and very detailed information.

LANGUAGE COURSES
Language schools teaching Hungarian to foreigners are in abundance, but they do vary tremendously in quality, approach and their success rates.

Hungarian Language School (☎ 1-351 1191, fax 351 1193; W www.hls.hu; VI Rippl-Rónai utca 4) is a good choice for those wanting to learn the basics.

Debrecen Summer University (*Debreceni Nyári Egyetem*; ☎/fax 52-489 117; W www .nyariegyetem.hu; Egyetem tér 1, PO Box 35, Debrecen 4010), in eastern Hungary, is the granddaddy of all the Hungarian language schools. It organises intensive two- and four-week courses during July and August and 80-hour, two-week advanced courses during winter. There is now a **Budapest branch** (☎/fax 1-320 5751; Jászai Mari tér 6) that puts on regular and intensive courses.

WORK

Travellers on tourist visas in Hungary are forbidden from taking any form of employment, but some end up teaching or even working for foreign firms without permits.

Check the English-language telephone book or ads for English schools in the *Budapest Sun*; there are also job listings but pay is generally low. You can do much better teaching privately (2000Ft to 4000Ft per hour).

Obtaining a work permit *(munkavállalási engedély)* involves a Byzantine paper chase. You'll need a letter of support from your prospective employer, copies of your birth certificate, academic record officially translated into Hungarian and results of a recent medical examination (including a test for HIV exposure). The employer then submits these to the local labour centre *(munkaügyi központ)*, and you *must* return to your country of residence and apply for the work permit (US$40) at the Hungarian embassy or consulate there.

ACCOMMODATION

Many cities and towns levy a local tourist tax of around 250Ft per person per night, though sometimes only after the first 48 hours. People under 18 years of age or staying at camping grounds may be exempt. Breakfast is usually included in the price of a hotel or hostel.

Camping

Hungary has more than 400 camping grounds. Small, private camping grounds are usually preferable to the large, noisy, 'official' sites. Prices vary widely and around Lake Balaton they can be exorbitant in summer.

Most camping grounds open from April or May to September or October and also rent small bungalows. In midsummer the bungalows may all be booked, so it check with the local Tourinform office before making the trip. A Camping Card International will sometimes get you a 10% discount. Camping 'wild' is prohibited in Hungary. Tourinform's *Camping Hungary* map/brochure lists every camping ground in the land.

Farmhouses

'Village tourism', which means staying at a farmhouse, can be cheap but most of the places are truly remote. Contact Tourinform or the **National Association of Village Tourism** *(FAOS; ☎/fax 1-268 0592; VII Király utca 93)* in Budapest for information.

Hostels & Student Dormitories

Despite all the places that are listed by the Budapest-based **Hungarian Youth Hostel Association** *(MISZSZ; ☎ 1-413 2065, fax 321 4851; W www.youthhostels.hu; VII Baross tér 15, 3rd floor)*, a hostel card isn't particularly useful as most of the associated hostels are remote, although it occasionally gets 10% off the quoted price.

There's no age limit at hostels and they stay open all day. Generally the only year-round hostels are in Budapest.

From 1 July to about 20 August, the cheapest rooms are in vacant student residences (dorm beds and sometimes private rooms too).

Private Rooms

Private rooms are usually assigned by travel agencies, which give you a voucher bearing the address and sometimes even the key to the house or flat. In Budapest, individuals at train stations approach anyone looking vaguely like a traveller and offer private rooms. Unless you find out the exact location, you're probably better off getting a room from an agency.

There's usually a 30% supplement on the first night if you stay less than four nights, and single rooms are hard to come by.

You'll probably share the house or flat with a Hungarian family. The toilet is usually communal but otherwise you can close your door and enjoy as much privacy as you please. Some places offer kitchen facilities. In Budapest and elsewhere, the distinction between the more expensive private rooms and pensions is becoming blurred.

In resort areas look for houses with signs reading *'szoba kiadó'* or the German *'Zimmer frei'* that advertise private rooms.

Pensions

Quaint, often family-run, pensions *(panziók)* are abundant across Hungary, and most towns have at least one. In Budapest they are mostly in the Buda Hills. Pensions are really just little hotels. They are usually new and clean and often have a restaurant attached.

Hotels

Hotels, called *szállók* or *szállodák*, run the gamut from luxurious five-star palaces to the run-down old communist-era hovels that still survive in some towns.

A cheap hotel will be more expensive than a private room, but it may be the answer if you're only staying one night or if you arrive too late to get a private room through an agency. Two-star hotels usually have rooms with a private bathroom; it's down the hall in a one-star place. Three- and four-star hotels, many of which are brand-new or are newly renovated old villas, can be excellent value compared with other European countries.

FOOD

Inexpensive by Western European standards and served in huge portions, traditional Hungarian food is heavy and rich. Meat, sour cream and fat abound and, except in season, *saláta* generally means a plate of pickled beets, cabbage and/or peppers. But things are improving for the health-conscious traveller, with vegetarian, 'New Hungarian' and ethnic cuisines more available (at least in Budapest).

The most famous traditional meal is *gulyás* (or *gulyásleves*), a thick beef soup cooked with onions and potatoes and usually eaten as a main course. *Pörkölt* (stew) is closer to what we call 'goulash' abroad. Pork, turkey and chicken are the most common meats and can be breaded and fried or baked.

Many dishes are seasoned with paprika, which appears on restaurant tables as a condiment beside the salt and pepper shakers. It's quite a mild spice and is used predominantly with sour cream or in *rántás*, a heavy roux of pork lard and flour added to cooked vegetables. Things stuffed *(töltött)* with meat and rice, such as cabbage or peppers, are cooked in rántás, tomato sauce or sour cream.

Another Hungarian favourite is *halászlé* (fisherman's soup), a rich mix of several kinds of poached freshwater fish, tomatoes, green peppers and paprika. Noodle dishes with cheese, such as *sztrapacska*, go well with fish.

Some dishes for vegetarians to request are *rántott sajt* (fried cheese), *gombafejek rántva* (fried mushroom caps), *gomba leves* (mushroom soup), *gyümölcs leves* (fruit soup), *sajtos kenyer* (sliced bread with soft cheese) and *túrós csusza* (Hungarian pasta with cheese). *Bableves* (bean soup) usually contains meat. *Palacsinta* (pancakes) may be savoury and made with *sajt* (cheese) or *gomba* (mushrooms) or sweet and prepared with *dió* (nuts) or *mák* (poppy seeds). *Lángos*, a deep-fried dough with various toppings, is a cheap meatless snack sold on streets throughout the land.

An *étterem* is a restaurant with a large selection. A *vendéglő* is smaller and is supposed to serve inexpensive regional dishes. An *étkezde* is even smaller, often with counter seating, while the over-used term *csárda*, originally a rustic country inn with Gypsy music, can now mean anything.

DRINKS

Wine has been produced in Hungary for thousands of years and you'll find it available by the glass or bottle everywhere. For dry whites, look for Badacsonyi Kéknyelű or Szürkebarát, Mőcsényi or Boglári Chardonnay or Debrői Hárslevelű. Olasz Rizling and Egri Leányka tend to be sweet , though nowhere near Tokaji Aszú dessert wines. Dependable reds include Villányi Merlot, Pinot Noir and Cabernet Sauvignon, Szekszárdi Kékfrankos and Nagyrédei Cabernet Franc. Celebrated Egri Bikavér (Eger Bull's Blood) is a full-bodied red high in acid and tannin. Hangover in a bottle.

A popular spirit is *pálinka*, a strong brandy distilled from a variety of fruits, but most commonly plums or apricots. Hungarian liqueurs are usually unbearably sweet and taste artificial, though the Zwack brand is reliable. Zwack also produces Unicum, a bitter aperitif that has been around since 1790.

Hungarian beers sold nationally include Dreher and Kőbanyai; others are distributed only near where they are brewed (eg, Kanizsai in Nagykanizsa and Szalon in Pécs). Bottled Austrian, German and Czech beers are readily available.

A *borozó* is a place (usually a dive) serving wine, a *pince* is a beer or wine cellar, while a *söröző* is a pub that offers *csapolt sör* (draught beer).

ENTERTAINMENT

Hungary is a paradise for culture vultures. In Budapest there are several musical events every night and excellent opera tickets cost between 600Ft and 7000Ft. Besides traditional opera, operetta and classical concerts, there are rock and jazz concerts, folk dancing, pantomime, puppet shows, movies in English, discos, floor shows and circuses to keep you entertained.

Excellent cultural performances can also be seen in provincial towns like Eger, Győr, Kecskemét, Pécs, Veszprém, Szombathely adn Szeged all of which have fine theatres. Information about events is readily available at Tourinform offices, in the monthly *Programme in Ungarn/in Hungary* and the *Pesti*

Est listings magazines available at the Tourinform offices and entertainment venues everywhere. The free *Pesti Est* listings magazine for Budapest publishes editions to almost 18 other cities and regions – from *Békés Est* to *Zalai Est*. You can pick them up for free in the tourist offices and at entertainment venues throughout the country. Some useful words to remember are *színház* (theatre), *pénztár* (box office), *jegy* (ticket) and *elkelt* (sold out).

In mid-June many theatres close for the summer holidays, reopening in late September or October. Summer opera, operetta and concert programmes specially designed for tourists are more expensive than the normal productions the rest of the year.

Be aware that many foreign films are dubbed into Hungarian, so try asking the ticket seller if the film retains the original soundtrack and has Hungarian subtitles *(feliratos)* or is dubbed *(szinkronizált* or *magyarul beszélő)*.

SHOPPING
Books and folk-music tapes and CDs are affordable, and there is an excellent selection. Traditional products include folk-art embroidery and ceramics, wall hangings, painted wooden toys and boxes, dolls, all forms of basketry and porcelain (especially Herend, Zsolnay or the cheaper Kalocsa). Feather or goose-down pillows and duvets (comforters) are of exceptionally high quality.

Foodstuffs that are expensive or difficult to buy elsewhere – goose liver (both fresh and potted), caviar and some prepared meats like Pick salami – make nice gifts (if you are allowed to take them home), as do the many varieties of paprika. Some of Hungary's 'boutique' wines – especially those that have imaginative labels – make good, inexpensive gifts. A bottle of dessert Tokay always goes down well.

Getting There & Away

AIR
Budapest's **Ferihegy airport** (☎ 1-296 9696), 24km southeast of the city centre, has two modern terminals side by side. Terminal 2A is reserved for the national carrier, **Malév Hungarian Airlines** (Ⓦ *www.malev.hu)*, and its code-share partners. Terminal 2B handles all other foreign airlines. For flight information at Terminal 2A, ring ☎ 1-296 7000 for departures or ☎ 1-296 8000 for arrivals. For Terminal 2B, ring ☎ 1-296 5882 (departures) or ☎ 1-296 5052 (arrivals).

Malév flies nonstop to Ferihegy from North America, the Middle East and many cities in Continental Europe and the British Isles. It has links to Asia and Australia via its European gateways. The airline has ticketing desks at Terminal 2A (☎ 1-296 7211) and at Terminal 2B (☎ 1-296 5767).

Malév doesn't offer student discounts on flights originating in Hungary, but youth fares are available to people aged under 26 (in summer only). These might not always be cheaper than a discounted ticket, however. Some sample return air fares to other cities in Eastern Europe include: Moscow (75,000Ft), Warsaw (63,000Ft) and Prague (63,000Ft).

LAND
Hungary has excellent land transport connections with its seven neighbours. Most of the departures are from Budapest, though other cities and towns closer to the various borders can also be used as springboards.

Bus
Most international buses are run by **Eurolines** (☎ *1-219 8080, 219 8000)* or its Hungarian associate, **Volánbusz** (☎ *1-485 2162, 485 2100;* ☎ *www.volanbusz.hu)*. The Eurolines passes include Budapest. For more information on these bus passes see the introductory Getting There & Away chapter.

Some Eurolines services between Budapest and Western Europe, with high-season (mid-June to mid-September) one-way fares quoted, include the following:

Amsterdam: 25,900Ft; 19 hours (1435km) via Frankfurt (21,900Ft) and Düsseldorf (23,500Ft), continuing on to Rotterdam (25,900Ft); four days a week year-round, six or seven weekly from early June to late September
Berlin: 19,900Ft; 15 hours (915km) via Prague (8900Ft), then continuing on to Hamburg (22,900Ft); three days a week year-round, five weekly from early June to late September
London: 33,900Ft; 26 hours (1755km) via Vienna (6390Ft) and Brussels (22,900Ft); four days a week year-round, five to seven weekly from early April to late October
Paris: 27,900Ft; 22 hours (1525km) via Strasbourg (25,900Ft) and Reims (27,900Ft); two to three days a week from April to late October

Rome: 23,500Ft; 15 hours (1330km) via Bologna (16,900Ft) and Florence (18,900Ft), continuing on to Naples (25,500Ft) four days a week year-round, five to six weekly from early April to late October to Rome; two days a week year-round to Naples

Vienna: 6390Ft; 3½ hours (254km) via Győr (4400Ft); three buses daily (four on Saturday)

To Romania, there are regularly scheduled buses on Saturday year-round to Arad (4000Ft, seven hours, 282km) and Timişoara (Hungarian: Temesvár; 4900Ft, eight hours).

Other useful international buses include those to: Bratislava (Pozsony; 3100Ft, four hours, 213km, daily year-round) in Slovakia; Prague (8900Ft, eight hours, 535km, three days a week year-round, five weekly from early June to late September) in the Czech Republic; Belgrade (4100Ft, nine hours, 422km, daily year-round) via Subotica (Szabatka; 3300Ft, four hours, 227km) in Yugoslavia; Pula (9900Ft, 14½ hours, 775km, Friday from late June to early September) via Rijeka (7900Ft, 10 hours, 546km) in Croatia; and Kraków (6900Ft, 10 hours, Saturday year-round) via Zakopane (5600Ft, 8½ hours, 387km) in Poland.

Train

Magyar Államvasutak (W *www.mav.hu),* which translates as Hungarian State Railways and is known as MÁV, links up with the European rail network in all directions, running trains as far as London (via Cologne and Brussels), Paris (via Frankfurt), Stockholm (via Hamburg and Copenhagen), Moscow, Rome and Istanbul (via Belgrade).

In Budapest, most international trains arrive at and depart from **Keleti station** *(Eastern;* ☎ *1-313 6835; VIII Kerepesi út 2-4);* trains to some places in Romania and Germany leave from **Nyugati station** *(Western;* ☎ *1-349 0115; VI Nyugati tér),* while **Déli station** *(Southern;* ☎ *1-355 8657; I Krisztina körút 37/a)* handles trains to/from Zagreb and Rijeka in Croatia. But these are not hard-and-fast rules, so *always* check from which station the train leaves when you buy a ticket. For 24-hour information on the international train services call ☎ 1-461 5500 in Budapest. For the domestic schedules, ring ☎ 1-461 5400.

Tickets & Discounts To avoid confusion, specify your train by the name listed under the following destinations or on the posted schedule when seeking information or buying a ticket. You can buy tickets at the three international train stations in Budapest, but it's easier at MÁV's central ticket office in Budapest (see Getting There & Away in that section).

There are big discounts on return fares only between Hungary and former communist countries: 30% to Bulgaria, the Czech Republic and Poland; 40% to Yugoslavia and the Baltic countries; 50% to Belarus, Russia and Ukraine; up to 65% to Slovakia and Slovenia; and up to 75% to Romania.

For tickets to Western Europe you'll pay the same as everywhere else unless you're aged under 26 and qualify for the 30% to 50% BIJ discount. Ask at MÁV, Express or the Wasteels office (☎ 1-210 2802) in Keleti Station in Budapest

The following are minimum return, 2nd-class fares from Budapest: Amsterdam €212; Berlin €126 (via Prague) and €198 (via Vienna); London €352; Munich €91; Rome (via Ljubljana) €172; and Vienna €41. Three daily EuroCity (EC) trains to Vienna and points beyond charge a supplement of 1000Ft to 1500Ft. The 1st-class seats are usually 50% more expensive than 2nd class. Costs for sleepers depend on the destination, and how many beds are in the carriage.

International seat reservation costs vary according to the destination (eg, €6.60 to Prague, €10.60 to Warsaw). Fines are levied on passengers without tickets or seat reservations on trains where they are mandatory. Tickets are valid for 60 days from the date of purchase, and stopovers are permitted.

MÁV sells Inter-Rail passes from one to eight zones to European nationals (or residents of at least six months). The price for any one zone is €226/158/113 for adult/youth 12 to 26/child four to 12. Hungary is in Zone D along with the Czech Republic, Slovakia, Poland and Croatia. Multizone passes are better value and are valid for one month: two zones cost €296/211/148 and three zones €336/239/168. All eight zones (a 'Global' pass) cost €398/281/199. Eurail passes are valid but not sold in Hungary.

Western Europe Seven trains a day link Vienna and Budapest (three hours, 273km) via Hegyeshalom and Győr. Most depart from Vienna's Westbahnhof, including the *Arrabona,* the EuroCity *Bartók Béla* and the EuroNight *Kálmán Imre* from Munich (7½ hours, 742km)

via Salzburg (six hours, 589km); the EC *Liszt Ferenc* from Cologne (11 hours, 1247km) via Frankfurt (10 hours, 1026km); the *Dacia Express* to Bucharest (15½ hours, 874km); and the InterCity *Avala* to Belgrade (10 hours, 647km). The early morning EC *Lehár* departs from Vienna's Südbahnhof. None requires a seat reservation, though they're highly recommended in summer.

Up to nine trains leave Vienna's Südbahnhof every day for Sopron (75 minutes, 76km) via Ebenfurt; as many as 10 a day also serve Sopron from Wiener Neustadt (easily accessible from Vienna). Some five milk trains daily make the four-hour, 136km trip from Graz to Szombathely.

The EC *Hungária* travels from Berlin (Zoo and Ostbahnhof stations) to Budapest (12½ hours, 1002km) via Dresden, Prague and Bratislava. The express *Spree-Donau Kurier* arrives from Berlin via Nuremberg.

Czech Republic, Slovakia & Poland In addition to being served by the EC *Hungária*, Prague (seven hours, 611km) can be reached from Budapest on the EC *Comenius*, the IC *Csárdás*, the *Slovan* and the *Pannónia Express*, which then carries on to Bucharest. The *Amicus* runs directly to/from Bratislava (three hours, 215km) every day.

Each day the EC *Polonia* and the *Báthory* head for Warsaw from Budapest (12 hours, 802km) passing through Katowice and either Bratislava or Štúrovo. The *Cracovia* runs to Kraków (10½ hours, 598km) via Kadice. From Miskolc in northern Hungary, you can pick up the *Karpaty* to Warsaw via Kraków and Košice.

Another train, the *Rákóczi*, links Budapest with Košice and Bratislava. The *Bem* connects Budapest with Szczecin (17 hours, 1019km) in northwestern Poland via Wrocław and Poznań.

Three local trains a day cover the 90km from Miskolc to Košice (two hours). The 2km journey from Sátoraljaújhely to Slovenské Nové Mesto (two a day) is only a four-minute ride by train.

Romania To Bucharest there are six trains: the EC *Traianus*, the *Dacia Express*, the *Ovidius*, the EN *Ister*, the *Muntenia* and the *Pannonia*. All go via Arad (5½ hours, 253km) and some require seat reservations. The *Karpaty* goes to Bucharest from Miskolc.

There are two daily connections to Cluj-Napoca (eight hours, 402km) via Oradea: the *Ady Endre* and the *Corona*. The *Partium* only goes as far as Oradea. All three trains require a seat reservation.

Two local trains a day link Budapest with Baia Mare (8¾ hours, 285km) in northern Romania via Satu Mare and Debrecen.

Bulgaria & Yugoslavia The *Transbalkan* links Budapest with Sofia (25 hours, 1366km) via Bucharest, before continuing on to Thessaloniki in Greece. Trains between Budapest and Belgrade (seven hours, 374km) via Subotica include the *Beograd*, the *Ivo Andri* and the IC *Avala*.

You must reserve your seats on some of these trains.

Two local trains a day make the 1¾-hour, 45km journey between Szeged and Subotica.

Croatia, Bosnia-Hercegovina & Slovenia You get to Zagreb (seven hours, 386km) on two trains that go via Siófok on Lake Balaton's southern shore: the *Maestral*, which ends in Split; and the *Venezia Express*, which carries on to Ljubljana (10 hours, 504km) and Venice. Two other trains to Ljubljana are the IC *Citadella* and the IC *Dráva*, which continues on to Venice. The IC *Kvarner* links Budapest with Rijeka (nine hours, 591km) via Siófok on Lake Balaton and Zagreb. The no-name train linking Budapest and Sarajevo (616km) via Pécs takes 14 hours.

Ukraine & Russia To Moscow (42 hours, 2106km) there's only the *Tisza Express*, which travels via Kyiv and Lviv in Ukraine.

Car & Motorcycle
Of the 50-odd international border crossings Hungary maintains with its neighbours, some 20 (mostly in the north and northeast) are restricted to local citizens on both sides of the border, though some allow EU citizens to cross as well.

For the latest list of border crossings check out w www.hungarytourism.hu, the website of Tourinform.

Walking & Cycling
Many border guards frown on walking across borders, particularly in Romania, Yugoslavia and Ukraine; in those places, try hitching a ride instead. Cyclists may have a problem

crossing at Hungarian border stations connected to main roads since bicycles are banned on motorways and national highways with single-digit route numbers.

If you're heading north, there are three crossings to and from Slovakia where you should not have any problems. Bridges link Esztergom with Štúrovo and Komárom with Komárno. At Sátoraljaújhely, northeast of Miskolc, there's a highway border crossing over the Ronyva River which links the centre of town with Slovenské Nové Mesto.

RIVER

A Danube hydrofoil service between Budapest and Vienna (5½ hours, 282km), with the possibility of disembarking at Bratislava (on request), runs daily between April and early November, with an extra sailing in August. Adult one-way/return fares for Vienna are €65/89 and for Bratislava €59/83. Students with ISIC cards pay €51/75, and children under six go free. A bicycle is €16 each way.

In Budapest, ferries arrive and depart from the International Ferry Pier (Nemzetközi hajóállomás) on V Belgrád rakpart, between Erzsébet and Szabadság Bridges on the Pest side. In Vienna, the boat docks at the Reichsbrücke pier near Mexikoplatz.

For detailed information and tickets, contact **Mahart PassNave** (☎ 1-484 4013; ⓦ www .maharttours.com) at the Belgrád rakpart in Budapest and **Mahart PassNave Wien** (☎ 01-72 92 161, 72 92 162; Handelskai 265/3/ 517) in Vienna.

DEPARTURE TAX

An air passenger duty of between 8000Ft and 10,000Ft is levied on all airline tickets issued in Hungary. The one exception is JFK airport in New York, which attracts a tax of 20,000Ft. The tax is usually included in the quoted fare.

Getting Around

AIR

There are no scheduled flights within Hungary. Domestic air taxis is a possibility but the cost is prohibitive – eg, 150,000Ft from Budapest to Szeged and back (you must pay the return) for up to three people – and the trips can take almost as long as an express train when you add the time required to get to/from the airports.

BUS

Volán buses are a good alternative to trains, and fares are only slightly more than comparable 2nd-class train fares. Bus fares average 994/1992/2974Ft per 100/200/300km.

In southern Transdanubia or parts of the Great Plain, buses are essential unless you are prepared to make several time-consuming changes on the train. For short trips in the Danube Bend or Lake Balaton areas, buses are also recommended. Tickets are usually available from the driver, but ask at the station to be sure. There are sometimes queues for intercity buses so it's probably wise to arrive early.

Timetables are posted at stations and stops. Some footnotes you could come across include *naponta* (daily), *hétköznap* (weekdays), *munkanapokon* (on work days), *munkaszüneti napok kivételével naponta* (daily except holidays), *szabadnap kivételével naponta* (daily except Saturday), *szabad és munkaszüneti napokon* (on Saturday and holidays), *munkaszüneti napokon* (on holidays), *iskolai napokon* (on school days) and *szabadnap* (on Saturday). Check carefully before buying.

A few large bus stations have left-luggage rooms, but they generally close by 6pm.

TRAIN

MÁV operates reliable, comfortable and not overcrowded train services on its 8000km of track, much of which converges in Budapest. For details on buying tickets, see that section under Budapest – Getting There & Away.

Second-class train fares are 302/732/1482/ 2390Ft for 50/100/200/400km. First class is 50% more. If you buy your ticket on the train rather than in the station, there's a 500Ft surcharge (1500Ft on InterCity trains). Seat reservations may be compulsory (indicated on the timetable by an 'R' in a box), mandatory on trains departing from Budapest (an 'R' in a circle) or simply available (just a plain 'R').

There are several types of train. The InterCity Express (ICE) and InterCityRapid (ICR) trains levy a supplement of 250Ft to 400Ft, which includes a seat. IC trains stop at main centres only and are the fastest and most comfortable trains. *Gyorsvonat* (fast trains) and *sebesvonat* (swift trains), indicated on the timetable by boldface type, a thicker route line and/or an 'S', often require a seat reservation (110Ft). *Személyvonat* (passenger trains) are the real milk runs and stop at every city, town, village and hamlet along the way.

If you plan to do a lot of travelling by train, get yourself a copy of MÁV's official timetable *(Menetrend)* to help with planning. It is available at most large stations and at the MÁV ticket office in Budapest for 650/1350Ft in small or large format.

In all stations a yellow board indicates departures *(indul)* and a white board arrivals *(érkezik)*. Express and fast trains are indicated in red, local trains in black. In some stations, large black-and-white schedules are plastered all over the walls. To locate the table you need, first find the posted railway map of the country, which indexes the route numbers at the top of the schedules.

All train stations have left-luggage offices (150Ft to 200Ft per item per day), some of which stay open 24 hours a day.

The following are distances and approximate times to provincial cities from Budapest (usually via express trains).

destination	duration	distance
Transdanubia		
Győr	1¾ hours	131km
Sopron	3 hours	216km
Szombathely	3½ hours	236km
Pécs	3 hours	228km
Danube Bend		
Esztergom	1½ hours	53km
Szentendre	40 minutes	20km
(HÉV commuter line)		
Vác	1½ hours	49km
Lake Balaton Area		
Siófok	1½ hours	115km
Balatonfüred	2 hours	132km
Veszprém	1¾ hours	112km
Székesfehérvár	50 minutes	67km
Great Plain		
Szolnok	1¼ hours	100km
Kecskemét	1½ hours	106km
Debrecen	3 hours	221km
Békéscsaba	2½ hours	196km
Szeged	2½ hours	191km
Northern Hungary		
Nyíregyháza	4 hours	270km
Eger	2 hours	143km
Miskolc	2¼ hours	183km
Sátoraljaújhely	3½ hours	267km

CAR & MOTORCYCLE

Motorways, preceded by an 'M', link Budapest with Lake Balaton and Vienna via Győr. They also run part of the way to Miskolc and Szeged and along the eastern bank of the Danube Bend. National highways are numbered by a single digit and fan out mostly from Budapest. Secondary and tertiary roads have two or three digits.

You must obtain a motorway pass to access the M1 and M3 (1500Ft for nine days). Passes are available at petrol stations, post offices and some motorway entrances and border crossings. The M5 is a toll road (400Ft to 1820Ft).

Petrol *(benzin)* of 91 and unleaded *(ólommentes)* 95 and 98 octane is available all over the country and costs 219/222/231Ft per litre respectively. Most stations also have diesel fuel *(gázolaj)* costing 203Ft. Payment by credit card is now possible.

Third-party insurance is compulsory. If your car is registered in the EU, it's assumed you have it. Other motorists must show a Green Card or will have to buy insurance at the border.

The so-called 'Yellow Angels' of the Hungarian Automobile Club do basic breakdown repairs for free if you belong to an affiliated organisation such as AAA in the USA or AA in the UK. You can telephone 24 hours a day on ☎ 188 nationwide.

Many cities and towns require that you 'pay and display' when parking. The cost averages about 100Ft an hour in the countryside, and up to 180Ft on central Budapest streets.

Road Rules

You must drive on the right. The use of seat belts in the front (and in the back, if fitted) is compulsory in Hungary, but this is often ignored. Motorcyclists must wear helmets.

Speed limits are strictly enforced: 50km/h in built-up areas, 80km/h on secondary and tertiary roads, 100km/h on highways and 120km/h on motorways. Exceeding the limit can earn you a fine of between 5000Ft and 30,000Ft.

All vehicles must have their headlights switched on throughout the day outside built-up areas. Motorcyclists must illuminate them at all times. Using a mobile phone while driving is prohibited in Hungary.

There is virtually a 100% ban on alcohol when you are driving, and this rule is *very* strictly enforced. Do not think you will get

HUNGARY

away with even one glass of wine at lunch; if caught with any – 0.001%! – alcohol in the blood, you will be fined up to 30,000Ft. If the level is high, you will be arrested and your licence almost certainly taken away.

Rental

In general, you must be at least 21 years old and have had your licence for at least a year to rent a car. Drivers under 25 sometimes have to pay a surcharge. All the big international firms have offices in Budapest, and there are scores of local companies throughout the country, but don't expect too many bargains. For more details, see Getting There & Away in the Budapest section.

HITCHING

Hitching is never entirely safe in any country in the world, and we don't recommend it. Travellers who decide to hitch are taking a small but potentially serious risk. Hitchhiking is, however, legal in Hungary except on the motorways. A service in Budapest matches drivers and passengers – see the Budapest Getting There & Away section for details.

BOAT

In summer there are regular passenger ferries on Lake Balaton and on the Danube from Budapest to Szentendre, Visegrád and Esztergom. Details of the schedules are given in the relevant destination sections.

LOCAL TRANSPORT

Public transport is efficient and cheap, with city bus and, in many towns, trolleybus services. Four cities, including Budapest and Szeged, also have trams, and there's an extensive metro (underground or subway) and a suburban commuter railway in Budapest. You must purchase tickets for all these at newsstands or ticket windows beforehand and validate them once aboard. Inspectors are everywhere.

Taxi

Taxis are plentiful and, if you are charged the correct fare, very reasonably priced. Flag fall varies, but a fair price is 150Ft to 200Ft, with the charge per kilometre about the same, depending on whether you book by telephone (cheaper) or hail a cab on the street. The best places to find taxis are in ranks at bus and train stations, near markets and around main squares. But you can flag down cruising taxis anywhere at any time. At night, vacant taxis have an illuminated sign on the roof.

In Budapest, and in touristy places outside the capital, it is not uncommon for taxi drivers to try to rip foreigners off. See Getting Around in the Budapest section for tips on how to avoid this.

Budapest

☎ 1 • pop 1.8 million

There's no other city in Hungary like Budapest. Home to almost a fifth of the national population, the *főváros* (capital) is also the country's administrative, business and cultural centre. For better or for worse, virtually everything in Hungary starts, finishes or is taking place in Budapest.

But it is the beauty of the city that makes it stand apart. More romantic than Warsaw and more cosmopolitan than Prague, Budapest straddles a gentle curve in the Danube, with the Buda Hills to the west and the start of the Great Plain to the east. Architecturally, it is a gem. Add to this parks brimming with attractions, museums filled with treasures, boats sailing upriver to the scenic Danube Bend and the Turkish-era thermal baths and you have one of Europe's most delightful cities to visit.

Strictly speaking, the story of Budapest begins only in 1873 when hilly, residential Buda and historic Óbuda (the oldest part of Buda) on the west bank of the Danube merged with flat, industrial Pest on the eastern side to form what was at first called Pest-Buda. But a lot of water had flowed under the Danube bridges by that time. The Romans built the settlement of Aquincum here, the Turks arrived uninvited and stayed for 150 years, the Austrians did the same and hung around for even longer. Today it is the increasingly sophisticated capital of a proud and independent republic that makes its own decisions and policies.

People come to Budapest for all sorts of reasons. Russians and Asians come here to make money or to get a taste of the West; Westerners revel in the affordable nightlife, theatres, museums, restaurants, cafés and bathhouses. Whatever your motives, there's no doubt that the 'Queen of the Danube' will be among the highlights of your travels around Eastern Europe.

ORIENTATION

Budapest is a well laid-out city and it is almost difficult to get lost. The Danube (Duna), the city's traditional artery, is spanned by nine bridges that link hilly, historic Buda with bustling, commercial and very flat Pest.

Two ring roads – the big one (Nagykörút) and the semicircular Kiskörút (little ring road) – link three of the bridges across the Danube and essentially define central Pest. Important boulevards such as Rákóczi út and leafy Andrássy út fan out from these, creating large squares and circles. The most central square in Pest is Deák tér. Buda is dominated by Castle and Gellért Hills; the main square is Moszkva tér.

Budapest is divided into 23 kerület (districts). The Roman numeral appearing before each street address signifies the district.

Maps

Lonely Planet's *Budapest City Map* covers the more popular parts of town in detail.

The best folding maps to the city are Cartographia's 1:20,000 (550Ft) and 1:28,000 (450Ft) *Budapest* ones. If you plan to see the city thoroughly, the *Budapest Atlas*, also from Cartographia, is indispensable. It comes in two scales: the pocket-size 1:25,000 (1900Ft) and the larger format 1:20,000 (2900Ft).

Many bookshops, including Libri Könyvpalota (see Bookshops later), stock a wide variety of maps, or go directly to **Cartographia** (☎ 312 6001; VI Bajcsy-Zsilinszky út 37; open 9am-5pm Mon-Wed, 9am-6.30pm Thur, 9am-3.30pm Fri).

INFORMATION
Tourist Offices

The best source of information about Budapest is **Tourinform** (☎ 438 8080, fax 356 1964; W www.hungarytourism.hu; V Vigadó utca 6; open 24hr). It has a nearby branch (Sütő utca 2; open 8am-8pm daily) and a 24-hour information hotline (☎ 06-80 66 0044).

See Travel Agencies later for details on other outfits that can book accommodation and transport and change money.

Discount Cards

The **Budapest Card** (☎ 266 0479; W www .budapestinfo.hu) offers free admission to most museums and galleries in town and unlimited travel on all forms of public transport. It also gives discounts on organised tours, at thermal baths and at selected shops and restaurants. A 48-/72-hour card costs 3700/4500Ft. The card is sold at Tourinform offices and travel agencies, hotels and train, bus and main metro stations.

Also worth considering is the Hungary Card (see Discount Cards under Planning in the Facts for the Visitor section).

Money

OTP bank (V Nádor utca 6; open 7.45am-5pm Mon, 7.45am-4pm Tues-Fri) has among the best exchange rates for cash and travellers cheques, but be sure to get there at least an hour before closing time to ensure the *bureau de change* counter is still open. **K&H** (V Váci utca 40; open 8am-5pm Mon, 8am-4pm Tues-Thur, 8am-3pm Fri) often offers good rates too.

There are ATMs all around the city, including in the train and bus stations, and quite a few foreign-currency exchange machines too, including ones at V Károly körút 20 and V Váci utca 40. In touristed areas private exchange offices such as Interchange are abundant, but they always give very poor rates.

American Express (☎ 235 4330; V Deák Ferenc utca 10; open 9am-5.30pm Mon-Fri, 9am-2pm Sat) changes its own travellers cheques without commission, but its rates are poor. Its commission on converting US dollar travellers cheques into cash dollars is 7%.

Tribus (see Private Rooms under Places to Stay later) is handy if you arrive late at night and need to change money.

Post & Communications

The **main post office** (V Petőfi Sándor utca 13-15 or V Városház utca 18; open 8am-8pm Mon-Fri, 8am-2pm Sat) is just a few minutes' walk from Deák tér and the Tourinform branch office. This is where you can pick up poste-restante mail.

The best place to make international phone calls is from a phone box with a phonecard. The phone boxes just inside the front door of the post office are relatively quiet.

Email & Internet Access

Internet cafés abound in Budapest.

Ami Internet Coffee (☎ 267 1644; W www .amicoffee.hu; V Váci utca 40; open 9am-2am daily) is very central and has 50 terminals. The costs are 200/400/700Ft for 15/30/60 minutes; five/10 hours cost 3250/6400Ft.

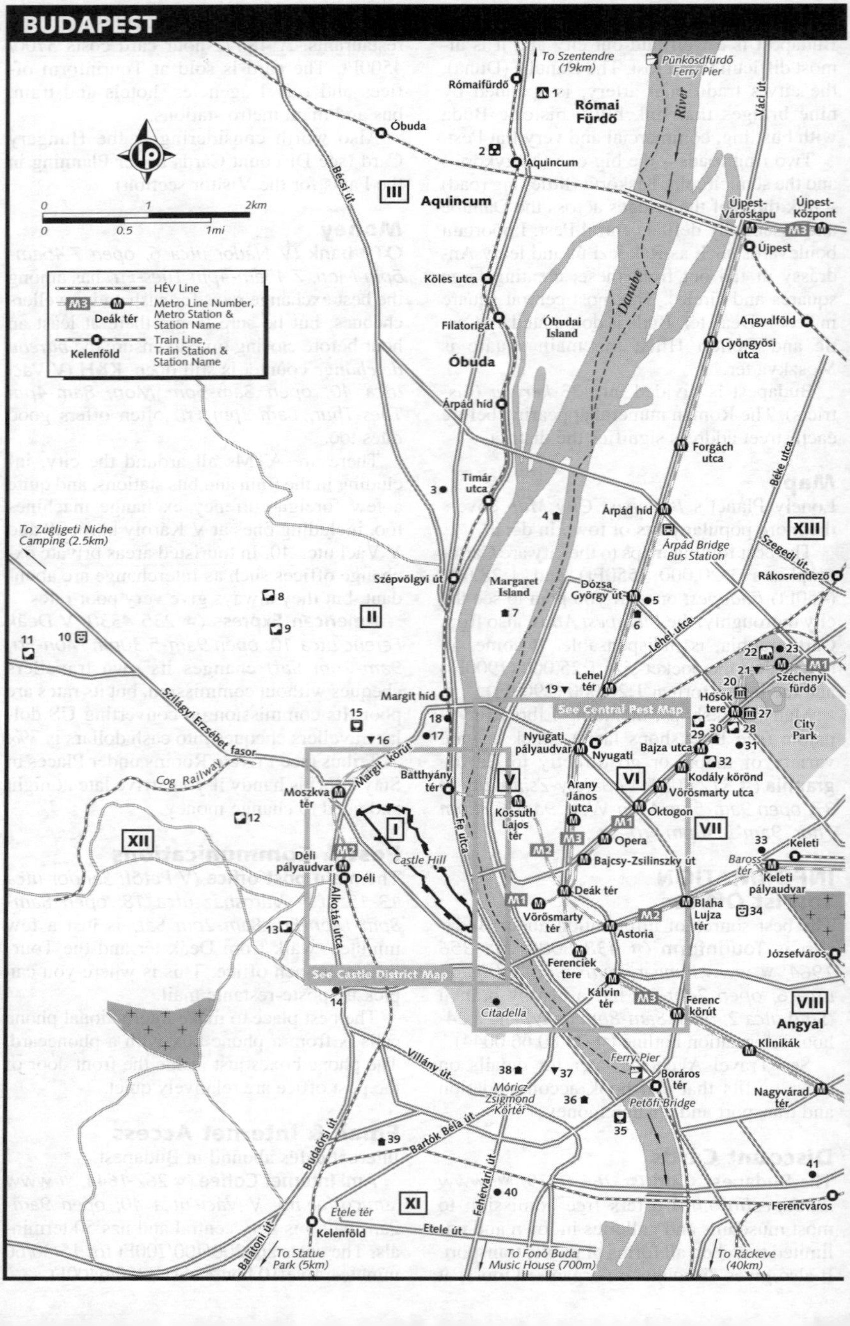

BUDAPEST

Map legend:

- HÉV Line
- **M3** **M** — Metro Line Number, Metro Station & Station Name — Deák tér
- Train Line, Train Station & Station Name — Kelenföld

Scale: 0 — 1 — 2km / 0 — 0.5 — 1mi

Map labels and features:

To Szentendre (19km)
Pünkösdfürdő Ferry Pier
Rómaifürdő
Római Fürdő
Váci út
Óbuda
2
Aquincum
III Aquincum
Újpest-Városkapu
M3 **M** Újpest
Köles utca
Filatorigát
Óbudai Island
Angyalföld
Óbuda
Gyöngyösi utca **M**
Árpád hid
Forgách utca **M**
Béke utca
Timár utca
3
4
Árpád hid **M**
XIII
Szegedi út
Árpád Bridge Bus Station
Rákosrendező
To Zugligeti Niche Camping (2.5km)
Szépvölgyi út
Margaret Island
II
Dózsa György út **M**
5
6
8
9
Lehel utca
22 23
21
M1
Széchenyi fürdő
11 10
Lehel tér
19
Hősök tere **M**
City Park
15
Margit hid
18
17
27
Szilágyi Erzsébet fasor
16
Margit körút
Nyugati pályaudvar **M** Nyugati
Bajza utca **M**
20
29
30 28
31
Cog Railway
Moszkva tér **M**
Battyány tér **M**
V
Arany János utca **M**
Kossuth Lajos tér
VI
Kodály körönd **M**
32
Vörösmarty utca **M**
VII
12
I
Fő utca
M3 **M** Opera
33
Keleti **M**
XII
Déli pályaudvar **M** Déli
Castle Hill
Bajcsy-Zsilinszky út **M**
Baross tér
Keleti pályaudvar
Alkotás utca
M2 Deák tér
Blaha Lujza tér **M2**
34
13
Vörösmarty tér **M**
Astoria **M**
Józsefváros
14
Ferenciek tere **M**
Kálvin tér **M**
Ferenc körút **M3**
VIII
Angyal
Citadella
See Castle District Map
See Central Pest Map
Villányi út
Klinikák **M**
38
37
Ferry Pier
Móricz Zsigmond Körtér
36
Boráros tér
Nagyvárad tér **M**
35
Petőfi Bridge
Bartók Béla út
39
41
XI
40
Fehérvári út
Ferencváros **M**
Etele tér
Kelenföld
Etele út.
To Statue Park (5km)
To Fonó Buda Music House (700m)
To Ráckeve (40km)
Budaörsi út
Balatoni út

Danube / River

BUDAPEST

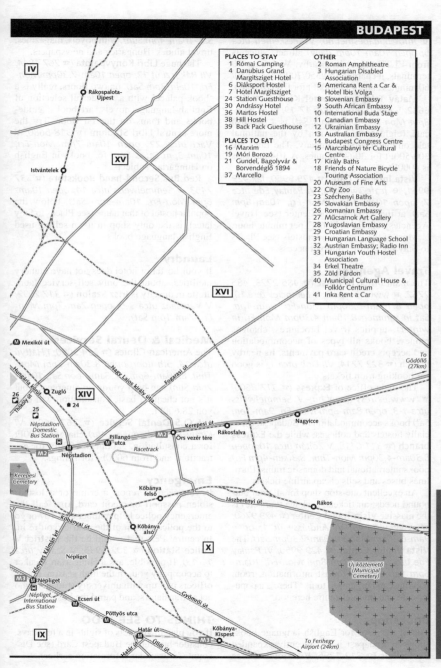

PLACES TO STAY
1 Római Camping
4 Danubius Grand Margitsziget Hotel
6 Diáksport Hostel
7 Hotel Margitsziget
24 Station Guesthouse
30 Andrássy Hotel
36 Martos Hostel
38 Hill Hostel
39 Back Pack Guesthouse

PLACES TO EAT
16 Marxim
19 Móri Borozó
21 Gundel, Bagolyvár & Borvendéglő 1894
37 Marcello

OTHER
2 Roman Amphitheatre
3 Hungarian Disabled Association
5 Americana Rent a Car & Hotel Ibis Volga
8 Slovenian Embassy
9 South African Embassy
10 International Buda Stage
11 Canadian Embassy
12 Ukrainian Embassy
13 Australian Embassy
14 Budapest Congress Centre
15 Marcibányi tér Cultural Centre
17 Király Baths
18 Friends of Nature Bicycle Touring Association
20 Museum of Fine Arts
22 City Zoo
23 Széchenyi Baths
25 Slovakian Embassy
26 Romanian Embassy
27 Műcsarnok Art Gallery
28 Yugoslavian Embassy
29 Croatian Embassy
31 Hungarian Language School
32 Austrian Embassy; Radio Inn
33 Hungarian Youth Hostel Association
34 Erkel Theatre
35 Zöld Párdon
40 Municipal Cultural House & Folklór Centrum
41 Inka Rent a Car

HUNGARY

Budapest Net (☎ 328 0292, fax 328 0294; e info@budapestnet.hu; V Kecskeméti utca 5; open 10am-10pm daily) attracts students from ELTE university nearby. With over 50 terminals, it charges 150/350/700Ft for 10/30/60 minutes and 2400/4600Ft for five/10 hours.

Matáv Telepont Internet Kávézó (☎ 485 6612; V Petőfi Sándor utca 17-19; open 9am-8pm Mon-Fri, 10pm-3pm Sat) is a smallish café (eight terminals) run by the national telecommunications company. The rates are 300/500Ft for 30/60 minutes. A 10-hour pass is 4000Ft.

Vista Internet Café (☎ 429 9950, fax 429 9951; e icafe@vista.hu; VI Paulay Ede utca 7; open 10am-10pm Mon-Fri, 10am-8pm Sat), at the Vista Visitor Center (see Travel Agencies), charges 11/660Ft per minute/hour.

Most of the year-round hostels (see Places to Stay later) offer Internet access.

Travel Agencies
The main office of **Ibusz** (☎ 485 2723, 485 2767; w www.ibusz.hu; V Ferenciek tere 10; open 8.15am-5.30pm Mon-Fri, 9am-1pm Sat in summer; 8.15am-4.30pm Mon-Fri in winter) supplies travel brochures, changes money, books all types of accommodation and accepts credit-card payments. Its nearby branch (☎ 322 7214; VII Dob utca 1) is good for booking train tickets.

The main office of **Express** (☎ 317 8600; w www.extress-travel.hu; V Semmelweiss utca 1-3; open 8am-6pm Mon-Fri, 9am-1pm Sat) books accommodation in Budapest, especially hostels and colleges; while the **Express branch** (☎ 311 6418; V Zoltán utca 10; open 8.30am-4.30pm Mon-Thur, 8.30am-4pm Fri) books international and domestic trains, Eurolines buses and sells cheap airline tickets.

An excellent one-stop shop for all your outbound needs (air tickets, package tours etc) is the massive **Vista Travel Center** (☎ 429 9760; w www.vista.hu; VI Andrássy út 1; open 9am-6.30pm Mon-Fri, 9am-2.30pm Sat). The **Vista Visitor Center** (☎ 429 9950; VI Paulay Ede utca 7; open 9am-8pm Mon-Fri, 10am-6pm Sat) handles tourist information, room bookings and organised tours. There's a popular café and Internet centre here too.

Bookshops
Top of the pops for English-language bookshops in Budapest is the recently expanded **Bestsellers** (☎ 312 1295; V Október 6 utca 11; open 9am-6.30pm Mon-Fri, 10am-5pm Sat, 10am-4pm Sun), with novels, magazines, travel guides, Hungarica and newspapers.

The huge **Libri Könyvpalota** (☎ 267 4844; VII Rákóczi út 12; open 10am-7.30pm Mon-Fri, 10am-3pm Sat), on two floors, really is a 'book palace' with a wonderful selection of English-language novels, art books, guidebooks and maps on the 1st floor. Try the more central **Libri Studium** (☎ 318 5680; V Váci utca 22; open 10am-7pm Mon-Fri, 10am-3pm Sat & Sun) for books in English on Hungarian subjects.

Red Bus Second-hand Bookstore (☎ 337 7453; V Semmelweiss utca 14; open 10am-6pm Mon-Fri, 10am-3pm Sat), below the popular hostel of that name (see Places to Stay later), is the only shop in town selling used English-language books.

Laundry
If your hostel or hotel does not have laundry facilities, about the only self-service laundrette in the city is **Irisz Szalon** (☎ 317 2092; V Városház utca 3-5; open 7am-7pm Mon-Fri, 7am-1pm Sat).

Medical & Dental Services
The **American Clinics** (☎ 224 9090; I Hattyú utca 14, 5th floor; open 8.30am-7pm Mon-Thur, 8.30am-6pm Fri, 8am-noon Sat, 10am-2pm Sun) can help you in an emergency but it's not cheap: a basic consultation will cost you 28,600Ft.

S.O.S Dental Service (☎ 267 9602; VI Király utca 14; open 24hr) charges 2000Ft for a consultation, 5000Ft to 6000Ft for extractions and from 6000Ft for fillings.

Emergency
If you need to report a crime or a lost or stolen passport or credit card, first call the emergency police help number at ☎ 107 or go to the police station of the district you're in. In central Pest that would be the **District V Police Station** (☎ 302 5935; V Szalay utca 11-13). If possible, ask a Hungarian speaker to accompany you. In the high season, police officers pair up with university students, who act as translators, and patrol the busiest areas.

THINGS TO SEE & DO
If you plan to visit lots of sights in a few days, consider buying the Budapest Card (see Discount Cards under Information earlier).

When your head begins to spin from all the museums, take a walk (or bus No 26 from Nyugati train station) over to **Margaret Island**, which is in the Danube between Buda and Pest, or to the **City Park** at the top of Andrássy út and accessible on the little yellow metro line (M1). Both of these 'green lungs' offer any number of sights and recreational facilities – from bicycle rentals, the ruins of two medieval monasteries and Olympic-size swimming pools on the island to the sprawling Széchenyi Baths (see the Thermal Baths section later), the **City Zoo** (☎ 363 3797; XIV Állatkerti körút; adult/child/student/family 900/650/750/2800Ft; open 9am-4pm daily Nov-Feb, 9am-5pm March & Oct, 9am-6pm Apr-Sept) and still more museums in the park.

Buda

Most of what remains of medieval Budapest is on **Castle Hill** (Várhegy) perched above the Danube and now on Unesco's list of World Heritage Sites. The easiest way to get there from Pest is to stroll across Chain Bridge and board the **funicular railway** (uphill/downhill ticket adult 450/250Ft, child 2-10 350/250Ft; open 7.30am-10pm daily) from Clark Ádám tér up to Szent György tér near the Royal Palace. The funicular does not run on the first and third Monday of the month.

Another option is to take the metro to Moszkva tér, cross the footbridge above the square and walk up Várfok utca to **Vienna Gate**. A minibus with a logo of a castle and labelled 'Várbusz' or 'Dísz tér' follows the same route from the start of Várfok utca.

At the Vienna Gate, turn west (right) onto Petermann bíró utca and walk past the **National Archives**, with its majolica-tiled roof, to Kapisztrán tér. The **Magdalen Tower** is all that's left of a Gothic church destroyed here during WWII. The white neoclassical building facing the square is the **Military History Museum** (☎ 356 9522; I Tóth Árpád sétány 40; adult/child 250/80Ft; open 10am-6pm Tues-Sun April-Sept, 10am-4pm Oct-Mar).

Walk southeast along Tóth Árpád sétány, the ramparts promenade, and to the east you'll glimpse the neo-Gothic tower of **Matthias Church** (☎ 489 0717; Szentháromság tér; adult/child 300/150Ft; open 9am-5pm Mon-Fri, 9am-1pm Sat, 1pm-5pm Sun). The church, rebuilt in 1896, has a colourful tiled roof and lovely murals inside. Franz Liszt's *Hungarian Coronation Mass* was played here

for the first time at the coronation of Franz Joseph and Elizabeth in 1867.

Just south of the church is an equestrian **statue of St Stephen**, Hungary's first king. Behind it is **Fishermen's Bastion** (adult/child 250/120Ft; open 8.30am-11pm daily), a neo-Gothic structure built in 1905 with stunning views of Pest and the Parliament building.

From the **Holy Trinity statue** in the centre of Szentháromság tér, Tárnok utca runs southeast to Dísz tér and the **Royal Palace**. The palace enjoyed its greatest splendour under King Matthias in the second half of the 15th century and has been destroyed and rebuilt half a dozen times since then.

Today it contains several important museums, including the **National Gallery** (☎ 375 7533; Wings B, C & D, Szent György tér 6; adult/child 600/300Ft; open 10am-6pm Tues-Sun Mar-Nov, 10am-4pm Dec-Feb), with a huge collection of Hungarian works of art from the Gothic period to the present, and the **Budapest History Museum** (☎ 375 7533; Wing E, Szent György tér 2; adult/child, student & senior/family 600/300/1000Ft; open 10am-6pm Wed-Mon Mar-mid-May, mid-Sept–Oct, 10am-6pm daily mid-May–mid-Sept, 10am-4pm daily Nov-Feb), which traces the city's 2000-year history.

To the south is Gellért Hill and the **Citadella** (admission 300Ft; open 8am-10pm daily) built by the Habsburgs after the 1848-49 revolution to 'defend' the city from further insurrection but never used as a fortress. To get there from Pest, cross Erzsébet Bridge and take the stairs leading up behind the waterfall and **statue of St Gellért** or go over Independence (Szabadság) Bridge and follow the path through the park opposite the entrance to the Gellért Baths. Bus No 27 runs almost to the top of the hill from Móricz Zsigmond körtér, southwest of the Gellért Hotel (and accessible using tram Nos 18, 19, 47 and 49).

The **Independence Monument**, the lovely lady with the palm leaf proclaiming freedom throughout the city at the eastern end of the Citadella, was erected as a tribute to the Soviet soldiers who died liberating Hungary in 1945, but both the victims' names in Cyrillic letters on the plinth and the memorial statues of Soviet soldiers were removed a decade ago. The most memorable views of Budapest and the Danube are from Gellért Hill; try to get up here at night.

HUNGARY

CENTRAL PEST

CENTRAL PEST

PLACES TO STAY
12 Best Hostel
13 Yellow Submarine Youth Hostel
15 Bánki Hostel
28 Hotel Medosz
64 Hostel Marco Polo
68 Carmen Mini Hotel
74 Inter-Continental Hotel
80 Budapest Marriott Hotel
81 Tribus Nonstop Hotel Service
87 Red Bus Hostel & Second-Hand Bookstore
95 Leo Panzió
111 Citadella Hotel & Hostel
117 Hotel Ibis Centrum
118 Museum Castle Guest House
127 Gellért Hotel & Baths
129 Hotels Corvin & Sissi

PLACES TO EAT
2 Rothschild Supermarket
3 Művész Bohém
6 Okay Italia
7 Wabisabi
9 Okay Italia Branch
14 Kaiser's Supermarket
17 Semiramis
29 Teaház a Vörös Oroszlánhoz
36 Café Vian
37 Fortuca
40 Felafel Faloda
41 Két Szerecsen
42 Művész
48 Kisharang
50 Gandhi
54 Coquan's Branch
60 Hannah
63 Match Supermarket
72 Gerbeaud
93 Múzeum
106 Centrál Kávéház
113 Rembetiko Piraeus
116 Marie Kristensen Sandwich Branch Bar
119 Stex Alfred
121 Teaház a Vörös Oroszlánhoz
122 Soul Café
123 Pink Cadillac
124 Coquan's
125 Shiraz Gyros Takeaway
126 Shiraz

BARS & CLUBS
5 Trocadero
10 Bank Music Club
16 Beckett's Irish Pub
30 Cactus Juice
34 Angyal
62 Old Man's Music Pub
75 Columbus Irish Pub
88 Café Eklektika
101 Capella Café
110 Limo Café
114 Közgáz Pince Klub

OTHER
1 Debrecen Summer University Branch
4 Gaiety Theatre
8 West End City Centre Shopping Mall
11 Post Office
18 District V Police Station
19 Parliament
20 Express Branch (Transport Tickets)
21 Hungarian Television Building
22 Soviet Army Memorial
23 US Embassy
24 National Bank Building
25 Irish Embassy
26 Hungarian Bicycle Touring Association
27 Cartographia Map Shop
31 House of Terror
32 Bábszínház (Budapest Puppet Theatre)
33 National Association of Village Tourism
35 Liszt Academy of Music
38 Budapest Operetta Theatre
39 MÁV Ticket Office
43 Hungarian State Opera House
44 Ticket Express
45 Budatours
46 St Stephen's Basilica
47 Bestsellers Bookshop
49 To-Ma Travel Agency
51 Central European University
52 Duna Palota
53 OTP Bank
55 La Boutique des Vins

56 Vista Travel Center
57 Vista Internet Café & Visitor Centre
58 S.O.S. Dental Service
59 Concerto Music Shop
61 BKV Office
65 Libri Könyvpalota Bookshop
66 Great Synagogue & Jewish Museum
67 Ibusz Branch
69 Lutheran Church
70 Tourinform Branch
71 American Express
73 UK Embassy
76 Tourinform (24 Hours)
77 Malév Ticket Office
78 Vigadó Jegyiroda (Ticket Office)
79 Pesti Vigadó (Concert Hall)
82 Rózsavölgyi Music Shop
83 Libri Studium Bookshop
84 Matáv Telepont Internet Kávézó
85 Main Post Office
86 Merlin Theatre
89 K&H Bank & Foreign Currency Exchange Machine
90 Express Main Office
91 East-West Business Centre
92 Kenguru (Car Pooling)
94 Irisz Szalon Laundrette
96 Ibusz Main Office
97 Inner Town Parish Church
98 St Gellért Statue
99 Rudas Baths
100 Mahart PassNave Ticket Office
102 Aranytíz Youth Centre & Kalamajka Táncház
103 Ami Internet Coffee
104 K&H Bank & Foreign Currency Exchange Machine
105 Pegazus Tours
107 National Museum
108 Budapest Net
109 Folkart Centrum
112 Independence Monument
115 Nagycsarnok (Great Market)
120 Hungarian Equestrian Tourism Association
128 Museum of Applied Arts

Many monuments to the Soviet liberators and socialist heroes that once filled Budapest's streets and squares are on display in the **Statue Park** (☎ 227 7446; XXII Szabadkai út; adult/ child 300/200Ft; open 10am-dusk daily Mar-Nov, 10am-dusk Sat & Sun Dec-Feb) in southwest Buda. To reach this socialist Disneyland, take tram No 19 or 49 (or a red-numbered bus

No 7 from Ferenciek tere in Pest) to the terminus at XI Etele tér. From there catch a yellow Volán bus from stand No 2 or 3 to Diósd-Érd. From June to August a direct bus (1250Ft, including admission to the park) leaves from in front of Hotel Le Meridien at V Erzsébet tér 9–10 at 9am, 10am and 11am and again at 3pm, 4pm and 5pm.

THE CASTLE DISTRICT

PLACES TO STAY
3 Büro Panzió
15 Art'otel Budapest
22 Burg Hotel
23 Kulturinnov

PLACES TO EAT
4 Nagyi Palacsintázója
9 Angelika
20 Fortuna Önkiszolgáló
25 Ruszwurm
26 Café Miró
27 Mongolian Barbecue
28 Caffè Déryné
36 Aranyszarvas

OTHER
1 Mammut II Shopping Mall
2 Mammut I Shopping Mall;
  Fény utca Market
5 American Clinics
6 Oscar's American Bar
7 Budapest Wine Society
  Shop
8 St Anne's Church
10 Vienna Gate
11 National Archives
12 Military History Museum
13 Magdalen Tower
14 Lutheran Church
16 Capuchin Church
17 Fishermen's Bastion
18 St Stephen Statue
19 Matthias Church
21 German Embassy
24 Holy Trinity Statue
29 Castle Theatre; Rivalda
  Café-Restaurant
30 Sándor Palace
31 Funicular (Lower Station)
32 Tram Stop No 19
33 National Gallery
34 Budapest History Museum
35 Ferdinand Gate

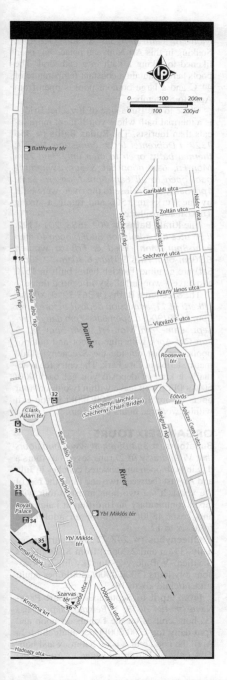

Pest

The most attractive boulevard in Budapest is leafy Andrássy út, which stretches northeast from Bajcsy-Zsilinszky út to Heroes' Square (Hősök tere) and City Park and is home to many important sights, including the neo-Renaissance **Hungarian State Opera House** (☎ 332 8197; VI Andrássy út 22), completed in 1884. Daily tours in English at 3pm and 4pm (1500/900Ft adult/student) are 'second-best' to attending a performance here. Many of the other great buildings along this section of Andrássy út date from Budapest's Golden Age, including **Drechsler House** (VI Andrássy út 25), now being turned into a hotel, and the sublime Art Nouveau **New Theatre** (VI Paulay Ede utca 35) around the corner.

A bit farther afield, Budapest's newest museum is the **House of Terror** (☎ 374 2600; Andrássy út 60; adult/child 1000/500Ft; open 10am-6pm Tues-Sun). Once the headquarters of the dreaded ÁVH secret police, it focuses on the crimes and atrocities committed by Hungary's fascist and Stalinist regimes.

The neo-Renaissance dome of **St Stephen's Basilica** (☎ 311 0839; V Szent István tér; treasury adult/child 200/150Ft; open 9am-7pm Mon-Sat, 1pm-4pm Sun) (1905) looms some 96m over Bajcsy-Zsilinszky út. The mummified right hand – the so-called Holy Right or Holy Dexter – of St Stephen is kept in the chapel at the rear of the church; take the passage on the left of the main altar. To reach the **dome** (adult/child 500/400Ft; open 10am-5pm daily Apr-May & Sept-Oct, 10am-6pm June-Aug) take the lift near the entrance and then scale 150-odd steps to the top.

To the northwest of the basilica, through stately Szabadság tér, is the neo-Gothic **Parliament** (☎ 441 4904; V Kossuth Lajos tér 1-3; adult/student 1700/800Ft), built in 1902 and housing the Crown of St Stephen, the nation's most important national icon. English language tours are held at 10am, noon and 2pm daily.

Several other museums in Pest are worth your time and consideration. The **National Museum** (☎ 338 2122; VIII Múzeum körút 14-16; adult/student 600/300Ft; open 10am-6pm Tues-Sun mid-Mar–mid-Oct, 10am-5pm mid-Oct–mid-Mar) contains the nation's most important collection of historical relics (including King Stephen's crimson silk coronation robe) in a large neoclassical building purpose-built in 1847.

HUNGARY

The **Museum of Applied Arts** (☎ 456 5100; IX Üllői út 33-37; adult/child 500/250Ft; open 10am-6pm Tues-Sun Apr-Oct, 10am-4pm Nov-Mar) has a wonderful array of Hungarian furniture dating from the 18th and 19th centuries, Art Nouveau and Secessionist artefacts and bric-a-brac. The building itself, built in 1896, is covered in colourful Zsolnay ceramic tiles and has a central hall of white marble modelled on the Alhambra in southern Spain.

Facing monument-filled **Heroes' Square**, which was constructed in 1896 to mark the millennium of the Magyar conquest of the Carpathian Basin, the **Museum of Fine Arts** (☎ 363 2675, 469 7100; adult/student & child 6-12 700/350Ft; open 10am-5.30pm Tues-Sun) houses Hungary's richest collection of foreign art. The collection of Old Masters is the most complete, and there are more works by El Greco here than anywhere outside Spain.

The twin-towered, Romantic-style **Great Synagogue** (☎ 324 1335; VII Dohány utca 2), dating from 1859, is the largest functioning synagogue in Europe. It contains the **Jewish Museum** (☎ 342 8949; adult/student 600/200Ft; open 10am-5pm Mon-Thur, 10am-3pm Fri, 10am-2pm Sun mid-April–Oct; 10am-3pm Mon-Thur, 10am-2pm Fri, 10am-2pm Sun Nov–mid-April), with a particularly harrowing exhibit on the Holocaust.

Thermal Baths

Budapest is a major spa centre with many thermal baths open to the public. The Danube follows the geological fault separating the Buda Hills from the Great Plain and over 40 million litres of warm mineral water gush forth daily from more than 120 thermal springs.

Some bathhouses require you to wear a bathing suit while others do not; take one just in case. Most of the public baths hire out bathing suits and towels (500Ft) if you don't have your own; bathing caps are provided for use in the swimming pools. Note that some of the baths become gay venues on male-only days – especially the Király and on Sunday the Gellért.

The city's most famous thermal spa is the **Gellért Baths** (☎ 466 6166; XI Kelenhegyi út; thermal baths admission 1600Ft, swimming pool & baths admission 2000-2400Ft; thermal baths open 6am-7pm Mon-Fri, 6am-5pm Sat & Sun May-Sept; 6am-7pm Mon-Fri, 6am-2pm Sat & Sun Oct-Apr; swimming pool open 6am-7pm daily May-Sept; 6am-7pm Mon-Fri, 6am-5pm Sat & Sun Oct-Apr). Soaking in this Art Nouveau palace has been likened to taking a bath in a cathedral. The pools here maintain a constant temperature of 44°C and a large outdoor pool is open from April to September.

Close to the Buda side of Erzsébet Bridge is a thermal bath where you'll meet more locals than tourists. The **Rudas Baths** (☎ 356 1322; I Döbrentei tér 9; admission 1000Ft; thermal baths open to men only 9am-7pm Mon-Fri, 6am-noon Sat & Sun; swimming pool open to all 6am-6pm Mon-Fri, 6am-1pm Sat & Sun), close to the river, were built by the Turks in 1566 and retain a strong Turkish atmosphere.

The **Király Baths** (☎ 202 3688, 201 4392; II Fő utca 84; admission 800Ft; open to men 9am-8pm Mon, Wed & Fri; to women 6.30am-6pm Tues & Thur, 6.30am-12.30pm Sat) are genuine Turkish baths built in 1570 and have a wonderful sky-lit central dome.

The **Széchenyi Baths** (☎ 363 3210; XIV Állatkerti út 11; admission deposit before/after 3pm 1500/900Ft; open 6am-7pm daily May-Sept; 6am-7pm Mon-Fri, 6am-5pm Sat & Sun Oct-Apr), with nine indoor and outdoor pools, are just outside the Széchenyi fürdő metro station in City Park. The entry fee is actually a kind of deposit; you get back 900/600/300Ft if you leave within two/three/ four hours before 3pm and 600/300Ft if you exit within two/three hours after 3pm.

ORGANISED TOURS

Budatours (☎ 353 0558; W www.budatours .hu; VI Andrássy út 2) runs seven bus tours a day in both open and covered coaches in July and August (between two and three the rest of the year). It's a two-hour nonstop tour with taped commentary in 16 different languages and costs 4800/2400Ft for an adult/child from six to 12.

Queenybus (☎ 247 7159) departs twice daily (11am and 2.20pm) from St Stephen's Basilica, V Bajcsy-Zsilinszky út, for two-hour city tours (5000/4000/2500Ft per adult/ student/child six to 16).

From April to September **Mahart Pass-Nave** (☎ 484 4013; V Belgrád rakpart) has 1½-hour cruises on the Danube at noon and 7pm daily for 1200/600Ft per adult/child. In April the noon cruise is on Saturday and holidays only, and from mid-June to August the evening programme begins at 7.45pm and includes music and dance (1500/750Ft). More expensive cruises also operate on the river, including **Legenda** (☎/fax 317 2203; ⓦ *www .legenda.hu*), which runs day (3400/1600Ft per adult/child) and night (4000Ft) tours with taped commentary in up to 30 languages.

Highly recommended for tours is **Absolute Walking Tours** (☎ 06-30 211 8861; ⓦ *www .budapestours.com*), a 3½-hour guided promenade through City Park, central Pest and Castle Hill. Tours (3500/3000Ft adult/student & under 26) depart at 9.30am and 1.30pm daily from the steps of the yellow Lutheran church on Deák tér and at 10am and 2pm from the steps of the Műcsarnok art gallery in the Heroes' Square from mid-May to September. During the rest of the year they leave from the Deák tér church at 10.30am and the Műcsarnok at 11am, with tours curtailed over Christmas and in January.

PLACES TO STAY
Camping
Római Camping (☎ 388 7167, fax 250 0426; III Szentendrei út 189; per person/tent site/caravan 990/1990/3300Ft, 2-bed cabins 3600-6000Ft; camping open year-round, cabins mid-Apr–mid-Oct) is a large site in a leafy park north of the city. To get there take the HÉV suburban railway from Batthyány tér metro station to the Rómaifürdő station, which is just about opposite the camping ground. Use of the adjacent swimming pool is included in the rates.

Zugligeti Niche Camping (☎ 200 8346; XII Zugligeti út 101; tent site for 2 people 2900-3000Ft, caravan 3950-4400Ft, bungalow for 2 people 4000Ft; open year-round) is in the Buda Hills at the bottom station of the chair lift (take bus No 158 from Moszkva tér to the terminus).

Hostels
There are two types of hostel in Budapest: year-round private hostels, many in old apartments in or near central Pest; and student dormitories open to travellers during summer holidays (July to late August). Year-round hostels generally have laundry facilities (about 1000Ft per load), a fully equipped kitchen, storage lockers, TV lounge, no curfew and computers for accessing the Internet.

Dormitory accommodation in both year-round and summer hostels ranges from 1700Ft

to 3300Ft; expect to pay from 2800Ft to 4700Ft for doubles (book these in advance). High season usually means April to October. Prices almost always include breakfast.

Express is the best travel agency to contact for hostel information (see Travel Agencies under Information earlier).

Year-Round Hostels – Buda The **Back Pack Guesthouse** (☎ 385 8946; ⓦ *www .backpackbudapest.hu*; XI Takács Menyhért utca 33; dorm beds 1800-2300Ft, doubles 2800Ft) is a colourful place with 50 beds and a friendly, much-travelled manager. There are dormitories with between five and 11 beds and one small double, a lovely garden and very laid-back clientele. It's in south Buda and not central, but transport is reliable. Get here on the black-numbered bus No 7 or 7A from Keleti train station, tram No 49 from the little ring road in central Pest, or tram No 19 from Batthyány tér in Buda.

Citadella Hotel (☎ 466 5794; ⓦ *www .citadella.hu*; XI Citadella sétány; dorm beds 2200Ft), in the fortress atop Gellért Hill, has a room with 14 beds as well as hotel rooms (see Hotels – Budget later). Solo travellers may prefer somewhere more central, as it's a bit isolated. To get here catch bus No 27 from XI Móricz Zsigmond körtér in Buda.

Student accommodation is available all year at the large **Martos Hostel** (☎ 209 4883, fax 463 3650; ⓔ *reception@hotel.martos.bme .hu*; XI Sztoczek utca 5-7; singles 3500Ft, doubles/triples/quads per person 2200Ft). It's reasonably well situated, near the Danube and a few minutes' walk from Petőfi Bridge (tram No 4 or 6). There are also doubles with shower and toilet (8000Ft) and small apartments with four beds (14,000Ft).

Year-Round Hostels – Pest The Travellers' Youth Hostels-Mellow Mood group, which runs a number of summer hostels (see that section following) for individuals and groups, also has two year-round hostels. More central (and expensive) is **Hostel Marco Polo** (☎ 413 2555; ⓦ *www.marcopolohostel.com*; VII Nyár utca 6; bed in 12-bed dorm low/high season €17/19, singles €46/51; doubles/triples/quads per person low season €31/26/22, high season €34/29/24). Almost like a mid-range hotel, it has telephones in the rooms, a lovely courtyard and bar and restaurant (set meals 1000Ft).

The same group operates **Diáksport Hostel** (☎ 340 8585, 413 2062; W www.backpackers .hu; XIII Dózsa György út 152; bed in 6-bed dorm 3300Ft, singles & doubles with bath per person 4600Ft, doubles/triples & quads with shared bath per person from 3600/3500Ft) is a bit far from the action (M3 metro stop: Dózsa György út), but compensates by having its own 24-hour bar. This is definitely a party place so go elsewhere if you've come to Budapest for a good rest. Student, youth and hostel card-holders get a 10% discount.

Another place a tad off the beaten track but with a great atmosphere is **Station Guesthouse** (☎ 221 8864; e station@matavnet.hu; XIV Mexikói út 36/b; bed in 14-/8-bed dorms 1700/2400Ft, doubles & triples/quads per person 3200/2700Ft). It's another party place with a 24-hour bar, pool table and occasional live entertainment. HI card-holders get 200Ft off the quoted prices and rates drop by 100Ft a night from the second to sixth night of stay. Get here on the M1 metro (stop: Mexikói út) or red-numbered bus No 7 from Keleti train station.

For a central, well-managed place, look no further than the **Red Bus Hostel** (☎/fax 266 0136; e redbusbudapest@hotmail.com; V Semmelweiss utca 14, 1st floor; dorm beds 2700Ft, singles 6000/7000Ft winter/summer, doubles 7000Ft), with large airy rooms cobbled from two flats, a modern kitchen and exceptionally friendly management.

Another very central place, close to the restaurants and bars of Ráday utca, is the **Museum Castle Guest House** (☎ 318 9508, 266 8879; e museumgh@freemail.C3.hu; VIII Mikszáth Kálmán tér 4, 1st floor; dorm beds 2800Ft), a poky but creatively decorated and friendly place, with six to nine dorm beds in three rooms.

Two similar places close to Nyugati station almost face one another on the intersection of Teréz körút and Podmaniczky utca. **Yellow Submarine Youth Hostel** (☎/fax 331 9896; W www.yellowsubmarinehostel.com; VI Teréz körút 56, 3rd floor; dorm beds 2500Ft, doubles/quads per person 3750/2800Ft) has lots of facilities. However, it overlooks one of Pest's busiest boulevards and there's no lift. The **Best Hostel** (☎ 332 4934; e bestyh@ mail.datanet.hu; VI Podmaniczky utca 27, 1st floor; dorm beds 2800Ft, doubles/quads per person 4000/3400Ft) is a bit dearer but rooms are bigger, airier and quieter.

Summer Hostels Affiliated with Hostelling International (HI), **Travellers' Youth Hostels-Mellow Mood** (☎ 413 2062, 215 0660; W www.backpackers.hu) runs many summer hostels in student accommodation. Its booths at Keleti train station (☎ 343 0748; open 7.30am-11pm daily during summer, 7.30am-9pm rest of year) make bookings and may arrange to transport you there. All the hostels are open 24 hours a day, and there's no curfew. An HI card is not required, but having one usually gets you a 10% discount.

The group's summer hostels include **Bánki Hostel** (VI Podmaniczky utca 8; bed in 8-bed dorms 3300Ft, quads/doubles per person from 3500/3800Ft), near Nyugati train station in Pest; and **Hill Hostel** (XI Ménesi út 5; doubles with shower 4700Ft per person) below leafy Gellért Hill in Buda.

Private Rooms

Private rooms in Budapest generally cost from 3600Ft to 5000Ft for a single, 5000Ft to 7000Ft for a double and 8000Ft to 14,000Ft for a small apartment, with a 30% supplement if you stay less than four nights. To get a room in the centre of town, you may have to try several offices. There are lots of rooms, and even in July and August you'll be able to find something. You'll probably need an indexed city map to find the flat housing your room.

Among the best places to try for private rooms are Ibusz and Vista (see Travel Agencies under Information earlier). Another good place is **To-Ma** (☎ 353 0819; W www.toma tour.hu; V Október 6 utca 22; open 9am-noon & 1pm-8pm Mon-Fri, 9am-5pm Sat & Sun). After hours try **Tribus Nonstop Hotel Service** (☎ 318 3925, 318 4848; W www .tribus.hu; V Apáczai Csere János utca 1; open 24hr) near the Budapest Marriott Hotel. It books all types of accommodation and cashes travellers cheques around the clock.

Hotels – Budget

In Buda, **Büro Panzió** (☎ 212 2929, fax 212 2928; e buro-panzio@axelero.hu; II Dékán utca 3; singles/doubles with shower 9000/ 13,500Ft), a pension just a block off the northern side of Moszkva tér, looks basic from the outside but its 10 rooms are comfortable and have TVs and telephones.

The 12-room **Citadella Hotel** (☎ 466 5794; W www.citadella.hu; XI Citadella sétány; doubles with/without bath from €55/50) has big, clean, dark-wood rooms, although we've heard complaints about the noisy dance club below.

In Pest, the most central cheap place is the **Hotel Medosz** (☎ 374 3000, fax 332 4316; VI Jókai tér 9; singles/doubles/triples 10,000/13,000/15,500Ft), right near Oktogon metro station and the restaurants and bars of Liszt Ferenc tér. The 70 rooms are well worn but have private bath and satellite TV; the best ones are in the main block, not in the labyrinthine wings.

Not very far from the square Deák tér, the **Carmen Mini Hotel** (☎ 352 0798, fax 318 3865; e carmen@axelero.hu; Károly körút 5/b, 2nd floor; singles/doubles €50/60) has nine large and spotless rooms all of which are protected from the noise of the little ring road by double-glazing.

Excellent value for its location and immaculate 14 rooms is **Leo Panzió** (☎ 266 9041, fax 266 9042; e panzioleo@mail .datanet.hu; V Kossuth Lajos utca 2/a, 2nd floor; singles €45-66, doubles €69-82).

Up close to leafy Andrássy út, the **Radio Inn** (☎ 342 8347, fax 322 8284; e radioinn@ elender.hu; VI Benczúr utca 19; singles €43-48, doubles €48-65) is a real find, with 33 large suites with bathroom, kitchen and bed (or beds).

Hotel Margitsziget (☎ 329 2949, fax 340 4846; e hotelmargitsziget@axelero.hu; XIII Margitsziget; singles €43-45, doubles €43-54), in the middle of Margaret Island, is good value and almost feels like a budget resort, with free use of tennis courts, swimming pool and sauna.

Hotels – Mid-Range

For location and price in Buda, you can't beat the **Kulturinnov** (☎ 355 0122, fax 375 1886; e mka3@axelero.hu; I Szentháromság tér 6; singles/doubles/triples €65/80/110), a 16-room hotel in the former Finance Ministry in the Castle District. Chandeliers and a sprawling marble staircase greet you on entry, though the rooms are not so nice.

The nearby **Burg Hotel** (☎ 212 0269, fax 212 3970; e hotel.burg@mail.datanet.hu; I Szentháromság tér 7-8; singles €73-97, doubles €85-109) is a new, 26-room hotel with all mod cons, opposite Matthias Church.

In Pest, two small three-star hotels sit side by side on a street close to the Ferenc körút metro station and the Danube. **Hotel Corvin**

(☎ 218 6566, fax 218 6562; e corvin@mail .datanet.hu; IX Angyal utca 31; singles/doubles/triples €80/100/120) has 40 very comfortable rooms with all the mod cons, while the 44-room **Hotel Sissi** (☎ 215 0082; w www .hotelsissi.hu; IX Angyal utca 33; singles €67-90, doubles €78-100) next door has nicer and cheaper rooms.

The appropriately named **Hotel Ibis Centrum** (☎ 215 8585; w www.ibishotel.com; IX Ráday utca 6; singles €78-98, doubles €85-106) faces central Kálvin tér. The rooms are light and airy and there's a pleasant garden.

Hotels – Top End

Choose any of the following for their location, special amenities and ambience: the old-world 234-room **Gellért Hotel** (☎ 385 2200; w www.danubiusgroup.com; XI Szent Gellért tér 1; singles €115-150, doubles €190-235); the almost-London **Art'otel Budapest** (☎ 487 9487; w www.parkplazaww.com; I Bem rakpart 16-19; singles & doubles from €198), a new trendy place with 165 rooms; the totally revamped Art Deco **Andrássy Hotel** (☎ 462 2100; w www.andrassyhotel.com; VI Andrássy út 111 or Munkácsy Mihály utca 5-7; singles €100-145, doubles €175-250), with 70 stunning rooms; or the 164-room **Danubius Grand Hotel Margitsziget** (☎ 452 6264; w www.danubiusgroup.com; XIII Margitsziget; singles €136-176, doubles €168-208), built in 1873 on Margaret Island along the Danube and connected to the thermal spa.

PLACES TO EAT
Buda

Restaurants If you are going to splash out in the touristy, expensive Castle District, choose **Rivalda** (☎ 489 0236; I Színház utca; mains 2900-5200Ft; open 11.30am-11.30pm daily), an international café-restaurant next to the Castle Theatre, with a thespian theme and garden courtyard. **Café Miró** (☎ 375 5458; I Úri utca 30; light meals 1200Ft; open 9am-midnight daily) is a bright, modern place, good for a light meal.

Aranyszarvas (☎ 375 6451; I Szarvas tér 1; mains 1500-2500Ft; open noon-11pm daily) is set in an old 18th-century inn at the foot of Castle Hill and serves game dishes. The outside terrace is lovely in summer.

Near Moszkva tér, **Marxim** (☎ 316 0231; II Kisrókus utca 23; pizzas 490-950Ft; open noon-10pm Mon-Sat) is a veritable temple of

HUNGARY

communist memorabilia and campy Stalinist decor. For more serious (but affordable) Italian fare head for **Marcello** (☎ 466 6231; XI Bartók Béla út 40; pizzas & pasta 720-850Ft; open 11am-midnight Mon-Thur, 11am-1pm Fri & Sat), popular with students from the nearby university and nonsmoking.

South of Déli train station, the **Mongolian Barbecue** (☎ 353 6363; XII Márvány utca 19/a; buffet before/after 5pm 1990/3690Ft) is another one of those all-you-can-eat pseudo-Asian places that includes as much beer and wine as you can sink too.

Cafés The perfect place for coffee and cakes in the Castle District is the very crowded **Ruszwurm** (☎ 375 5284; I Szentháromság utca 7; open 10am-7pm daily). Two other charming cafés are **Angelika** (☎ 212 3784; I Batthyány tér 7; open 9am-midnight daily) and the untouristed **Caffè Déryné** (☎ 212 3864; I Krisztina tér 3; open 8am-10pm Mon-Fri, 8am-9pm Sat, 9am-9pm Sun).

Fast Food For a cheap and quick weekday lunch while in the Castle District try **Fortuna Önkiszolgáló** (☎ 375 2401; I Hess András utca 4; open 11.30am-2.30pm Mon-Fri), a self-service place above the Fortuna. **Nagyi Palacsintázója** (Granny's Palacsinta Place; ☎ 201 8605, 212 4866; I Hattyú utca 16; menus 568-888Ft; open 24hr) serves Hungarian pancakes – both savoury (148Ft to 248Ft) and sweet (78Ft to 248Ft) – throughout the day.

Self-Catering Budapest counts some 20 markets though the lion's share of them are in Pest. The **Fény utca market** (II Fény utca) is conveniently located next to the huge Mammut shopping mall.

Pest

Restaurants For good, old-fashioned Hungarian home cooking try **Móri Borozó** (☎ 349 8390; XIII Pozsonyi út 37; mains 500-750Ft; open 10am-8pm Mon-Thur, 10am-3pm Fri), a little wine bar-restaurant just a short walk north of Szent István körút.

If you want a bit more style (antique furniture, photos of Magyar actors on the walls and piano music), head for the **Művész Bohém** (☎ 339 8008; XIII Vígszínház utca 5; mains 750-1700Ft; open 11am-11pm daily), directly behind the Gaiety Theatre.

Stex Alfred (☎ 318 5716; VIII József körút 55-57; mains 710-1980Ft; open 8am-6am daily) is a big, noisy place. The extensive menu includes soups, sandwiches, pasta, fish and meat dishes and it transforms into a lively bar late at night. Best of all there's breakfast (320Ft to 860Ft).

Two pedestrian areas in Pest popular with Budapest's young-bloods are Ráday utca and Liszt Ferenc tér. On or near the former, try the upbeat **Pink Cadillac** (☎ 216 1412; IX Ráday utca 22; pizzas 650-1055Ft; open 11am-12.30am Sun-Thur, 11am-1am Fri & Sat) for pizza; or **Shiraz** (☎ 218 0881; IX Mátyás utca 22; mains 1350-1950Ft; open noon-midnight daily), a Persian restaurant with a **gyros take-away** (☎ 217 4547; IX Ráday utca 21; gyros 460-550Ft) round the corner.

Soul Café (☎ 217 6989; IX Ráday utca 11-13; mains 1200-2300Ft; open noon-1am daily) is a good choice for inventive Continental food and decor.

Of the many places on Liszt Ferenc tér, **Café Vian** (☎ 268 1164; VI Liszt Ferenc tér 9; open 9am-midnight daily), with an eight-page drinks menu, is a good choice. **Fortuca** (☎ 413 1612; VI Liszt Ferenc tér 10; pizzas & pasta 990-1290Ft; open 11am-1am daily) is the recommended new kid on the block. Nearby, but more subdued, is **Két Szerecsen** (☎ 343 1984; VI Nagymező utca 14; mains 800-2000Ft; open 8am-1am Sun-Thur, 11am-1am Fri & Sat), which also serves breakfast (from 600Ft).

Okay Italia (☎ 349 2991; XIII Szent István körút 20; pizzas & pasta 1090-1640Ft, mains 1390-2480Ft) is a perennially popular Italian-run place with a nearby **branch** (☎ 332 6960; V Nyugati tér 6). For excellent Greek food go to the **Rembetiko Piraeus** (☎ 266 0292; V Fővám tér 2-3; mains 990-2990Ft; open noon-midnight) overlooking a leafy square and the Great Market Hall.

Budapest has some decent vegetarian restaurants. **Gandhi** (☎ 269 1625; V Vigyázó Ferenc utca 4; set menu small/large 980/1680Ft; open noon-10pm Mon-Sat), in a cellar near Chain Bridge, serves a daily Sun and Moon plate set menu as well as wholesome salads, soups and desserts. **Wabisabi** (☎ 412 0427; XIII Visegrádi utca 2; mains 1080-1480Ft; open 9am-11pm Mon-Sat) offers wonderful Asian-inspired vegan dishes.

For a kosher meal, head for **Hannah** (☎ 342 1072; VII Dob utca 35; lunch 2500Ft; open

11.30am-3pm Sun-Fri), in a courtyard near the Great Synagogue.

If you want to dine in style, the **Múzeum** (☎ 338 4221; *VIII Múzeum körút 12; mains 1700-4100Ft; open noon-midnight Mon-Sat)* is still going strong after more than a century at the same location near the National Museum.

Gundel (☎ 468 4040; *XIV Állatkerti út 2; mains 3500-8800Ft; open noon-4pm & 6.30pm-midnight)* is Budapest's fanciest eatery, but these days the cognoscenti eschew it for its little sister and brother next door: **Bagolyvár** (☎ 343 0217; *mains 1180-2380Ft; open noon-11pm)*, with excellent reworked classics; and **Borvendéglő 1894** (☎ 468 4044; *mains 1600-2100Ft; open noon-11pm Tues-Sat)*, a new wine cellar and restaurant.

Cafés & Teahouses Try Gerbeaud (☎ 429 9000; *V Vörösmarty tér 7; open 9am-9pm daily)*, which has been the city's most fashionable café for the city's elite since 1870. **Művész** (☎ 352 1337; *VI Andrássy út 29; open 9am-11pm daily)*, almost opposite the State Opera House, is a more interesting place to people-watch and has cheaper (though with inferior) cakes.

Centrál Kávéház (☎ 266 4572; *V Károlyi Mihály utca 9; mains 1990-3590Ft; open 8am-1am Mon-Sat, 8am-midnight Sun)* is another reopened grande dame jostling to reclaim her title as *the* place to sit and look intellectual. It serves meals as well as fine coffee and cakes.

Budapest has a growing number of hip modern cafés and teahouses whose patrons take their hot beverages very seriously indeed. For the former, try **Coquan's** (☎ 215 2444; *IX Ráday utca 15; open 7.30am-7pm Mon-Fri, 9am-5pm Sat)*, with a long list of brews, cakes, bagels and a second branch (☎ 266 9936; *V Nádor utca 5; open 9am-7pm Mon-Fri, 9am-5pm Sat)*. One of the best teahouses in the city (usually nonsmoking) is **Teaház a Vörös Oroszlánhoz** *(Teahouse at the Red Lion;* ☎ 269 0579; *VI Jókai tér 8; open 11am-11pm Mon-Sat, 3pm-11pm Sun)*, with an Asian vibe and a **branch** (☎ 215 2101; *IX Ráday utca 9)* that keeps the same hours.

Fast Food American fast-food joints proliferate in Budapest but a much better choice are the wonderful little *étkezde* serving simple dishes that change every day. A central one is

Kisharang (☎ 269 3861; *V Október 6 utca 17; mains 500-820Ft; open 11am-8pm Mon-Fri, 11.30am-4.30pm Sat & Sun)*.

An inexpensive place to nosh Israeli-style is **Falafel Faloda** (☎ 267 9567; *VI Paulay Ede utca 53; large/small sandwiches 450/270Ft, salads 420-1050Ft; open 10am-8pm Mon-Fri, 10am-6pm Sat)*, where you pay a fixed price to stuff a piece of pita bread or fill a plastic container from the great assortment of salad options. Cheaper Middle Eastern food can be found at **Semiramis** (☎ 311 7627; *V Alkotmány utca 20; open noon-9pm Mon-Sat)*.

If you're craving for a Western-style sandwich, **Marie Kristensen Sandwich Bar** (☎ 218 1673; *IX Ráday utca 7; sandwiches 220-550Ft; open 8am-9pm Mon-Fri, 11am-8pm Sat)* has a large selection and does salads (from 490Ft) too.

Self-Catering Budapest's biggest market, the **Nagycsarnok** *(Great Market; IX Fővám tér)*, has become a bit of a tourist trap. Still, plenty of locals head here for fruit and vegetables, deli items, fish and meat. There are good food stalls on the upper level.

Large supermarkets are everywhere in Pest, including **Match** *(VIII Rákóczi út; open 6am-9pm Mon-Fri, 7am-8pm Sat, 7am-4pm Sun)* facing Blaha Lujza tér; and **Kaiser's** *(VI Nyugati tér 1-2; open 7am-8pm Mon-Sat, 7am-3pm Sun)* opposite Nyugati train station. **Rothschild** *(XIII Szent István körút 4; open 6am-8pm Mon-Fri, 7am-4pm Sat, 9am-5pm Sun)* is another chain, with a good supply of kosher products.

ENTERTAINMENT
Ticket Agencies

Tickets for concerts, dance performances and theatre are available from **Vigadó Jegyiroda** (☎ 327 4322; *V Vörösmarty tér 1; open 9am-7pm Mon-Fri, 10am-5pm Sat)*. **Ticket Express** *(information* ☎ 312-0000, *bookings* ☎ 06-30 303 0999; Ⓦ *www.tex.hu)* has half a dozen outlets, including a District VI branch *(VI Andrássy út 18; open 9.30am-6.30pm Mon-Fri, 9am-1pm Sat)*.

Classical Music

Koncert Kalendárium lists all concerts in town each month. Major venues include the **Liszt Academy of Music** (☎ 342 0179; *VI Liszt Ferenc tér 8)* in Pest and the **Budapest Congress Centre** (☎ 372 57000; *XII Jagelló út 1-3)* in

Buda. The **Pesti Vigadó** (☎ 318 9167; V Vigadó tér 2) usually has light classical music and touristy musical revues. Concerts are also held regularly in the city's churches, including **Matthias Church** on Castle Hill.

Opera

You should pay at least one visit to the **State Opera House** (☎ 332 7914; W www.opera .hu; VI Andrássy út 22) to see a performance and the incredible interior decor. Budapest's second opera house is the modern (and ugly) **Erkel Theatre** (☎ 333 0540; III Köztársaság tér 30). The **Budapest Operetta Theatre** (☎ 269 0118; VI Nagymező utca 17) puts on operettas – always a riot, particularly campy ones like the *Queen of the Csárdás* composed by Imre Kálmán.

Folk & Traditional Performance

Authentic folk-music workshops (*táncház*, literally 'dance house') are held at various locations throughout the week but less frequently in summer. Venues in Buda include the **Fonó Buda Music House** (☎ 206 6296; W www.fono.hu; XI Sztregova utca 3), the **Folklór Centrum** (☎ 203 3868; XI Fehérvári út 47) in the Municipal Cultural House and the **Marczibányi tér Cultural Centre** (☎ 212 2820; W www.marczi.hu; II Marczibányi tér 5/a). In Pest there is the wonderful **Kalamajka Táncház** (☎ 317 5928; V Molnár utca 9) at the Aranytíz Youth Centre.

Hungária Koncert (☎ 317 1377) organises folk and Gypsy concerts featuring the Hungarian State Folk Ensemble and two other groups at the **Duna Palota** (V Zrínyi utca 5) and the **Bábszínház** (Budapest Puppet Theatre; VI Andrássy út 69) throughout the year. Tickets cost 5600Ft (5100Ft for students).

Theatre

In Pest, **Merlin Theatre** (☎ 317 9338; W www .szinhaz.hu/merlin; V Gerlóczy utca 4) regularly stages comedies and dramas in English. A more recent arrival, the **International Buda Stage** (☎ 391 2525; II Tárogató út 2-4; tickets 300-800Ft) in Buda has English-language theatre, films and music programmes.

Pubs & Clubs

Budapest has a number of 'Irish' pubs, including **Becketts** (☎ 311 1035; V Bajcsy-Zsilinszky út 72; open 10am-1am Sun-Thur, 10am-3am Fri & Sat) and **Columbus** (☎ 266 9013; open noon-1am daily), which sits on a boat moored in the Danube opposite the Inter-Continental hotel.

In Pest, **Cactus Juice** (☎ 302 2116; VI Jókai tér 5; open 11am-2am Mon-Thur, 11am-4am Fri & Sat, 4pm-2am Sun) is in 'American rustic' drag and a good place to sip and sup with no distractions. There's dancing at weekends.

Old Man's Music Pub (☎ 322 7645; VII Akácfa utca 13; open 3pm-4am daily) pulls in the best live blues and jazz acts in town; shows are from 9pm to 11pm.

In Buda, **Oscar's American Bar** (☎ 212 8017; I Ostrom utca 14; open 5pm-2am Sun-Thur, 5pm-4am Fri & Sat), with some film memorabilia on the wood-panelled walls and leather directors' chairs on the floor, is a cocktail oasis up from the desert of Moszkva tér.

A wonderful spot to chill out along the banks of the Danube is **Zöld Párdon** (W www .zp.hu), an outdoor dancing and drinking venue on the Buda side of Petőfi Bridge. The 'world's longest summer festival' runs from 9am to 6am daily from May to September. Concerts begin at 8pm and then DJs take over until dawn.

Bank Music Club (☎ 414 5025; VI Teréz körút 55; open 9pm-5am Thur-Sat), in the south wing of Nyugati train station next to McDonald's, has a floor with international hits and another with Hungarian pop music and concerts. The **Közgáz Pince Klub** (☎ 218 6855; IX Fővám tér 8; open 9pm-5am Mon-Sat) has fewer frills and charges cheap covers but there's plenty of room to dance.

Trocadero (☎ 311 4691; VI Szent István körút 15; open 9pm-2am Tues-Thur, 9pm-5am Fri & Sat) attracts one of the most diverse crowds in Budapest with its great canned Latin, salsa and concert nights. Best parties are at weekends.

Gay & Lesbian Venues Budapest's flagship gay club is **Angyal** (☎ 351 6490; VII Szövetség utca 33; open 10pm-5am Fri-Sun), which welcomes girlz on Friday and Sunday. **Capella Café** (☎ 318 6231; V Belgrád rakpart 23; open 10pm-5am Wed-Sat) and its new extension, **Limo Café** (☎ 266 5455; V Belgrád rakpart 9; open noon-5am Sun-Thur, noon-6am Fri & Sat), are twin clubs frequented by gays, lesbians and fellow travellers.

The only real lesbian venue is **Café Eklektika** (☎ 266 3054; V Semmelweiss utca 21;

HUNGARY

open noon-midnight Mon-Fri, 5pm-midnight Sat & Sun), though it attracts a mixed crowd.

SHOPPING

Upstairs at the **Nagycsarnok** *(IX Fővám tér)* there are dozens of stalls selling Hungarian folk costumes, dolls, painted eggs, embroidered tablecloths and so on. If you prefer your prices clearly labelled, head for the **Folkart Centrum** *(☎ 318 4697; V Váci utca 58; open 10am-7pm daily)*.

There's an excellent selection of Hungarian wines at the **Budapest Wine Society Shop** *(☎ 212 2569; I Batthyány utca 59; open 10am-8pm Mon-Fri, 10am-6pm Sat)* in Buda and **La Boutique des Vins** *(☎ 317 5919; V József Attila utca 12; open 10am-6pm Mon-Fri, 10am-3pm Sat)* in Pest.

Many record shops sell CDs and tapes of traditional folk music, including **Rózsavölgyi** *(☎ 318 3500; V Szervita tér 5; open 9.30am-7pm Mon-Fri, 10am-5pm Sat)*. For locally produced classical CDs, tapes and vinyl, try **Concerto** *(☎ 268 9631; VII Dob utca 33; open noon-7pm Mon-Fri, noon-4pm Sun)*.

GETTING THERE & AWAY
Air

In Budapest, the main ticket office for **Malév Hungarian Airlines** *(☎ 235 3534, 235 3417; W www.malev.hu; V Dorottya utca 2; open 8.30am-5.30pm Mon-Wed & Fri, 8.30am-6pm Thur)* is near Vörösmarty tér. Other major carriers and their locations include:

Aeroflot *(☎ 318 5892)* V Váci utca 4
Air France *(☎ 318 0441)* V Kristóf tér 6
British Airways *(☎ 411 555)* VIII Rákóczi út 1–3 (East-West Business Centre)
KLM Royal Dutch Airlines *(☎ 373 7737)* VIII Rákóczi út 1–3 (East-West Business Centre)
Lufthansa *(☎ 266 4511)* V Váci utca 19–21
SAS *(☎ 266 2633)* V Bajcsy-Zsilinszky út 12
Swiss International Air Lines/Brussels Airlines *(☎ 328 5000)* V Kristóf tér 7–8

For details of international flights to/from Budapest, see the general Getting There & Away section earlier in this chapter. For information on getting to/from Ferihegy airport, see the Getting Around section later.

Bus

For details of international bus services see the general Getting There & Away section earlier in this chapter.

All international buses and some – but not all – buses to/from southern and western Hungary now arrive at and depart from the new **Népliget bus station** *(☎ 264 3939; IX Üllői út 131; metro Népliget)* in Pest. The **ticket office** *(open 6am-6pm Mon-Fri, 6am-4pm Sat & Sun)* is upstairs. **Eurolines** *(☎ 219 8080, 219 8000)* is represented here, as is its Hungarian associate, **Volánbusz** *(☎ 1-485 2162, 485 2100; W www.volanbusz.hu)*. There's a **left-luggage office** *(open 6am-9pm daily)* downstairs, which charges 150Ft per piece per day.

Népstadion bus station *(☎ 252 4498; XIV Hungária körút 48-52; metro Népstadion)* in Pest now serves most buses to domestic destinations. Things were in a state of flux at the time of research while the adjacent Budapest Sportcsarnok, destroyed by fire in 1999, was being rebuilt, but you should find the **ticket office** *(open 6am-6pm Mon-Fri, 6am-noon Sat & Sun)* as well as the **left-luggage office** *(open 6am-6pm daily)* here.

Most buses to the Danube Bend and parts of northern Hungary (eg, Balassagyarmat, Szécsény) arrive at and leave from the **Árpád Bridge bus station** *(☎ 329 1450, off XIII Róbert Károly körút; metro Árpád híd; ticket office open 7am-4pm Mon-Fri)* in Pest. The small **Széna tér bus station** *(☎ 201 3688, I Széna tér 1/a; metro Moszkva tér)* in Buda handles some traffic to and from the Pilis Hills and towns northwest of the capital, with some departures to Esztergom.

Train

For details of international trains, see the introductory Getting There & Away section earlier in this chapter. For general information on intercity train travel within Hungary, see the introductory Getting Around section.

The three main train stations are each on a metro line. **Keleti station** *(Eastern; ☎ 333 6342, 313 6835; VIII Kerepesi út 2-4; metro Keleti pályaudvar)* handles most (but not all) international trains, plus domestic trains to/from the north and northeast. For some Romanian and German destinations as well as domestic ones to/from the Great Plain and the Danube Bend, head for **Nyugati station** *(Western; ☎ 349 0115; VI Nyugati tér; metro Nyugati pályaudvar)*. For trains bound for Transdanubia and Lake Balaton, go to **Déli station** *(Southern; ☎ 375 6293, 355 8657; I Krisztina körút 37/a; metro Déli pályaudvar)*. Some trains to/from western and southern

Transdanubia also pass through Budapest's 'fourth' station – Kelenföld in Buda – but most of these services start or end at Déli or Keleti stations. Always check which station the train leaves from when you buy a ticket.

Buying Tickets Go to the **MÁV ticket office** (☎ 461 5500, 461 5400; W www.mav.hu; VI Andrássy út 35; open 9am-6pm Mon-Fri Apr-Sept, 9am-5pm Oct-Mar) for international train tickets and to make advance seat reservations for domestic express trains. The prices are the same as you would pay at the station and it accepts credit cards.

MÁV, Express (see Travel Agencies under Information earlier) and **Wasteels** (☎ 210 2802; open 8am-7pm Mon-Fri, 8am-1pm Sat) in Keleti station sell BIJ train tickets to those under 26, giving a 25% to 50% discount on fares to Western Europe. You must show your passport as proof of age.

You must have an ISIC card to get the student fare on international tickets. There are no student fares on domestic train travel.

Car & Motorcycle

Car rental costs have risen in recent years and are now usually charged in euros. One of the cheapest companies for renting cars is **Inka Rent a Car** (☎ 456 4666, fax 456 4699; e mail@inkarent.hu; IX Könyves Kálmán körút; open 8am-7pm Mon-Sat, 8am-2pm Sat). Although it is more expensive than Inka, **Americana Rent a Car** (☎ 350 2542, fax 320 8287; e americana@mail.matav.hu; XIII Dózsa György út 65) in the Ibis Volga hotel is reliable and has American cars with automatic transmissions.

The 25% ÁFA (value-added tax) on car rentals doesn't apply to nonresidents paying with foreign currency or credit card.

Hitching

Kenguru (☎ 266 5837, 483 0105; W www .kenguru.hu; VIII Kőfaragó utca 15; open 8am-6pm Mon-Fri, 10am-2pm Sat & Sun) matches up drivers and riders for a fee – mostly to points abroad. Approximate one-way fares include: Amsterdam 13,800Ft, London 15,200Ft, Munich 7300Ft, Paris 14,400Ft, Prague 5400Ft and Vienna 2800Ft.

Boat

Hydrofoils linking Budapest with Vienna via Bratislava run daily between April and early November; see River in the introductory Getting There & Away section of this chapter.

Mahart ferries link Budapest with the towns of the Danube Bend – see Getting There & Away under Szentendre in The Danube Bend section later in this chapter for fares and schedules. In Budapest, boats leave from below Vigadó tér on the Pest side. The first stop is at Batthyány tér in Buda.

GETTING AROUND
To/From the Airport

The **Airport Minibus Service** (☎ 296 8555, fax 296 8993) ferries passengers in eight-seat vans from the airport directly to their hotel, hostel or residence. The fare is 1800/3300Ft one way/return, and tickets are available at a clearly marked desk in the arrival halls. You need to book your journey *to* the airport 24 hours in advance.

The cheapest but most time-consuming method to get into town is to take the airport bus (look for the stop marked 'BKV Plusz Reptér Busz' on the pavement between terminals 2A and 2B), which terminates at Kőbánya-Kispest metro station. From there take the blue metro line (M3) into the centre. The total cost should be 190Ft.

If you want to take a taxi to the airport, telephone **Tele 5** (☎ 355 5555). There is a flat fare of 2800Ft to or from the airport from Pest (3200Ft or from Buda).

Public Transport

All public transport in Budapest is run by **BKV** (Budapest Public Transport Company; ☎ 342 2335, 06-80 406 688; W www.bkv.hu).

The three underground metro lines meet at Deák tér: the little yellow line (M1) from Vörösmarty tér to Mexikói út; the red line (M2) from Déli train station to Örs vezér tere; and the blue line (M3) from Újpest-Központ to Kőbánya-Kispest. A possible source of confusion on the yellow line is that one stop is called Vörösmarty tér and another is Vörösmarty utca. The HÉV above-ground suburban railway, which runs north from Batthyány tér, is almost like a fourth metro line.

There's also an extensive network of buses, trams and trolleybuses. On certain bus lines the same numbered bus may have a black or a red number. The red-numbered bus is the express, which makes limited stops. A useful transit map detailing all services is available at most metro ticket booths.

The metro operates from 4.30am until 11.30pm. There are also some 17 night buses (marked with an É after the designated number) running every half-hour or so along the main routes.

Travelling 'black' (without a valid ticket) is risky; with better surveillance (especially in the metro), there's a good chance you'll get caught. The on-the-spot fine is 1600Ft, which rises to 4000Ft if you pay later at the **BKV office** (☎ 461 6800; VII Akácfa utca 22; open 6am-8pm Mon-Fri, 8am-2pm Sat).

Fares & Travel Passes To travel on the metro, trams, trolleybuses, buses and the HÉV (as far as the city limits, which is the Békásmegyer stop to the north) you must have a valid ticket, which you can buy at kiosks, newsstands or metro entrances. The basic fare for all forms of transport is 106Ft (1000/1910Ft for a block of 10/20 tickets), allowing you to travel as far as you like on the same metro, bus, trolleybus or tram line without changing. A ticket allowing unlimited stations with one change in 90 minutes costs 190Ft.

On the metro exclusively, the 106Ft base fare drops to 75Ft if you are just going three stops within 30 minutes. For 120Ft you can travel five stops and transfer at Deák tér to another metro line within one hour. Unlimited stations travelled with one change within 60 minutes costs 175Ft. You must always travel in one continuous direction on a metro ticket; return trips are not allowed. Tickets have to be validated in machines at metro entrances and on other forms of transport – inspectors will also fine you for not validating your ticket.

Life is much simpler if you buy a pass. Passes are valid on all trams, buses, trolleybuses, HÉV (within the city limits) and metro lines, and you don't have to worry about validating your ticket each time you get on.

A one-day pass is poor value at 850Ft, but the three-day pass (touristajegy, or tourist ticket) for 1700Ft and the seven-day pass (hetijegy, or one week) for 2100Ft are worthwhile for most people. You'll need a photo for the fortnightly (2650Ft) or monthly (4050Ft) passes.

Taxi

Overcharging (due to rigged meters or long detours) is quite common in Budapest. Never get into a taxi that does not have a yellow licence plate (as required by law), the logo of a reputable taxi firm on the side doors and a table of fares posted prominently.

Taxi firms apply different tariffs, but prices cannot exceed the legally enforced ceiling rates. Between 6am and 10pm the maximum flag fall allowed is 200Ft, the per-kilometre fee is 200Ft, and the waiting fee 50Ft a minute. From 10pm to 6am, the maximum charges are 280/280/70Ft. Hungarians rarely flag down taxis in the street – they almost always ring for them, and fares are actually cheaper if you book. Make sure you know the number of the landline phone you're calling from as that's how they establish your address (though you can call from a mobile too). Dispatchers usually speak English.

Following are the telephone numbers of several reliable taxi firms in order of preference: **City** (☎ 211 1111), **Fő** (☎ 222 2222), **Tele 5** (☎ 355 5555), **Rádió** (☎ 377 7777) and **Buda** (☎ 233 3333).

Boat

Between May and mid-September **BKV passenger ferries** (☎ 369 1359; w www.ship-bp.hu) depart from Boráros tér beside Petőfi Bridge and head to Pünkösdfürdő north of Aquincum, with many stops along the way. Tickets (500/400Ft adult/child from end to end or 400/200Ft from intermediate stops) are usually sold on board. The ferry stop closest to the Castle District is Batthyány tér, and Petőfi tér is not far from Vörösmarty tér, a convenient place to pick up the boat on the Pest side.

The Danube Bend

Between Vienna and Budapest, the Danube breaks through the Pilis and Börzsöny Hills in a sharp bend. Here medieval kings once ruled Hungary from majestic palaces overlooking the river at Esztergom and Visegrád. East of Visegrád, the river divides, with Szentendre and Vác on different branches and long, skinny Szentendre Island in the middle. Today the historic monuments, easy access, good facilities and forest trails combine to put this scenic area at the top of any visitor's list.

SZENTENDRE
☎ 26 • pop 21,400
Szentendre (St Andrew in English) is a pretty little town 19km north of Budapest on an arm of the Danube. With its charming old centre,

HUNGARY

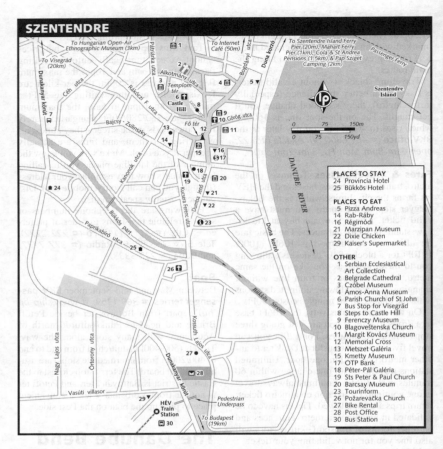

SZENTENDRE

PLACES TO STAY
24 Provincia Hotel
25 Bükkös Hotel

PLACES TO EAT
5 Pizza Andreas
14 Rab-Ráby
16 Régimódi
21 Marzipan Museum
22 Dixie Chicken
29 Kaiser's Supermarket

OTHER
1 Serbian Ecclesiastical
  Art Collection
2 Belgrade Cathedral
3 Czóbel Museum
4 Ámos-Anna Museum
6 Parish Church of St John
7 Bus Stop for Visegrád
8 Steps to Castle Hill
9 Ferenczy Museum
10 Blagoveštenska Church
11 Margit Kovács Museum
12 Memorial Cross
13 Metszet Galéria
15 Kmetty Museum
17 OTP Bank
18 Péter-Pál Galéria
19 Sts Peter & Paul Church
20 Barcsay Museum
23 Tourinform
26 Požarevačka Church
27 Bike Rental
28 Post Office
30 Bus Station

Serbian Orthodox churches, art and craft galleries and easy accessibility from the capital, the place swells with tourists during the summer. Just try to avoid it at weekends.

Orientation & Information

From the HÉV and bus stations, it's a short walk under the subway and up Kossuth Lajos utca to Fő tér, the centre of the old town. The Duna korzó – the river embankment – is a block east of this square. There are no left-luggage offices at the HÉV or bus stations.

Tourinform (☎ 317 965; **e** szentendre@ tourimform.hu; Dumtsa Jenő utca 22; open 9.30am-4.30pm Mon-Fri year-round, 10am-2pm Sat & Sun in summer) has brochures and information. The **OTP bank** (Dumtsa Jenő utca 6) is just off Fő tér, and the main **post**

office (Kossuth Lajos utca 23-25) is across from the bus and train stations.

There's an **Internet café** (Bogdányi utca 40), north of Fő tér, with Web access for 500Ft an hour.

Things to See

Begin your sightseeing at Fő tér, the town's central focus. Many of the buildings around this colourful square date from the 18th century, as does the **memorial cross** (1763) in the centre and the 1752 Greek Orthodox **Blagoveštenska Church** (☎ 310 554; admission 100Ft; open daily mid-Mar–Oct) on the northeastern corner.

The **Ferenczy Museum** (☎ 310 790; Fő tér 6; adult/child 300/150Ft; open 10am-6pm Wed-Sun Apr-Sept) displays artwork of the influential Ferenczy clan; paintings from Károly Ferenczy and sculptures, weaving and paintings from his three children.

Just east of Fő tér is the **Margit Kovács Museum** (☎ 310 244; Vastagh György utca 1; adult/child 450/220Ft; open 10am-6pm daily Feb-Oct). Kovács (1902–77) was a ceramicist who combined Hungarian folk, religious and modern themes to create Gothic-like figures. Narrow stepped lanes lead up from between Fő tér 8 & 9 to Castle Hill and the **Parish Church of St John** (rebuilt in 1710), from where you get great views of the town. Just north, the tall red tower of the Serbian **Belgrade Cathedral** (Pátriárka utca), from 1764, casts its shadow over the next-door **Serbian Ecclesiastical Art Collection** (☎ 312 399; adult/child 200/100Ft; open 10am-6pm Tues-Sun May-Oct, 10am-4pm Tues-Sun Mar & Apr, 10am-4pm Fri-Sun Jan & Feb).

The large **Hungarian Open-Air Ethnographic Museum** (☎ 502 500; adult/child 600/300Ft; open 9am-5pm Tues-Sun Apr-Oct, 9am-7pm July & Aug), which includes reassembled houses and buildings from around the country, is quite a way northwest on Sztaravodai út. Guided tours in English, French and German are available for 7000Ft. There's often a seasonal festival or everyday village activities going on; Tourinform stocks brochures with details. Up to 15 buses daily leave for the museum from stand No 7 at the bus station (about a 15-minute trip).

Szentendre has a plethora of museums and galleries not mentioned here; check with Tourinform for more details.

Activities

Szentendre Island has oodles of kilometres of uncrowded cycling – **rental bicycles** are available in the courtyard behind Kossuth Lajos utca 17-19 from 400Ft for one hour to 2500Ft for the day. **Canoes** and **motor boats** can be rented from **Dunabogdány** (☎/fax 390 086) for 1700Ft and 6000Ft per day respectively; boats are delivered, for which there's a minimal charge.

Places to Stay & Eat

You can easily see Szentendre on a day trip from Budapest, but if you want to stay the options range from inexpensive camping to pricey hotels.

About 2km north of Szentendre on Pap Island is **Pap Sziget Camping** (☎ 310 697; bus No 1, 2 or 3; camp sites per tent/adult/child 1900/900/500Ft, hostel singles/doubles 2600/3800Ft, bungalows & 4-person motel rooms 6000Ft; open May–mid-Oct). Generally the accommodation options of this leafy camping ground has shared bathrooms.

For rooms in **private houses** head west of the town centre around the Dunakanyar körút ring road, and look for 'Zimmer frei' signs.

If pensions are more your style there are a couple of places not far north. Take your pick between **Cola** (☎ 310 410, fax 500 539; Dunakanyar körút 50; singles/doubles €23/32), with comfy rooms (some with terrace), but is on a busy road; and **St Andrea** (☎ 311 989, fax 500 804; Egres utca 22; singles/doubles €20/25), which has simpler rooms but is on a quiet street.

More a pension than a hotel, **Bükkös Hotel** (☎ 312 021, fax 310 782; Bükkös part 16; singles/doubles €40/45) is central and has good rooms.

The three-star **Provincia Hotel** (☎ 301 082, fax 301 085; Paprikabíró utca 21-23; singles/doubles €50/61) has modern rooms and a sauna, swimming pool and garage.

In a tourist hub like Szentendre, you're not going to starve. **Régimódi** (☎ 311 105; Dumtsa Jenő utca 2), just down from the Margit Kovács Museum, has a filling Hungarian set menu for 1500Ft. Another old stand-by is **Rab-Ráby** (☎ 310 819; Péter-Pál utca 1; mains 1000-2000Ft).

For a simple affair with outdoor seating try **Pizza Andreas** (☎ 310 530; Duna korzó 5; pizzas from 700Ft).

Dixie Chicken (☎ 311 008; Dumtsa Jenő utca 16; burgers from 240Ft) is your standard fast-food joint, but it does have a salad bar. A large **Kaiser's supermarket** is next to the HÉV station if you want to give Szentendre's touristy restaurants a miss and have a riverside picnic.

The unusual **Marzipan Museum** (☎ 310 931; Dumtsa Jenő utca 12; admission to museum 250Ft) is a good place to stop for cake and ice cream.

Getting There & Away

Bus & Train Take the HÉV from Budapest's Batthyány tér metro station to the end of the line (40 minutes). You'll never wait longer than 20 minutes, and the last train leaves Szentendre for Budapest at 11.10pm. Some HÉV trains run only as far as Békásmegyer, where you cross the platform to catch the Szentendre train.

Buses from Budapest's Árpád híd bus station, which is on the blue metro line, also run to Szentendre frequently. Some buses continue on to Visegrád (eight buses daily) and Esztergom (17 a day).

Boat From late May to early September, one daily Mahart ferry plies the Danube to/from Budapest's Vigadó tér (830/1660Ft one way/return), departing from Budapest at 9am and Szentendre at 11.45am and 5.55pm. From mid-June to early September two extra ferries leave Budapest at 10.30am (express hydrofoil; 1300Ft one way; Tuesday to Sunday only) and 2pm and one from Szentendre at 5.45pm (express hydrofoil; Tuesday to Sunday only). From April to late May and September until seasonal shutdown, one boat daily leaves Budapest at 9am and Szentendre at 5.15pm. There is one departure from Szentendre (10.40am) to Visegrád during the low season and two in the high season (10.40am and 3.30pm). The 3.30pm departure continues on to Esztergom. The riverboat terminal is 1km north of town at the end of Czóbel Béla sétány.

VISEGRÁD
☎ 26 • pop 1540

Visegrád is superbly situated on the Danube's abrupt loop between the Pilis and Börzsöny Hills. After the 13th-century Mongol invasions, Hungarian kings built a mighty citadel on the hill top and a lower castle near the river. In the 14th century a royal palace was built on the flood plain at the foot of the hills and in 1323 King Charles Robert of Anjou, whose claim to the local throne was being fiercely contested in Buda, moved the royal household here. For nearly two centuries Hungarian royalty alternated between Visegrád and Buda.

The destruction of Visegrád came with the Turks and later the Habsburgs who destroyed the citadel to prevent Hungarian independence fighters from using it. All trace of the palace was lost until 1934 when archaeologists, by following descriptions in literary sources, uncovered the ruins that you can visit today.

The small town has two distinct areas; one to the north around Mahart ferry pier and another, the main town, about 1km to the south. There's a bank in the main centre at Rév utca, but it isn't always open and doesn't have an ATM.

Things to See & Do

The partly reconstructed **Royal Palace** (☎ 398 026; Fő utca 29; adult/child 400/200Ft; open 9am-4.30pm Tues-Sun), 400m south of the Mahart pier, doesn't come anywhere near its former glory, but is still worth a look. Highlights include the working Hercules Fountain in the Gothic courtyard and a small museum devoted to the history of the palace and its reconstruction.

The palace's original Gothic fountain is in the museum at **Solomon's Tower** (☎ 398 233; adult/child 400/200Ft; open 9am-4.30pm Tues-Sun May-Sept), a few hundred metres north of the palace ruins. This was part of a lower castle controlling river traffic.

Visegrád Citadel (adult/child 500/250Ft; open 9.30am-6pm daily mid-Mar–mid-Oct, weekends only rest of year) is high on a hill directly above Solomon's Tower. While the citadel (1259) itself is not particularly spectacular, the view of the Danube Bend from the walls is well worth the climb. There's a small museum on torture and some quasi-medieval activities. From the town centre a trail leads to the citadel from behind the Catholic church on Fő tér; this is less steep than the arduous climb from Solomon's Tower. **Citibus** (☎ 311 996), a local bus service, runs up to the citadel from the Mahart ferry pier three times daily (more often in July and August).

Places to Stay & Eat

On Mogyoróhegy (Hazelnut Hill), just about 2km northeast of the citadel, **Jurta Camping** (☎ 398 217; camp sites per tent/adult/child 420/550/350Ft; open May-Sept) is nicely situated but far from the centre, and buses only run there between June and August.

Visegrád Tours (☎ 398 160; Rév utca 15), near the bank, can organise private rooms starting at 4000/5900Ft for singles/doubles. Many houses along Fő utca and Széchenyi utca in the main centre have signs advertising 'Zimmer frei'.

Haus Honti (☎ 398 120, fax 397 274; Fő utca 66; singles/doubles 7000/8000Ft) is a friendly pension with homely rooms. Backing onto the pension, and accessible from the main road to Esztergom, is the pension's newer and more expensive cousin, **Hotel Honti** (singles/doubles 9000/10,000Ft), with its modern, spacious rooms.

If you go in for men in tights and silly hats, the medieval-style **Reneszánsz** (☎ 398 081;

Fő utca 11; mains 900-1500Ft), opposite the Mahart pier, can be a lot of fun. A better and cheaper deal is **Grill Udvar** (Rév utca 6; pizzas & mains from 500Ft), opposite the bank. **Gulás Csárda** (☎ 398 329), in town at the start of Mátyás király utca, serves reliable Hungarian standards for around 1000Ft.

Getting There & Away

Bus & Train Buses are very frequent (up to 16 daily) to and from Budapest's Árpád híd station, the Szentendre HÉV station and Esztergom. No railway line reaches Visegrád, but you can take one of many trains bound for Szob from Budapest's Nyugati station. Get off at Nagymaros-Visegrád, and hop on the ferry across to Visegrád.

Boat Between mid-June and early September, three daily Mahart ferries (7.30am, 9am and 2pm) leave Budapest for Visegrád (870/1740Ft one way/return, 3½ hours). Two of these ferries continue on to Esztergom at 10.55am and 5pm. Ferries to Budapest depart from Visegrád at 10.30am, 4.30pm and 5.30pm; only the first two stop in Szentendre on the way. On weekends from July to mid-August there is a high-speed hydrofoil from Budapest to Visegrád (1790/2990Ft, one hour), departing from Budapest at 9.30am and Visegrád at 3.55pm.

Hourly ferries cross the Danube to Nagymaros (170/170/700Ft per person/bicycle/car). The ferry operates all year except when the Danube freezes over or fog descends.

ESZTERGOM

☎ 33 • pop 29,300

Esztergom, at the western entrance to the Danube Bend, is one of Hungary's most historically important cities and has been the seat of Roman Catholicism here for more than a millennium. Second-century Roman emperor-to-be Marcus Aurelius wrote his *Meditations* while he camped here. Stephen I, founder of the Hungarian state, was born and crowned at Esztergom, and it was the royal seat from the late 10th to the mid-13th centuries. Originally the clerics lived by the river bank while royalty lived in the hill-top palace. When the king departed for Buda after the Mongol invasion, the archbishop moved up and occupied the palace, maintaining Esztergom's prominence. In 1543 the Turks ravaged the town and much of it was rebuilt in the 18th and 19th centuries.

Orientation & Information

The train station is on the southern edge of town, about a 10-minute walk south of the bus station. From the train station, walk north on Baross Gábor út, then along Ady Endre utca to Simor János utca. The ticket clerk at the train station holds luggage (open 24 hours).

Gran Tours (☎/fax 502 000; Széchenyi tér 25; open 8am-6pm Mon-Fri, 9am-noon Sat June-Aug, 8am-4pm Mon-Fri Sept-May) is best in town for information. You could also try **Cathedralis Tours** (☎ 415 260; cnr Bajcsy-Zsilinszky utca & Batthyány Lajos utca; open 8am-5pm Mon-Fri, 9am-noon Sat).

The **OTP bank** (Rákóczi tér) does foreign exchange transactions. The **post office** (Arany János utca 2) is just off Széchenyi tér.

Things to See & Do

You can't miss **Esztergom Basilica** (☎ 411 895; admission free; open 7am-6pm daily), built on a hill high above the Danube – it's the largest church in Hungary. The colossal building was rebuilt in the neoclassical style in the 19th century, but the white and red marble **Bakócz Chapel** (1510) on the south side was moved here from an earlier church. Underneath the cathedral is a large **crypt** (admission 50Ft; open 9am-5pm daily); among those buried in the crypt is the controversial Cardinal Mindszenty who, among other things, was imprisoned by the communists for refusing to allow Hungary's Catholic schools to be secularised. The **treasury** (adult/child 250/150Ft; open 9am-4.30pm daily mid-Mar–Oct, 11am-3.30pm Nov–mid-Mar) contains priceless and beautiful medieval objects, including the 13th-century Hungarian coronation cross. It's worth making the twisting climb up to the **cupola** (admission 100Ft) for outstanding views over the city – this is not for the faint-hearted, particularly when it's windy.

At the southern end of the hill is the **Castle Museum** (☎ 415 986; adult/child 400/200Ft; open 9am-4.30pm Tues-Sun Apr-Oct, 10am-4pm Nov-Mar), with partially reconstructed remnants of the medieval royal palace (1215) and archaeological finds from the region.

Southwest of the cathedral along the banks of the Little Danube is the pretty Víziváros (Watertown) district, home to the **Watertown Parish Church** (1738), with its fairy-tale air. Esztergom's **Christian Museum** (☎ 413 880; Berényi Zsigmond utca 2; adult/child 250/150Ft; open 10am-6pm Tues-Sun) is in the

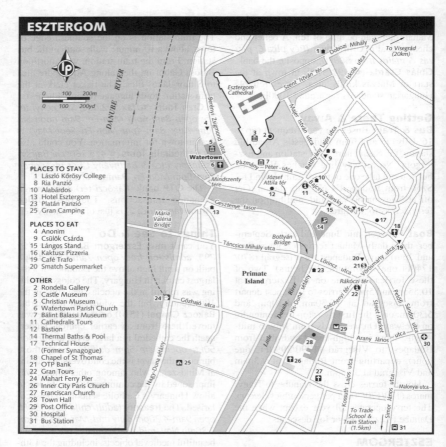

ESZTERGOM

PLACES TO STAY
1 László Kőrösy College
8 Ria Panzió
10 Alabárdos
13 Hotel Esztergom
23 Platán Panzió
25 Gran Camping

PLACES TO EAT
4 Anonim
9 Csülök Csárda
15 Lángos Stand
16 Kaktusz Pizzeria
19 Café Trafo
20 Smatch Supermarket

OTHER
2 Rondella Gallery
3 Castle Museum
5 Christian Museum
6 Watertown Parish Church
7 Bálint Balassi Museum
11 Cathedralis Tours
12 Bastion
14 Thermal Baths & Pool
17 Technical House
  (Former Synagogue)
18 Chapel of St Thomas
21 OTP Bank
22 Gran Tours
24 Mahart Ferry Pier
26 Inner City Paris Church
27 Franciscan Church
28 Town Hall
29 Post Office
30 Hospital
31 Bus Station

adjacent Primate's Palace (1882). It houses the best collection of medieval religious art in the country. Nearby is the **Bálint Balassi Museum** (☎ 412 185; Pázmány Péter utca 13; adult/child 100/50Ft; open 9am-5pm Tues-Sun), with objects of local interest.

Cross the bridge south of Watertown Parish Church and about 100m farther south is the recently completed **Mária Valéria Bridge**. Destroyed during WWII, it once again connects Esztergom with the Slovakian city of Štúrovo.

The Moorish Romantic-style **Technical House** (Imaház utca 4), dating from 1888, once served as a synagogue for Esztergom's Jewish community, the oldest in Hungary.

Esztergom has some outdoor **thermal baths** (☎ 312 249; Bajcsy-Zsilinszky utca 14; adult/child 350/150Ft; open 9am-6pm daily May-Sept). You can use the **indoor pool** (open 6am-6pm Mon & Sat, 6am-7pm Tues-Fri, 9am-4pm Sun) the rest of the year.

Places to Stay

Gran Camping (☎ 411 953, fax 402 513; Nagy-Duna sétány 3; camp sites per tent/adult/child/car 950/950/500/1000Ft, dorm beds 1700Ft, bungalows 9000-13,000Ft, doubles 6500Ft; open May-Sept), down a quiet lane by the Danube, is small and central. Bungalows sleep four to six.

Contact Gran Tours (see Information earlier) for **private rooms** (from 2000Ft) or **apartments** (about 6000Ft). From July to late August dormitory rooms become available at the **trade school** (☎ 411 746; Budai Nagy

HUNGARY

Antal utca 38; dorm beds 1200Ft) near the train station; and at the **László Kőrösy College** *(☎ 400 005; Szent István tér 16; dorm beds 2700Ft)*, opposite the cathedral.

The large, plain **Platán Panzió** *(☎ 411 355; Kis-Duna sétány 11; rooms from 4200Ft)* has doubles with a shared bathroom. It's central and relatively cheap.

Comfortable **Alabárdos** *(☎/fax 312 640; Bajcsy-Zsilinszky utca 49; singles/doubles 6000/9000Ft)* is close to the basilica. The nearby but flashier **Ria Panzió** *(☎ 313 115; fax 401 429, Batthyány Lajos utca 11; singles/ doubles 8500/10,500Ft)* has private parking and good-sized rooms.

Hotel Esztergom *(☎ 412 555, fax 412 853; Nagy-Duna sétány; singles/doubles €42/56)* looks like it might be a 1970s hotel in decline, but it's actually quite good. There's a rather fancy restaurant, roof terrace and sports centre.

Places to Eat

The cheapest place in town to grab a bite to eat is the small **lángos stand** at the entrance to the baths.

For something less casual try **Csülök Csárda** *(☎ 312 420; Batthyány Lajos utca 9; mains from 850Ft)*, popular with both visitors and locals and serving good home cooking and huge main courses.

Anonim *(☎ 411 880; Berényi Zsigmond utca 4; mains 1000-2400Ft; open until 10pm daily)*, in a historical townhouse, serves small but excellent dishes. For pizza, pasta and salads, head to the small **Kaktusz Pizzeria** *(Bajcsy-Zsilinszky utca 25-27; pizzas from 450Ft; open until 10pm daily)*.

Modern **Cafe Trafó** *(Vörösmarty utca 15; coffee from 100Ft)* is a little island oasis (literally) – *the* place to take a breather, sit back and relax. There's a **Smatch supermarket** on Bajcsy-Zsilinszky utca.

Getting There & Away

Bus & Train Buses to/from Budapest's Árpád híd bus station run about every half-hour from around 4am to 6.30pm. Buses from Budapest to Esztergom may travel via Dorog (75 minutes) or Visegrád and Szentendre (two hours). Buses to Visegrád and Szentendre depart almost hourly from 6am to 8.40pm and to Sopron and Győr once daily.

Trains to Esztergom depart from Budapest's Nyugati train station (1½ hours) up to 13 times a day. To get to western Transdanubia

from Esztergom, take one of the three daily trains to Komárom (1½ hours) where you can pick up connecting trains to Győr, Sopron and Lake Balaton.

Boat Mahart riverboats travel to/from Budapest (910/1820Ft one way/return, five hours) once a day from late May to mid-June, and twice a day beween mid-June and late September. From April to late May and late September to seasonal shutdown, they only run on Saturday and bank holidays, leaving Budapest at 8am and Esztergom at 3pm. A speedy hydrofoil makes the run from Budapest to Esztergom (1990/3390Ft, 1½ hours) weekends only between early July and mid-August, departing from Budapest at 9.30am and from Esztergom at 3.30pm.

Western Transdanubia

Beyond the Bakony Hills, northwest of Lake Balaton, lies western Transdanubia, a region that's bounded by the Danube and the Alps. Conquered by the Romans but never fully occupied by the Turks, this enchanting corner of Hungary contains picturesque small towns and cities with a decidedly Central European air. The old quarters of Sopron and Győr are brimming with what were once the residences of prosperous burghers and clerics, Kőszeg offers an intact medieval castle, Fertőd a magnificent baroque palace and Pannonhalma a functioning Benedictine monastery.

GYŐR
☎ 96 • pop 129,500

Győr (pronounced **jyeur**) is Hungary's third-largest industrial centre, but you'd never know it standing in its charming old centre. This historic city, midway between Budapest and Vienna at the point where the Mosoni-Danube, Rábca and Rába Rivers meet, was the site of a Roman town named Arrabona. In the 11th century, Stephen I established a bishopric here and in the 16th century a fortress was erected to hold back the Turks.

Orientation & Information

The large neobaroque City Hall (1898) rises up across from the train station. The **left-luggage office** *(open 5am-11pm daily)* at the

GYŐR

To István Széchenyi
University (200m)

Kálóczy tér

To Amnesia
(500m)

Mosoni-Danube River

Mosoni-Danube River

Móricz Zsigmond rakpart

Bástya utca

Vörösmarty utca

Dunakapu tér

Apáca utca

Rákóczi Ferenc utca

Nefelejcs utca

Káptalandomb

8 · Apor Vilmos püspök tere 7 +

6 ·

4 ·

5 ·

Jedlik Ányos utca

Liszt Ferenc utca

Teleki László utca

11 · 12 ·

Széchenyi tér

17 ·

16 ·

Káptalandomb

9 ·

Király utca

13 ·

14 · 15 ·

Iskola utca

Kisfaludy utca

20 ·

19 18 ·

10 ·

Rába kettős híd

Bécsi kapu tér

Kazinczy utca

27 ·

Czuczor Gergely utca

21 ·

26 ·

Schweidel utca

31 ·

32 ·

Kisfaludy utca

Aradi vértanúk útja

Arany János utca

28 ·

Baross Gábor utca

22 ·

23 ·

33 ·

34 · Virágpiac

29 ·

30 ·

25 ·

24 ·

Kossuth Lajos utca

Petőfi tér

35 ·

Zechmeister utca

Bajcsy-Zsilinszky út

38 ·

39 ·

To Kiskút-liget
Camping (3km) &
Budapest (109km)

36 ·

37 ·

Jókai utca

Árpád út

Market

40 ·

Városháza tér

Szent István út

Baross híd

Honvéd liget

42 · 43 ·

Révai Miklós út

Train Station

Eszperantó utca

Zrínyi utca

44 ·

To Pannonhalma
Abbey (21km)

Kálvária utca

Hunyadi utca

Hunyadi utca

Ország útja

Rába River

PLACES TO STAY	
2	Duna
12	Katalinkert
20	Kertész
21	Teátrum
26	Kuckó
31	Ibusz
33	Hotel Klastrom
42	Hotel Szárnyaskerék

PLACES TO EAT	
1	Veszti
18	24-Hour Shop
29	Komédiás
29	Szürkebarát Borozó
30	Kaiser's Supermarket
36	Rábaparti
37	Cake Shop
38	Márka

OTHER	
3	Péter Váczy Museum
4	János Xánthus Museum
5	Imre Patkó Collection; Iron Stump House
6	Ark of the Covenant
7	Cathedral
8	Bishop's Castle; Diocesan Treasury
9	Thermal Baths

10	Captain Drakes Pub
11	Archaeology Museum
13	Napoleon House
14	Jesuit Pharmacy
15	St Ignatius Church
16	Column of the Virgin
17	Széchenyi Cultural Centre
19	20th Century Café
22	Győr National Theatre
23	Main Post Office
24	Béla Bartók Cultural Centre
27	Internet Café
28	OTP Bank
32	Carmelite Church
34	Flower Market
35	Synagogue
39	Tourinform
40	City Hall
41	Stop for Bus No 8 to Camping Ground
43	Post Office
44	Bus Station

HUNGARY

station is next to the exit from one of the two tunnels under the tracks (the one directly opposite the start of Aradi vértanúk útja). This same tunnel leads directly through to the main bus station, just south of the train station.

Baross Gábor utca, which leads to the old town and the rivers, lies diagonally across from City Hall. Much of central Győr is pedestrianised, making parking difficult but walking the city a real pleasure.

There's a **Tourinform** (☎ 311 771; e gyor@tourinform.hu; Árpád út 32; open 8am-8pm Mon-Fri, 9am-6pm Sat & Sun June–mid-Sept; 8am-6pm Mon-Fri, 9am-2pm Sat Apr & May; 9am-4pm Mon-Fri, 9am-2pm Sat mid-Sept–Mar) office on the corner of Árpád út and Baross Gábor utca.

OTP bank (Baross Gábor 16) has a branch on the main pedestrian street. There are several ATMs around the town centre.

There's a post office next to the train station and the **main post office** (Bajcsy-Zsilinszky út 46) is to the northeast of this. A small **Internet café** (Czuczor Gergely utca 6) is bizarrely located above a clothes shop and charges 200Ft per hour.

Things to See

The enchanting **Carmelite church** (1725) and many fine baroque palaces line Bécsí kapu tér. On the northwestern side of the square are the fortifications built in the 16th century to stop the Turks. A short distance east is **Napoleon House** (Király utca 4), where Bonaparte spent his only night in Hungary in 1809.

Head north along one of the narrow, pedestrianise lanes that lead up to Chapter Hill (Káptalandomb), the oldest part of Győr. The solid baroque **Cathedral** (open 10am-noon & 2pm-5pm daily) on the hill was originally Romanesque, but most of what you see inside dates from the 17th and 18th centuries. Don't miss the Gothic **Hédervary Chapel** on the southern side of the cathedral, which contains a glittering 15th-century bust of King (and St) Ladislas. West of the cathedral is the fortified **Bishop's Castle** in a mixture of styles, which now houses the **Diocesan Treasury** (☎ 312 153; adult/child 300/100Ft; open 10am-4pm Tues-Sun).

The streets behind the cathedral are full of old palaces, and at the bottom of the hill on Jedlik Ányos utca is the **Ark of the Covenant**, an outstanding baroque statue dating from 1731. From here you can head north to a bridge overlooking the junction of the city's three rivers.

One of the nicest things about Győr is its atmospheric old streets. Stroll down Bástya utca, Apáca utca, Rákóczi Ferenc utca, Liszt Ferenc utca and Király utca, where you'll see many fine buildings. The late-Renaissance palace was once a charity hospital, and now houses the **Péter Váczy Museum** (☎ 318 141; Rákóczi Ferenc utca 6; admission free; open 10am-6pm Tues-Sun Mar-Oct, 10am-5pm Nov-Feb). Enter around the back at Nefelejcs utca 3.

Széchenyi tér is the heart of Győr and features the **Column of the Virgin** (1686) in the middle. **St Ignatius Church** (1641) is the finest in the city with a superb pulpit, pews and ceiling frescoes. The **Jesuit Pharmacy** (☎ 320 954; Széchenyi tér 9; admission free; open 7.30am-4pm Mon-Fri) is a fully operational baroque institution.

Cross the square to the **János Xantus Museum** (☎ 310 588; Széchenyi tér 5; adult/child 400/200Ft; open 10am-6pm Tues-Sun), which is in a palace built in 1743. Beside it is the **Iron Stump House** (Széchenyi tér 4), which still sports the beam onto which itinerant artisans would drive a nail to mark their visit. The building now houses the **Imre Patkó Collection** (☎ 310 588; adult/child 300/150Ft; open 10am-6pm Tues-Sun) of paintings and Asian and African art, one of Hungary's finest small museums.

Pannonhalma Abbey If you have a half-day to spare, it's worth visiting Pannonhalma Abbey (☎ 570 191; open 8.30am-6pm daily June-Sept, 8.30am or 9.30am-4.30pm or 5pm Tues-Sun Oct-May), a Unesco World Heritage listed site on top of a 282m hill some 21km south of Győr. Highlights include the Gothic cloister (1486), the Romanesque basilica (1225) and the 11th-century crypt.

Because it's a working monastery, the abbey must be visited with a guide. Tours in Hungarian with foreign-language text cost 1000/300Ft per adult/child, while tours in foreign languages are 2000/1000Ft. From late March to mid-November tours are available at 11am and 1pm in English, Italian, German, French and Russian. In the low season, tours in foreign languages are available only by request. The entry fee includes the tour.

Pannonhalma is best reached from Győr by bus (almost every hour) as the train station is

HUNGARY

2km southwest of the abbey. To be safe, allow one hour to travel the 18km by bus.

Activities

Győr's **thermal baths** (☎ 522 646; Ország út 4; adult/child 500/400Ft; open 9am-6pm daily May-Sept), west of the Rába River, was undergoing a major face-lift at the time of research, but should be ready by the end of 2003. There is also a **covered pool** (open 6am-8pm Mon-Fri year-round).

Places to Stay

Camping Some 3km northeast of town is the **Kiskút-liget Camping** (☎ 318 986; camp sites including tent & one person 1470Ft, 4-person bungalows 4300Ft, motel doubles 3800Ft; bungalows open mid-Apr–mid-Oct, motel open year-round) in suburban Győr. Take bus No 8 from beside City Hall.

Private Rooms & Hostels Private rooms are available from the friendly **Ibusz** (☎ 311 700; Kazinczy utca 3) office from 2000Ft per person. Dormitory accommodation is available year-round at the huge **István Széchenyi University** (☎ 503 447; Héderváry út 3; dorm beds around 1000Ft) north of the town centre. Check with Tourinform for other possibilities.

Pensions Győr is full of small private pensions and, while not the cheapest places to stay, they are usually very central and in some of the city's most atmospheric old buildings.

Kuckó (☎ 316 260, fax 312 195; Arany János utca 33; singles/doubles 5900/7490Ft) has nine rooms with private bath in a lovely old townhouse. The new kid on the block is **Katalinkert** (☎/fax 542 088; Sarkantyú köz 3; singles/doubles 5800/7500Ft), with six nice modern rooms tucked away above a pleasant courtyard restaurant.

Kertész (☎/fax 517 461; Iskola utca 11; singles/doubles 6000/8000Ft) is bigger with nine rooms, all with bath. Other fine choices, and under the same management, are **Teátrum** (☎ 310 640, fax 328 827; Schweidel utca 7; singles/doubles/triples 6200/7900/9500Ft), on a pedestrianised mall; and the pretty **Duna** (☎/fax 329 084; Vörösmarty utca 5; singles/doubles/triples 6200/7900/9500Ft).

Hotels Convenient to the train and bus stations is **Hotel Szárnyaskerék** (☎ 314 629; Révai Miklós utca 5; doubles with/without bath 6900/4650Ft), a large, institutional-like place. Only four rooms have en suite baths.

If your budget is bigger, you shouldn't go past **Hotel Klastrom** (☎ 516 910, fax 327 030; e klastrom@arrabonet.gyor.hu; Zechmeister utca 1; singles/doubles/triples €49/66/76), wonderfully positioned by the river just off Bécsí kapu tér. It has rooms in a beautifully restored 250-year-old Carmelite convent, and a sauna and solarium for guests.

Places to Eat

Komédiás (☎ 527 217; Czuczor Gergely utca 30; mains around 1000Ft) is a cellar restaurant worth a try, as is atmospheric **Veszti** (☎ 337 700; Móricz Zsigmond rakpart 3; pizzas from 390Ft, mains from 760Ft; open 11am-1pm daily). Situated on an old paddle-steamer on the Mosoni-Duna River, it has a huge range of pizzas and Tex-Mex/Americana mains.

For a cheap and filling meal, try **Rábaparti** (Zechmeister utca 15; mains from 700Ft), an unpretentious (though rather gloomy) restaurant. For a self-service meal, head for **Márka** (☎ 320 800; Bajcsy-Zsilinszky út 30; salads & mains around 430Ft; buffet open 11am-5pm Mon-Sat).

A decent wine cellar is **Szürkebarát Borozó** (☎ 311 548; Arany János utca 20; mains from 600Ft). A stairway in the courtyard leads down into this vaulted restaurant. There's an excellent ice-cream stand in the same courtyard. For cakes, don't go past the tiny **cake shop** at Jókai utca 6. It's so popular people line up along the footpath.

A massive **Kaiser's supermarket** (cnr Arany János utca & Aradi vértanúk útja) and department store takes up much of the block on this corner.

There's a **24-hour shop** on the corner of Teleki László utca and Schweidel utca and another at the train station.

Entertainment

The celebrated Győr Ballet and the city's opera company and philharmonic orchestra all perform at the modern **Győr National Theatre** (☎ 314 800; Czuczor Gergely utca 7), a technically advanced though rather unattractive structure covered in op art tiles by Victor Vasarely.

In summer there's a month-long festival of music, theatre and dance from late June to late July. In March, Győr hosts many events in conjunction with Budapest's Spring Festival.

Captain Drakes Pub *(Radó sétány)* on the little island in the Rába River is a great spot for a drink on balmy summer evenings. **Amnesia** *(Héderváry utca 16)* is a club/bar north of the city centre that attracts a student crowd, while the **20th Century Café** *(Schweidel utca 25)* is central and caters to a more mature audience.

Getting There & Away

Bus Buses travel to Balatonfüred (four daily), Budapest (every hour), Esztergom (one per day), Hévíz (two daily), Keszthely (five daily), Pannonhalma (hourly), Pécs (two daily) and Vienna (one to three daily). To get to Fertőd, you must take the Sopron bus to Kapuvár (up to 12 a day) and change there.

Train Győr is well connected by express train to Budapest's Déli, Kelenföld and Keleti train stations (1½ hours) and to Sopron (1½ hours). Other trains go to Szombathely (1¾ hours) via Celldömölk. To go to Lake Balaton take one of the six trains daily heading south to Veszprém (2½ hours) via Pannonhalma.

For Vienna's Westbahnhof you may have to change trains at Hegyeshalom since some express trains don't pick up passengers at Győr. Another route to Austria requires a change at Sopron and passes through Wiener Neustadt before arriving at Vienna's Südbahnhof.

SOPRON

☎ 99 • pop 55,000

Sopron (Ödenburg in German) sits right on the Austrian border, only 69km south of Vienna. In 1921 the town's residents voted in a referendum to remain part of Hungary, while the rest of Bürgenland (the region to which Sopron used to belong) went to Austria.

Sopron has been an important centre since the time of the Romans, who called it Scarbantia. The Mongols and Turks never got this far, so numerous medieval structures remain intact. In the small, horseshoe-shaped old town, still partially enclosed by medieval walls built on Roman foundations, almost every building is historically important.

Orientation & Information

From the main train station, walk north on Mátyás király utca, which becomes Várkerület after a few blocks. Várkerület and Ógabona tér form a loop right around the old town, following the line of the former city walls. Előkapu (Front Gate) and Hátsókapu (Back Gate) are the two main entrances to the old town and Fő tér, the town's central square.

The bus station is northwest of the old town on Lackner Kristóf utca. There is a **left-luggage office** *(open 3am-11pm daily)* in the main train station. There's no left-luggage area at the bus station.

Tourinform *(☎/fax 338 892;* |e| *sopron@ tourinform.hu; Előkapu 11; open 9am-5pm daily June-Aug, 9am-4pm daily Sept-May)* is right near the Fire Tower.

There is an **OTP bank** *(Várkerület 96/a)* outside the old town. For Internet access head to **Internet Sopron** *(Új utca 3; open 11am-8pm Mon-Fri, 10am-5pm Sat)*, which charges 400Ft for an hour's surfing.

Things to See

The 60m-high **Fire Tower** *(☎ 311 327; Fő tér; adult/child 300/150Ft; open 10am-6pm Tues-Sun Apr-Oct)*, above the old town's northern gate, is a true architectural hybrid. The 2m-thick square base, built on a Roman gate, dates from the 12th century, the middle cylindrical and arcaded balcony was built in the 16th century and the baroque spire was added in 1680. You can climb up to the top for a marvellous view of the city. **Fidelity Gate** at the bottom of the tower pictures Hungary receiving the *civitas fidelissima* (most loyal citizenry) of Sopron. It was erected in 1922 after that crucial plebiscite.

In the centre of Fő tér is the magnificent **Holy Trinity Column** (1701) and beyond this the 13th-century **Goat Church**, whose name comes from the heraldic animal of its chief benefactor. Below the church is the **Chapter Hall** *(☎ 338 843; Templom utca 1; admission free; open 10am-noon & 2pm-5pm Tues-Sun May-Sept)*, part of a 14th-century Franciscan monastery with frescoes and stone carvings.

Of the several excellent museums on Fő tér, two stand out (both are open 10am to 6pm Tuesday to Sunday April to September, and 10am to 2pm October to March). **Fabricius House** *(☎ 311 327; adult/child 300/150Ft)* at No 6 is a comprehensive historical museum with rooms on the upper floors that are devoted to domestic life in the 17th and 18th centuries and has impressive Roman sculpture in the Gothic cellar. **Storno House** *(☎ 311 327; adult/child 500/250Ft)* at No 8 is a famous Renaissance palace (1560) that is now a museum and gallery of Romanesque and Gothic decorative art.

HUNGARY

SOPRON & THE LŐVÉR HILLS

A unique museum of Jewish life is housed in the 14th-century **Old Synagogue** *(Új utca 22; adult/child 200/100Ft; open 9am-5pm Wed-Mon Mar-Sept)*, and it is in better condition than many others scattered throughout the country.

In the Ikva district north of the old town are several more interesting museums, including the excellent **Zettl-Langer Collection** *(☎ 335 123; Balfi út 11; admission 200Ft; open 10am-noon Tues-Sun)* of ceramics, paintings and furniture; and the hunger-inducing **Bakery Museum** *(☎ 311 327; Bécsí út 5; adult/child 200/100Ft; open 10am-2pm Tues-Sun May-Aug)*.

To visit the hills surrounding Sopron, take bus No 1 or 2 to the Szieszta Hotel and hike up through the forest to the **Károly Lookout** (394m) for the view. To the northwest is the slightly bizarre **Taródi Castle** *(Csalogány köz 8)*, a 'self-built private castle' owned by the obsessed Taródi family.

Places to Stay

On Pócsi-domb about 2.5km south of the city centre is **Lővér Camping** *(☎/fax 311 715; Kőszegi út; bus No 12 from bus & train stations; camping per adult/child 600/300Ft, bungalow doubles 2688Ft; open mid-Apr–mid-Oct)* in a quiet rural spot. The bungalows and camp sites are shaded.

The **Brennbergi Hostel** *(☎/fax 313 116; Brennbergi út; bus No 3; dorm beds 1200Ft, bungalows per person 2000Ft; open mid-Apr–mid-Oct)* is pretty far west of the city centre, but a bed is cheap and there are also bungalows here.

Ciklámen Tourist *(☎ 312 040; Ógabona tér 8)* travel agency has private rooms for about 3000/4000Ft a single/double, though singles are scarce in summer.

Sopron has plenty of pensions and hotels to choose from. A good bet is **Jégverem** *(☎/fax 510 113; e haspart@axelero.hu; Jégverem utca 1; singles/doubles 4000/8000Ft)*, with five large rooms in an 18th-century ice warehouse and cellar, in the Ikva district.

Bástya *(☎ 325 325, fax 334 061; Patak utca 40; singles/doubles 6000/8000Ft)* has 16 modern rooms and is a 10-minute walk north of the old town. Another wise choice but out near the Lővér Hills is **Diana** *(☎ 329 013; Lővér körút 64; singles/doubles 5400/8000Ft)*. Its eight rooms are large and comfortable, and there's a restaurant.

Hotel Palatinus *(☎ 523 816; Új utca 23; singles/doubles €40/52)* couldn't be more central, but it's not a particularly attractive place. Sopron's grand old dame is the 100-year-old **Pannónia Med Hotel** *(☎ 312 180, fax 340 766; Várkerület 75; singles/doubles from 16,800/18,900Ft)*. It's a nice place with all the trimmings, but is a tad overpriced.

Places to Eat

Generális-Corvinus *(☎ 314 841; Fő tér 7-8; mains 1000-1900Ft)*, with its café tables on the square, is a great place for a meal in the warm months. Opposite is **Gambrinus** *(☎ 339 966; Fő tér 3; mains 800-1500Ft; open to midnight daily)*, with solid Hungarian and Austrian fare. **Fórum Pizzéria** *(☎ 340 231; Szent György utca 3; dishes under 1000Ft)* is a good bet for decent pizza, pasta and salads.

The burgers at **Speedy Burger** *(Várkerület 36; burgers 260-380Ft)* are big, filling and served before you know it. A great place for an inexpensive lunch or light meal is **Cézár Pince** *(☎ 311 337; Hátsókapu 2; dishes 330-690Ft; open to 11pm daily)*, in a medieval cellar off Orsolya tér. Around the corner is **Papa Joe's Steakhouse** *(☎ 340 933; Várkerület 108; mains 900-1500Ft)*, with grills, steaks, soups and salads and an inviting courtyard.

Stop in at **Várkapu Café** *(Várkerület 108/a; cakes from 50Ft)* for cake and coffee on the corner of Hátsókapu. For ice cream, line up at the old-world ice creamery and cake shop **Dömötöri** *(Széchenyi tér 13; ice cream 60Ft per scoop)*, by far the most popular in town.

For self-catering heading for the **Smatch supermarket** *(Várkerület 100)*.

Entertainment

The **Hungarian Cultural House** *(Széchenyi tér)*, undergoing renovation at the time of research, is usually the place for music and other cultural events. The beautiful **Petőfi Theatre** *(☎ 511 700; Petőfi tér 1)*, with its National Romantic-style decor, is in constant use. Its **ticket office** *(☎ 511 730; open 9am-5pm Mon-Fri, 9am-noon Sat)* is at Széchenyi tér 17.

For less highbrow entertainment, head to the **Music Café** *(Várkerület 49)*, which often has live jazz in the evenings. If you're feeling a bit more raucous you can head to the 'saloon bar' at **Papa Joe's Steakhouse** (see Places to Eat). But before leaving town be sure to sample Sopron's wines in the deep, deep cellar of **Gyógy-gődőr** *(Fő tér 4)*.

HUNGARY

Getting There & Away

Bus Bus connections are good. There are hourly buses (sometimes more) to Fertőd and Győr, and less frequent buses to Balatonfüred (two daily), Budapest (four), Esztergom (two), Hévíz and Keszthely (three), Kőszeg (eight), Pécs (one) and Szombathely (nine). There is an 8am bus to Vienna daily, plus an extra 9.25am departure on Monday and Thursday, and 8.55am and 9.25am on Friday. Two buses a week make the trip to Munich and Stuttgart (8.05pm Thursday and 9.05pm Sunday).

Train Express trains en route to Vienna's Südbahnhof pass through Sopron up to nine times daily; five local services a day depart for Wiener Neustadt (where you can transfer for Vienna). Eight express trains a day depart for Keleti in Budapest, travelling via Győr and Komárom, and seven to nine trains to Szombathely.

FERTŐD
☎ 99 • pop 2700

Don't miss the 126-room **Esterházy Palace** (☎ 537 640; adult/child 1000/600Ft; open 10am-6pm Tues-Sun mid-Mar–Oct, 10am-4pm Fri-Sun Nov–mid-Mar) at Fertőd, 27km east of Sopron and easily accessible by bus. Built in 1766, this magnificent Versailles-style baroque palace, easily the finest in Hungary, must be visited with a guide, and information sheets in various languages are available. From May to October piano and string quartets perform in the concert hall regularly, and the Haydn Festival takes place here in early September (Joseph Haydn was court musician to the Esterházy family from 1761 to 1790). Programmes are available from the palace or from **Tourinform** (☎ 370 544; e fertod@tourinform.hu; Madách Sétány 1), opposite the palace inside the old Grenadier House.

Places to Stay & Eat

Dori Hotel & Camping (☎/fax 370 838; Pomogyi út 1; camp sites per tent €2-2.60, per person €1.20-1.70; bungalow singles €17-21, doubles €30-34; hotel singles €15-19, doubles €27-30) has a good range of accommodation possibilities 100m north of the palace. Price depends on the season.

You can spend the night in the palace at the **Kastély Hotel** (☎ 537 640; doubles/triples/quads 4200/5800/6600Ft), but don't

expect palace standards. The rooms are clean, simple and booked well in advance.

Two decent restaurants occupying the palace's Grenadier house are **Gránátos** and **Kastélykert** (mains around 1000-1500Ft at both). For ice cream head to **Elit** (Fő utca 1; ice cream from 80Ft), west of the palace in town.

KŐSZEG
☎ 94 • pop 11,900

Kőszeg (Güns in German) is a small town at the foot of the Kőszeg Hills just 3km from the Austrian border. Mt Írottkő (882m), southwest of town and straddling the border, is the highest point in Transdanubia. At Kőszeg's centre is the old town, a well-preserved medieval precinct with a main square that's hardly changed since the 18th century. The Várkör rings the centre along the old castle walls.

In 1532 Kőszeg's castle garrison held off a Turkish army of 100,000, and this delay gave the Habsburgs time to mount a successful defence of Vienna, ensuring Kőszeg's place in Hungarian history.

Orientation & Information

The train station is a 15-minute walk to the southeast of the old town on Alsó körút; buses stop just a block from Várkör on Liszt Ferenc utca. The train station doesn't have a left-luggage office, but the staff will probably agree to hold your bags for the usual fee.

There's a helpful **Tourinform** office (☎ 563 120; e koszeg@tourinform.hu; Jurisics tér 7; open 8am-6pm Mon-Fri, 10am-6pm Sat & Sun mid-June–mid-Sept; 8am-4pm Mon-Fri mid-Sept–mid-June) on the main square. The **OTP bank** (Kossuth Lajos utca 8) has a foreign currency exchange machine.

Things to See

Heroes' Gate, leading into Jurisics tér, was erected in 1932 to mark the 400th anniversary of the Turkish onslaught. In the General's House next to the gate is the **Városi Museum** (☎ 360 240; Jurisics tér 4-6; adult/child 100/50Ft; open 10am-5pm Tues-Sun), containing exhibits on folk art, trades and crafts, and the natural history of the area.

Buildings of note on the town's main square include the striking **Town Hall** at No 8, the **Church of St Henry** (1615) and behind it the **Church of St James** (1403), a splendid Gothic structure with three 15th-century frescoes. There's a baroque **pharmacy** (☎ 360 337;

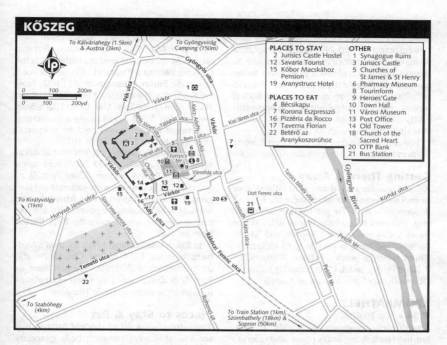

KŐSZEG

To Kálváriahegy (1.5km) & Austria (3km)
To Gyöngyvirág Camping (150m)
Gyöngyös utca
Pék utca
Várkör
Rajnis József utca · Táblaházi utca
Chernel utca
Várkör
Bem J utca
Kiss János utca
Jurisics tér
Városház utca
Chernel utca
Várkör
Ady E utca
Hunyadi János utca
Szent Imre herceg utca
Temető utca
To Királyvölgy (1km)
To Szabóhegy (4km)
Liszt Ferenc utca
Tanos Mihály utca
Gyöngyös River
Kórház utca
Kossuth Lajos utca
Rákóczi Ferenc utca
Petőfi tér
Rohonci út
To Train Station (1km), Szombathely (18km) & Sopron (50km)

0   100   200m
0   100   200yd

PLACES TO STAY
2 Jurisics Castle Hostel
12 Savaria Tourist
15 Kóbor Macskához Pension
19 Aranystrucc Hotel

PLACES TO EAT
4 Bécsikapu
7 Korona Eszpresszó
16 Pizzéria da Rocco
17 Taverna Florian
22 Betérő az Aranykoszorúhoz

OTHER
1 Synagogue Ruins
3 Jurisics Castle
5 Churches of St James & St Henry
6 Pharmacy Museum
8 Tourinform
9 Heroes'Gate
10 Town Hall
11 Városi Museum
13 Post Office
14 Old Tower
18 Church of the Sacred Heart
20 OTP Bank
21 Bus Station

Jurisics tér 11; admission free; open 10am-5pm Tues-Sun), which is now a museum. The square also contains a statue of the Virgin Mary (1739) and the town fountain (1766).

The other main highlight of Kőszeg is the Gothic and baroque **Jurisics Castle** (☎ 360 240; Rajnis utca 9; adult/child 100/60Ft; open 10am-5pm Tues-Sun), dating from 1263 and now a historical museum.

A pleasant way to spend a few hours is walking in the hills west of the town. Of particular interest in this area is the baroque chapel on 393m **Kálváriahegy** (Calvary Hill), the vineyards of **Királyvölgy** (King's Valley) and 458m **Szabóhegy** (Tailor's Hill). A copy of Cartographia's *A Kőszegi-hegység és környéke* (The Kőszeg Hills & Surrounds) 1:40,000 map (No 13; 650Ft) will prove useful when exploring the area.

Places to Stay
Gyöngyvirág Camping (☎ 360 454, fax 364 574; Bajcsy-Zsilinszky utca 6; camp sites per adult/child/tent/car 500/300/300/300Ft, pension rooms from 3500Ft; open year-round), by the little Gyöngyös River, has a basic camping ground and clean, modern rooms.

Jurisics Castle Hostel (☎ 360 113; Rajnis József utca 9; doubles 3000Ft), in a small building near the entrance to the castle, is well worn, but the location makes it attractive.

Savaria Tourist (☎ 563 048; Várkör 69) can arrange private rooms from about 4000Ft a double and pensions from 4000Ft to 8000Ft. Plus every second restaurant seems to have some pension rooms upstairs.

Kóbor Macskához (☎/fax 362 273; Várkör 100; singles/doubles 5000/6300Ft) has nine charming rooms with bath. It is above a sometimes noisy restaurant-cum-pub. **Aranystrucc Hotel** (☎ 360 323, fax 563 330; Várkör 124; singles/doubles 4700/7700Ft), in an 18th-century building overlooking Fő tér, has large rooms with bath and TV, which can also be rather noisy.

Places to Eat
Pizzéria da Rocco (☎ 362 379; Várkör 55; pizzas 400-1500Ft; open 10am-midnight daily), with its huge garden inside the old castle walls, is a great place for pizza or just a drink. For fine dining, head next door to **Taverna Flórián** (☎ 563 072; Várkör 59; pasta around 700Ft, mains around 1500Ft),

HUNGARY

which serves quality Mediterranean food in beautiful cellar-like surroundings.

Bécsikapu (☎ 360 297; Rajnis József utca 5; mains around 800Ft), almost opposite St James Church, is a pleasant place close to the castle. **Betérő az Aranykoszorúhoz** (Temető utca 59; open daily; mains around 800Ft) proves quite a mouthful not only in name (literally 'Visitor at the Sign of the Golden Wreath'), but also with its dishes.

For coffee and cakes you can't beat **Korona Eszpresszó** (Várkör 18; open 8am-6pm daily).

Getting There & Away

Kőszeg is at the end of an 18km railway spur from Szombathely, to which there are 14 to 15 departures a day. To get to/from anywhere else, you must take a bus. At least half a dozen buses a day run to/from Sopron and Szombathely, and there is one daily to Keszthely. Three buses a week (7.05am Wednesday, 8.10am Friday and 4.45am Saturday) head for Oberpullendorf and Vienna in Austria.

SZOMBATHELY
☎ 94 ● pop 85,600

Szombathely (pronounced roughly as **som**-bot-hay) means 'Saturday place' and refers to the important weekend markets held here in the Middle Ages. It's a pretty, relaxed city and, though it's not packed with sights, you might find yourself passing through as it is a transport crossroad.

Orientation & Information

Szombathely is made up of narrow streets and squares with the town centre at leafy Fő tér, one of the largest squares in Hungary. The train station is five blocks east of Mártírok tere at the end of Széll Kálmán út. The bus station is north of the cathedral at Petőfi Sándor utca.

There's a **Tourinform** office (☎ 514 451; [e] szombathely@tourinform.hu; Király utca 11; open 9am-6pm Mon-Fri, 9am-5pm Sat & Sun June–mid-Sept; 9am-5pm Mon-Fri mid-Sept–May), north of Fő tér, which may have moved to the **City Hall** (Kossuth Lajos utca) by the time you read this.

OTP bank has branches at Király utca 10 and on Fő tér.

Things to See

The rebuilt **Szombathely Cathedral** (1797) is on Templom tér. Behind the cathedral is the

Garden of Ruins (☎ 313 369; Templom tér; adult/child 300/150Ft; open 9am-5pm Tues-Sun Mar-Nov), with Roman Savaria relics. On the other side of the cathedral is the baroque **Bishop's Palace** (1783), and beyond this is the **Smidt Museum** (☎ 311 038; Hollán Ernő utca 2; adult/child 300/150Ft; open 10am-5pm Tues-Sun Mar-Dec, 10am-5pm Tues-Fri Jan & Feb), containing a fascinating assortment of things collected by a squirrel physician before his death in 1975.

Szombathely Gallery (☎ 508 800; Rákóczi Ferenc utca 12; adult/child 300/150Ft; open 10am-5pm Tues & Fri-Sun, 10am-7pm Thur) is one of the best modern art galleries in Hungary. The lovely twin-towered Moorish-style building (1881) across the street at No 3, a former synagogue, now houses the **Béla Bartók Concert Hall**.

In **Ják**, a small village 12km south of Szombathely, is the 1214 **Abbey Church** (☎ 356 217; adult/child 200/100Ft; open 8am or 9am-5pm daily), one of the finest examples of Romanesque architecture in Hungary.

Places to Stay & Eat

Tourinform has a list of **student hostels** that are available over summer; beds generally cost between 800Ft and 1400Ft. **Savaria Tourist** (☎ 511 435; Mártírok tere 1) and **Ibusz** (☎ 314 141; Fő tér 44) may have private rooms available (doubles from 3000Ft).

Liget Hotel (☎ 509 323; Szent István park 15; singles/doubles from 5000/6000Ft), west of the centre and accessible on bus No 27 from the train station, is a quiet hotel that's more like a motel.

The faded Art Nouveau splendour of the **Hotel Savaria** (☎ 311 440; Mártírok tere 4; singles/doubles without bath, 4900/6900Ft, singles with bath 7900-12,900Ft doubles with bath 10,900-15,900Ft), well positioned in the very centre of town, is reasonable value.

Surprisingly for a town of this size, there isn't a big selection of eateries. For a cheap meal head to **Mensa** (Mártírok tere 5/b; light meals from 300Ft) near Hotel Savaria, or for something more substantial and upmarket try **Paradicsom** (☎ 342 012; Belső Uránia Udvar; mains 600-1500Ft), an above-average Italian restaurant off Mártírok tere.

Getting There & Away

Bus Up to 16 buses leave every day for Ják (they drop you at the bottom of the hill, a short walk from the church) and there are half-hourly departures to Kőszeg. Other destinations include: Budapest (three departures daily), Győr (six), Keszthely via Hévíz (two), Pécs (three) and Sopron (four). One bus a week departs for Graz in Austria (7am Friday) and three to Vienna (6.40am Wednesday, 7am Friday and 3.55am Saturday).

Train Express trains to Déli and Kelenföld stations in Budapest go via Veszprém and Székesfehérvár. Up to four express trains run to Győr via Celldömölk daily, and up to three to Pécs. Frequent local trains run to Kőszeg and Sopron.

Szombathely is only 13km from the Austrian border, and there are direct trains that travel to/from Graz.

Lake Balaton

Lake Balaton, which is 77km long, is the largest freshwater lake in Europe, outside Scandinavia. The southeastern shore is quite shallow and in summer the warm, sandy beaches are a favourite holiday spot. Better scenery, more historic sites and deeper water are found on the northwestern side. Balaton's very popularity is its main drawback, with the southeastern shore particularly crowded during July and August.

The lake is also a favourite centre for yachting enthusiasts. Other common activities are horse riding, cycling and hiking – *A Balaton* 1:40,000 map (No 41; 550Ft) is handy for this. The thermal baths of Hévíz are also nearby. Many towns and villages on the lake, particularly along its northern shore, are important wine-making centres.

Getting Around

From April to mid-October, Mahart ferries run between Siófok, Balatonfüred and Tihany, as well as Fonyód and the Badacsony area. During the main summer season (between mid-May and early September), ferries ply the entire length of the lake from Balatonkenese to Keszthely and make frequent stops on both shores.

There are also car ferries across the lake between Tihanyi-rév and Szántódi-rév from March to mid-November. It costs 280/230/460/920Ft per person/bicycle/motorcycle/car.

BALATONFÜRED
☎ 87 • pop 13,200

Balatonfüred, a spa town with the easy-going grace that highly commercialised Siófok on the opposite shore totally lacks, has attracted heart patients for centuries because of its curative thermal waters. It has been the most fashionable bathing resort on the lake since the late 18th century, when a medicinal bathing centre

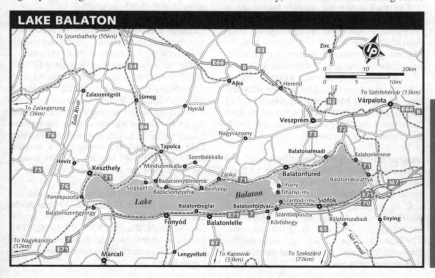

LAKE BALATON

was established here. Unfortunately the mineral baths are now reserved for patients. During the early 19th century it became an important meeting place for many of Hungary's intellectuals, and some parts of town still bear an aristocratic air.

Orientation & Information

The adjacent bus and train stations are on Dobó István utca, 1km northwest of the spa centre and lake. From the stations it's an easy walk to the lakefront, first northeast along Dobó István utca, then southeast along Jókai Mór utca.

Tourinform (e *balatonfured@tourinform .hu*) has two offices in Balatonfüred. One is inconveniently located 1km northwest of the centre (☎ 580 480; *Petőfi Sándor utca 68; open 9am-2pm or 4pm Mon-Fri*) and another annoyingly situated about 1.5km to the southwest (☎ 580 480; *Széchenyi utca 47; open 9am-5pm Mon-Fri, 9am-1pm Sat May-Sept; 9am-3pm Mon-Fri Oct-Apr*).

The **OTP bank** (*Petőfi Sándor utca 8*) and **post office** (*Zsigmond utca 14*) are northwest of the ferry pier.

Things to See

The heart of the old spa town is **Gyógy tér**. In the centre of this leafy square, **Kossuth Spring** (1853) dispenses slightly sulphuric water that you can drink.

The **park** along the nearby lakeshore is worth a promenade. Near the wharf you'll encounter a bust of the Bengali poet Rabindranath Tagore before a lime tree that he planted in 1926 to mark his recovery from illness after treatment in Balatonfüred.

Diagonally opposite the **Round Church** (1846), on the corner of Jókai Mór utca and Honvéd utca, is **Mór Jókai Museum** (☎ 343 426; *adult/child 200/100Ft; open 10am-6pm Tues-Sun May-Oct*), in the acclaimed novelist's former summer house.

Veszprém The picturesque buildings and surrounding area of Veszprém (pop 63,900), 16km north of Balatonfüred, make it a worthwhile day trip from the lake area. You'll be able to get information about attractions at **Tourinform** (☎ 88-404 548; e *veszprem@ tourinform.hu; Vár utca 4*) in the old town. The best way to get here is by bus, as the bus station in Veszprém is central and the train station is 3km from town.

Activities

Balatonfüred has three **public beaches** (*adult/ child 260/160Ft*); the best is Kisfaludy Strand along Aranyhíd sétány northeast of the pier. There are other beaches attached to various places to stay.

In July the Anna Ball is held at the Sanatorium, near Gyógy tér, and it's a prime event on the Hungarian social calendar. Tickets cost from 25,000Ft. Concerts and other events accompany the ball; keep your eyes peeled if you're here in July.

Places to Stay

Camping Massive **Füred Camping** (☎ 580 241; *Széchenyi utca 24; camp sites 2900-4900Ft, adult 600-1300Ft, child 500-1050Ft, 3-4 person bungalows or motel rooms 5460-22,490Ft; open Apr–mid-Oct*) is about 2km southwest of the train station. It has every type of accommodation you need, but is ridiculously expensive during the summer months.

Hostels & Private Rooms The **Lajos Lóczy Gymnasium** (☎ 343 428; *Bartók Béla utca 4; dorm beds 1500Ft*), near the stations, and the far-flung **Ferenc Széchenyi College** (☎ 343 844; *dorm beds 1500Ft*), on Hősök tere, 3km to the northeast of the resort, usually have accommodation in summer.

Balatontourist (☎ 580 031; *Petőfi Sándor utca 2*), near the OTP Bank, has private rooms for €25-30 per double.

Pensions & Hotels Prices for accomodation fluctuate throughout the year and usually peak between early July and late August.

The friendly **Ring Pension** (☎ 342 884; *Petőfi Sándor utca 6a; singles/doubles from 7200/8000Ft*) is so-named because the owner was a champion boxer. Neat, clean rooms with shared bathrooms vary in price, depending on the size of the room and its amenities. Closer to the lake is another excellent choice, **Zöld Tető** (☎ 341 701; *Huray utca 4; singles/ doubles €35.50/45.50*). It's more expensive, but the rooms are a cut above and there's a lovely garden.

One of the nicest places in town, and also reasonably priced, is the central **Hotel Blaha Lujza** (☎ 581 210; *Blaha Lujza utca 4; singles 7300-8200Ft, doubles 9300-12,300Ft*). This hotel was once the holiday home of the much-loved 19th-century Hungarian actress-singer Lujza Blaha.

HUNGARY

With less soul, but right on the water, is the high-rise **Hotel Uni** (☎ 581 360; Széchenyi utca 10; singles 4520-9880Ft, doubles 5610-11,850Ft). Every room in the nearby **Tagore Hotel** (☎ 342 603; Deák Ferenc utca 56; singles €22-35, doubles €29-50) has a balcony, and it's also close to the lake.

Places to Eat
The eastern end of Tagore sétány is a strip of pleasant bars and terraced restaurants, including **Bella** (☎ 481 815; pizzas 600-800Ft), with good pizza and pasta. For cheap eats, head west along the lake and Zákonyi Ferenc utca where you'll come across a plethora of **food stalls**.

Balaton (☎ 481 319; Kisfaludy utca 5; mains 1000-2000Ft), just north of the pier, isn't the cheapest place in town but the selection is wide and so is the shaded terrace. **Halászkert** (☎ 343 039; Zákonyi Ferenc utca 3; mains 800-1000Ft), west of Vitorlás tér and the pier, still serves one of the best 'drunkard's fish soups' (korhely halászlé) in Hungary.

Escape the crowds down by the lake and head to popular **Cafe Bergman** (☎ 341 087; Zsigmond utca 3) near the post office for cake and ice cream.

Getting There & Away
Buses to and from Tihany and Veszprém leave continually throughout the day, and there are also departures for Hévíz (six daily), Győr (seven), Esztergom (one), Sopron (two) and Kecskemét (one).

Balatonfüred is 2½ hours by express train from Déli and Kelenföld stations in Budapest and three hours by local train. The line goes to Tapolca via Badacsony. There are a number of towns on the train line with 'Balaton' or 'Füred' somewhere in the name, so double-check which station you're getting off at.

Mahart ferries travel on the lake from Balatonfüred to Badacsony (900ft), Siófok (760Ft) and Tihany (480Ft).

SIÓFOK
☎ 84 • pop 22,200
Siófok is the largest and busiest settlement on Balaton's southeastern shore. It's a useful transit point, but there's no reason to stay. A strip of pricey high-rise hotels, a half-dozen large camping grounds, holiday cottages, tacky discos and a sleazy nightlife attract big crowds. In midsummer, bedlam reigns; in winter Siófok is all but dead.

Siófok can be convenient, however, if you're just passing through, as the train and bus stations are adjacent in the centre of town on Váradi Adolf tér, just off Fő utca (the main drag), and the Mahart ferry pier is an easy 10-minute walk to the northwest. The **Tourinform** (☎ 315 355; e siofok@tourinform.hu; Szabadság tér) office is in the base of the landmark water tower in the town centre.

TIHANY
☎ 87 • pop 1300
Tihany village sits on a peninsula of the same name, which juts 5km into Lake Balaton, almost linking its northern and southern shores. The whole peninsula is a nature reserve, and many people consider it the most beautiful place on the lake. After visiting the quaint town and famous Abbey Church, you can easily shake the tourist hordes by hiking to the Inner Lake (Belsőtó) or the reedy (and almost dried up) Outer Lake (Külsőtó). Both have abundant birdlife.

Orientation & Information
Tihany village sits on a ridge on the eastern side of the peninsula's high plateau. The Inner Harbour (Belső kikötő), where ferries to/from Balatonfüred and Siófok dock, is below the village. Car ferries to/from Szántódi-rév and passenger ferries to/from Balatonföldvár dock at Tihanyi-rév, the port at the southern end of the peninsula.

For information, there is a **Tourinform** (☎ 448 804; e tihany@tourinform.hu; Kossuth Lajos utca 20; open 9am-8pm Mon-Fri, 9am-6pm Sat & Sun June-Aug; 9am-5pm Mon-Fri, 9am-3pm Sat May & Sept; 9am-3pm Mon-Fri Oct-Apr) office in the centre. The **post office** (Kossuth Lajos utca 37) has an ATM and will exchange money.

Things to See & Do
Tihany's twin-towered **Abbey Church** (☎ 448 405; adult/child 260/130Ft; open 9am-6pm daily May-Sept, 10am-5pm Apr & Oct, 10am-3pm Nov-Mar), dating from 1754, is outstanding for its carved baroque altars, pulpit and organ. The 11th-century **crypt** below the front of the church contains the tomb of the abbey's founder, King Andrew I. The abbey's Deed of Foundation, now in the archives of the Benedictine Abbey at Pannonhalma near Győr, is the earliest document in existence containing Hungarian words.

HUNGARY

The monastery beside the church contains the **Abbey Museum**, with exhibits relating to Lake Balaton and a library of manuscripts. Archaeological finds are in the cellar. The view of Lake Balaton from behind the abbey is superb. The admission fee includes entry to the museum and crypt.

Pisky sétány, a promenade running along the ridge north from the church to Echo Hill, passes a cluster of folk houses, which have now been turned into a small **open-air museum** (☎ 714 960; adult/child 200/100Ft; open 10am-6pm Tues-Sun May-Sept).

From Echo Hill you can descend Garay utca to the inner harbour or continue up to a couple of **hiking trails**. The red-marked trail crosses the peninsula between the two lakes to **Csúcs Hill** (two hours), which offers fine views over the surrounding countryside.

Following the green trail northeast of the church for an hour will bring you to a **Russian Well** (Oroszkút) and the ruins of the **Old Castle** (Óvár), where the Russian Orthodox monks, brought to Tihany by Andrew I, hollowed out cells in the soft basalt walls. Study the map near the front of the Abbey Church before heading off.

Places to Stay & Eat

Tihany Tourist (☎ 448 481; Kossuth Lajos utca 11) has **private rooms** from 4000Ft per double in the low season and 5000Ft in the high season. Many houses along Kossuth Lajos utca and on the little streets north of the Abbey Church have 'Zimmer frei' signs.

The swish, 16-room **Erika** (☎ 448 010; Batthyány utca 6; doubles €60) has rooms with bath and all the mod cons. It also has a small swimming pool.

Club Tihany (☎ 538 500; Rév utca 3; bungalows from €50, singles/doubles from €45/56) is a 13-hectare resort near the car ferry. Bungalows accommodate two to four people, and prices skyrocket during the summer months of July and August.

Rege Café (☎ 448 280; Kossuth Lajos utca 22; mains 1000-2000Ft), in the former monastery stables next to the Abbey Church, is modern and expensive but offers a panoramic view from its terrace. Also good are **Kecskeköröm Csárda** (Kossuth Lajos utca 13; mains around 1200Ft), a few hundred metres northwest of Rege Café on the main road, and **Kakas Csárda** (☎ 448 541; Batthyány utca 1; mains around 1500Ft).

Getting There & Away

Buses cover the 11km from Balatonfüred's train station to and from Tihany about 20 times every day.

Passenger ferries to/from Siófok and Balatonfüred stop in Tihany from late April to late October. Catch them at the pier below the abbey or at Tihanyi-rév. From early March to late November the car ferry crosses the narrow stretch of water between Tihanyi-rév and Szántódi-rév.

BADACSONY
☎ 87 • pop 2600

Four different towns actually make up the Badacsony region, but when Hungarians say Badacsony, they usually mean the little resort at the Badacsony train station, near the ferry pier southwest of Badacsonytomaj. Lying between Balatonfüred and Keszthely, this picturesque region of basalt peaks can claim some of the best hikes in Hungary. Vineyards hug the sides of Badacsony's extinct volcanic cone, and the gentle climate and rich soil make this an ideal wine-making area.

Orientation & Information

Route No 71, the main road along Balaton's northern shore, runs through Badacsony as Balatoni út; this is where the bus lets you off. The ferry pier is on the south side of this road; almost everything else is north. Above the village, several pensions and houses with private rooms ring the base of the hill on Római út. Szegedi Róza utca branches off to the north from Római út through the vineyards to Kisfaludy House and the base of the hill.

Tourinform (☎ 431 046; e badacsony tomaj@tourinform.hu; Park utca 6; open 9am-6pm Mon-Fri, 9am-1pm Sat & Sun June-Aug; 8am-4pm Mon-Fri Sept-May), northwest of the bus stops and pier, is the first port of call for information. From October to April or as late as mid-May almost the whole town shuts up shop.

You can change money at the nearby **post office** (Park utca 3). The ticket clerk at the train station will mind your bags for a fee.

Things to See & Do

The **József Egry Museum** (Egry sétány 12) in town is normally devoted to the Balaton region's leading painter (1883–1951), but it was in meltdown mode at the time of research, and no one is sure when it will reopen.

The slopes and vineyards above the town are sprinkled with little press houses and 'folk-baroque' mansions. One of these is the **Róza Szegedi House** (1790), which belonged to the actress wife of the poet Sándor Kisfaludy of Sümeg. It contains a literature museum.

If you'd like a running start on your hiking, catch one of the topless jeeps marked 'Badacsony hegyi járat'. They depart from diagonally opposite Tourinform from 9am to dusk from May to September whenever at least six paying passengers climb aboard (600/1000Ft one way/return). The jeep will drop you at Kisfaludy House, where a map of the trails is posted by the parking lot. **Kisfaludy Tower**, 1km or so above, offers splendid views.

The tiny **beach** *(adult/child 300/150Ft)* is reedy; you would do better to head a few kilometres east to Badacsonytomaj or Badacsonyörs for a swim.

Places to Stay & Eat

The closest camping ground is **Badacsony Camping** *(☎ 531 041; camp sites per tent 655-990Ft, per adult 655-930Ft, per child 520-700Ft; open May-early Sept)*, at the water's edge, about 1km west of the ferry pier. Price depends on the season.

There are plenty of travel agencies organising **private rooms**, including **Miditourist** *(☎ 431 028; Egry sétány 3)* and **Balatontourist** *(☎ 531 021; Park utca 4)*, both near Tourinform; doubles are around €18 to €25. There are several small **pensions** in town and among the vineyards on Római út.

The best place for a meal or drink is the terrace of **Kisfaludy House** *(☎ 431 016; Szegedi Róza utca 87; mains 1000-2500Ft)*, on the hill overlooking the vineyards and the lake. **Halászkert** *(☎ 431 054; Park utca 5; mains around 1500Ft)* is crowded and touristy, but the fish dishes are excellent.

There are **food stalls** with picnic tables dispensing sausage and fish soup between the train station and Park utca.

Getting There & Away

Three buses a day head for Balatonfüred. Other destinations include: Budapest (once daily), Hévíz (one), Keszthely (one) and Veszprém (one).

Badacsony is on the rail line linking all the towns on Lake Balaton's northern shore with Déli and Kelenföld stations in Budapest and Tapolca. To get to Keszthely you must change

at Tapolca, but there's often an immediate connection.

Ferries to Fonyód are fairly frequent and reasonably regular to Keszthely between late April and late October; in Fonyód you can get a connection to southern Transdanubia by taking a train direct to Kaposvár. Other ferry destinations include Tihany and Balatonfüred.

KESZTHELY

☎ 83 • pop 23,000

Keszthely (pronounced **kest**-hay) is a fairly large old town, which boasts the incredible Festetics Palace, some good facilities and boat services on the lake from June to early September. It's the only town on Lake Balaton that has a life of its own; since it isn't entirely dependent on tourism, it's 'open' all year.

Orientation & Information

The bus and train stations, side by side at the end of Mártírok útja, are fairly close to the ferry pier. There is a **left-luggage office** *(open 24hr)* at the train station. From the stations follow Mártírok útja up the hill, then turn right onto Kossuth Lajos utca into town.

Tourinform *(☎/fax 314 144;* [e] *keszthely@ tourinform.hu; Kossuth Lajos utca 28; open 9am-8pm Mon-Fri, 9am-6pm Sat mid-June–mid-Sept; 9am-5pm Mon-Fri, 9am-1pm Sat mid-Sept–mid-June)* is an excellent source of information on the whole Balaton area.

There's a huge **OTP bank** facing the park south of the Catholic church and close by is the **main post office** *(Kossuth Lajos utca 48)*.

Things to See

Keszthely's most impressive sight is the **Festetics Palace** *(☎ 312 190; Kastély utca 1; adult/student 1500/750Ft; open 9am-6pm daily July-Aug, 9am-5pm Tues-Sun Sept-May)*, the one-time residence of the wealthy Festetics family, which was built in 1745 and extended 150 years later. The palace boasts 100 rooms, but only the **Helikon Palace Museum** and the renowned **Helikon Library**, in the baroque south wing, are open to visitors. One-hour guided tours of the palace will set you back 5000Ft.

In 1797 Count György Festetics, an uncle of the reformer István Széchenyi, founded Europe's first agricultural institute, the Georgikon, here in Keszthely. Part of the original school is now the **Georgikon Farm Museum** *(☎ 311 563; Bercsényi Miklós utca*

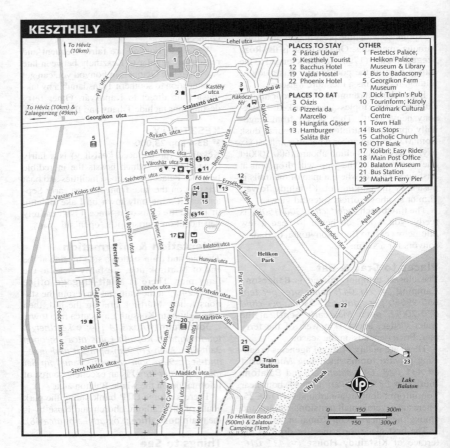

KESZTHELY

PLACES TO STAY	OTHER
2 Párizsi Udvar	1 Festetics Palace;
9 Keszthely Tourist	Helikon Palace
12 Bacchus Hotel	Museum & Library
19 Vajda Hostel	4 Bus to Badacsony
22 Phoenix Hotel	5 Georgikon Farm
	Museum
PLACES TO EAT	7 Dick Turpin's Pub
3 Oázis	10 Tourinform; Károly
6 Pizzeria da	Goldmark Cultural
Marcello	Centre
8 Hungária Gösser	11 Town Hall
13 Hamburger	14 Bus Stops
Saláta Bár	15 Catholic Church
	16 OTP Bank
	17 Kolibri; Easy Rider
	18 Main Post Office
	20 Balaton Museum
	21 Bus Station
	23 Mahart Ferry Pier

67; adult/child 300/150Ft; open 10am-5pm Mon-Sat, 10am-6pm Sun May-Oct).

The **Balaton Museum** (☎ 312 351; *Múzeum utca 2; adult/child 200/150Ft; open 10am-6pm Tues-Sat May-Oct, 10am-5pm Nov-Apr)* has exhibits on the history of navigation on the lake and photographs of summer frolickers at the lake early in the 20th century.

Places to Stay

Zalatour Camping (☎/fax 312 782; *Ernszt Géza sétány; camp sites per tent 650-790Ft, per adult 650-790Ft, per child 270-300Ft; bungalows 3000-4200Ft, apartments 7900-9300Ft)*, about 1km south of town, is a big place with large bungalows for four people and smaller but better equipped apartments. There are also tennis courts, and the site has

access to Helikon Beach. Prices depend on the season.

Vajda Hostel (☎ 311 361; *Gagarin utca 4; dorm beds 1000-1200Ft; open mid-June–late Aug)* is what János Vajda College becomes over the summer break.

Private rooms are available from **Keszthely Tourist** (☎ 312 031; *Kossuth utca 25; doubles around 4000Ft)*. If the agencies are closed, a good place to look for a room is Móra Ferenc utca, to the east of the town centre near the lake. Look out for the usual '*szoba kiadó*' or '*Zimmer frei*' signs.

In the off season it's worth checking for specials at the upmarket hotels along the lakefront. **Phoenix Hotel** (☎ 312 631; *Balatonpart 5; singles €20-24, doubles €25-40)* is a two-star place with low off-season rates.

Párizsi Udvar (☎/fax 311 202; Kastély utca 5; rooms from 6900Ft) pension is a good choice near the Festetics Palace. Its 14 rooms were originally part of the palace complex.

Bacchus Hotel (☎/fax 314 097; W www .bacchushotel.hu; Erzsébet királyné utca 18; singles €28-41, doubles €36-54) has 26 lovely rooms and houses a wine museum where you can have tastings. Prices for rooms vary depending on the season.

Places to Eat
Burgers, salads and outdoor seating are available at the **Hamburger Saláta Bár** (Erzsébet királyné utca; burgers from 300Ft). **Pizzeria da Marcello** (☎ 313 563; Városház utca 4; pizzas from 650Ft), in a cellar with rustic furniture, has made-to-order pizzas and salads.

Oázis (☎ 311 023; Rákóczi tér 3; open 11am-4pm Mon-Fri; mains 650-950Ft), incredibly for this carnivorous country, serves only vegetarian dishes. A real oasis.

Hungária Gösser (☎ 312 265; Kossuth Lajos utca 35; mains from 800Ft) is a pub-restaurant in a lovely historical building with stained-glass windows. It has German and Hungarian dishes and a salad bar.

Entertainment
On Sunday at 8.30pm between July and mid-August, there's Hungarian folk dancing in the courtyard of the **Károly Goldmark Cultural Centre** (☎ 314 286; Kossuth Lajos utca 28).

There are several interesting places for a drink along Kossuth Lajos utca. **Easy Rider** at No 79 attracts the local young bloods, while **Kolibri** cocktail bar at No 81 is for an older crowd. **Dick Turpin's Pub** (Városház utca 2) plays the best music and is more central.

Getting There & Away
There are about 10 daily buses to Hévíz and Veszprém, one to Szombathely and two to Siófok. Other towns served by buses include Badacsony (three daily), Budapest (six), Győr (two), Pécs (three) and Sopron (three).

Some of these buses – including those to Hévíz – can be boarded at the bus stops in front of the Catholic church on Fő tér. For buses to the lake's northern shore you can catch the bus along Tapolcai út.

Keszthely is on a branch rail line linking Tapolca and Balatonszentgyörgy, from where up to 17 daily trains continue along the southern shore to Siófok and Budapest. To reach Szombathely or towns along Lake Balaton's northern shore by train, change at Tapolca.

Mahart ferries link Keszthely with most places on the lake from late May to early September.

HÉVÍZ
☎ 83 • pop 4400
Hévíz, 7km northwest of Keszthely, is the site of Europe's largest thermal lake, Gyógytó. The people of this town have made use of the warm mineral water for centuries, first as a tannery in the Middle Ages and later for curative purposes (it was developed as a private resort in 1795).

The bus station is on Somogyi Béla utca, opposite the northern entrance to the thermal lake. For information head to the travel agency **Hévíz Tourist** (☎ 341 348; Rákóczi utca 2; open 8.30am-5.30pm Mon-Fri, 9am-1pm Sat). The town has an **OTP bank** (Erzsébet királynő utca 7) in the centre of town, and a **post office** (Kossuth Lajos utca 4) northwest of the lake.

Thermal Lake
The Gyógytó (admission 3 hours/whole day 600/1200Ft; open 8.30am-5.30pm daily in summer, 9am-4.30pm in winter) is an astonishing sight: a milky blue-green surface of about five hectares, covered for most of the year in water lilies. The spring is a crater some 40m deep that disgorges up to 80 million litres of warm water a day, renewing the lake every two days or so. The surface temperature here averages 33°C and never drops below 26°C, allowing bathing throughout the year. The water and the mud on the bottom are slightly radioactive and are said to alleviate various medical conditions. A covered bridge leads to the pavilion, from where catwalks and piers fan out. Hold onto your ticket for the lake as you will have to show it to get out. There is an **indoor spa** (adult/child 490/270Ft; open 7am-4pm daily year-round) not far from the lake to the northwest.

Places to Stay & Eat
During the summer period, accommodation may prove a problem and it is generally more expensive.

Castrum Camping (☎ 343 198; Tó-part; camp site per tent 580-860Ft, per adult 720-1150Ft, per child 430-720Ft; pension singles 5800-10,100Ft, doubles 7200-11,500Ft) is close to the lake's southern end and is the most central of Hévíz's several camping grounds.

Hévíz Tourist can find you a **private room** for around €20 to €25 a double. You'll see *'Zimmer frei'* and *'szoba kiadó'* signs on Kossuth Lajos utca and Zrínyi utca, to the west of the lake.

One kilometre northwest of the lake is **Pannon Hotel** (☎ *340 482; Széchenyi utca 23; singles €29, doubles €40-54*), with colourful rooms and a pleasant garden. Across the road is another good option, **Hotel Napfény** (☎ *340 642; Széchenyi utca 21; singles 4200-5600Ft, doubles 7100-9900Ft)*. The high-rise **Hotel Panoráma** (☎ *341 074; Petőfi Sándor utca 9; singles €29-39, doubles €38-46)* is closer to the lake but less personal.

The best places for a quick bite are the **food stalls** selling *lángos* (dough snack), sausages and other fast-food treats at the bottom of Rákóczi utca.

For a proper meal, try **Liget** (*Dr Moll Károly tér; pizzas and mains around 1000-1200Ft*) in the centre of town; or **Piroska** (☎ *343 942; Kossuth Lajos utca 10; mains 700-1400Ft*), a quiet spot west of the lake with a shady terrace. For cake and ice cream the **Astoria** (*Rákóczi utca 13; ice cream 80Ft*) is popular, with a terrace for watching the passing parade.

Getting There & Away

Hévíz doesn't have a train station, but a bus goes to Keszthely almost every half-hour from stand No 3 in the bus station. There are frequent departures to towns such as Badacsony (eight daily), Balatonfüred (seven) and Veszprém (eight). Other destinations include Budapest (five), Győr (three), Pécs (two), Sopron (two) and Szombathely (three).

Southern Transdanubia

Southern Transdanubia is bordered by the Danube River to the east, the Dráva River, Croatia and Slovenia to the south and west, and Lake Balaton to the north. It's generally flatter than Western Transdanubia, with the Mecsek and Villány Hills rising in isolation from the plain.

Near Mohács on the Danube in 1526, the Hungarian army under young King Lajos II was routed by a vastly superior Ottoman force. The gracious city of Pécs still bears the imprint of Turkish rule.

PÉCS
☎ 72 ● pop 166,500

Pécs (pronounced **paich**) was an important historical city early – for 400 years the settlement was the capital of the Roman province of Lower Pannonia. Christianity flourished here in the 4th century and by the 9th century the town was known as Quinque Ecclesiae for its five churches (it's still called Fünfkirchen in German). In 1009 Stephen I made Pécs a bishopric. The first Hungarian university was founded here in the mid-14th century.

City walls were erected after the Mongol invasion of 1241, but 1543 marked the start of almost a century and a half of Turkish domination. The Turks left their greatest monuments at Pécs and these, together with imposing churches and a lovely synagogue, over a dozen museums, possibilities for hiking through the Mecsek Hills and a lively student atmosphere, make Pécs the perfect place to spend a couple of days.

Orientation

The bus and train stations are three blocks apart on the southern side of the centre of town. Find your way north to Széchenyi tér, the centre of the old town where a dozen streets meet.

The **left-luggage office** at the main train station is in a separate building, to the west of the station. It's open 4am to midnight, while the one at the bus station is open 6am to 6pm.

Information

For information about attractions **Tourinform** (☎ *213 315;* e *baranya-m@tourinform.hu; Széchenyi tér 9; open 9am-7pm Mon-Fri, 9am-6pm Sat & Sun mid-June–mid-Sept; 8am-4pm Mon-Fri, 9am-2pm Sat mid-Sept–mid-June)* has copious amounts on Pécs and Baranya County. Unless otherwise indicated, museums and other sites are open 10am to 6pm Tuesday to Saturday and 10am to 4pm Sunday from April to October and 10am to 4pm the rest of the year. They generally cost 200Ft to 400Ft for adults and 100Ft to 200Ft for children.

There are plenty of ATMs scattered around town. The main **OTP bank** (*Rákóczi út*) has a currency-exchange machine and there's a branch on Király utca. The **M&M Exchange**

HUNGARY

(Király utca 16; open 8.30am-5pm Mon-Fri, 8.30am-1pm Sat) offers decent rates.

The **main post office** *(Jókai Mór utca 10)* is in a beautiful Art Nouveau building (1904). **Mac Café**, inside the Dante Café (see Entertainment later), charges 500Ft for Internet connection.

Things to See

Széchenyi tér is the bustling heart of Pécs, dominated to the north by the former Gazi Kassim Pasha Mosque, the largest Turkish building in Hungary. Today it's the Inner Town Parish Church and more commonly known as the **Mosque Church** *(☎ 321 976; open 10am-4pm Mon-Sat, 11.30am-4pm Sun mid-Apr–mid-Oct; 10am-noon Mon-Sat, 11.30am-2pm Sun mid-Oct–mid-Apr)*. Islamic elements inside, such as the mihrab (prayer niche) on the southeastern side, are easy to spot. Behind the Mosque Church is the **Archaeology Museum** *(☎ 312 719; Széchenyi tér 12; open 10am-4pm Tues-Sun Apr-Oct, 10am-2pm Nov-Mar)*. Southwest of Széchenyi tér is another important Turkish building, the 16th-century **Hassan Jakovali Mosque** *(Rákóczi út 2)*. It comes complete with minaret and a small museum of Ottoman history.

From the Hassan Mosque head northeast to Szent István tér where you'll find an excavated 4th-century **Christian tomb** *(☎ 312 7190)*, with striking frescoes of Adam and Eve, and Daniel in the lion's den. The **Roman mausoleum** *(Apáca utca 14)* a little farther south, and the **Jug mausoleum** *(Dom tér)* to the north, are other fine examples of underground tombs – all three have been declared World Heritage Sites by Unesco.

A stone's throw east of the Christian tomb is the **Csontváry Museum** *(☎ 310 544; Janus Pannonius utca 11)*, displaying the work of the incomparable painter Tivadar Kosztka Csontváry (1853–1919).

Dóm tér is dominated by the huge four-towered **Basilica of St Peter**. The oldest part of is the 11th-century crypt, but the whole complex was rebuilt in a neo-Romanesque style in 1881. The **Bishop's Palace** (1770) is in front of the cathedral, and west is a 15th-century **barbican**, the only stone bastion to survive from the old city walls.

Káptalan utca, which climbs northeast from here, is lined with museums. Behind the **Endre Nemes Museum** *(☎ 310 172; open 10am-2pm Tues-Sun)* at No 5 is the Erzsébet Schaár Utca or 'Street', a complete artistic environment in which the sculptor has set her whole life in stone. The **Vasarely Museum** *(☎ 324 822)* at No 3 houses the op art of Victor Vasarely, who was born here in 1908. The cellar labyrinth of the Vasarely Museum hosts the **Mecsek Mine Museum**. Across the street at No 2 is the **Zsolnay Porcelain Museum**, which has examples of famous porcelain from the factory's early days in the mid-19th century to the present.

Attractions in the eastern part of the city include the neo-rococo **National Theatre** and **Church of St Stephen** (1741), both on Király utca. If you turn right from Király utca into Felsőmalom utca, you'll find an excellent **City History Museum** *(☎ 310 165; open 10am-4pm Tues-Sat)* at No 9.

Pécs' beautifully preserved 1869 **synagogue** *(☎ 315 881; Kossuth tér; adult/child 150/50Ft; open 9am-5pm Sun-Thur, 9am-4pm Fri May-Oct)* is south of Széchenyi tér.

Mecsek Hills Bus No 35 from in front of the train station (or from Aradi vértanúk útja) climbs hourly to the 194m **TV Tower** *(adult/child 280/180Ft; open 9am-9pm Sun-Thur, 9am-11pm Fri & Sat June-Aug, 9am-7pm rest of year)* on Misina Peak (534m) in the Mecsek Hills.

Well-marked hiking trails fan out from the TV Tower – the 1:40,000 *A Mecsek* topographical map (No 15; 650Ft) shows them all. Armed with this map, you could also take a bus from the bus station to **Orfű** (with an attractive lake) or **Abaliget** (with a 450m-long cave) and hike back over the hills. Much of this area has been logged, but doesn't attract many visitors, so it is quite peaceful.

Places to Stay

Camping Up in the Mecsek Hills, **Mandulás Camping** *(☎ 315 981; Ángyán János utca 2; bus No 34; tent sites 600Ft, motel doubles 3500Ft, bungalows per person 1600Ft, hotel doubles with bath 6000Ft; open mid-Apr–mid-Oct)* has a good selection of accommodation options.

Hostels & Private Rooms During July and August, central **Mátyás Kollégium** *(☎ 315 846; Széchenyi tér 11; dorm beds around 1200Ft)* and **János Kollégium** *(☎ 251 234; Szántó Kovács János utca 1/c; dorm beds around 1000Ft)*, both west of the town centre,

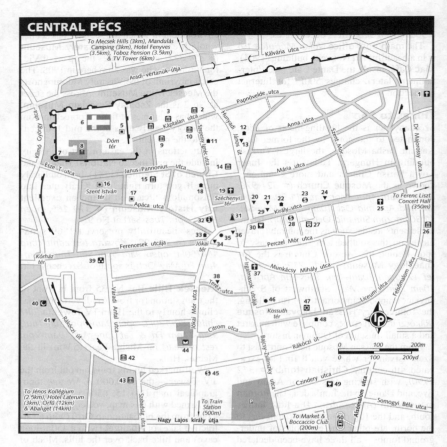

CENTRAL PÉCS

accommodate travellers in dormitory rooms with two to five beds. Ask Tourinform about other college dorms.

Ibusz (☎ 212 157; Apáca utca 1) arranges **private rooms** from 2000Ft per person and apartments for a little bit more.

Pensions & Hotels The **Centrum** (☎/fax 311 707; Szepessy Ignác utca 4; singles/doubles 4500/5600Ft) has seven rooms that aren't particularly modern, but it's a friendly place and very central.

Another central place to try is **Főnix Hotel** (☎ 311 682, fax 324 113; Hunyadi János út 2; singles/doubles 4790/7290Ft), with 15 accommodating rooms. South of the synagogue is the friendly **Diana** (☎ 328 594, fax 333 373; Tímár 4a; dorm beds 2000Ft,

singles/doubles 5600/8600Ft), with eight excellent hotel-style rooms and dorm rooms that sleep up to four.

The big 1960s-style **Hotel Laterum** (☎ 252 108, fax 252 131; bus No 4; Hajnóczy utca 37-39; dorm beds 2000-2500Ft, doubles 5500-8000Ft) is on the far western side of town. Dorm-bed rates depend on the season and doubles on the amenities.

The landmark **Hotel Palatinus** (☎ 514 260, fax 514 738; Király utca 5; singles/doubles from €51/58) is an opulent old place, but it's overpriced considering the rooms aren't nearly as grand as the impressive foyer.

Up in the Mecsek Hills, the lovely **Toboz Pension** (☎ 510 555, fax 510 556; Fenyves sor 5; singles/doubles 7600/10,200Ft) has a retreat feel to it and good rooms. The nearby

CENTRAL PÉCS

PLACES TO STAY
11 Centrum
12 Főnix Hotel
18 Mátyás
    Kollégium
22 Hotel Palatinus
33 Ibusz
48 Diana

PLACES TO EAT
13 Cellárium
20 Mecsek Cukrászda
21 Dóm Vendéglö
24 Oazis
29 Dóm Snack
34 Az Elefánthoz;
    Morik Caffè
36 Virág
38 Tex-Mex Café
41 Nonstop Grocery
    Store

OTHER
1   St Augustine Church
2   Zsolnay Porcelain Museum
3   Modern Hungarian Art
    Gallery I
4   Ferenc Martyn Museum
5   Jug Mausoleum
6   Basilica of St Peter
7   Barbican
8   Bishop's Palace
9   Endre Nemes Museum
10 Vasarely Museum &
    Mecsek Mine Museum
14 Archaeology Museum
15 Csontváry Museum;
    Dante Café; Mac Café
16 Christian Tomb
17 Roman Mausoleum
19 Mosque Church
23 OTP Bank
25 Church of St Stephen

26 City History Museum
27 National Theatre
28 M&M Exchange
30 Murphy's Pub
31 Trinity Column
32 Tourinform
35 Artists' House; Corvina
    Art Bookshop
37 Church of the Good
    Samaritan
39 Pasha Memi Bath Ruins
40 Hassan Jakovali Mosque
42 Ethnology Museum
43 Modern Hungarian Art
    Gallery II
44 Main Post Office
45 Main OTP Bank
46 Town Hall
47 Synagogue
49 Soul 6
50 Bus Station

Hotel Fenyves (π/fax 315 996; Szőlő utca 64; singles/doubles from 6800/9800Ft) has fading rooms, compensated by great views of the city and terraces. Take bus No 34 or 35 from the train station for both places.

Places to Eat
Király utca is lined with eateries. **Dóm Snack** (Király utca 3; dishes around 700Ft) has pizza and pasta. Down the alleyway next door, **Dóm Vendéglö** (π 210 088; mains 800-1600Ft) is the place to splurge on fine food and ornate surrounds. Further east at No 17 is **Oázis** (kebabs & dishes 500-800Ft), a small takeaway spot (it also has pavement seating) serving Middle Eastern dishes at the right price.

Housed in an attractive cellar is **Tex-Mex Café** (π 215 427; Teréz utca 10; mains 900-1500Ft), with tasty enchiladas and fajitas, and tequila to wash it down.

Az Elefánthoz (π 215 026; Jókai tér 6; mains around 1000Ft) is a bustling Italian restaurant with excellent pizza, pasta and meal-sized salads. Occupying the same building and sharing a terrace is the **Morik Caffè** (π 215 026), a great place to people-watch. Behind the Főnix Hotel, the underground **Cellárium** (π 314 453; Hunyadi János út 2; mains 800-1200Ft) is a reliable choice.

For coffee and cake, try **Mecsek Cukrászda** (π 315 444; Széchenyi tér 16) near to the Mosque Church or **Virág** (π 313 793; Irgalmasok utcája) not far south.

There are several **nonstop grocery stores**, including one at Rákóczi út 8.

Entertainment
The biweekly freebie *Pécsi Est* will tell you what's on in Pécs and surrounding towns. Pécs has well-established opera and ballet companies. If tickets to the **National Theatre** (π 310 539; Király utca) are sold out, try for a cancellation an hour before the performance.

The **Artists' House** (π 315 388; Széchenyi tér 7-8) advertises its many programmes outside. This is the place to ask about classical music concerts. Another venue is the **Ferenc Liszt Concert Hall** (π 311 557; Király utca 83), east of the centre.

There are pubs and bars along Király utca, many with outside tables in summer. **Murphy's Pub** (Király utca 2) is a poor attempt at an Irish pub, but it attracts the crowds. **Dante Café** (Janus Pannonius 11), occupying the ground floor of the Csontváry Museum, is a good place to meet local students, and has a huge garden and occasional live music. Clubs worth checking include **Boccaccio** (Bajcsy-Zsilinszky utca 45), a large place with three dance floors; and **Soul 6** (Czindery utca 6), a small but popular venue.

Getting There & Away
There are hourly buses in summer to Abaliget and Orfű in the Mecsek Hills, but only seven to 10 a day during winter. Other destinations

include Hévíz (two daily), Keszthely (three), Kecskemét (two), Siklós (12 or more), Siófok (four), Sopron (one) and Szeged (seven). Buses run three to four times every day from Barcs on the border to Zagreb in Croatia. There are also three buses dailyy (at 11.50am, 4.30pm and 4.45pm) from Pécs to Osijek, which is in Croatia.

Up to 13 trains a day connect Pécs with Budapest. You can reach Nagykanizsa and other points northwest via a rather circuitous but scenic line along the Dráva River. From Nagykanizsa, up to eight trains a day continue on to Szombathely. One early morning express (at 5.35am) follows this route from Pécs all the way to Szombathely. Two daily trains run from Pécs (10.50am and 1pm) to Osijek.

HARKÁNY
☎ 72 • pop 3500

The hot springs at Harkány, 26km south of Pécs, have medicinal waters with the richest sulphuric content in Hungary. There are large outdoor thermal pools open in summer and indoor baths open year-round.

For information on the town and the area go to **Tourinform** (☎ 479 624; e harkany@ tourinform.hu; Kossuth Lagos utca 2/a; open 9am-6pm Mon-Fri, 10am-6pm Sat & Sun mid-June– mid-Sept; 9am-4pm Mon-Fri mid-Sept–mid-June). **K&H Bank** has an exchange office at the entrance to the spa.

There's not much to see in town, but **Siklós**, 6km east of Harkány, is surrounded by the wine-producing Villány Hills. On a hill top stands a well-preserved 15th-century castle, now the **Castle Museum** (adult/child 450/250Ft; open 9am-4pm or 6pm Tues-Sun), with a Gothic chapel and a dungeon.

Places to Stay & Eat
Thermál Camping (☎ 480 117; Bajcsy-Zsilinszky utca 6; camp sites per tent/person 700/700Ft, 4-person bungalows 8000Ft, motel rooms 3500Ft, hotel rooms 5000Ft; open mid-Mar–mid-Oct) occupies a leafy space just north of the baths.

Tourinform has a comprehensive list of **private rooms** (from 3000Ft), but doesn't make bookings. If the office is shut, Bartók Béla utca has a proliferation of 'Zimmer frei' signs.

There's a bunch of hotels along Bajcsy-Zsilinszky utca opposite the baths entrance. The **Baranya Hotel** (☎/fax 480 160; singles/doubles €18/36) is typical.

You're not going to starve in this town of sausage stands and wine counters, but if you want to sit down, go to **Robinson** (Kossuth Lajos utca 7; mains 1000-1500Ft). For something cheaper, try **Éden** (Kossuth Lajos utca 7; pizzas 750-1000Ft) just across the road.

Getting There & Away
All buses between Pécs and Siklós stop in Harkány. Harkány is a transit point for people travelling between Croatia and Yugoslavia. Three buses a day link Harkány with Croatia: two go to Osijek (at 12.30pm and 5.30pm) and one to Našice (10am weekdays).

The Great Plain

The Great Plain (Nagyalföld) of southeastern Hungary is a wide expanse of level *puszta* (prairie) drained by the Tisza River. For many centuries it has appeared in poems, songs, paintings and stories. Parts of the plain have been turned into farmland, but other regions are little more than grassy, saline deserts.

Visitors to the region are introduced to the lore of the Hungarian horse, cow and shepherds and their unique animals: Nonius horses, long-horned grey cattle and *racka* sheep. Two national parks protect the unique environment: Kiskunság in the Bugac Puszta and Hortobágy in the Hortobágy Puszta, which was listed as a World Heritage Site by Unesco in 1999.

KECSKEMÉT
☎ 76 • pop 108,500

Lying exactly halfway between Budapest and Szeged and near the geographical centre of Hungary, Kecskemét is a clean, leafy city famous for its apricots, potent *barack pálinka* (apricot brandy), fine architecture and level puszta. A vast quantity of average-quality wine is also produced here.

Orientation & Information
Kecskemét is a city of squares running into one another. The main bus and train stations are opposite each other in József Katona Park. A 10-minute walk southwest along Nagykőrösi utca will bring you to the first of the squares, Szabadság tér. The train station has a **left-luggage office** (open 7am-7pm).

Tourinform (☎ 481 065; e kecskemet@ tourinform.hu; Kossuth tér 1; open 8am-8pm Mon-Fri, 9am-1pm Sat & Sun July-Aug;

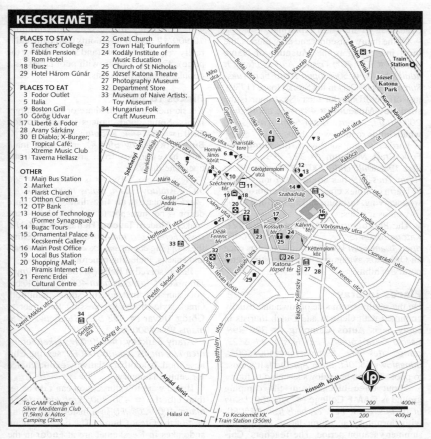

KECSKEMÉT

PLACES TO STAY
6   Teachers' College
7   Fábián Pension
8   Rom Hotel
18 Ibusz
29 Hotel Három Gúnár

PLACES TO EAT
3   Fodor Outlet
5   Italia
9   Boston Grill
10 Görög Udvar
17 Liberté & Fodor
28 Arany Sárkány
30 El Diablo; X-Burger;
    Tropical Café;
    Xtreme Music Club
31 Taverna Hellasz

OTHER
1   Main Bus Station
2   Market
4   Piarist Church
11 Otthon Cinema
12 OTP Bank
13 House of Technology
    (Former Synagogue)
14 Bugac Tours
15 Ornamental Palace &
    Kecskemét Gallery
16 Main Post Office
19 Local Bus Station
20 Shopping Mall;
    Piramis Internet Café
21 Ferenc Erdei
    Cultural Centre

22 Great Church
23 Town Hall; Tourinform
24 Kodály Institute of
    Music Education
25 Church of St Nicholas
26 József Katona Theatre
27 Photography Museum
32 Department Store
33 Museum of Naive Artists;
    Toy Museum
34 Hungarian Folk
    Craft Museum

8am-5pm Mon-Fri, 9am-1pm Sat May, June & Sept; 8am-5pm Mon-Fri Oct-Apr) is on the northeastern corner of the Town Hall.

The **OTP bank** (Szabadság tér 1/a), on the corner of Arany János utca, does foreign exchanges. There are plenty of ATMs around town. The **main post office** (Kálvin tér 10) is to the southeast. **Piramis Internet Café** (Csányi utca 1-3; open 10am-8pm Mon-Fri, noon-8pm Sat & Sun) is upstairs in the small shopping mall at the western end of Szabadság tér. Surfing costs 480Ft per hour.

Things to See
Kossuth tér is surrounded by historic buildings. Dominating the square is the massive Art Nouveau **Town Hall** (1897), which is flanked by the **Great Church** (1806) and the

earlier **Church of St Nicholas**, dating (in parts) from the 13th century. Nearby is the magnificent 1896 **József Katona Theatre** (Katona József tér) with a baroque statue of the Trinity (1742) in front of it.

Facing Szabadság tér, the Art Nouveau **Ornamental Palace** (1902) is covered in multicoloured majolica tiles. It houses the **Kecskemét Gallery** (☎ 480 776; Rákóczi út 1; adult/child 260/130Ft; open 10am-5pm Tues-Sat, 1.30pm-5pm Sun), but more impressive than the art is the building's aptly named **Decorative Hall**, with its amazing stucco peacock, bizarre windows and tiles.

A few doors up, the imposing Moorish-style **House of Technology** (☎ 487 611; Rákóczi út 2; open 10am-6pm Mon-Fri) was once a synagogue and now holds exhibitions. The little

HUNGARY

streets (some paved with brick) northwest of Szabadság tér are worth exploring.

Of the many museums and art galleries, the most interesting is the **Museum of Naive Artists** (☎ 324 767; Gáspár András utca 11; adult/child 150/50Ft; open 10am-5pm Tues-Sun mid-Mar–Oct) in the Stork House (1730), just off Petőfi Sándor utca. Next door is the small **Toy Museum** (☎ 481 469; adult/child 200/100Ft; open 10am-5pm Tues-Sun), which holds regular workshops.

Farther to the southwest, the **Hungarian Folk Craft Museum** (☎ 327 203; Serfőző utca 19a; adult/child 200/100Ft; open 10am -5pm Tues-Sat) has around 10 rooms of an old farm complex crammed with embroidery, woodcarving, furniture and agricultural tools, as well as textiles.

The **Photography Museum** (☎ 483 221; Katona József tér 12; adult/child 150/100Ft; open 10am-5pm Wed-Sun) in what was once an Orthodox synagogue has interesting temporary exhibits.

Places to Stay

On the southwestern side of town and usually crammed with German and Dutch tourists in caravans is **Autós Camping** (☎ 329 398; Csabai Géza körút 5; bus Nos 1, 11 & 22; camp sites per tent/person 500/600Ft, bungalows 5500Ft; open Apr-Oct). It's close to pools and the bungalows sleep up to four.

About three blocks from the camping ground is **GAMF College** (☎ 510 300; Izsáki út 10; bus Nos 1, 11 & 22; beds from 1250Ft), with dormitory accommodation during the summer vacation period. The **Teachers' College** (☎ 486 977; Piaristák tere 4; beds 1600Ft) is more central. Both colleges are open mid-June to August, but you can sometimes get a bed at other times. Tourinform has a list of other colleges.

Ibusz (☎ 486 955; Kossuth tér 3) has private rooms from 1500Ft to 2500Ft per person.

Fábián Pension (☎ 477 677, fax 477 175; Kápolna utca 14; singles/doubles 5500/7500Ft) is a fab place – all 10 rooms are modern, clean and have a bath and the friendly staff speak a multitude of languages.

Rom Hotel (☎ 483 174; Széchenyi tér 14; rooms 5000Ft, apartment 10,000Ft) is above a solarium in a small shopping plaza, across from the local bus station. The apartment, which sleeps four and has a small kitchen, is great value.

The charming **Hotel Három Gúnár** (☎ 483 611; Batthyány utca 1-7; singles/doubles 10,900/12,000Ft) has rooms with bath and is really very comfortable (and should be for the price). The hotel's bar, with pool tables, is a popular place with guests.

Places to Eat

Kecskemét has its fair share of cheap burger joints. Some good choices include **Boston Grill** (☎ 484 444; Kápolna utca 2) and **X-Burger** (Kisfaludy utca 4), in a small mall. Both have burgers from around 250Ft and open late daily.

Next door to X-Burger is **El Diablo** (☎ 500 922; Kisfaludy utca 4; mains 1000-2000Ft), a Mexican place with fine dishes and bizarre decor – be sure not to step on the plastic snakes. Modern **Taverna Hellasz** (☎ 417 213; Deák Ferenc tér; mains from 750Ft), behind the shopping centre, has excellent Greek meals and snacks, including generous gyros.

Pizzas served at **Italia** (☎ 484 627; Hornyik János körút 4; pizzas from 400Ft) are OK but you can opt instead for some mammoth Greek-style dishes by crossing the street to **Görög Udvar** (☎ 492 513; Széchenyi tér 9; mains 950-1500Ft).

Arany Sárkány (☎ 320 037; Erkel Ferenc utca 1/a; mains around 1000Ft), serving Chinese food, is another relatively exotic choice for central Hungary.

If you want to splurge, you can't do better than **Liberté** (☎ 480 350; Szabadság tér 2; mains 1000-2000Ft) in a historical building east of the Great Church. The best ice cream and cakes in Kecskemét are at **Fodor** in the same building as Liberté. Fodor has another outlet at Nagykőrösi utca 15.

Entertainment

The **Ferenc Erdei Cultural Centre** (☎ 484 594; Deák Ferenc tér 1) sponsors some events and is a good source of information. The 19th-century **József Katona Theatre** (☎ 483 283; Katona József tér) stages dramatic works as well as operettas and concerts by the Kecskemét Symphony Orchestra.

A chilled-out place for a drink in the evenings is the **Tropical Café** (Kisfaludy utca 4); once you're ready to go clubbing, head next door to the **Xtreme Music Club** or the to the student-friendly **Silver Mediterrán Club** (Izsáki út 2) near GAMF College (see Places to Stay).

Getting There & Away

There are buses almost hourly to Budapest, every couple of hours to Szeged and at least two a day to Pécs and Eger.

Kecskemét is on the rail line that links Budapest's Nyugati station with Szeged. To get to Debrecen and other cities and towns east, you must change at Cegléd.

KISKUNSÁG NATIONAL PARK

Totalling 76,000 hectares, Kiskunság consists of half a dozen 'islands' of land. Much of the park's alkaline ponds, dunes and grassy 'deserts' are off limits to casual visitors, but you can get a close look at this environmentally fragile area – and see the famous horse herds go through their paces – at **Bugac**, 30km southwest of Kecskemét.

Bugac Tours (☎ 482 500; Szabadság tér 5; open 8am-4.30pm Mon-Fri) in Kecskemét is the place to go for bus timetables, tour prices and general information. It also has an office at the park entrance.

The main attraction at the park is the **horse show** (adult/child 1100/550Ft, with horse-drawn carriage tour 2200/1100Ft; 3.15pm daily June-Aug, 1.15pm daily May & Sept). The horse herders crack their whips, race one another bareback and ride 'five-in-hand', a breathtaking performance in which one csikós (cowboy) gallops five horses at full speed while standing on the backs of the rear two. The show takes place 3km from the park entrance; you can either walk or catch a ride with the horse-drawn carriage.

Bugaci Karikás Csárda (☎ 482 500; mains from 1000Ft), with its folk-music ensemble and goulash, is a lot more fun than it might appear. It has horse riding (2000Ft per hour), a **camping ground** (camp sites per person 500Ft) and also rustic **cottages** (per double 8000Ft) nearby.

The best way to get there on your own is by bus from Kecskemét. The 11am bus from the main terminal gets you to the park entrance around noon. After the show, the first bus back to Kecskemét passes by the park entrance at 4pm on weekdays, and 6.35pm on weekends (a change at Jakabszállás is required). More convenient on weekends is the narrow-gauge train; it leaves from Bugac felső station, 15 minutes' walk south of the park entrance, at 6.20pm and will get you to Kecskemét KK train station (south of the town centre) around 7.45pm.

SZEGED

☎ 62 • pop 175,500

Szeged (Segedin in German), the most important city on the southern Great Plain, straddles the Tisza River just before it enters Yugoslavia. The Maros River from Romania enters the Tisza just east of the centre.

But all this water has been known to prove hazardous. Disaster struck in 1879 when the Tisza swelled its banks and almost washed the city off the map. Szeged was redesigned with concentric boulevards and radial avenues. Flooding can still be a problem; in April 2000 the river burst its banks again, causing most damage in New Szeged.

Szeged is more architecturally homogeneous than many other cities, with few modern buildings intruding on the stately city centre. It's large and lively with lots of students, and produces paprika and Pick, which is Hungary's finest salami.

Orientation & Information

The main **train station** (Indóház tér) is south of the city centre; tram No 1 will take you to the centre of town. The **bus station** (Mars tér) is to the west of the centre and is within easy walking distance via pedestrian Mikszáth Kálmán utca. There is a **left-luggage office** (open 4am-11pm) at the train station.

Tucked away in a quiet courtyard is **Tourinform** (☎ 488 690; e szeged@tourinform .hu; Dugonics tér 2; open 10am-6pm Mon-Fri May-Sept, 9am-4pm Oct-Apr). It also has a pavilion (open 9am-9pm daily May-Sept) on the square.

The **K&H Bank** (Klauzál tér 2) has a foreign currency exchange machine. Next door is an **OTP Bank** (Klauzál tér 4).

There is a **main post office** (Széchenyi tér 1) in the centre of town. **Cyber Café** (Dugonics tér 11; open until midnight daily) is a dark basement bar where Internet use costs 480Ft per hour.

Things to See & Do

Begin your tour of Szeged in Dóm tér, dominated by the twin-towered **Votive Church**, an ugly brown brick structure that was pledged after the flood of 1879 but not completed until 1930. The Romanesque **St Demetrius Tower** nearby is all that remains of a church dating from the 13th century, which was demolished to make room for the present one. Running along three sides of the square is the **National**

SZEGED

Pantheon – statues and reliefs of 80 Hungarian notables. The **Szeged Open-Air Festival** is held here from mid-July to late August.

Inside the **Serbian Orthodox Church** *(adult/child 100/80Ft)*, dating from 1778 and behind the Votive Church, have a look at the fantastic iconostasis – a central gold 'tree' with 60 icons hanging off its 'branches'. Get the key at Somogyi utca 3 (flat I/5) towards the river.

Head north to the **Ferenc Móra Museum** *(☎ 549 040; Várkert; adult/child 300/150Ft; open 10am-3pm Tues, 10am-5pm Wed-Sun)*, in a huge neoclassical building (1896). Downstairs is a good collection of Hungarian paintings and an exhibit on the Avar people, who occupied the Carpathian Basin from the 5th to 8th centuries. The upper floor is dedicated to folk art.

There are many fine buildings around Széchenyi tér in the centre of town, including the **Town Hall**. Don't miss the **Reök Palace** *(Kölcsey utca)*, a mind-blowing Art Nouveau structure from 1907.

The 1903 **Great Synagogue** *(☎ 423 849; Gutenberg utca 13; adult/child 200/100Ft; open 10am-noon & 1pm-5pm Sun-Fri Apr-Sept, 9am-2pm Oct-Mar)* is the most beautiful Jewish house of worship in Hungary and is still in use. Free organ concerts here are common on summer evenings.

Places to Stay

The most central camping ground is **Partfürdő Camping** *(☎ 430 843; Közép-kikötő sor; camp sites per tent/adult/child 600/600/430Ft, bungalows from 6000Ft)* on the eastern banks of the Tisza and near the public swimming pools and thermal baths.

Plenty of student accommodation is open to travellers in July and August, including the central **István Apáthy College** *(☎ 545 896; Eötvös utca 4; dorm beds 1250Ft, rooms per person from 2500Ft)* near the Votive Church. **Ottó Hermann College** *(☎ 544 309; Temesvári körút 52; bus No 2; dorm beds from 700Ft, doubles 2000Ft)* is a cheaper option but is east of the town centre in New Szeged.

Contact **Szeged Tourist** *(☎ 420 428; Klauzál tér)* for **private rooms** from 2000Ft to 3000Ft per person.

If you arrive by bus you'll be within walking distance of **Pölös Panzió** *(☎/fax 498 208; Pacsirta utca 17a; singles/doubles 4500/5500Ft)*, which has well-worn yet comfortable

rooms. The rooms at **Csirke Panzió** *(☎ 426 188; Bocskai utca 3b; singles/doubles 5000/6000Ft)* are quite large but are often taken, so call ahead.

The grand old three-star **Hotel Tisza** *(☎/fax 478 278; Wesselényi utca 1; singles 5880-11,900Ft, doubles 8760-14,900Ft)*, just off Széchenyi tér, is a glorious place to stay and its large bright rooms are still reasonable value (price depends on bathroom facilities).

Places to Eat

Jumbo Grill *(Mikszáth Kálmán utca 4; dishes from 270Ft)*, with salads and excellent grilled chicken, is a good spot for a cheap meal.

The **Leső Harcsa Halászcsárda** *(Eager Catfish Fishermen's Inn; ☎ 555 980; Roosevelt tér 14; mains around 1500Ft)* is a little on the expensive side but is a Szeged institution and serves up *halászlé* (fisherman's soup) by the cauldron.

Nearby **Régi Hídhoz** *(At the Sign of the Old Bridge; ☎ 420 910; Oskola utca 4; mains 800-1200Ft)* serves standard Hungarian fare and has a pleasant garden.

A popular Chinese restaurant is **Hong Kong** *(Deák Ferenc utca 24; mains 700-1000Ft)*. Head here at lunchtime, when there's a great set menu (990Ft). **Numero Uno Pizza** *(☎ 424 745; Széchenyi tér 5; pizzas from 275Ft)* has good pizzas and its garden is a fine place for a drink.

Zodiákus *(☎ 420 914; Oskola utca 13; mains 1000-2000Ft)* is a cut above, with an excellent international menu and zodiac symbols everywhere you look.

For coffee, cake and a bit of peace and quiet, head to **Grand Café** *(☎ 420 578; Deák Ferenc utca 18, 2nd floor)*.

Entertainment

The best sources of information in culturally active Szeged are the **Cultural Centre** *(☎ 479 566; Vörösmarty utca 3)* and the free bi-weekly *Szegedi Est*. The **National Theatre** *(☎ 479 279; Deák Ferenc utca 12-14)* has always been the centre of cultural life in the city and usually stages opera and ballet.

There's a vast array of bars, clubs and other nightspots in this student town, especially around Dugonics tér. The cover charge for these clubs ranges from free entry to 500Ft. The clubs generally open until 4am almost daily. **JATE Club** *(Toldy utca 1)* is the best place to meet students on their own turf.

HUNGARY

Sing Sing Disco (cnr Mars tér & Dr Baross József utca; open Wed-Sat) has lots of rave parties, while Soho Music Club (Londoni körút 3) is best for drum & bass. The huge Tiszagyöngye Disco (Közép-kikötő sor) in New Szeged is another popular hangout.

Getting There & Away

Bus Bus services are good, with departures to Budapest (seven daily), Eger (two), Győr (two), Kecskemét (10) and Pécs (seven).

If you're heading for Romania, buses run to Arad at 6.30am daily, with extra departures at 8.45am on Friday, 10.10am on Saturday and 8.10am on Sunday. There are buses to Timișoara on Tuesday and Friday at 6.30am and Saturday at 10.10am. Buses run to the Yugoslavian destinations of Novi Sad once daily and Subotica three times daily. A 9.30am bus on Friday departs for Vienna.

Train Szeged is on the main train line to Nyugati station in Budapest. Another line connects the city with Hódmezővásárhely and Békéscsaba, where you can change trains for Gyula or Romania. Southbound local trains leave Szeged for Subotica twice daily (6.35am and 4.20pm).

Northern Hungary

Northern Hungary is the most mountainous part of the country. The southern foothills of the Carpathian Mountains stretch east along the Slovakian border in a chain of wooded hills (maximum height 1000m) from the Danube Bend almost as far as Ukraine. Historic Eger offers an ideal base for sightseers and wine-tasters; Szilvásvárad, the Hungarian home of the snow-white Lipizzaner horses, is just to the north. To the northeast is Tokaj, celebrated for its legendary sweet wines.

EGER

☎ 36 • pop 61,500

Eger (Erlau in German) is a lovely baroque city full of historic buildings. It was here in 1552 that Hungarian defenders temporarily stopped the Turkish advance into Western Europe and helped preserve Hungary's identity. The Turks returned in 1596 and managed to capture Eger Castle but were evicted in 1687. Eger played a central role in Ferenc Rákóczi II's attempt to overthrow the Habsburgs early

in the 18th century, and it was then that a large part of the castle was razed by the Austrians.

Credit goes to the bishops of Eger for erecting most of the town you see today. Eger has some of Hungary's finest architecture, especially examples of Copf (Zopf in Hungarian), a transitional style between late baroque and neoclassicism found only in Central Europe.

Today Eger is famous for its potent Bull's Blood (Egri Bikavér) red wine. Dozens of wine cellars are to be found in Szépasszonyvölgy (Valley of the Beautiful Women), just a 20-minute walk southwest of the centre.

Orientation & Information

The **main train station** (Vasút utca) is a 15-minute walk south of town, just east of Deák Ferenc utca. The **Egervár train station** (Vécseyvölgy utca), which serves Szilvásvárad and other points north, is a five-minute walk north of the castle along Bástya utca. The **bus station** (Pyrker János tér) is west of Széchenyi István utca, Eger's main drag.

The friendly staff at Tourinform (☎ 517 715, fax 518 815; e eger@tourinform.hu; Bajcsy-Zsilinszky utca 9; open 9am-7pm Mon-Fri, 10am-6pm Sat & Sun June-Aug; 9am-5pm Mon-Fri, 9am-1pm Sat Sept-May) can supply lots of information and recommend agencies for finding private rooms.

Due west is a branch of **OTP bank** (Széchenyi István utca 2; open 7.45am-5pm Mon, Tues, Thur & Fri, 7.45am-6pm Wed). The main **post office** (Széchenyi István utca 20-22; open 8am-8pm Mon-Fri, 8am-1pm Sat) is 350m to the north. **Egri Est Café** (see Entertainment later) doubles as an Internet café (300/500Ft for 30/60 minutes).

Things to See & Do

The first thing you see as you come into town from the bus or train station is the neoclassical **Eger Cathedral** (Pyrker János tér 1), built in 1836. Directly opposite is the Copf-style **Lyceum** (☎ 520 400; Eszterházy tér 1; open 9.30am-3pm Tues-Sun Apr-Sept, 9.30am-1.30pm Sat & Sun Oct-Mar), dating from 1765, with a 20,000-volume frescoed **library** (adult/student 300/150) on the 1st floor and an 18th-century **observatory** and **Astronomy Museum** (adult/student 300/150Ft) on the 6th floor. Climb three more floors up to the observation deck for a great view of the city and to try out the **camera obscura**, the 'eye of Eger', designed in 1776 to entertain the locals.

HUNGARY

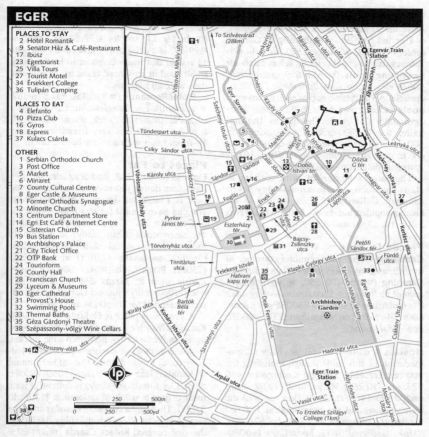

EGER

PLACES TO STAY
2 Hotel Romantik
9 Senator Ház & Café-Restaurant
17 Ibusz
23 Egertourist
25 Villa Tours
27 Tourist Motel
34 Érsekkert College
36 Tulipán Camping

PLACES TO EAT
4 Elefánto
10 Pizza Club
16 Gyros
18 Express
37 Kulacs Csárda

OTHER
1 Serbian Orthodox Church
3 Post Office
5 Market
6 Minaret
7 County Cultural Centre
8 Eger Castle & Museums
11 Former Orthodox Synagogue
12 Minorite Church
13 Centrum Department Store
14 Egri Est Café & Internet Centre
19 Cistercian Church
19 Bus Station
20 Archbishop's Palace
21 City Ticket Office
22 OTP Bank
24 Tourinform
26 County Hall
28 Franciscan Church
29 Lyceum & Museums
30 Eger Cathedral
31 Provost's House
32 Swimming Pools
33 Thermal Baths
35 Géza Gárdonyi Theatre
38 Szépasszony-völgy Wine Cellars

Kossuth Lajos utca to the south has some superb buildings, including the rococo **Provost's House** at No 4, the baroque **County Hall** at No 9 (check out the frilly wrought-iron gates in the passageway) and the former **Orthodox synagogue** (1893) at No 17.

At the northern end of Kossuth Lajos utca, across Dózsa György tér, a cobblestone lane leads to **Eger Castle** (☎ 312 744; Vár 1; adult/student combined ticket 500/250Ft, grounds only 200/100Ft; open 8am-8pm Tues-Sun Apr-Aug, 8am-7pm Sept, 8am-6pm Oct & Mar, 8am-5pm Nov-Feb), erected in the 13th century after the Mongol invasion. Inside are the foundations of St John's Cathedral, which was destroyed by the Turks. Models and drawings in the **István Dobó Museum**, housed in the former Bishop's Palace (1470), show how

the cathedral once looked. Beneath the castle are underground **casemates** hewn from solid rock, which you may tour with a Hungarian-speaking guide (included in the admission price; English-language guide 400Ft extra). Other exhibits include the **Waxworks** (adult/student 250/150Ft) and **Minting Exhibit** (adult/student 100/50Ft). You can still tour the castle grounds for 200/100Ft on Monday, when all the other exhibits are closed.

The **Minorite church** (Dobó István tér), built in 1771, is one of the most glorious baroque buildings in the world. In the square in front are statues of national hero István Dobó and his comrades-in-arms routing the Turks in 1552. Due north in the old town is the 40m **Minaret** (Knézich Károly utca; admission 100Ft; open 9am-6pm daily Apr-Oct), topped

HUNGARY

with a cross. Only non-claustrophobes will brave the 97 narrow spiral steps to the top.

Unwind in the **Archbishop's Garden** (*enter from Petőfi Sándor tér 2*), once the private reserve of papal princes. It has **open-air swimming pools** (☎ *411 699; adult/child 500/350Ft; open 6am-8pm Mon-Fri, 8am-7pm Sat & Sun May-Sept*) as well as **covered pools** (*adult/child 500/350Ft; open 9am-7pm daily Oct-Apr*). The nearby **thermal baths** (☎ *413 356; Fürdő utca 1-3; admission 500Ft; open to women noon-6pm Wed & Fri; to men noon-6pm Tues & Thur, 10am-2pm Sat*) date from Turkish times.

The huge selection of **wine cellars** to chosse between at Szépasszony-völgy can be daunting. Cellars 16, 17, 29, 42 and 48 are always popular, but there's better wine at Nos 5, 13, 18, 23, 31 and 32.

Places to Stay

Camping Within easy stumbling distance of the Szépasszony-völgy wine cellars is **Tulipán Camping** (☎/*fax 410 580;* **W** *www.home/ zonnet.hu/tulipan; Szépasszony-völgy utca 71; tent/caravan sites 600/800Ft, per person 600Ft, 4-/5-person bungalows 5000/9000Ft; open year-round*).

Hostels A number of colleges offer accommodation in July and August, including the 400-bed **Erzsébet Szilágyi College** (☎ *410 571, fax 310 259; Mátyás király út 62; dorm beds 1100-1500Ft*), about 1km south of the train station; and the more central 132-bed **Érsekkert College** (☎ *413 661, fax 520 440; Klapka György utca 12; beds 1200-1400Ft*).

Private Rooms Agencies that can organise private rooms for between 2100Ft and 2500Ft a night per person include: **Egertourist** (☎ *510 270, fax 411 225; Bajcsy-Zsilinszky utca 9; open 9am-5pm Mon-Fri, 9am-1pm Sat Jun-Sept*); **Ibusz** (☎ *311 451, fax 312 652; Széchenyi István utca 9; open 8am-4pm Mon-Fri, 9am-1pm Sat June-Sept*); and **Villa Tours** (☎ *410 215, fax 518 038; Jókai utca 1; open 8am-4pm Mon-Fri*).

Hotels The **Tourist Motel** (☎ *411 101, fax 429 014; Mekcsey István utca 2; singles/ doubles/triples with shared bathroom 3000/ 5000/6000Ft*) is a frayed though spotlessly clean place south of the castle with 34 rooms. Breakfast costs 500Ft extra.

In Eger's main square, **Senator Ház** (☎/*fax 320 466;* **e** *hotelsen@axelero.hu; Dobó István tér 11; singles €27.50-48, doubles €39-57*) is a delightful 18th-century inn with 11 rooms that many consider to be the finest small hotel in provincial Hungary. Would that they were all like this...

Hotel Romantik (☎ *310 456, fax 516 362;* **e** *romantik-eger@axelero.hu; Csíky Sándor utca 26; singles €35-55, doubles €40-65, triples €50-75*) is a very friendly and cosy 16-room hotel with a pretty back garden.

Places to Eat

Express (☎ *517 920; Barkóczy utca 4; open 7am-8pm daily*), just northeast of the bus station, is a large self-service restaurant where you can have a meal for less than 400Ft.

Gyros (☎ *310 135; Széchenyi István utca 10; open noon-10pm daily*) is a friendly local café-restaurant with Greek salads (360Ft), moussaka (750Ft) and souvlaki (750Ft). **Pizza Club** (☎ *427 606; Dr Hibay Károly utca 8; pizzas 650-1200Ft; open noon-10pm daily*), just off Dobó István tér, is recommended for its pizzas and pasta.

A great new place is **Elefanto** (☎ *411 031; Katona István tér 2; mains 950-1800Ft; open noon-midnight daily*), high above the market, with a nonsmoking interior and covered balcony for al fresco dining. The café-restaurant at **Senator Ház** hotel (*mains 1050-1800Ft; open 11am-midnight daily*) is delightful for a meal or just a snack of *palacsinta* (130Ft to 350Ft). There are a couple of *csárdas* amid the wine cellars of Szépasszony-völgy, including the vine-covered **Kulacs Csárda** (☎ *311 375; Szépasszony-völgy utca; mains 900-1500Ft; open noon-11pm Tues-Sun*).

Entertainment

The Tourinform office, the **County Cultural Centre** (☎ *510 020; Knézich Károly utca 8*) opposite the minaret, or the city's **ticket office** (☎ *518 347; Széchenyi István utca 5; open 9am-4pm Mon-Fri*) can tell you what concerts and plays are on. Venues are the **Géza Gárdonyi Theatre** (☎ *310 026; Hatvani kapu tér 4*), the Lyceum and Eger Cathedral (see Things to See & Do). From mid-May to mid-October there are half-hour organ concerts at 11.30am daily from Monday to Saturday and at 12.45pm on Sunday in the cathedral.

Of the many cafés and bars in the centre, among the best is **Egri Est Café** (☎ *411 105;*

Széchenyi István utca 16; open 11am-midnight Sun-Thur, 11am-4am Fri & Sat), with parties at the weekend.

Getting There & Away

Buses leave Eger for Szilvásvárad about every half-hour, for Budapest and Miskolc about once an hour, for Szeged twice a day, for Kecskemét three times a day and for Debrecen five times a day.

Eger is on a minor train line linking Putnok and Füzesabony; for Budapest, Miskolc or Debrecen you usually have to change at Füzesabony. There are up to five direct trains a day to and from Budapest's Keleti station (2½ hours) that do not require a change.

SZILVÁSVÁRAD

☎ 36 • pop 1950

The Bükk Hills, most of which falls within the 43,000-hectare Bükk National Park, lie to the north of Eger. A good place to begin a visit is the village of Szilvásvárad, 28km from Eger. It's an ideal base for hiking and the centre of horse breeding in Hungary, with some 250 prize Lipizzaners in local stables.

Orientation & Information

Arriving in Szilvásvárad, get off the train at Szilvásvárad-Szalajkavölgy, the first of the town's two stations, and follow Egri út northeast for about 10 minutes to town. The bus from Eger will drop you off in the centre.

There's no tourist office, but Tourinform in Eger can provide information and sells Cartographia's three 1:40,000 maps of the Bükk region (1250Ft each): A Bükk-fennsík (Bükk Plateau; No 33); A Bükk – északi rész (Bükk – northern section; No 29); and A Bükk – déli rész (Bükk – southern section; No 30).

Along the main drag, you'll find an **OTP bank** (Egri út 30a; open 8am-4pm Mon-Fri) and the **post office** (Egri út 12; open 8am-4pm Mon-Fri).

Things to See & Do

Some people come to Szilvásvárad just to ride the open-air **narrow-gauge railway** (☎ 355 197; adult/child one way 160/80Ft, steam train 320/240Ft) into the Szalajka Valley. It departs seven times a day from May to September (10 times at the weekend), with three daily departures in April and October. The station is approximately 300m south of Egri út at Szalajka-völgy 6.

The little train chugs along for about 5km to **Szalajka-Fátyolvízesés**. Stay on the train for the return trip or you can walk back along well-trodden, shady paths, taking in the sights along the way, including the trout-filled streams. On the way, the **Forestry Museum** (☎ 355 112; open 8.30am-4.30pm Tues-Sun mid-Apr–Sept, 8.30am-3pm Tues-Sun Oct, 9am-2pm daily Nov–mid-Apr) deals with everything that the forest contains or surrenders: timber, game, plant life etc.

From Szalajka-Fátyolvízesés, you can walk for 15 minutes to the **Istállóskő Cave**, where Palaeolithic pottery shards have been discovered, or climb 958m **Mt Istállóskő**, the highest peak in the Bükk.

In Szilvásvárad, both the covered and open **racecourses** (adult/child 150/100Ft) put on Lipizzaner parades and coach races on weekends throughout the summer, but times are not fixed.

For horse riding (1800-2500Ft per hour) or coach rides (from 4300Ft), head for the **Lipizzaner Stud Farm** (☎ 355 155; Fenyves utca; open 8am-4pm daily) to the northwest. You'll learn more about these intelligent creatures at the **Horse Museum** (☎ 355 135; Park utca 8; adult/child 80/50Ft; open 9am-noon & 1pm-4pm daily) in an 18th-century working stable.

Mountain Bike Rentals (☎ 06-30 335 2695; Szalajka-völgy) rents out bicycles from a stand opposite the narrow-gauge train station. The rates are 700/900/1100/1300/1500Ft for 1/2/3/4/5 hours, or 1800Ft per day.

Places to Stay & Eat

Hegyi Camping (☎/fax 355 207; W www.hegyicamping.com; Egri út 36/a; tent site per person 550-750Ft, caravan 2000Ft, 2-/3-/4-bed houses 3900/4900/5600Ft; open mid-Apr–mid-Oct) is on the way to the centre from Szilvásvárad-Szalajkavölgy train station.

Hotel Lipicai (☎ 355 100, fax 355 200; Egri út 12-14; singles/doubles 5100/6100Ft) is a basic-looking place that's a little bit on the dark and dingy side, although the rooms are reasonable.

The **Hotel Szilvás** (☎ 355 159, fax 355 324; e reserve@hotelszilvas.hunguest.hu; Park utca 6; singles 4600-6300Ft, doubles 6900-9200Ft) is a 40-room hotel just beyond the Horse Museum in the former Palavicini mansion. Prices depend on the season and if your room has a bath, shower and/or toilet.

HUNGARY

Szalajka-völgy is lined with food stalls and restaurants, including the pretty **Lovas** (☎ 355 555; mains 860-2620Ft; open noon-10pm daily). Many of them serve trout (45Ft to 50Ft/100g), the speciality of the area.

Getting There & Away
Buses to/from Eger are frequent and faster than the train. Up to eight trains a day link Szilvásvárad with Egervár station.

TOKAJ
☎ 47 • pop 4650

Although it's just a picturesque little town at the bottom of the Zemplén Hills, Tokaj has been synonymous with fine wine since the 17th century. Tokaj is, in fact, just one of 28 towns and villages of the Tokaj-Hegyalja, a 6600-hectare vine-growing region that produces wine along the southern and eastern edges of the Zemplén Hills. In 2002 it was the eighth site in Hungary to be added to the Unesco World Heritage List.

King Louis XIV famously called Tokaj 'the wine of kings and the king of wines'; to modern tastes it's often overly sweet and oxidised. The dessert wines are especially sugary and rated based on the number of *puttony* (butts) of sweet Aszú added. Tokaj also produces less-sweet wines: Szamorodni (like dry sherry), Furmint and Háslevelú, the driest of all.

Information
Tourinform (☎ 552 070, fax 352 259; e tokaj@tourinform.hu; Serház utca 1; open 9am-4pm Mon-Fri) is just off Rákóczi út. It sits between the **OTP bank** (Rákóczi út 35; open 8am-4pm Mon-Fri) and the **post office** (Rákóczi út 24; open 8am-5pm Mon-Fri, 8am-noon Sat).

Things to See & Do
The **Tokaj Museum** (☎ 352 636; Bethlen Gábor utca 13; adult/child 300/200Ft; open 9am-4pm Tues-Sun May-Nov) leaves nothing unsaid about the history of Tokaj, the region and its wines. Just up the road in an 18th-century Greek Orthodox church, the **Tokaj Gallery** (☎ 352 003; Bethlen Gábor utca 17; admission free; open 10am-4pm daily May-Oct) exhibits works by local artists. The Eclectic **Great Synagogue** (Serház utca 55) is a short distance to the east.

Private cellars (*pincék*) offering **wine tastings** are scattered throughout town, including those at Rákóczi út 2 and 6, Óvári utca 40 and Bem József utca 2 and 16. For the ultimate in tasting venues head for the 600-year-old **Rákóczi Cellar** (☎ 352 408; Kossuth tér 15; open 10am-7pm or 8pm daily Apr-Oct), where bottles of wine mature in long corridors (one measures 28m by 10m). Tastings of six Tokaj wines cost 1800Ft or, if you prefer only Aszú, 2750Ft.

The correct order of sampling Tokaj wines is: Furmint, dry Szamorodni, sweet Szamorodni and then the Aszú wines – from three to six puttony.

Places to Stay
Pelsőczi-Tiszavirág Camping (☎ 352 626, fax 352 017; Horgász út 11; tent/caravan sites 450/900Ft, per person 40Ft, 2-/3-bed bungalows 4000/6000Ft) is along the river just north of Tisza Bridge opposite town.

North of the Tourinform office, **Lux** (☎/fax 352 145; Serház utca 14; doubles 4550Ft) is a friendly six-room pension.

Tokaj Hotel (☎ 352 344, fax 352 759; Rákóczi út 5; singles 4600-5700Ft, doubles 5000-6200Ft), at the confluence of the Bodrog and Tisza Rivers, has 42 no-frills rooms. Come armed with insect repellent.

Places to Eat
Makk Marci (☎ 352 336; Liget köz 1; pizzas 430-900Ft; open 8am-10pm daily) is a cheap and friendly pizzeria. **Róna** (☎ 352 116; Bethlen Gábor utca 19; starters 290-450Ft, mains 700-1650Ft; open 11am-10pm daily) specialises in fish dishes.

Tokaj can now boast one of provincial Hungary's finest restaurants. **Degenfeld** (☎ 553 050; Kossuth tér 1; mains 950-2200Ft; open 11.30am-10pm daily), in a lovely 19th-century townhouse on the main square, has inventive New Hungarian cuisine, an excellent wine list and lovely decor.

Getting There & Away
Up to nine buses a day go to Szerencs, the chocolate capital of Hungary, with two to Nyíregyháza and one to Debrecen.

Up to 14 trains a day connect Tokaj with Miskolc and Nyíregyháza; change at the latter for Debrecen. To travel north to Sárospatak and Sátoraljaújhely, take the Miskolc-bound train and change at Mezőzomb. Only two direct trains a day travel to and from Budapest's Keleti station.

Liechtenstein

Blink and you might miss Liechtenstein; the country measures just 25km from north to south and an average of 6km from west to east. In some ways you could be forgiven for mistaking it for a part of Switzerland. The Swiss franc is the legal currency, all travel documents valid for Switzerland are also valid for Liechtenstein, and the only border regulations are on the Austrian side. Switzerland also represents Liechtenstein abroad, subject to consultation.

But a closer look reveals that Liechtenstein is quite distinct from its neighbour. Ties with Switzerland began only in 1923 with the signing of a customs and monetary union. Before that, it had a similar agreement with Austria-Hungary. Although Liechtenstein shares the Swiss postal system, it issues its own postage stamps. Unlike Switzerland, Liechtenstein joined the United Nations (UN; 1990) and, in 1995, the European Economic Area (EEA). Despite going separate ways over the EEA issue, the open border between Liechtenstein and Switzerland remains intact. Liechtenstein has no plans to seek full EU membership.

Liechtenstein is a prosperous country, with a high standard of living and the wealthiest royal family in Europe. In 2000 its unemployment rate was a measly 1.1% – 290 people!

Facts about Liechtenstein

Liechtenstein was created by the merger of the domain of Schellenberg and the county of Vaduz in 1712 by the powerful Liechtenstein family. It was a principality under the Holy Roman Empire from 1719 to 1806 and, after a spell in the German Confederation, it achieved full sovereign independence in 1866. A modern constitution was drawn up in 1921, but even today the prince retains the power to dissolve parliament and must approve every act before it becomes law. Prince Franz Josef II was the first ruler to live in the castle above the capital city of Vaduz. He died in 1989 after a reign of 51 years, and was succeeded by his son, Prince Hans-Adam II, who has since clashed with the government over his proposed constitutional reforms that would limit government power.

At a Glance

- **Vaduz** – 400km-worth of hiking trails through stunning Alpine scenery
- Sending postcards home stamped by the country's postal service

Capital	Vaduz
Population	32,860
Official Language	German
Currency	1 Swiss franc (Sfr) = 100 centimes
Time	GMT/UTC+0100
Country Phone Code	☎ 423

Liechtenstein has no military service and its minuscule army (80 men!) was disbanded in 1868. It is best known for wine production, postage stamps, dentures (an important export) and its status as a tax haven. In 2000, Liechtenstein's financial and political institutions were rocked by allegations that money laundering was rife in the country.

In response to international outrage, banks agreed to stop allowing customers to bank money anonymously.

Despite its small size, Liechtenstein has two political regions (upper and lower) and three distinct geographical areas: the Rhine Valley in the west, the edge of the Tirolean Alps in the southeast, and the northern lowlands. The population is 32,860, a third of which are foreign residents.

LIECHTENSTEIN

Facts for the Visitor

See the Switzerland chapter for practical details not covered here.

Liechtenstein's telephone country code is ☎ 423, and there are no regional telephone codes.

Getting There & Away

Liechtenstein has no airport (the nearest is in Zürich), and only a few trains stop within its borders, at Schaan. Getting there by postbus is easiest. There are usually three buses an hour from the Swiss border towns of Buchs (Sfr2.40) and Sargans (Sfr3.60) that stop in Vaduz. Buses run every 30 minutes from the Austrian border town of Feldkirch; you sometimes have to change at Schaan to reach Vaduz (the Sfr3.60 ticket is valid for both buses).

Emergency Services

The same emergency numbers apply as in Switzerland: dial ☎ 117 for the police, ☎ 144 for an ambulance, or ☎ 118 in the event of fire.

By road, route 16 from Switzerland passes through Liechtenstein via Schaan and terminates at Feldkirch. The N13 follows the Rhine along the Swiss/Liechtenstein border; minor roads cross into Liechtenstein at each motorway exit.

Getting Around

Postbus travel within Liechtenstein is cheap and reliable; all fares cost Sfr2.40 or Sfr3.60, and a weekly/monthly pass is only Sfr10/20 (half-price for students and seniors).

The only drawback is that some services finish early; the last of the hourly buses from Vaduz to Malbun, for example, leaves at 6.20pm. Grab a timetable from the post office.

Vaduz

pop 4930

Although it's the capital of Liechtenstein, Vaduz is little more than a village. Two adjoining streets – Äulestrasse and pedestrian-only Städtle – enclose the centre of town. Everything of importance is within this small area, including the bus station.

Liechtenstein Tourism (☎ 239 63 00; e touristinfo@liechtenstein.li; Städtle 37; open 8am-noon & 1.30pm-5.30pm Mon-Fri year-round, 10am-noon & 1.30pm-4pm Sat Apr-Oct, 10am-noon & 1.30pm-5pm Sun May-Sept) has plenty of useful information (ask for the Liechtenstein in Figures brochure); for Sfr2, staff will stamp your passport with a souvenir entry stamp.

Send postcards at the **main post office** (Äulestrasse 38; open 7.45am-6pm Mon-Fri, 8am-11am Sat), which has the same postal rates as Switzerland.

The **Telecom FL shop** (☎ 237 74 74; Austrasse 77; open 9am-noon & 1.30pm-6.30pm Mon-Fri, 9am-1pm Sat), 1km south of Vaduz, provides free Internet access.

For medical attention, contact the hospital, **Liechtensteinisches Landesspital** (☎ 235 44 11; Heiligkreuz 25).

Things to See & Do

Many tourists come to Liechtenstein for the stamps – a stamp in the passport and stamps on a postcard for the folks back home. But it's also worthwhile heading for the hills, with some 400km of **hiking trails** through Alpine scenery; see the tourist office for the *Liechtenstein Hiking Map* 1:25,000 (Sfr15.50).

Although the **castle** is not open to the public, you can climb the hill for a closer look. There are views of Vaduz and the mountains, and a network of marked walking trails along the ridge.

Liechtenstein Kunstmuseum *(☎ 235 030 00;* **w** *www.kunstmuseum.li; Städtle 32; adult/student/child Sfr8/5/5; open 10am-5pm Tues-Wed & Fri-Sun, 10am-8pm Thur)* houses the national art collection in a rather sleek modern building, with works from the 16th to 18th centuries from the prince's private collection.

Philatelists will lick their lips in anticipation of the **Postage Stamp Museum** *(☎ 236 61 05; Städtle 37; admission free; open 10am-noon & 1pm-5pm daily),* which exhibits 300 frames of national stamps issued since 1912. The **National Museum** *(Städtle 43)* reopens – after major renovations – in spring 2003.

Look out for processions and fireworks on 15 August, Liechtenstein's national holiday. The bands performing at the **Little Big One** *(***w** *www.littlebigone.com)* open-air music festival sweep into town on the third June weekend.

Places to Stay

The country's minute dimensions mean you can base yourself anywhere and still be within easy cycling or postbus distance of the centre. Ask the tourist office for a list of private rooms and chalets outside Vaduz.

Triesenberg, on a hillside terrace overlooking the Rhine Valley, has **Camping Mittagspitz** *(☎ 392 26 86; adult/child/tent/car Sfr8.50/4/5/4, dorm beds for adult/child Sfr22/13).* The **SYHA hostel** *(☎ 232 50 22, fax 232 58 56;* **e** *schaan@youthhostel.ch; Untere Rütigasse 6; dorm beds from Sfr28.60, doubles without/with toilet Sfr74.20/86.20; open mid-Mar–Nov)* is in a quiet rural setting between Vaduz and nearby Schaan. Take the postbus to the Muhleholz stop; it's a five-minute walk (signposted) from there.

Another cheapie outside Vaduz is **Hotel Falknis** *(☎ 232 63 77; Landstrasse 92; singles/doubles Sfr55/110),* a 20-minute walk from the centre (or take the postbus). There's a pub below and basic rooms with hall showers above.

Gasthof Au *(☎ 232 11 17, fax 232 11 68; Austrasse 2; singles/doubles Sfr60/96, with bathroom Sfr80/120),* on the main road into town, has rudimentary rooms and a garden restaurant.

Places to Eat

Pedestrian-only Stadtle street has a clutch of pavement restaurants and cafés. Popular options include **Hotel Engel** *(Städtle 13),* with standard international fare; and **Beat** *(Städtle 5),* a stylish eatery for local suits.

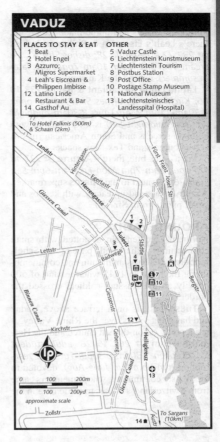

VADUZ

PLACES TO STAY & EAT	OTHER
1 Beat	5 Vaduz Castle
2 Hotel Engel	6 Liechtenstein Kunstmuseum
3 Azzurro;	7 Liechtenstein Tourism
Migros Supermarket	8 Postbus Station
4 Leah's Eiscream &	9 Post Office
Philippen Imbisse	10 Postage Stamp Museum
12 Latino Linde	11 National Museum
Restaurant & Bar	13 Liechtensteinisches
14 Gasthof Au	Landesspital (Hospital)

For an odd but delicious mix of authentic Philippino dishes and home-made ice cream, there's **Leah's Eiscream & Philippen Imbiss** (☎ 232 72 00; *Städtle 28; dishes Sfr9.50, ice cream from Sfr2; open 10am-7pm daily, later in summer*), behind the Kunstmuseum.

Latino Linde Restaurant & Bar (☎ 233 10 05; *Kirchstrasse 2; dishes Sfr17.50-25; open 8.30am-11pm Mon-Thur, 8.30am-midnight Fri, 4pm-midnight Sat*) is a local haunt with bamboo screens and South American rugs. It serves burgers and Tex-Mex snacks.

For a quick bite, there's **Azzurro** (☎ 232 48 18; *open 8am-7pm Mon-Fri, 8am-6pm Sat, 10am-6pm*), next to the **Migros** supermarket. Azzurro is a stand-up eatery with kebabs and small pizzas from Sfr7.50.

AROUND VADUZ

Northern Liechtenstein is dotted with small communities with a gentle pace of life. **Schellenberg** has a Russian monument, commemorating the night in 1945 when a band of 500 heavily armed Russian soldiers crossed the border.

Triesenberg is on a terrace above Vaduz and has great views over the Rhine Valley. It has a pretty onion-domed church and the **Heimatmuseum** (☎ 262 19 26; *adult/student Sfr2/1; open 1.30pm-5.30pm Tues-Sat year-round, 2pm-5pm Sun June-Aug*), devoted to the Walser community, whose members came from Switzerland's Valais to settle here in the

13th century. Apparently, the Walser dialect is still spoken here. **Balzers**, in the extreme south of the country, is dominated by the soaring sides of Gutenberg Castle (not open to public).

MALBUN

Liechtenstein's ski resort, Malbun, perches at 1600m in the southeast. It has some good **mountain runs** for novices (as well as two ski schools) and more difficult runs. A one-day pass for all the ski lifts costs Sfr35 (students/seniors Sfr29). Skis, shoes and poles cost Sfr43 for a day, and can be hired from the **sports shop** (☎ 263 37 55).

During summer, skis give way to mountain boots as the **hiking** fraternity hits town. Worthwhile treks include the Panorama and Furstin-Gina paths, which start and finish in Malbun. See birds of prey at close quarters at **Galina Hotel** (☎ 263 34 24; *adult/child Sfr6/3*), which runs a 40-minute falconry show at 3pm daily during summer.

The road from Vaduz terminates at Malbun. The **tourist office** (☎ 263 65 77; *open 9am-noon & 1.30pm-5pm Mon-Fri, 9am-noon & 1pm-4pm Sat, closed mid-Apr–May & Nov–mid-Dec*) is by the first bus stop.

The village has eight hotels, each with a restaurant, including the **Alpenhotel Malbun** (☎ 263 11 81, fax 263 96 46; *singles/doubles from Sfr45/90*) and **Turna** (☎ 265 50 40, fax 265 50 41; e turna@adon.li; *singles/doubles Sfr70/110*).

Poland

Travellers to Poland will delight in its heroic past, urban vitality and natural beauty.

The enduring character of Poland's cities is displayed in the old-world splendour of regal Kraków, in the modern clamour of ambitious Warsaw and in the resilient spirit of maritime Gdańsk. Outdoor enthusiasts will surely be impressed by the undeveloped coastline and intricate waterways in the north, as well as the rugged mountains in the south.

Poland may not be as cheap as it used to be, but it remains excellent value and tourist facilities are often very good. And unlike some countries in Eastern Europe, foreigners are charged the same as locals for everything.

In rural areas, you will certainly still see horse-drawn ploughs and carts, but the cities are as dynamic and cosmopolitan as those found in Western Europe. Over the past decade, Poland has developed into a modern, vibrant and progressive state, yet it has maintained its traditional culture. Poland is now reasserting itself after centuries of occupation and subversion, so now is a great time to visit.

Facts about Poland

HISTORY

The region now known as Poland was first settled in the Neolithic period (4000 to 2000 BC) and later invaded by such diverse groups as the Celts, Balts and Huns, as well as various Germanic tribes.

In the early Middle Ages, Western Slavs moved into the flatlands between the Vistula and Odra Rivers, and became known as Polanians, or 'people of the plains'. When the ambitions of a local tribal chief converged with those of Roman missionaries, Poland as a political entity was born. In AD 966 Mieszko I, Duke of the Polanians, adopted Christianity in exchange for official recognition from Rome of his status as regional overlord. The Church formally expanded into the area in 1000, when bishoprics were established in Kołobrzeg (Pomerania), Kraków and Wrocław. Mieszko founded the Piast dynasty, which ruled Poland for over 400 years. His son Bolesław Chrobry (Boleslaus the Brave) was crowned Poland's first king by a papal edict in 1025.

At a Glance

- **Warsaw** – Poland's cosmopolitan melting pot, with a rebuilt Old Town and Chopin's house
- **Kraków** – incredible royal capital packed with untouched centuries-old architecture
- **Auschwitz** – a shocking, emotional and essential visit
- **Zakopane & the Tatra Mountains** – amazing alpine location, offering outdoor fun for all seasons
- **Toruń** – historic city of narrow back lanes, burgher mansions and Gothic churches

Capital	Warsaw
Population	39 million
Official Language	Polish
Currency	1 złoty (zł) = 100 groszy
Time	GMT/UTC+0100
Country Phone Code	☎ 48

Warsaw Maps
Warsaw p452
Central Warsaw p454

Kraków Maps
Kraków p466
Kraków–Old Town & Wawel p468
Kraków–Kazimierz p470

RUSSIA LITHUANIA
Gdańsk p506
Olsztyn p515
The Great Masurian Lakes p518
Toruń p501
BELARUS
GERMANY
Poznań p496
Warsaw
Lublin p484
Wrocław p491
Zamość p489
CZECH REPUBLIC
Kraków
UKRAINE
Zakopane p473
SLOVAKIA

Following the battlefield exploits of Mieszko and Bolesław, the Polish kingdom in the early 11th century comprised Wielkopolska, the original Polanian core near Poznań; Pomerania to the north; Silesia to the south; and Małopolska, east of the Vistula. (While Poland subsequently underwent innumerable territorial reconfigurations, its contemporary

429

POLAND

borders, drawn by Stalin at the end of WWII, closely resemble those of a millennium ago.)

Poland's early success as a regional power was short-lived. German encroachment in the west led to the relocation of the royal capital from Poznań to Kraków in 1038. In the absence of a strong king, rapacious nobles split the realm into four principalities in the mid-12th century. Things did not improve in 1226 when the Prince of Mazovia invited a band of Germanic crusaders to help convert the pagan tribes still living in the north. Subsequently, the Teutonic Knights quickly slashed their way to a sizable swathe of the Baltic coast, and the pagans and Poles were harshly dealt with. The south had its own problems to contend with as marauding Tatars overran Kraków twice in the mid-13th century.

The kingdom was finally reconstituted under Kazimierz III Wielki (the Great), who reigned from 1333 to 1370. Reunified and reinvigorated, Poland prospered. Scores of new towns sprang up, while Kraków blossomed into one of the leading cultural centres in Europe. Unfortunately, his legacy remained etched in stone, not blood: Kazimierz failed to produce a legitimate male heir, so the Piast dynasty reached the end of the line.

Lithuania at this time was a formidable political force and the last pagan stronghold in Eastern Europe, so Poland's nobles decided that Jadwiga, the 10-year-old daughter of Kazimierz's nephew, should marry the Grand Duke of Lithuania, Jagiełło. The union of Poland and Lithuania created a great continental power. It encompassed a vast territory, which stretched from the Baltic to the Black Sea, and assembled a fearsome army, which defeated the Teutonic Knights in 1410.

During the 16th century, the enlightened King Zygmunt I ushered in the Renaissance, lavishly patronising the arts and sciences. Nicolaus Copernicus was busy revolutionising the field of astronomy and, in so doing, reordering the cosmos. In 1569 Poland and Lithuania formally merged into a single state, with Poland acting as senior partner, and both countries remained politically entwined until the late 18th century.

The Jagiellonian dynasty at last expired with the death of Zygmunt II in 1572. The nobility reasserted its dominance over the throne by making the king an elected official of the parliament, known as the *Sejm*. In the absence of a serious Polish contender for king, the Sejm's aristocratic members considered foreigners (over whom the nobles could wield more control). Consequently, seven of Poland's 11 kings in the 17th and 18th centuries were foreigners. Zygmunt's imported Swedish successor, Zygmunt III, moved the capital to Warsaw in 1596.

Throughout the 17th century, the regional rivals of Sweden and Russia marched back and forth across Polish territory, whittling away at the northern and eastern possessions. In the late 18th century, Russia, Prussia and Austria greedily conspired to carve up the politically inept and militarily weak Polish state. In a series of three partitions between 1773 and 1795, Poland was systematically removed from the map of Europe.

From the late 18th to the mid-19th century, Poland, now subject to three empires, experienced a nationalist revival. The romantic movement in the arts preserved folk traditions, recounted past glories and lamented independence lost. National revolutionaries plotted insurrections. Fresh from the American War of Independence, Tadeusz Kościuszko led patriotic forces in an unsuccessful armed rebellion against Russia in 1794. The oppressed Poles fought alongside Napoleon, who in 1807 established a duchy in Warsaw, from where he led his Grand Army to Moscow. Napoleon was eventually crushed by the Russians, as were Polish uprisings in 1831 and 1863.

In the early 20th century the empires of Eastern Europe were finally dismembered after five exhausting years of war and revolution. In 1919 the Treaty of Versailles declared Poland once again to be a recognised sovereign state. No sooner restored, Poland was again at war. Under the command of Marshal Jozef Piłsudski, Poland sought to reclaim its eastern territories from long-time nemesis Russia, now under the Bolsheviks. After two years of inconclusive fighting, the exhausted combatants agreed on a compromise, which returned Vilnius and Lviv to Poland.

But peace didn't last long. On 1 September 1939, a Nazi blitzkrieg poured down on the Polish city of Gdańsk and WWII started. Hitler used Poland as a headquarters and staging ground for the Nazi offensive against the Soviet Union. When the German advance finally stalled and the Red Army's counteroffensive began, Poland became host to a relentlessly grinding campaign of utter devastation. And the Soviets did not come as liberators, but as occupiers of another sort.

Six million Polish inhabitants (roughly 20% of the population) died during WWII. Nazi Germany relegated the Slavic Poles to the role of slave labourers, while Poland's three million Jews were brutally annihilated in death camps. Finally, Poland's borders were redrawn yet again. The Soviet Union claimed the eastern territories and extended the western boundary at the expense of Germany. These border changes were accompanied by the forced resettlement of more than a million Poles, Germans and Ukrainians.

Poland's four decades of Soviet-dominated communist rule were punctuated by waves of protests to which the regime responded with a mix of coercion and concessions. Each round left the communists in power, but more isolated, and the opposition beaten, but more confident. This cycle culminated in the paralysing strikes of 1980–81, led by the Solidarity trade union. This time the regime survived only by imposing martial law.

In the late 1980s, Soviet leader, Mikhail Gorbachev, authorised the Polish communist leader, General Wojciech Jaruzelski, to explore a compromise solution to the political stalemate. In 1989 the communists, Solidarity and the Church held round-table negotiations, which yielded new parliamentary elections. The communists failed to win one seat in open competition, while Solidarity became the political embodiment of Polish nationalism.

The Polish elections of June 1989 triggered a succession of events that soon brought about the collapse of communism across

POLAND

Eastern Europe. In 1990, the communist party in Poland disbanded and Solidarity leader, Lech Wałęsa, became Poland's first democratically elected president.

However, the exultations over the demise of communism were soon tempered by the uncertainties of the road ahead. The postcommunist transition brought radical changes, which induced new social hardships and political crises. But within a decade Poland appeared to have successfully consolidated a democratic polity, built the foundations for a market economy, and reoriented its foreign relations towards the West. In March 1999, Poland was granted full membership of NATO. Poland is also focussed on joining the EU in the next expansion.

GEOGRAPHY

Bordered by seven states and one sea, Poland covers an area of 312,677 sq km. It is approximately as large as the UK and Ireland put together and less than half as big as Texas.

The northern edge of Poland meets the Baltic Sea. This broad, 524km-long coastline is spotted with sand dunes and seaside lakes. Also concentrated in the northeast are many postglacial lakes – more than any country in Europe except Finland.

The southern border is defined by the mountain ranges of the Sudetes and Carpathians. Poland's highest mountains are the rocky Tatras, a section of the Carpathian Range it shares with Slovakia. The highest peak of the Polish Tatras is Mt Rysy (2499m).

The area in between is a vast plain, sectioned by wide north-flowing rivers. Poland's longest river is the Vistula (Wisła), which winds 1047km from the Tatras to the Baltic.

CLIMATE

Poland has a moderate continental climate with considerable maritime influence along the Baltic coast. As a result, the weather can

be unpredictable. Summer is usually warm and sunny, with July the hottest month, but it's the season with the highest rainfall. Spring and autumn are pleasantly warm but can also be rainy. You can expect snow anywhere in Poland between December and March, lingering until April or even May in the mountains.

FLORA & FAUNA

Forests cover about 28% of Poland and, admirably, up to 130 sq km of new forest is planted each year. Some 60% of the forests are pine trees, but the share of deciduous species, such as oak, beech and birch, is increasing.

Poland's fauna includes hare, red deer, wild boar and, less abundant, elk, brown bear and wildcat. European bison, which once inhabited Europe in large numbers, were brought to the brink of extinction early in the 20th century and a few hundred now live in Białowieża National Park. The Great Masurian Lakes district attracts a vast array of bird life, such as storks and cormorants. The eagle, though rarely seen today, is Poland's national bird and appears on the Polish emblem.

Poland has 23 national parks, but they cover less than 1% of the country. No permit is necessary to visit these parks, but most have admission fees (about 5zł per person). Camping in the parks is sometimes allowed, but only in specified sites. Poland also has a network of not-so-strictly preserved areas called 'landscape parks'. About 105 of these parks, covering 6% of Poland, are scattered throughout the country.

GOVERNMENT & POLITICS

The political left, repackaged as Social Democrats, made a startling comeback in parliamentary elections held only three years after the fall of the communists in Poland. In 1995, Lech Wałęsa was narrowly defeated by Aleksander Kwaśniewski of the Democratic Left Alliance (SLD). In October 2000, Kwaśniewski was re-elected as president, while Wałęsa collected just 1% of the vote. In the parliamentary elections a year later, the SLD again won and Solidarity failed to win a even one seat. Leszek Miller, a former senior Communist Party official, became prime minister.

The president is directly elected for a five-year term and nominates the prime minister. The parliament consists of two houses: a 460-seat lower house (the Sejm) and a 100-seat upper house (the Senat). With the imposition

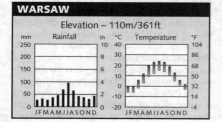

WARSAW
Elevation – 110m/361ft

of a 5% threshold for parliamentary representation, Poland's splintered political groupings have realigned into a relatively coherent multiparty system.

ECONOMY

The economic legacy of the communists included burdensome nanational debt and stagnant production. In 1990 the new government launched a radical 'shock therapy' campaign to build a market economy. Initially the reforms caused hyperinflation and a sharp fall in production, but the economy finally stabilised by the mid-1990s and has since experienced positive growth.

Over 60% of the workforce is in the private sector, with small businesses leading the way. Poland's numerous small farms keep food shelves well stocked, though trade barriers have limited export potential. Many of the mammoth communist-era industries, such as coal and steel, remain under state tutelage.

In mid-2002, the annual inflation rate was only 3.3%, but the GDP growth rate was still alarmingly low (1.1%) and unemployment was unacceptably high (18%). Poland remains desperate to join the EU, and to be part of its monetary union (unlikely until at least 2007).

POPULATION & PEOPLE

Poland was for centuries a multinational country and home to large Jewish, German and Ukrainian communities. However, because of ethnic cleansing and forced resettlements after WWII, Poland became an ethnically homogeneous country – about 98% of the population are now Poles. Poland's Jewish population once numbered more than three million but today it's between 5000 and 10,000.

Over 60% of the citizens live in towns and cities. Warsaw is by far the largest city, followed by Łódź, Kraków, Wrocław, Poznań and Gdańsk. Upper Silesia (around Katowice) is the most densely inhabited area while the northeastern border regions remain the least populated.

Between five and 10 million Poles live outside Poland. This emigre community, known as 'Polonia', is located mainly in the USA (particularly Chicago).

ARTS

Poland's rich literary tradition dates from the 15th century and claims four Nobel laureates. Its modern voice was shaped during the 19th century during the period of foreign subjugation. Nationalist-inspired writers thrived, including the poet Adam Mickiewicz (1798–1855), and Henryk Sienkiewicz (1846–1916), who won a Nobel Prize in 1905 for *Quo Vadis?*. This nationalist tradition was again revived during the communist period when Czesław Miłosz was awarded the Nobel Prize in 1980 for *The Captive Mind*.

At the turn of the 20th century, the avant-garde 'Young Poland' movement in art and literature developed in Kraków. The most notable representatives of this movement were the writer Stanisław Wyspiański (1869–1907), also famous for his stained-glass work; the playwright, Stanisław Ignacy Witkiewicz (1885–1939), commonly known as Witkacy; and the Nobel laureate Władysław Reymont (1867–1925). In 1996, Wisława Szymborska (1923–) also received a Nobel Prize for her ironic poetry.

Unquestionably, Poland's most famous musician was Frédéric Chopin (1810–49), whose music displays the melancholy and nostalgia that became hallmarks of the Polish national style. Stanisław Moniuszko (1819–72) 'nationalised' 19th-century Italian opera music by introducing Polish folk songs and dances onto the stage. His *Halka* (1858), about a peasant girl abandoned by a young noble, is a staple of the national opera houses.

Jan Matejko (1838–93) is Poland's best-known painter. His monumental historical paintings hang in galleries throughout the country. Wojciech Kossak (1857–1942) is another who documented Polish history; he is best remembered for the colossal *Panorama of Racławicka*, on display in Wrocław.

Poland claims several world-renowned film directors. The most notable is Andrzej Wajda, who received an Honorary Award at the 1999 Academy Awards. Western audiences are probably more familiar with the work of Roman Polański, who directed critically acclaimed films such as *Rosemary's Baby* and *Chinatown*. The late Krzysztof Kieślowski is best known for the trilogy *Three Colours: Blue/White/Red*.

SOCIETY & CONDUCT

Poles are friendly and polite, but not overly formal. The way of life in large urban centres increasingly mimics Western styles and manners. In the countryside, however, a more conservative culture dominates, evidenced by

POLAND

traditional gender roles and strong family ties. In both urban and rural settings, Poles are devoutly religious.

The Poles' sense of personal space may be a bit cosier than you are accustomed to – you may notice this trait when queuing for tickets or manoeuvring along city streets. When greeting each other, Polish men are passionate about shaking hands. Polish women, too, often shake hands with men, but the man should always wait for the woman to extend her hand first.

RELIGION

Over 80% of Poles are practising Roman Catholics. The Orthodox church exists along a narrow strip on the eastern frontier and its adherents constitute about 1% of the population.

The election of Karol Wojtyła, the archbishop of Kraków, as Pope John Paul II in 1978, and his triumphal visit to his homeland a year later, significantly enhanced the status of the church in Poland. The country is proud of its 'Polish Pope': his image is prominently displayed in public places and private homes throughout the country.

The overthrow of communism was as much a victory for the Church as it was for democracy. The fine line between the Church and the state is often blurred in Poland. The Church today is a powerful lobby on social issues. Legislation has been passed that mandates Catholic religious instruction in public schools and 'Christian values' in broadcasting. Some Poles have recently grown wary of the Church's increasing influence in society and politics.

LANGUAGE

Polish is a western variant of the group of Slavonic languages (which includes Czech and Slovak). Visually, Polish looks daunting (how do you possibly pronounce Wrzeszcz, a suburb near Gdańsk?) and is not an easy language to master. However, it is phonetic and there are few dialects or variations.

While Polish is overwhelmingly the major language, some older Poles, especially in the west, speak German, while many of the younger set speak English. Most tourist offices and upmarket hotels have at least one English-speaker, but visitors will do well to learn a few key phrases in Polish. To, umm, polish up on your Polish, see the Language chapter at the back of this book.

Facts for the Visitor

HIGHLIGHTS

Nature buffs will love Poland's pristine Baltic beaches, majestic snowcapped peaks and secluded forest-lined lakes. The beaches of Łeba, perhaps the most inspiring on the coast, are surrounded by miles of unending, desertlike sand dunes. Mikołajki is a charming town that provides access to the Great Masurian Lakes, ideal for biking, sailing and kayaking. Zakopane is the base for hiking and skiing in the Tatras, Poland's most magnificent mountain range. And the Unesco-listed Białowieża National Park is a gorgeous pocket of forest with a bison reserve.

Poland's rich history is recounted by its imposing medieval castles and charming old town squares. Many of them, such as those in Gdańsk and Wrocław, were lovingly rebuilt after WWII. The royal grandeur of Poland's past is best preserved in Kraków's Old Town, which was virtually undamaged during WWII. Visitors can also imagine medieval life at Malbork Castle, the largest Gothic castle in Europe.

Auschwitz is the most vivid reminder of the atrocities that occurred during WWII, while the Nazis left haunting reminders, such as Hitler's former bunker at Wolf's Lair, not far from Olsztyn.

SUGGESTED ITINERARIES

Your itinerary obviously depends on the amount of time available, your interests, where you will arrive and/or depart, and the season, but you may wish to use the list below as a guide:

One Week
Warsaw (two days), Kraków (two), Oświęcim (one), Wrocław (one) & Toruń (one)

Two Weeks
Follow the suggestions above, but add more days to each place. With any extra time, visit Zakopane and the Tatra Mountains (two to three days), Gdańsk and around (two to three), the Great Masurian Lakes (two to three) or Białowieża National Park (one to two).

One Month
Spend longer at the places listed for 'Two Weeks' and include Łódź (one), Częstochowa (one), Poznań and around (three to four), Olsztyn and around (one to two), and places in the southeast such as Lublin and around (three to four) and Zamość (two).

POLAND

Two Months
All of the above, plus maybe a trek in the Tatras or Sudeten Mountains, or spend more time exploring the Great Masurian Lakes or Białowieża National Park.

PLANNING
When to Go
The tourist season runs roughly from May to September and peaks in July and August. Many Poles – and their children – go on holidays during these two months, so transport is crowded and accommodation is often limited. Most theatres and concert halls are also closed at this time.

The best time to visit Poland is either spring (late April to late June) or early autumn (September to mid-October). These periods are pleasantly warm and ideal for general sightseeing and outdoor activities. Many cultural events still take place in both periods.

Mid-autumn to mid-spring is colder, darker and perhaps less attractive for most visitors. However, it's not a bad time to visit city sights and enjoy the cultural life. Except for skiing (from December to March), outdoor activities are less prominent in this period and many camping grounds and youth hostels are closed.

Maps
Maps of all cities, towns and tourist attractions in Poland are easy to buy throughout the country. Three of the best publishers of maps are Copernicus, Eurocity and Shell, but few are translated into English. Copernicus' *Polska Atlas Samochodowy* (1:200,000) is the most detailed for driving and cycling, but it's bulky.

What to Bring
The days when shelves in Poland were empty is happily long over. You can now buy almost anything, including clothes, toiletries, stationery, sports and camping equipment, and prices are lower than in Western Europe.

RESPONSIBLE TOURISM
In some popular places (such as Kraków and Zakopane), the summer influx of tourists puts a real strain on local infrastructure and the environment. One way to minimise your own impact – and perhaps enjoy yourself more – is to avoid visiting in the high season. Also, spending money in less-visited areas is another way to even out the inequitable financial input caused by tourism while simultaneously broadening your enjoyment and understanding of the country.

TOURIST OFFICES
Local Tourist Offices
Almost everywhere of interest in Poland has a regional tourist office. These offices are usually more helpful, and often open longer hours, than those of the Polish Tourists Association (PTTK), which are more like organisations of travel agencies offering tours, guides and car hire. However, in some places PTTK offices act as de facto regional tourist offices. Staff at both usually speak English (and often German) and sell maps and guidebooks.

Orbis Travel, the largest travel agency in Poland, has offices and operates upmarket hotels throughout the country. It is often the best place to buy tickets for domestic and international trains and airlines, and for international ferries. Orbis does not focus on providing free information to travellers, but staff are helpful and often speak English.

Tourist Offices Abroad
Polish National Tourist Offices in other countries include:

France (☎ 01 47 42 07 42, **W** www.tourisme .pologne.net) 49 ave de l'Opéra, 75002 Paris
Germany (☎ 030-21 00 92 11, **W** www.polen -info.de) Marburger Strasse 1, 10789 Berlin
Netherlands (☎ 020-625 35 70) Leidsestraat 64, 1017 PD Amsterdam
UK (☎ 020-7580 8811, **W** www.pnto.dial.pipex .com) 1st floor, Remo House, 310-312 Regent St, London W1R 5AJ
USA (☎ 212-338 9412, **W** www.polandtour.org) 275 Madison Ave, Suite 1711, New York, NY 10016

VISAS & DOCUMENTS
Citizens of the European Union, Switzerland, Japan, the UK and the USA can receive a visa for up to 90 days (Britons up to 180 days) at all major borders, and international airports and sea ports. Citizens of Australia, Canada, New Zealand, South Africa and Israel must obtain a tourist visa from a Polish embassy or consulate before coming to Poland.

Tourist visas from Polish embassies or consulates are issued for up to 180 days. The price varies between countries, but is usually about US$50. You can obtain a 48-hour transit visa (onward visa required) if you need to pass through Poland. Visas are generally issued in a few days, but an 'express same-day service' is available at some embassies/consulates if you hand over an additional 50% fee.

If you apply for a visa outside your own country (eg, if you're Aussie and received your visa from the Polish embassy in London), keep all documentation – particularly a copy of your visa application form if possible – to show the immigration officials in Poland.

All visas for Poland – whether obtained at a border, airport, sea port, embassy or consulate – are only valid for the period specified and normally *cannot* be extended. If you want to extend your visa, simply leave the country and get another one.

Student Cards

ISIC cards provide discounts on almost all museums (up to 50%), local transport (50%) in Warsaw (but nowhere else), Polferries services (20%), domestic flights on LOT (10%), PKS buses (30%) from Tuesday to Thursday, and some buses run by Polski Express (30%). ISIC cards, however, *cannot* be used for domestic or international train tickets bought in Poland. ISIC cards are available (with the correct documentation) from Almatur, which has offices in every city in Poland.

EMBASSIES & CONSULATES
Polish Embassies & Consulates

For details about Polish diplomatic missions in other East European countries, refer to the relevant chapters elsewhere in this book.

Australia
Embassy: (☎ 02-6273 1208) 7 Turrana St, Yarralumla, ACT 2600
Consulate: (☎ 02-9363 9816) 10 Trelawney St, Woollahra, NSW 2025

Canada
Embassy: (☎ 613-789 0468) 443 Daly Ave, Ottawa 2, Ontario K1N 6H3
Consulate: (☎ 514-937 9481) 1500 Ave des Pins Ouest, Montreal, Quebec PQ H3G 1B4
Consulate: (☎ 416-252 5471) 2603 Lakeshore Blvd West, Toronto, Ontario M8V 1G5
Consulate: (☎ 604-688 3530) 1177 West Hastings St, Suite 1600, Vancouver, BC V6E 2K3

France
Embassy: (☎ 01 43 17 34 22) 5 rue de Talleyrand, 75007 Paris
Consulates in Lille and Lyons

Germany
Embassy: (☎ 030-22 31 30) Lassenstrasse 19–21, 14193 Berlin
Consulates in Cologne, Hamburg and Leipzig

Netherlands
Embassy: (☎ 070-360 28 06) Alexanderstraat 25, 2514 JM The Hague

Russia
Embassy: (☎ 095-231 15 00) ul Klimashkina 4, 123447 Moscow
Consulate: (☎ 812-274 41 70) ul 5 Sovietskaya 12/14, 193130 St Petersburg
Consulate: (☎ 0112-27 33 77) ul Kashtanova 51, 236000 Kaliningrad

UK
Embassy: (☎ 020-7580 0475) 73 New Cavendish St, London W1N 7RB
Consulate in Edinburgh

USA
Embassy: (☎ 202-234 3800) 2640 16th St NW, Washington, DC 20009
Consulates in New York, Chicago and Los Angeles

Embassies & Consulates in Poland

All diplomatic missions that are listed below are in Warsaw (☎ area code 022) unless stated otherwise.

Australia (☎ 521 34 44, W www.australia.pl) ul Nowogrodzka 11
Belarus (☎/fax 617 84 11) ul Ateńska 67
  Consulate-General: (☎/fax 058-341 00 26) ul Jaśkowa Dolina 50, Gdańsk
Canada (☎ 584 31 00, e wsaw@dfait.maeci.gc .ca) Al Jerozolimskie 123
Czech Republic (☎ 628 72 21, e warsaw@ embassy.mzv.cz) ul Koszykowa 18
France (☎ 529 30 00, e ambassade@sunik .pagi.pl) ul Puławska 17
  Consulate-General: (☎ 012-424 53 00) ul Stolarska 15, Kraków
Germany (☎ 617 30 11, W www .ambasadaniemiec.pl) ul Dąbrowiecka 30
  Consulate-General: (☎ 012-421 84 73, fax 421 76 28) ul Stolarska 7, Kraków
  Consulate-General: (☎ 058-341 43 66) Al Zwycięstwa 23, Gdańsk
Ireland (☎ 849 66 55, W www.irlandia.pl) ul Humańska 10
Lithuania (☎ 625 33 68, e litwa.amb@waw.pdi .net) Al Szucha 5
Netherlands (☎ 849 23 51, fax 849 83 45) ul Chocimska 6
Russia (☎ 621 34 53, fax 625 30 16) ul Belwederska 49
  Consulate: (☎ 012-422 26 47, fax 422 90 66) ul Biskupia 7, Kraków
Slovakia (☎ 525 81 10, e slovakia@waw.pdi .net) ul Litewska 6
UK (☎ 628 10 01, W www.britishembassy.pl) Al Róż 1
Ukraine (☎ 625 01 27, e emb_pl@mfa.gov.ua) Al Szucha 7

Consulate: (☎ 012-429 60 66, fax 429 29 36) ul Krakowska 41, Kraków
USA (☎ 628 30 41, Ⓦ www.usinfo.pl) Al Ujazdowskie 29/31
Consulate: (☎ 012-424 51 00) ul Stolarska 9, Kraków

CUSTOMS

Customs procedures are usually a formality when both entering and leaving Poland, and your luggage will probably only receive a cursory glance.

When entering Poland, you're allowed to bring duty-free articles for personal use. Every foreigner can bring in or take out of Poland the equivalent (in any currency) of up to €5000. If you wish to leave the country with more than €5000 (in any currency), complete a Currency Declaration form on arrival and have it stamped by customs officials. In practice, it is unlikely anyone will ask you how much money you have.

When leaving the country, you may take out duty-free gifts and souvenirs to a total value of up to €90. Note that the export of items manufactured before 9 May 1945 is prohibited.

MONEY
Currency

The official Polish currency is the złoty ('zwo-ti'), abbreviated to zł. (For reasons unclear, the currency is often abbreviated to PLN in English-language publications and documents.) The złoty is divided into 100 groszy, abbreviated to gr. Denominations of notes are 10, 20, 50, 100 and 200 zł (rare), and coins come in one, two five, 10, 20 and 50 gr, and one, two and five zł. Polish currency is convertible so the black market for currency exchange has all but disappeared.

Exchange Rates

At the time of writing, the approximate exchange rates were:

country	unit		złoty
Australia	A$1	=	2.21zł
Canada	C$1	=	2.60zł
Czech Republic	1 Kč	=	0.12zł
Euro Zone	€1	=	3.70zł
Japan	¥100	=	3.15zł
NZ	NZ$1	=	1.89zł
Russia	R1	=	0.11zł
Slovakia	10 Sk	=	0.85zł
UK	UK£1	=	5.85zł
Ukraine	1 hrn	=	0.74zł
USA	US$1	=	4.03zł

Exchanging Money

For maximum flexibility, travellers should bring cash and one or two credit cards. Cash is easy to change and convenient, especially since Poland is a relatively low-crime destination. Private foreign-exchange offices – called *kantor* – are *everywhere*; in fact, there are often so many that we don't need to show them on our maps. Kantors require no paperwork and charge no commission. Exchange rates rarely vary, but rates at kantors in the midst of major tourist attractions, in top-end hotels and at airports are generally poor.

The most widely accepted currencies are the US dollar, the euro and the pound sterling (in that order). Foreign banknotes should be in perfect condition or kantors may refuse to accept them.

Travellers cheques are obviously more secure than cash, but they're also less convenient. Kantors very rarely change travellers cheques. Not all banks do either and most also charge a commission of 2% to 3%. The best place to change travellers cheques are branches of Bank Pekao or PKO Bank. In a remote region, finding an open bank that cashes travellers cheques may be tricky, especially on weekends.

Ask your local bank about the possibility of cashing Eurocheques while in Poland, because some readers have recently had success.

Automated teller machines (ATMs) – called a *bankomat* – are a convenient way of obtaining local currency. ATMs, which accept up to 17 different international credit cards, are now strategically located in the centre of all cities and most smaller towns. Banks without an ATM may provide cash advances over the counter on credit cards, especially Visa. Bank Pekao will give cash advances with Visa and MasterCard; rates are set and charged by your own bank. Credit cards are increasingly useful for buying goods and services, though their use is still limited to upmarket establishments.

Costs

Travellers must pay for everything in Poland (except visas and international airfares) in the local currency, even if prices are quoted to you (and listed in this chapter) in US dollars and euros. Happily, foreigners pay the same price as Poles for everything.

If you use camping grounds and/or youth hostels, and self-cater or eat at cheap cafeterias, it's possible manage on the złoty equivalent of US$15 per person per day. Increase this to $30/25 per person per day travelling as a single/double if you want to stay in decent budget accommodation and eat meals in acceptable restaurants. To add in some cultural events, a few beers, a taxi or two and some 1st-class train travel, allow US$40/35.

Tipping & Bargaining

If a 'service charge' is added to the restaurant bill there is no obligation to tip. In budget-priced restaurants guests rarely leave a tip; in upmarket establishments it is customary to tip 10% of the bill. Tipping taxi drivers is not necessary unless the driver has been particularly helpful – the driver may reward himself with a 'tip' anyway by not giving you the correct change. Bargaining is rare; perhaps only in outdoor markets in smaller towns.

Taxes & Refunds

A Value Added Tax (VAT) of 3% to 22% is added to most goods and services. It is always included in the prices quoted to you and the prices listed in this chapter.

Visitors not from Poland or an EU country are entitled to a refund of VAT paid on goods taken home if they spend more than 200zł in one day at any shop displaying the sign 'Global Refund' (W www.globalrefund.pl). Ask staff at any of the shops about the complicated (but worthwhile) procedures, so you can claim tax reimbursements at international airports, sea ports and borders when you leave.

POST & COMMUNICATIONS
Post

Postal services are operated by Poczta Polska. Most cities have a dozen or more post offices, of which the Poczta Główna (main post office) has the widest range of facilities, including poste restante, fax and, sometimes, Internet.

Letters and postcards sent by air from Poland take about one week to reach a European destination and up to two weeks if sent to anywhere else. Receiving mail via the poste restante system only reliable in large cities such as Warsaw, Kraków and Gdańsk. Poste-restante mail is held for 14 working days, then returned to the sender.

The cost of sending a normal-sized letter (up to 20g) or a postcard to just about anywhere outside Poland is 2zł, plus a surcharge up to 60g for the 'airmail express' service.

Telephone

Major telecommunications facilities in Poland are provided by Telekomunikacja Polska (TP), which usually has a telephone centre near or inside the main post office. Most of the public telephones now use magnetic phonecards, which are available at post offices, kiosks and grocery stores. Phonecards are available in units of 25 (11.30zł), 50 (20.40zł) and 100 (37.20zł) – one unit represents one three-minute local call. The cards can be used for domestic and international calls. Make sure you tear off the perforated corner before placing it into the telephone.

Not long ago, TP upgraded the telephone system so that all numbers throughout Poland have seven digits. (Numbers included in this chapter are currently correct.) If you ring a six-digit number, the new number should be provided in English (eventually) by the operator. Otherwise, if the number starts with:

1 or 2 – add 4 to the beginning
3, 4 or 5 – add 6
6, 7, 81, 82, 83, 84 or 85 – add 2
86, 87, 88 or 89 – add 3

When calling a number from another telephone district within Poland you must add a prefix of 0; then an 'operator code' of 1033, 1044, 1055 or 1066 depending on which telephone operator you choose to use; then the area code (which is listed in the destination sections later); and, eventually, the actual number. It doesn't matter which operator (and code) you use, and operator codes are not used for international calls.

The three mobile (cell) telephone providers are Idea (W www.idea.pl), Era and Plus GSM. Mobile phones are extremely popular as a status symbol and a more reliable alternative to the jammed land lines and occasionally inoperable public phones.

Direct dialling is possible to just about anywhere in the world. Collect calls are also possible to most countries. Inquire at any TP office for the toll-free number to the operator in the country you want to call. These numbers include:

Australia	☎ 00 800 61 111 61
Canada	☎ 00 800 11 141 18
France	☎ 00 800 33 111 33
Germany	☎ 00 800 49 111 49
UK	☎ 00 800 44 111 44
USA (AT&T)	☎ 00 800 11 111 11

To call Poland from abroad, dial the country code (☎ 48), then the two-digit area code (drop the initial '0' and don't use an operator code), and then the seven-digit local number. The Polish international access code for overseas calls from Poland is 00. If you need help, try the operators for local numbers (☎ 913), national numbers and codes (☎ 912) and international codes (☎ 908), but don't expect anyone to speak English.

The cost of a call from a telephone booth using a phonecard to Europe and the UK is about 3zł per minute, about 6zł to North America, and about 9zł to Australia and New Zealand. If you want to use an international operator (☎ 901), you must pay for at least three minutes.

Fax
Faxes can be sent and received at any main post office for the cost of the equivalent telephone call (minimum of three minutes), but with the advent of mobile phones and the Internet, the old-fashioned fax machine is fast becoming obsolete.

Email & Internet Access
Poland is now truly part of the 'cyber world' and several Polish Internet service providers compete for the growing market. Internet centres can be found all over Poland; smaller towns often have a couple of computers in the main post office, while cities offer a wide choice of trendy cyberpubs and Internet cafés. Sending/receiving emails and/or surfing the Net usually costs about 10zł per hour.

DIGITAL RESOURCES
Before you travel – or while you're in Poland – you may wish to access one of the following websites.

ⓦ www.poland.pl – excellent place to start surfing
ⓦ www.polishpages.com.pl – best for anything business-related
ⓦ www.insidepoland.com – current affairs & reasonable links
ⓦ www.polishworld.com – directories & travel bookings

BOOKS
Jews in Poland by Iwo Cyprian Pogonowski provides a comprehensive record of half a millennium of Polish-Jewish relations in Poland.

God's Playground: A History of Poland by Norman Davies offers an in-depth analysis of Polish history. The condensed version, *The Heart of Europe: A Short History of Poland*, also by Davies, has greater emphasis on the 20th century. *The Polish Way: A Thousand-Year History of the Poles and their Culture* by Adam Zamoyski is a superb cultural overview of Poland. It's crammed with maps and illustrations that bring the past 1000 years to life. *The Polish Revolution: Solidarity 1980–82* by Timothy Garton Ash is entertaining and thoroughly researched.

NEWSPAPERS & MAGAZINES
Warsaw's major English-language publication *The Warsaw Voice* (ⓦ www.warsawvoice.pl) is a well-edited but rather too serious weekly providing a useful insight into national politics and business.

The excellent *Welcome to...* series of magazines covers Poznań, Wrocław, Kraków, Gdańsk and Warsaw individually. Just as good are the *What, Where, When* magazines covering (individually) Warsaw, Kraków and Gdańsk. These publications are free.

Recent copies of newspapers and magazines from the UK, the USA, Germany and France are readily available in the cities. Look for them at EMPiK bookshops, which are *everywhere*, and at newsstands in the lobbies of upmarket hotels.

RADIO & TV
The state-run Polish Radio (Polskie Radio) is the main broadcaster, while Warsaw-based Radio Zet and Kraków-based RFM are two nationwide private broadcasters. Plenty of other private competitors operate locally on FM. Almost every word spoken on radio is in Polish, but most music is in English. Major stations in Warsaw include Radio Kolor (103FM) and Radio Pagoda (100.1FM).

Poland has several private TV channels, including PolSat, and two state-owned countywide channels, but none of them provides any regular foreign-language programmes. Many programmes are so badly overdubbed – with one male voice covering all actors (including children and women) – that you can often still hear the original language. Most

POLAND

POLAND

major hotels have satellite dishes that allow access to various European and US channels.

TIME

All of Poland lies within the same time zone, ie, GMT/UTC+1 hour. Poland puts its clocks forward one hour in late March and turns them back again in late September.

LAUNDRY

Do-it-yourself laundrettes are rare, but dry-cleaners *(pralnia)* can be found in larger cities. Expect to pay 5zł to 8zł per garment. Top-class hotels offer a faster – but more expensive – dry-cleaning service for guests.

TOILETS

Toilets are labelled *toaleta* or simply 'WC'. Gentlemen should use the door labelled *męski* and/or marked with an inverted pyramid, and the ladies should look for the door labelled *damski* and/or marked with a circle. Public toilets can be found inside all transport terminals and tourist attractions, and cost the user about 1zł. Restaurants often allow nonpatrons to use their facilities for about the same price.

WOMEN TRAVELLERS

Travel for women in Poland is hassle-free except for occasional encounters with drunks. Harassment of this kind is almost never dangerous, but can be annoying. Simply take the usual precautions.

Women travellers may wish to contact the **International Professional Women of Poland** organisation *(☎/fax 022-606 03 14)* or the **International Women's Group** *(☎ 022-630 72 21)*, both based in Warsaw.

GAY & LESBIAN TRAVELLERS

The Polish gay and lesbian movement is less underground than it used to be. Warsaw and Kraków have the most open scene and are the easiest places to make contacts.

The best sources of information in Warsaw are the **Pride Society** *(e pridesociety@yahoo .com)* and the monthly *Warsaw Insider* magazine, which lists current gay and lesbian clubs in the capital. The website w www.gej .net is also a useful source of information.

DISABLED TRAVELLERS

Poland is not well set up for people with disabilities, although there have been significant improvements over recent years. Wheelchair ramps are only available at some upmarket hotels and public transport will be a real challenge for anyone with mobility problems.

SENIOR TRAVELLERS

Travelling around Poland causes few problems for mobile senior travellers, especially if you choose upmarket hotels and travel 1st class on trains.

Senior visitors (with the appropriate cards) can receive discounts on domestic flights with LOT (20%), buses operated by PKS (30%) from Tuesday to Thursday and, possibly, all of the three international ferry services.

TRAVEL WITH CHILDREN

Parents travelling with children in Poland should not have any particular problems. Children (under 14) often receive discounts to museums and can usually sleep in the same hotel room as adults for little extra cost. Any of the endless things required by children of all ages are readily available throughout Poland.

USEFUL ORGANISATIONS

You may wish to contact one or more of the following organisations before or during your visit to Poland. Each of these is based in Warsaw (☎ area code 022).

American Friends in Warsaw (☎ 816 70 94)
British Council (☎ 695 59 00, fax 621 99 55) Al Jerozolimskie 59
French Institute (☎ 827 76 40) ul Senatorska 38
Goethe Institute (☎ 656 60 50) 10th floor, Palace of Culture & Science
Polish Community (☎ 826 20 41) ul Krakowskie Przedmieście – for Polish expats
UNICEF (☎/fax 628 03 01) Al Szucha 16/15

DANGERS & ANNOYANCES

Poland is a relatively safe country, though crime has increased steadily since the fall of

---

Emergency Services

The nationwide, toll-free, 24-hour emergency telephone numbers are ☎ 911 for a pharmacy, ☎ 998 for the fire brigade and ☎ 999 for ambulance.

For the police dial ☎ 997 – but call ☎ 112 from a mobile (cell) phone.

Roadside Assistance is available on ☎ 981.

Don't expect the operators for any of these services to speak English, however.

communism. Take care when walking alone at night, especially in the city centre and in the suburb of Praga. Be particularly alert at any time in the Warszawa Centralna (central) train station, the favourite playground for thieves and pickpockets. Theft from cars is becoming a plague, so keep your vehicle in a guarded car park whenever possible. Heavy drinking is common and drunks can be disturbing, though rarely dangerous. Smoking is common in all public places, especially on public transport.

Poland is an ethnically homogeneous nation. Travellers who look racially different may attract some stares from locals, but this is more likely to be curiosity than anything hostile or ostensibly racist. Football (soccer) hooligans are not uncommon, so avoid travelling on public transport with them (especially if their team has lost!).

LEGAL MATTERS

Foreigners are, of course, subject to the laws of Poland, but there are no laws specific to Poland or not obvious to visitors.

BUSINESS HOURS

Most grocery shops are open weekdays (Monday to Friday) 7am or 8am to 6pm or 7pm and until about 2pm on Saturday. Larger stores stay open for a few hours longer. Banks in larger cities are open from about 8am to 5pm weekdays (sometimes until 2pm on Saturday), but open for fewer hours in smaller towns. Kantors generally operate from 9am to 6pm on weekdays and until about 2pm on Saturday.

Larger post offices are normally open 8am to 8pm weekdays, and one post office in the larger cities will often stay open for 24 hours. Government departments operate about 8am to 4pm on weekdays.

The opening hours of museums and other tourist attractions vary greatly. They tend to open any time between 9am and 11am and close some time from 3pm to 6pm. Most museums are open on weekends, but many close on Monday and also stay closed on the day following a public holiday. Most museums also shut their doors one or two hours earlier in the low season (October to April).

PUBLIC HOLIDAYS & SPECIAL EVENTS

Poland's public holidays include New Year's Day (1 January), Easter Monday (March or April), Labour Day (1 May), Constitution Day (3 May), Corpus Christi (one Thursday in May or June), Assumption Day (15 August), All Saints' Day (1 November), Independence Day (11 November) and Christmas (25 and 26 December).

Cultural, musical and religious events are held regularly in Warsaw, Wrocław, Kraków, Częstochowa, Poznań and Gdańsk – refer to the relevant sections later for details.

ACTIVITIES

Hikers and long-distance trekkers can enjoy any of the thousands of kilometres of marked trails across the Tatra and Sudeten Mountains, around Białowieża National Park and the Great Masurian Lakes district, and at places near Poznań and Świnoujście – refer to the relevant sections later for details. Trails are easy to follow and detailed maps are available at most larger bookshops.

Poland is fairly flat and ideal for cyclists. Bicycle routes along the banks of the Vistula River are popular in Warsaw, Toruń and Kraków. Many of the national parks – including Tatra (near Zakopane), Wolin (near Świnoujście) and Słowinski (near Łeba) – offer bicycle trails, as does the Great Masurian Lakes district. Bikes can be rented at most resort towns and larger cities. (Also see Cycling in the Getting Around section later.)

Zakopane will delight skiers from December to March. Facilities tend to be significantly cheaper – though not as developed – as the ski resorts in Western Europe.

Throngs of yachties, canoeists and kayakers enjoy the network of waterways in the Great Masurian Lakes district every summer; boats are available for rent from all lakeside towns. Windsurfers can head to the windswept beaches of the Hel Peninsula.

COURSES

Polish-language courses are available in most major cities, but some only operate in summer. In Kraków, look for posters plastered around major tourist attractions; in Warsaw, check out *The Warsaw Voice*. Otherwise, contact one of the following organisations before you leave home.

The Centre for Polish Studies (☎ 058-550 68 59, ⓦ www.learnpolish.edu.pl) ul Podgorna 8, Sopot
Polonia Institute of the Jagiellonian University (☎ 012-429 76 32, fax 429 93 51) ul Jodłowa 13, Kraków

POLAND

'Polonicum' Institute of Polish Language & Culture for Foreigners (☎/fax 022-826 54 16), Warsaw University, ul Krakowskie Przedmieście 26/28

Schola Polonica (☎ 022-625 26 52, **W** www .schola.pl) ul Jaracza 3 m 19, Warsaw

WORK

Travellers hoping to find paid work in Poland will probably be sorely disappointed. The complex paperwork required for a working visa is enough to put most people off the idea. Also, wages are low and you'll probably have to compete for casual work with other Eastern Europeans, who may be willing to work for a relative pittance.

ACCOMMODATION
Camping

Poland has hundreds of camping grounds and many offer good-value cabins and bungalows. Theoretically, most are open from May to September, but some really only bother opening their gates between June and August.

Hostels

Youth hostels (schroniska młodzieżowe) in Poland are operated by Polskie Towarzystwo Schronisk Młodzieżowych (PTSM), a member of Hostelling International. Currently Poland has about 130 hostels open all year and about 450 only open in July and August. The all-year hostels are more reliable and have more facilities, such as a kitchen and dining room. The seasonal hostels are usually installed in suburban schools (while the students are off for their holidays) and amenities can be basic. Annoyingly, many hostels have no actual names or use names that are ambiguous.

Many previously strict hostel rules have been relaxed or abandoned. Youth hostels are now open to all, members and nonmembers alike, with no age limit. Curfew is often 10pm, but some hostel staff may be flexible. Most hostels are closed between 10am and 5pm.

A bed in a hostel dormitory costs about 20zł to 25zł per person per night. Single and double rooms, if available, cost about 45/70zł. The youth hostel card gives a 10% to 25% discount on these prices for nationals and, sometimes, for foreigners. Hostels can also provide sheets for about 5zł per person.

Given the low prices, hostels are popular and often full. A particularly busy time is early May to mid-June, when the hostels are often crowded with groups of rowdy Polish school kids.

In most major cities, a few student dorms open as hostels in summer, though they're often in the suburbs. Regional tourist offices are the best places to find out which student hostels are available and how to get there.

Mountain Refuges

PTTK (see the Tourist Offices section earlier) runs a chain of mountain refuges (schroniska górskie) for trekkers. They are usually simple, but the price is right and the atmosphere is welcoming. They also serve cheap, hot meals. The more isolated refuges are obliged to accept everyone, regardless of how crowded they get. As a result, in the high season even a space on the floor can be hard to find. Refuges are normally open all year, but confirm with the nearest PTTK office before setting off.

Hotels

Most cities and towns offer a variety of old and new hotels ranging from ultrabasic to extraplush. Rooms with a private bathroom can be considerably more expensive than those with shared facilities, sometimes twice as much. Hotel prices often vary according to the season and are usually posted (but rarely in English) at hotel reception desks. Rates quoted in this chapter include all taxes.

If possible, check the room before accepting. Don't be fooled by the hotel reception areas, which may look great in contrast to the rest of the establishment.

Two reliable companies can that can arrange accommodation over the Internet are **W** www.poland4u.com and **W** www.hotels poland.com. These sometimes have substantial discount offers.

Private Rooms & Apartments

Some cities and tourist-oriented towns have agencies – usually called a biuro zakwaterowania or biuro kwater prywatnych – which arrange accommodation in private homes. Rooms cost about 55/90zł for singles/doubles depending on the season, amenities provided and distance from the city centre. The most important factor to consider is location; if the home is in the suburbs, find out how far it is from reliable public transport.

During the high season, home owners also directly approach tourists. Prices are often lower (and open to bargaining), but you're more likely to be offered somewhere out in the sticks. Also, private homes in smaller resorts and villages often have signs outside their gates or doors offering a *pokoje* (room) or *noclegi* (lodging).

In Warsaw and Kraków a few agencies offer self-contained apartments (with a kitchen and, sometimes, a laundry). Discounts for more than five days are often attractive so they're an affordable alternative to mid-range and top-end hotels. And the price is per apartment, so you can squeeze in as many people as you want (within reason!).

FOOD

Poles start off their day with breakfast *(śniadanie)*, which is roughly similar to its Western counterpart. The most important and substantial meal of the day, *obiad*, is normally eaten between 2pm and 5pm. *Obiad* usually includes a hearty soup as well as a main course. The third meal is supper *(kolacja)*, which is often similar to breakfast.

Etiquette and table manners are much the same as in the West. When beginning a meal, whether it's in a restaurant or at home, wish your fellow diners *smacznego* ('bon appetit'). When drinking a toast, the Polish equivalent of 'cheers' is *na zdrowie* ('to the health').

Regional Dishes

Polish cuisine has been influenced by various cultures, including Jewish, Ukrainian, Russian, Hungarian and German. Polish food is hearty and filling, abundant in potatoes and dumplings, and rich in meat but not vegetables.

Poland's most famous dishes are *bigos* (sauerkraut with a variety of meats), *pierogi* (ravioli-like dumplings stuffed with cottage cheese or minced meat or cabbage and wild mushrooms) and *barszcz* (red beetroot soup originating from Russian *borshch*).

Hearty soups such as *żurek* (sour soup with sausage and hard-boiled eggs) are a highlight of Polish cuisine. Main dishes are often made with pork, including *golonka* (boiled pig's knuckle served with horseradish) and *schab pieczony* (roast loin of pork seasoned with prunes and herbs). *Gołącbki* (cabbage leaves stuffed with minced beef and rice) is a tasty alternative.

Potato pancakes *(placki ziemniaczane)* and crepes *(naleśniki)* are popular snacks. The favourite Polish summer dessert is fresh berries with cream.

Places to Eat

The gastronomic scene in Poland has developed dramatically over the last decade. A constellation of Western-style eating outlets – almost nonexistent in communist Poland – have sprung up to serve culinary delights that were previously unobtainable. Most of the famous international fast-food chains have already conquered all Polish cities and a myriad of Polish imitations has settled in.

The cheapest place to eat is a milk bar *(bar mleczny)*, a no-frills, self-service cafeteria. They're open at around 7am to 8am (for breakfast) and close between 6pm and 8pm (earlier on Saturday); only a handful are open on Sunday. Milk bars are normally self-serve, so it means that you can see what's cooking, and point, pay and enjoy without speaking a word of Polish.

Most top-class restaurants have menus in English and/or German, but don't expect any foreign-language menus or English-speaking waiters in cheaper eateries. Most staff don't speak English, so we haven't included telephone numbers for restaurants in this chapter.

Menus are usually have several sections: soups *(zupy)*, main courses *(dania drugie)* and accompaniments *(dodatki)*. The price of the main course may not include a side dish – such as potatoes, French fries and salads – which you choose separately (and pay extra for) from the *dodatki* section. Also note that the price for some dishes (particularly fish and poultry) is often listed per 100g, so the price will depend on the *total* weight of the fish/meat.

DRINKS

Wódka (vodka) is the national drink, which the Poles claim was invented in their country. In Poland, vodka is usually drunk neat and comes in a number of colours and flavours, including *myśliwska* (flavoured with juniper berries), *wiśniówka* (with cherries) and *jarzębiak* (with rowanberries). The most famous variety is *żubrówka* (bison vodka), flavoured with grass from the Białowieża Forest and often drunk with apple juice. Other notable spirits include *krupnik* (honey liqueur), *śliwowica* (plum brandy) and *winiak* (grape brandy).

Poles also appreciate the taste of a cold beer *(zimne piwo)*. Polish beer is cheap and palatable and particularly enjoyable while sitting at an outdoor café in a city's old town. The top brands found throughout the country (and a lot of research was done on this topic!) include

Żywiec, Okocim and EB, while the regional brands are available in every city. Imported beers can be bought at upmarket establishments, particularly any of the plethora of Irish pubs in the cities.

The quantity and quality of Polish wine is nothing to get excited about, but Hungarian and Bulgarian wines are acceptable and cheap. Wines from elsewhere will be expensive.

ENTERTAINMENT

Every city and town has several cinemas offering recently released films. Thankfully, all films are screened with the original soundtrack (normally English) and Polish subtitles (unlike Polish television). Tickets cost from 6zł to 13zł depending on the city, film shown, session time and comfort of the cinema.

Polish theatre continues to impress foreign audiences. Language is obviously an obstacle for foreigners, but theatre buffs may want to visit some of the better theatres just to watch the acting. Most theatres are closed on Monday and every day in July and August. Tickets cost about 15zł to 25zł. If possible, try to get rid of the jeans and sneakers for the evening or you'll definitely be 'frowned upon' by the other patrons.

Some of the largest cities have opera houses and those in Warsaw and Łódź arguably offer the best productions. For classical music, the Filharmonia Narodowa (National Philharmonic) usually holds concerts on Friday and Saturday nights in most major cities. Again, tickets are very cheap.

Warsaw and Kraków have lively jazz scenes. Discos are popular and usually open from 9pm to late on Thursday, Friday and Saturday. And there's no shortage of places for a drink at any time of the day or night.

SPECTATOR SPORTS

Poland's most popular sport is football (soccer). Although the Polish national team did qualify for the World Cup in 2002, it didn't fare as well as the long-suffering Polish fans had hoped. The most prominent teams in the Polish Football Federation are Legia Warszawa, Widzew Łódź and Wisła Kraków.

The most prestigious international sporting event in Poland is the Tour de Pologne, a long-distance cycling race that takes place every September. Other popular sports include basketball and boxing (Poland boasts the WBO light-heavyweight world champion).

SHOPPING

Amber is a fossil resin of vegetable origin that comes primarily from the Baltic region and appears in a variety of colours from pale yellow to reddish brown. The best places to buy jewellery made from amber are Gdańsk, Kraków and Warsaw.

Polish contemporary paintings, original prints and sculptures are sold by private commercial art galleries, especially in Warsaw and Kraków. Polish poster art has received international recognition; the best selection of poster galleries is also in Warsaw and Kraków.

Other ideas for mementoes include crystal glass, handmade pottery (especially from the villages within an hour's drive from Wrocław), chessboards (from shops at the main square in Kraków), and original paintings of Kraków and other picturesque old towns.

Getting There & Away

AIR

The national carrier, **LOT** (w *www.lot.com*), flies to all major European cities, as well as almost everywhere in Germany. LOT and other regional airlines also link Warsaw with Kyiv, Odesa and Lviv (Ukraine), Rīga (Latvia), Minsk (Belarus), Tallinn (Estonia), Vilnius (Lithuania) and Moscow. Warsaw is also serviced by most major European carriers, such as Air France, Alitalia, British Airways, KLM-Royal Dutch Airlines and Lufthansa Airlines. Other regional airlines with flights to/from Warsaw include Aeroflot, Aerosvit, Czech Airlines, Malév Hungarian Airlines, Tarom (from Romania) and Turkish Airlines.

A few flights from Europe also regularly go to/from Gdańsk, Kraków, Poznań, Szczecin and Wrocław – see the relevant sections later in this chapter for details.

From the USA, LOT offers frequent direct flights to Warsaw from Chicago and New York and has a code-share agreement with American Airlines for other US cities. In summer, there are also direct flights on LOT to Kraków from Chicago (April to September) and New York (June to September). For Canadians, LOT flies several days a week directly from Toronto to Warsaw.

From Australia (and New Zealand), the cheapest and most direct way to Poland is by

Qantas to Bangkok, and from there to Warsaw on LOT.

Regular fares to Warsaw are not cheap. However, advance-purchase excursion fares can be good value if you can be flexible and work around the restrictions. Bucket shops in Europe and Asia sell LOT tickets at large discounts, usually from Asia to Western Europe or vice versa with a free stopover in Warsaw. Ask around the budget agencies in Singapore, Penang, Bangkok, London or Amsterdam. Also, an increasing number of travel agencies in Poland try to offer competitive fares. Warsaw is the best place to shop around.

LAND
Border Crossings

Below is a list of major road border crossings that accept foreigners and are open 24 hours.

Belarus – south to north Terespol & Kuźnica Białostocka

Czech Republic – west to east Porajów, Zawidów, Jakuszyce, Lubawka, Kudowa-Słone, Boboszów, Głuchołazy, Pietrowice, Chałupki & Cieszyn

Germany – north to south Lubieszyn, Kołbaskowo, Krajnik Dolny, Osinów Dolny, Kostrzyn, Słubice, Świecko, Gubin, Olszyna, Łęknica, Zgorzelec & Sieniawka

Lithuania – east to west Ogrodniki & Budzisko

Russia – east to west Bezledy & Gronowo

Slovakia – west to east Chyżne, Chochołów, Łysa Polana, Niedzica, Piwniczna, Konieczna & Barwinek

Ukraine – south to north Medyka, Hrebenne, Dorohusk & Zosin

Train

Every day, dozens of trains link Poland with every neighbouring country and beyond. International train travel is not cheap, however, especially for longer routes. To save money on train fares, look into the choice of special train tickets and rail passes – refer to the Getting Around chapter at the beginning of this book. Domestic trains in Poland are significantly cheaper than international ones, so you'll save money if you buy a ticket to the first city you arrive at inside Poland and then take a local train. The official website **w** www.wars.pl has information and you can also buy tickets for some services online.

Please note that some international trains to/from Poland have recently become notorious for theft. Some Poles are now too afraid to take any overnight train to/from Poland.

Keep a grip on your bags, particularly on the Berlin-Warsaw, Prague-Warsaw and Prague-Kraków overnight trains, and on *any* train travelling to/from Gdańsk. Several readers have been gassed while in their compartments and have had everything stolen while they 'slept'. Always reinforce your carriage and, if possible, sleep in a compartment with others. First-class trains, in theory, should be safer.

UK & Germany Train travel from London to Warsaw is either via the Channel Tunnel or Ostend. Tickets can be bought from British Rail ticket offices or travel centres. You may find a cheaper fare from an agency that specialises in travel and tours to Poland, such as **Fregata Travel** (☎ 020-7247 8484; **w** www.fregata travel.co.uk; 83 White Chapel High St, London E1 7QX) or **Polorbis** (☎ 020-7636 4701; **w** www.polorbis.co.uk; Suite 530-2 Walmar House, 288/300 Regent St, London W1B 3AL).

The Warsaw-Berlin route (via Frankfurt/Oder and Poznań) is serviced by several trains a day, including three EuroCity express trains (€33 2nd class, 6½ hours). There are also numerous connections between Warsaw and Cologne, Dresden, Frankfurt-am-Main and Leipzig; between Kraków and Berlin, via Wrocław; and between Gdańsk and Berlin, via Szczecin.

Czech Republic & Austria Four trains a day travel between Prague and Warsaw (10 to 12 hours) via either Wrocław or Katowice. Every day, four trains also travel between Prague and Wrocław (seven hours) and one plies the route between Prague and Kraków (nine hours).

Two trains a day travel between Vienna and Warsaw (about 10 hours) and one goes between Vienna and Kraków (seven hours).

Slovakia & Hungary Two trains travel daily between Budapest and Warsaw (12 hours), via Bratislava. These trains are routed through a short stretch of the Czech Republic, so get a Czech visa if necessary. The daily train that runs between Budapest and Kraków (11 hours) follows a different route through Košice in eastern Slovakia.

Elsewhere in Eastern Europe Warsaw has direct train links with Kyiv (Ukraine), Minsk (Belarus), Vilnius (Lithuania), and

POLAND

Moscow and St Petersburg. (These trains only have sleeping cars.) There are also daily trains between Gdańsk and Kaliningrad (five hours) in Russia.

Remember that you may need transit visas for the countries you'll be passing through en route. For example, the Warsaw–Vilnius–St Petersburg train line goes via Hrodna in Belarus. The Belarus border guards will awaken ignorant travellers and demand a US$30 visa fee – or may even send you back from whence you came. You can avoid this by taking a direct bus between Poland and Lithuania.

Bus

International bus services throughout Western and Eastern Europe are offered by dozens of Polish and international companies. Prices for international buses are generally cheaper than for trains, but you will undoubtedly find it more comfortable, and probably quicker, to travel to/from Poland by train.

One of the major bus operators is Eurolines, a consortium of affiliated European bus companies including the Polish national bus company **PKS** (**W** www.pekaesbus.com.pl).

Western Europe PKS operates dozens of buses each week to all major cities in Germany, as well as to Copenhagen on Sunday, from the Dworzec Zachodnia (Western Bus Station) in Warsaw.

Three or four days every week (and daily during summer), **Eurolines** (☎ 0990-808 080; **W** www.gobycoach.com) has services from London (Victoria) to Zamość, via Poznań, Łódź, Warsaw (Zachodnia) and Lublin; and from London to Kraków, via Wrocław and Częstochowa.

Three times a week, Eurolines goes from Paris (place de la Concorde) to Białystok, via Poznań and Warsaw; from Paris to Kraków, via Wrocław and Częstochowa; and Paris to Gdynia, via Poznań, Toruń and Gdańsk. Book at **Polka Service** (☎ 01 49 72 51 51; 28 vve du Général de Gaulle, Bagnolet).

Eurolines also has regular buses from Hamburg to Częstochowa, via Wrocław; and from Cologne to Warsaw, via Poznań and Łódź.

Elsewhere in Eastern Europe PKS has regular buses from Warsaw to Rīga (Friday), to Minsk (Tuesday, Friday and Sunday), to Kyiv (Tuesday, Thursday and Saturday) and to Vilnius (daily). These routes should not

normally take more than 12 to 15 hours each, though the actual time depends on traffic lines at the border and customs.

Also, PKS buses run six times a day between Przemyśl and Lviv (three hours), weekly between Suwałki and Vilnius (five hours), regularly between Zakopane and Budapest (nine hours), and twice a day between Gdańsk and Kaliningrad (five hours).

To Kraków, a few buses a week depart from Budapest (10 hours), and one a week makes the long haul from St Petersburg, via Minsk, Warsaw (Dworzec Zachodnia) and Częstochowa.

Car & Motorcycle

To drive a car into Poland you will first need your driving licence from home – you can use this for six months after arrival in Poland, but then you'll have to apply for a local licence. Also required are vehicle registration papers and liability insurance ('green card'). If your insurance is not valid for Poland you must buy an additional policy at the border. The car registration number will be entered in your passport.

SEA

Three companies operate passenger and car ferries all year.

Polferries (**W** www.polferries.pl) offers services between Gdańsk and Nynäshamn (19 hours) in Sweden every day in summer (three times a week in the low season). It also has daily services from Świnoujście to Ystad (9½ hours) in Sweden, to Rønne (five hours) in Denmark on Saturday, and to Copenhagen (10½ hours) five times a week.

Stena Line (**W** www.stenaline.com) operates between Gdynia and Karlskrona (11 hours) in Sweden at least six times a week.

Unity Line runs ferries between Świnoujście and Ystad (eight hours) every day.

Deck tickets normally do not need to be booked in advance. Cabins, which range in standard and therefore price, should be reserved in the high season. Cars should also be booked in advance at any time. Bicycles go free. A return ticket costs about 20% less than two singles and is valid for six months. Any travel agency in Scandinavia will sell tickets. In Poland, inquire at any Orbis Travel office. Orbis can also book tickets for other European ferries, eg, between Italy and Greece.

In summer, passenger boats ply the Baltic coast from Świnoujście to Ahlbeck, Heringsdorf, Bansin and Sassnitz in Germany.

ORGANISED TOURS
A number of tours to Poland can be arranged from abroad.

USA
Affordable Poland (☎ 800 497 9929, W www .s-traveler.com) 1600 Saratoga Ave, Suite 609, San Jose, CA 95129
Pat Tours (☎ 413-747 7702, 800 388 0988, W www.polandtours.com) 1285 Riverdale St, West Springfield, MA 01089
UK
Polorbis (☎ 020-7636 4701, W www.polorbis .co.uk) Suite 530-532 Walmar House, 288/300 Regent St, London W1B 3AL
Martin Randall Travel (☎ 020-8742 3355, W www.martinrandall.com) 10 Barley Mow Passage, Chiswick, London W4 4PH

DEPARTURE TAX
International departure tax for flights from Warsaw is US$10 and approximately $8 for departures from other Polish airports. The tax is automatically added to the cost of the ticket whether you buy it in or outside Poland.

Getting Around

AIR
The only domestic carrier, LOT, operates flights several times a day from Warsaw to Gdańsk, Kraków, Łódź, Poznań, Szczecin and Wrocław. So, flying between, for example, Kraków and Gdańsk means a connection in Warsaw and connections are not necessarily convenient. All flights to/from Warsaw cost 171/268zł one way/return – except between Warsaw and Szczecin, which costs about 30% more – but must be booked and paid for at least two weeks in advance. Tickets can be bought at LOT offices and most travel agencies, including the nationwide Orbis Travel.

Promotional fares (eg, early or late flights, weekend flights etc) are often worth looking out for – check the English-language newspapers and magazines.

TRAIN
Trains will be your main means of transport, especially for long distances. They are cheap, fairly reliable and rarely overcrowded (except for peak times in July and August). The Polish State Railways (PKP) operates more than 27,000km of railway lines and almost every place listed in this chapter (and many, many more) is accessible by train.

Express trains (*pociąg ekspresowy*) are a faster but more expensive way to travel, while fast trains (*pociąg pospieszny*) are a bit slower and maybe more crowded. Slow passenger trains (*pociąg osobowy*) stop at every tree at the side of the track and should be used only for short trips. Express and fast trains do not normally require seat reservations except at peak times; seats on passenger trains cannot be reserved.

InterCity trains operate on some major routes out of Warsaw, including Gdańsk, Kraków, Poznań and Szczecin. They only stop at major cities en route and are faster than express trains (averaging about 100km/h). These trains require seat reservations and a light meal is included in the fare.

Almost all trains carry two classes: 2nd class (*druga klasa*) and 1st class (*pierwsza klasa*), which is 50% more expensive. The carriages on long-distance trains are usually divided into compartments: 1st-class compartments have six seats and 2nd-class ones contain eight seats. There is often little difference in the standard between the two classes except that fewer people travel on 1st class so you'll always have more room.

In a couchette on an overnight train, compartments have four/six beds in 1st/2nd class. Sleepers have two/three people (1st/2nd class) in a compartment which is fitted with a washbasin, sheets and blankets. Most 2nd-class and all 1st-class carriages have nonsmoking compartments.

Train Stations
Most train stations in the cities are reasonably modern and convenient. The main train station in every city is often identified by the name 'Główny' ('main') – don't make the mistake of getting off at a suburban station if you don't want to.

Large train stations have left-luggage rooms (*przechowalnia bagażu*), which are usually secure. They operate 24 hours, but generally close once or twice a day for an hour or so. The daily storage charge per item is about 4zł per day or 'part thereof', though some rooms demand that you also pay a percentage (about 1%) of the 'declared value of

POLAND

your baggage' for some unspecified 'insurance' purposes.

Timetables

Train departures *(odjazdy)* are listed on a yellow board and arrivals *(przyjazdy)* on a white board. Ordinary trains are marked in black print; fast trains in red. An additional 'Ex' indicates an express train and InterCity trains are identified by the letters 'IC'. The letter 'R' in a square indicates the train has compulsory seat reservation. The timetables clearly show the time of the train's arrival and departure and which platform *(peron)* it's using.

Timetables for services to/from Warsaw (7zł) and for all of Poland (45zł) are available from major train stations. Although written in Polish, these timetables are useful and easy to use. The same information is available on the PKP's official website **w** www.pkp.pl, but it's in Polish.

Train stations in the larger cities normally have an information desk, but it's rarely staffed with anyone who speaks English.

Tickets

Most large train stations are now computerised, so buying a ticket *(bilety)* is now less of a hassle than it used to be. However, be at the station at least half an hour before the departure time of your train and make sure you're queuing at the right ticket window *(kasa)*. Better still, buy a ticket up to 30 days in advance (for no extra charge) from the train station or (for any trip more than 100km) from any larger Orbis Travel office. (Orbis has offices in the city centres and can issue a ticket in less than a minute.) Sleepers *(miejsca sypialne)* and couchettes *(kuszetki)* can be booked at special counters in larger train stations or from Orbis; advance reservations are advisable.

If a seat reservation is compulsory on your train, you will automatically be sold a reserved seat ticket *(miejscówka)*. It's important to note that if you do not make a seat reservation, you can travel on *any* train (of the type requested, ie, passenger, fast or express) to the destination indicated on your ticket and on the date specified.

Your ticket will list the class *(klasa)*; the type of train *(poc)*; the places the train is travelling from *(od)* and to *(do)*; the major town or junction the train is travelling through *(prez)*; and the total price *(cena)*. If more than one place is listed under the heading

prez (via), find out from the conductor *early* if you have to change trains at the junction listed or be in a specific carriage (the train may separate later).

If you get on a train without a ticket, you can buy one directly from the conductor for a small supplement – but do it right away. If the conductor finds you first, you'll be fined for travelling without a ticket. You can always upgrade from 2nd to 1st class for a small extra fee (about 5zł), plus the additional fare.

Fares

Tickets for fast trains are 50% to 60% more expensive than those for passenger trains, and tickets for express trains are 33% to 50% more than for fast trains. Only 2nd-class fares are listed in this book – for 1st-class fares, add another 50%. A reserved seat, which costs an additional 7zł to 12zł, may be useful for 2nd-class carriages on busy routes at peak times, but is not necessary for 1st-class carriages where a seat is guaranteed. A 1st-/2nd-class couchette costs an extra 50/65zł and a sleeper is an additional 90/140zł.

Note: PKP does not offer discounts on domestic and international trains to foreign students, ISIC card-holders or senior travellers.

Polrail Pass

This pass provides unlimited travel on trains throughout Poland. It is valid for all domestic passenger, fast and express trains, but you'll have to pay a surcharge to use the InterCity and EuroCity services. Passes come in durations of eight days (€162/108 for 1st/2nd class), 15 days (€192/128), 21 days (€216/144) and one month (€273/182). Persons aged under 26 on the first day of travel can buy a 'Junior' pass for 25% to 30% less. Seat reservation fees (when required) are included.

The pass is available from North American travel agencies through Rail Europe and travel agencies in Western Europe. It can also be bought at the **Wasteels** office (☎ *022-620 21 49)* in the underground mezzanine level at the Warszawa Centralna train station in the capital, and at **Orbis Travel** (☎ *022-827 72 65, fax 827 76 05; ul Bracka 16, Warsaw)*.

BUS & MINIBUS

Sometimes buses are convenient, especially on short routes and around the mountains in southern Poland. However, trains are almost always quicker and more comfortable for

POLAND

longer distances, and minibuses are far quicker and more direct for short trips. If you can, avoid using buses altogether because they can be frustratingly slow and indirect.

Most buses are operated by the state bus company, PKS, which has bus terminals (*dworzec autobusowy PKS*) in all cities and towns. PKS provides two kinds of service: ordinary buses (marked in black on timetables), which cover mostly regional routes and stop anywhere and everywhere along the way; and fast buses (marked in red), which cover mainly long-distance routes and ignore minor stops.

Timetables are posted on boards either inside or outside PKS bus terminals. Always check any additional symbols next to the departure time of your bus; these symbols often indicate that the bus runs only on certain days or in certain seasons. Terminals in the larger cities normally have an information desk, but it's rarely staffed with anyone who speaks English.

The largest private bus operator is Polski Express, a joint venture with Eurolines National Express based in the UK. Polski Express operates several major long-distance routes to/from Warsaw (see that section later for details) and is faster, more comfortable and often cheaper than PKS buses. Polski Express buses normally arrive at/depart from or near the PKS bus terminals – exceptions are mentioned in the relevant Getting There & Away sections.

Tickets for PKS buses must be bought at the terminal. On long routes serviced by fast buses tickets can be bought up to 30 days in advance, but for short local routes tickets are only available on the same day. Tickets for Polski Express buses can be bought up to 14 days in advance at the terminals or stops where they arrive/depart.

For shorter trips, minibuses usually provide a better alternative to PKS buses. Minibuses always travel faster than buses, usually leave more frequently (normally at set times and not when the minibus is full) and stop *far* less often. The cost of travelling on a minibus is almost the same as on a bus.

CAR & MOTORCYCLE

Poland's 220,000km of sealed roads are in an acceptable condition for leisurely driving. Over the next 15 years Poland had planned to build a 2600km network of toll motorways stretching from the Baltic coast to the Czech border and from Germany to Ukraine, but this has been stalled indefinitely through a lack of funds.

Petrol is readily available at petrol stations, which have mushroomed throughout the country. These places sell several kinds and grades of petrol, including 94-octane leaded, 95-octane unleaded, 98-octane unleaded and diesel. Most petrol stations are open 6am to 10pm (7am to 3pm Sunday), though some operate around the clock.

Car theft is a problem in Poland, so always try to park your vehicle at a guarded car park (*parking strzeżony*). Otherwise, hide or remove your bags so the car looks empty. The radio/cassette player in the car is usually the first thing that attracts thieves' attention.

Also see under Car & Motorcycle in the Getting There & Away section earlier in this chapter.

Road Rules

The speed limit is 130km/h on motorways, 100km/h or 110km/h on two- or four-lane highways, 90km/h on other open roads and 60km/h in built-up areas (50km/h in Warsaw). If the background of the sign bearing the town's name is white you must reduce speed to 60km/h; if the background is green there's no need to reduce speed (unless road signs indicate otherwise). Radar-equipped police are very active, especially in villages with white signs. (Approaching cars often flash their lights in warning.)

Unless signs state otherwise, cars may park on pavements as long as a minimum 1.5m-wide walkway is left for pedestrians. Parking in the opposite direction to the flow of traffic is allowed. The permitted blood alcohol level is 0.02%, so it's best not to drink at all if you're driving.

Seat belts are compulsory in the front seats, but most Polish drivers think its actually safer to drive *without* a belt! Motorbike helmets are also compulsory. Between 1 October and the end of February, all drivers must use their car (and motorbike) headlights during the day (and night!)

Rental

Most of the major international car rental companies, like **Avis** (W *www.avis.pl*), **Hertz** (W *www.hertz.pl*) and **Europcar** (W *www .europcar.com.pl*), are represented in larger cities and have smaller offices at the airports. The rates offered by these companies are not cheap: the prices are comparable to, or even higher than, full-price rental in Western Europe, and promotional discounts are not very often available.

The increasing number of local operators, such as **Payless Car Rental** (w *www.payless carrental.pl)*, provide a reliable and more affordable alternative. It charges about €55 per day (for one to five days with unlimited kilometres) or €44 per day (eight to 13 days with unlimited kilometres), plus petrol and insurance (from €14 per day).

Some companies offer one-way rentals, but almost all will insist on keeping the car within Poland. And no agency will allow you to drive their precious vehicle into Russia, Ukraine or Belarus. There is nowhere in Poland to rent a motorcycle.

Rental agencies will need to see your passport, your local driving licence (which must be held for at least one year) and a credit card (for the deposit). You need to be at least 21 or 23 years of age to rent a car; sometimes 25 for a more expensive car.

It's usually cheaper to prebook a car in Poland from abroad rather than to front up at an agency inside Poland. It would be even cheaper to rent a car in Western Europe, eg, Berlin or Geneva, and drive it into Poland, but few rental companies will allow this. If they do, special insurance is required.

HITCHING
Lonely Planet does not recommend hitchhiking, but it does take place in Poland. Car drivers rarely stop to pick up hitchhikers, and large commercial vehicles (which are easier to wave down) expect to be paid the equivalent of a bus fare.

BOAT
Sadly, no passenger-boat services regularly travel along the major rivers or the Baltic, despite Poland's long coastline. Several places, such as Kraków and Kazimierz Dolny, offer local river cruises, and from Gdańsk and other ports nearby boats take tourists along the Baltic coast, but these only operate during the peak summer season.

On the Great Masurian Lakes, excursion boats operate in summer between Giżycko, Mikołajki, Węgorzewo and Ruciane-Nida. The most unusual boat trip is the full-day cruise along the Elbląg-Ostróda Canal. There is also rafting in the Dunajec Gorge.

CYCLING
Cycling is not great for getting around cities, but is often a perfect way to travel between villages. Major roads are busy but generally flat, while minor roads can be bumpy. If you get tired, or want to avoid the mountains in the south or travel a long distance in a short time, it's easy to place your bike in the special luggage compartment of a train. These compartments are at the front or rear of slow passenger trains, but rarely found on fast or express trains, and never on InterCity or EuroCity services. You'll need a special ticket for your bike from the railway luggage office.

LOCAL TRANSPORT
Most cities have buses *(autobus)* and trams *(tramwaj)*, and some have trolleybuses *(trolejbus)*. Public transport throughout Poland runs daily from around 5am to 11pm, and may be crowded during rush hours. Larger cities also have night-time services on buses and trams. Timetables are usually posted at the stops, but don't expect the times to be too accurate.

Most cities and towns have a flat-rate fare of about 2zł for local transport, but if you change trams, buses or trolleybuses you'll need another ticket. Passes for unlimited travel on all public transport for one day, one week or one month are often available but only valid in that particular town or city. For bulky luggage, buy an additional ordinary ticket.

Tickets should be bought beforehand from nearby kiosks – often marked RUCH – and *must* be punched or stamped in a machine upon boarding. You can usually buy tickets on board the bus, tram or trolleybus for a small extra charge, but if the driver doesn't have any tickets or change, you'll have to get off at the next stop and buy a ticket at a kiosk.

Plain-clothed inspectors check tickets more often than they used to and backpackers are their favourite prey. If you're caught without a ticket, pay the fine straight away – but ask for identification and a receipt. *Never* give an inspector your passport; if they threaten you with police intervention, volunteer to accompany them to the nearest police station.

At long last, Warsaw has installed a metro system. However, it's of minimal interest or use to travellers.

Taxi
Taxis in Poland are plentiful and not too expensive by Western standards. Legitimate

taxis are usually recognisable by large boards on the roof with the company's name and telephone number. And by law these taxis must display a sign on the window with their fares.

Pirate taxis (called the 'Mafia' by Poles) do not have a sign on top with a name and phone number, nor do they list their fares. (To add to the confusion, some legitimate taxis may have no name or telephone on top of the vehicle, in which case check that the fares are listed on the windows.) For some 'convenient' reason, these illegal taxis often have prime positions outside major tourist haunts, transport terminals and top-end hotels. They tend to charge several times more than the normal fare and should be avoided.

Legitimate taxis can be waved down from along the street or taken from a taxi stand (postój taksówek). Your hotel will happily order a taxi for you; you won't be charged for this by the hotel or taxi.

All legitimate taxis have meters. When you get into a taxi, make sure the driver turns on the meter (and keeps it on) at the correct fare:

tariff 1 – the day time rate (6am-10pm), which is about 2zł per kilometre plus a flag fall (which includes the first kilometre) of about 5zł

tariff 2 – the rate for night-time, Sunday and public holidays (about 50% more)

tariff 3 – the long-distance daytime rate

tariff 4 – the long-distance night-time rate

ORGANISED TOURS

A new breed of travel agencies based in Poland focuses on Western tourists and happily sells tours abroad (often through other agencies). The three listed below are reliable, offer interesting alternatives to the predictable 'cultural tours around Kraków' and other essential services. Some foreign travel agencies are included in the Getting There & Away section earlier, and a few local agencies are also included in the sections later for Warsaw, Kraków and the Great Masurian Lakes district.

Almatur – has offices in most Polish cities. It offers budget-priced sailing, kayaking and horse-riding holidays (mainly July and August). It also operates student hostels in summer, sells tickets on international buses and issues ISIC cards (see the relevant section under Visas & Documents earlier).

Kampio (☎ 022-823 70 70, fax 823 71 44, e kampio@it.com.pl) ul Maszynowa 9 m 2, Warsaw – focuses on ecotourism, eg, kayaking, biking and bird-watching trips, around the interesting

regions, such as Białowieża National Park and the Great Masurian Lakes. Guides speak English and German.

Orbis Travel (w www.orbis.pl) – the previously government-run dinosaur, which is now privatised. This competent organisation has offices in all cities and towns in Poland, operates 56 hotels around the country and offers package tours to Poles and foreigners in and outside Poland. Major Orbis offices also sell advance tickets for domestic and international trains, and tickets for international ferries and all domestic and international airlines.

Warsaw

☎ 022 • pop 1.75 million

Warsaw, or Warszawa ('vah-SHAH-vah') in Polish, is the geographical, political and economic heart of the country. It's a large, cosmopolitan and modern city, which was mostly rebuilt after WWII, and certainly has enough museums and other attractions to keep most visitors happy for several days.

Warsaw began its life in the 14th century as a stronghold of the Mazovian dukes. When Poland and Lithuania were unified in 1569, Warsaw's strategic central location came to the fore and the capital was transferred here from Kraków. Paradoxically, the 18th century – a period of catastrophic decline for the Polish state – witnessed Warsaw's greatest prosperity. A wealth of splendid churches, palaces and parks were built and cultural and artistic life flourished. The first constitution in Europe, however short-lived, was instituted in Warsaw in 1791.

The 19th century was a period of decay for Warsaw, which became a mere provincial town in the Russian empire. After WWI Warsaw was reinstated as the capital of a newly independent Poland and began to thrive once more. In WWII, however, 700,000 residents perished (over half of the city's population) and 85% of its buildings were destroyed. Very few of the 350,000 Jews living in Warsaw in 1939 escaped the death camps. No other city in Eastern European suffered such immense loss of life or devastation.

Immediately after the war the gigantic task of restoration began and Warsaw re-emerged like a phoenix from the ashes. Parts of the historic city, most notably the Old Town, have been meticulously rebuilt to their previous condition.

POLAND

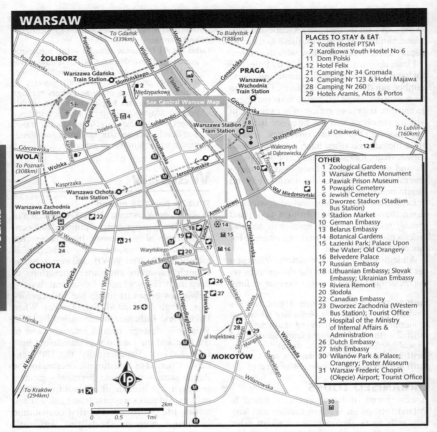

WARSAW

PLACES TO STAY & EAT
2 Youth Hostel PTSM
7 Karolkowa Youth Hostel No 6
11 Dom Polski
12 Hotel Felix
21 Camping Nr 34 Gromada
24 Camping Nr 123 & Hotel Majawa
28 Camping Nr 260
29 Hotels Aramis, Atos & Portos

OTHER
1 Zoological Gardens
3 Warsaw Ghetto Monument
4 Pawiak Prison Museum
5 Powązki Cemetery
6 Jewish Cemetery
8 Dworzec Stadion (Stadium Bus Station)
9 Stadion Market
10 German Embassy
13 Belarus Embassy
14 Botanical Gardens
15 Łazienki Park; Palace Upon the Water; Old Orangery
16 Belvedere Palace
17 Russian Embassy
18 Lithuanian Embassy; Slovak Embassy; Ukrainian Embassy
19 Riviera Remont
20 Słodoła
22 Canadian Embassy
23 Dworzec Zachodnia (Western Bus Station); Tourist Office
25 Hospital of the Ministry of Internal Affairs & Administration
26 Dutch Embassy
27 Irish Embassy
30 Wilanów Park & Palace; Orangery; Poster Museum
31 Warsaw Frederic Chopin (Okęcie) Airport; Tourist Office

Information

Tourist Offices The official **tourist organisation** (☎ 9431, ⓦ www.warsawtour.pl) has several branches: opposite the Royal Castle at Plac Zamkowy (open 9am-5pm daily); in the arrivals hall of the airport (open 8am-8pm daily May-Oct, 8am-6pm Nov-Apr); next to the ticket office at the Dworzec Zachodnia (Western Bus Station; open 6am-9.30pm daily); and in the main hall of the Warszawa Centralna train station (open 8am-6pm daily). Each can provide free city maps of Warsaw, sell maps of other Polish cities, and help you book a hotel room (but not a room in a private home).

Another state-run tourist office, **Warsaw Tourist & Cultural Information** (☎ 656 68 54; Plac Defilad; open 9am-6pm daily) is on the ground floor of the Palace of Culture & Science building.

These official tourist offices should not be confused with the many offices signposted 'Warsaw Center of Tourist Information' (one of which is also in the Old Town). These private agencies are helpful, but rarely keen to freely dispense independent information.

Books & Magazines If you're staying here a few days, pick up a copy of the free monthly magazines *Warszawa: What, Where, When* and *Welcome to Warsaw*. Both are a mine of information about cultural events and provide reviews of new restaurants, bars and nightclubs. They're available in the lobbies of most top-end hotels – most reliably, the Hotel Gromada Centrum and Hotel MDM (see Places to Stay later). The comprehensive monthly *Warsaw Insider* (9zł), and the free bimonthly *The Visitor*, are also both published in English and worth finding.

Money Foreign-exchange offices, known as kantors, and ATMs are easy to find around the city centre. Kantors open 24 hours can be found at the Warszawa Centralna train station, and either side of the immigration counters at the airport, but exchange rates at these places are about 10% lower than in the city centre. Avoid changing money in the Old Town where the rates are even lower.

Bank Pekao has a dozen branches in the city, including one along ul Krakowskie Przedmieście, next to the Church of the Holy Cross. Also, useful is the **PBK Bank** *(ground floor, Palace of Culture & Science bldg)* and the **PKO Bank** *(Plac Bankowy 2)*. These banks change major-brand travellers cheques, offer cash advances on Visa and MasterCard and have ATMs that take just about every known credit card. Another place to cash major travellers cheques is **American Express** *(Marriott Hotel, Al Jerozolimskie 65/79)*.

Post & Communications The best place to send and receive letters and faxes is the **main post office** *(ul Świętokrzyska 31/33; open 24hr)*. The poste restante is at window No 12. Letters should be addressed to Poste Restante, Poczta Główna, ul Świętokrzyska 31/33, 00-001 Warszawa 1.

For telephone calls, use a phonecard at any of the plethora of telephone booths around the city or inside the main post office.

Email & Internet Access Internet centres and cafés are springing up all around Warsaw. The most atmospheric places are **Casablanca** *(ul Krakowskie Przedmieście 4/6)* and **Studio.tpi** *(ul Świętokrzyska 3)*.

Several very convenient but dingy **Internet centres** are also found along the underground mezzanine level of the Warszawa Centralna train station.

Travel Agencies Refer to Organised Tours later in this section for information about travel agencies based in Warsaw.

Bookshops The **American Bookstore** *(ul Nowy Świat 61)* offers a wide selection of Lonely Planet titles, English publications and maps. The largest array of foreign newspapers and magazines is in the **EMPiK Megastore** *(ul Marszałkowska 116/122)*. For trashy novels in English, visit **Co-Liber** bookshop *(cnr Marszałkowska & ul Widok)*, next to Max Bar restaurant.

Laundry Take your dirty clothes to **Alba Dry Cleaning** *(ul Chmielna 26)*.

Medical Services Some of the many pharmacies throughout the city stay open all night, including one in the Warszawa Centralna train station.

The **Hospital of the Ministry of Internal Affairs & Administration** *(☎ 602 15 78; ul Wołoska 137)* is a private hospital preferred by important government officials and diplomats. **CM Medical Center** *(☎ 458 70 00; 3rd floor, Marriott Hotel, Al Jerozolimskie 65/79)* offers specialist doctors, carries out laboratory tests and makes house calls. Otherwise, ring your embassy for other recommendations.

Things to See & Do

Old Town All places listed below – and many more – are detailed (in English and on a map) in the free pamphlet *Warsaw: The Old Town*, available from the official tourist offices.

The main gateway to the Old Town is **Plac Zamkowy** (Castle Square). Amazingly, all of the 17th- and 18th-century buildings around this square were completely rebuilt from their foundations after WWII. (Compare the square now with photos taken immediately after WWII; these photos are on postcards today.) The reconstruction was so superb that the Old Town has been included on Unesco's World Heritage List. In the centre of the square is the **Monument to Sigismund III Vasa**, who moved the capital from Kraków to Warsaw.

The square is dominated by the massive 13th-century **Royal Castle** *(admission free to the courtyards; open 10am-4pm Mon-Sat, 11am-4pm Sun, closed Mon 1 Oct-15 Apr)*. The castle developed over the centuries as successive Polish kings added wings and redecorated the interior, but it was nothing more than a pile of rubble in 1945. The castle was completely rebuilt between 1971 and 1984.

The highlights of the castle's interior are the **King's Apartments** *(admission 14zł)* and the **Art Gallery** *(admission 9zł)*. Both can only be visited on a guided tour (in Polish); a

POLAND

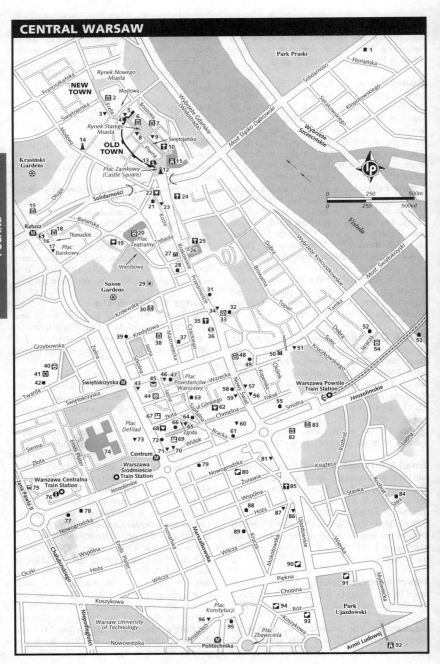

CENTRAL WARSAW

CENTRAL WARSAW

PLACES TO STAY
1 Hotel Praski
21 Old Town Apartments
28 Hotel Orbis Europejski
32 Hotel Harenda; Pub Harenda
37 Hotel Mazowiecki
47 Hiotel Warszawa
52 Hotel Belfer
53 Hotel Na Wodzie
55 Smolna Youth Hostel No 2
63 Hotel Gromada Centrum
78 Marriott Hotel; CM Medical Centre; American Express
84 Hotel Powiśle
88 City Apartments
89 Biuro Podróy Syrena (Private Rooms)
95 Hotel MDM

PLACES TO EAT
3 Restauracja Pod Samsonem
5 Bar Mleczny Pod Barbakanem
8 Karczma Gessler
9 Restauracja Bazyliszek
17 Salad Bar Tukan
23 Restauracja Siedem Grzechow
34 Bar Mleczny Uniwersytecki
43 McDonald's; Grocery Shop
46 Restaurant Varsovia
51 Salad Bar Tukan
56 Restaurancja Wegetariańska; Bar Co Tu
57 Mata Hari
59 Bar Mleczny Familijny
60 Restaurant Polska
65 Bar Turecki; Bar Krokiecik
70 Pizza Hut; KFC

71 Max Bar; Co-Liber Bookshop
73 MarcPol Supermarket
81 Bar Mleczny Szwajcarski
86 Café Ejlat
87 Adler Bar & Restaurant
96 Bar Hoa Lan

OTHER
2 Marie Skłodowska-Curie Museum
4 Barbican
6 Warsaw Historical Museum
7 Adam Mickiewicz Museum of Literature
10 St John's Cathedral
11 Royal Castle
12 Monument to Sigismund III Vasa
13 Tourist Office
14 Monument to the Warsaw Uprising
15 State Archaeological Museum
16 PKO Bank
18 Jewish Historical Institute
19 Barbados
20 Teatr Wielki
22 Irish Pub
24 St Anne's Church
25 Carmelite Church (Seminary Church)
26 Radziwiłł Palace
27 Połocki Palace
29 Tomb of the Unknown Soldier
30 Zachęta Contemporary Art Gallery
31 Warsaw University
33 Casablanca
35 Church of the Holy Cross

36 Bank Pekao
38 Ethnographic Museum
39 Trakt
40 Jewish Theatre
41 Nożyk Synagogue
42 Our Roots
44 Filharmonia Narodowa
45 Main Post Office
48 Studio.tpi
49 Almatur
50 Chopin Museum; Morgan's Irish Pub
54 Teatr Ateneum
58 American Bookstore
61 Orbis Travel
62 Pub Krista
64 Cepelia
66 Alba Dry Cleaning
67 Kino Relax
68 Hybrydy
69 Kino Atlantic
72 EMPiK Megastore
74 Palace of Culture & Science; Warsaw Tourist & Cultural Information Office; PBK Bank; Centrum Sztuki Studio
75 Polski Express Bus Stop
76 Tourist Office
77 LOT Head Office
79 ZASP Kasy Teatralne
80 Australian Embassy
82 National Museum
83 Museum of the Polish Army
85 St Alexander's Church
90 US Embassy
91 French Embassy
92 Ujazdów Castle; Center of Contemporary Art
93 British Embassy
94 Czech Embassy

POLAND

tour in English, German or French costs an extra 75zł per group. Entry to the whole complex is free on Sunday, when no guides are available in any language, but you still need to line up for (free) tickets to the apartments and/or gallery. On any day in summer, arrive at the castle early and be prepared to wait.

From the Castle head down ul Świętojańska to the 15th-century Gothic **St John's Cathedral** (ul Świętojańska 8; admission free; open 10am-1pm & 3pm-5.30pm Mon-Sat), the oldest church in Warsaw. This road continues to the magnificent **Rynek Starego Miasta** (Old Town Square).

Alongside this square is the **Warsaw Historical Museum** (Rynek Starego Miasta 42; admission 5zł, free Sun; open 11am-6pm Tues & Thur, 10.30am-4pm Wed, Fri, Sat &

Sun). Make sure you're there at midday to see the English-language film (included in the admission fee), which unforgettably depicts the wartime destruction of the city. Nearby is the **Adam Mickiewicz Museum of Literature** (Rynek Starego Miasta 20; admission 5zł; open 10am-3pm Mon, Tues & Fri, 11am-6pm Wed, Thur & Sun). It features displays about the history of Polish literature and exhibits about this revered Polish writer.

Walk west for one block to the **Barbican**, part of a medieval wall that encircled Warsaw and was built on a bridge over a moat. To the north along ul Freta is the **Rynek Nowego Miasta** (New Town Square). On the way, perhaps pop into the **Marie Skłodowska-Curie Museum** (ul Freta 16; admission 5zł; open 10am-4pm Tues-Sat, 10am-2pm Sun).

POLAND

It features modest displays about the great lady in the house where she was born. Many Polish streets are named after Marie Curie, but she has been given the Polish-French name, Marie Skłodowska-Curie.

Marie Curie laid the foundations for radiography, nuclear physics and cancer therapy. She was born in Warsaw, then part of Russia, in 1867. Curie lived in Poland for 24 years before being forced (under Russian law) to leave Poland (because she was a woman) to further her studies.

In Paris, she and her French husband Pierre Curie discovered two new radioactive chemical elements: radium and polonium (named after her homeland). She won numerous awards and distinctions, including two Nobel Prizes. Tragically, she died at the age of 67 from leukaemia caused by prolonged exposure to radiation.

If you're interested, take a detour to the **State Archaeological Museum** (ul Długa 52; admission 6zł; open 9am-4pm Mon-Fri, 10am-4pm Sun), based in a 17th-century former arsenal. It houses some unremarkable bits and pieces excavated from all over Poland.

The Royal Way (Szlak Królewski) This 4km route links the Royal Castle with Łazienki Park (see the next section) via ul Krakowskie Przedmieście, ul Nowy Świat and Al Ujazdowskie. The places mentioned here (and numerous others) are detailed in English and on a map in the free pamphlet, *Warsaw: The Royal Route*, available from the official tourist offices. If you want to save time and energy, jump on and off bus No 180, which stops at most places along this route and continues to Wilanów Park (see the later section).

Just south of the Royal Castle is the 15th-century **St Anne's Church** (ul Krakowskie Przedmieście 68; admission free; open daylight hours), one of the most ornate churches in the city. You can climb the **tower** (admission 3.50zł; open 10am-6pm Tues-Sun) for views of Plac Zamkowy and the castle. About 300m further south is the former **Carmelite Church** (ul Krakowskie Przedmieście 52/54; admission free; open daylight hours), also known as the Seminary Church. Nearby, the **Radziwiłł Palace** (not open to the public) is occupied by the Polish president. Opposite, **Połocki Palace** (ul Krakowskie Przedmieście 15/17; admission free; open 10am-6pm Tues-Sun) houses a modern art gallery.

To the west of the neoclassical Hotel Orbis Europejski are the **Saxon Gardens** (admission free; permanently open). At the entrance is the small but poignant **Tomb of the Unknown Soldier** (admission free; permanently open), which occupies a fragment of an 18th-century royal palace destroyed in WWII. The ceremonial changing of the guard takes place here on Sunday at noon.

South of the tomb, the **Zachęta Contemporary Art Gallery** (ul Królewska; admission 10zł, free Fri; open 10am-6pm Tues-Sun) features modern painting, photography and sculpture, and many excellent special exhibits. About 200m further south is the **Ethnographic Museum** (ul Kredytowa 1; admission 5zł; open 9am-4pm Tues, Thur & Fri, 11am-7pm Wed, 10am-5pm Sat & Sun). This large building displays various traditional Polish costumes, crafts and folk art.

Back on the Royal Way is the 17th-century **Church of the Holy Cross** (ul Krakowskie Przedmieście 3; admission free; open most afternoons). This is where Chopin's heart is preserved (in the second pillar on the left-hand side of the main nave). It was brought from Paris, where Chopin died of tuberculosis aged only 39, in accordance with his will. If you want to know more, head along ul Tamka towards the river to the small **Chopin Museum** (ul Okólnik 1; admission 7zł; open about 10am-4pm Mon-Sat), which features, among other things, the great man's last piano and a collection of his manuscripts.

Return to the Royal Way and head south along ul Nowy Świat to the roundabout at the junction of Al Jerozolimskie. On the way to the river is the enormous **National Museum** (Al Jerozolimskie 3; museum admission 11zł, temporary exhibitions 15zł, free Sat; open 10am-4pm Tues, Wed & Fri, noon-5pm Thur, 10am-5pm Sat & Sun). It houses a magnificent collection of Polish sculptures and art from the medieval period to the present. Next door, and in the same massive complex, is the **Museum of the Polish Army** (Al Jerozolimskie 3; admission 8zł, free Fri; open about 11am-5pm Wed-Sun). The huge collection of weapons, medals and so on is probably only of interest to military buffs.

Continue south along Al Ujazdowskie and cross busy ul Armii Ludowej. Over the road is the cutting-edge **Center of Contemporary Art** (Al Ujazdowskie 6; admission 10zł, free Thur; open about 11am-6pm Tues-Sun). It's housed in the reconstructed **Ujazdów Castle**, built during the 1620s. Further down (towards the south) is the small **Botanical Gardens** *(admission 4zł; open 9am-7pm Mon-Fri, 10am-8pm Sat & Sun)*.

Łazienki Park This park *(admission free; open daylight hours)* is large (74 hectares), shady and popular. It's best known for the 18th-century **Palace upon the Water** *(admission 11zł, free Thur; open 9am-3.30pm Tues-Sun)*. It was the summer residence of Stanisław August Poniatowski, the last king of Poland, who was deposed by a Russian army and confederation of Polish magnates in 1792. The park was once a royal hunting ground attached to Ujazdów Castle.

The **Old Orangery** *(admission 6zł, free Tues; open 9am-4pm Tues-Sun)* contains a gallery of sculpture and also an 18th-century theatre. Between noon and 4pm every Sunday in summer (May to September) piano recitals are held here among the rose gardens.

Wilanów Park This equally splendid park *(ul Wisłostrada; admission free; open 9.30am-dusk daily)* is about 6km southeast of Łazienki Park. The centrepiece is the magnificent **Wilanów Palace** *(admission 18zł, free Thur; open 9.30am-4.30pm Wed-Mon)*. The palace was the summer residence of King Jan III Sobieski who defeated the Turks at Vienna in 1683, thereby ending the Turkish threat to Central Europe. In summer, arrive early and be prepared to wait. The last tickets are sold two hours before closing time.

In the well-kept park behind the palace is the **Orangery** *(admission free; open 9.30am-4.30pm Wed-Mon)*, which houses an art gallery. The **Poster Museum** *(admission 8zł, free Wed; open 10am-4pm Tues-Sun)*, in the former royal stables, is one of the best places to see Poland's world-renowned poster art.

To reach Wilanów, take bus No 180 from anywhere along the Royal Way (see earlier section).

Palace of Culture & Science This giant eyesore *(Plac Defilad; open 8am-8pm daily)* is an apocalyptic piece of Stalinesque architecture. This 'gift of friendship' from the Soviet Union to the Polish nation was built in the early 1950s and is still Poland's largest and tallest (234m) building. It has a huge congress hall, three theatres and a cinema.

The **observation terrace** *(admission 15zł; open 9am-6pm daily)* on the 30th floor provides a panoramic view, which is perhaps best appreciated at the coffee shop. Poles often joke that this is the best view of Warsaw because it's the only one that doesn't include the Palace of Culture & Science itself!

Jewish Heritage

The vast suburbs northwest of the Palace of Culture & Science were once predominantly inhabited by Polish Jews. During WWII the Nazis established a Jewish ghetto in the area but razed it to the ground after crushing the Warsaw Ghetto Uprising in April 1943. This tragic event is immortalised by the **Monument to the Warsaw Uprising** *(cnr ul Długa & ul Miodowa)*.

The **Warsaw Ghetto Monument** *(cnr ul Anielewicza & ul Zamenhofa)* also commemorates victims using pictorial plaques. The nearby **Pawiak Prison Museum** *(ul Dzielna 24/26; admission free; open about 10am-4pm Wed-Sun)* occupies the former building used as a Gestapo prison during the Nazi occupation. Moving exhibits include letters and other personal items.

Arguably the most dramatic remnant of the Jewish legacy is the vast **Jewish Cemetery** *(ul Okopowa 49/51; admission free; open 9am-4pm Sun-Fri May-Sept, 9am-3pm Sun-Fri Oct-Apr)*. Founded in 1806, it still has over 100,000 gravestones and is the largest collection of its kind in Europe. Visitors must wear a head covering before entering the cemetery, which is accessible from the Old Town on tram Nos 22, 27 and 29.

The **Jewish Historical Institute** *(ul Tłomackie 3/5; admission 10zł; open 9am-4pm Mon-Wed & Fri, 11am-6pm Thur)* features permanent exhibits about the Warsaw Ghetto, as well as art and photographs relating to local Jewish history. Tucked away behind the **Jewish Theatre** is the neo-Romanesque **Nożyk Synagogue** *(ul Twarda; admission 3.50zł; open 10am-8pm Sun-Thur, 10am-4pm Fri)*. Warsaw's only synagogue that managed to survive WWII, albeit in a sorry state. It has subsequently been restored and is still used today for religious services.

A walking tour of these – and around 20 other – Jewish sites are detailed (in English and with a map) in the free pamphlet, *Historical Sites of Jewish Warsaw*, available from the official tourist offices.

Organised Tours

The following companies offer tours around Warsaw.

Almatur (☎/fax 826 26 39, e dot@almatur.pl) ul Kopernika 23 – see Organised Tours in the Getting Around section earlier.

Orbis Travel (☎ 827 72 65, fax 827 76 05) ul Bracka 16 – has branches all over Warsaw, as well as at the airport. See Organised Tours in the Getting Around section earlier.

Our Roots (☎/fax 620 05 56) ul Twarda 6 – Warsaw's primary agency for anyone interested in tours about local Jewish heritage.

Trakt (☎ 827 80 68, W www.trakt.com.pl) ul Kredytowa 6 – guided tours of Warsaw in English and 21 other languages. Walking tours cost about 40zł per group per hour.

Special Events

Warsaw's major annual events include the International Book Fair (May), the Warsaw Summer Jazz Days (late June/early July), the Mozart Festival (June-July), 'Art of the Street' International Festival (July) and the 'Warsaw Autumn' Festival of Contemporary Music (September).

Places to Stay

Warsaw is the most expensive city in Poland for accommodation. The number of upmarket hotels is rising, while trying to find anywhere cheap within 30 minutes of the city centre by tram is increasingly difficult. If you're having trouble finding a room anywhere, one of the official tourist offices will help you (see the Information section earlier).

Camping The largest and most central camping ground in Warsaw is **Camping Nr 34 Gromada** (☎ 825 43 91; ul Żwirki i Wigury 32; camping per tent 11zł, electricity 9zł, cabins per person 20zł; open Apr-Oct). Staff are friendly and helpful, and the camping ground is clean and popular. It's accessible from the airport on bus Nos 175 and 188, and from Warszawa Centralna train station on bus Nos 136 and 175.

Set in extensive and secure grounds, **Camping Nr 123** (☎/fax 823 37 48, e camp123@friko6.onet.pl; ul Warszawskiej 1920r 15/17; camping per person/tent 10/10zł; open year-round) features bungalows and hotel rooms and is close to the Dworzec Zachodnia bus station. The complex also features indoor tennis courts and an outdoor swimming pool (all open to the public).

Camping Nr 260 (☎ 842 27 68; ul Inspektowa 1; camping per person/tent 12/5zł; open May-Sept) is a lifeless and treeless place, accessible on any bus heading towards Wilanów Park from the Old Town.

Hostels Each hostel listed below closes between at least 10am and 4pm each day.

Smolna Youth Hostel No 2 (☎/fax 827 89 52; ul Smolna 30; dorm beds 33zł; singles/doubles with TV & shared bathroom 60/110zł; open year-round) is the best and most central. For singles or doubles, book in advance and book dorm beds in summer. The three-night maximum is often waived when it's not so busy.

Karolkowa Youth Hostel No 6 (☎/fax 632 97 46; ul Karolkowa 53a; dorm beds from 35zł; open year-round) is in the Wola suburb and accessible by tram No 12, 22 or 24 from the Warszawa Centralna train station. This well-established and friendly place has laundry and Internet facilities. It also offers rooms and apartments comparable to the hotels that charge twice as much, ie, singles without/with bathroom for 80/130zł, doubles with TV and shared bathroom from 130zł and apartments for two with kitchen, TV and bathroom for 160zł.

Youth Hostel PTSM (☎ 831 17 66; ul Międzyparkowa 4/6; dorm beds 35zł; open Apr-Oct) is in parkland in the northern suburbs. The rates are cheaper, but the standards are far lower than the other two hostels, and there are no single or double rooms. Take bus No 175 from the central train station or airport.

Private Rooms & Apartments Rooms in private homes can be arranged through **Biuro Podróży Syrena** (☎/fax 629 49 78; e office@syrena-pl.com; ul Krucza 17). Singles/doubles with shared bathroom in the city centre cost 79/110zł for one or two nights and as little as 68/96zł for three or more nights. Apartments with a double bed, kitchen, bathroom and TV are available for 250zł to 320zł per night.

If you're going to stay in Warsaw for a while a private apartment may end up being cheaper than a mid-range hotel. Apartments are furnished with a kitchen, bathroom, laundry and (usually) cable TV, and fit as many people as you can squeeze in.

Old Town Apartments (☎/fax 826 78 63; ul Kozia 3/5) offers, well, apartments in the Old Town. The 'studios' cost US$70/350 per day/week and apartments from US$95/475 (one bedroom) to US$110/550 (two bedrooms).

The agency **City Apartments** *(☎/fax 628 76 11;* e *info@hotelinwarsaw.com; ul Hoża 38)* offers large apartments (mostly in the Old Town) for less: 'studios' cost US$60/300 per day/week and apartments US$85/425 (one bedroom) and US$100/500 (two bedrooms).

Hotels – Budget The best value in the capital can be found at **Hotel Majawa** *(☎/fax 823 37 48;* e *camp123@friko6.onet.pl; ul Warszawskiej 1920r 15/17; hotel singles/ doubles with shared bathroom 80/109zł; double bungalows without/with bath from 79/109zł).* The bungalows at this camping ground are private and clean, while the hotel rooms are quiet, spotless and bright.

Hotel Na Wodzie *(☎/fax 628 58 83; ul Wybrzeże Kościuszkowskie; single/double cabins with shared bathroom 65/85zł; open Apr-Nov)* is actually in two boats – the *Aldona* and *Anita* – both anchored along the Vistula River between the railway and Poniatowski bridges. The living quarters are adequate, but the location leaves something to be desired.

The best choice of budget accommodation is along ul Mangalia, where three one-star hotels are virtually next door to each other – perhaps check out all three and then decide. They all belong to Hotel Felix (see next section) and information is available on its website. Singles/doubles with bath at all three cost 120/150zł, and they are accessible by bus Nos 118, 403, 503 and 513 along ul Sobieskiego.

Hotel Aramis *(☎ 842 09 74;* e *aramis@ felix.com.pl; ul Mangalia 3b)* is the largest and best equipped. **Hotel Atos** *(☎ 841 43 95;* e *atos@felix.com.pl; ul Mangalia 1)* only has nine rooms, but is cosy. **Hotel Portos** *(☎ 842 68 51;* e *portos@felix.com.pl; ul Mangalia 3a)* is also fairly good value for the price.

Hotels – Mid-Range All hotels listed in this section include breakfast in the room rates.

A former army dorm, **Hotel Mazowiecki** *(☎ 827 23 65;* w *www.mazowiecki.com.pl; ul Mazowiecka 10; singles/doubles from 150/ 200zł, with bath 210/270zł)* was once reserved for military officers. The classy foyer belies the ordinary rooms, but it's pleasant enough and convenient.

Hotel Praski *(☎/fax 818 49 89;* w *www .praski.pl; Al Solidarności 61; singles/doubles with shared bathroom from 150/200zł)* is on

the other side of the river, but little more than 1km from the Old Town. It has been renovated in recent years and is one of the best two-star places in the capital.

Hotel Powiśle *(☎ 628 00 14, fax 621 66 57; ul Szara 10a; singles/doubles from 180/ 250zł)* is a quiet and friendly place, but a little out of the way of the better bars and restaurants. The rooms are large and feature new bathrooms, TVs and some have fridges.

Hotel Belfer *(☎/fax 625 51 85; ul Wybrzeże Kościuszkowskie 31/33; singles/ doubles 110/246zł, with bath 169/250zł)* was formerly a teachers hotel. Rooms on the upper floors provide good views of the Vistula River, but the place is run down and the rooms are generally small and poorly furnished. A last resort.

Hotel Warszawa *(☎ 826 94 21;* e *hotel .warszawa@syrena.com.pl; Plac Powstańców Warszawy 9; singles/doubles 170/250zł, with bath 250/360zł)* is a multistorey Stalinesque monstrosity. Although stuck in the 1960s, it's comfortable and convenient and staff are pleasingly friendly. The buffet breakfast will probably fill you up until dinnertime.

Hotel Felix *(☎ 810 06 91;* w *www.felix .com.pl; ul Omulewska 24; singles/doubles from 200/235zł)* is an unexciting Soviet-style block, but is spotlessly clean and good value. Take tram No 9, 24 or 44 from the Warszawa Centralna train station.

Hotels – Top End Places listed below offer all the amenities you would expect for these prices, including breakfast. It's worth asking about 'weekend rates' (ie, Friday, Saturday and Sunday nights), which are often 20% to 30% less.

Hotel Harenda *(☎ 826 00 71, fax 826 26 25; ul Krakowskie Przedmieście 4/6; singles/ doubles 320/370zł)* boasts a pleasant location in the Old Town and an appealing ambience. The singles are remarkably small, however, but all the bathrooms are spotless. It's far nicer than the communist-era throwbacks still operating elsewhere.

The **Hotel Orbis Europejski** *(☎ 826 50 51;* e *europej@orbis.pl; ul Krakowskie Przedmieście 13; singles/doubles €120/150)* is in a charming location near the Saxon Gardens. Most rooms are uninspiring, but the place just oozes charm and history.

Hotel Gromada Centrum *(☎ 625 15 45, fax 625 21 40; Plac Powstańców Warszawy 2;*

POLAND

singles/doubles 400/480zł) has an excellent location and efficient and friendly staff. The bathrooms are outstanding.

Hotel MDM *(☎ 621 62 11, fax 621 41 73; Plac Konstytucji 1; singles/doubles 415/545zł)* is large and unremarkable, but convenient and staffed with friendly folk.

Places to Eat

Warsaw has a wider range of eating places than any other Polish city. There's been a virtual explosion of modern bistros, pizzerias, snack bars and international fast-food chains in recent years, yet a number of genuine milk bars still exist and have the cheapest food in town.

The free booklet *Warszawa Restaurants*, available from the official tourist offices, lists hundreds of restaurants serving every conceivable cuisine, while the English-language newspapers and magazines (see Information section earlier) provide reviews of what's currently in vogue.

Polish Restaurants The Old Town boasts some of Warsaw's best restaurants specialising in Polish cuisine, but prices are predictably high. Each is likely to offer a menu in English.

Karczma Gessler *(Rynek Starego Miasta 21/21a; mains from 45zł)* continues to be recommended by satisfied patrons. The food and decor in this romantic cellar are spectacular, though it's not cheap and vegetarians will not find much to satisfy their taste buds.

Restauracja Bazyliszek *(Rynek Starego Miasta 3/9; mains 38-75zł)* is one of the longest standing Polish restaurants in the capital and continues to maintain high standards. It serves hearty, traditional fare (including lots of meaty game) in old-world surroundings.

Restauracja Siedem Grzechów *(ul Krakowskie Przedmieście 45; mains 35-55zł)* is a quaint downstairs place decorated with 1920s memorabilia. It's a lively place and ideal for an evening meal and/or drink.

Restaurant Polska *(ul Nowy Świat 21; mains from 35zł)* is another favourite situated in an elegant basement. The Polish dishes are more for tourist palates, but still authentic, and the choice is mouthwatering. Enter gate No 21 and walk straight ahead for 100m.

Dom Polski *(ul Francuska 11; mains from 30zł)* is perennially popular with tour groups and out-of-towners looking for tasty food and reasonable prices. It's worth the pleasant walk over the bridge.

Restaurant Varsovia *(ul Świętokrzyska 15; meals about 15zł)* is a reasonably classy place with a range of Polish and Western meals listed on a menu in English. It's just around the corner from Hotel Warszawa.

Bar Krokiecik *(ul Zgoda 1; meals 8-10zł)*, near Bar Turecki, is a central option for more affordable Polish meals.

Other Restaurants Offering a large array of tasty Chinese meals and a menu in English, **Bar Co Tu** *(just off ul Nowy Świat; most meals under 10zł)* is a small but popular eatery. It's not far down (south) from the Restauracja Wegetariańska

Bar Hoa Lan *(ul Śniadeckich 12; mains 8-15zł)* is much like the Co Tu – small, cosy, friendly and cheap – but it leans more to Vietnamese and doesn't have a menu in English.

Adler Bar & Restaurant *(ul Mokotowska 69; starters 15zł, mains about 35zł)* is a tiny oasis among the concrete jungle. It's worth a splurge for impeccable service and the variety of Polish and Bavarian *nouvelle cuisine.*

Café Ejlat *(Al Ujazdowskie 47; mains 24-42zł)* offers large portions of authentic Jewish food, as well as live music (mostly on Saturday and Sunday nights).

Restauracja Pod Samsonem *(ul Freta 3/5; mains 19-27zł)*, which is opposite the Marie Skłodowska-Curie Museum, is frequented by locals for inexpensive and tasty meals with a combined Polish and Jewish flavour. Daily specials are listed in crayon on the side of the wooden door.

Vegetarian For adventurous vegetarians **Mata Hari** *(ul Nowy Świat 52; soups 5zł & mains 7-12zł)* is a superb option offering delicious and cheap Indian food.

Restauracja Wegetariańska *(just off Nowy Świat; soups & salads from 5zł)* is another enticing place for healthy, meat-free food.

Salad Bar Tukan *(sandwiches about 3zł, salads from 5zł)* has several outlets around the capital, including Plac Bankowy 2 (in the blue skyscraper) and ul Tamka 37. The Tukan probably offers the widest choice of salads in Poland.

Cafeterias Opposite the Barbican, **Bar Mleczny Pod Barbakanem** *(ul Mostowa 27/29; mains 8-12zł)* is a popular milk bar that has survived the fall of the Iron Curtain and continues to serve cheap, unpretentious food. It's position would be the envy of many upmarket eateries.

Three milk bars along the Royal Way are at comfortably short walking intervals.

Bar Mleczny Uniwersytecki (*ul Krakowskie Przedmieście 20; mains 8-12zł*) is packed with students – probably there for the cheap prices rather than the food itself.

Bar Mleczny Familijny (*ul Nowy Świat 39; soups 3-4zł, mains 6-11zł*) is incongruously in the fashionable shopping district.

Bar Mleczny Szwajcarski (*ul Nowy Świat 5; mains 7-12zł*) is another rock-bottom, no-frills eatery.

Fast Food Junk-food junkies will not suffer withdrawal symptoms while in Warsaw.

Pizza Hut (*ul Widok*) offers the normal array of pizzas and a salad bar, and has a menu in English and German. Next door, the smiling face of Colonel Sanders looms large over an outlet of **KFC**. The golden arches of **McDonald's** are *everywhere* – most noticeably on the corner of ul Świętokrzyska and ul Marszałkowska.

Turkish food is increasingly popular and reasonably cheap and healthy. **Bar Turecki** (*ul Zgoda 3; meals 8-13zł*) is one of the best – seek out the tempting aroma wafting across the street.

For more choice, try one of the self-serve cafeterias around town – ideal for seeing what you want and pointing at it without a word of Polish. **Max Bar** (*cnr Marszałkowska & ul Widok; lunch specials 7.50zł*) offers a wide array of food and is popular.

Self-Catering The most convenient places to shop for groceries are the **MarcPol Supermarket**, in front of the Palace of Culture & Science building, and the **grocery shop** (*cnr ul Świętokrzyska & ul Marszałkowska*) downstairs and next to McDonald's.

Entertainment

For more information about what to do, and where and when to go, check out *The Buzz* section of *The Warsaw Voice* and the informative *Warszawa: What, Where, When.*

Pubs & Bars Warsaw is now flooded with all sorts of pubs and bars. The most charming places for a drink are around Rynek Starego Miasta in the Old Town, but the prices are predictably high.

Two authentic Irish pubs are great spots to meet expats and enjoy a Guinness (or three). **Irish Pub** (*ul 3 Miodowa*) is popular and near the Old Town, with live music most nights. **Morgan's Irish Pub** (*ul Tamka 40*), under the Chopin Museum, is busy, especially with sports nuts glued to the large-screen TVs.

Pub Harenda (*ul Krakowskie Przedmieście 4/6*), at the back of Hotel Harenda, is often crowded. It provides an appealing beer garden and equally appealing happy hours. Live jazz music is performed here during the week and there's dance music on weekends.

Pub Krista (*ul Górskiego 8*), along the extension of ul Złota, has been recommended by some of our readers for its fine ales and cellar atmosphere.

Nightclubs The following two student clubs are popular and cheap, but only open from June to September. **Riviera Remont** (*ul Waryńskiego 12*) has live music (often jazz) on Thursday and Saturday nights. **Słodoła** (*ul Batorego 10*) is another popular student club which pulsates with techno music most nights.

Hybrydy (*ul Złota 7/9*) has been going for some 45 years and is still trendy! It features all sorts of taped and live music most nights.

Barbados (*ul Wierzbowa 9; open Wed-Sat*), over the road from the Teatr Wielki, is where the 'beautiful people' of Warsaw come.

The official tourist offices have updated lists of what's hot and what's not, and the *Warsaw Insider* is always a great source.

Cinemas To fill in a rainy afternoon, or to avoid watching Polish TV in your hotel room, try catching a film at one of the 40 cinemas across the city. Two central options are **Kino Atlantic** (*ul Chmielna 33*) and **Kino Relax** (*ul Złota 8*).

Theatre, Opera & Ballet Advance tickets for most events at most theatres can be bought at **ZASP Kasy Teatralne** (*Al Jerozolimskie 25; open 11am-6pm Mon-Fri, 11am-2pm Sat*) or at the **EMPiK Megastore** (*ul Marszałkowska 116/122*). Otherwise, same-day tickets may be available at the box offices. Remember, most theatres close in July and August.

Centrum Sztuki Studio (*Palace of Culture & Science building*) and **Teatr Ateneum** (*ul Jaracza 2*) lean towards contemporary Polish-language productions. **Teatr Wielki** (*Grand Theatre; Plac Teatralny 1*) is the main venue for opera and ballet. **Filharmonia Narodowa** (ul Jasna 5) has concert and chamber halls.

In **Łazienki Park**, piano recitals are held every Sunday from May to September and chamber concerts are staged there in summer at the **Old Orangery**.

Shopping

An impressive display of Poland's relatively new free-market enthusiasm is the huge bazaar at the **Stadion Market** (Al Jerozolimskie) in the suburb of Praga. It's open daily from dawn until around noon and busiest on weekends. Beware of pickpockets.

Reasonably priced handicrafts are available from several outlets of the nationwide **Cepelia** chain, including one at ul Chmielna 8. Stalls in and around Rynek Starego Miasta sell charming mementos, such as paintings of the Old Town, jewellery and traditional dolls.

Getting There & Away

Air The Warsaw Frederic Chopin Airport is more commonly called the Okęcie Airport, after the suburb, 10km southwest of the city centre, where it's based. This small and barely functional airport has international arrivals downstairs and departures upstairs. Domestic arrivals and departures occupy a small separate part of the same complex.

The useful tourist office is on the arrivals level of the international section. It sells city maps and can help find a place to stay. At the arrivals level, there are also a few ATMs that accept major international credit cards, and several kantors. Avoid the Orbis Travel office because of its astronomical fees and low exchange rates. There are also several car-rental companies, a left-luggage room and a newsagent where you can buy public transport tickets. Buses and taxis depart from this level.

Domestic and international flights on LOT can be booked at the **LOT** head office (☎ 657 80 11, Al Jerozolimskie 65/79) in the Marriott Hotel complex or at any travel agency, including the Orbis Travel. Other airline offices are listed in the *Warszawa: What, Where, When* and *Welcome to Warsaw* magazines.

Information about international and domestic flights to/from Warsaw is included in the introductory Getting There & Away and Getting Around sections earlier.

Bus Warsaw has two major bus terminals for PKS buses.

Dworzec Zachodnia (Western Bus Station; Al Jerozolimskie 144) handles all domestic buses heading south, north and west of the capital, including Częstochowa (31zł), Gdańsk (55zł), Kazimierz Dolny (17zł), Kraków (36zł), Olsztyn (30zł), Toruń (31zł), Wrocław (41zł) and Zakopane (49zł). This complex is southwest of the city centre and adjoins the Warszawa Zachodnia train station. Take the commuter train that leaves from Warszawa Śródmieście station.

Dworzec Stadion (Stadium Bus Station; ul Sokola 1) adjoins the Warszawa Stadion train station. It is also easily accessible by commuter train from Warszawa Śródmieście. Dworzec Stadion handles a few domestic buses to the east and southeast, eg, Lublin (24zł), Białystok (20zł) and Zamość (35zł), as well as Kazimierz Dolny.

Polski Express (☎ 620 03 26) operates coaches from the airport, but passengers can get on/off and buy tickets at the obvious stall along Al Jana Pawła II, next to the Warszawa Centralna train station. Polski Express buses travel daily to Białystok (30zł); Częstochowa (34zł); Gdynia, via Sopot and Gdańsk (53zł); Kraków (54zł); Lublin (31zł); Toruń (35zł); and Wrocław (35zł).

International buses depart from and arrive at Dworzec Zachodnia or, occasionally, outside the Warszawa Centralna train station. Tickets for the international buses are available from the bus offices at Dworzec Zachodnia, from agencies at Warszawa Centralna or from any of the major travel agencies in the city, including Almatur.

Train Warsaw has several train stations, but the one that most travellers will use almost exclusively is **Warszawa Centralna** (Warsaw Central; Al Jerozolimskie 54); it handles the overwhelming majority of domestic trains and all international services. Refer to the Getting There & Away section earlier for details about international trains to/from Warsaw, and to the relevant Getting There & Away sections later in this chapter for information about domestic services to/from Warsaw.

Remember, Warszawa Centralna is often *not* where domestic and international trains start or finish, so make sure you get on or off the train at this station in the few minutes allotted. And watch your belongings closely at all times, because pickpocketing and theft is an increasing problem.

On the street level of the central station, the spacious main hall houses ticket counters, ATMs and snack bars, as well as a post office, a newsagent (for public-transport tickets) and also a tourist office. Along the underground mezzanine level leading to the tracks and platforms are a dozen kantors (one of which is open 24 hours), a **left-luggage office** *(open 7am-9pm daily)*, lockers, eateries, several other places to buy tickets for local public transport, Internet centres and bookshops.

Tickets for domestic and international trains are available from counters at the station (but allow at least an hour for possible queuing) or, in advance, from any major Orbis Travel office (see under Organised Tours earlier). Tickets for immediate departures on domestic and international trains are also available from numerous, well-signed booths in the underpasses leading to Warszawa Centralna.

Some domestic trains also stop at Warszawa Śródmieście station, 300m east of Warszawa Centralna, and Warszawa Zachodnia, next to Dworzec Zachodnia bus station.

Getting Around

To/From the Airport The cheapest way of getting from the airport to the city centre (and vice versa) is on bus No 175. This bus leaves every 10 to 15 minutes for the Old Town, via ul Nowy Świat and the Warszawa Centralna train station. It operates daily from 5am to 11pm. If you arrive in the wee hours, night bus No 611 links the airport with Warszawa Centralna every 30 minutes.

The taxi fare between the airport and the city centre is about 25zł. Make sure you take one of the official taxis with a name and telephone number on top and fares listed on the window; you can arrange this at one of the three official taxi counters on the arrivals level of the international section of the terminal. The 'Mafia' cabs still operate at the airport and charge astronomical rates.

Public Transport Warsaw's public transport is frequent, cheap and operates daily from 5am to 11pm. The fare (2.40zł) is a flat rate for any bus, tram, trolleybus or metro train anywhere in the city – ie, one 2.40zł fare is valid for one ride on one form of transport. Warsaw is the only place in Poland where students with an ISIC card get a discount (50%). Bulky luggage (anything that exceeds 60cm x 40cm x 20cm) costs an extra 2.40zł.

Tickets (valid on all forms of public transport) for 60/90 minutes are 3.60/4.50zł, and passes (for all public transport) are available for one day (7.20zł), three days (12zł), one week (26zł) and one month (66zł). Daily tickets are actually valid for 24 hours and start from the time you first use it. Tickets should be purchased before boarding from kiosks (including those marked RUCH) and punched in one of the small machines on-board. Ticket inspectors are not uncommon and fines are high.

One very useful bus is the 'sightseeing route' No 180, which links Powązki Cemetery with Wilanów Park. It stops at most attractions listed in the Royal Way section earlier, as well as Łazienki Park, and travels via ul Krakowskie Przedmieście and ul Nowy Świat.

A metro line operates from the Ursynów suburb (Kabaty station) at the southern city limits to Ratusz (Town Hall), via the city centre (Centrum), but is of limited use to visitors. Local commuter trains head out to the suburbs from the Warszawa Śródieście station.

Taxi Taxis are a quick and easy way to get around – as long as you use official taxis and drivers use their meters. Beware of 'Mafia' taxis parked in front of top-end hotels, at the airport, outside Warszawa Centralna train station and in the vicinity of most tourist sights.

Car Rental There is little incentive to drive a rented car through Warsaw's horrific traffic and confusing streets, and you're likely to get serious migraines looking for car parks anyway. But there are lots of good reasons to hire a car in Warsaw for jaunts around the countryside. Offices for major car-rental companies are listed in the local English-language newspapers and magazines, and these companies also have counters at the airport. Alternatively, book through a travel agency. More details about car rental is under Car & Motorcycle in the Getting Around section earlier.

Mazovia & Podlasie

Mazovia only came to the fore when the capital was transferred to Warsaw in 1596. It has never been a fertile region, so there are few historic towns – the notable exception is Poland's second largest city, Łódź. To the east along the Belarus border is Podlasie, which literally means 'land close to the forest'. The highlight of the region is the magnificent Białowieża National Park.

ŁÓDŹ
☎ 042 • pop 840,000

Łódź ('Woodge') is slowly cleaning up its dull image and pollution-stained buildings. It offers several elegant malls and plenty of parklands, and is worth a visit if you're getting sick of the tourist hordes in Kraków.

Many of the attractions – and most of the life-support systems, such as banks, kantors and ATMs – are along, or just off, the backbone of ul Piotrkowska. The **tourist office** (☎/fax 633 71 69, ul Traugutta 18) is 300m east of the main street.

The **Historical Museum of Łódź** (ul Ogrodowa 15; admission 6zł; open 10am-2pm Tues & Thur-Sun, 2pm-6pm Wed) is 200m northwest of Plac Wolności, which is at the northern end of the main drag. Also worthwhile is the **Museum of Ethnography & Archaeology** (Plac Wolności 14; admission 6zł; open about 10am-4pm Tues-Sun).

Herbst Palace (ul Przędalniana 72; admission 6zł; open about noon-4pm Tues-Sun) has been converted into an appealing museum. It's accessible by bus No 55 heading east from the cathedral at the southern end of ul Piotrkowska. The **Jewish Cemetery** (ul Bracka 40; admission 2zł; open 9am-5pm Sun-Thur, 9am-3pm Fri; enter from ul Zmienna) is one of the largest in Europe. It's 3km northeast of the city centre and accessible by tram No 1 or 6 from near Plac Wolności.

The tourist office can provide information about camping grounds and private rooms. The **youth hostel** (☎ 630 66 80, fax 630 66 83, ul Legionów 27; dorm beds 30-60zł) is one of the best in Poland, so book ahead. It's only 250m west of Plac Wolności.

Hotel Urzędu Miasta (☎ 640 66 09, fax 640 66 45, ul Bojowników Getta Warszawskiego 9; singles/doubles with bathroom 110/145zł) is good value and only 500m north of Plac Wolności.

LOT (☎ 633 48 15; ul Piotrkowska 122) flies to Warsaw four times a week. From the Łódź Kaliska train station, 1.2km southwest of central Łódź, trains go regularly to Wrocław, Poznań, Toruń and Gdańsk. For Warsaw and Częstochowa, use the Łódź Fabryczna station, 400m east of the city centre. Buses go in all directions from the bus terminal, next to the Fabryczna train station.

BIAŁOWIEŻA NATIONAL PARK
☎ 085

Białowieża ('Byah-wo-VYEH-zhah') is Poland's oldest national park and the only one registered by Unesco as a Biosphere Reserve and a World Heritage Site. The 5346 hectares protect the primeval forest, as well as 120 species of birds. Animal life includes elk, wild boar, wolf and, the uncontested king of the forest, the rare European bison (which was once thought to be extinct).

The ideal base is the charming village of Białowieża. The main road to Białowieża from Hajnówka leads to the southern end of Palace Park; alternatively, a slight detour around the park leads to the village's main street, ul Waszkiewicza. Along this street is a **post office** and **Internet centre**, but there's nowhere to change money. (The nearest kantor is in Hajnówka.)

You'll find the **PTTK office** (☎/fax 681 26 24, W www.pttk.sitech.pl; open 8am-4pm daily) is at the southern end of Palace Park. Serious hikers should contact the **National Park Office** (☎ 681 29 01; open 9am-4pm daily) inside Palace Park. Most maps of the national park (especially the one published by PTOP) details several enticing **hiking trails**.

Things to See & Do

A combined ticket (12zł) allows you entry to the museum, the bison reserve and the nature reserve. Alternatively, you can pay for each attraction separately.

The elegant and compact **Palace Park** (admission free; open daylight hours) is only accessible on foot, bicycle or horse-drawn cart across the bridge from the PTTK office. Over the river is the excellent **Natural & Forestry Museum** (admission 5zł; open 9am-4pm Tues-Sun June-Sept, 9am-3pm Oct-May), one of the best of its kind the country. Unfortunately, the adjacent **lookout tower** isn't tall enough to get any decent views of the surrounding national park.

The **European Bison Reserve** (admission 5zł; open 9am-5pm daily) is a small park containing many of these mighty beasts, as well as wolves, strange horse-like tarpans and mammoth żubroń (hybrids of bisons and cows). Entrance to the reserve is just north of the Hajnówka-Białowieża road, about 4.5km west of the PTTK office – look for the signs along the żebra żubra trail or follow the green or yellow marked trails.

The main attraction is the **Strict Nature Reserve** *(admission 5zł; open 9am-5pm daily)*, which starts about 1km north of the Palace Park. It can only be visited on a three-hour (Polish-language) tour with a licensed guide along a 6km trail. If you want a guide who speaks English or German you'll be slugged 150zł per group. Licensed guides (in any language) can be arranged at the PTTK office or any travel agency in the village. Note that the reserve does close sometimes due to inclement weather.

A more comfortable way to visit the nature reserve is by horse-drawn cart (with a guide), which costs 100zł (three hours) and holds four people. Otherwise, it may be possible (with permission from the PTTK office) to visit the reserve by bicycle (with a guide).

The PTTK office and **Zimorodek** *(☎ 681 26 09, ul Waszkiewicza 2)*, opposite the post office, rent bikes. Contact Wejmutka (see Places to Stay & Eat) about hiring a **canoe** for a leisurely paddle along the river.

Places to Stay & Eat
Plenty of homes along the road from Hajnówka offer private rooms for about 30/50zł for singles/doubles.

Youth Hostel *(☎/fax 681 25 60; ul Waszkiewicza 6; dorm beds 17zł, rooms per person 25zł; open year-round)* is one of the best in the region. The bathrooms are clean and the kitchen is excellent.

Dom Wycieczkowy PTTK *(☎/fax 681 25 05; singles from 50zł, doubles with bath 80zł)* boasts a serene location inside the Palace Park. It has seen better days, but the position and rates are hard to beat. It has a **restaurant**.

Pension Gawra *(☎ 681 28 04, fax 681 24 84, ul Poludnlowa 2; rooms without/with bath 60/100zł)* is excellent value. This quiet, homely place with large rooms overlooking a typically pretty garden is just off the main road from Hajnówka, about 400m southwest of Palace Park.

Pensjonacik Unikat *(☎/fax 681 27 74, ul Waszkiewicza 39; singles/doubles from 40/ 80zł)* is charmingly decorated (complete with bison hides on the wall) and good value. The **restaurant** offers traditional food at reasonable prices and has a menu in both German and English.

Wejmutka *(meals 7-12zł)*, alongside the river opposite the PTTK office, has one of the nicest settings in eastern Poland.

Getting There & Away
From Warsaw, take the express train (at 2.07pm) from Warszawa Centralna to Siedlce (1½ hours), wait for a connection on the slow train to Hajnówka (two hours), and then catch one of the nine daily buses to Białowieża. Back to Warsaw, the only sensible option is the 11.06am train from Hajnówka to Siedlce, with an immediate connection to Warszawa Centralna.

Five buses a day travel from the Dworzec Stadion station in Warsaw to Białystok (four hours), from where buses regularly go to Białowieża (2½ hours) – but you may need to stay overnight in Białystok. To Warsaw, a bus leaves Białowieża for Białystok at 5.55am.

Małopolska

Małopolska (literally 'little Poland') encompasses the whole of southeastern Poland, from the Lublin Uplands in the north down to the Carpathian Mountains along the borders with Slovakia and Ukraine. Kraków became the royal capital of Małopolska in 1038 and remained so for over 500 years. Visitors to the region can admire the royal dignity of Kraków, explore the rugged beauty of the Tatra Mountains and witness the tragic remnants of the Jewish heritage.

KRAKÓW
☎ 012 • pop 770,000

Kraków is Poland's third-largest city and one of its oldest, dating from the 7th century. The city was founded by Prince Krak, who, according to legend, secured its prime location overlooking the Vistula River after outwitting the resident dragon.

In 1000 the bishopric of Kraków was established here. By 1038 the city became the capital of the Piast kingdom, and the kings ruled from Wawel Castle until 1596. Even after the capital was moved to Warsaw, Polish royalty continued to be crowned and buried at the Wawel Cathedral.

At this crossing of trade routes from Western Europe to Byzantium and from southern Europe to the Baltic sea, a large medieval city developed. Particularly good times came with the reign of King Kazimierz the Great, a generous patron of the arts.

Kraków is the only large city in Poland whose old architecture survived WWII intact.

POLAND

POLAND

KRAKÓW

To Częstochowa (114km)
To Warsaw (295km)

Radzikowskiego
Jasnogórska
Al 29 Listopada

Conrada
Opolska
Lublańska
Bora-Komorowskiego

Balicka
To Airport (7km)
Bronowicka

ul Szablowskiego
Wesele
Al Armii Krajowej
Słowackiego
ul Biskupia

To Airport (8km)
Reymonta
Kraków Główny Train Station
Al Jana Pawła II

Królowej Jadwigi
ul Oleandry
5
OLD TOWN
Mogilska
Al Pokoju

Piłsudski Mound
Zoo
Kościuszko Mound
Blonia
4
See Old Town & Wawel Map

Las Wolski
ZWIERZYNIEC
ul Kamendulska
KAZIMIERZ
Nowohucka

To Oświęcim (Auschwitz) & Birkenau (54km)
3
Księcia Józefa
See Kazimierz Map
7
Saska

Vistula
PODGÓRZE
Lipska

Praska Tyniecka
Krakus Mound
Kraków Płaszów Train Station

Konopnickiej
Kamieńskiego
Wielicka
ul Grochowa
8

Kobierzyńska
Nowogródzka
Zakopiańska

1 PFC Camping Nr 45
2 Schronisko Szkolne
3 Camping Nr 46 Smok
4 National Museum's Main Building
5 Youth Hostel PTSM
6 Russian Consulate
7 Former Schindler's Factory
8 Youth Hostel (ul Grochowa)
9 Former Płaszów Concentration Camp
10 Camping Nr 171 Krakowianka

Żywiecka Boczna
Babińskiego
9
10

0   1   2km
0   0.5   1mi

To Zakopane (103km)
To Wieliczka Salt Mine (8km)

In January 1945 a sudden encircling man-oeuvre by the Soviet Red Army forced the Germans to evacuate the city, so Kraków was saved from destruction.

No other city in Poland better captures its intriguing history: the Old Town harbours towering Gothic churches and the splendid Wawel Castle, while Kazimierz, the now-silent Jewish quarter, recounts a more tragic story. Kraków is also home to world-class museums and a lively cultural scene. In 1978 Unesco included the Old Town of Kraków on its first World Heritage list. This historic core has changed little.

Information
Tourist Offices & Publications There is a confusing array of tourist offices in Kraków.

Kraków's **Municipal Tourism Information Centre** (*Rynek Główny 1/3; ☎ 428 36 00; open 8am-6pm Mon-Fri, 9am-3pm Sat & Sun*) is the major office. There is also a smaller and less busy **tourist office** (*☎ 432 01 10,* e *it-krakow@wp.pl; open 8am-8pm Mon-Fri, 9am-5pm Sat & Sun*) along the path between ul Szpitalna and the main train station. Another **tourist counter** (*☎ 421 50 31,* e *ap2info@interia.pl; open about 6am-10am & 3pm-8pm daily*) is at the far end of the main train station building.

The Kazimierz **tourist office** (*☎ 432 08 40,* e *biuro@kazimierzbiuro.kraknet.pl; ul Józefa 7; open 10am-4pm Mon-Fri*) provides information about Jewish heritage in that area.

The **Culture Information Centre** (*☎ 421 77 87,* w *www.karnet.krakow2000.pl; ul Św*

Jana 2; open 10am-6pm Mon-Fri, 10am-4pm Sat) is the best place to get information about (and tickets for) the plethora of cultural events in the city.

Two free monthly magazines, *Welcome to Cracóv & Małopolska* and *Kraków: What, Where, When* (the latter also in German), are available at the tourist offices and some travel agencies and upmarket hotels. The *Kraków Insider* booklet (6.50zł) is also very useful.

The tourist offices, as well as some hotels and travel agencies, sell the 'Cracóv Tourist Card' (45/65zł for two/three days). This card provides free admission to all museums and attractions in Kraków and access on all public buses and trams, as well as various discounts (up to 40%) for organised tours and at selected restaurants.

Money Kantors and ATMs can be found all over the city centre. It's worth noting, however, that most kantors close on Sunday and areas near Rynek Główny square and the main train station offer terrible exchange rates. There are also exchange facilities at the airport. For travellers cheques, try **Bank Pekao** *(Rynek Główny 31)*, which also provides cash advances on MasterCard and Visa.

Post & Communications The **main post office** *(ul Westerplatte 20; open 8am-8pm Mon-Fri, 8am-2pm Sat, 9am-noon Sun)* has a poste-restante bureau. Mail addressed to Poste Restante, Poczta Główna, ul Westerplatte 20, 31-045 Kraków 1, Poland, can be collected at window No 1. Telephone calls can be made at the **telephone centre** *(ul Wielopole; open 24hr)*, next to the Main Post Office, or from the **post & telephone office** *(ul Lubicz 4; open 24hr)*, conveniently opposite the main train station building.

Email & Internet Access The most atmospheric place to check emails is downstairs at **Cyber Café U Luisa** *(Rynek Główny 13)*. Otherwise, try **Centrum Internetowe** *(Rynek Główny 9)*, where views of the square from the window are so exceptional that it's hard to concentrate on the computer screen, or **Looz Internet Café** *(ul Mikołajska 13)*, a dingy Internet café-cum-pub.

Bookshops The widest selection of regional and city maps, as well as Lonely Planet titles, is in **Sklep Podróżnika** *(ul Jagiellońska 6)*. As usual, the **EMPiK Megastore** *(Rynek Główny 5)* sells foreign newspapers and magazines. For literature and trashy novels (in English and German), check the **Columbus Bookshop** *(ul Grodzka 60)* or **Księgarnia Językowa** *(Plac Matejki 5)*. For publications related to Jewish issues visit the **Jarden Jewish Bookshop** *(ul Szeroka 2)* in Kazimierz.

Things to See & Do

Old Town The magnificent **Rynek Główny** is the largest (roughly 800m wide and 1200m long) medieval town square in the whole of Europe. Dominating the square is the 16th-century Renaissance **Cloth Hall** (Sukiennice). On the ground floor is a large **craft market** and upstairs is the **Gallery of 19th-Century Polish Painting** *(admission 5zł, free Sun; open 10am-3.30pm Tues, Wed, Fri-Sun, 10am-6pm Thur)*, which includes several famous works by Jan Matejko.

The ostentatious 14th-century **St Mary's Church** *(Rynek Główny 4; admission 2.50zł; open noon-6pm Mon-Sat)* fills the northeastern corner of the square. The huge main altarpiece by Wit Stwosz (Veit Stoss) of Nuremberg is the finest Gothic sculpture in Poland. Every hour a *hejnał* (bugle call) is played from the highest tower of the Church. Today, it's a musical symbol of the city; the melody based on five notes was played in medieval times as a warning call. It breaks off abruptly to symbolise when, according to legend, the throat of a 13th-century trumpeter was pierced by a Tatar arrow.

West of the Cloth Hall is the 15th-century **Town Hall Tower** *(admission 3zł; open 10am-5pm Wed-Fri, 10am-4pm Sat & Sun)*, which you can climb. Also worth a visit is the **Historical Museum of Kraków** *(Rynek Główny 35; admission 5zł; open 9am-3.30pm Tues, Wed & Fri, 11am-6pm Thur)*.

From St Mary's Church, walk up (northeast) ul Floriańska to the 14th-century **Florian Gate**, the only one of the original eight gates. Behind the gate is the **Barbican** *(admission 5zł; open 9am-5pm daily May-Sept)*, a defensive bastion built in 1498. Nearby, the **Czartoryski Museum** *(ul Św Jana 19; admission 5zł; open about 10am-3.30pm Tues-Sun)* features an impressive collection of European art, including some works by Leonardo da Vinci and Rembrandt.

South of Rynek Główny, Plac Wszystkich Świętych is dominated by two 13th-century

POLAND

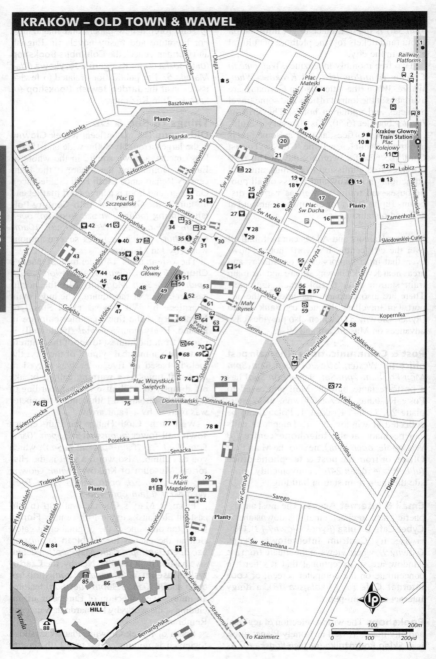

KRAKÓW – OLD TOWN & WAWEL

KRAKÓW – OLD TOWN & WAWEL

PLACES TO STAY

5	Pokoje Gościnne Jordan; Jordan (Travel Agency)
9	Biuro Turystyki i Zakwaterowania Waweltur (Private Rooms)
10	Jordan Tourist Information & Accommodation Center
13	Hotel Europejski
14	Hotel Polonia
26	Hotel Pollera
34	Hotel Saski
57	Hotel Wit Stwosz
58	Hotel Wyspiański
67	Hotel Rezydent
78	Hotel Wawel Tourist
84	Pensjonat Rycerski

PLACES TO EAT

18	Bistro Rożowy Słoń
19	Restauracja Sąsiedzi
28	Restaurant Orient Lychee
29	Bar Mleczny Dworzanin
30	Café Camelot
31	Restauracja Chłopskie Jadło
44	Jadłodajnia Kuchcik
45	Salad Bar Chimera
47	Restauracja Sphinx
55	Ipanema
60	Green Way Bar Wegetariański; Jadłodajnia U Stasi
62	Bistro Rożowy Słoń
77	Pod Aniołami
80	Restauracja U Literatów

OTHER

1	Underground Passage to Buses to Oświecim (Auschwitz & Birkenau)
2	Bus No 208 to Airport
3	Minibuses to Wieliczka
4	Księgarnia Językowa Bookshop
6	LOT Office
7	Bus Terminal
8	Private Buses to Zakopane
11	Post & Telephone Office
12	Bus B to Airport
15	Tourist Office
16	Church of the Holy Cross
17	Teatr im Słowackiego
20	Barbican
21	Florian Gate
22	Czartoryski Museum
23	Equinox
24	Irish Pub Pod Papugami
25	Piwnica Pod Złotą Pipą
27	Indigo Jazz Club
32	Kino Sztuka
33	Kino Apollo
35	Culture Information Centre
36	Orbis Travel
37	Historical Museum of Kraków
38	Bank Pekao
39	Klub Pasja
40	Sklep Podróżnika Bookshop
41	Stary Teatr
42	Klub Kulturalny
43	St Anne's Church

46	Police Station
48	Town Hall Tower
49	Cloth Hall; Craft Market
50	Gallery of 19th-Century Polish Painting
51	Municipal Tourism Information Centre
52	Statue of Adam Mieckiewicz
53	St Mary's Church
54	Jazz Club U Muniaka
56	Black Gallery
59	Looz Internet Café
61	EMPiK Megastore
63	Pub Bastylia
64	Centrum Internetowe
65	St Adalbert's Church
66	Cyber Café U Luisa
68	Almatur
69	US Consulate
70	German Consulate-General
71	Main Post Office
72	Telephone Centre
73	Dominican Church
74	French Consulate-General
75	Franciscan Church
76	Filharmonia Krakówska
79	Church of SS Peter & Paul
81	Wyspiański Museum
82	St Andrew's Church
83	Columbus Bookshop
85	Cathedral Museum
86	Wawel Cathedral
87	Wawel Castle
88	Dragon's Cave

POLAND

monastic churches: the **Dominican Church** (ul Stolarska 12; admission free; open 9am-6pm daily) to the east and the **Franciscan Church** (Plac Wszystkich Świętych 5; admission free; open 9am-5pm daily) to the west. The latter is noted for its stained-glass windows.

South along ul Grodzka is the early-17th-century Jesuit **Church of SS Peter & Paul** (ul Grodzka 64; admission free; open dawn-dusk daily), the first baroque church built in Poland. The Romanesque 11th-century **St Andrew's Church** (ul Grodzka 56; admission free; open 9am-6pm Mon-Fri) was the only building in Kraków to withstand the Tatars' attack of 1241.

Along ul Kanonicza – probably Kraków's most picturesque street – is the **Wyspiański Museum** (ul Kanonicza 9; admission 5zł, free Sun; open 11am-6pm Tues-Thur, 9am-3.30pm Wed & Fri, 10am-3.30pm Sat & Sun). It is dedicated to Poland's renowned poet, painter, playwright and stained-glass designer.

Wawel Hill South of the Old Town is the dominant Wawel Hill (admission to grounds free; open 6am-8pm daily May-Sept, 6am-5pm Oct-Apr). This hill is crowned with a castle and cathedral, both of which are the very symbols of Poland and the guardians of its national history.

Inside the extensive grounds are several worthwhile attractions; all are open from about 9.30am to 3pm Tuesday to Friday and from 10am to 3pm on Saturday and Sunday. Each place has different opening hours on Monday (as indicated below). Currently, entry to the Treasury & Armoury and Lost Wawel is free on Monday, but check this at the ticket office because the allocated days with free entry (and regulations about it) change regularly.

Allow at least three hours to explore the castle and cathedral and come early, especially in summer. As soon as you arrive, stop at the kasa (ticket office) in the grounds; entry to most attractions is limited and only available by ticket (even when admission is free you'll still need a ticket).

Inside the magnificent **Wawel Castle**, the largest and most popular exhibits are the **Royal Chambers** (admission 15zł; closed Mon) and the **Royal Private Apartments** (admission 15zł; closed Mon). Entry to the latter is only allowed on a guided tour (included in the admission fee), but if you want a guide who speaks English, French or German contact the **guides office** (☎ 422 09 04) along the laneway up to the hill.

Dominating the hill is the 14th-century **Wawel Cathedral** (admission free, but total of 6zł admission to tombs & bell tower; open 9am-5pm Mon). For four centuries it was the coronation and burial place of Polish royalty, as evidenced by the **Royal Tombs** where 100 kings and queens have been buried. The golden-domed **Sigismund Chapel** (1539), on the southern side of the cathedral, is considered to be the finest Renaissance construction in Poland, and the **bell tower** houses the country's largest bell (11 tonnes). More exhibits about the cathedral are in the **Cathedral Museum** (admission 5zł; closed Mon).

Other attractions in the complex include the **Museum of Oriental Art** (admission 6zł; closed Mon); the **Treasury & Armoury** (admission 12zł; open 9.30am-1pm Mon); the **Lost Wawel** (admission 6zł; open 9.30am-noon Mon), which has some archaeological exhibits; and the quirky **Dragon's Cave** (admission 3zł; open 9am-5pm Mon).

Kazimierz Founded by King Kazimierz the Great in 1335, Kazimierz was until the 1820s an independent town with its own municipal charter and laws. In the 15th century, Jews were expelled from Kraków and forced to resettle in a small prescribed area in Kazimierz, separated by a wall from the larger Christian quarter. The Jewish quarter later became home to Jews fleeing persecution from all corners of Europe.

By the outbreak of WWII there were 65,000 Jews in Kraków (around 30% of the city's population), and most lived in Kazimierz. During the war the Nazis relocated Jews to a walled ghetto in Podgórze, just south of the Vistula River. They were exterminated in the nearby **Płaszów Concentration Camp**, as portrayed in Steven Spielberg's haunting film *Schindler's List*. The current Jewish population in Kraków is about 100.

These days Kazimierz is undergoing a renaissance as citizens of all creeds and religions realise the benefit of living in such a charming place so close to the city centre.

Kazimierz has two historically determined sectors. Its western Catholic quarter is dotted with churches. The 14th-century Gothic **St Catherine's Church** (ul Augustian 7; admission free; open only during services) boasts a

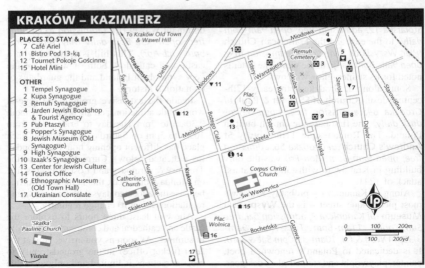

KRAKÓW – KAZIMIERZ

PLACES TO STAY & EAT
7 Café Ariel
11 Bistro Pod 13-ką
12 Tournet Pokoje Gościnne
15 Hotel Mini

OTHER
1 Tempel Synagogue
2 Kupa Synagogue
3 Remuh Synagogue
4 Jarden Jewish Bookshop & Tourist Agency
5 Pub Ptaszyl
6 Popper's Synagogue
8 Jewish Museum (Old Synagogue)
9 High Synagogue
10 Izaak's Synagogue
13 Center for Jewish Culture
14 Tourist Office
16 Ethnographic Museum (Old Town Hall)
17 Ukrainian Consulate

singularly imposing 17th-century gilded high altar, while the 14th-century **Corpus Christi Church** (ul Bożego Ciała 26; admission free; open 9am-5pm Mon-Sat) is crammed with baroque fittings. The **Ethnographic Museum** (Plac Wolnica; admission 4zł; open 10am-6pm Mon & Wed-Sat, 10am-2pm Sun) in the Old Town Hall has a reasonably interesting collection of regional crafts and costumes.

The eastern Jewish quarter is dotted with synagogues, many of which miraculously survived the war. The most important is the 15th-century **Old Synagogue**, the oldest Jewish religious building in Poland. It now houses the **Jewish Museum** (ul Szeroka 24; admission 6zł; open 9am-3pm Wed-Thur, 11am-7pm Fri, 9am-4pm Sat & Sun).

A short walk north is the small 16th-century **Remuh Synagogue** (ul Szeroka 40; admission 5zł; open 9am-4pm Mon-Fri), the only one still used for religious services. Behind it, the **Remuh Cemetery** (admission free; open 9am-4pm Mon-Fri) boasts some extraordinary Renaissance gravestones. Nearby, the restored **Izaak's Synagogue** (ul Jakuba 25; admission 6zł; open 9am-7pm Sun-Fri) shows documentary films about life in the Jewish ghetto.

It's easy to take a self-guided walking tour around Kazimierz (and other parts of Kraków) with the booklet *Retracing Schindler's List* (in German or English). It contains a map and plenty of explanations and is available from the **Jarden Jewish Bookshop** (ul Szeroka 2, Kazimierz).

Wieliczka Salt Mine Wieliczka ('Vyeh-LEECH-kah'), 15km southeast of the city centre, is famous for the **Wieliczka Salt Mine** (W www.kopalnia.pl; ul Daniłowicza 10; admission 29zł; camera permit 13zł, 20% discount Nov-Feb; open 8am-8pm daily Apr-Oct, 8am-4pm Nov-March). Remarkably, this eerie world of pits and chambers is all hewn out by hand from solid salt, and every single element, from chandeliers to altarpieces, is made of salt. Appropriately, the mine is included on Unesco's World Heritage list.

The highlight of a mine visit is the richly ornamented **Chapel of the Blessed Kinga**, which is actually a church measuring 54m by 17m and is 12m high. Construction of this underground temple took more than 30 years (1895–1927), resulting in the removal of 20,000 tonnes of rock salt. The **museum** (admission 12zł) is on the 3rd floor of the mine.

The obligatory guided tour (included in the admission fee) through the mine takes about two hours (a 2km walk). Tours in English operate at 10am, 12.30pm and 3pm, but only between June and August; one or two tours a day (June to August) also run in German (depending on demand). If you're visiting independently, you must wait for a tour to start, but the management guarantees that you'll wait no more than one hour. If you join a Polish-language tour, buy an English-language booklet (7zł) at the mine. Otherwise, prebook a private tour (about 85zł for a small group) in English or German. Last admission to the mine is about three hours before closing time.

Minibuses to Wieliczka town depart every 15 minutes between 6am and 8pm from near the bus terminal in Kraków and drop passengers outside the salt mine (but ask the driver to do this). Trains between Kraków and Wieliczka leave every 45 minutes throughout the day, but the train station in Wieliczka is a fair walk from the mine.

Organised Tours
The following companies operate tours of Kraków and surrounding areas.

Almatur (☎ 422 09 02, ul Grodzka 2) – all sorts of interesting outdoor activities in and around Kraków during summer.

Jordan (☎ 421 21 35, W www.jordan.krakow.pl) ul Długa 9 – tours to Auschwitz and Wieliczka

Jarden Tourist Agency (☎/fax 421 71 66, W www .jarden.pl) ul Szeroka 2 – the best agency for tours of Jewish heritage. Guided walking tours around Kazimierz cost 25/30zł per person (two/three hours). It's showpiece – 'Retracing Schindler's List' – (two hours by car) costs 45zł per person. All tours require a minimum of three and must be arranged in advance. All tours are in English, but French- and German-speaking guides can be organised.

Orbis Travel (☎ 422 40 35, W www.orbis.travel .krakow.pl) Rynek Główny 41 – with a number of agencies around town including one at the Old Town square

Zeluga Krakowska (☎ 422 08 55) – boat trips along the Vistula between May and September from near Wawel Hill.

Special Events
Kraków boasts one of the richest cycles of annual events in Poland. Major cultural festivals include the Jewish Culture Festival (June/July) and International Festival of Street Theatre (July). Major musical events include the

Organ Music Festival (March/ April) and the Summer Jazz Festival (July). Contact the helpful Culture Information Centre (see under Tourist Offices earlier) for full programme details and bookings.

Seven days after Corpus Christi (a Thursday in May or June), Kraków has a colourful pageant headed by Lajkonik, a legendary figure disguised as a Tatar riding a hobbyhorse.

Places to Stay

Kraków is unquestionably Poland's premier tourist destination, so booking any form of accommodation between April and October is strongly recommended – and *essential* in July and August. If you can't find any accommodation anywhere, contact the tourist offices in the main train station building and along the path near ul Szpitalna.

Camping Four kilometres west of the Old Town is **Camping Nr 46 Smok** (☎ 429 72 66; ul Kamedulska 18; camping per person/tent 15/10zł; open June-Sept). It's small, quiet and pleasantly located. To get here frrom outside the Kraków Główny train station building, take tram No 2 to the end of the line in Zwierzyniec and change for any westbound bus (except No 100).

Camping Nr 171 Krakowianka (☎ 266 41 91; ul Żywiecka Boczna 4; camping per person/tent 15/10zł; open May-Sept) is on the road to Zakopane 5km south of the Old Town. Take tram No 19 or bus No 119 from the main train station.

PFC Camping Nr 45 (☎ 637 21 22; ul Radzikowskiego 99; camping per person/tent 15/14zł; open June–mid-Sept) is beside the Motel Krak on the Katowice road about 4km northwest of the Old Town. It's large and well equipped, but the traffic noise can be considerable. To get here, take bus No 501 from the main train station.

Hostels The largest hostel in Poland, **Youth Hostel PTSM** (☎ 633 88 22, e smkrakow .pro.onet.pl; ul Oleandry 4; dorm beds 14-24zł; open year-round) is only 1km west of the Old Town. Although it has 380 beds, it's sometimes full – and always noisy. Take tram No 15 from outside the main train station building and get off just past Hotel Cracovia.

Another **Youth Hostel** (☎/fax 653 24 32; ul Grochowa 21; dorm beds 15-25zł; doubles with shared bathroom per person 50zł;

open year-round) is on the 3rd floor of a student dormitory. It's in a quiet suburb 5km southeast of the Old Town and quite remote. Take bus No 115 from the train station.

Schronisko Szkolne (☎ 637 24 41; ul Szablowskiego 1c; dorm beds 15-25zł; open year-round) is 3.5km northwest of the Old Town. This place is not too convenient either, but it's more likely to have space in July and August (when some 200 extra beds become available). Take tram No 4 or 13 from the train station.

The tourist offices will have information about the current availability of accommodation in **student hostels** during the summer months (July to September), though some hostels offer a few rooms all year. Singles/doubles with a shared bathroom are cheap – from 60/80zł – but the hostels are invariably far from the Old Town.

Private Rooms In summer, you may be accosted by intimidating old ladies offering private rooms. As always, check the location before making any decision.

Biuro Turystyki i Zakwaterowania Waweltur (☎/fax 422 16 40; ul Pawia 8; open 8am-8pm Mon-Fri, 8am-2pm Sat) arranges private rooms. Singles cost from 64zł to 75zł and doubles from 96zł to 128zł. The rates are cheaper the further away you stay from the Old Town.

Jordan Tourist Information & Accommodation Centre (☎ 422 60 91; w www.jordan .krakow.pl; ul Pawia 12; open 8am-6pm Mon-Fri, 9am-1pm Sat-Sun) is next door. It offers slightly better rooms for higher prices: about 90/110zł for singles/doubles.

The tourist counter in the main train station building can arrange double rooms (no singles) in the Old Town for about 100zł and well-appointed single/double apartments (with bathroom and kitchen) close to the Old Town for 110/130zł. The tourist office in Kazimierz can also arrange **private rooms** in that area.

Hotels – Budget Note that one of the youth hostels, and most student hostels, have individual rooms and that private rooms and apartments are often better value than hotels. See the sections earlier for details.

Kazimierz is only a short walk from the Old Town and almost feels like a separate village. Most places in Kazimierz are expensive, but a couple of cheapies can be found.

Tournet Pokoje Gościnne (☎ 292 00 88; W www.nocleg.krakow.pl; ul Miodowa 7; singles/doubles 140/180zł) is a new place offering simple but comfortable and quiet rooms. The bathrooms are tiny, however.

Hotel Mini (☎ 430 61 00, fax 430 59 88; Plac Wolnica 7; singles/doubles 130/220zł) is central but quiet, just back from the Ethnographic Museum. The singles are small, but the doubles are large and attic-style and contain some lounge furniture. All are spotlessly clean. Your leg muscles will get a workout going up and down the stairs.

Hotels – Mid-Range & Top End Unless stated otherwise, all rooms listed below contain a TV and rates include breakfast.

Near the bus and train stations, **Hotel Polonia** (☎ 422 12 33; e polonia@bci.krakow .pl; ul Basztowa 25; singles/doubles 99/ 119zł, with bath 250/285zł) is in a grand old building. The newer rooms are not great value and face the noisy main road, but the ones with a shared bathroom are excellent value – but book ahead.

The **Pokoje Gościnne Jordan** (☎ 421 21 25; W www.jordan.krakow.pl; ul Długa 9; singles/doubles from 140/210zł) is about the best value within walking distance of the Old Town, so book ahead. The rooms are modern but unremarkable. The reception is in the travel agency next door.

Pensjonat Rycerski (☎ 422 60 82, fax 422 33 99; Plac Na Groblach 22; doubles without/ with bath from 195/270zł) is one of the surprisingly few places close to Wawel Hill – and it charges accordingly. Still it's popular and often booked out.

Hotel Saski (☎ 421 42 22, fax 421 48 30; ul Sławkowska 3; singles/doubles 160/170zł, with bath 200/260zł) is ideally located in an historic house just off Rynek Główny. It's comparatively good value and the rooms feature ornate furniture, but readers have complained about late-night noise from nearby cinemas and cafés. Breakfast is additional to the room rate.

Formerly the drab Dom Turysty PTTK hostel, the **Hotel Wyspiański** (☎ 422 95 66; e wyspianski@janpol.com.pl; ul Westerplatte 15; singles/doubles Mon-Thur from 250/310zł, Fri-Sun from 220/260zł) has now been completely renovated. It's no longer the bargain it was, but prices are marginally acceptable on weekends.

Hotel Pollera (☎ 422 10 44; W www .pollera.com.pl; ul Szpitalna 30; singles/ doubles 295/345zł) is a classy place with large rooms crammed with elegant furniture. The singles are unexciting, but the doubles are far nicer. It's central and quiet (except for the squeaky floors). Substantial discounts are available between October and March.

Near the main square, **Hotel Wawel Tourist** (☎ 424 13 00; W www.wawel-tourist.com .pl; ul Poselska 22; doubles 190zł, singles/ doubles with bath from 195/280zł) is in a recently renovated 16th-century building. It's quiet and well furnished (though some rooms are small) and staff are friendly.

Hotel Rezydent (☎ 429 54 95, fax 429 55 76; ul Grodzka 9; singles/doubles US$85/ 120) is a newish place with modern facilities only a stone's throw from the main square.

Hotel Wit Stwosz (☎ 429 60 26; W www .wit-stwosz.hotel.krakow.pl, ul Mikołajska 28; singles/doubles 320/360zł) is in a historic town house along a quiet street. It's comfortable, stylish and remarkably good value for a top-end hotel.

Places to Eat

By Polish standards, Kraków is a food paradise. The Old Town is tightly packed with good gastronomic venues, ranging from rockbottom to top-notch. Privatisation has pretty much eliminated the dirt-cheap proletarian milk bars, but many excellent affordable alternatives have popped up in their place.

One local speciality is *obwarzanki*, a ringshaped pretzel powdered with poppy seeds, and available from vendors dozing next to their pushcarts.

Almost every proper restaurant that is listed below can provide menus in English and, possibly, German.

Polish Restaurants Recommended by several readers, **Restauracja Chłopskie Jadło** (ul Św Jana 3; mains 18-35zł) is arranged as an old country inn and serves scrumptious Polish food from the 'Peasant's Kitchen'.

Restauracja U Literatów (ul Kanonicza 7; mains from 12zł) may look uninviting with the plastic tables but it's a tiny oasis of greenery with a courtyard setting (hidden from the main street).

Jadłodajnia Kuchcik (ul Jagiellońska 12; mains 8-15zł) offers substantial portions of home-cooked Polish food in unpretentious surroundings. You may have to wait for a table between noon and 2pm.

Bistro Pod 13-ką (*ul Miodowa 13; mains 10-15zł*) is arguably the best place in Kazimierz to try tasty authentic Polish cooking at affordable prices.

Restauracja Sąsiedzi (*ul Szpitalna 40; mains from 10zł*) is a popular split-level place with cafeteria-style food at sensible prices.

Pod Aniolami (*ul Grodzka 35; mains from 30zł*) delighted at least one reader who says this restaurant serves the 'best meals in Kraków'. There are plenty of meat dishes and the surroundings are cosy, if a little smoky.

Other Restaurants For large helpings (with the obligatory dollop of sliced Polish cabbage), **Restaurant Orient Lychee** (*ul Floriańska 27; meals with rice about 10zł*) is one of several Chinese-cum-Vietnamese eateries located in the Old Town. The service is quick and informal.

Café Camelot (*ul Św Tomasza 17; salads about 8zł, mains from 12zł*) has a cosy interior, but if the weather's fine or it's too smoky indoors some tables are set up among the ferns outside. It's perfect for enjoying a sandwich, salad and/or decent coffee while perusing a few day-old English-language newspapers.

Ipanema (*ul Św Tomasza 28; mains about 16zł*) is a newish place that has been recommended by readers for its authentic Brazilian cuisine at reasonable prices.

Café Ariel (*ul Szeroka 18; mains 18-25zł*) is a quaint place in the heart of Kazimierz, which offers a mouthwatering array of authentic Jewish meals.

Restauracja Sphinx (*Rynek Główny 26; mains from 15zł*) is one of several identical places found throughout Poland. As usual, the portions are large, the service is quick and the restaurant is located in a prime position. It's one of the few places around the main square with reasonably priced drinks.

Vegetarian In an attractive cellar along an arcade, **Salad Bar Chimera** (*ul Św Anny 3; salads from 5zł*) offers some of the best salads in Kraków – all listed alphabetically (in Polish) from 'A to Z'.

Green Way Bar Wegetariański (*ul Mikołajska 16; snacks from 6zł, mains from 10zł*) has outlets in several Polish cities. It rarely fails to satisfy anyone looking for something healthy and/or meat-free.

Fast Food Undoubtedly the cheapest place in the middle of the Old Town is **Bar Mleczny Dworzanin** (*ul Floriańska 19; mains from 8zł*). It's often standing room only and the lines of hungry patrons are long.

Bistro Różowy Słoń (*ul Sienna 1 & ul Szpitalna 38; meals about 6zł*) is recognisable by the bright pink chairs and cartoon-painted walls. The 'Pink Elephant' offers, among other tasty treats, a huge selection of pancakes (about 20 types!) and a salad bar – all at remarkably low prices.

Jadłodajnia U Stasi (*ul Mikołajska 16; mains 6-12zł*), near the Green Way Bar Wegetariański, is one of the oldest and best-known eateries. This unpretentious place is very popular for its *pierogi* (stuffed dumplings), but it's only open at lunchtime.

Self-Catering There are no supermarkets or even major grocery shops in the Old Town, so the best place for self-catering is any of the number of **delikatessy** found along the streets.

Entertainment

The comprehensive (free) English-language booklet, *Karnet*, published by the Culture Information Centre (see Tourist Offices earlier), lists almost every event in the city.

Pubs & Bars There are more than 100 pubs and bars in the Old Town alone. Many are housed in ancient vaulted cellars, but non-smokers beware: all have poor ventilation and most patrons seem to take delight in chain-smoking. Some of the best places to relax with a drink are any of the plethora of places around Rynek Główny, but prices are high.

Irish Pub Pod Papugami (*ul Św Jana 18*) was recently refurbished and is now a charming underground watering hole decorated with old motorcycles (among other strange items).

Klub Kulturalny (*ul Szewska 25*) is set in a labyrinthine array of beautiful medieval brick vaults. It's long established and popular, with good music and pleasant atmosphere.

Piwnica Pod Złotą Pipą (*ul Floriańska 30*) is another place located that's inside an inviting cellar. It's more suited to conversation than listening to music.

Pub Bastylia (*ul Stolarska 3*) is a bizarre place on five levels with some floors decorated like a French jail!

Pub Ptaszyl (*ul Szeroka 10*) is an artsy place to check out if you're in Kazimierz.

Nightclubs For foot-tapping jazz head to **Jazz Club u Muniaka** *(ul Floriańska 3)* or the **Indigo Jazz Club** *(ul Floriańska 26)*.

Black Gallery *(ul Mikołajska 24)* is a crowded underground pub-cum-nightclub that only gets going after midnight and stays open *really* late.

Klub Pasja *(ul Szewska 5)* occupies vast brick cellars. It's trendy and attractive and popular with foreigners for its Western music and billiard tables.

Equinox *(ul Sławkowska 13/15)* has long been one of the most popular haunts in the Old Town. Discos are held most nights.

Cinemas Two of the better and more convenient cinemas showing recent films are **Kino Apollo** *(ul Św Tomasza 11a)* and **Kino Sztuka** *(cnr Św Tomasza & Św Jana)*.

Theatre The best-known venue, **Stary Teatr** *(ul Jagiellońska 1)*, consistently offers quality productions. **Teatr im Słowackiego** *(Plac Św Ducha 1)*, built in 1893, focuses on Polish classics and large-scale productions. It was totally renovated in 1991 and its interior is spectacular. **Filharmonia Krakówska** *(ul Zwierzyniecka 1)* boasts one of the best orchestras in the country; concerts are usually held on Friday and Saturday.

Getting There & Away

For information about travelling from Kraków to Zakopane, Częstochowa or Oświęcim (for Auschwitz), refer to the relevant Getting There & Away sections later.

Also see the Getting There & Away section earlier in this chapter for information about the international bus and train services to and from Kraków.

Air The John Paul II International Airport is more often called the Balice Airport, after the suburb in which it's located about 15km west of the Old Town. LOT flies between Kraków and Warsaw six times a day, and offers direct flights from Kraków to Frankfurt, London, Paris, Rome and Zurich.

In summer, LOT also flies directly from Chicago (April-Sept) and New York (June to September). In addition, Austrian Airlines flies directly between Kraków and Vienna several times a week. Bookings for all flights can be made at the **LOT** office *(☎ 422 4215; ul Basztowa 15)*.

Bus The main **bus terminal** *(Plac Kolejowy)* is conveniently opposite the main train station building and only minutes on foot from the Old Town. However, trains are more frequent and faster so bus services are limited to the regional centres of minimal interest to travellers, as well as Lublin (three a day), Zamość (two), Warsaw (four), Wrocław (two) and Cieszyn (eight) on the Czech border.

Polski Express buses to Warsaw depart from a spot opposite the bus terminal.

Train The lovely old **Kraków Główny** train station *(Plac Dworcowy)*, on the northeastern outskirts of the Old Town, handles all international trains and almost all domestic rail services. (Note that the railway platforms are about 150m north of the station building.)

Each day from Kraków, five InterCity trains speed to Warsaw (2¾ hours) and about four express (46zł in 2nd class) and five fast trains also travel to the capital. Also every day from Kraków there are three trains to Wrocław, two to Poznań, two to Lublin and six to Gdynia, via Gdańsk.

Advance tickets for international and domestic trains can be booked directly at the Kraków Główny station building or from **Orbis Travel** (see Organised Tours earlier).

Getting Around

The airport is accessible on Bus No 208, which leaves from a spot just north of the bus terminal in Kraków every 30 to 40 minutes. More frequent and faster is 'Bus B', which leaves from a stop along ul Lubicz and opposite Hotel Europejski. A taxi to or from the airport will cost about 50zł.

Any of the numerous travel agencies in Kraków can arrange car rental. Alternatively, most companies, like **Payless** *(☎ 639 32 62, fax 639 32 63)*, have counters at the airport.

Kraków is ideal for cycling. The bike paths along both sides of the Vistula River from Wawel Hill are very pleasant (if a little crowded on summer weekends). If you want to escape the city, head out to the **Kościuszko Mound** in Zwierzyniec, where the hilly roads are less busy and more pleasant. Bikes can be rented from the **Jordan Tourist Information & Accommodation Centre** *(ul Pawia 12)*.

AB City Tour offers tours on tiny, train-like electric cars around Rynek Główny (5zł per person) and Kazimierz (20zł). They leave hourly from the main square.

POLAND

POLAND

OŚWIĘCIM
☎ 033 • pop 48,000

The name of Oświęcim ('Osh-FYEN-cheem'), about 60km west of Kraków, may be unfamiliar to outsiders, but the German name, Auschwitz, is not. This was the scene of the most extensive experiment in genocide in the history of humankind.

The Auschwitz camp was established in April 1940 in the prewar Polish army barracks on the outskirts of Oświęcim. Originally intended to hold Polish political prisoners, the camp eventually developed into the largest centre for the extermination of European Jews. Towards this end, two additional camps were subsequently established: the much larger Birkenau (Brzezinka), or Auschwitz II, 3km west of Auschwitz; and Monowitz (Monowice), several kilometres west of Oświęcim. These death factories eliminated 1.5 to two million people of 27 nationalities – about 90% of whom were Jews.

Auschwitz
Auschwitz was only partially destroyed by the fleeing Nazis, so many of the original buildings remain as a bleak document of the camp's history. A dozen of the 30 surviving prison blocks house sections of the **State Museum Auschwitz-Birkenau** (admission free; open 8am-7pm daily June-Aug, 8am-6pm May & Sept, 8am-5pm Apr & Oct, 8am-4pm March & 1 Nov-15 Dec, 8am-3pm Dec 16-end Feb).

About every half-hour, the cinema in the **Visitors' Centre** at the entrance to Auschwitz shows a 15-minute documentary film (admission 2zł) about the liberation of the camp by Soviet troops on 27 January 1945. It's shown in several different languages throughout the day; check the schedule at the information desk as soon as you arrive at the camp. The film is not recommended for children under 14 years old. The Visitors' Centre also has a cafeteria, kantor and left-luggage room, and several bookshops.

Some basic explanations in Polish, English and Hebrew are provided on site, but you'll understand more if you buy the small Auschwitz Birkenau Guide Book (translated into about 15 languages) from the bookshops at the Visitors' Centre. English-language tours (3½ hours; 25zł per person) of Auschwitz and Birkenau are guaranteed to leave daily at 11.30am, while another starts at 1pm if there's enough demand. Tours in German commence when a group of seven or eight can be found. But make sure that you receive your allotted time; some guides tell you to wander around Birkenau by yourself and to make your own way back to Auschwitz.

Birkenau
It was actually at Birkenau (admission free; same opening hours), not Auschwitz, where the extermination of huge numbers of Jews took place. This vast (175 hectares), purpose-built and efficient camp had over 300 prison barracks and four huge gas chambers complete with crematoria. Each gas chamber held 2000 people, and electric lifts raised the bodies to the ovens. The camp could hold 200,000 inmates at one time.

Although much of the camp was destroyed by retreating Nazis, the size of the place, fenced off with barbed wire stretching almost as far as the eye can see, provides some idea of the scale of this heinous crime. The viewing platform above the entrance also provides further perspective. In some ways, Birkenau is even more shocking than Auschwitz and there are far fewer tourists.

Places to Stay & Eat
For most visitors, Auschwitz and Birkenau is an easy day trip from Kraków.

The **cafeteria** in the Visitors' Centre is sufficient for a quick lunch.

Centrum Dialogu i Modlitwy (☎ 843 10 00, fax 843 10 01; ul Kolbego 1; camping/rooms with breakfast per person 20/65zł) is 700m southwest of Auschwitz. It's comfortable and quiet, and most rooms have a private bathroom.

Hotel Glob (☎/fax 843 06 43; ul Powstańców Śląskich 16; singles/doubles with breakfast 100/150zł) is an ugly building about 100m from the train station in Oświęcim. The rooms are decent enough but a little noisy.

Getting There & Away
From Kraków Główny station, eleven trains go to Oświęcim (two hours) each day, though more depart from Kraków Płaszów station. Check the schedules the day before so you can plan your visit properly. The most convenient departure from Kraków Płaszów is at 7.20am, and at 7.45am from Kraków Główny.

Far more convenient are the 12 buses (10zł, 90 minutes) per day to Oświęcim which depart from the small bus stop on ul Bosacka in

Kraków; the stop is at the end of the underpass below the railway platforms. Get off at the final stop (outside the PKS bus maintenance building), 200m from the entrance to Auschwitz. The return bus timetable to Kraków is displayed at the Birkenau Visitors' Centre.

Every hour on the hour from 11am to 4pm (inclusive) between 15 April and 31 October buses shuttle passengers between the visitors' centres at Auschwitz and Birkenau. Otherwise, between both places follow the signs for an easy walk (3km) or take a taxi. Auschwitz is also linked to central Oświęcim and the town's train station by bus Nos 19 and 24-29 every 30 to 40 minutes.

Most travel agencies in Kraków offer organised tours of Auschwitz (including Birkenau). However, some tours do not provide private transport, so it's often easier (and far cheaper) to use the public transport system and join an official tour from the Visitors' Centre in Auschwitz.

CZĘSTOCHOWA
☎ 034 • pop 260,000

Częstochowa ('Chen-sto-HO-vah'), 114km northwest of Kraków, is the spiritual heart of Poland. This likeable town owes its fame to the miraculous Black Madonna kept in the Jasna Góra monastery. The Paulites of Hungary founded the Jasna Góra monastery in 1382 and received the Black Madonna shortly thereafter. In 1430 the holy icon was stolen by the Hussites, who slashed the face of the Madonna. The wounds began to bleed, so the frightened thieves abandoned the icon and ran off. The monks who found the panel wanted to clean it, and a spring miraculously bubbled from the ground. The spring exists to this day, and St Barbara's Church was founded on the site. The picture was restored and repainted, but the scars on the face of the Virgin Mary were left as a reminder of the miracle.

Early in the 17th century the monastery was fortified, and it was one of the few places in the country to withstand the Swedish sieges of the 1650s. This miracle was again attributed to the Black Madonna. In 1717 the Black Madonna was crowned 'Queen of Poland'.

From the train station, and adjacent bus terminal, turn right (north) up Al Wolności – along which there are several Internet centres – to the main thoroughfare, Al Najświętszej Marii Panny (sensibly simplified to Al NMP). At the western end of this broad avenue is the monastery and at the eastern end is Plac Daszyńskiego. Between both is the **tourist office** (☎/fax 368 22 60; Al NMP 65; open 9am-5pm Mon-Fri, 10am-2pm Sat), several banks, kantors and travel agencies, including **Orbis Travel** (Al NMP 40/42).

Things to See
The **Paulite Monastery on Jasna Góra** (admission free; open dawn-dusk daily) retains the appearance of a hill-top fortress. Inside the grounds are three **museums** (admission free but donations welcome; all open 9am-5pm daily): **The Arsenal**, with a variety of old weapons; the **600th-Anniversary Museum** (Muzeum Sześćsetlecia), which contains Lech Wałęsa's 1983 Nobel Peace Prize; and **The Treasury** (Skarbiec), featuring offerings presented by the faithful.

The **tower** (open 8am-4pm daily Apr-Nov) is the tallest (106m) historic church tower in Poland. The baroque church is beautifully decorated. The image of the Black Madonna on the high altar of the adjacent chapel is hard to see, so a copy is on display in the **Knights' Hall** (Sala Rycerska) in the monastery.

On weekends and in holidays expect long queues for all three museums. The crowds in the chapel may be so thick that you're almost unable to enter, much less get near the icon.

In the Town Hall the **Częstochowa Museum** (Plac Biegańskiego 45; admission 2.50zł; open 8.30am-4pm Wed-Sat, 10am-4pm Sun) features an ethnographic collection and modern Polish paintings.

Special Events
The major Marian feasts at Jasna Góra are 3 May, 16 July, 15 August (especially), 26 August, 8 September, 12 September and 8 December. On these days the monastery is packed with pilgrims.

Places to Stay & Eat
Camping Oleńka (☎/fax 324 74 95; ul Oleńki 10/30; camping per person/tent 15/10zł, 3-/4-bed rooms with shared bathroom 25/50zł, bungalows with bath 80/100zł; open year-round) is only 100m west of the monastery. It would get unbearably noisy here in midsummer and when there's a pilgrimage.

The **youth hostel** (☎ 324 31 21; ul Jasnogórska 84/90; open July-Aug; dorm beds about 18zł), two blocks north of the tourist office, has modest facilities.

POLAND

Dom Pielgrzyma *(☎ 324 70 11; ul Wys-zyńskiego 1/31; singles/doubles from 70/ 90zł)* is a huge place behind the monastery. It offers numerous quiet and comfortable rooms, and is remarkably good value.

Plenty of **eateries** can be found near the Dom Pielgrzyma. Better restaurants are dotted along Al NMP, such as the classy **Restaurant Polonus** *(Al NMP 75; mains from 14zł)* near the path up to the monastery. **Bar Viking** *(cnr Waszyngtona & ul Nowowiejskiego; mains from 11zł)*, about 200m south of the Często-chowa Museum, is cheap and cheerful.

Getting There & Away

Every day from the **bus terminal** *(Al Wolności 45)* three buses go to Kraków, three travel to Wrocław, one heads for Zakopane and three speed off to Warsaw. International buses also often pass through Częstochowa – see the Getting There & Away section earlier in this chapter.

From the impressive **train station** *(Al Wolności 21)*, eleven trains a day go to War-saw (51zł 2nd-class express). There are also four to five daily trains to Gdynia, via Gdańsk, Łódź, Olsztyn and Zakopane; six to Kraków; and nine to Wrocław.

ZAKOPANE
☎ 018 • pop 30,000

Nestled at the foot of the Tatra Mountains, Zakopane is the most famous resort in Poland and the major winter-sports capital. Although essentially a base for skiing and hiking in the Tatras, Zakopane itself has an enjoyable, laid-back atmosphere, even if it is overbuilt, overpriced and commercialised.

In the late 19th century, Zakopane became popular with artists, many of whom came to settle and work here. The best known are the composer Karol Szymanowski and the writer and painter, Witkacy. The father of the latter, Stanisław Witkiewicz (1851–1915), was in-spired by traditional local architecture and experimented with the so-called Zakopane style. Some buildings he designed still remain.

Information

The **Tourist Information Centre** *(☎ 201 22 11; ul Kościuszki 17; open 8am-8pm Mon-Sat, 9am-7pm Sun May-Sept, 8am-5pm daily Oct-Apr)* is helpful. The knowledgable English-speaking staff can arrange private rooms, inquire on your behalf about hotel vacancies, organise car rental and sell hiking and city maps. The centre can also arrange rafting trips down the Dunajec River (see the Dunajec Gorge section later) and guides for the Tatra Mountains (see later), as well as one-day trips to Slovakia (60zł per person).

Dozens of **kantors** can be found along the main streets. Several banks along the pedes-trian mall, such as **PKO Bank** *(ul Krupówki 19)*, handle foreign exchange, as does **Bank Pekao** *(cnr ul Staszica & Al 3 Maja)*. The com-bined **main post office** and **telephone centre** *(ul Krupówki)* is along the mall. **GraNet Inter-net Café** *(ul Krupówki 2)* is a convenient place to surf the Net.

Centrum Przewodnictwa Tatrzańskiego *(Tatra Guide Centre; ☎ 206 37 99; ul Chału-bińskiego 42/44)* and **Biuro Usług Turystyc-znych PTTK** *(☎ 201 58 48; ul Krupówki 12)* can arrange English- and German-speaking mountain guides with advance notice. **Orbis Travel** *(☎ 201 48 12; ul Krupówki 22)* offers the usual services, as well as accommodation in private homes.

Księgarnia Górska, in the reception area of the Dom Turysty PTTK (see later), is by far the best place for regional hiking maps.

Things to See & Do

The **Tatra Museum** *(ul Krupówki 10; admis-sion 4zł; open 9am-5pm Tues-Sat, 9am-3pm Sun)* has exhibits about regional history, eth-nography and geology, and plenty of displays about the flora and fauna of the Tatras.

Head southwest on ul Kościeliska to **Villa Koliba** *(ul Kościeliska 18)*, the first design (1892) by Witkiewicz in the Zakopane style. Predictably, it now houses the **Museum of Zakopane Style** *(admission 4zł; open 9am-5pm Wed-Sat, 9am-3pm Sun)*. About 350m southeast is **Villa Atma** *(ul Kasprusie 19)*. In-side is **Szymanowski Museum** *(admission 4zł; open about 10am-4pm Tues-Sun)*, dedi-cated to the great musician who once lived there. There are piano recitals here in summer.

The **Tatra National Park Natural Museum** *(ul Chałubińskiego 42a; admission 4zł; open 9am-2pm Mon-Sat)*, near the Rondo en route to the national park, has some mildly interest-ing exhibits about the park's natural history.

A short walk northeast up the hill leads to **Villa Pod Jedlami** *(ul Koziniec 1)*, another splendid house in the Zakopane style (the in-terior cannot be visited). Perhaps Witkiewicz's greatest achievement is the **Jaszczurówka**

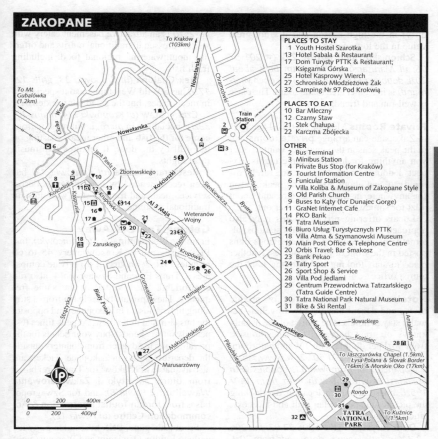

ZAKOPANE

To Kraków
(103km)

To Mt
Gubałówka
(1.2km)

Train
Station

PLACES TO STAY
1 Youth Hostel Szarotka
13 Hotel Sabała & Restaurant
17 Dom Turysty PTTK & Restaurant;
    Księgarnia Górska
25 Hotel Kasprowy Wierch
27 Schronisko Młodzieżowe Żak
32 Camping Nr 97 Pod Krokwią

PLACES TO EAT
10 Bar Mleczny
12 Czarny Staw
21 Stek Chałupa
22 Karczma Zbójecka

OTHER
2 Bus Terminal
3 Minibus Station
4 Private Bus Stop (for Kraków)
5 Tourist Information Centre
6 Funicular Station
7 Villa Koliba & Museum of Zakopane Style
8 Old Parish Church
9 Buses to Kąty (for Dunajec Gorge)
11 GraNet Internet Cafe
14 PKO Bank
15 Tatra Museum
16 Biuro Usług Turystycznych PTTK
18 Villa Atma & Szymanowski Museum
19 Main Post Office & Telephone Centre
20 Orbis Travel; Bar Smakosz
23 Bank Pekao
24 Tatry Sport
26 Sport Shop & Service
28 Villa Pod Jedlami
29 Centrum Przewodnictwa Tatrzańskiego
    (Tatra Guide Centre)
30 Tatra National Park Natural Museum
31 Bike & Ski Rental

Słowackiego

Kozieniec

28

To Jaszczurówka Chapel (1.5km),
Łysa Polana & Slovak Border
(16km) & Morskie Oko (17km)

29

Rondo

30

31

TATRA
NATIONAL
PARK

32

To Kuźnice
(1.5km)

Marusarzówny

0   200   400m
0   200   400yd

POLAND

Chapel, about 1.5km further east along the road to Morskie Oko.

Mt Gubałówka (1120m) offers excellent views over the Tatras and is a favourite destination for tourists who don't feel like *too* much exercise. The **funicular** (one way/return 8/14zł) covers the 1388m-long route in less than five minutes and climbs 300m from the funicular station just north of ul Krupówki. It operates between 9am and 9pm from 1 May to 30 September, but at other times it only runs on weekends. An all-day pass for skiers costs 70zł; a one-day pass at other times for 10 rides costs 50zł.

Places to Stay

Like all seasonal resorts, accommodation prices fluctuate considerably between the low season and high season (December to February and July to August). It is always wise to book accommodation in advance at these peak times, especially on weekends. Rates for the high seasons are listed below.

Camping You'll find that **Camping Nr 97 Pod Krokwią** (*☎ 201 22 56; ul Żeromskiego 34; camping per person 15zł; bungalows per person 35-45zł; open year-round)* is convenient and clean. Take any bus or minibus to Kuźnice and get off at the Rondo.

Hostels The friendly and homely **Youth Hostel Szarotka** (*☎ 206 62 03; ul Nowotarska 45; dorm beds 35-50zł; doubles 140zł; open year-round)* is along a noisy road about a 10-minute walk from the town centre. It does get packed (and untidy and sometimes dirty) in the high season and it's not great value in the low season.

Schronisko Młodzieżowe Żak (☎ 201 57 06; ul Marusarzówny 15; dorm beds about 20zł; doubles per person from 35zł; open year-round) is in a quiet area to the south. The place is well-run and friendly.

Private Rooms Most of the travel agencies in Zakopane can arrange **private rooms**, but in the peak season they may not want to offer you anything for less than three nights. Expect a double room (singles are rarely offered) to cost about 50zł in the peak season for anywhere in the town centre and about 40zł for somewhere a little further out.

Locals offering private rooms may also approach you at the bus or train stations; alternatively, just look out for the obvious signs posted in the front of private homes. Another place to start looking and booking is at the tourist office.

Hotels Given the abundance of private rooms and decent hostels, few travellers actually stay in hotels. The tourist office usually knows of great bargains for guesthouses: from 40zł per double with TV and bathroom.

Hotel Sabala (☎ 201 50 92; w www.sabala .zakopane.pl; ul Krupówki 11; doubles with breakfast & without/with bath from 140/ 195zł) boasts a superb location overlooking the picturesque pedestrian mall and has cosy, attic-style rooms.

Dom Turysty PTTK (☎ 206 32 07, fax 206 32 84; ul Zaruskiego 5; dorm beds from 20zł, doubles 80zł; singles/doubles with bath from 70/120zł) is a renovated former hostel. It offers heaps of different types of rooms, so check a few out first. The **restaurant** on the ground floor is open early for breakfast.

Hotel Kasprowy Wierch (☎/fax 201 27 38; ul Krupówki 50b; doubles with TV & breakfast 200zł) is comfortable, central and cosy.

Places to Eat
The central pedestrian mall, ul Krupówki, is lined with all sorts of eateries. **Bar Mleczny** (ul Krupówki 1; mains from 6zł) is about the only milk bar in town these days.

Downstairs from the Orbis Travel office, **Bar Smakosz** (ul Krupówki 22; mains 8-10zł) offers some outdoor tables and reasonable prices in a central location.

Karczma Zbójecka (ul Krupówki 28; mains 18-25zł) is an attractive basement eatery with waiters dressed in traditional outfits and offering mouthwatering regional food, including fresh fish.

Stek Chałupa (ul Krupówki 33; grills 12-17zł) has a Wild West theme, so it specialises in meat dishes, but the salad bar is extensive.

Czarny Staw (ul Krupówki 2/4; mains 20-38zł) specialises in pierogi, but most patrons come for the fish and other meats roasting on the grill by the door. It features live music most nights.

Restaurant Sabala (ul Krupówki 11) has been recommended by readers for its decor, service, meals and friendly staff who dress in traditional costume.

Getting There & Away
From the **bus terminal** (ul Chramcówki), fast PKS buses run to Kraków every 45 to 60 minutes (9zł, 2½ hours). Two private companies – Trans Frej and Szwagropol – also run comfortable buses (10zł) at the same frequency. These private buses leave from a stop along ul Kościuszki in Zakopane, and opposite the bus terminal in Kraków. At peak times (especially on weekends), buy your tickets for the private buses in advance from counters outside the departure points in Zakopane. Tickets are also available in Kraków: for Trans Frej buses from **Biuro Turystyki i Zakwaterowania Waweltur** (ul Pawia 8); and for Szwagropol buses from **Jordan Tourist Information & Accommodation Centre** (ul Pawia 12).

From Zakopane, PKS buses also go twice daily to Lublin, Oświęcim and Warsaw (eight hours) and once to Przemyśl and Sanok. A couple of buses per week (daily in summer) also go to Budapest (nine hours) in Hungary.

PKS buses – and minibuses from opposite the bus terminal – regularly travel to Lake Morskie Oko (see next section) and on to Polana Palenica. To cross into Slovakia, get off this bus/minibus at Łysa Polana, cross the border on foot and take another bus to Tatranská Lomnica in Slovakia. Buses and minibuses to Kuźnice also leave every 20 minutes.

From the **train station** (ul Chramcówki), trains for Kraków (42zł 2nd-class express, 3½ hours) leave every two hours or so, but avoid the passenger train, which takes up to five hours. Between one and three trains a day go to Częstochowa, Gdynia via Gdańsk, Lublin, Łódź and Poznań, and five head to Warsaw.

THE TATRA MOUNTAINS
☎ 018

The Tatras, 100km south of Kraków, is the highest range of the Carpathian Mountains. Roughly 60km long and about 15km wide, this mountain range stretches across the Polish-Slovak border. A quarter is in Poland and is now mostly part of the Tatra National Park (about 212 sq km). The Polish Tatras contain more than 20 peaks over 2000m, the highest of which is Mt Rysy (2499m).

Cable Car to Mt Kasprowy Wierch

Almost every Polish tourist has made the cable car trip *(return 28zł; open 7.30am-8pm daily in summer, 7.30am-4pm in winter)* from Kuźnice (3km south of central Zakopane) to the summit of Mt Kasprowy Wierch (1985m). At the end of the trip, you can get off and stand with one foot in Poland and the other in Slovakia. The one-way journey takes 20 minutes and climbs 936m. The cable car normally shuts down for a few weeks in May, June and November, and won't operate if the snow and, particularly, the winds are dangerous.

The view from the top is spectacular (clouds permitting). Two chair lifts transport skiers to and from various slopes between December and April. A small **cafeteria** serves skiers and hikers alike. In the summer, many people return to Zakopane on foot down the Gąsienicowa Valley, and the most intrepid walk the ridges all the way across to Lake Morskie Oko via Pięciu Stawów, a strenuous hike taking a full day in good weather.

If you buy a return ticket, your trip back is automatically reserved for two hours after your departure, so buy a one-way ticket to the top (18zł) and another one down (10zł) if you want to stay longer. Mt Kasprowy Wierch is popular, so the lines for tickets are long; in summer, arrive early and expect to wait. PKS buses and minibuses to Kuźnice frequently leave from Zakopane.

Lake Morskie Oko

One of the most popular destinations in the Tatras is the emerald-green Lake Morskie Oko (Eye of the Sea), among the loveliest in the Tatras. The easiest way to reach the lake is by road from Zakopane. PKS buses and minibuses regularly depart from Zakopane for Polana Palenica (30 minutes), from where a road (9km) continues uphill to the lake. Cars,

bikes and buses are not allowed up this road, so you'll have to walk, but it's not steep (allow about two hours one way). Alternatively, take a horse-drawn carriage (32/15zł uphill/downhill, but very negotiable) to within 2km of the lake. In winter, transport is by horse-drawn four-seater sledge, which is more expensive. The last minibus to Zakopane returns between 5pm and 6pm.

Hiking

If you're doing any hiking in the Tatras get a copy of the *Tatrzański Park Narodowy* map (1:25,000), which shows all hiking trails in the area. Better still, buy one or more of the 14 sheets of *Tatry Polskie* (available at the bookshop in the Dom Turysty PTTK in Zakopane). In July and August these trails can be overrun by tourists, so late spring and early autumn are the best times. Theoretically you can expect better weather in autumn (September to October) when rainfall is lower.

Like all alpine regions, the Tatras can be dangerous, particularly during the snowy time (November to May). Always use common sense and remember that the weather can be unpredictable. Bring proper hiking boots, warm clothing and waterproof rain gear – and be prepared to use occasional ropes and chains (provided along the trails) to get up and down some rocky slopes. Guides are not necessary because many of the trails are marked, but guides can be arranged in Zakopane (see that section for details) for about 180zł per day.

Several picturesque valleys south of Zakopane include the **Dolina Strążyska**. You can continue from the Strążyska by the red trail up to **Mt Giewont** (1909m), 3½ hours from Zakopane, and then walk down the blue trail to Kuźnice in two hours.

Two long and beautiful forested valleys, the **Dolina Chochołowska** and the **Dolina Kościeliska**, are in the western part of the park, known as the Tatry Zachodnie (West Tatras). These valleys are also ideal for cycling. Both valleys are accessible by PKS buses and private minibuses from Zakopane.

The Tatry Wysokie (High Tatras) to the east offer quite different scenery: bare granite peaks and glacial lakes. One great way to get there is to take the cable car to **Mt Kasprowy Wierch** (see earlier) and then hike eastward along the red trail to Mt Świnica (2301m) and on to the Zawrat pass (2159m) – a toughish three to four hours from Mt Kasprowy. From

POLAND

Zawrat, descend northwards to the Dolina Gąsienicowa along the blue trail and then back to Zakopane.

Alternatively, head south (also along the blue trail) to the wonderful **Dolina Pięciu Stawów** (Five Lakes Valley) where there is a mountain refuge 1¼ hours from Zawrat. The blue trail heading west from the refuge passes **Lake Morskie Oko**, 1½ hours from the refuge.

Skiing

Zakopane boasts four major ski areas (and several smaller ones) with over 50 ski lifts. **Mt Kasprowy Wierch** and **Mt Gubałówka** offer the best conditions and most challenging slopes in the area, with the ski season extending until early May. Lift tickets cost about 7zł per ride. Alternatively, you can buy an all-day pass (70zł), which is expensive but allows you to skip the queues. Take the funicular or cable car (see earlier) and purchase your lift tickets on the mountain.

Ski equipment rental is available at all facilities except Mt Kasprowy Wierch. Otherwise, stop off on your way to Kuźnice at the **ski rental** place near the Rondo in Zakopane. Other places in Zakopane, such as **Tatry Sport** (ul Piłsudskiego 4) and **Sport Shop & Service** (ul Krupówki 52a), also rent ski gear.

Cycling

Cycling is a pleasant way to get around Zakopane and to see some of the less steep parts of the Tatras. Bicycles can be rented at several places in Zakopane, particularly near the Rondo. The **Dolina Chochołowska** and the **Dolina Kościeliska**, in the Tatry Zachodnie, are the best places in the park for cycling. The service road, which marks the northern boundary of the park, Droga pod Reglami, also offers a pleasant and picturesque ride.

Places to Stay

Tourists are not allowed to take their own cars into the park; you must walk in, take the cable car or use an official vehicle owned by the park or a hotel/hostel.

Camping is also not allowed in the park, but eight PTTK mountain refuges/hostels provide simple accommodation. Most refuges are small and fill up fast; in midsummer and midwinter they're invariably packed beyond capacity. No one is ever turned away, however, though you may have to crash on the floor if all the beds are taken. Do not arrive

too late, and bring along your own bed mat and sleeping bag. All refuges serve simple hot meals, but the kitchens and dining rooms close early (sometimes at 7pm).

The refuges listed here are open all year, but some may be temporarily closed for renovations or because of inclement weather. Check the current situation at the Dom Turysty PTTK in Zakopane or the regional **PTTK headquarters** (☎/fax 018-438 610) in Nowy Sącz.

The easiest refuge to reach from Zakopane is the large and decent **Kalatówki Hostel** (☎/fax 206 36 44; dorm beds 35zł, doubles with bathroom & breakfast about 145zł), a 40-minute walk from the Kuźnice cable-car station. About 30 minutes beyond Kalatówki on the trail to Giewont is **Hala Kondratowa Hostel** (☎ 201 52 14; dorm beds 20-22zł). It's in a great location and has a great atmosphere, but it is small.

Hikers wishing to traverse the park might begin at the **Roztoka Hostel** (☎ 207 74 42; dorm beds 22-30zł), accessible by the bus/minibus to Morskie Oko. An early start from Zakopane, however, would allow you to visit Morskie Oko in the morning and stay at the **Morskie Oko Hostel** (☎ 207 76 09; dorm beds from 35zł), or continue through to the **Dolina Pięciu Stawów Hostel** (☎ 207 76 07; dorm beds from 25zł). This is the highest (1700m) and most scenically located refuge in the Polish Tatras.

A leisurely day's walk northwest of Pięciu Stawów is the **Murowaniec Hala Gąsienicowa Hostel** (☎ 201 26 33; dorms 20-30zł), from where you can return to Zakopane.

Getting There & Away

Refer to the Zakopane section earlier for details about travelling to the national park.

DUNAJEC GORGE

An entertaining and leisurely way to explore the Pieniny Mountains is to go **rafting** on the Dunajec River, which winds its way along the Polish-Slovak border through a spectacular and deep gorge. Adrenalin junkies may be disappointed, however, because this is *not* a white-water rafting experience. In recent years, the course of the river has changed so it now cuts through Slovakia for a few kilometres, but Polish and Slovak immigration officials don't wait on rafts to check passports.

The trip starts at the wharf (Przystań Flisacka) in Kąty, 46km northeast of Zakopane, and finishes at the spa town at Szczawnica. The 17km (2½-hour) raft trip operates between May and October, but only starts when there's a minimum of 10 passengers.

The gorge is an easy day trip from Zakopane. In summer, 10 PKS buses leave from a spot along ul Kościeliska. Alternatively, catch a regular bus to Nowy Targ (30 minutes) from Zakopane and one of six daily buses (one hour) to Kąty. From Szczawnica, take the bus back to Zakopane or change at Nowy Targ. Each day, five buses also travel between Szczawnica and Kraków.

To avoid waiting around in Kąty for a raft to fill up, organise a trip at any travel agency in Zakopane or at the tourist office. The cost is about 60zł per person, and includes transport, equipment and guides, as well as a visit to the timber Gothic church in **Debno Podhalanskie** and the ruined castle at **Czorsztyn**.

SANOK
☎ 013 • pop 40,000
Sanok is noted for its unique **Museum of Folk Architecture** (ul Rybickiego 3; admission 8zł; open about 9am-4pm daily), which features architecture from regional ethnic groups. Walk north from the town centre for 1.5km along ul Mickiewicza. The **Historical Museum** (ul Zamkowa 2; admission 6zł; open 9am-3pm daily) is housed in an obvious 16th-century castle and contains Poland's most impressive collection of Ruthenian icons.

Sanok is also an excellent base to explore surrounding villages, many of which have some lovely old churches. The best way to get around is along the marked **Icon Trail**. This **hiking** or **cycling** trail commences in Sanok and completes a 70km loop, passing by 10 village churches as well as picturesque and pristine mountain countryside. More information and maps (in English) are available from the **PTTK office** (☎ 463 21 71; ul 3 Maja 2), near the main square, Plac Św Michała.

Convenient budget accommodation is available at **Hotel Pod Trzema Różami** (☎/fax 463 09 22; ul Jagiellońska 13; singles/doubles with bathroom 85/120zł), about 200m south of the main square. Further south (about 400m) and up the scale is **Hotel Jagielloński** (☎/fax 463 12 08; ul Jagiellońska 49; singles/doubles with bathroom from 85/110zł). Both have an attached **restaurant**.

The **bus terminal** and adjacent **train station** are about 1km southeast of the main square. Four buses go daily to Przemyśl, and buses and fast trains go regularly to Kraków and Warsaw.

PRZEMYŚL
☎ 016 • pop 70,000
Perched on a hillside overlooking the San River and dominated by four mighty historic churches, Przemyśl ('PSHEH-mishl') is a picturesque town with a sloping and well-preserved **Rynek** (town square). The **tourist office** (☎/fax 675 16 64; ul Ratuszowa) is one block north of the Rynek.

About 350m southwest of the Rynek are the ruins of a 14th-century **castle** (ul Zamkowa), built by Kazimierz Wielki. The **Regional Museum** (Plac Czackiego 3; admission 5zł; open 10.30am-5.30pm Tues & Fri; 10am-2pm Wed, Thur, Sat & Sun) houses a splendid collection of Ruthenian icons. It's about 150m southeast of the Rynek.

Przemyśl has a wide selection of inexpensive accommodation, including the well-kept **Youth Hostel Matecznik** (☎/fax 670 61 45; ul Lelewela 6; dorm beds 18-22zł; open year-round). It's a 20-minute walk northwest down ul Kościuszki from the Rynek or take one of the city buses. **Hotelik Pod Basztą** (☎ 678 82 68; ul Królowej Jadwigi 4; singles/doubles with shared bathroom 60/78zł) is just below the castle.

Bar Rubin (ul Kazimierza Wielkiego 19; mains 9-15zł), 250m east from the Rynek, is inexpensive and friendly.

From Przemyśl, buses run to Lviv (95km) in Ukraine six times a day and regularly to all towns in southeastern Poland. Trains run regularly from Przemyśl to Lublin, Kraków and Warsaw and stop here on the way to/from Lviv. The bus terminal and adjacent train station in Przemyśl are about 1km northeast of the Rynek.

LUBLIN
☎ 081 • pop 360,000
Throughout its history, Lublin has seen repeated invasions by Swedes, Austrians, Russians and Germans. During WWII the Nazis established a death camp at nearby Majdanek, but Lublin does boast happier remnants of its Jewish heritage. The city didn't experience significant wartime damage so the Old Town has retained much of its historic architectural fabric – though parts are in serious need of restoration.

POLAND

LUBLIN

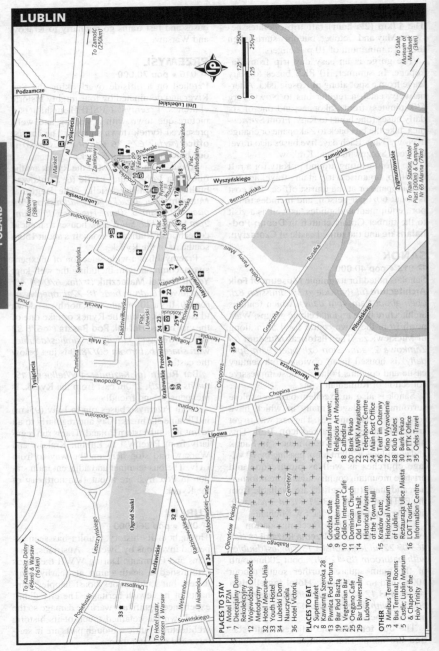

To Zamość (250km)

Podzamcze

Unii Lubelskiej

Al Tysiąclecia

Market

Plac Zamkowy

Podwale

Plac Po Farze

Ul Dominikańska

Plac Katedralny

Lubartowska

Grodzka

Rynek

Królewska

Łokietka

Jezuicka

Wyszyńskiego

Bernardyńska

Zamojska

To Train Station, Hotel
Piast (300m) & Camping
Nr 65 Marina (7km)

To State
Museum of
Majdanek
(3km)

To Kozłówka
(38km)

Wodopojna

Świętoduska

Radziwiłłowska

Niecała

Dolna Panny Marii

Kapucyńska

Narutowicza

Górna

Rusałka

Prusa

Plac Litewski

3 Maja

Chmielna

Tysiąclecia

Kościuszki

Prowiałów

Kołłątaja

Hempla

Krakowskie Przedmieście

Ogrodowa

Chopina

Szopena

Piłsudskiego

Graniczna

Narutowicza

Okopowa

Ogród Saski

Leszczyńskiego

Lipowa

Chopina

Skłodowskiej-Curie

Obrońców Pokoju

Radziszewskiego

Cemetery

To Kazimierz Dolny
(45km) & Warsaw
(161km)

Ul Akademicka

Weteranów

Sowińskiego

Racławickie

Długosza

Popiełuszki

To Hotel Huzar;
Skansen (4km)

To Warsaw

PLACES TO STAY
1 Motel PZM
7 Diecezjalny Dom
  Rekolekcyjny
12 Wojewódzki Ośrodek
  Metodyczny
30 Hotel Mercure-Unia
32 Youth Hostel
34 Lubelski Dom
  Nauczyciela
36 Hotel Victoria

PLACES TO EAT
2 Supermarket
8 Kawiarnia Szeroka 28
19 Piwnica Pod Fortuną
21 Bar Pod Basztą
25 Vegetarian Bar
29 Oregano Cafe
  Bar Uniwersalny
  Ludowy

OTHER
3 Minibus Terminal
4 Bus Terminal; Rooms
5 Castle; Lublin Museum
  & Chapel of the
  Holy Trinity
6 Grodzka Gate
9 Klub Internetowy
10 Odilon Internet Cafe
11 Dominican Church
14 Old Town Hall;
  Historical Museum
  of the Town Hall
15 Kraków Gate;
  Historical Museum
  of Lublin;
  Restauracja Ulice Miasta
16 LOIT Tourist
  Information Centre
17 Trinitarian Tower;
  Religious Art Museum
18 Cathedral
20 Bank Pekao
22 EMPiK Megastore
23 Telephone Centre
24 Main Post Office
26 Teatr im Osterwy
27 Kino Wyzwolenie
28 Klub Hades
30 Bank Pekao
31 PTTK Office
35 Orbis Travel

POLAND

Information

The **LOIT Tourist Information Centre** (☎ 532 44 12, ⓔ loit@inetia.pl; ul Jezuicka 1/3; open 10am-6pm Mon-Sat, 10am-3pm Sun) has helpful English-speaking staff. It's also a good place to pick up maps of Lublin and other Polish and Ukrainian cities. The **PTTK office** (☎ 532 96 54; ul Krakowskie Przedmieście 78; open 9am-4pm Mon-Fri) can help with guides, car rental and organised tours. Both offices sell the handy *Lublin: A Tourist Guidebook* (10zł), ideal if you're going to explore the Old Town in depth.

Bank Pekao (ul Królewska 1 • ul Krakowskie Przedmieście 64) changes travellers cheques and gives cash advances on Visa and MasterCard. Plenty of ATMs can be found on ul Krakowskie Przedmieście, but most kantors seem to be along ul Peowiaków.

The **main post office** (ul Krakowskie Przedmieście 50) is easy to find, but the adjacent **telephone centre** is back from the main road. For cybermail, try **Klub Internetowy** (ul Swietoduska 16), at the back of a small laneway off ul Wodopojna, or **Odilon Internet Café** (Plac po Farze) in the Old Town. Maps and books are available from the **EMPiK Megastore** (ul Krakowskie Przedmieście 16).

Things to See

Old Town The compact historic quarter is centred around the **Rynek**, the irregularly shaped main square surrounding the oversized neoclassical **Old Town Hall** (1781). Downstairs, the **Historical Museum of the Town Hall** (admission 5zł; open 9am-4pm Wed-Sat, 9am-5pm Sun) is about as unexciting as it sounds.

The more enticing **Historical Museum of Lublin** (Plac Łokietka 3; admission 3zł; open 9am-4pm Wed-Sat, 9am-5pm Sun) is inside the 14th-century **Kraków Gate**, the only significant remnant of the medieval fortifications. At noon every day, a bugler comes from nowhere and plays a special tune from on top of the gate. (If you just love bugling, come here for the annual **National Bugle Contest** on 15 August.)

For an expansive **view** of the Old Town, climb the **Trinitarian Tower** (1819), which houses the **Religious Art Museum** (Plac Kathedralny; admission 8zł; open 10am-5pm daily Apr-Oct). According to legend, the metal rooster on top of the tower will crow when a virgin walks past! Next to the tower is the

16th-century **cathedral** (Plac Kathedralny; admission free; open dawn-dusk daily) with its impressive baroque frescoes all over its interior. The painting of the Virgin Mary is said to have shed tears in 1945 so it's a source of pride and reverence for local believers.

Castle Built on a hill northeast of the Old Town is a magnificent 14th-century castle (admission free; open dawn-dusk daily). It was mostly destroyed, so what remains was rebuilt as a prison during the 1820s and remained as such until 1944. During the Nazi occupation, more than 100,000 people passed through this prison before being deported to the death camps. Most of the edifice is now occupied by the **Lublin Museum** (Ⓦ www.zamek-lublin .pl; admission 6zł; open 9am-4pm Wed-Sat, 9am-5pm Sun). This extensive museum contains a number of sections realting to archaeology, ethnography, decorative art, paintings, arms and coins.

At the eastern end of the castle – but only accessible through the museum entrance – is the exquisite 14th-century **Chapel of the Holy Trinity** (admission 10zł; open 9am-4pm Mon-Sat, 9am-5pm Sun). Its interior is entirely covered with amazing Russo-Byzantine frescoes painted in 1418 – possibly the finest medieval wall paintings in Poland. Admittance to the chapel is restricted, so tickets (which also allow you entry to the museum) must be bought in advance at the museum entrance.

Majdanek About 4km southeast from the Old Town is the **State Museum of Majdanek** (Ⓦ www.majdanek.pl; admission free; open 8am-6pm daily May-Sept, 8am-3pm Oct-Apr). It commemorates one of the largest death camps in Europe, and was the first such memorial in the world. About 235,000 people, representing 51 nationalities from 26 countries (including over 100,000 Jews), were exterminated here. Barracks, guard towers and barbed wire fences remain as they were more than 50 years ago; even more chilling are the crematorium and gas chambers.

At the entrance to the site is a **Visitors' Centre** (admission free; open 8am-4pm daily May-Sept, 8am-3pm Oct-Apr), where a short film (admission 2zł) can be seen. From the Centre, the marked 'visiting route' (5km) passes the massive stone **Monument of Fight & Martyrdom** and finishes at the domed **mausoleum** holding the ashes of many victims.

This is a vast area so allow at least two hours. And note that children under 14 years old are *not* permitted anywhere in the camp. Trolleybus No 156 from near the Bank Pekao along ul Królewska goes to the entrance of Majdanek.

Pick up the free *Heritage Trail of the Lublin Jews* pamphlet (in English) from the tourist office if you want to walk along the marked **Jewish Heritage Trail** around Lublin.

Places to Stay

Camping Lublin's only camping ground is **Camping Nr 65 Marina** (*☎/fax 744 10 70; ul Kręznicka 6; camping per person/tent 10/10zł, cabins from 65zł; open May-Sept).* It's serenely located on a lake about 8km south of the Old Town – take Bus No 17, 20 or 21 from the train station to Stadion Sygnał and then catch bus No 25.

Hostels The **Youth Hostel** (*☎/fax 533 06 28; ul Długosza 6; dorm beds 20-32zł; open year-round)* is modest but well run. It's 50m up a lane off ul Długosza and in the heart of the university district.

The **Wojewódzki Ośrodek Metodyczny** (*☎ 532 92 41, fax 534 46 34; ul Dominikańska 5; dorm beds about 40zł)* is good value and often busy, so book ahead. Look for the sign 'Wojewódzki Ośrodek Doskonalenia Nauczycieli' outside.

Diecezjalny Dom Rekolekcyjny (*☎ 532 41 38; ul Podwale 15; dorm beds about 30zł)* is a Catholic institution, so please behave appropriately. There is a 10pm curfew.

Hotels Opposite the train station, **Hotel Piast** (*☎ 532 16 46; ul Pocztowa 2; dorm beds 25zł, singles/doubles with shared bathroom 50/ 75zł)* is ideal for a late-night arrival or an early-morning departure. However, it's a long way from anywhere else and not in a pleasant part of town. Similarly unappealing are the musty and noisy **rooms** *(singles/doubles 43/60zł)* at the bus terminal (see under Getting There & Away later).

Lubelski Dom Nauczyciela (*☎ 533 82 85, fax 533 03 66; ul Akademicka 4; singles/ doubles from 80/83zł, doubles with bath 150zł)* is a teachers hostel. Most of the rooms are tiny, but clean and perfectly acceptable, while the renovated rooms have a bathroom.

The **Motel PZM** (*☎ 533 42 32; ul Prusa 8; singles/doubles with bathroom & breakfast 150/190zł)* is probably the best value in the mid-range. The rooms are modern and the hotel is handy to the castle and bus terminal.

Hotel Victoria (*☎ 532 70 11, fax 532 90 26; ul Narutowicza 58/60; singles with toilet & sink 80zł, singles/doubles with bath & TV 200/300zł)* has been renovated, despite its outward appearances, and is convenient and comfortable. You can probably find better value than the rooms with bath, but it's ideal for the single traveller who can live without a shower. (There is no communal shower either.)

Hotel Mercure-Unia (*☎ 533 72 12; e mer .unia@orbis.pl; Al Racławickie 12; singles/ doubles with bath, TV & breakfast 376/450zł)* is modern and convenient.

Places to Eat

Patronised by city workers and university students, **Bar Uniwersalny Ludowy** *(ul Krakowskie Przedmieście 60; mains 8-12zł)* is a long-established milk bar.

Bar Pod Basztą *(ul Królewska 6; meals from 8zł)* is a clean and modern place, which is ideal for a budget-priced lunch of hamburgers or *pierogi ruskie*.

A few **takeaway joints** along Plac Zamkowy have set up outdoor (plastic) tables, but more appealing are the atmospheric bars and restaurants lining the Rynek. **Piwnica Pod Fortuna** *(Rynek 8; mains from 28zł)* is one of several charming places to enjoy Polish and Western food, but like most others in this area prices are high.

Restauracja Ulice Miasta *(Plac Łokietka 2; mains from 12zł)* has a great position adjoining the Kraków Gate. Enjoy one of its daily three-course specials (about 20zł) or just relax with a drink after traipsing around the Old Town.

Kawiarnia Szeroka 28 *(ul Grodzka 21; mains about 20zł)* offers artistic charm, Jewish cuisine and economical dining if you stick to soups (6zł) and salads (8zł). Other attractions are the terrace views and live Jewish music on summer weekends.

Oregano Café *(ul Kościuszki; main meals from 14zł)* has a menu in English. Most main courses are pricey, but soups (8zł) and pasta dishes (14zł to 19zł) are great value and tasty.

Vegetarian Bar *(ul Narutowicza 3)* is downstairs along a courtyard off the main road. It's a popular place with young locals who want cheap, meatless food. There is a **supermarket** and **market** near the bus terminal.

Entertainment

The main venue for drama is **Teatr im Osterwy** (ul Narutowicza 17), which features mostly classical plays with some emphasis on national drama. **Klub Hades** (ul Hempla) features live music (including rock and jazz) most nights and a disco on Friday. Ask around the hostels about the best **student nightclubs**. The quaint but unpronounceable **Kino Wyzwolenie** (ul Peowiaków 6) shows recent English-language films.

Getting There & Away

The **bus terminal** (Al Tysiąclecia), opposite the castle, handles most of the traffic. At least one bus a day heads to Białystok, Kraków, Łódź, Olsztyn, Toruń and Zakopane. Each day, six buses also go to Przemyśl, nine head to Zamość and 12 to 15 travel to Warsaw (three hours). From the same terminal, Polski Express offers eight daily buses to Warsaw.

The **Lublin Główny** train station (Plac Dworcowy) is 1.2km south of the Old Town and accessible by trolleybus No 160. At least six trains go daily to Warsaw (45zł 2nd-class express, 2½ hours) and two fast trains travel to Kraków (four hours). Tickets can be purchased at the station or from **Orbis Travel** (☎ 532 22 56; e orbis.lublin@pbp.com.pl; ul Narutowicza 33a).

For more information about transport to places near Lublin, see the Around Lublin section next.

AROUND LUBLIN
Kozłówka

The hamlet of Kozłówka ('Koz-WOOF-kah'), 38km north of Lublin, is famous for its sumptuous late-baroque **palace**, which now houses the **Museum of the Zamoyski Family** (admission 12.50zł; open 10am-4pm Tues, Thur & Fri, 10am-5pm Wed, Sat & Sun Mar-Nov). It featrues original furnishings, ceramic stoves and an unusually large collection of paintings.

The palace is also noted for its **Socialist-Realist Art Gallery** (admission 4zł; same opening hours). It has an overwhelming number of portraits and busts of the revolutionary communist leaders, and also features scenes of farmers, factory workers and family members building communism, as well as communist political and satirical posters.

You can stay in the **palace rooms** (☎ 081-852 83 10, fax 852 83 50), but contact staff ahead about availability and current costs.

From Lublin, two buses head to Kozłówka each morning, usually on the way to Michóv. Only a few buses return directly to Lublin in the afternoon, so check the timetable before visiting the museum. Alternatively, you can catch one of the frequent buses to/from Lubartów, which is regularly connected by bus and minibus to Lublin.

Kazimierz Dolny
☎ 081 • pop 4000

Set on the bank of the Vistula River at the foot of wooded hills, Kazimierz Dolny (usually just known locally as Kazimierz) is a charming village with fine historic architecture and museums. During the week, Kazimierz is a lethargic place, but it has become a fashionable destination and does get unreasonably crowded on summer weekends. (It attracts about 1.5 million visitors each year!) For some, the highlight is the annual **National Festival of Folk Bands & Singers** in June.

From the **bus stop** follow ul Tyszkiewicza (and the crowds) southwest for 100m. Then turn left at the post office to the Rynek town square (about two minutes' walk) or continue straight ahead and over the creek to ul Senatorska. From the Rynek, ul Nadwiślańska heads northwest towards the Vistula and ul Klasztorna heads southwest over the creek to ul Krakowska.

The **PTTK tourist office** (☎/fax 881 00 46; Rynek 27) has local bus timetables posted on the window. It also sells the useful *Mapa Turystyczna 2001*, which details (in English) the main attractions, and arranges accommodation in private rooms. The small **PKO Bank** (ul Senatorska) may change money; otherwise, try the **post office** (ul Tyszkiewicza 2), which has a foreign-exchange counter.

Things to See & Do All museums listed below are open 10am and 4pm Tuesday to Sunday from May to September and 10am and 3pm from October to April).

The elegant 15th-century **Rynek** is lined with merchants homes. The finest example is the **House of the Celej Family** (ul Senatorska 11/13), which accommodates the **Town Museum** (admission 5zł).

Obvious cobblestoned laneways from the Rynek lead up to the ruins of the 14th-century **castle**, the 13th-century **watch tower** and several abandoned **granaries**. All provide fine **panoramas** of the town and river.

POLAND

Several marked **walking trails** originate at the Rynek. The *Mapa Turystyczna 2001*, available at the tourist office, has details.

At the end of ul Nadwiślańska, there are motorised 'gondolas' offering **boat trips** (7zł, 45 minutes) on the Vistula. From the same point, a boat regularly crosses the river to **Janowiec** from May to September. Otherwise, from a point about 10 minutes' further southwest along the river (also accessible from ul Krakowska), a car/passenger ferry also crosses the river to Janowiec all year. Janowiec is home to an elegant 16th-century castle and the **Castle Museum** (*admission 6zł*).

About 600m northeast along the river from the end of ul Nadwiślańska is the **Natural Museum** (*ul Puławska 54; admission 5.50zł*). It's easy to spot along the road from Lublin.

Places to Stay & Eat Although Kazimierz has many places to stay, you may face a shortage on summer weekends. Look for signs outside homes and in shop windows, and expect to pay about 30/50zł per person in low/high season. The tourist office can also help.

Strażnica Youth Hostel (*☎ 881 04 27; ul Senatorska 25; dorm beds with breakfast 28-35zł; open year-round*) boasts a position and building the envy of many other expensive pensions. It's clean and friendly, and should be booked ahead at all times.

Pensjonat Pod Wietrzną Górą (*☎/fax 881 05 43; ul Krakowska 1; singles/doubles with bathroom & breakfast from 85/175zł*) is one of several charming pensions within a stone's throw of the Rynek.

Dziunia (*☎ 0603-635 746; accommodation per person about 50zł; open May-Sept*) offers something a little different – cabins in a boat moored along the river at the end of ul Nadwiślańska. Facilities are shared and basic, however. It's one of several other adjacent boats with a **bar** and **restaurant**.

Piekarnia Artystyczna (*ul Nadrzeczna 6*), along the southeastern extension of ul Senatorska, sells delicious bread and pastries. It's also an ideal place for a hot drink or ice cream.

Tables and chairs spill out into the village square from several enticing English-style pubs. **Bistro Mars** (*Rynek 11; meals from 10zł*) sells cold beers, tasty *pierogi* and pizzas.

Getting There & Away Kazimierz is an easy day trip from Lublin. Buses to Puławy, via Kazimierz Dolny, leave Lublin every 90 minutes or so, but the hourly minibuses from near the bus terminal in Lublin are quicker and cheaper. From Kazimierz, six buses go directly to Warsaw Stadion station (three hours) and two for Warsaw Zachodnia station.

ZAMOŚĆ
☎ 084 • pop 65,000

Zamość ('ZAH-moshch') was founded in 1580 by Jan Zamoyski, the chancellor and commander-in-chief of Renaissance Poland, who intended to create an ideal urban settlement and impregnable barrier against Cossack and Tatar raids from the east. During WWII, the Nazis renamed the town 'Himmlerstadt' and imported German colonists to create what Hitler had hoped would become an eastern bulwark for the Third Reich. The Polish inhabitants were expelled from the town and its environs, and most of the Jewish population was exterminated.

Fortunately, the Old Town of Zamość escaped war destruction. Restoration work, which has been inching along for decades, has returned the central square to its former splendour and the Old Town was added to Unesco's World Heritage list in 1992.

Information
The **Tourist Information Centre** (*☎ 639 22 93; e zoit@zamosc.um.gov.pl; Rynek Wielki 13; open 8am-6pm Mon-Fri, 10am-3pm Sat & Sun May-Sept, 8am-4pm Mon-Fri Oct-Apr*) is in the town hall. It sells the handy *Along The Streets of Zamość* (5zł), in English and French, and international bus tickets.

Bank Pekao (*ul Grodzka 2*) has an ATM, cashes travellers cheques and gives advances on Visa and MasterCard. There's a 24-hour **foreign-exchange counter** in Hotel Zamojski. There's also a **kantor** in the Market Hall. The quaint **main post office** (*ul Kościuszki*) is near the cathedral. If you find an Internet centre in the Old Town, please send us an email and let us know! The unnamed **bookshop** (*cnr ul Staszica & ul Bazyliańska*) sells maps.

Things to See
Rynek Wielki is an impressive Renaissance square (exactly 100m by 100m) dominated by the lofty **Town Hall** and surrounded by arcaded burghers' houses. Many of these houses have preserved the fancy stucco design on their interiors and exteriors. The **Museum of Zamość** (*admission 5.50zł; open 9am-2pm*

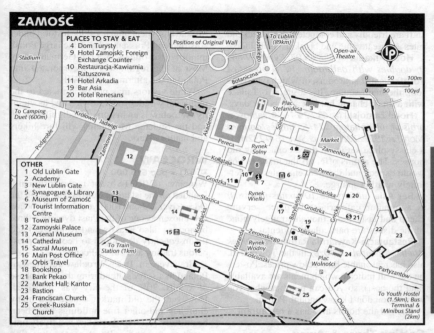

ZAMOŚĆ

PLACES TO STAY & EAT
4 Dom Turysty
9 Hotel Zamojski; Foreign Exchange Counter
10 Restauracja-Kawiarnia Ratuszowa
11 Hotel Arkadia
19 Bar Asia
20 Hotel Renesans

OTHER
1 Old Lublin Gate
2 Academy
3 New Lublin Gate
5 Synagogue & Library
6 Museum of Zamość
7 Tourist Information Centre
8 Town Hall
12 Zamoyski Palace
13 Arsenal Museum
14 Cathedral
15 Sacral Museum
16 Main Post Office
17 Orbis Travel
18 Bookshop
21 Bank Pekao
22 Market Hall; Kantor
23 Bastion
24 Franciscan Church
25 Greek-Russian Church

POLAND

Mon-Fri) is based in two of the loveliest buildings at Rynek Nos 24 and 26.

Southwest of the square is the mighty 16th-century **cathedral** *(ul Kolegiacka; admission free; open dawn-dusk daily)*, which holds the tomb of Zamoyski in the chapel to the right of the high altar. In the grounds, the **Sacral Museum** *(admission 2.50zł; open 10am-4pm Mon-Fri, 10am-1pm Sat & Sun May-Sept, 10am-1pm Sat & Sun only Oct-Apr)* features various robes, paintings and sculptures.

Zamoyski Palace (not open to the public) lost much of its character when it was converted into a military hospital in the 1830s. Nearby, the **Arsenal Museum** *(ul Zamkowa 2; admission 5.50zł; open 9am-4pm Mon-Fri)* is an unremarkable military museum. To the north of the palace stretches a beautifully landscaped **park**.

Before WWII, Jews accounted for 45% of the town's population (of 12,000) and most lived in the area north and east of the palace. The most significant Jewish architectural relic is the Renaissance **synagogue** *(cnr ul Zamenhofa & ul Bazyliańska)*, built in the 1610s. It's now used as a public library, so you can go inside and see the decorative walls.

On the eastern edge of the Old Town is the antiquated **Market Hall**. Behind it is the best surviving **bastion** from the original wall that encircled Zamość.

Places to Stay & Eat
Camping Duet *(☎/fax 639 24 99; ul Królowej Jadwigi 14; camping per person/tent 6.50/ 10zł, single/double bungalow 75/93zł; open year-round)* is about 1km west of the Old Town. It also has tennis courts, and a **restaurant**, swimming pool, sauna and Jacuzzi.

The **Youth Hostel** *(☎ 627 91 25; ul Zamoyskiego 4; dorm beds 22-30zł; open July & Aug)* is in a school about 1.5km east of the Old Town and not far from the bus terminal. It's basic but adequate.

Dom Turysty *(☎ 639 26 39; ul Zamenhofa 11; doubles with shared bathroom 45zł)* can't quite decide which of several alternative names to use, but everyone knows it as simply Dom Turysty. The rooms are unexceptional but the price and location are attractive.

Hotel Renesans *(☎ 639 20 01, fax 638 51 74; ul Grecka 6; singles/doubles Mon-Fri 128/183zł, Sat & Sun 105/152zł)* offers spacious, modern rooms with a fridge, desk and separate seating area. It's in a top location and staff are friendly and competent. The weekend rates are great value and breakfast is included.

Hotel Arkadia (☎ 638 65 07; Rynek Wielki 9; doubles with bathroom, TV & breakfast 100zł) has just six rooms, of which two overlook the main square. It's a grand old place with a lot of charm, but has seen better days.

Hotel Zamojski (☎ 639 25 16; e zamosc@ orbis.pl; ul Kołłątaja 2/4/6; singles/doubles Mon-Fri 192/272zł, Sat & Sun 164/232zł) is a classy place set up in three connecting old houses. The rooms offer all the luxuries you would expect, and the weekend rates are definitely worth a splurge.

Bar Asia (ul Staszica 10; mains from 8zł) is a popular cafeteria-style place serving cheap and tasty food, though strangely none of the dishes are particularly Oriental.

Restauracja-Kawiarnia Ratuszowa (Rynek Wielki 13; meals 9-10zł), in the Town Hall, also has reasonable food at low prices. Posters on the wall indicate which meals are available (and the cost), so you can point at what you want if you don't know enough Polish.

Each of the hotels also has a **restaurant**.

Getting There & Away

Buses are normally more convenient and quicker than trains. The **bus terminal** (ul Hrubieszowska) is 2km east of the Old Town and linked by frequent city buses. Daily, two fast buses go to Kraków, four or five to Warsaw (five hours) and nine to Lublin (two hours).

Far quicker, and surprisingly cheaper, are the minibuses that travel every 30 minutes between Lublin and Zamość. They leave from the minibus stand across the road from the bus terminal in Zamość and from a disorganised corner northwest of the bus terminal in Lublin.

From the **train station**, about 1km southwest of the Old Town, several slow trains head to Lublin (about four hours) every day and three slow trains plod along to Warsaw (six hours). **Orbis Travel** (☎ 639 30 01; ul Grodzka 18) sells train tickets.

Silesia

Silesia in southwestern Poland includes Upper Silesia, the industrial heart of the country; Lower Silesia, a fertile farming region with a cultural and economic centre in Wrocław; and the Sudeten Mountains, a forested range that runs for over 250km along the Czech border. Silesia has spent much of its history under Austrian and Prussian rule, so the large Polish minority was often subject to Germanisation. Most of the region was reincorporated into Poland in the aftermath of WWII.

While visitors may not be attracted to the industrial wonders of Katowice and its vicinity, Wrocław is an historic and dignified city, and the Sudeten Mountains will lure hikers and nature lovers.

WROCŁAW
☎ 071 • pop 675,000

Wrocław ('VROTS-wahf') was originally founded on the island of Ostrów Tumski in the Odra River. About 1000 years ago, Wrocław was chosen as one of the Piast dynasty's three bishoprics (also Kraków and Kołobrzeg) and it subsequently developed to become a prosperous trading and cultural centre.

However, in 1945 Wrocław returned to Poland in a sorry state; during the final phase of WWII, 70% of the city was destroyed. However, the old market square and many churches and other fine buildings have been beautifully restored. Wrocław is a lively university town and cultural centre, boasting many theatres, museums and annual festivals.

Information

The **Tourist Information Centre** (☎ 344 11 11; w www.wroclaw.pl; Rynek 14; open 9am-7pm Mon-Fri, 9am-5pm Sat) is helpful and sells some souvenirs. A **tourist information counter** (☎ 369 54 97) is in the Wrocław Główny train station. The practical Welcome to Wrocław magazine (in English or German) is available free from the tourist offices, as well as travel agencies and upmarket hotels.

Bank Pekao (ul Oławska 2) cashes travellers cheques and gives advances on Visa and MasterCard. There are kantors all over the city centre and a number in the bus and train stations. ATMs are also plentiful, including at the train station.

The **main post office** (Rynek) conveniently overlooks the main square. The **Cyber & Tea Tavern** (ul Kuźnicza 29) offers visitors the chance to surf the Net while indulging in a drink or two. Alternatively, try the busy little **W Sercu Miasta** down a laneway in the middle of the Rynek.

The best place for maps and guidebooks is **Księgarnia Podróżnika** (ul Wita Stwosza

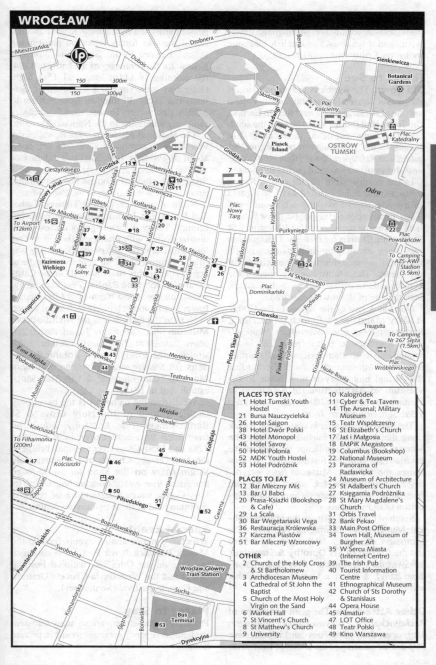

WROCŁAW

POLAND

PLACES TO STAY
1 Hotel Tumski Youth Hostel
21 Bursa Nauczycielska
26 Hotel Saigon
38 Hotel Dwór Polski
43 Hotel Monopol
46 Hotel Savoy
50 Hotel Polonia
52 MDK Youth Hostel
53 Hotel Podróżnik

PLACES TO EAT
12 Bar Mleczny Miś
13 Bar U Babci
20 Prasa-Książki (Bookshop & Cafe)
29 La Scala
30 Bar Wegetariaski Vega
36 Restauracja Królewska
37 Karczma Piastów
51 Bar Mleczny Wzorcowy

OTHER
2 Church of the Holy Cross & St Bartholomew
3 Archdiocesan Museum
4 Cathedral of St John the Baptist
5 Church of the Most Holy Virgin on the Sand
6 Market Hall
7 St Vincent's Church
8 St Matthew's Church
9 University
10 Kalogródek
11 Cyber & Tea Tavern
14 The Arsenal; Military Museum
15 Teatr Współczesny
16 St Elizabeth's Church
17 Jaś i Małgosia
18 EMPiK Megastore
19 Columbus (Bookshop)
22 National Museum
23 Panorama of Racławicka
24 Museum of Architecture
25 St Adalbert's Church
27 Księgarnia Podróżnika
28 St Mary Magdalene's Church
31 Orbis Travel
32 Bank Pekao
33 Main Post Office
34 Town Hall; Museum of Burgher Art
35 W Sercu Miasta (Internet Centre)
39 The Irish Pub
40 Tourist Information Centre
41 Ethnographical Museum
42 Church of Sts Dorothy & Stanislaus
44 Opera House
45 Almatur
47 LOT Office
48 Teatr Polski
49 Kino Warszawa

19/20). **EMPiK Megastore** *(Rynek 50)* offers the widest choice of foreign-language newspapers and magazines. For English-language books, try **Columbus** *(ul Kuźnicza 57).*

Things to See

Old Town The **Rynek** is the second-largest old market square (after Kraków) in Poland and one of the largest (3.7 hectares) in Europe. The **Town Hall** (built 1327–1504) on the south side is certainly one of the most beautiful in Poland. Inside, the **Museum of Burgher Art** *(admission 4zł; open about 10am-4pm Tues-Sun)* shows off its splendid period interiors.

In the northwestern corner of the Rynek are two small houses called **Jaś i Małgosia** *(ul Św Mikołaja)* linked by a baroque gate. (They're not open to the public.) Just behind them looms the monumental, 14th-century **St Elizabeth's Church** *(ul Elżbiety 1; admission free; open about 8am-6pm daily)* with its 83m-high tower, which you can climb for city **views**. The southwestern corner of the Rynek spills into **Plac Solny** (Salt Square), once the site of the town's salt trade.

One block east of the Rynek is the Gothic **St Mary Magdalene's Church** *(ul Łaciarska; admission free; open 9am-4pm Mon-Sat)* with a Romanesque portal from 1280 incorporated into its southern external wall. Further east, the 15th-century former Bernardine church and monastery is now home to the **Museum of Architecture** *(ul Bernardyńska 5; admission 5zł; open 10am-4pm Tues, Wed & Sat-Sun, noon-6pm Thur).*

The university quarter is north of the Rynek along the river bank. Further around is **The Arsenal**, the most significant remnant of the town's 15th-century fortifications. It now houses the **Military Museum** *(ul Cieszyńskiego 9; admission 4zł; open 10am-4pm Tues-Sun)*, which features a predictable collection of old weapons.

South of the Old Town are the **Ethnographical Museum** *(ul Kazimierza Wielkiego 35; admission 4zł; open 10am-4pm Tues-Sun)* and the **Church of Sts Dorothy & Stanislaus** *(ul Świdnicka; admission free; open dawn-dusk daily)*, a massive Gothic complex that was built in 1351.

Other Attractions The giant **Panorama of Racławicka** *(ul Purkyniego 11; admission 19zł; open 9am-4pm Tues-Sun)* is a massive 360-degree painting of the Battle of Racławice

(1794). In this battle near Kraków the Polish peasant army led by Tadeusz Kościuszko defeated Russian forces intent on partitioning Poland. Created by Jan Styka and Wojciech Kossak for the centenary of the battle in 1894, the painting is 114m long and 15m high. Obligatory tours (in English, French or German) run every 30 minutes from 9.30am to 3.30pm (inclusive). The entrance fee includes same-day admission to the National Museum.

The **National Museum** *(Plac Powstańców Warszawy 5; admission 10zł, free Sat; open about 10am-4pm Tues-Sun)* has exhibits of Silesian medieval art and one of the country's finest collections of modern Polish painting. Entry is free with a ticket to the Panorama.

North of the river, Ostrów Tumski (Cathedral Island) has been inhabited since the 8th century. Today it's a markedly ecclesiastical district dotted with churches, though it's no longer an island (an arm of the Odra River was filled in during the 19th century). The focal point is the mighty two-towered Gothic **Cathedral of St John the Baptist** *(Plac Katedralny; admission free; open 10am-6pm Mon-Sat).* A **tower** (admission 5zł) offers wonderful **views**.

Next to the cathedral is the **Archdiocesan Museum** *(Plac Katedralny 16; admission 2zł; open 9am-3pm Tues-Sun).* Further north stretches the lovely, restful **Botanical Gardens** *(ul Sienkiewicza 23; open 8am-6pm Mon-Fri, 10am-6pm Sat & Sun May-Sept)*, established in 1811.

West from the cathedral is the two-storey Gothic **Church of the Holy Cross & St Bartholomew** *(Plac Kościelny; admission free; open 9am-6pm daily)*, built between 1288 and 1350. Cross over the small bridge to the 14th-century **Church of the Most Holy Virgin Mary on the Sand** *(ul Św Jadwigi; admission free; erratic opening hours)* with its lofty Gothic vaults. Classical music concerts are often held in these two divine venues.

Special Events

Wrocław's major annual events include the Musica Polonica Nova Festival (February), the Jazz on the Odra International Festival (May) and the Wratislavia Cantans Oratorio and Cantata Festival (September).

Places to Stay

Probably because there are so many transient students, no agency arranges rooms in private homes.

Camping Camping Nr 267 Ślęża (☎/fax 343 44 42; ul Na Grobli 16/18; camping per person/tent 14/3zł, double bungalows with shared/private bathroom 75/150zł; open year-round) is on the bank of the Odra, 2km east of the Old Town. No local transport goes all the way, so take tram No 4 to Plac Wróblewskiego from the train station and walk about 1km further east.

Camping AZS-AWF Stadion (☎ 348 46 51; ul Paderewskiego 35; camping per person/tent 10/4zł, double bungalows with shared bathroom 41zł; open May-Sept) is near the Olympic stadium in Park Szczytnicki, 4km east of the Old Town. Take tram No 9 from the train station.

Hostels Not far from the train station, **MDK Youth Hostel** (☎ 343 88 56; e mdk .kopernik.wp.pl; ul Kołłątaja 20; dorm beds about 25zł) is in a grand (but poorly signed) mustard-coloured building. It's almost always full, so book ahead.

Hotel Tumski Youth Hostel (☎ 322 60 99; w www.hotel-tumski.com.pl; ul Słodowy 10; dorm beds from 25zł) is convenient and staff are friendly. It's good value, but some rooms are cramped. It's attached to the bright orange Hotel Tumski.

Bursa Nauczycielska (☎ 344 37 81; ul Kotlarska 42; singles/doubles with shared bathroom 55/90zł) is a teachers hostel ideally located just one block northeast of the Rynek. Rooms are clean and well kept.

Hotels Unless stated otherwise, all hotels listed below offer rooms with a bathroom and TV, and rates include breakfast. Many places offer substantial discounts for weekends (Saturday and Sunday night) and some may offer the same discount on Friday night if requested.

Hotel Podróżnik (☎ 373 28 45; ul Sucha 1; singles/doubles 90/130zł) is on the 1st floor of the bus terminal. It's obviously convenient and noisy, yet surprisingly pleasant.

Hotel Polonia (☎ 343 10 21; e polonia@ odratourist.pl; ul Piłsudskiego 66; singles/ doubles Mon-Fri from 155/188zł, Sat & Sun from 116/142zł) is handy to the train and bus stations. It's a bit musty and old-fashioned but good value.

Hotel Savoy (☎/fax 372 53 79; Plac Kościuszki 19; singles/doubles Mon-Fri about 110/130zł, Sat & Sun about 90/110zł) is in an excellent spot midway between the train station and Old Town. It's good value, especially on weekends. Breakfast is an extra 10zł.

Hotel Saigon (☎/fax 344 28 81; ul Wita Stwosza 22/23; singles/doubles Mon-Fri 155/188zł, Sat & Sun 139/169zł) has some bizarre Chinese-style decorations in the foyer, but the rooms are bland and unexciting. It's convenient but a little noisy. The highlight is the outstanding breakfast.

Beside the Opera House, **Hotel Monopol** (☎ 343 70 41; e monopol@orbis.pl; ul Modrzejewskiej 2; singles/doubles from 115/150zł, with bath from 180/260zł) is particularly good value and guests have the dubious honour of staying in the same hotel that was once frequented by the infamous Austrian former house painter with the funny moustache.

Hotel Dwór Polski (☎/fax 372 34 15, ul Kiełbaśnicza 2; singles/doubles Mon-Fri 300/360zł, Sat & Sun 220/280zł) is worth a splurge – but book ahead. This gorgeous place set back from the road is nicely furnished with old-fashioned beds. Guests can luxuriate in the large bathrooms or the (free) sauna.

Places to Eat

For hearty, hot dishes at cheap prices, **Bar Mleczny Wzorcowy** (ul Piłsudskiego 86; mains from 8zł) is a typical milk bar with a long menu (in Polish).

Bar Mleczny Miś (ul Kuźnicza 45-47; mains 8-12zł), in the university area, is basic but popular with frugal university students.

Bar U Babci (ul Więzienna 16; meals about 12zł) is a cosy, family-run place serving honest Polish food at prices that suit students. Only four or five dishes are offered every day, but each is delicious.

Bar Wegetariański Vega (Rynek 1/2; snacks from 5zł, meals about 12zł) is in the centre of the Rynek and offers the best value in the Old Town. It doesn't have any outdoor tables, but the healthy treats that are on offer are excellent value. It's open from 8am for a breakfast of muesli or omelettes.

Most places around the Rynek are classy, with outdoor tables and impeccably dressed waiters, but expect to pay *at least* 20zł for a main course.

Restauracja Królewska (Rynek 5; mains from 28zł), in the gastronomic complex of the Dwór Polski (Polish Court), continues to be Wrocław's top spot for traditional Polish cuisine in a historic setting. **Karczma Piastów** (ul Kiełbaśnicza; mains from 18zł), at the back of

POLAND

the same complex, also serves authentic Polish food, but is cheaper and less formal.

La Scala *(Rynek 38; mains from 25zł)* offers authentic Italian food and, according to those in the know, the best cappuccino in town. It's pricey, but worth a splurge.

Prasa-Ksiażki *(ul Kuźnicza; open 10am-7pm Mon-Fri, 10am-2pm Sat)* is a bookshop-cum-café. It's ideal for meeting locals while getting a caffeine fix.

Entertainment

Wrocław is an important cultural centre, so there's always something going on somewhere. Check out the (free) bimonthly *Wrocław Cultural Guide* for details (in English) of what's on and where. It's available from the tourist offices and upmarket hotels.

The Irish Pub *(Plac Solny 5)* is certainly one of the more authentic Celtic-style drinking establishments in Poland, but like most places around the Rynek it's expensive. There's live music most nights.

Kalogródek *(ul Kuźnicza 29)* is a poky beer garden in a concrete jungle, but popular among students. The surrounding streets are packed with other cheap and friendly haunts.

Teatr Polski *(ul Zapolskiej 3)* is the major mainstream city venue and stages classic Polish and foreign drama. **Teatr Współczesny** *(ul Rzeźnicza 12)* tends more towards contemporary productions.

Filharmonia *(ul Piłsudskiego 19)* hosts concerts of classical music, mostly on Friday and Saturday night.

Kino Warszawa, at the back of a laneway off ul Piłsudskiego, shows recent English-language films.

Getting There & Away

Orbis Travel *(☎ 343 26 65; Rynek 29)* and **Almatur** *(☎ 344 47 28; ul Kościuszki 34)* offer the usual services. If you're travelling to/from Wrocław on Friday, Saturday or Sunday, book your bus or train ticket as soon as possible because thousands of itinerant university students travel to/from the city most weekends.

Refer to the Getting There & Away section earlier in this chapter for information about international buses and trains to/from Wrocław.

Air Every day, LOT flies about eight times between Wrocław and Warsaw and once between Wrocław and Frankfurt-am-Main. Most days, SAS also flies to Copenhagen

(April to October only) and Eurowings goes to Munich (all year). Tickets for all airlines can be bought at the **LOT office** *(☎ 343 90 31; ul Piłsudskiego 36)*.

The airport is in Strachowice, about 12km west of the Old Town. Bus No 406 links the airport with Wrocław Główny train station and bus terminal, via the Rynek.

Bus The **bus terminal** *(ul Sucha 11)* is just south of the main train station. Several PKS buses a day go to Warsaw, Poznań, Częstochowa and Białystok (seven hours). Polski Express also offers several buses a day to Warsaw. For most travel, however, the train is more convenient.

Train The **Wrocław Główny** station *(ul Piłsudskiego 105)* was built in 1856 and is a historical monument in itself. Every day, fast trains to Kraków depart every one or two hours, and several InterCity and express trains (62zł 2nd class) go to Warsaw (six hours), usually via Łódź. Wrocław is also regularly linked by train to Poznań, Częstochowa, Szczecin and Lublin.

SUDETEN MOUNTAINS

The Sudeten Mountains (Sudety) run for over 250km along the Czech-Polish border. The Sudetes feature dense forests, amazing rock formations and deposits of semiprecious stones, all of which can be explored along any of the extensive network of trails for **hiking** or **mountain biking**. The highest part of this old and eroded chain is Mt Śnieżka (1602m). Both the following towns offer the normal tourist facilities.

Szklarska Poréba in the northwestern end of the Sudetes offers superior facilities for **hiking** and **skiing**. It's at the base of Mt Szrenica (1362m), and the town centre is at the upper end along ul Jedności Narodowej. The small **tourist office** *(☎/fax 075-717 24 49; W szklarskaporeba.pl; ul Jedności Narodowej 3)* has accommodation information and maps. Nearby, several trails begins at the intersection of ul Jedności Narodowej and ul Wielki Sikorskiego. The red trail goes to Mt Szrenica (two hours) and offers a peek at Wodospad Kamieńczyka, a spectacular waterfall.

Karpacz to the southeast has a bit more to offer in terms of nightlife, though it attracts fewer serious mountaineers. It's loosely clustered along a 3km road winding through

Łomnica Valley at the base of Mt Śnieżka. The **tourist office** (☎/fax 075-761 97 16; ul Konstytucji 3 Maja 25A) should be your first point of call. To reach the peak of Mt Śnieżka on foot, take one of the trails (three to four hours) from Hotel Biały Jar. Some of the trails pass by one of two splendid postglacial lakes, Mały Staw and Wielki Staw.

The bus is the fastest way of getting around the region. Every day from Szklarska Poręba, about four buses head to Wrocław and one slow train plods along to Warsaw. From Karpacz, get a bus to Jelenia Góra, where plenty of buses and trains go in all directions.

For the Czech Republic, take a bus from Szklarska Poręba to Jakuszyce, cross the border on foot to Harrachov (on the Czech side) and take another bus from there.

Wielkopolska

Wielkopolska ('Great Poland') is the cradle of the Polish nation. In the 6th and 7th centuries AD, Slavic tribes settled the flatlands in this region, from which they eventually derived the name Polanians, or 'inhabitants of the plain'. Despite the royal seat moving to Kraków in 1038, Wielkopolska remained as Poland's most important province until the second partition in 1793, when it was annexed to Prussia. The region then passed back and forth between Polish and German hands several times, culminating in the liberation battles of 1945, which devastated the area. Today, Poznań has been rebuilt and is the region's major commercial and cultural centre.

POZNAŃ
☎ 061 • pop 610,000

Poznań, midway between Berlin and Warsaw, is the focal point of early Polish history. In the 9th century the Polanian tribes built a wooden fort on the island of Ostrów Tumski, and from 968 to 1038 Poznań was the de facto capital of Poland. By the 15th century Poznań was already a trading centre and famous for its fairs. This commercial tradition was reinstituted in 1925, and today the fairs – held for a few days each month – dominate the economic and cultural life of the city.

Information
The **Tourist Information Centre** (☎/fax 855 33 79; Stary Rynek 59/60; open 9am-5pm

Mon-Fri, 10am-2pm Sat) is helpful. The **City Information Centre** (☎ 851 96 45; ul Ratajczaka 44; open 10am-7pm Mon-Fri, 10am-5pm Sat & Sun) handles bookings for cultural events. The free bi-monthly Welcome to Poznań magazine is available at most of the decent hotels.

Bank Pekao (ul Św Marcin 52/56 • ul 23 Lutego) is probably the best place for travellers cheques and credit cards. A few of the kantors in the city centre are shown on the map; there's also one in the bus terminal and another (open 24 hours) in the train station.

For old-fashioned communication visit the **main post office** (ul Kościuszki 77) or the **telephone centre** (Stary Rynek). Check your emails at the **Internet Café** (Plac Wolności 8) or at **Klik** (ul Szkolna – enter from off ul Jaskółcza), a funky pub-café-Internet centre that offers some pleasing privacy.

EMPiK Megastore (Plac Wolności) offers the largest choice of foreign magazines and newspapers. For maps and Lonely Planet guidebooks, visit the excellent **Turystyczna Globtrotter** (ul Żydowska) or **Glob-Tour** inside the train station.

Things to See
Old Town The Old Market Square, **Stary Rynek**, has been beautifully restored to its historic shape. The focal point is the Renaissance **Town Hall** (built 1550–60) with its decorative facade facing east. In accordance with a strange custom, every day at noon two metal goats high above the clock butt their horns together 12 times. Inside the building, the **Poznań Historical Museum** (admission 5.50zł, free Sat; open about 10am-4pm Mon-Tues, Fri & Sun, noon-6pm Wed) reveals the city's past through splendid period interiors.

The square also features the **Wielkopolska Military Museum** (Stary Rynek 9; admission 5.50zł; open about 10am-3pm Tues-Sun) and the unique **Museum of Musical Instruments** (Stary Rynek; 45/47; admission 5.50zł; open 11am-5pm Tues-Sun). The **Archaeological Museum** (ul Wodna 27; admission 3zł; open about 10am-4pm Tues-Sun) features displays about the ancient history of the region, as well as some Egyptian artefacts.

The 17th-century **Franciscan Church** (ul Franciszkańska 2; admission free; open about 8am-8pm daily), one block west of the Rynek, has an ornate baroque interior, complete with wall paintings and rich stucco work. On a hill

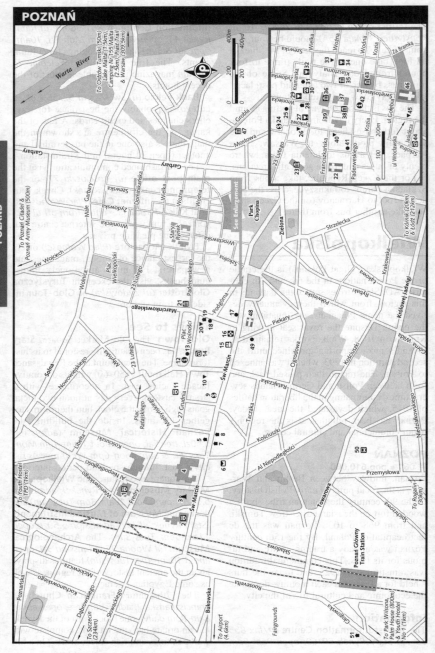

POZNAŃ

POZNAŃ

PLACES TO STAY
5 Hotel Lech
7 Hotel Royal
8 Hotel Wielkopolska
19 Hotel Rzymski
28 Dom Turysty
51 Biuro Zakwaterowania
Przemysław (Private Rooms)

PLACES TO EAT
10 Spaghetti Bar Piccolo
20 Bar Caritas
26 Spaghetti Bar Piccolo
33 Pizzeria di Luigi
40 Restauracja Sphinx
45 Bar Wegetariański; Bar
Pasibruzch

OTHER
1 Teatr Wielki
2 Filharmonia
3 Monument to the Victims
of June 1956

4 Palace of Culture
6 Main Post Office
9 Bank Pekao
11 Teatr Polski
12 City Information Centre
13 EMPiK Megastoreq
14 Internet Cafe
15 Kino Muza
16 Shopping Centre Pasaz
17 Kantor
18 Orbis Travel
21 National Museum:
Paintings & Sculpture
Gallery
22 Franciscan Church
23 Museum of Applied Arts
24 Bank Pekao
25 Kantor
27 Galaxy Klub; Bee Jay's
29 El Otro Muchos Patatos
30 Telephone Centre;
Gospoda Pod
Koziołkami

31 Turystyczna Globtrotter
(Bookshop)
32 O'Morgan's Irish Pub
34 Deja Vu
35 Museum of Musical
Instruments
36 Town Hall; Poznań Historical
Museum
37 Souvenir Stalls
38 Wielkopolska Military
Museum
39 Weigh House
41 Kantor
42 Tourist Information Centre
43 Archaeological Museum
44 Klik (Internet Cafe)
46 Parish Church of St
Stanislaus
47 Wielkopolska Ethnographic
Museum
48 St Martin's Church
49 LOT Office
50 Bus Terminal

POLAND

above the church is the **Museum of Applied Arts** *(admission 3zł; open about 10am-4pm Tues, Wed, Fri-Sun)*.

The nearby **National Museum: Paintings & Sculpture Gallery** *(Al Marcinkowskiego 9; admission 10zł, free Sat; open about 10am-5pm Tues-Sun)* holds a typical collection of art, including medieval church woodcarving and Polish paintings.

Two blocks south of Stary Rynek is the large, pink baroque **Parish Church of St Stanislaus** *(ul Gołębia 1; admission free; open erratic hours)* with a three-naved interior with monumental altars built in the mid-17th century. A short stroll to the southeast is the **Wielkopolska Ethnographic Museum** *(ul Grobla 25; admission 5.50zł; open about 10am-4pm Tues, Wed, Fri-Sun)*, which features a worthwhile collection of woodcarving and traditional costumes of the area.

Other Attractions About 1.3km north of the Old Town is the 19th-century Prussian **Poznań Citadel**, where 20,000 German troops held out for a month in February 1945. The fortress was destroyed by artillery fire but a park was laid out on the site, which incorporates the **Poznań Army Museum** *(Al Armii Poznań; admission 4zł; open 9am-4pm Tues-Sat, 10am-4pm Sun)*.

The massive 1956 strike by the city's industrial workers was the first major popular

upheaval in communist Poland. The strike was cruelly crushed by tanks, leaving 76 dead and over 600 wounded. In a park in the new city centre, the moving **Monument to the Victims of June 1956** commemorates the event.

In **Park Wilsona**, less then 1km southwest of the train station, is the **Palm House** *(ul Matejki 18; admission 5.50zł; open about 9am-4pm Tues-Sun)*. This huge greenhouse (built in 1910) contains 19,000 species of tropical and subtropical plants, including a remarkable collection of giant cacti and towering bamboo trees.

Ostrów Tumski is 1km east of the Old Town (take any eastbound tram from Plac Wielkopolski). This river island is dominated by the monumental, double-towered **Poznań Cathedral** *(ul Ostrów Tumski)*, originally built in 968 but rebuilt several times since. The Byzantine-style **Golden Chapel** (1841), and the **mausoleums** of Mieszko I and Boleslaus the Brave, are behind the high altar. Opposite the cathedral is the 15th-century **Church of the Virgin Mary** *(ul Panny Marii 1/3)*, possibly the purest Gothic building in the city.

Further out from Ostrów Tumski and about 2.5km east of the Old Town is **Lake Malta**. This 64-hectare artificial lake is a favourite weekend destination for Poles, and holds sailing regattas, outdoor concerts and other events in summer. The carnival atmosphere is enhanced by games, food and souvenir stands.

To get to the lake hop on tram No 1, 4 or 8 from Plac Wielkopolski.

Special Events

Poznań's trade fairs are its pride. The largest take place in January, June, September and October. A dozen additional smaller fairs also occur throughout the year. Major cultural events include the St John's Fair (June) and the Malta International Theatre Festival (late June).

Places to Stay

During trade fairs, the rates of Poznań's hotels and private rooms tend to increase (and in some cases double) and accommodation may be difficult to find. (The hard part is knowing when a fair is actually taking place.) The tourist office will help you find a room if you're having trouble; otherwise, it pays to book ahead. Prices given in this section are for off-fair periods.

Camping On the northeastern shore of Lake Malta. **Camping Nr 155 Malta** (☎ 876 62 03, fax 867 62 83; ul Krańcowa 98; camping per person/tent 7/5zł, single/double bungalows 150/180zł; open year-round) is 3.5km east of the Old Town. One reader claimed that this was the 'most beautiful camping ground in Poland', but it's not accessible by public transport (so take a taxi).

Hostels A 15-minute walk southwest of the train station along ul Głogowska, **Youth Hostel No 1** (☎/fax 866 40 40; ul Berwińskiego 2/3; dorm beds 16zł; open year-round) is adjacent to Park Wilsona. It's small and basic, but fills up fast.

Youth Hostel TPD (☎/fax 848 58 36; ul Drzymały 3; dorm beds 16-28zł; open year-round) is newer and more comfortable. It's 3km north of the train station (take tram No 11), and 3km northwest of the Old Town (tram No 9).

The tourist office should know which **student hostels** and **worker hostels** are open, but most of these are in the outer suburbs.

Private Rooms In the main hall of the train station, **Glob-Tour** (☎/fax 866 06 67) offers cheap singles from 40zł to 50zł and doubles from 50zł to 60zł. The agency is open 24 hours, but private rooms can only be arranged between 7am and 10pm daily.

Not too far from the train station is **Biuro Zakwaterowania Przemysław** (☎ 866 35 60; W www.przemyslaw.com.pl; ul Głogowska 16; open 8am-6pm Mon-Fri, 10am-2pm Sat) who can organise singles/doubles starting from 55/75zł.

Hotels The rates for each hotel listed below include breakfast. Many places offer substantial discounts on weekends, but not during trade fairs.

Dom Turysty (☎/fax 852 88 93; W www .domturysty-hotel.com.pl; Stary Rynek 91; dorm beds about 60zł, singles/doubles 125/182zł, with bath 190/310zł) is set in an 18th-century former palace. It's a bit musty and old-fashioned, but boasts the best location in Poznań. The breakfast is hardly worth getting up for, however.

Hotel Lech (☎/fax 853 01 51; ul Św Marcin 74; singles/doubles Mon-Fri 181/270zł, Sat & Sun 122/220zł) is stuck in the 1960s, but the bathrooms are modern and spotless.

Hotel Wielkopolska (☎ 852 76 31, fax 851 54 92; ul Św Marcin 67; singles/doubles 130/170zł, with bath & TV 180/230zł) is better value. The rooms are overdue for some renovation, but it's quiet and comfortable.

The **Hotel Royal** (☎ 858 23 00; W www .hotel-royal.com.pl; ul Św Marcin 71; singles/doubles Mon-Fri 290/370zł Sat & Sun, 232/296zł) has been extensively renovated. This gorgeous place set back from the main road offers rooms with a huge bed and excellent bathroom. It's certainly worth a splurge, especially on weekends.

Hotel Rzymski (☎ 852 81 21, fax 852 89 83; Al Marcinkowskiego 22; singles/doubles Mon-Fri 182/246zł, Sat & Sun 164/221zł) doesn't look like too much from the outside, but it offers large, comfortable rooms in a good central location.

Places to Eat

You can point at what you want without resorting to your phrasebook at **Bar Caritas** (Plac Wolności 1; mains 8-12zł), a cheap and convenient milk bar.

Bar Pasibruzch (ul Wrocławska 23; lunch specials 8zł) is another cafeteria with plenty of tasty, hot food waiting to be dolloped onto your plate.

Bar Wegetariański (ul Wrocławska 21; meals from 10zł), a funky vegetarian place in a cellar off the main road. Staff are happy to recommend one or more of their delicious healthy wonders.

Gospoda Pod Koziołkami *(Stary Rynek 95; main meals from 20zł)* is worth a splurge. If you don't want any of the typically heavy grills, try the salad bar and lighter meals offered upstairs.

Spaghetti Bar Piccolo *(ul Rynkowa 1 • ul Ratajczaka 37; meals about 4zł)* is the best of several similar places offering plastic dishes of pasta and a modest choice of salads at remarkably cheap prices.

Pizzeria di Luigi *(ul Woźna; pizzas 10zł, pasta 10-12zł)* serves some of the tastiest pasta northeast of Italy. The owners may not be Italian, but the food is authentic and the setting is cosy.

Bee Jay's *(Stary Rynek 87; meals from 15zł)*, next to the Galaxy Klub, is one of the more reasonably priced eateries around the main square. It offers passable Indian meals and pricey Mexican fare, among other items – all listed on a menu in English. There's live music on weekends.

Restaurant Sphinx *(Stary Rynek 77; mains about 15zł)* is part of a nationwide chain that offers grills with the trimmings, and a menu in English. The line for the colossal takeaway burgers is predictably long.

Entertainment

O'Morgan's Irish Pub *(ul Wielka 7)* is *the* place to go for a beer or two, but beware: any drinking or eating establishment around or near the Rynek is way overpriced.

Déjà Vu *(ul Woźna 21)* is a very small but cosy bar, popular with students who take advantage of discounted drinks.

Galaxy Klub *(Stary Rynek 85)* is a well-frequented place to let your hair down (if you have any). **El Otro Muchos Patatos** *(Stary Rynek 92; entrance opposite Dom Turysty)* features taped and live Latin music (sometimes even performed by the Polish owners!) most nights.

Teatr Polski *(ul 27 Grudnia 8/10)* is the major centre for plays and dances, while **Teatr Wielki** *(ul Fredry 9)* is where opera and ballet are more likely to be held. **Filharmonia** *(ul Św Marcin 81)* offers classical concerts at least every Friday night.

Kino Muza *(Św Marcin 30)* is one of several cinemas offering current films in comfortable surroundings.

Getting There & Away

LOT flies five times a day between Warsaw and Poznań. Also, LOT has flights from Poznań to Hanover and Düsseldorf most days; LOT and SAS fly daily to Copenhagen; and Austrian Airlines goes regularly to Vienna. Tickets for all airlines are available from the **LOT** office (☎ 858 55 00; ul Piekary 6) or from **Orbis Travel** (☎ 853 20 52, Al Marcinkowskiego 21). The airport is in the western suburb of Ławica, 7km from the Old Town and accessible by bus Nos 59 and 78.

The **bus terminal** *(ul Towarowa 17)* is a 10-minute walk east of the train station. Bus services are poor, however, and really only useful for regional towns, such as Kórnik and Rogalin (see Around Poznań next). Buses do travel from Poznań four or five times a day to Łódź, once to Toruń and thrice to Wrocław, but the trains are better.

The busy **train station** *(ul Dworcowa 1)* is well set up. Every day, it offers nine trains to Kraków (74zł 2nd-class express, 6½ hours), a dozen to Szczecin (half of which continue to Świnoujście), seven to Gdańsk, four to Toruń and seven to Wrocław. About 15 trains a day also head to Warsaw (46zł 2nd-class express, five hours), including several Inter-City services (three hours).

For information about international buses and trains to/from Poznań, refer to the Getting There & Away section earlier in this chapter.

AROUND POZNAŃ

Kórnik, about 20km southeast of Poznań, is noted for the **Castle of Kórnik**. Inside, the **museum** *(ul Zamkowa 5; admission 8zł; open about 9am-4pm Tues-Sun)* displays fabulous 19th-century furnishings and interiors. Behind the castle is the large, English-style **Arboretum** *(admission 5zł; open 9am-5pm daily May-Sept, 9am-3pm Oct-Apr)*, with some 3000 plant species. Buses connect Poznań with Kórnik every 30 minutes or so.

The popular and well-established **Trasa Kornicka** (Kórnik Route) is an 80-km hiking and cycling trail from Poznań to Szreniawy via Kórnik, Rogalin and the Wielkopolska National Park. Details are available from the tourist office in Poznań.

Rogalin, about 30km south of Poznań, boasts the large 18th-century baroque **Palace of Rogalin**, which houses an extensive **museum** *(admission 6.50zł; open 10am-4pm*

Tues-Sun). Some visitors come just to wander around the **gardens** surrounding the castle. Buses travel about every two hours between Poznań and Rogalin, but use several different routes. Buses between Kórnik and Rogalin are infrequent, however, so check the timetables if you plan to visit both destinations in one day from Poznań.

THE PIAST TRAIL

A popular tourist route winding east from Poznań to Inowrocław is the Piast Trail (Szlak Piastowski), which includes places and monuments relating to early Polish history.

Lake Lednica

Lake Lednica is 30km east of Poznań on the road to Gniezno. The **Museum of the First Piasts** *(admission 5.50zł; open about 10am-5pm Tues-Sun; closed 16 Nov-14 Feb)* is on the lakeshore. From the museum, the island of **Ostrów Lednicki**, which was the site of a stronghold built by the first Piasts in the 10th century, is accessible by boat between mid-April and early November. Visitors can see the remains of a church and a stone palace, where researchers claim Duke Mieszko I was probably baptised in 966.

About 2km south of the museum, and 500m north of the Poznań-Gniezno road is the **Wielkopolska Ethnographic Park** *(admission 6.50zł; open about 9am-5pm Tues-Sun; closed 16 Nov-14 Feb)*. It features some 19th-century rural architecture from the region.

From Poznań, take one of the eight daily buses (fewer on weekends) to Gniezno via Pobiedziska – *not* via Kostrzyn. Buy your ticket for Lednogóra, which is the closest village on this road, and ask the driver to let you off.

Gniezno

Gniezno ('GNYEZ-no'), 50km east of Poznań, is commonly considered the first capital of the Polish nation. About 1000 years ago an archbishopric was established here, and in 1025 Boleslaus the Brave was crowned in the local cathedral to become the first Polish king.

The first stop for all visitors should be the **tourist office** *(☎ 428 41 00; ul Tumska 12)*, which is one block northwest of the Rynek (old town square).

Gniezno's pride and joy is the **cathedral** *(ul Tumska; admission free; open about 9am-5.30pm Mon-Sat, 1pm-5.30pm Sun)*, a large, twin-towered Gothic structure rebuilt in the

14th century. The **Museum of the Origins of the Polish State** *(ul Kostrzewskiego 1; admission 5.50zł; open 10am-5pm Tues-Sun)*, on the western side of Lake Jelonek from the Rynek, recounts some regional history.

Internat Medycznego Studium Zawodowego *(☎ 426 34 09; ul Mieszka I 27; singles/doubles with shared bathroom 35/ 70zł)* is excellent value. It's located approximately 200m south of the southeastern end of the mall (ul Tumska).

The **City Hotel** *(☎ 425 35 35; Rynek 15; doubles without/with bathroom 85/122zł)* is in a prime location. The rooms are cramped, but it's good value.

The train and bus stations are both 1km southeast of the Rynek and accessible from along the extension of ul Tumska. Trains run regularly to Poznań and Toruń, and buses travel to Poznań via Lake Lednica.

Pomerania

Pomerania (Pomorze) stretches along the Baltic coast from the German frontier to the lower Vistula Valley in the east. The region rests on two large urban pillars: Szczecin at its western end and Gdańsk to the east. Between them stretches the sandy coastline dotted with beach resorts. Further inland is a wide belt of rugged, forested lakeland sprinkled with medieval castles and towns, and the charming city of Toruń.

TORUŃ

☎ 056 • pop 208,000

Toruń is a historic city, characterised by its narrow streets, burgher mansions and mighty Gothic churches. The compact Old Town was built on the slopes of the wide Vistula and is one of the most appealing in central Poland. Toruń is famous as the birthplace of Nicolaus Copernicus, who spent his youth here and after whom the local university is named.

In 1233 the Teutonic Knights established an outpost in Toruń. Following the Thirteen Years' War (1454–66), the Teutonic Order and Poland signed a peace treaty here, which returned to Poland a large area of land stretching from Toruń to Gdańsk. In the following centuries, Toruń suffered a fate similar to that of the surrounding region: Swedish invasions and Prussian domination until the early 20th century.

POLAND

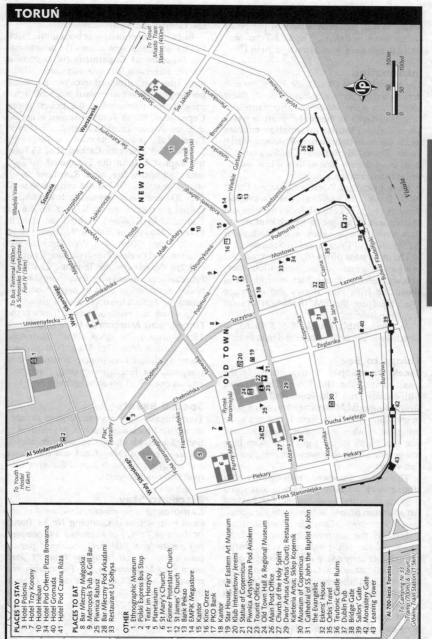

TORUŃ

To Toruń
Miasto Train
Station (400m)

To Bus Terminal (400m)
& Schronisko Turystyczne
Fort IV (3km)

To Youth
Hostel
(1.6km)

NEW TOWN

OLD TOWN

Vistula

To Camping Nr 33
Tramp (700m) & Toruń,
Główny, Train Station (1.5km)

To 700-lecia Torunia

Fortunately, the city suffered little damage during WWII, so Toruń is the best-preserved Gothic town in Poland. The Old Town was added to Unesco's World Heritage list in 1997.

Information

The **tourist office** (☎ 621 09 31; Ⓦ www.it .torun.com.pl; Rynek Staromiejski 1; open about 9am-4pm Mon-Sat, also 9am-1pm Sun May-Sept) is certainly worth a visit. There's also a **tourist information counter** inside the main train station. The free, glossy Toruń Tourist & Business Guide, available from most decent hotels, lists a few worthwhile eateries and nightclubs.

Bank Pekao (ul Wielkie Garbary 11) and **PKO Bank** (ul Szeroka) cash travellers cheques and give cash advances on Visa and MasterCard. A couple of handy **kantors** are shown on the map. There's no shortage of ATMs along ul Różana and ul Szeroka.

The **main post office** (Rynek Staromiejski) overlooks the main square, while **Klub Internetowy Jeremi** (Rynek Staromiejski 33) is above the Irish Pub. Books and maps are available from the **EMPiK Megastore** (ul Królowej-Jadwigi).

As usual, **Orbis Travel** (☎ 655 48 63; ul Mostowa 7) can help with air and train tickets.

Things to See

Rynek Staromiejski is unquestionably the focal point of the Old Town. The massive 14th-century brick **Old Town Hall** now shelters the **Regional Museum** (admission 8.50zł; open 10am-4pm Tues-Sun). It features some historical exhibits and regional artwork, and you can climb to the top of the 40m-high **tower** (from May to September only) for the fine **views**.

The richly decorated, 15th-century **Star House**, with its Baroque facade and spiral wooden staircase, contains the **Far Eastern Art Museum** (Rynek Staromiejski 35; admission 5.50zł; open 10am-4pm Tues-Sun).

Just off the northwestern corner of the square is the late-13th-century **St Mary's Church** (ul Panny Marii; admission free; open dawn-dusk daily), a Gothic building with magnificent 15th-century stalls. Behind the church is the **Planetarium** (ul Franciszkańska 15; admission 8zł; open 9am-6pm Tues-Fri, 11am-5pm Sat & Sun). Rather dated presentations take place six times a day from Monday to Friday and three times on both Saturday and Sunday. A few shows are offered in English and German during the summer.

In 1473, Copernicus was born in the brick Gothic house that now houses the disappointing **Museum of Copernicus** (ul Kopernika 15/17; admission 9zł, free Sun; open 10am-4pm Tues-Sun) stretched over two adjoining buildings. A short audiovisual 'sound & light' presentation (included in the ticket) about Copernicus' life in Toruń is shown every 30 minutes. A soundtrack in English – and even Esperanto! – is available during summer.

One block east is the **Cathedral of SS John the Baptist & John the Evangelist** (ul Żeglarska; admission free; open 8am-6pm daily), started around 1260 but not completed until over 200 years later. Its massive **tower** houses Poland's second-largest bell (after the Wawel Cathedral in Kraków). Behind the church, **Eskens' House** (ul Ciasna 4/6; admission 4.50zł; open 10am-4pm Wed-Sun) has old weapons and modern Polish paintings. Further east are the ruins of the **Teutonic Castle** (ul Przedzamcze; admission free; permanently open), destroyed in 1454 by angry townsfolk protesting against the oppressive regime.

In a park just north of the Old Town is the **Ethnographic Museum** (ul Wały Sikorskiego 19; admission 8zł; open about 10am-4pm daily, closed Mon Oct-Mar). It showcases many traditional customs, costumes and weapons. An English-speaking guide will cost an extra 30zł per small group.

Special Events

Toruń breaks out of its comparative slumber during the Probaltica Music & Art Festival of Baltic States (May), the Contact International Theatre Festival (May/June) and the Music and Architecture International Summer Festival (July and August).

Places to Stay

Camping A five-minute walk west of the main train station is **Camping Nr 33 Tramp** (☎/fax 654 71 87; ul Kujawska 14; camping per person/tent 10/15zł, doubles/4-person cabins with shared bathroom from 71/95zł; open mid-May–mid-Sept). The cabins and rooms are simple and it's alarmingly close to the train line.

Hostels The **Youth Hostel** (☎ 654 45 80; ul Św Józefa 22/24; dorm beds 15-25zł; open year-round) is 2km northwest of the Rynek.

It's accessible on bus No 11 from the main train station and the Old Town.

Schronisko Turystyczne Fort IV (☎ 655 82 36, fax 655 81 34; ul Chrobrego; dorm beds from 20zł; open year-round) is charmingly located in an old Prussian fort. Although not convenient, it's relatively easy to reach on bus No 14 leaving from the bus terminal and main train station.

Hotels All hotels listed (except the Polonia) are charming, old-fashioned pensions, which are both convenient and quiet. Unless stated otherwise, each offers rooms with a bathroom and TV, and rates include breakfast.

Hotel Polonia (☎ 622 30 28; Plac Teatralny 5; singles/doubles 150/180zł) has been recently renovated (at last!), but is no longer a bargain. It is, however, still a good mid-range option.

Hotel Trzy Korony (☎/fax 622 60 31; Rynek Staromiejski 21; singles/doubles 90/110zł, with bath 150/190zł) is not quite as nice as the outside would suggest. It does boast a superb location, however, overlooking the main square so ask for a room with a view.

For good value try the **Hotel Pod Orłem** (☎/fax 622 50 24; W www.hotel.torun.pl; ul Mostowa 17; singles/doubles 110/140zł, breakfast per person 15zł). The rooms are smallish and have squeaky wooden floors, and some contain poky bathrooms, but the service is good and the scrumptious breakfast will take your mind off its other (minor) faults.

Hotel Pod Czarna Róża (☎/fax 621 96 37; ul Rabiańska 11; singles/doubles 170/210zł) is extremely cosy. The rooms feature lovely antique-style furniture, and staff are pleasingly friendly and helpful.

The **Hotel Heban** (☎ 652 15 55; W www .hotel-heban.com.pl; ul Małe Garbary 7; doubles 250zł) is over a classy restaurant of the same name. Rooms are lovingly furnished and have a modern bathroom. It's worth a splurge, but not if you're travelling alone.

Hotel Gromada (☎ 622 60 60; ul Żeglarska 10/14; singles/doubles Mon-Thur 185/240zł, Fri-Sun 150/195zł) is not great value compared to the others, except on weekends. Dinner in the classy restaurant attached costs a reasonable 30zł (guests only).

Places to Eat
Bar Mleczny Małgośka (ul Szczytna 10/12; meals from 7zł) is a clean and convenient milk bar that also offers passable hamburgers and pizzas.

Bar Mleczny Pod Arkadami (ul Różana 1; meals from 8zł), just off Rynek Staromiejski, is much the same.

Several decent Italian restaurants are along ul Mostowa. **Pizza Browarna** (ul Mostowa 17; mains 10-12zł), under Hotel Pod Orłem, is very popular with locals. Nearby, **Restaurant u Sołtysa** (ul Mostowa; mains from 15zł) serves traditional Polish food.

Metropolis Pub & Grill Bar (ul Podmurna 28; mains 9-12zł) is a dark but inviting place (complete with indoor waterfall!) that serves pasta, pizza and Polish food. Daily specials (from 6zł) are advertised on sandwich boards along ul Szeroka.

Piwnica Ratusz (Rynek Staromiejski; mains about 12zł) is probably the best-value eatery around the main square. Look out for the daily specials (5zł to 8zł).

Restaurant-Kafeteria Artus (Rynek Staromiejski 6; soups 5zł, mains 9-12zł), inside Dwór Artusa (Artus Court), is the most charming place in Toruń. Set up inside an elegant indoor courtyard, the prices are not as high as the setting would suggest. The menu is in English and German.

Toruń is famous for its gingerbread (pierniki), produced here since, well, forever. It comes in a variety of shapes, including figures of local hero Copernicus, and can be bought at **Sklep Kopernik** (Rynek Staromiejski 6) in Dwór Artusa.

Entertainment
Piwnica Artystyczna Pod Aniołem (Rynek Staromiejski 1), set in a splendid spacious cellar in the Old Town Hall, offers live music some nights. Other great places for a drink include the quasi-Irish **Dublin Pub** (ul Mostowa) and **Piwnica Ratusz** (see Places to Eat), which offers a few outdoor tables in the square and a huge cavernous area downstairs.

Teatr im Horzycy (Plac Teatralny 1) is the main stage for theatre performances, while **Dwór Artusa** (Artus Court; Rynek Staromiejski 6) often presents classical music.

Kino Orzez (ul Strumykowa 3) shows recent films.

Getting There & Away
The **bus terminal** (ul Dąbrowskiego) is a about a 10-minute walk north of the Old Town. It offers regular services to regional

villages of minimal interest to travellers and surprisingly few long-distance buses. **Polski Express** (Al Solidarności) has hourly services to Warsaw (four hours) and two a day to Szczecin. Refer to the Getting There & Away section earlier in this chapter for information about international buses to/from Toruń.

The main **Toruń Główny** train station (Al Podgórska) is on the opposite side of the Vistula River and linked to the Old Town by bus Nos 22 and 27. Some (but not all) trains stop and finish at the more convenient **Toruń Miasto** train station, about 500m east of the New Town.

From the Toruń Główny station, there are services to Poznań (three a day), Gdańsk (six), Kraków (three), Łódź (seven), Olsztyn (nine), Szczecin (one) and Wrocław (two). Five trains a day head towards Warsaw (51zł 2nd-class express, four hours). Trains travelling between Toruń and Gdańsk often change at Bydgoszcz, and between Toruń and Kraków you may need to get another connection at Inowrocław.

GDAŃSK
☎ 058 • pop 475,000

Gdańsk is an important port and shipbuilding centre along the Baltic coast. In existence since the 9th century, Gdańsk came to the fore after the Teutonic Knights seized it in 1308. Within half a century it became a thriving medieval town known as Danzig.

In 1454, many inhabitants staged an armed protest against economic restrictions imposed by the rulers and destroyed the Teutonic Knights' castle and pledged loyalty to the Polish monarch. In return, Gdańsk was given numerous privileges by the Poles, including a monopoly over the grain trade and a degree of political independence. So, by the mid-16th century, Gdańsk controlled three-quarters of Poland's foreign trade; it was then the country's largest city and the Baltic's greatest port.

In 1793 Gdańsk fell under Prussian dominion and this lasted until the 20th century, when, in the aftermath of WWI, it became the virtually autonomous Free City of Danzig. The importance of this strategic port was emphasised when the Nazis bombarded Westerplatte and, thereby, started WWII. The war devastated most of Gdańsk, but the historic quarters have been almost completely rebuilt.

Today, Gdańsk is most famous as the birthplace (in 1980) of the Solidarity trade union, which was the catalyst for the fall of communism in Poland and in the rest of the former Soviet bloc.

Information
The helpful **PTTK office** (☎/fax 301 13 43; e pttkgda@gdansk.com.pl; ul Długa 45; open 10am-6pm daily) is conveniently opposite the Main Town Hall. The free monthly magazines *Welcome to Gdańsk, Sopot, Gdynia* and *Gdańsk, Gdynia, Sopot: What, Where, When* are annoyingly hard to find; try the top-end hotels in the city centre.

Bank Gdański (Wały Jagiellońskie 14/16 • Długi Targ 14/16) also has other offices at central locations. **Bank Pekao** (ul Garncarska 23) will provide cash advances on Visa and MasterCard. Some **kantors** are located on the map; one is open 24 hours in the main train station. There are plenty of ATMs all over the city centre.

For snail mail, go to the **main post office** (ul Długa 22). The poste restante is in the same building but the entrance is through the back door from ul Pocztowa. Mail should be addressed to: Your Name, Poste Restante, ul Długa 22/28, 80-801 Gdańsk 50, Poland. Next to the main entrance of the post office is the **telephone centre** (ul Długa 26).

The most convenient place to check your emails is **Rudy Kot** (ul Garncarska 18/20). It's also a decent pub that offers inexpensive meals and occasionally features live music. Otherwise, try **Jazz 'n' Java** (ul Tkacka), which also offers music and drinks.

Almatur (☎ 301 24 24; Długi Targ 11) and **Orbis Travel** (☎ 301 45 44; ul Podwale Staromiejskie 96/97) both provide the usual services to travellers. The PTTK office also offers (expensive) walking tours around the Old Town, and tours of Oliwa, Westerplatte, Gdynia and Sopot.

English Books Unlimited (ul Podmłyńska 10) has the best choice of English-language books and dictionaries. The widest selection of foreign-language press is in the **EMPiK Megastore** (ul Podwale Grodzkie 8), across the road from the main train station; a smaller **EMPiK** (Długi Targ) is in the Main Town.

Things to See
Main Town The richest architecture and most thorough restoration are found in this historic quarter. Ul Długa (Long Street) and Długi Targ (Long Market) form the city's main

thoroughfare; both are now pedestrian malls. They are known collectively as the **Royal Way**, along which Polish kings traditionally paraded during their periodic visits. They entered the Main Town through the **Upland Gate** (built in the 1770s on a 15th-century gate), passed through the **Golden Gate** (1614) and proceeded east to the Renaissance **Green Gate** (1568). This gate was intended to be the kings' residence though none of them stayed here (they preferred the cosier houses nearby).

Inside the towering Gothic **Main Town Hall** (*ul Długa 47*) is the **Gdańsk History Museum** (*admission 5zł, free Wed; open about 10am-4pm Tues-Sun*). It, well, provides a history of Gdańsk, including photos of the damage caused during WWII.

Near the Town Hall is **Neptune's Fountain** (1615), behind which stands the **Artus Court Museum** (*ul Długi Targ 43/44; admission 5zł, free Wed; open 10am-4pm Tues-Sat, 11am-4pm Sun*) where local merchants used to congregate. The adjacent **Golden House** (1618) has perhaps the richest facade in town. A little further west, the 18th-century **Dom Uphagena** (*ul Długa 12; admission 5zł, free Sun; open about 10am-4pm Tues-Sun*) features the sort of ornate furniture typical of the houses along this old street.

Two blocks north of Green Gate along the waterfront is the 14th-century **St Mary's Gate**, which houses the **Archaeological Museum** (*ul Mariacka 25/26; admission 5.50zł, free Sat; open about 10am-4pm Tues-Sun*). It features plenty of displays about amber, and offers **river views** from the adjacent tower. Through this gate, the most picturesque street in Gdańsk – **ul Mariacka** (St Mary's St) – is lined with 17th-century burgher houses.

At the end of ul Mariacka is the gigantic 14th-century **St Mary's Church** (*admission free; open about 8am-8pm daily*), possibly the largest old brick church in the world. Inside, the 14m-high astronomical clock is certainly unique: its maker had his eyes gouged out to prevent him from creating a rival. The fabulous **panorama** from the 82m tower is well worth the climb (405 steps). West along ul Piwna (Beer St) is the Dutch Renaissance **Arsenal** (1609), now occupied by a market.

Further north along the waterfront is the 15th-century **Gdańsk Crane**, the largest of its kind in medieval Europe and capable of hoisting loads of up to 2000kg. It's now part of the

Central Maritime Museum (*ul Szeroka 67/68 & ul Ołowianka 9; open 10am-4pm Tues-Sun*). The museum has several sections either side of the river, including the obvious **Sołdek Museum Ship**. A ticket to each of the three sections costs 5zł or 12zł to the entire museum complex.

Old Town Almost totally destroyed in 1945, the Old Town has never been completely rebuilt apart from a handful of churches. The largest and most remarkable of these is **St Catherine's Church** (*ul Wielke Młyny; admission free; open about 8am-6pm Mon-Sat*), Gdańsk's oldest church (begun in the 1220s). Opposite, the **Great Mill** (*ul Wielke Młyny*) was built by the Teutonic Knights in around 1350. It used to produce 200 tonnes of flour per day and continued to operate until 1945. More recently, it has been converted into a modern shopping complex.

Right behind St Catherine's is **St Bridget's Church** (*ul Profesorska 17; admission free; open about 10am-6pm Mon-Sat*). Formerly Lech Wałęsa's place of worship, the church was a strong supporter of the shipyard workers and its priest often spoke about political issues during his sermons in the 1980s.

At the entrance to the Gdańsk Shipyards to the north stands the **Monument to the Shipyard Workers** (*Plac Solidarności*). It was erected in late 1980 in memory of 44 workers killed during the riots of December 1970. Down the street is the evocative **Roads to Freedom Exhibition** (*ul Doki 1; admission 5zł, free Wed; open 10am-4pm Tues-Sun*), also known as the **Solidarity Museum**.

Old Suburb This section of Gdańsk was also reduced to rubble in 1945. Little of the former urban fabric has been reconstructed, except for the former Franciscan monastery that now houses the **National Museum** (*ul Toruńska 1; admission 12zł, free Sat; open 10am-5pm Tues-Sun*). The museum is famous for its Dutch and Flemish paintings, especially Hans Memling's 15th-century *Last Judgement*. If the museum looks deserted, open the gate yourself; a member of staff will soon find you and demand a ticket.

Adjoining the museum is the former Franciscan **Church of the Holy Trinity** (*ul Św Trójcy; admission free; open about 10am-8pm Mon-Sat*), which was built at the end of the 15th century.

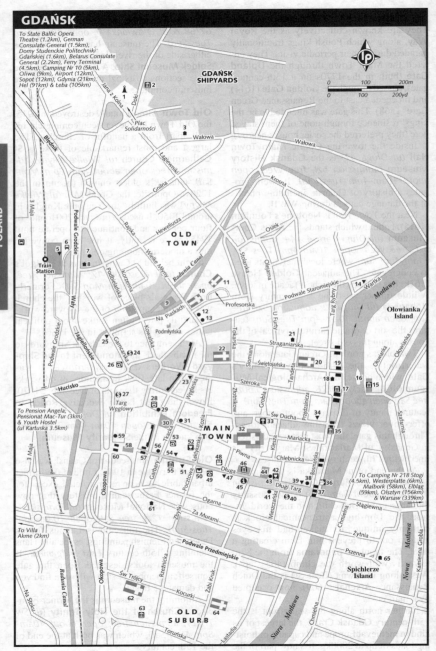

GDAŃSK

To State Baltic Opera
Theatre (1.2km), German
Consulate General (1.5km),
Domy Studenckie Politechniki
Gdańskiej (1.6km), Belarus Consulate
General (2.2km), Ferry Terminal
(4.5km), Camping Nr 10 (5km),
Oliwa (9km), Airport (12km),
Sopot (12km), Gdynia (21km),
Hel (91km) & Łeba (105km)

GDAŃSK
SHIPYARDS

Plac
Solidarności

Wałowa

Wałowa

Krosna

OLD
TOWN

Osiek

Ołowianka
Island

Main Town

OLD
SUBURB

Spichlerze
Island

To Camping Nr 218 Stogi
(4.5km), Westerplatte (6km),
Malbork (58km), Elbląg
(59km), Olsztyn (156km)
& Warsaw (339km)

GDAŃSK

POLAND

Oliwa About 9km northwest of the Main Town in the suburb of Oliwa is **Park Oliwski** (ul Cystersów). This lovely piece of greenery surrounds the soaring **Oliwa Cathedral** (admission free; open about 8am-8pm daily), built in the 13th century with a Gothic facade and a long, narrow central nave. The famous Baroque organ is used for recitals each hour between 10am and 3pm Monday to Saturday in June, July and August. Elsewhere in the park is the **Ethnographic Museum** (admission 4zł; open about 10am-4pm Tues-Sun) in the Old Granary, and the **Modern Art Gallery** (admission 8zł; open about 9am-4pm Tues-Sun) in the former Abbots' Palace.

To reach the park, take the commuter train to the Gdańsk Oliwa station. From there, it's a 10-minute walk; head (west) up ul Poczty Gdańsk, turn right (north) along the highway and look for the signs (in English) to 'Ethnographic Museum' and 'Cathedral'.

Westerplatte When the German battleship Schleswig-Holstein began shelling the Polish naval post at Westerplatte at 4.45am on 1 September 1939, World War II had officially started. The 182-man Polish garrison held out against ferocious attacks for seven days before surrendering.

A park at Westerplatte, 7km north of the Main Town, now features a hill-top **memorial** (admission free; permanently open), a small **museum** (ul Sucharskiego; admission 2zł; open about 10am-4pm Tues-Sun May-Sept) and plenty of other **ruins** caused by the Nazi bombardment. The café at the bus stop serves light meals and drinks.

Bus No 106 (25 minutes) goes to the park every 15 minutes from a stop outside the main train station in Gdańsk. Alternatively, excursion boats (33/46zł one way/return) to and around Westerplatte leave from a dock near the Green Gate in Gdańsk between 1 April and 30 October.

Special Events

The Dominican Fair (first two weeks in August) is an annual shopping fair dating back to 1260. Organ recitals are held at the Oliwa Cathedral twice a week (mid-June-late Aug) as part of the International Organ Music Festival. St Nicholas' and St Bridget's Churches also host organ recitals.

St Mary's Church is the stage for the International Organ, Choir & Chamber Music Festival (every Friday in July and August). Also popular is the International Street & Open-Air Theatre Festival (July).

POLAND

Places to Stay

If you're having trouble finding accommodation, the PTTK Office (see the Information section earlier) is happy to ring around a few hotels and hostels (for no charge). Also refer to the Around Gdańsk section later for details of a few (of the many) places to stay in nearby Sopot and Gdynia.

Camping About 5.5km northeast of the Main Town, **Camping Nr 218 Stogi** (☎ 307 39 15, fax 343 55 47; ul Wydmy 9; camping per person/tent sites 10/10zł, beds in cabins from 23zł; open May-Sept) is only 200m from the excellent beach in the seaside holiday centre of Stogi. Take tram No 8 from the main train station in Gdańsk.

Camping Nr 10 (☎/fax 343 55 31; ul Hallera 234; camping per person/tent 10/11.50zł, beds in cabins about 30zł; open May-Sept) is in the suburb of Brzeźno, about 1km from the beach. It's accessible by tram No 13 from the main train station in Gdańsk and by tram No 15 from the ferry terminal in Westerplatte.

Hostels The main **Youth Hostel** (☎/fax 301 23 13; ul Wałowa 21; dorm beds 15zł; singles/doubles with shared bathroom from 25/50zł; open year-round) is only five minutes' walk northeast of the main train station. It's in a quiet, old building back from the road. It's often full, particularly in summer, so book ahead. The noticeboard next to the reception is a mine of local information.

Another **Youth Hostel** (☎ 302 60 44, fax 302 41 87; ul Kartuska 245b; dorm beds 17-33zł; open year-round) is 3.5km west of the main train station; take bus No 161 or 167 along ul 3 Maja from the back of the station.

Domy Studenckie Politechniki Gdańskiej (☎ 347 25 47; ul Wyspiańskiego 7a; singles/doubles from 30/48zł) opens about 10 of its student dorms as travellers' hostels between early July and late September. A bed will vary in price depending on the facilities and standards (some even have private bathrooms). All are in the suburb of Gdańsk Wrzeszcz and accessible by public transport.

Private Rooms Opposite the main train station, **Grand Tourist** (☎ 301 26 34, e tourist@ gt.com.pl; ul Podwale Grodzkie 8; open 8am-7pm Mon-Fri, 8am-2pm Sat) is below the street level. It offers private singles/doubles in

the city centre for 55/90zł and rooms in the suburbs from 43/75zł. The apartments with a kitchen, bathroom and double bed are good value for 180zł per night. When making your choice, work out the distance from the house to the frequent and inexpensive local commuter train line.

Hotels The rooms are small but cosy, and the bathrooms are clean at **Dom Harcerza** (☎ 301 36 21; e domharcerza@go2.pl; ul Za Murami 2/10; doubles with shared bathroom 60zł), which offers the best value and location for any budget-priced hotel. It's popular (so get there early or book ahead) and it can get noisy when large groups are staying there.

Three charming, family-run pensions offering comfortable rooms with a bathroom and breakfast are located 3km or less west of the city centre.

Pension Angela (☎/fax 302 23 15; ul Beethowena 12; doubles about 100zł) is cosy and the breakfasts are admirably large. It's accessible by bus No 130 or 184 from the main train station.

Another friendly place is **Pensionat Mac-Tur** (☎/fax 302 41 70; w www.mactur.gda .pl; ul Beethowena 8; rooms per person 70-120zł). It is located only just a few metres from Angela's.

Villa Akme (☎/fax 302 40 21; w www .akme.gda.pl; ul Drwęcka 1; singles/doubles about 110/150zł) has been renovated and is very nice. It's 2km southwest of the main train station and accessible by bus No 118, 155 or 208.

Dom Aktora (☎/fax 301 61 93; ul Straganiarska 55/56; singles/doubles with shared bathroom 200/250zł, apartments from 300zł) is a quaint place offering seven apartments (with TV, sitting room and bathroom) but only two rooms. It's always popular, so be sure to book ahead.

Hotel Hanza (☎ 305 34 27; w www.hanza -hotel.com.pl; ul Tokarska 6; singles/doubles with bathroom & breakfast from 580/650zł) is attractively perched along the waterfront near the Gdańsk Crane. Some rooms have views and all are comfortable and quiet, but you would hope so for this sort of price.

On Spichlerze Island, the **Hotel Novotel Gdańsk** (☎ 300 27 50; e ngdansk@orbis.pl; ul Pszenna 1; singles/doubles with breakfast from 292/366zł), is popular with businessmen and families and offers affordable luxury.

Places to Eat

Bar Mleczny Neptun *(ul Długa 33/34; meals about 12zł)* is classier than your run-of-the-mill milk bar. It's open at 7am for breakfast, but closes at 6pm.

Bar Mleczny Turystyczny *(ul Węglarska 1/4; meals about 10zł)* is more basic than the Neptun, but food is displayed cafeteria-style so it's easier to point at what you want without speaking Polish.

Karzcma Hevelius *(ul Długa 18; soups 5zł, mains from 12zł)* is a favourite: it's cosy and friendly, and you can choose hearty Polish food from a menu in German and English. The lunch specials (from 8zł) are worth looking out for.

Restauracja Kubicki *(ul Wartka 5; mains from 20zł)* is a decent mid-priced place to try Polish food from an English menu. It claims to be one of the oldest places in Gdańsk (established 1918), and offers appropriately old-fashioned decor and service.

Pub Duszek *(ul Św Ducha 119/121; soups 7zł, mains from 12zł)* is one of several similarly quaint and quiet eateries in the back streets offering tasty food. It has a tiny basement and a few tables outside. The menu is in English.

Restaurant Sphinx *(ul Długi Targ 31/32; mains about 14zł)* serves pizzas, as well as large grills with all the trimmings. The long line of people next door are queuing for a 'Sphinx Burger' (5zł), which is so big that a plastic fork is also provided to help you shovel the salads into your mouth.

Green Way *(ul Garncarska 4/6; meals 7-10zł)* is always popular with local vegetarians for sandwiches, crepes and salads.

Pizza Hut and **KFC** are joint tenants at ul Długa 75/76. **McDonald's** *(ul Podwale Grodzkie 1)* is inside the main train station. For self-catering, visit the **supermarket** inside the former Arsenal facing Targ Węglowy.

Entertainment

State Baltic Opera Theatre *(Al Zwycięstwa 15)* is in the suburb of Wrzeszcz, not very far from the commuter train station at the Gdańsk Politechnika.

Teatr Wybrzeże *(Targ Węglowy 1)*, next to the Arsenal, is the main city theatre. Both Polish and foreign classics (all in the Polish language) are often part of the repertoire.

Jazz Club *(Długi Targ 39/40)* is the main jazz venue and has live music on weekends.

Celtic Pub *(ul Lektykarska 3)* is authentic, popular and doesn't try too hard to be too Irish.

Kino Helikon and **Kino Neptun** *(ul Długa 57)*, which share the same premises, both offer newish films in relatively comfortable surroundings.

Getting There & Away

Refer to the Getting There & Away section earlier in this chapter for information about international bus and train services to/from Gdańsk, and international ferry services to/from Gdańsk and Gdynia. For travel to surrounding places, see Around Gdańsk next.

Air From Gdańsk, LOT flies to Warsaw about eight times a day and once a day to Frankfurt and Hamburg. SAS also flies daily to Copenhagen. Tickets for all airlines can be bought at the **LOT** office *(☎ 301 28 21; ul Wały Jagiellońskie 2/4)*.

Bus The **bus terminal** *(ul 3 Maja 12)* handles all domestic and international services. It's behind (west of) the main train station and connected to ul Podwale Grodzkie by an underground passageway. Every day, there are four buses to Olsztyn, four to Toruń, six to Warsaw (50zł, six hours) and one or two to Białystok and Świnoujście. Polski Express also offers daily buses to Warsaw from this bus terminal.

Train The city's main train station, **Gdańsk Główny** *(ul Podwale Grodzkie 1)*, is conveniently located on the western outskirts of the Old Town. Most long-distance trains actually start or finish at Gdynia, so make sure you get on/off quickly at the Gdańsk Główny station.

Each day about 18 trains head to Warsaw, including 10 express trains (59zł 2nd class, five hours) and five InterCity services (3½ hours). Also each day, there are six trains to Olsztyn, 10 to Kraków, five to Wrocław via Poznań, seven to Toruń and four to Szczecin. Trains also head to Białystok and Lublin once or twice a day.

Boat Polferries uses the **ferry terminal** *(ul Przemysłowa)* in Nowy Port, about 5km north of the Main Town but only a short walk from the local commuter train station at Gdańsk Brzeźno. Orbis Travel and the PTTK Office in Gdańsk can provide information and sell tickets.

POLAND

Between 1 May and 30 September, excursion boats leave regularly each day from the dock near the Green Gate in Gdańsk for Sopot (33/46zł one way/return) and Gdynia (39/54zł) – and you can even go to Hel (46/59zł)! From the same dock, boats also head out to Westerplatte (33/46zł) between 1 April and 30 October.

Getting Around
The airport is in Rębiechowo, about 12km northwest of Gdańsk. It's accessible by bus No 110 from the Gdańsk Wrzeszcz local commuter train station or less frequently by Bus B from outside the Gdańsk Główny train station. Taxis will cost about 30zł one-way.

The local commuter train, known as the SKM, runs every 15 minutes almost all day and night between the Gdańsk Główny and Gdynia Główna Osobowa train stations, via the Sopot and Gdańsk Oliwa stations. (Note: the line to Gdańsk Nowy Port, via Gdańsk Brzeźno, is a separate branch line that leaves less regularly from Gdańsk Główny.) Buy tickets at any station and validate them in the machines at the platform entrance.

Cars can be rented from a number of agencies at the airport or organised at any travel agency in Gdańsk.

AROUND GDAŃSK
Gdańsk is part of the so-called Tri-City Area, which stretches 30km along the coast from Gdynia to Gdynia and includes Sopot. Gdynia and Sopot are easy day trips from Gdańsk and both provide cheaper and nicer accommodation options.

Sopot
☎ 058 • pop 43,000
Sopot, 12km north of Gdańsk, has been one of Poland's most fashionable seaside resorts since the 19th century. It has an easy-going atmosphere and there are long tidy stretches of sandy **beach**.

From the train station, turn left (north) and walk about 200m to the **tourist office** (☎ 550 37 83; ul Dworcowa 4; open 8am-7pm Mon-Fri, 10am-6pm Sat-Sun May-Sept, 8am-4pm Mon-Fri Oct-Apr). From there, head down ul Bohaterów Monte Cassino, one of Poland's most attractive pedestrian malls, past the church to Poland's longest **pier** (515m). Signposted from along this mall is an Internet centre, **www.c@fe** (ul Chmielewskiego 5a).

Opposite Pension Wanda (see below), the **Museum Sopotu** was being renovated at the time of research.

Places to Stay & Eat There is little in the way of budget options, but the tourist office can arrange **private rooms** from 50/100zł for singles/doubles.

Camping Nr 19 (☎ 550 04 45; ul Zamkowa Góra 25; camping per person/tent 15/15zł, 3-bed cabins about 100zł; open May-Sept) is the largest and best camping ground in Sopot. It's at the north end of town near the Sopot Kamienny Potok commuter train station, which is one stop north of the Sopot station.

Pension Wanda (☎ 550 30 37, fax 551 57 25; ul Poniatowskiego 7; singles/doubles with bathroom & breakfast from 150/210zł) has a handy location (about 500m southeast of the pier) and some rooms with views.

Hotel Eden (☎/fax 551 15 03; ul Kordeckiego 4/6; doubles without/with bathroom from 120/180zł) is a quiet pension overlooking the town park one street from the beach.

Grand Hotel Orbis (☎ 551 00 41; e sograd@orbis.pl; ul Powstańców Warszawy 12/14; singles/doubles with bathroom & breakfast 330/450zł) is next to the pier overlooking the beach. It has just been renovated and is worth a splurge. The elegant **restaurant** offers marvellous views and impeccable service.

Bistros and **cafés** serving almost every conceivable cuisine sprout up in summer along the mall and the promenades. **Restaurant Irena** (ul Chopina 36; mains from 12zł), two blocks south of the tourist office, continues to be popular among holiday-makers for its hearty Polish food and friendly service.

Getting There & Away From the **Sopot train station** (ul Dworcowa 7), local commuter trains run every 15 minutes to Gdańsk Główny and Gdynia Główna Osobowa stations. Excursion boats leave several times a day (May to September) from the Sopot pier to Gdańsk, Gdynia and Hel.

Gdynia
☎ 058 • pop 260,000
Gdynia, 9km north of Sopot, is the third part of the Tri-City Area. It has nothing of the historic splendour of Gdańsk, nor relaxed beach ambience of Sopot; it's just a busy, young city with an omnipresent port atmosphere.

From the main Gdynia Główna Osobowa train station – where there is a **tourist office** – follow ul 10 Lutego east for about 1.5km to the pier. At the end of the pier is the recommended **Oceanographic Museum & Aquarium** (admission 8.50zł; open 10am-5pm daily), which houses a vast array of sea creatures, both alive and embalmed.

A 20-minute walk uphill (follow the signs) from Teatr Muzyczny on Plac Grunwaldzki (about 300m southwest of the start of the pier) leads to **Kamienna Góra**. This hill offers wonderful **views**, best enjoyed while sipping a drink at the **Major Restaurant**.

Places to Stay & Eat To be honest, no hotel in central Gdynia is worth recommending. Those on a budget can try the **Youth Hostel** (☎ 627 10 05, ul Energetyków 13a; dorm beds about 20zł; open year-round). It's about 3km northwest of the city centre and accessible by bus Nos 104 or 150 from ul Jana z Kolna near the bus terminal.

Alternatively, contact **Biuro Zakwaterowań Turus** (☎ 621 82 65; ul Starowiejska 47; entrance from ul Dworcowa), opposite the train station, about a private room. Singles/doubles cost from 65/95zł, but a minimum booking of three nights is often required.

There are plenty of **milk bars** in the city centre and several upmarket **fish restaurants** along the pier. **Bistro Kwadrans** (Skwer Kościuszki 20; mains 8-12zł), one block north of the median strip along ul 10 Lutego, is recommended for tasty Polish food.

Getting There & Away Local commuter trains link the **Gdynia Główna Osobowa** station (Plac Konstytucji) with Sopot and Gdańsk every 15 minutes. From the same station, trains regularly go each day to Hel (in summer) and Lębork (for Łeba). From the small **bus terminal** outside this train station, minibuses also go to Hel and Łeba, and two buses run daily to Świnoujście.

Stena Line uses the **Terminal Promowy** (ul Kwiatkowskiego 60), about 5km northwest of Gdynia. Ask about the free shuttle central bus between Gdańsk and here, via Gdynia and Sopot, when you book your ticket, or take bus No 150 from outside the main train station.

Between May and September, excursion boats leave regularly throughout the day to Gdańsk, Sopot and Hel from a point halfway along the pier in Gdynia.

Hel

This old fishing village at the tip of the, umm, phallic Hel Peninsula north of Gdańsk is now a popular beach resort. The pristine, windswept **beach** on the Baltic side stretches the length of the peninsula. On the other (southern) side the sea is popular for **windsurfing**; equipment can be rented at the villages of Władysławowo and Jastarnia. Hel is a popular day trip from Gdańsk and worth visiting – if only to say that you've 'been to Hel and back'!

The odd-sounding **Fokarium** (ul Morska 2), along the main road, is home to many endangered Baltic grey seals. The 15th-century **Gothic church** (bul Nadmorksi 2), along the esplanade near the Fokarium, houses the **Museum of Fishery** (admission 5.50zł; open about 10am-4pm Tues-Sun).

The best places to stay are any of the numerous **private rooms** offered in local houses (mostly from May to September). Expect to pay about 75zł per double.

To Hel, minibuses leave every hour or so from outside the main train station in Gdynia and several slow trains depart from Gdańsk and Gdynia daily from May to September. Hel is also accessible by excursion boat from Gdańsk, Sopot and Gdynia – see those sections earlier for details.

Łeba

☎ 059 • pop 4100

Łeba ('WEH-bah') is a sleepy fishing village that turns into a popular seaside resort between May and September. The wide sandy **beach** stretches in both directions and the water is reputedly the cleanest along the Polish coast – ideal if you're looking for a beach resort.

From the train station, and adjacent bus stop, head east along ul 11 Listopada as far as the main street, ul Kościuszko. Then turn left (north) and walk about 1.5km to the better eastern beach via the esplanade (ul Nadmorska); if in doubt, follow the signs to the beachside Hotel Neptune.

The **tourist office** (☎ 866 25 65; open 8am-4pm Mon-Fri May-Sept) is inside the train station. There are several **kantors** along ul 11 Listopada.

Słowiński National Park This 186-sq-km park begins just west of Łeba and stretches along the coast for 33km. It contains a diversity of habitats, including forests, lakes, bogs and beaches, but the main attraction is the

POLAND

huge number of massive (and shifting) **sand dunes** that create a desert landscape. The wildlife and birdlife is also remarkably rich.

From Łeba to the sand dunes, follow the signs from near the train station northwest along ul Turystyczna and take the road west to the park entrance in the hamlet of Rąbka. Minibuses ply this road in summer from Łeba; alternatively, it's a pleasant walk or bike ride (8km). No cars or buses are allowed beyond the park entrance.

Places to Stay & Eat Many houses offering **private rooms** open their doors all year, but finding a room during the summer tourist season can be tricky.

Camping grounds include the **Intercamp 84** (*☎ 866 12 06; ul Turystyczna 10*) and **Camping Nr 41 Ambré** (*☎ 866 24 72, ul Nadmorska 9a*) – but bring mosquito repellent if you don't want to be eaten alive.

Biuro Wczasów Przymorze (*☎ 866 13 60; ul Dworcowa 1*), diagonally opposite the train station, also arranges private rooms.

Hotel Wodnik (*☎ 866 13 66; **w** www .wodnik.leba.pl; ul Nadmorska 10; singles/ doubles with bathroom & breakfast from 120/150zł*) is one of several pensions along the esplanade on the eastern side of the beach.

There are plenty of decent **eateries** in the town centre and along ul Nadmorska.

Getting There & Away The usual transit point is Lębork, 29km south of Łeba. To Lębork, slow trains run every hour or two from Gdańsk, via Gdynia, and there are buses every hour from Gdynia. Between Lębork and Łeba, you have a choice of four trains or eight buses a day. In summer (June to August), two buses and two trains run directly between Gdynia and Łeba and one train a day travels to/from Warsaw (eight hours).

Malbork
☎ 055 • pop 42,000

Malbork, 58km southeast of Gdańsk, boasts the **Malbork Castle** (*admission 15.50zł; grounds open 9am-4pm, rooms 9am-3pm Tues-Sun*), the largest Gothic castle in Europe. It was built by the Teutonic Knights in 1276 and became capital of the Grand Master of Teutonic Knights in 1309. It was badly damaged during WWII, but has been almost completely rebuilt since. It was placed on the Unesco World Heritage list in 1997.

Admission includes a compulsory three-hour tour (in Polish). Tours in English, French or German are available for an additional 126zł per group, but should be arranged in advance. The last tickets are sold at 2.30pm.

The **Youth Hostel** (*☎ 272 24 08; ul Żeromskiego 45; dorms beds about 25zł; open year-round*) is in a local school about 500m south of the castle.

Hotel & Restaurant Zbyszko (*☎ 272 26 40, fax 272 33 95; ul Kościuszki 43; singles/ doubles with bathroom & breakfast 120/ 170zł*) is conveniently located along the road to the castle. The rooms are fairly unremarkable but serviceable for one night.

Hotel & Restaurant Zamek (*☎/fax 272 33 67; singles/doubles with bathroom, TV & breakfast 190/210zł*) is inside a restored medieval building in the Lower Castle. The rooms are a bit old-fashioned, but the bathrooms are new.

The train and bus stations are about 1km southeast of the castle. As you leave the train station, turn right, cut across the highway, head down ul Kościuszki and follow the signs to the castle. Malbork is on the busy Gdańsk-Warsaw railway line, so it's an easy day trip from Gdańsk. There are buses every hour to Malbork from Gdynia and five daily from Gdańsk. From Malbork, trains also regularly go to Elbląg, Toruń and Olsztyn.

ŚWINOUJŚCIE
☎ 091 • pop 45,000

In a remote northwestern corner of Poland, Świnoujście ('Shvee-no-OOYSH-cheh') is quite a detour from other major destinations in Poland. However, if you're passing through on your way to/from Germany or Scandinavia, it's an enjoyable stopover.

Świnoujście sits on two islands at the mouth of the Świna River. Wolin Island on the southeastern side of the river has the port and bus and trains stations, while the town centre is across the river to the northwest on Uznam Island. A free ferry connects both sides every 15 minutes.

The **Tourist Information Centre** (*☎/fax 322 49 99, **e** cit@fornet.com.pl; open 9am-5pm daily*) is inside one of the two adjacent townside ferry terminals on Uznam Island. From either townside terminal, walk 400m west along the waterfront and then continue 300m northwest on ul Armii Krajowej to Plac Wolności. Here are the **post office**, **kantors**

Gdańsk's Main Town Hall tower looms above the pedestrian Długi Targ – once part of the Royal Way

Polish folk dancers in traditional costume twirl in medieval Rynek Główny, Kraków

Top of the world, Mt Rysy, High Tatras, Slovakia

The modern Nový most, Bratislava, Slovakia

Ruins of Spišský hrad, Slovakia's largest castle

Štrbské pleso, one of many glacial lakes in the Vysoké Tatry (High Tatras) of Slovakia

and **Internet centres**. From the square, the **beach** is 700m north along ul Piłsudskiego.

Things to See & Do

The self-explanatory **Museum of Seafishing** *(Plac Rybaka 1; admission 4.50zł; open 9am-4pm Tues-Fri, 11am-4pm Sat-Sun)* is about 400m west of the ferry terminals in town.

Locally available maps indicate pleasant **cycling** paths all around the town and countryside. Bikes can be rented from around the two ferry terminals in town.

About 15km east of Świnoujście, **Międzyzdroje** is a popular seaside resort with a lovely **beach** surrounded by the thickly forested **Wolin National Park**. This park features many lakes, including the horseshoe-shaped **Lake Czajcze** and the aptly named **Lake Turkusowe** (Turquoise). There's a small **bison reserve** *(admission 5zł; open 10am-6pm Tues-Sun June-Sept)* 2km east of Międzyzdroje.

Places to Stay & Eat

The rates given below are for the very busy high season.

Camping Nr 44 Relax *(☎/fax 321 39 12; ul Słowackiego 1; camping per person/tent 10/5zł, 3-bed cabins about 135zł; open June-Sept)* enjoys an excellent location along a secluded piece of the beach. Turn right (east) from along ul Piłsudskiego.

The **Youth Hostel** *(☎/fax 327 06 13; ul Gdyńska 26; dorm beds 22zł; open all year)* is a long way from the beach – to get there follow the signs along ul Grunwaldzka from Plac Wolności.

Dom Rybaka *(☎/fax 321 29 43; ul Wybrzeże Władysława IV 22; singles/doubles 36/66zł, doubles with bathroom 110zł)* is pleasantly located about 500m west of the townside ferry terminals.

The best places to eat and drink in Świnoujście are the two **food centres** along the promenade, ul Żeromskiego.

Getting There & Away

The border crossing for Germany is 2km northwest along ul Konstytucji 3 Maja from Plac Wolności.

From Świnoujście, buses regularly go to Gdynia and Międzyzdroje, but trains are more frequent. Every day, slow trains go every two hours to Szczecin (2¼ hours), via Międzyzdroje, and fast trains go to Warsaw (summer only), Kraków, Poznań and Wrocław.

International ferries depart from the **ferry terminal** near Świnoujście Port train station, one stop beyond the main Świnoujście station. **Morskie Biuro Podróży PŻB** *(☎ 322 43 96; ul Brema 9/2)* sells tickets for Polferries; **Biuro Podróży Partner** *(☎ 322 43 97; ul Bohaterów Września 83/14)* handles tickets for Unity Line. Both are only a few paces from the post office. See the Getting There & Away section earlier in this chapter for information about ferries from Denmark and Sweden to Świnoujście, and boats from there to Germany.

SZCZECIN

☎ 091 • pop 425,000

Szczecin ('SHCHEH-cheen') is the main urban centre and port in northwestern Poland. It has a colourful and stormy history, but sadly most remnants were destroyed during WWII. Therefore, Szczecin has none of the charm of Toruń or Poznań, but it's a worthwhile stopover if you're travelling to/from Germany.

The **tourist information office** *(☎ 434 04 40, Al Niepodległości 1)* is helpful but the **tourist office** *(☎ 434 02 86; open 10am-6pm daily)* in the castle is better set up. The **post office** and most **kantors** and **Internet centres** are along the main street, Al Niepodległości.

The city's major attraction is undoubtedly the huge and rather austere **Castle of the Pomeranian Princess** *(ul Korsazy 34; admission free; open dawn-dusk daily)*, 500m northeast of the tourist office. Originally built in the mid-14th century, it was enlarged in 1577 and rebuilt after WWII. Inside the grounds, the **Castle Museum** *(admission 8zł; open about 10am-4pm Tues-Sun)* features displays about the bizarre history of the castle.

A short walk down (south) from the castle is the 15th-century **Old Town Hall** *(Plac Rzepichy)*, which contains the **Historical Museum of Szczecin** *(admission 6zł; open about 10-4pm Tues-Sun)*. Nearby is the charmingly rebuilt 'old town' with cafés and bars. Three blocks northwest of the castle is the **National Museum** *(ul Staromłyńska 27; admission 5.50zł; open about 10am-4pm Tues-Sun)*.

Places to Stay & Eat

Camping PTTK Marina *(☎/fax 460 11 65, ul Przestrzenna 23; camping per person/tent 10/5zł, double cabins from 85zł; open May-Sept)* is on the shore of Lake Dąbie – get off at the Szczecin Dąbie train station and ask for directions (2km).

POLAND

Youth Hostel PTSM (☎ *422 47 61; ul Monte Cassino 19a; dorm beds 10-35zł; open year-round*) is located 2km northwest of the tourist office.

Hotel Promorski (☎ *433 61 51; Plac Brama Portowa 4; singles/doubles with shared bathroom from 60/64zł*) is fairly basic but it is perfectly adequate. It's central (200m west of Al Niepodłegłości), but a little noisy.

Hotel Podzamcze (☎/fax *812 14 04; ul Sienna 1/3; singles/doubles with bathroom & breakfast 180/230zł*) is in a charming location near the Old Town Hall.

Two restaurants about 200m west along ul Obrońców Stalingradu from the northern end of Al Niepodłegłości are popular: **Bar Turysta**, at No 6a, is a standard milk bar, while **Bar Rybarex**, at No 6 next door, is ideal for fresh fish with salad and chips.

Dublin Pub (*ul Kaszubska 57*), around the corner from the Promorski, is popular and offers a limited range of meals.

Getting There & Away

LOT flies between Szczecin and Warsaw about seven times a day and most days to Copenhagen. Book at the **LOT** office (☎ *433 50 58; ul Wyzwolenia 17*), about 200m up from the northern end of Al Niepodłegłości.

The **bus terminal** (*Plac Grodnicki*), and the nearby **Szczecin Główny** train station (*ul Kolumba*), are 600m southeast of the tourist office. Two buses a day head for Gdynia, but there's little else of use to travellers. Express and fast trains travel regularly to Poznań, Gdańsk and Warsaw (34zł 2nd-class express, seven hours), and slow trains plod along every two hours to Świnoujście.

Advance tickets for trains and ferries are available from **Orbis Travel** (☎ *434 26 18; Plac Zwycięstwa 1*), about 200m west of the main post office.

Warmia & Masuria

Warmia and Masuria are in northeastern Poland, to the east of the lower Vistula Valley. Here the Scandinavian glacier left behind a typical postglacial landscape characterised by some 3000 lakes, many linked by rivers and canals, creating a system of waterways enjoyed by yachties and canoeists. The winding shorelines are surrounded by hills and forests, making this picturesque lake district one of the most attractive areas in the country. There's little industry and so little pollution.

OLSZTYN

☎ 089 • pop 165,000

Olsztyn ('OL-shtin') is a likeable transport hub with an attractive old town of cobblestoned streets, art galleries, cafés, bars and restaurants. It's also the obvious base from where to explore the region, including the Great Masurian Lakes district (see later).

Olsztyn's history has been a successive overlapping of Prussian and Polish influences. From 1466 to 1773 the town belonged to the kingdom of Poland. Nicolaus Copernicus, administrator of Warmia, commanded Olsztyn Castle from 1516 to 1520. With the first partition of Poland, Olsztyn became Prussian Allenstein and remained so until 1945. The city was badly damaged during WWII, but has been mostly rebuilt.

Everyone should stop at the helpful **tourist office** (☎/fax *535 35 65;* e *oldtur@praca.gov .pl; ul Staromiejska 1; open 8am-3.30pm Mon-Fri*). The few **kantors** around town are marked on the map; otherwise, try the **PKO Bank** (*cnr ul 1 Maja & ul 11 Listopada*).

For snail mail, go to the **main post office** (*ul Pieniężnego*); for 'cybermail', try the **Internet centre** inside the **telephone office** (*ul Pieniężnego*) opposite. Books and maps are sold at **EMPiK** (*ul 1 Maja*) and the quaint little **Ambassador Bookshop** in the Gazeta Olsztyńska Museum.

Things to See

The **High Gate** (or Upper Gate) is all that remains of the 14th-century city walls. A little further west, the 14th-century **Castle of the Chapter of Warmia** (*ul Zamkowa 2*) contains the **Museum of Warmia & Mazury** (*admission 6zł; open 9am-5pm Tues-Sun May-Sept, 10am-4pm Tues-Sun Oct-Apr*). It features plenty of exhibits about Copernicus, who made some astronomical observations here in the early 16th century, as well as some coins and art.

The **Rynek** (Market Square) was destroyed during WWII and rebuilt in a style only superficially reverting to the past. To the east, the red-brick Gothic **Cathedral of Św Jakuba Większego** (*ul Długosza*) dates from the 14th century. Its 60m tower was added in 1596. **Gazeta Olsztyńska Museum** (*ul Targ Rybny 1; admission 5zł; open 9am-4pm Tues-Sun*)

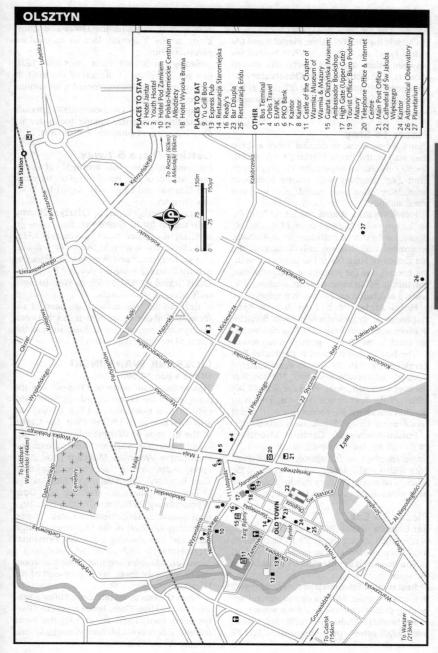

OLSZTYN

PLACES TO STAY
2 Hotel Jantar
3 Youth Hostel
10 Hotel Pod Zamkiem
12 Polsko-Niemieckie Centrum
15 Młodzieży
18 Hotel Wysoka Brama

PLACES TO EAT
9 Yu Grill Boro
13 Express Pub
14 Restauracja Staromiejska
16 Ready's
23 Bar Dziupla
25 Restauracja Eridu

OTHER
1 Bus Terminal
4 Orbis Travel
5 EMPIK
6 PKO Bank
7 Kantor
11 Castle of the Chapter of
   Warmia; Museum of
   Warmia & Mazury
15 Gazeta Olsztyńska Museum;
   Ambassador Bookshop
17 High Gate (Upper Gate)
19 Tourist Office; Biuro Podróży
   Mazury
20 Telephone Office & Internet
   Centre
21 Main Post Office
22 Cathedral of Sw Jakuba
24 Kantor
26 Astronomical Observatory
27 Planetarium

is a town museum housed in a building once occupied by the local newspaper.

Outside the Old Town, the **Planetarium** (*Al Piłsudskiego 38; admission 7zł*) has shows between 10am and 4pm every day except Monday. The **Astronomical Observatory** (*ul Żołnierska 13; admission 7zł*) offers tours between 9am and 3.30pm every day but Monday – get tickets from the Planetarium.

Places to Stay

Conveniently between the Old Town and the train station, the **Youth Hostel** (*☎ 527 66 50, fax 527 68 70; ul Kopernika 45; dorm beds from 24zł, doubles with shared bathroom from 56zł; open year-round*) is a well-run place and tidy.

Hotel Wysoka Brama (*☎/fax 527 36 75, ul Staromiejska 1; dorm beds 16zł, singles/doubles with shared bathroom from 45/58zł, apartment 160zł*) is superbly located in the old section of High Gate. The dorms are nothing special and the rooms are unremarkable, but the large apartment (with kitchen, TV, seating and bathroom) is worth a splurge.

Hotel Jantar (*☎ 533 54 52; ul Kętrzyńskiego 5; singles/doubles from 50/80zł, doubles with bath from 100zł*) is convenient but stuck in the 1960s – perhaps a last resort.

The best option in town is the **Hotel Pod Zamkiem** (*☎ 535 12 87; e hotel@olsztyn .com.pl; ul Nowowiejskiego 10; singles/doubles with bathroom, TV & breakfast 130/180zł*) is the best option in town. This cosy pension has charming rooms in a convenient spot near the castle. Breakfast is excellent.

Polsko-Niemieckie Centrum Młodzieży (*☎ 534 07 80, fax 527 69 33; ul Okopowa 25; singles/doubles with bathroom & breakfast 160/180zł*) is also ideally situated next to the castle. The rooms are very comfortable (some have views of the castle) and staff are friendly.

Places to Eat

Bar Dziupla (*Rynek 9/10; mains from 10zł*) is renowned among locals for its tasty Polish food, such as *pierogi*. The restaurant is small so you may need to order takeaway and eat in the square.

Restauracja Staromiejska (*ul Staromiejska 4/6; mains about 18zł*) is one of several appealing cafés facing the tiny town square.

Restauracja Eridu (*ul Prosta 3/4; mains from 12zł*) offers some inexpensive Middle Eastern choices.

Yu Grill Boro (*ul Nowowiejskiego; grills about 15zł*), opposite the Hotel Pod Zamkiem, serves Yugoslav fare in an outdoor parkside setting.

Ready's (*ul Staromiejska; grills from 12zł*) is a popular place at the top of the mall. It serves mainly grills, smothered with various sauces and salads.

Express Pub (*ul Okopowa; daily specials about 8zł*) is popular among locals for its cosy interior and authentic Polish food.

Getting There & Away

Each day from the **bus terminal** (*ul Partyzantów*) four or five buses travel to Białystok and Gdańsk, and another 10 depart for Warsaw (five hours).

Also every day from the **Olsztyn Główny** train station (*ul Partyzantów*), four trains go to Białystok, three head to Warsaw (33zł 2nd-class express), eight leave for Gdańsk, two go to Poznań and Wrocław, and six depart for Toruń (a route not covered by buses). **Orbis Travel** (*☎ 527 44 55; Al Piłsudskiego*) sells advance train tickets.

Refer to the relevant sections later for information about buses and trains between Olsztyn and regional attractions, such as the Great Masurian Lakes district.

LIDZBARK WARMIŃSKI
☎ 089 • pop 18,000

This town, 46km north of Olsztyn, was the main seat of the Warmian bishops from 1350 until Prussia took over in 1773. Copernicus also lived here from 1503 to 1510. The **Castle of the Bishops of Warmia** miraculously survived numerous wars and now houses the entertaining **Warmian Museum** (*Plac Zamkowy; admission 8.50zł; open 9am-5pm Tues-Sun May-Sept, 10am-4pm Oct-Apr*).

The best places to stay are the **Dom Wycieczkowy PTTK** (*☎ 767 25 21; ul Wysoka Brama 2; singles/doubles with shared bathroom 42/65zł*) in the 15th-century **High Gate**; and the charming, but small, **Pensjonat Pizza Hotel** (*☎ 767 52 59; ul Konstytucji 3 Maja 26; doubles without/with bathroom 98/132zł*), only about 500m northeast of the High Gate.

From the bus terminal, about 500m northwest of the High Gate, buses travel to Olsztyn every hour. There are also regular buses travelling between Lidzbark Warmiński and Frombork and Gdańsk.

FROMBORK

☎ 055 • pop 2600

This small, sleepy town on the shore of the Vistula Lagoon was founded in the 13th century. A fortified ecclesiastical township was later erected on Cathedral Hill overlooking the lagoon. Frombork is most famous, however, as the place where Copernicus wrote his astounding *On the Revolutions of the Celestial Spheres*.

Cathedral Hill is now occupied by the extensive **Nicolaus Copernicus Museum**, with several sections requiring separate tickets. Perhaps the highlight is a red-brick Gothic **cathedral** (*admission 5zł; open 9.30am-5pm Mon-Sat May-Sept, 9am-4pm Oct-Apr*) built in the 14th century.

Youth Hostel Copernicus (☎ *243 74 53; ul Elbląska 11; dorm beds about 15zł; open year-round*) also allows camping. It's 500m west of Cathedral Hill on the road to Elbląg.

Dom Wycieczkowy PTTK (☎ *243 72 52; ul Krasickiego 2; dorm beds from 25zł; singles/ doubles with bathroom from 45/65zł*) is large and only 80m west of Cathedral Hill.

The bus and train stations are along the riverfront about 300m northwest of the castle. Frombork can be directly reached by bus from Elbląg (hourly), Gdańsk, Lidzbark Warmiński and Malbork. From Olsztyn, get a connection in Elbląg.

ELBLĄG-OSTRÓDA CANAL

This 82km waterway between Elbląg and Ostróda is the longest navigable canal still used in Poland. Built between 1848 and 1876, it was used for transporting timber from the rich inland forests to the Baltic Sea. To resolve the 99.5m difference in water levels, the canal utilises an unusual system of five water-powered slipways so that boats are actually sometimes carried across dry land on rail-mounted trolleys.

Normally, **excursion boats** (mid-May to late September) depart from both Elbląg and Ostróda daily at 8am (80zł, 11 hours), but actual departures depend on the number of willing passengers. For information, call the **boat operators** (*in Elbląg* ☎ *055-232 43 07, in Ostróda 089-646 38 71*).

In Elbląg, **Camping Nr 61** (☎*/fax 055-232 43 07; ul Panieńska 14; cabins 75zł; open May-Sept*), right at the boat dock, is pleasant. **Hotel Galeona** (☎*/fax 055-232 48 08; ul Krótka 5; singles/doubles without bathroom

52/65zł*) in the city centre is good value. In Ostróda, try **Dom Wycieczkowy Drwęci** (☎*/fax 646 30 35, ul Mickiewicza 7; singles/ doubles with shared bathroom 55/65zł*), 500m east of the bus and train stations.

Elbląg is easily accessible by train and bus from any of the cities of Gdańsk, Malbork, Frombork and Olsztyn. Ostróda is also regularly connected by train to Olsztyn and Toruń and by bus to Olsztyn and Elbląg.

THE GREAT MASURIAN LAKES

The Great Masurian Lakes district east of Olsztyn is a verdant land of rolling hills interspersed with glacial lakes, peaceful farms and dense forests. The district has over 2000 lakes, the largest of which is **Lake Śniardwy** (110 sq km), Poland's largest lake. About 200km of canals connect these lakes, so the area is a prime destination for yachties and canoeists, as well as those who prefer to hike, fish and mountain-bike.

The detailed *Wielkie Jeziora Mazurskie* map (1:100,000) is essential for anyone exploring the region by boat, canoe, bike, car or foot. The *Warmia i Mazury* map (1:300,000), published by Vicon and available at regional tourist offices, is perfect for anyone using private or public transport, and has explanations in English.

Getting Around

Yachties can sail the larger lakes all the way from Węgorzewo to Ruciane-Nida. Expect to pay between $25 and $100 per day for a boat for four to five people with mattresses.

Canoeists will perhaps prefer the more intimate surroundings along rivers and smaller lakes. The most popular kayak route takes about 10 days (106km) and follows rivers, canals and lakes from Sorkwity to Ruciane-Nida with places to stay and eat along the way. Brochures explaining this route are available at regional tourist offices. There's also an extensive network of trails – ideal for **hiking** and **mountain biking** – around the lakes.

Most travellers prefer to enjoy the lakes in comfort on the **excursion boats**. Boats run daily (May to September) between Giżycko and Ruciane-Nida, via Mikołajki; and daily (June to August) between Węgorzewo and Ruciane-Nida, via Giżycko and Mikołajki. In practice, however, services are more reliable from late June to late August. Schedules and fares are clearly posted at the lake ports.

POLAND

THE GREAT MASURIAN LAKES

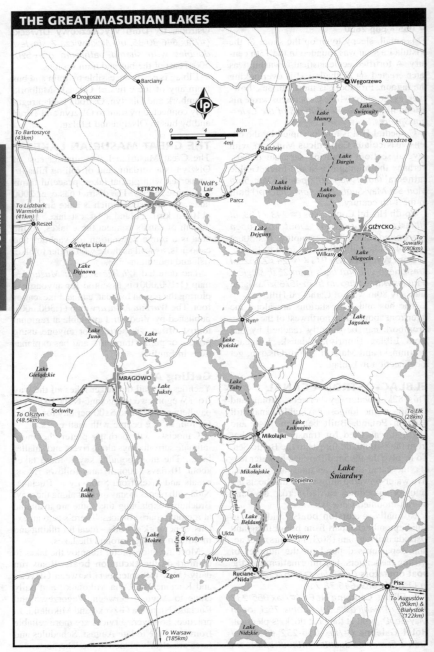

Travelling around the lakes district by train and bus is not very convenient, so allow plenty of time. Otherwise, you can organise a tour with **Diuna** (☎/fax 087-423 02 09; e diuna@post.pl; Pisz), or **Biuro Podróży Mazury** (☎/fax 089-527 40 59; e postmaster@ pttkmazury.pl; ul Staromiejska 1, Olsztyn).

Reszel

Reszel, about 60km northeast of Olsztyn, has an old town dominated by the massive 14th-century **Reszel Castle** (admission 1zł; open dawn-dusk daily). It has been partially converted into an **art gallery** and **restaurant**. It also houses the **Zamek Reszel Kreativ Hotel** (☎ 089-755 01 09, fax 755 15 97; singles/ doubles with bathroom & breakfast 180/ 230zł), which offers nicely furnished rooms with lovely views. Plenty of buses link Reszel with Kętrzyn, Święta Lipka and Olsztyn.

Święta Lipka

This hamlet boasts an exquisite 17th-century **church** (admission free; open 7am-7pm daily), considered one of the purest examples of late-baroque architecture in Poland. One highlight of the interior is the lavishly decorated organ. The angels adorning the 5000 pipes play their instruments and dance to the music when the organ is sounded. This mechanism is demonstrated several times daily from May to September and recitals are held Friday nights from June to August.

Ask any of the regional tourist offices for a list of homes in Święta Lipka offering **private rooms**. There are several places to eat and drink near the church.

Buses run to Kętrzyn and Reszel every hour or so, but less often to Olsztyn and Lidzbark Warmiński.

Kętrzyn

The 14th-century **castle** (admission free; permanently open) in this charming village houses the worthwhile **Regional Museum** (admission 3zł; open about 9am-4pm Mon-Fri, 9am-3pm Sat & Sun).

Hotel Koch (☎ 089-752 20 58, fax 752 23 90; ul Traugutta 3; singles/doubles 125/ 180zł), in the centre, is the best place to stay.

Zajazd Pod Zamkiem (☎ 089-752 31 17, fax 752 20 41; ul Struga 3) is a classy restaurant next to the castle. It also offers a few sumptuous singles/doubles with bathroom and breakfast for 90/130zł.

Buses leave regularly for most places in the lake district, as well as Olsztyn. A few trains a day go to Gdańsk, via Elbląg, and Olsztyn.

Wolf's Lair

Hitler's wartime headquarters was at Gierłoż, 8km east of Kętrzyn, in Wolf's Lair (admission 7zł; open 8am-dusk daily). Hitler arrived here on 26 June 1941 (four days after the invasion of the Soviet Union) and stayed until 20 November 1944, except for a few short trips to the outside world.

In July 1944 a group of pragmatic, high-ranking German officers tried to assassinate Hitler. The leader of the plot, Claus von Stauffenberg, arrived from Berlin on 20 July on the pretext of informing Hitler of the newly formed reserve army. As a frequent guest he had no problems entering the meeting with a bomb in his briefcase. He placed his briefcase a few feet from Hitler and left to take a pre-arranged phone call. The explosion killed two staff members and wounded half a dozen others, but Hitler suffered only minor injuries. Stauffenberg and some 5000 people involved in the plot were subsequently executed.

On 24 January 1945, as the Red Army approached, the Germans blew up Wolfsschanze (as it was known in German), so most bunkers were destroyed. However, cement slabs – some 8.5m thick – and twisted metal remain, giving this hideous place an eerie feel.

A large map is posted at the entrance and the remaining bunkers are clearly labelled in English. Guides speaking English and German also wait at the entrance and charge about 65zł per group for a 90-minute tour of the site. Booklets allowing a self-guided walking tour are available in English and German at the kiosk in the car park.

Hotel Wilcze Gniazdo (☎ 089-752 44 29, fax 752 44 92; singles/doubles with bathroom & breakfast 60/80zł) is charmless but functional. A **restaurant** is attached.

Catch one of several daily buses from Kętrzyn to Węgorzewo and get off at the entrance. Between May and September, bus No 1 from the train station in Kętrzyn also goes to the site.

Giżycko
☎ 087

Set on the northern shore of Lake Niegocin, Giżycko ('Ghee-ZHITS-ko') is the largest lakeside centre in the region. There are some significant ruins of the **Boyen Fortress** (admission free; permanently open), built by the Prussians between 1844 and 1855 to protect the border with Russia.

Near the main square (Plac Grunwaldzki) are the **tourist information office** (☎ 428 52 65, [e] infoturyst@wp.pl; ul Warszawska 17, enter from ul Kętrzyńskiego) and **Bank Pekao** (ul Olsztyńska 17). There are some **kantors** in the town centre, including one at **Orbis Travel** (ul Dąbrowskiego 3), about 250m east of the main square.

Sailing boats are available from **Almatur** (☎ 428 33 88; ul Moniuszki 24), 700m west of the fortress, **Centrum Mazur** at Camping Nr 1 Zamek and **Orbis Travel**.

Hotel Wodnik (see next) rents out bicycles and kayaks, sell tickets for the excursion boats and arranges car rental.

Places to Stay & Eat Just west of the canal, **Camping Nr 1 Zamek** (☎ 428 34 10; ul Moniuszki 1; camping per person/tent 15/10zł, cabins about 22zł per person; open mid-June–early Sept) is simple but central. **Motel Zamek** (☎ 428 24 19; doubles 120zł; open May–Sept) is part of the same complex.

The **Youth Hostel** (☎ 428 29 59; dorm beds 18zł; open year-round) is in the Boyen Fortress.

Hotel Wodnik (☎ 428 38 72, fax 428 39 58; ul 3 Maja 2; singles/doubles with bathroom & breakfast from 88/129zł), just off the main square, is good value.

Café Bar Ekran (Plac Grunwaldzki; mains from 12zł) serves some very tasty home-made Polish food.

Getting There & Away From the train station, on the southern edge of town near the lake, around eight trains run daily to Kętrzyn and Olsztyn, and two head to Gdańsk.

From the adjacent bus terminal, buses travel regularly to Węgorzewo, Mikołajki, Kętrzyn and Olsztyn. Also, one or two buses go daily to Lidzbark Warmiński and six head to Warsaw.

Mikołajki
☎ 087
Mikołajki ('Mee-ko-WAHY-kee'), 86km east of Olsztyn, is a picturesque little village

and probably the best base for exploring the lakes. The **tourist office** (☎/fax 421 68 50; Plac Wolności 3) is in the town centre. There are several **kantors** nearby, but there is nowhere to change travellers cheques or get cash advances.

Sailing boats – and often **canoes** – can be hired from **Wioska Żeglarska** (☎ 421 60 40; ul Kowalska 3) at the waterfront, and also from the **Hotel Wałkuski** (☎ 421 64 70; ul 3 Maja 13a).

Lake Śniardwy and Lake Łuknajno are ideal for **cycling**. The tourist office can provide details and maps, and bikes can be rented from **Hotel Wałkuski** or **Pensjonat Mikołajki** (☎ 421 64 37, ul Kajki 18).

Places to Stay & Eat Across the bridge, **Camping Nr 2 Wagabunda** (☎ 421 60 18; ul Leśna 2; camping per person/tent 15/12zł, cabins about 75zł; open May-Sept) is a 10-minute walk southwest of the town centre.

The **Youth Hostel** (☎ 421 64 34; ul Łabędzia 1; dorm beds about 16zł; open July-Aug) is next to the stadium about 500m from the main square on the Łuknajno road.

Several charming pensions and homes that offering **private rooms** are dotted all along ul Kajki, the main street leading around Lake Mikołajskie; another collection of pensions can be found along the roads to Ruciane-Nida and Ełk.

Hotel & Restaurant Mazur (☎ 421 69 41; Plac Wolności; singles/doubles with bathroom & breakfast 150/200zł) is an enticing place overlooking the town square.

Plenty of **eateries** spring up in summer along the waterfront and around the town square to cater for peak-season visitors.

Getting There & Away From the bus terminal, next to the train station on the southern edge of the town near the lake, four buses go to Olsztyn each morning. Otherwise, get a bus (hourly) to Mrągowo and change there for Olsztyn and Kętrzyn. Several buses also go daily to Giżycko and two or three depart in summer for Warsaw.

From the sleepy train station, a few slow trains shuttle along daily to Olsztyn and Kętrzyn, and two fast trains head to Gdańsk and Białystok.

Slovakia

Slovakia's rugged High Tatra mountains, the gentler natural beauty of the Malá Fatra hills, and the canyons of the Slovenský raj offer some of the best terrain in Europe for outdoor activities. Best of all, these places are off the beaten track as most visitors don't get further than Bratislava.

Slovakia is also rich in architecture, arts and folk culture. Bratislava is a lively, cosmopolitan city with a rich cultural life, while East Slovakia boasts a treasury of unspoiled medieval towns. There are about 180 castles in Slovakia, the largest and most photogenic being Spišský hrad, east of Levoča.

Rural Slovaks still preserve their peasant traditions, evident in the colourful crafts and folk costumes you'll see in remote Slovak villages. The majority of Slovaks are warm and friendly people prepared to go out of their way to help you enjoy their country.

Facts about Slovakia

HISTORY

Slavic tribes first occupied what is now Slovakia in the 5th century AD. In 833, the prince of Moravia captured Nitra and formed the Great Moravian Empire, which included all of present Central and West Slovakia, the Czech Republic and parts of neighbouring Poland, Hungary and Germany. The empire converted to Christianity with the arrival of the missionaries, Cyril and Methodius, in 863.

In 907, the Great Moravian Empire collapsed as a result of the political intrigues of its rulers, and invasion by Hungary. By 1018 the whole of Slovakia was annexed to Hungary and remained so for the next 900 years (although the Spiš region of East Slovakia belonged to Poland from 1412 to 1772).

The Hungarians developed mining (silver, copper and gold) and trade (gold, amber and furs). After a Tatar invasion in the 13th century, the Hungarian king invited the Saxon Germans to settle the depopulated northeastern borderlands.

When the Turks overran Hungary in the early 16th century, the capital moved from Buda to Bratislava. After the creation of the

At a Glance

- **Bratislava** – wonderful museums and architecture, stunning vistas of the Carpathian Mountains
- **Malá Fatra** – beautiful mountain valley of Vrátna dolina with endless hiking possibilities
- **Vysoké Tatry** – wide glacial valleys; precipitous mountain walls; clear mountain lakes
- **Levoča** – fine walled town; Renaissance buildings; atmospheric central square
- **Bardejov** – medieval town with preserved moats, towers and bastions

Capital	Bratislava
Population	5.4 million
Official Language	Slovak
Currency	1 koruna (Sk) = 100 halier
Time	GMT/UTC+0100
Country Phone Code	☎ 421

dual Austro-Hungarian monarchy in 1867, a policy of enforced Magyarisation was instituted in Slovakia. In 1907 Hungarian became the sole language of elementary education.

As a reaction to this, Slovak intellectuals cultivated increasingly closer cultural ties with the Czechs, who were themselves dominated by the Austrians. The concept of a single Czecho-Slovakian political entity was born

521

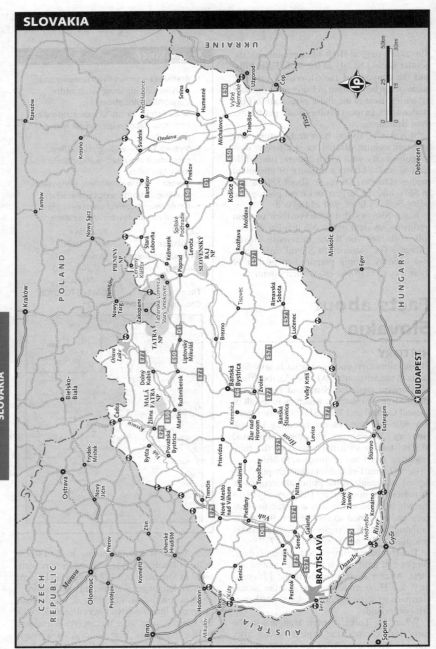

SLOVAKIA

and, after the Austro-Hungarian defeat in WWI, Slovakia, Ruthenia, Bohemia and Moravia were united as Czechoslovakia.

The centralising tendencies of the sophisticated Czechs alienated many Slovaks. After the 1938 Munich Pact that forced Czechoslovakia to cede territory to Germany, Slovakia declared autonomy within a federal state. Hungary took advantage of this instability to annex a strip of southern Slovakia including Košice and Komárno. The day before Hitler's troops invaded Czech territory in March 1939, a fascist puppet state headed by Jozef Tiso (executed in 1947 as a war criminal) was set up, and Slovakia became a German ally.

In August 1944 Slovak partisans instigated the Slovak National Uprising (Slovenské národné povstanie, or SNP) against the Tiso regime, an event that is now a source of national pride. It took the Germans several months to crush the uprising. In the wake of Soviet advances in early 1945, a Czechoslovak government was established at Košice two months before the liberation of Prague.

The Czechoslovakia established after the war was to have been a federal state, but after the communist takeover in February 1948 power once again became centralised in Prague. Many of those who resisted the new communist dictatorship were ruthlessly eliminated by execution, torture and starvation in labour camps.

Although the 1960 constitution granted Czechs and Slovaks equal rights, only the 1968 'Prague Spring' reforms introduced by Alexander Dubček (a rehabilitated Slovak communist) implemented this concept. In August 1968, Soviet troops quashed democratic reform, and although the Czech and Slovak Republics theoretically became equal partners in a federal Czechoslovakia in 1969, the real power remained in Prague.

The Velvet Revolution of 1989 led to a resurgence of Slovak nationalism. In February 1992 the Slovak parliament rejected a treaty that would have perpetuated a federal Czechoslovakia.

The rift deepened with the June 1992 elections, which brought to power the nationalist Movement for a Democratic Slovakia (HZDS) headed by Vladimír Mečiar. In July the Slovak parliament voted to declare sovereignty. Mečiar held negotiations with his Czech counterpart Václav Klaus, but they could not reach a compromise. They subsequently agreed that the federation would peacefully dissolve on 1 January 1993.

Mečiar dominated Slovak politics for the next five years. His authoritarian rule gained control of most of the media, and the passing of antidemocratic laws (and the mistreatment of Slovakia's Hungarian and Roma minorities) attracted criticism from human rights groups, the EU and the US government.

Mečiar's controversial reign ended when Mikuláš Džurinda, leader of the right-leaning Slovak Democratic Coalition (SDK), was elected prime minister in 1998. Yet Slovak society remains deeply polarised. There is still strong support for Mečiar, who took 43% of the vote in the 1999 presidential election, narrowly losing to former communist Rudolf Schuster. Parliamentary elections held in September 2002 returned the ruling coalition of centre-right parties. Mr Mečiar's HZDS party gained the largest single vote at 19.5%, its poorest showing in a decade, but could not form a majority government.

The centre-right coalition, led by Džurinda, includes a new pro-business party ANO (New Citizens Alliance) headed by media mogul Pavol Rusko. The new government is expected to boost ties with the West and the path appears clear for Slovakia's entry into NATO by 2003 and the EU in 2004 or 2005.

GEOGRAPHY

Slovakia sits in the heart of Europe, straddling the northwestern end of the Carpathian Mountains. This hilly 49,035 sq km country forms a clear physical barrier between the plains of Poland and Hungary. Almost 80% of Slovakia is more than 750m above sea level, and forests, mainly beech and spruce, cover 40% of the country.

Southwestern Slovakia is a fertile lowland stretching from the foothills of the Carpathians down to the Danube (Dunaj in Slovak), which forms the border with Hungary from Bratislava to Štúrovo.

Central Slovakia is dominated by the Vysoké Tatry (High Tatras) mountains along the Polish border, Gerlachovský štít (2654m), the highest peak in the Carpathians, and the forested ridges of the Nízke Tatry, the Malá Fatra and the Veľká Fatra. South are the limestone ridges and caves of Slovenský raj and Slovenský kras. The longest river, the Váh, rises in the Tatras and flows 390km west and south to join the Danube at Komárno.

SLOVAKIA

CLIMATE

Slovakia generally experiences hot summers and cold winters. The warmest, driest and sunniest area is the Danube lowland, which is east of Bratislava.

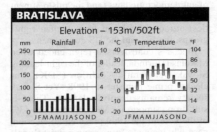

ECOLOGY & ENVIRONMENT

The Slovak environment is not as badly polluted as other European countries. The larger towns that have seen rapid industrialisation since WWII suffer most, especially Bratislava and Košice, but also Žilina and Trenčín. According to government figures, pollution has decreased since 1996.

Slovakia's first (Soviet-designed) nuclear power station was built at Bohunice nearby Trnava in the 1970s and supplies about a third of the country's electricity; the government has agreed to close it down by 2008. A second plant at Mochovce, east of Nitra, came online in June 1998, attracting protest from Austria.

The Gabčíkovo hydroelectric project on the Danube west of Komárno became highly controversial after Hungary backed out of the joint project in 1989 due to environmental considerations. Both countries are still negotiating on the project. Gabčíkovo produces enough electricity to cover the needs of every home in Slovakia and its canal allows the largest river vessels to reach Bratislava all year.

NATIONAL PARKS

Slovakia's national parks contain bears, marmots, wolves, lynxes, chamois, otters and minks. Deer, pheasants, partridges, ducks, wild geese, storks, grouse, eagles and other birds of prey can be seen across the country.

There are five national parks: Malá Fatra (east of Žilina), Nízke Tatry (between Banská Bystrica and Poprad), Tatra National Park (north of Poprad), Pieniny (along the Dunajec River) and Slovenský raj (near Spišská Nová Ves). In this chapter we cover all of these except Nízke Tatry.

GOVERNMENT & POLITICS

Slovakia is a parliamentary republic headed by the president (currently Rudolf Schuster), who is elected for a five-year term by the National Council; the next presidential election is in 2004. The president appoints and dismisses ministers. The cabinet is headed by the prime minister. The single-chamber National Council has 150 members, elected every four years by proportional representation.

ECONOMY

Since the break-up of Czechoslovakia in 1993 the Slovak economy has lagged behind its neighbour's. Following a slump from 1998 to 2001, growth was projected at 4% for 2002 and 2003. Unemployment remains very high at 18% (but up to 90% among the Roma), and the average monthly salary is just US$400.

Slovakia's manufacturing sector produces ceramics, chemicals, machinery, petroleum products, steel, textiles and weapons, and agriculture remains an important part of the economy with over one-third of the country under cultivation. Slovakia's main trading partners are Germany, the Czech Republic, Russia and Italy.

POPULATION & PEOPLE

Slovakia has a population of 5.4 million, of which 86% are Slovaks, 10% Hungarians and 1% Czechs. The 600,000 ethnic Hungarians live mostly in southern and eastern Slovakia. Official census figures from 1999 put the Roma population at just 1.7% (90,000), but the true figure is thought to be between 200,000 and 400,000.

The nomadic culture of the Roma has been destroyed by its assimilation into mainstream Slovak life under communist rule. Recently, as heavy industrial jobs have disappeared, many Slovak Roma have moved abroad. As elsewhere in Eastern Europe, there is much prejudice against Roma.

The largest cities are Bratislava (population 441,500), Košice (235,000), Prešov (92,000), Nitra (86,500) and Žilina (84,000).

ARTS

Slovakia has many outstanding buildings, paintings and sculptures by both foreign and local artists. Some of the most notable Gothic masterpieces can be found in St James' Church in Levoča, and there are magnificent Renaissance buildings in Bardejov.

Slovak cinema first made its mark as part of the Czechoslovak 'New Wave' of the 1960s, with classic films like *Smrt si rika Engelchen* (Death Calls Itself Engelchen; 1963) directed by Ján Kádar and *Obchod na korze* (The Shop on the Main Street; 1965) by Elmar Klos. The Czechoslovak film industry stagnated after the 1968 Soviet invasion, and lack of funding has meant that little serious movie-making has been done since 1993. Martin Sulík is Slovakia's most promising new director, winning an Oscar nomination for *Všetko, čo mám rád* (Everything I Like, 1992), and receiving international acclaim for *Záhrada* (The Garden; 1995) and *Krajinka* (The Landscape; 2000).

Music
Traditional Slovak folk instruments include the *fujara* (a 2m-long flute), the *gajdy* (bagpipes) and the *konkovka* (a strident shepherd's flute). Folk songs helped preserve the Slovak language during Hungarian rule, and in East Slovakia ancient folk traditions are a living part of village life.

In classical music, the 19th-century works of Ján L Bela and the symphonies of Alexander Moyzes receive world recognition. A small rock and pop scene has produced the young singer-songwriter Jana Kirschner, whose second album *V Cudzom Meste* (In A Strange Town; 1999) went platinum.

SOCIETY & CONDUCT
Despite the surliness that Slovaks sometimes show to each other in service industries, they are generally friendly and hospitable. It is customary to say 'good day' (*dobrý den*) when you enter a shop, hotel or restaurant, and 'goodbye' (*do videnia*) when you leave. On public transport, younger people will readily give up their seats to the elderly and infirm.

If you are invited to someone's home, bring flowers for your hosts (an odd number – even numbers are for funerals!). If your hosts remove their shoes you should do the same. For a classical concert or theatre, men wear a suit and tie, while women wear a dinner dress. Casual dress is fine in contemporary venues, such as theatre or rock/jazz concerts.

RELIGION
Religion is taken seriously, with Roman Catholics forming the majority and Evangelicals also numerous; East Slovakia has many Greek Catholics and Orthodox believers.

LANGUAGE
Although many people working in tourism have a good knowledge of English, in rural Slovakia very few people speak anything other than Slovak. German is probably the most useful non-Slavic language. Any effort to communicate in Slovak will be appreciated.

Slovak is a West Slavic language, very closely related to Czech – the two languages are mutually comprehensible. See the Language chapter at the end of this book for details on Slovak pronunciation and some useful words and phrases. Lonely Planet's *Eastern Europe phrasebook* has a complete chapter on Slovak.

Facts for the Visitor

HIGHLIGHTS
Bratislava's old town and castle are worth exploring, as are the picturesque, historic towns of Bardejov, Levoča and Košice. Spišší hrad, towering above Spišské Podhradie, is the largest castle in the country.

The rocky peaks of the Vysoké Tatry and the wooded hills of the Slovenský raj offer excellent hiking and mountaineering, while the Malá Fatra has good hiking and skiing.

SUGGESTED ITINERARIES
Depending on the length of your stay, you could do the following things:

Two days
　Visit Bratislava and Devín Castle
One week
　Visit Bratislava, the Vysoké Tatry, Levoča and Košice

PLANNING
When to Go
Locals take their holidays in July and August, when the mountain areas like the Tatras and Malá Fatra are at their most crowded, but cities like Bratislava have lower hotel prices and cheap student dorm beds available. The accommodation options in the mountain resorts is cheapest from May to June and again from September to October.

Maps
The Austrian publisher Freytag & Berndt has a good map of Slovakia (*Slovenská republika*, 1:500,000). The whole country is covered by excellent 1:50,000 hiking maps published by

Vojenský kartografický ústav (VKÚ), which also produces more detailed skiing and hiking maps (1:25,000) and plans of major towns and cities.

TOURIST OFFICES
Local Tourist Offices
Slovakia has quite an extensive network of **municipal information centres** (*Mestské in-formačné centrum;* ☎ *16 186)* belonging to the Association of Information Centres of Slovakia (AiCES). The staff speak English, organise sightseeing tours and guides, and can also assist with accommodation. Offices are normally open 8am to 6pm weekdays and to noon Saturday during summer (June to August), 9am to 5pm weekdays only the rest of the year.

Branches of the commercial agency Satur can also help with accommodation, and ISIC, Euro<26 and IYTC cards are available from some major offices.

Tourist Offices Abroad
The **Slovak Tourist Board** *(☎/fax 224 94 60 82; Purkyňova 4)* has an office in central Prague, but there is no representation of the Board in other countries.

VISAS & DOCUMENTS
Nationals of Canada, New Zealand and most European countries do not need a visa for tourist visits of up to 90 days (UK citizens up to 180 days; US, Italian and South African citizens up to 30 days). At the time of research, Australians *do* need a visa.

EMBASSIES & CONSULATES
Slovak Embassies
Slovak embassies abroad include:

Australia (☎ 02-6290 1516) 47 Culgoa Circuit, O'Malley, ACT 2606
Austria (☎ 01-318 90 55211) Armbrustergasse 24, 1-1190 Wien
Canada (☎ 613-749 4442) 50 Rideau Terrace, Ottawa, Ontario K1M 2A1
Czech Republic (☎ 233 32 54 43) Pod Hrad-bami 1, 160 00 Praha 6
France (☎ 01 45 20 78 75) 125 rue de Ranelagh, 75016 Paris
Germany (☎ 030-889 26 20) Pariser Strasse 44, Berlin 107 07 Berlin
Hungary (☎ 01-273 35 00) Stefania ut 22-24, H-1143 Budapest XIV
Netherlands (☎ 070-416 7773) Parkweg 1, 2585 JG The Hague

Poland (☎ 022-525 81 10) Litevska 6, 00-581 Warszawa
UK (☎ 020-7313 6490) 25 Kensington Palace Gardens, London W8 4QY
Ukraine (☎ 044-229 79 22) Jaroslavov val 34, 252 034 Kyiv
USA (☎ 202-237 1054) 3523 International Court NW, Washington, DC 20008

Embassies & Consulates in Slovakia
Australia and New Zealand do not have embassies in Slovakia; the nearest are in Vienna and Berlin respectively. The following are all in Bratislava (area code ☎ 02).

Austria (☎ 54 43 29 85) Ventúrska 10
Czech Republic (☎ 59 20 33 03) Hviezdoslavovo 8
France (☎ 59 34 71 11) Hlavné nám 7
Germany (☎ 54 41 96 40) Hviezdoslavovo nám 10
Hungary (☎ 54 43 05 41) Sedlárska 3
Poland (☎ 54 41 31 96) Hummelova 4
UK (☎ 54 41 96 32) Panská 16
Ukraine (☎ 59 20 28 16) Radvanská 35
USA (☎ 54 43 08 61) Hviezdoslavovo nám 4

CUSTOMS
If you're over 18 years of age, you can bring in 2L of wine, 1L of spirits and 250 cigarettes, along with reasonable personal effects and up to 3000 Sk worth of gifts and other noncommercial goods.

You cannot export genuine antiques. The customs officers are very strict and will readily confiscate goods that are even slightly suspect. If you have any doubts about what you are planning to take out of the country, check with the curatorial staff at the National Museum in Bratislava.

Arriving visitors may be asked to prove they have at least US$50 a day for each day of their stay (or a credit card), but this is rarely enforced. You may also be asked for proof of medical insurance.

MONEY
Currency
Slovakia's currency is the Slovak crown (*Slovenská koruna*; Sk), containing 100 hellers *(halier)*. There are coins of 10, 20 and 50 hellers, and one, two, five and 10 crowns (Sk). Banknotes come in denominations of 20, 50, 100, 200, 500, 1000 and 5000 crowns.

Exchange Rates
As this book went to print, the Slovenská koruna (Sk) was officially worth:

country	unit		koruna
Australia	A$1	=	24.55 Sk
Canada	C$1	=	28.86 Sk
Euro Zone	€1	=	44.52 Sk
Japan	¥100	=	37.91 Sk
NZ	NZ$1	=	21.31 Sk
UK	UK£1	=	70.93 Sk
USA	US$1	=	45.38 Sk

Exchanging Money

The easiest place to change cash and travellers cheques is at a branch of the Všeobecná úverová banka (VÚB; General Credit Bank), Slovenská sporiteľňa (Slovak Savings Bank) or Investičná banka (Investment Bank) where there's a standard 1% commission. Satur offices and the post office exchange windows charge 2% commission. Banks often give a slightly better rate for travellers cheques than for cash. Most banks are open 8am or 9am to 4pm or 5pm weekdays (some close for 30 minutes between noon and 1.30pm).

Credit cards (Visa, MasterCard, Eurocard and AmEx) can be used in most major hotels, restaurants and shops. Some of the larger branches of major banks give cash advances on credit cards. ATMs (bankomat) are easily found in most towns, and most accept Visa, MasterCard, Eurocard, Plus and Cirrus.

Some exchange places may not accept damaged US dollar notes.

Costs

Slovakia is still a bargain compared to the Czech Republic. You'll find food, admissions and transport are cheap and accommodation is manageable, except in Bratislava. If you camp or stay in hostels, eat in local pubs and take local transport, expect to spend about US$15 to US$20 a day. Students usually get 50% off the entry price at museums and galleries.

POST & COMMUNICATIONS
Post

Airmail is fairly reliable, but don't post anything valuable. Express Mail Services are available from most post offices, but if you are mailing a parcel over 2kg from Slovakia, it has to be sent from a customs office (colnica; open 8am to 3pm weekdays); post office staff will direct you to the nearest one. Poste restante mail can be sent to major post offices in larger cities and will be kept for one month; it should be addressed to Poste Restante, Pošta 1.

A postcard/letter (20g) to European countries is 10/14 Sk and elsewhere 14/18 Sk by airmail). A 2kg parcel to most European countries costs 650 Sk airmail. Most post offices are open 7am or 8am to 5pm or 8pm weekdays and to noon Saturday. In large cities and towns they also open 8am to noon Sunday.

Telephone

Slovakia's telephone system has been overhauled and modernised in the last few years. All the area codes were changed in July 2001; the old codes (beginning with ☎ 07 to 09) no longer work, but still appear on some signs and publicity materials. For directory inquiries call ☎ 120 (for the region you are calling from) or ☎ 121 (for numbers elsewhere in Slovakia). For international enquiries call ☎ 0149.

Direct-dial international calls can be made at post offices, telephone centres and most public phones on the street (look for the green or blue sticker saying 'international'). Most public telephones now accept phonecards only, though a few still take coins. Phonecards (telefónna karta) costing 60 Sk, 100 Sk, 140 Sk, 180 Sk or 350 Sk are available from post offices and any shop displaying the phonecard logo. A peak-rate (7am to 7pm weekdays), three-minute direct-dial call from Slovakia will cost about 30 Sk to the UK, France, Canada and USA; 30 Sk to South Africa; 38 Sk to Australia; and 90 Sk to New Zealand.

To call Slovakia from abroad, dial the international access code, then dial ☎ 421 (the country code for Slovakia), then the area code (minus the initial zero) and the number. The international access code in Slovakia is ☎ 00. For further information and a list of country and access codes see 'Appendix – Telephones' at the back of this book.

The Country Direct service is available in Slovakia (get a full list of countries and numbers from any telephone office or directory). Useful numbers include:

Australia Direct	☎ 0800 006101
Canada Direct	☎ 0800 000151
Canada (AT&T)	☎ 0800 000152
Deutschland Direct	☎ 0800 004949
France Direct	☎ 0800 003301
Netherlands	☎ 0800 003101
UK Direct (BT)	☎ 0800 004401
USA (AT&T)	☎ 0800 000101
USA (MCI)	☎ 0800 000112
USA (Sprint)	☎ 0800 087187

SLOVAKIA

Fax & Telegram

Telegrams can be sent from most post offices, while faxes can only be sent from certain major post offices.

Email & Internet Access

There are Internet cafés in most large towns and tourist centres.

DIGITAL RESOURCES

The Slovakia Document Store at **w** slovakia .eunet.sk contains links to a wealth of information on Slovakia. For up-to-date news and current affairs check out the websites of The Slovak Spectator (**w** www.slovakspectator .sk) and Slovakia.org (**w** www.slovakia.org). Most Slovak towns maintain a website; eg, **w** www.kosice.sk for Košice's.

BOOKS

For a very readable history try Stanislav J Kirschbaum's *A History of Slovakia – The Struggle for Survival*. William Shawcross' *Dubček & Czechoslovakia* is a biography of the late leader and an account of the 1968 Prague Spring. One of the few fictional works readily available in English translation is *The Year of the Frog* by Martin Šimečka, a story about a young intellectual who is made a social outcast by the communist government for his political views.

Lonely Planet's *Czech & Slovak Republics* by Richard Nebeský & Neil Wilson gives extensive information on the nuts and bolts of travelling in Slovakia.

NEWSPAPERS & MAGAZINES

The Slovak Spectator (35 Sk) is a weekly Bratislava-based, English-language paper that includes the latest information on what's happening in the city. In Bratislava and most major tourist centres the main European and US newspapers and magazines are available.

RADIO & TV

BBC English-language programmes are available 24 hours in Bratislava on FM 93.8 and in Košice on FM 103.2. Hotel room TVs with satellite connections can receive English-language channels such as Sky News, Eurosport and BBC World.

TIME

The time in Slovakia is GMT/UTC plus one hour. At the end of March Slovakia goes on summer time and clocks are set forward an hour. At the end of October they're turned back an hour.

WOMEN TRAVELLERS

Slovakia's rate of sexual violence is low in comparison to that of Western countries and assaults on solo female travellers are rare.

GAY & LESBIAN TRAVELLERS

Homosexuality has been legal since the 1960s and the age of consent is 16, but gay or lesbian partners do not have the same legal status as heterosexual partners.

There is a gay-support organisation called **Ganymedes** (**☎** 02-52 49 57 96; PO Box 4, 830 00 Bratislava). The lesbian organisation is **Museion** (**e** vamo@ba.psg.sk; Saratovská 3, 841 02 Bratislava for postal inquiries only).

DISABLED TRAVELLERS

There are very few facilities for disabled people. Transport is a major problem as buses and trams have no wheelchair access. KFC and McDonald's entrances and toilets are wheelchair friendly. For more information contact the **Alliance of Organisations of Disabled People in Slovakia** (Asociácia organizácií zdravotne postihnutých občanov SR; **☎** 02-52 44 41 19; **w** www.zutom.sk/ aozpo; Žabotova 2, 811 04 Bratislava).

DANGERS & ANNOYANCES

Crime is low compared with the West. Some Bratislava taxi drivers have been known to overcharge foreigners and in touristy places some waiters occasionally overcharge. Another problem is the increasing number of robberies on international trains passing through the country. Sometimes the passengers are gassed to sleep in their compartments and then relieved of their valuables.

Bad driving – especially dangerous overtaking – is a widespread problem.

Confusingly, buildings on some streets have two sets of numbers. The blue number is the actual street number while the red number

---

Emergency Services

In the event of an emergency call **☎** 158 for state police, **☎** 150 for fire, **☎** 155 for ambulance, **☎** 154 for car breakdown assistance. These numbers can be dialled nationwide.

is the old registration number. The streets themselves are sometimes poorly labelled.

Recent years have seen a rise in violent racist attacks by skinhead gangs on Roma people, and also on dark-skinned tourists.

BUSINESS HOURS

On weekdays, shops open at around 8am or 9am and close at 5pm or 6pm. Many small shops, particularly those in country areas, close for up to an hour for lunch between noon and 2pm, and almost everything closes on Saturday afternoon and all day Sunday. Major department stores open on weekends and stay open until 7pm on Thursday and Friday. Most restaurants are open every day but smaller ones often close by 9pm or even earlier.

Most museums and castles are closed on Monday and the day following a public holiday. Many tourist attractions are closed from November to March and open on weekends only in April and October. Staff at some isolated sights take an hour off for lunch. The main town museums stay open all year.

PUBLIC HOLIDAYS & SPECIAL EVENTS

Public holidays are New Year's and Independence Day (1 January), Three Kings Day (6 January), Good Friday and Easter Monday (March/April), Labour Day (1 May), Cyril and Methodius Day (5 July), SNP Day (29 August), Constitution Day (1 September), Our Lady of Sorrows Day (15 September), All Saints' Day (1 November) and Christmas (24 to 26 December).

During late June or early July folk dancers from all over Slovakia meet at the Východná Folklore Festival, 32km west of Poprad. There are folk festivals in June in Červený Kláštor and Kežmarok, and in many other towns from June to August. The two-week Bratislava Music Festival is held from late September to early October, and the Bratislava Jazz Days weekend is in late October.

ACTIVITIES

Slovakia is one of Eastern Europe's best areas for hiking (see the Malá Fatra, Vysoké Tatry and Slovenský raj sections for details). There is excellent rock climbing and mountaineering in the Vysoké Tatry, and paragliding is also becoming popular. Contact the **Mountain Guide** (Horský Vodca; ☎ 052-442 22 60) office in Starý Smokovec for more information.

Slovakia offers some of the best cycling terrain in Central Europe, with uncrowded roads and beautiful scenery. East Slovakia especially is prime cycling territory. Mountain biking in the Vysoké Tatry and Slovenský raj is excellent. **Tatrasport** (☎ 055-442 52 41) has branches in Starý Smokovec, Štrbské Pleso and Tatranská Lomnica and rents out mountain bikes for 299 Sk a day.

Slovakia has some of Europe's cheapest ski resorts, but the skiable areas are small and few lifts are linked. The season runs from December to April in the Vysoké Tatry, Nízke Tatry and Malá Fatra. There is good downhill and cross-country skiing in the Vysoké Tatry and the Malá Fatra. Ski and snowboard gear is available for hire at very competitive rates, but the waits at uplift can be excruciatingly long during the peak season.

Some of Slovakia's major rivers such as the Váh, Hron and Nitra offer good canoeing and kayaking. **T-Ski** (☎ 055-442 32 00) in Starý Smokovec can arrange rafting trips (from 580 Sk per person). For information on rafting on the Dunajec River in Pieniny National Park, see the Dunajec Gorge section.

WORK

The unemployment rate in Slovakia is high and there are not many job opportunities for non-Slovak speakers. Your best bet is to find a job teaching English. The **British Council** (☎ 02-54 43 17 93; Panská 17, Bratislava) has a teaching centre in Bratislava, or try the **Berlitz Language Centre** (☎ 02-54 43 37 96; Na vŕšku 6, Bratislava).

ACCOMMODATION

Foreigners can often pay 30% to 100% more for accommodation than Slovaks. Unless otherwise stated, all prices quoted for rooms are for a single/double/triple/quad.

Accommodation in the mountain resorts can be up to 50% cheaper in the low season (usually May to June and October to November); prices quoted in this chapter are for the high season.

Camping

There are several hundred camping grounds around the country, usually open from May to September. They're often accessible on public transport, but there's usually no hot water. Most have a small snack bar and many have small cabins for rent that are cheaper than a hotel room. Camping wild in national parks is prohibited.

Hostels

The Hostelling International (HI) handbook lists an impressive network of hostels, but they're mostly open in July and August only, and usually full. In July and August many student dormitories become temporary hostels. Satur and municipal information offices usually have information on hostels and can make advance bookings for you.

Tourist hostels (*Turistické ubytovňy*), which provide very basic and cheap dormitory accommodation, are not connected to the HI network. You should ask about them at information offices.

Private Rooms & Pensions

Private rooms (look for signs reading '*privát*' or '*Zimmer frei*') are usually available in tourist areas (from 200 Sk per person). AiCES tourist information offices and travel agencies like Satur can book them. Some have a three-night minimum-stay requirement.

Many small pensions (often just glorified private rooms) exist in tourist regions, and these offer more personalised service and cheaper rates than hotels.

Hotels

Hotels in Bratislava are considerably more expensive than in the rest of the country. There are five categories, from one star (budget) to five star (luxury). Two-star rooms are typically US$15/20, three-star around US$25/40 (but up to US$60 in Bratislava).

FOOD

The cheapest eateries are the self-service restaurants called *jedáleň* or *bistro*, which sometimes have tasty dishes like barbecued chicken or hot German-style sausage. Train station buffets and busy beer halls are also cheap. If the place is crowded with locals, is noisy and looks chaotic, chances are it will have great lunch specials at low prices.

Lunches are generally bigger and cheaper than dinners. Dinner is usually eaten early, between 6pm and 7pm. Don't expect to be served at any restaurant if you arrive within half an hour of closing time.

The Slovak for menu is *jedálny lístok*. The main categories are *predjedlá* (starters), *polievky* (soups), *hotová jedlá* (ready-to-serve dishes), *jedlá na objednávku* (dishes prepared as they are ordered), *mäsité jedlá* (meat dishes), *ryby* (fish), *zelenina* (vegetables), *šaláty* (salads), *ovoce* (fruit), *zákusok* (dessert) and *nápoje* (drinks). Anything that comes with *knedle* (dumplings) will be a hearty meal.

Vegetarians are catered for at a small but increasing number of restaurants and health-food shops, although in small towns you might be restricted to salads and *vysmážaný syr* (deep-fried cheese). Note that many of the innocent-looking vegetable-based soups may use a ham or beef stock, and dishes advertised as 'vegetarian' *(bezmasa)* may actually contain meat!

Tipping is optional. If you were happy with the service, you could round up the bill to the next 5 Sk (or to the next 10 Sk if the bill is over 100 Sk).

Cafés (*kaviáreň* or *cukráreň*) offer cakes, puddings and coffee as good as anything you'll find in neighbouring Austria at a fraction of the price.

Local Specialities

Soups include *cesnaková polievka* (garlic soup), a treat that is not to be missed. Slovakia's traditional dish is *bryndžové halušky* (dumplings baked with sheep's-milk cheese and bits of bacon).

Meat dishes come with potatoes – either boiled, fried or as chips. Goulash or *segedín* (also known as *koložárska kapusta* – a beef goulash with sauerkraut in cream sauce) comes with *knedle*. *Kapor* (carp) or *pstruh* (trout) can be crumbed and fried or baked. *Ovocné knedle* or *guľky* (fruit dumplings), with whole fruit inside, come with cottage cheese or crushed poppy seeds, as well as melted butter.

DRINKS

Slovak wine is good and cheap. Well-known brands include Tokaj from southern Slovakia, and Kláštorné (a red) and Venušíno čáro (a white), both from the Modra region north of Bratislava.

Slovak *pivo* (beer) is as good as Czech – try Zlatý Bažant from Hurbanovo or Martiner from Martin.

Coffee is usually served Turkish-style *(turecká káva)* with sludgy grounds in the cup. For ordinary black/white coffee order *espresso/espresso s mliekom*. Tea (*čaj*) can be enjoyed in a tearoom (*čajovňa*).

SHOPPING

Good buys include china, Bohemian crystal, jewellery, folk ceramics, garnets, fancy leather goods, special textiles, lace, embroidery, shoes, colour-photography books and souvenirs. Antiques and valuable-looking artworks are closely scrutinised by customs.

Getting There & Away

AIR

Bratislava's MR Štefanik airport receives only a small number of flights from continental Europe. Vienna's Schwechat airport is just 60km from Bratislava, and is served by a vast range of much cheaper international flights.

Czech Airlines (ČSA) flies between Bratislava and Prague several times every day with connections to major European cities, New York, Montreal and Toronto. Return flights from New York to Bratislava (via Prague) can cost as little as US$600, and London to Bratislava (via Prague) from £225. See also Air under Getting There & Away in the Bratislava section.

LAND
Bus

Seven buses a day (four at the weekend) link Bratislava to Schwechat airport in Vienna (€7.20, one hour) and central Mitte Busbahnhof (€10.90, 1½ hours). See also Getting There & Away in the Bratislava section.

Train

There are trains from Bratislava to Vienna (Südbahnhof) five times daily (one hour). From Vienna there are connections to most Western European cities and there are several express trains daily from Bratislava to Budapest (three hours). See Getting There & Away in the Bratislava section. Daily sleeper services travel to Kyiv, Ukraine, changing at Košice (30 hours, 1443km), and to Moscow, changing at Warsaw (33 hours, 1991km).

There are three expresses a day between Košice and Muszyna (1¼ hours) in Poland. From Muszyna trains travel to Nowy Sącz and (less frequently) to Kraków. There's also a daily train from Košice to Bucharest (15½ hours). See also the Košice Getting There & Away section in this chapter.

Car & Motorcycle

There is only one border crossing to/from Austria (at Berg, southwest of Bratislava) and to/from Ukraine (at Vyšne nemecké), but there are plenty of options to/from the Czech Republic, Hungary and Poland.

RIVER

See Boat under Getting There & Away in the Bratislava section.

Getting Around

BUS

Intercity bus travel, operated by the various branches of Slovenská autobusová doprava (SAD), is generally slower and less comfortable than the train, and not much cheaper. Departures are less frequent, and weekend services are more sharply reduced than rail services. One-way bus tickets cost around 24/46/96/190 Sk for 25/50/100/200km. It is advisable to arrive at least 10 minutes before departure time.

When trying to decipher bus schedules beware of departure times bearing footnotes you don't completely understand. Check the time at the information window whenever possible. It is helpful to know that *premáva* means 'it operates' and *nepremáva* means 'it doesn't operate'.

TRAIN

Slovak Republic Railways (*Železnice Slovenskej republiky* or *ŽSR*) provides a cheap and efficient service. One-way fares (2nd class) are 24/48/98/196 Sk for 25/50/100/200km; the surcharge for express services is around 20 Sk to 70 Sk. Most of the places covered in this chapter are on or near the main railway line between Bratislava and Košice.

By express train from Bratislava it's 1¾ hours to Trenčín, almost three hours to Žilina, five hours to Poprad, 5½ hours to Spišská Nová Ves, and 6½ hours to Košice.

Most train stations in Slovakia have a left-luggage office (*úschovňa*) where you can leave your bag for 10 Sk to 20 Sk, and/or lockers for 5 Sk. When using lockers, remember to set the combination dial inside the door *before* you close it.

The Czech website **w** www.vlak-bus.cz has Slovakia's national railway and bus timetables online.

SLOVAKIA

CAR & MOTORCYCLE

There are plenty of petrol stations. Leaded petrol is available as *special* (91 octane) and *super* (96 octane), unleaded as *natural* (95 octane) or *natural plus* (98 octane); diesel is *nafta* or just *diesel*. Natural 95 costs around 33 Sk a litre, diesel 30 Sk.

Road Rules

You can drive in Slovakia using your own licence. Speed limits are 40km/h to 60km/h in built-up areas, 90km/h on open roads and 130km/h on motorways; motorbikes are limited to 90km/h. At level crossings over railway lines the speed limit is 30km/h. Beware of speed traps (usually just outside the city limits) as the police can levy on-the-spot fines of up to 2000 Sk.

In order to use the motorways in Slovakia (which are denoted by green signs), all drivers must purchase a motorway sticker *(nálepka)*, which should be displayed in the windscreen. You can buy stickers at border crossings, petrol stations or Satur offices (100 Sk for 15 days, 600 Sk for a year, for vehicles up to 1.5 tonnes). You can be fined 5000 Sk if you don't have a sticker.

Rental

Avis has offices in Bratislava and Košice. Its cheapest cars cost around 1650 Sk a day including unlimited kilometres and Collision Damage Waiver. There are much cheaper local companies (see Getting Around in the Bratislava section). Cars hired in the Czech Republic can usually be driven into Slovakia without extra insurance, but not vice versa – check with the rental company.

BICYCLE

Cyclists should be aware that roads are often narrow and potholed, and in towns the cobblestones and tram tracks can be a dangerous combination, especially when it has been raining. Theft is a problem in large cities, so a good chain and lock are a must.

It's fairly easy to transport bikes on trains. First purchase your train ticket and then take it with your bicycle to the railway luggage office. There you fill out a card, which will be attached to your bike. You will be given a receipt that should list all the accessories on your bike, such as lights and dynamo. The cost of transporting a bicycle is usually 10% of the train ticket.

HITCHING

Slovakia is no safer than other European countries when it comes to hitching: many hitchers are assaulted and/or raped, and each year a few are killed. Despite these dangers many Slovaks, including young women travelling alone, choose to hitch.

LOCAL TRANSPORT

City buses and trams operate from around 4.30am to 11.30pm daily. Tickets are sold at public transport offices, from ticket machines and newsstands and must be validated once you're aboard.

Bratislava

☎ 02 • pop 441,500

Bratislava is Slovakia's capital and largest city. Here the Carpathian Mountains, which stretch 1200km from the Iron Gate of Romania, finally slope down to the Danube. The Austrian border is almost within sight of the city and Hungary is just 16km away.

Founded in AD 907, Bratislava was already a large city in the 12th century. Commerce developed in the 14th and 15th centuries, and in 1467 the Hungarian Renaissance monarch Matthias Corvinus founded a university here, the Academia Istropolitana. The city became Hungary's capital in 1541, after the Turks captured Buda, and remained so from 1563 to 1830. In St Martin's Cathedral 11 Hungarian kings and seven queens were crowned. Bratislava flourished during the reign of Maria Teresa of Austria (1740–80) when some imposing baroque palaces were built. In 1918 the city was included in the newly formed Republic of Czechoslovakia, in 1969 it became the state capital of a federal Slovak Republic, and in 1993 it was named the capital of an independent Slovakia.

Many beautiful monuments survive in the old town to tell of its past under Hungarian rule, and Bratislava's numerous museums are surprisingly rich. The opera productions of the Slovak National Theatre rival anything in Europe. Bratislava isn't as swamped by Western tourism as are Budapest and Prague (except on weekends when the Austrians invade).

Orientation

Hviezdoslavova nám is a convenient reference point, with the old town to the north, the

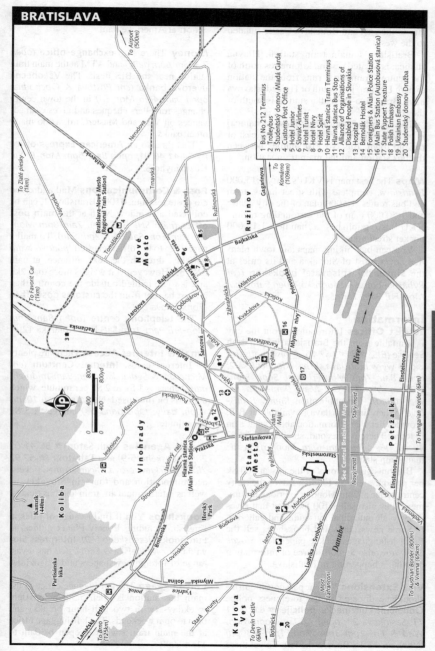

BRATISLAVA

To Airport (500m)

To Komárno (105km)

To Zlaté piesky (11km)

To Favorit Car (1km)

To Brno (125km)

Bratislava-Nové Mesto (Regional Train Station)

Nové Mesto

Ružinov

Rosťmská

Nerudova

Trnavská

Vajnorská

Tomášikova

Driehova

Ružinská

Bajkalská

Račianska

Gagarinova

River

Jarošova

Bajkalská

Trnavská

Pluhová

Miletičova

Prievozská

Košická

Jaskový rad

Račianska

Šancová

Krížna

Kvetná

Polná

Karadžičova

Mlynské nivy

Mýtna

Mlynské nivy

Dunajská

Stare most

To Hungarian Border (6km)

Petržalka

See Central Bratislava Map

Nový most

Einsteinova

Koliba

Kamzík (440m)

Partizánska lúka

Vinohrady

Stromová

Brnianska

Horský Park

Búdková

Mudroňova

Jantova

Ludvíka Svobodu

Staré grunty

Lamačská cesta

Vydrica potok

Mlynská dolina

Botanická

Karlova Ves

To Devín Castle (6km)

Danube

Most Lafranconi

To Austrian Border (800m) & Vienna (65km)

Staré Mesto

Nám 1 Mája

Štefánikova

Staromestská

Palisády

Šulekova

N 0 400 800m
0 400 800yd

SLOVAKIA

1 Bus No 212 Terminus
2 Trolleybus
3 Študentský domov Mladá Garda
4 Customs Post Office
5 Hotel Junior
6 Slovak Airlines
7 Hotel Turist
8 Hotel Nivy
9 Hotel Spirit
10 Hlavná stanica Tram Terminus
11 Hlavná stanica Bus Stop
12 Alliance of Organisations of Disabled People in Slovakia
13 Hospital
14 Bernolák Hostel
15 Foreigners & Main Police Station
16 Main Bus Station (Autobusová stanica)
17 State Puppet Theatre
18 Polish Embassy
19 Ukrainian Embassy
20 Študentský domov Družba

Hlavná stanica (Main Train Station)

Pražská

Záhradnícka

Odbojárov

Vajnorská

Podjavorinská

Jesenová

Legionárska

Karadžičova

Mýtna

Žabotova

Vištuk

Danube to the south, the Slovak National Theatre to the east and Bratislava Castle siutated to the west.

Bratislava's main train station, Hlavná stanica, is located several kilometres north of the centre. Tram No 1 runs from the station to nám L Štúra, just south of Hviezdoslavova nám. Bratislava-Petržalka station is south of the river.

The main bus station (autobusová stanica) is on Mlynské nivy, a little over 1km east of the old town. Bus No 210 shuttles between the bus station and the main train station.

Maps The best map is VKÚ's hefty 1:15,000 *Bratislava*, complete with street index, tram and bus routes, 1:5000 plan of the city centre and 1:50,000 map of the surrounding region. VKÚ also publishes a handier 1:15,000 pocket street atlas.

You can buy hiking maps and town plans that cover most of Slovakia and its cities at the **Slovenský spisovatel bookshop** *(cnr Rybárska brána & Laurinská; open 9am-6pm Mon-Fri, 9am-1pm Sat).*

Information

Tourist Offices Information about the city is available from the **Bratislava Information Service** *(BIS; ☎ 54 43 37 15; e bis@bratislava .sk; w www.bratislava.sk/bis; Klobučnícka 2; open 8am-7pm Mon-Fri June-Sept, 9am-5.30pm Mon-Fri Oct-May, 9am-1pm Sat year-round)*. The publication *Kam v Bratislave* (Where in Bratislava), available at BIS, provides detailed information about what's on in town. There is a second, smaller **BIS** *(☎ 52 49 59 06; open 9am-6pm Mon-Fri)* at the main train station.

BIS runs guided tours of the city at 300 Sk per person; a tour in English leaves their city centre office at 2pm Monday to Friday in summer. They also sell a 100 Sk ticket that gives entry to all municipal museums and galleries.

Some newsstands and bookshops sell the English-language weekly paper *The Slovak Spectator*, also a good source of information on what's happening in Bratislava.

Visa Extensions Visa or passport inquiries should be directed to the foreigners police **Oddelenie cudzineckej polície** *(☎ 61 01 11 11; Sasinkova 23; open 7.30am-noon Mon, Wed & Fri, 1pm-3pm Mon, 1pm-5.30pm Wed)*, on the 1st floor to the left. To get there

take tram No 4, 6, 7 or 11 from Špitalská and get off at Americké nám.

Money There's an **exchange office** *(open 7.30am-6pm daily)* and ATM at the main train station near the BIS desk. The **Všeobecná úverová banka** *(cnr Poštová & Obchodná; open 9am-4pm Mon-Fri)* in the town centre changes travellers cheques and gives cash advances on Visa and MasterCard, as do many other banks.

There's also an **American Express office** *(☎ 54 41 40 01; open 8am-5pm Mon-Fri)* at Kuzmányho 8.

Post & Communications Mail addressed c/o poste restante, 81000 Bratislava 1, can be collected at window No 6 at the **main post office** *(nám SNP 34; open 7am-8pm Mon-Fri, 7am-6pm Sat, 9am-2pm Sun)*. To mail a parcel, go to the office marked *'podaj a výdaj balíkov'*, through the next entrance, at nám SNP 35. However, if it weighs more than 2kg and is to be mailed outside the country then it must be sent from the **customs post office** *(Tomášikova 54)*.

The **telephone centre** *(open 8am-7pm Mon-Fri, 9am-1pm Sat)* is at Kolárska 12.

Email & Internet Access There are plenty of Internet cafés. **Internet Centrum** *(cnr Michalská & Sedlárska; open 9am-midnight daily)* charges 1 Sk to 2 Sk per minute, which depends on time used. **Netcafe** *(open 10am-10pm daily; Obchodná 53)* charges 1.5 Sk per minute.

Travel Agencies Both **Satur** *(☎ 55 41 01 28; Jesenského 5-9)* and **Tatratour** *(☎ 52 92 78 88; Mickiewiczova 2)* can arrange tickets, accommodation and tours in Slovakia, as well as international air, train and bus tickets.

Bookshops You'll find a range of titles in English, including Lonely Planet guides, at **Eurobooks** *(Jesenského 5-9)*. **Interpress Slovakia** *(cnr Michalská & Sedlárska)* has a vast range of foreign newspapers and magazines.

Left Luggage The left-luggage office at the main bus station is open 5.30am to 10pm weekdays (with two half-hour breaks) and 6am to 6pm weekends. The left-luggage office at the main train station is open 6.30am to 11pm daily.

Medical & Emergency Services For
medical emergencies call ☎ 155. The main
outpatient clinic is at the hospital on Mýtna
5. There's a 24-hour pharmacy (lekáreň) at
nám SNP 20.

The main police station (polícia) is located
at Sasinkova 23.

Things to See & Do

You could begin your exploring at the Slovak
National Museum (adult/child 20/10 Sk, free
last Sun of month; open 9am-5pm Tues-Sun),
built in 1928, opposite the hydrofoil terminal
on the river. The museum features anthropol-
ogy, archaeology, natural history and geology
exhibits, with a large relief map of Slovakia.

Further west along the riverfront is the
overhanging facade of the Slovak National
Gallery (Rázusovo nábrežie 2; adult/child
20/10 Sk; open 10am-6pm Tues-Sun), which
houses Bratislava's major art collection. The
controversial modern building daringly incorporates an 18th-century palace.

Backtrack slightly to nám L Štúra where
you'll find the neobaroque Reduta Palace
(1914), which is now Bratislava's main concert hall. Go north up Mostová to the recently
renovated Hviezdoslavovo nám, a broad,
tree-lined space dominated by the flamboyant
Slovak National Theatre (1886) on the right,
with Ganymede's Fountain (1888) in front.

Crowded, narrow Rybárska brána runs
through the old town to Hlavné nám; at the
centre is Roland's Fountain (1572). To one
side is the old town hall (1421), now the
Municipal Museum (admission 25 Sk; open
10am-5pm Tues-Sun), with torture chambers
in the cellar and an extensive historical collection housed in finely decorated rooms. You
enter the museum from the picturesque inner
courtyard, where concerts are held in summer.

Leave the courtyard through the east gate
and you'll be on the square in front of the Primate's Palace (1781). Enter to see the Hall of
Mirrors where Napoleon and the Austrian emperor Franz I signed a peace treaty in 1805. In
the municipal gallery on the 2nd floor are rare
English tapestries (1632). St George's Fountain stands in the courtyard. On Saturday, the
palace is crowded with couples being married,
but it's still open to visitors.

Return through the old town hall courtyard
and turn left into Radničná 1 to find the Museum of Wine Production (adult/child 20/
10 Sk; open 9.30am-4.30pm Wed-Mon) in

the Apponyi Palace (1762). You can buy a
museum guidebook in English. Next, head
north on Františkánske nám to the Franciscan
Church (1297). The original Gothic chapel,
with the skeleton of a saint enclosed in glass,
is accessible through a door on the left near
the front. Opposite this church is the Mirbach
Palace (Františkánske nám 11; adult/child
40/20 Sk, free 1st Sat of month; open 10am-
5pm Tues-Sun), built in 1770, which is a
beautiful rococo building that now houses a
good collection of art.

From the palace continue along narrow
Zámočnícka to the Michael Tower (adult/
child 20/10; open 10am-5pm Tues-Fri,
11am-6pm Sat & Sun May-Sept, 9.30am-
4.30pm Tues-Sun Oct-Apr), with a collection
of antique arms and a great view from the top.
Stroll south down Michalská to the Palace of
the Royal Chamber (Michalská 1), built in
1756. Now the university library, this building was once the seat of the Hungarian parliament. In 1848 serfdom was abolished here.

Take the passage west through the palace
to the Gothic Church of the Clarissine
Order, which has a pentagonal tower (1360)
supported by buttresses. Continue west on
Farská, then turn left into Kapitulská and go
straight ahead to the 15th-century coronation
church, St Martin's Cathedral. Inside is a
bronze statue (1734) of St Martin cutting off
half his robe for a beggar.

The busy motorway in front of St Martin's
follows the moat of the former city walls. Construction of this route and the adjacent bridge
was controversial as several of the city's historic structures had to be pulled down and vi-
brations from the traffic have structurally
weakened the cathedral. Find the passage
under the motorway and head up towards
Bratislava Castle, built above the Danube on
the southernmost spur of the Little Carpathian
Mountains.

From the 1st to the 5th centuries, Bratislava
Castle was a frontier post of the Roman Empire. Since the 9th century the castle has been
rebuilt several times; it was the seat of Hungarian royalty until it burnt down in 1811.

Reconstructed between 1953 and 1962, the
castle now has a large Historical Museum
(adult/child 40/20 Sk; open 9am-5pm Tues-
Sun) in the main building, and the interesting
Museum of Folk Music (adult/child 40/20
Sk; open 9am-5pm Tues-Sun) in a northern
wing. Climb up to the castle grounds for a

SLOVAKIA

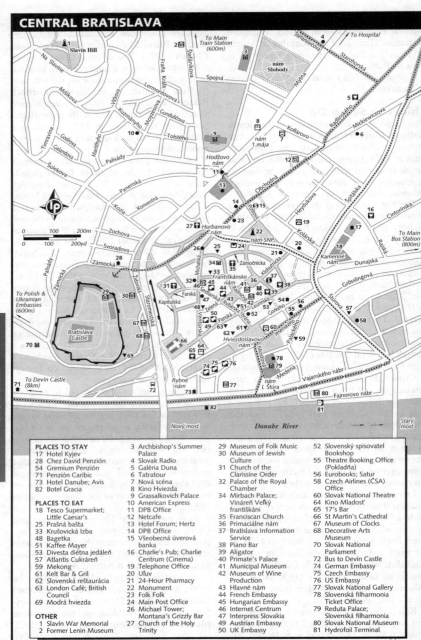

CENTRAL BRATISLAVA

PLACES TO STAY
17 Hotel Kyjev
28 Chez David Penzión
54 Gremium Penzión
71 Penzión Caribic
73 Hotel Danube; Avis
82 Botel Gracia

PLACES TO EAT
18 Tesco Supermarket;
   Little Caesar's
25 Prašná bašta
33 Krušovická Izba
48 Bagetka
51 Kaffee Mayer
53 Divesta diétna jedáleň
57 Atlantis Cukráreň
59 Mekong
61 Kelt Bar & Gril
62 Slovenská reštaurácia
63 London Café; British
   Council
69 Modrá hviezda

OTHER
1 Slavín War Memorial
2 Former Lenin Museum

3 Archbishop's Summer
   Palace
4 Slovak Radio
5 Galéria Duna
6 Tatratour
7 Nová scéna
8 Kino Hviezda
9 Grassalkovich Palace
10 American Express
11 DPB Office
12 Netcafe
13 Hotel Forum; Hertz
14 DPB Office
15 Všeobecná úverová
   banka
16 Charlie's Pub; Charlie
   Centrum (Cinema)
19 Telephone Office
20 Uľuv
21 24-Hour Pharmacy
22 Monument
23 Folk Folk
24 Main Post Office
26 Michael Tower;
   Montana's Grizzly Bar
27 Church of the Holy
   Trinity

29 Museum of Folk Music
30 Museum of Jewish
   Culture
31 Church of the
   Clarissine Order
32 Palace of the Royal
   Chamber
34 Mirbach Palace;
   Vináreň Veľký
   františkáni
35 Franciscan Church
36 Primaciálne nám
37 Bratislava Information
   Service
38 Piano Bar
39 Aligator
40 Primate's Palace
41 Municipal Museum
42 Museum of Wine
   Production
43 Hlavné nám
44 French Embassy
45 Hungarian Embassy
46 Interpress Slovakia
47 Interpress Slovakia
49 Austrian Embassy
50 UK Embassy

52 Slovenský spisovateľ
   Bookshop
55 Theatre Booking Office
   (Pokladňa)
56 Eurobooks; Satur
58 Czech Airlines (ČSA)
   Office
60 Slovak National Theatre
64 Kino Mladosť
65 17's Bar
66 St Martin's Cathedral
67 Museum of Clocks
68 Decorative Arts
   Museum
70 Slovak National
   Parliament
72 Bus to Devín Castle
74 German Embassy
75 Czech Embassy
76 US Embassy
77 Slovak National Gallery
78 Slovenská filharmonia
   Ticket Office
79 Reduta Palace;
   Slovenská filharmonia
80 Slovak National Museum
81 Hydrofoil Terminal

great view. The **Slovak National Parliament** meets in the modern complex that overlooks the river just beyond the castle.

At the foot of the hill is the **Decorative Arts Museum** *(adult/child 20/10 Sk; open 11am-5pm Wed-Mon)* and almost opposite is the **Museum of Clocks** *(adult/child 20/10 Sk; open 9.30am-4.30pm Wed-Mon)*. Further north is the **Museum of Jewish Culture** *(Židovská 17; adult/child 30/15 Sk; open 10am-5pm Sun-Fri)*.

As you return from the castle, take a stroll across the Danube on one of the pedestrian walkways on the sweeping **Nový most** (New Bridge), built in 1972. On the far side you can take a lift up one of the pylons to an expensive café that sits 80m above the river.

Communist Bratislava From nám SNP, where there is a monument to the heroes of the Slovak National Uprising, head north to Hodžovo nám and along Mýtna to the corner with Štefanovičova, where the chunky **Slovak Radio** (Slovenský rozhlas) building, like an upside-down stepped pyramid, sits among the housing estates.

West from nám Slobody along Spojná and north up Štefánikova, you will come to the former **Lenin Museum**, now an art gallery. Continue north a little, then west up the steps of Puškinova towards the **Slavín War Memorial** (1965). This is where 6847 Soviet soldiers who died in the battle for Bratislava in 1945 are buried. There's a good view of modern Bratislava from here, especially of the prefabricated suburb of Petržalka to the south.

Hiking

To get out of the city and up into the forested Little Carpathian Mountains, take trolleybus No 203 northeast from Hodžovo nám to the end of the line at Koliba, then walk up the road for about 20 minutes to the **TV tower** on Kamzík hill (440m). There is a viewing platform and a revolving café at the top.

Maps posted at the tower outline the many hiking possibilities in the area, including a 6km walk that goes down the Vydrica Valley to Partisan Meadow. Continue down the road to Vojenská hospital from where bus No 212 runs back to Hodžovo nám.

Places to Stay

Satur can book private rooms (from 400 Sk per person), pensions and hotels. BIS can assist in finding accommodation in private rooms, student dormitories (open during summer only, from 200 Sk per person), hostels, pensions (from about 1200 Sk a double) and hotels. Reservations are recommended year-round.

Camping A lake resort that's 7km northeast of Bratislava – **Zlaté piesky** (Golden Sands) – has bungalows, a motel, a hotel and a camping ground. Tram Nos 2 (from the main train station) and 4 (from the city centre) terminate here. You can hire rowing boats and sailboards in summer and there are also tennis courts.

As you cross the pedestrian bridge from the tram stop you'll see the Hotel Flora (see Hotels – Suburbs, following) just to your left. Bear left past the hotel to find the lakeside **Intercamp Zlaté piesky** *(☎/fax 44 25 73 73; e kempi@netax.sk; camp sites 40-60 Sk, plus per person 70 Sk, per car 70 Sk; 4-bed bungalows 830 Sk; open mid-Apr–mid-Oct)*.

Hostels The following places offer accommodation in July and August only; the BIS desk at the train station will help you arrange hostel accommodation, if you can resist their attempts to sell you a private room, which are often a long way from the city centre and no cheaper than hostels.

The 12-storey **Bernolák Hostel** *(☎ 52 49 71 84, fax 52 49 77 24; Bernolákova 1; beds per person from 130 Sk)*, about five blocks east of the main train station, is closest to the city centre. There's a swimming pool and disco (audible throughout the building).

Študentský domov Mladá Garda *(☎ 44 25 30 20, fax 44 45 96 90; e ubytovacie@ garda.sk; Račianska 103; beds per person 140-200 Sk; open mid-July–end Aug)* is 4km northeast of town; take tram No 3, 5, 7 or 11. The 24-hour reception has both English- and German-speaking staff.

Študentský domov Družba *(☎ 65 42 00 65; Botanická 25; singles/doubles 500/900 Sk)* is 20 minutes west of the city centre near the Danube (take tram No 1 from the train station, No 4 or 12 from nám L Štúra). It has comfortable, well-equipped rooms with bathroom and TV.

Hotels & Pensions – Centre The best deal near the centre of Bratislava is **Penzión Caribic** *(☎ 54 41 83 34, fax 54 41 83 33; Žižkova 1/A; singles/doubles 800/1500 Sk)*, beneath the castle.

A good place in the heart of town is **Gremium Penzión** (☎ 54 13 10 26, fax 54 43 06 53; Gorkého 11; singles/doubles 890/1600 Sk), with rooms that include breakfast. You'll need to book ahead to get one of the few rooms available.

The friendly, welcoming **Hotel Spirit** (☎ 54 77 75 61, fax 54 77 78 17; e univ@stonline .sk; Vančurova 1; singles/doubles/triples 900/1300/1600 Sk) is ... well, colourful. Descend the steps behind the tram terminus at the train station, turn left under the railway bridge, then left again. You can't miss it; in fact, wear your sunglasses.

Botel Gracia (☎ 54 43 21 32, fax 54 43 21 31; singles/doubles 1750/2400 Sk) has comfy en suite cabins in a former cruise boat moored near the Hotel Danube on Rázusovo nábrežie.

Hotel Kyjev (☎ 52 96 10 82, fax 52 92 68 20; e rezervacia@kyjev-hotel.sk; singles/doubles 2200/2400 Sk) is a graceless tower block overlooking the Tesco department store on Špitálska, but it's central. Rooms with bathroom and TV are reasonable value and include breakfast.

In the splurge category is **Chez David Penzión** (☎ 54 41 38 24, fax 54 41 26 42; Zámocká 13; doubles 4700 Sk), a modern hotel built on the site of the old Jewish ghetto below the castle.

If you feel like really splashing out, the luxury **Hotel Danube** (☎ 59 34 08 33, fax 54 41 43 11; e danube@internet.sk; Rybné nám 1; singles/doubles €146/166) has a swimming pool and riverside location.

Hotels – Suburbs There is lots of soulless but perfectly acceptable accommodation in modern hotels a short bus or tram ride away from the centre.

Friendly **Hotel Turist** (☎ 55 57 27 89, fax 55 57 31 80; e hotel@turist.sk; Ondavská 5; singles/doubles/triples 1020/1250/1500 Sk) has dated but functional rooms with bathroom and balcony. Take bus No 61 or 74 from the main train station to the Zimný štadión stop; Ondavská is the third street on the right after the stop. **Hotel Nivy** (☎ 55 41 03 90, fax 55 41 03 89; e hotel@hotelnivy.sk; Líščie nivy 3; doubles/quads 1300/2400 Sk) is a bigger place with slightly nicer accommodation just two blocks past the Turist.

Hotel Junior (☎ 43 33 80 00, fax 43 33 80 65; e recepcia@juniorhotel.sk; Drieňová 14; singles/doubles 1970/2480 Sk) overlooks a small lake in the eastern suburbs (take tram No 8, 9 or 12, or bus No 34, 38 or 54).

The slightly seedy **Hotel Flora** (☎ 44 25 79 26, fax 44 25 79 45; Zlaté piesky; doubles from 620 Sk) is next to the camping ground (see Camping earlier) at Zlaté piesky. While the Flora is cheap and clean, it's not recommended for lone females.

Places to Eat

Restaurants – Budget If you fancy a cheap and filling sandwich, try **Bagetka** (sandwiches 30-95 Sk; open 9am-9pm Mon-Sat, 2pm-9pm Sun), in a passage between Zelená and Venturská. Busy **Divesta diétna jedáleň** (Laurinská 8; mains 54-64 Sk; open 11am-3pm Mon-Fri) provides low-calorie and vegetarian lunches.

Two good inexpensive pubs serving typical Slovak food for lunch and dinner are **Prašná bašta** (Zámočnícka 11; mains 105-185 Sk; open 11am-11pm daily) and the **Krušovická Izba** (Biela 5; mains 80-130 Sk; open 9am-midnight Mon-Fri, 10am-10pm Sat & Sun).

Little Caesar's on the ground floor in Tesco (see Self-Catering following) does great pizza by the slice, to eat in or take away.

Restaurants – Mid-Range The **Kelt Bar & Gril** (Hviezdoslavovo nám 26; mains 95-250 Sk; open 11am-11pm daily) serves an international menu that ranges from pasta to nachos to New York steaks.

The delicious Thai dishes served at the elegant **Mekong** (Palackého 18; mains 90-220 Sk; open 11am-11pm Mon-Sat, 11am-10pm Sun) make a welcome change from pork and dumpling meals.

Also worth trying is the wine restaurant **Vináreň Veľký františkáni** (Františkánske nám 10; mains 100-200 Sk; open 11am-11pm daily) in the old monastery beside the Mirbach Palace, where Romani musicians often perform.

Modrá hviezda (Beblavého 14; mains 80-150 Sk; open 11.30am-11pm Mon-Sat), on the way up to the castle, is a wine bar and restaurant that features Slovak cuisine.

Restaurants – Top End The master chef in **Slovenská reštaurácia** (Hviezdoslavovo nám 20; mains 95-295 Sk; open 11am-11pm daily) serves gourmet Slovak cuisine; wash it down with a bottle of Slovakian Modrá or Tokaj wine.

Cafés The streets of central Bratislava have been taken over by countless cafés in the last few years. The classy **Kaffee Mayer** (*Hlavné nám 4; open 9am-1am daily*) has excellent but pricey coffee, cakes and light meals. For a cheaper cappuccino, try the **London Café** (*Panská 17; open 10am-9pm Mon-Fri*) in the British Council's courtyard.

Atlantis Cukráreň (*Štúrova 13; open 9am-9pm Mon & Wed-Fri, 10am-7pm Sat & Sun*) sells Bratislava's best ice cream for just 6 Sk a scoop; on Sunday afternoon the queue runs out the door and along the street.

Self-Catering There is a good **supermarket** (*open 8am-9pm Mon-Fri, 8am-7pm Sat, 9am-7pm Sun*) in the basement of Tesco on the square Kamenné nám.

Entertainment

Opera and ballet are presented at the **Slovak National Theatre** (*Hviezdoslavovo nám*), except during August. The local opera and ballet companies are outstanding. Tickets are sold at the **booking office** (*pokladňa; cnr Jesenského & Komenského; open 8am-5.30pm Mon-Fri, 9am-noon Sat*) behind the theatre. Tickets are sold in the theatre itself an hour before the performance, but they're usually sold out (*vypredané*) by then, especially on weekends.

Nová scéna (*Kollárovo nám 20*) presents operettas, musicals and drama (the latter in Slovak). The ticket office is open 12.30pm to 7pm weekdays and an hour before performances (by when they're usually sold out).

The **Slovenská filharmonia** (*cnr nám L Štúra & Medená*) is based in the Reduta Palace, across the park from the National Theatre. The **ticket office** (*Palackého 2; open 1pm-7pm Mon, Tues, Thur & Fri, 8am-2pm Wed*) is inside the building.

Štátne Bábkové divadlo (*State Puppet Theatre; Dunajská 36*) puts on puppet shows for kids, usually at 9am or 10am and sometimes again at 1.30pm or 2.30pm.

Bars & Clubs For loud music and a young crowd, try **Charlie's Pub** (*Špitálska 4; open 6pm-4am Sun-Thur, 6pm-6am Fri & Sat*), one of the city's most popular drinking places.

Montana's Grizzly Bar (*Michalská 19; open 11am-midnight daily*), at the base of the Michael Tower, is the meeting place for English-speaking expats. It has an attractive beer garden.

Two bars that have live jazz several times a week are **17's Bar** (*Hviezdoslavovo nám 17; open 11.30am-1am Mon-Thur, 11.30am-2am Fri & Sat, 4pm-11pm Sun*) and **Aligator** (*Laurinská 7; open 4pm-3am Mon-Sat*). The **Piano Bar** (*Laurinská 11*) is the place for a pleasant and quiet drink.

Galéria Duna (Ⓦ *www.duna.sk; Radlinského 11*) is a club that hosts rock bands, dance music or whatever the alternative scene has to offer – coming events are posted on its website (in Czech, but usable).

Cinemas In the same complex as Charlie's Pub is the four-screen **Charlie Centrum** cinema, which shows the films in their original language. Other cinemas in the city centre are **Kino Mladosť** (*Hviezdoslavovo nám 17*) and **Kino Hviezda** (*nám 1.mája 9*).

Shopping

For folk handicrafts head to **Uľuv** (*nám SNP*) or **Folk Folk** (*Obchodná 10*).

Getting There & Away

Air There are daily flights from Bratislava to Prague with **ČSA** (☎ *52 96 13 25; Štúrova 13*) and to Košice with **Slovak Airlines** (☎ *44 45 00 96; Trnavská cesta 56*). The best prices out of Bratislava are available by booking online with the no-frills **SkyEurope Airlines** (☎ *48 50 48 50*; Ⓦ *www.skyeurope.com*), which flies to Košice (740 Sk one way), Prague (from 1525 Sk) and Split (2525 Sk) in Croatia.

Bus Buy your ticket from the ticket windows, not the driver at Bratislava's **main bus station** (*SAD/Eurolines information* ☎ *0984-222 222, international lines* ☎ *55 56 73 49; Mlynské nivy*), east of the city centre. Reservations for the buses marked 'R' on the posted timetable can be bought from the AMS counter. The footnotes on the timetables in this station are in English.

Seven buses a day connect Bratislava to Vienna (Mitte Busbahnhof; €10.90, 1½ hours). Ten express buses a day run to Prague (4¾ hours). Other buses leaving Bratislava daily include nine to Košice (334 Sk, seven hours), three to Bardejov (468 Sk, 9½ hours) and one to Starý Smokovec (336 Sk, 7¾ hours). There's a weekly bus to Győr (200 Sk, 2½ hours), Hungary.

Eurolines buses to Bratislava include five a week from Brussels (€122 one way, 16 hours)

SLOVAKIA

via Vienna, one daily from Zürich (65 Sfr, 13 hours) and three every week (five in summer) from London (UK£78, 22 hours). The Zürich bus continues to Košice twice a week (21 hours, 94 Sfr).

There are also buses from Bratislava to Belgrade (9½ hours) on Monday and Friday, Budapest (four hours, daily), and Kraków (eight hours, weekly). Tickets can be bought either at the international ticket window in the bus station or at the adjacent Eurolines office, depending on the destination. Beware of buses that transit the Czech Republic, as you could be put off at the border if you need a visa and don't have one.

Train All express trains between Budapest (380 Sk, 2¾ hours) and Prague (528 Sk, 4½ hours) call at Bratislava. There are frequent trains from Bratislava to Košice (414 Sk, six hours) via Trenčín, Žilina and Poprad.

There are hourly trains between Vienna (Südbahnhof) and Bratislava's main train station (1½ hours). One nightly train departs for Moscow (33 hours).

Boat An interesting way to enter or leave Slovakia is on the hydrofoils that ply the Danube between Bratislava and Vienna once a day Wednesday to Sunday from mid-April to October (twice daily on Friday and Saturday in May to September and on Thursday in July and August). These 1¾-hour trips cost €19/29 one way/return. Buy tickets at the hydrofoil terminal (Fajnorovo nábrežie 2). In late summer the service can be interrupted because of low water levels.

There is also a daily (twice daily in August) hydrofoil service between Bratislava and Budapest from mid-April to October. The trip downstream to Budapest takes four hours (40 minutes longer upstream to Bratislava), and costs €59/83 one way/return (10% off for ISIC holders).

Getting Around

To/From the Airport Bratislava's airport (Letisko MR Štefánika) is 7km northeast of the city centre. The only way to get there is on city bus No 61 from the train station or by taxi (around 280 Sk).

Tram & Bus Bratislava's public transport (Dopravný podnik Bratislava or DPB) is based on an extensive tram network complemented by bus and trolleybus. You can buy tickets (12/14/20 Sk for 10/30/60 minutes) at DPB offices and from machines at main tram and bus stops – validate the ticket in the little red machines on the bus or tram when you board.

Tourist tickets (turistické cestovné lístky) valid for one/two/three/seven days (75/140/170/255 Sk) are sold at DPB offices at the train and bus stations, in the underground passageway below Hodžovo nám (open 6am to 7pm weekdays) and on Obchodná near the Hotel Forum (open 9.30am to 5.30pm weekdays). The one- and two-day tickets can also be bought from ticket machines.

Note that bags larger than 30cm x 40cm x 60cm need a half-fare ticket. Travellers have reported being fined up to 1200 Sk for not having a ticket for their backpacks.

Taxi Bratislava's taxis all have meters and drivers are far less likely to try to overcharge you than those in Prague. To order one call **Fun Taxi** (☎ 16 777) or **Otto Taxi** (☎ 16 322).

Car There are several inexpensive local car-rental companies (contact BIS or Satur for others), such as **Favorit Car** (☎ 44 88 41 52; Pri vinohradoch 275), that rent out a Škoda Felicie for around 580 Sk per day plus 3 Sk per kilometre; weekly rates with unlimited kilometres begin at around 7000 Sk including collision-damage waiver, but the office is 8km out of town. **Avis** (☎ 53 41 61 11) has a desk in the Hotel Danube, while **Hertz** (☎ 43 63 66 62) has a desk in the lobby of the Hotel Forum; both have desks at Bratislava's airport, but renting from these outlets costs two to three times more than a local agency.

AROUND BRATISLAVA

From the 1st to the 5th centuries AD, **Devín Castle** (open Tues-Sun May-Oct) was a frontier post of the Roman Empire. During the 9th century the castle was a major stronghold of the Great Moravian Empire. The castle withstood the Turks but was blown up in 1809 by the French. Today it is regarded as a symbol of the Slovaks who maintained their identity despite a millennium of foreign rule. The Gothic ruins contain an exhibit of artefacts found on site. Austria is just across the river.

Getting There & Away

Catch bus No 29 (two an hour) from the Nový most bus terminal to the castle, on a hill where the Morava and Danube Rivers meet. Stay on the bus to the end of the line and walk back to the castle. Remember to take a bus ticket for the journey back; there's no ticket machine at the Devín stop.

West Slovakia

TRENČÍN
☎ 032 • pop 57,000

For many centuries, where the Váh River valley begins to grow narrow between the White Carpathians and the Strážov Hills, Trenčín Castle guarded one of the main trade routes between the Danube River and the Baltic Sea. Laugaricio, a Roman military post (the northernmost Roman camp in Eastern Europe) was set up here in the 2nd century AD; a rock inscription that is dated AD 179 mentions the Roman 2nd Legion and its victory over the Germanic Kvad tribes.

The mighty castle that now towers above the town was first noted in a Viennese chronicle in 1069. In the 13th century the castle's master Matúš Čák held sway over much of Slovakia, and in 1412 Trenčín obtained the

rights of a free royal city. The present castle dates from that period, and although both the castle and town were destroyed by fire in 1790, much has been restored. Today Trenčín is a centre of Slovakia's textile industry.

Orientation & Information

From the adjacent bus and train stations walk west through the city park and underneath the highway to the Tatra Hotel, from which a street bears left uphill to Mierové nám, the main square.

The helpful, well-informed staff at the **AiCES information centre** (☎ 743 35 05; Štúrovo nám 10; open 8am-6pm Mon-Fri, 8am-1pm Sat) can assist you to find accommodation; during the summer months ask about the student dormitories.

The **Všeobecná úverová banka** (Mierové nám 48) cashes travellers cheques, and there is an ATM at another VÚB branch across the street at No 37.

The telephone centre is in the **main post office** (Mierové nám). Check your email at the **Internet Klub Modra Linka** (open 10am-10pm daily), next to the information centre, for 1 Sk per minute.

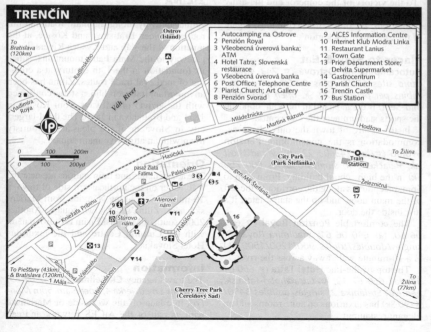

TRENČÍN

1	Autocamping na Ostrove
2	Penzión Royal
3	Všeobecná úverová banka; ATM
4	Hotel Tatra; Slovenská restaurace
5	Všeobecná úverová banka
6	Post Office; Telephone Centre
7	Piarist Church; Art Gallery
8	Penzión Svorad
9	AiCES Information Centre
10	Internet Klub Modra Linka
11	Restaurant Lanius
12	Town Gate
13	Prior Department Store; Delvita Supermarket
14	Gastrocentrum
15	Parish Church
16	Trenčín Castle
17	Bus Station

Things to See

At the western end of Mierové nám are the baroque **Piarist Church** and the 16th-century **town gate**, which contains a clock that plays old-fashioned tunes on the hour. The **art gallery** (*admission 10 Sk; open 9am-5pm Tues-Sun*), in the former Piarist convent next to the church, features works by local artists, notably the realist painter MA Bazovský.

A covered stairway from the corner of the square opposite Piarist Church leads to the Gothic **parish church** and the entrance to **Trenčín Castle** (*admission 80 Sk; open 9am-5pm daily Apr-Sept*). The highlight of the tour (no English) – mostly dreary 18th-century paintings of the ruling family – is the view from the tower. The so-called Well of Love on the first terrace is 70m deep. At night-time the castle is lit with green and purple fairy lights. The two-hour Medieval Days show includes sword fighting and ghosts (9pm every second Friday or Saturday from May to September).

The famous **Roman inscription** of AD 179 is on the cliff behind the Hotel Tatra and can only be seen through a viewing window on the hotel's staircase – ask at reception for permission to see it. The translation reads: 'To the victory of the emperor and the army which, numbering 855 soldiers, resided at Laugaricio. By order of Maximianus, legate of the 2nd auxiliary legion'.

Places to Stay & Eat

Autocamping na Ostrove (*☎ 743 40 13; camp sites 65 Sk, plus 65 Sk per person; cabins per person 120 Sk; open mid-May–mid-Sept*) is on an island in the Váh, opposite the sports stadium near the city centre.

In the centre of town the only cheap accommodation is the nonsmoking **Penzión Svorad** (*☎/fax 743 03 22; e svorad@host.sk; Palackého 4; singles/doubles 500/750 Sk*) in the high school building. From 7am to 4pm, reception is along the corridor to the left of the main door, and up the stairs; later, it's just inside the door.

The comfortable **Penzión Royal** (*☎ 640 06 60, fax 640 06 61; Vladimíra Roya 19; singles/doubles/triples 900/1200/1500 Sk*) is a 10-minute walk away across the river.

The top-of-the-line **Hotel Tatra** (*☎ 650 61 11, fax 650 62 13; e tatra@hotel-tatra.sk; gen MR Štefánika 2; singles/doubles 3490/4490 Sk*) has luxurious en suite rooms and an elegant restaurant.

Gastrocentrum (*mains 35-65 Sk; open 7am-5pm Mon-Fri*) is a self-service cafeteria serving filling hot meals. You'll find better, but pricier, food and a pleasant atmosphere at **Restaurant Lanius** (*Mierové nám 22; mains 65-110 Sk; open 10am-10pm Sun-Thur, 10am-11pm Fri & Sat*).

Slovenská restaurace (*mains 80-120 Sk; open 11am-midnight daily*), in the basement of the Tatra Hotel, serves traditional Slovak food, though you run the risk of being serenaded at your table by a violinist.

There's a **Delvita supermarket** (*open 8am-6pm Mon-Wed, 8am-7pm Thur & Fri, 8am-1pm Sat*) in the Prior department store, two blocks west of the square.

Getting There & Away

All express trains on the main railway line from Bratislava (142 Sk, 1¾ hours) to Košice via Žilina stop here. There are six buses a day to Bratislava, Žilina and Košice, and several to Brno in the Czech Republic.

Central Slovakia

ŽILINA
☎ 41 • pop 84,000

Žilina, midway along the main road and rail routes between Bratislava and Košice, at the junction of the Váh and Kysuca Rivers, is the gateway to the Malá Fatra mountains. Since its foundation in the 13th century at a crossing of medieval trade routes, Žilina has been an important transport hub, a status confirmed with the arrival of railways from Košice in 1871 and Bratislava in 1883. The third-largest city in Slovakia, it's a pleasant, untouristy town with an attractive main square.

Orientation

The adjacent bus and train stations are near the Váh River on the northeastern side of town, a 10-minute walk along Národná from Mariánské nám, Žilina's old town square. Another 200m south of Mariánské nám is Štúrovo nám, with the Cultural Centre and the luxurious Hotel Slovakia.

Information

The travel agency **CK Selinan** (*☎ 562 07 89; Burianova medzierka 4; open 9am-5pm Mon-Fri*), in a lane off the west side of Mariánské nám, is part of the AiCES network and can provide information about Žilina and the Malá Fatra area.

The **Všeobecná úverová banka** (Na bráne 1; open 7.30am-4.30pm Mon-Wed & Fri, 7.30am-noon Thur), two blocks south from Mariánské nám changes travellers cheques and has an ATM.

The **post office** (Sladkovičova 1) is three blocks north of Mariánské nám. There's an **Internet Klub** (open 10am-10pm daily) in the south end of the Dom Kultúry on Šturovo nám, which charges 1 Sk a minute.

Things to See

Apart from the renovated old town square, with its picturesque church and covered arcade, the only sight worth seeking out is the collection of naive art figures made of metal and wire at the dilapidated **Regional Museum** (admission 30 Sk; open 8am-4pm open Tues-Sun), in the Renaissance castle across the river in Budatín, a 15-minute walk northwest from the train station.

Places to Stay & Eat

Pension GMK Centrum (☎ 562 21 36; Mariánské nám 3; singles/doubles from 790/1290 Sk) has smallish rooms, and is tucked away in an upstairs passage off the square. **Penzión Majovey** (☎ 562 41 52, fax 562 52 39; Jána Milca 3; singles/doubles 700/900 Sk) is nicer.

If these places are full, you can always resort to the comfortable if slightly run-down **Hotel Polom** (☎ 562 11 51; Hviezdoslavova 22; singles/doubles 820/1050 Sk) opposite the train station, where the renovated rooms come with en suite bathroom and TV. Older rooms with no frills cost 390/530 Sk.

Bageteria (Jána Milca 1) on the corner of Národná is a good place for hefty sandwiches and inexpensive buffet food.

Radničná vináreň (Mariánské nám 28; mains 100-140 Sk; open 10am-midnight Mon-Sat, noon-midnight Sun) has outdoor tables and a cellar restaurant serving good, inexpensive Slovak dishes.

Campari Pizza (Zaymusova 4; pizza 50-100 Sk; open 11am-9pm Mon-Fri), on the north side of Šturovo nám, has a nice back terrace where you can down pseudo-pizza and cheap red wine.

Getting There & Away

Žilina is on the main railway line from Bratislava to Košice via Trenčín and Poprad, and is served by frequent express trains. Most trains between Prague and Košice also stop at Žilina. Express trains from Žilina take 6¼ hours to Prague (466km), 1¼ hours to Trenčín (92 Sk), 2¾ hours to Bratislava (212 Sk), two hours to Poprad (158 Sk) and three hours to Košice (250 Sk).

There are also daily direct trains to Kraków in Poland (provided you don't need a visa to transit the Czech Republic). You can avoid Czech territory by going through Poprad and the Javorina/-ysa Polana border crossing on to Zakopane.

There are several buses a day to Brno (134km) and Prague.

MALÁ FATRA
☎ 041

The Malá Fatra (Little Fatra) mountain range stretches 50km across northwestern Slovakia; Veľký Kriváň (1709m) is the highest peak. Two hundred square kilometres of this scenic range, north of the Váh River and east of Žilina, are included in Malá Fatra National Park. At the heart of the park is the Vrátna dolina, a beautiful mountain valley with forested slopes on all sides.

Noted for its rich flora, Vrátna dolina has something for everyone. The hiking possibilities vary from easy tourist tracks through the forest to scenic ridge walks, and in winter there is downhill and cross-country skiing and snowboarding. There are plenty of places to stay and eat, though in midsummer and winter accommodation is tight. The valley is an easy day trip from Žilina. The mountains are accessible by road, trail and chairlift for anyone with the urge to enjoy their beauty.

Information

There's an **AiCES Information Centre** (☎ 599 31 00; e ztt@terchova.sk; 10am-3.45pm Mon-Fri, open 10am-4pm Sat, 10am-2pm Sun) in the Obecni úrad (regional offices) in Terchová. The **Slovenská sporiteľňa** bank next door has an exchange counter and an ATM. The **post office** is 100m further east on the main road.

The **Mountain Rescue Service** (Horská služba; ☎ 569 52 32), on the access road to Hotel Boboty, can provide detailed information on the national park.

If you plan to hike, you should get the VKÚ's 1:50,000 Malá Fatra – Vrátna map (sheet No 110).

SLOVAKIA

MALÁ FATRA

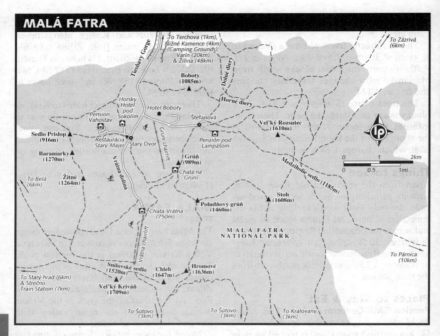

SLOVAKIA

Things to See & Do

The road enters the Vrátna dolina just south of Terchová, where it runs through the **Tiesňavy Gorge** with rocky crags on both sides. One rock resembles a person praying (turn and look back after you've passed through the gorge).

From **Chata Vrátna** (750m) at the head of the valley, a two-seater chairlift (110/140 Sk one way/return) climbs 770m to Snilovské sedlo (1520m), a saddle midway between Chleb (1647m) and Veľký Kriváň (1709m). Take along warm clothes as it will be a lot cooler on top.

From Snilovské sedlo you can follow the red trail southeast along the mountain ridges past Hromové (1636m), then northeast to Poludňový grúň (1460m) and Stoh (1608m) to Medziholie sedlo (1185m), below the rocky summit of Veľký Rozsutec (1610m). An orange trail skirting the side of Stoh avoids a 200m climb.

From Medziholie it's easy to descend via another green trail to **Štefanová**, a picturesque village of log houses. You can do the hike from Snilovské sedlo to Štefanová via Medziholie in about four hours. Other possible hikes from Snilovské sedlo are the blue trail to Starý Dvor via Baraniarky (1270m; three hours) and the red trail west to Strečno train station via the Starý hrad ruins (6½ hours).

Skiing There is good downhill skiing and snowboarding for all levels, with some 20 inexpensive lifts at various places in the valley (few are linked, though). Reasonable skis, boots and snowboards are available for hire. The best time is from late December to March.

Places to Stay & Eat

No camping is allowed in the Vrátna dolina. The nearest **camping grounds** are at Nižné Kamence, 3.5km west of Terchová, and at Varín, another 11km towards Žilina.

There are lots of **private rooms** in Terchová from 200 Sk per person.

The friendly **Hotel Terchová** (☎ 569 56 25, fax 569 56 30; e vratna@hotel-terchova.sk; singles/doubles 720/1440 Sk), at the Vrátna junction in Terchová, is new and comfortable.

Horsky Hotel pod Sokolím (☎/fax 569 53 26), on the hill above the good **Reštaurácia Starý Majer**, and **Pension Vahostav** (☎ 569 53 06), about 1km further up the valley, have beds for 200 Sk to 300 Sk per person.

Spectacular views across Lake Bled to the island church and the Karavanke Range beyond, Slovenia

Venetian-style houses, Piran harbour, Slovenia

Ljubljana's Franciscan Church and Triple Bridge

Lively scenes from Lucerne's celebration of Fasnacht, a Shrovetide carnival in Switzerland

The traditional painted architecture in Appenzell village, Switzerland, is a favourite with tourists

A unique way of enjoying the beauty of the Vaud Alps of Switzerland during International Balloon Week

Chata Vrátna (☎ 569 57 39, fax 569 57 31; e chatavratna@icos.sk; dorm beds 150 Sk, double/triple/quads 460/590/690 Sk), a large wooden chalet at the head of the valley, is usually full with hikers in summer and skiers in winter. In spring and late autumn, groups of school children pack the dormitories. There are regular hotel rooms as well as dorm beds.

There's a big **potraviny** (grocery; open 6am-6pm Mon-Fri, 6am-2pm Sat, 8am-noon Sun) beside the Hotel Terchová.

Štefanová Friendly **Chata vo Vyhnana** (☎/fax 569 51 24; e chatavyhnana@stonline .sk; half/full board per person 160/300 Sk) in Štefanová has good dorm accommodation. A few minutes' walk up the green trail in Štefanová village is **Chata pod Skalným mestom** (☎ 569 53 63; beds per person 300 Sk). A few hundred metres beyond is the slightly posher **Penzión pod Lampášom** (☎ 569 53 92; full board per person 700 Sk). There are also several private rooms (privaty) around the village – look for the 'zimmer frei' signs.

The comfortable **Hotel Boboty** (☎ 569 52 28, fax 569 57 37; singles/doubles 800/1000 Sk) is a five-minute walk up from the bus stop near Štefanová. The hotel, with a sauna, swimming pool and restaurant, was being renovated and extended at the time of research.

Getting There & Around
The bus from Žilina to Chata Vrátna (one hour, 32km) leaves from platform No 10 at Žilina bus station nine times a day. If you come on a day trip, check the times of return trips at the information counter at Žilina bus station before setting out.

You can hire bicycles in Terchová – ask at the information centre for details.

East Slovakia

East Slovakia is one of the most attractive touring areas in Central Europe. In one compact region you can enjoy superb hiking in the Vysoké Tatry (High Tatra) mountains, rafting on the Dunajec River, historic towns such as Levoča and Bardejov, the great medieval castle at Spišské Podhradie, the charming spa of Bardejovské Kúpele and city life in Košice. Getting around is easy, with frequent trains and buses to all these sights plus easy access to Poland and Hungary. In spite of all these attractions, the region still feels somewhat off the beaten track.

VYSOKÉ TATRY
☎ 0969
The Vysoké Tatry (High Tatras) are the only truly alpine mountains in Central Europe. This 27km-long granite massif covers 260 sq km, forming the northernmost portion of the Carpathian Mountains. The narrow, rocky crests soar above wide glacial valleys with precipitous walls. At 2654m, Gerlachovský štít (Mt Gerlach) is the highest mountain in the entire 1200km Carpathian range, and several other peaks exceed 2500m.

Enhancing the natural beauty packed into this relatively small area are clear mountain lakes, thundering waterfalls and dazzling snowfields. The lower slopes are covered by dense forest; from 1500m to 1800m lies a belt of shrubs and dwarf pines, and above are alpine flora, bare rock and snow.

Since 1949, most of the Slovak part of this jagged range has been included in the Tatra National Park (Tanap), the first national park to be created in former Czechoslovakia, complementing a similar park in Poland. A 600km network of hiking trails reaches all the alpine valleys and many peaks. The red-marked Tatranská magistrála trail follows the southern slopes of the Vysoké Tatry for 65km through a variety of striking landscapes. Other routes are also colour-coded and easy to follow. Park regulations require you to keep to the marked trails and to refrain from picking flowers.

Climate & When to Go
When planning your trip, keep in mind that the higher trails are closed from November to mid-June, to protect the delicate environment. There's snow by November (on the highest passes as early as September), and many snowfields linger until May or even June. Beware of sudden thunderstorms, especially on ridges and peaks where there's no protection. Always wear hiking boots and carry warm clothing. Remember that the assistance of the Mountain Rescue Service is not free. July and August are the warmest (and most crowded) months, while August and September are the best for high-altitude hiking. Hotel prices are lowest from April to mid-June.

The **Tanap Mountain Rescue Service office** next to Satur in Starý Smokovec can give you a weather report for the next day.

SLOVAKIA

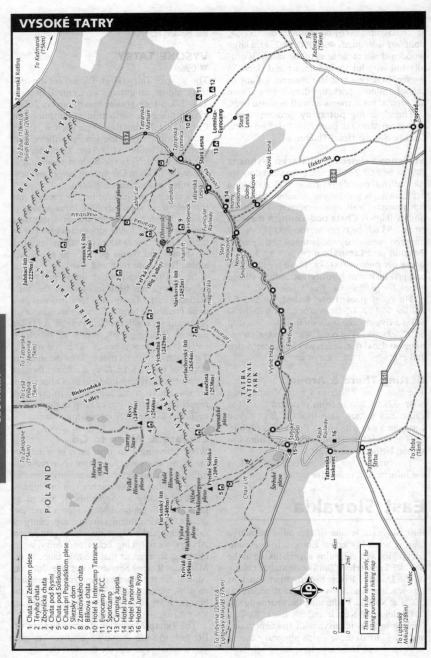

VYSOKÉ TATRY

To Kežmarok (15km)

To Ždiar (10km) & Polish Border (20km)

Tatranská Kotlina

Belianske Tatry

537

Tatranská Matliare

Skalnaté pleso

Cable Car

Jahňací štít (2229m)

Lomnický štít (2634m)

Gondola

Lomnická

Tatranská Lomnica

Tatranská Lesná

Lomnica-Eurocamp

To Kežmarok (16km)

To Poprad

Stará Lesná

Nová Lesná

Električka

Skalnaté pleso

magistrála

Trebielovka

Obrovský vodopád

Veľká Studená (Big Valley)

chairlift

Funicular Railway

Horný Smokovec

Dolný Smokovec

Starý Smokovec

Nový Smokovec

Tatranská Lesná

Električka

534

Slavkovský štít (2452m)

Východná Vysoká (2429m)

magistrála

Gerlachovský štít (2655m)

Tatranská

Kончistá (2538m)

TATRA NATIONAL PARK

Vyšné Hágy

Električka

To Tatranská Javorína (5km)

To Lysá Poľana (5km)

Bielovodská Valley

High Tatras

(Vysoké Tatry)

Rysy (2499m)

Vysoká (2560m)

Popradské pleso

Štrbské Pleso

Rack Railway

To Štrba (1km)

To Zakopane (15km)

Morskie (Oko) Lake

Čierny Staw

POLAND

Veľké Hincovo pleso

Malé Hincovo pleso

Predné Solisko (2093m)

Chair Lift

Nižné Wahlenbergovo pleso

Srbské pleso

Tatranská Lieskovec

Tatranská Štrba

Furkotský štít (2405m)

Vyšné Wahlenbergovo pleso

Kriváň (2494m)

To Pribylina (20km) & Liptovský Mikuláš (37km)

To Liptovský Mikuláš (28km)

To Važec

Važec

SLOVAKIA

1 Chata pri Zelenom plese
2 Téryho chata
3 Zbojnícka chata
4 Chata pod Rysmi
5 Chata pod Soliskom
6 Chata pri Popradskom plese
7 Sliezsky dom
8 Zamkovského chata
9 Bilíkova chata
10 Hotel & Intercamp Tatranec
11 Eurocamp FICC
12 Športcamp
13 Camping Jupela
14 Hotel Junior
15 Hotel Panoráma
16 Hotel Junior Rysy

4km
2mi
0   2
0   1   2

This map is for reference only, for hiking purchase a hiking map

Orientation

Starý Smokovec, an early 20th-century resort that is well connected to the rest of the country by road and rail, makes a pleasant base camp. Small electric trains trundle frequently between here and Štrbské Pleso, Tatranská Lomnica and Poprad, where they link up with the national railway system. Buses also run frequently between the resorts. Cable cars, chairlifts and a funicular railway carry you up the slopes to hiking trails that soon lead you away from the throng. During winter, skiers flock to the area. All three main train stations have left-luggage offices.

Maps Our Vysoké Tatry map is intended for initial orientation only. Buy a proper VKÚ 1:25,000 or 1:50,000 Vysoké Tatry hiking map when you arrive. Good maps are usually available at hotels, shops and newsstands inside the park. When buying your map, make sure you get a green one with summer hiking trails and not a blue one with winter ski routes.

Information

Tourist Offices The main AiCES Tatra information centre (☎ 442 34 40; ℮ tik .vysoketatry@sinet.sk; open 8am-6pm daily Dec–mid-Apr, 8am-4.30pm Mon-Sat rest of year) in the Dom služieb shopping centre, northwest of Starý Smokovec train station, has plenty of information on the region but does not book accommodation. There's another office (☎ 449 23 91; open 8.30am-6pm daily Dec–mid-Apr, 8.30am-11.30am & noon-4pm Mon-Fri rest of year) next to Obchodný dom Toliar department store, opposite the Štrbské Pleso train station.

The helpful staff at the **Satur office** (☎ 442 24 97; ℮ smokovec@satur.sk; open 8am-4pm Mon-Fri), just above the train station at Starý Smokovec, provide general advice, mountain guides and tours, and can book beds in local hotels, pensions and mountain huts.

Check out the website maintained by the **Tatra National Park** (ⓦ www.tanap.sk) as it is packed with useful information on accommodation, mountain guides, equipment rental and trail conditions.

Money The **Všeobecná úverová banka** (open 8am-noon & 1pm-4pm Mon-Wed & Fri, 8am-noon Thur), in the commercial centre above the bus station in Starý Smokovec, changes travellers cheques and has an ATM.

Post & Communications The post office (open 7.30am-noon & 1am-4pm Mon-Fri, 8am-10am Sat), near Starý Smokovec train station, has coin and cardphones, and sells phonecards. You can check email at the café next door to Starý Smokovec information centre, and in Hotel Toliar in Štrbské Pleso.

Things to See & Do

Above Starý Smokovec From Starý Smokovec a funicular railway, built in 1908, takes you up to **Hrebienok** (1280m; 60 Sk one way), a ski resort with a view into the Veľká Studená (Big Valley). Alternatively, it takes less than an hour to walk up to Hrebienok (green trail). If you catch the funicular railway, a 20-minute walk north from the top station along the red Tatranská magistrála trail takes you to the **Obrovský vodopád** (waterfall).

For great scenery, fork left before the waterfall on the blue trail that leads to Zbojnícka chata in the Veľká Studená (three hours). Beyond Zbojnícka, the blue trail climbs over a 2373m pass and descends the long Bielovodská valley towards the Polish border.

Zamkovského chata is just off the Magistrála, less than an hour north from Hrebienok. From here a green trail leads northwest to Téryho chata in the Malá Studená (three hours). The round trip from Hrebienok to Zamkovského, Téryho and Zbojnícka and then back to Hrebienok takes about eight hours. The trail from Téryho to Zbojnícka is one-way only, in that direction, and involves some steep ascents with the aid of chains and ladders.

Štrbské Pleso From the modern ski resort of Štrbské Pleso with its glacial lake (1346m), take the red-marked Magistrála trail for about an hour up to **Popradské pleso**, an idyllic lake at 1494m. The Magistrála runs along the south shore of Štrbské pleso lake – just head uphill from the train station to find it. From Popradské pleso the Magistrála zigzags steeply up the mountainside then traverses east towards Sliezský dom and Hrebienok (four hours). A shorter option is to hike up the blue trail from Popradské pleso to the Hincovo lakes (1½ hours).

Tatranská Lomnica In 1937 a 30-person cable car (lanová dráha) opened from Tatranská Lomnica to the mountain lake of **Skalnaté pleso** (1751m). The **cable car** (120 Sk one way; open Wed-Mon) is very popular with the

SLOVAKIA

tourists, so during the peak seasons of July to September and December to April get to the ticket office early. Note that it's often closed for maintenance in November and May.

A modern gondola with four-seat cabins (120 Sk one way; closed 1st Mon June-Aug) also runs to Skalnaté pleso via Štart, leaving from above the Horec Hotel in Tatranská Lomnica – it is faster and has shorter queues than the cable car.

There's a big observatory at Skalnaté pleso, where a smaller 15-person **cable car** carries you to the summit of **Lomnický štít** at 2632m (300 Sk one way) for a sweeping view of the entire Vysoké Tatry range. You're only allowed 30 minutes at the top, and if you miss your car down, you'll have to wait until another car has room for you. From Skalnaté pleso it's two hours' walk down Magistrála trail to Hrebienok and the funicular railway down to Starý Smokovec.

The **Tatra National Park Museum** (open 8am-noon & 1pm-4.30pm Mon-Fri, 8am-noon Sat & Sun), a few hundred metres from the bus station, has an exhibition on the area's natural and human histories.

Activities
Mountain Climbing You can reach the summit of Slavkovský štít (2452m) via the blue trail from Starý Smokovec (seven to eight hours return). Mt Rysy (2499m), right on the Polish border, is a nine-hour return trip from Štrbské pleso (via Popradské pleso and chata pod Rysmi). You can do these routes on your own, but to scale the peaks without marked hiking trails (Gerlachovský štít included) you must hire a mountain guide. Members of recognised climbing clubs are exempt from this requirement.

Satur in Starý Smokovec books guides from the Tanap Mountain Rescue Service office for 4000 Sk to 5000 Sk per day for a guide for up to five people.

Skiing & Snowboarding Štrbské Pleso, Starý Smokovec and Tatranská Lomnica all have lifts offering fairly average downhill skiing and snowboarding, as well as good cross-country skiing trails. Štrbské Pleso and Starý Smokovec are much better suited to beginners and intermediates, while Tatranská Lomnica is more suitable for intermediates and experts. Ski/snowboard hire costs from 249/390 Sk a day.

Places to Stay
Camping No wild camping is permitted within Tatra National Park. **Camping Jupela** (☎ 446 74 93; camp sites 80 Sk, plus 90 Sk per person; open May-Sept) is 10 minutes' walk downhill from Stará Lesná train station.

There are three camping grounds 2km from Tatranská Lomnica (near Tatranská Lomnica-Eurocamp train station on the line to Studený potok). The largest is **Eurocamp FICC** (☎ 446 77 41, fax 446 73 46; camp sites 90 Sk, plus 120 Sk per person, bungalows 1050-1500 Sk; open year-round), five minutes' walk from the train station, with four-person luxury bungalows with private bath. The Eurocamp has restaurants (which include the good folkloric Koliba Restaurant), bars, shops, a supermarket, a swimming pool, tennis, sauna, disco, hot water and row upon row of parked caravans.

An eight-minute walk south of Eurocamp is the less-expensive **Športcamp** (☎ 446 72 88; open June-Sept) where there are also four- or five-person bungalows that must be booked ahead in summer. A 10-minute walk north of Eurocamp, towards Tatranská Lomnica, is the **Hotel & Intercamp Tatranec** (☎ 446 70 92).

Chaty Up on the hiking trails are nine mountain chalets (chaty), but given their limited capacity and the popularity of the area, they may all be full in midsummer. Many of the chalets close for maintenance in November and May. Although food is available at the chalets, you should bring some of your own supplies. A stay in a chata is one of the best mountain experiences the Tatras have to offer.

Satur in Starý Smokovec can reserve beds at most of the chalets. High-season prices are around 300 Sk to 500 Sk per person.

The following are the main chalets on the upper trails, from west to east:

Chata pod Soliskom (1800m) At the top of the Štrbské Pleso chairlift, it is small and very busy.
Chata pri Popradskom plese (1500m; ☎ 449 21 77) Eight-bed, six-bed and double rooms with restaurant
Chata pod Rysmi (2250m) Open June to October. This chata was destroyed by an avalanche in winter 1999 to 2000, and again in February 2001, and was being rebuilt – in a safer location! – at the time of writing.
Sliezský dom (1670m; ☎ 442 52 02; e gotravel@ neta.sk) Large mountain hotel with restaurant and cafeteria
Zbojnícka chata (1960m; ☎ 0903-619 000) Alpine bunks and restaurant

Téryho chata (2015m; ☎ 442 52 45) Alpine bunks and restaurant

Zamkovského chata (1475m; ☎ 442 26 30) Alpine bunks and restaurant

Bilíkova chata (1220m; ☎ 442 24 39) Attractive wooden chalet with double rooms

Chata pri Zelenom plese (1540m; ☎ 446 74 20) Dorm accommodation with restaurant

Private Rooms Satur can help out with private rooms (250 Sk to 500 Sk per person) and apartments. You can also check out the website for the **Tatra National Park** (w www .tanap.sk/homes.html).

Hotels In the high seasons (mid-December to February and mid-June to September), hotel prices almost double compared with the low seasons (March to mid-June and October to mid-December). Most prices quoted in this section are high season.

The Satur office at Starý Smokovec can help you to find a room in all categories, from budget to deluxe. They do not always know about last-minute cancellations in hotels so if they can't direct you to any accommodation, then tramp around to see what you can find.

Starý Smokovec & Around One of the best deals at Starý Smokovec is the friendly, family-run **Pension Vesna** (☎ 442 27 74, fax 442 31 09; e vesna@sinet.sk; apartments per person 700 Sk), behind the large sanatorium below Nový Smokovec train station. Spacious three-bed apartments with private bath are available, and the owner speaks English. You can take a short cut through the sanatorium grounds to get there (ask), or follow the red signs west from the train station.

Hotel Smokovec (☎ 442 51 91, fax 442 51 94; e smokovec@tatry.net; doubles/quads 1980/3560 Sk), located immediately below Starý Smokovec train station, has spacious rooms including a bath and TV; breakfast is 130 Sk extra. It also has a swimming pool.

The majestic and century-old **Grand Hotel** (☎ 442 21 54, fax 442 21 57; singles/doubles 1700/2900 Sk), opposite Hotel Smokovec, has a certain old-fashioned elegance. Use of the indoor swimming pool is included.

The cheapest place to stay if you have an HI or ISIC card is **Hotel Junior** (☎ 442 26 61, fax 442 24 93; singles/doubles/triples/quads 350/680/840/1010 Sk), just below the Horný Smokovec train station. The hotel is often full of noisy school groups.

The 96-room **Park Hotel** (☎ 442 23 42, fax 442 23 04; singles/doubles 550/1100 Sk) above Nový Smokovec train station, and the **Hotel MS 70** (☎ 442 29 72, fax 442 29 70; doubles/triples 920/1330 Sk), west of the Park Hotel, are good mid-range choices.

Tatranská Lomnica The best value in town is the **Penzión Bélin** (☎/fax 446 77 78; e belin@tatry.sk; rooms per person 240 Sk), on the main road just a few minutes' walk north of the train station.

The squat, monolithic **Hotel Slovan** (☎ 446 78 51, fax 446 76 27; e slovan@tatry.sk; singles/doubles 950/1420 Sk) is five minutes' uphill behind Hotel Slovakia. It lacks character, but is not bad value for rooms with private bath and satellite TV.

One of Slovakia's most romantic hotels is the 89-room **Grandhotel Praha** (☎ 446 79 41/5, fax 446 78 91; e grandpraha@ tatry.sk; singles/doubles 2100/3100 Sk), built in 1905 and hidden in the forest up the hill beside the cable-car terminal.

Štrbské Pleso The 11-storey **Hotel Panoráma** (☎ 449 21 11, fax 449 28 10; e hotel@ hotelpanorama.sk; singles/doubles 985/ 1770 Sk) is the pyramidal eyesore next to the shopping centre above the Štrbské Pleso train station. The rooms are good, all have baths, and the view is much nicer looking out.

You'll find some cheaper options down the hill in Tatranská Štrba, including **Hotel Junior Rysy** (☎ 4484 845, fax 448 42 96; e hotel .rysy@ke.telecom.sk; singles/doubles 700/ 900 Sk), just a few minutes' walk from the Tatranská Lieskovec stop on the rack-railway between Tatranská Štrba and Štrbské Pleso.

Places to Eat
Almost all the hotels and chalets in this region have their own restaurants. Just above the bus station at Starý Smokovec is **Bistro-Fast Food Tatra** (open 10am-7pm daily), but the self-service **bistro** (open 8am-7pm daily) in Hotel Smokovec is better.

For typical Slovak food with a Roma band, head for the mid-range **Restaurant Koliba** (open 5pm-midnight), just southwest of the train station.

The friendly **restaurant** (mains 130-190 Sk; open 11.30am-11pm daily), above the Tatrasport shop opposite the bus station, is the nicest place in town.

SLOVAKIA

There's a good self-service restaurant in the **Obchodný dom Toliar** *(open 8am-7pm daily)* next to Štrbské Pleso train station.

There are **supermarkets** in Starý Smokovec, Tatranská Lomnica and Štrbské Pleso, all open 7.45am to 5.45pm Monday to Friday, and 8am to noon Saturday and Sunday; the *potraviny* (grocery), just east of the Hotel Smokovec, is open noon to 6pm on Saturday.

Getting There & Away

Bus There are regular express buses from Bratislava to Starý Smokovec (seven hours) and Tatranská Lomnica. From Starý Smokovec there are eight buses a day to -ysa Polana; six to Levoča; two to Bardejov; four to Žilina (125 Sk, 3¼ hours); three to Trenčín; and one to Brno and Prague (11 hours) in the Czech Republic. The Hungarian Volánbusz bus from Budapest to Tatranská Lomnica runs twice a week (seven hours).

Train To reach Vysoké Tatry, take any of the express trains running between Prague, Bratislava and Košice, and change at Poprad. There are frequent narrow-gauge electric trains between Poprad and Starý Smokovec.

Alternatively, get off the express at Tatranská Štrba, a main-line station west of Poprad, and take the rack-railway up to Štrbské Pleso.

The booking offices in Starý Smokovec and Tatranská Lomnica train stations can reserve sleepers and couchettes from Poprad to Bratislava and to Prague, Karlovy Vary and Brno in the Czech Republic.

Walking into Poland For anyone who is interested in walking between Slovakia and Poland, there's a highway border crossing near Javorina, an hour from Starý Smokovec by bus (46 Sk). The bus is occasionally crowded and the bus stop is 100m from the border (bus times posted). On the Polish side, buses can fill up with people on excursions between Morskie Oko Lake and Zakopane, so it's easier southbound than northbound.

You'll find a bank where you can change money at -ysa Polana on the Polish side, but there's no Slovak bank at Javorina. The rate offered at the border is about 10% worse than in Zakopane. Southbound travellers should buy a few dollars worth of Slovak crowns at an exchange office in Poland to pay the onward bus fare to Starý Smokovec or Poprad, as this may not be possible at the border.

A bus direct from Poprad to Zakopane, Poland, leaves Starý Smokovec bus station at 6.15am on Thursday and Saturday (two hours). Also ask Satur about its excursion buses to Zakopane and Kraków.

Getting Around

Electric trains travel from Poprad to Starý Smokovec (16 Sk, 30 minutes) and Štrbské Pleso (26 Sk, one hour) about every half-hour, and from Starý Smokovec to Tatranská Lomnica (11 Sk, 15 minutes) about every 30 to 60 minutes. These trains make frequent stops along their routes; when there isn't a ticket window at the station, go immediately to the conductor on boarding to buy your ticket.

A rack-railway connects Štrba (on the main Žilina-Poprad road and train line) with Štrbské Pleso (22 Sk, 5km). A two-/six-day ticket giving unlimited travel on the Tatra trains costs 136/262 Sk.

You can hire **mountain bikes** from Tatrasport in Starý Smokovec for 299 Sk a day.

POPRAD

☎ 052 • pop 53,000

Poprad is a modern industrial city with little to interest visitors; however, it's an important transportation hub. The electric railway from here to Starý Smokovec was built in 1908 and extended to Štrbské Pleso in 1912.

The **AiCES information centre** *(☎ 772 17 00; nám Sv Egídia 2950/114; open 8.30am-noon & 1pm-5pm Mon-Fri, 9am-1pm Sat)* covers the whole Tatry region, and rents bicycles for 200 Sk a day.

There's a 24-hour left-luggage desk at the Poprad train station.

Places to Stay & Eat

If you arrive late, you could stay at the run-down **Hotel Európa** *(☎ 772 18 83; singles/doubles/triples 250/400/550 Sk)* just outside of the Poprad train station.

In town, **Tatratour** *(☎ 776 37 12; nám Sv Egídia 9)* can arrange smarter pension accommodation from 350 Sk per person.

Ulica 1.mája, north of the main square, has several good eateries including **Slovenská reštaurácia** *(mains 45-65 Sk; open 11am-11pm daily)* and a cheap **pizzeria** *(open 9.30am-7pm Mon-Sat)*.

There's also a **supermarket** above the Prior department store at the western end of the town square.

Getting There & Away

Bus There are buses to almost everywhere in Slovakia departing from the large bus station next to the train station, including Bratislava (336 Sk, four hours), Košice (158 Sk, two hours), Červený Kláštor (62 Sk, 1¾ hours), Levoča (26km), Spišské Podhradie (41km) and Bardejov (125km).

Train Poprad is a major junction on the main train line from Prague and Bratislava to Košice. Express trains run to Žilina (two hours) and Košice (1½ hours) every couple of hours. Electric trains climb 13km to Starý Smokovec, the main Vysoké Tatry resort, every hour or so. A branch line runs to Plaveč (two hours by local train), where you can get a connection to Muszyna, five times a day.

KEŽMAROK
☎ 052 • pop 21,100

Over the centuries this fiercely independent town, its northwestern skyline dominated by the mighty Vysoké Tatry range, was the second most important in the region after Levoča. In the 13th century it was colonised by the Germans and was granted royal status in 1380. The citizens of Kežmarok declared an independent republic in 1918 but almost immediately the town was incorporated into Czechoslovakia. These days Kežmarok has a well-preserved old town with a castle and three interesting churches to admire.

If you can make it to Kežmarok on the second weekend in July, don't miss the Festival of European Folk Crafts, with exhibits of craft making, folk dancing and singing.

Orientation & Information

The bus and train stations are side by side northwest of the old town, just across the Poprad River.

There's a useful **AiCES information office** (☎ 452 40 47; open 8.30am-noon & 1.30pm-5pm Mon-Fri, 9am-2pm Sat year-round, 9am-2pm Sun June-Sept) located at Hlavné nám 46 for tourist help.

Things to See

The **New Evangelical Church** (cnr Toporcerova & Hviezdoslavova; open 9am-noon & 2pm-5pm daily May-Sept), built in 1894, is a huge red and green pseudo-Moorish structure housing the mausoleum of Imre Thököly, who fought with Ferenc Rákóczi against the Habsburg takeover of Hungary. Next door, the **Wooden Articulated Church** (open 9am-noon & 2pm-5pm daily May-Sept) was built in 1717 without a single iron nail and has an amazing cross-shaped interior of carved and painted wood.

North of Hlavné nám is the 15th-century Gothic **Church of the Holy Cross** (nám Požárnikov), with its beautifully carved wooden altars supposedly crafted by students of Master Pavol of Levoča.

The **Kežmarok Museum** (admission 50 Sk; open 9am-4pm Tues-Sun), inside the 15th-century Kežmarok Castle, features history, archaeology and period-furniture.

Places to Stay & Eat

The basic **Karpaty Camping** (☎ 452 24 90) is about 4km southwest of the town centre on the road to Poprad. **Private rooms** through AiCES cost from 200 Sk per person.

Beneath the castle walls is **Penzión Hubert** (☎ 0905-248 460; Hradská cesta 8; rooms per person 300 Sk), while **Hotel Štart** (☎ 452 29 15; rooms per person from 290 Sk) is 10 minutes' walk north of the castle.

The **Kežmarská Restaurant** (Hradné nám 5; mains 60-120 Sk; open 9am-10pm daily) opposite the castle is reasonable, or try **Pizza Palermo** (Hlavné nám 8; mains 60-100 Sk; open 10am-10pm daily) for pizza and pasta.

Getting There & Away

Buses are faster and more plentiful than trains – they run about hourly from Poprad, and there are eight daily from Starý Smokovec. There are also five daily buses to Červený Kláštor.

DUNAJEC GORGE
☎ 052

The Pieniny National Park (21 sq km), created in 1967, combines with a similar park in Poland to protect the 9km Dunajec Gorge between the Slovak village of Červený Kláštor and Szczawnica, Poland. The river here, flowing between 500m limestone cliffs, forms the international boundary.

At the mouth of the gorge is a 14th-century fortified **Carthusian monastery** (admission 25 Sk; open 9am-5pm daily May-Sept, 9am-4pm Tues-Sat Oct-Apr), now used as a park administrative centre and museum with a good collection of statuary and old prints of the area. Near the monastery is an **information centre** (open 9am-5pm daily May-Sept).

From May to October, river trips (200 Sk per person) on wooden rafts depart from two locations at Červený Kláštor: opposite the monastery, and 1km upriver west of the village. A raft will set out only when enough passengers appear. When business is slow you may have to wait. Note that this is not white-water rafting – the Dunajec is a rather sedate experience.

From the downriver terminus you can hike back to the monastery in a little over an hour. The rafting operation on the Polish side is larger and better organised (see Dunajec Gorge in the Poland chapter for details), and the Slovak raft trip is much shorter than the Polish one.

Even if you don't go rafting, it's still worth hiking along the riverside trail through the gorge on the Slovak side (no such trail exists on the Polish side).

Places to Stay

Across a small stream from the monastery is a **camping ground** *(open mid-June–mid-Sept)*. No bungalows are available.

There are several pensions in Červený Kláštor plus the **Hotel Pltník** *(☎ 482 25 25;*

beds per person 500 Sk), which can often be booked up in summer.

One kilometre up the road to Veľký Lipník from the monastery is **Hotel Dunajec** *(☎ 482 20 27)*, with some inexpensive bungalows across the road.

Close to Lesnica, which is just 2km east of Cerveny Klastor, near the downstream end of the rafting trip, is the inexpensive **Pieniny chata** *(☎/fax 439 75 30; beds 150 Sk, doubles with breakfast 430 Sk)*, which is often full during the summer.

Getting There & Away

Direct buses run between Červený Kláštor and both Poprad and Stara Ľubovňa, and there are buses from Stará Ľubovňa to Bardejov, Prešov and Košice.

Although Poland is just across the river, there's no official border crossing here. You can take a bus to Stará Ľubovňa and then a train to Plaveč, where a local train departs three times daily for Muszyna in Poland, 16km away. Alternatively, you can use the -ysa Polana crossing (see Getting There & Away in the Vysoké Tatry section) to make your way to Zakopane.

SPIŠSKÁ NOVÁ VES & SLOVENSKÝ RAJ

SLOVENSKÝ RAJ
☎ 053

South of Poprad lies the Slovenský raj (Slovak Paradise), a national park created in 1988. This mountainous karst area features forests, cliffs, caves, canyons, waterfalls and 1896 species of butterfly, and is prime hiking territory.

Orientation & Information

The nearest town is **Spišská Nová Ves**, 23km southeast of Poprad. The main trailheads on the northern edge of the national park are at Čingov, 5km west of Spišská Nová Ves, and Podlesok, 1km southwest of Hrabušice.

The **AiCES information centre** (*☎ 442 82 92;* **W** *www.slovenskyraj.sk; Letná 49; open 8.30am-5.30pm Mon-Fri, 9.30am-1pm Sat June-Sept; 9.30am-4pm Mon-Fri Oct-May)* in Spišská Nová Ves can help with accommodation and national park information. You can buy VKÚ's 1:25,000 *Slovenský raj* hiking map (sheet No 4) here.

You can cash travellers cheques or use the 24-hour ATM at the **Slovenská sporiteľňa** (*nám MR Štefánika*). The telephone centre is in the **main post office** (*nám MR Štefánika 7; open 7am-7pm Mon-Fri, 7am-11am Sat*).

Things to See & Do

From Čingov a blue trail leads up the **Hornád River gorge**, passing below Tomášovský výhľad, to Letanovský mlýn. The trail up the river is narrow and there are several ladders and ramps where hikers can only pass one by one. During peak periods hikers are allowed to travel only in an upstream direction from Čingov, returning over Tomášovský výhľad.

One kilometre beyond Letanovský mlýn, a green trail leaves the river and climbs sharply up to **Kláštorisko**, where there's a **restaurant** (*☎ 449 33 07; cabins per person 200 Sk; open daily year-round)*, with chalet *(chaty)* accommodation. To stay here in midsummer, you should call ahead to check availability. From Kláštorisko you can follow another blue trail back down the ridge towards Čingov. You'll need around six hours to do the entire circuit, lunch at Kláštorisko included.

From Podlesok, an excellent day's hike heads up the **Suchá Belá gorge** (with several steep ladders), then east to Kláštorisko on a yellow then red trail. From here, take the blue trail down to the Hornád River, then follow the river gorge upstream to return to Podlesok. Allow six to seven hours.

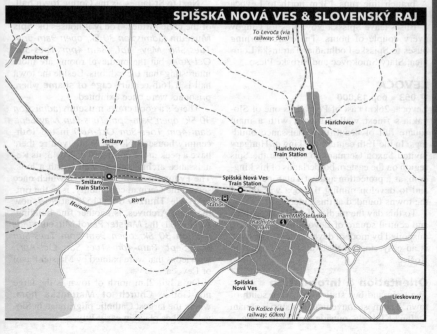

SPIŠSKÁ NOVÁ VES & SLOVENSKÝ RAJ

Arnutovce

To Levoča (via railway; 5km)

Harichovce

Smižany

Harichovce Train Station

Smižany Train Station

Hornád

River

Spišská Nová Ves Train Station

Bus Station

nám MR Štefánika

Radničné nám

Spišská Nová Ves

Lieskovany

To Košice (via railway; 60km)

SLOVAKIA

Places to Stay

You can camp at the **Autocamping Ďurkovec** (☎ 429 71 05, fax 429 71 06; [e] durkovec@durkovec.sk; camp sites 40 Sk, plus per person 50 Sk, dorm beds 150 Sk, bungalows 1800 Sk), about 20 minutes' walk west from Čingov bus stop, and at **Autocamp Podlesok** (☎ 449 02 81; [e] slovrajbela@globtelnet.sk; camp sites 100 Sk, huts per person 300 Sk).

The family-oriented **Hotel Flora** (☎ 449 11 31, fax 449 11 30; singles/doubles with bath 550/800 Sk) is just east of Čingov. Nearby is the comfortable, chalet-style **Hotel Čingov** (☎ 443 36 33, fax 443 36 30; [e] hotelcingov@slovanet.sk; singles/doubles 750/900 Sk).

Getting There & Away

Slovenský raj trailheads are accessible by bus from Spišská Nová Ves at Čingov, and by car at Podlesok. The closest train station is Spišské Tomášovce, an hour's walk from Letanovský mlýn on a green-marked trail. Only local trains stop at this station (about nine a day between Poprad and Spišská Nová Ves).

Spišská Nová Ves is on the main railway line from Žilina to Košice, with trains from Poprad every hour or so. All trains stop here. A branch line runs 13km north to Levoča with services every two hours or so.

Buses leave Spišská Nová Ves for Čingov every couple of hours. There are morning buses to Spišské Podhradie, Tatranská Lomnica, Starý Smokovec and Štrbské Pleso.

LEVOČA
☎ 053 • pop 13,000

Levoča, 26km east of Poprad, is one of Slovakia's finest walled towns, with a main square full of beautiful Renaissance buildings. In the 13th century the king of Hungary invited Saxon Germans to colonise the Spiš region on the eastern borderlands of his kingdom, as a protection against Tatar incursions and to develop mining. Levoča was one of the towns founded at this time.

To this day the medieval walls, street plan and central square of Levoča have survived, unspoiled by modern development. The town is an easy stop on the way from Poprad to Košice.

Orientation & Information

The train and bus stations are 1km south of town. The most convenient bus stop is at nám Štefana Kluberta, outside the Košice Gate.

The **AiCES information centre** (☎ 451 37 63; nám Majstra Pavla 58; open 9am-5pm Mon-Fri, 9.30am-2pm Sat) is at the top of the square. **Slovenská sporiteľňa** (nám Majstra Pavla 56; open 8am-3pm Mon-Fri, 8am-4pm Wed) changes travellers cheques and also has an ATM.

The **telephone centre** is in the **post office** (nám Majstra Pavla 42; open 8am-noon & 1pm-4.30pm Mon-Fri, 8am-11.30am Sat). You can check email at **System House** (Košická 3; open 8am-11.30am & 12.30pm-4.30pm Mon-Fri) for 1.50 Sk per minute.

Things to See

Nám Majstra Pavla, Levoča's central square, is filled with superb Gothic and Renaissance buildings. The 15th-century **St James' Church** (admission 40 Sk; open 2pm-5pm Mon, 9am-5pm Tues-Sat, 1pm-5pm Sun June-Sept; 8am-4pm Tues-Sat Oct-May) contains a towering Gothic altar (1517) by Majster Pavol (Master Paul) of Levoča, one of the largest and finest of its kind in Europe. The Madonna on this altar appears on the 100 Sk banknote. Buy tickets in the Municipal Weights House opposite the north door.

Next to St James' is the Gothic **town hall**, enlivened by Renaissance arcades and murals of the civic virtues. Today it houses the **Spiš Museum** (admission 30 Sk; open 9am-5pm Tues-Sun May-Sept, 8am-4pm Tues-Sun Oct-Apr), but the medieval rooms are more interesting than the exhibits. Beside the town hall is a 16th-century **cage of shame** where prisoners were once exhibited.

There's a good **crafts museum** (admission 30 Sk; open 9am-5pm Tues-Sun May-Sept, 8am-4pm Tues-Sun Oct-Apr) in the 15th-century house at No 40. While you're there have a peek in the courtyard of No 43; its Renaissance architecture is well worth a look. The **Evangelical church** (1837), which once served the German community, is in the Empire style. **Thurzov dom** (1532) at No 7, now the State Archives, is another fine building. At No 20 is the **Majster Pavol Museum** (admission 30 Sk; open 9am-5pm Tues-Sun May-Sept, 8am-4pm Tues-Sun Oct-Apr), with icons that were painted by Majster Pavol of Levoča.

On a hill 2km north of town is the large neo-Gothic **Church of Mariánska hora**, where the largest Catholic pilgrimage in Slovakia takes place in early July.

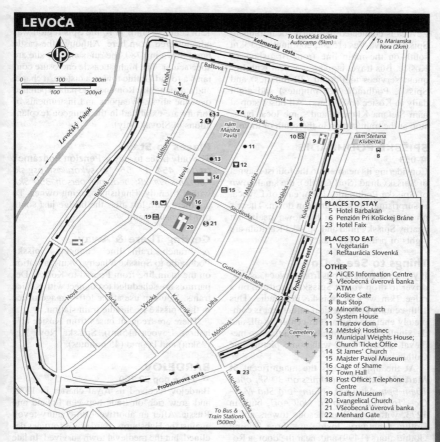

LEVOČA

PLACES TO STAY
5 Hotel Barbakan
6 Penzión Pri Košickej Bráne
23 Hotel Faix

PLACES TO EAT
1 Vegetarián
4 Reštaurácia Slovenká

OTHER
2 AiCES Information Centre
3 Všeobecná úverová banka ATM
7 Košice Gate
8 Bus Stop
9 Minorite Church
10 System House
11 Thurzov dom
12 Mestský Hostinec
13 Municipal Weights House; Church Ticket Office
14 St James' Church
15 Majster Pavol Museum
16 Cage of Shame
17 Town Hall
18 Post Office; Telephone Centre
19 Crafts Museum
20 Evangelical Church
21 Všeobecná úverová banka
22 Menhard Gate

SLOVAKIA

Places to Stay

The **Levočská Dolina Autocamp** (☎ 451 27 05; open mid-June–Aug) is 5km north of nám Štefana Kluberta on the road to Závada. Bungalows are available.

AiCES can book accommodation for travellers, including **private rooms** from 250 Sk per person. Most of the rooms are outside the old town; those inside are more expensive, around 300 Sk to 400 Sk.

The slightly run-down, 25-room **Hotel Faix** (☎ 451 23 35; Probstnerova cesta 22; doubles 700 Sk), which is between the train station and the old town, has basic doubles with a shower or toilet.

Penzión Pri Košickej Bráne (☎ 451 28 79; Košická 16; 450 Sk per person) is just inside the Košice Gate.

The best-value hotel within the city walls is the charmingly old-fashioned **Hotel Barbakan** (☎ 451 4310, fax 451 3609; e recepcia.hot@ barbakan.sk; Košická 15; singles/doubles 1150/1450 Sk). The rates include breakfast and the rooms have an en suite bathroom, TV and minibar.

Places to Eat

The best place for a meal is the homely and inexpensive **Reštaurácia Slovenká** (nám Majstra Pavla 62; mains 70-110 Sk; open 9am-10pm daily). The popular **Vegetarián** (Uhoľná 137; mains 30-70 Sk; open 10am-3.15pm Mon-Fri), is off the northwest corner of the main square. For a beer, try the Slovenká or the lively **Mestský hostinec** (nám Majstra Pavla 11).

Getting There & Away

Levoča is connected by hourly local trains to Spišská Nová Ves (15 Sk, 20 minutes), 13km south on the main line from Bratislava to Košice. Bus travel is more practical with frequent services to Poprad (30 minutes) and Spišské Podhradie (20 minutes) and eight daily to Košice (two hours). All buses stop at nám Štefana Kluberta and some local buses stop at the train station in the south of town.

SPIŠSKÉ PODHRADIE
☎ 053

Considering its nearness to the tourist magnet of Spišský hrad (Spiš Castle), the small town of Spišské Podhradie, 15km east of Levoča, is surprisingly dismal and run down. There's no reason to linger in the town itself, but nearby Spišský hrad and Spišská Kapitula are sights of prime importance.

Things to See & Do

If you're arriving by bus from Levoča, ask the driver to drop you at **Spišská Kapitula**, on a ridge 1km west of Spišské Podhradie. This 13th-century ecclesiastical settlement is completely encircled by a 16th-century wall, and the single street running between the two medieval gates is lined with some picturesque Gothic houses.

At the upper end is the magnificent **St Martin's Cathedral** (admission 30 Sk; open 10am-5pm Mon-Sat, 11am-4pm Sun May-Oct, 1pm-3pm Mon-Fri Nov-Apr), built in 1273, with twin Romanesque towers and a Gothic sanctuary. Inside are three folding Gothic altars (1499) and, near the door, a Romanesque white lion. On either side of the cathedral are the seminary and the Renaissance bishop's palace (1652).

Crowning a ridge on the far side of Spišské Podhradie is the 180m-long **Spišský hrad** (admission 50 Sk; open 9am-6pm daily May-Sept, 9am-3pm daily Nov-Apr), the largest castle in Slovakia. In 1993 it was added to Unesco's world heritage list. The castle is directly above the train station, 1km south of Spišské Podhradie's bus stop. Cross at the tracks near the station and follow the yellow markers up to the castle. The first gate is always locked, so carry on to the second one higher up. (If you're driving or cycling, the access road is off the Prešov highway east of town.)

The castle was founded in 1209 – the defenders of Spišský are said to have repulsed

the Tatars in 1241 – and reconstructed in the 15th century. Until 1710 the Spiš region was administered from here. Although the castle burnt down in 1780, the ruins and the site are spectacular. The highest castle enclosure contains a round Gothic tower, a cistern, a chapel and a rectangular Romanesque palace perched over the abyss. Weapons and instruments of torture are exhibited in the dungeon (explanations in Slovak only).

Places to Stay

The only place to stay is **Penzión Podzámok** (☎/fax 454 17 55; e sykora@sn.psg.sk; Podzámková 28; beds per person 350 Sk), with a friendly, English-speaking owner. To get there, turn left after the bridge just south of Mariánské nám.

Getting There & Away

A branch train line connects Spišské Podhradie to Spišské Vlachy (9km), a station on the main line from Poprad to Košice. Departures are scheduled to connect with Košice trains. You can use the left-luggage office in the Spišské Podhradie train station.

There are frequent buses from Košice (1½ hours), Levoča (15km), Spišská Nová Ves (25km) and Poprad (45 minutes).

BARDEJOV
☎ 054 • pop 32,200

Bardejov received its royal charter in 1376, and grew rich on trade between Poland and Russia. After an abortive 17th-century revolt against the Habsburgs, Bardejov's fortunes declined, but the medieval town survived. In late 1944 heavy fighting took place at the Dukla Pass on the Polish border, 54km northeast of Bardejov on the road to Rzeszów (preserved WWII Soviet tanks can be seen from the road).

The sloping central square lined with the Gothic-Renaissance houses built by wealthy merchants has been carefully preserved. Much of the town's walls, including the moat, towers and bastions, remain intact. The town hosts several festivals, one of the liveliest being The Market (jarmok), when Radničné nám turns into one big market with lots of food, drink and good times included.

Orientation

The bus and train station (left-luggage office open 7am to 6.30pm Monday to Saturday, 11am to 8pm Sunday) is a five-minute walk

northeast from Radničné nám, the main square in Bardejov.

Information

The helpful **AiCES information centre** (☎ 472 62 73; Radničné nám 21; open 9am-4.30pm Mon-Fri) can assist with accommodation and guided tours.

The **Investičná banka** (Radničné nám; open 8am-4.30pm Mon, Tues, Thur & Fri, 8am-2pm Wed) changes travellers cheques and has an ATM.

The **telephone centre** is in the **main post office** (Dlhý rad 14).

Things to See

The 14th-century **Church of St Egídius** is one of the most remarkable buildings in the country, with no less than 11 tall Gothic altarpieces, built from 1460 to 1510, all with their own original paintings and sculptures. The structural purity of the parish church and the 15th-century bronze baptismal font are very striking.

There are four branches of the **Šariš Museum** (admission 25 Sk; open 8.30am-noon & 12.30pm-5pm daily May-Sept) on the main square. In the centre is the **old town hall** (1509), the first Renaissance building in Slovakia, now a museum with more altarpieces and a historical collection. Two museums face one another on Rhodyho at the southern end of the square: one has an excellent natural history exhibit, the other a collection of icons. A fourth branch at Radničné nám 13 has temporary art exhibits.

Places to Stay

There's not a lot to choose from. First choice is the excellent **Penzión Semafor** (☎ 474 44 33, 0905-830 984; e semafor@stonline.sk; cnr Kellerova & BS Timravy; singles/doubles 500/1000 Sk) is a few minutes' walk north of the old town.

Šport Hotel (☎ 472 49 49; Kutuzovova 31; rooms per person 500 Sk), a slightly worn out, two-storey block overlooking the Topľa River, is aimed mainly at Slovak families, but may take you in if they have room.

If you have some cash to spare, the flashy **Hotel Bellevue** (☎ 472 84 04, fax 472 84 09; Mihalov; singles/doubles 1800/2200 Sk) sits on a hilltop 3km southwest of the centre; take bus No 8 westbound from Dlhý rad.

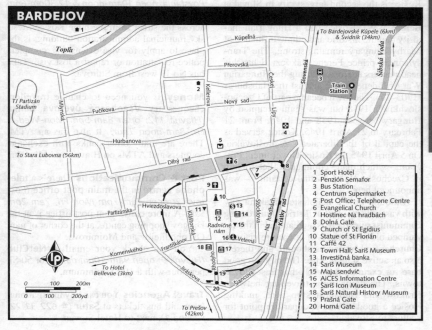

BARDEJOV

1 Sport Hotel
2 Penzión Semafor
3 Bus Station
4 Centrum Supermarket
5 Post Office; Telephone Centre
6 Evangelical Church
7 Hostinec Na hradbách
8 Dolná Gate
9 Church of St Egídius
10 Statue of St Florián
11 Caffé 42
12 Town Hall; Šariš Museum
13 Investičná banka
14 Šariš Museum
15 Maja sendvič
16 AiCES Information Centre
17 Šariš Icon Museum
18 Šariš Natural History Museum
19 Prašná Gate
20 Horná Gate

SLOVAKIA

Places to Eat

Again, there is not much choice. Apart from a few pizza restaurants there is the beer hall **Hostinec Na hradbách** *(Stöcklova 16; mains 50-90 Sk; open 10am-10pm Mon-Fri, 11am-3pm Sat & Sun).*

Maja sendvič *(Radničné nám 15; open 8am-9pm Mon-Thur, 8am-11pm Fri, 3pm-11pm Sat, 3pm-8pm Sun)* sells huge baguette sandwiches for around 30 Sk. Popular cafés on and around the square include **Caffé 42** at the corner of Hviezdoslavova.

There's a supermarket at **Centrum** *(cnr Slovenská & Dlhý rad; open 6am-6pm Mon-Thur, 6am-8pm Fri, 6am-4pm Sat).*

Getting There & Away

There are frequent buses from Bardejov to Košice (79 Sk, 1¾ hours). If you want to go to the Vysoké Tatry, there are hourly buses to Poprad (120 Sk, two hours); there are also two buses daily direct to Starý Smokovec (three hours), six to Bratislava (10 hours) and six to Žilina (five hours).

KOŠICE

☎ 055 • pop 235,000

Košice is the second-largest city in Slovakia and capital of the eastern part of the country. Before WWI, Košice had a Hungarian majority and the historic and ethnic influence of nearby Hungary remains strong. The Transylvanian prince Ferenc Rákóczi II had his headquarters at Košice during the Hungarian War of Independence against the Habsburgs (1703–11). The town became part of Czechoslovakia in 1918 but was again occupied by Hungary between 1938 and 1945. From 21 February to 21 April 1945, Košice served as the capital of the liberated Czechoslovakia. On 5 April 1945 the Košice Government Program – which made communist dictatorship in Czechoslovakia a virtual certainty – was announced here.

Although now a major steel-making city with vast new residential districts built during communist rule, there is a great deal in the revamped old town that is of interest to visitors. Churches and museums abound, and there's also an active state theatre. The city is a good base for excursions on to other East Slovak towns. The daily trains travelling between Kraków and Budapest stop here, making Košice a good arrival or departure point for visitors to Slovakia.

Orientation

The adjacent bus and train stations are just east of the old town. A five-minute walk along Mlynská will bring you into Hlavná (Main Street), which broadens to accommodate the squares of Hlavné nám and nám Slobody.

The left-luggage office in the train station is open 24 hours a day, except for three 45-minute breaks.

Information

Tourist Offices The **AiCES information centre** (☎ 16 168; e *mic@pangea.sk; open 8am-5pm Mon-Fri, 9am-1pm Sat)*, in the Dargov department store, opposite the Hotel Slovan sells maps, guidebooks and concert tickets, and also provides information about accommodation.

The **municipal information centre** *(☎ 625 88 88; Hlavná 59; open 9am-6pm Mon-Fri, 9am-1pm Sat)* in the town hall provides much the same services, and also sells parking tickets.

Visa Extensions The **police and passport office** *(Úradovňa cudzineckej polície a pasovej služby; trieda Slovenského Národného Povstania; open 10am-noon & 12.30pm-6pm Mon & Wed, 7am-noon Tues, Thur & Fri)*, across the street from the huge Košice/Mestský municipal administration building, is the place to apply for visa extensions, complete police registration or report a lost visa. Take bus No 19 west from Štúrova.

Money If you need to change travellers cheques try **Všeobecná úverová banka** *(Hlavná 112; open 8am-5pm Mon-Wed & Fri, 8am-noon Thur)*. It also has an ATM. There are many other banks with exchange counters and ATMs on Hlavná and Mlynská.

Post & Communications There's a **telephone centre** in the **main post office** *(Poštová 2; open 7am-7pm Mon-Fri, 7am-2pm Sat)*. A more convenient post office is at the Dargov shopping centre, at the corner of nám Osvoboditeľov and Mojmirova.

You can check your email at **NetClub** *(Hlavná 9; open 9am-10pm daily)* for 50 Sk per hour with a 10 Sk minimum.

Travel Agencies You can buy international train and bus tickets at **Satur** *(☎ 622 31 22; Hlavná 1)*, next to Hotel Slovan.

KOŠICE

PLACES TO STAY
1 Hotel Alessandria
27 Penzión Platz
40 Hotel Slovan
46 TJ Metropol turistická ubytovňa

PLACES TO EAT
9 Reštauráciá Kohút
11 Cukráreň Aida
12 Bakchus
14 Bagetéria
21 Gastrodom Supermarket
22 Pizzeria Venezia
24 Kaviáreň Slavia
35 Reštaurácia Ajvega/Ajmexica

OTHER
2 Zoology Museum
3 East Slovak Museum
4 Všeobecná úverová banka
5 Tesco Supermarket
6 Konzervatórium
7 Slovak Technical Museum
8 Franciscan Church
10 Jazz Klub
13 Uľuv Crafts Shop
15 Main Post Office; Telephone Centre
16 Plague Column
17 Jesuit Church
18 Mikluš Prison
19 Weapons Museum; Ferenc Rákóczi House Museum
20 Bus Station
23 Municipal Information Centre; Town Hall
25 State Theatre
26 Dominican Church
28 Musical Fountain
29 Marsab Bookshop
30 AF Knihupectvo
31 Urban Tower; Kaviáreň Urbana
32 Cathedral of St Elizabeth
33 St Michael's Chapel
34 East Slovak Art Gallery
36 Evangelical Church
37 NetClub
38 Bomba Klub
39 Satur
41 Dargov Shopping Centre
42 AiCES Information Centre
43 Post Office
44 Thália Hungarian Theatre
45 State Philharmonic Hall

SLOVAKIA

Bookshops The **Marsab Bookshop** *(Hlavná 41; open 8am-6pm Mon-Fri, 9am-noon Sat)* has a good range of hiking maps and town plans. **AF Kníhupectvo** *(Mlynská)* has a small but welcome selection of fiction in English.

Things to See

Unless noted otherwise, admission to the museums and galleries is 20 Sk.

Košice's top sight is the recently renovated **Cathedral of St Elizabeth** (1345–1508), a magnificent late-Gothic edifice. In a crypt on the left side of the nave is the tomb of Duke Ferenc Rákóczi, who was exiled to Turkey after the failed 18th-century Hungarian revolt against Austria. Only in 1905 was he officially pardoned and his remains reburied here.

On the southern side of the cathedral is the 14th-century **St Michael's Chapel**, and to the north is the 14th-century **Urban Tower**, which now houses a café. Nearby is the **East Slovak Art Gallery** *(Východoslovenská galéria; nám Slobody 27; open 10am-6pm Tues-Sat, 10am-2pm Sun)*, housed in a building that dates from 1779 and from which the 1945 Košice Government Program was proclaimed.

Most of Košice's other historic sites are north along Hlavná. In the centre of the square is the ornate **State Theatre** (1899) with a kitsch musical fountain in front. Facing it at Hlavná 59, is the rococo former **town hall** (1780), and north of the theatre is a large baroque **plague column** (1723). Further north is the fascinating **Slovak Technical Museum** *(Hlavná 88; open 8am-5pm Tues-Fri, 9am-2pm Sat, noon-5pm Sun)*, full of interesting examples of old technology.

The **East Slovak Museum** *(nám Maratónu mieru; open 9am-5pm Tues-Sat, 9am-1pm Sun)*, at the northern end of Hlavná, is dedicated to regional culture, history and archaeology. Don't miss the Košice Gold Treasure in the basement, a hoard of almost 3000 gold coins dating from the 15th to the 18th centuries and discovered by chance in 1935. In the park behind the museum building is an old wooden church. Across the square is the **Zoology Museum** (same hours).

Walk back along Hlavná to the State Theatre and turn left on narrow Univerzitná to **Mikluš Prison** (under renovation at the time of research). This connected pair of 16th-century houses once served as a prison equipped with medieval torture chambers and cells. The ticket office that's behind the nearby gate at

Hrnčiarska 7 also sells tickets for **Ferenc Rákóczi House Museum** and the **Weapons Museum**; these are in the Executioner's Bastion (Katova bašta), which was a part of Košice's 15th-century fortifications. All three can only been seen on a guided tour (20 Sk), but a minimum of 10 visitors is needed.

Ask at the municipal information office about tours of the **Lower Gate**, the archaeological remnants of the old city walls that lie beneath nám Slobody south of the cathedral.

Places to Stay

Camping South of the city is **Autocamping Salaš Barca** *(☎ 623 33 97, fax 625 83 09; camp sites 60 Sk, plus per person 70 Sk, cars 80 Sk, 3-bed bungalows 720 Sk; open 15 Apr-30 Sept)*. Take tram No 3 south along Južná trieda from the train station to the Juh SAD stop (about 200m before an overpass), then head right (west) on Alejová (the Rožňava Hwy) for about 500m until you see the entrance to the camping ground on the left. New road building has made the site awkward to get to by car – the access road is only accessible from the eastbound carriageway, so coming from the city you have to continue to the next roundabout and come back again.

Hostels The dilapidated **Domov mládeže** *(☎ 642 90 52; Medická 2; beds per person 150 Sk)* has beds in two- and three-bed rooms (student card not required). It's a 15-minute hike west of the centre along Poštová and Vojenská, then up the steps on the left where the road bends sharp right.

TJ Metropol turistická ubytovňa *(☎ 625 59 48, fax 76 31 10; Štúrova 32; rooms per person 300 Sk)* is an attractive sports complex with bright but basic rooms. You get a lot of tram noise in the very early morning.

Hotels & Pensions There's a handful of pensions within the old town, including the attractive **Penzión Platz** *(☎/fax 622 34 50; Dominikánske nám 23; doubles 1200 Sk)*. The information centre can suggest others.

The renovated **Hotel Alessandria** *(☎ 622 59 03, fax 622 59 18; Jiskrova 3; singles/ doubles 1150/1790 Sk)* is hidden away on a quiet back street, and has four-star facilities with a quaint, 1970s feel to it.

With secure parking, luxurious, business-oriented **Hotel Slovan** *(☎ 622 73 78, fax 622 84 13; e reserve@hotelslovan.sk; Hlavná 1;*

singles/doubles from 2250/3100 Sk) is the best and priciest place in town, with an elegant restaurant.

Places to Eat

A popular place to eat on the main square is the inexpensive **Bakchus** *(Hlavná 8; mains 55-90 Sk; open 9am-11pm Mon-Fri, 10am-midnight Sat & Sun)*, with an international menu and an open courtyard in summer.

Reštaurácia Ajvega/Ajmexica *(Orlia 10; mains 90-135 Sk; open 11am-10pm daily)* combines a tasty vegetarian menu with carnivorous Mexican fare. **Reštauraciá Kohút** *(Hrnčiarska 23; mains 100-180 Sk; open 11.30-midnight daily)* serves chicken dishes and kebabs, and has a nice summer garden out back.

Pizzeria Venezia *(Mlynská; mains 80-110 Sk; open 11am-10pm daily)* with pleasant outdoor tables, has good pizzas and pasta.

Elegant **Kaviáreň Slavia** *(Hlavná 59)*, all dark wood and art-nouveau detailing, is a good place for coffee and cakes, while **Cukráreň Aida** *(cnr Hlavná & Biela)*, has the best ice cream in town. **Kaviáreň Urbana** *(open Mon-Fr)* is set in the 14th-century Gothic Urban Tower and serves coffee, drinks and cakes.

You can get cheap baguette sandwiches at **Bagetéria** *(Hlavná 74; open 8.30am-9pm Mon-Thur, 8.30am-10pm Fri, 9am-9pm Sat, 10am-8pm Sun)*.

There are supermarkets at **Tesco** *(Hlavná; open 8am-8pm Mon-Wed, 8am-9pm Thur & Fri, 8am-6pm Sat & Sun)* and **Gastrodom** *(Mlynská; open 6am-7pm Mon-Fri, 6am-1pm Sat)*.

Entertainment

The renovated **State Theatre** *(Hlavné nám)* stages regular performances. The **Thália Hungarian Theatre** and **State Philharmonic** are in the southwestern corner of the old town; performances are held once or twice a week. Recitals are sometimes given at the **Konzervatórium** *(Hlavná 89)*.

Bars & Clubs The cellar bar **Bomba klub** *(Hlavná 5; open 10am-midnight Mon-Thur, 10am-1am Fri, 11am-midnight Sat, noon-midnight Sun)* is a popular bar with both locals and English-speaking visitors. **Jazz Klub** *(Kováčska 39; open 4pm-2am daily)* has live

jazz twice a week; the café-bar is open from 11am Monday to Friday.

Shopping

Uľuv *(Hlavná 76)* has a good selection of local handicrafts.

Getting There & Away

Train A sleeper train leaves Košice daily at 7.10am for Kyiv (22 hours, 998km). Overnight trains with sleepers and couchettes are also available between Košice and Bratislava (seven hours, 445km) and Prague (11 hours, 708km), Plzeň (896km), Brno (493km) and Karlovy Vary (897km) in the Czech Republic. Daytime express trains connect Košice to Poprad (122 Sk, two hours), Žilina (250 Sk, three hours), Bratislava and Prague.

The daily *Cracovia* express train between Budapest (four hours) and Kraków (five hours) passes through Košice (reservations are required). Northbound, the *Cracovia* departs Košice at 1.05am, and southbound at 5.38am.

Bus For shorter trips to Levoča (two hours), Bardejov (1½ hours) and Spišské Podhradie (1½ hours), you're better off taking a bus. A bus to Užgorod, Ukraine (2½ hours), leaves Košice every afternoon. There's also a daily bus to Prague (12 hours).

Heading for Poland, there's a bus from Košice to Nowy Targ (four hours) at 5.45am every Thursday and Saturday, and to Krosno every Wednesday, Friday and Saturday. In both cases the fare is paid to the driver.

There's a bus from Košice to Miskolc (Hungary) at 6.30am on Wednesday, Friday and Saturday (two hours), and at 5.40pm Monday to Thursday. You should book your ticket the day before at window No 1 in the bus station. On Wednesday this bus continues to Budapest (five hours).

Car You will find **Hertz** *(☎ 633 06 56)* has offices at Watsonova 5, while **Avis** *(☎ 632 58 63)* is at Prešovská 69; both have desks at Košice airport. Satur can suggest cheaper local agencies.

Getting Around

Bus and tram tickets are available for 8 Sk from tobacconists, newsstands and public transport kiosks.

SLOVAKIA

Slovenia

Slovenia (Slovenija) is one of the most over-looked gems in all of Europe. The wealthiest nation of former Yugoslavia, Slovenia – an Alpine country – has much more in common with its Central European neighbours than with the Balkan countries it split from in a 10-day war in 1991. The two million Slovenes were economically the most well-off among the peoples of what was once Yugoslavia, and the relative affluence and orderliness of this nation is immediately apparent. Many of its cities and towns bear the imprint of the Habsburg Empire and the Venetian Republic, and the Julian Alps are reminiscent of Switzerland.

Fairy-tale Bled Castle, breathtaking Lake Bohinj, the scenic caves at Postojna and Škocjan, the lush Soča Valley, the coastal towns of Piran and Koper and thriving Ljubljana are great attractions. All are accessible at much less than the cost of similar places in Western Europe. The amazing variety that is packed into one small area makes this country truly a 'Europe in miniature'. An added bonus is that Slovenia is a nation of polyglots, and communicating with these friendly, helpful people is never difficult.

Facts about Slovenia

HISTORY

The early Slovenes settled in the river valleys of the Danube Basin and the eastern Alps during the 6th century AD. Slovenia was brought under Germanic rule in 748, initially by the Frankish empire of the Carolingians, who converted the population to Christianity, and then as part of the Holy Roman Empire in the 9th century. The Austro-German monarchy took over control in the early 14th century and ruled (as the Habsburg Empire from 1804) right up until the end of WWI in 1918 – with only one brief interruption.

Over those six centuries, the upper classes became totally Germanised, though the peasantry retained their Slovenian identity. The Bible was translated into the vernacular during the Reformation in 1584, but Slovene did not come into common usage as a written language until the early 19th century.

In 1809, in a bid to isolate the Habsburg Empire from the Adriatic, Napoleon set up the Illyrian Provinces (Slovenia, Dalmatia and part of Croatia) with Ljubljana as the capital. Though the Habsburgs returned in 1814, French reforms in education, law and public administration endured. The democratic revolution that swept Europe in 1848 also brought increased political and national consciousness among Slovenes and, following WWI and the dissolution of the Austro-Hungarian Empire,

Slovenia was included in the Kingdom of Serbs, Croats and Slovenes.

During WWII much of Slovenia was annexed by Germany, with Italy and Hungary taking smaller bits of territory. The Slovenian Partisans fought courageously from mountain bases against the invaders, and Slovenia joined the Socialist Federal Republic of Yugoslavia in 1945.

Moves by Serbia in the late 1980s to assert its leading role culturally and economically among the Yugoslav republics was a big concern to Slovenes. When Belgrade abruptly ended the autonomy of Kosovo (where 90% of the population is ethnically Albanian) in late 1988, Slovenes feared the same could happen to them. For some years, Slovenia's interests had been shifting to the capitalist west and north; the Yugoslav connection, on the other hand, had become not only an economic burden but a political threat as well.

In the spring of 1990, Slovenia became the first Yugoslav republic to hold free elections and shed 45 years of communist rule; in December the electorate voted by 88% in favour of independence. The Slovenian government began stockpiling weapons, and on 25 June 1991 it pulled the republic out of the Yugoslav Federation. Slovenia took control of the border crossings and a 10-day war ensued. Resistance from the Slovenian militia was determined and, as no territorial claims or minority issues were involved, the Yugoslav government agreed to a truce brokered by the European Community (EC).

Slovenia got a new constitution in late December 1991, and on 15 January 1992 the EC formally recognised the country. Slovenia was admitted to the UN in May 1992 and is currently negotiating to become a member of the EU. Accession is expected to be granted in January 2004.

GEOGRAPHY

Slovenia is wedged between Austria and Croatia and shares much shorter borders with Italy and Hungary. With an area of just 20,256 sq km, Slovenia is the smallest country in Eastern Europe, about the size of Wales or Israel. Much of the country is mountainous, culminating in the northwest with the Julian Alps and the nation's highest peak, Mt Triglav (2864m). From this jagged knot, the main Alpine chain continues east along the Austrian border, while the Dinaric Range runs southeast along the coast into Croatia.

Below the limestone plateau of the Karst region lying between Ljubljana and Koper is Europe's most extensive network of karst caverns, which gave their name to other such caves around the world.

The coastal range forms a barrier isolating the Istrian Peninsula from Slovenia's corner of the Danube Basin. Much of the interior east of the Alps is drained by the Sava and Drava Rivers, both of which empty into the Danube. The Soča flows through western Slovenia into the Adriatic.

CLIMATE

Slovenia is temperate with four distinct seasons, but topography creates three individual climates. The northwest has an alpine climate with strong influences from the Atlantic as well as abundant precipitation. Temperatures in the Alpine valleys are moderate in summer but cold in winter. The coast and western Slovenia, as far north as the Soča Valley, have a Mediterranean climate with mild, sunny weather much of the year, though the *burja*, a cold and dry northeasterly wind from the Adriatic, can be fierce at times. Most of eastern Slovenia has a continental climate with hot summers and cold winters.

Most of the rain falls in March and April and again in October and November. January is the coldest month with an average temperature of -2°C and July the warmest (21°C).

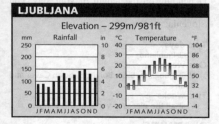

LJUBLJANA
Elevation – 299m/981ft

ECOLOGY & ENVIRONMENT

Slovenia is a very green country – over half its total area is covered in forest – and is home to 2900 plant species; Triglav National Park is particularly rich in indigenous flowering plants. Common European animals (deer, boar, chamois) abound, and rare species include *Proteus anguinus*, the unique 'human fish' that inhabits pools in karst caves.

GOVERNMENT & POLITICS

Slovenia's constitution provides for a parliamentary system of government. The National Assembly, which has exclusive jurisdiction over passing of laws, consists of 90 deputies elected for four years by proportional representation. The 40 members of the advisory Council of State are elected for five-year terms by regions and special-interest groups. The head of state, the president, is elected directly for a maximum of two five-year terms. Executive power is vested in the prime minister and the 15-member cabinet.

In parliamentary elections in November 2000, a centrist alliance of the Liberal Democrats, the People's Party, Social-Democrats and the Democratic Party of Pensioners of Slovenia garnered more than two-thirds of the vote, seating 62 MPs. Liberal Democrat Party leader Janez Drnovšek, prime minister from the first elections in 1992, again was elected head of government. Milan Kučan – a former Communist, elected as Slovenia's first president in November 1992, received a second five-year term in 1997. The most recent presidential elections were held during November 2002.

ECONOMY

Slovenia has emerged as one of the strongest economies of the former socialist countries of Eastern Europe in the years since independence. Inflation has dropped, employment is on the rise and the per-capita GDP has hovered around US$10,000 for the past few years.

For many Slovenes, however, the economic picture remains unclear. Real wages continue to grow – but faster than inflation, which puts Slovenia's international competitiveness at a disadvantage. Inflation rocketed up to 200% after independence and has steadily declined since; it is currently at 8.4%. The official unemployment rate is around 8%.

POPULATION & PEOPLE

Slovenia was the most homogeneous of all the Yugoslav republics; about 88% of the population are Slovenes. About 5% of the population is considered Croat, Serbian or Bosnian (mostly recent immigrants) and small ethnic enclaves of Italians (3000) and Hungarians (8500) still live in border areas. Some towns are officially bilingual; you'll see Italian in Piran, Koper and Portorož, and Magyar (Hungarian) in Murska Sobota and

Lendava. There are some 2300 Roma (Gypsies), mostly in the northeast.

ARTS

Slovenia's best-loved writer is the Romantic poet France Prešeren (1800–49), whose lyric poetry set new standards for Slovenian literature and helped to raise national the consciousness. Disappointed in love, Prešeren wrote sensitive love poems but also satirical verse and epic poetry.

Many notable bridges, squares and buildings in Ljubljana and elsewhere in Slovenia were designed by the architect Jože Plečnik (1872–1957), who studied under Otto Wagner in Vienna.

Postmodernist painting and sculpture has been more or less dominated since the 1980s by the multimedia group Neue Slowenische Kunst (NSK) and the five-member artists' cooperative IRWIN. Avante-garde dance is best exemplified by Betontanc, an NSK dance company that mixes live music and theatrical elements (called 'physical theatre' here) with sharp political comment.

Since WWII, many Slovenian folk traditions have been lost, but compilations by the trio Trutamora Slovenica (available at music shops in Ljubljana) examine the roots of Slovenian folk music. Folk groups – both 'pure' and popular – to watch out for include the Avseniki, Ansambel Lojzeta Slaka, the Alpski Kvintet led by Oto Pestner, and the Roma band Šukar.

Popular music runs the gamut from Slovenian *chanson* (best exemplified by Vita Mavrič) and folk to jazz and techno. Three punk groups from the late 1970s and early 1980s, Pankrti, Borghesia and Laibach, hailed from Slovenia.

Literature is extremely important to Slovenes; the last census marked a 99.6% literacy rate. Popular fiction writers include Drago Jančar and Boris Pahor. *Afterwards: Slovenian Writing 1945–1995*, edited by Andrew Zawacki, showcases the talents of the modern Slovenian *literati* (available in English at all large Ljubljana bookshops).

RELIGION

About 70% of Slovenes consider themselves Roman Catholic, but churches are hardly full on Sunday. Most weddings are now civil ceremonies. Yugoslav immigrants have brought a small Muslim population of about 5%.

LANGUAGE

Slovene is a South Slavic language written in the Roman alphabet and closely related to Croatian and Serbian. It is grammatically complex with lots of cases, genders and tenses and has something that is very rare in linguistics: singular, dual and plural forms. It's one *miza* (table) and three or more *mize* (tables) but two *mizi*.

Virtually everyone in Slovenia is able to speaks at least one other language: Croatian, Serbian, German, English and/or Italian. English is definitely the preferred language of the young.

See the Language section at the end of the book for pronunciation guidelines and useful words and phrases. Lonely Planet's *Eastern Europe phrasebook* contains a chapter on Slovene.

Facts for the Visitor

HIGHLIGHTS

Ljubljana, Piran and Koper have outstanding architecture; the hill-top castles at Bled and Ljubljana are impressive. The Škocjan and Postojna Caves are among the world's foremost underground wonders. The Soča Valley is indescribably beautiful in spring, while the frescoed Church of St John the Baptist is in itself worth the trip to Lake Bohinj.

SUGGESTED ITINERARIES

Depending on the length of your stay, you might want to see and do the following in Slovenia:

Two days
    Visit Ljubljana
One week
    Visit Ljubljana, Bled, Bohinj, Škocjan Caves and Piran
Two weeks
    Visit all the places covered in this chapter

PLANNING
When to Go

Snow can linger in the mountains as late as June, but May and June are great months to be in the lowlands and valleys when everything is fresh and in blossom. (April can be a bit wet though.) In July and August, hotel rates go up and there will be lots of tourists, especially on the coast, but all the youth hostels are open. September is an excellent month to visit as the days are long and the weather still warm, and it's the best time for hiking and climbing. October and November can be quite rainy, and winter (December to March) is definitely for skiers.

Maps

The Geodesic Institute of Slovenia (Geodetski Zavod Slovenije; GZS), the country's principal cartographic agency, produces national (1:300,000), regional (1:50,000) and topographical maps of the entire country (64 sheets at a scale of 1:50,000) as well as city plans. The Alpine Association of Slovenia (Planinska Zveza Slovenije; PZS) has some 30 different hiking maps, with scales as large as 1:25,000.

TOURIST OFFICES
Local Tourist Offices

Located in the World Trade Centre, the **Slovenian Tourist Board** (STO; ☎ 01-589 18 40, fax 589 18 41; ⓦ www.slovenia-tourism.si; Dunajska cesta 156) is the umbrella organisation for tourist offices in Slovenia. It handles requests for information in writing or you can check out its excellent website.

The best office for face-to-face information in Slovenia is the **Ljubljana Tourist Information Centre** (TIC). Most of the destinations that are described in this chapter have some form of tourist office but if the place you're visiting doesn't, seek some assistance at a branch of one of the big travel agencies (eg, Kompas or Globtour) or from museum or from hotel staff. You can find comprehensive sites on most towns in this chapter on the Internet by typing in the city name, such as ⓦ www .ljubljana.si or ⓦ www.ptuj.si.

Tourist Offices Abroad

The Slovenian Tourist Board maintains tourist offices in the following countries:

Austria (☎ 01-715 4010, fax 713 8177) Hilton Center, Landstrasser Hauptstrasse 2, 1030 Vienna
Croatia (☎ 01-457 2118, fax 457 7921, ⓔ kompas-zagreb@zg.tel.hr) Hotel Esplanade, Mihanovičeva 1, 10000 Zagreb
Germany (☎ 089-2916 1202, fax 2916 1273, ⓔ slowenien.fva@t-online.de) Maximiliansplatz 12a, 80333 Munich
Hungary (☎ 1-269 6879, fax 268 1454, ⓔ tourism.and.travel@kompas.hu) Rakoczi ut 14, 1072 Budapest

Italy (☎ 022 951 1187, fax 022 951 4071, ⓔ slovenia@tin.it) Galeria Buenos Aires 1, 20124 Milan
Netherlands & Belgium (☎ 010-465 3003, fax 465 7514, ⓔ kompasnl@euronet.nl) Benthuizerstraat 29, 3036 CB Rotterdam
Switzerland (☎ 01-212 6394, fax 212 5266, ⓔ adria.slo@bluewin.ch) Löwenstrasse 54, 8001 Zürich
UK (☎ 020-7287 7133, fax 7287 5476, ⓔ slovenia@cpts.fsbusiness.co.uk) 49 Conduit St, London W1S 2YS
USA (☎ 212-358 9686, 358 9025, ⓔ slotouristboard@sloveniatravel.com) 345 East 12th St, New York, NY 10003

In addition, the Kompas travel agency has representative offices in many cities around the world, including:

Canada (☎ 514-938 4041) 4060 Ste-Catherine St West, Suite 535, Montreal, Que H3Z 2Z3
France (☎ 01-53 92 27 80) 14 Rue de la Source, 75016 Paris
USA (☎ 954-771 9200) 2929 East Commercial Blvd, Suite 201, Ft Lauderdale, FL 33306

VISAS & DOCUMENTS

Passport-holders from Australia, Canada, Israel, Japan, New Zealand, Switzerland, USA and EU countries do not require visas for stays in Slovenia of up to 90 days; those from the EU as well as Switzerland can also enter on a national identity card for a stay of up to 30 days. Citizens of other countries requiring visas (including South Africans) can get them at any Slovenian embassy or consulate. They cost the equivalent of €20 for a single entry and €40 for multiple entries.

EMBASSIES & CONSULATES
Slovenian Embassies & Consulates

Slovenia has diplomatic representation in the following countries; the website ⓦ www.gov .si/mzz/eng contains further listings.

Australia (☎ 02-6243 4830) Advance Bank Centre, Level 6, 60 Marcus Clark St, Canberra, ACT 2601
Austria (☎ 01-586 1309) Nibelungengasse 13, 1010 Vienna
Canada (☎ 613-565 5781) 150 Metcalfe St, Suite 2101, Ottawa, Ontario K2P 1P1
Croatia (☎ 01-631 1000) Savska cesta 41/IX, 10000 Zagreb
Germany (☎ 030-206 1450) Hausvogteiplatz 3-4, 10117 Berlin

SLOVENIA

Hungary (☎ 1-438 5600) Cseppkő ut 68, 1025 Budapest
Italy (☎ 068 091 4310) Via Leonardo Pisano 10, 00197 Rome
UK (☎ 020-7495 7775) Suite 1, Cavendish Court, 11-15 Wigmore St, London W1H 9LA
USA (☎ 202-667 5363) 1525 New Hampshire Ave NW, Washington, DC 20036

Embassies & Consulates in Slovenia

Selected countries that have representation in Ljubljana (area code ☎ 01) appear in the following list. Citizens of countries not listed here should contact their embassies in Vienna or Budapest.

Albania (☎ 432 23 24) Ob Ljubljanici 12
Australia (☎ 425 42 52) Trg Republike 3/XII
Austria (☎ 479 07 00) Prešernova cesta 23
Bosnia-Hercegovina (☎ 432 40 42) Kolarjeva 26
Canada (☎ 430 35 70) Miklošičeva cesta 19
Croatia (☎ 425 62 20) Gruberjevo nab 6
France (☎ 426 45 25) Barjanska 1
Germany (☎ 251 61 66) Prešernova cesta 27
Hungary (☎ 512 18 82) ul Konrada Babnika 5
Ireland (☎ 308 12 34) temporary office at Grand Hotel Union, Miklošičeva cesta 1
Netherlands (☎ 420 14 61) Palača Kapitelj, Poljanski nasip 6
Romania (☎ 505 82 94) Podlimbarskega 43
Slovakia (☎ 425 54 25) Tivolska cesta 4
South Africa (☎ 200 63 00) Pražakova ul 4
UK (☎ 200 39 10) Trg Republike 3/IV
USA (☎ 200 55 00) Prešernova cesta 31

CUSTOMS

Travellers are allowed to bring in the usual personal effects, a couple of cameras and electronic goods for their own use, as well as 200 cigarettes, a generous 4L of spirits and 1L of wine.

MONEY
Currency

Slovenia's currency, the tolar, is abbreviated as SIT. Prices in shops and restaurants, and train and bus fares are always in tolars, but because of inflation, a few hotels, guesthouses and even camping grounds use the euro. For that reason, some accommodation and a few other items are listed in this book in euros. You are always welcome to pay in tolars, though.

Money includes coins of one, two, five and 10 tolars and the banknotes are in denominations of 10, 20, 50, 100, 200, 500, 1000, 5000 and 10,000 tolars.

Exchange Rates

Conversion rates for major currencies at the time of publication are listed below:

country	unit		tolar
Australia	A$1	=	135.65 SIT
Canada	C$1	=	155.21 SIT
Euro Zone	€1	=	228.88 SIT
Japan	¥100	=	192.05 SIT
NZ	NZ$1	=	116.81 SIT
UK	UK£1	=	355.39 SIT
USA	US$1	=	237.10 SIT

Exchanging Money

Cash & Travellers Cheques It is simple to change cash at banks, travel agencies, any *menjalnica* (private exchange bureau) and certain post offices. Slovenia recently had a problem with travellers-cheque fraud, so it's difficult to exchange them, even at banks, but restaurants and hotels will still accept them.

There's no black market and exchange rates vary little, but watch out for a commission (*provizija*) of up to 3% tacked on by some tourist offices, hotels and travel agencies.

ATMs & Credit Cards Visa, MasterCard/Eurocard and American Express credit cards are widely accepted at most restaurants, shops, hotels, car-rental firms and travel agencies; Diners Club less so.

Automated teller machines (ATMs) linked to Cirrus or Plus now blanket Slovenia; their locations are noted in the Information sections of the individual destinations. Clients of Visa can get cash advances in tolars from any A Banka branch; MasterCard and Eurocard can be used any branch of **Nova Ljubljanska Banka** (*☎ 01-425 01 55; Trg Republike 2, Ljubljana*); and **American Express** (*☎ 01-431 90 20; Trubarjeva, Ljubljana*).

Costs

Slovenia remains much cheaper than neighbouring Italy and Austria, but don't expect the low prices you'd see in Eastern European countries like Hungary or Bulgaria.

If you stay in private rooms or at guesthouses, eat at medium-priced restaurants and travel 2nd class on the train or by bus, you should get by for under US$40 a day. Staying at hostels or college dormitories, eating takeaway at lunch and at self-service restaurants at night will cut costs considerably.

Travelling in a little more style and comfort – occasional restaurant splurges with bottles of wine, an active nightlife, staying at small hotels or guesthouses with 'character' – will cost about US$65 a day.

Tipping & Bargaining

Tipping isn't customary in Slovenia, but no-one's going to complain if you leave your change at the table in a restaurant.

Unlike some of its Eastern European neighbours, bargaining is not commonplace in Slovenia. You can try it at street markets, but you run the risk of offending someone.

Taxes & Refunds

A 'circulation tax' (prometni davek) not unlike Value-Added Tax (VAT) applies to the purchase of most goods and services here. Visitors can claim refunds on total purchases of 15,000 SIT or more (certain tobacco products and spirits are exempt) through Kompas MTS, which has offices at Brnik airport and some two dozen border crossings. Ask for a DDV-VP form at the time of purchase.

Most towns and cities levy a 'tourist tax' on overnight visitors of between 150 SIT and 300 SIT per person per night (less at camping grounds), which is included in the prices listed in this chapter.

POST & COMMUNICATIONS
Post

Poste restante is sent to the main post office in a city or town (in the capital, it goes to the branch at Slovenska cesta 32, 1101 Ljubljana) where it is held for 30 days. American Express card-holders can have their mail addressed c/o Atlas Express, Trubarjeva cesta 50, 1000 Ljubljana.

Domestic mail costs 31 SIT for up to 20g and 56 SIT for up to 100g. Postcards are 31 SIT. For international mail, the base rate is 95 SIT for 20g or less, 221 SIT for up to 100g and 83 SIT to 107 SIT for a postcard, depending on the size. Then you have to add on the airmail charge: 30 SIT for every 10g. An aerogramme is 125 SIT.

Telephone

The easiest place to make long-distance calls and send faxes and telegrams is from a post office or telephone centre; the one at Trg Osvobodilne Fronte (Trg OF) near the train and bus stations in Ljubljana is open 24 hours.

Public telephones on the street do not accept coins; they require a phonecard (telefonska kartica) available at all post offices and some newsstands.

Phonecards cost 700/1000/1700/3500 SIT for 25/50/100/300 pulses. A local one-minute call absorbs one pulse, and a three-minute call from Slovenia will cost about 126 SIT to most of Western Europe, the USA, Canada and Croatia; 162 SIT to Eastern Europe; 342 SIT to Australia; and 486 SIT to Japan, South Africa and New Zealand. International rates are 20% cheaper between 7pm and 7am Monday to Saturday, and all day Sunday.

The international access code in Slovenia is ☎ 00. The international operator or directory inquiries can be reached on ☎ 115. To call Slovenia from abroad dial the international access code, ☎ 386 (Slovenia's country code), the area code (without the initial zero, eg, 1 in Ljubljana) followed by the number.

Email & Internet Access

There is now an Internet café in almost every town in Slovenia. Ljubljana has 11 places to check your email. If you can't find an Internet café (in Ptuj, for example), try the local university or library. They will usually let travellers log on to the Internet for free or at little cost.

DIGITAL RESOURCES

The official Slovenian tourist information website is W www.slovenia-tourism.si. You can find information on accommodation, traffic conditions, the different regions etc.

The site W www.matkurja.com is a comprehensive overview of Slovenian websites, including resources for travellers. Many sites are in English.

See the Digital Resources section in the Ljubljana section for more useful websites.

BOOKS

Books can be expensive in Slovenia. Lonely Planet's Slovenia is the only complete and independent English-language guide to this country. Discover Slovenia, published annually by the Cankarjeva Založba bookshop in Ljubljana (3500 SIT), is a colourful and easy introduction available in seven languages, including English, German, and French, and Zoë Brân's After Yugoslavia, part of the Lonely Planet Journeys series, retraces the author's 1978 trip through the former Yugoslavia.

SLOVENIA

NEWSPAPERS & MAGAZINES

Slovenia publishes four daily newspapers, the most widely read being *Delo* (Work), *Večer* (Evening) and *Slovenske Novice* (a tabloid with Slovenian news). The entertainment and culture magazine *Ljubljana Life* is published monthly and is available in hotels and at the TIC. There are no local English-language newspapers, though the *International Herald Tribune*, *Guardian International*, *Financial Times* and *USA Today* are available in the afternoon on the day of publication at hotels and department stores in Ljubljana.

RADIO & TV

News, weather, traffic and tourist information in English, German and Italian follows the Slovene-language news, on Radio Slovenija 2 during the weekends in July and August. Also in July and August, Radio Slovenija 1 and 2 broadcast a report on the weather, including conditions on the sea and in the mountains, in the same languages. There's a nightly news bulletin in English and German at 10.30pm throughout the year on Radio 1. Most Slovene hotels have English- or German-language cable channels.

TIME

Slovenia is one hour ahead of GMT/UTC. The country goes onto summer time (GMT/UTC plus two hours) on the last Sunday in March when clocks are advanced by one hour. On the last Sunday in October they're turned back one hour.

LAUNDRY

Commercial laundrettes are rare in Slovenia. The best places to look for do-it-yourself washers and dryers are hostels, college dormitories and camping grounds, and there are a couple of places in Ljubljana that will do your laundry reasonably quickly (see Laundry under Information in the Ljubljana section).

PHOTOGRAPHY

Film is plentiful and fairly inexpensive in Slovenia. A roll of 24 exposures costs about 900 SIT.

WOMEN TRAVELLERS

Women are unlikely to encounter problems while travelling in Slovenia. Crime is low and harassment is rare. There is a **women's crisis helpline** (☎ 080 11 55) for emergencies.

Emergency Services

In the event of an emergency call ☎ 113 for the police and ☎ 112 for the fire, first aid or ambulance services.

The automobile assistance (AMZS) information number is ☎ 530 53 00. For road emergency and towing services ring ☎ 1987. These numbers can be dialled nationwide.

GAY & LESBIAN TRAVELLERS

The gay association **Roza Klub** (☎ 01-430 47 40; *Kersnikova ul 4, Ljubljana*), organises a disco every Sunday night at Klub K4 in Ljubljana. Roza Klub is made up of a gay branch of the S/vKUC (Student Cultural Centre), Magnus, as well as a lesbian branch, LL (the same contact details as Roza Klub).

The **GALfon** (☎ 01-432 40 89) is a hotline and source of general information for gays and lesbians. It operates daily from 7pm to 10pm. The **Slovenian Queer Resources Directory** (W www.ljudmila.org/siqrd) leaves no stone unturned.

Gay and lesbian travellers should encounter no major problems in Slovenia.

DISABLED TRAVELLERS

Slovenia's government is currently working on making public spaces more accessible to the disabled, but it's still a pretty tough go. A group that looks after the interests and special needs of physically challenged people is the **Zveza Paraplegikov Republike Slovenije** (ZPRS; ☎ 01-432 71 38) in Ljubljana.

SENIOR TRAVELLERS

Senior citizens may be entitled to discounts in Slovenia on things like museum admission fees, provided they show proof of age.

DANGERS & ANNOYANCES

Slovenia is hardly a violent or dangerous place. Police say that 90% of all crimes reported involve theft so travellers should take the usual precautions. Bike theft is fairly common in Ljubljana.

BUSINESS HOURS

Shops, groceries and department stores open 7.30am or 8am to 7pm on weekdays and to 1pm on Saturday. Bank hours are generally 8am to 4.30pm or 5pm on weekdays (often with a lunch break) and till noon on Saturday.

Main post offices are open 7am to 8pm on weekdays, till 1pm on Saturday and occasionally 9am to 11am on Sunday.

PUBLIC HOLIDAYS & SPECIAL EVENTS

Public holidays in Slovenia include two days at New Year (1 and 2 January), National Culture Day (8 February), Easter Sunday and Monday (March/April), Insurrection Day (27 April), two days for Labour Day (1 and 2 May), National Day (25 June), Assumption Day (15 August), Reformation Day (31 October), All Saints' Day (1 November), Christmas (25 December) and Independence Day (26 December).

Though cultural events are scheduled throughout the year, the highlights of the Slovenian summer season (July and August) are the International Summer Festival in Ljubljana; the Piran Musical Evenings; the Primorska Summer Festival at Piran, Koper, Izola and Portorož in July; and Summer in the Old Town in Ljubljana, with three or four cultural events a week taking place.

ACTIVITIES
Skiing

Skiing is by far the most popular sport in Slovenia, and every fourth Slovene is an active skier. The country has many well-equipped ski resorts in the Julian Alps, especially Vogel (skiing up to 1840m) above Lake Bohinj, Kranjska Gora (1600m), Kanin (2300m) above Bovec, and Krvavec (1970m), northeast of Kranj.

All these resorts have multiple chairlifts, cable cars, ski schools, equipment rentals and large resort hotels.

Hiking

Hiking is almost as popular as skiing in Slovenia, and there are approximately 7000km of marked trails and 165 mountain huts. Visitors can experience the full grandeur of the Julian Alps in the Triglav National Park at Lake Bohinj, and for the veteran mountaineer there's the Slovenian Alpine Trail, which crosses all the highest peaks in the country.

Kayaking, Canoeing & Rafting

The best white-water rafting is on the Soča, one of only half a dozen rivers in the European Alps whose upper waters are still unspoiled. The centre is at Bovec.

Fishing

Slovenia's rivers and Alpine lakes and streams are teeming with trout, grayling, pike and other fish. The best rivers for angling are the Soča, the Krka, the Kolpa and the Sava Bohinjka near Bohinj. Lake fishing is good at Bled and Bohinj.

Cycling

Mountain bikes are available for hire at Bled and Bohinj. You can also rent bikes on the coast and in Ljubljana.

WORK

Employment of foreigners in Slovenia is among the most restricted in Europe. Even foreign businesses have difficulty obtaining working visas for their employees. This is likely to change when Slovenia is accepted into the EU, expected 1 January 2004. Legislation will be changed to reflect that in the more liberalized EU countries.

ACCOMMODATION
Camping

In summer, camping is the cheapest way to go, and you'll find there are convenient camping grounds all over the country. You don't always need a tent as some camping grounds have inexpensive bungalows or caravans. Two of the best camping grounds are Zlatorog on Lake Bohinj and Jezero Fiesa near Piran, though they can be very crowded in summer. It is forbidden to camp 'rough' in Slovenia.

Hostels & Student Dormitories

Slovenia has only a handful of 'official' hostels, including two in Ljubljana and excellent ones in Bled and Piran, but many others aren't open year-round. You'll find that some college dormitories accept travellers in the summer months.

Private Rooms & Apartments

Private rooms arranged by tourist offices and travel agencies can be inexpensive, but a surcharge of up to 50% is often levied on stays of less than three nights. You can often bargain for rooms without the surcharge by going directly to any house with a sign reading 'sobe' (rooms).

Pensions & Guesthouses

A small guesthouse (called a *penzion* or *gostišče*) can be good value, though in July and

SLOVENIA

August you may be required to take at least one meal and the rates are higher.

Farmhouses

The agricultural cooperatives of Slovenia have organised a unique program to accommodate visitors on working farms. Prices are about 3500 SIT per night for bed and breakfast (30% more if less than a two-night stay) to about 5000 SIT per night with full-board during high season (July, August and around Christmas). Contact the **Association of Tourist Farms of Slovenia** (☎ 03-491 64 80; ⓔ ztks@siol.net). Bookings can be made through **ABC Farm & Countryside Holidays** (☎ 01-507 61 27, fax 519 98 76; Ul Jožeta Jame 16, Ljubljana).

Hotels

Hotel rates vary according to the time of year, with July and August the peak season and May/June and September/October the shoulder seasons. In Ljubljana, prices are constant all year. Many hotels in Slovenia includes breakfast in the price, and many offer free admission or discounts to the spa in town.

FOOD

Slovenian cuisine is heavily influenced by the food of its neighbours. From Austria, there's *klobasa* (sausage), *zavitek* (strudel) and *Dunajski zrezek* (Wiener schnitzel). *Njoki* (potato dumplings), *rižota* (risotto) and the ravioli-like *žlikrofi* are obviously Italian, and Hungary has contributed *golaž* (goulash), *paprikaš* (chicken or beef 'stew') and *palačinke* (thin pancakes filled with jam or nuts and topped with chocolate). And then there's that old Balkan stand-by, *burek*, a greasy, layered cheese, meat or even apple pie served at takeaway places everywhere.

No Slovenian meal can be considered complete without soup, be it the very simple *goveja juha z rezanci* (beef broth with little egg noodles), *zelenjavna juha* (vegetable soup) or *gobova juha* (mushroom soup). There are several types of Slovenian dumplings called *štruklji* that are made with various types of local cheese.

Also try the baked delicacies, including *potica* (walnut roll) and *gibanica* (pastry filled with poppy seeds, apple and/or sultanas and cottage cheese and topped with cream). Traditional dishes are best tried at an inn (*gostilna* or *gostišče*).

Many restaurants have set lunches for 900 to 1600 SIT. These can be great value, as some are upmarket restaurants where dinner can cost three or four times as much.

DRINKS

Wine-growing regions of Slovenia are Podravje in the east, noted for such white wines as Renski Rizling (a true German Riesling), Beli Pinot (Pinot Blanc) and Traminec (Traminer); Posavje in the southeast (try the distinctly Slovenian light-red Cviček); and the area around the coast, which produces a hearty red called Teran made from Refošk grapes. *Vinska cesta* means 'wine road', and wherever you see one of these signs, you'll find wineries and vineyards open for tasting. They cover the area around Maribor, where it's said that every house has its own vineyard.

Žganje is a strong brandy or *eau de vie* that is distilled from a variety of fruits, but most commonly plums. The finest brandy is Pleterska Hruška, made from pears.

SPECTATOR SPORTS

For skiing enthusiasts, World Cup slalom and giant slalom events are held at Kranjska Gora in late December. In early January, women's World Cup skiing takes place in Maribor.

SHOPPING

Slovenia isn't famous for its handicrafts, but there are some beautiful things available, especially antiques. Every Sunday, the **antique flea market** takes place along the Ljubljanica River. You'll find furniture, stamps, art, knickknacks and every imaginable item. Most of the best craft stores, including **Dom** and **365**, and the best antique shops can be found on Mestni trg (square) near the Town Hall.

Getting There & Away

AIR

Slovenia's national air carrier, **Adria Airways** (in Ljubljana ☎ 01-231 33 12, at Brnik airport ☎ 04-202 51 11; ⓦ www.adria.si) has nonstop flights to Ljubljana from cities including Amsterdam, Brussels, Copenhagen, Frankfurt, Istanbul, London, Moscow, Munich, Ohrid, Paris, Sarajevo, Skopje, Split, Tirana, Vienna and Zürich. You can check out the website for the schedules. From May to October, Adria flies to Dublin, Manchester and Tel Aviv.

Lufthansa flies from Frankfurt and Munich and Swiss from Zürich.

LAND
Bus

Buses from Ljubljana serve a number of international destinations, including the following cities and towns: Belgrade (7100 to 7400 SIT, three daily); Frankfurt (17,550 SIT, daily at 7.30pm); Munich (7900 SIT, daily at 7.30pm); Rijeka (2880 SIT, daily at 7.40pm); Split (7140 SIT, daily at 7.40pm); Trieste (2110 SIT, daily at 6.25am) and Zagreb (2570 SIT, three daily).

Italy Nova Gorica is the easiest departure point from Slovenia to Italy, as you can catch up to five buses a day to/from the Italian city of Gorizia or simply walk across the border at Rožna Dolina. Take one of 17 daily buses (2020 SIT). Koper also has good connections with Italy – some 17 buses a day on weekdays go to/from Trieste, 21km to the northeast. There's also a daily bus from Trieste to Ljubljana (2110 SIT, daily at 6.25am).

Hungary There is no direct bus that links Ljubljana to Budapest. Instead, take one of up to five daily buses to Lendava; the Hungarian border is 5km to the north. The first Hungarian train station, Rédics, is only 2km beyond the border.

Train

The main train routes into Slovenia from Austria are Vienna/Graz to Maribor and Ljubljana and Salzburg to Jesenice. Tickets cost 8000 SIT from Ljubljana to Salzburg (four hours) and 11,558 SIT to Vienna (six hours). But it's cheaper to take a local train to Maribor (1380 SIT) and buy your ticket on to Vienna from there. Similarly, from Austria you should only buy a ticket as far as Jesenice or Maribor, as domestic fares are much lower than the international fares.

There are three trains a day between Munich and Ljubljana (12,806 SIT, seven hours). Take the EuroCity *Mimara* via Salzburg or the *Lisinski* express, which leaves at 11.30pm (a sleeping carriage is available). A 1000 SIT supplement is payable on the *Mimara*. Seat reservations (600 SIT) are available on both.

Two trains a day travel from Trieste to Ljubljana (4400 SIT, three hours) via the towns of Divača and Sežana. From Croatia it's Zagreb to Ljubljana (2500 SIT, 2½ hours) via Zidani Most, or Rijeka to Ljubljana (2099 SIT, 2½ hours) via Pivka. The InterCity *Drava* and *Venezia Express* trains link Ljubljana with Budapest (9900 SIT, eight hours, two daily) via northwestern Croatia and Zagreb respectively. Three trains a day go to Belgrade (8000 SIT).

Border Crossings

Slovenia maintains some 150 border crossings with Italy, Austria, Hungary and Croatia, but only 26 are considered international or interstate crossings. The rest are minor crossings only open to Slovenian citizens or others with special permits.

SEA

From late March to November on Friday, Saturday and Sunday, the *Prince of Venice*, a 39m Australian-made catamaran seating some 330 passengers, sails between Izola and Venice (return ticket 15,000/13,500/9500 SIT high/ shoulder/off season). The boat departs from Izola at 8am and returns at 5.30pm. There's an additional sailing on Tuesday and Saturday in July and August. The price of the boat trip includes a sightseeing tour in Venice. From Izola there are frequent buses to Portorož, Piran and Koper. Another catamaran, the *Marconi*, links Trieste with Piran (see Cruises in the Piran section).

DEPARTURE TAX

A departure tax of 2700 SIT is levied on all passengers leaving Slovenia by air, though this is almost always included in your airline ticket price.

Getting Around

BUS

Except for long journeys, the bus is preferable to the train in Slovenia. Departures are frequent. In some cases you don't have much of a choice; travelling by bus is the only practical way to get from Ljubljana to Bled and Bohinj, the Julian Alps and much of the coast.

In Ljubljana you can buy your ticket with seat reservation (600 SIT, depending on the destination) the day before, but many people simply pay the driver on boarding. The one

SLOVENIA

time you really might need a reservation is Friday afternoon, when many students travel from Ljubljana to their homes or people leave the city for the weekend. There is a 220 SIT charge for each bag placed underneath the bus.

Useful footnotes that you might see on the Slovenian bus schedules include: *vozi vsak dan* (runs daily); *vozi ob delavnikih* (runs on working days – Monday to Friday); *vozi ob sobotah* (runs on Saturday); and *vozi ob nedeljah in praznikih* (runs only on Sunday and holidays).

TRAIN

Slovenske Železnice (SŽ; Slovenian Railways) operates on just over 1200km of track. The country's most scenic rail routes run along the Soča River from Jesenice to Nova Gorica via Bled (Bled Jezero station) and Bohinjska Bistrica (89km) and from Ljubljana to Zagreb (160km) along the Sava River.

On posted timetables in Slovenia, *odhod* or *odhodi vlakov* means 'departures' and *prihod* (or *prihodi vlakov*) is 'arrivals'. If you don't have time to buy a ticket, seek out the conductor who will sell you one for an extra charge of 200 SIT.

CAR & MOTORCYCLE

Even though it's a small country, having your own wheels will help if you're planning some outdoor activities, as the buses don't run frequently off the beaten path. The use of seat belts in the front seats is compulsory in Slovenia, and a new law requires all vehicles to have their headlights on throughout the day outside built-up areas. Speed limits for cars are 50km/h in built-up areas, 90km/h on secondary roads, 100km/h on main highways and 130km/h on motorways.

Tolls are payable on several motorways, but they're not terribly expensive. For example, Ljubljana to Postojna will cost 440 SIT. Petrol remains relatively cheap: 187.00/195.20 SIT per litre for 95/98 octane (both unleaded). Diesel costs 154.60 SIT.

Slovenia's automobile club, the **Avto Moto Zveza Slovenije** (AMZS; ☎ 01-530 53 00), may be a helpful contact.

The permitted blood-alcohol level for motorists is 0.05% or 0.5g/kg of blood (the level is zero for professional drivers) and the law is strictly enforced. Anything over that could earn you a fine of 25,000 SIT and one to three demerit points.

Car Rental

Car rentals from international firms like Avis, National, Budget and Kompas Hertz vary widely in price, but expect to pay from about 14,750/73,920 SIT a day/week with unlimited mileage, collision damage waiver, theft protection and personal accident insurance for a compact (like a Ford Fiesta). Add 20% VAT.

Some car-rental agencies have minimum-age rules (21 or 23 years) and/or require that you've had a valid licence for one or even two years. Three international chains are **Kompas Hertz** (☎ 01-231 12 41; Miklošičeva ul 11), **National** (☎ 01- 588 44 50; Baragova ul 5) and **Avis** (☎ 01- 430 80 10; Čufarjeva ul 2). They also have counters at the airport. Two excellent smaller agencies, with more competitive rates, are **ABC Rent a Car** (☎ 04-236 79 90; open 24hr) at Brnik airport and **Avtoimpex** (☎ 01- 519 72 97; Celovška cesta 252) in Ljubljana.

HITCHING

Hitchhiking is legal everywhere except on motorways and some major highways and is generally easy; even young women do it. But hitching is never a totally safe way of getting around and, although we mention it as an option, we don't recommend it.

Ljubljana

☎ 01 • pop 280,000

Ljubljana (Laibach in German) is by far the largest and most populous city in Slovenia. However, in many ways the city, the name of which almost means 'beloved' (ljubljena) in Slovene, doesn't feel like an industrious municipality of national importance but a pleasant, self-contented town with responsibilities only to itself and its citizens. The most beautiful parts of the city are the Old Town below the castle and the embankments designed by Plečnik, along the narrow Ljubljanica River.

Ljubljana began as the Roman town of Emona, and legacies of the Roman presence can still be seen throughout the city. The Habsburgs took control of Ljubljana in the 14th century and later built many of the pale-coloured churches and mansions that earned the city the nickname 'White Ljubljana'. From 1809 to 1814 Ljubljana was the capital of the Illyrian Provinces, Napoleon's short-lived springboard to the Adriatic.

Despite the patina of imperial Austria, contemporary Ljubljana has a vibrant Slavic air all its own. It's like a little Prague without the hordes of tourists but with all the facilities you'll need. Almost 50,000 students attend Ljubljana University's 20 faculties and three art academies, so the city always feels young.

Orientation

The tiny bus station and renovated train station are opposite each other on the square Trg Osvobodilne Fronte (known as Trg OF) at the northern end of the town centre (called Center).

Information

Tourist Offices The Ljubljana **Tourist Information Centre** (*TIC;* ☎ *306 12 15, fax 306 12 04;* e *pcl.tic-lj@ljubljana.si; Stritarjeva ul 2; open 8am-8pm Mon-Fri, 10am-6pm Sat, Sun & holidays in summer; to 6pm daily low season*) is in the historical Kresija building southeast of Triple Bridge. The **branch office** (*☎/fax 433 94 75; open 9am-9pm daily in summer, 10am-5.30pm Mon-Fri Oct-May*) is at the train station. The TIC is worth visiting to pick up free maps and brochures, organise sightseeing trips or inquire about accommodation options.

The main office of the **Alpine Association of Slovenia** (*☎ 434 30 22;* w *www.pzs.si; Dvoržakova ul 9*) is in a small house set back from the street. It can help plan trekking or hiking trips anywhere in the country, including the Julian Alps.

Money There are more than 50 ATMs in Ljubljana. Many are in the Center, including an **A Banka** (*Trg Osvobodilne Fronte 2*) opposite the train station and another one at Slovenska 58 (where card-holders can get cash advances). There are branches of Banka Koper outside the Globtour agency in the Maximarket passageway connecting Trg Republike with Plečnikov trg and at Cigaletova ul 4.

You can get cash advances on MasterCard at **Nova Ljubljanska Banka** (*Trg Republike 2; open 8am-5pm Mon-Fri, 9am-noon Sat*). Next to the SKB Banka on Trg Ajdovščina is a currency exchange machine that changes the banknotes of 18 countries into tolar at a good rate. **Hida exchange bureau** (*Pogarčarjev trg 1; open 7am-7pm Mon-Fri, 7am-2pm Sat*) is inside the Seminary building near the open-air market.

Post & Communications Poste-restante mail will only be held for 30 days at the **post office** (*☎ 426 46 68; Slovenska cesta 32; postal code 1101; open 7am-8pm Mon-Fri, 7am-1pm Sat*). Make international telephone calls or send faxes from here or the **main post office** (*Pražakova ul 3; same hours*).

To mail a parcel you must go to the **special customs post office** (*Trg OF 5; open 24hr*) opposite the bus station. Do not seal your package until after it has been inspected; the maximum weight is about 15kg, depending on the destination.

Email & Internet Access Internet access is free at **Klub K4 Café** (*☎ 431 70 10; Kersnikova ul 4*). **Cyber Café** (*Slovenska cesta 10*) sells drinks and has five terminals for 200/400/600 SIT for 15/30/60 minutes; students pay half price.

Kavarna Čerin (*☎ 232 09 90, Trubarjeva 52*) is a full-service café with free Internet access (and peanuts) for the purchase of a drink. Hotel Turist (see Places to Stay later in this section) has an Internet connection, free for guests, 220 SIT per 20 minutes for all others (available 24 hours).

Digital Resources Useful websites for Ljubljana include:

- w **www.ljubljana.si** City of Ljubljana
- w **www.uni-lj.si** Ljubljana University (check out the Welcome page with practical information in English for foreign students)
- w **www.geocities.com/ljubljanalife** The English -language magazine for expatriates and visitors

Travel Agencies Backpackers and students should head for the **ZMT Infopoint** (*☎ 438 03 12; Kersnikova ul 6*), which sells ISIC cards, **Mladi Turist** (*☎ 425 92 60; Salendrova ul 4*), the office of the Slovenian Youth Hostel Association, or **Erazem Travel Office** (*☎ 433 10 76; Trubarjeva cesta 7*).

There is also an **American Express** representative (*☎ 431 90 20; Trubarjeva 50*) in the city centre.

Bookshops Ljubljana's largest bookshop is **Mladinska Knjiga** (*Slovenska cesta 29*). It has an extensive collection of books in English. There's also **DZS** (*☎ 200 80 42; Mestni tri 26*). **Kod & Kam** (*Trg Francoske Revolucije 7*) is excellent for travel guides and maps, especially if you plan to go hiking.

SLOVENIA

LJUBLJANA

To Avtoimpex Car Rental,
Hound Dog Disco, Casa
del Papa & Brnik Airport (23km)

To Dijaški Dom Bežigrad (2km),
National Car Rental, Camping
Ježica (6km), World Trade
Centre (11km) & Kamnik (23km)

Train Station &
Tourist Office
Branch

Trg Osvobodilne Fronte

To
Metelkova,
Club Tiffany,
Monokel Club, Orto
Bar, Vegodrom &
Zdravstveni Medical Center

Tivoli
Park

Dunajska c

Celovška c

Tivolska c

Dvoržakova ul

Pražakova ul

Cigaletova ul

Trdinova ul

Kolodvorska ul

Čufarjeva ul

Kersnikova ul

Vošnjakova ul

Gosposvetska c

Slovenska c

Tavčarjeva ul

Resljeva c

Komenskega ul

To Čerin, Birdland, American
Express Office (100m),
Dijaški Dom Tabor (250m),
Park Hotel (300m), Rog
Bicycle Rental (500m)
& Emergency Medical
Centre (800m)

Argentinski
Park

Miklošičev
Park

Puharjeva ul

Štefanova

Cankarjeva c

Tomšičeva ul

Župančičeva

Beethovnova ul

Dalmatinova c

Trg
Ajdovščina

Center

Miklošičeva c

Nazorjeva ul

Čopova ul

Trubarjeva c

Mala ul

Prešernova

Tomšičeva ul

Trg
Narodnih
Herojev

Subičeva ul

Slovenska c

Petkovškovo nabrežje

Dragon
Bridge

Prešernov
trg

Triple
Bridge

Plečnik Colonnade

Adamič-Lundrovo nab

Pogačarjev

Vodnikov
trg

Trg
Republike

Wolfova ul

Mačkova ul

Ribji
trg

Ciril-Metodov trg

Krekov
trg

To Dijaški
Dom Ivana
Cankarja (2:1km)

subway

Kongresni
trg

Dvorni
trg

Študentovska
ul

Old
Town

To Rožnik
Hill & Zoo

Erjavčeva c

Cankarjeva

Gregorčičeva c

Igriška ul

Vegova ul

Mestni
trg

Castle Hill
(376m)

Castle Tunnel

Shoemaker
Bridge

Rimska c

Pod Trančo

Stari trg

Aškerčeva c

Slovenska

Turjaška ul

Novi trg

Reber
ul

Ul na Grad

Trg
Francoske
Revolucije

Salendrova ul

Breg

Ljubljanica

Gornji trg

Levstikov
trg

Rožna ul

To Botanical
Garden

Krakovo

Zoisova c

Gosposka ul

Karlovška c

Kovinarska ul

Subičeva ul

To Tivoli Castle

To Rožnik
Hill & Zoo

LJUBLJANA

PLACES TO STAY		12	Kompas Cinema	52	Hida Exchange Bureau;
40	Hotel Turist; Klub Central	14	Avis		Seminary
46	Grand Hotel Union	15	Kinoteka Cinema	54	Tourist Information Centre (TIC)
80	Pri Mraku	16	Kompas Hertz Car Rental	55	Prešeren Monument
		17	Banka Koper	56	Chemoexpress Laundry
PLACES TO EAT		18	A Banka	58	Robba Fountain
5	Burek Stand	20	K4 Café; Roza Klub;	59	Town Hall
13	Burek Stand		University Student Centre	60	Vinoteka Movia
19	Evropa Café	21	ZMT Infopoint	61	DZS Bookshop
35	Quick	22	Adria Airways	62	Bicycle Rentals
38	Šestica	23	Lufthansa Ticket Office	63	365
44	Napoli	24	National Gallery	64	Maček
53	Ribca	25	Church of Sts Cyril &	66	Filharmonija
57	Zvezda Café		Methodius	69	Ljubljana University
65	Žibila	26	Museum of Modern Art	70	Ursuline Church of the Holy
67	Ljubljanski Dvor	27	US Embassy		Trinity
68	Burja	28	National Museum	71	Brewery Pub
77	Prema	29	Opera House	72	Maximarket Department Store
79	Foculus	30	Parliament Building		& Supermarket; Banka Koper
87	Pri Viteza	31	Jazz Club Gajo	73	Globtour Agency
88	Najboljski Gyros	32	Mladinska Knjiga Bookshop	74	Nova Ljubljanska Banka
94	Špajza	33	Post Office (Poste Restante)	75	UK Embassy; Australian
95	Pri sv Florianu; Moro	34	Komuna Cinema		Consulate
		36	Kompas Travel Agency;	76	Cankarjev Dom
OTHER			Holidays' Pub	78	Cyber Cafe
1	Tivoli Recreation Centre &	37	Cankarjeva Založba Bookshop	81	Ilirija Column
	Zlati Klub	39	SKB Banka	82	Križanke Booking Office
2	Ilirija Swimming Pool	41	Tour As	83	Križanke Theatre
3	Alpine Association of Slovenia	42	Patrick's Irish Pub	84	Kod & Kam Bookshop
4	City Bus Ticket Kiosks	43	Salon	85	National & University Library
6	Main Post Office	45	Art Nouveau Bank Buildings	86	Mladi Turist
7	Canadian Consulate	47	Union Cinema	89	Dom
8	City Airport Buses	48	Franciscan Church	90	Castle Tower
9	Post Office (Customs)	49	Erazem Travel Office	91	Ljubljana Castle
10	Bus Station	50	Produce Market	92	Pentagonal Tower
11	A Banka	51	Cathedral of St Nicholas	93	Church of St Florian

The best places to buy English and other foreign-language newspapers and magazines are the newsstands in the lobby of the **Grand Hotel Union** (Miklošičeva cesta 1) and in the basement of the **Maximarket department store** (Trg Republike).

Laundry The student dormitory **Dijaški Dom Kam** (Kardeljeva ploščad 14), north of the Center in Bežigrad, has washing machines and dryers that you can use (Building C), as does **Camping Ježica** (Dunajska cesta 270).

Chemoexpress (Wolfova ul 12; open 7am-6pm Mon-Fri) near Prešernov trg is an old-style laundry and dry cleaner.

Left Luggage The 24-hour left-luggage office (garderoba; 400 SIT per piece) at the train station is on platform No 1. There is a smaller garderoba (open 5.30am to 8.15pm) inside the bus station.

Medical Services In a medical emergency, dial ☎ 112, or go to the **emergency medical centre** (☎ 232 30 60; Bohoričeva 9). If you need to see a doctor, try the **Zdravstveni dom Center** (☎ 472 37 00; Metelkova 9).

Things to See & Do

The most picturesque sights of old Ljubljana are along the banks of the Ljubljanica, a tributary of the Sava that curves around the foot of Castle Hill.

Opposite the tourist information centre and the Kresija building is the celebrated **Triple Bridge**. In 1931, Jože Plečnik added the side bridges to the original central span, which dates from 1842. On the northern side of the bridge is Prešernov trg with its pink **Franciscan church** (1660), a **statue** (1905) of poet France Prešeren and some wonderful Art Nouveau buildings. A lively pedestrian street, **Čopova ul**, runs northwest.

SLOVENIA

On the southern side of the bridge in Mestni trg, the baroque **Robba Fountain** stands in front of the **Town Hall** (Magistrat; 1718). Italian sculptor Francesco Robba designed this fountain in 1751 and modelled it after one in Rome. Enter the town hall to see the double Gothic courtyard. South of Mestni trg is **Stari trg**, full of atmosphere day and night. Northeast are the twin towers of the **Cathedral of St Nicholas** (1708), which contains impressive frescoes. Behind the cathedral is Ljubljana's colourful open-air **produce market** (closed Sunday) and an arch-fronted **colonnade** along the riverside designed by Plečnik.

Ljubljana Castle has finally been renovated, so you can now climb the 19th-century Castle Tower to the west, view the exhibits in the Gothic chapel and the **Pentagonal Tower** (open Tues-Sun). There's a new virtual **museum** (adult/child 700/400 SIT; open 10am-9pm daily). Študentovska ul, opposite the Vodnik statue in the market square, offers a panoramic path to the castle, or try Reber ul between Stari trg 17 and 19. You can take the tram, which leaves Prešernov trg (next to the Triple Bridge) daily during the winter at 20 past the hour from 10am to 3pm, and May to September from 10am to 8pm. The train costs 500/350 SIT for adults/children and students.

Near the now-closed Municipal Museum is the 1941 **National & University Library** (Gosposka ul 14), designed by Plečnik, and north on Gosposka ul is the main building (1902) of **Ljubljana University** (Kongresni trg 12), which was formerly the regional parliament. The elegant **Filharmonija** (Philharmonic Hall), at No 10 on the southeastern corner of the square, is home to the Slovenian Philharmonic Orchestra. The **Ursuline Church of the Holy Trinity** (1726), with an altar by Robba, faces Kongresni trg to the west.

Walk west along Šubičeva ul to several fine museums. The **National Museum** (Muzejska ul 1; adult/child 500/300 SIT; open 10am-6pm Tues-Sun), built in 1885, has prehistory and natural history collections. The highlight is a Celtic *situla*, a kind of pail, from the 6th century BC sporting a fascinating relief.

The **National Gallery** (Prešernova cesta 24; adult/child 700/500 SIT, free Sat afternoon; open 10am-6pm Tues-Sun) displays European portraits and landscapes from the 17th to 19th centuries, as well as copies of medieval frescoes. The gallery's north wing has a permanent collection of European paintings from the Middle Ages to the 20th century and is used for temporary exhibits.

Diagonally opposite the National Gallery is the **Museum of Modern Art** (Cankarjeva ul 15; adult/senior 1000/500 SIT, children free; open 10am-6pm Tues-Sun) where a part of the International Biennial of Graphic Arts is held summers of odd-numbered years.

The Serbian Orthodox **Church of Sts Cyril & Methodius** (open 3pm-6pm Tues-Sat), opposite the Museum of Modern Art, is worth visiting to see the beautiful modern frescoes. The subway from the Museum of Modern Art leads to Ljubljana's green lung, **Tivoli Park**.

Activities

The **Tivoli Recreation Centre** (☎ 431 51 55; Celovška cesta 25) in Tivoli Park has bowling alleys, tennis courts, an indoor swimming pool, a fitness centre and a roller-skating rink. In summer, there's minigolf. The **Zlati Klub** at this centre has several saunas, a steam room, warm and cold splash pools and even a small outside pool surrounded by high walls so you can sunbathe in the nude (mixed sexes, but Friday mornings 9am-1pm are women only).

The outdoor **Ilirija pool** (Celovška cesta 3; open 9am-11am Mon-Fri, 6.30pm-10pm Tues-Thur, 10am-8pm Sat & Sun in summer) is opposite the Tivoli hotel.

Organised Tours

Guided tours (€5.50, half-price for students, pensioners and children) of Ljubljana are available in Slovene and English from in front of the Town Hall at Mestni trg 1. Tours leave at 5pm daily from 1 June to 30 September and at 11am Sunday from 1 October to 31 May.

Places to Stay

Camping Some 6km north of Center on the Sava is **Camping Ježica** (☎ 568 39 13; Dunajska cesta 270; bus No 6 or 8; tent or caravan sites per adult/child low season €6/5, high season €8/6; bungalow singles/doubles/triples €25/40/50), a shady camping area open year-round with a restaurant and swimming pool that accommodates 300 people.

Hostels & Student Dormitories Three student dormitories (dijaški dom) are open to foreign travellers in July and August. Most central is **Dijaški Dom Tabor** (☎ 234 88 40, fax 234 88 55; e ssljddta1s@guest.arnes.si; Vidovdanska ul 7; singles 4000 SIT, doubles or triples per bed 2900/3400 SIT members/ nonmembers) across from the Park Hotel and affiliated with Hostelling International (HI). Rates include breakfast.

Dijaški Dom Bežigrad (☎ 534 28 67; e dd .lj-bezigrad@guest.arnes.si; Kardeljeva pl 28; bus No 6; singles/shared per person 3800/ 3300 SIT, breakfast 460 SIT) another HI member, is in the Bežigrad district 2km north of the train and bus stations. The Bežigrad has 50 rooms available in July and August.

Dijaška Dom Ivana Cankarja (☎ 474 86 00; e dd.lj-ic@guest.arnes.si; Polanski cesta 26; accommodation per person €10-14, including breakfast €12-15) is just east of the town centre (10% less for students).

Private Rooms & Apartments The TIC has about 40 private rooms on its list, but just a handful are in Center. Most of the others would require a bus trip up to Bežigrad. Prices range from 3500 SIT for singles and 5000 SIT for doubles. It also has eight apartments and one studio – four of which are central – for one to four people costing from 9700 SIT to 16,700 SIT. Whether you're looking for an apartment for one day or several months, try **Tour As** (☎ 434 26 60; e info@apartmaji.si; Mala ul 8) by Hotel Turist.

Hotels The best deal for location and quality is **Pri Mraku** (☎ 433 40 49; e mrak@daj-dam .si; Rimska cesta 4, singles/doubles 13,950/ 19,200 SIT). For 8450 SIT per person, up to four people can have a 5th-floor room with shared bathroom. The Mraku also has an excellent restaurant.

The 122-room **Park Hotel** (☎ 433 13 06, fax 433 05 46; e hotel.park@siol.net; Tabor 9; singles/doubles from €37/50) is where most people usually end up, as it's the city's only large budget hotel close to Center and the Old Town. It's pretty depressing, but the price is right and rates include breakfast. Students with cards get a 20% discount.

Bit Center Hotel (☎ 548 00 55, fax 548 00 56; w www.bit-center.net; Litijska 57; bus No 9 from the railway station; singles/ doubles or triples 5490/8190 SIT, breakfast 800 SIT), one small step up from a hostel, is also a possibility. Hotel guests get a 50% discount on sauna and health-club services, available in the same building.

A reasonable alternative in the town centre is the three-star **Hotel Turist** (☎ 234 91 30,

fax 234 91 40; e info@hotelturist.si; Dalmatinova; 15 singles/doubles from €66/90).

Places to Eat

Restaurants There are several excellent restaurants in Ljubljana that are relatively good value. **Šestica** (Slovenska cesta 40; lunch menus 1000-1400 SIT, mains 1100-2000 SIT) is a 200-year-old stand-by with a pleasant courtyard.

If you're in the mood to try horse meat, visit **Pri Vitezu** (Breg 4), a pricey but highly rated restaurant along the Ljubljanica.

Pri sv Florijanu (☎ 351 22 14; Gornji trg 20; set lunch 1690 SIT) has creative modern Slovenian food, including a great vegetable soup and leek risotto. The set lunch is good value. **Moro**, the happening new Moroccan themed bar and restaurant, is downstairs.

The capital abounds in Italian restaurants and pizzerias. Among the best in town are **Ljubljanski Dvor** (Dvorni trg 1) on the west bank of the Ljubljanica and **Foculus** (Gregorčičeva ul 3; small/large pizzas 800/1100 SIT) next door to the Glej Theatre. Other pizzapasta places include **Napoli** (Prečna ul 7) off Trubarjeva cesta and **Čerin** (Trubarjeva 52), which also has Internet access in its next-door Kavarna Čerin.

Špajza (Gornji trg 28) is popular with locals. **Casa del Papa** (☎ 434 31 58; Celovška 54) serves Latin-influenced lunch and dinner in a Hemingway-inspired setting.

The delicious vegetarian restaurant **Vegodrom** (☎ 459 17 50, Maistrova 10) also serves Indian cuisine like samosas and palak paneer.

Cafés For coffee and cakes you might try the elegant **Evropa Café** (Gosposvetska cesta 2) on the corner of Slovenska cesta or the trendy **Zvezda Café** (Wolfova 14).

Self-Service & Fast Food For hamburgers, to-go coffee and other fast food visit **Quick** (Cankarjeva cesta 12; open 6.30am-11pm Mon-Sat, 4pm-10pm Sun), with a play area for kids. For a quick and tasty lunch, try **Ribca** (Pogarčarjev trg), a seafood bar below the Plečnik Colonnade. **Najboljski Gyros** (Stari trg 19; open 9am-1am Mon-Thurs, noon-1am Fri & Sat) sells gyros, pizzas and crepes, all under 1000 SIT.

There are **burek stands** (about 500 SIT) at several locations in Ljubljana. The one at Kolodvorska ul 20 is open 24 hours.

SLOVENIA

Self-Catering In the basement of the Maxi-market shopping arcade, the **supermarket** (*Trg Republike; open 9am-8pm Mon-Fri, to 3pm Sat & Sun*) has about the largest selection in town. The best places for picnic supplies are the city's many delicatessens, including **Žibila** (*Kongresni trg 9*) and **Burja** (*Kongresni trg 11*). For healthy snacks and vegetarian food, try **Prema** (*Gregorčičeva 9*).

Entertainment

Ask the TIC for its monthly programme of events in English – it is called *Where to? in Ljubljana* – or check out *Ljubljana Life*, the English-language monthly magazine available at the TIC and in hotels and restaurants.

Pubs & Bars A fun place to try Slovenian wine is **Vinoteka Movia** (*Mestni trg 2*), a wine bar next to the Town Hall. Pleasant and congenial places for a *pivo* (beer) or glass of *vino* (wine) include **Salon** (*Trubarjeva cesta 23*), **Patrick's Irish Pub** (*Prečna ul 6*) and **Holidays' Pub** (*Slovenska cesta 36*) next to the Kompas travel agency. Along the river, the most popular bar for locals and tourists is **Maček** (*Cankarjevo nab 19*).

Clubs Two of the most popular conventional clubs are **Klub Central** (*Dalmatinova ul 15*) next to the Turist Hotel and **Hound Dog** (*Trg Prekomorskih Brigad 4*) in the Hotel M, both populated by a young crowd. The student hang-out **K4** (*Kersnikova ul 4*) has a disco every night, open until the wee hours on Friday and Saturday nights and until around midnight on other nights. A popular place is **Metelkova mesto** (along Metelkova cesta near Maistrova ul), where squatters have turned former Yugoslav army barracks into the hippest spot in town, with several nightclubs and bars.

Gay & Lesbian Venues A popular spot for both gays and lesbians on Sunday night is **Roza Klub** (*open 10pm-4am*) at K4. At the Metelkova squat, there's a café/pub for gays called **Club Tiffany**. **Monokel Club** (*open Thur-Mon*) is a popular spot for lesbians in the same building.

Rock & Jazz Ljubljana has a number of excellent rock clubs with canned or live music including **Orto Bar** (*Grablovičeva ul 1*) and the **Brewery Pub** (*Plečnikov trg 1*). For jazz, you cannot beat the **Jazz Club Gajo** (*Beethovnova ul 8*) near the Parliament building. **Birdland** (*Trubarjeva cesta 50*) also has a jam session on Wednesday night and occasional jazz concerts on the weekend.

Classical Music, Opera & Dance Ljubljana is home to two orchestras. Concerts are held in various locations all over town, but the main venue – with up to 700 cultural events every year – is **Cankarjev Dom** (*Trg Republike*). The **ticket office** (☎ 241 71 00; *open 10am-2pm & 4.30pm-8pm Mon-Fri, 10am-1pm Sat & 1hr before performances*), is in the basement of the nearby Maximarket mall. Tickets will cost anywhere between 1500 SIT and 3000 SIT with gala performances worth as much as 6000 SIT. Also check for any concerts performed at the beautiful **Filharmonija** (*Kongresni trg 10*).

At the ticket office of the **Opera House** (☎ 425 48 40; *Župančičeva ul 1; open 2pm-5pm Mon-Fri, 6pm-7pm Sat & 1hr before performances*) you can also buy ballet tickets.

For tickets to the Ljubljana Summer Festival and anything else that is staged at the Križanke, go to the **booking office** (☎ 252 65 44; *Trg Francoske Revolucije 1-2; open 10am-2pm & 4.30pm-8pm Mon-Fri, 10am-1pm Sat & 1hr before performances*) behind the Ilirija Column.

Cinemas For first-run films, try the **Komuna** (*Cankarjeva cesta 1*), **Kompas** (*Miklošičeva cesta 38*) or **Union** (*Nazorjeva ul 2*). All three generally have three screenings a day. The **Kinoteka** (*Miklošičeva cesta 28*) shows art and classic films. Cinema tickets generally cost around 800 SIT, and there are discounts usually available for the first session on weekday screenings.

Getting There & Away

Bus You can reach virtually anywhere in the country by bus from the capital. The timetable in the shed-like **bus station** (☎ 090 42 30; *Trg OF*) lists all routes and times.

Some sample destinations and one-way fares are: Bled (1220 SIT, hourly); Bohinj (1730 SIT, hourly); Jesenice (1310 SIT, hourly); Koper (2200 SIT, eight a day); Maribor (2370 SIT, 10 a day); Murska Sobota (3570 SIT, five a day); Novo Mesto (1390 SIT, hourly); Piran (3370 SIT, seven a day); Postojna (1120 SIT, 25 a day) Ptuj (connect in Maribor); and Rogaška Slatina (1950 SIT, daily at 9.30am).

Train All domestic and international trains arrive at and depart from the station (☎ 291 33 32; Trg OF 6). Local trains leave Ljubljana regularly for Bled (680 SIT, 51km); Jesenice (800 SIT, 64km); Koper (1380 SIT, 153km); Maribor (1380 SIT, 156km); Murska Sobota (2100 SIT, 216km); and Novo Mesto (950 SIT, 75km).

There is a 260 SIT surcharge on domestic InterCity train tickets. For more details on international trains to/from Ljubljana, see the introductory Getting There & Away section of this chapter.

Getting Around

To/From the Airport The city bus from lane No 28 leaves every hour for Brnik airport (680 SIT), 23km to the northwest, hourly at 10 minutes past the hour Monday to Friday and weekends on odd hours. There's also an **airport shuttle** (☎ 040-887 766) for about 2500 SIT. A taxi will cost between 5000 SIT and 6500 SIT. Brnik is about 40 to 45 minutes from the city centre.

Bus Ljubljana's bus system (☎ 582 24 60) is excellent and very user-friendly. There are 22 lines; five (Nos 1, 2, 3, 6 and 11) are considered to be main lines. These start to operate at 3.15am and run until midnight, while the rest run from 5am to 10.30pm.

You can either pay on board the bus (230 SIT) or use the tiny yellow plastic tokens (170 SIT) that are available from the bus station, newsstands, tobacconists, post offices and the two kiosks on the pavement in front of Slovenska cesta 55. An all-day ticket is also available for 660 SIT.

Taxi You can call a taxi on one of 10 numbers: ☎ 9700 to 9709. Flag fall is 150 SIT, and rates are 100 to 300 SIT per kilometre, depending on time of day. A taxi from the bus or train station to downtown runs at about 700 SIT, and 2000 SIT to outlying hotels.

Bicycle Visitors can rent bicycles from **Rog** (☎ 520 03 10; open 8am-7pm Mon-Fri, 8am-noon Sat), next to Rozmanova ul 1. From June to the end of September, you can also rent bikes near **Café Maček** (☎ 041-696 515) on Cankarjevo nab.

Julian Alps

Slovenia shares the Julian Alps in the northwestern corner of the country with Italy. The tri-peaked Mt Triglav (2864m), the country's highest summit, is climbed regularly by thousands of weekend warriors, but there are countless less ambitious hikes on offer in the region. Lakes Bled and Bohinj make ideal starting points – Bled with its comfortable resort facilities, Bohinj right beneath the rocky crags themselves. Most of this spectacular area falls within the boundaries of the Triglav National Park, which was established in 1924.

BLED
☎ 04 • pop 5400

Bled, a fashionable resort at just over 500m, is set on an idyllic, 2km-long emerald-green lake with a little island and church in the centre and a dramatic castle towering overhead. Trout and carp proliferate in the clear water, which is surprisingly warm and a pleasure for swimming or boating. To the northeast, the highest peaks of the Karavanke Range form a natural boundary with Austria, and the Julian Alps lie to the west. Bled has been a favourite destination for travellers for decades. All in all, it is beautiful but be warned that it can get very crowded – and pricey – in season.

Orientation

Bled village is at the northeastern end of the lake below Bled Castle. The bus station is also here on Cesta Svobode, but the main Lesce-Bled train station is about 4km to the southeast. In addition there's Bled Jezero, a branch-line train station northwest of the lake, not far from the camping ground.

Information

Tourist Offices Beld **tourist office** (☎ 574 11 22, fax 574 15 55; **w** www.bled.si; Cesta Svobode 15; open 9am-7pm Mon-Sat, 9am-3pm Sun Apr-Oct; 9am-5pm Mon-Sat, 9am-2pm Sun Nov-Mar) is next to the Park Hotel. In July and August the office stays open till 10pm Monday to Saturday and to 8pm on Sunday. Ask for the useful booklet Bled Tourist Information (300 SIT), available in English or German, which is reproduced on the town's useful website.

In Triglav shopping centre, **Kompas** (☎ 574 15 15; Ljubljanska cesta 4) sells some good

SLOVENIA

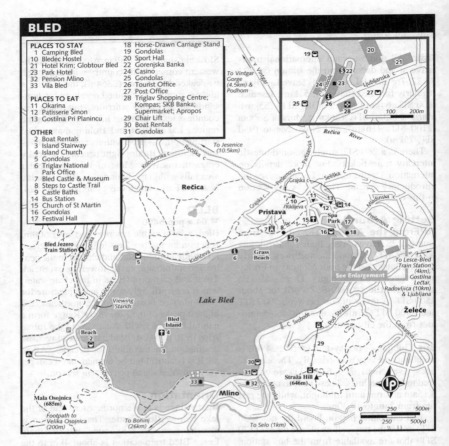

BLED

PLACES TO STAY
1 Camping Bled
10 Bledec Hostel
21 Hotel Krim; Globtour Bled
23 Park Hotel
32 Pension Mlino
33 Vila Bled

PLACES TO EAT
11 Okarina
12 Patisserie Šmon
13 Gostilna Pri Planincu

OTHER
2 Boat Rentals
3 Island Stairway
4 Island Church
5 Gondolas
6 Triglav National
  Park Office
7 Bled Castle & Museum
8 Steps to Castle Trail
9 Castle Baths
14 Bus Station
15 Church of St Martin
16 Gondolas
17 Festival Hall

18 Horse-Drawn Carriage Stand
19 Gondolas
20 Sport Hall
22 Gorenjska Banka
24 Casino
25 Gondolas
26 Tourist Office
27 Post Office
28 Triglav Shopping Centre;
   Kompas; SKB Banka;
   Supermarket; Apropos
29 Chair Lift
30 Boat Rentals
31 Gondolas

hiking maps. The **Triglav National Park office** (☎ 578 02 00; Kidričeva cesta 2; open 7am-3pm Mon-Fri) is located on the lake's northern shore.

Email & Internet Access Internet access is available at the **Bledec Hostel** at a cost of 500 SIT for 30 minutes. In the Triglav shopping centre, **Apropos** (Ljubljanska cesta 4; open 8am-midnight Mon-Sat) charges 1000 SIT for one hour, 500 SIT for 30 minutes.

Money Gorenjska Banka (Cesta Svobode 15; open 9am-11.30am & 2pm-5pm Mon-Fri, 8am-11am Sat), in the Park Hotel shopping complex, has an ATM for MasterCard/Cirrus holders. SKB Banka ATM (Ljubljanska cesta 4; open 8.30am-noon & 2pm-5pm Mon-Fri)

accepts all cards. Kompas and the tourist office change money.

Post & Communications The **post office** (Ljubljanska cesta 10; open 7am-7pm Mon-Fri, to noon Sat) is also in the centre of town.

Things to See

There are several trails to **Bled Castle** (adult/child 700/400 SIT; open 9am-8pm daily May-Sept, 9am-5pm Oct-Apr), the easiest is the one south from behind Bledec Hostel at Grajska cesta 17. The castle was the seat of the Bishops of Brixen (South Tirol) for over 800 years. Atop a steep cliff 100m above the lake, it offers magnificent views in clear weather. The **museum** presents the history of the area and allows a peep into a small 16th-century chapel. The expensive restaurant serves drinks on a terrace with a magnificent view.

Bled's other striking feature is tiny **Bled Island** (Blejski Otok) at the western end of the lake. The tolling 'bell of wishes' echoes across the lake from the tall white belfry rising above the dense vegetation. It's said that all who ring it will get their wish; naturally it chimes constantly. Underneath the present baroque church are the foundations of what was a pre-Romanesque chapel, unique in Slovenia. Most people reach the island on a *pletna*, a large gondola hand-propelled by a boatman. The price (1800 SIT per person) includes a half-hour visit to the island, church and belfry. If there are two or three of you it would be cheaper and more fun to hire a rowing boat (2000 SIT an hour for up to four) from the Castle Baths on the shore below the castle, in Mlino on the southern lakeshore or in front of the **Casino** (*Cesta Svobode 15*).

Hiking

An excellent half-day hike from Bled features a visit to the most impressive **Vintgar Gorge** (*adult/child 500/300 SIT; open daily May-Oct*), 4.5km to the northwest. Head northwest on Prešernova cesta then north on Partizanska cesta to Cesta v Vintgar. This will take you to Podhom, where signs point the way to the gorge entrance. A wooden footbridge hugs the rock wall for 1600m along the Radovna River, crisscrossing the raging torrent four times over rapids, waterfalls and pools before reaching **Šum Waterfall**.

From there a trail leads over Hom Hill (834m) east to the ancient pilgrimage **Church of St Catherine**. The trail then leads due south through Zasip and back to Bled. From late June to mid-September an Alpetour bus makes the run from Bled's bus station to Vintgar daily, or take the hourly Krnica bus to Spodnje Gorje which is 1km from the entrance; in summer there are two daily buses from Spodnje Gorje to the gorge entrance.

Places to Stay

Camping At the western end of the lake **Camping Bled** (*☎ 575 20 00; adult/child low season 1250/875 SIT, high season 1840/1290 SIT; open Apr–mid-Oct*) is in a quiet valley about 2.5km from the bus station. The location is good and there's even a beach, tennis courts, a large restaurant and a supermarket, but it fills up very quickly in summer.

Hostels The **Bledec Hostel** (*☎ 574 52 50; Grajska cesta 17; beds low/high season with ISIC/IYHF card €14/15, without card €17/19*) has a total of 55 beds in 13 rooms. Self-service laundry facilities are available for 800 SIT. Breakfast is included.

Private Rooms Finding a private room in Bled is easy. Travel agencies have extensive lists, and there are lots of houses around the lake with '*sobe*' or '*Zimmer frei*' signs indicating rooms to rent. **Kompas** (*☎ 574 15 15; e kompas.bled@siol.net; Ljubljanska cesta 4 singles €14-21, doubles €18-34, 2-person apartments €24-38*) is a good place to start. Rooms or apartments are also available from the tourist office or **Globtour Bled** (*☎ 574 41 86, fax 574 41 85; Ljubljanska cesta 7*) at Krim Hotel. All charge similar prices.

Hotels Most of Bled's hotels are pretty expensive affairs. Among the cheapest is the 212-bed **Hotel Krim** (*☎ 579 70 00, fax 574 37 29; e hotelkrim@hotel-krim.si; Ljubljanska cesta 7; singles/doubles high season €48/68*) in the town centre.

Central **Park Hotel** (*☎ 579 30 00; e info@gp-hoteli-bled.si; Cesta Svobode 15; singles/doubles €91/98 low season, €107/114 high season*) has attractive rooms, some with a wonderful lake view.

Across from the boat rentals and just a little way out of town, is the attractive **Pension Mlino** (*☎ 574 14 04, fax 574 15 06; Cesta Svobode 45; doubles summer 6600 SIT, off season 4400 SIT*).

For a splurge and a little history, check out **Vila Bled** (*☎ 579 15 00; Cesta Svobode 26; e vilabled@robas.si; singles/doubles low season €95/135, high season €115/155*), a grand resort hotel that was once Tito's summer home. It's been a hotel since the 80s, and includes tennis courts, a private boathouse, and Communist-era artwork.

Places to Eat

Bled's best choice for an affordable meal is the homy **Gostilna Pri Planincu** (*Grajska cesta 8; meals from 2000 SIT*), which is just a stone's throw from the bus station. The menu includes some excellent dishes such as mushroom soup and grilled chicken with fries and salad.

Okarina (*☎ 574 14 58; Riklijeva cesta 9*) has top-rate Indian cuisine with an assortment of vegetarian dishes as well as offering its Slovenian specialities.

Patisserie Šmon *(Grajska 3)* offers scrumptious desserts and coffee.

There's a **supermarket** in the Triglav shopping centre.

A few miles out of town in Radovljica is **Gostilna Lečtar** *(☎ 537 48 00; Linhartov trg 2; closed Tuesday)*. This traditional restaurant is one of the most famous in Slovenia, and Radovljica is a charming small town with frescoed buildings. Take the main highway towards Ljubljana and you'll see signs for Radovljica.

Getting There & Around

If you're coming from Ljubljana, take the bus not the train. The train from Ljubljana will leave you at the Lesce-Bled station, 4km southeast of Bled while the bus takes you to the town centre. There are buses to Ljubljana (hourly), Bohinj (hourly starting at 7.20am), Radovljica (every 30 minutes) and Kranjska Gora via Lesce (eight daily). One bus a day from July to mid-September goes to Bovec via Kranjska Gora and the heart-stopping Vršič Pass.

Lesce-Bled train station handles up to 20 trains a day from Ljubljana (55 minutes). About eight cross the Austrian border, continuing on to Germany. There are six trains daily to Jesenice, six to Nova Gorica, 10 to Bohinj, and one a day at 6.14am during the summer to Skofja Loca.

Kompas *(☎ 574 15 15; Ljubljanska cesta)* rents out bicycles and mountain bikes for 4700/1500/2200 SIT per hour/half-day/day.

BOHINJ
☎ 04

Bohinj is a larger and much less developed glacial lake, 26km southwest of Bled. It is exceedingly beautiful, with high mountains that rise directly from the basin-shaped valley. There are secluded beaches for swimming just off the trail along the northern shore and there are many hiking possibilities, including an ascent of Mt Triglav.

Orientation

There is no town called Bohinj; the name actually refers to the entire valley, its settlements and the lake. The largest town in the Bohinj area is Bohinjska Bistrica (population 3080), 6km east of the lake. The main settlement on the lake is Ribčev Laz at the southeastern corner. All in a row just up from the bus stop, are the post office, tourist office, a supermarket, a pizzeria and the Alpinum travel agency.

About 1km north across the Sava Bohinjka River and at the mouth of the Mostnica Canyon sits the town of Stara Fužina. The Zlatorog Hotel is situated at Ukanc at the western end of the lake near the camping ground and the cable car, which takes visitors up Mt Vogel and to the ski lifts (1922m).

Information

There's a helpful and very efficient **tourist office** *(☎ 572 33 70, fax 572 33 30; w www .bohinj.si; Ribčev Laz 48; open 7.30am-8pm daily July–mid-Sept, 8am-6pm Mon-Sat, 9am-3pm Sun mid-Sept–Jun)*. Its website contains much useful information.

The tourist office can change money but there's a 3% commission. There's an ATM at the post office next door. There are braches of **Gorenjska Banka** at Trg Svobode 2b and in Bohinjska Bistrica.

The **post office** *(Ribčev Laz 47; open 8am-6pm Mon-Fri, 8am-noon Sat)* is open during the listed hours but with a couple of half-hour breaks during the day.

Alpinum travel agency *(☎ 572 34 41; Ribčev Laz 50)* organises sporting activities in Bohinj and rents rooms.

Things to See & Do

The **Church of St John the Baptist**, on the northern side of the Sava Bohinjka across the stone bridge from Ribčev Laz, has exquisite 15th-century frescoes and can lay claim to being the most beautiful and evocative church in Slovenia. The **Alpine Dairy Museum** *(adult/child 400/300 SIT)*, at house No 181 in Stara Fužina about 1.5km north of Ribčev Laz, has a small but interesting collection related to Alpine dairy farming in the Bohinj Valley, once the most important such centre in Slovenia. If you have time, take a walk over to **Studor**, a village a couple of kilometres to the east renowned for its *kozolci* and *toplarji*, single and double hayracks that are unique to Slovenia.

Sporting equipment is available to rent from **Alpinsport kiosk** *(☎ 572 34 86; Ribčev Laz 53)*, just before the stone bridge to the church. Canoes & kayaks cost from 800/3100 SIT per hour/day. It also organises **guided mountain tours** (4600 SIT) and **canoe trips** (3600 SIT) on the Sava, as well as 'canyoning' through the rapids of the Mostnica Gorge stuffed into a neoprene suit, life jacket and helmet starting at 7900 SIT.

The **Vogel cable car** *(adult/child return 1000/700 SIT)*, above the camping ground at the western end of Lake Bohinj about 5km from Ribčev Laz, will whisk you 1000m up into the mountains. It runs every half-hour year round except in November, from 8am to 6pm (till 8pm in July and August). From the upper station (1540m) you can scale **Mt Vogel** in a couple of hours for a sweeping view of the surrounding region.

Savica Waterfall

An hour's hike west of the Zlatorog Hotel at Ukanc is the **Savica Waterfall** *(adult/child 300/150 SIT)*, the source of the Sava River, which gushes from a limestone cave and falls 60m into a narrow gorge. It costs 500 SIT for the car park, but the receipt can be redeemed for a drink at the restaurant.

Places to Stay

Autocamp Zlatorog *(☎ 572 34 82, fax 572 34 83; camp sites per person 1100-2100 SIT; open year-round)* caters mostly to camper vans, but its location on the lake near the Zlatorog Hotel can't be beaten.

The tourist office can arrange **private rooms** *(singles/doubles with shower low season 1920/3200 SIT, July & August to 2400/4000 SIT)* in neighbouring villages. There is usually a 30% surcharge for if you are staying fewer than three days.

Places to Eat

Pizza Center *(Ribčev Laz 50)*, next to the Alpinum travel agency, is very popular year-round.

For a truly different lunch, try **Planšar** *(Stara Fužina 179)* opposite the Alpine Dairy Museum. It specialises in home-made dairy products, and you can taste a number of local specialities for about 700 SIT.

There's a **Mercator supermarket** *(Ribčev Laz 49; open 7am-7pm Mon-Fri, 7am-5pm Sat)* for self-caterers.

Getting There & Around

There are hourly buses between Ribčev Laz and Ljubljana via Bled, Radovljica, Kranj and Bohinjska Bistrica. There are also about six local buses a day to Bohinjska Bistrica. All of these buses stop near the post office on Triglavska cesta in Bohinjska Bistrica and in Ribčev Laz (500m from the TIC towards Pension Kristal) before carrying on to Zlatorog Hotel in Ukanc. The closest train station is at Bohinjska Bistrica, which is on the Jesenice to Nova Gorica line.

Mountain bikes and helmets can be rented from **Alpinsport kiosk** *(☎ 572 34 86; Ribčev Laz 53)* for 800/3100 SIT per hour/day.

KRANJSKA GORA

☎ 04 • pop 1530

Known primarily for the best skiing in Slovenia, Kranjska Gora is also a worthy summer and off-season sporting ground. Climbing, fishing, ice-skating, hiking, bicycling – it's all here.

The Kranjska Gora **tourist office** *(☎ 588 17 68; e turisticno.drustvo.kg@siol.net; Tičarjeva 2; open 8am-8pm Mon-Sat, 9am-6pm Sun; off-season to 3pm Mon-Fri, to 6pm Sat & 1pm Sun)* has useful handouts and sells maps and guides to surrounding areas.

A good ski school and rental place is **Bernik** *(☎ 588 14 70; e sport@s5.net; Borovška cesta 88a)*.

Places to Stay & Eat

For **private rooms**, you can contact the tourist office. A decent, well-priced hotel that's in the centre of town is the **Hotel Prisank** *(☎ 588 41 70; e info@htp-gorenjka.si; Borovška 93; depending on season singles 5100-9400 SIT, doubles 7200-13,500 SIT)*.

Pizzeria Pino *(☎ 588 15 64; Borovška 75)* sells good meat and vegetarian pizzas for 700 to 1200 SIT.

There is also the **Mercator supermarket** *(Borovška 92)* in the same street.

HIKING MT TRIGLAV

The Julian Alps are among the finest hiking areas in Central and Eastern Europe. None of the 150 mountain huts *(planinska koča or planinski dom)* is more than five hours' walk from the next. The huts in the higher regions are open from July to September, and in the lower regions from June to October. You'll never be turned away if the weather looks bad, but some huts on Triglav get very crowded at weekends, especially in August and September. A bed for the night should cost about 2500 SIT per person. Meals are also available, so you don't need to carry a lot of gear. Leave most of your things below, but warm clothes, sturdy boots and good physical condition are indispensable.

The best months for hiking are August to October, though above 1500m you can encounter winter conditions at any time. Keep to the trails that are well marked with a red circle and a white centre, rest frequently and never *ever* try to trek alone.

For good information about the mountain huts and detailed maps, contact the **Alpine Association of Slovenia** (see the Information section under Ljubljana) or the TICs in Bled, Bohinj, Kranjska Gora (all excellent places to start a mountain-hut hike) or Ljubljana. You will also be able to pick up a copy of the 1:20,000 *Triglav* map or the 1:50,000-scale *Julijske Alpe – Vzhodni Del (Julian Alps – Eastern Part)*, which is published by the Alpine Association and available at bookshops and tourist offices.

The *Dnevnik S Slovenske Planinske Poti*, a mountain hut 'passport', is a booklet published by the Alpine Association and available at any Triglav area tourist office. Hikers can bring this booklet with them to any of the 150 huts and try to collect as many stamps as possible.

Soča Valley

BOVEC & KOBARID
☎ 05 • pop 1775 & 1460

The Soča Valley, defined by the bluer-than-blue Soča, stretches from the Triglav National Park to Nova Gorica and is one of the most beautiful and peaceful spots in Slovenia. Of course it wasn't always that way. During much of WWI, this was the site of the infamous Soča (or Isonzo) Front, which claimed the lives of an estimated one million people and was immortalised by the American writer Ernest Hemingway in his novel *A Farewell to Arms*. Today visitors flock to the town of Kobarid to relive these events at the award-winning **Kobarid Museum** (☎ 389 00 00; *Gregorčičeva ul 10; adult/student & child 700/500 SIT*) or, more commonly, head for Bovec, 21km to the north, to take part in some of the best whitewater rafting in Europe. The season lasts from April to October.

In Bovec, the people to see for any sort of water sports are **Soča Rafting** (☎ 389 62 00; **e** *soca.rafting@arctur.si*), 100m from the Alp Hotel (across from the post office) or **Bovec**

Rafting Team (☎ 388 61 28; *Trg Golobarskih Žrtev*) in the small kiosk opposite the Martinov Hram restaurant. Rafting trips on the Soča lasting about 1½ hours start at 7000 SIT (students receive a discount). The cost of the trip includes all necessary safety equipment and gear. A kayak costs from 4500 SIT for four hours including equipment; a two-person canoe is 5500 SIT per person. There are kayaking lessons in summer (eg, a two-day intensive course for beginners costs 24,000 SIT without equipment).

In Kobarid, the **tourist office** in the Kobarid Museum and, in Bovec, the **Avrigo Tours agency** (☎ 388 60 22; *Trg Golobarskih Žrtev 47*), next to the Alp hotel, can organise **private double rooms** from 2500 SIT per person.

There are four camping grounds in Bovec – the closest is **Polovnik** (☎ 388 60 69) – and there is one in Kobarid – **Koren** (☎ 388 53 12).

Getting There & Away
There are up to six buses between Kobarid and Bovec and to Tolmin daily. Other destinations include Ljubljana (two to five buses daily), Nova Gorica (four to six) and Cerkno (up to five). In July and August there's a daily bus to Ljubljana via the Vršič Pass and Kranjska Gora. From Bled there are three trains every day to Most na Soči (55 minutes) from where you can catch regular buses to Kobarid and Bovec (45 minutes).

Karst Region

POSTOJNA
☎ 05 • pop 8200

Vying with Bled as the top tourist spot in Slovenia, **Postojna Cave** (*adult/student & child 2400/1200 SIT*) continues to attract the hordes. The electric train ride into the cave (to breeze through the less attractive parts) makes a visit seem a bit like Disneyland. Visitors get to see about 5.7km of the cave's over 20km on a 1½-hour tour in Slovenian, English, German or Italian. About 4km are covered by an electric train that will shuttle you through colourfully lit karst formations along the so-called Old Passage; the remaining 1700m is on foot. The tour ends with a viewing of a tank full of *Proteus anguinus*, the 'human fish' inhabiting Slovenia's karst caves. Dress warmly as the cave is a constant 9.5°C (with 95% humidity) all year.

From May to September, tours leave on the hour between 9am and 6pm daily. In March, April and October there are tours at 10am, noon, 2pm and 4pm with an extra daily one at 5pm in April and additional tours on the weekend in October at 11am. 1pm, 3pm and 5pm. Between November and February, tours leave at 10am and 2pm on weekdays, with extra ones added at noon and 4pm on the weekend and public holidays.

If you have the chance, visit the **Predjama Castle**, an awesome 16th-century fortress perched in the gaping mouth of a hill-top cavern 9km northwest of Postojna. As close as you'll get from Postojna by local bus (and during the school year only), though, is Bukovje, a village about 2km north of Predjama. Visiting the castles and the moderately impressive caves costs 1300/650 SIT for adults/students and children. A taxi from Postojna plus an hour's wait at the castle costs 12,000 SIT.

Orientation & Information

Postojna Cave is about 2km northwest of the town's bus station while the train station is 1km southeast of the centre. The caves are well signposted from the town centre and taxis are available from the bus and train stations.

The **tourist office** (☎ 726 51 83; Jamska cesta 9; e td.tic.postojna@siol.net; open 8am-6pm Mon-Fri, to 7pm in summer, 8am-noon Sat year-round) is in the shopping centre beneath the Hotel Jama.

Kompas (☎ 726 42 81; e info@kompas -postojna.si; Titov trg 2a) can arrange **private rooms** from 2800 SIT per person.

Getting There & Away

Postojna is a day trip from Ljubljana or a stopover on the way to/from the coast or Croatian Istria; almost all buses between the capital and the coast stop here. There are direct trains to Postojna from Ljubljana (one hour, 67km, 21per day) and Koper (1½ hours, 86km, 13 per day) but the bus station is closer to the caves.

ŠKOCJAN CAVES
☎ 05

Škocjan Caves (adult/student/child 1700/ 1000/800 SIT), which some travellers consider a highlight of their visit, are close to the village of Matavun, 4km southeast of Divača (between Postojna and Koper). They have been heavily promoted since 1986 when they were first entered on Unesco's World Heritage List. There are seven two-hour tours a day at 10am, and 11.30am and on the hour from 1pm to 5pm from June to September. Tours leave at 10am, 1pm and 3.30pm in April, May and October. There's a daily tour at 10am and an extra one at 3pm on Sunday and holidays from November to March.

These caves are in located in more natural surroundings than the Postojna Cave but are tough to reach without your own transport. From the train station at Divača (there are up to a dozen trains daily to/from Ljubljana), you can follow a path leading southeast through the village of Dolnje Ležeče to Matavun. The driver of any bus heading along the highway to or from the coast will let you off at the access road (there are huge signs announcing the caves) if you ask in advance. From where the bus drops you, walk the remaining 1.5km to the caves' entrance.

LIPICA
☎ 05 • pop 130

The famous Lipizzaner horses of the imperial Spanish Riding School in Vienna have been bred here since the 18th century and now perform at numerous equestrian events around the world. You can tour the 311-hectare **Lipica Stud Farm** (☎ 739 15 80, fax 734 63 70; e lipica@siol.net; adult/student & child €6/2; open year-round); there are between four and nine tours a day, depending on the season. A tour combined with an exhibition (€12/4), in which the snow-white creatures go through their paces is available at 3pm Tuesday, Friday and Sunday from May to October but Friday and Sunday only in April. If you've made prior arrangement, you can ride the horses all year or take a riding lesson (€17 to €60, depending on the season and length).

There are several expensive hotels available on the premises, or try the **Pension Risnik** (☎ 763 00 08; Kraška cesta 24; accommodation per person 2200 SIT) in nearby Divača.

For dinner, try the excellent Italian cuisine at **Gostilna Malovec** (☎ 763 12 25; Kraška cesta 30a).

Lipica is 10km southwest of Divača and 10km south of Sežana, which are both on the main train line from Trieste to Ljubljana. From Monday to Friday there are five buses a day from Sežana to Lipica.

SLOVENIA

The Coast

KOPER
☎ 05 • pop 24,000

Koper, only 21km south of Trieste, is an industrial port town with a quaint city centre. The town's Italian name, Capodistria, recalls its former status as capital of Istria under the Venetian Republic in the 15th and 16th centuries. After WWII, the port was developed to provide Slovenia with an alternative to Italian Trieste and Croatian Rijeka. Once an island but now firmly connected to the mainland by a causeway, the Old Town's medieval flavour lingers despite the industry, container ports, high-rise buildings and motorways beyond its 'walls'. This administrative centre is the largest town on the Slovene coast and makes a good base for exploring the region.

Orientation

The bus and train stations are combined in a modern structure about a kilometre southeast of the Old Town at the end of Kolodvorska cesta. There's a left luggage facility open 5.30am to 10pm that costs 400 SIT.

Information

Tourist Offices You will find the **tourist office** (☎/fax 627 37 91; Ukmarjev trg 7; open 9am-9pm Mon-Sat, 9am-1pm Sun June-Sept; 9am-2pm & 5pm-7pm Mon-Fri, 9am-1pm Sat Oct-May) opposite the marina.

Money The fairly central **Nova Ljubljanska Banka** (Pristaniška ul 45; open 8.30am-noon, 3.30pm-6pm Mon-Fri) has an ATM. There are also a couple of private exchange offices on Pristaniška ul, including **Maki** (open 8am-7pm Mon-Fri, to 1pm Sat). The ATM on the southeastern corner of Titov trg takes Visa, MasterCard, Maestro and Cirrus. The ATM at the post office accepts MasterCard and Cirrus.

Post & Communications The **post office** (Muzejski trg 3; open 8am-7pm Mon-Fri, 8am-noon Sat) is near the regional museum.

Email & Internet Access Travellers can use the five computers at **PINA** (Gregorčičeva ul 6, 3rd floor), a cultural and educational centre, for free. The computers are available on weekdays 10am to 2pm and 6pm to 10pm, and 6pm to 10 pm on Saturday.

Things to See

From the stations you enter Prešernov trg through the **Muda Gate** (1516). Walk past the bridge-shaped **Da Ponte Fountain** (1666), into Župančičeva ul and then right onto Čevljanka ul. This leads to Titov trg, the medieval central square. Most of the things to see in Koper are clustered here.

The 36m-high **City Tower** (1480), which you can climb daily in summer, stands beside the **Cathedral of St Nazarius**, dating mostly from the 18th-century. The lower portion of the cathedral's facade is Gothic, and the upper part is Renaissance. North is the sublime **Loggia** (1463), now a café and gallery, and to the south is the 1452 **Praetorian Palace** (free guided visits 10.15am and 5pm), both good examples of Venetian Gothic style. On the narrow lane behind the cathedral is a 12th-century Romanesque baptistry called the **Carmine Rotunda**. Trg Brolo to the east of the cathedral contains several more old Venetian buildings, including **Brutti Palace**, now a library, at No 1 and the **Fontico**, a 14th-century granary, at No 4.

The **Koper Regional Museum** (Kidričeva ul 19; adult/student & child 350/250 SIT; open 8am-3pm Mon-Fri, 8am-1pm Sat year-round, 6pm-8pm Mon-Fri in summer) is in the Belgramoni-Tacco Palace. It contains old maps and photos of the port and coast, an Italianate sculpture garden and paintings from the 16th to 18th centuries, and copies of medieval frescoes.

Places to Stay

The closest camping grounds are **Adria** (☎ 652 83 23), at Ankaran about 10km to the north by road, and **Jadranka** (☎ 640 23 00) at Izola 8km to the west.

Both the tourist office and **Kompas** (☎ 627 15 81; Pristaniška ul) opposite the vegetable market have private rooms for about 2700 to 3100 SIT per person, depending on the category and season. Apartments for three/four people start at 10,000/16,000 SIT. Most of the rooms are in the new town beyond the train station.

In July and August the **Dijaški Dom Koper** (☎ 627 32 52; Cankarjeva ul 5; beds per person 3500 SIT), an official hostel in the Old Town east of Trg Brolo, rents out 380 beds in triple rooms. The rest of the year only three beds are available. An HI card will get you a 10% discount.

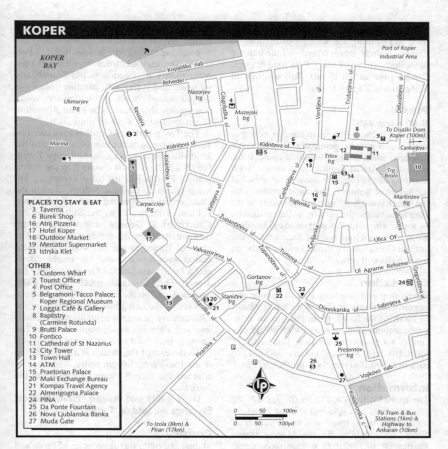

KOPER

PLACES TO STAY & EAT
3 Taverna
6 Burek Shop
16 Atrij Pizzeria
17 Hotel Koper
18 Outdoor Market
19 Mercator Supermarket
23 Istrska Klet

OTHER
1 Customs Wharf
2 Tourist Office
4 Post Office
5 Belgramoni-Tacco Palace;
  Koper Regional Museum
7 Loggia Café & Gallery
8 Baptistry
  (Carmine Rotunda)
9 Brutti Palace
10 Fontico
11 Cathedral of St Nazarius
12 City Tower
13 Town Hall
14 ATM
15 Praetorian Palace
20 Maki Exchange Bureau
21 Kompas Travel Agency
22 Almerigogna Palace
24 PINA
25 Da Ponte Fountain
26 Nova Ljublanska Banka
27 Muda Gate

The only hotel in the Old Town is the renovated **Hotel Koper** (☎ 610 05 00, fax 610 05 94; e koper@terme-catez.si; Pristaniška ul 3; singles/doubles off season 10,700/17,200 SIT, July & Aug 13,000/20,800 SIT), with its business-like facilities.

Places to Eat

For fried dough on the go, head for the **burek shop** (Kidričeva ul 8). **Pizzeria Atrij** (Triglavska ul 2; open to 10pm daily) has a courtyard out the back.

One of the most colourful places for a meal in Koper is **Istrska Klet** (Župančičeva ul 39; mains around 1200 SIT), in an old palace. This is a good place to try Teran, the hearty red (almost purple) wine from the Karst and coastal wine-growing areas.

Taverna (Pristaniška ul 1; lunch 850/1000 SIT), in a 15th-century salt warehouse opposite the marina, has some decent fish dishes and lunch menus.

The large shopping centre and outdoor **market** (Pristaniška ul; open 7am-2pm) is open most days and contains a **Mercator supermarket** and various **food shops**.

Getting There & Away

There are buses almost every 20 minutes on weekdays to Piran (17km) and Portorož via Izola, and every 40 minutes on weekends. Buses also leave every hour or 90 minutes for Ljubljana (2400 SIT, 2¼ hours) via Divača and Postojna. You can also take the train to Ljubljana (1700 SIT, 2¼ hours), which is much more comfortable.

SLOVENIA

Up to 17 buses a day depart for Trieste (600 SIT) during the week. Destinations in Croatia include Buzet (three or four buses a day), Poreč (three or four), Pula (one or two); Rijeka (one at 10.10am), Rovinj (one at 3.55pm) and Zagreb (two).

PIRAN
☎ 05 • pop 4400

Picturesque Piran (Pirano in Italian), sitting at the tip of a narrow peninsula, is everyone's favourite town on the Slovenian coast. It's a gem of Venetian Gothic architecture with narrow little streets, but it can be mobbed at the height of summer. The name derives from the Greek word for 'fire', *pyr*, referring to the ones lit at Punta, the very tip of the peninsula, to guide ships to the port at Aegida (now Koper). Piran's long history dates back to the ancient Greeks, and remnants of the medieval town walls still protect it to the east.

Orientation

Buses stop just south of Piran Harbour and next to the library on Tartinijev trg, the heart of Piran's Old Town. Piran charges an exorbitant amount of money to park inside the city centre, so go to the car park just south of town. It's 1600 SIT for 24 hours (3400 SIT to park in town), and there's a shuttle into Piran.

Information

The **tourist office** (☎ *673 25 07, fax 673 25 09; Stjenkova ul*) opposite the Piran Hotel essentially rents out rooms and keeps very brief hours. Instead head for the **Maona travel agency** (☎ *673 12 91;* e *maona@siol.net; Cankarjevo nab 7; open Apr-Oct*), where the helpful and knowledgable staff can organise accommodation, an endless string of activities and boat cruises. During the months when the office is closed, ask at the agency in nearby Portorož (see that section later in the chapter).

Banka Koper (*Tartinijev trg 12; open 8.30am-noon & 3pm-5pm Mon-Fri, to noon Sat*) changes cash and has an ATM.

There's a **post office** (*Cankarjevo nab 5; open 8am-7pm Mon-Fri, 8am-noon Sat*) on the harbourfront.

Things to See & Do

The exhibits of Piran's **Maritime Museum** (*Cankarjevo nab 3; adult/student 500/400 SIT; open 9am-noon & 3pm-6pm Tues-Sun*), in a 17th-century harbourside palace, focus on the three 'Ss' that have shaped Piran's development over the centuries: the sea, sailing and salt-making (at Sečovlje just southeast of Portorož). The antique model ships are first-rate; other rooms are filled with old figureheads, weapons and votive folk paintings placed in the pilgrimage church at Strunjan for protection against shipwreck. The **Piran Aquarium** (*Tomšičeva ul 4*) is closed until 2004.

The **Town Hall** and **Court House** stand on Tartinijev trg, which contains a statue of the local violinist and composer Giuseppe Tartini (1692–1770). A short distance to the northwest is Prvomajski trg (also known as Trg Maja 1) and its baroque **cistern**, used in the 18th century to store the town's fresh water.

Piran is dominated by the tall tower of the **Church of St George**, a Renaissance and baroque structure on a ridge above the sea north of Tartinijev trg. It's wonderfully decorated with frescoes and has marble altars and a large statue of the George slaying the dragon. The free-standing **bell tower** (1609) was modelled on the campanile of San Marco in Venice; the octagonal **Baptistry** from the 17th century next to it contains altars, paintings and a Roman sarcophagus from the 2nd century, later used as a baptismal font.

To the east of the church is a 200m stretch of the 15th-century **town walls**, which can be climbed for superb views of Piran and the Adriatic.

During July and August, **Piran Musical Evenings** are held on Tartini trg.

Cruises

Maona and other travel agencies in Piran and Portorož can book you on any number of cruises – from a loop that takes in the towns along the coast to day-long excursions to Venice, Trieste, Rovinj or Brioni National Park in Croatia.

From late-May to October, the large catamaran *Marconi* sails down the Istrian Coast in Croatia as far as the Brioni Islands and the national park there. All-day excursions cost €54/29 return for adults/children aged four to 12; lunch is extra. To Rovinj the cost is €27/18. The boat leaves at 10am and returns at about 6.45pm except in September when it departs and returns 20 minutes earlier. At 8.35pm (6.50pm in September) on the same days, the *Marconi* heads for Trieste (35 minutes, one way €16/12 for adults/children) and returns the following morning at 9am.

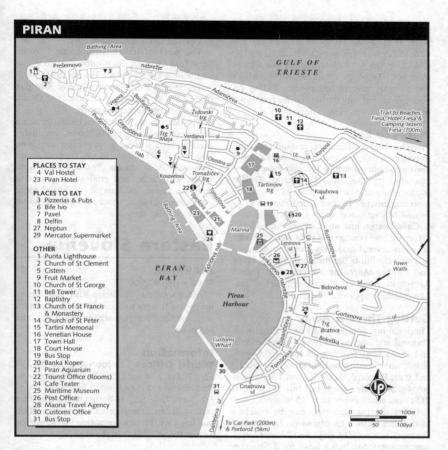

PIRAN

GULF OF TRIESTE

PIRAN BAY

Piran Harbour

Town Walls

PLACES TO STAY
4 Val Hostel
23 Piran Hotel

PLACES TO EAT
3 Pizzerias & Pubs
6 Bife Ivo
7 Pavel
8 Delfin
27 Neptun
29 Mercator Supermarket

OTHER
1 Punta Lighthouse
2 Church of St Clement
5 Cistern
9 Fruit Market
10 Church of St George
11 Bell Tower
12 Baptistry
13 Church of St Francis & Monastery
14 Church of St Peter
15 Tartini Memorial
16 Venetian House
17 Town Hall
18 Court House
19 Bus Stop
20 Banka Koper
21 Piran Aquarium
22 Tourist Office (Rooms)
24 Cafe Teater
25 Maritime Museum
26 Post Office
28 Maona Travel Agency
30 Customs Office
31 Bus Stop

To Car Park (200m) & Portorož (5km)

To Beaches, Fiesa, Hotel Fiesa & Camping Jezero Fiesa (700m)

Places to Stay

Camping The closest camping ground is **Camping Jezero Fiesa** (☎ 674 62 30, fax 674 64 26; *open June-Sept*) at Fiesa, 4km by road from Piran (but less than a 1km walk on the coastal trail east of the Church of St George). It's in a quiet valley by two small ponds, and close to the beach, but can be crowded.

Private Rooms & Hostels The tourist offices (☎ 674 70 15; **w** *www.portoroz.si*) in Piran and Portorož as well as the **Maona travel agency** (☎ 674 64 23; **e** *maona@ siol.net*) can arrange private rooms and apartments throughout the year. Single rooms cost 3100 to 3800 SIT, depending on the category and the season, while doubles are 4600 to 6600 SIT and triples 5800 SIT to 7700 SIT.

Apartments for two are 6200 SIT to 7700 SIT. They usually levy a 50% surcharge for rooms if you stay fewer than three nights.

A very central, relatively cheap place is the **Val Hostel** (☎ 673 25 55, fax 673 25 56; **e** *yhostel.val@siol.net; Gregorčičeva ul 38a; beds off-season per person €16, summer & holidays €18; open year-round*) at Vegova ul. It has 56 beds with shared shower; breakfast is included in the rates.

Hotels Not in Piran itself, but definitely one of the nicest places to stay on the coast is **Fiesa** (☎ 671 22 00, fax 671 22 23; **e** *hotel.fiesa@ amis.net; singles/doubles €35/52, July & Aug €50/89*). The hotel is a pleasant, four-storey, 22-room place overlooking the sea near the Jezero Fiesa camping ground.

SLOVENIA

With a position right at the edge of the water is the **Piran Hotel** (☎ *676 21 00, fax 676 25 22;* e *recepcija.piran@hoteli-piran.si; Kidričeva nab 4; singles/doubles low season from €41/66, high season €58/98*), which has recently refurbished rooms. Sitting on your private balcony during sunrise makes the higher-priced, sea-view rooms worth it.

Places to Eat

Piran has plenty of seafood restaurants along Prešernovo nab, but you do pay for location. Two good ones are **Bife Ivo** and **Pavel**. You can also try the local favourites: **Delfin** (*Kosovelova ul 4*) near Prvomajski trg or the more expensive **Neptun** (*Župančičeva ul 7*) behind Maona travel agency.

Cafe Teater, just south of the Piran Hotel, offers six beers on tap and light snacks. There are also several pizzerias along Prešernovo nab near the Punta lighthouse including **Flora** and **Punta**. **Mercator supermarket** (*open 7am-8pm Mon-Fri, 7am-1pm Sat, 7am-11am Sun*) is opposite Trg Bratsva 8.

Getting There & Away

The local bus company I&I links Piran with Portorož and Lucija (bus No 1); with Portorož and Fiesa (bus No 2; mid-June to August only); with Strunjan and Portorož (bus No 3); and with Portorož, Sečovlje and Padna (bus No 4). Schedules vary, but bus No 1 (210 SIT) runs about every 10 to 15 minutes.

Other destinations that can be reached from Piran include Ljubljana via Divača and Postojna (six to 10 a day) and Nova Gorica (one or two). Six buses head for Trieste on weekdays, and there are two daily departures for Zagreb. One bus daily heads south for Croatian Istria at 4.25pm, stopping at the coastal towns of Umag, Poreč and Rovinj.

PORTOROŽ
☎ 05 • pop 2950

The 'Port of Roses' is essentially a solid strip of high-rise hotels, restaurants, bars, travel agencies, shops, discos, beaches with turnstiles, parked cars and tourists. It's not to everyone's taste, but it does have the best beaches in Slovenia and tons of places to stay and eat. The **tourist office** (☎ *674 02 31, fax 674 82 61;* w *www.portoroz.si; Obala 16; open 9am-9pm high season*) is also the TIC for Piran. It has information on the Primorska Summer Festival, a celebration of music and dance that takes place in Portorož, Piran, Koper and Izola throughout July.

The **post office** (*K Stari cesta 1; open 8am-7pm Mon-Fri, 8am-noon Sat*) is opposite the now empty Palace Hotel (1891).

Try at either the tourist office or **Kompas** (☎ *617 80 00;* e *portoroz@kompas.si; Obala 41*) for private accommodation.

The beaches at Portorož, including the main one accommodating 6000 bodies, are 'managed' so you'll have to pay anywhere from 300 to 800 SIT to use them. They are open 9am to dusk in season. You can rent cabin space, umbrellas and chaise lounges, and there's a variety of activities to spend more money on, including water skiing, paragliding and water bike rentals.

Eastern Slovenia

MARIBOR
☎ 02 • pop 96,900

Maribor straddles the Drava River, but everything you'll want to access is on the northern side, between the train station and 'Lent,' the old town.

Information

Tourist Offices The **tourist office** (☎ *234 66 11, fax 234 66 13;* e *matic@maribor.si; Partinzanska cesta 47; open 9am-6pm Mon-Fri, 9am-1pm Sat*) is across from the train station. It can arrange private accommodation and has a wealth of information on the *vinska cestas* (wine routes) in the area.

Money There's an ATM in the train station. **Nova KBM Banka** has an ATM opposite Maribor Castle on Slovenska ul. **Ljubljanska Banka** (*Ventrinjska 2; open 9am-1pm & 3pm-5pm Mon-Fri*) exchanges cash with no commission.

Post & Communications The main **post office** (*Partinzanska cesta 54*) is next to the train station. The exchange desk is open 7am to 7pm Monday to Saturday and 9am to 1pm Sunday for cash transactions only.

Email & Internet Access If you don't mind the smoke, **Kibla multimedijski center** offers free Internet access. Enter the Narodni Dom building at Kneza Koljca ul 9 and go through the first door on the left.

Things to See and Do

Maribor is the second largest city in Slovenia, industrial but with a charming pedestrian city centre, largely free of tourists. Although not readily available outside the country, some connoisseurs say Slovenian wines equal French or Italian. The 2,400-year-old viticulture tradition in this region is most evident in the hills around Maribor. The city is also the starting point for winery tours of the surrounding area. There's no public transport in these areas, so you'll need a rental car (see the Getting There & Around section later).

The oldest living grapevine, **Stara Trta** (*Vojašniška 8*), has been continuously producing wine for over 400 years. Across from the castle in Trg Svobode is the **Vinag** wine cellar, a 20,000-sq-metre cellar that can store seven million litres of wine.

Enjoy the 'green treasure' Pohorje area on a day trip using local bus No 6, which departs from the train station. The bus drops you at the Pohorje cable car, which will take you to areas for hiking and skiing.

The **Lent Festival** takes over Maribor for two weeks in the end of June and start of July.

Places to Stay

HI hostel **Dijaski Dom 26 Junij** (*☎ 480 17 10; Zeleznikova ul 12; bus No 3; accommodation per person 2700 SIT*) is only open July and August.

A fairly central and inexpensive hotel is **Club VIP** (*☎ 229 62 00, fax 229 62 10; Tomšičeva 10; singles/doubles €36/55*). To take advantage of the free entry into the Fontana spa, try the pleasant, central **Orel Hotel** (*☎ 250 67 00, fax 251 84 97; e orel@ termemb.si; Grajski trg 3a; singles/doubles 12,000/19,000 SIT*).

Places to Eat

Bolarič deli (*Juličeva ul 3; light meals 450-900 SIT open 7am-7pm Mon-Fri, to 1pm Sat*) is the cheapest place around. Decent pizza can be found at **Verdi** (*Dravska ul*), next to the river. Around the corner is **Grill Ranca** (*Vojašniška ul 4*), serving Balkan favourites.

The **Mercator supermarket** (*open 7am-8pm Mon-Fri, 7am-6pm Sat, 8am-11am Sun*) is a few steps away from the bus station.

Getting There & Away

Ten buses a day go to Ljubljana, starting at 5am and ending at 5.50pm. This is the best

jump-off point for Rogaška Slatina (three daily) or Ptuj (20 daily). Take local bus No 6 to get to the Pohorje cable car.

Trains link Maribo to many cities in neighbouring countries: Vienna (7489 SIT, four hours, two a day); Graz (2358 SIT, one hour, two a day); and Zagreb (3100 SIT, three hours, two a day at 12.10pm and 7.55pm); Budapest (7000 SIT, seven hours, two daily at 9.10am and 3.20pm; change at Pragersko). Trains also go to Ljubljana (2½ hours, eight daily).

Getting Around

To follow the *vinska cesta*, try **Avis** (*☎ 228 79 10; Partizanska cesta 24; open 8am-4pm Mon-Fri, to noon Sat*).

If you want to get around the area without a car, you can rent bicycles at **Café Promenada** (*☎ 613 13 10; Lackova u 45*).

PTUJ
☎ 02 • pop 19,100

Charming and compact Ptuj is Slovenia's version of an Italian hill town. It's first incarnation was as *Poetovio*, a Roman village. Remnants of its Roman past still dot the town, and there's a hill-top castle with a magnificent museum.

Information

The helpful Ptuj **tourist office** (*☎ 779 60 11; w www.ptuj.si; Slovenski trg 3; open 8am-5pm Mon-Fri, to 1pm Sat*) also opens a branch at No 14 during the summer.

Things to See & Do

The hill-top castle features the **Ptuj Regional Museum** (*adult/child 600/300 SIT; open 9am-5pm winter, to 6pm in summer, to 8pm Sat & Sun July & Aug*), with exhibits on musical instruments, weaponry, the Kurentovanje Festival and Ptuj's history. Call ahead to arrange an English-speaking guide (250 SIT).

About 1.5km from the centre of town is **Terme Ptuj** (*☎ 782 72 11; Pot v Toplice 9; adult/child 1800/1200 SIT*), a giant spa complex with four swimming pools, water slides, massage treatments and eight tennis courts.

The **library** (*Prešernova ul 33-35*) is in the building complex known in the 1700s as the *Small Castle*. You can also check your email for free for up to one hour on the 2nd floor. The ornate **Town Hall** (*Mestni trg 1*) was built in 1907 to resemble the earlier late-Gothic version. The **Town's Tower** (*Slovenski trg*) stands

SLOVENIA

in front of the **Provost's Church**. The tower was mentioned as early as 1376 in city documents, and has been rebuilt many times down through the centuries.

Every February for the 10 days surrounding Mardi Gras, Ptuj hosts the **Kurentovanje Festival**, a district-wide party that attracts visitors from all over the world.

Places to Stay & Eat

The TIC arranges **private accommodation** starting at around 3500 SIT per person.

The **Terme Ptuj camping ground** (☎ 782 72 11; *adult/child €8.60/6.10*) offers free access to the spa complex. It also has **apartments** *(singles/doubles/rooms for up to 6 people €40/65/82)*.

The central **Garni Hotel Mitra** (☎/fax 774 21 01; *e fredi@zerak.com; Prešernova ul 6; singles/doubles/triples 7700/11,000/13,500 SIT*) offers pleasant rooms.

A great place to try Slovenian seafood dishes is **Ribič** (☎ 771 46 71; *Dravska ul 9*). It serves fresh fish for 4000 SIT per kilo and a host of Slovene specialities.

There's an **open-air market** *(Novi trg; open 7am to 3pm daily)* for self-caterers.

Getting There & Away

Ptuj is on the line to many European destinations. There are trains to Munich (10 hours, two per day), Venice (eight hours, one daily), Zagreb (three hours, five a day) and Ljubljana

(2½ hours, 11 a day). By bus, you can get to Maribor (680 SIT, 40 minutes, at least hourly), Rogaška Slatina (3.10pm daily) and Ljubljana (2½ hours, 11 daily).

THERMAL SPAS

Slovenia was once a Roman protectorate, and this is evident in Slovenian devotion to spa culture. Nearly every town in this chapter boasts a spa, and there are a multitude of spas off the beaten track as well. The famous healing properties of the region's thermal waters have brought visitors to Slovenia for centuries. For information about spas in Slovenia, contact the **Slovenian Spas Community** (☎ 03-544 21 11; **w** *www.terme-giz.si*).

Rogaška Slatina

The most famous and oldest spa town in Slovenia, Rogaška Slatina is past its heyday as the premier spot to 'take the waters', but it's in beautiful surroundings and has several good spas.

In the middle of the town there's a **tourist office** (☎ 03-811 50 13; *e tic.rogaska@siol .net; Zdraviliški trg 1*) near several hotels and spas. A good bet for a bed is the **Zdraviliški Dom** (☎ 03-811 20 00; *doubles from €35*).

To get to Rogaška Slatina, take either the bus or train to Celje and transfer. The bus drops you off next to the town centre, which is pedestrian-only, and the train stops about 200m away.

Switzerland

Chocolate, cheese and clocks; strait-laced bankers and big business – the cliches paint only a limited picture of Switzerland. Broader brushstrokes might add elegant cities buzzing with nightlife, a taste for eclectic culture, and some of the most exquisite natural beauty on the continent. The poet and novelist Goethe's description of the country as a combination of 'the colossal and the well-ordered' still fits, typified by awe-inspiring Alps set against tidy, efficient, watch-precise towns and cities.

Switzerland has one of the highest standards of living in the world, so even generous budgets will take a beating here, but the payoff is a super-slick infrastructure giving quick and easy access to everything the country has to offer. Switzerland blends the flavours of Germany, France and Italy to create a three-cultures-in-one experience.

Its distinct regional personalities are all the while united by a sophisticated sensibility and financial savvy.

Add an unassailable independent streak born of an obsession with getting along with the neighbours and it's plain why Switzerland remains an oasis of stability hardly touched by the political storms around it. The cynics who say that Switzerland is wasted on the Swiss are just jealous.

At a Glance

- **Neuchâtel** – cross-country skiing and horse riding in the Jura Mountains
- **Geneva** – cosmopolitan ambience and thriving arts scene
- **Zermatt** – skiing, mountaineering and hiking mecca with stupendous views of the Matterhorn
- **Zürich** – museums, art galleries and elegant shops
- **Lucerne** – historic covered bridges, cruise on Lake Lucerne

Capital	Bern
Population	7.28 million
Official Language	French, German & Italian
Currency	1 Swiss franc (Sfr) = 100centimes
Time	GMT/UTC+0100
Country Phone Code	☎ 41

Facts about Switzerland

HISTORY

The first inhabitants of the region were a Celtic tribe, the Helvetii. The Romans arrived in 107 BC via the Great St Bernard Pass, but were gradually driven back by the Germanic Alemanni tribe, which settled in the region in the 5th century. Burgundians and Franks also came to the area, and Christianity was gradually introduced.

The territory was united under the Holy Roman Empire in 1032, but central control was never tight, and neighbouring nobles fought each other for local influence. The Germanic Habsburg expansion was spearheaded by Rudolph I, who gradually brought the squabbling nobles to heel.

The Swiss Confederation

Upon Rudolph's death in 1291, local leaders saw a chance to gain independence. The forest communities of Uri, Schwyz and Nidwalden formed an alliance on 1 August 1291, which is seen as the origin of the Swiss Confederation (their struggles against the Habsburgs are idealised in the legend of William Tell). This union's success prompted

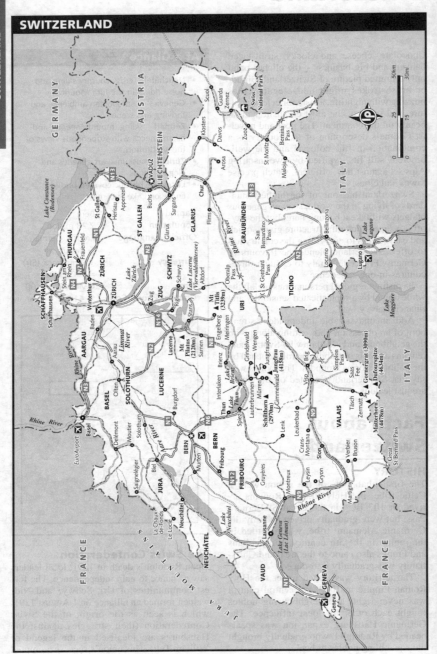

SWITZERLAND

GERMANY

AUSTRIA

LIECHTENSTEIN

★ VADUZ

N13

Schaffhausen

Stein am Rhein

SCHAFFHAUSEN

St Gallen

Appenzell

Henisau

THURGAU

Frauenfeld

ST GALLEN

Buchs

Sargans

Chur

GLARUS

Glarus

Films

GRAUBÜNDEN

Scuol

Guarda

Zernez

Swiss National Park

Klosters

Davos

Zuoz

Arosa

St Moritz

Bernina Pass

Maloja

Lake Constance (Bodensee)

Baden

ZÜRICH

Winterthur

ZÜRICH

Lake Zürich

Zug

ZUG

Rigi

SCHWYZ

Schwyz

Lake Lucerne (Vierwaldstättersee)

Altdorf

URI

Oberalp Pass

St Gotthard Pass

San Bernardino Pass

Bellinzona

Locarno

Lugano

TICINO

Lake Lugano

Lake Maggiore

ITALY

AARGAU

Aarau

Limmat River

Olten

Lucerne

Stans

Mt Pilatus (2120m)

Sarnen

Mt Titlis (3239m)

Engelberg

Meiringen

Brienz

Lake Brienz

Grindelwald

Wengen

Jungfraujoch

Jungfrau (4158m)

Brig

Visp

Simplon Pass

Saas Fee

Täsch

Zermatt

Gornergrat (3090m)

Dufourspitze (4634m)

Matterhorn (4477m)

VALAIS

BASEL

Basel

EuroAirport

Delémont

Moutier

Solothurn

SOLOTHURN

Burgdorf

LUCERNE

Thun

Lake Thun

Spiez

Interlaken

Lauterbrunnen

Mürren

Schilthorn (2970m)

Grimmelwald

Lenk

Leukerbad

Crans-Montana

Sion

Verbier

Bruson

Martigny

Great St Bernard Pass

Rhône River

Rhine River

Aare River

Saignelégier

Biel

JURA

Delémont

Neuchâtel

La Chaux-de-Fonds

Le Locle

NEUCHÂTEL

Lake Neuchâtel

Murten

FRIBOURG

Fribourg

Gruyères

Montreux

Leysin

Gryon

BERN

BERN

Lausanne

Lake Geneva (Lac Léman)

VAUD

GENEVA

Geneva

FRANCE

JURA MOUNTAINS

N1 N2 N3 N4 N5 N6 N9 N11 N12 N13

0 25 50km
0 15 30mi

other communities to join: Lucerne (1332) was followed by Zürich (1351), Glarus and Zug (1352), and Bern (1353).

Encouraged by successes against the Habsburgs, the Swiss acquired a taste for territorial expansion. More land was seized. Fribourg, Solothurn, Basel, Schaffhausen and Appenzell joined the confederation, and the Swiss gained independence from the Holy Roman Emperor Maximilian I after their victory at Dornach in 1499.

Finally the Swiss over-reached themselves. They took on a superior force of French and Venetians at Marignano in 1515 and lost. Realising they could no longer compete against larger powers with better equipment, they declared their neutrality. Even so, Swiss mercenaries continued to serve in other armies for centuries, and earned an unrivalled reputation for skill and courage.

The Reformation during the 16th century caused upheaval throughout Europe. The Protestant teachings of Luther, Zwingli and Calvin spread quickly, although the inaugural cantons remained Catholic. This caused internal unrest that dragged on for centuries.

The French Republic invaded Switzerland in 1798 and established the Helvetic Republic. The Swiss vehemently resisted such centralised control, causing Napoleon to restore the former confederation of cantons in 1803. Yet France still retained overall jurisdiction. Following Napoleon's defeat by the British and Prussians at Waterloo, Switzerland finally gained independence.

The Modern State

Throughout the gradual move towards one nation, each canton remained fiercely independent, to the extent of controlling coinage and postal services. The cantons lost these powers in 1848, when a new federal constitution was agreed upon, with Bern as the capital. The Federal Assembly was set up to take care of national issues, but the cantons retained legislative (Grand Council) and executive (States Council) powers to deal with local matters.

Having achieved political stability, Switzerland could concentrate on economic and social matters. Poor in mineral resources, it developed industries dependent on highly skilled labour. A network of railways and roads was built, opening up previously inaccessible regions of the Alps and helping the development of tourism.

The Swiss carefully guarded their neutrality in the 20th century. Their only involvement in WWI was organising units of the Red Cross (founded in Geneva in 1863 by Henri Dunant). Switzerland joined the League of Nations after peace was won, however, only if its involvement was financial and economic rather than military. Apart from some accidental bombing, WWII left Switzerland largely unscathed.

While the rest of Europe underwent the painful process of rebuilding from the ravages of war, Switzerland expanded its already powerful commercial, financial and industrial base. Zürich developed as an international banking and insurance centre. Many international bodies, such as the World Health Organisation, based their headquarters in Geneva. Workers and employers struck agreements under which industrial weapons such as strikes and lockouts were renounced. Social reforms, such as old-age pensions (1948), were also introduced.

Afraid that its neutrality would be compromised, Switzerland managed to avoid joining the United Nations (UN) for over 50 years, restricting itself to observer status. However, in a March 2002 referendum, after much lobbying by government, economists and the media, the Swiss people finally voted in favour of membership. The government proudly announced that Switzerland's days of sitting on the sidelines were over.

The Swiss aren't quite as keen on joining the EU, however. Switzerland's 1992 application remains frozen, after voters twice failed to endorse the federal government's strategy. Nevertheless, the 1999 bilateral agreements promised market access, and free movement of people and transport between Switzerland and the EU.

In the 1990s the country's WWII record came under critical scrutiny. Swiss banks were accused of holding huge sums deposited by Jews who later became victims of the Holocaust. In 1998, facing a class action lawsuit in the US by Holocaust survivors, the banks agreed to pay US$1.25 billion to settle all outstanding claims. In 2002 an independent commission of historians set up by the Swiss government confirmed that tens of thousands of Jewish refugees were turned back from Switzerland's border, and left to face their fate in Nazi Germany. Swiss banks were also accused of banking Nazi plunder during WWII. A sum of at least US$400 million (US$3.8 billion today) was deposited.

Despite its long-standing military neutrality, Switzerland maintains a 400,000-strong civilian army. Every able-bodied male undergoes national service at 20 and stays in the reserves for 22 years, all the while keeping his rifle and full kit at home. Some complain of the high cost of keeping the civilian army going, and a 2001 referendum was held to decide whether the army should be scrapped. However, the people gave the army a reprieve...for now.

GEOGRAPHY
Mountains make up 70% of Switzerland's 41,290 sq km. Not a square inch of land is wasted in this compact country, with 30% meadow and pasture, 32% forest, 10% arable and 28% put to other use. Farming of cultivated land is intensive and cows graze on the upper slopes in summer as soon as the retreating snow line permits.

The Alps occupy the central and the southern regions of the country. The Dufourspitze (4634m), a peak on the Monte Rosa massif, is the highest point, although the Matterhorn (4478m) is more famous.

Glaciers account for an area of 2000 sq km, most notably the Aletsch Glacier, which at 169 sq km is the largest valley glacier in Europe.

The St Gotthard Massif, in the centre of Switzerland, is the source of many lakes and rivers, such as the Rhine and the Rhône. The Jura Mountains straddle the border with France, and peak at around 1700m. Between the two mountain systems is the Mittelland, also known as the Swiss Plateau, a region of hills crisscrossed by rivers, ravines and winding valleys.

CLIMATE
Ticino in the south has a hot, Mediterranean climate, and Valais in the southwest is noted for being dry.

Elsewhere the temperature is typically from 20° to 25°C in summer and 2° to 6°C in winter, with spring and autumn temperatures hovering around the 7° to 14°C mark. Summer tends to bring a lot of sunshine, however, it also brings the most rain. You will need to be prepared for a range of temperatures depending on your altitude.

Look out for the *Föhn*, a hot, dry wind that sweeps into the valleys, can be oppressively uncomfortable and can strike at any time of year.

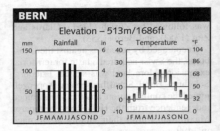

ECOLOGY & ENVIRONMENT
Switzerland has long been an environmentally aware nation. Its citizens diligently recycle household waste and cities encourage the use of public transport. The policy in the mountains is to contain rather than expand existing resorts.

GOVERNMENT & POLITICS
The modern Swiss Confederation is made up of 23 cantons; three are subdivided, bringing the total to 26. Each has its own constitution and legislative body for dealing with local issues.

National legislative power is in the hands of the Federal Assembly, which has two chambers. The lower chamber, the National Council, has 200 members elected by proportional representation. The upper chamber, the States Council, has 46 members, two per full canton. The Federal Assembly elects seven members to form the Federal Council, which holds executive power. All elections are for a four-year term except the posts of president and vice-president of the confederation, which are rotated annually. The vice-president always succeeds the president.

Under the 1874 constitution, Swiss citizens enjoy direct democracy: 50,000 signatories are needed to force a full referendum on proposed laws, and 100,000 to initiate legislation. Citizens regularly vote in referendums on national, local and communal issues. Yet surprisingly, women only won the right to vote in federal elections in 1971. It was 1991 before women gained a cantonal vote in Appenzell, the last remaining canton that still conducts votes by a show of hands in an Landsgemeinde (open-air parliament).

ECONOMY
Though poor in natural resources, Switzerland has a strong and stable market economy thanks to international trade and banking.

High prices in Switzerland are matched by high wages, and a good proportion of the wealth generated is channelled back into the community via social-welfare programmes. The Swiss generally enjoy moderate tax rates, low inflation (0.6% in 2002) and negligible unemployment rates (2.2% in 2002).

Due to the absence of other raw materials, hydroelectric power is the main source of energy. Chemicals, machine tools, and watches and clocks are the most important exports, and Swiss banks are a magnet for foreign funds attracted to political and monetary stability. Tourism is the country's third-biggest industry and an excellent infrastructure makes life easy for visitors. Swiss breakthroughs in science and industry include vitamins, DDT, gas turbines and milk chocolate.

POPULATION & PEOPLE

With a population of 7.28 million, Switzerland averages 174 people per square kilometre. Alpine districts are sparsely populated, while the Mittelland is very densely settled, especially around the shores of the larger lakes. Zürich is the largest city (339,300) followed by Geneva (176,000), Basel (163,800) and Bern (122,000). Most of the people are of Germanic origin, as reflected in the breakdown of the four national languages (see Language later in this section). Around 20% of the people living in the country are residents but not Swiss citizens; the foreign influx started after WWII, particularly from southern Europe.

ARTS

Switzerland does not have a very strong tradition in the arts, though there are several noteworthy exceptions. Paul Klee (1879–1940), the best-known native painter, created bold, hardlined abstract works. The writings of philosopher Jean-Jacques Rousseau (1712–78) in Geneva played an important part in the development of democracy. Critically acclaimed postwar dramatists and novelists, Max Frisch (1911–91) and Friedrich Dürrenmatt (1921–90), entertained readers with their dark tragicomedies, satire and morality plays. On the musical front, Arthur Honegger (1892–1955) is Switzerland's most recognised composer. The tranquillity of the mountains and lakes also seduced many foreign writers and artists (such as Voltaire, Byron and Shelley), who made their homes in Switzerland.

Gothic and Renaissance architecture are prevalent in urban areas, especially Bern. Rural Swiss houses vary according to region, but are generally characterised by ridged roofs with wide, overhanging eaves, and balconies and verandas enlivened by colourful floral displays, especially geraniums.

SOCIETY & CONDUCT

The Swiss are polite, law-abiding people who usually see no good reason to break the rules. You'll see few local litterbugs or jaywalkers here. Living quietly with your neighbours is a national obsession, with strict rules about noise levels (no baths or flushing toilets after 10pm – tourist accommodation excepted). Lunch is another designated quiet time, when many businesses shut up shop, and most workers and schoolchildren head home to eat with the family.

Good manners infuse the national psyche, and politeness is the cornerstone of all social intercourse. Always shake hands when being introduced to a Swiss, and kiss on both cheeks to greet and farewell friends. Don't forget to greet shopkeepers when entering shops. Remember to say *Grüezi* (hello) before launching into your question or request.

When drinking with Swiss, always wait until everyone has their drink and toast each of your companions, looking them in the eye and clinking glasses. Drinking before the toast is unforgivable, and will lead to seven years of bad sex...or so the superstition goes. Don't say you weren't warned.

Switzerland is a dog-friendly country, and some travellers may be surprised to find them everywhere – on trains, in restaurants and cafés, even hanging out with their owners in late-night bars. For a nation of such fit and active people, the Swiss are no more enlightened than the rest of Europe when it comes to smoking. A pungent blue haze hovers in most bars, restaurants and cafés.

In a few mountain regions such as Valais, people still wear traditional rural costumes, but dressing up is usually reserved for festivals. Yodelling, playing the alp horn and Swiss wrestling are also part of the Alpine tradition.

RELIGION

Protestantism and Roman Catholicism are equally widespread, though their concentration varies between cantons. Strong Protestant areas are Bern, Vaud and Zürich, whereas

Valais, Ticino and Uri are mostly Catholic. Most Swiss make a financial contribution by way of a *Kirchensteuer* (church tax), a percentage of their income tax that the government distributes to the churches through state subsidies.

LANGUAGE

Located in the corner of Europe where Germany, France and Italy meet, Switzerland is a linguistic melting pot with three official federal languages: German (spoken by 64% of the population), French (19%) and Italian (8%). A fourth language, Rhaeto-Romanic, or Romansch, is spoken by less than 1% of the population, mainly in the canton of Graubünden. Derived from Latin, it's a linguistic relic that has survived in the isolation of mountain valleys. Romansch was recognised as a national language by referendum in 1938 and given federal protection in 1996.

Though German-speaking Swiss have no trouble with standard High German, they use *Schwyzertütsch* (Swiss German) in most non-official situations. Swiss German covers a wide variety of melodic dialects that differs markedly from High German. Visitors will probably note the frequent use of the suffix *-li* to indicate the diminutive, or as a term of endearment.

English-speakers will have few problems being understood in the German-speaking parts. However, it is simple courtesy to greet people with the Swiss-German *Grüezi* and to inquire *Sprechen Sie Englisch?* (Do you speak English?) before launching into English.

In French Switzerland you shouldn't have too many problems either, though the locals' grasp of English probably will not be as good as the German-speakers'. Italian Switzerland is where you will have the greatest difficulty.

Most locals speak some French and/or German in addition to Italian. English has a lower priority, but you'll still find that the majority of hotels and restaurants have at least one English-speaking staff member.

See the Language chapter at the back of the book for German, French and Italian pronunciation guidelines and useful words and phrases.

Facts for the Visitor

HIGHLIGHTS

For mountain vistas you'll never forget the Jungfrau region, with the Schilthorn (2970m) and its neighbour, the Jungfrau (4158m). Challenging hikes and dazzling views can be enjoyed from the peaks overlooking Lake Lucerne and at Zermatt, in the shadow of the Matterhorn. Catch a lake steamer to Château de Chillon, on Lake Geneva, justifiably the most famous castle in Switzerland. For buzzing nightlife and medieval town centres creaking with history, head to Bern and Zürich. Culture buffs will find plenty of interest in Basel and Geneva, with many fine museums and galleries. But whatever you do, wherever you go, remember to stop and taste the chocolate!

SUGGESTED ITINERARIES

Depending on the length of your stay, you might want to see and do the following:

Two days
Visit Interlaken and the Jungfrau, with an excursion to the mountains.

One week
Spend two days in the Jungfrau, two days in Lucerne taking a lake steamer and going on mountain hikes, and a few days on Lake Geneva, visiting Château de Chillon.

Two weeks
As above, but spend longer in the mountains, and visit Bern, Basel and Zürich.

One month
As above, but make time for Geneva, Zermatt and the Matterhorn, and the Italian towns in Ticino.

Two months
As above, but take your time. Include visits to Neuchâtel and the Jura Mountains, St Moritz and Graubünden, and the northeast towns of Schaffhausen, Appenzell and St Gallen.

LANGUAGE AREAS

Romansch
German
French
Italian

Basel   Zürich

Bern   Lucerne
Lausanne   Chur
St Moritz
Geneva   Bellinzona

PLANNING
When to Go

Visit Switzerland from December to April for winter sports, and May to October for general sightseeing and hiking. Alpine resorts all but close down in late April, May and November.

Maps

Michelin covers the whole country with four maps. The *Landeskarte der Schweiz* (Topographical Survey of Switzerland) series is larger in scale and especially useful for hiking. Kümmerly + Frey maps are also good for hikers. All these maps are sold throughout Switzerland. Swiss banks, especially the UBS branches, are a good source of free maps.

What to Bring

Take a sturdy pair of boots if you intend to walk in the mountains, and warm clothing for those cold nights at high altitude. Hostel membership is invaluable and it's cheaper to join before you get to Switzerland.

TOURIST OFFICES
Local Tourist Offices

Verkehrsbüro or *Tourismus* (tourist offices) are extremely helpful. They have reams of literature to give out, including maps (nearly always free), and staff invariably speak English. Offices can be found everywhere tourists are likely to go and will often book hotel rooms and organise excursions. If you are staying in resorts, ask the local tourist office whether there's a Visitor's Card, which is excellent for discounts.

Switzerland Tourism also sells the **Swiss Museum Passport** (w *www.museums.ch; adult/student Sfr30/25*), which will save big bucks if you plan to visit more than a handful of museums.

Tourist Offices Abroad

Switzerland Tourism has a free-phone number for **Europe** (☎ *00800 100 200 30*) and the **USA/Canada** (☎ *011800 100 200 30*). Offices can be found in:

UK (☎ 020-7734 1921, fax 7437 4577; e info .uk@switzerland.com) 10th Floor, Swiss Centre, 10 Wardour St, London W1D 6QF
USA (☎ 1-877-794-8037; e info.usa@switzer landtourism.ch) 608 Fifth Ave, New York, NY 10020

Canadian queries are now handled through the US office.

VISAS & DOCUMENTS

Visas are not required for passport holders of the UK, USA, Canada, Australia, New Zealand or South Africa. A maximum three-month stay applies although passports are rarely stamped.

EMBASSIES & CONSULATES
Swiss Embassies & Consulates

Swiss embassies can be found in:

Australia (☎ 02-6273 3977, fax 6273 3428; e vertretung@can.rep.admin.ch) 7 Melbourne Ave, Forrest, Canberra, ACT 2603
Canada (☎ 613-235 1837, fax 563 1394; e vertretung@ott.rep.admin.ch) 5 Marlborough Ave, Ottawa, Ontario K1N 8E6
New Zealand (☎ 04-472 1593, fax 499 6302; e vertretung@wel.rep.admin.ch) 22 Panama St, Wellington
UK (☎ 020-7616 6000, fax 7724 7001; e swiss embassy@lon.rep.admin.ch) 16-18 Montague Place, London W1H 2BQ
USA (☎ 202-745 7900, fax 387 2564; e vertretung@was.rep.admin.ch) 2900 Cathedral Ave NW, Washington, DC 20008-3499

Embassies & Consulates in Switzerland

All embassies are in Bern (the Bern tourist office lists them in the free *Bern Aktuell*). They include:

Canada (☎ 031 357 32 00) Kirchenfeldstrasse 88
France (☎ 031 359 21 11) Schosshaldenstrasse 46
Germany (☎ 031 359 41 11) Willadingweg 83
Ireland (☎ 031 352 14 42) Kirchenfeldstrasse 68
Italy (☎ 031 350 07 77) Elfenstrasse 14
UK (☎ 031 359 77 00) Thunstrasse 50
USA (☎ 031 357 70 11) Jubiläumsstrasse 93

Foreign consulates include:

Australia (☎ 022 799 91 00) Chemin des Fins 2, Geneva
Canada (☎ 022 919 92 00) Ave de l'Ariana 5, Geneva
France (☎ 022 319 00 00) Rue Imbert Galloix 11, Geneva
Germany (☎ 022 730 11 11) Chemin du Petit-Saconnex 28C, Geneva
New Zealand (☎ 022 734 95 30) Chemin du Petit-Saconnex 28A, Geneva
UK (☎ 022 918 24 00) Rue de Vermont 37-39, Geneva
USA (☎ 022 840 51 60) Rue Versonnex 7, Geneva; (☎ 01 422 25 66) Dufourstrasse 101, Zürich

CUSTOMS

Visitors from Europe may import 200 cigarettes, 50 cigars or 250g of pipe tobacco (twice as much for visitors from non-European countries). The allowance for alcoholic beverages is the same for everyone: 1L of alcohol above 15% and 2L below 15%. Tobacco and alcohol may only be brought in by people aged 17 or older.

MONEY
Currency

Swiss francs (Sfr, written CHF locally) are divided into 100 centimes (called *rappen* in German-speaking Switzerland). There are notes for 10, 20, 50, 100, 500 and 1000 francs, and coins for five, 10, 20 and 50 centimes, and one, two and five francs.

All major travellers cheques and credit cards are accepted. Virtually all train stations have money-exchange facilities open daily. Commission is not usually charged for changing cash or cheques but it's gradually creeping in. Shop around for the best exchange rates. Hotels usually have the worst rates.

Having money sent to Switzerland should be straightforward. No charge is made at Swiss American Express (AmEx) offices for receiving Moneygram transfers. Likewise for money sent to Western Union offices, of which there are many, particularly at larger train stations. Automatic teller machines (ATMs), known as Bancomats in banks and Postomats in post offices, are everywhere, and many give credit-card advances.

There are no restrictions on the amount of currency that can be brought in or taken out of Switzerland.

Exchange Rates

country	unit		Swiss franc
Australia	A$1	=	Sfr0.89
Canada	C$1	=	Sfr1.03
euro zone	€1	=	Sfr1.47
Japan	¥100	=	Sfr1.26
New Zealand	NZ$1	=	Sfr0.75
UK	UK£1	=	Sfr2.29
USA	US$1	=	Sfr1.57

Costs

Affluent Switzerland has one of the highest standards of living in Europe, and prices are inevitably high. Some travellers can scrimp by on about Sfr60 a day after buying a rail pass. This is survival level – camping or hostelling, self-catering when possible and allowing nothing for nonessentials. If you want to stay in pensions, see some sights and have a beer, count on spending twice as much. Minimum prices per person are around Sfr25/50 in a hostel/hotel and Sfr10/15 for lunch/dinner (excluding drinks).

Tipping & Bargaining

Tipping is not strictly necessary as hotels, restaurants and bars are required by law to include a 15% service charge on bills. Nevertheless, locals often 'round up' and a few extra francs for good service is appreciated. Prices are fixed, but travellers have successfully haggled for lower hotel rates in the low season.

Taxes & Refunds

VAT (MWST or TVA) on goods and services is levied at a rate of 7.5% (3.5% for hotel bills). Nonresidents can claim back the tax on purchases over Sfr500 (not hotel/restaurant bills). This can be done by presenting the goods and an export declaration to customs officials at airports and major border crossings when leaving the country. Ask for the documentation when making the purchase.

Switzerland has a motorway tax (see Car & Motorcycle in the Getting There & Away section later in this chapter).

POST & COMMUNICATIONS
Post

Postcards and letters to Europe cost Sfr1.30/1.20 priority/economy; to elsewhere they cost Sfr1.80/1.40. The term poste restante is used nationwide or you could use the German term, *Postlagernde Briefe*. Mail can be sent to any town with a post office and is held for 30 days; show your passport to collect mail. AmEx also holds mail for one month for people who use its cheques or cards.

Post office opening times vary but typically are 7.30am to noon and 2pm to 6.30pm Monday to Friday and until 11am Saturday. The largest post offices offer services outside normal hours (to late evening daily), but some transactions are subject to a Sfr1 to Sfr2 surcharge.

Telephone & Fax

The privatised Swisscom is the main telecommunications provider. The minimum charge in Swisscom payphones is Sfr0.60, though per-minute rates are low. Swisscom charges the same rate for national or local calls. During the day it's Sfr0.08 per minute, and during evenings and weekends it drops to Sfr0.04. Most phone boxes also allow you to send short emails worldwide for Sfr1.50 each.

The country code for Switzerland is ☎ 41. In March 2002 regional codes were incorporated into the subscriber number to create 10-digit numbers (with the exception of Zürich, which has nine-digit numbers). Drop the initial zero on the subscriber number when dialling from overseas.

International call prices have dropped substantially in recent years. A standard-rate call to the USA/Australia/UK costs Sfr0.12/0.25/0.12 per minute. Standard rates apply on weekdays (day or night), and there are reduced rates on weekends and public holidays. Many telephone boxes no longer take coins; the prepaid *taxcard* comes in values of Sfr5, Sfr10 and Sfr20, and is sold in post offices, kiosks and train stations.

Hotels can charge as much as they like for telephone calls, and they usually charge a lot, even for direct-dial calls.

To send a one-page fax at post offices costs Sfr7/8/9 for Switzerland/Europe/elsewhere, plus Sfr1/4/5 for each following page.

Email & Internet Access
Most large towns have an Internet café, and most cities have several. Rates range from reasonable (Sfr8 per hour) to ridiculous (Sfr24 per hour!!). Youth hostel Internet corners are often the best places to do a quick email check. Keep an eye out for cyber happy hours elsewhere.

DIGITAL RESOURCES
Switzerland has a strong presence on the Internet, with most tourist-related businesses having their own website; a good place to start is **Switzerland Tourism** (w *www.myswitzerland.com*), with many useful links. For current news, try the w www.sri.ch website, and for in-depth coverage of major cities, check out w www.swisstownguide.ch.

BOOKS
See Lonely Planet's *Switzerland* and *Walking in Switzerland* guides for more detailed information on Switzerland and its walks. *Living and Working in Switzerland* by David Hampshire is an excellent practical guide. *Why Switzerland?* by Jonathan Steinberg explores

the country's history and culture, and enthusiastically argues that Switzerland is *not* a boring country. Paul Bilton's slim volume *The Xenophobe's Guide to the Swiss* is informative and amusing. *The Swiss, the Gold and the Dead* by Jean Ziegler details shady banking deals during WWII. Fiction about Switzerland is surprisingly scarce, but Anita Brookner won the Booker Prize in 1984 for *Hotel du Lac*, a novel set around Lake Geneva.

English-language books are widely available in Switzerland, though for foreign titles you always pay more than the cover price. Check second-hand bookshops in cities.

NEWSPAPERS & MAGAZINES
Various English-language newspapers and magazines (*The Times, International Herald Tribune, Newsweek, Time*) are widely available and cost around Sfr3 to Sfr6.

RADIO & TV
Swiss Radio International broadcasts in English. Pick it up on 3985kHz, 6165kHz and 9535kHz. The English-language World Radio Geneva is on the FM band at 88.4mHz. Multichannel, multilingual cable TV is widespread; nearly all hotels have it.

TIME
Swiss time is GMT/UTC plus one hour. Daylight savings comes into effect at midnight on the last Saturday in March, when the clocks are moved forward one hour; they go back again on the last Saturday in October.

LAUNDRY
It usually costs about Sfr10 to wash and dry a 5kg load in a coin-operated or service laundrette. Many hostels also have washing machines (around Sfr8).

TOILETS
Public toilets are invariably spick-and-span, with a vast array of whizz-bang, self-cleaning models. Urinals are usually free but there's often a pay slot for cubicles. Note that the McClean chain of toilets in train stations charges as much as Sfr2 for a pee.

WOMEN TRAVELLERS
Women travellers should experience few problems with sexual harassment in Switzerland. However, some Ticino males suffer from machismo leanings, so you may experience

SWITZERLAND

unwanted attention in the form of whistles and catcalls. It's best to ignore the perpetrators.

GAY & LESBIAN TRAVELLERS

Attitudes to homosexuality are reasonably tolerant and the age of consent is 16. Zürich has a lively gay scene and hosts the Christopher Street Day march in late June. It's also home to *Cruiser* magazine (☎ *01 388 41 54;* e *info@cruiser.ch;* w *www.cruiser.ch),* which lists significant gay and lesbian organisations, and has extensive listings of bars and events in Switzerland (Sfr4.50). For more insights into gay life in Switzerland, check out **Pink Cross** (w *www.pinkcross.ch).*

DISABLED TRAVELLERS

Many hotels have disabled access and most train stations have a mobile lift for boarding trains. For useful travel information, you can contact Switzerland Tourism or the **Swiss Invalid Association** (*Schweizerischer Invalidenverband;* ☎ *062 206 88 88, fax 062 206 88 89;* w *www.siv.ch; Froburgstrasse 4, Olten CH-4601).*

DANGERS & ANNOYANCES

Crime rates are low, but that's no reason to forget your street smarts. Remember to be security-conscious and keep your valuables safely tucked away. Take special care in the mountains as **helicopter rescue** (☎ *1414)* is expensive (make sure your travel insurance covers alpine sports).

BUSINESS HOURS

Most shops are open 8am to 6.30pm Monday to Friday, with a 90-minute or two-hour break for lunch at noon. In towns there's often a late shopping day till 9pm, typically on Thursday or Friday. Closing times on Saturday are usually 4pm or 5pm. At some places, such as large train stations, you may find shops are open daily. Banks are open 8.30am to 4.30pm weekdays, with some local variations.

Emergency Services

Emergency telephone numbers are: police ☎ 117, fire brigade ☎ 118, and ambulance (most areas) ☎ 144. The national 24-hour number for roadside assistance in the event of breakdown is ☎ 140.

PUBLIC HOLIDAYS & SPECIAL EVENTS

National holidays are 1 January, Good Friday, Easter Monday, Ascension Day, Whit Monday, 1 August (National Day), and 25 and 26 December. Some cantons observe 2 January, 1 May (Labour Day), Corpus Christi and 1 November (All Saints' Day). Many events take place at a local level throughout the year (check with the local tourist offices). Dates often vary from year to year. This is just a brief selection:

Costumed Sleigh Rides Experience archetypal Swiss kitsch in the Engadine in January.
Fasnacht In February, a lively spring carnival of wild parties and parades is celebrated countrywide, but with particular enthusiasm in Basel and Lucerne.
Combats de Reines From March to October, the lower Valais stages traditional cow fights.
Landsgemeinde On the last Sunday in April, Appenzellers gather in the main square to take part in a unique open-air parliament.
Montreux Jazz Festival Big-name rock/jazz acts hit town in July for this famous festival.
National Day On 1 August, celebrations and fireworks mark the country's National Day.
Street Parade In early August, Zürich lets its hair down with an enormous techno parade with 30 lovemobiles and more than half a million ravers.
Vintage Festivals You can down a couple in wine-growing regions such as Neuchâtel and Lugano in October.
Onion Market In late November, Bern takes on a carnival atmosphere for a unique market day.
Escalade Festival This historical festival held in Geneva celebrates deliverance from would-be conquerors.

ACTIVITIES

There are dozens of ski resorts throughout the Alps, the pre-Alps and the Jura, with some 200 ski schools. Resorts favoured by the package-holiday companies don't necessarily have better skiing facilities, but they do tend to have more off-slope activity when it comes to après-ski. Equipment hire is available at resorts and ski passes allow unlimited use of mountain transport.

There's no better way to enjoy Switzerland's spectacular scenery than to walk through it. There are 50,000km of designated paths, often with a convenient inn or café en route. Yellow signs marking the trail make it difficult to get lost, and each gives an average walking time to the next destination. Slightly more strenuous mountain paths have white-red-white markers. The **Schweizer Alpen-Club** (*SAC;* ☎ *031 370 1818, fax 031 370 18 00;* w *www.sac-cas.ch; Monbijoustrasse 61, Bern*) maintains huts for overnight stays at altitude and can help with extra information. Lonely Planet's *Walking in Switzerland* contains track notes for walking in the Swiss countryside.

You can water-ski, sail and windsurf on most lakes. Courses are usually available, especially in Central Switzerland. There are over 350 lake beaches. Anglers should contact the local tourist office for a fishing permit valid for lakes and rivers. The Rotsee near Lucerne is a favourite place for rowing regattas. Rafting is possible on many Alpine rivers, including the Rhine and the Rhône.

Bungy-jumping, paragliding, canyoning and other high-adrenalin sports are widely available throughout Switzerland, especially in the Interlaken area.

WORK

Switzerland's bilateral agreement with the EU on the free movement of persons has eased regulations for EU citizens. Non-EU citizens officially need special skills to work legally but people still manage to find casual work in ski resorts – anything from snow clearing to washing dishes. Hotel work has the advantage of including meals and accommodation.

In theory, jobs and work permits should be sorted out before arrival, but if you find a job once you're in the country the employer may well have unallocated work permits. The seasonal 'A' permit is valid for up to nine months, and the elusive and much sought-after 'B' permit is renewable and valid for a year. Many resort jobs are advertised in the Swiss weekly newspaper *hotel + tourismus revue*. Casual wages are higher than in most other European countries.

ACCOMMODATION
Camping

There are about 450 camping grounds, classified from one to five stars depending upon amenities and the convenience of location. Nightly charges are around Sfr7 per person plus Sfr5 to Sfr10 for a tent, and around Sfr5 for a car. Many sites offer a slight discount if you have a Camping Carnet (earned by membership of a camping club). Free camping is discouraged and you should be discreet. Contact the **Schweizerischer Camping und**

Caravanning-Verband (*Swiss Camping & Caravanning Federation;* ☎ *041 210 48 22; Habsburgerstrasse 35, Lucerne CH-6004*) for more information.

Hostels

There are 63 official Swiss Youth Hostels (*Jugendherberge, auberge de jeunesse, alloggio per giovani*) that are automatically affiliated to the international network. Nearly all youth hostels include breakfast and sheets in the price. Average high-season prices are Sfr30/50/80 for dorm beds/singles/doubles. Most hostels charge a few francs less during the low season (this chapter quotes high-season prices). Many places have double or family rooms available (with single or bunk beds), and around half of the Swiss hostels have kitchen facilities. Reception desks are often closed during the day, with check-in usually available from mid-late afternoon. It's wise to ring ahead to check on suitable check-in times.

Membership cards must be shown at hostels. Nonmembers pay a Sfr6 'guest fee' to stay in Swiss hostels; six of these add up to a full international membership card. Buying an international membership before you leave home is usually cheaper.

Hostels do get full, so it's wise to book ahead. Bookings can made by phone, email or via the website w www.youthhostel.ch (you'll need a credit card to book online). You can also ask your Swiss hostel to reserve ahead for your next one (Sfr1 plus a Sfr9 refundable deposit). A map, giving full details of all hostels, is available free from hostels and some tourist offices. For more information contact the **Schweizer Jugendherbergen** (*Swiss Youth Hostel Association or SYHA;* ☎ *01 360 14 14;* e *marketing@youthhostel.ch; Schaffhauserstrasse 14, Zürich CH-8042*).

Some of the best budget accommodation you'll find is in independent 'backpacker hostels' – they're listed in *Swiss Backpacker News*, free from hostels and some tourist offices, and on the website w www.backpacker.ch. Prices are similar to SYHA hostels and membership is not required. The independents often have a more laid-back atmosphere and allow you to escape the bane of hostel living – noisy school groups. Many offer double rooms and kitchens and some have their own bars and clubs.

In ski resorts, some hotels have an annexe with a dormitory (*Touristenlager* or *Massenlager* in German, *dortoir* in French).

Schweizer Alpen-Club maintains around 150 dormitory-style mountain huts at higher altitudes.

Hotels

Swiss accommodation is geared towards value for money rather than low costs, so even budget rooms are fairly comfortable (and pricey). The high-season prices quoted in this chapter could be reduced by 10% (towns) to 40% (alpine resorts) during the low season. Hotels are star rated. Prices start at around Sfr50/90 for a basic single/double. Count on at least Sfr10 more for a room with a private shower. Rates generally include breakfast, which tends to be a buffet in mid-range and top-end hotels. Half-board (ie, including dinner) is common in ski resorts. 'Hotel Garni' means a B&B establishment without a restaurant. Note that some train stations have hotel information boards with a free telephone. For more information contact the **Schweizer Hotelier-Verein** (Swiss Hotel Association; ☎ 031 370 41 11; Ⓦ www .swisshotels.ch; Monbijoustrasse 130, Bern CH-3001).

Other Accommodation

Private houses in rural areas sometimes offer inexpensive rooms; look out for signs saying Zimmer frei (rooms vacant). Some farms also take paying guests. Self-catering accommodation is available in holiday chalets, apartments or bungalows. Local tourist offices have lists of everything on offer in the area.

FOOD

Lactose intolerants will struggle in this dairy-obsessed country, where cheese is a way of life. The best-known Swiss dish is fondue, in which melted Emmental and Gruyére are combined with white wine, served in a large pot and eaten with bread cubes. Another popular artery-hardener is Raclette, melted cheese, served with potatoes. Rösti (fried, buttery, shredded potatoes) is German Switzerland's national dish, and is served with everything.

Many dishes are meaty, and veal is highly rated throughout the country; in Zürich it is thinly sliced and served in a cream sauce (Geschnetzeltes Kalbsfleisch). Bündnerfleisch is dried beef, smoked and thinly sliced. Like their northern neighbours, the Swiss also munch on a wide variety of Wurst (sausage).

Vegetarians won't have any trouble in the cities and larger towns, where there are often several dedicated vegetarian restaurants. Most eateries will also offer a small selection of nonmeat options, including large salad plates and the less appealing 'Toast Hawaii'. Soups are popular and are often a meal in themselves.

International fast-food chains proliferate, but better quality budget meals can often be found in markets and street stalls. In German-speaking Switzerland, pretzel shops and bratwurst stands abound, but thanks to an influx of Middle Eastern and North African communities, more exotic fare is easy to come by.

Buffet-style restaurant chains, such as Manora, have a huge selection of freshly cooked food at low prices. Their salad and dessert buffet bars are particularly tempting. Many budget travellers rely on picnic provisions from the supermarkets. Migros and Coop are the main supermarket chains (closed Sunday, except at some train stations). Larger branches have good quality self-service restaurants, which are typically open until around 6.30pm on weekdays and to 4pm or 5pm on Saturday.

Eating out in restaurants can be pricey. Look out for the fixed-menu dish of the day (Tagesteller plat du jour, or piatto del giorno), which often has several courses and is much cheaper than à la carte choices. Main meals are eaten at noon, and restaurants tend to have a closing day, often Monday.

Finally, Switzerland makes some of the most delectable chocolate in the world – don't miss it!

DRINKS

Rivella is a refreshing soft-drink alternative, made from the milk by-product whey (it's much nicer than it sounds). For simpler tastes, mineral water is readily available and tap water is drinkable everywhere.

Buying drinks in restaurants is inevitably expensive. Head to the local supermarkets if you're on a tight budget. Lager comes in 0.5L or 0.3L bottles, or on draught (vom Fass or à la pression) with measures ranging from 0.2L to 0.5L. Cardinal is a popular local brand, though small breweries all over the country serve up their own brews.

Wine is considered an essential accompaniment to lunch and dinner. Local vintages are generally good quality, but you might never have heard of them, as they are rarely exported. The main growing regions are the Italian- and French-speaking areas, particularly in Valais and by lakes Neuchâtel and Geneva. Both red and white wines are produced, and each region has its speciality (eg, Merlot in Ticino). There is also a choice of locally produced fruit brandies, often served with or in coffee.

ENTERTAINMENT
In the cities, nightlife centres on a thriving café culture and an ever-changing wave of hip bars and clubs. Check free newspapers or city listing guides for the latest hotspots. Many places open early for breakfast and stay open all day, transforming from cafés/restaurants into bars/clubs at night. There's a robust alternative scene, with old factories and warehouses being converted into clubs, restaurants, art spaces and live-music venues. Ski resorts have a distinctive atmosphere, with the après-ski scene keeping things buzzing until late. Cinemas usually show films in their original language. Check posters for the upper-case letter: for instance, E/d/f indicates English with both German and French subtitles. In French Switzerland you might see 'VO' instead, which signifies 'original version'.

SPECTATOR SPORTS
Switzerland might not breed bands of obsessive sports fanatics, but football (soccer) still has a strong following, with most towns having their own professional teams. Ice hockey is also popular and tennis has won its fair share of fans, particularly since naturalised Swiss Martina Hingis started hitting winners on the world circuit. Not surprisingly, winter sports are where the Swiss really come into their own, with most ski resorts hosting popular annual events, including long-distance cross-country contests and dramatic downhill races.

SHOPPING
Switzerland is known for producing high-quality luxury items such as watches, jewellery and exquisite chocolates. Swiss army knives are popular, whether it's a simple blade (Sfr10) or a mini-toolbox (Sfr100 or more); the larger youth hostels sell them at below-list price. Textiles and embroidery are best bought in St Gallen or Appenzell, and for woodcarvings head to Brienz. For a country that prides itself on quality and style, a surprising amount of tacky tourist gear fills the souvenir shops. Lovers of kitsch will be in their element, with a vast array of cuckoo clocks and cowbells to choose from.

Getting There & Away
AIR
The busiest international airports are Zürich and Geneva, each with several nonstop flights a day to major transport hubs such as London, Paris and Frankfurt. Budget airline **easyJet** (w www.easyjet.com) offers regular services from London to/from Zürich and Geneva. EuroAirport, near Mulhouse in France, serves Basel, while both Bern and Lugano have small airports.

After a 2001 crisis in the airline industry, Swissair's subsidiary Crossair was rebadged Swiss International Air Lines (known simply as 'Swiss'), becoming the new national airline. Swiss luggage check-in facilities are at major train stations around the country. For reservations throughout Switzerland, call ☎ 0848-85 2000 (local rate).

Airport departure taxes range from Sfr15 for Lugano up to Sfr24.50 for Zürich, and are always included in the ticket price.

LAND
Bus
With such cheap flights available, few people travel to Switzerland by bus these days. The trip from London to Geneva (UK£145 return, three to seven per week) or Zürich (UK£100 return, one to two per week, via Basel) is an exhausting 18- to 20-hour journey. For those with Busabout passes, there are stops in Geneva, Interlaken, Lucerne and Lauterbrunnen. For more information, see the website (w www.busabout.com). Geneva also has bus connections to Barcelona, and Zürich has various services to Eastern Europe. See the Geneva and Zürich entries later in this chapter for details.

Train
Located in the heart of Europe, Switzerland is a hub of train connections to the rest of the continent. Zürich is the busiest international terminus. It has two direct day trains and one night train to Vienna (nine hours). There are several trains daily to both Geneva and Lausanne from Paris (three to four hours by superfast TGV). Travelling from Paris to Bern takes 4½ hours by TGV. Most connections from Germany pass though Zürich or Basel. Nearly all connections from Italy pass through Milan

SWITZERLAND

before branching off to Zürich, Lucerne, Bern or Lausanne. Reservations on international trains are subject to a surcharge of Sfr5 to Sfr30, which depends upon the date and the service.

Car & Motorcycle

Roads into Switzerland are good despite the difficulty of the terrain, but special care is needed to negotiate mountain passes. Some, such as the N5 route from Morez (France) to Geneva, are not recommended if you have not had previous mountain-driving experience. Upon entering Switzerland you will need to decide whether you wish to use the motorways (there is a one-off charge of Sfr40). Arrange to have some Swiss francs ready, as you might not always be able to change money at the border. Better still, pay for the tax in advance from Switzerland Tourism or a motoring organisation. The sticker (called a *vignette*) you receive is valid for a year and must be displayed on the windscreen. A separate fee must be paid for trailers and caravans (motorcyclists must pay too). Some Alpine tunnels incur additional tolls.

BOAT

Switzerland can be reached by lake steamers: from Germany via Lake Constance (Bodensee); from Italy via Lake Maggiore; and from France via Lake Geneva (Lac Léman).

Getting Around

PASSES & DISCOUNTS

Swiss public transport is an efficient, fully integrated and comprehensive system which incorporates trains, buses, boats and funiculars. Convenient discount passes make the system even more appealing.

The Swiss Pass is the best deal for people planning to travel extensively, offering unlimited travel on Swiss Federal Railways, boats, most Alpine postbuses, and trams and buses in 35 towns. Reductions of 25% apply to funiculars and mountain railways. These passes are available for four days (Sfr240), eight days (Sfr340), 15 days (Sfr410), 22 days (Sfr475) and one month (Sfr525); prices are for 2nd-class tickets. The Swiss Flexi Pass allows free, unlimited trips for three to eight days within a month and costs Sfr230 to Sfr420 (2nd class).

With either pass, two people travelling together get 15% off.

The Swiss Card allows a free return journey from your arrival point to any destination in Switzerland, 50% off rail, boat and bus excursions, and reductions on mountain railways. It costs Sfr165 (2nd class) or Sfr240 (1st class) and it is valid for a month. The Half-Fare Card is a similar deal minus the free return trip. It costs Sfr99 for one month.

Except for the Half-Fare Card, these passes are best purchased before arrival in Switzerland from Switzerland Tourism or a travel agent. The Family Card gives free travel for children aged under 16 if they're accompanied by a parent and is available free to pass purchasers.

Regional passes, valid for a specific tourist region, provide free travel on certain days and half-price travel on other days within a seven or 15-day period.

All the larger lakes are serviced by steamers, for which rail passes are usually valid (Eurail is valid; Inter-Rail often gets 50% off).

AIR

Internal flights are not of great interest to most visitors, owing to the short distances and excellent ground transport. **Swiss International Air Lines** (W *www.swiss.com*) is the local carrier, linking major towns and cities several times daily, including Zürich, Geneva, Basel, Bern and Lugano.

BUS

Yellow postbuses are a supplement to the rail network, following postal routes and linking towns to the more inaccessible regions in the mountains. In all, routes cover some 8000km of terrain. Services are regular, and departures tie in with train arrivals. Postbus stations are next to train stations, and offer destination and timetable information.

TRAIN

The Swiss rail network covers 5000km and is a combination of state-run and private lines. Trains are clean, reliable, frequent and as fast as the terrain will allow. Prices are high, though the travel passes mentioned earlier will cut costs. All fares quoted in this chapter are for 2nd class; 1st-class fares are about 65% higher. In general, Eurail passes are not valid for private lines and Inter-Rail pass holders get a 50% discount. All major stations are connected by hourly departures, but services stop from around midnight to 6am.

Train stations offer luggage storage, either at a counter (usually Sfr5 per piece) or in 24-hour lockers (Sfr2 to Sfr7). They also have excellent information counters that give out free timetable booklets and advice on connections. Train schedules are revised yearly, so double-check details before travelling. For train information, consult the excellent website for the **Schweizerische Bundesbahnen** *(SBB,* **w** *www.sbb.ch)* or phone ☎ 0900-300 300 (Sfr1.19 per minute).

CAR & MOTORCYCLE

Be prepared for winding roads, high passes and long tunnels. Normal speed limits are 50km/h in towns, 120km/h on motorways, 100km/h on semi-motorways (designated by roadside rectangular pictograms showing a white car on a green background) and 80km/h on other roads. Don't forget you need a vignette to use motorways and semi-motorways (see the Getting There & Away section earlier in this chapter). Mountain roads are good but stay in low gear whenever possible and remember that ascending traffic has right of way over descending traffic, and postbuses always have right of way. Snow chains are recommended in winter. Use dipped lights in *all* road tunnels. Some minor Alpine passes are closed from November to May – check with tourist offices or motoring organisations such as the **Swiss Touring Club** *(TCS;* ☎ 022-417 2727; **w** *www.tcs.ch).*

Switzerland is tough on drink-driving; if your blood alcohol level is over 0.05% you face a large fine or imprisonment.

Rental

For the best deals, you have to prebook – see the Getting Around chapter. One-way drop-offs are usually free of charge within Switzerland, though collision-damage waiver costs extra. Multinationals provide similar rates – around Sfr100 to Sfr130 for one day's rental (unlimited kilometres and the lowest-category car), with reductions beyond three days. Look out for special weekend deals. Local operators may have lower prices (the local tourist office will have details), though you won't get a 'one-way drop-off' option.

BICYCLE

Despite the hilly countryside, many Swiss choose to get around on two wheels. You can hire bikes from most train stations (adult/child Sfr30/25 per day) and return to any station with a rental office, though this incurs a Sfr6 surcharge. Bikes can be transported on most trains; SBB rentals travel free (maximum five bikes per train). If you have your own wheels you'll need a bike pass (one day Sfr15, with Swiss travel pass Sfr10). Look for the *Cycling in Switzerland* booklet (Sfr37.80) in bookshops, which covers nine routes and 3300km of bike paths. Local tourist offices often have good cycling information. Bern, Basel, Geneva and Zürich offer free bike loans – see the city sections.

HITCHING

Lonely Planet does not recommend hitchhiking. Indigenous Swiss are not very forthcoming with lifts and most hitchers will be picked up by foreigners. Although illegal on motorways, hitching is allowed on other roads. A sign is helpful. Make sure you stand in a place where vehicles can stop. To try to get a ride on a truck, ask around the customs post at border towns.

LOCAL TRANSPORT
City Transport

All local city transport is linked together on the same ticketing system and you need to buy tickets before boarding. One-day passes are usually available and are much better value than paying per trip. There are regular checks for fare dodgers; those caught without a ticket pay an on-the-spot fine of Sfr40 to Sfr60.

Taxis are always metered and tend to wait around train stations, but beware – they are expensive!

Mountain Transport

Vertigo sufferers will be challenged by the five main modes of transport used in steep Alpine regions. A funicular *(Standseilbahn, funiculaire)* is a pair of counterbalancing cars on rails, drawn by cables. A cable car *(Luftseilbahn, téléphérique)* is dramatically suspended from a cable high over a valley. A gondola *(Gondelbahn, télécabine)* is a smaller version of a cable car except that the gondola is hitched onto a continuously running cable as soon as the passengers are inside. A cable chair *(Sesselbahn, télésiège)* is likewise hitched on to a cable but is not enclosed. A ski lift *(Schlepplift, téléski)* is a T-bar hanging from a cable, which the skiers hold on to while their feet slide along the snow (these are gradually being phased out because of safety concerns).

ORGANISED TOURS

Tours are booked through local tourist offices. The country is so compact that excursions to the major national attractions are offered from most towns. A trip up to Jungfraujoch, for example, is available from Zürich, Geneva, Bern, Lucerne and Interlaken.

Bern

pop 122,000

Bern, the nation's capital, is the fourth-largest city and retains a relaxed, small-town charm. Surrounded on three sides by the deep-green Aare River, its medieval old town features 6km of covered arcades and countless historic fountains and monuments. Founded in 1191 by Berchtold V, Bern was named for the unfortunate bear (*Bärn* in local dialect) who was Berchtold's first hunting victim. Today, the bear remains the heraldic mascot of the city.

Orientation

The compact centre of the old town is contained within a sharp U-bend of the Aare River. On the western edge of the old town, the main train station is within easy reach of all the main sights, and offers bike rental and airline check-in.

Information

Tourist Offices Located in the train station, **Bern Tourismus** (☎ 031 328 12 28; e info -res@bernetourism.ch; open 9am-8.30pm daily June-Sept, 9am-6.30pm Mon-Sat & 10am-5pm Sun Oct-May) offers a two-hour city tour by coach (Sfr25; daily April to October, weekly November to March) and an on-foot version (Sfr14; daily June to September) in summer. Its free booklet, *Bern aktuell*, has plenty of useful information, and the online **Bern Youth Guide** (w www.youthguide.ch) has some excellent tips and links. There's another tourist office by the bear pits.

Money The **SBB exchange office** (open 6.30am-9pm daily) is in the lower level of the train station.

Post & Communications The **main post office** (Schanzenstrasse; open 7.30am-6.30pm

Mon-Fri, 8am-noon Sat) has convenient automatic stamp machines if you get there after hours.

ispace (☎ 031 327 76 77; e info@compe rio.ch; Zeughausgasse 14; free/Sfr4/6 for 10/ 30/45min; open 9am-5.30pm Mon-Fri), in the basement of the Medienhaus, is a good place to do a quick email check for free. **Loeb department store** (Spitalgasse 47-51; Sfr5/10 for 30/60min) has an Internet café in the basement. There are two free terminals, but you'll have to wait during busy times.

Bycom Internet Pub (☎ 031 313 81 91; Aarbergergasse 46; Sfr5 per hour; open 6am-11.30pm Mon-Thur & Sun, 6am-3am Fri, 9am-3am Sat) is a two-level lounge bar-cum-Internet café with 50 coin-operated computer terminals, a fully stocked bar and a groovy atmosphere.

Travel Agencies The budget and student travel agency **STA Travel** (☎ 031 302 03; 12 Falkenplatz 9 • 031 312 07 24; Zeughausgasse 18; both open 9.30am-6pm Mon-Fri, 10am-1pm Sat) can help with travel advice.

Bookshops English-language books fill an entire floor at **Stauffacher** (☎ 031 311 24 11; Neuengasse 25). You can also browse the second-hand bookshops of Rathausgasse or Kramgasse.

Medical Services There is a **university hospital** (☎ 031 632 21 11; Freiburgstrasse). For help in locating a doctor or dentist call ☎ 0900 57 67 47.

Things to See & Do

The city map available from the tourist office (Sfr1) sends you on a sightseeing stroll through the old town. The core of the walk is Marktgasse and Kramgasse, with their covered arcades, colourful fountains, and cellars with hidden shops, bars and theatres.

Check out the **ogre fountain** in Kornhausplatz, depicting a giant enjoying a meal of wriggling children.

Dividing Marktgasse and Kramgasse is the **Zytglogge**, a colourful clock tower with revolving figures that herald the chiming hour. People gather a few minutes before the hour on the eastern side to watch them twirl. Nearby is **Einstein House** (☎ 031 312 00 91; Kramgasse 49; adult/student/child Sfr3/2/2; open 10am-5pm Tues-Fri, 10am-4pm Sat

BERN

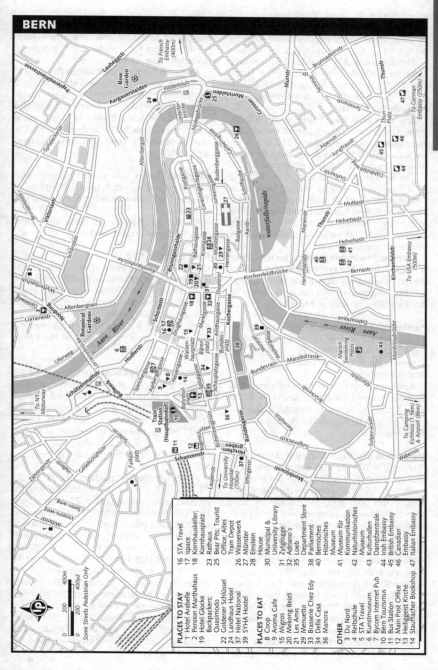

PLACES TO STAY
1   Hotel Arabelle
2   Pension Marthahaus
19 Hotel Glocke
22 Backpackers;
    Quasimodo
24 Goldener Schlüssel
37 Landhaus Hotel
37 Hotel National
39 SYHA Hostel

PLACES TO EAT
8   Coop
9   Aroma Cafe
15 Migros
20 Mekong Beizli
21 Les Amis
29 Menuetto
33 Brasserie Chez Edy
34 Della Casa
36 Manora

OTHER
3   Du Nord
4   Reitschule
5   STA Travel
6   Kunstmuseum
7   Bycom Internet Pub
10 Bern Tourismus
11 Bus Station
12 Main Post Office
13 Heiliggeist Kirche
14 Stauffacher Bookshop

16 STA Travel
17 ispace
18 Kornhauskeller;
    Kornhausplatz
23 Rathaus
25 Bear Pits; Tourist
    Office; Altes
    Tram Depot
26 Wasserwerk
27 Münster
28 Einstein
    House
30 Municipal &
    University Library
31 Zytglogge
32 Adriano's
35 Loeb
    Department Store
38 Parlament
40 Bernisches
    Historisches
    Museum
41 Museum für
    Kommunikation
42 Naturhistorisches
    Museum
43 Kulturhallen
    Dampfzentrale
44 Irish Embassy
45 British Embassy
46 Canadian
    Embassy
47 Italian Embassy

Mar-Oct, 1pm-5pm Tues-Fri, 12pm-4pm Sat Feb & Nov), where the physicist lived when he developed his theory of relativity.

The unmistakably Gothic, 15th-century **Münster** *(cathedral; open 10am-5pm Tues-Sat, 11.30am-5pm Sun)* features imposing, 12m-high, stained-glass windows and an elaborate main portal.

Just across the Aare River are the **Bärengraben** (bear pits). Though bears have been the entertainment at this site since 1857, it's sad to see such majestic beasts doing tricks for treats in such a cramped, concrete environment.

The adjoining **Tourist Centre** *(☎ 031 328 12 12; open 10am-4pm daily Mar-May & Oct, 9am-6pm daily June-Sept, 11am-4pm Fri-Sun Nov-Feb)* has a free multimedia show of the city's history. Up the hill is the **Rose Garden**, with 200 varieties of roses and an excellent view of the city.

Open-air swimming pools, such as those at Marzili, have free entry (open May to September). On steamy days locals walk upriver and fling themselves into the swift current of the Aare, floating back to Marzili.

Parliament The **Bundeshäuser**, home of the Swiss Federal Assembly, is worth a look. There are free tours (six daily) when the parliament is not in session (watch from the public gallery when it is).

Arrive early and reserve a place (don't forget your passport for ID purposes). A multilingual guide takes you through the impressive chambers and highlights the development of the Swiss constitution.

Museums The **Kunstmuseum** *(Museum of Fine Arts; ☎ 031 328 09 44; w www.kunst-museumbern.ch; Hodlerstrasse 8-12; adult/student/child Sfr7/5/free; open 10am-9pm Tues, 10am-5pm Wed-Sun)* holds the Paul Klee collection and an interesting mix of Italian masters, Swiss and modern art.

Many museums are clustered on the southern side of the Kirchenfeldbrücke. **Bernisches Historisches Museum** *(☎ 031 350 77 11; w www.bhm.ch; Helvetiaplatz 5; adult/student Sfr5/3; open 10am-5pm Tues & Thur-Sun, 10am-8pm Wed)* features the original sculptures from the Münster doorway depicting the *Last Judgment* and Niklaus Manuel's macabre *Dance of Death* panels.

The kid-friendly **Naturhistorisches Museum** *(☎ 031 350 71 11; w www.nmbe.ch;*

Bernastrasse 15; adult/student/child Sfr5/3/ free; open 2pm-5pm Mon, 9am-5pm Tues-Fri, 10am-5pm Sat-Sun) has animals depicted in realistic dioramas.

Museum für Kommunikation *(☎ 031 357 55 55; w www.mfk.ch; Helvetiastrasse 16; adult/student/child Sfr6/4/2; open 10am-5pm Tues-Sun)* takes visitors on an interactive journey through the history of communications, including radio, TV and new media. The museum also runs some fascinating temporary exhibitions.

Markets An open-air market groaning with fresh fruit and veg is held at Bärenplatz on Tuesday and Saturday mornings, or daily in summer.

On the last Monday in November, Bern hosts its famous onion market.

Places to Stay
Camping Nestled by the river Aare is **Camping Eichholz** *(☎ 031 961 26 02; Strandweg 49; e camping.eichholz@swissonline.ch; camp site per person/small tent Sfr6.90/5, bungalow rooms 2/3/4 beds Sfr15/17/22; open 20 April-30 Sept)*. It's a half-hour walk from the centre, or the weary can ride tram No 9 from the station to Wabern.

Hostels The **SYHA hostel** *(☎ 031 311 63 16, fax 031 312 52 40; w www.jugibern.ch; Weihergasse 4; dorm beds from Sfr29.80, singles/doubles Sfr42.80/75.60)* is in a quiet riverside spot below Parliament (signposted). Lunch (Sfr12.50) and dinner (Sfr11.50) are available, and there's an Internet surfing happy hour (midnight to 7am) for the bargain-basement Sfr2.50 per hour.

Hotel Glocke Backpackers *(☎ 031 311 37 71, fax 031 311 10 08; e info@chilisback packers.com; Rathausgasse 75; dorm beds Sfr27, singles/doubles Sfr75/110)*, renovated in 2000, has a prized position in the old town, spotless rooms and tiny, sparkling-white hall bathrooms.

Landhaus Hotel *(☎ 031 331 41 66, fax 031 332 69 04; e landhaus@spectraweb.ch; Altenbergstrasse 4; dorm beds Sfr30, doubles without/with bathroom from Sfr110/140)*, near the bear pits, offers modern minimalist rooms and a slick restaurant/bar downstairs (live jazz Thursday evenings). Private room prices include bedding and breakfast, but dorm dwellers pay extra.

Hotels Near the train station there's the **National** (☎ 031 381 19 88, fax 031 381 68 78; e info@nationalbern.ch; Hirschengraben 24; singles/doubles from Sfr60/95, with bathroom from Sfr85/130), a grand, old-world, family-run hotel, kept in the style of 100 years ago.

Pension Marthahaus (☎ 031 332 41 35, fax 031 333 33 86; e info@marthahaus.ch; Wyttenbachstrasse 22a; bus No 20 to Gewerbeschule; singles/doubles/triples Sfr60/95/120, with bathroom Sfr90/120/150), 1km out of town in a quiet residential area, is warm and welcoming, with comfy rooms, Internet access and a share kitchen.

Goldener Schlüssel (☎ 031 311 02 16, fax 031 311 56 88; e info@goldenerschluessel .ch; Rathausgasse 72; singles/doubles Sfr82/115, with bathroom Sfr108/145, half-/full board Sfr24/40), once a horse market, is now faded but functional. Its bustling ground-floor restaurant serves fondue and other favourites.

Hotel Arabelle (☎ 031 301 03 05, fax 031 302 42 62; e info@arabelle.ch; Mittelstrasse 6; bus No 12 to Mittelstrasse; singles/doubles Sfr105/155), near the university, has modern, bright and breezy rooms.

Places to Eat

Wall-to-wall cafés and restaurants line the popular meeting places of Bärenplatz and Theaterplatz, as well as the more upmarket Gerechtigkeitsgasse.

For both convenience and delicious fresh food, try the **Manora** (Bubenbergplatz 5a; salads Sfr4.40-9.40, pizzas Sfr6.90-8.90; open 6.30am-10.45pm Mon-Sat, 8.30am-10.45pm Sun), a busy, two-level, buffet-style restaurant.

Aroma (Genfergasse 8; snacks Sfr4.90-13.50; open 7am-9pm Mon-Fri, 7am-7pm Sat, 11am-8pm Sun) is a popular coffee stop. Its carefully crafted mugs of coffee sport lovehearts in the froth.

Brasserie Chez Edy (☎ 031 311 38 93; Bärenplatz; mains Sfr24-34; open 11am-11pm) is the best of the Bärenplatz bunch. Try the speciality mussels (served 10 different ways), or the Bernese Platter, with more sauerkraut and sausages than you can finish.

Don't be fazed by the dingy entrance to **Della Casa** (☎ 031 311 21 42; Schauplatzgasse 16; lunch menu from Sfr18.50, mains Sfr22.50-42; open 8am-11.30pm Mon-Fri, 9am-3pm Sat). Inside you'll find an old but cosy eatery with floral curtains, leadlight lamps and traditional Swiss specialities.

Menuetto (☎ 031 311 14 48; Herrengasse 22; meals Sfr13.80-23.50; open 11.15am-2.15pm & 5.30pm-10pm Mon-Sat) is a mecca for vegetarians, serving up seriously wholesome dishes to a seriously wholesome crowd.

Hidden below a popular grungy bar, **Les Amis** (☎ 031 311 51 87; Rathausgasse 63; mains Sfr30-37.50; open 6.30pm-12.30am Tues-Sat) specialises in French and Italian dishes.

MeKong Beizli (☎ 031 311 26 00; Chindlifrässer-Passage, Kornhausplatz 7; starters Sfr10.50, mains Sfr21-29; open 10am-11pm daily), at the entrance to an arcade, is perfect for a chilli fix, with spicy Thai soups and Chinese stir-fries.

Self-caterers can buy up big at **Coop** (Neuengasse) and **Migros** (Marktgasse 46), which also have cheap self-service restaurants.

Entertainment

Bern has a thriving nightlife, with countless bars and clubs to choose from. See the website w www.bernbynight.ch for an extensive list.

Du Nord (☎ 031 332 23 38; Lorrainestrasse 2; open 8am-12.30pm Mon-Fri, 9am-12.30pm Sat, 4pm-12.30pm Sun) is a spacious, semi-grungy, bar-restaurant with a laid-back atmosphere and a social conscience.

Altes Tramdepot (☎ 031 368 14 15; Am Bärengraben; open 11am-12.30am daily), beside the bear pits, brews its own beer on the premises (sample three types for Sfr9.50). This cavernous converted tram depot has snacks and monster meals, and sweeping views across the river.

Adriano's (☎ 031 318 88 31; Theaterplatz 2; open 7am-12.30pm Mon-Sat, 10am-11.30pm Sun) transforms from hip bar with black-clad regulars at night to mellow prework breakfast niche the next morning.

Kornhauskeller (☎ 031 327 72 72; Kornhausplatz 18; open 6pm-1am Mon-Wed, 6pm-2am Thur-Sat, 6pm-12.30am Sun) is a magnificent, underground gallery bar and restaurant with vaulted ceilings, frescoes and comfy sofas overlooking diners below. Drinks are dear, but it's worth sipping slowly on a fruit juice (Sfr5) to soak up the atmosphere.

Wasserwerk (☎ 031 312 12 31; w www .wasserwerk.ch; Wasserwerkgasse 5; gigs free-Sfr30; open 9pm-1.30am Sun-Thur, 9pm-2.30am Fri-Sat), in a converted riverside warehouse, is a favourite hang-out for local pool-players and clubbers, with international DJs and regular special events. See the website for the latest programme.

Quasimodo (☎ *031 311 13 81; Rathausgasse 75; admission free; open 4pm-1.30am Mon-Wed, 4pm-3.30am Thur-Sat)*, underneath Hotel Glocke, is a dimly lit techno bar/club pumping out a hard electronic pulse.

There's almost always something interesting on at **Kulturhallen Dampfzentrale** (☎ *031 311 63 37;* w *www.dampfzentrale.ch; Marzilistrasse 47; bus No 30 to Marzili)*, with an eclectic mix of acts from jazz and flamenco to classical and club DJs. The late-night Moonlinerbus shuttles from Dampfzentrale to the station on weekends.

The **Reitschule** (☎ *031 306 69 69;* w *www .reitschule.ch; Schützenmattstrasse)*, a graffiti-covered alternative arts centre in a grotty area, attracts a left-leaning crowd looking for dance, theatre, cinema and live music. There's also a bar, restaurant and women's centre. It's rather run-down. There are plans for renovation.

Getting There & Away

There are daily flights to/from Lugano, London, Paris, Amsterdam and other European destinations from Bern-Belp airport. Postbuses depart from the western side of the train station. There are at least hourly train connections to most Swiss towns, including Geneva (Sfr50, 1¾ hours), Basel (Sfr37, 70 minutes), Interlaken (Sfr25, 50 minutes) and Zürich (Sfr48, 70 minutes).

There are three motorways that intersect at the northern part of the city. The N1 runs from Neuchâtel in the west and Basel and Zürich in the northeast. The N6 connects Bern with Thun and the Interlaken region in the southeast. The N12 is the route from Geneva and Lausanne in the southwest.

Getting Around

Belp airport is some 9km southeast of the city centre. A bus links the airport to the train station (Sfr14). It takes 30 minutes and is coordinated with flight arrivals and departures.

Bus and tram tickets cost Sfr1.60 (maximum six stops) or Sfr2.50. A day pass for the city and regional network is Sfr8. A 24/48/72-hour pass for the city costs Sfr6.50/10.50/14.50. Buy single-journey tickets at stops and passes from the tourist office or the **BernMobil office** *(Bubenbergplatz 5)*.

Many taxis wait by the train station. They charge Sfr6.80 plus Sfr3.10 per kilometre (Sfr3.40 after 8pm daily and on Sunday).

From May to October there are *free* daily loans of city bikes outside the train station. ID and Sfr20 deposit are required.

AROUND BERN

There are some excellent excursions close to Bern. About 30km west of Bern is **Murten**, a historic walled town overlooking a lake. There are hourly trains from Bern (Sfr11.80).

Fribourg, to the southwest, has an enticing old town-centre and an **Art & History Museum** which is well stocked with late-Gothic sculpture and painting. It's easily accessible by train (Sfr11.80, 30 minutes).

Further south is **Gruyéres**, about an hour away from either Fribourg or Montreux, with a 13th-century **castle** on the hill. Fromage fanciers flock to **La Maison du Gruyére** (☎ *026 921 84 00;* w *www.lamaisondu gruyere.ch; tours Sfr5; open 9am-7pm daily June-Sept, 9am-6pm daily Oct-May)*, which offers daily cheese-making tours. Fans of the *Alien* movie can pay homage to its designer at the **Musée HR Giger** (☎ *026 921 22 00; adult/child Sfr10/5; open 10am-6pm daily summer, 10am-5pm Tues-Sun daily winter)*.

Neuchâtel & the Jura

The northwest corner of the country hugs the border with France, sharing its language, food and sensibility. Neuchâtel is a wine-making region featuring rolling hills and a postcard-perfect lake as well as a proud watch-making heritage. The Jura region is often overlooked by foreign visitors but attracts its fair share of Swiss holidaymakers. Dominated by the Jura mountain range, its landscape of forests, pastures and gentle slopes makes it ideal territory for a range of sports and outdoor activities.

NEUCHÂTEL
pop 32,000

Neuchâtel is the canton's capital, on the northwest shore of the large lake that shares its name. This laid-back French-style resort, surrounded by vineyards, has a cruisey café culture and an inviting medieval old town.

The train station (Gare CFF) has daily money exchange and bike rental. The central pedestrian zone and Place Pury (the hub of local buses) are about 1km away down the hill along Ave de la Gare.

The **tourist office** (☎ 032 889 68 90; e tourisme.neuchatelois@ne.ch; Place du Port; open 9am-7pm daily mid-May–mid-Oct, 9am-noon & 1.30pm-5.30pm Mon-Fri, 9am-noon Sat mid-Oct–mid-May) is in the main post office by the lake.

Things to See & Do

The centrepiece of the old town is the 12th-century **Chateau de Neuchâtel** (tours daily Apr-Sept), now housing cantonal offices, and the adjoining **Collegiate Church**. The church features a striking cenotaph of 15 statues dating from 1372. Nearby, the **Prison Tower** (admission Sfr1; open Apr-Aug) offers broad views of the town and lake.

Visit the **Musée d'Art et d'Histoire** (Museum of Art & History; ☎ 032 717 79 20; Esplanade Léopold-Robert 1; adult/student Sfr7/4, free Wed; open 10am-6pm Tues-Sun), on the waterfront, to see the museum's beloved 18th-century clockwork figures.

Tropical Gardens Papiliorama/Nocturama (☎ 038 33 43 44; adult/student/child Sfr11/9/5; open 9am-6pm daily summer, 10am-5pm daily winter) has a complex of lush vegetation with colourful butterflies and tropical birds, as well as a faux moonlit world for Latin American night creatures. It's 6km east of Neuchâtel at Marin (take bus No 1 from Place Pury).

The tourist office has information on nearby walking trails and boat trips on the lake.

Places to Stay

Oasis Neuchâtel (☎ 032 731 31 90, fax 032 730 37 09; e auberge.oasis@bluewin.ch; Rue du Suchiez 35; dorm beds Sfr25-32, twins Sfr64; open Apr-Oct) is 2km from the centre; take bus No 1 (Cormondrèche) to Vauseyon, then follow the signs towards Centre Sportive. This friendly, independent hostel is a bit of a hike, but rewards you with glorious views. At the time of writing there was talk of renovation or closure, so ring ahead before traipsing uphill.

Hôtel Marché (☎ 032 723 23 30, fax 032 723 23 33; e info@hoteldumarche.ch; Place des Halles 4; singles/doubles/triples Sfr70/100/125) offers basic rooms right in the thick

of it, overlooking the cafés of bustling Place des Halle.

Hotel des Arts (☎ 032 727 61 61, fax 032 727 61 62; e info@hotel-des-arts.ch; Rue Pourtales 3; singles/doubles/suites from Sfr108/150/200), a couple of blocks from the main drag, was spruced up in early 2002, and has bright, cheerful rooms.

The **Hôtel Alpes et Lac** (☎ 032 723 19 19, fax 032 723 19 20; e hotel@alpesetlac.ch; station-side singles/doubles from Sfr120/180, lakeside from Sfr145/207), opposite the train station, is an elegant option with renovated rooms and a generous breakfast buffet. It's worth paying an extra Sfr20 for panoramic views over Neuchâtel's rooftops.

Places to Eat

Bach et Buck Creperie (☎ 032 725 63 53; Ave du 1er-Mars 22; crepes Sfr6-10.50; open 11.30am-1.45pm & 5.30pm-9.45pm Mon-Thur, 11.30am-1.45pm & 5.30pm-11.30pm Fri-Sat, 5pm-9.45pm Sun) has a menu of 130 crepes and good vegie options in a café dominated by refreshing green-themed decor.

Cafe des Halles (☎ 032 724 31 41; Rue du Trésor 4; mains Sfr14-23; open 8am-midnight Mon-Sat, 10am-midnight Sun), in an impressive high-ceilinged historic house on the main square, has scrumptious pizzas, pastas and a large shaded terrace.

Night owls should keep an eye out for Neuchâtel's **restaurants de nuit** (all-night eateries; open 9pm-6am), which are strung all over town.

Self-caterers can stock up on local wines and cheeses at **Coop** (Rue de la Treille 4) and **Aux Gourmets** (cnr Rue de Seyon & Rue de L'Ancien Hotel-de-Ville), both near Place Pury.

Entertainment

Chauffage Compris (☎ 032 721 43 96; Rue des Moulins 37; open 7am-1am Mon-Thur, 7am-2am Fri, 8am-2am Sat, 3pm-midnight Sun) is a funky café/bar with quality coffee, a range of spirits and beers and a daily lunch menu. Grab a board game from the bar and settle in for a few hours.

Café du Cerf (☎ 724 27 44; Rue de L'Ancien Hotel-de-Ville 4; open 8am-midnight Mon-Fri, 8am-1am Sat & Sun) is a friendly, popular beer-lover's paradise (150 choices) with Cambodian specialities from the linked restaurant Le Lotus upstairs.

Also worth a look are **Bar de L'Univers** (☎ 032 721 43 40; Rue du Coq d'Inde 22), a cool, smoky, studied-grunge bar for all ages, tucked into the corner of a quiet square; and **Brasserie Cafe du Theatre** (☎ 032 725 29 77; Faubourg du Lac 1), a glass-fronted place attracting all types for a chat and a late supper.

Getting There & Around

There are hourly fast trains to Geneva (Sfr42, 70 minutes) and Bern (Sfr17.20, 35 minutes). Postbuses heading to the Jura leave from the station.

Local buses cost Sfr1.60 to Sfr2.60 per trip, or Sfr7 for a 24-hour pass.

AROUND NEUCHÂTEL
La Chaux-de-Fonds

Watch- and clock-making have a long history here, and the town even boasts its own **Musée International D'Horlogerie** (Horology Museum; ☎ 032 967 68 61; Rue des Musées 29; adult/student Sfr8/4; open 10am-6pm Tues-Sun Jun-Sept, 10am-noon & 2pm-5pm Oct-May), with over 4500 timekeeping exhibits being displayed. Just 20km northwest of Neuchâtel and accessible by train in 30 minutes (Sfr10.40), it's an ideal day trip.

JURA CANTON

The youngest canton in Switzerland is the Jura, which only broke away from the Bern canton in 1974. Though the capital is Delémont, outdoor enthusiasts head to Franches-Montagnes (Free Mountain), a magnet for mountain-bikers, hikers and cross-country skiers. Some 1500km of hiking trails and 200km of prepared cross-country ski trails lead through scenic pastures and woodlands.

It's also horse country, with over 30 towns and villages boasting equestrian centres that offer all-inclusive weeks, weekends or simply hourly rides.

The main town in Franches-Montagnes is Saignelégier, where you will find **Jura Tourisme** (☎ 032 952 19 53, fax 032 952 19 50; w www.juratourisme.ch; Place du 23-Juin 6, Saignelégier). Staff can help with accommodation and outdoor activities.

Saignelégier can be reached by train from La Chaux-de-Fonds (Sfr12.60, 40 minutes) and Basel (Sfr27, 95 minutes with change at Glovelier).

Geneva

pop 176,000

Geneva (Genève, Genf, Ginevra), Switzerland's third-largest city, sits comfortably on the shore of Lake Geneva (Lac Léman). The canton is surrounded by France on three sides and the Gallic influence is everywhere. Birthplace of the Red Cross, once League of Nations headquarters and now European home of the UN, Geneva has been an important centre of both diplomacy and business for decades. The city belongs not so much to Switzerland as to the whole world. More than 40% of residents are non-Swiss and this city of bankers, diplomats and transients has a truly international flavour. Despite the obvious affluence of the city and its impressive lakeside position, take a step into the backblocks and you'll find a scruffier, seedier side.

Orientation

The Rhône River runs through the city, dividing it into *rive droite* (right bank, ie, north of the Rhône) and *rive gauche* (left bank). On the northern side is the main train station, Gare de Cornavin; south of the river lies the old town. In summer, Geneva's most visible landmark is the **Jet d'Eau**, a giant fountain on the southern shore.

In France, **Mont Saléve** yields an excellent view of the city and Lake Geneva. Take bus No 8 to Veyrier and walk across the border. The cable car costs Sfr19 return and runs daily in summer, but infrequently in winter.

Information

Tourist Offices For advice on accommodation or attractions, go to **Genéve Tourisme** (☎ 022 909 70 00; e info@geneve-tourism .ch; Rue du Mont-Blanc 18; open 9am-6pm Mon-Sat, plus 9am-6pm Sun summer). Grab a copy of the excellent (and free) *Vélo-Cité* map or the budget-conscious brochure *Genève info-jeunes*. There's also the **city information office** (☎ 022 311 98 27; Pont de la Machine; open noon-6pm Mon, 9am-6pm Tues-Fri, 10am-5pm Sat) and **Centre d'Accueil et de Renseignements** (CAR; ☎ 022 731 46 47; open 9am-11pm daily mid-June–mid-Sept), with youth-oriented information dispensed from a bus parked at the station end of Rue du Mont-Blanc.

Money There is an **exchange office** (open 6.45am-9.30pm daily summer, 6.50am-7.40pm Mon-Sat, 6.50am-6.40pm Sun rest of year) in Gare de Cornavin.

Post & Communications Not far from the station is the **main post office** (Rue du Mont-Blanc 18; open 7.30am-6pm Mon-Fri, 8.30am-noon Sat).

Near the tourist office you'll find excellent Internet rates (Sfr1/3/4 for 10/30/60 minutes) at **Video Club** (☎ 022 731 47 48; Rue des Alpes 19; open 11am-midnight Mon-Thur, 11am-2am Fri-Sat, noon-midnight Sun). In the train station, **Internet Cafe de la Gare** offers bargain nightly rates between 9pm and 11pm (Sfr3 per hour), but prices rise at other times.

Travel Agencies Among a string of travel agents and airline offices is **American Express** (☎ 022 731 76 00; Rue du Mont-Blanc 7; open 8.30am-5.45pm Mon-Fri year-round, 9am-noon Sat-Sun in summer). On the other side of town, there's a branch of **STA Travel** (☎ 022 329 97 33; Rue Vignier 3; open 9.15am-6pm Mon-Fri, 9am-noon Sat).

Medical Services Ring ☎ 111 for medical information. For medical services there's the **Cantonal Hospital** (☎ 022 372 33 11; Rue Micheli-du-Crest 24) or a private 24-hour clinic, **Permanence Médico Chirurgicale** (☎ 022 731 21 20; Rue de Chantepoulet 1-3). The **Servette Clinique** (☎ 022 733 98 00; Ave Wendt 60) offers emergency dental treatment.

Things to See & Do

The city centre is so compact that it's easy to see many of the main sights on foot. Start a scenic walk through the old town at the **Île Rousseau**, home to a statue in honour of the celebrated free thinker. Head west along the southern side of the Rhône until you reach the 13th-century **Tour de L'Île**, once part of the medieval city fortifications. Walk south down the narrow, cobbled Rue de la Cité until it becomes Grand-Rue. **Rousseau's birthplace** is at No 40.

A short detour off Grand-Rue there's the part-Romanesque, part-Gothic **Cathédrale St Pierre**, where John Calvin preached from 1536 to 1564. There are good views from the **tower** (admission Sfr3; open 9am-5pm daily June-Sept, 10am-noon & 2pm-5pm Mon-Sat, 11am-12.30pm & 1.30pm-5pm Sun

Oct-May). The cathedral location has been a place of worship since the 4th century, and you can witness evidence of this in the **archaeological site** (adult/student Sfr5/3; open Tues-Sun).

Grand-Rue terminates at **Place du Bourg-de-Four**, which is the site of a medieval marketplace that features both a fountain and street cafés.

Take Rue de la Fontaine to reach the lakeside. Anticlockwise round the shore is the **Jet d'Eau**. Calling this a fountain is an understatement. The water shoots up with incredible force (200km/h, 1360HP), to create a 140m-high plume. At any one time there are seven tonnes of water is in the air, and much of it falls on spectators who venture out on the pier. It's not activated in winter or in high winds.

United Nations The European arm of the UN and the home of 3000 international civil servants is the Art-Deco **Palais des Nations** (☎ 022 907 48 96; Ave de la Paix 9-14; tour adult/student Sfr8.50/6.50; open 10am-5pm daily July-Aug, 10am-noon & 2pm-4pm daily Apr-June & Sept-Oct, 10am-noon & 2pm-4pm Mon-Fri Nov-Mar). You can see where decisions about world affairs are made on the hour-long tour (bring your passport to get in). Take Bus No 5 or 8 from the station.

Museums There are plenty of museums (many free) to keep you busy on a rainy day. **Musée d'Art et d'Histoire** (Museum of Art and History; ☎ 022 418 26 00; Rue Charles-Galland 2) has a vast collection of paintings, sculpture, weapons and archaeological displays. **Musée d'Histoire Naturelle** (Museum of Natural History; ☎ 022 418 63 00; Route de Malagnou 1) delights the kiddies with dioramas and anthropological displays. **Maison Tavel** (☎ 022 418 37 00; 6 Rue du Puits Saint Pierre) gives visitors an insight into the everyday, with a focus on the history of urban life in Geneva. These museums are free and are open 9.30am or 10am to 5pm Tuesday to Sunday.

The **International Red Cross & Red Crescent Museum** (☎ 022 748 95 25; Av de la Paix 17; Bus No 5 or 8; adult/student Sfr10/5; open 10am-5pm Wed-Mon), next to the UN, proudly tells the story of the world's first humanitarian organisation, and keeps you up to date with current work in the field.

SWITZERLAND

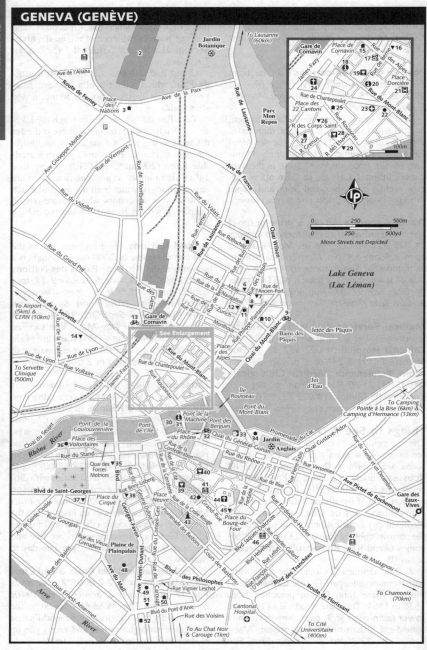

GENEVA (GENÈVE)

To Lausanne (60km)

Jardin Botanique

Route de Ferney

Ave de l'Anana

Ave de la Paix

Place des Nations

Ave de la Paix

Parc Mon Repos

Rue de Lausanne

Ave de Vermont

Ave Giuseppe-Motta

Rue de Vermont

Rue de Montbrillant

Ave de France

Quai Wilson

Rue du Vidollet

Rue de Lausanne

Rue du Grand Pré

Rue des Gares

Rue de la Servette

To Airport (5km) & CERN (10km)

Rue de la Prairie

Rue de Lyon

Rue de Lyon

Rue Voltaire

To Servette Clinique (500m)

Gare de Cornavin

See Enlargement

Rue du Mont-Blanc

Rue de Chantepoulet

Rue Rousseau

Place des Alpes

Lake Geneva (Lac Léman)

Bains des Pâquis

Jetée des Pâquis

0   250   500m
0   250   500yd

Minor Streets not Depicted

Île Rousseau

Jet d'Eau

To Camping Pointe à la Bise (6km) & Camping d'Hermance (13km)

Pont du Mont-Blanc

Pont de la Machine

Pont des Bergues

Pont de l'Île

Quai du Seujet

Rhône River

Pont de la Coulouvrenière

Place des Volontaires

Rue du Stand

Quai des Forces Motrices

Blvd de Saint-Georges

Place du Cirque

Rue Gourgas

Rue des Vieux Grenadiers

Plaine de Plainpalais

Rue de Carouge

Ave Henri-Dunant

Blvd des Philosophes

Rue Vignier Leschot

Quai des Bains

Quai Ernest-Ansermet

Arve River

Blvd du Pont d'Arve

Rue des Voisins

To Au Chat Noir & Carouge (1km)

Cantonal Hospital

To Cité Universitaire (400m)

Promenade du Lac

Jardin Anglais

Quai Gustave-Ador

Ave Pictet de Rochemont

Gare des Eaux-Vives

To Chamonix (70km)

Route de Florissant

Route de Malagnou

Blvd des Tranchées

Enlargement (inset)

Gare de Cornavin

Place de Cornavin

Rue de Berne

Rue des Alpes

James-Fazy

Rue de Chantepoulet

Place des 22 Cantons

Place Dorcière

Rue du Mont-Blanc

Rue Rousseau

R des Corps-Saint

R Grenus

R des Étuves

0   100m

GENEVA

PLACES TO STAY		35	La Mamounia	23	Permanence Médico
3	Centre Masaryk	37	Le The		Chirurgicale
4	SYHA Hostel	38	Victoria	24	Notre-Dame
5	City Hostel	45	Chez Ma Cousine	28	Mulligans
10	Hôtel de la Cloche	51	Café Universal	30	Tour de l'Île
15	Hôtel Bernina			31	City Information Office
25	Hôtel Excelsior	**OTHER**		32	Free Bicycle Rental
27	Hotel Saint-Gervais	1	International Red Cross &	33	MGN boat departure
50	Hôtel le Prince		Red Crescent Museum	34	CGN Ticket Booth
52	Hôtel Carmen	2	Palais des Nations (UN)	36	L'Usine
		9	Free Bicycle Rental	39	Flanagan's Irish Bar
PLACES TO EAT		11	Sixt	40	Alhambar
6	Migros	13	Genev' Roule	41	Maison Tavel
7	L'amalgam	17	Video Club	42	Rousseau's Birthplace
8	Edelweiss	18	CAR Information Centre	43	Reformation Monument
12	Espresso Club	19	Post Café	44	Cathédrale St Pierre
14	Kong Restaurant	20	Genéve Tourism;	46	Musée d'Art et d'Histoire
16	Al-Amir		Main Post Office	47	Musée d'Histoire Naturelle
26	Manora	21	International Bus Terminal	48	Fruit market
29	Sugar Hut	22	American Express	49	STA Travel

Parks & Gardens Geneva has more parkland than any other Swiss city, much of it along the lakefront.

There's the **Jardin Anglais**, near the jet, featuring a large flower clock; and, in the north of the city, the impressive **Jardin Botanique** (admission free; open 9.30am-5pm daily winter, 8am-7.30pm daily rest of year), with exotic plants and an aviary.

South of Grand-Rue is **Promenade des Bastions**, containing a massive monument to the Reformation: the giant figures of Bèze, Calvin, Farel and Knox are flanked by smaller statues of other important figures, and depictions of events instrumental in the spread of the movement.

CERN Some 10km northwest of the centre is the European Centre for Nuclear Research (CERN; ☎ 022 767 84 84; e visits.service@ cern.ch; Route de Meyrin; bus No 9 from train station; admission free; open 9am-5pm Mon-Sat). Its educational Microcosm exhibition covers particle accelerators and the Big Bang; real enthusiasts can get up close to the large hadron collider on one of the guided tours that run at 9am and 2pm (take your passport and book well in advance).

Special Events

The Geneva Festival, a 10-day event in early August, features parades, fireworks and live music, most of it along the lake. In early December, L'Escalade celebrates the foiling of an invasion by the Duke of Savoy in 1602 with a costumed parade and day of races around the old town.

Places to Stay

Camping Some 7km northeast of the centre, on the southern lakeshore, is **Camping Pointe á la Bise** (☎ 022 752 12 96; Chemin de la Bise 19; camp site per adult/child/tent Sfr6.70/ 3.10/6; open Apr-Oct) in Vesenaz. Take bus E from Rive. Further away, but a cheaper option, is **Camping d'Hermance** (☎ 022 751 14 83; Rue de Nord 44; open Apr-Oct) at the terminus of bus E, 14km from the centre.

Hostels Above an International School for tots near the UN, **Centre Masaryk** (☎ 022 733 07 72; Ave de la Paix 11; Bus No 5 or 8; dorm beds Sfr30, singles/doubles/triples Sfr40/76/ 99) has large rooms with lots of character, creaky floorboards and wonderful views over parkland. Get a key for late access and beware of stray building blocks.

Closer to the centre is the **SYHA hostel** (☎ 022 732 62 60, fax 022 738 39 87; w www .yh-geneva.ch; Rue Rothschild 28-30; dorm beds from Sfr25, doubles without/with bath Sfr70/80), a big, busy, concrete box of a building with helpful staff. Breakfast is included and dinners cost Sfr12.50.

The independent **City Hostel** (☎ 022 901 15 00; e info@cityhostel.ch; Rue Ferrier 2; dorm beds in 4-/3-/2-bed rooms Sfr25/28/31, singles/doubles Sfr55/80) is in a charmless

'70s-style building. It offers adequate rooms, kitchen and Internet access (Sfr4 for 30 minutes).

Cité Universitaire (☎ 022 839 22 22, fax 022 839 22 23; Ave de Miremont 46; dorm beds Sfr20, singles for students/nonstudents Sfr42/49, studios Sfr75), south of the Rhône, is an enormous jumble of student accommodation with Internet, reading room and restaurant (open 7am to 10pm; breakfast Sfr7). Basic dorms are only available from mid-June to September, but ask for affordable singles at other times. Take bus No 3 from Gare de Cornavin to the terminus at Champel.

Hotels Geneva has a huge number of five- and four-star hotels that fill quickly with business clientele.

See the tourist office, or w www.geneva -tourism.ch, for some upmarket choices. For the budget-conscious, there are a few good-value options in town.

Hôtel de la Cloche (☎ 022 732 94 81, fax 022 738 16 12; e hotelcloche@span.ch; Rue de la Cloche 6; singles/doubles Sfr60/85, doubles with shower & toilet Sfr120) is a small, old-fashioned hotel with expansive rooms, ageing furniture, dramatic chandeliers and towering ceilings. It's liable to be full so call ahead.

Hotel Saint-Gervais (☎/fax 022 732 45 72; Rue des Corps-Saints 20; singles/doubles from Sfr62/78) is a tiny place with tiny rooms, but its convenient location and unorthodox design (one room has tartan-covered ceiling, door and floor) have won fans.

Near the university, **Hôtel Carmen** (☎ 022 329 11 11, fax 022 781 59 33; Rue Dancet 5; singles/doubles Sfr55-100, doubles Sfr75-126) is a friendly, family-run place with some of the best-value rooms in town. Studio apartments are available for longer stays. If Carmen is booked out, try the nearby **Hôtel le Prince** (☎ 022 807 05 00, fax 022 807 05 29; w www.hotel-le-prince.ch; 16 Rue des Voisins; singles/doubles from Sfr85/110), with modest but comfortable rooms.

If you're looking for convenience, there are several tourist-class hotels clustered near the train station. Reliable options include **Hôtel Bernina** (☎ 022 908 49 50, fax 022 908 49 51; e info@bernina-geneve.ch; Place de Cornavin 22; singles/doubles from Sfr130/160), offering renovated rooms directly across the road; and **Hôtel Excelsior**

(☎ 022 732 09 45, fax 022 738 43 69; Rue Rousseau 34; singles/doubles from Sfr120/180), around the corner.

Places to Eat

Geneva is the cuisine capital of Switzerland, with a wide range of choices, from Chinese to Lebanese to North African. You'll find cheapish Asian and Middle Eastern eateries in the seedy streets north of Rue des Alpes, or on Boulevard de Saint-Georges south of the river. Don't miss the best kebab in town from the hole-in-the-wall Lebanese takeaway **Al-Amir** (Rue de Berne 22; kebabs Sfr8; open 11am-2am daily).

For tasty dishes and extensive salad and dessert bars, head to **Manora** (Rue de Cornavin 4; small/large meals Sfr6.90/8.90; open 7.30am-9.30pm Mon-Sat, 9am-9.30pm Sun).

Restaurants Tuck into the plentiful plat du jour (Sfr16) at **La Mamounia** (☎ 022 329 55 61; Blvd Georges-Favon 10; dishes Sfr23-29; open noon-2pm & 7pm-midnight daily) and you won't need dinner. The Moroccan eatery has generous melt-in-your-mouth couscous dishes with an array of condiments; weekend diners often score a belly-dancer bonus.

West of the station, **Kong Restaurant** (Rue de la Servette 31; mains Sfr10-26; open noon-2pm & 6.45pm-10pm Mon-Sat, 6.45pm-10pm Sun) satisfies the biggest appetites with its all-you-can-eat buffet (Sfr17.50; available Tuesday to Friday).

At the other end of the scale, there's **Le The** (☎ 079 436 77 18; Rue des Bains 65; tea Sfr4, dishes Sfr4-8), a tiny boutique teahouse with exquisite Chinese infusions (61 varieties) and bite-size delicacies.

For flavoursome Thai food, there's the busy, intimate **Sugar Hut** (☎ 022 731 4613; Rue des Etuves 16; mains Sfr22-28; open noon-2pm & 7pm-2am Mon-Fri, 7pm-2am Sat-Sun), with a good seafood selection.

Road-testing Swiss specialities in Geneva is not out of the question either. **Victoria** (☎ 022 807 11 99; Rue Bovy-Lisberg 2; dishes Sfr21-49; open 10.30am-3pm & 5.30pm-midnight Mon-Sat) is a stylish brasserie run by gourmet chefs specialising in Genevese food. Or go the whole hog at kitschy **Edelweiss** (☎ 022 731 49 40; Place de la Navigation 2), with pots of steaming fondue (from Sfr23) in a Swiss-chalet setting and a folklore show (from 7pm nightly).

Cafés In the old town, terrace cafés and restaurants crowd along the medieval Place du Bourg-de-Four. **Chez Ma Cousine** (☎ 022 310 96 96; Place du Bourg-de-Four 6; meals Sfr13.90; open 7am-midnight Mon-Fri, 11am-midnight Sat, 11am-11pm Sun) entices local lunchers with its country-cottage decor and plates piled high with its signature dish (half-chicken, potatoes and salad).

The walk-in-wardrobe-sized **Espresso Club** (☎ 022 738 84 88; Rue des Paquis 25; meals Sfr13-22; open 6am-2am Mon-Fri, 7am-2am Sat, 8am-7pm Sun) is a popular cruisey café serving up pizza, pasta, salads and industrial-strength coffee.

Around the corner is **L'amalgam** (Rue de l'Ancien-Port 13; meals Sfr16-18) which is all African art, palms and ochre tones, with simple fusion food and a mellow mood.

Café Universal (☎ 022 781 18 81; Blvd du Pont d'Arve 26; mains Sfr24-32, plat du jour Sfr17-18) is French, smoky and cool, and features monster mirrors, 1920s posters, glittering chandeliers and an arty crowd.

Self-Catering Stock up at **Migros** (Rue des Pâquis; open 8am-7pm Mon-Fri, 8am-6pm Sat), which also sells baguettes (Sfr2) and sandwiches (Sfr3.60) from its self-service restaurant. **Aperto** (open 6am-10pm daily), in the train station, has fresh produce and a mini bakery. You can pick up seasonal goodies at the fruit and vegie markets scattered around (the one at Plainpalais operates five days a week).

Entertainment

The latest nightclubs, live music venues and theatre events are well covered in the weekly *Genève Agenda*, free from the tourist office.

Alhambar (☎ 022 312 13 13; 1st floor, Rue de la Rôtisserie 10; open noon-2pm Mon, noon-2pm & 6pm-2am Tues-Fri, 5pm-2am Sat, 11am-midnight Sun) is an oasis of theatricality in an otherwise staid shopping district, with a buzzing atmosphere, an eclectic music programme and the best Sunday brunch in town.

An odd blend of Brit fixtures and loud blues music attracts a mixed crowd at the **Post Café** (Rue de Berne 7), near the tourist office. Other pubs popular with the city's English-speakers are **Mulligans** (14 Rue Grenus) and **Flanagan's Irish Bar** (Rue du Cheval-Blanc). Both open daily at 5pm and

keep the Guinness flowing well into the wee hours.

L'Usine (☎ 022 328 08 18; Place des Volontaires 4), a converted factory, contains an art-house cinema, experimental theatre and a venue for local and visiting bands.

Described by tourist boffins as the 'Greenwich Village' of Geneva, Carouge (south of town) is full of groovy shops, bars and clubs. One of the most popular is **Au Chat Noir** (☎ 022 343 49 98; Rue Vautier 13, Carouge; entry free-Sfr15; open 6pm-4am Mon-Thur, 6pm-5am Fri, 9pm-5am Sat-Sun), serving up funk, African beats, jazz and DJs.

Getting There & Away

Air Geneva airport is an important transport hub and has frequent connections to every major European city.

Bus International buses depart from **Place Dorcière** (☎ 022 732 02 30), off Rue des Alpes.

There are several buses a week to London (Sfr145, 17 hours) and Barcelona (Sfr100, 10 hours).

Train There are more or less hourly connections to most Swiss towns; the Zürich trip takes three hours (Sfr76), as does Interlaken (Sfr63), both via Bern.

There are regular international trains going to Paris (Sfr95 by TGV, 3½ hours; reservations essential), Hamburg (Sfr280, 10 hours), Milan (Sfr81, four hours) and Barcelona (Sfr100, nine hours). **Gare des Eaux-Vives** is the best station for Annecy and Chamonix. To get there from the Gare de Cornavin, take tram No 16.

Car & Motorcycle An autoroute bypass skirts Geneva, with major routes intersecting southwest of the city: the N1 from Lausanne joins with the E62 to Lyon (130km) and the E25 heading southeast towards Chamonix. Toll-free main roads follow the course of these motorways.

Sixt (☎ 022 732 90 90; Place de la Navigation 1) has the best daily car rental rates (from Sfr89 per day, unlimited kilometres). Its 72-hour weekend deal is Sfr159.

Boat Next to Jardin Anglais is a ticket booth for **Compagnie Générale de Navigation** (CGN; ☎ 022 312 52 23; w www.cgn.ch), which operates a steamer service to all towns and major villages bordering Lake Geneva, including those in France.

Boats operate throughout the year, but the busy summer timetable runs from May to September. Destinations include Lausanne (Sfr34.80, 3½ hours) and Montreux (Sfr40.80, 4½ hours).

Eurail and Swiss passes are valid on CGN boats or there are CGN boat day passes for Sfr55 and circular excursions.

Getting Around

To/From the Airport Getting from the airport is easy with regular trains into Gare de Cornavin (Sfr5.20, six minutes). Bus No 10 (Sfr2.20) does the same 5km trip. A taxi would cost Sfr25 to Sfr35.

Public Transport The city is efficiently serviced by buses, trams, trains and boats, and ticket dispensers are found at all stops. Tickets cost Sfr1.80 (within one zone, 30 minutes) and Sfr2.20 (two zones, 60 minutes). A day pass costs Sfr6 for the city or Sfr12 for the whole canton. Tickets and passes are also valid for MGN boats that travel along the city shoreline.

Taxi Taxis are Sfr6.30 flag fall and Sfr2.90 per kilometre (Sfr3.50 per kilometre from 8.30pm to 6.30am).

Bicycle You can rent bikes from **Genev' Roule** (☎/fax 022 740 13 43; Place de Mont-brillant 17; Sfr10/42 per day/week; open 8am-6pm Mon-Sat, 10am-6pm Sun), right next to the station.

If you're willing to ride a bike covered in advertising, it will only cost you Sfr7. From May to October, Genev' Roule even has bikes free of charge, available here and at Bains des Pâquis, Place du Rhône and Plaine de Plainpalais. Some ID and Sfr50 deposit is required.

Boat In addition to CGN (see under Getting There & Away earlier in this section), smaller companies operate excursions on the lake between April and October (no passes valid). Ticket offices and departures are along the Quai du Mont-Blanc and next to the Jardin Anglais. Trips range from 45 minutes (Sfr8) to two hours (Sfr20), with commentary in English.

Lake Geneva Region

LAUSANNE
pop 115,500

Capital of the Vaud canton, Lausanne is a beautiful hillside city overlooking Lake Geneva, with several distinct personalities. There's the former fishing village, Ouchy, with its summer beach-resort feel; Place St-Francois, with stylish, cobblestoned shopping streets; and Flon, a warehouse district of bars, galleries and boutiques.

On the lake south of the train station is Ouchy, while to the north is Place St François (the main hub for local transport). The **main tourist office** (☎ 021 613 73 21; e informa tion@lausanne-tourisme.ch; open 9am-6pm daily Oct-Mar, 9am-8pm Apr-Sept) is in the Ouchy metro station. The train station also has a **tourist office** (open 9am-7pm daily), as well as bicycle rental and money exchange.

The **main post office** (open 7.30am-6.30pm Mon-Fri, 8am-noon Sat) is by the train station. Across the road is **Quanta** (open 9am-midnight daily), a video-games centre offering Internet access for Sfr4/8 for 30/60 minutes.

Things to See & Do

Worth the hill climb is the glorious Gothic **Cathedrale de Lausanne** (open 7am-7pm Mon-Fri, 8am-7pm Sat-Sun Apr-Sept; closes 5.30pm Oct-Mar), built in the 12th and 13th centuries. Highlights include the stunningly detailed carved portal, vaulted ceilings and archways, and carefully restored stained-glass windows.

Musée de l'Art Brut (☎ 021 647 54 35; w www.artbrut.ch; Ave de Bergiéres 11; adult/student Sfr6/4; open 11am-1pm & 2pm-6pm Tues-Fri, 11am-6pm Sat-Sun) is a fascinating amalgam of 15,000 works of art created by untrained artists – psychiatric patients, eccentrics and incarcerated criminals. Biographies and explanations are in English.

The Olympic movement is alive and well in Lausanne, home of the IOC headquarters. Sports aficionados can immerse themselves in archive footage, interactive computers and memorabilia at information-packed **Musée Olympique** (☎ 021 621 65 11; w www.olym pic.org; Quai d'Ouchy 1; adult/student/child Sfr14/9/7; open 9am-6pm Mon-Wed & Fri-Sun, 9am-8pm Thur May-Sept; closed Mon Oct-Apr).

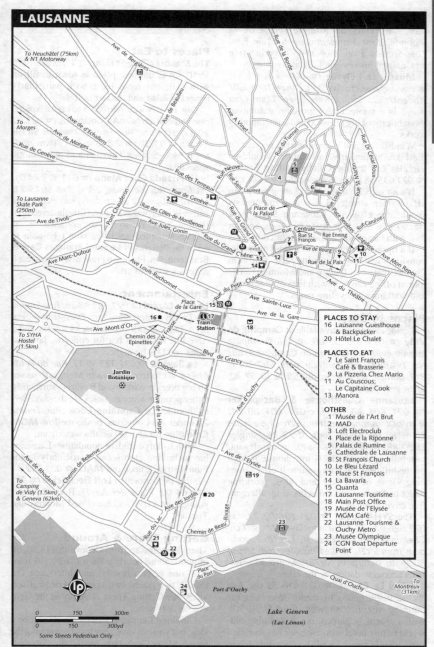

LAUSANNE

PLACES TO STAY
16 Lausanne Guesthouse & Backpacker
20 Hôtel Le Chalet

PLACES TO EAT
7 Le Saint François Café & Brasserie
9 La Pizzeria Chez Mario;
11 Au Couscous; Le Capitaine Cook
13 Manora

OTHER
1 Musée de l'Art Brut
2 MAD
3 Loft Electroclub
4 Place de la Riponne
5 Palais de Rumine
6 Cathédrale de Lausanne
8 St François Church
10 Le Bleu Lézard
12 Place St François
14 La Bavaria
15 Quanta
17 Lausanne Tourisme
18 Main Post Office
19 Musée de l'Elysée
21 MGM Café
22 Lausanne Tourisme & Ouchy Metro
23 Musée Olympique
24 CGN Boat Departure Point

To Neuchâtel (75km) & N1 Motorway
To Morges
To Lausanne Skate Park (250m)
To SYHA Hostel (1.5km)
To Camping de Vidy (1.5km) & Geneva (62km)
To Montreux (31km)

Ave de Bergières
Ave de Beaulieu
Ave A Vinet
Rue de la Borde
Rue du Tunnel
Rue Dr César Roux
Ave de Echallens
Ave de Morges
Rue de Genève
Rue des Terreaux
Rue Neuve
Rue Saint-Laurent
Rue de Genève
Place de la Palud
Rue Louis Curtat
Rue St Martin
Rue Bessières
Rue Caroline
Rue Langallerie
Ave de Tivoli
Ave Jules Gonin
Rue des Côtes-de-Montbenon
Port Chauderon
Ave de Beaulieu
Rue du Grand Pont
Rue Centrale
Rue St François
Rue Enning
Ave Marc-Dufour
Ave Louis-Ruchonnet
Ave du Grand Chêne
Rue de Bourg
Rue de la Paix
Ave Mon Repos
Ave du Théâtre
Place de la Gare
Rue du Petit-Chêne
Ave Sainte-Luce
Ave de la Gare
Ave Mont d'Or
Chemin des Epinettes
Ave W Fraisse
Blvd de Grancy
Jardin Botanique
Ave Dapples
Ave d'Ouchy
Ave de la Harpe
Ave de l'Elysée
Ave de Rhodanie
Chemin de Bellerive
Ave des Jordils
Ave du Lac
Chemin de Beau-Rivage
Place du Port
Port d'Ouchy
Quai d'Ouchy
Lake Geneva (Lac Léman)

Train Station

0   150   300m
0   150   300yd

Some Streets Pedestrian Only

For a range of museum subjects under one roof, the **Palais de Rumine** (Place de la Riponne 6; most museums open 11am-5pm Tues-Sun) is a one-stop shop covering fine arts, natural history, geology and zoology.

Musée de l'Elysée (☎ 021 316 99 11; w www.elysee.ch; Ave de L'Elysée 18; adult/ student/child Sfr8/4/free; open 11am-6pm daily) is a photography museum exhibiting thought-provoking classical and contemporary works.

Windsurfing and waterskiing are popular on the lake, particularly in summer. Would-be yachties can try the **Ouchy Sailing School** (☎ 021 635 58 87; w www.ecole-de-voile.ch).

It's no surprise that inline skating has taken off in steep-streeted Lausanne. Enthusiasts should check out the **Lausanne Skate Park** (☎ 021 626 37 93; w www.fievre.ch; Sévelin 36), with large indoor and outdoor courses.

If a tipple (not a topple) is more your style, consider walking the **vineyard trails** in Lavaux, between Ouchy and Montreux. The tourist office can help with lists of vineyards, and walking and cycling maps.

Places to Stay

Lakeside camping is available at **Camping de Vidy** (☎ 021 622 50 00; e info@camping lausannevidy.ch; Chemin du Camping 3; bus No 1; adult/child/tent/car park Sfr7.70/5/ 8/3, bungalows 2/4 persons Sfr55.30/87.30; open year-round).

Lausanne Guesthouse & Backpacker (☎ 021 601 80 00, fax 021 601 80 01; e info@lausanne-guesthouse.ch; Chemin des Epinettes 4; dorm beds Sfr29-34, singles Sfr80-88, doubles Sfr86-98), in an elegant, tastefully renovated 1894 townhouse, is high on the hill near the train station. It offers stunning views of the lake and Alps, sparkling white bathrooms and a nonsmoking, allergenfree environment.

The **SYHA hostel** (☎ 021 626 02 22, fax 021 626 02 26; e lausanne@youthhostel.ch; Chemin du Bois-de-Vaux 36; bus No 2; dorm beds from Sfr28, singles/doubles from Sfr53/ 80, with bathroom Sfr78/94) provides nofrills accommodation by the lake.

Hôtel Le Chalet (☎ 021 616 52 06; Ave d'Ouchy 49; metro to Jordils stop; singles/ doubles with hall showers from Sfr50/90), with a charming garden, is a welcoming oldworld family hotel whose owner has an infectious joie de vivre. Swedish playwright Johan

August Strindberg lived here in the late 19th century.

Places to Eat

The **Manora** (Place St François 17; meals from Sfr10.40) is the best place in town to fill up with delicious fresh food, with particularly tempting salad and dessert buffets.

Dig into North African sausages, spiced rice and couscous at **Au Couscous** (☎ 021 22 20 17; 1st floor, Rue Enning 2; meals Sfr19-34; open 11.30am-2.30pm & 6.30pm-midnight Mon-Sun), a Tunisian and macrobiotic specialist.

La Pizzeria Chez Mario (☎ 021 323 74 01; 1st floor, Rue de Bourg 28; dishes Sfr13-21; open 11.30am-12.30am daily) serves up pasta and delicious pizzas in a graffiti-plastered den. Follow the scrawl to find the entrance.

Sweet-toothed aesthetes won't be able to resist the delights of **Le Saint François Café & Brasserie**, on Place St-François, where each cake is a work of art.

Entertainment

Le Bleu Lézard (☎ 021 321 38 35; Rue Enning 10; La Cave open 8pm-1am Tues-Thur & Sun, 8pm-3am Fri-Sat) offers snacks by day and a cave-like basement bar for concerts, jam sessions and DJs by night.

La Bavaria (☎ 021 323 39 13; Rue du Petit-Chêne 10; open 8am-1am Mon-Sat) serves up big beers in dark-wood Bavarian surrounds. Other popular watering holes are the shoulder-to-shoulder **Le Capitaine Cook** (Rue Enning 2), under Au Couscous; or the mellow **MGM Café** (Rue du Lac 14) on the waterfront.

With its large student population, Lausanne has a thriving club scene, particularly in the Flon district. Check out **MAD** (☎ 021 312 11 22; Rue de Genéve) or **Loft Electroclub** (☎ 021 311 64 00; Place Bel Air 1). Both clubs get going from 11pm and are closed Monday and Tuesday.

Getting There & Around

There are trains to/from Geneva (Sfr18.80, 50 minutes, three hourly), Bern (Sfr30, 70 minutes, one or two hourly) and Interlaken Ost (Sfr52, two hours, two hourly). For boat services, see Getting There & Away in the Geneva section earlier.

Climbing Lausanne's steep streets can be a slog, but you can save your legs by catching the metro. Many locals buzz around on mopeds.

MONTREUX
pop 22,300

Centrepiece of the 'Swiss Riviera', Montreux is an affluent lakeside town with stunning views of the French Alps, excellent lakeside walks and the ever-popular Château de Chillon.

The **train station** and **main post office** are on Ave des Alpes, with the town centre to the left (south). The **tourist office** (☎ 021 962 84 36; e tourism@montreuxtourism.ch; open 9am-12.30pm & 1.30pm-6pm Mon-Fri, 10am-2pm Sat-Sun) is in the pavilion on the lakeshore (descend the stairs or lift opposite the post office).

Things to See & Do

The **Château de Chillon** (☎ 021 966 89 10; w www.chillon.ch; adult/student/child Sfr8.50/6.50/4; open 9am-7pm daily Apr-Sept, 9.30am-5pm Mar & Oct, 10am-4pm Jan-Feb & Nov-Dec) deservedly receives more visitors than any other historical building in Switzerland. The fortress was originally constructed on the shores of Lake Geneva in the 11th century, and caught the public imagination when Lord Byron wrote *The Prisoner of Chillon* about Bonivard, a prior chained in the dungeons for almost four years in the 16th century.

You can easily spend a couple of hours touring the tower, courtyards, dungeons and staterooms containing weapons, frescoes and furniture.

The castle is a pleasant 45-minute walk along the lakefront from Montreux. It's accessible by local train (Sfr2.60; Veytaux-Chillon stop) or bus No 1 (Sfr2.60; Veytaux stop).

Montreux's idyllic location has attracted writers, musicians and artists for hundreds of years. To learn more about such icons as Noel Coward, Vladimir Nabokov and Charlie Chaplin and their local connections, ask for the **Hemingway Trail** walking tour map from the tourist office. Or take the **Poet's Ramble** along the shoreline from Vevey to Montreux, featuring a series of 'speaking benches' which quote famous texts in several languages.

Montreux also has many famous music links. You may already know it as the subject of Deep Purple's famous *Smoke on the Water*. Queen's Freddy Mercury was a regular visitor, recording most of his music here (see the statue on the waterfront). And then there's the annual **Jazz Festival** (☎ 021 963

82 82; w www.montreuxjazz.com), which transforms the town every July. Visit the website for a full programme.

Places to Stay

The modern **SYHA hostel** (☎ 021 963 49 34, fax 021 963 27 29; Passage de l'Auberge 8, Territet; bus No 1; dorm beds Sfr30, doubles without/with bathroom Sfr76/84; open mid-Feb–mid-Nov), a 30-minute walk from the centre, is on the waterfront just 15 minutes from Château de Chillon.

Hotel Wilhelm (☎ 021 963 14 31, fax 021 963 32 85; e hotel.wilhelm@span.ch; Rue de Marché 13-15; singles/doubles Sfr60/100, with bathroom Sfr70/120) is a traditional family-run hotel a few paces from the train station.

Hostellerie du Lac (☎ 021 963 32 71, fax 021 963 18 35; Rue du Quai 12; singles Sfr50-140, doubles Sfr150; open Mar-Nov) has a faded grandeur and a prime lakeside position. Rooms vary dramatically in price, style and facilities – some even have lakeside balconies.

If you can't secure a lakeside spot, try **Hotel Elite** (☎ 021 966 03 03; Ave du Casino 25; singles/doubles with breakfast from Sfr70/130), a small, quiet alternative with friendly staff and spacious renovated rooms.

Places to Eat

Paradise (☎ 021 963 19 35; Grand-Rue 58; meals from Sfr8; open 7am-1am Tues-Thur, 7am-2am Fri-Sat) has a sprawling salad buffet with 40 dishes (Sfr2.80 per 100g) and flavoursome kebabs and souvlakis.

Delicious buttery perch fillets are a highlight at the **Hostellerie du Lac restaurant** (mains Sfr31; open 11.30am-9.30pm Wed-Mon). Its large, open terrace which overlooks the lakeside promenade is just perfect for people-watching.

For pizza and pasta, try the wood-panelled **Brasserie des Alpes** (☎ 021 963 21 20; Ave des Alpes 23; pizzas Sfr14-22). Coffee lovers can get a caffeine fix at **Mokaccino**, a busy café in the Forum shopping centre on Ave du Casino. In the same centre is **piMi**, the fast-food section of Migros supermarket, with good-value croissants and baguettes.

Getting There & Away

There are trains to/from Geneva (Sfr26, 70 minutes, hourly) and Lausanne (Sfr9.80, 25 minutes, three hourly). Make the scenic journey to Interlaken via the **GoldenPass Panoramic**, with changeovers at Zweisimmen and Spiez (Sfr54, rail passes valid, three hours).

The track winds its way up the hill for excellent views over Lake Geneva. For boat services, see the Geneva Getting There & Away section earlier.

VEVEY
pop 15,400

Another popular pitstop on the Swiss Riviera is Vevey, a few kilometres west of Montreux. Its sprawling square on the waterfront becomes a bustling **marketplace** on summer Saturdays, with traditionally dressed merchants selling local handicrafts and wines.

For overnight stays, try the independent hostel **Yoba Riviera Lodge** (☎ *021 923 80 40, fax 021 923 80 41;* e *info@rivieralodge .ch; Place du Marché; dorm beds Sfr24-29, doubles Sfr80),* in a 19th-century townhouse near the waterfront.

Some of the best budget eating in town is at the **Manora**, opposite the train station, or the **Migros restaurant** on Rue de Lausanne.

Sip on a coffee or beer at **Charly's Bar** (☎ *021 921 50 06; Rue du Lac 45; open 8am-1.30am Mon-Thur, 8am-2.30am Fri-Sat, 10am-midnight Sun),* which is a busy glass-fronted place with fantastic views.

VAUD ALPS

To get off the beaten track and enjoy the Alpine experience, consider staying in quiet, untouristed **Gryon** (1130m), southeast of Montreux. It's close to the ski fields of Villars and 30 minutes by train from Bex (on the Lausanne–Sion rail route).

The popular **Swiss Alp Retreat** (☎ *024 498 33 21, fax 024 498 35 31;* e *info@gryon.com; dorm beds/doubles from Sfr18/50)* is a homely wooden chalet with kitchen, sundeck and log fire. Phone ahead for check-in.

Another tranquil Alpine spot, **Leysin** attracts skiiers, snowboarders, hikers and meditators. It is accessible from Aigle on the Lausanne-Sion route.

For an overnight stay, head to the **Hiking Sheep** (☎/*fax 024 494 35 35;* e *hiking sheep@leysin.net; dorm beds/doubles from Sfr23/60).* This 19th-century guesthouse provides breathtaking views, combined with a pine-forested back yard and a friendly laid-back atmosphere.

Valais

The dramatic Alpine scenery of Valais (Wallis in German) once made it one of the most inaccessible regions of Switzerland. Today, the mountains and valleys have been opened up for keen skiers and hikers by an efficient network of roads, railways and cable cars. It's an area of extraordinary natural beauty and, naturally enough, each impressive panorama has spawned its own resort.

Valais villages are also well known for the bizarre cow fights waged to determine the best beast to lead the herd to summer pastures. Far from a blood sport, the bovine battles merely leave the beasts exhausted. The unfortunate winner is rewarded with an enormous bell to lug around. Fights are held on selected Sundays from late March to October; for an up-to-date programme, see the Valais Tourism website (w www.matterhornstate.com).

SION
pop 27,500

With two ancient fortifications that dominate the town, the capital of the Lower Valais is worth a stop en route from Montreux to Zermatt. **Château de Tourbillon** and the 11th-century church **Basilique de Valère** sit atop twin hills and offer excellent views of the Rhône Valley below. Several Valais regional museums are also based in the town. Overnighters will find basic four-bed dorms at the modern **SYHA hostel** (☎ *027 323 74 70, fax 027 323 74 38; Rue de l'Industrie 2; dorm beds from Sfr28),* behind the station.

ZERMATT
pop 5340

This skiing, mountaineering and hiking mecca bathes in the reflected glory of the most famous peak in the Alps, the Matterhorn (4478m). The town is small and easy to navigate, and it's car-free except for tiny electric taxis and vans that whisk guests around the streets. The main street is Bahnhofstrasse, but street names are rarely used.

Zermatt Tourismus (☎/*fax 027 966 81 00;* e *zermatt@wallis.ch; open 8.30am-noon & 1.30pm-6pm Mon-Fri, 8.30am-noon Sat)* is beside the train station. During high season it's also open Saturday afternoon and Sunday. Next door is **Zermatt Tour**, a travel agency that also changes money.

Alpin Center (☎ 027 966 24 60; open 8am-11.30am & 4pm-6.30pm daily), on Bahnhofstrasse near the post office, is a one-stop shop for all adventure needs, whether it be ski passes, heli-skiing, mountain guiding or snowboard lessons.

Activities

Zermatt is arguably the country's best ski resort, with many demanding slopes to test the experienced skier and panoramic views at every turn (beginners have fewer possibilities). February to April is peak time, but high-altitude ski fields make **skiing** possible right through summer. Stunning vistas of Monte Rosa and the Matterhorn can be seen from the network of cable cars and gondolas.

The cog-wheel railway to **Gornergrat** (3090m; Sfr63 return; departures every 20 minutes) is a particular highlight. Topped by the highest cable station in Europe (3820m), the Klein Matterhorn provides access to summer skiing slopes, as well as the ski route down to Cervinia in Italy (don't forget your passport). A day pass for all ski lifts, excluding Cervinia, costs Sfr64. Ski shops open daily for rental – for one day, hire prices are Sfr28 for skis and stocks and Sfr15 for boots.

Of course, in summer, Zermatt becomes a hub for **hikers**, attracted by 400km of trails through high-Alpine scenery with views of Europe's highest mountains.

A walk in the **cemetery** is a sobering experience for any would-be mountaineers, with many monuments and gravestones commemorating deaths on Monte Rosa and the Matterhorn. The **Hinter Dorf**, just north of the church, is another interesting part of town. Here, the touristy chalets make way for traditional Valais wooden huts.

Places to Stay & Eat

Tourism is big business in Zermatt, and holiday chalets and apartments dominate the town. The tourist office can help with a full list. Be warned that many hotels and restaurants close between seasons.

The **SYHA hostel** (☎ 027 967 23 20, fax 027 967 53 06; e zermatt@youthhostel.ch; dorm beds with half-board from Sfr48; closed mid-Apr–June), a 20-minute walk from the station, is a five-storey chalet high on the hill with excellent views of the Matterhorn.

Matterhorn Hostel (☎ 027 968 19 19, fax 027 968 1915; w www.matterhornhostel.com; Schluhmattstrasse 32; dorm beds Sfr29, doubles Sfr78; open year-round), a short walk from the station, is the independent option, with Internet access (Sfr2 for 10 minutes), its own restaurant and après-ski bar.

Directly opposite the station is **Hotel Bahnhof** (☎ 027 967 24 06, fax 027 967 72 16; e welcome@hotelbahnhof.com; dorm beds Sfr30, singles/doubles Sfr56/86, with shower Sfr68/96), with an impressive industrial-size kitchen, ski storage room in the basement, large dorms, and twins with balconies facing the Matterhorn.

Squeezed between old mountain huts on cobblestoned streets, **Hotel Gabelhorn** (☎ 027 967 22 35; singles/doubles from Sfr40/80; closed May, Jun & Oct), in the Hinter Dorf area, is a traditional family-run pension. It's full of character but a little cramped.

A favourite hang-out for resort workers is the **Brown Cow** (Hotel de la Poste; ☎ 027 967 19 32; snacks Sfr6-14; open 9am-1.30am daily), with great music, hearty food and cowhide decor. Don't miss the monster vegie burger with chunky chips for Sfr10.50. Within the same complex underneath the Hotel de la Poste is the **Old Spaghetti Factory** (open 7pm-11pm daily) and **Broken's Pizza Factory** (open 7pm-1.30am).

For Valais specialities, there's **Walliserkanne** (☎ 027 966 46 10; Bahnhofstrasse; meals from Sfr15), by the post office. Or fill up with raclette and rosti at **Restaurant Weisshorn** (meals Sfr12.50-30) and **Café du Pont** (meals Sfr11-22), which sit side by side beyond the church on Bahnhofstrasse.

Head to the **North Wall Bar** (☎ 027 967 28 63; open 6.30pm-12.30am daily) for cheap beer, inspirational ski videos and 'the best pizza in town' (from Sfr12). Or catch the latest Hollywood blockbuster at **Vernissage Cultural Centre** (☎ 027 967 66 36; Hofmattstrasse 4; open 5pm-2am), with a cinema, bar and nightclub just off the main drag.

Getting There & Away

Hourly trains depart from Brig, calling at Visp en route, a steep, scenic journey (Sfr35/69 one way/return, 80 minutes). Swiss Passes are valid and Inter-Rail passes give 50% off for those under 26. The only way out is to backtrack, but if you're going to Saas Fee you can divert there from Stalden-Saas. The popular scenic Glacier Express travels to/from St Moritz from Zermatt (see the St

Moritz Getting There & Away section later in this chapter for details).

As Zermatt is car-free, you need to park cars at Täsch (Sfr4.50 to Sfr12 per day) and take the train from there (Sfr7.40). Parking is free near Visp station if you take the Zermatt train.

OTHER RESORTS

Saas Fee, the self-styled 'Pearl of the Alps', is in the valley adjoining its more famous neighbour, Zermatt, ringed by 4000m peaks. It has summer skiing and the highest metro in the world to **Mittelallalin** (3500m), where there's an **ice pavilion** (admission Sfr7) and fabulous views. Summer hikers have access to 280km of marked **trails**. The **tourist office** (☎ 027 958 18 68; e to@saas-fee.ch/), opposite the bus station, can help with hiking maps and accommodation options. Car-free Saas Fee cannot be reached by train. Buses depart from Brig via Visp (Sfr17.20, one hour, hourly). Travelling to/from Zermatt, you must transfer at Stalden-Saas. There are car parks at the village entrance.

Other popular ski resorts include **Verbier**, in west Valais, with 400km of ski runs (ski passes Sfr51 per day); and the lesser-known **Leukerbad**, west of Brig (Sfr43 per day), which also boasts Europe's largest alpine **thermal baths**.

Ticino

South of the Alps, Ticino (Tessin in German) enjoys a Mediterranean climate and an unmistakable Italian flavour. Indeed, it belonged to Italy until the Swiss Confederation seized it in 1512.

Cuisine, architecture and plantlife mirrors that of its southern neighbour, and Italian is the official language of the canton. Many people also speak French and German, but English is less widely spoken.

The region also boasts spectacular Swiss scenery, with dramatic gorges in the north and languid, lakeside towns in the south. Free open-air music festivals include Bellinzona's Piazza Blues (late June), and Lugano's Estival Jazz (early July) and Blues to Bop Festival (late August).

BELLINZONA
pop 16,700

Ticino's capital is a city of castles situated in a valley at the southern side of the San

Bernardino and St Gotthard Alpine Passes. World Heritage-listed in 2000, Bellinzona's imposing battlements and towers at one time played a significant role in fortifiying the region and still dominate the town today. You can roam the ramparts of the two larger castles, **Castelgrande** or **Castello di Montebello**, and visit the **museums** (admission Sfr4 each; open Tues-Sun), however, there's limited English translation. The smallest castle, set high on the hill, is **Castello di Sasso Corbaro**.

The **tourist office** (☎ 091 825 21 31, fax 825 38 17; e bellinzona.turismo@bluewin.ch; Viale Stazione 18; open 9am-6.30pm Mon-Fri, 9am-noon Sat), in the post office, can provide information on Bellinzona and the whole canton.

Places to Stay & Eat

The **SYHA hostel** (☎ 091 825 15 22; e bellinzona@youthhostel.ch; Via Nocca 4; dorm beds from Sfr35, singles/doubles Sfr50/90) shares the grand old Villa Montebello with a private school and a catering company (which supplies the inclusive buffet breakfast). At the foot of the Montebello Castle, it's a 10-minute walk from the station.

For budget rooms closer to the station, there's **Garni Moderno** (☎/fax 091 825 13 76; Viale Stazione 17b; singles/doubles Sfr55/90, doubles with bath Sfr120), part of Caffé della Posta (closed Sunday).

Ristorante Corona (☎ 091 825 28 44; Via Camminata 5; pizzas Sfr11-17; open 7am-midnight Mon, 7am-1am Tues-Sat) serves enormous thin-crust pizzas in the friendly front pub area. For fancier fare, there's a formal restaurant behind.

As usual, the best budget eats can be found in **Manora** (Manor department store, Viale Stazione); there's also a good self-service restaurant at the **Coop** (Via H Guisan).

Getting There & Away

Bellinzona is on the train route connecting Locarno (Sfr7.20, 25 minutes) and Lugano (Sfr11.40, 30 minutes).

It's also on the Zürich-Milan route. Postbuses head northeast to Chur; please note that you will need to reserve your postbus seat the day before on ☎ 091 825 77 55, or at the train station.

There is a scenic cycling track along the Ticino River to Lake Maggiore and Locarno.

LOCARNO
pop 14,600

Locarno, at the northern end of Lake Maggiore, has a quaint old town with Italianate townhouses, piazzas and arcades, and a laid-back summer-resort atmosphere.

Piazza Grande is the centre of town and the location of the **main post office**. In the nearby casino complex is the **tourist office** (☎ 091 751 03 33, fax 091 751 90 70; e locarno@ ticino.com; open 9am-6pm Mon-Fri, 10am-5pm Sat, 10am-noon & 1pm-3pm Sun). It stocks brochures on many parts of Switzerland.

A five-minute walk east is the train station, where there's an **Aperto supermarket**, **money exchange** and **bike rental**. You can gulp down shots and smoke Cuban cigars while checking your email at the Latino-style **Pardo Bar** (☎ 091 752 21 23; Via della Motta 3; Sfr4 for 20min; open 11am-1am Mon-Sat, 4pm-1am Sun). On Piazza Imbarcadero, near the waterfront, the Visitors Center offers Internet access at the **Cyberbox** and charges Sfr2/5 for 10/30 minutes.

Things to See & Do

Don't miss the formidable **Madonna del Sasso**, up on the hill with panoramic views of the lake and town. The sanctuary was built after the Virgin Mary appeared in a vision in 1480. It features a church with 15th-century paintings, a small museum and several distinctive statues. There is a funicular from the town centre, but the 20-minute climb is not demanding (take Via al Sasso off Via Cappuccini) and you pass some shrines on the way.

In the old town, there are a couple of churches worth visiting, including the 17th-century **Chiesa Nuova** (Via Cittadella), with an ornate ceiling and frolicking angels.

Locarno has more hours of sunshine than anywhere else in Switzerland, perfect for strolls and bike rides around the lake. **Giardini Jean Arp** is a small lakeside park off Lungolago Motta, where sculptures by the surrealist artist are scattered among palm trees and springtime tulips.

In August, over 150,000 film buffs hit town for the **Locarno International Film Festival**, with a huge open-air screen in Piazza Grande. For more information see w www.pardo.ch.

Places to Stay

Delta Camping (☎ 091 751 60 81; camp sites low/high season Sfr21/47, plus Sfr11/18 per person; open Mar-Oct) is family friendly but pricey. There are plenty of cheaper options on Lake Maggiore outside Locarno; ask the tourist office for the Camping Ticino brochure.

The **SYHA hostel** (☎ 091 756 15 00, fax 091 756 15 01; e locarno@youthhostel.ch; Via Varenna 18; dorm beds/doubles Sfr32/72), 500m west of Piazza Grande, is in the charmless Palagiovani (Palace of Youth), which also houses a radio station, music school and youth bureau.

The staff are all smiles at **Pensione Città Vecchia** (☎/fax 091 751 45 54; e cittavecc hia@datacomm.ch; Via Toretta 13; dorm beds Sfr28-35, singles/doubles Sfr37/74; open Mar-Nov), a nonsmoking hostel with basic dorms (breakfast included). It's uphill from Piazza Grande via a lane next to the Manor department store.

Convenient to the station and lake is clean, clinical **Garni Montaldi** (☎ 091 743 02 22, fax 091 743 54 06; Piazza Stazione; singles/ doubles Sfr58/110, with shower from Sfr60/ 120). Rates include continental breakfast; ask for deals out of season. The reception is also here for **Stazione** (singles/doubles from Sfr44/ 88; open Apr-Oct), an older building to the rear with spacious, rudimentary rooms.

Places to Eat

Manora (Via Stazione 1; meals from Sfr6.90; open 7.30am-9pm Mon-Sat, 8am-9pm Sun), by the train station, has excellent self-service hot meals and salad plates.

Lungolago (Lungolago Motta; pizza from Sfr12.50; open 7am-1am daily), a popular haunt for snackers and beer-guzzlers, is perfect for steamy summer evenings. The more sophisticated **Hotel Ristorante Zurigo** (☎ 091 743 16 17; Via Verbano 9; mains Sfr16-37; open 7am-11pm daily) has moreish Mediterranean meals and a lakeside outlook.

In the backblocks, **Ristorante Cittadella** (☎ 091 751 58 85; Via Cittadella 18; dishes Sfr35-50; open 8am-2pm & 5.30pm-midnight daily) has a ground-floor trattoria with pizzas and pastas, and an elegant upstairs eatery serving seafood.

On Piazza Grande there's a **Coop supermarket** and a **Migros De Gustibus** snack bar opposite.

Getting There & Away

The St Gotthard Pass provides the road link (N2) to central Switzerland. There are trains every one to two hours from Brig, passing through Italy en route (Sfr50, 2½ hours). You change trains at Domodóssola across the border, so take your passport.

One-day travel passes for boats on Lake Maggiore cost Sfr12 to Sfr21, depending on the coverage. For more information, contact **Navigazione Lago Maggiore** (NLM; ☎ 091 751 18 65). There is a regular boat and hydrofoil service from Italy (except in winter).

LUGANO
pop 25,900

Switzerland's southernmost tourist town is a sophisticated slice of Italian life, with colourful markets, upmarket shops, pedestrian-only piazzas and lakeside parks. Resting on the shore of Lake Lugano with Montes San Salvatore and Bré rising on either side, it's also a great base for lake trips, water sports and hillside hikes.

The train station has **money exchange**, **bike rental** and an **Aperto supermarket**, all open daily. The old town is a 10-minute walk down the hill to the east. On the lake side of the Municipio building is the **tourist office** (☎ 091 913 32 32, fax 091 922 76 53; e info@lugano -tourism.ch; Riva Albertolli; open 9am-6.30pm Mon-Fri, 9am-12.30pm & 1.30pm-5pm Sat, 10am-3pm Sun; closed weekends in winter). The **main post office** (Via della Posta 7) is in the centre of the old town. There are four stand-up Internet terminals (Sfr5 for 30 minutes) on the 3rd floor of the **Manor** department store (Piazza Dante).

Things to See & Do

Stroll through the winding alleyways of Lugano's old town and go window-shopping along the stylish arcade-lined **Via Nassa** (street of fishing nets).

At the end, pop into the **Santa Maria degli Angioli Church** (Piazza Luini), featuring a vivid 1529 fresco of the Crucifixion by Bernardino Luini.

There are many worthwhile museums in the waterfront town and the surrounding region. Art lovers can get their fix of 19th- and 20th-century works at the **Museo Cantonale d'Arte** (☎ 091 910 47 80; w www.museo-can tonale-arte.ch; Via Canova 10; adult/student Sfr7/5; open 2pm-5pm Tues, 10am-5pm Wed-Sun), with examples by Renoir, Hodler and Klee. The café set can pay homage at the **Coffee Museum** in Balerna or the **Alpenrose**

Chocolate Museum in Caslano. Ask the tourist office for a full museum list.

Waterbabies will love the **Lido** (adult/child Sfr6/4; open 9am-7pm May-Sept), east of the Cassarate River, with a swimming pool and sandy beaches.

Take a **boat trip** to one of the many photogenic villages hugging the shoreline of Lake Lugano. One of the most popular is car-free **Gandria**, a tiny hillside village with historic homes and shops and narrow winding alleyways right down to the water. If you hit town at mealtimes you can tuck into a traditional Ticinese dish in one of the many **grotti**. You can also see how the smugglers plied their trade at the **Swiss Customs Museum** (☎ 091 910 48 11; admission free; open 1.30pm-5.30pm daily Apr-mid-Oct), across the water.

Swissminiatur (adult/child Sfr12/7, including boat trip Sfr27.80/14.40; open 9am-6pm daily mid-Mar-Oct), in Melide, is a kitschy display of 1:25 scale models of national attractions. You can get there by bus, train or boat.

There are excellent hikes and views from **Monte San Salvatore** and **Monte Bré**. The **funicular** (one-way/return ticket Sfr12/18) from Paradiso up Monte San Salvatore operates from mid-March to mid-November. To ascend Monte Bré, take the year-round **funicular** (one-way/return Sfr13/19) from Cassarate. The tourist office can help with hiking information.

If you've got some spare francs, you can pick up bargain Prada and Versace at **Foxtown** (Via A Maspoli; w www.foxtown.ch; open 11am-7pm daily), an enormous, discount, factory-outlet complex 15km south of Lugano.

Places to Stay

An excellent budget option close to the station is **Hotel Montarina** (☎ 091 966 72 72, fax 091 966 00 17; e info@montarina.ch; Via Montarina 1; dorm beds Sfr25, sheets Sfr4 for whole stay, singles/doubles Sfr70/100, with bathroom Sfr80/120; open mid-Mar-Oct). This lovingly renovated 19th-century villa is heaven in summer, with a swimming pool, large dorms and a garden with palm trees.

The **SYHA hostel** (☎ 091 966 27 28, fax 091 968 23 63; Via Cantonale 13; dorm beds/doubles Sfr31/72; open mid-Mar-Nov) is a hard 20-minute walk uphill from the train station (signposted), or take bus No 5 to Crocifisso. Breakfast is included and you can cool off in the swimming pool.

Closer to the old town is **Albergo Ristorante Pestalozzi** (☎ 091 921 46 46, fax 091 922 20 45; e pestalo@bluewin.ch; Piazza Indipendenza 9; singles/doubles Sfr60/100, with bathroom from Sfr92/144), an inviting Art Nouveau hotel with a variety of renovated rooms.

In Paradiso, near the foot of Monte San Salvatore, there's the homely **Hotel Dischma** (☎ 091 994 21 31, fax 091 994 15 03; e dischma@swissonline.ch; Vicolo Geretta 6; bus No 1; singles/doubles from Sfr60/106).

Places to Eat

Head to the pedestrian-only **piazzas** to tempt the tastebuds, with panini (Sfr5) and gelati (Sfr3) from street stalls, or larger meals in the pizzerias and cafés spilling on to the streets.

You can produce your own pizzettes at the sprawling **Manora** (meals from Sfr8.90; open 7.30am-10pm Mon-Sat & 10am-10pm Sun), with a wide range of self-service food. It's up the stairs on the northern side of Piazza Cioccaro.

On the southern side is **Sayonara** (☎ 091 922 01 70; Via Soave 10; pasta from Sfr10, pizza Sfr15.50-20.50; open 6.30am-midnight daily), with delicious Italian cuisine and a good wine list (try the Ticinese white Merlot).

Panino Gusto (☎ 091 922 51 51; Via Motta 7a; panini Sfr9-19; open 11am-7pm Mon-Wed, 11am-midnight Thur-Sat) offers panini with smoked meats, salmon and cheeses.

Ristorante Pestalozzi (see Places to Stay earlier in the Lugano section; meals from Sfr11; open 11am-9.30pm daily) has a changing daily menu with plenty of vegie options in a large alcohol-free dining room.

The critically acclaimed **La Tinéra** (Via dei Gorini; dishes Sfr11-27; open 8.30am-3pm & 5.30pm-11pm Mon-Sat), off Piazza della Riforma, is a tiny cellar restaurant serving local specialities to a jam-packed crowd.

For drinks, pitta bread and tapas amid tropical decor, try **Ethnic** (Quartiere Maghetti; tapas Sfr4-8, meals Sfr8-18; open 6pm-midnight Mon-Sat). Self-caterers can stock up at the large **Migros** (Via Pretorio) opposite Via Emilio Bossi.

Getting There & Away

Lugano is on the same road and rail route as Bellinzona. Two postbuses run to St Moritz daily in summer, cut back to one during winter (and only on Friday, Saturday and Sunday

during some weeks). It costs Sfr50 (plus Sfr12 reservation fee) and takes 4½ hours. Reserve your seat the day before at the **bus station** or the **train information office**, or by phoning ☎ 091 807 85 20. Buses leave from the bus station on Via Serafino Balestra, though the St Moritz bus also calls at the train station. A three-/seven-day regional holiday pass costs Sfr72/92 and is valid for all regional public transport, including funiculars and boats on Lake Lugano.

Graubünden

Graubünden (Grisons, Grigioni, Grishun) is the largest Swiss canton and it has some of the most developed winter sports centres in the world, including Arosa, Davos, Klosters, Flims and, of course, famous St Moritz. Away from the international resorts, Graubünden is a relatively unspoiled region of rural villages, alpine lakes and hill-top castles. Dazzling scenery and outdoor pursuits are the region's main attractions, and tourism is one of its biggest money-spinners. In the north, the locals speak German, in the south Italian, and in between mostly Romansch.

CHUR
pop 31,800

Chur, the canton's capital and largest town, is also one of the oldest settlements in Switzerland, tracing its history back some 3000 years. Today it serves as a gateway for the region. For a town map and accommodation options see the **tourist office** (☎ 081 252 18 18; Grabenstrasse 5; open 1.30pm-6pm Mon, 8.30am-noon & 1.30pm-6pm Tues-Fri, 9am-noon Sat). For information on the canton, try the **regional tourist office** (☎ 081 254 24 24; e contact@graubuenden.ch; Alexanderstrasse 24; open 8am-6pm Mon-Fri).

The old town features 16th-century buildings, fountains and alleyways. Worth a visit are the 1491 **Church of St Martin**, with stained-glass windows created by Augusto Giacometti, and the imposing **cathedral**, dating from 1150. The **Kunstmuseum** (Postplatz; adult/student Sfr10/7; open 10am-noon & 2pm-5pm Tues-Wed & Fri-Sun, 10am-noon & 2pm-8pm Thur) has a collection of artwork by the three Giacomettis (Alberto, Augusto and Giovanni), and exhibits by local sci-fi artist HR Giger (of Alien fame).

Chur is only 90 minutes by fast train from Zürich (Sfr35) and two hours from St Moritz (Sfr38). It's on the *Glacier Express* route (see the St Moritz Getting There & Away section later), and there are also rail connections to Davos, Klosters, Arosa, and Sargans (Sfr9.80, 25 minutes), the station for Liechtenstein.

ST MORITZ
pop 5600

St Moritz has built its reputation as the playground of the international jet set for more than a century, but the curative properties of its waters have been known for 3000 years. The plush main town, St Moritz Dorf, lounges on the slopes overlooking Lake St Moritz. In winter, superb skifields are the main drawcard; in summer, visitors come for the hiking, windsurfing, 'kitesurfing' and inline skating.

Orientation & Information

Hilly St Moritz Dorf is above the train station, with luxury hotels, restaurants and shops. To the southwest, 2km around the lake, lies the more downmarket St Moritz Bad; buses run between the two. St Moritz is seasonal and becomes a ghost town during November and late April to early June.

The **train station** near the lake rents out bikes in summer and changes money from 6.50am to 8.10pm daily. Up the hill on Via Serlas is the **post office** and five minutes further on is the **tourist office** (☎ 081 837 33 33, fax 081 837 33 77; e information@stmoritz.ch; Via Maistra 12; open 9am-6pm Mon-Sat, 4pm-6pm Sun high season; 9am-noon & 2pm-6pm Mon-Fri, 9am-noon Sat low season), with friendly, helpful staff.

You can check your favourite websites at **Bobby's Pub** (☎ 081 834 42 83; Via dal Bagn 50a; open 9am-1.30am Mon-Sat, 2pm-1.30am Sun) which charges Sfr2 for 10 minutes of Net access.

Activities

There are 350km of **downhill runs** around St Moritz, although the choice for beginners is limited. A one-day ski pass costs Sfr63, and ski and boot rental is about Sfr43 per day. There are also 160km of **cross-country trails** (equipment rental Sfr20) and 120km of marked **hiking paths**.

Sporting activities abound both in winter and summer. You can try golf (including on the frozen lake in winter), tennis, inline skating,

fishing, horse riding, sailing, windsurfing and river rafting, to mention a few. The tourist office has a list of prices and contacts. People-watching in St Moritz is another great sport and it's fun and free. If a touch of rest and recovery is on the agenda, try a health treatment in the spa (W www.stmoritz-spa.ch).

Places to Stay & Eat

The **Olympiaschanze camping ground** (☎ 081 833 40 90; camp site per adult/tent Sfr8/6.30; open late May-late Sept) is 1km southwest of St Moritz Bad.

Naturally, cheaper digs are found in the 'Bad' part of town. Backing on to forest and the cross-country ski course is the **SYHA hostel** (☎ 081 833 39 69, fax 081 833 80 46; Via Surpunt 60; W www.youthhostel.ch/st.moritz; dorm beds with half-board Sfr45.50, doubles without/with bathroom Sfr117/140), a large, modern, ochre-coloured centre with excellent facilities. There's mountain bike rental, compulsory half-board, a ski room and Internet access (Sfr4 for 15 minutes).

If the hostel is full, head next door to the **Hotel Stille** (☎ 081 833 69 48, fax 081 833 07 08; e hotel.stille@bluewin.ch; singles/twins Sfr57/114 in summer, Sfr72/144 in winter), which attracts a young, sporty crowd. Breakfast is included and dinner is available in winter for Sfr19.

You'll get basic budget rooms in a convenient lakeside location at **Bellaval** (☎ 081 833 32 45, fax 081 833 04 06; e hotel-bellaval@bluewin.ch; Via Grevas 55; singles/doubles from Sfr55/110, with bathroom from Sfr80/140). Prices include breakfast.

The pretty, peach-coloured **Hotel Languard Garni** (☎ 081 833 31 37, fax 081 833 45 46; e languard@bluewin.ch; Via Veglia 14; singles/doubles from Sfr105/190) is a three-star, family hotel in St Moritz Dorf overlooking the lake. It's worth paying Sfr20 extra for a room with a view.

Heading into St Moritz Bad, there's a clutch of good-value pizzerias and Italian restaurants, including **La Fontana** (☎ 081 833 12 66; Via dal Bagn 16; mains Sfr12-28; open 9am-10.30pm Mon-Sat), a cosy rustic restaurant with candles; and **Pizzeria La Botte** (☎ 081 833 39 88; Via dal Bagn 15; mains Sfr16-24; open 11am-2pm & 4pm-1am daily), with rich, buttery Italian dishes. Next to La Fontana, there also is a **Coop supermarket** for self-caterers.

Getting There & Away

The *Glacier Express* plies one of Switzerland's most famous scenic train routes, connecting St Moritz to Zermatt via the 2033m Oberalp Pass. It takes 7½ hours to cover 290km and cross 291 bridges (Sfr138, plus a Sfr9 to Sfr12 supplement depending on the season). Novelty drink glasses in the dining car have sloping bases to compensate for the hills – but remember to keep turning them around!

Two postbuses run to/from Lugano daily in summer – in winter, there's a daily bus on Friday, Saturday and Sunday. You must reserve a seat the day before on ☎ 081 837 67 64.

Nine daily trains travel south to Tirano in Italy with connections to Milan.

AROUND ST MORITZ

The Engadine Valley, running northeast and southwest of St Moritz, has an interesting combination of plush resorts and unspoilt villages. In **Guarda** and **Zuoz** you can see homes displaying traditional **sgraffito** designs (patterns scratched on wall plaster) that are characteristic of the Engadine.

In the **Davos/Klosters** region there are 320km of ski runs, mostly medium to difficult, including one of the hardest runs in the world, the **Gotschnawang**. **Arosa** is another top-notch resort, easily reached by train from Chur. Most other ski resorts in Graubünden have easy to medium runs. Ski passes for the top resorts average Sfr50 for one day (cheaper by the week); passes for smaller places cost less.

The annual Engadine Cross-country Ski Marathon between Maloja and Zuoz is on the second Sunday in March. The route crosses ice-covered lakes and passes by St Moritz Lake. Trains and buses run regularly along the valley.

Flora and fauna abound in the 169 sq km **Swiss National Park** (☎ 081-856 13 78; W *www.nationalpark.ch; open June-Oct)*. The park information centre near Zernez has details of hiking routes and the best places to see particular animals. Call or check the website.

Zürich

pop 339,300

Switzerland's most populous city offers an ambience of affluence, style and culture. Banks and art galleries greet you at every turn in a marriage of finance and aesthetics, and at night, the pinstripe brigade yields the streets to bar-hoppers and clubbers.

Zürich started life as a Roman customs post and graduated to the status of free city under the Holy Roman Empire in 1218. The city's reputation as a cultural and intellectual centre began after it joined the Swiss Confederation in 1351, and Huldrych Zwingli brought the Reformation doctrines to the city in the early 16th century. Zürich's status as a business centre was boosted by the energetic administrator and railway magnate Alfred Escher in the 19th century. WWI saw Switzerland become temporary home to luminaries such as Lenin, Trotsky and James Joyce; and Tristan Tzara and Hans Arp, key figures in the founding of Dadaism in 1916 at Cabaret Voltaire.

Orientation

Zürich is at the northern end of Lake Zürich (Zürichsee), with the city centre split by the Limmat River. Like many Swiss cities, it is compact and easy to navigate. The main train station (Hauptbahnhof) is on the western bank of the river, close to the old centre.

Information

Tourist Offices The **Zürich Tourist Service** (☎ *01 215 40 00, fax 01 215 40 44;* e *infor mation@zurichtourism.ch; open 8.30am-8.30pm Mon-Fri, 8.30am-6.30pm Sat & Sun Nov-Mar, 8.30am-7pm Mon-Fri, 9am-6.30pm Sat & Sun Apr-Oct)* is in the train station's main hall. There's a free city map, but Sfr3 gets you a more detailed map with a street index.

Money There's no shortage of choice when exchanging money in this banking city. Banks are open 8.15am to 4.30pm Monday to Friday (until 6pm Thursday). There is an **exchange office** (open 6.30am-10pm daily) in the main train station.

Post & Communications The main post office is **Sihlpost** (☎ *01 296 21 11; Kasernen-strasse 95-97; open 7.30am-8pm Mon-Fri, 8am-4pm Sat)*, but there's a more convenient post office at the main train station.

Several tables of terminals vie for space with video games in **Quanta Virtual Fun Space** (cnr Niederdorfstrasse & Mühlegasse) where Net access costs Sfr10 an hour.

Stars Bistro (open 11am-11pm Mon-Sat, 10am-11pm Sun), in the main hall of the train

SWITZERLAND

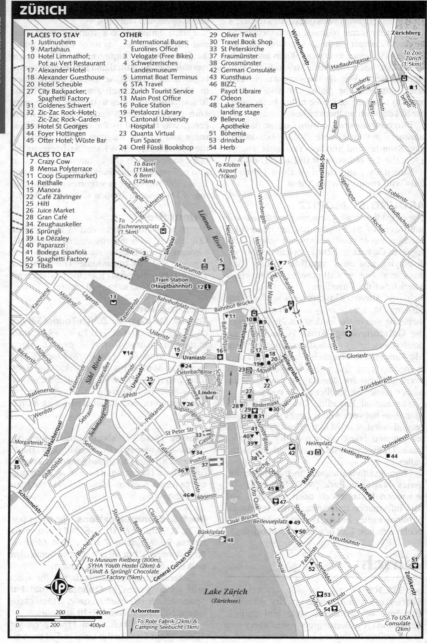

ZÜRICH

PLACES TO STAY
1 Justinusheim
9 Martahaus
10 Hotel Limmathof;
   Pot au Vert Restaurant
17 Alexander Hotel
18 Alexander Guesthouse
20 Hotel Scheuble
27 City Backpacker;
   Spaghetti Factory
31 Goldenes Schwert
32 Zic-Zac Rock-Hotel;
   Zic-Zac Rock-Garden
35 Hotel St Georges
44 Foyer Hottingen
45 Otter Hotel; Wüste Bar

PLACES TO EAT
7 Crazy Cow
8 Mensa Polyterrace
11 Coop (Supermarket)
14 Reithalle
15 Manora
22 Café Zähringer
25 Hiltl
26 Juice Market
28 Gran Café
34 Zeughauskeller
36 Sprüngli
39 Le Dézaley
40 Paparazzi
41 Bodega Española
50 Spaghetti Factory
52 Tibits

OTHER
2 International Buses;
   Eurolines Office
3 Velogate (Free Bikes)
4 Schweizerisches
   Landesmuseum
5 Limmat Boat Terminus
6 STA Travel
12 Zurich Tourist Service
13 Main Post Office
16 Police Station
19 Pestalozzi Library
21 Cantonal University
   Hospital
23 Quanta Virtual
   Fun Space
24 Orell Füssli Bookshop

29 Oliver Twist
30 Travel Book Shop
33 St Peterskirche
37 Fraumünster
38 Grossmünster
42 German Consulate
43 Kunsthaus
46 BIZZ;
   Payot Libraire
47 Odeon
48 Lake Steamers
   landing stage
49 Bellevue
   Apotheke
51 Bohemia
53 drinxbar
54 Herb

To Basel
(113km)
& Bern
(125km)

To Kloten
Airport
(10km)

To
Escherwyssplatz
(1.5km)

Limmat River

Train Station
(Hauptbahnhof)

Lindenhof

Rindermarkt

Heimplatz

Lake Zürich
(Zürichsee)

Zürichberg

To Zoo
Zürich
(1.5km)

Bürkliplatz

Bellevueplatz

Arboretum

To Museum Rietberg (800m),
SYHA Youth Hostel (2km) &
Lindt & Sprüngli Chocolate
Factory (5km)

To Rote Fabrik (2km) &
Camping Seebucht (3km)

To USA
Consulate
(2km)

0   200   400m
0   200   400yd

station, is a sprawling smoky café with Internet access (Sfr5 for 20 minutes).

Travel Agencies For help with travel suggestions and budget fares there's **STA Travel** (☎ 01 261 97 57; Leonhardstrasse 10; open 10am-6pm Mon-Wed & Fri, 10am-8pm Thur, 10am-1pm Sat).

Bookshops & Libraries A great source of fiction, nonfiction and travel books in English is **Orell Füssli Bookshop** (☎ 01 211 04 44; Bahnhofstrasse 70). **Payot Libraire** (☎ 01 211 54 52; Bahnhofstrasse 9) specialises in both English- and French-language titles.

Travel Book Shop (☎ 01 252 38 83; Rindermarkt 20) sells English-language travel books and maps. You can also read English-language newspapers in the **Pestalozzi Library** (☎ 01 261 78 11; Zähringerstrasse 17; open 10am-7pm Mon-Fri, 10am-4pm Sat).

Medical & Emergency Services For medical and dental help, ring ☎ 01 269 69 69. The **Cantonal University Hospital** (☎ 01 255 11 11; Rämistrasse 100) has a casualty department, and there's a 24-hour chemist at **Bellevue Apotheke** (☎ 01 252 56 00; Theaterstrasse 14). **Police HQ** (☎ 01 216 71 11; Bahnhofquai 3) is in an impressive building overlooking the river.

Things to See & Do

The cobblestoned pedestrian streets of the old town on each side of the Limmat River are worth a wander. Explore intimate alleyways with surprises at every turn – 16th- and 17th-century houses and guildhalls, tiny boutiques and cafés, courtyards and fountains.

For a brief history lesson, the tourist office runs two-hour **walking tours** (adult/student/child Sfr20/15/10; daily May-Oct).

Elegant **Bahnhofstrasse** is simply perfect for window-shopping and affluent Zürcher-watching. The bank vaults beneath the street are said to be crammed with gold and silver. Above ground, you'll find luxury shops selling the best Switzerland can offer, from watches and clocks to chocolates, furs, porcelain and fashion labels galore.

Walks around Lake Zürich are a pleasant diversion from city crowds. Wander down the west bank and concrete walkways give way to parkland in the **Arboretum**. On the eastern bank, the **Zürichhorn** park has sculptures and a

Chinese Garden. In summer, the lakeside park buzzes with food stalls and entertainment. Take the S10 train to **Uetliberg** (813m) for hikes and sweeping views.

Places of Worship The 13th-century tower of **St Peterskirche** (St Peter's Church) is hard to miss, with the largest clock face in Europe (8.7m in diameter). Also west of the Limmat River, the part Romanesque, part Gothic **Fraumünster** features *The Heavenly Paradise* window by Augusto Giacometti and magnificent stained-glass works created by surrealist Marc Chagall when in his 80s. Across the river, the dual-towered **Grossmünster** looms. Highlights are the choir windows designed by Augusto Giacometti (1933) and an imposing statue of Charlemagne (1107) with giant crown and sword in the crypt. Zwingli preached here in the 16th century.

Museums With one of the best collections in the country, **Kunsthaus** (Museum of Fine Arts; ☎ 01 253 84 84; W www.kunsthaus.ch; Heimplatz 1; adult/student/child Sfr10/6/free, free Wed; open 10am-9pm Tues-Thur, 10am-5pm Fri-Sun) has works by Dali, Man Ray, Hockney, Renoir, Monet and Marc Chagall. Temporary exhibitions incur an extra charge.

Schweizerisches Landesmuseum (Swiss National Museum; ☎ 01 218 65 11; W www.musee-suisse.ch; Museumstrasse 2; adult/student/child Sfr5/3/free; open 10am-5pm Tues-Sun) delves into cultural history, with sections on church art, weapons, coins and room interiors, all housed in a mock castle built in 1898.

Museum Rietberg (☎ 01 202 45 28; W www.rietberg.ch; Gablerstrasse 15; tram No 7; adult/student from Sfr12/6; open 10am-5pm Tues & Thur-Sun, 10am-8pm Wed) has wonderful collections of art and artefacts from Africa and Asia. Also keep an eye out for numerous private galleries around the city.

Other Attractions The **Lindt & Sprüngli chocolate factory** (☎ 01 716 22 33; Seestrasse 204; bus No 165 from Bürkliplatz to Schooren; admission free; open 10am-noon & 1pm-4pm Wed-Fri) has a small exhibit and corny documentary; free chocolate samples abound. For choc fanatics only.

Zoo Zürich (☎ 01 254 25 00; Zürich-bergstrasse 221; tram No 6; adult/student

Sfr14/7; open 8am-6pm daily Mar-Oct, 8am-5pm daily Nov-Feb) exhibits 1800 animals nestled within Zürichberg, a beautiful wood ideal for walks away from the city.

Special Events

On the third Monday in April, Zürich celebrates the arrival of warmer weather with Sechseläuten. The guild members parade the streets in historical costume and tour the guildhalls, playing music. A fireworks-filled 'snowman' (the Böögg) is ignited at 6pm.

Zürich lets its hair down in August, with the techno Street Parade (second only to Berlin's Love Parade), attracting well over half a million ravers who flock to the city to party. A three-hour parade is followed by all-night parties around the city.

In February, just after Ash Wednesday, the city celebrates Fasnacht, with parades and festive costumes. Zürcher Festspiele, from mid-June to mid-July, offers a programme of music, dance and theatre.

Places to Stay

Accommodation can be hard to find, particularly from August to October. Cheaper hotels fill early. Book ahead or use the information board and free phone in the train station. The tourist office can sometimes get lower rates (no booking fee).

Camping On the west shore of the lake 4km from the centre (signposted), **Camping Seebucht** *(☎ 01 482 16 12; Seestrasse 559; bus No 161 or 165 from Bürkliplatz; camp sites per adult/tent/car park/camper van Sfr8.50/12/3/16; open May-Sept)* has good facilities including a shop and café.

Hostels The SYHA hostel *(☎ 01 482 35 44, fax 01 480 17 27;* e *zurich@youthhostel.ch; Mutschellenstrasse 114, Wollishofen; dorm beds from Sfr32, singles/doubles from Sfr69/90)* is large and modern with two- to six-bed dorms, 24-hour service and excellent facilities. Take tram No 6 or 7 to Morgental, or S-Bahn 8 to Wollishofen.

Bar-hoppers will feel reallt at home at the **City Backpacker** *(☎ 01 251 90 15, fax 01 251 90 24;* e *backpacker@access.ch; Niederdorfstrasse 5; dorm beds without/with sheets Sfr29/32, singles/doubles/triples/quads Sfr66/92/126/164)*, in the heart of the busy Niederdorfstrasse. Take a wander up the

narrow steps to the 2nd floor to find reception. Facilities include Internet access (Sfr5 for 25 minutes) and a rooftop area.

Removed from the busy city streets is the tranquil student home **Justinusheim** *(☎ 01 361 38 06, fax 01 362 29 82; Freudenbergstrasse 146; singles/doubles/triples Sfr50/80/120, with shower Sfr60/100/140)*. Overlooking carefully tended gardens, spartan but spacious rooms are available during student holidays (particularly mid-July to mid-October), though there are vacancies during term too. A few paces from the Zürichberg woods, it has views of the city and lake far below. Take tram No 10 from the train station to Rigiblik, then the frequent Seilbahn (every six minutes) to the top station, opposite the hostel.

Foyer Hottingen *(☎ 01 256 19 19, fax 01 256 19 00;* e *info@foyer-hottingen.ch; Hottingerstrasse 31; dorm beds Sfr35, singles/doubles/triples Sfr70/110/140, with bathroom Sfr105/150/190)* has sparkling, white, minimalist rooms and a peaceful pace, away from the hubbub. Dorm beds are available for women only.

Hotels On the west bank of the Sihl River, **Hotel St Georges** *(☎ 01 241 11 44, fax 01 241 11 42;* e *st-georges@bluewin.ch; Weberstrasse 11; singles/doubles Sfr78/102, with bathroom Sfr104/136)* is a bit of a hike, but it's quiet, comfortable and includes continental breakfast.

A more convenient option is the recently renovated **Martahaus** *(☎ 01 251 45 50, fax 01 251 45 40;* e *info@martahaus.ch; Zähringerstrasse 36; dorm beds Sfr37, singles/doubles/triples from Sfr75/98/129)*, just a five-minute walk from the station. Privacy even prevails in the six-bed dorms with individual cubicles fashioned from partitions and curtains. Book ahead as it's often full.

Hotel Limmathof *(☎ 01 261 42 20, fax 01 262 02 17; Limmatquai 142; singles/doubles/triples with bathroom Sfr110/168/198)* is an easy stumble from Niederdorfstrasse's nightlife, but is inevitably noisy. The **pot au vert** vegetarian restaurant is on the 1st floor.

Zic-Zac Rock-Hotel *(☎ 01 261 21 81, fax 01 261 21 75;* e *rockhotel.ch@bluewin.ch; Marktgasse 17; singles from Sfr75, doubles without/with bathroom Sfr120/160)*, features a bold paint job, rock-star room names and gold discs, and is a bit of a novelty, but it is cramped.

Alexander Hotel (☎ 01 251 82 03, fax 01 252 74 25; e info@hotel-alexander.ch; Niederdorfstrasse 40; singles/doubles Sfr160/220, guesthouse Sfr95/140) offers three-star accommodation with mod cons and breakfast, but ask about its linked two-star **guesthouse** in Zähringerstrasse, with much simpler, better-value rooms.

Goldenes Schwert (☎ 01 266 18 18, fax 01 266 18 88; e hotel@rainbow.ch; Marktgasse 14; singles/doubles from Sfr130/155) is a gay-friendly hotel with murals and mirror balls in some rooms and a disco downstairs.

Otter Hotel (☎ 01 251 22 07, fax 01 251 22 75; Oberdorfstrasse 7; singles/doubles from Sfr100/130), on fashionable Oberdorfstrasse, is flamboyantly quirky, with 17 room choices including hot pink, desert-island and Arabian-nights themes – a basic breakfast is included.

Simple and elegant, **Hotel Scheuble** (☎ 01 251 87 95, fax 01 251 76 78; e info@scheuble.ch; Mühlegasse 17; singles Sfr140-210, doubles 190-400) offers newly renovated rooms and sleek modern furniture.

Places to Eat
Zürich has a thriving café culture and hundreds of restaurants serving all types of local and international cuisine. A good place to start exploring is Niederdorfstrasse and the backstreets nearby, with wall-to-wall cafés, restaurants and bars of every description.

Restaurants With a fun, buzzing atmosphere, **Spaghetti Factory** (☎ 01 251 94 00; Niederdorfstrasse 5; pasta Sfr13.50-22; open 11am-2am daily) serves big, steaming bowls of its namesake dish (22 choices). Night owls with the munchies can fill up at a second **branch** (Theaterstrasse 10; open all night Fri-Sat).

For melt-in-your-mouth garlic mushrooms and other delicious tapas, head to the ground-level café section of **Bodega Española** (☎ 01 251 23 10; Münstergasse 15; tapas Sfr4.80; open 11.45am-2pm & 6pm-11pm).

Hiltl (☎ 01 227 70 00; Sihlstrasse 28; mains Sfr20-25; open 7am-11pm Mon-Sat, 11am-11pm Sun) is an institution, serving tasty vegie meals to Zürchers since 1898 (when vegetarians were commonly thought of as crackpots). Try the Indian buffet (Sfr4.60 per 100g, Sfr42 all-you-can-eat; from 5pm nightly).

Another local eatery with a long history is the touristy **Zeughauskeller** (☎ 01 211 26 90; Bahnhofstrasse 28a; mains Sfr15-30; open 11.30am-11pm daily), a meat-lovers' heaven (with Swiss specialities and 'sausage of the month') which is housed in a 500-year-old former armoury.

In the shadow of Grossmünster is stylish **Le Dézaley** (☎ 01 251 61 29; Römergasse 7; dishes from Sfr22; open 11am-2pm & 5pm-11pm Mon-Sat), the locals' choice for fondue and Vaudois specialities.

Dining becomes entertainment at the big, bright, irreverent **Crazy Cow** (☎ 01 261 40 55; Leonhardstrasse 1; dishes from Sfr17; open 6.30am-midnight daily). There's a giant Toblerone pillar and an unreadable 'Swiss-German' menu as well as delicious chicken wings served in toy supermarket trolleys.

Reithalle (☎ 01 212 07 66; Theaterhaus Gessneralle; Gessnerallee 8; mains Sfr20-25; open 11am-midnight Mon-Fri, 6pm-4am Sat, 5pm-11pm Sun), in a large converted horse stable, has a mixed menu (pastas and curries) and is often packed with theatre-goers. The Saturday-night diners get in free to the disco.

Cafés Next to the Polybahn (funicular) top station, **Mensa Polyterrace** (Leonhardstrasse 34; dishes Sfr10.50; open 7am-7pm Mon-Fri during term) is an enormous, bustling university cafeteria.

Pile your plate high with tasty fresh food at the buffet-style **Manora** (5th floor, Manor department store, Bahnhofstrasse; mains from Sfr8.90; open 9am-8pm Mon-Fri, 9am-5pm Sat).

Creative vegetarian options are a highlight at **Tibits** (☎ 01 260 32 22; Seefeldstrasse 2; open 6.30am-midnight Mon-Fri, 8am-midnight Sat, 9am-midnight Sun), a sprawling modern vegie restaurant with purple walls and comfy lounges. The salad bar has 30 different choices for Sfr3.50 per 100g.

If you need to detox after a night on the fondue, **Juice Market** (☎ 01 211 69 33; Augustinergasse 42; juices Sfr6.50-9; open 8am-7pm Mon-Fri, 8am-5pm Sat) makes fresh protein shakes and smoothies, and a range of healthy snack alternatives.

Run by a collective, **Café Zähringer** (☎ 01 252 05 00; Zähringerplatz 11; snacks Sfr5.50-7.50, meals Sfr10.50-22; open 6pm-midnight Mon, 8am-midnight Tues-Thur, 8am-12.30am Fri-Sat, 8am-midnight Sun) provides mellow music, a relaxed atmosphere and scrumptious low-fat soups and snacks.

Paparazzi (☎ 01 250 55 88; Nägelihof 1, Limmatquai; snacks Sfr5-14; open 8.30am-10pm Mon-Thur, 8.30am-midnight Fri-Sat) is a fun place to hang out among old movie posters, cameras and early paparazzi snaps.

Old photos of famous folk also adorn the **Gran Café** (☎ 01 252 31 19; Limmatquai 66; open 6am-11.30pm Mon-Fri, 7am-midnight Sat, 7.30am-11.30pm Sun), by the river, with a bargain all-you-can-eat spaghetti for Sfr10.90 (from 6pm).

Sprüngli (☎ 01 244 47 11; Bahnhofstrasse 21; open 7am-6.30pm Mon-Fri, 7.30am-5.30pm Sat, 10am-5pm Sun) is a must for chocoholics. Choose from a huge range of truffles and cakes from display cases downstairs, or mingle with the well-heeled crowd in the elegant 1st-floor tearooms for a rather special experience.

Self-Catering Cheap eats abound around the train station, especially in the underground Shopville, which has a **Migros** (open 7am-8pm Mon-Fri, 8am-8pm Sat-Sun). Above ground by the station, there is a large **Coop** supermarket. Niederdorfstrasse has a string of **snack bars** offering pretzels, bratwurst, kebabs and Oriental food.

Entertainment

Like most big cities, Zürich has a fickle, ever-changing entertainment scene. Pick up the free events magazine *Züritipp* from the tourist office or check daily listings at [w] www.zueritipp .ch. Tickets for many events are available from **Billettzentrale** (BIZZ; ☎ 01 221 22 83; Bahnhofstrasse 9; open 10am-6.30pm Mon-Fri, 10am-2pm Sat).

Late-night pubs, clubs and discos clutter Niederdorfstrasse and its adjoining streets. English speakers gravitate towards the Irish pub **Oliver Twist** (Rindermarkt 6) and the constantly crowded, American-style **Zic-Zac Rock-Garden** (Marktgasse 17).

Lenin and James Joyce once downed drinks at the **Odeon** (☎ 01 251 16 50; Am Bellevue; open 7am-2am Mon-Thur & Sun, 7am-4am Fri-Sat), a swish, smoky bar packed with an arty crowd. More laid-back is **Bohemia** (☎ 01 383 70 60; am Kreuzplatz; open 7am-1am Mon-Fri, 9am-2am Sat, 10am-1am Sun), a spacious, Cuban-themed café/bar. **Wüste Bar** (☎ 01 251 22 07; Oberdorfstrasse 7; open

10am-midnight Mon-Thur, 10am-2am Fri-Sat), underneath the Otter Hotel, is small and groovy with plush red seats and a cowhide bar.

You'll pay around Sfr15 admission for most clubs, however a couple of small, central establishments have no cover charge. Try **Herb** (Kreuzstrasse 24; open 9pm-2am Mon-Wed, 9pm-3am Thur-Sat) and **drinxbar** (Dufourstrasse 24; 5pm-midnight Mon-Wed, 5pm-2am Thur-Sat, 5pm-midnight Sun).

Factories in the industrial quarter, west of the train station, are gradually being taken over by a wave of hip bars, clubs and restaurants. Head to Escherwyssplatz (tram No 4 or 13) and follow your ears. The **Peugeot Bar** (☎ 01 273 11 25; Pfingstweidstrasse 6) draws big crowds with its unpretentious atmosphere and produce-market setting. Nearby, **Moods Jazz Club** (☎ 01 276 80 00; Schiffbaustrasse 6), in a former ship-building factory, shares its cavernous postmodern space with a theatre, bar and stylish restaurant.

Rote Fabrik (☎ 01 481 9143; Seestrasse 395; bus No 161 or 165 from Bürkliplatz), once a cutting-edge centre for alternative arts, is more mainstream these days. It offers a range of music, original-language films, theatre, dance and a bar/restaurant.

Cinema prices are around Sfr15, reduced to Sfr11 on Monday. There's also an **open-air cinema** in Zürichhorn park from mid-July to mid-August. The **Comedy Club** performs plays in English – check venues in events magazines or free newspapers by tram stops.

Getting There & Away

Air Kloten airport is 10km north of the city centre and has several daily flights to/from all major destinations. **Swiss** (☎ 0848 85 2000; open 8.30am-6.30pm Mon-Fri, 9.30am-2.30pm Sat) has an office in the main train station.

Bus Various buses head east to Budapest, Belgrade, Dubrovnik and other destinations. The **Eurolines office** (☎ 01 272 40 42) is behind the train station, and is open daily, but intermittently.

Train There are direct trains to Stuttgart (Sfr62, three hours), to Munich (Sfr89, 4½ hours), to Innsbruck (Sfr69, four hours) and to Milan (Sfr75, four hours), as well as many other international destinations. There are also at least hourly departures to most of the Swiss towns including Lucerne (Sfr22, 50 minutes), Bern (Sfr48, 70 minutes) and Basel (Sfr32, 65 minutes).

Car & Motorcycle The N3 approaches Zürich from the south along the shore of Lake Zürich. The N1 is the fastest route from Bern and Basel and the main entry point from the west. The N1 also services routes to the north and east of Zürich.

Getting Around

To/From the Airport Regular trains make the 10-minute trip from the airport to the main train station (Sfr5.40). Taxis cost around Sfr50.

Public Transport There's a comprehensive, unified bus, tram and S-Bahn service in the city that includes boats plying the Limmat River. All tickets must be bought in advance from dispensers at stops. Short trips under five stops are Sfr2.30. A one-hour/24-hour pass for the city costs Sfr3.60/7.20, while a 24-hour pass including travel to/from the airport is Sfr10.80. For unlimited travel within the canton, including extended tours of the lake, a day pass costs Sfr28.40, or Sfr20 after 9am (9-Uhr-Pass).

Lake steamers depart from Bürkliplatz from early April to late October (Swiss Pass and Eurail valid, Inter-Rail 50% discount). A popular option is the two-hour journey to Rapperswill (round trip Sfr20). For more information, contact **Zürichsee-Schifffahrtsgesellschaft** (ZSG; ☎ 01 487 13 33; w www.zsg.ch).

Taxi & Bicycle Taxis in Zürich are expensive, even by Swiss standards, at Sfr6 plus Sfr3.50 per kilometre. Use of city bikes is free of charge from **Velogate** (platform 18, main train station; open 7.30am-9.30pm year-round). Bring photo ID and Sfr20 deposit.

Central Switzerland

This is the region that many visitors consider the 'true' Switzerland. Rich in typical Swiss features – mountains, lakes, tinkling cowbells and alpine villages – it's also where Switzerland began as a nation 700 years ago. The original pact of 1291, which was signed by the communities of Uri, Schwyz and Nidwalden, can be viewed in the **Bundesbriefarchiv hall** in Schwyz town centre.

LUCERNE
pop 57,100

Ideally situated in the historic and scenic heart of Switzerland, Lucerne (Luzern in German) is an excellent base for mountain excursions, with easy access to the towering peaks of Mt Pilatus and Mt Rigi. It also has a great deal of character in its own right, particularly the medieval town centre.

The mostly pedestrian-only old town is on the northern bank of the Reuss River. The train station is centrally located on the southern bank. Beside platform three is **Luzern Tourismus** (☎ 041 227 17 17; e luzern@luzern.org; Zentralstrasse 5; open 8.30am-7.30pm Mon-Fri, 9am-7.30pm Sat & Sun Apr-Oct; closes 6pm Nov-Mar). In front of the train station is the **boat landing stage** and across the road is the **main post office** (open 7.30am-6.30pm Mon-Fri, 8am-noon Sat).

Internet access can be pricey in Lucerne. For the best deal (Sfr2 for 30 minutes) head to the **Stadtbibliothek** (Library; Löwenplatz 10; open 1.30pm-6.30pm Mon, 10am-6.30pm Tues-Wed & Fri, 10am-9pm Thur, 10am-4pm Sat).

American Express (☎ 041 410 00 77; Schweizerhofquai 4; open 8.30am-5pm Mon-Fri, plus 8.30am-noon Sat in summer) has an ATM and money exchange.

Ask for the visitor's booklet (available from your accommodation) for various discounts on excursions.

Things to See

Your first port of call should be the medieval **old town**, with ancient rampart walls and towers, 15th-century buildings with painted facades and the two much-photographed covered bridges. **Kapellbrücke** (Chapel Bridge), dating from 1333, is Lucerne's best-known landmark, famous for its distinctive water tower and the spectacular 1993 fire that nearly destroyed it. Though it has been rebuilt, fire damage is still obvious on the 17th-century pictorial panels under the roof. In better condition, but rather dark and dour, are the *Dance of Death* panels under the roofline of **Spreuerbrücke** (Spreuer Bridge).

There's a fine view of the town and lake from the Gütsch Hotel; climb uphill for 20 minutes or treat your feet by taking the clunky **Gütschbahn** (Sfr3).

Make sure that you set aside a few hours for the fascinating **Gletschergarten** (Glacier Garden; ☎ 041 410 43 40; Denkmalstrasse 4;

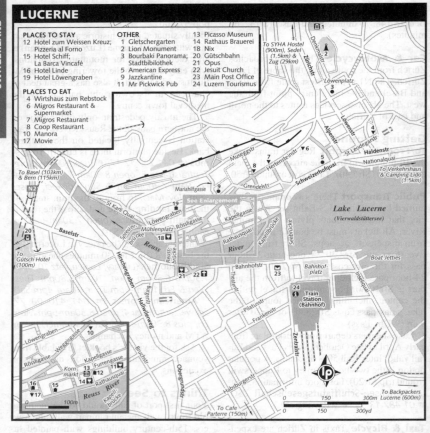

LUCERNE

PLACES TO STAY
12 Hotel zum Weissen Kreuz;
   Pizzeria al Forno
15 Hotel Schiff;
   La Barca Vincafé
16 Hotel Linde
19 Hotel Löwengraben

PLACES TO EAT
4 Wirtshaus zum Rebstock
6 Migros Restaurant &
  Supermarket
7 Migros Restaurant
8 Coop Restaurant
10 Manora
17 Movie

OTHER
1 Gletschergarten
2 Lion Monument
3 Bourbaki Panorama;
  Stadtbibilothek
9 Jazzkantine
11 Mr Pickwick Pub

13 Picasso Museum
14 Rathaus Brauerei
18 Nix
20 Gütschbahn
21 Opus
22 Jesuit Church
23 Main Post Office
24 Luzern Tourismus

---

w www.gletschergarten.ch; adult/student/
child Sfr9/7/5.50; open 9am-6pm daily Apr-
Oct, 10am-5pm daily Nov-Mar). Most visitors come here to peer into the giant glacial
potholes that prove Lucerne's prehistory as a
subtropical palm beach, but don't miss Am-
rein's House, with collections of antique
maps and paintings, and the entertaining,
century-old Alhambra Hall of Mirrors.

Nearby is the poignant **Lion Monument**,
carved in natural rock in 1820 and dedicated
to the Swiss soldiers who died in the French
Revolution. Another moving historical exhibit is the **Bourbaki Panorama** (☎ 041 412
30 30; Löwenplatz 11; **w** www.panorama
-luzern.ch; adult/student/child Sfr7/6/5;
open 9am-6pm daily), an 1100 sq metre circular painting with commentary depicting the

first Red Cross efforts during the Franco-
Prussian War.

The **Picasso Museum** (☎ 041 410 35 33;
Furrengasse 21; adult/student/child Sfr6/3/3;
open 10am-6pm daily Apr-Oct, 11am-1pm &
2pm-4pm daily Nov-Mar) has a small artwork
exhibit, but the main attraction is its collection
of intimate black-and-white photos of the
artist, his muse Jacqueline and his children.

Verkehrshaus (Transport Museum; ☎ 041
370 44 44; Lidostrasse 5; bus No 6, 8 or 24
from Bahnhofplatz; adult/student/child Sfr21/
19/12; open 10am-6pm daily Apr-Oct, 10am-
5pm daily Nov-Mar), east of the city centre, is
a huge complex devoted to Switzerland's
proud transport history. There are trains, planes
and automobiles, a communications display,
simulators, planetarium and IMAX theatre

(costs extra). For unrivalled views of the town and lake, take off in the Hiflyer, a captive balloon you can ride for an extra Sfr20 (15 minutes' duration).

Culture buffs should consider buying the Lucerne museums pass (Sfr29, valid for one month).

From mid-August through mid-September, Lucerne hosts the annual **Internationale Musikfestwochen** (*International Festival of Music;* ☎ *041 226 44 00;* **w** *www.lucerne -music.ch*).

Activities
If you want an adrenalin rush, contact **Outventure** (☎ *041 611 14 41;* **w** *www.outven ture.ch*), which has a wide range of adventure sports (eg, bungy-jumping, paragliding and canyoning in the Lucerne/Engelberg region).

Organised Tours
There are many options for scenic cruises on the lake, including on old-fashioned paddle-steamers. Swiss and Eurail passes are valid on all boat trips and Inter-Rail pass holders travel half-price. A 2nd-class day pass for unlimited boat travel is Sfr44. Also popular are trips to the nearby mountains (ask tourist office staff about special deals in winter).

A popular option is the **Golden Roundtrip** (*Sfr78.20*), which includes a lake steamer to Alpnachstad, a steep cog railway (open May to November) up craggy Mt Pilatus (2120m), a cable car down to Kriens and bus back to Lucerne.

To visit Mt Titlis (3020m), Central Switzerland's highest lookout, there's the tourist office's all-inclusive **guided tour** (*Sfr95*), including coach trip, Titlis rotating cable car and guide. If you prefer to go it alone, you'll pay Sfr88 for the return journey to Titlis, including cable cars and a train to Engelberg.

Nearby Mt Rigi offers 100km of excellent hiking trails. A combination lake steamer, cog railway and cable-car excursion up Mt Rigi (1797m) costs Sfr87. Rail pass holders should ask about reductions on tour prices.

Places to Stay
Camping Lido (☎ *041 370 21 46; Lidostrasse 8; bus No 6, 8 or 24; camp site per adult/ tent/car Sfr8.70/5/5, bunk in cabin Sfr15; open mid-Mar–Oct*) entices happy campers with its tranquil spot near the Lido and transport museum.

Backpackers Lucerne (☎ *041 360 04 20, fax 041 360 04 42; Alpenquai 42; dorm beds in 4-/2-bed rooms Sfr24/30*), a 12-minute walk southeast of the station, is a cheerful independent with sprawling parkland frontage and a scrap of lakefront beach nearby.

The **SYHA hostel** (☎ *041 420 88 00, fax 041 420 56 16;* **e** *luzern@youthhostel.ch; Sedelstrasse 12; bus No 18 from Bahnhofplatz; dorm beds from Sfr31.50, singles/doubles Sfr64/78, with bathroom Sfr70/90*), around 1km north of the city walls, is a large, modern, reliable option.

Good for novelty value is **Hotel Löwengraben** (☎ *041 417 12 12, fax 041 417 12 11;* **e** *hotel@loewengraben.ch; Löwengraben 18; dorm beds from Sfr30, singles/twins/doubles with breakfast Sfr120/165/190, suites Sfr250-300*), a converted prison with basic, white-washed, 'cell-like' rooms and some fancier suites (albeit with bars on the windows). Its transformation comes complete with a stylish restaurant (see Places to Eat later), trendy bar and nightclub, and Internet access.

Simple but central is **Hotel Linde** (☎ *041 410 31 93; Metzgerrainle 3; singles/doubles Sfr44/88; open Apr-Oct*), off Weinmarkt in the old town, offering six cheap and cheerful rooms with crisp white linen. Check-in is through the ground-floor Italian restaurant.

At the three-star **Hotel zum Weissen Kreuz** (☎ *041 418 82 20, fax 041 418 82 30;* **e** *wkreuz@tic.ch; singles/doubles with breakfast from Sfr100/180*), nestled in a cobble-stoned alleyway, there are casual, comfortable rooms a few paces from the water.

Hotel Schiff (☎ *041 418 52 52, fax 041 418 52 55;* **e** *contact@hotel-schiff-luzern.ch; Unter der Egg 8; singles/doubles with breakfast from Sfr80/120, with bathroom from Sfr150/190*), overlooking the Reuss River, has mostly spacious, renovated rooms, though they vary in style and price.

Places to Eat
Good eating is easy to find in Lucerne, particularly along the Reuss River, around Kornmarkt or in the winding maze of streets in the old town.

A fairly reliable cheapie is the buffet-style **Manora** (*5th floor, Weggisgasse 5; salads Sfr4.40-9.40; open 9am-6.30pm Mon-Wed, 9am-9pm Thur-Fri & 8am-4pm Sat*), with a small rooftop terrace with mountain vistas.

For speedy service, try **Pizzeria al Forno** *(1st floor, Hotel zum Weissen Kreuz; pizza/pasta from Sfr14/13; open 11am-11.30pm Tues-Sat, 11am-10pm Sun-Mon)*, with 34 varieties of mouthwatering wood-fired pizza. At the converted prison, **Hotel Löwengraben** *(mains Sfr24-28; open 11am-2pm Mon-Fri, 6pm-12.30am Tues-Sat)*, bread and water has been replaced by tasty Asian dishes. Try the daily menu (Sfr17 to Sfr18).

Movie *(☎ 041 410 36 31; Metzgerrainle 9; mains Sfr18.50-36; open 11.30am-2.30pm & 5.30pm-1.30am Mon-Fri, 11.30am-1.30am Sat, 10am-11pm Sun)* is a popular lighthearted theme restaurant with an elaborate film-studio decor, a movie-reel menu and American-style food. Be prepared for intermittent trailers of mainstream flicks on the diner's big screen.

Wirtshaus zum Rebstock *(☎ 041 410 35 81; St Leodegarstrasse 3; dishes Sfr16-42)*, in an ivy-covered historic building, has an eclectic blend of cuisine, from the Rebstock Teller, a meat-fest of fillets (Sfr42.80), to creative vegie dishes such as ravioli curry with shitake mushroom sauce (Sfr17.50).

Wander in and smell the coffee at **La Barca Vincafé**, hidden away under the Hotel Schiff, an antipasto bar serving up super-strong Italian blends.

Self-caterers should head to Hertensteinstrasse, where cheap eats are plentiful. There are numerous **hole-in-the-wall shops** selling pretzels (from Sfr2) and baguettes (from Sfr5). There's also a **Coop restaurant**, two **Migros restaurants** and a **supermarket**.

Entertainment

Jazzkantine *(☎ 041 410 73 73; Grabengasse 8; open 7am-12.30am Mon-Sat, 4pm-12.30am Sun)* is a groovy hang-out frequented by the young, creative types from the adjoining jazz school. There's cool music, counter meals and Saturday-night gigs and weeknight jazz workshops.

More laid-back is **Cafe Parterre** *(☎ 041 210 40 93; Mythenstrasse 7; open 7am-12.30am Mon-Fri, 9am-12.30am Sat & Sun)*, south of the train station, with industrial decor, beer garden and pool tables in the back bar. Breakfast is served into the afternoon for late risers.

Bar-hoppers can choose from the **Rathaus Brauerei** *(Unter der Egg 2)*, serving big home brews on the waterfront; **Nix** *(Mühlenplatz 4)*, a low-key wine bar with abstract artwork and tasty bar snacks; **Mr Pickwick Pub** *(Rathausquai 6)* for Brit beer, food and footy; or the upmarket **Opus** *(Bahnhofstrasse 16)*, with a choice of 600 wines (25 by the glass).

Behind Lake Rotsee near the youth hostel there is **Sedel** *(☎ 041 420 63 10)*, a former women's prison with rock concerts and DJs at the weekend.

Getting There & Around

Hourly trains connect Lucerne to Zürich (Sfr11, 50 minutes), Interlaken (Sfr29, two hours), Bern (Sfr32, 1½ hours), Lugano (Sfr58, 2½ hours) and Geneva (Sfr70, 3¼ hours). The N2/E9 motorway which connects Basel and Lugano passes by Lucerne, and the N14 provides the road link to Zürich.

INTERLAKEN
pop 15,000

Interlaken, flanked by the stunning Lakes Thun and Brienz and within yodelling distance of the mighty peaks of the Jungfrau, Mönch and Eiger, is a popular base for exploring the delights of the Jungfrau region. Lovers of kitsch will have a field day in the town itself, with horse-drawn carriages and the souvenir shops overflowing with tacky tourist mementoes. Interlaken is also a mecca for thrillseekers. It has a flourishing adventure-sports industry offering a range of white-knuckle, high-adrenalin sports.

Orientation & Information

Most of Interlaken lies between its two train stations, Interlaken Ost and West, which both offer bike rental and daily money-exchange facilities. Behind each station is a landing for lake boat services. The main shopping street, Höheweg, runs between the stations, and you can walk from one to the other in 20 minutes.

Near Interlaken West is the **main post office** *(cnr Marktgasse & Höheweg)* and **Interlaken Tourismus** *(☎ 033 826 53 00; e mail@interlakentourism.ch; Höheweg 37; 8am-6.30pm Mon-Fri, 8am-5pm Sat, 10am-noon & 4pm-6pm Sun July-Aug; shorter hours & closed Sun between seasons)*. There's a hotel board and free phones outside the tourist office and at both train stations. You can check your email at **Buddy's Pub** *(Höheweg 33)*, where the costs are Sfr5/9/16 for 15/30/60 minutes of Net access, but the hostels (particularly Backpackers Villa; see Places to Stay later in this section) often have cheaper access.

Things to See & Do

Interlaken is an active town, bursting with options for hiking, rafting, bungy-jumping, heli-skiing, skydiving and paragliding. The adventure-sports industry continues to thrive, despite the tragic canyoning disaster in 1999 in which 21 people lost their lives. Local operators include **Alpin Raft** (☎ 033 823 41 00; W www.alpinraft.ch) and the **Alpin Center** (☎ 033 823 55 23; W www.alpincenter.ch). One of the more bizarre summer activities is **zorbing** (offered by Alpin Center for Sfr95), where you are enclosed in an enormous transparent ball and sent plummeting down a snow-covered hill.

Hiking trails dot the area surrounding Interlaken, all with signposts giving average walking times. For an excellent panorama and more signposted hiking trails, catch the funicular up to **Harder Kulm** (Sfr21 return; open May to October).

Find time to get out on a lake if possible. Ferries chug along to several towns and villages (Swisspass and Eurail valid, Inter-Rail 50% off). **Lake Thun** has the greater number of resorts and villages, including Spiez (Sfr13/8.60 by steamer/train) and Thun (Sfr19.20/13.60). Medieval castles dominate both towns. Another fine castle is the 13th-century **Schloss Oberhofen** – boats stop right outside.

St Beatus Höhlen (Caves; ☎ 033 841 16 43; adult/student/child Sfr16/14/8; W www .beatushoehlen.ch; open 10.30am-5pm daily Apr-Oct) has some impressive stalagmite formations, a small museum, and a rather feeble reconstruction of a prehistoric settlement. The caves are a 90-minute walk, or save your legs by catching the boat (Sfr5.80).

Lake Brienz has a more rugged shoreline and fewer resorts than its neighbour. The enormous **Freilichtmuseum Ballenberg** (Ballenburg Open-Air Museum; W www.ballenberg.ch; adult/child Sfr16/8; open 10am-5pm daily mid-Apr–Oct) gives visitors a taste of Swiss rural life, with farm animals, craftsmen at work and 100 century-old houses. A shuttle bus operates from the train station at Brienz (Sfr12.40/6 by steamer/train).

Places to Stay

The Guest Card (available from accommodation places) provides useful discounts.

There are a dozen camping grounds in and around Interlaken. Most convenient is **Sackgut** (☎ 033 822 44 34; e sackgut@swisscamps.ch; Brienzstrasse; adult/child/tent from Sfr8.20/5.20/6.50; open Apr-Oct), behind Interlaken Ost station. For alternatives, visit the website at W www.campinginterlaken.ch.

The **SYHA hostel** (☎ 033 822 43 53, fax 033 823 20 58; e boenigen@youthhostel.ch; Aareweg 21, am See, Bönigen; bus No 1; dorm beds from Sfr27.70, singles/doubles Sfr40.70/81.40; closed early Nov–mid-Dec), a 20-minute walk around Lake Brienz from Interlaken Ost, has large dorms and breakfast buffet. What this hostel lacks in elegance it makes up for with its fantastic view over the marine-green Lake Brienz.

For 50 years now, young Americans have flocked to **Balmer's Herberge** (☎ 033 822 19 61, fax 033 823 32 61; e balmers@tcnet.ch; Hauptstrasse 23-25; dorm beds Sfr24-26, singles/doubles/triples/quads Sfr40/68/90/120). It has excellent facilities (games rooms, kitchen, bar and restaurant) and a raucous summer-camp feel, but it's definitely not for everyone. It's a 15-minute walk (signposted) from either station.

For a similarly raucous but Australasian flavour, head to the **Funny Farm** (☎ 079-652 61 27; e james@funny-farm.ch; dorm beds from Sfr25), a converted farmhouse behind the Mattenhof Hotel. The perfect antidote to Swiss-style regimentation, this free-and-easy place has basic, colourful rooms, didgeridoo workshops, swimming pool, bar and party atmosphere. Rooms with better facilities are available in the linked **Mattenhof** (dorm beds Sfr35).

If you need some shut-eye, try the **Backpackers Villa** (☎ 033 826 71 71, fax 033 826 71 72; e backpackers@villa.ch; Alpenstrasse 16; dorm beds Sfr32, doubles Sfr88), an ordered Christian hostel with spacious, renovated rooms. It's well worth the extra Sfr5 surcharge for a 'Jungfrau room' with balcony and mountain view.

The aptly named **Happy Inn Lodge** (☎ 033 822 32 25, fax 033 822 32 68; e info@happy-inn.com; Rosenstrasse 17; dorms Sfr19-30, singles/doubles from Sfr30/60 per person) has basic rooms and a merry bartender/owner serving drinks in the pub below.

Choose between the old and new at **Hotel Alphorn** (☎ 033 822 30 51, fax 033 823 30 69; e accommodation@hotel-alphorn.ch; Rugenaustrasse 8; singles/doubles Sfr90/150), where rooms are either minimalist and modern or filled with florals and antiques. It's in a quiet residential street near the West train station, and some spacious three-star options are available in the linked **Hotel Eiger** (singles/doubles Sfr110/180).

Each room is different in the **Hotel Splendid** (☎ 033 822 76 12, fax 033 822 76 79; e info@splendid.ch; Höheweg 33; singles/ doubles Sfr135/210), above Buddy's Pub, which offers three-star comfort in the heart of town.

Places to Eat

Brasserie 17 (open 8.30am-12.30am Mon-Sat, 5pm-12.30am Sun), underneath Happy Inn Lodge, is a fun local hang-out serving up chicken wings, spareribs and live music on Thursday night.

For simple Italian home cooking, try **Ristorante Arobaleno** (☎ 033 823 12 43; Hotel Post Hardimannli, Hauptrasse 18; mains Sfr20.50-35.50; open 9am-12.30am daily), with an excellent two-course daily menu.

The ravenous can fill up with tasty thin-crust pizzas and plentiful pasta plates at **Pizzeria Mercato** (☎ 033 827 87 71; Postgasse 1; pizzas from Sfr14; open 10am-midnight daily mid-Apr–Sept, 10am-2.30pm & 5-11.30pm daily Oct–mid-Apr).

Gasthof Hirschen (☎ 822 15 45; Hauptrasse 11; mains Sfr16.50-34; open Mon & Thur-Fri from 2pm, Sat-Sun from 11am) is a wisteria-strewn rustic chalet with fondue, rosti and a meaty menu. More central is **Hotel Splendid** (open 6pm-late daily summer, 6pm-late Fri-Sat in winter; closed April & Nov), with a popular 1st-floor restaurant serving steaming fondue (from Sfr19.50) and other local specialities.

More exotic options include **Spice of India** (Postgasse 6), serving delicious dishes with a kick; or **El Azteca** (Jungfraustrasse 30), with friendly waitresses and passable Mexican food.

Self-caterers can pick up all their supplies at **Migros** (cnr Rugenparkstrasse & General Guisan-Strasse) and **Coop**, with branches on Bahnhofstrasse and opposite Interlaken Ost.

Entertainment

If too much kitsch is not enough, catch the Swiss Folklore Show at the **Kursaal** (Casino; ☎ 033 827 61 00; show Sfr20, with dinner Sfr39-59.50; 7.30pm daily May-Sept). Sip on a cocktail and enjoy the sweeping mountain views from **Top o'Met** (18th floor, Höheweg 37). Other popular watering holes include the

tiny, English-style **Buddy's Pub** (Höheweg 33; 10am-1am Sun-Thur, 10am-1.30am Fri-Sat); the larger, rowdier **Café-Bar Hüsi** (Postgasse 3; open 4pm-12.30am Tues-Sun); and the grungy **Postiv Einfach** (Centralstrasse; open 5pm-12.30am Mon-Thur & Sun, 5pm-1.30am Fri-Sat), with DJs, live music and black-clad crowd. Most of the hostels also have their own bars and bistros. For house music, check out the Hotel Mattenhof's **Club Caverne** in summer.

Getting There & Away

Trains to Lucerne (Sfr30, two hours) depart hourly from Interlaken Ost. Trains to Brig and Montreux (via Bern or Zweisimmen) depart from Interlaken West or Ost. Main roads head east to Lucerne and west to Bern, but the only way south for vehicles, without a major detour around the mountains, is the car-carrying train from Kandersteg, south of Spiez.

JUNGFRAU REGION

The views get better the further south you go from Interlaken. Outdoor enthusiasts will find it hard to tear themselves away. The region's most popular peaks are the Jungfrau and the Schilthorn, but you can also enjoy marvellous vistas and hikes from Schynige Platte, Männlichen and Kleine Scheidegg. In winter, the Jungfrau is a magnet for skiers and snowboarders, with 200km of pistes, ranging from amateur slopes to intermediate to demanding runs down the Schilthorn. Ski passes cost Sfr52/95 for one/two days (discounts for seniors and teens).

Grindelwald

Once a simple farming village, Grindelwald is now the largest ski resort in the Jungfrau, nestled in a valley under the north face of the Eiger. In the First region there are 90km of **hiking trails** above 1200m, with 48km open year-round. The First is the main **skiing** area in winter, with runs stretching from **Oberjoch** at 2486m to the village at 1050m. You can catch the longest **cable car** in Europe from Grindelwald-Grund to Männlichen, where there are more extraordinary views and hikes (one-way/return Sfr29/46).

Grindelwald Tourism (☎ 033 854 12 12; e touristcenter@grindelwald.ch; open 8am-7pm Mon-Fri, 8am-6pm Sat, 9am-noon & 2pm-5pm Sun July-Sept; shorter hours & closed Sun between seasons) is in the centre at the Sportzentrum, 200m from the train station.

Places to Stay & Eat Grindelwald has several **camping grounds** and countless **holiday apartments** and **chalets** from which to choose. Ask the tourist office for a complete list.

The **SYHA hostel** (☎ 033 853 10 09, fax 033 853 50 29; e grindelwald@youthhostel .ch; Terrassenweg; dorm beds from Sfr29.50), a hillside wooden chalet above the town, has magnificent views. The bad news is it's a tough 20-minute climb from the station. Avoid the slog by taking the Terrassenweg-bound bus to the Gaggi Säge stop.

If the hostel's full, try the nearby **Naturfreundehaus** (☎ 033 853 13 33, fax 033 853 43 33; e nfhostel@grindelwald.ch; Terrassenweg; dorm beds from Sfr27, with breakfast/ half-board Sfr33/50). Both hostels are closed between seasons.

Near the Mälichen cable-car station, the modern **Mountain Hostel** (☎ 033 853 39 00; e mhostel@grindelwald.ch; dorm beds/ doubles with breakfast from Sfr34/88) is a good base for sports junkies eager to get to the slopes. Big, bright and blue, it's impossible to miss.

Lehmann's Herberge (☎/fax 033 853 31 41; singles/doubles from Sfr40/80), in the village centre, provides spartan rooms and a buffet breakfast. It's situated just off the main street (signposted).

The **Hirschen Hotel** (☎ 033 854 84 84; e hirschen.grindelwald@bluewin.ch; singles/ doubles Sfr105/180), on the main street, is a friendly and family-run three-star hotel with cheerful, wood-panelled rooms.

Most hotels in town have their own restaurants and some also have bars and clubs. For tasty traditional food and staggering views of the Eiger, try **Rendez-vous Restaurant** (☎ 033 853 11 81; mains Sfr13.50-27; closed Tues) on the main street. Fondue is Sfr21.50, or launch yourself into a platter of Grindelwald cheese or cold meats.

Onkel Tom's Hütte (☎ 033 853 52 39; pizza from Sfr10; open 6pm-10.30pm Tues, noon-11.30pm Wed-Sat, noon-9pm Sun), on the way out of town, is a cosy California-style barn with cheap tucker and an excellent wine list.

Self-caterers can stock up at **Coop supermarket** opposite the tourist office.

Getting There & Away Grindelwald is only 40 minutes by train from Interlaken Ost (Sfr9.40 each way), and is easily reached by road.

Lauterbrunnen Valley

The Lauterbrunnen Valley branches out from Interlaken with sheer rockfaces and towering mountains on either side, attracting an army of hikers and mountain bikers. Cow bells echo in the valley and every house and hostel has a postcard-worthy view. The first village reached by car or rail is **Lauterbrunnen**, known mainly for the trickling **Staubbach Falls** and the much more impressive **Trümmelbach Falls** (admission Sfr10; open Apr-Oct), 4km out of town. Find out more from the **tourist office** (☎ 033 855 19 55; e info@lauterbrunnen.tourismus .ch), on the main street.

Above the village (via the funicular) there's Grütschalp, where you switch to the train to **Mürren** (Sfr9.40 total), a skiing and hiking resort. The ride yields tremendous unfolding views across the valley to the Jungfrau, Mönch and Eiger peaks. Mürren's efficient **tourist office** (☎ 033 856 86 86; e info@muerren.ch) is in the sports centre. A pleasant 40-minute walk downhill from Mürren is tiny **Gimmelwald**, a minute rural village with a pungent barnyard aroma.

Gimmelwald and Mürren can also be reached from the valley floor by the **Stechelberg cable car**, which runs up to **Schilthorn** (2971m). From the top there's a fantastic panorama, and film shows will remind you that James Bond performed his stunts here in *On Her Majesty's Secret Service*. The standard return fare for Schilthorn is Sfr89, but ask about low-season or first/last ascent of the day discounts.

Places to Stay & Eat Gimmelwald and Lauterbrunnen have some of the cheapest accommodation in the region. Another base with plenty of appeal is Wengen, a hiking and skiing centre clinging to the eastern side of the valley. It has several hotels and the reader-recommended backpacker hostel **Hot Chili Peppers** (☎ 033 855 50 20; e chilis@wengen .com; dorm beds/doubles Sfr26/99), with chatty staff and a popular ground-floor bar.

Lauterbrunnen With views of the falls, **Camping Schützenbach** (☎ 033 855 12 68; adult/child/tent Sfr8.40/3.90/14, dorm beds

Sfr18.50) and **Camping Jungfrau** *(☎ 033 856 20 10; adult/child/tent Sfr10.60/5/15, dorm beds Sfr22)* offer excellent facilities and a range of accommodation.

You won't get much cheaper than **Matratzenlager Stocki** *(☎ 033 855 17 54; dorm beds Sfr13; closed Nov & Dec)*, a cosy, mountain cabin with a homely feel and extremely close quarters.

Another excellent option is the newish **Valley Hostel** *(☎/fax 033 855 20 08; e valley hostel@bluewin.ch; dorm beds/doubles from Sfr22/52)*, which offers comfy rooms (many with balconies) and a mellow, nonsmoking environment.

Chalet im Rohr *(☎ 033 855 21 82; singles/ doubles Sfr26/52)*, across from the church, is a large, creaky wooden chalet with balconies and overflowing flowerboxes.

Cheap eats are harder to track down. Stock up in the **Coop** near the tourist office, or try one of the **hotel restaurants**. For a snack, beer, email check or serious game of darts, head to the **Horner Pub/Hotel** *(☎ 033 855 16 73; open 9am-1.30am daily)*.

Gimmelwald Close to the cable-car station, **Mountain Hostel** *(☎ 033 855 17 04, fax 033 855 26 88; e mountainhostel@tcnet.ch; dorm beds Sfr18)* has jaw-dropping views, snacks and beer for hungry guests, Internet access and a pool table. If you don't mind the occasional roll in the hay, **Esther's Guesthouse** *(☎ 033 855 54 88; e evallmen@bluewin.ch)* offers beds of straw in a big, old barn (Sfr20, including a generous breakfast of organic food). Health nuts can pick up biodynamic farm produce from Esther's 'Little Farmer Shop'.

Restaurant-Pension Gimmelwald *(☎/fax 033 855 17 30; e pensiongimmelwald@ tcnet.ch; dishes from Sfr14)* has hearty home cooking, including fondue and farmers' barley soup. Five minutes up the hill there's the **Mittaghorn** *(Walter's; ☎ 033 855 16 58; dorm beds/doubles Sfr25/70)*, with basic accommodation and a small café.

Mürren By the train station is **Eiger Guesthouse** *(☎ 033 855 35 35, fax 033 855 35 31; e eigerguesthouse@muerren.ch; dorm beds Sfr45, singles Sfr65-90, doubles Sfr110-150)*, with a bar, restaurant and games room. **Hotel Edelweiss** *(☎ 033 855 13 12, fax 033 855 42 02; e edelweiss@muerren.ch; singles Sfr90-120, doubles Sfr190-240)* offers comfortable

three-star rooms with views of the Eiger and Jungfrau (ask for a balcony). Don't leave town without trying the hearty home cooking at **Staegerstübli**, with generous helpings of delicious traditional food. Self-caterers can stock up at the **Coop supermarket** next door.

Jungfraujoch

The trip to Jungfraujoch by train (the highest in Europe) is excellent – if it's a clear day. Unfortunately, the price is as steep as the track and you're at the mercy of the weather gods (call ☎ 033 855 10 22 for taped forecasts or check cable TV). From Interlaken Ost, trains go via Grindelwald or Lauterbrunnen to Kleine Scheidegg. From here, the line is less than 10km long but took 16 years to build. Opened in 1912, the track powers through both the Eiger and the Mönch, pausing briefly for travellers to take happy snaps of views from two windows blasted in the mountainside, before terminating at Jungfraujoch (3454m).

On the summit, there is free entry to the **ice palace** (exhibition rooms cut within the glacier) and free use of plastic disks for sliding down glacial slopes. From the terrace of the **Sphinx Research Institute** (a weather station) the panorama of peaks and valleys is unforgettable, including the **Aletsch Glacier** to the south, and mountains as distant as the Jura and the Black Forest. Take warm clothing and sunglasses (for glacier walking).

From Interlaken Ost, the journey is 2½ hours each way (Sfr162 return). Allow at least three hours at the site. There's a cheaper 'good morning ticket' of Sfr125 if you can drag yourself out of bed for the early train (6.35am from Interlaken) and leave the summit by noon. From 1 November to 30 April the reduction is valid for the 6.35am and 7.35am trains, and the noon restriction does not apply. Eurail passholders get 25% off, and Swisspass holders slightly more.

Northern Switzerland

This region is important for industry and commerce, yet by no means lacks tourist attractions. Take time to explore the tiny rural towns set among green rolling hills, and Lake Constance (Bodensee) and the Rhine on the German border.

BASEL
pop 163,800

Basel (Bâle in French) is an affluent city squeezed into the top left corner of the country, bordering France and Germany. Although a major hub of commerce and industry, it has an idyllic old town and many enticing museums. The famous Renaissance humanist, Erasmus of Rotterdam, was associated with the city and his tomb rests in the cathedral.

Orientation & Information

Basel's strategic position on the Rhine, beside France and Germany, has been instrumental in its development. On the northern bank of the river is Kleinbasel (Little Basel), surrounded by German territory. The pedestrian-only old town and most popular sights are on the south bank in Grossbasel (Greater Basel).

The **Basel Tourismus** (☎ *061 268 68 68;* e *office@baseltourismus.ch; Schifflände 5; open 8.30am-6pm Mon-Fri & 10am-4pm Sat)* is by the Mittlere Brücke. There's a hole-in-the-wall **tourist office** in the main **SBB train station**, which also has **bike rental** and **money exchange** *(open 6am-9pm daily)* and a **Migros supermarket** *(open 6am-10pm Mon-Fri, 7.30am-10pm Sat-Sun & holidays).*

The **main post office** *(Freie Strasse; open 7.30am-6.30pm Mon-Wed & Fri, 7.30am-10pm Thur, 8am-noon Sat)* is situated in the city centre and there's another **branch** by the train station.

You can check your emails in quiet, modern comfort at the **Tiscali Internet Center** (☎ *0844 89 19 91;* e *info@tiscalinet.ch; Steinentorstrasse 11; open 9am-10pm Mon-Thur, 9am-8pm Fri, 9am-5pm Sat)* where Net access costs Sfr5/8 for 30/60 minutes. With better hours, but sharing space with noisy computer games, there's **Domino** (☎ *061 271 13 50;* e *ngc@ net-generation.ch; Steinenvorstadt 54; open 9.30am-midnight Mon-Thur, 9.30am-1am Fri-Sat, 1pm-midnight Sun)* where Net access costs Sfr10/60 for an hour/day.

Things to See & Do

Take a self-guided walk through the **old town**, with its cobbled streets, colourful fountains, and Middle-Age churches and stately buildings. The tourist office distributes leaflets with suggested routes, and it can also arrange two-hour **guided walks** *(adult/child Sfr15/7.50; 2.30pm daily May–mid-Oct, 2.30pm Sat mid-Oct–Apr).*

In Marktplatz is the impressive rust-coloured **Rathaus** (town hall), with frescoed courtyard. The 12th-century **Münster** (cathedral) is another highlight, with Gothic spires and Romanesque St Gallus doorway. Don't miss the stunning view of the Rhine behind the Münster, where office workers lunch and visitors gaze across the river to Kleinbasel.

Theaterplatz is a crowd-pleaser, with a curious **fountain**, designed by Swiss sculptor Jean Tinguely. His madcap scrap-metal machines perform a peculiar water dance, delighting children and weary travellers alike. Also check out the 700-year-old **Spalentor** gate tower, a remnant of the town's old city walls, with a massive portal and grotesque gargoyles.

Basel has over 30 museums from which to choose – the BaselCard costs Sfr25/33/45 for one/two/three days and gives free entry to them all.

The **Kunstmuseum** *(Art Museum;* ☎ *061 206 62 62;* w *www.kunstmuseumbasel.ch; St Albangraben 16; adult/student/child Sfr10/ 8/free, free 1st Sun of month; open 10am-5pm Tues-Sun)* features religious and local art, a cubism collection including a palette of Picassos, and a copper-etchings gallery. Admission also grants entry to the **Museum für Gegenwartskunst** (☎ *061 272 81 83; St Alban-Rheinweg 60; same hours),* in a converted factory, exhibiting contemporary art pieces including works by Andy Warhol and Joseph Beuys.

Contemporary-art devotees should also make sure to visit the **Museum Jean Tinguely Basel** (☎ *061 681 93 20;* w *www.tinguely.ch; Grenzacherstrasse/Solitude-Park; adult/child Sfr7/5; open 11am-7pm Wed-Sun),* east of the city centre, a shrine to the mechanical work of the local artist.

For a change of pace, the BaselCard provides free entry to Basel's **zoo** (☎ *061 295 35 35; Binningerstrasse;* w *www.zoobasel.ch; adult/child/family Sfr14/5/30; open 8am-6pm daily),* known locally as the 'Zolli'.

Of interest, but possibly more for novelty value than anything else, is Drei Länder Eck (Three Countries Corner), where the Swiss, German and French borders meet. Take tram No 8 to the last stop, from where it's a 10-minute walk.

If you're lucky enough to be in town on the Monday after Ash Wednesday you'll be treated to Fasnacht, a three-day spectacle of parades, masks, music and costumes, all starting at 4am.

SWITZERLAND

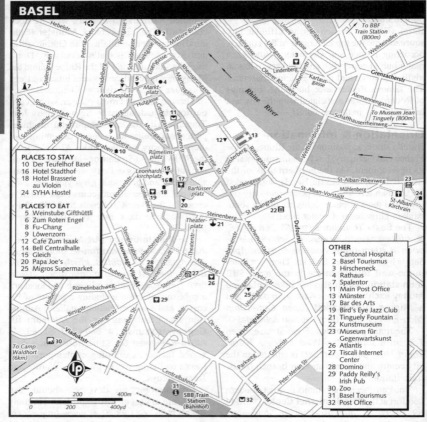

BASEL

PLACES TO STAY
10 Der Teufelhof Basel
16 Hotel Stadthof
18 Hotel Brasserie
au Violon
24 SYHA Hostel

PLACES TO EAT
5 Weinstube Gifthüttli
6 Zum Roten Engel
8 Fu-Chang
9 Löwenzorn
12 Cafe Zum Isaak
14 Bell Centralhalle
15 Gleich
20 Papa Joe's
25 Migros Supermarket

OTHER
1 Cantonal Hospital
2 Basel Tourismus
3 Hirscheneck
4 Rathaus
7 Spalentor
11 Main Post Office
13 Münster
17 Bar des Arts
19 Bird's Eye Jazz Club
21 Tinguely Fountain
22 Kunstmuseum
23 Museum für
Gegenwartskunst
26 Atlantis
27 Tiscali Internet
Center
28 Domino
29 Paddy Reilly's
Irish Pub
30 Zoo
31 Basel Tourismus
32 Post Office

Places to Stay

Hotels are often full during Basel's numerous trade fairs and conventions, so book ahead. The tourist offices offer a reservation service for a fee (Sfr10/15 for Basel/out-of-town) and can help with cheaper, out-of-town accommodation. Don't forget to ask your accommodation for the Mobility Card, which entitles you to free local transport.

Camp Waldhort (☎ 061 711 64 29; e camp.waldhort@gmx.ch; Heideweg 16, Reinach; adult/child/tent/camper van Sfr7/4.50/11/17; open Mar-Oct) is in a small village, 6km south of the train station.

The **SYHA hostel** (☎ 061 272 05 72, fax 061 272 08 33; St Alban Kirchrain 10; dorm beds Sfr30-32, singles/doubles Sfr80/100), 10 minutes from the centre, is in a converted

textiles factory in St Alban, a quiet, leafy, old-money part of town. It has small spick-and-span rooms and Internet access (Sfr5 for 20 minutes).

Hotel Stadthof (☎ 061 261 87 11, fax 061 261 25 84; e info@stadthof.ch; Gerbergasse 84; singles/doubles from Sfr70/120) offers rudimentary rooms with shared hall shower. Tucked in the corner of buzzing Barfüsserplatz, its bar and **restaurant** do a roaring trade.

Climb the ancient stone stairs to **Hotel Brasserie au Violon** (☎ 061 269 87 11, fax 061 269 87 12; e auviolon@iprolink.ch; Im Lohnhof 4; singles/doubles from Sfr90/140), a majestic former monastery and prison with tastefully decorated rooms. There's an elegant **restaurant** downstairs for breakfast (Sfr14) and other meals.

Der Teufelhof Basel (☎ 061 261 10 10, fax 061 261 10 04; e info@teufelhof.com; Leonhardsgraben 47; singles/doubles from Sfr250/277, in Galeriehotel annexe from Sfr180/255) is a unique option for more creative souls. Each of the nine rooms features theme-based 'environmental art' created by a different artist. The Galeriehotel annexe has cheaper rooms, and there's a small theatre, stylish **restaurant** and wine shop.

Places to Eat
For a quick, cheap bite on the run, the daily **market** on Marktplatz has tasty bratwurst (Sfr5) and delicious breads (Sfr3 to Sfr7). Alternatively, there's pedestrian-only **Steinenvorstadt**, with its countless fast-food outlets, cafés and restaurants.

Cafe Zum Roten Engel (☎ 061 261 20 08; Andreasplatz 15; meals Sfr9-14; open 9am-midnight Mon-Sat, 10am-10pm Sun), hidden away in a quiet, leafy courtyard, is a busy student hang-out serving delicious vegie snacks and gigantic mugs of coffee.

Gleich (☎ 061 261 48 83; Leonhardsberg 1; mains Sfr16-26; open 10.30am-9.30pm Mon-Fri), in a laneway off Gerbergasse, is another favourite haunt for nonmeat-eaters.

Zum Isaak (☎ 061 25 77 11; Kaffihaus am Munsterplatz 16; open 9am-10.30pm Tues-Sat, 9am-6pm Sun; tea/coffee Sfr4.30, meals Sfr8-18) blends quirky artwork with a laid-back atmosphere and a range of 20-plus teas.

For Basel specialities and a traditional atmosphere, try **Weinstube Gifthüttli** (☎ 061 261 16 56; Schneidergasse 11; mains Sfr25-38; open 9am-11.30pm Mon-Sat) or **Löwenzorn** (☎ 061 261 42 13; Gemsberg 2; mains Sfr27.50-44; open 9am-11.45pm Mon-Sat). Both restaurants offer a meaty daily lunch menu for Sfr17 to Sfr20.

Papa Joe's (☎ 061 274 04 04; am Barfi; meals Sfr22.50-48.50; open 11.30am-2pm & 5pm-late Mon-Fri, 5pm-late Sat & Sun) is a Tex-Mex-style restaurant serving burgers, ribs and nachos to appreciative locals. Its adjoining bar, with terracotta tiles, plastic toucans and American paraphernalia, attracts a cocktail-quaffing crowd.

Fu-Chang (☎ 061 261 98 71; Schützenmattstrasse 1; lunches Sfr12.50-15; open 11.30am-3pm & 5.30pm-10pm Mon-Fri, 11am-3pm Sat), a stone's throw from the towering Spalentor, serves generous helpings of tasty Asian dishes.

For self-caterers, there's the local **Migros** (Sternengasse 17; open 7.30am-6.30pm Mon-Wed & Fri, 7.30am-10pm Thur, 7.30am-5pm Sat). Or for a huge selection of organic local produce (including 200 different cheeses), try the **Bell Centralhalle** (cnr Streitgasse & Weisse Gasse; open 8am-6pm Mon-Fri, 8am-10pm Thur, 8am-5pm Sat).

Entertainment
In Steinenvorstadt, there's a string of **cinemas** with latest-release movies. There's also a bar/café/restaurant to suit every taste. **Paddy Reilly's Irish Pub** (☎ 061 281 33 36; Steinentorstrasse 45; bar meals Sfr5-12.50; open 11.30am-1am Sun-Wed, 11.30am-2am Thur-Sat) entices expats with Brit beers and big-screen TV. The spacious, stylish **Bar des Arts** (☎ 061 273 57 37; Am Barfüsserplatz 6; open 11am-1am Mon-Wed, 11am-2am Thur, 11am-3am Fri-Sat, 3pm-midnight Sun) has a piano player tickling the ivories and an extensive drinks menu (happy hour 5pm to 7pm).

For everything from house to pop, soul and R&B, there's **Atlantis** (☎ 061 228 96 96; Klosterberg 13). Wrapped in garish gold, it's impossible to miss. In Kleinbasel, there's the grungier **Hirscheneck** (☎ 061 692 73 33; Lindenberg 23; entry Sfr8-15) which is a melting pot of nonconservatives, with DJs and thrashy live music on weekends and the occasional weekday.

For smoother grooves, try the **Bird's Eye Jazz Club** (☎ 061 263 33 41; Kohlenberg 20; entry from Sfr10; open 8pm-1am Tues-Wed & Sun, 8pm-2am Thur-Sat).

Getting There & Away
Basel is a major European rail hub. On most international trains you pass through the border controls in the station, so allow extra time. Trains to France leave from the **SNCF section** of SBB station; there are seven daily to Paris (Sfr69, five hours). Germany-bound trains stop at **Badischer Bahnhof** (BBF) on the northern bank; local trains to the Black Forest stop only at BBF, though fast EC services stop at SBB, too.

Main destinations along this route are Amsterdam (Sfr180, eight hours), Frankfurt (Sfr80, three hours) and Hamburg (Sfr198, 6½ hours). Services within Switzerland leave from SBB: there are two fast trains hourly to both Geneva (Sfr71, three hours; via Bern or Biel/Bienne) and Zürich (Sfr30, 70 minutes).

By motorway, the E25/E60 heads from Strasbourg and passes by the EuroAirport, and the E35/A5 hugs the German side of the Rhine.

Getting Around

For the EuroAirport, catch bus No 50 from in front of the SBB Station (Sfr6.60). City buses and trams run every six to 10 minutes (Sfr1.80 for four or fewer stops, Sfr2.80 for central zone, Sfr8 for day pass). By the SBB station is a **hut** offering *free* bike loans in summer.

SCHAFFHAUSEN
pop 32,900

Schaffhausen is a quaint medieval town on the northern bank of the Rhine, surrounded by German territory. Beautiful oriel windows, painted facades and ornamental fountains crowd the streets of the **old town**. See the finest examples of these in Vordergasse and Vorstadt, which intersect at Fronwagplatz. **Schaffhausen Tourism** (☎ 052 625 51 41; e tourist@swissworld.com) can help with a map and sightseeing options.

For the best views around, climb up to the 16th-century hill-top **Munot fortress** (admission free; open 8am-10pm daily May-Sept, 9am-5pm daily Oct-Apr). By the cathedral is the **Allerheiligen Museum** (☎ 052 633 07 77; Klosterstrasse; admission free; open noon-5pm Tues-Wed & Fri-Sun, noon-8pm Thur), with art and archaeological exhibits.

Rhine Falls (Rheinfall) is a 40-minute stroll westward along the river, or take bus No 1 to Neuhausen. Though the drop is only 23m, the waterfall is considered the largest in Europe, with an extraordinary amount of water thundering over it. The 45km of the Rhine from Schaffhausen to Constance is one of the river's most stunning stretches, passing by meadows, castles and ancient villages, including **Stein am Rhein**, 20km to the east, where you could easily wear out your camera in Rathausplatz.

Places to Stay & Eat

Schaffhausen is an easy day trip from Zürich, but overnighters won't regret a stay at the **SYHA hostel** (☎ 052 625 88 00, fax 052 624 59 54; Randenstrasse 65; dorm beds from Sfr24; open Mar-Nov), in an impressive 16th-century former manor house.

If you've got the munchies, look for pretzel and bratwurst **stalls** on Vordergasse. There are also cheap eats at **Migros** (Vorstadt 39), **China**

Town Take Away (Vorstadt 36) or **Manora** (Manor department store, Vordergasse).

Getting There & Away

Hourly trains run to Zürich (Sfr17.20, 50 minutes). Constance and Basel can be reached by either Swiss or (cheaper) German trains. **Untersee Und Rhein** (☎ 052 634 08 88; e info@urh.ch) operates steamers to/from Constance (Sfr38, four hours, four daily May to October). Schaffhausen has good roads in all directions.

ST GALLEN
pop 70,300

In AD 612, an itinerant Irish monk called Gallus fell into a briar. An irritating mishap, most people would think, but Gallus interpreted it as a sign from God and decided to stay put and build a hermitage. From this inauspicious beginning the town of St Gallen evolved and developed into an important medieval cultural centre.

The **main post office** is opposite the train station. Two minutes away there's **St Gallen-Bodensee Tourismus** (☎ 071 227 37 37; e info@stgallen-bodensee.ch; Bahnhofplatz 1a; open 9am-noon & 1pm-6pm Mon-Fri, 9am-noon Sat).

St Gallen has an interesting pedestrian-only **old town**. Many buildings have distinctive oriel windows, with the best on Gallusplatz, Spisergasse and Kugelgasse. Don't miss the twin-tower **Kathedrale**, with an ostentatious interior which includes dark ceiling frescoes by Josef Wannenmacher and the marine-green stucco-work by the Gigel brothers. Also note the pulpit, arches and woodcarvings around the confessionals.

Bookworms will treasure a sticky-beak through the nearby **Stiftsbibliothek** (Abbey Library; ☎ 071 227 34 16; adult/student Sfr7/5; closed three weeks in Nov), one of the oldest libraries of the Western world. It contains some manuscripts from the Middle Ages and an opulent rococo interior.

Places to Stay & Eat

The modern **SYHA hostel** (☎ 071 245 47 77, fax 071 245 49 83; Jüchstrasse 25; dorm beds Sfr26, singles/doubles Sfr46.50/72; open Mar–mid-Dec) is a signposted 15-minute walk east of the old town; take the Trogenerbahn from the station to 'Schülerhaus' (Sfr2.40).

Closer to town is the **Hotel Vadian Garni** (☎ 071 228 18 78, fax 071 228 18 79;

Gallusstrasse 36; singles/doubles from Sfr70/ 100, with bathroom Sfr92/140), a friendly and alcohol-free, family-run hotel close to the cathedral. The recently renovated **Weisses Kreuz** (*☎/fax 071 223 28 43; Engelgasse 9; singles/doubles from Sfr61/108)* is central and good value, with reception in the mellow bistro-bar downstairs.

Fast-food stalls proliferate around the old town, selling St Gallen sausage and bread for around Sfr6. There's also a buffet-style **Manora** *(4th floor, Manor department store, Marktplatz)*, with a wide selection of freshly cooked meals.

Restaurant Marktplatz (*☎ 071 222 36 41; Neugasse 2; mains Sfr14.50-19.80; open 8.30am-midnight Mon-Sat, 10am-midnight Sun)* is a rowdy beer-hall-style restaurant serving beer, pizza and local meaty dishes.

For a calmer atmosphere and traditional Swiss food, try **Wirtschaft Zur Alten Post** (*☎ 071 222 66 01; Gallusstrasse 4; mains Sfr20-42; open 11am-2pm & 5.30pm-11pm Tues-Sat)*, near the cathedral. Small and cosy, it fills quickly so reserve ahead.

Getting There & Away
St Gallen is a short train ride from Lake Constance (Bodensee), upon which boats sail to Bregenz in Austria, and to Constance and Lindau in Germany (but not in winter). There are also regular trains to Bregenz (Sfr16, 40 minutes), Constance (Sfr16.60, one hour) and Zürich (Sfr26, 70 minutes).

APPENZELL
Parochial Appenzellers, inherently resistant to change, are often the butt of Swiss jokes. Appenzell village, nestled in the middle of lush farmland, reflects this conservatism, with an old-fashioned ambience that's popular with tourists. Cobblestoned streets are lined with traditional old houses with painted facades, and souvenir shops selling everything from cowbells and chocolate to embroidered linen.

The streets are bedecked with flags and flowers on the last Sunday in April, when the locals vote on cantonal issues by a show of hands in the open-air parliament (Landsgemeinde). Many men carry swords or bayonets (often heirlooms) as proof of citizenship, but the women produce a simple licence to vote (they only won the right to vote in cantonal affairs in 1991).

There are hourly connections from St Gallen by narrow-gauge train, which meanders along, mostly following the course of the road (45 minutes). There are also trains to/ from Zürich (Sfr32, two hours), changing at Gossau or St Gallen.

Appendix – Telephones

Dial Direct

You can dial directly from public telephone boxes from almost anywhere in Europe to almost anywhere in the world. This is usually cheaper than going through the operator. In much of Europe, public telephones accepting phonecards are becoming the norm and in some countries coin-operated phones are difficult to find.

To call abroad simply dial the international access code (IAC) for the country you are calling from (most commonly ☎ 00 in Europe but see the following table), the country code (CC) for the country you are calling, the local area code (usually dropping the leading zero if there is one) and then the number. If, for example, you are in Italy (international access code ☎ 00) and want to make a call to the USA (country code ☎ 1), San Francisco (area code ☎ 415), number ☎ 123 4567, then you dial ☎ 00-1-415-123 4567. To call from the UK (☎ 00) to Australia (☎ 61), Sydney (☎ 02), number ☎ 1234 5678, you dial the following: ☎ 00-61-2-1234 5678.

Home Direct

If you would rather have somebody else pay for the call, you can, from many countries, dial directly to your home country operator and then reverse charges; you can also charge the call to a phone company credit card. To do this, simply dial the relevant 'home direct' or 'country direct' number to be connected to your own operator. For the USA there's a choice of AT&T, MCI or Sprint Global One home direct services. Home direct numbers vary from country to country – check with your telephone company before you leave, or with the international operator in the country you're ringing from. From phone boxes in some countries you may need a coin or local phonecard to be connected with the relevant home direct operator.

In some places (particularly airports), you may find dedicated home direct phones where you simply press the button labelled USA, Australia, Hong Kong or whatever for direct connection to the operator. Note that the home direct service does not operate to and from all countries, and that the call could be charged at operator rates, which makes it expensive for the person paying. Placing a call on your phone credit card is more expensive than paying the local tariff.

Dialling Tones

In some countries, after you have dialled the international access code, you have to wait for a second dial tone before dialling the code for your target country and the number. Often the same applies when you ring from one city to another within these countries: wait for a dialling tone after you've dialled the area code for your target city. If you're not sure what to do, simply wait three or four seconds after dialling a code – if nothing happens, you can probably keep dialling.

Phonecards

In major locations phones may accept credit cards: simply swipe your card through the slot and the call is charged to the card, though rates can be very high. Phone-company credit cards can be used to charge calls via your home country operator.

Stored-value phonecards are now almost standard all over Europe. You usually buy a card from a post office, telephone centre, newsstand or retail outlet and simply insert the card into the phone each time you make a call. The card solves the problem of finding the correct coins for calls (or lots of correct coins for international calls) and generally gives you a small discount.

Call Costs

The cost of international calls varies widely from one country to another: a US$1.20 call from Britain could cost you US$6 from Turkey. The countries shown in the 'Telephone Codes & Costs' table that follows are rated from * (cheap) to *** (expensive), but rates can vary depending on which country you are calling to (for example, from Italy it's relatively cheap to call North America, but more expensive to call Australia). Reduced rates are available at certain times, usually from mid-evening to early morning, though it varies from country to country – check the local phone book or ask the operator for more details. Calling from hotel rooms can be very expensive.

Telephone Codes & Costs

	CC	cost (see text)	IAC	IO
Albania	355	***	00	12
Andorra	376	**	00	821111
Austria	43	*	00	09
Belarus	375	***	8(w)10	(017) 233 2971
Belgium	32	**	00	1224 (private phone)
				1223 (public phone)
Bosnia-Hercegovina	387	**	00	900/901/902
Bulgaria	359	**	00	0123 (calls)
				0124 (inquiries)
Croatia	385	**	00	901
Cyprus	357	***	00	
Cyprus (Turkish)	90+392		00	
Czech Republic	420	*	00	1181/0149
Denmark	45	**	00	141
Estonia	372	***	000	165
Finland	358	**	00, 990, 994, 999	020222
France	33	*	00(w)	12
Germany	49	*	00	11834
Gibraltar	350	***	00	100
Greece	30	*	00	161
Hungary	36	*	00(w)	199
Iceland	354	***	00	5335010
Ireland	353	*	00	114
Northern Ireland	44+28	*	00	155
Italy	39	**	00	15
Latvia	371	***	00	115
Liechtenstein	423	***	00	114
Lithuania	370	***	00	194/195
Luxembourg	352	**	00	0010
Macedonia	389	***	99	901
Malta	356	**	00	194
Moldova	373	***	8(w)10	973
Morocco	212	***	00(w)	12
Netherlands	31	**	00	0800-0410
Norway	47	**	00	181
Poland	48	**	00	901
Portugal	351	*	00	099
Romania	40	***	00	971
Russia	7	**	8(w)10	
Slovakia	421	**	00	0149
Slovenia	386	**	00	115
Spain	34	**	00(w)	025
Sweden	46	**	00	0018
Switzerland	41	**	00	114
Tunisia	216	**	00	
Turkey	90	***	00	115
UK	44	*	00	155
Ukraine	380	**	810	079/073
Yugoslavia	381	***	99	901

CC – Country Code (to call into that country)
IAC – International Access Code (to call abroad from that country)
IO – International Operator (to make inquiries)
(w) – wait for dialling tone

Other country codes include: Australia ☎ 61, Canada ☎ 1, Hong Kong ☎ 852, India ☎ 91, Indonesia ☎ 62, Israel ☎ 972, Japan ☎ 81, Macau ☎ 853, Malaysia ☎ 60, New Zealand ☎ 64, Singapore ☎ 65, South Africa ☎ 27, Thailand ☎ 66, USA ☎ 1

Language

This Language Guide contains pronunciation guidelines and basic vocabulary to help you get around Central Europe. For background information about the languages, see the Language sections under Facts for the Visitor in the relevant country chapters.

For a more detailed guide to all the languages included here, get a copy of Lonely Planet's *Eastern Europe* and *German phrasebooks*.

Czech

Pronunciation

Many Czech letters are pronounced as per their English counterparts. An accent lengthens a vowel and the stress is always on the first syllable. Words are pronounced as written, so if you follow the guidelines below you should have no trouble being understood. When consulting indexes on Czech maps, be aware that **ch** comes after **h**. An accent over a vowel indicates that it is lengthened.

c	as the 'ts' in 'bits'
č	as the 'ch' in 'church'
ch	as in Scottish *loch*
ďʼ	as the 'd' in 'duty'
ě	as the 'ye' in 'yet'
j	as the 'y' in 'you'
ň	as the 'ni' in 'onion'
ř	as the sound 'rzh'
š	as the 'sh' in 'ship'
ťʼ	as the 'te' in 'stew'
ž	as the 's' in 'pleasure'

Basics

Hello/Good day.	*Dobrý den.* (pol)
Hi.	*Ahoj.* (inf)
Goodbye.	*Na shledanou.*
Yes.	*Ano.*
No.	*Ne.*
Please.	*Prosím.*
Thank you.	*Dekuji.*
That's fine/You're welcome.	*Není zač/Prosím.*
Sorry. (forgive me)	*Promiňte.*
I don't understand.	*Nerozumím.*
What is it called?	*Jak se to jmenuje?*
How much is it?	*Kolik to stojí?*

Getting Around

What time does the ... leave/arrive?	*Kdy odjíždí/přijíždí ...?*

Signs – Czech

Vchod	**Entrance**
Východ	**Exit**
Informace	**Information**
Otevřeno	**Open**
Zavřeno	**Closed**
Zakázáno	**Prohibited**
Policie	**Police Station**
Telefon	**Telephone**
Záchody/WC/ Toalety	**Toilets**

boat	*loď*
city bus	*městský autobus*
intercity bus	*meziměstský autobus*
train	*vlak*
tram	*tramvaj*

arrival	*příjezdy*
departure	*odjezdy*
timetable	*jízdní řád*
Where is the bus stop?	*Kde je autobusová zastávka?*
Where is the station?	*Kde je nádraží?*
Where is the left-luggage room?	*Kde je úschovna zavazadel?*
Where is it?	*Kde je to?*
Please show me on the map.	*Prosím, ukažte mi to na mapě.*
left	*vlevo*
right	*vpravo*
straight ahead	*rovně*

Around Town

the bank	*banka*
the chemist	*lékárna*
the church	*kostel*
the market	*trh*
the museum	*muzeum*
the post office	*pošta*
the tourist office	*turistické informační centrum (středisko)*
travel agency	*cestovní kancelář*

Accommodation

hotel	*hotel*
guesthouse	*penzión*
youth hostel	*ubytovna*
camping ground	*kemping*
private room	*privát*

Emergencies – Czech

Help!	*Pomoc!*
Call a doctor/ ambulance/police!	*Zavolejte doktora/ sanitku/policii!*
Go away!	*Běžte pryč!*
I'm lost.	*Zabloudil jsem.* (m)
	Zabloudila jsem. (f)

single room	*jednolůžkový pokoj*
double room	*dvoulůžkový pokoj*
Do you have any rooms available?	*Máte volné pokoje?*
How much is it?	*Kolik to je?*
Does it include breakfast?	*Je v tom zahrnuta snídane?*

Time, Days & Numbers

What time is it?	*Kolik je hodin?*
today	*dnes*
tonight	*dnes večer*
tomorrow	*zítra*
yesterday	*včera*
in the morning	*ráno*
in the evening	*večer*

Monday	*pondělí*
Tuesday	*úterý*
Wednesday	*středa*
Thursday	*čtvrtek*
Friday	*pátek*
Saturday	*sobota*
Sunday	*neděle*

1	*jeden*
2	*dva*
3	*tři*
4	*čtyři*
5	*pět*
6	*šest*
7	*sedm*
8	*osm*
9	*devět*
10	*deset*
100	*sto*
1000	*tisíc*

one million	*jeden milión*

German

Pronunciation

Vowels

As a rule, German vowels are long before one consonant and short before two consonants, eg, the **o** is long in the word *Dom*, 'cathedral', but short in the word *doch*, 'after all'.

au	as the 'ow' in 'vow'
ä	short, as in 'cat' or long, as in 'care'
äu	as the 'oy' in 'boy'
ei	as the 'ai' in 'aisle'
eu	as the 'oy' in 'boy'
ie	as the 'brief'
ö	as the 'er' in 'fern'
ü	similar to the 'u' in 'pull' but with lips stretched back

Consonants

Most German consonants sound similar to their English counterparts. One important difference is that **b**, **d** and **g** sound like 'p', 't' and 'k', respectively when word-final.

ch	as in Scottish *loch*
j	as the 'y' in 'yet'
qu	as 'k' plus 'v'
r	can be trilled or guttural, depending on the region
s	as in 'sun'; as the 'z' in 'zoo' when followed by a vowel
sch	as the 'sh' in 'ship'
sp, st	as 'shp' and 'sht' when word-initial
tion	the 't' is pronounced as the 'ts' in 'its'
v	as the 'f' in 'fan'
w	as the 'v' in 'van'
z	as the 'ts' in 'its'

Basics

Good day.	*Guten Tag.*
Hello. (in Bavaria and Austria)	*Grüss Gott.*
Goodbye.	*Auf Wiedersehen.*
Bye.	*Tschüss.* (informal)
Yes.	*Ja.*
No.	*Nein.*
Please.	*Bitte.*
Thank you.	*Danke.*
You're welcome.	*Bitte sehr.*
Sorry. (excuse me, forgive me)	*Entschuldigung.*
What's your name?	*Wie heissen Sie?*
My name is ...	*Ich heisse ...*
Do you speak English?	*Sprechen Sie Englisch?*
How much is it?	*Wieviel kostet es?*

Getting Around

What time does ... leave/arrive?	*Wann (fährt ... ab/ kommt ... an)?*
the boat	*das Boot*
the city bus	*der Bus*
the intercity bus	*der überland Bus*

the train	*der Zug*
the tram	*die Strassenbahn*

What time is the next ...?	*Wann fährt das nächste ...?*
I'd like to hire a car/bicycle.	*Ich möchte ein Auto/ Fahrrad mieten.*
I'd like a one-way/ return ticket.	*Ich möchte eine Einzel- karte/Rückfahrkarte.*

1st/2nd class	*erste/zweite Klasse*
left luggage lockers	*Schliessfächer*
timetable	*Fahrplan*
bus stop	*Bushaltestelle*
tram stop	*Strassenbahnhaltestelle*
train station	*Bahnhof (Bf)*
ferry terminal	*Fährhafen*

Where is the ...?	*Wo ist die ...?*
Go straight ahead.	*Gehen Sie geradeaus.*
Turn left.	*Biegen Sie links ab.*
Turn right.	*Biegen Sie rechts ab.*
near/far	*nahe/weit*

Around Town

I'm looking for ...	*Ich suche ...*
a bank	*eine Bank*
the ... embassy	*die ... Botschaft*
my hotel	*mein Hotel*
the market	*der Markt*
the newsagency	*der Zeitungshändler*
the pharmacy	*die Apotheke*
the post office	*das Postamt*
the stationers	*der Schreibwaren- geschäft*
the telephone centre	*die Telefonzentrale*
the tourist office	*das Verkehrsamt*
What time does it open/close?	*Um wieviel Uhr macht es auf/zu?*

Accommodation

hotel	*Hotel*
guesthouse	*Pension, Gästehaus*

Signs – German

Eingang	**Entrance**
Ausgang	**Exit**
Zimmer Frei	**Rooms Available**
Auskunft	**Information**
Offen	**Open**
Geschlossen	**Closed**
Polizeiwache	**Police Station**
Toiletten (WC)	**Toilets**
Herren	**Men**
Damen	**Women**

Emergencies – German

Help!	*Hilfe!*
Call a doctor!	*Holen Sie einen Arzt!*
Call the police!	*Rufen Sie die Polizei!*
Go away!	*Gehen Sie weg!*
I'm lost.	*Ich habe mich verirrt.*

youth hostel	*Jugendherberge*
camping ground	*Campingplatz*

Do you have any rooms available?	*Haben Sie noch freie Zimmer?*
a single room	*ein Einzelzimmer*
a double room	*ein Doppelzimmer*
Is breakfast included?	*Ist Frühstück in- begriffen?*

How much is it ...?	*Wieviel kostet es ...?*
per night	*pro Nacht*
per person	*pro Person*

Time, Days & Numbers

What time is it?	*Wie spät ist es?*
today	*heute*
tomorrow	*morgen*
yesterday	*gestern*
in the morning	*morgens*
in the afternoon	*nachmittags*

Monday	*Montag*
Tuesday	*Dienstag*
Wednesday	*Mittwoch*
Thursday	*Donnerstag*
Friday	*Freitag*
Saturday	*Samstag, Sonnabend*
Sunday	*Sonntag*

0	*null*
1	*eins*
2	*zwei/zwo*
3	*drei*
4	*vier*
5	*fünf*
6	*sechs*
7	*sieben*
8	*acht*
9	*neun*
10	*zehn*
11	*elf*
12	*zwölf*
13	*dreizehn*
100	*hundert*
1000	*tausend*

one million	*eine Million*

Hungarian

Pronunciation

The pronunciation of Hungarian consonants can be simplified by pronouncing them more or less as in English; the exceptions are listed below. Double consonants **ll**, **tt** and **dd** aren't pronounced as one letter as in English but lengthened so you can almost hear them as separate letters. Also, **cs**, **zs**, **gy** and **sz** (consonant clusters) are separate letters in Hungarian and appear that way in telephone books and other alphabetical listings. For example, the word *cukor*, (sugar) appears in the dictionary before *csak* (only).

c	as the 'ts' in 'hats'
cs	as the 'ch' in 'church'
gy	as the 'j' in 'jury'
j	as the 'y' in 'yes'
ly	as the 'y' in 'yes'
ny	as the 'ni' in 'onion'
r	like a slightly trilled Scottish 'r'
s	as the 'sh' in 'ship'
sz	as the 's' in 'set'
ty	as the 'tu' in British English 'tube'
w	as 'v' (found in foreign words only)
zs	as the 's' in 'pleasure'

Vowels are a bit trickier, and the semantic difference between **a**, **e** or **o** with and without an accent mark is great. For example, *hát* means 'back' while *hat* means 'six'.

a	as the 'o' in hot
á	as in 'father'
e	a short 'e' as in 'set'
é	as the 'e' in 'they' with no 'y' sound
i	as in 'hit' but shorter
í	as the 'i' in 'police'
o	as in 'open'
ó	a longer version of o above
ö	as the 'o' in 'worse' with no 'r' sound
ő	a longer version of ö above
u	as in 'pull'
ú	as the 'ue' in 'blue'
ü	similar to the 'u' in 'flute'; purse your lips tightly and say 'ee'
ű	a longer, breathier version of ü above

Basics

Hello.	*Jó napot kívánok.* (pol)
	Szia/Szervusz. (inf)
Goodbye.	*Viszontlátásra.* (pol)
	Szia/Szervusz. (inf)

Yes.	*Igen.*
No.	*Nem.*
Please.	*Kérem.*
Thank you.	*Köszönöm.*
Sorry. (forgive me)	*Sajnálom/Elnézést.*
Excuse me.	*Bocsánat.*
What's your name?	*Hogy hívják?* (pol)
	Mi a neved? (inf)
My name is ...	*A nevem ...*
I don't understand.	*Nem értem.*
Do you speak English?	*Beszél angolul?*
What is it called?	*Hogy hívják?*
How much is it?	*Mennyibe kerül?*

Getting Around

What time does the ... leave/arrive?	*Mikor indul/érkezik a ...?*
boat/ferry	*hajó/komp*
city bus	*helyi autóbusz*
intercity bus	*távolsági autóbusz*
plane	*repülőgép*
train	*vonat*
tram	*villamos*

arrival	*érkezés*
departure	*indulás*
timetable	*menetrend*

Where is ...?	*Hol van ...?*
the bus stop	*az autóbuszmegálló*
the station	*a pályaudvar*
the left-luggage room	*a csomagmegőrző*

Please show me on the map.	*Kérem, mutassa meg a térképen.*
(Turn) left.	*(Forduljon) balra.*
(Turn) right.	*(Forduljon) jobbra.*
(Go) straight ahead	*(Menyen) egyenesen elore.*
near/far	*közel/messze*

Signs – Hungarian

Bejárat	**Entrance**
Kijárat	**Exit**
Információ	**Information**
Nyitva	**Open**
Zárva	**Closed**
Tilos	**Prohibited**
Rendőrőr-Kapitányság	**Police Station**
Telefon	**Telephone**
Toalett/WC	**Toilets**
Férfiak	**Men**
Nők	**Women**

Around Town

Where is ...?	Hol van ...?
a bank	bank
a chemist	gyógyszertár
the market	a piac
the museum	a múzeum
the post office	a posta
a tourist office	idegenforgalmi iroda

| What time does it open? | Mikor nyit ki? |
| What time does it close? | Mikor zár be? |

Accommodation

hotel	szálloda
guesthouse	fogadót
youth hostel	ifjúsági szálló
camping ground	kemping
private room	fizetővendég szoba

Do you have rooms available?	Van szabad szobájuk?
How much is it per night/ per person?	Mennyibe kerül éjszakánként/ személyenként?
Does it include breakfast?	Az ár tartalmazza a reggelit?
single room	egyágyas szoba
double room	kétágyas szoba

Time, Days & Numbers

What time is it?	Hány óra?
today	ma
tonight	ma este
tomorrow	holnap
yesterday	tegnap
in the morning	reggel
in the evening	este

Monday	hétfő
Tuesday	kedd
Wednesday	szerda
Thursday	csütörtök
Friday	péntek
Saturday	szombat
Sunday	vasárnap

1	egy
2	kettő
3	három
4	négy
5	öt
6	hat
7	hét
8	nyolc
9	kilenc
10	tíz
100	száz
1000	ezer

| one million | millió |

Polish

Pronunciation

Written Polish is phonetically consistent, which means that the pronunciation of letters or clusters of letters doesn't vary from word to word. The stress almost always goes on the second-last syllable.

Vowels

a	as the 'u' in 'cut'
e	as in 'ten'
i	similar to the 'ee' in 'feet' but shorter
o	as in 'lot'
u	a bit shorter than the 'oo' in 'book'
y	similar to the 'i' in 'bit'

There are three vowels unique to Polish:

ą	a nasal vowel sound like the French un, similar to 'own' in 'sown'
ę	also nasalised, like the French un, but pronounced as 'e' when word-final
ó	similar to Polish u

Consonants

In Polish, the consonants b, d, f, k, l, m, n, p, t, v and z are pronounced more or less as they are in English. The following consonants and clusters of consonants sound distinctly different to their English counterparts:

c	as the 'ts' in 'its'
ch	similar to the 'ch' in the Scottish loch
cz	as the 'ch' in 'church'
ć	much softer than Polish c (as 'tsi' before vowels)
dz	similar to the 'ds' in 'suds' but shorter
dź	as dz but softer (as 'dzi' before vowels)

dż	as the 'j' in 'jam'
g	as in 'get'
h	as **ch**
j	as the 'y' in 'yet'
ł	as the 'w' in 'wine'
ń	as the 'ny' in 'canyon' (as 'ni' before vowels)
r	always trilled
rz	as the 's' in 'pleasure'
s	as in 'set'
sz	as the 'sh' in 'show'
ś	as **s** but softer (as 'si' before vowels)
w	as the 'v' in 'van'
ź	softer version of **z** (as 'zi' before vowels)
ż	as **rz**

Basics

Hello. (inf)	*Cześć.*
Hello/	*Dzień dobry.*
Good morning.	
Goodbye.	*Do widzenia.*
Yes/No.	*Tak/Nie.*
Please.	*Proszę.*
Thank you.	*Dziękuję.*
Excuse me/	*Przepraszam.*
Forgive me.	
I don't understand.	*Nie rozumiem.*
What is it called?	*Jak to się nazywa?*
How much is it?	*Ile to kosztuje?*

Getting Around

What time does the ... leave/arrive?	*O której godzinie przychodzi/odchodzi ...?*
plane	*samolot*
boat	*statek*
bus	*autobus*
train	*pociąg*
tram	*tramwaj*
arrival	*przyjazd*
departure	*odjazd*
timetable	*rozkład jazdy*
Where is the bus stop?	*Gdzie jest przystanek autobusowy?*
Where is the station?	*Gdzie jest stacja kolejowa?*
Where is the left-luggage room?	*Gdzie jest przecho-walnia bagażu?*
Please show me on the map.	*Proszę pokazać mi to na mapie.*
straight ahead	*prosto*
left	*lewo*
right	*prawo*

Around Town

the bank	*bank*
the chemist	*apteka*
the church	*kościół*
the city centre	*centrum miasta*
the market	*targ/bazar*
the museum	*muzeum*
the post office	*poczta*
the tourist office	*informacja turystyczna*
What time does it open/close?	*O której otwierają/ zamykają?*

Accommodation

hotel	*hotel*
youth hostel	*schronisko młodzieżowe*
camping ground	*kemping*
private room	*kwatera prywatna*
Do you have any rooms available?	*Czy są wolne pokoje?*
How much is it?	*Ile to kosztuje?*
Does it include breakfast?	*Czy śniadanie jest wliczone?*
single room	*pokój jednoosobowy*
double room	*pokój dwuosobowy*

Time, Days & Numbers

What time is it?	*Która jest godzina?*
today	*dzisiaj*
tonight	*dzisiaj wieczorem*
tomorrow	*jutro*
yesterday	*wczoraj*
in the morning	*rano*
in the evening	*wieczorem*
Monday	*poniedziałek*
Tuesday	*wtorek*
Wednesday	*środa*
Thursday	*czwartek*
Friday	*piątek*
Saturday	*sobota*
Sunday	*niedziela*

Signs – Polish

Wejście	**Entrance**
Wyjście	**Exit**
Informacja	**Information**
Otwarte	**Open**
Zamknięte	**Closed**
Wzbroniony	**Prohibited**
Posterunek Policji	**Police Station**
Toalety	**Toilets**
Panowie	**Men**
Panie	**Women**

Emergencies – Polish

Help!	Pomocy!/Ratunku!
Call a doctor!	Proszę wezwać lekarza!
Call the police!	Proszę wezwać policję!
I'm lost.	Zgubiłem się. (m)
	Zgubiłam się. (f)

1	jeden
2	dwa
3	trzy
4	cztery
5	pięć
6	sześć
7	siedem
8	osiem
9	dziewięć
10	dziesięć
20	dwadzieścia
100	sto
1000	tysiąc

one million	milion

Slovak

Pronunciation

The 43 letters of the Slovak alphabet have similar pronunciation to those of Czech. There are thirteen vowels (a, á, ä, e, é, i, í, o, ó, u, ú, y, ý), three semi-vowels (l, ľ, r) and five diphthongs (ia, ie, iu, ou, ô). Letters and diphthongs which may be unfamiliar to native English speakers include the following:

c	as the 'ts' in 'its'
č	as the 'ch' in 'church'
dz	as the 'ds' in 'suds'
dž	as the 'j' in 'judge'
ia	as the 'yo' in 'yonder'
ie	as the 'ye' in 'yes'
iu	as the word 'you'
j	as the 'y' in 'yet'
ň	as the 'ni' in 'onion'
ô	as the 'wo' in 'won't'
ou	as the 'ow' in 'know'
š	as the 'sh' in 'show'
y	as the 'i' in 'machine'
ž	as the 'z' in 'azure'

Basics

Hello.	Ahoj.
Goodbye.	Dovidenia.
Yes.	Áno.
No.	Nie.
Please.	Prosím.
Thank you.	Ďakujem.
Excuse me/	Prepáčte mi/
Forgive me.	Odpuste mi.
I'm sorry.	Ospravedlňujem sa.
I don't understand.	Nerozumiem.
What is it called?	Ako sa do volá?
How much is it?	Koľko to stojí?

Getting Around

What time does the ... leave/arrive?	Kedy odchádza/ prichádza ...?
boat	loč
city bus	mestský autobus
intercity bus	medzimestský autobus
plane	lietadlo
train	vlak
tram	električka

arrival	príchod
departure	odchod
timetable	cestovný poriadok
Where is the bus stop?	Kde je autobusová zastávka?
Where is the station?	Kde je vlaková stanica?
Where is the left-luggage room?	Kde je úschovňa batožín?
Please show me on the map.	Prosím, ukážte mi to na mape.
left	vľavo
right	vpravo
straight ahead	rovno

Around Town

the bank	banka
the chemist	lekárnik
the church	kostol
the city centre	stred (centrum) mesta

Signs – Slovak

Vchod	Entrance
Východ	Exit
Informácie	Information
Otvorené	Open
Zatvorené	Closed
Zakázané	Prohibited
Polícia	Police Station
Telefón	Telephone
Záchody/WC/ Toalety	Toilets

the market	*trh*
the museum	*múzeum*
the post office	*pošta*
the telephone centre	*telefónnu centrálu*
the tourist office	*turistické informačné centrum*

Accommodation

hotel	*hotel*
guesthouse	*penzion*
youth hostel	*mládežnícka ubytovňa*
camping ground	*kemping*
private room	*privat*

Do you have any rooms available?	*Máte voľné izby?*
How much is it?	*Koľko to stojí?*
Does it include breakfast?	*Sú raňajky zahrnuté v cene?*

single room	*jednolôžková izba*
double room	*dvojlôžková izba*

Time, Days & Numbers

What time is it?	*Koľko je hodín?*
today	*dnes*
tonight	*dnes večer*
tomorrow	*zajtra*
yesterday	*včera*
in the morning	*ráno*
in the evening	*večer*

Monday	*pondelok*
Tuesday	*utorok*
Wednesday	*streda*
Thursday	*štvrtok*
Friday	*piatok*
Saturday	*sobota*
Sunday	*nedeľa*

1	*jeden*
2	*dva*
3	*tri*
4	*štyri*
5	*päť*
6	*šesť*
7	*sedem*
8	*osem*
9	*deväť*
10	*desať*
100	*sto*
1000	*tisíc*

one million	*milión*

Emergencies – Slovak

Help!	*Pomoc!*
Call a doctor!	*Zavolajte doktora/ lekára!*
Call an ambulance!	*Zavolajte záchranku!*
Call the police!	*Zavolajte políciu!*
Go away!	*Chod preč! (sg)/ Chodte preč! (pl)*
I'm lost.	*Nevyznám sa tu.*

Slovene

Pronunciation

The Slovene alphabet consists of 25 letters, most of which are very similar to English. It doesn't have the letters 'q', 'w', 'x' and 'y', but the letters ê, é, ó, ò, č, š and ž are added. Each letter represents only one sound, with very few exceptions, and the sounds are pure and not diphthongal. The letters l and v are both pronounced like English 'w' when they occur at the end of syllables and before vowels. Though words like *trn* (thorn) look unpronounceable, most Slovenes (depending on dialect) add a short vowel like an 'a' or the German 'ö' in front of the 'r' to give a Scot's pronunciation of 'tern' or 'tarn'.

c	as the 'ts' in 'its'
č	as the 'ch' in 'church'
ê	as the 'a' in 'apple'
e	as the 'a' in 'ago' (when unstressed)
é	as the 'ay' in 'day'
j	as the 'y' in 'yellow'
ó	as the 'o' in 'more'
ò	as the 'o' in 'soft'
r	a rolled 'r' sound
š	as the 'sh' in 'ship'
u	as the 'oo' in 'good'
ž	as the 's' in 'treasure'

Basics

Hello.	*Pozdravljeni.* (pol) *Zdravo/Živivo.* (inf)
Good day.	*Dober dan!*
Goodbye.	*Nasvidenje!*
Yes.	*Da* or *Ja.* (inf)
No.	*Ne.*
Please.	*Prosim.*
Thank you (very much).	*Hvala (lepa).*
You're welcome.	*Prosim/Ni za kaj!*
Excuse me.	*Oprostite.*
What's your name?	*Kako vam je ime?*

My name is ...	*Jaz sem ...*
Where are you from?	*Od kod ste?*
I'm from ...	*Sem iz ...*

Getting Around

What time does ... leave/arrive?	*Kdaj odpelje/ pripelje ...?*
boat/ferry	*ladja/trajekt*
bus	*avtobus*
train	*vlak*
one-way (ticket)	*enosmerna (vozovnica)*
return (ticket)	*povratna (vozovnica)*

Around Town

Where is the/a ...?	*Kje je ...?*
bank/exchange	*banka/menjalnica*
embassy	*konzulat/ambasada*
post office	*pošta*
telephone centre	*telefonska centrala*
tourist office	*turistični informa- cijski urad*

Accommodation

hotel	*hotel*
guesthouse	*gostišče*
camping ground	*kamping*
Do you have a ...?	*Ali imate prosto ...?*
bed	*posteljo*
cheap room	*poceni sobo*
single room	*enoposteljno sobo*
double room	*dvoposteljno sobo*

Signs – Slovene

Vhod	**Entrance**
Izhod	**Exit**
Informacije	**Information**
Odprto	**Open**
Zaprto	**Closed**
Prepovedano	**Prohibited**
Stranišče	**Toilets**

Emergencies – Slovene

Help!	*Na pomoč!*
Call a doctor!	*Pokličite zdravnika!*
Call the police!	*Pokličite policijo!*
Go away!	*Pojdite stran!*

How much is it per night?	*Koliko stane za eno noč?*
How much is it per person?	*Koliko stane za eno osebo?*
for one/two nights	*za eno noč/za dve noči*
Is breakfast included?	*Ali je zajtrk vključen?*

Time, Days & Numbers

today	*danes*
tonight	*nocoj*
tomorrow	*jutri*
in the morning	*zjutraj*
in the evening	*zvečer*
Monday	*ponedeljek*
Tuesday	*torek*
Wednesday	*sreda*
Thursday	*četrtek*
Friday	*petek*
Saturday	*sobota*
Sunday	*nedelja*

1	*ena*
2	*dve*
3	*tri*
4	*štiri*
5	*pet*
6	*šest*
7	*sedem*
8	*osem*
9	*devet*
10	*deset*
100	*sto*
1000	*tisoč*
one million	*milijon*

Thanks

Many thanks to the travellers who used the last edition and wrote to us with helpful hints, useful advice and interesting anecdotes:

Nick Adlam, Carolyn Agardy, Bashar Amso, Josee Archambault, Elena Arriero, Saara Arvo, Kyle Austen, Andrei Avram, Ivan Babiuk, Monika Bailey, Steve Barnett, Montse Baste-Kraan, Ken Baxter, Szirti Bea, Gregory Becker, Matt Beks, Tony Bellette, Fletcher Benton, Alisa Bieber, Chris Bolger, Bela Borsos, Melissa Bowtell, Ben Brehmer, Dylan Browne, Stefan Brunnsteiner, Rod George Bryant, Doris Calhoun, Samantha Campbell, Fred Carreon, Kent Carter, Romelle Castle, Tara Castle, Sandy Ceniseros, Andrea Cervenka, Matt Chaffe, Greg Chandler, Anthi Charalambous, Kah Chong, Vincent Choo, K M Chow, Niko Cimbur, Erica Clarke, Stephen Coast, Martha W Connor, Dave Conway, Catalin Coroama, Alma Cristina, Susan Cubberly, Phil Cubbin, Sigal Dabach, Paul Dalton, Harry Davidson, Christine Davis, Robert Davison, Johan de Vetti, Mike Dean, Philippe Dennler, Luc Desy, Stelios N Deverakis, Nathan Dhillon, Kathleen Diamond, Floris Dirks, Mathew Dolenac, James Done, Nicola Doran, Ryan Dougherty, Loretta Dupuis, John Dynan, Jariko Eastvold, Ben Edmunds, Katie Elder, Robert Essenyi, Martin Fagerer, Teresa Fanning, Anne Fenerty, Nate Findley, Deborah Fink, Kristine Flora, Karen Forster, Joao fraga, Helen Frakes, Viola Franke, Wes Galt, Sarit Gelbart, Tim Gilley, Paul W Gioffi, Ian Glennon, Antonio Gonzalez-Avila, Martin & Margaret Goodwin, Samantha Gordon, Phyllis Grant, Ania Gruba, Frederik Grufman, Karen Grunow, Gabriel Gruss, Jerry Gwee, Mikael Hanas, Sue Harrison, Shona Hawkes, Catherine Hegyi, Irene Herrera, Peter Hertrampf, Marrianne Hoeyland, Peter Hoogland, Karen Howat, Petr Hruska, Michael Huber, Loryn Hunter, Mark Huntsman, Steuart Hutchinson, Bruce & Kay Ikawa, Victor & Agnes Isaacs, Charles Jans, Rok Jarc, Marie Javins, Prashant Jayaprakash, Janaka Jayasingha, Ida Johansson, David John, John Johnson, Andrew Jones, Jenny Jones, Benno Kaestli, Judith Kahan, Markus Kaim, David Katz, Christoph Kessel, John Killick, Kerry King, Seamus King, Rob Kingston, Wim Klumpenhouwer, David Klur, Timo Knaebe, J E Knowles, Helke Knuetter, Barbara Kocot, Gertie Korevaar, Igor Korsic, Richard Kort, Juraj Kosticky, Donna Krupa, Francesca Lanaro, San Lauw, Antonio Lee, Steve Lees, Desmond Leow, Ralf Liebau, Lisa Long, Simon Looi, Maria Lopez, Stephen Lowe, Deirdre MacBean, Alessandro Maccari, Alex MacKenzie, Andrea MacLeod, Kevin Madden, Dee Mahan, John marquis, Alberto Martin, Antoinette & Gerald Martin, Phillip Matthews, Eileen Mazur, Glenn McAllister, Florence & Michael McBride, Judie McCourt, Andrea McEneaney, David McGowan, Claire McKee, Ian McLoughlin, Gunnar Merbach, Lin Merry, Julian Mettler, Robin Meyerhoff, Vicky Michels, Eric Milsom, David Minkin, Basit Mirza, Martin Mischkulnig, Dr Michael Mittler, Lee Gerard Molloy, Jason Mote, Grainne Murphy, Kathryn Murphy, Roberta Murray, Petra Naavalinna, Jonas Nahm, Jan Nesnidal, Borut Nikolas, Jen Noble, Jamie Norris, Jacqui O'Connell, Robin O'Donoghue, Mick Ogrizek, Elka (Alice) Olsen, Andre Oord, Gustavo Orlando-Zon, Carlos Ortiz, Michaela Osborne, Megan Packer, Manuel Padilla, Rolf Palmberg, Michael Parsons, James Payne, Justin Peach, Jan M Pennington, Steve Penny, Claus Penz, Sam Perry, Bill Petrovic, Suzanne Pfouts, Eric Philpott, Stacey Piesner, Michel Pinton, Scott Plimpton, Magdalena Polan, Kevin Presto, Anna Ptaszynska, Marc Purnal, Catherine Rentz, Grant Reynolds, Helen Richards, Tony Richmond, Jason Rodrigues, Clare Rose, Vicki Roubicek, Jaroslaw Rudnik, Melissa Russel, Ian Rutt, Kym Ryan, Marcin Sadurski, Rachel Samsonowitz, Claudio Sandroni, Karl Scharbert, Sabine Schmitz, Larry Schwarz, Eric Schwenter, Paola Sconzo, Rick Seymour, Brett Shackelford, Tal Shany, Jessica Sherwood, Bogdan Siewierski, Helen Silverberg, Carol & Ron Simmons, Alec Sirken, Ella Smit, Ann Snyder, Raewyn Somerville, David Spiers, Kevin Stanes, David Staunton Lambert, Julie Stenberg, Samo Stritof, Clare Szilagyi, Amanda Fay Szumutku, Patricia Tandy, Iain Taylor, Nicky Taylor, Vera ten Hacken, Ivo Tence, Kate Thomas, Julia Tobey, Chester A Troy, Dave Upton, Boaz Ur, Caroliena van den Bos, Mathieu Vandermissen, Maarten Vermeulen, Knut Vold, Anne Volmari, Jost Wagner, A Watson, Valda White, Kate Wierciak, Hanna Wilhelm, Ernst Williams, Fiona Wilson, David Young, Choi Young Min, Holger Zimmermann, Paul Zoglin, Attila Zsunyi, Will Zucker

LONELY PLANET

Guides by Region

Lonely Planet is known worldwide for publishing practical, reliable and no-nonsense travel information in our guides and on our Web site. The Lonely Planet list covers just about every accessible part of the world. Currently there are 16 series: Travel guides, Shoestring guides, Condensed guides, Phrasebooks, Read This First, Healthy Travel, Walking guides, Cycling guides, Watching Wildlife guides, Pisces Diving & Snorkeling guides, City Maps, Road Atlases, Out to Eat, World Food, Journeys travel literature and Pictorials.

AFRICA Africa on a shoestring • Botswana • Cairo • Cairo City Map • Cape Town • Cape Town City Map • East Africa • Egypt • Egyptian Arabic phrasebook • Ethiopia, Eritrea & Djibouti • Ethiopian Amharic phrasebook • The Gambia & Senegal • Healthy Travel Africa • Kenya • Malawi • Morocco • Moroccan Arabic phrasebook • Mozambique • Namibia • Read This First: Africa • South Africa, Lesotho & Swaziland • Southern Africa • Southern Africa Road Atlas • Swahili phrasebook • Tanzania, Zanzibar & Pemba • Trekking in East Africa • Tunisia • Watching Wildlife East Africa • Watching Wildlife Southern Africa • West Africa • World Food Morocco • Zambia • Zimbabwe, Botswana & Namibia
Travel Literature: Mali Blues: Traveling to an African Beat • The Rainbird: A Central African Journey • Songs to an African Sunset: A Zimbabwean Story

AUSTRALIA & THE PACIFIC Aboriginal Australia & the Torres Strait Islands •Auckland • Australia • Australian phrasebook • Australia Road Atlas • Cycling Australia • Cycling New Zealand • Fiji • Fijian phrasebook • Healthy Travel Australia, NZ & the Pacific • Islands of Australia's Great Barrier Reef • Melbourne • Melbourne City Map • Micronesia • New Caledonia • New South Wales • New Zealand • Northern Territory • Outback Australia • Out to Eat – Melbourne • Out to Eat – Sydney • Papua New Guinea • Pidgin phrasebook • Queensland • Rarotonga & the Cook Islands • Samoa • Solomon Islands • South Australia • South Pacific • South Pacific phrasebook • Sydney • Sydney City Map • Sydney Condensed • Tahiti & French Polynesia • Tasmania • Tonga • Tramping in New Zealand • Vanuatu • Victoria • Walking in Australia • Watching Wildlife Australia • Western Australia
Travel Literature: Islands in the Clouds: Travels in the Highlands of New Guinea • Kiwi Tracks: A New Zealand Journey • Sean & David's Long Drive

CENTRAL AMERICA & THE CARIBBEAN Bahamas, Turks & Caicos • Baja California • Belize, Guatemala & Yucatán • Bermuda • Central America on a shoestring • Costa Rica • Costa Rica Spanish phrasebook • Cuba • Cycling Cuba • Dominican Republic & Haiti • Eastern Caribbean • Guatemala • Havana • Healthy Travel Central & South America • Jamaica • Mexico • Mexico City • Panama • Puerto Rico • Read This First: Central & South America • Virgin Islands • World Food Caribbean • World Food Mexico • Yucatán
Travel Literature: Green Dreams: Travels in Central America

EUROPE Amsterdam • Amsterdam City Map • Amsterdam Condensed • Andalucía • Athens • Austria • Baltic States phrasebook • Barcelona • Barcelona City Map • Belgium & Luxembourg • Berlin • Berlin City Map • Britain • British phrasebook • Brussels, Bruges & Antwerp • Brussels City Map • Budapest • Budapest City Map • Canary Islands • Catalunya & the Costa Brava • Central Europe • Central Europe phrasebook • Copenhagen • Corfu & the Ionians • Corsica • Crete • Crete Condensed • Croatia • Cycling Britain • Cycling France • Cyprus • Czech & Slovak Republics • Czech phrasebook • Denmark • Dublin • Dublin City Map • Dublin Condensed • Eastern Europe • Eastern Europe phrasebook • Edinburgh • Edinburgh City Map • England • Estonia, Latvia & Lithuania • Europe on a shoestring • Europe phrasebook • Finland • Florence • Florence City Map • France • Frankfurt City Map • Frankfurt Condensed • French phrasebook • Georgia, Armenia & Azerbaijan • Germany • German phrasebook • Greece • Greek Islands • Greek phrasebook • Hungary • Iceland, Greenland & the Faroe Islands • Ireland • Italian phrasebook • Italy • Kraków • Lisbon • The Loire • London • London City Map • London Condensed • Madrid • Madrid City Map • Malta • Mediterranean Europe • Milan, Turin & Genoa • Moscow • Munich • Netherlands • Normandy • Norway • Out to Eat – London • Out to Eat – Paris • Paris • Paris City Map • Paris Condensed • Poland • Polish phrasebook • Portugal • Portuguese phrasebook • Prague • Prague City Map • Provence & the Côte d'Azur • Read This First: Europe • Rhodes & the Dodecanese • Romania & Moldova • Rome • Rome City Map • Rome Condensed • Russia, Ukraine & Belarus • Russian phrasebook • Scandinavian & Baltic Europe • Scandinavian phrasebook • Scotland • Sicily • Slovenia • South-West France • Spain • Spanish phrasebook • Stockholm • St Petersburg • St Petersburg City Map • Sweden • Switzerland • Tuscany • Ukrainian phrasebook • Venice • Vienna • Wales • Walking in Britain • Walking in France • Walking in Ireland • Walking in Italy • Walking in Scotland • Walking in Spain • Walking in Switzerland • Western Europe • World Food France • World Food Greece • World Food Ireland • World Food Italy • World Food Spain **Travel Literature:** After Yugoslavia • Love and War in the Apennines • The Olive Grove: Travels in Greece • On the Shores of the Mediterranean • Round Ireland in Low Gear • A Small Place in Italy

LONELY PLANET

Mail Order

Lonely Planet products are distributed worldwide.They are also available by mail order from Lonely Planet, so if you have difficulty finding a title please write to us. North and South American residents should write to 150 Linden St, Oakland, CA 94607, USA; European and African residents should write to 10a Spring Place, London NW5 3BH, UK; and residents of other countries to Locked Bag 1, Footscray, Victoria 3011, Australia.

INDIAN SUBCONTINENT & THE INDIAN OCEAN Bangladesh • Bengali phrasebook • Bhutan • Delhi • Goa • Healthy Travel Asia & India • Hindi & Urdu phrasebook • India • India & Bangladesh City Map • Indian Himalaya • Karakoram Highway • Kathmandu City Map • Kerala • Madagascar • Maldives • Mauritius, Réunion & Seychelles • Mumbai (Bombay) • Nepal • Nepali phrasebook • North India • Pakistan • Rajasthan • Read This First: Asia & India • South India • Sri Lanka • Sri Lanka phrasebook • Tibet • Tibetan phrasebook • Trekking in the Indian Himalaya • Trekking in the Karakoram & Hindukush • Trekking in the Nepal Himalaya • World Food India **Travel Literature:** The Age of Kali: Indian Travels and Encounters • Hello Goodnight: A Life of Goa • In Rajasthan • Maverick in Madagascar • A Season in Heaven: True Tales from the Road to Kathmandu • Shopping for Buddhas • A Short Walk in the Hindu Kush • Slowly Down the Ganges

MIDDLE EAST & CENTRAL ASIA Bahrain, Kuwait & Qatar • Central Asia • Central Asia phrasebook • Dubai • Farsi (Persian) phrasebook • Hebrew phrasebook • Iran • Israel & the Palestinian Territories • Istanbul • Istanbul City Map • Istanbul to Cairo • Istanbul to Kathmandu • Jerusalem • Jerusalem City Map • Jordan • Lebanon • Middle East • Oman & the United Arab Emirates • Syria • Turkey • Turkish phrasebook • World Food Turkey • Yemen **Travel Literature:** Black on Black: Iran Revisited • Breaking Ranks: Turbulent Travels in the Promised Land • The Gates of Damascus • Kingdom of the Film Stars: Journey into Jordan

NORTH AMERICA Alaska • Boston • Boston City Map • Boston Condensed • British Columbia • California & Nevada • California Condensed • Canada • Chicago • Chicago City Map • Chicago Condensed • Florida • Georgia & the Carolinas • Great Lakes • Hawaii • Hiking in Alaska • Hiking in the USA • Honolulu & Oahu City Map • Las Vegas • Los Angeles • Los Angeles City Map • Louisiana & the Deep South • Miami • Miami City Map • Montreal • New England • New Orleans • New Orleans City Map • New York City • New York City City Map • New York City Condensed • New York, New Jersey & Pennsylvania • Oahu • Out to Eat – San Francisco • Pacific Northwest • Rocky Mountains • San Diego & Tijuana • San Francisco • San Francisco City Map • Seattle • Seattle City Map • Southwest • Texas • Toronto • USA • USA phrasebook • Vancouver • Vancouver City Map • Virginia & the Capital Region • Washington, DC • Washington, DC City Map • World Food New Orleans **Travel Literature**: Caught Inside: A Surfer's Year on the California Coast • Drive Thru America

NORTH-EAST ASIA Beijing • Beijing City Map • Cantonese phrasebook • China • Hiking in Japan • Hong Kong & Macau • Hong Kong City Map • Hong Kong Condensed • Japan • Japanese phrasebook • Korea • Korean phrasebook • Kyoto • Mandarin phrasebook • Mongolia • Mongolian phrasebook • Seoul • Shanghai • South-West China • Taiwan • Tokyo • Tokyo Condensed • World Food Hong Kong • World Food Japan **Travel Literature:** In Xanadu: A Quest • Lost Japan

SOUTH AMERICA Argentina, Uruguay & Paraguay • Bolivia • Brazil • Brazilian phrasebook • Buenos Aires • Buenos Aires City Map • Chile & Easter Island • Colombia • Ecuador & the Galapagos Islands • Healthy Travel Central & South America • Latin American Spanish phrasebook • Peru • Quechua phrasebook • Read This First: Central & South America • Rio de Janeiro • Rio de Janeiro City Map • Santiago de Chile • South America on a shoestring • Trekking in the Patagonian Andes • Venezuela **Travel Literature**: Full Circle: A South American Journey

SOUTH-EAST ASIA Bali & Lombok • Bangkok • Bangkok City Map • Burmese phrasebook • Cambodia • Cycling Vietnam, Laos & Cambodia • East Timor phrasebook • Hanoi • Healthy Travel Asia & India • Hill Tribes phrasebook • Ho Chi Minh City (Saigon) • Indonesia • Indonesian phrasebook • Indonesia's Eastern Islands • Java • Lao phrasebook • Laos • Malay phrasebook • Malaysia, Singapore & Brunei • Myanmar (Burma) • Philippines • Pilipino (Tagalog) phrasebook • Read This First: Asia & India • Singapore • Singapore City Map • South-East Asia on a shoestring • South-East Asia phrasebook • Thailand • Thailand's Islands & Beaches • Thailand, Vietnam, Laos & Cambodia Road Atlas • Thai phrasebook • Vietnam • Vietnamese phrasebook • World Food Indonesia • World Food Thailand • World Food Vietnam

ALSO AVAILABLE: Antarctica • The Arctic • The Blue Man: Tales of Travel, Love and Coffee • Brief Encounters: Stories of Love, Sex & Travel • Buddhist Stupas in Asia: The Shape of Perfection • Chasing Rickshaws • The Last Grain Race • Lonely Planet ... On the Edge: Adventurous Escapades from Around the World • Lonely Planet Unpacked • Lonely Planet Unpacked Again • Not the Only Planet: Science Fiction Travel Stories • Ports of Call: A Journey by Sea • Sacred India • Travel Photography: A Guide to Taking Better Pictures • Travel with Children • Tuvalu: Portrait of an Island Nation

LONELY PLANET

You already know that Lonely Planet produces more than this one guidebook, but you might not be aware of the other products we have on this region. Here is a selection of titles that you may want to check out as well:

Prague map
ISBN 1 86450 012 3
US$5.95 • UK£3.99

Vienna
ISBN 1 86450 195 2
US$14.99 • UK£8.99

Central Europe phrasebook
ISBN 1 86450 226 6
US$7.99 • UK£4.50

Prague Condensed
ISBN 1 74059 349 9
US$11.99 • UK£5.99

Europe on a shoestring
ISBN 1 74059 314 6
US$24.99 • UK£14.99

German phrasebook
ISBN 1 86450 153 7
US$7.99 • UK£3.99

Read This First: Europe
ISBN 1 86450 136 7
US$14.99 • UK£8.99

Western Europe
ISBN 1 74059 313 8
US$27.99 • UK£16.99

Walking in Switzerland
ISBN 0 86442 737 9
US$19.99 • UK£12.99

Eastern Europe
ISBN 1 74059 289 1
US$27.99 • UK£15.99

Paris
ISBN 1 74059 306 5
US$15.99 • UK£9.99

Bavaria
ISBN 1 74059 013 9
US$17.99 • UK£11.99

Available wherever books are sold

Index

Abbreviations

Text

Bold indicates maps.

Bold indicates maps.

MAP LEGEND

CITY ROUTES

Freeway .... Freeway	⹋⹋⹋⹋ .... Unsealed Road
Highway ...... Primary Road	▬▬▬→ .... One Way Street
Road ...... Secondary Road	▬▬▬▬ .... Pedestrian Street
Street .... Street	⊓⊓⊓⊓⊓⊓ .... Stepped Street
Lane .... Lane	)= = = ... Tunnel
▬▬▬ ...... On/Off Ramp	▬▬▬ .... Footbridge

HYDROGRAPHY

~~ ...... River, Creek	◯ ◖◗ .... Dry Lake; Salt Lake
▬·▬·▬ .... Canal	◉ ↝ ..... Spring; Rapids
◯ .... Lake	◐ ⤶ ≈ ...... Waterfalls

REGIONAL ROUTES

▬▬▬▬ .... Tollway, Freeway
▬▬▬▬ .... Primary Road
▬▬▬▬ .... Secondary Road
▬▬▬▬ .... Minor Road

TRANSPORT ROUTES & STATIONS

▬▬●▬ .... Train	----⬚ ...... Ferry
●●●●●● ...... Underground Train	▬ ▬ ▬ ...... Walking Trail
▬ ▬Ⓜ .... Metro	·········· ...... Walking Tour
▬▬▬▬▬ .... Tramway	░░░░░ ...... Path
╫─╫─╫─╫ ..... Funicular Railway	▬▬▬ ...... Pier or Jetty

BOUNDARIES

▬·▬··▬· .... International
▬··▬··▬·· .... State
▬ ▬ ▬ .... Disputed
▬▬◼▬▬ .... Fortified Wall

AREA FEATURES

▒▒ .... Building	▒▒ .... Market	∿∿∿ ...... Beach	∿∿∿ ...... Forest
⊛ ...... Park, Gardens	◯ ...... Sports Ground	+ + + ... Cemetery	▭ ...... Plaza

POPULATION SYMBOLS

✪ **CAPITAL** ...... National Capital	● **CITY** ...... City	● Village ...... Village
◉ **CAPITAL** ...... State Capital	○ **Town** ...... Town	▒▒ ...... Urban Area

MAP SYMBOLS

▲ .... Place to Stay	▼ .... Place to Eat	● .... Point of Interest

✈ ...... Airport	▦ ...... Cinema	✚ ...... Police Station	🏊 ...... Swimming Pool
⊖ ...... Bank	🛂 .. Embassy, Consulate	✉ ...... Post Office	✡ ...... Synagogue
⊕ ...... Border Crossing	⚓ ...... Fountain	🍺 ...... Pub or Bar	🚕 ...... Taxi Rank
▣ ...... Bus Station	✚ ...... Hospital	🍺 ...... Pub or Bar (Ire)	☎ ...... Telephone
▣ ... Cable Car, Funicular	🖥 ...... Internet Cafe	✕ ...... Ruins	▤ ...... Theatre
🏰 ...... Castle, Chateau	▲ ...... Mounment	✪ ...... Shopping Centre	❶ .. Tourist Information
▰▰❶ ... Cathedral, Church	🏛 ...... Museum	⚴ ...... Ski Field	🖼 ...... Zoo

Note: not all symbols displayed above appear in this book

LONELY PLANET OFFICES

Australia
Locked Bag 1, Footscray, Victoria 3011
☎ 03 8379 8000 fax 03 8379 8111
email: talk2us@lonelyplanet.com.au

UK
10a Spring Place, London NW5 3BH
☎ 020 7428 4800 fax 020 7428 4828
email: go@lonelyplanet.co.uk

USA
150 Linden St, Oakland, CA 94607
☎ 510 893 8555 TOLL FREE: 800 275 8555
fax 510 893 8572
email: info@lonelyplanet.com

France
1 rue du Dahomey, 75011 Paris
☎ 01 55 25 33 00 fax 01 55 25 33 01
email: bip@lonelyplanet.fr
www.lonelyplanet.fr

World Wide Web: www.lonelyplanet.com *or* AOL keyword: lp
Lonely Planet Images: lpi@lonelyplanet.com.au